Sealy and Worthington's Text, Cases, and Materials in Company Law

Eleventh edition

Sarah Worthington QC(Hon), FBA

Downing Professor of the Laws of England
Fellow of Trinity College, University of Cambridge
Bencher of Middle Temple

OXFORD
UNIVERSITY PRESS

OXFORD
UNIVERSITY PRESS

Great Clarendon Street, Oxford, OX2 6DP,
United Kingdom

Oxford University Press is a department of the University of Oxford.
It furthers the University's objective of excellence in research, scholarship,
and education by publishing worldwide. Oxford is a registered trade mark of
Oxford University Press in the UK and in certain other countries

Eighth edition 2008
Ninth edition 2010
Tenth edition 2013

Impression: 1

Published in the United States of America by Oxford University Press
198 Madison Avenue, New York, NY 10016, United States of America

British Library Cataloguing in Publication Data
Data available

Library of Congress Control Number: 2016936817

ISBN 978-0-19-872205-2

Printed in Italy by
L.E.G.O. S.p.A.

Preface

The ambitions with this book remain as they have always been: to take the broad subject matter of company law and present it as simply as possible, and in a manner which informs and challenges; which reveals its distinctive goals and its underlying structure; and which prompts questions and provokes deeper understanding and insight. To generations of students and teachers this book is simply 'Sealy'. Nevertheless, with a further tweak to the title, this eleventh edition becomes *Sealy and Worthington's Text, Cases, and Materials in Company Law*. The nod to 'text' in the title does little more than acknowledge the mechanism by which Len Sealy always sought to deliver his own ambitions for this book. As in previous editions, I have aimed to continue this.

This edition also marks a change in formatting (and in paper—perhaps in line with the new plastic banknotes). As the subject matter of company law becomes increasingly vast, the job of exposing its underlying structure becomes correspondingly more important. To that end, two of the less obvious presentational changes are more important than they might at first seem. Firstly, each chapter begins with a headline excerpt of its 'contents'. This is intended to serve as a succinct identification of the legal issues to be addressed. Secondly, and more importantly—even if less often appreciated as such—the 'Contents' pages at the start of the book (at pp vii–xviii) set out in full all the headings and sub-headings in each chapter. These pages thus provide a detailed diagram of the skeleton of the subject of company law on which the substance of each chapter then hangs.

Turning from the form of presentation to the subject's essential substance, both the legislature and the courts have been active. The Companies Act 2006 continues to be revised and updated to reflect modern needs and commercial practices. On this front, perhaps the most noteworthy change, in both philosophy and content, is the new requirement for all companies to compile a public register of 'people with significant control' (a PSC Register: see Chapter 14). This PSC Register must disclose the names of people who are able to exert 'significant influence or control' over the company's business: it matters not whether the 'person' is corporate or human, a company shareholder or not, and, if a shareholder, whether the legal owner of the shares or not. This change from earlier practices was introduced, along with other important changes (such as to the CDDA 1986), by the Small Business, Enterprise and Employment Act 2015 (SBEEA 2015).

In addition, corporate governance has remained firmly under the microscope, with further revisions to the UK Corporate Governance Code and the UK Stewardship Code; and continued attention to the issues addressed in the Kay Report (including problems of short-termism) and the Davies Report (gender diversity on boards).

The courts too have proved a significant source of further change. The Supreme Court has been particularly active. Its major decisions include those on the separate legal personality of companies (*Prest v Petrodel Resources Ltd* [2013] UKSC 34, included in the last edition only by way of late addendum); on attribution in corporate activity, especially corporate wrongdoing (*Bilta (UK) Ltd (In Liq) v Nazir* [2015] UKSC 23); on directors' duties and proper purposes (*Eclairs Group Ltd v JKX Oil & Gas Plc* [2015] UKSC 71); and on remedies (*AIB Group (UK) Plc v Mark Redler & Co Solicitors* [2014] UKSC 58; *FHR European Ventures LLP v Cedar Capital Partners LLC* [2014] UKSC 45). The lower courts, too, have been equally active.

All of this serves as a pointed reminder that companies are not mere abstractions. Everything done by a company and everything done within a company is done by human beings. Every case that comes to court involves real people facing real pressures. It is this that brings the subject alive, fills it with events and characters and makes it fun to study and to teach. The 2006 Act, as amended, may have introduced some new concepts and changed some of the rules, but its role will only be, as before, to serve the same needs of commerce and the people who engage in it: the same problems and questions will arise, and there will be no better way for students to understand the law and to test how it will work in practice than by examining how it would apply to the facts of known cases.

In this eleventh edition there has been some major restructuring of individual chapters. In particular, Chapter 2 (on corporate personality and limited liability) and Chapter 3 (on corporate activity and legal liability) have been completely revised, with much extended text and commentary and the addition and reorganisation of relevant case extracts. Chapter 7 (on directors' duties) and Chapter 8 (on auditor liability) have also been modified. Extracts from the judgments in a good few older cases have again had to be discarded or shortened in favour of newer substitutes.

Apart from statute and cases, other major influences on corporate law and practice continue to grow in importance, and need inclusion in order to give a balanced view: the regulation of the financial services industry, the rules of the Stock Exchange, new rulings of the European Court, and directives and reform proposals from the European Commission.

Finally, I must record my thanks to a number of people. First and foremost, Michael Lok has once again provided unparalleled research assistance on all the areas addressed in this book, and managed to do that while conducting an increasingly busy and successful practice in Hong Kong. I am enormously grateful to him. Joy Ruskin-Tompkins as copy editor and Jonathan Price as proof reader have provided admirably rigorous, effective, prompt, and professional service. And John Carroll and Sarah Stephenson at Oxford University Press have provided thoughtful, careful and proactive help at all stages of production. Thank you to all of you.

This eleventh edition endeavours to state the law as at 31 March 2016, with some minor additions at proofs stage.

Sarah Worthington

June 2016

New to this edition

Key revisions in the 11th edition include:

- Complete updating of statutory, regulatory and case law materials, including the major changes introduced by SBEEA 2015, but also including changes to the core legislation in CA 2006 and to the various corporate governance codes requiring 'comply or explain' adherence.

- Major rewriting of Chapter 2 (Corporate personality and limited liability) in the light of *Prest v Petrodel Resources Ltd* (2013, SC): ie changed structure, considerable new text, and new cases.

- Major rewriting of Chapter 3 (Corporate activity and legal liability) to take into account a number of recent cases: ie changed structure, considerable new text, and new cases.

- Supreme Court cases including:
  - *Prest v Petrodel Resources Ltd*
  - *Bilta (UK) Ltd v Nazir*
  - *AIB Group (UK) plc v Mark Redler & Co Solicitors*
  - *Eclairs Group Ltd v JKX Oil & Gas Plc*
  - *FHR European Ventures LLP v Cedar Capital Partners LLC*
  - *Braganza v BP Shipping Ltd*
  - *Re Nortel GmbH; Re Lehman Bros International (Europe)*

- Court of Appeal cases including:
  - *Re Coroin Ltd*
  - *Antonio Gramsci Shipping Corporation v Recoletos Ltd*
  - *Brumder v Motornet Service and Repairs Ltd*
  - *Speechley v Allott*
  - *Smithton Ltd v Naggar*
  - *Burry & Knight Ltd v Knight*
  - *Relfo Ltd (In Liquidation) v Varsani*

- Additional coverage of statutory derivative actions, with excerpts from leading recent HCt and CA cases.

- Additional coverage of insolvency and proprietary issues, including notes on leading recent HCt and CA cases.

Source acknowledgements

Grateful acknowledgement is made to all the authors and publishers of copyright material which appears in this book, and in particular to the following for permission to reprint material from the sources indicated:

The Government of the Hong Kong Special Administrative Region: for extracts from the following cases—*Thanakharn Kasikorn Thai Chamkat (Mahachon) v Akai Holdings Ltd (In Liquidation)* FACV 9/2010; *Moulin Global Eyecare Trading Ltd (In Liquidation) (formerly known as Moulin Optical Manufactory Ltd) v The Commissioner of Inland Revenue* FACV5/2013.

The Judgment published in this text is reproduced from those posted on the Judiciary's website with the permission of the Government. The Government accepts no liability or responsibility for the accuracy or completeness of any judgment being published in this text.

The Incorporated Council of Law Reporting: for extracts from the *Appeal Cases* (AC), *Chancery Reports* (Ch), *Court of Appeal* (EWCA), *High Court* (EWHC), *King's Bench Reports* (KB), *Queen's Bench Reports* (QB), and the *Weekly Law Reports* (WLR).

Informa Law: for an extract from *Lloyd's Law Reports*.

RELX (UK) Limited, trading as LexisNexis: for extracts from the *All England Law Reports* (ALL ER) and *Butterworths Company Law Cases* (BCLC).

Thomson Reuters (Professional) UK Limited: for extracts from *British Company Law Cases* (BCLC) and *British Company Cases* (BCC).

Extracts from unreported case reports, Law Commission Reports, Consultation papers, and Home Office reports and statistics are Crown copyright material and are reproduced under Class Licence Number C2006010631 with the permission of the Controller of OPSI and the Queen's Printer for Scotland. Extracts from House of Lords Reports (UKHL) are Parliamentary copyright and are reproduced by permission of the Controller of HMSO on behalf of Parliament.

Every effort has been made to trace and contact the copyright holders but this has not been possible in all cases. If notified, the publisher will undertake to rectify any errors or omissions at the earliest opportunity.

Contents

List of abbreviations

Abbreviation	Detail
APPCGG	All Party Parliamentary Corporate Governance Group
BERR	Department for Business, Enterprise and Regulatory Reform*
BIS	Department for Business, Innovation and Skills*
CA 1985	Companies Act 1985
CA 1989	Companies Act 1989
CA 2006	Companies Act 2006
C(AICE)A 2004	Companies (Audit, Investigations and Community Enterprise) Act 2004
CDDA 1986	Company Directors Disqualification Act 1986
CEO	Chief executive officer
CIC	Community interest company
CJEU	Court of Justice of the European Union
CLR	The collective publications of the DTI's Company Law Review
COMI	Centre of main interest
CPR	Civil Procedure Rules
CVA	Company voluntary arrangement
DTI	Department of Trade and Industry*
EA 2002	Enterprise Act 2002
ECtHR	European Court of Human Rights
EEIG	European Economic Interest Grouping
FCA	Financial Conduct Authority**
FPC	Financial Policy Committee
FRC	Financial Reporting Council
FSA	Financial Services Authority**
FSA 1986	Financial Services Act 1986
FSA 2012	Financial Services Act 2012
FSMA 2000	Financial Services and Markets Act 2000
IA 1986	Insolvency Act 1986
IR 1986	Insolvency Rules 1986
LLP	Limited liability partnership
MiFID	Markets in Financial Instruments Directive (2004/39/EC)
NED	Non-executive director
PIE	Public-Interest Entities
PRA	Prudential Regulation Authority**
PSC	People with significant control
RIE	Recognised investment exchange
SBEEA 2015	Small Business, Enterprise and Employment Act 2015
SE	*Societas Europaea*
UKLA	United Kingdom Listing Authority
UNCITRAL	United Nations Commission on International Trade Law

* These are recent successor government departments (always including responsibility for companies, although other responsibilities have been added and subtracted with each change). The DTI ceased to exist in 2007, replaced by BERR, which itself was replaced by BIS in June 2009.

** The FSA 2012 abolished the FSA with effect from 1 April 2013, and its responsibilities were then split between two new agencies, the FCA and the PRA, and the Bank of England.

Table of statutes

Table of secondary legislation

Table of cases

Paragraph numbers in **bold** *indicate case extracts with the relevant page numbers in italics*

AUSTRALIA

HONG KONG

NEW ZEALAND

USA

1

THE COMPANY AND ITS INCORPORATION

Introduction

A company is very easily defined.[1] In typical legal usage it is the kind of legal entity or corporate body which is brought into being by the registration procedures laid down by the Companies Act 2006 (CA 2006) and its predecessors.[2] Its creation is evidenced by the issue of a certificate of incorporation by the Registrar of Companies. Except in a few rare cases the last word of its name will be 'Ltd' (Limited) or, in the case of a public company, the unpronounceable abbreviation 'plc' (public limited company).[3] In the United States, the word corresponding to company is 'corporation', and the corporation's name normally terminates in that word (Corpn) or 'Incorporated' (Inc), although 'Limited' is sometimes used there, too.

Companies are encountered everywhere. They provide most of the goods and services we use every day. They own large and small stores; run transport, telephone and communication systems; supply water and power; and run schools and hospitals. When thinking of companies, we usually think of large organisations, although 'one man companies' are perfectly possible.

What makes companies remarkable is that they are 'legal persons' in their own right, not simply groups of individuals working together in a common enterprise. In the study of

---

[1] Of course, the word 'company' has other meanings in everyday speech; and note in particular the abbreviation 'Co' (and especially '& Co'), which is commonly used as part of the name of an unincorporated partnership that is not a 'company' in any strict legal sense, and is also occasionally used by an individual trader.

[2] A company may also be created by Royal Charter or by special Act of Parliament. Most of these companies are a century or more old. Few such companies still exist, and the rules of 'company law' as derived from the Companies Acts and common law may not always apply to them, eg neither the *ultra vires* doctrine nor the winding-up procedure has traditionally applied to chartered companies (though there are now some exceptions). Beyond this, these types of company are mainly of interest in helping to explain some of the more arcane rules of the subject which evolved long ago and have been allowed to survive into modern times.

[3] CA 2006 ss 58–60. Exceptions are unlimited companies, charitable companies and companies granted a dispensation under ss 60 and 61. There are Welsh equivalents for 'Limited' and 'plc'. The word 'limited' is also used by co-operatives and similar bodies registered under the Industrial and Provident Societies Act 1965, and by limited liability partnerships ('LLP'), under the Limited Liability Partnerships Act 2000.

company law, therefore, it is not only necessary to address the types of rules that enable groups of people to work together in an organisation, but also to address the rules that enable a non-human 'person' to perform a wide variety of acts for itself. The fascination of companies and company law lies in both these aspects.

Companies in action: special features and key parties

Company law is about the interactions between a *company* (as a legal person in its own right), the company's *members* (and since most companies are limited by shares, these are generally its *shareholders*[4]), its *directors* and its *creditors* (both *secured* and *unsecured*).

The relevant law must provide rules to deal with the creation of companies; the ways companies deal with outsiders (eg how companies contract with their suppliers and customers, how they commit torts and crimes and how they sue and are sued, etc); how people come to be directors and shareholders; the powers and duties of directors and shareholders in their various relationships with the company, the creditors and each other; the regulation of disputes *within* these groups (eg how directors make decisions, how battles between majority and minority shareholders are resolved, how priorities between secured and unsecured creditors are determined); and, finally, how companies 'die', or cease to exist.

The key players in all of this are the directors and the members. The task of the directors is to manage the company (although what this means in practice is determined by the constitution of the company, which in turn is governed by the members). The directors generally act collectively, via a *board of directors*. The boards of directors in medium-sized and larger companies will typically comprise both *executive directors*, who are employed by the company and intimately involved in the day-to-day management of the company, and *non-executive directors* (NEDs), who are not so employed or intimately involved in day-to-day issues.

The members are not often closely involved in the day-to-day management of the company (unless they are also its directors), but they do exercise ultimate control over the company. They too act collectively, via the *general meeting*, usually (but not always) by majority vote. The members have the power to dismiss the directors and, often, the power to appoint them. The rights of members are essentially a matter of contract between the members and the company (agreed in the company's constitutional documents, supplemented by any subsequent agreements).

If the company has shares, the members of the company are its shareholders. These shareholders provide '*equity funding*' to the company by way of paying for their shares (and can be contrasted with the *debt funding* provided by bank loans, etc). The rights that the shareholders receive in return are set out in the terms of the share issue. Generally there are rights to *vote*, to receive *dividends* out of the company's profits while the company is a going concern (*if* the directors recommend dividends), and to share in any

---

[4] Companies may also be limited by guarantee. In a company limited by guarantee, the members do not usually pay any money to the company at the outset, but they promise (they 'guarantee') that if the company becomes insolvent, they will pay the amount specified in their guarantee to the company, for the company's use in paying off its creditors. In a company limited by shares, by contrast, the shareholders promise to provide funds to the company by way of the price paid for the share, usually paid in full at the time the share is purchased. That sum is the limit of the shareholder's obligation to contribute to the capital of the company, so if the company becomes insolvent, all the shareholder is required to pay to support the company is the amount (if any) still unpaid on the shares. See Insolvency Act 1986 (IA 1986) s 74.

surplus assets of the company (ie assets remaining after all of the company's creditors have been paid in full) when the company is *wound up*. There may be more than one *class* of shareholder, with different classes having different rights to vote or to receive particular financial benefits. All these matters are settled by agreement between the company and its shareholders.

Companies are used as vehicles for all sorts of activities. Typically, they are used for conducting business, from the small corner grocery store to the large multinational corporation. Companies are also used for running many non-profit ventures. Despite the varied size and function of companies, there are certain core features that are common to most companies. Two are of central significance: the *separate legal personality* of companies (ie a company is a separate legal person, distinct from its directors and its members), and the *limited liability* of its members.[5] Both of these features are dealt with in detail in the next chapter, but deserve a word of explanation here.

The fact that a company is a legal person in its own right is fundamental to the whole structure of company law. And yet there is no fanfare about this in the Act itself: all that CA 2006 s 7 says is that 'A company is formed under this Act by . . . [and then describes how a company is formed].' But the separate legal personality of the company ensures that *it* owns property, *it* contracts with third parties, *it* is owed duties by its directors, *it* makes constitutional commitments to its members, and so on. Crucially, this independence enables the company's business assets and liabilities (and attendant risks) to be segregated from the personal assets and liabilities of the company's members and directors. This partitioning of assets is crucial to the attractiveness of companies as commercial vehicles.

The limited liability of a company's members is related to the company's separate personality, but does not follow automatically from it (after all, it is possible to have companies whose members have *unlimited* liability (CA 2006 s 3(4))[6]). Where liability of members is limited, it is either limited 'by shares' to the price of the shares or 'by guarantee' to the commitment embodied in the guarantee.[7] What this means is that the company's liabilities to third parties can *only* be met out of the *company's* assets (including, of course, the company's receipts of the full share price and the benefit of the guarantees provided by members). The company's creditors cannot seek satisfaction from the company members personally, even if the company has insufficient funds to pay its own liabilities in full. Notice that although we typically use the shorthand expression that a company is a 'limited liability company', the *company's* liability is not in fact limited at all; only its members' liability is.[8]

Sources of company law

Registered companies can only be created because legislation permits it. That same legislation is also the primary source of the rules that govern the operation of companies. Most of the relevant provisions are now to be found within the 1,300 plus provisions and 16 Schedules of CA 2006. This Act received Royal Assent on 8 November 2006, and was

[5] Unless the company is an unlimited company (see 'Limited and unlimited companies: CA 2006 s 3', p 21).

[6] Some risky corporate ventures (eg historically, mining ventures) are set up this way to persuade outside funders of the confidence of the members in the likely success of the planned venture. But it is more usual now, in these types of cases, to set up a company limited by shares and require the shareholders (and directors) to provide unlimited personal guarantees of the company's debts. The two structures are functionally equivalent.

[7] See fn 4.

[8] For further reading, see PL Davies, *Introduction to Company Law* (2nd edn, 2010); and RH Kraakman et al (eds), *The Anatomy of Corporate Law* (2nd edn, 2009).

then slowly introduced over almost three years, from January 2007 to October 2009. In the transition phase, the relevant provisions from the predecessor Companies Acts 1985 and 1989 (CA 1985 and CA 1989) continued to govern. Now virtually every provision in CA 2006 is in force, and the Act is fully operational. It replaces CA 1985 and CA 1989, other than Parts 14 and 15 of CA 1985 (company investigations).

In addition to UK legislation in the form of the Companies Acts, companies are regulated by other statutes,[9] common law rules, European law (especially harmonisation Directives), and certain other special rules (eg the Listing Rules of the London Stock Exchange). There are also non-binding codes of best practice (eg the UK Corporate Governance Code and the UK Stewardship Code, both issued by the Financial Reporting Council) which require certain listed companies to 'comply or explain [why they have not]'; these are assuming a greater role generally, particularly in the fields of corporate governance and corporate reporting.

UK Companies Acts

CA 2006 (especially Parts 1 to 39) either restates or amends almost all of the predecessor legislation. It also codifies certain aspects of the case law, especially that relating to directors' duties. Note that CA 2006 s 2 defines 'the Companies Acts' (note the plural) to mean CA 2006 itself (but only the Parts specified in s 2(2)), and parts of other specified Acts that remain in force (s 2(1)(b) and (c)).

CA 2006 is the product of the most extensive revision of company law since 1856. It arises from a consultation carried out over seven years, from 1998 to 2005, by the Company Law Review (CLR), which was set up by the Department of Trade and Industry (DTI). That consultation was itself preceded by substantial work and two reports delivered by the Law Commissions on directors' duties and shareholder remedies.[10] (Note that the DTI no longer exists. Early in 2007 it became the Department for Business, Enterprise and Regulatory Reform (BERR), which in 2009 became the Department for Business, Innovation and Skills (BIS). Each change of name reflects a change in the functions undertaken by the department.)

The CLR produced eight substantial consultation documents, followed by a two-volume final report in 2001.[11] In response to this, in July 2002, the government published a two-volume White Paper, *Modernising Company Law* (Cm 5553), and then in March 2005, after another three years' work, a second and substantially revised White Paper, *Company Law Reform* (Cm 6456). The Company Law Reform Bill, which resulted from all this work, was introduced into the House of Lords in November 2005 and, as indicated earlier, received Royal Assent a year later in November 2006. It is reputedly the longest Bill ever considered by Parliament.

---

[9] Especially the IA 1986 and the Financial Services and Markets Act 2000 (FSMA 2000), and the company-specific Company Directors Disqualification Act 1986, but also by statutes that apply generally to 'legal persons', such as the Sale of Goods Act 1979 and various Property Law Acts.

[10] Law Commission, *Company Directors: Regulating Conflicts of Interests and Formulating a Statement of Duties* (Law Com No 261, 1999) (available at: www.lawcom.gov.uk/wp-content/uploads/2015/03/lc261_Company_Directors.pdf). This was preceded by a Consultation Paper (LCCP 153, September 1998) which is available at: www.lawcom.gov.uk/wp-content/uploads/2015/06/cp153_Company_Directors_Consulation.pdf and which usefully sets out the Commission's understanding of the current law. Also Law Commission, *Shareholder Remedies* (Law Com No 246, 1997) available at: www.lawcom.gov.uk/wp-content/uploads/2015/03/lc246_Shareholder_Remedies.pdf, and the preceding Consultation Paper (LCCP 142, 1996), available at: www.lawcom.gov.uk/wp-content/uploads/2015/03/cp142_Shareholder_Remedies_Consultation.pdf.

[11] All of these documents may be downloaded from the BIS website: http://webarchive.nationalarchives.gov.uk/20121029131934/http://www.bis.gov.uk/policies/business-law/company-and-partnership-law/company-law/publications-archive.

According to a BIS Consultation Report published in August 2010, the key policy objectives of CA 2006 include:[12]

- to enhance stakeholder engagement and a long-term investment culture (promoting wider participation, and ensuring decisions are based on a long-term view rather than immediate return);
- to ensure better regulation and a 'think small first' approach;
- to make it easier to set up and run a company.

Regulatory amendments to CA 2006

The process of major company law reform is considered later. But many provisions in CA 2006 give the Secretary of State the power to make any necessary regulations by statutory instrument. This is done, as specified, by either the *affirmative resolution procedure* (s 1290) or the *negative resolution procedure* (s 1289).

The affirmative procedure requires the proposed statutory instrument to be laid before Parliament and approved by both Houses; the negative procedure does not require this, but the regulations may be annulled by resolution of either House. The latter procedure is reserved for regulations that do not increase the burdens on the affected parties (eg regulations introducing exemptions from audit requirements), the former for cases where Parliament needs to retain greater control over the delegated amendment process.

History of legislative reform

The first Companies Act was passed in 1844. It was not concerned with the creation of companies per se: 'joint stock companies' already existed in considerable numbers, and had done so for over a century. This Act provided for the registration of the 'deed of settlement' of such companies (ie registration of their principal constitutional document). In return for registration, they were accorded corporate status (ie recognised by the law as entities in their own right). 'Joint stock' companies formed on the basis of a deed of settlement were different from the chartered corporations like the Hudson's Bay Company and the Bank of England, and different again from the statutory companies which sprang up in great numbers early in the nineteenth century to build the nation's railways and canals and docks.[13] They were outsized, unincorporated partnerships, running sometimes into hundreds of members, carefully set up by the skills of clever equity draftsmen so that large-scale ventures could be organised on the basis of a common fund or 'joint stock' pooled by the participants, and run by directors and managers for the benefit of all concerned. By 1844, they were too important to be ignored or outlawed and too unwieldy to fit at all easily into normal legal procedures such as litigation. The 1844 Act was the first step in giving these companies legal recognition.

A decade later, in 1855, a further Act was passed which allowed the shareholders who invested in a company to limit their liability; and a year after that a revised statute, the Joint Stock Companies Act 1856, established the framework for the modern-style company, incorporated by the process of registration and enjoying limited liability. The old 'deed of settlement' gave way to the 'memorandum and articles of association', which in the 2006 Act gave way to a simple one-document constitution, the 'articles'.

There have not been any paradigm shifts in either the institution of 'the company' or in the legislation dealing with it from 1856 to the present day. That also includes the 2006 Act: for all its welcome changes, it does not fundamentally alter the structure of

---

[12] www.gov.uk/government/publications/companies-act-2006-executive-summary-of-evaluation-report.

[13] The Companies Clauses Consolidation Act 1845, which is still in force, applies to these 'statutory' companies. This Act contains standard provisions which may be incorporated by reference into the particular Act, so making the procedure shorter and cheaper.

the subject. Of course, Parliament has been busy in company affairs from time to time, passing, amending and consolidating Acts, each bigger than the last one. Until the recent review (noted earlier), the last fundamental reassessment of the subject took place at the time of the Crimean War.

CA 1985 and CA 1989 are the immediate predecessors of CA 2006. Parts of these Acts remained in force during the transition to full operation of CA 2006; indeed, some minor parts which were not re-enacted in CA 2006 are still operational.[14] The 1985 statute was the result of parliamentary efforts to make a fresh start by consolidating all the company-related statutory provisions that were then operative into one major Act, the Companies Act 1985, and three minor ones, the Company Securities (Insider Dealing) Act 1985,[15] the Company Directors Disqualification Act 1986 (CDDA 1986) and the Companies Consolidation (Consequential Provisions) Act 1985.

But this tidying up exercise achieved very little. CA 1985 (747 sections and 25 Schedules) did not survive intact for long. In the same year it was enacted, the Insolvency Act 1985 (now almost entirely repealed and replaced by the Insolvency Act 1986) superseded nearly a third of it with sweeping new provisions. Further changes were made by the Financial Services Act 1986 (itself now superseded by the Financial Services and Markets Act 2000), and by CA 1989 (again, a substantial piece of legislation containing 216 sections and 24 Schedules).

It is an unhappy fact that the volume of companies legislation almost quadrupled in the course of the 1980s. And the process continues. Even in the lead up to the reforms embodied in CA 2006, there was a steady flow of new measures. These included some reforms of considerable importance, such as the provisions which authorise the formation of single member companies ('Classifications based on size', p 23) and those which have introduced a new regime to regulate the issue of prospectuses inviting the public to invest in a company's shares ('Prospectuses', p 764).

This complexity creates its own risks. When the law is embodied in a number of different statutes, and especially when those statutes are long and complicated, there is a risk that parties will not be aware of the relevant rules. For example, in *British Racing Drivers' Club Ltd v Hextall Erskine and Co* [1996] 3 All ER 667 (Ch), over £2.8 million was awarded in damages against an experienced commercial lawyer who wrongly advised that it was not necessary for a company to obtain the approval of its members for a substantial property transaction (now see CA 2006 s 190 at 'Transactions with directors requiring the approval of members', p 464). And in *Brady v Brady* **[10.08]**, the lawyers did not appreciate which statutory provision was relevant to the case until it reached the House of Lords.

The Company Law Review (CLR)

In March 1998, the DTI commissioned a fundamental review of company law. An independent Steering Group led the CLR. Its terms of reference required it to consider how core company law could be modernised in order to provide a simple, efficient and cost-effective framework for British business in the twenty-first century.

The CLR presented its Final Report to the Secretary of State for Trade and Industry on 26 July 2001. This report contained a range of recommendations for substantive changes to many areas of company law, and a set of principles to guide the development of the law more generally. Most notably it proposed that the law should be as simple and as accessible as possible for smaller firms and their advisers and should avoid imposing unnecessary burdens on the ways companies operate (ie 'think small first'). See 'The process of company law reform', p 18. Many, but not all, of the provisions of CA 2006 implement CLR recommendations.

---

[14] Eg on company investigations, see Chapter 14.
[15] Since repealed and replaced by the Criminal Justice Act 1993 Pt V.

The most important documents produced as a result of the CLR law reform process are:

(i)   White Paper, *Company Law Reform* (Cm 6456, March 2005);

(ii) White Paper, *Modernising Company Law* (Cm 5553-I and Cm 5553-II, July 2002);

(iii) DTI, *Modern Company Law for a Competitive Economy: Final Report* (URN 01/942 and 01/943, 2001).

These, and all the other consultation papers, are available on the BIS website.[16]

Case law

In all these years of reform, no Companies Act has ever been a complete code. Much of company law goes back to the days of the deed of settlement companies and the chartered and statutory corporations which flourished in earlier centuries. A great deal of the essence and spirit of the present company law is derived from this old case law rather than from anything in the Companies Acts themselves. Indeed, these Acts always assumed the existence of companies, and took for granted matters of everyday practice in company affairs, and the body of judicial precedent that has grown up over the years. The influence of these background factors has been remarkably persistent, even, sometimes, on matters where business circumstances today are quite different.

In addition to the principles of common law and equity that have evolved independently of statute (eg on directors' duties, although that has now been codified in CA 2006), there are of course many other rulings of the courts based on the Companies Acts themselves. These are sometimes on the literal wording of particular sections and sometimes on the broader interpretations of the general institutional framework that is established by the Acts (eg the 'maintenance of capital' rules ('Dividend distributions', pp 565ff)). In addition, there are decisions concerned with the interpretation of documents such as the company's constitutional documents or shareholders' resolutions of individual companies. Many of these are of a common or standard type (eg provisions in articles defining the functions of the board of directors, or the terms on which preference shares are issued) and so have significance for company law generally as well as for the parties in the case in question.

In some areas, practice is almost as important as the law itself. A student of English company law who did not know something of 'the City' and those bodies which have traditionally been self-regulating, such as the Stock Exchange, would gain only an imperfect impression of such matters as public issues of shares and takeover bids. It is true that the financial services legislation of 1986 and its successors have slowly put much of this regulation on a full statutory basis, but the older rules and practices of these various bodies remain instructive.

European law

There are many ways in which the UK's membership of the EU influences its company law. The objectives of the Treaty of Rome (now renamed as the Treaty on the Functioning of the European Union, under the Treaty of Lisbon) include the facilitating of trade and

---

[16] The DTI's Review (Modern Company Law for a Competitive Economy): published Consultation Documents: No 1 (February 1999): *The Strategic Framework* (URN 99/654)

No 2 (October 1999): *Company General Meetings and Shareholder Communication* (URN 99/1144)

No 3 (October 1999): *Company Formation and Capital Maintenance* (URN 99/1145)

No 4 (October 1999): *Reforming the Law Concerning Overseas Companies* (URN 99/1146)

No 5 (March 2000): *Developing the Framework* (URN 00/656)

No 6 (June 2000): *Capital Maintenance—Other Issues* (URN 00/880)

No 7 (October 2000): *Registration of Company Charges* (URN 00/1213)

No 8 (November 2000): *Completing the Structure* (URN 00/1335). See fn 11.

the removal of barriers to people's freedom to establish their businesses and invest their capital on a basis of equality throughout the EU. To this end, a programme for the 'harmonisation' of the domestic company laws of the member states was instituted. It seeks to remove the differences of detail between those local laws which might act as impediments to such equality. The Treaty expressly authorises and empowers its organs to issue 'Directives' for this purpose.

These harmonisation Directives are referred to as the 'First Directive', 'Second Directive', and so on, in the order in which they were proposed by the Commission and then jointly approved by the Council and the European Parliament following Art 251 of the EC Treaty. Of the 13 proposals so far, the fifth and tenth have not yet been adopted, and the ninth has been withdrawn. In addition to these 13 company-specific Directives, there are of course other EU Directives which impact on company law issues.[17]

Directives

In principle, a Directive is binding only on the member state, which must implement it by its own legislation;[18] it does not immediately or directly affect individual companies or citizens as a 'source' of law. However, a number of rulings given by both the European Court and English courts have made inroads into this principle. In the first place, if a Directive has been implemented by domestic legislation, recourse may be had to the text of the Directive as an aid to resolve questions of statutory interpretation in relation to that legislation. This will normally require the court to give a 'purposive' rather than a restrictive construction to the statute or regulations in question, in keeping with the usual approach of the European Court (*Litster v Forth Dry Dock and Engineering Co Ltd* [1990] 1 AC 546, HL).

Even where the local legislation does not itself implement a Directive, but merely covers similar ground, the European Court has ruled that it must be interpreted in the light of the wording and purpose of the Directive (*Marleasing SA v La Comercial Internacional de Alimentación SA* **[1.01]**), although not where this would distort the natural meaning of the legislation (*Duke v GEC Reliance Ltd* [1988] AC 618, HL).

And if a member state has implemented a Directive, or has failed to do so within the time limit fixed for implementation, the terms of the Directive may be relied on as against the member state itself or a government agency or public body. Thus, in *Karella v Ministry of Industry, Energy and Technology* **[1.02]**, it was held that an individual could invoke the Second EU Company Law Directive for the purpose of having legislation of the Greek Parliament declared unlawful.

By and large, the object of a Directive is to set *minimum* standards: there is ordinarily nothing to stop a member state from enacting legislation which goes further than the Directive prescribes. Thus, most of the provisions of the Second Company Law Directive are made to apply only to public companies, but under the UK legislation many of them were made to apply to private companies as well. And in *Siemens AG v Nold* [1997] 1 BCLC 291, the Court of Justice of the European Union held that it was in order for German law to give shareholders greater protection than was required by the Directive when a company makes an issue of new shares. Even when a Directive or proposed Directive is only in a draft stage, it may be important to know about it, since it may indicate the lines along which tomorrow's law is likely to develop.

---

[17] See the European Commission's Justice website on company law and corporate governance: http://ec.europa.eu/justice/civil/company-law/index_en.htm.

[18] A range of SIs continue the technical implementation of Regulations and Directives.

Regulations

EU law may also be made by Regulations. A Regulation, in contrast to a Directive, has direct effect as part of the domestic law of each member state, although local legislation may be necessary to supplement a Regulation by, for instance, providing administrative facilities.

A Directive does not have direct effect so as to impose obligations on an individual. Domestic legislation of a member state must be interpreted so far as possible in the light of the wording and purpose of any relevant Directive.

[1.01] Marleasing SA v La Comercial Internacional de Alimentación SA (1990) C-106/89, [1992] 1 CMLR 305 (Court of Justice of the European Union)

Marleasing sued a number of companies, including La Comercial. It alleged, inter alia, that the formation of La Comercial was void because it had been formed for the purpose of defrauding the creditors of one of its founding shareholders. The Court ruled that even though this might have been a ground for declaring that a company's incorporation was a nullity under Spanish domestic law (because the civil code provided that contracts for unlawful purposes had no legal effect), it was not consistent with Art 11 of the First EU Company Law Directive, so that the defence could not be relied on.

The Court delivered the following judgment:

> . . . [T]he national court referred the following question to the Court:
>
> Is Article 11 of Council Directive 68/151/EEC of 9 March 1968, which has not been implemented in national law, directly applicable so as to preclude a declaration of nullity of a public limited company on a ground other than those set out in the said Article? . . .
>
> With regard to the question whether an individual may rely on the directive against a national law, it should be observed that, as the Court has consistently held, a directive may not of itself impose obligations on an individual and, consequently, a provision of a directive may not be relied upon as such against such a person (judgment in Case 152/84, *Marshall v Southampton and South-West Hampshire Area Health Authority.*[19])
>
> However, it is apparent from the documents before the Court that the national court seeks in substance to ascertain whether a national court hearing a case which falls within the scope of Directive 68/151 is required to interpret its national law in the light of the wording and the purpose of that directive in order to preclude a declaration of nullity of a public limited company on a ground other than those listed in Article 11 of the directive.
>
> In order to reply to that question, it should be observed that, as the Court pointed out in its judgement in Case 14/83, *Von Colson and Kamann v Land Nordrhein-Westfalen,*[20] the Member States' obligation arising from a directive to achieve the result envisaged by the directive and their duty under Article 5 of the Treaty to take all appropriate measures, whether general or particular, to ensure the fulfilment of that obligation, is binding on all the authorities of Member States including, for matters within their jurisdiction, the courts. It follows that, in applying national law, whether the provisions in question were adopted before or after the directive, the national court called upon to interpret it is required to do so, as far as possible, in the light of the wording and the purpose of the directive in order to achieve the result pursued by the latter and thereby comply with the third paragraph of Article 189 of the Treaty.

[19] [1986] ECR 723, [1986] 1 CMLR 688.
[20] [1984] ECR 1891, [1986] 2 CMLR 430 at [26].

> It follows that the requirement that national law must be interpreted in conformity with Article 11 of Directive 68/151 precludes the interpretation of provisions of national law relating to public limited companies in such a manner that the nullity of a public limited company may be ordered on grounds other than those exhaustively listed in Article 11 of the directive in question....
>
> [Those grounds include] the ground that the objects of the company are unlawful or contrary to public policy.
>
> According to the Commission, the expression 'objects of the company' must be interpreted as referring exclusively to the objects of the company as described in the instrument of incorporation or the articles of association. It follows, in the Commission's view, that a declaration of nullity of a company cannot be made on the basis of the activity actually pursued by it, for instance defrauding the founder's creditors....

> ➤ Note

It will be seen that Art 11 of the Directive allows a judicial declaration of nullity to be made on the ground that a company's objects are unlawful or contrary to public policy. When the UK implemented this Directive by domestic legislation, no steps were taken to include any provision based on Art 11, for the reasons given at Note 1 following *HA Stephenson & Son Ltd v Gillanders, Arbuthnot & Co* [1.08], p 31. But, as the case of *R v Registrar of Companies, ex p AG* [1.09] shows, such a declaration is not unknown in the UK.

A Directive may be invoked by an individual directly against a member state or government agency.

[1.02] Karella v Ministry of Industry, Energy and Technology [1991] ECR I-2691, [1993] 2 CMLR 865 (Court of Justice of the European Union)

Legislation enacted by the Greek Parliament (Law No 1386/1983) empowered a governmental authority called the Business Reconstruction Organisation (OAE) to take over control of a company and to increase the capital of such a company by administrative decision. The OAE took control of a company called Klostiria Velka AE and decided to increase its capital from Dr 220 million to Dr 400 million. Two shareholders successfully argued that this was contrary to the Second EU Company Law Directive Art 25(1), which requires an increase of capital, except in limited circumstances, to be effected by a resolution of the shareholders.

The Court delivered the following judgment:

> The national court's questions essentially raise two issues. The first is concerned with Article 25(1) of the Second Directive. The national court wishes to establish whether, having regard to Article 41(1) of the Second Directive, Article 25(1) may be relied upon against the administration by individuals in the national courts. It then asks whether Article 25(1), in conjunction with Article 21(1), is applicable with regard to public rules, such as those provided for in Law No 1386/1983, which govern the completely exceptional cases of undertakings which are of particular economic and social importance for society and are undergoing serious financial difficulties.
>
> The second issue is concerned with Article 42 of the Second Directive. The national court asks whether that provision may be relied upon by individuals and whether it has to be interpreted as precluding national rules of the type referred to above . . .
>
> *The direct effect of Article 25(1) of the Second Directive*
>
> As the Court has consistently held, wherever the provisions of a directive appear, as far as their subject matter is concerned, to be unconditional and sufficiently precise, individuals are entitled

to invoke them against the State (see, in particular, the judgment in Case 8/81 *Becker v Finanzamt Muenster-Innenstadt* [1982] ECR 53).

Consequently, it should be examined whether Article 25(1) of the Second Directive, which provides that any increase in capital must be decided upon by the general meeting, satisfies those conditions.

It must be held in that connection that that provision is clearly and precisely worded and lays down, unconditionally, a rule enshrining the general principle that the general meeting has the power to decide upon increases in capital.

The unconditional nature of that provision is not affected by the derogation provided for in Article 25(2) of the Second Directive to the effect that the company's instrument of incorporation or the general meeting may authorise an increase in the subscribed capital up to a maximum amount which is to be fixed with due regard for any maximum amount provided for by law. That individual, clearly defined derogation does not leave Member States any possibility of making the principle of the power of the general meeting subject to any exceptions other than that for which express provision is made. . . .

It is appropriate therefore to answer the national court by stating that Article 25(1) of the Second Directive may be relied upon by individuals against the public authorities before national courts.

The scope of Article 25(1) of the Second Directive

As for the scope of Article 25(1) of the Second Directive with respect to a law, such as Law No 1386/1983, it should be examined in the first place whether such a law falls within the field of application of the directive, since that legislation does not set out the basic rules on increases of capital and merely seeks to deal with exceptional situations. If that legislation falls within the field of application of the Second Directive, it should then be considered whether it can qualify for the benefit of the derogation provided for in Article 41(1) of that directive.

As far as the field of application of the Second Directive is concerned, it should be stated first of all that, in accordance with Article 54(3)(g) of the Treaty, it seeks to coordinate the safeguards which, for the protection of the interests of members and others, are required by Member States of companies and firms within the meaning of the second paragraph of Article 58 of the Treaty with a view to making such safeguards equivalent. Consequently, the aim of the Second Directive is to provide a minimum level of protection for shareholders in all the Member States.

That objective would be seriously frustrated if the Member States were entitled to derogate from the provisions of the directive by maintaining in force rules—even rules categorised as special or exceptional—under which it is possible to decide by administrative measure, outside any decision by the general meeting of shareholders, to effect an increase in the company's capital which would have the effect either of obliging the original shareholders to increase their contributions to the capital or of imposing on them the addition of new shareholders, thus reducing their involvement in the decision-taking power of the company.

However, that observation does not signify that Community law prevents Member States from derogating from those provisions in any circumstances. The Community legislature has made specific provision for well-defined derogations and for procedures which may result in such derogations with the aim of safeguarding certain vital interests of the Member States which are liable to be affected in exceptional situations. Instances of this are Articles 19(2) and (3), Article 40(2), Article 41(2) and Article 43(2) of the directive.

In this connection, it must be held that no derogating provision which would allow the Member States to derogate from Article 25(1) of the directive in crisis situations is provided for either in the EEC Treaty or in the Second Directive itself . . .

It follows that, in the absence of a derogation provided for by Community law, Article 25(1) of the Second Directive must be interpreted as precluding the Member States from maintaining in force rules incompatible with the principle set forth in that article, even if those rules cover only exceptional situations . . .

➤ Note

Despite the extensive programme for the harmonisation of companies legislation within the EU, some quite fundamental differences remain—and in many cases are likely to continue. See 'The market for corporate law: country of incorporation, "seat" and "COMI"', p 13 on the different means of determining 'home' for a company. What is more, these are often differences in the commercial practice or 'culture' as between one country and another, which are likely to survive any kind of legislative reform. For instance, in some jurisdictions such as the UK, a relatively high proportion of the shares in the larger companies are held by members of the public and institutional investors (eg pension funds) and are actively traded on the Stock Exchange; in others, there is extensive use of shares in 'bearer' form which can be transferred from one owner to another by simply handing over the relevant share certificate; and in yet others, major shareholdings in the leading companies are held by banks, either in their own right or as nominees for the real owners. It is very difficult to frame a single set of rules which will take account of these variations in practice. For example, it is only in a jurisdiction like the UK where there is an extensive market for shares that a 'takeover bid' can be made to work effectively; in other countries, the different patterns of shareholding (and differences in accounting practice, etc) create 'barriers' to takeovers which are every bit as insurmountable as a prohibition imposed by statute would be.

European Directives and Regulations relating to company law

The Directives that have already been implemented by the European Parliament and Council cover a wide range of company law matters, although noticeably only those where member states have a vested self-interest in harmonisation. These include Directives on formation of single member private limited liability companies, formation of public limited liability companies and the maintenance and alteration of their capital, requirements for annual accounts and consolidated accounts, prospectus requirements, cross-border mergers of limited liability companies, transparency and disclosure Directives, a takeovers Directive, a market abuse Directive and a shareholder rights Directive. Once agreed, lobbying for further changes commonly continues: for instance, there are current proposals to amend the existing Shareholder Rights Directive (Directive 2007/36/EC) so as to improve the corporate governance, competitiveness and long-term sustainability of companies.[21]

Other Directives never proceeded past the proposal stage. For example, a *Fifth Directive* has never been adopted, largely because of opposition from the UK. It would have required all companies with a workforce above a certain size to institute a system of employee participation in management decisions, and would have included provisions governing directors' duties and the function of auditors. Similarly, a draft *Ninth Directive* would have introduced rules governing the conduct of corporate groups, including intra-group liabilities on insolvency. Like many other Directives, it was based on a German model, but this has not worked well even in Germany itself, and so the Directive has now been formally withdrawn.

There are noticeably fewer Regulations. Two merit special comment, since they allow for different formal company structures. Regulation (EC) 2137/85 permits the establishment of *European Economic Interest Groupings* (EEIGs),[22] intended to be used for non-profit-making cross-border ventures for purposes such as joint research and development.

Regulation (EC) 2157/2001[23] (supplemented by Directive 2001/86/EC on the involvement of employees) provides a Statute for a European Company that enables the formation of

---

[21] http://ec.europa.eu/internal_market/company/shareholders/indexa_en.htm.

[22] Supplemented by the EEIG Regulations (SI 1989/638), which set out in Sch 1 the full text of the EU Regulation, as amended by the European Economic Interest Grouping and European Public Limited-Liability Company (Amendment) Regulations 2014 (SI 2014/2382).

[23] For a recent report published as part of a review process on the functioning of the SEs by the European Commission: http://eur-lex.europa.eu/LexUriServ/LexUriServ.do?uri=COM:2010:0676:FIN:EN:PDF.

supranational companies governed in important respects by EU rather than local law. This proposal was stalled for over 30 years, partly because some of its provisions (eg as regards worker participation) were met by the same self-interested objections that had stood in the way of adoption of the Directives mentioned earlier. Eventually political agreement on an amended text was reached. A company operating in more than one EU country can now incorporate as a *'European Company'* (SE or *'Societas Europaea'*), rather than a company formed under the law of an individual member state, so avoiding the need to establish subsidiaries under all the different national laws. Many details, however, from the mechanics of registration to the rules of insolvency, are delegated to the law of the member state where the company has its main base, rather than administered from Brussels and governed by provisions of EU law. [24] In that sense, the Regulation is less ambitious than originally intended. And the vexed question of the involvement of employees is dealt with in a separate Directive.

In the area of insolvency law, Regulation (EC) 1346/2000 establishes common rules to deal with cross-border insolvency proceedings.[25] See 'The market for corporate law: country of incorporation, "seat" and "COMI"', p 13.

Finally, various Recommendations have been advanced. The Company Law Slim Working Group made Recommendations on the simplification of the First and Second Directives; the Commission has made Recommendations on statutory audit (2001/256/EC and 2002/590/EC) and on the recognition, measurement and disclosure of environmental issues in the annual accounts and annual reports of companies. More recently, there has been a Recommendation on the quality of corporate governance reporting ('comply or explain') (2014/208/EU).[26]

European law harmonisation

The EU company law harmonisation programme has attracted criticism because many of its measures have been seen as too prescriptive and regulatory in their approach, and too detailed in form, leading to widespread proliferation of rules and increases in compliance costs. This may have been true, but recent moves aim to reduce the burden, particularly for small and medium enterprises (SMEs), by (for instance) relaxing the accounting requirements and, for some, removing altogether the obligation to have accounts audited.

Of course, what for one person may be an additional constraint may for another be a positive benefit: the standardisation of accounting formats may seem tiresome for those who have to comply but makes the reading easier for those relying on the accounts; and the general tightening up of the rules governing entry to the financial services markets has led not only to a 'level playing field', but more importantly to the opening up of these markets to users based anywhere in the EU—a development from which UK firms probably have stood to gain more than those of any other country.

The market for corporate law: country of incorporation, 'seat' and 'COMI'

In all this talk of European harmonisation, it is important to note that there are also legal rules in particular jurisdictions which may be regarded as inviolate. One such rule divides the EU member states into two groups: those which take the country of incorporation as the state whose law is, for most purposes, the governing law, and those which consider that this should be determined by the country where the company's main establishment

---

[24] See, eg, the guidance issued by the UK Companies House on the European Company in November 2014: www.gov.uk/government/uploads/system/uploads/attachment_data/file/395911/se-gpo6.pdf.

[25] As amended by Regulation 2015/848 of 20 May 2015. Also see *Re Arm Asset Backed Securities SA* [2013] EWHC 3351 (Ch), in which David Richards J left open the possibility that the Regulation be applied in proceedings not based on the insolvency of the company: [23]–[26].

[26] http://eur-lex.europa.eu/legal-content/EN/TXT/?uri=CELEX%3A32014H0208. See Chapter 5.

or 'seat' (*Sitz* or *siège réel*) is located. The UK and Ireland are typical of the former; France and Germany of the latter, and it can fairly be said that 'never the twain shall meet'. So, a company cannot be incorporated in France if its main business is to be based in another country, and if a French-registered company were to move its main activities abroad then under French law it would have to be wound up. But a company incorporated in the UK can have its centre of business anywhere.

This dichotomy seems to be far too firmly entrenched to make radical change at all likely. Even so, the following case shows that there may be rather more freedom of choice than might have been expected.

The country of incorporation.

[1.03] Centros Ltd v Erhvervs-og Selskabsstryrelsen (1999) C-212/97, [1999] 2 CMLR 551, [2000] Ch 446 (Court of Justice of the European Union)

Danish law requires that all companies should be formed with a prescribed minimum capital and that a substantial sum should be paid up on that capital prior to incorporation. Mr and Mrs Bryde, Danish citizens, formed a company in England with a nominal capital of £100 on which nothing was ever paid up. It never traded in the UK. They then sought to register a branch of this company in Denmark but the Danish authority (referred to in the report as 'the Board') refused, on the ground that this was a way of avoiding the Danish rules as to capital. The court held that the authority's refusal to register the branch was an obstacle to the freedom of establishment conferred by Arts 52 and 58 of the Treaty of Rome.

The Court delivered the following judgment:

> As a preliminary point, it should be made clear that the Board does not in any way deny that a joint stock or private limited company with its registered office in another Member State may carry on business in Denmark through a branch. It therefore agrees, as a general rule, to register in Denmark a branch of a company formed in accordance with the law of another Member State. In particular, it has added that, if Centros had conducted any business in England and Wales, the Board would have agreed to register its branch in Denmark.
>
> According to the Danish Government, Article 52 of the Treaty is not applicable in the case in the main proceedings, since the situation is purely internal to Denmark. Mr and Mrs Bryde, Danish nationals, have formed a company in the United Kingdom which does not carry on any actual business there, with the sole purpose of carrying on business in Denmark through a branch and thus of avoiding application of Danish legislation on the formation of private limited companies. It considers that in such circumstances the formation by nationals of one Member State of a company in another Member State does not amount to a relevant external element in the light of Community law and, in particular, freedom of establishment.
>
> In this respect, it should be noted that a situation in which a company formed in accordance with the law of a Member State in which it has its registered office desires to set up a branch in another Member State falls within the scope of Community law. In that regard, it is immaterial that the company was formed in the first Member State only for the purpose of establishing itself in the second, where its main, or indeed entire, business is to be conducted.
>
> That Mr and Mrs Bryde formed the company Centros in the United Kingdom for the purpose of avoiding Danish legislation requiring that a minimum amount of share capital be paid up has not been denied either in the written observations or at the hearing. That does not, however, mean that the formation by that British company of a branch in Denmark is not covered by freedom of establishment for the purposes of Articles 52 and 58 of the Treaty. The question of the application of those articles of the Treaty is different from the question whether or not a Member State may adopt

measures in order to prevent attempts by certain of its nationals to evade domestic legislation by having recourse to the possibilities offered by the Treaty.

As to the question whether, as Mr and Mrs Bryde claim, the refusal to register in Denmark a branch of their company formed in accordance with the law of another Member State in which it has its registered office constitutes an obstacle to freedom of establishment, it must be borne in mind that that freedom, conferred by Article 52 of the Treaty on Community nationals, includes the right for them to take up and pursue activities as self-employed persons and to set up and manage undertakings under the same conditions as are laid down by the law of the Member State of establishment for its own nationals. Furthermore, under Article 58 of the Treaty companies or firms formed in accordance with the law of a Member State and having their registered office, central administration or principal place of business within the Community are to be treated in the same way as natural persons who are nationals of Member States.

The immediate consequence of this is that those companies are entitled to carry on their business in another Member State through an agency, branch or subsidiary. The location of their registered office, central administration or principal place of business serves as the connecting factor with the legal system of a particular State in the same way as does nationality in the case of a natural person.

Where it is the practice of a Member State, in certain circumstances, to refuse to register a branch of a company having its registered office in another Member State, the result is that companies formed in accordance with the law of that other Member State are prevented from exercising the freedom of establishment conferred on them by Articles 52 and 58 of the Treaty.

Consequently, that practice constitutes an obstacle to the exercise of the freedoms guaranteed by those provisions.

According to the Danish authorities, however, Mr and Mrs Bryde cannot rely on those provisions, since the sole purpose of the company formation which they have in mind is to circumvent the application of the national law governing formation of private limited companies and therefore constitutes abuse of the freedom of establishment. In their submission, the Kingdom of Denmark is therefore entitled to take steps to prevent such abuse by refusing to register the branch.

It is true that according to the case law of the Court a Member State is entitled to take measures designed to prevent certain of its nationals from attempting, under cover of the rights created by the Treaty, improperly to circumvent their national legislation or to prevent individuals from improperly or fraudulently taking advantage of provisions of Community law.

However, although, in such circumstances, the national courts may, case by case, take account—on the basis of objective evidence—of abuse or fraudulent conduct on the part of the persons concerned in order, where appropriate, to deny them the benefit of the provisions of Community law on which they seek to rely, they must nevertheless assess such conduct in the light of the objectives pursued by those provisions.

In the present case, the provisions of national law, application of which the parties concerned have sought to avoid, are rules governing the formation of companies and not rules concerning the carrying on of certain trades, professions or businesses. The provisions of the Treaty on freedom of establishment are intended specifically to enable companies formed in accordance with the law of a Member State and having their registered office, central administration or principal place of business within the Community to pursue activities in other Member States through an agency, branch or subsidiary.

That being so, the fact that a national of a Member State who wishes to set up a company chooses to form it in the Member State whose rules of company law seem to him the least restrictive and to set up branches in other Member States cannot, in itself, constitute an abuse of the right of establishment. The right to form a company in accordance with the law of a Member State and to set up branches in other Member States is inherent in the exercise, in a single market, of the freedom of establishment guaranteed by the Treaty . . .

The other concept of 'place of business' which is increasingly important, if only on the insolvency of a company, is 'centre of main interest' (COMI). This is a term which describes the jurisdiction with which a company (or a person) is most closely associated for the purposes of cross-border insolvency proceedings. It is used in both the EC Regulation on Insolvency Proceedings (Insolvency Regulation) (1346/2000 ([2000] OJ L160/1)) and the UNCITRAL Model Law on Cross-Border Insolvency (Model Law), although it is not defined in either. The former uses the concept of COMI to determine which member state of the EU (other than Denmark) takes precedence if competing company insolvency procedures are commenced in different member states. The latter uses the concept to determine the degree to which the courts of one jurisdiction are obliged to recognise and assist insolvency proceedings commenced in a different jurisdiction.

COMI is thus an EU concept, not a feature of national law. It *must* therefore be given a consistent EU-wide interpretation: *Interedil Srl v Fallimento Interedil Srl* (Case C-396/09) [2012] BCC 851. The fact that this measure is embodied in a Regulation with direct applicability and effect, as opposed to a Directive, helps to promote consistency of application.

Although COMI is not defined in the Insolvency Regulation or the Model Law, the preamble to the EC Insolvency Regulation states that it should correspond to the place where the debtor conducts the administration of his interests on a regular basis and is therefore ascertainable by third parties (para 13, Preamble). In both the Insolvency Regulation and the Model Law, there is a rebuttable presumption that a corporate debtor's COMI is the location of the company's registered office (Art 3, Insolvency Regulation and Art 16(3), Model Law). But, at least in the Insolvency Regulation, that is a weak presumption, regularly displaced in practice.

The leading case on identifying COMI is still *Eurofood IFSC Ltd* (Case C-341/04) [2006] ECR I-3813, [2006] BCC 397 (as endorsed by the Court of Justice in *Rastelli Davide e C Snc v Jean-Charles Hidoux* [2011] EUECJ C-191/10). Here the European Court of Justice indicated that the presumption that a company has its COMI in the member state where it is registered is not rebutted simply because it is a subsidiary subject to a degree of economic control from a parent located in another member state. All factors need to be considered, in particular where its presence is *objectively* ascertainable to creditors.

More significantly, COMI need not be static. And, indeed, a deliberate change of COMI may reflect a concerted attempt to forum shop, typically to relocate to the UK at the eleventh hour to take advantage of the UK's more debtor-friendly insolvency rules. See, for example, *Shierson v Vlieland-Boddy* [2005] EWCA Civ 974, [2005] BCC 949. This has been sufficiently lucrative to national professional practices, that overseas jurisdictions have moved to amend their own insolvency laws to align better with UK practices. In this field, as in many others, however, the legislation does not deal effectively with corporate groups, and that remains an area of significant controversy: see, for example, *Eurofood* (in the previous paragraph); *Re Daisytek-ISA Ltd* [2003] BCC 562.

There is also the comity mechanism located in Insolvency Act 1986 s 426 which is available to the courts in a number of scheduled jurisdictions with an English common law heritage. *Re Integrated Medical Solutions Ltd* [2012] BCC 215 examines the interrelationship between the IA 1986 and the Insolvency Regulation, and applied the former in the light of the latter. Indeed, the Insolvency Regulation has become even more important given the Supreme Court's recent retrenchment of the common law position: *Rubin v Eurofinance SA* [2012] UKSC 46, [2012] 3 WLR 1019, which, perhaps unexpectedly, disapproved of *Cambridge Gas Transport Corp v Official Committee of Unsecured Creditors of Navigator Holdings plc* [2006] UKPC 26, [2007] 1 AC 508.

Human rights legislation

The UK has been a signatory to the European Convention on Human Rights from as long ago as 1950, but the principles of the Convention were not incorporated into its domestic law until the enactment of the Human Rights Act 1998. Until this Act came into force, very few cases which had implications for company law were taken to the European Court of Human Rights in Strasbourg—one notable exception being *Saunders v UK* (1996) 23 EHRR 313.[27]

However, there is now a far greater awareness of these principles and their effect. See, for example, amendments made to the law which now restrict the use of self-incriminating statements made under compulsion in a later prosecution, and changes to the City Code on Takeovers and Mergers.

Applying human rights legislation to companies.

[1.04] Exmoor Coast Boat Cruises Ltd v Revenue and Customs Commissioners [2014] UKFTT 1103 (First-tier Tribunal (Tax Chamber))

This case held, that, on the facts, a company did not qualify for relief from being required to file its VAT form online (under the exemption in the Value Added Tax Regulations 1995 reg 25A) because even if its director's beliefs were accepted as those of the company, the director was not a practising member of a religious society or order whose beliefs were incompatible with the use of electronic communications. The reasoning merits consideration.

JUDGE BARBARA MOSEDALE:

71. My conclusion from *Pine Valley* [*Pine Valley Developments Ltd* [1991] ECHR 12742/87] is that a company has human rights if and to the extent it is the alter ego of a person (or, potentially, a group of people). Therefore, it must be seen as being in the shoes of that person and must possess the same human rights because any other decision would deny that person his human rights.

72. Therefore, while it is ludicrous to suggest a company has a religion, or private life or family, nevertheless a company which is the alter ego of a person can be a victim of a breach of A9 (the right to manifest its religion) if, were it not so protected, that person's human rights would be breached.

73. HMRC say that this is not right: the remedy is for that person to take an action in their own name claiming that the treatment of his company is a breach of his personal human rights. But it is also HMRC's position that the owner of the company would not have the right ('*locus standi*') to bring an action in the Tribunal against the notice to file online served on the company. In HMRC's view, all Mr Oxenham could do would be to make a complaint direct to the European Court of Human Rights.

74. HMRC's position is unappealing: the Convention itself provides that in the determination of his civil rights a person is entitled to a fair and public hearing within a reasonable time. HMRC's position would deny him any national remedy at all for this alleged breach of his human rights. Further, if HMRC were right it would means the Convention itself discriminates between a person who trades in their own name and a person who trades via a company. Yet, it is clear from *Pine Valley* that the Court cannot see a good reason to make such a distinction. I do not think the Convention does make such a distinction. Mr Oxenham's rights are the appellant company's rights and can be relied on by the appellant in this Tribunal.

Self-regulation

Finally, mention should be made of various initiatives taken independently of government which have led to reforms of a self-regulatory nature, some of them of considerable significance. The City Code on Takeovers and Mergers used to be the most notable of these, although now this work has been put on a statutory basis. Before these changes, however,

---

[27] See 'Inspections and subsequent fair trials—criminal and civil cases', p 777.

the Code, and the Panel on Takeovers and Mergers which administered it, which had been set up by the Bank of England and representatives of various professional and financial bodies without the backing of legislation, had discharged the important public function of regulating the conduct of takeovers for several decades.

Now the most important self-regulatory regime is found in the UK Corporate Governance Code. This is a statement of principles of good governance and a code of best practice, appended to the listing rules of the Stock Exchange. It must be adhered to by all listed companies on a 'comply or explain' basis (see Chapter 5). The Code is regularly reviewed and updated. The current version was issued in September 2014 by the Financial Reporting Council (FRC), the UK's independent regulator responsible for promoting confidence in corporate reporting and governance. It revises previous versions, which themselves can be traced back to a 1998 version prepared by the Committee on Corporate Governance chaired by Sir Ronald Hampel, which in turn built on the 1992 work of the Cadbury Committee and others. Again, this Code operates without legislative backing. This 'comply or explain' model is becoming more widely used. See too the UK Stewardship Code, also issued by the Financial Reporting Council (see Chapter 5).

The process of company law reform

Company law, perhaps more so than any other branch of commercial law, is not a field where finality is ever to be expected. There is always pressure for it to be modernised so as to take account of new developments in business practice, or for it to be reformed for some other reason (eg because the drafting of an earlier statute has proved to be defective, or because a ruling of the courts is thought to have left the law in an unsatisfactory state). The substantive aspects of the various statutory changes were summarised at 'Sources of company law', pp 3ff. However, the *process* of company law reform also merits attention.

In the past, a practice developed of establishing a committee, appointed by the government every 20 years or so, with a general brief to look at the subject as a whole and make recommendations for reform. This would be followed shortly after by an amending Act, which in turn was very soon consolidated with the previous Act so that it was all brought together. The last of such committees was the Jenkins Committee, which reported in 1962. But at that point the pattern was broken. No amending legislation was introduced to implement the committee's proposed reforms (apart from an abortive Bill in the late 1970s, and some piecemeal measures in the ensuing decade), and the practice of setting up such committees was abandoned.

Besides these committees with a general brief, there were others appointed from time to time to look at a particular topic, such as the Bodkin Committee on sharepushing (1937). These reports (many never followed by legislation) contain some material of great interest, although they are now rather dated. They do, however, serve as a pointed reminder that some problems have been in need of a solution for decades.[28]

---

[28] These reports include: Loreburn Committee, reported 1906, leading to Companies Acts of 1907–08; Wrenbury Committee, reported 1918; Greene Committee, reported 1926, leading to Companies Acts of 1928–29; Bodkin Committee, reported 1937 (sharepushing), leading to Prevention of Fraud (Investments) Act 1939; Anderson Committee, reported 1936 (unit trusts); Cohen Committee, reported 1945, leading to Companies Acts of 1947–48; Gedge Committee, reported 1954 (no par value shares); Jenkins Committee, reported 1962; Bullock Committee, reported 1977 (employee representation); Wilson Committee, reported 1980 (financial institutions); Cork Committee, reported 1982 (insolvency), leading to Insolvency Acts of 1985 and 1986; Gower, *Review of Investor Protection*, reported 1984, leading to Financial Services Act 1986; Prentice, *Reform of the Ultra Vires Rule*, reported 1986, leading to reforms in CA 1989; Dearing, *The Making of Accounting Standards*, reported 1988; Diamond, *A Review of Security Interests in Property*, reported 1989 (company charges).

From the 1980s onwards, all the initiative for reform came from within government, and legislation was usually put in place after the publication of a consultative document inviting comments from members of the public and interested bodies. The driving force behind many statutory changes was the need to implement numerous EU Directives. Time constraints meant that amendments to the primary legislation were often made by statutory instrument, frequently by enacting additional 'layers' of law which left the existing legislation in place and supplemented or qualified it with further rules.

In the course of the 1990s, the DTI set up a succession of working groups to examine possible reforms of particular topics, and also published a number of discussion documents inviting comments and suggestions from the public at large. In a few cases amending legislation followed, usually where this could be done by statutory instrument. But other reforms were simply left in abeyance until time could be found in the parliamentary schedule for a Bill. Significantly, the DTI also adopted an occasional practice of referring certain specific areas of company law to the Law Commissions. They were in a position to examine the subjects in depth, consult widely and publish reports containing recommendations for reform. Unhappily, these recommendations, too, were put on hold until an opportunity arose to enact primary legislation.[29]

It was widely accepted that, as a result of this piecemeal approach to reform, the UK companies legislation had become very untidy, complex and difficult to understand. A thorough overhaul was thought to be essential. This was eventually initiated in 1998 with the creation of the Company Law Review (see 'The Company Law Review', p 6).

The ambitious nature of this review helped to determine the reform *process*. Mrs Margaret Beckett, then Secretary of State for Trade and Industry, published a consultation paper with the challenging title *Modern Company Law for a Competitive Economy*. The focus was to be on the framework of 'core' company law,[30] reviewing every aspect of the subject, even the foundations which were put in place by the Victorians in the mid-nineteenth century. The emphasis was on clarity, simplification, consistency, predictability and transparency, with the aim of promoting competitiveness in the modern commercial and technological environment.

The project involved very large numbers of people, many of them serving on 'working groups' charged with examining separate areas of the law. At the head of all these bodies was a 'Steering Group' whose members included representatives of commerce, the professions, the judiciary, academics and the DTI itself. There was, in addition, a Consultative Committee of some 40 members, and, beyond this, others assisted by undertaking research or providing information from overseas jurisdictions. All in all, the Review was the most thorough and comprehensive undertaking since the introduction of limited liability and the other reforms of the 1850s.

All these outputs then had to be converted into legislation. This was an enormous task, although one advantage of comprehensive redrafting is the opportunity to eliminate accumulated legislative flaws. These were numerous. From the 1970s, many corporate law reforms were effected by statutory instrument under provisions such as the European Communities Act 1972 and the Deregulation and Contracting Out Act 1994. These Acts, exceptionally, authorise the amendment of primary legislation by subordinate 'regulations' that by-pass the usual full parliamentary procedure (see 'Regulatory amendments to CA 2006', p 5). This has certain advantages—for instance, it enables the UK government to

---

[29] See especially the consultations on directors' duties and the remedies available to minority shareholders.

[30] 'Core' company law was taken to include the essential principles of company law that are common to all companies, or at least to large categories of companies such as public companies or private companies. The intention was that new legislation would exclude provisions that only applied to companies that fell into a special class for reasons unrelated to company law (eg charitable companies), or that were better treated in other statutes, eg the rules governing the offering of shares to the public, which are now dealt with as part of the securities regulation.

honour its obligations to implement EU Directives promptly without taking up precious parliamentary time—but it also has its drawbacks. There is not the same opportunity for scrutiny and debate that a normal Bill receives. And the amendments are necessarily restricted to doing no more than the empowering Act permits: the statutory instrument cannot effect related changes to other parts of company law, however logical or desirable such further measures might be. As a consequence, before the enactment of CA 2006, the companies legislation had become progressively more and more diffuse and untidy.

Despite acknowledging this, any future reforms of CA 2006 will still have to pursue these familiar and rather unsatisfactory reform routes. The CLR had usefully recommended that there should be a permanent Company Law Reporting Commission to keep company law and governance under review and submit an annual report to the Secretary of State. In turn, the Secretary of State would be under a duty to consult the Commission on proposed secondary legislation (*Final Report*, Vol 1, paras 5.21–5.37). The government rejected this suggestion, however, saying it preferred a flexible approach, and had already shown its commitment to reform and consultation by setting up the CLR itself (White Paper, Cm 5553-I, 2002, part II, paras 5.25–5.27).

In its 2005 White Paper, the government countered with its own proposal (Cm 6456, para 6.1). It suggested that after CA 2006 was enacted, future reform and restatement of company law should be made by a special form of secondary legislation, using a procedure like that for regulatory reform orders under the Regulatory Reform Act 2001. This would have involved consultation by the Secretary of State, examination by committees of both Houses and final approval by a resolution of each House. However, despite widespread earlier support, this proposal was defeated as an inappropriate process for large and potentially controversial reforms.

Failing such formal processes, company law reform continues to rely on ad hoc interventions or other more coordinated but independent interventions. For example, the Bank of England sponsors an independent body, the Financial Markets Law Committee, whose role is to identify issues of legal uncertainty or misunderstanding, both present and future, in the framework of the wholesale financial markets which might give rise to material risks, and to consider how such issues should be addressed. The Committee also acts as a bridge to the judiciary to help UK courts remain up to date with developments in financial markets practice. This is certainly good as far as it goes, but is not focused on 'core company law'.

But change does happen. The government has recently engaged in a series of reforms aimed at simplifying processes, making it easier for businesses and reducing bureaucracy. In 2015 and 2016, a number of amendments were (or will be) delivered by the Deregulation Act 2015 and the Small Business, Enterprise and Employment Act 2015 (SBEEA 2015).[31] These changes are particularly significant for company registration and filing, directors duties and disqualification, and corporate insolvency, and are discussed in the relevant pages which follow.

> Question

What are the advantages and disadvantages of these different models for law reform in ensuring that the UK has a 'modern company law for a competitive economy'?[32]

---

[31] The government has provided an overview of the changes under SBEEA 2015, together with their respective dates of commencement: www.gov.uk/government/news/the-small-business-enterprise-and-employment-bill-is-coming.

[32] See B Manning, 'Thinking Straight About Corporate Law Reform' (1977) 4 *Law and Contemporary Problems* 3 (written in the US context, but the points raised about the proper focus of corporate law reform are perfectly general).

The purpose of company law: enabling or regulatory?

Legal scholars, economists and social scientists have between them established an extensive body of literature that focuses on variants of the question: what is company law *for*?—or, perhaps, what *should* it be for? At the one extreme, there are those who advocate that its role should be primarily that of *enabling* those engaged in commerce to order their affairs in whatever way suits their purpose best, with minimal interference from the state. A strong belief in the principle of freedom of contract and in the power of market forces characterises this philosophy. At the other extreme, it is contended that the potential for abuse inherent in the concept of limited liability and in the massive economic power wielded by the largest corporations requires the imposition of strong *regulatory* measures by the lawmakers—or, alternatively, that rules of a similar prescriptive nature can be used to make the company a powerful instrument of social engineering, supplementing the law in other areas such as employment law, environmental law, and so on.[33]

To some extent linked with these debates is a well-established classification of the rules of company law into those which are permissive ('may'), those which are presumptive ('may waive') and those which are mandatory ('must' or 'must not'). This analysis was pioneered by the doyen of American company law scholars, Professor Eisenberg, in an article in (1989) 89 Colum LR 1461.

The corporation laws of the United States jurisdictions are generally regarded as the most liberal and permissive, and those of Germany as among the most prescriptive. So far as English law is concerned, it is fair to say that while much of the nineteenth-century legislation was enabling, the innovations of the twentieth century have been increasingly more regulatory in nature. Typically, the more recent reform packages have been introduced with the avowed intention of striking a balance between interfering with business as little as possible, on the one hand, and ensuring that adequate measures are in place to curb abuse and sharp practice, on the other. But invariably caution seems to have dictated that the scales should be tipped heavily in the latter direction. CA 2006 has clearly followed this pattern in some respects, but reversed it in others. Where the overall balance now lies is not so clear.

Classification of companies

The Companies Acts recognise a number of types and classifications of company, as described in the following sections.

Limited and unlimited companies: CA 2006 s 3

CA 2006 s 3 defines a 'limited company' and an 'unlimited company'. A company may be limited by shares or by guarantee by an appropriate limiting provision in the company's constitution. Where there is no such limiting provision on the liability of the company's members, a company is an 'unlimited company'.

---

[33] The CLR terms this topic the 'scope' issue, putting the question: 'For what purpose and in whose interests should companies be operated and controlled?' It is more commonly referred to as the 'stakeholder' debate, and in this book is discussed under the heading of directors' duties, at Chapter 7.

An *unlimited company* has no limit on the liability of its members. In other words, members can be called upon to satisfy personally the whole of its liabilities to its creditors. In a *limited company*, this liability is restricted by law to an amount fixed by the terms of issue of the shares or by the company's constitutional documents. Unlimited companies are exempt from the statutory obligation to publish their accounts and reports (s 448).

Companies limited by shares and companies limited by guarantee

There are two types of limited company. In a company *limited by shares* a member is not liable for the company's debts beyond the amount remaining unpaid on his or her shares. This is, of course, in addition to what he or she (or a previous owner of the shares) has already paid on those shares. Thus, if a company allots to Smith a share of nominal value £1 'at par' (ie for a price of £1), and 60p is paid to the company by Smith on the issue of that share to him, the maximum potential liability of Smith or any later holder of that share to meet the company's debts is the outstanding balance of 40p.

In a company *limited by guarantee* a member is only liable to make a contribution to the assets of the company in the event of its being wound up, and the amount of this contribution (very commonly a nominal sum such as £5) is fixed at the outset by the company's constitution.

Companies limited by guarantee are used mainly for non-profit-making purposes, ranging all the way from some of the major charities to the local golf club. Since they must be formed without any share capital, they have to look elsewhere for their funding, for example to subscriptions or fees.

Public and private companies: CA 2006 s 4

CA 2006 s 4 defines 'private' and 'public' companies in the following terms: a 'private company' is any company that is not a public company; and a 'public company' is a company with a certificate of incorporation that states it is a public company, and that has complied with all the necessary provisions of the Act (or former Companies Acts) as regards registration or re-registration as a public company. There is a minimum share capital requirement (the 'authorised minimum'), currently £50,000 (CA 2006 ss 761 and 763). This authorised minimum may be satisfied in sterling or the euro equivalent of the prescribed sterling amount (s 763).

Only a company limited by shares may be a public company. Public companies have the advantage of being able to offer their shares by advertisement to the public for investment (s 755); but they are subject to a greater degree of regulation by the law.

A *private company* is any company that is not a public company. The legislation makes a number of concessions for private companies—for example, a private company may have only one director while a public company must have at least two (s 154), and a public company is subject to minimum capital requirements (ss 761ff). Only private companies may take advantage of the written resolutions procedure for decision-making (ss 288ff).

The name of a public company ends with the designation 'plc', and that of a private company with the word 'Limited' (ss 58ff).

English company law, unlike that of most other European countries, deals with both public and private companies in the same Act. From time to time there have been suggestions that the law should be reframed so that each category has its own statute, or that the law should go even further to accommodate the special needs of the smallest businesses by having a separate, simplified, legislative regime especially designed for them (as was done for a short time by the Close Corporations Act in South Africa). However, neither the CLR nor the Law Commissions considered that there was any great support for such a proposal in this country, and it is unlikely to be advanced further.

Change of company status

CA 2006 ss 89ff permit a company to alter its status (eg from limited to unlimited, or from private to public) by re-registration.

In each case various conditions have to be met. These relate to: (i) the agreement of the company's members to the change of status (eg sometimes it is necessary to have the unanimous support of members, sometimes the support of a special resolution (ie 75% vote) of the members agreeing to the change); (ii) satisfying the conditions necessary for the new status; and (iii) ensuring there are no historical circumstances that militate against the change.

Charitable and community interest companies

A company of the types already mentioned may also be a charity (if it meets the legal requirements to attract that classification) or a community interest company (if it meets the requirements of Pt 2 of C(AICE)A 2004).

A limited company wishing to register as a community interest company (CIC) must be approved by the Regulator of Community Interest Companies, who must be satisfied that the company meets the 'community interest' test and is not an excluded company. A company meets the community interest test if a reasonable person might consider that its activities are being carried out for the benefit of the community (C(AICE)A 2004 s 35(2)). Excluded companies are companies devoted to political campaigning. CICs are subject to limitations on the dividends they may pay to their members.

European public limited-liability companies (SEs)

It is possible to register a European public limited-liability company (*Societas Europaea* or SE) in any EU state under Regulation (EC) 2157/2001. There are strict preconditions to be met, so that in effect the formation of an SE requires collaboration between at least two companies registered in different member states. Together they may then register as an SE. The SE must register as an SE in the member state in which it has its registered office, and it then will be treated in every state as if it were a public limited liability company formed in accordance with the law of the member state in which it has a registered office.

Classifications based on size

The categories noted in the previous sections are classifications of companies formally set out by CA 2006—companies are *registered* within these categories. In addition, a division of private companies and groups is made on the basis of *size* by CA 2006 ss 444ff, and 465ff, which give dispensations from certain of the accounting requirements to 'small' and 'medium-sized' companies and groups, and by CA 2006 ss 475ff, which exempt 'very small' companies from the obligation to have their accounts audited. Going still further, SBEEA 2015 s 33 now provides definitions for 'small businesses' and 'micro businesses', based on staff headcount and other matters such as turnover and balance sheet totals. These definitions are in line with the EU definitions of 'small enterprise' and 'microenterprise', and are intended to be relied upon in secondary legislation.

'Single member' companies

Since 1992, it has been possible for private companies to have a single member. (The minimum number was formerly two.) These companies are subject to some special rules under the Act (eg CA 2006 s 357, which requires decisions taken by the single member to be recorded in writing). Thus single member companies may be regarded as a further sub-species of company for classification purposes.

Parent and subsidiary companies: CA 2006 s 1159

Larger enterprises often operate as corporate groups, or in structures where the parent company or holding company owns (either wholly or partially) a number of subsidiary companies. CA 2006 s 1159 defines one company to be a 'subsidiary' of another (the 'holding' company) where the holding company (i) holds a majority of the voting rights in it; or (ii) is a member of it and has the right to appoint or remove a majority of its board of directors; or (iii) is a member of it and controls alone, pursuant to an agreement with other members, a majority of the voting rights in it; or (iv) is a subsidiary of a company that is itself a subsidiary of the holding company. Although holding companies and subsidiaries are separate legal persons, CA 2006 makes certain special provisions in relation to corporate groups, in at least partial recognition of the practical intuition that the 'group' acts as a combined enterprise.

The Supreme Court decision in *Enviroco Ltd v Farstad Supply A/S* [2011] UKSC 16 provides a rather dramatic illustration of these rules in operation. A contractor and its affiliates (which included its co-subsidiaries) were all covered by an indemnity clause in a charterparty. At the time the damage was incurred, the parent company had mortgaged the shares it owned in the subsidiary, so that the lender rather than the parent was their registered legal owner (albeit only by way of security).[34] This was enough to deny the relationship of parent and subsidiary according to the statutory definition, and so was also enough to deny the protection of the indemnity clause in relation to the damage caused by the subsidiary.

Companies and other business structures

There are many types of organisation which have structures that are to a greater or lesser degree similar to those of companies, but which are governed by separate legislation. Some of these are regarded in law as being 'persons' in their own right, distinct from their members: for example, building societies, friendly societies and industrial and provident societies (ie the co-operatives). Others are not, the most familiar example being trade unions. Partnerships generally have no separate personality (although they do in Scotland, and see later).

The most important business alternatives to adopting a corporate structure are sole traders and partnerships. Neither typically has limited liability, although there are some exceptions with partnerships. Partnerships may be divided into three categories: 'ordinary' partnerships, in which every member has unlimited liability for the debts and obligations of the firm; *limited partnerships*, in which the active partners have unlimited liability but the 'sleeping' partners' liability is limited; and *limited liability partnerships*, formed and

---

[34] This was in Scotland. In England, the lender would typically have taken a charge, and so there would have been no transfer of legal ownership of the shares. See Chapter 12.

registered under the Limited Liability Partnerships Act 2000, which do have separate personality and whose members enjoy limited liability.[35]

Incorporation, registration and the role of the registrar

Incorporation

To incorporate a company under CA 2006 ss 7ff, it is necessary to draw up two basic documents, the *memorandum of association* and the company's constitution or *articles of association* (to the extent that this is not supplied by default application of the Model Articles, see s 20). (Note that the memorandum here is not part of the company's constitution; it is not at all the same type of document as the memorandum under the previous Companies Acts legislation.)

The memorandum must be signed or authenticated by the first member or members ('subscribers') and delivered by them or their agent[36] to the Registrar of Companies, together with the prescribed fee and certain supporting documents (see ss 9ff). These include statements of the company's proposed name, registered office, whether members' liability is to be limited, proposed company directors (and secretary, if there is one[37]), assertions that these people consent to act,[38] initial share capital (if it is a company with shares), proposed articles of association (or, by default, the Model Articles will apply) and, finally, a statement of compliance (s 13).

Since the documents have to include the company's name, it is prudent to check in advance that a proposed name is likely to be available. See the rules on names in CA 2006 ss 53ff.

If the registrar is satisfied that the requirements of the Act as to registration are met, he will register the documents (s 14), and issue a certificate of incorporation, signed by the registrar and authenticated by his seal (s 15). Note that a company may not be formed for an unlawful purpose, so this can be grounds for refusing registration (see s 7(2)).

The certificate of incorporation is conclusive evidence that the requirements of the Act have been complied with and that the company is duly registered (s 15(4)).[39]

The effects of incorporation are set out in s 16, including that the body corporate is capable of exercising all the functions of an incorporated company (s 16(3)).

All of this recitation of the Companies Act provisions for incorporation, along with many textbooks, encourage the belief that companies are formed by a genuine 'association' of people with a real business that they wish to incorporate, who have constitutional documents drawn up for that specific purpose, subscribe to them and send them off to the

---

[35] Provisions from CA 2006 (with modifications) have been applied to limited liability partnerships by virtue of the Limited Liability Partnerships (Application of Companies Act 2006) Regulations 2009 (SI 2009/1804). See also D Sutherland, 'Limited Liability Partnerships: All Change with the Companies Act 2006?' (2008) 7 JIBFL 340.

[36] Incorporation documents may be filed electronically.

[37] This is only compulsory for public companies: CA 2006 s 12.

[38] Since October 2015, the directors need not provide individual formal statements that they consent to act; instead, there is a simpler 'consent to act' procedure in which newly appointed officers simply agree to the filing of a statement indicating that they have consented to act, incorporated as part of the relevant appointment and incorporation form (SBEEA 2015 s 100).

[39] And can therefore only be questioned by the AG, because the Act does not bind the Crown (per Lord Parker of Waddington in *Bowman v Secular Society Ltd* **[1.07]** at 438–440, and *Cotman v Brougham* [1918] AC 514 at 519). For an example of a request for reversal of a decision to register a company, see *R v Registrar of Companies, ex p AG* **[1.09]**.

registrar for registration. But this is not true. Most companies formed in the UK today are bought 'off the shelf': the incorporation procedure has been executed as a purely paper exercise by people who have no intention of using the company themselves. The initial subscribers and officers will be clerks in the firm's employment, and the company's name a figment of someone's imagination. All these details will then be amended by the shelf-company's purchasers.

Memorandum of association

CA 2006 s 8 deals with the memorandum of association, replacing s 3(1) of the 1985 Act. Under the new legislation the memorandum serves a more limited, but nonetheless important, purpose: it evidences the intention of the subscribers to the memorandum to form a company and become members of that company on formation. In the case of a company that is to be limited by shares, the memorandum also provides evidence of the members' agreement to take at least one share each in the company. It is not possible, or necessary, to amend or update the memorandum; if the members want to change the company's constitution, they do that by changing the articles ('History', p 27 and Chapter 4).

All of the companies formed under the old Acts (such as CA 1985) will have been formed with an 'old-style memorandum' and articles. The memorandum was the primary public constitutional document of the company, setting out the company's fixed financial information, and its objects (or powers). This document was supplemented by the articles of association, which generally dealt with the internal management of the company. CA 2006 s 28 provides that any provisions in the memoranda of existing companies that are not of the type described in CA 2006 s 8 will be treated as if they were provisions in the company's articles. This includes both substantive provisions and also any provisions for their entrenchment. Existing companies will, therefore, not be required to amend their articles to reflect these statutory changes in CA 2006, but they may do so if they wish.

Constitutional documents: articles of association and the company's objects

The articles of association (as amended from time to time) provide the company with its constitution (s 17). Every company must have articles. These will be either articles registered by the company itself on its incorporation (s 9(5)(b)), or the Model Articles for limited companies that are deemed by CA 2006 s 20 to apply if no articles are registered, or, if articles are registered, to the extent that the Model Articles are not specifically excluded or modified. The default provisions are 'Model Articles' in CA 2006, and 'Tables A–F' for CA 1985.

Under previous legislation (CA 1985 and its predecessors), all companies were required to have *objects*, and these objects had to be specified in the ('old-style') memorandum. So, for example, a company's objects might be the running of schools, the building of canals or the pursuit of research into medical diseases. The 'objects' were the activities that the company had been formed to pursue. Their statement was intended to provide comfort to members and creditors, who could rest secure in the knowledge of the ventures the company would pursue. It was also intended to constrain the directors, preventing them exercising their powers for unauthorised ends. But the courts soon came to the view that purported activities outside the company's objects were void, being *ultra vires*, or outside the company's capacity to act. This had a significant and detrimental effect on both the company and those it had dealings with: contracts entered into in good faith were rendered void, with all that followed from that. This was commercially unacceptable, and statutory provisions were enacted to protect third parties while still restraining directors.

The public role played by a statement of the company's objects was recognised as inessential, and CA 2006 s 31(1) now provides that a company will have unrestricted objects unless the objects are specifically restricted by the articles. This means that unless a company makes a deliberate choice to restrict its objects, the objects will have no bearing on what a company can do. If a statement restricting the objects is made, it must be made as part of the company articles of association (s 31(2)).

CA 2006 s 33 provides that the company's constitution binds the company and its members to the same extent as if there were covenants on the part of the company and of each member to observe the provisions. This has significant ramifications: see Chapter 4.

History

Prior to the Joint Stock Companies Act 1856, companies were formed on the basis of a *deed of settlement*—an elaborate form of partnership deed. The Act of 1844 provided for the registration of the deed of settlement and the grant of corporate status in return. The 1856 Act introduced a new constitutional framework based on two documents—the *memorandum of association* and the *articles of association*—and this pattern continued under successive Companies Acts. The memorandum was the more fundamental document: the articles could not modify the memorandum, and if there was any inconsistency, the terms of the memorandum prevailed (*Guinness v Land Corpn of Ireland* (1822) 22 Ch D 349, CA). In addition, statutory provisions such as CA 1985 s 125 (CA 2006 s 22) made it possible to 'entrench' rights by writing them into the memorandum with a prohibition or restriction on their alteration.

Under CA 2006, this question of primacy as between the company's two constitutional documents, its memorandum and its articles, does not arise, as all the company's constitutional provisions are contained in the articles; the memorandum is nothing more than a statement by the first members that they intend to form a legal entity.

The question of alterability was, originally, perhaps the most important distinction between the two documents: apart from changing its name (in very limited circumstances) and increasing its capital, a company could do nothing under the Act of 1856 to alter any of the terms of the memorandum, while the articles could be changed simply by a special resolution of the members. With time it became possible to alter virtually all the provisions of the memorandum by one procedure or another, and so this distinction was of subsidiary importance. Broadly speaking, however, we can say that by its memorandum a company proclaimed to the world the *external* aspects of its constitution, such as its name, domicile, objects, status (as limited or unlimited, public or private, etc) and capital structure, while the articles were concerned with matters of *internal* organisation, which are primarily of interest to its own members and officers, for example the procedures for paying the subscription price for shares and for transferring shares, the convening and conduct of members' and directors' meetings, the appointment, removal and remuneration of directors and the payment of dividends.

Under CA 2006 s 21(1), as in CA 1985, the general rule is that provisions of a company's articles of association (its constitution) may be altered by special resolution. Through entrenchment provisions, however, more restrictive procedures can be introduced: CA 2006 s 22. Note that CA 2006 s 22(2) has not been brought into force because of concerns that it would prevent the alteration of class rights contained in the articles (see CA 2006 and Limited Liability Partnerships (Transitional Provisions and Savings) (Amendments) Regulations 2009 (SI 2009/2476) reg 2(1)).

Company names

CA 2006 introduced a system of company name adjudication to deal with problems of confusingly similar names. An application to the Companies Name Adjudicator stating the objection must be made. Two possible grounds for an application are specified in CA 2006 s 69: (i) it is the same as a name associated with the applicant in which he has goodwill; or (ii) it is sufficiently similar to such a name that its use in the UK would be likely to mislead by suggesting a connection between the company and the applicant. An objection will be upheld if either of these grounds is satisfied, unless the defendant company can establish one of the defences listed in s 69(4). The cases on 'passing off' are likely to be material in interpreting this provision (see, eg, *Reckitt & Coleman Ltd v Borden Inc* [1990] 1 All ER 873; *Exxon Corpn v Exxon Insurance Consultants International Ltd* [1982] Ch 119; *Asprey & Garrard Ltd v WRA (Guns) Ltd* [2001] EWCA Civ 1499, CA).

The registrar's decision to register

There are two issues to be addressed: Can the registrar refuse to register? And what is the effect of registration, even if procured by fraud?

The registrar cannot refuse registration if the objects of the company are lawful and the documents are in order.

[1.05] R v Registrar of Companies, ex p Bowen [1914] 3 KB 1161 (King's Bench Divisional Court)

Application was made to register a proposed company named The United Dental Service Ltd. The subscribers to the memorandum were seven unregistered dental practitioners. The registrar refused to register the company unless either the memorandum was altered so as to provide that the work of the company should be undertaken only by registered dentists, or the name of the company was amended so as not to include the word 'dental' or 'dentist'. The applicants sought a writ of mandamus to compel the registrar to register the company. It was held that the registrar's refusal was unjustified, and mandamus was granted.

> LORD READING CJ: In my opinion the question turns in the main . . . upon whether the use of these words, 'The United Dental Service', would amount to an offence under the Dentists Act 1878 . . . I think these words, 'United Dental Service', imply a description of the acts to be performed, and do not imply that the persons who will perform them are persons specially qualified under the statute of 1878. The Registrar of Companies would be entitled, if the use of the proposed name would be an offence under the statute (either under this or any other statute), to refuse to register the company with that name; but, having arrived at the conclusion that that would not be the effect of the use of the words 'United Dental Service', I hold that the registrar was wrong in refusing registration upon that ground . . .
>   AVORY J delivered a concurring judgment.
>   BANKES J concurred.

➤ Notes

1. There is one statutory exception to the principle that incorporation is freely available: the Trade Union and Labour Relations (Consolidation) Act 1992 s 10(3) states that a trade union shall not be registered as a company under CA 2006, and that any such registration is void.[40]

---

[40] See R Drury, 'Nullity of Companies in English Law' (1985) 48 MLR 625.

2. The registrar's powers in relation to company names have varied under successive Companies Acts. For the present law, see CA 2006 ss 53ff. The use of the word 'Dental' is now restricted by regulations made under the previous CA 1985 s 29 (now see CA 2006 ss 55 and 56) and requires the consent of the General Dental Council.

The registrar may refuse to register a company whose objects are unlawful.

[1.06] R v Registrar of Joint Stock Companies, ex p More [1931] 2 KB 197 (Court of Appeal)

The registrar refused to register a company formed to sell tickets in an Irish lottery. The Court of Appeal held that the lottery was illegal in England and that his refusal was right.

> SCRUTTON LJ: This is a short point involving the construction of, s 41 of the Lotteries Act 1823. Two gentlemen proposed to sell tickets in England in connection with an Irish lottery. For some reason they did not propose to do this themselves; they proposed to form a private company to do it. It is merely conjecture on my part that this may be due to the fact that the provisions in the Act of 1823 making offenders liable to be punished as rogues and vagabonds do not apply to a company, and so the two gentlemen intending to form this company wished in this way to avoid the risk of being prosecuted under the Act. They accordingly lodged the memorandum and articles of association of the proposed company with the Registrar of Companies, who, when he saw that the object of the company was to sell tickets in a lottery known as the Irish Free State Hospitals Sweepstake, refused to register the company. Whereupon an application was made to the court for a writ of mandamus directing the registrar to register the company. To succeed in that application the applicant must show that it is legal to sell in England tickets for the Irish Free State Hospital Sweepstake authorised by an Act of the Irish Free State. The only Act which can be supposed to authorise the selling in England is an Irish Act, but the Irish Parliament has no jurisdiction in England, and that being so, the Irish Parliament cannot authorise lottery tickets to be sold in England. The authority to sell in any place must be given by the Parliament having jurisdiction in that place, and the Imperial Parliament has given no authority to sell lottery tickets in England . . . . The appeal must be dismissed.
>   GREER and SLESSER LJJ delivered concurring judgments.

Registration does not establish conclusively that the objects of a company are lawful, but after the issue of a certificate of incorporation the regularity of the incorporation cannot be challenged on the grounds of illegality except in proceedings specially brought in the name of the Crown to have the registration cancelled.

[1.07] Bowman v Secular Society Ltd [1917] AC 406 (House of Lords)

The main object of the society, which was registered as a company limited by guarantee, was 'to promote . . . the principle that human conduct should be based upon natural knowledge, and not upon super-natural belief, and that human welfare in this world is the proper end of all thought and action . . .'. It was alleged that this object, involving a denial of Christianity, was against public policy, so that a bequest to the society was invalid. The House of Lords upheld the view of the courts below that this object was not unlawful. This extract from the speech of Lord Parker of Waddington is concerned with the incidental point of the conclusiveness of the certificate of incorporation. His views were supported by Lords Dunedin and Buckmaster.

LORD PARKER OF WADDINGTON: My Lords, in the present case . . . the testator has given his residuary estate through the medium of trustees for sale and conversion to the Secular Society Limited, and the question is as to the validity of this gift. There is no doubt as to the certainty of the subject-matter, or as to the testator's disposing power, or as to the validity of his will. So far as the conditions essential to the validity of the gift are concerned, the only doubt is as to the capacity of the donee.

The Secular Society Limited was incorporated as a company limited by guarantee under the Companies Acts 1862 to 1893, and a company so incorporated is by, s [18] of the Act of 1862 [CA 2006 s 16(3)] capable of exercising all the functions of an incorporated company. Prima facie, therefore, the society is a corporate body created by virtue of a statute of the realm, with statutory power to acquire property by gift, whether *inter vivos* or by will. The appellants endeavour to displace this prima facie effect of the Companies Acts in the following manner. If, they say, you look at the objects for which the society was incorporated, as expressed in its memorandum of association, you will find that they are either actually illegal or, at any rate, in conflict with the policy of the law. This being so, the society was not an association capable of incorporation under the Acts. It was and is an illegal association, and as such incapable of acquiring property by gift. I do not think this argument is open to the appellants, even if their major premise be correct. By the first section of the Companies Act 1900 [CA 2006 s 15(4)] the society's certificate of registration is made conclusive evidence that the society was an association authorised to be registered—that is, an association of not less than seven persons associated together for a lawful purpose. The section does not mean that all or any of the objects specified in the memorandum, if otherwise illegal, would be rendered legal by the certificate. On the contrary, if the directors of the society applied its funds for an illegal object, they would be guilty of misfeasance and liable to replace the money, even if the object for which the money had been applied were expressly authorised by the memorandum. In like manner a contract entered into by the company for an unlawful object, whether authorised by the memorandum or otherwise, could not be enforced either in law or in equity. The section does, however, preclude all His Majesty's lieges from going behind the certificate or from alleging that the society is not a corporate body with the status and capacity conferred by the Acts. Even if all the objects specified in the memorandum were illegal, it does not follow that the company cannot on that account apply its funds or enter into a contract for a lawful purpose. Every company has power to wind up voluntarily, and moneys paid or contracts entered into with that object are in every respect lawfully paid or entered into. Further, the disposition provided by the company's memorandum for its surplus assets in case of a winding up may be lawful though all the objects as a going concern are unlawful. If there be no lawful manner of applying such surplus assets they would on the dissolution of the company belong to the Crown as bona vacantia: *Cunnack v Edwards*.[41]

My Lords, some stress was laid on the public danger, or at any rate the anomaly, of the courts recognising the corporate existence of a company all of whose objects, as specified in its memorandum of association, are transparently illegal. Such a case is not likely to occur, for the registrar fulfils a quasi-judicial function,[42] and his duty is to determine whether an association applying for registration is authorised to be registered under the Acts. Only by misconduct or great carelessness on the part of the registrar could a company with objects wholly illegal obtain registration. If such a case did occur it would be open to the court to stay its hand until an opportunity had been given for taking the appropriate steps for the cancellation of the certificate of registration. It should be observed that neither, s 1 of the Companies Act 1900, nor the corresponding section of the Companies (Consolidation) Act 1908, is so expressed as to bind the Crown, and the

---

41 [1896] 2 Ch 679.

42 The use of the term 'quasi-judicial' is misleading. This function of the registrar can only be described as 'ministerial': as we have seen earlier, in the matter of registration, he exercises no discretionary powers, still less is he concerned to adjudicate any dispute.

Attorney-General, on behalf of the Crown, could institute proceedings by way of certiorari to cancel a registration which the registrar in affected discharge of his quasi-judicial duties had improperly or erroneously allowed. But . . . I do not think that the present is a case requiring such action on the part of your Lordships' House.

My Lords, it follows from what I have already said that the capacity of the Secular Society Limited to acquire property by gift must be taken as established, and, all the conditions essential to the validity of the gift being thus fulfilled, the donee is entitled to receive and dispose of the subject-matter thereof . . .

LORDS DUNEDIN, SUMNER and BUCKMASTER delivered concurring opinions.

LORD FINLAY LC dissented.

[1.08] HA Stephenson & Son Ltd v Gillanders, Arbuthnot & Co (1931) 45 CLR 476 (High Court of Australia)

EVATT J: [The] effect of formal incorporation is not regarded by the legislature as empowering the registrar to ignore compliance with the Act; but the legislature wishes to ensure that after the new legal entity has been brought into existence by the formal act of a state functionary, it will not be necessary for persons dealing with the company to ascertain at their peril whether the various statutory requirements have been complied with . . . It is not so much a power given to the registrar by the legislature, as a protection given to the public who may be dealing with the company because of the assumption that the registrar will be careful in the matter . . .

See also *Salomon v Salomon & Co Ltd* **[2.02]** and *Scott v Frank F Scott (London) Ltd* **[4.01]**.

➤ Notes

1. Put another way, a conclusive evidence provision such as CA 2006 s 15(4) means what it says. See *Bank of Beirut SAL v Prince El-Hashemite* [2015] EWHC 1451 (Ch), a case on the registration of limited partnerships. Nugee J relied on *Bowman* to conclude that the certificates of registration of each partnership constituted conclusive evidence that each partnership came into existence, despite the fact that the registration had been procured by fraud and forgery.

2. This makes plain that it is not up to the registrar to check the accuracy or validity of the documents delivered to him, but simply to register (or not) as appropriate. However, in *registering*, the registrar owes a duty of care to the company (and only to the company—not to third parties relying on the register) to ensure that what is registered corresponds with what ought to be registered given the documents delivered to the registrar. In *Sebry v Companies House* [2015] EWHC 115 (QB), the court found the registrar in breach of this duty of care, and liable to compensate the company, after negligently entering a winding-up order on the register against a viable company with a similar name; as a result, the creditors refused to deal with the company, which had then gone into administration.

3. CA 2006 s 15(4) thus appears to make it unnecessary for English company law students to consider the topics of defective incorporation and declaration of nullity which have traditionally occupied a substantial amount of space in the textbooks in other European countries and in parts of the United States. It was not considered necessary for the UK to take any steps to implement Arts 11 and 12 of the First EU Company Law Directive, which deal with these questions. However, this may have been a misjudgement, in the light of the next case, *R v Registrar of Companies, ex p AG* **[1.09]**.

The registrar's decision to incorporate a company is subject to judicial review at the suit of the Crown.

[1.09] R v Registrar of Companies, ex p AG [1991] BCLC 476 (Queen's Bench Divisional Court)

The facts appear from the judgment.

ACKNER LJ: This application has many of the indicia that one might expect to find in a students' end of term moot. It appears indirectly to have been stimulated by the action of the Policy Division of the Inland Revenue.

The Attorney-General applies to quash the incorporation and registration by the Registrar of Companies nearly a year ago, that is on 18 December 1979, of Lindi St Claire (Personal Services) Ltd as a limited company under the provisions of the Companies Act 1948 to 1976.

The grounds of the application, to state them quite briefly, are these. In certifying the incorporation of a company and in registering the same the Registrar of Companies acted ultra vires or mis-directed himself or otherwise erred in law, in particular as to the proper construction and application of, s 1(1) of the Companies Act 1948 in that the company was not formed for any lawful purpose but, on the contrary, was formed expressly with the primary object of carrying on the business of prostitution, such being an unlawful purpose involving the commission of acts which are immoral and contrary to public policy.

The first point to consider is the validity of the procedure which has been adopted in this case, that is by way of application for judicial review, such application being made by the Attorney-General.

[His Lordship referred to *Bowman v Secular Society Ltd* **[1.07]** and continued:] So clearly the Attorney-General is entitled to bring these proceedings.

Now as to the facts, these come within a very short compass and they amount to the following. A firm of certified accountants, Gilson Clipp & Co, on 16 August 1979 wrote to the Registrar of Companies at Companies House, Crown Way, Maindy, Cardiff pointing out that they had received a letter from the Inland Revenue Policy Division, who stated that they considered prostitution to be a trade which is fully taxable, and that they, the certified accountants, saw no reason why their client should not be able to organise her business by way of a limited company. They asked whether the name 'Prostitute Ltd' was available for registration as a limited company, pointing out the main object of the company would be that of organising the services of a prostitute.

The registrar did not like that name and did not accept it, nor did he accept another name 'Hookers Ltd' which was offered. But subsequently two further names were offered, 'Lindi St Claire (Personal Services) Ltd' and 'Lindi St Claire (French Lessons) Ltd', and it was the former which he registered.

The memorandum of association said in terms that the first of the objects of the company was 'To carry on the business of prostitution'.

The only director of the company is Lindi St Claire, Miss St Claire describing herself specifically as 'Prostitute'. The other person who owns also one share is a Miss Duggan, who is referred to as 'the cashier'.

Leave having been obtained to apply for judicial review, Miss St Claire wrote in these terms:

I would like to say that prostitution is not at all unlawful, as you have stated, and I feel it is most unfair of you to take this view, especially when I am paying income tax on my earnings from prostitution to the government Inland Revenue.

Furthermore, I feel it is most unfair of you to imply that I have acted wrongly, as I was most explicit to all concerned about the sole trade of the company to be that of prostitution and nothing more. If my company should not be deemed valid, then it should have not been granted in the first place by the Board of Trade. It is most unfair of the government to allow me to go ahead with my company one moment, then quash it the next . . . .

It is well settled that a contract which is made upon a sexually immoral consideration or for a sexually immoral purpose is against public policy and is illegal and unenforceable. The fact that it does not involve or may not involve the commission of a criminal offence in no way prevents the contract being illegal, being against public policy and therefore being unenforceable. Here, as the documents clearly indicate, the association is for the purpose of carrying on a trade which involves illegal contracts because the purpose is a sexually immoral purpose and as such against public policy.

Mr Simon Brown submits that if that is the position, as indeed it clearly is on the authorities, then the association of the two or more persons cannot be for 'any lawful purpose'.

To my mind this must follow. It is implicit in the speeches in the Bowman case to which I have just made reference. In my judgment, the contention of the Attorney-General is a valid one and I would order that the registration be therefore quashed.

SKINNER J concurred.

➤ Questions

1. Tom, Dick and Harry wish to incorporate the plumbing business which they have carried on in partnership for some years. What would you say might be (i) the advantages and (ii) the disadvantages for them in buying a ready-made company rather than having one incorporated by their own solicitor?

2. If they do decide to use a ready-made company, what steps will have to be taken in order to transfer the company to them and to make it fit for their needs?

3. What might be the consequences of the court's order in Miss St Claire's case, in the previous extract [1.09], so far as concerns acts done in the year that the company was on the register?

▨ Further reading

BRATTON, W, 'Corporate Law's Race to Nowhere in Particular' (1994) 44 *University of Toronto Law Journal* 401.

BRATTON, W, 'The Nexus of Contract Corporation: A Critical Appraisal' (1989) 74 *Cornell Law Review* 407.

DAVIES, PL, *Introduction to Company Law* (2nd edn, 2010), especially ch 1.

DRURY, R, 'The "Delaware Syndrome": European Fears and Reactions' [2005] JBL 709.

HANSMANN, H and KRAAKMAN, RH, 'The Essential Role of Organizational Law' (2000) 110 *Yale Law Journal* 387.

KAHN-FREUD, O, 'Some Reflections on Company Law Reform' (1944) 7 MLR 54.

KEAY, A, 'Ascertaining the Corporate Objective: An Entity Maximisation and Sustainability Model' (2008) 71 MLR 663.

KRAAKMAN, RH et al (eds), *The Anatomy of Corporate Law* (2nd edn, 2009), especially ch 1.

MILMAN, D, 'The Courts and the Companies Acts: The Judicial Contribution to Company Law' [1990] LMCLQ 401.

STOKES, M, 'Company Law and Legal Theory' in W Twining (ed), *Legal Theory and Common Law* (1986), p 155, and also in S Wheeler (ed), *A Reader on the Law of Business Enterprises* (1994), p 80.

WEDDERBURN, KW, 'The Social Responsibility of Companies' (1985) 15 *Melbourne University Law Review* 4.

WOLFF, M, 'On the Nature of Legal Persons' (1938) 54 LQR 494.

2

CORPORATE PERSONALITY AND LIMITED LIABILITY

General issues

We saw in the previous chapter that the separate legal personality of a company and the limited liability of its members are two pillars on which much of company law and corporate practice rests. Both of these ideas are examined in more detail here.[1]

The most important legal feature of a company is that it is a legal person in its own right, separate from the legal persons that are its members (or shareholders) and its directors. It is important to understand exactly what this means and what consequences inevitably follow from it. We typically use the word 'person' to refer to an individual human being, but in law the word has a more technical meaning: 'a subject of rights and duties'.[2] In this sense it is possible to speak of a corporation as a 'person' and recognise its separate 'personality'.

---

[1] There is a considerable body of writing on the theory, or theories, of corporate personality. No attempt has been made to select material representing the various schools of thought for inclusion in this book. For the interested reader, the following are amongst the best-known writings in English on the subject: FW Maitland, *Introduction to Gierke's Political Theories of the Middle Age* (1900); M Radin, 'The Endless Problem of Corporate Personality' (1932) 32 *Columbia Law Review* 643; AA Berle and GC Means, *The Modern Corporation and Private Property* (1932); RH Coase, 'The Nature of the Firm' (1937) 4 *Economica NS* 386; M Wolff, 'On the Nature of Legal Persons' (1938) 54 LQR 494; HLA Hart, 'Definition and Theory in Jurisprudence' (1954) 70 LQR 37, 45ff; MC Jensen and WH Meckling, 'Theory of the Firm: Managerial Behaviour, Agency Costs and Ownership Structure' (1976) 3 J Fin Econ 305; M Stokes, 'Company Law and Legal Theory' in W Twining (ed), *Legal Theory and Common Law* (1986); DD Prentice, 'The Theory of the Firm: Minority Shareholder Oppression: Sections 459–461 of the Companies Act 1985' (1988) 8 OJLS 55; CA Riley, 'Contracting Out of Company Law: Section 459 of the Companies Act 1985' (1992) 55 MLR 782; FH Easterbrook and DR Fischel, 'The Corporate Contract' (1989) 89 *Columbia Law Review* 1416; WW Bratton, 'The New Economic Theory of the Firm: Critical Perspectives from History' (1989) 41 Stan L Rev 1471; R Flannigan, 'The Economic Structure of the Firm' (1995) 33 *Osgoode Hall Law Journal* 105; BR Cheffins, *Company Law: Theory, Structure and Operation* (1997).

[2] In this sense 'person' can, eg, include such inanimate entities as a fund (*Arab Monetary Fund v Hashim (No 3)* [1991] 2 AC 114, [1991] BCLC 180, HL), or a Hindu temple (*Bumper Development Corpn Ltd v Metropolitan Police Comr* [1991] 1 WLR 1362, CA). Note that neither a fund nor a temple is regarded as a corporation under English law, where typically corporate personality is recognised only in a group, a municipality or an office (eg the Crown). In the two cases referred to, the court was applying the accepted rule of the conflict of laws which states that the question whether or not a group or entity should be accorded corporate status is to be decided by the law of the jurisdiction in which it is situated or domiciled.

To say that a company is a legal person suggests that it can be subjected to legal liabilities and entitled to advance legal claims in own name, that it can own property, enter into contracts, hold legal rights and commit legal wrongs, all as its own person. This is typically precisely what the shareholders who incorporate their business want: they want the *company* to run the business, and the *company* to carry the associated liabilities and have *its* assets at risk should the business suffer a downturn; they do *not* want their own assets at risk. This is what we mean by 'limited liability' for the shareholders. This idea of asset partitioning between the company and its shareholders is important.[3] In this way, the shareholders are insulated from corporate losses, but will benefit from corporate successes: should the business grow, the shareholders will receive increased dividends and enjoy enhanced share values; but should the business fail, the losses are the company's.

Third parties dealing with the business are usually equally keen on the corporate form, if only for ease of monitoring. Companies are required to make a good deal of financial information publicly available, and this provides useful (if only partial) information on the company's standing. Certainly it is easier to monitor a company than to monitor all the various individuals who might be associated in some way with running the company's business.

But sometimes this status quo looks less attractive, and the paper tiger of a company with its own legal personality is seen as frustrating. The outsiders want to ignore the corporate entity—which is invisible anyway—and instead claim access to the property and legal rights of those standing behind the company pulling the strings, typically the company's shareholders. This was precisely the issue in perhaps the most famous case in all of company law, *Salomon v A Salomon & Co Ltd* [1897] AC 22 (House of Lords) **[2.02]**. Salomon was a bootmaker who operated initially as a sole trader, and later converted the business to one run by a company. When the business suffered a downturn and the company was unable to pay its debts, the company's creditors sought to impose liability on Mr Salomon himself, the man behind the company as its majority shareholder. The creditors' claims succeeded in the lower courts but failed before the House of Lords. This is the case which settled—very firmly—the idea that a company is an independent legal person, separate from its shareholders, even shareholders who wield complete control over the company's activities.

But the creditors' failure in this case, now well over 100 years ago, did not stop other claimants seeking to achieve the same ends. The stakes are often high. The cases extracted in this chapter include examples of outsiders suing in negligence for the harm caused by asbestosis, making their claims against the wealthy holding company (ie the rich corporate shareholder) rather than the undercapitalised subsidiary; or divorcing wives asserting interests in family homes held not by their ex-husbands but by companies controlled by them.

In these sorts of cases, the claimants invariably want to look to the person (human or corporate) behind the company and assert claims against those individuals which seem to involve ignoring the corporate intermediary standing between the two parties; as metaphor would have it, they want to 'pierce the corporate veil': that is, ignore the corporate form, and go behind it (behind its veil) to the individuals—human or corporate—who are the shareholders. The law in this area was until very recently exceptionally messy, and seemingly impossible to rationalise. In 2013, however, the Supreme Court took the opportunity to review the jurisdiction in *Prest v Petrodel Resources Ltd* [2013] UKSC 34 **[2.12]**.

---

[3] H Hansmann and R Kraakman, 'The Essential Role of Organizational Law' (2000) 110 *Yale Law Journal* 387, esp 393–395; H Hansmann, R Kraakman and R Squire, 'Law and the Rise of the Firm' (2006) 119 *Harvard Law Review* 1333, esp 1337–1356.

Although the judges deciding *Prest v Petrodel Resources Ltd* did not deny the existence of the doctrine of 'piercing the veil', they came as close as possible to doing so. Despite a good number of older cases using the terminology of 'piercing the veil', Lord Neuberger PSC remarked that 'there is not a single instance in this jurisdiction where the doctrine has been invoked properly and successfully' ([64]), and he suggested that orthodox legal analysis, respecting the corporate form, would invariably deliver the result that was warranted. This could be done by paying proper attention to all the possible relationships a company (as a separate entity) might have with its shareholders and with other parties. In the right circumstances these relationships could suffice to make those shareholders or other parties the subject of legal claims. Note that these claims would then be made without ignoring the corporate form; indeed, the existence of the company would typically be essential in establishing the necessary relationship on which litigation was based.

Because of *Prest v Petrodel Resources Ltd*, the analysis underpinning this area of the law can be explained in a much simpler and more intelligible way than was previously possible. There are three broad aspects of the law to be addressed: the consequences of separate legal personality; the idea of 'piercing the corporate veil'; and the various ways of connecting the company with other parties, particularly the company's shareholders, so that those other parties can be made liable in appropriate circumstances. Each of those aspects is considered in turn.

In all of this, two cases are particularly important: *Salomon v A Salomon & Co Ltd* **[2.02]** and *Prest v Petrodel Resources Ltd* **[2.12]**. They deserve serious attention and are extracted at length here. Together they provide the building blocks on which separate legal personality and its various consequences are built. Other cases provide illustration and guidance on the sometimes dramatic consequences of separate legal personality.

Given the approach now mandated by *Prest v Petrodel Resources,* a good number of the older cases in this area must be treated with caution. Many of the cases appearing in earlier editions of this book have been culled. Of the ones which remain, it is important to keep firmly in mind the idea that these older cases often use the terminology 'piercing the corporate veil' when all they mean is that, in the circumstances, the company's members can be made liable to third parties. This may often be done on perfectly orthodox legal grounds, without in any way ignoring the company's corporate personality. By contrast, the Supreme Court in *Prest v Petrodel Resources* confines the expression to circumstances where the separate legal personality of the company is *ignored*. As Lord Neuberger noted, even in the cases where this is what the judges say they are doing (two successful cases only, it seems: see 'Illustrating "evasion"', p 71), there are alternative, orthodox analyses to reach the same ends.

This limited meaning of 'piercing the corporate veil' is adopted here. Other less graphic terminology is used when corporate personality is not ignored at all, but the company's members are nevertheless found to be liable to outsiders on the basis of calling into play other general legal principles: see 'Connections between the company and other persons', p 75ff.

Separate corporate personality

The next extracts establish this foundational principle. Once that is done, we will examine the ramifications.

A company is a legal person separate and distinct from its members.

[2.01] Prest v Petrodel Resources Ltd [2013] UKSC 34, [2013] 2 AC 415 (Supreme Court)

The facts are immaterial at this stage, but see **[2.12]**.

> LORD SUMPTION SCJ:
>
> 8....The separate personality and property of a company is sometimes described as a fiction, and in a sense it is. But the fiction is the whole foundation of English company and insolvency law. As Robert Goff LJ once observed [in discussing 'corporate groups' as 'economic units'], in this domain 'we are concerned not with economics but with law. The distinction between the two is, in law, fundamental': *Bank of Tokyo Ltd v Karoon (Note)* [1987] AC 45, 64. He could justly have added that it is not just legally but economically fundamental, since limited companies have been the principal unit of commercial life for more than a century. Their separate personality and property are the basis on which third parties are entitled to deal with them and commonly do deal with them.

[2.02] Salomon v A Salomon & Co Ltd [1897] AC 22 (House of Lords)

The facts and arguments appear from the speech of Lord Macnaghten.[4] The extended detail is included here to illustrate a typical sole trader to small business incorporation. The process is instructive. Modern practice would be for the sole trader to be incorporated from the outset, although similar injections of assets and capital are usually needed from the incorporators/shareholders.

> LORD MACNAGHTEN: Mr Salomon, who is now suing as a pauper, was a wealthy man in July 1892. He was a boot and shoe manufacturer trading on his own sole account under the firm of 'A Salomon & Co', in High Street, Whitechapel, where he had extensive warehouses and a large establishment. He had been in the trade over thirty years. He had lived in the same neighbourhood all along, and for many years past he had occupied the same premises. So far things had gone very well with him. Beginning with little or no capital, he had gradually built up a thriving business, and he was undoubtedly in good credit and repute.
>
> It is impossible to say exactly what the value of the business was. But there was a substantial surplus of assets over liabilities. And it seems to me to be pretty clear that if Mr Salomon had been minded to dispose of his business in the market as a going concern he might fairly have counted upon retiring with at least £10,000 in his pocket.
>
> Mr Salomon, however, did not want to part with the business. He had a wife and a family consisting of five sons and a daughter. Four of the sons were working with their father . . . But the sons were not partners: they were only servants. Not unnaturally, perhaps, they were dissatisfied with their position. They kept pressing their father to give them a share in the concern. 'They troubled me,' says Mr Salomon, 'all the while.' So at length Mr Salomon did what hundreds of others have done under similar circumstances. He turned his business into a limited company. He wanted, he says, to extend the business and make provision for his family. In those words, I think, he fairly describes the principal motives which influenced his action.
>
> All the usual formalities were gone through; all the requirements of the Companies Act 1862 were duly observed. There was a contract with a trustee in the usual form for the sale of the

---

[4] The centenary of *Salomon*'s case was marked by a number of conferences and publications. See, eg, CEF Rickett and RB Grantham (eds), *Corporate Personality in the Twentieth Century* (1998), and a series of articles in (1998) 16 C & SLJ.

business to a company about to be formed. There was a memorandum of association duly signed and registered, stating that the company was formed to carry that contract into effect, and fixing the capital of £40,000 in 40,000 shares of £1 each. There were articles of association providing the usual machinery for conducting the business. The first directors were to be nominated by the majority of the subscribers to the memorandum of association. The directors, when appointed, were authorised to exercise all such powers of the company as were not by statute or by the articles required to be exercised in general meeting; and there was express power to borrow on debentures, with the limitation that the borrowing was not to exceed £10,000 without the sanction of a general meeting.

The company was intended from the first to be a private company;[5] it remained a private company to the end. No prospectus was issued; no invitation to take shares was ever addressed to the public.

The subscribers to the memorandum were Mr Salomon, his wife, and five of his children who were grown up. The subscribers met and appointed Mr Salomon and his two elder sons directors. The directors then proceeded to carry out the proposed transfer. By an agreement dated 2 August 1892 the company adopted the preliminary contract, and in accordance with it the business was taken over by the company as from 1 June 1892. The price fixed by the contract was duly paid. The price on paper was extravagant. It amounted to over £39,000—a sum which represented the sanguine expectations of a fond owner rather than anything that can be called a businesslike or reasonable estimate of value. That, no doubt, is a circumstance which at first sight calls for observation; but when the facts of the case and the position of the parties are considered, it is difficult to see what bearing it has on the question before your Lordships. The purchase-money was paid in this way: as money came in, sums amounting in all to [£20,000][6] were paid to Mr Salomon, and then immediately returned to the company in exchange for fully paid shares. The sum of £10,000 was paid in debentures[7] for the like amount. The balance, with the exception of about £1,000 which Mr Salomon seems to have received and retained, went in discharge of the debts and liabilities of the business at the time of the transfer, which were thus entirely wiped off. In the result, therefore, Mr Salomon received for his business about £1,000 in cash, £10,000 in debentures, and half the nominal capital of the company in fully paid shares for what they were worth. No other shares were issued except the seven shares taken by the subscribers to the memorandum, who, of course, knew all the circumstances, and had therefore no ground for complaint on the score of overvaluation.

The company had a brief career: it fell upon evil days. Shortly after it started there seems to have come a period of great depression in the boot and shoe trade. There were strikes of workmen too; and in view of that danger contracts with public bodies, which were the principal source of Mr Salomon's profit, were split up and divided between different firms. The attempts made to push the business on behalf of the new company crammed its warehouses with unsaleable stock. Mr Salomon seems to have done what he could: both he and his wife lent the company money; and then he got his debentures cancelled and reissued to a Mr Broderip, who advanced him £5,000, which he immediately handed over to the company on loan. The temporary relief only hastened ruin. Mr Broderip's interest was not paid when it became due. He took proceedings at once and got a receiver appointed. Then, of course, came liquidation and a forced sale of the company's assets. They realised enough to pay Mr Broderip, but not enough to pay the debentures in full: and the unsecured creditors were consequently left out in the cold.

---

[5] This expression is used descriptively. The 'private company' was first made the subject of separate statutory provision in the Companies Act 1907.

[6] The report reads '£30,000', but this is plainly an error. The figure of £20,000 appears in other reports of the case, eg 66 LJ Ch 35 at 49.

[7] This means that the sum of £10,000 was advanced by Salomon to the company as a loan, secured by a charge over the assets of the company.

In this state of things the liquidator met Mr Broderip's claim by a counter-claim, to which he made Mr Salomon a defendant. He disputed the validity of the debentures on the ground of fraud. On the same ground he claimed rescission of the agreement for the transfer of the business, cancellation of the debentures, and repayment by Mr Salomon of the balance of the purchase-money. In the alternative, he claimed payment of £20,000 on Mr Salomon's shares, alleging that nothing had been paid on them.

When the trial came on before Vaughan Williams J [*Broderip v Salomon* [1895] 2 Ch 323], the validity of Mr Broderip's claim was admitted, and it was not disputed that the 20,000 shares were fully paid up. The case presented by the liquidator broke down completely; but the learned judge suggested that the company had a right of indemnity against Mr Salomon. The signatories of the memorandum of association were, he said, mere nominees of Mr Salomon—mere dummies. The company was Mr Salomon in another form. He used the name of the company as an alias. He employed the company as his agent; so the company, he thought, was entitled to indemnity against its principal. The counter-claim was accordingly amended to raise this point; and on the amendment being made the learned judge pronounced an order in accordance with the view he had expressed.

The order of the learned judge appears to me to be founded on a misconception of the scope and effect of the Companies Act 1862. In order to form a company limited by shares, the Act requires that a memorandum of association should be signed by seven persons, who are each to take one share at least. If those conditions are complied with, what can it matter whether the signatories are relations or strangers? There is nothing in the Act requiring that the subscribers to the memorandum should be independent or unconnected, or that they or any one of them should take a substantial interest in the undertaking, or that they should have a mind and will of their own, as one of the learned Lords Justices seems to think, or that there should be anything like a balance of power in the constitution of the company. In almost every company that is formed the statutory number is eked out by clerks or friends, who sign their names at the request of the promoter or promoters without intending to take any further part or interest in the matter.

When the memorandum is duly signed and registered, though there be only seven shares taken, the subscribers are a body corporate 'capable forthwith', to use the words of the enactment, 'of exercising all the functions of an incorporated company'. Those are strong words. The company attains maturity on its birth. There is no period of minority—no interval of incapacity. I cannot understand how a body corporate thus made 'capable' by statute can lose its individuality by issuing the bulk of its capital to one person, whether he be a subscriber to the memorandum or not. The company is at law a different person altogether from the subscribers to the memorandum; and, though it may be that after incorporation the business is precisely the same as it was before, and the same persons are managers, and the same hands receive the profits, the company is not in law the agent of the subscribers or trustee for them. Nor are the subscribers as members liable, in any shape or form, except to the extent and in the manner provided by the Act. That is, I think, the declared intention of the enactment. If the view of the learned judge were sound, it would follow that no common law partnership could register as a company limited by shares without remaining subject to unlimited liability.

Mr Salomon appealed; but his appeal was dismissed with costs, though the appellate court did not entirely accept the view of the court below [*Broderip v Salomon* [1895] 2 Ch 323]. . . .

Among the principal reasons which induce persons to form private companies, as stated very clearly by Mr Palmer in his treatise on the subject, are the desire to avoid the risk of bankruptcy, and the increased facility afforded for borrowing money. By means of a private company, as Mr Palmer observes, a trade can be carried on with limited liability, and without exposing the persons interested in it in the event of failure to the harsh provisions of the bankruptcy law. A company, too, can raise money on debentures, which an ordinary trader cannot do. Any member of a company, acting in good faith, is as much entitled to take and hold the company's debentures as any outside creditor. Every creditor is entitled to get and to hold the best security the law allows him to take.

If, however, the declaration of the Court of Appeal means that Mr Salomon acted fraudulently or dishonestly, I must say I can find nothing in the evidence to support such an imputation. The purpose for which Mr Salomon and the other subscribers to the memorandum were associated was 'lawful'. The fact that Mr Salomon raised £5,000 for the company on debentures that belonged to him seems to me strong evidence of his good faith and of his confidence in the company. The unsecured creditors of A Salomon and Co Ltd may be entitled to sympathy, but they have only themselves to blame for their misfortunes. They trusted the company, I suppose, because they had long dealt with Mr Salomon, and he had always paid his way; but they had full notice that they were no longer dealing with an individual . . .

It has become the fashion to call companies of this class 'one man companies'. That is a taking nickname, but it does not help one much in the way of argument. If it is intended to convey the meaning that a company which is under the absolute control of one person is not a company legally incorporated, although the requirements of the Act of 1862 may have been complied with, it is inaccurate and misleading: if it merely means that there is a predominant partner possessing an overwhelming influence and entitled practically to the whole of the profits, there is nothing in that that I can see contrary to the true intention of the Act of 1862, or against public policy, or detrimental to the interests of creditors. If the shares are fully paid up, it cannot matter whether they are in the hands of one or many. If the shares are not fully paid, it is as easy to gauge the solvency of an individual as to estimate the financial ability of a crowd.

One argument was addressed to your Lordships which ought perhaps to be noticed, although it was not the ground of decision in either of the courts below. It was argued that the agreement for the transfer of the business to the company ought to be set aside, because there was no independent board of directors, and the property was transferred at an overvalue. There are, it seems to me, two answers to that argument. In the first place, the directors did just what they were authorised to do by the memorandum of association. There was no fraud or misrepresentation, and there was nobody deceived. In the second place, the company have put it out of their power to restore the property which was transferred to them [ie the company could not make *restitutio in integrum* because the assets had already been sold in the liquidation of the company] . . .

LORD HALSBURY LC: My Lords, the important question in this case, I am not certain it is not the only question, is whether the respondent company was a company at all—whether in truth that artificial creation of the legislature had been validly constituted in this instance; and in order to determine that question it is necessary to look at what the statute itself has determined in that respect. I have no right to add to the requirements of the statute, or to take from the requirements thus enacted. The sole guide must be the statute itself.

Now, that there were seven actual living persons who held shares in the company has not been doubted. As to the proportionate amounts held by each I will deal presently; but it is important to observe that this first condition of the statute is satisfied, and it follows as a consequence that it would not be competent to any one—and certainly not to these persons themselves—to deny that they were shareholders.

I must pause here to point out that the statute enacts nothing as to the extent or degree of interest which may be held by each of the seven, or as to the proportion of interest or influence possessed by one or the majority of the shareholders over the others. One share is enough. Still less is it possible to contend that the motive of becoming shareholders or of making them shareholders is a field of inquiry which the statute itself recognises as legitimate. If they are shareholders, they are shareholders for all purposes; and even if the statute was silent as to the recognition of trusts, I should be prepared to hold that if six of them were [trustees for] the seventh, whatever might be their rights inter se, the statute would have made them shareholders to all intents and purposes with their respective rights and liabilities, and, dealing with them in their relation to the company, the only relations which I believe the law would sanction would be that they were corporators of the corporate body.

I am simply here dealing with the provisions of the statute, and it seems to me to be essential to the artificial creation that the law should recognise only that artificial existence—quite apart from the motives or conduct of individual corporators. In saying this, I do not at all mean to suggest that if it could be established that this provision of the statute to which I am adverting had not been complied with, you could not go behind the certificate of incorporation to show that a fraud had been committed upon the officer entrusted with the duty of giving the certificate, and that by some proceeding in the nature of *scire facias* you could not prove the fact that the company had no real legal existence. But short of such proof it seems to me impossible to dispute that once the company is legally incorporated it must be treated like any other independent person with its rights and liabilities appropriate to itself, and that the motives of those who took part in the promotion of the company are absolutely irrelevant in discussing what those rights and liabilities are.

I will for the sake of argument assume the proposition that the Court of Appeal lays down—that the formation of the company was a mere scheme to enable Aron Salomon to carry on business in the name of the company. I am wholly unable to follow the proposition that this was contrary to the true intent and meaning of the Companies Act. I can only find the true intent and meaning of the Act from the Act itself; and the Act appears to me to give a company a legal existence with, as I have said, rights and liabilities of its own, whatever may have been the ideas or schemes of those who brought it into existence.

I observe that the learned judge (Vaughan Williams J) held that the business was Mr Salomon's business, and no one else's, and that he chose to employ as agent a limited company; and he proceeded to argue that he was employing that limited company as agent, and that he was bound to indemnify that agent (the company). I confess it seems to me that that very learned judge becomes involved by this argument in a very singular contradiction. Either the limited company was a legal entity or it was not. If it was, the business belonged to it and not to Mr Salomon. If it was not, there was no person and no thing to be an agent at all; and it is impossible to say at the same time that there is a company and there is not.

Lindley LJ, on the other hand, affirms that there were seven members of the company; but he says it is manifest that six of them were members simply in order to enable the seventh himself to carry on business with limited liability. The object of the whole arrangement is to do the very thing which the legislature intended not to be done.[8]

It is obvious to inquire where that intention of the legislature manifested in the statute is. Even if we were at liberty to insert words to manifest that intention, I should have great difficulty in ascertaining what the exact intention thus imputed to the legislature is, or was. In this particular case it is the members of one family that represent all the shares; but if the supposed intention is not limited to so narrow a proposition as this, that the seven shareholders must not be members of one family, to what extent may influence or authority or intentional purchase of a majority among the shareholders be carried so as to bring it within the supposed prohibition? It is, of course, easy to say that it was contrary to the intention of the legislature—a proposition which, by reason of its generality, it is difficult to bring to the test; but when one seeks to put as an affirmative proposition what the thing is which the legislature has prohibited, there is, as it appears to me, an insuperable difficulty in the way of those who seek to insert by construction such a prohibition into the statute.

As one mode of testing the proposition, it would be pertinent to ask whether two or three, or indeed all seven, may constitute the whole of the shareholders? Whether they must be all independent of each other in the sense of each having an independent beneficial interest? And this is a question that cannot be answered by the reply that it is a matter of degree. If the legislature intended to prohibit something, you ought to know what that something is. All it has said is that one share is sufficient to constitute a shareholder, though the shares may be 100,000 in number.

---

[8] In *Re Baglan Hall Colliery Co* (1870) LR 5 Ch App 346, Giffard LJ states that it 'is the policy of the Companies Act to enable business people to incorporate their businesses and so avoid incurring further personal liability'.

Where am I to get from the statute itself a limitation of that provision that that shareholder must be an independent and beneficially interested person? . . .

My Lords, the learned judges appear to me not to have been absolutely certain in their own minds whether to treat the company as a real thing or not. If it was a real thing; if it had a legal existence, and if consequently the law attributed to it certain rights and liabilities in its constitution as a company, it appears to me to follow as a consequence that it is impossible to deny the validity of the transactions into which it has entered. . . .

LORDS WATSON and DAVEY delivered concurring opinions. LORD MORRIS concurred.

➤ Questions

1. List the various arguments advanced, and rejected, by the House of Lords in reaching their conclusion that Mr Salomon was not personally liable to the company's creditors. What factors might have altered the conclusions reached? The answer to this question remains of vital importance. Modern analyses of the potential to look beyond the company itself to fund liabilities turn on these issues. See the later discussions in 'Connections between the company and other persons', pp 75ff.

2. To what do you think Lord Macnaghten was alluding when he said that the unsecured creditors of the company 'had full notice that they were no longer dealing with an individual'? Was it fair to say that 'they have only themselves to blame for their misfortunes'?

3. Was there a 'very singular contradiction' in the reasoning of Vaughan Williams J, as Lord Halsbury said? (See later on the circumstances in which a company *will* be held to be carrying on business as the agent of its principal shareholder: 'Agency rules and third parties', pp 76ff.)

4. *Salomon*'s case has been described as a 'calamitous decision' (O Kahn-Freund (1944) 7 MLR 54). Would you agree?

➤ Note

It makes no difference to the rule in *Salomon* that one member owns all or substantially all of the shares. Until 1992, when the Twelfth EU Directive on Single-Member Companies was implemented in the UK, it was necessary for a company to have at least two members. (The number in 1844 was originally set at 25, but this number was reduced to seven by the Companies Act 1862—the Act under which Mr Salomon's company was registered—and later to two.) However, even under the former law it was possible for one person to own all the shares in a company *beneficially* and at the same time comply with the legislation by the simple expedient of vesting one or more shares in nominees who held the shares on his behalf and acted at his direction. In many other jurisdictions, the one person company has been recognised for a long time.

The consequences of separate legal personality

Having established that a company *is* an independent legal person, it is necessary to consider the consequences. We start with the specifics: that a company, as a legal person, can own property, enter into contracts, run its own business and sue and be sued on its own liabilities. Once these concrete ideas have been addressed, some consideration is given to broader generalities. For example, not every law applies to companies (eg companies cannot smoke, or drive a car), so how do we determine whether a particular legal rule, be it common law or statute, applies or not? Similarly, how is a company's corporate nationality, residence, domicile, or indeed any other question of status, determined?

The company owns its own property

It should be unsurprising that a legal person can own and manage its own property. What typically does come as a surprise, however, is the necessary corollary that the shareholders then do *not* own this property. This is true even if the shareholders have ultimate control over the company, and can therefore determine, in a practical sense, what is done with the company's property. This degree of control does not make the company's property their property. The next two cases illustrate that to dramatic effect.

The property of a company belongs to it and not to its members. Neither a member nor a creditor of a company (unless a secured creditor) has an insurable interest in the assets of the company.

[2.03] Macaura v Northern Assurance Co [1925] AC 619 (House of Lords)

Macaura was the owner of the Killymoon estate in County Tyrone. He sold the whole of the timber on the estate to Irish Canadian Sawmills Ltd in consideration of the allotment to him of 42,000 fully paid £1 shares. Macaura and his nominees owned all the shares in the company, and Macaura was also an unsecured creditor of the company for an amount of £19,000. Following the sale of the timber, Macaura took out insurance policies in his own name with the respondent insurance company and others, covering the timber against fire. Two weeks later, almost all of the timber was destroyed in a fire. A claim brought by Macaura on the policies was dismissed on the ground that he had no insurable interest in the timber.

LORD SUMNER: My Lords, this appeal relates to an insurance on goods against loss by fire. It is clear that the appellant had no insurable interest in the timber described. It was not his. It belonged to the Irish Canadian Sawmills Ltd, of Skibbereen, co Cork. He had no lien or security over it and, though it lay on his land by his permission, he had no responsibility to its owner for its safety, nor was it there under any contract that enabled him to hold it for his debt. He owned almost all the shares in the company, and the company owed him a good deal of money, but, neither as creditor nor as shareholder, could he insure the company's assets. The debt was not exposed to fire nor were the shares, and the fact that he was virtually the company's only creditor, while the timber was its only asset, seems to me to make no difference. He stood in no 'legal or equitable relation to' the timber at all. He had no 'concern in' the subject insured. His relation was to the company, not to its goods, and after the fire he was directly prejudiced by the paucity of the company's assets, not by the fire. . . .

My Lords, I think this appeal fails.

LORDS BUCKMASTER and WRENBURY delivered concurring opinions.

LORDS ATKINSON and PHILLIMORE concurred.

➤ Notes

1. Similarly in *JJ Harrison (Properties) Ltd v Harrison* [2001] EWCA Civ 1467, [2002] 1 BCLC 162, the court stated that there is no rule of company law which constitutes a company the trustee of its property and its members or shareholders as beneficiaries of that trust.

2. In *Prest v Petrodel Resources Ltd* [2013] UKSC 34 **[2.12]**, the divorcing parties were litigating over the division of an estate worth more than £50 million, but held by nominee companies. The Supreme Court confirmed that an order in respect of a company's

property (houses in London and overseas) could not be made in favour of the wife under the Matrimonial Causes Act 1973 s 24(1)(a), even though the husband owned 100% of the shares and had complete control of the companies, unless there were legitimate grounds for 'piercing the corporate veil', which there were not here (see '"Piercing the corporate veil" vs separate legal personality', pp 63ff). Mere ownership and control of the shares did not give the husband an interest in the houses. (Note, however, that the Supreme Court went on to find that the companies here could be regarded as holding the properties on trust for the husband, not by virtue of his status as sole shareholder and controller, but in the particular circumstances of this case. The Matrimonial Causes Act 1973 was thus applicable to enable orders to be made against the husband in relation to his beneficial interest in the houses.)

3. In *Acatos & Hutcheson plc v Watson* [1995] BCLC 446, A Ltd owned nearly 30% of the shares in A & H plc but had no other assets. It would have been unlawful for A & H plc to acquire these shares because the 'rule in *Trevor v Whitworth*' forbids a company to own shares in itself (the rule is not the same now, see 'Redemptions and repurchases of shares', p 542). But Lightman J said that it was permissible for it to purchase all the shares in A Ltd, which of course meant that for all practical purposes it did, indirectly, own 30% of its own shares. He added, however, that he might have thought it appropriate to pierce the veil and declare the transaction unlawful if A Ltd had been *deliberately* set up by A & H plc to acquire the shares as the first of two stages in a single scheme to evade the rule. See R Nolan, 'The Veil Intact' (1995) 16 Co Law 180.

The property of a company belongs to it and not to its members. Orders for disclosure of the company's documents must be made against the company: the company's members cannot generally be ordered to make such disclosure.

[2.04] Lonrho Ltd v Shell Petroleum Co Ltd [1980] QB 358 (Court of Appeal), affd [1980] 1 WLR 627 (House of Lords)

Lonrho sought an order for discovery (ie disclosure) of certain documents which it claimed (as the rules on disclosure required) were in the 'power' of two multinational oil companies, Shell and BP. These documents were held in Rhodesia (now Zimbabwe) and South Africa by local subsidiaries of Shell and BP, the subsidiaries being in each case wholly owned and controlled by Shell and BP. The application was refused.

SHAW LJ: This appeal poses as its principal issue a compact question as to the application and scope of RSC, Ord 24. When is a document in the power (as distinct from the possession or control) of a party to litigation so as to require him to disclose it if it relates to matters in question in that litigation?

The question seems elementary, but it poses for me at any rate a difficult philosophical problem as to what constitutes power, and I must confess to some vacillation as the arguments on either side proceeded. In the end I have come to the view that a document can be said to be in the power of a party for the purpose of disclosure only if, at the time and in the situation which obtains at the date of discovery, that party is, on the factual realities of the case virtually in possession (as with a one man company in relation to documents of the company) or otherwise has a present indefeasible legal right to demand possession from the person in whose possession or control it is at that time.

In the present case no such sure or direct route to acquiring possession existed or exists. The relationship between Shell and BP, on the one hand, and, on the other hand, the various subsidiaries, including those which are wholly owned by the two parent companies, may afford an ultimate but not an immediate or certain prospect of acquiring possession of documents which belong to and are in the possession and control for the time being of a subsidiary. The realisation of that prospect might involve the alteration of the articles of an unwilling or recalcitrant subsidiary followed by the removal of its then directors and their substitution by others more compliant. This would involve a radical transformation of the local scene within the subsidiary company. It would involve not merely raising the corporate veil, but committing an affront on the persona of the company itself. Even then, the directors who are substituted for the recalcitrant ones may find that there exists a conflict of duty so that they have no right to comply with the requirement. It would follow that the outcome of such a procedure would be at the best dubious . . .

There are no doubt situations, such as existed in *B v B (Matrimonial Proceedings: Discovery)*[9] where on the established facts a company is so utterly subservient or subordinated to the will and the wishes of some other person (whether an individual or a parent company) that compliance with that other person's demands can be regarded as assured. Each case must depend upon its own facts and also upon the nature, degree and context of the control . . .

LORD DENNING MR and BRANDON LJ delivered concurring judgments.

The company enters into its own contracts

The second feature associated with legal personality is that the company can enter into contracts on its own account. When it does, both the benefits *and* the liabilities under the contract are the company's; they do not belong to the company's controllers. As the next case makes plain, this is true even if the contract is between the company and its sole director and shareholder in circumstances where that individual must have acted for himself on one side of the transaction and for the company on the other side of the transaction.

A company may make a valid and effective contract with one of its members. It is possible for a person to be at the same time wholly in control of a company (as its principal shareholder or member and its sole director) and an employee of that company.

[2.05] Lee v Lee's Air Farming Ltd [1961] AC 12 (Privy Council)

Lee, the appellant's late husband, had formed the respondent company to carry on his business of spreading fertilisers on farmland ('top-dressing') from the air. He held 2,999 of its 3,000 shares, and was by its articles of association appointed sole governing director and (also pursuant to the articles) employed at a salary as its chief pilot. He was killed in an aircraft crash while flying for the company. If he was a 'worker' (defined as 'any person who has entered into or works under a contract of service . . . with an employer . . . whether remunerated by wages, salary, or otherwise') then his widow was entitled to be paid compensation by his employer under the Workers' Compensation Act 1922 (NZ). The company, as required by statute, was insured against liability to pay its workers such compensation. Mrs Lee appealed successfully against the ruling of the Court of Appeal of New Zealand that Lee could not be a 'worker' when he was in effect also the employer.

The opinion of their Lordships was delivered by LORD MORRIS OF BORTH-Y-GEST: The Court of Appeal recognised that a director of a company may properly enter into a service agreement with his company, but they considered that, in the present case, inasmuch as the deceased was the

[9] [1978] Fam 181, [1979] 1 All ER 801.

governing director in whom was vested the full government and control of the company he could not also be a servant of the company. . . . [After discussing the facts of the case:] Their Lordships find it impossible to resist the conclusion that the active aerial operations were performed because the deceased was in some contractual relationship with the company. That relationship came about because the deceased as one legal person was willing to work for and to make a contract with the company which was another legal entity. A contractual relationship could only exist on the basis that there was consensus between two contracting parties. It was never suggested (nor in their Lordships' view could it reasonably have been suggested) that the company was a sham or a mere simulacrum. It is well established that the mere fact that someone is a director of a company is no impediment to his entering into a contract to serve the company. If, then, it be accepted that the respondent company was a legal entity their Lordships see no reason to challenge the validity of any contractual obligations which were created between the company and the deceased . . .

Nor in their Lordships' view were any contractual obligations invalidated by the circumstance that the deceased was sole governing director in whom was vested the full government and control of the company. Always assuming that the company was not a sham then the capacity of the company to make a contract with the deceased could not be impugned merely because the deceased was the agent of the company in its negotiation. . . . In their Lordships' view it is a logical consequence of the decision in *Salomon's* case **[2.02]** that one person may function in dual capacities. There is no reason, therefore, to deny the possibility of a contractual relationship being created as between the deceased and the company.... [I]t is [then] said that the deceased could not both be under the duty of giving orders and also be under the duty of obeying them. But this approach does not give effect to the circumstance that it would be the company and not the deceased that would be giving the orders. Control would remain with the company whoever might be the agent of the company to exercise it. The fact that so long as the deceased continued to be governing director, with amplitude of powers, it would be for him to act as the agent of the company to give the orders does not alter the fact that the company and the deceased were two separate and distinct legal persons.... Just as the company and the deceased were separate legal entities so as to permit of contractual relations being established between them, so also were they separate legal entities so as to enable the company to give an order to the deceased . . .

> ➤ Notes

1. Although *Lee*'s case is undoubtedly correct as a ruling in company law, the question whether a person should be regarded as an 'employee' of a company which he can control as a director or major shareholder may not always be so clear-cut. Arguments that the employment contract is a sham may be raised (*Secretary of State for Business, Enterprise and Regulatory Reform v Neufeld* [2009] EWCA Civ 280, although the contract was upheld); and claims for unfair or wrongful dismissal obviously require careful attention (*Secretary of State for Trade and Industry v Bottrill* [1999] ICR 592, CA).

2. There is one crucial limitation to actions by employee/managers against their companies. The wrongdoing employee/manager cannot insist that his or her own wrongful conduct, attributed to the company (see Chapter 3), then counts as the *company's* wrong for which the company is then liable to the injured wrongdoer: see *Brumder v Motornet Service and Repairs Ltd* **[3.32]**.

The company runs its own business

The third aspect of separate legal personality is that the company runs its own business. As in *Salomon v A Salomon & Co Ltd* **[2.02]**, the fact that one person controls the company and every aspect of its business does not make that business the controller's; it is still the company's.

The fact that one person holds all, or substantially all, of the shares in a company does not, without more, make the company's business that person's business in the eyes of the law.

[2.06] Gramophone and Typewriter Co Ltd v Stanley [1908] 2 KB 89 (Court of Appeal)

All the shares in a German company (Deutsche Grammophon Aktiengesellschaft) were held by the appellant company, which was resident for tax purposes in England. The appellant was assessed for income tax not only upon the profits of the German company actually remitted to the English holding company in England, but also on a sum of £15,000 retained by the German company and transferred by it to a depreciation fund. The unremitted profits were taxable in England only if they were the profits or gains of a business 'carried on' *by the English company*. The Court of Appeal held they were not.

BUCKLEY LJ: The question is, I think, one of fact . . . The question of fact is whether the business in Germany is carried on by the appellant company. If it is, the [appellants] do not dispute that the Attorney-General [for the Inland Revenue] is right. If, on the contrary, the German business is not carried on by the English company, then equally the Attorney-General cannot dispute but that the English company is assessable only upon the dividends which it may receive upon its shares in the German company.

In order to succeed the Attorney-General must, I think, make out either, first, that the German company is a fiction, a sham, a simulacrum, and that in reality the English company, and not the German company, is carrying on the business; or, secondly, that the German company, if it is a real thing, is the agent of the English company. As regards the former of these, there are no facts at all to show that the German company is a pretence.... The only remaining question, therefore, is whether the German company is agent of the English company, whether the English company is really carrying on the business and is employing the German company to do so on its behalf. Upon this point the Attorney-General relies principally upon the fact that . . . the appellant company now holds all the shares of the German company. In my opinion this fact does not establish the relation of principal and agent between the English company and the German company. It is so familiar that it would be a waste of time to dwell upon the difference between the corporation and the aggregate of all the corporators.... [I]it cannot seriously be suggested that each time one person becomes the holder of all the shares an agency comes into existence which dies again when he parts with some of them.

Further it is urged that the English company, as owning all the shares, can control the German company in the sense that the German company must do all that the English company directs. In my opinion this again is a misapprehension. This court decided not long since, in *Automatic Self-Cleansing Filter Syndicate Co Ltd v Cuninghame* **[4.05]** that even a resolution of a numerical majority at a general meeting of the company cannot impose its will upon the directors when the articles have confided to them the control of the company's affairs. The directors are not servants to obey directions given by the shareholders as individuals; they are not agents appointed by and bound to serve the shareholders as their principals. They are persons who may by the regulations be entrusted with the control of the business, and if so entrusted they can be dispossessed from that control only by the statutory majority which can alter the articles. Directors are not, I think, bound to comply with the directions even of all the corporators acting as individuals. Of course the corporators have it in their power by proper resolutions, which would generally be special resolutions,[10] to remove directors who do not act as they desire, but this in no way answers the

---

10   An ordinary resolution is now sufficient in all cases: CA 2006 s 168.

question here to be considered, which is whether the corporators are engaged in carrying on the business of the corporation. In my opinion they are not. To say that they are involves a complete confusion of ideas . . .

COZENS-HARDY MR and FLETCHER MOULTON LJ delivered concurring judgments.

The company sues and is sued on its own liabilities

Fourthly, again as a characteristic of legal personality, the company sues and is sued on its *own* legal rights and liabilities. This has two aspects. The first is procedural: it is the *company* which brings its own legal claims. This, we shall see, can cause some practical problems when the company's controllers (typically the directors) disagree with the company's members about whether the company should litigate.[11] The second is substantive: the legal rights and obligations in issue belong to the company; in particular, the company carries its own liabilities, and members cannot generally be sued on these liabilities.[12] This is the central legal principle in *Salomon* [2.02]. Yet contrary claims are often brought before the courts for the very practical reason that the company is unable to fund its admitted liabilities in circumstances where the members of the company have deep pockets and could do so. This may be because the company is a 'one man company' and the shareholder a rather wealthier individual (as in *Salomon*) or is an undercapitalised subsidiary of a far wealthier parent company.

The next case is an illustration. Prior to the Supreme Court decision in *Prest v Petrodel Resources Ltd* [2.12], this case was a leading authority on 'piercing the corporate veil'. Its treatment now can be rather more succinct, but both the context and its key legal points remain important and instructive.

[2.07] Adams v Cape Industries plc [1990] Ch 433 (Court of Appeal)

Cape, an English company, headed a group which included many wholly owned subsidiaries. Some of these mined asbestos in South Africa and others marketed the asbestos in various countries, including the United States. Several hundred plaintiffs had been awarded damages by a Texas court for personal injuries suffered as a result of exposure to asbestos dust. The defendants included one of Cape's subsidiaries, NAAC, which was based in Illinois. The Court of Appeal held that the judgment could not be enforced against the far wealthier English parent, Cape, rejecting arguments: (i) that Cape and the relevant subsidiaries should be treated as a single economic unit; (ii) that the subsidiaries were used as a 'façade' concealing the true facts; and (iii) that an agency relationship existed between Cape and NAAC.

The judgment of the court (SLADE, MUSTILL and RALPH GIBSON LJJ) was delivered by SLADE LJ:

The 'single economic unit' argument

There is no general principle that all companies in a group of companies are to be regarded as one. On the contrary, the fundamental principle is that 'each company in a group of companies (a relatively modern concept) is a separate legal entity possessed of separate legal rights and liabilities': *The Albazero*,[13] per Roskill LJ.

---

[11] See Chapter 4, 'Dividing corporate power between members and directors', p 189; and Chapter 13, 'Company claims and the statutory derivative action: CA 2006 ss 260ff', p 671.

[12] Unless there is some legal reason why they too should be made liable. The following cases discuss some of the options, but see especially 'Connections between the company and other persons', p 75.

[13] [1977] AC 774 at 807.

It is thus indisputable that each of Cape, Capasco, NAAC and CPC were in law separate legal entities. Mr Morison did not go so far as to submit that the very fact of the parent-subsidiary relationship existing between Cape and NAAC rendered Cape or Capasco present in Illinois. Nevertheless, he submitted that the court will, in appropriate circumstances, ignore the distinction in law between members of a group of companies treating them as one, and that broadly speaking, it will do so whenever it considers that justice so demands. In support of this submission, he referred us to a number of authorities. . . .

We have some sympathy with Mr Morison's submissions in this context. To the layman at least the distinction between the case where a company itself trades in a foreign country and the case where it trades in a foreign country through a subsidiary, whose activities it has full power to control, may seem a slender one . . .

It is [therefore] not surprising that in many cases . . . the wording of a particular statute or contract has been held to justify the treatment of parent and subsidiary as one unit, at least for some purposes. . . .

Mr Morison described the theme of all these cases as being that where legal technicalities would produce injustice in cases involving members of a group of companies, such technicalities should not be allowed to prevail. We do not think that the cases relied on go nearly so far as this. As Sir Godfray [counsel for Cape] submitted, save in cases which turn on the wording of particular statutes or contracts, the court is not free to disregard the principle of *Salomon v A Salomon & Co Ltd* **[2.02]** merely because it considers that justice so requires. Our law, for better or worse, recognises the creation of subsidiary companies, which though in one sense the creatures of their parent companies, will nevertheless under the general law fall to be treated as separate legal entities with all the rights and liabilities which would normally attach to separate legal entities.

In deciding whether a company is present in a foreign country by a subsidiary, which is itself present in that country, the court is entitled, indeed bound, to investigate the relationship between the parent and the subsidiary. In particular, that relationship may be relevant in determining whether the subsidiary was acting as the parent's agent and, if so, on what terms. However, there is no presumption of any such agency. There is no presumption that the subsidiary is the parent company's alter ego. In the court below the judge refused an invitation to infer that there existed an agency agreement between Cape and NAAC comparable to that which had previously existed between Cape and Capasco and that refusal is not challenged on this appeal. If a company chooses to arrange the affairs of its group in such a way that the business carried on in a particular foreign country is the business of its subsidiary and not its own, it is, in our judgment, entitled to do so. Neither in this class of case nor in any other class of case is it open to this court to disregard the principle of *Salomon v A Salomon & Co Ltd* **[2.02]** merely because it considers it just so to do.

[His Lordship reviewed the evidence, and concluded that, although Cape was in a position to exercise overall control over the general policy of NAAC, this control did not extend to the subsidiary's day-to-day running. The contention that the group was a 'single economic unit' was accordingly rejected.]

The 'corporate veil' point

Quite apart from cases where statute or contract permits a broad interpretation to be given to references to members of a group of companies, there is one well-recognised exception to the rule prohibiting the piercing of 'the corporate veil'. . . . [That is where special circumstances exist indicating that the company is a mere façade concealing the true facts.] . . .

Mr Morison submitted that the court will lift the corporate veil where a defendant by the device of a corporate structure attempts to evade (i) limitations imposed on his conduct by law; (ii) such rights of relief against him as third parties already possess; and (iii) such rights of relief as third parties may in the future acquire. Assuming that the first and second of these three conditions will suffice in law to justify such a course, neither of them apply in the present case. It is not suggested that the arrangements involved any actual or potential illegality or were intended to deprive anyone of their existing rights. Whether or not such a course deserves moral approval, there was nothing illegal as such in Cape arranging its affairs (whether by the use of subsidiaries or otherwise) so as to attract the minimum publicity to its involvement in the sale of Cape asbestos in the United States of America. As to condition (iii), we do not accept as a matter of law that the court is entitled to lift the corporate veil as against a defendant company which is the member of a corporate group merely because the corporate structure has been used so as to ensure that the legal liability (if any) in respect of particular future activities of the group (and correspondingly the risk of enforcement of that liability) will fall on another member of the group rather than the defendant company. Whether or not this is desirable, the right to use a corporate structure in this manner is inherent in our corporate law. Mr Morison urged on us that the purpose of the operation was in substance that Cape would have the practical benefit of the group's asbestos trade. in the United States of America without the risks of tortious liability. This may be so. However, in our judgment, Cape was in law entitled to organise the group's affairs in that manner and . . . to expect that the court would apply the principle of *Salomon v A Salomon & Co Ltd* in the ordinary way. . . .

We reject the 'corporate veil' argument.

The 'agency argument'

We now proceed to consider the agency argument in relation to NAAC on the footing, which we consider to be the correct one, that NAAC must for all relevant purposes be regarded as a legal entity separate from Cape.

[His Lordship reviewed the evidence and concluded:] Having regard to the legal principles stated earlier in this judgment, and looking at the facts of the case overall, our conclusion is that the judge was right to hold that the business carried on by NAAC was exclusively its own business, not the business of Cape . . . We see no sufficient grounds for disturbing this finding of fact.

➤ Question

The plaintiffs in *Adams* were tort victims. Some commentators argue that there is a stronger case for looking to the members or shareholders behind the corporate framework in such cases because the tort victims, unlike creditors with claims based in contract, were never in a position to negotiate or to take the risk of the company's potential insolvency into account in settling the terms of their bargain. However, it is observed by others that *all* tort victims face this risk that their tortfeasor may be impecunious. *Should* the law adopt a different approach to corporate personality, or to the limited liability of members, in dealing with contract and tort claimants? (Note that the law could do either *without* ignoring the separate corporate person, although most of these early cases argued for 'piercing [ie ignoring] the corporate veil'.)

➤ Notes

1. In *Yukong Lines Ltd of Korea v Rendsburg Investments Corpn of Liberia* [1998] 1 WLR 294, Toulson J adopted a very similar line of reasoning where the question was whether the *Salomon* principle should be disregarded so as to make Mr Ramvrias, the sole shareholder of the defendant company (Rendsburg), personally liable for damages for breach of a contract to charter a ship which had ostensibly been entered into by that company. He rejected an argument that the charterparty had in reality been entered into by Rendsburg as Ramvrias's agent (indeed, to the contrary, the document had been signed by Ramvrias as Rendsburg's agent), and also further arguments that the company was a 'sham' or, alternatively, that the corporate veil should be pierced in the interests of justice. (The real complaint was that Ramvrias had caused Rendsburg to transfer most of its funds to another of his companies so that it would not be in a position to meet any award of damages

that might be made against it. But, as the judge observed, there were other ways in which these funds might be recouped—for example, in an action by Rendsburg's liquidator for breach by Ramvrias of his duty *as a director* (note, not as a member): see 'The functions, powers and duties of the liquidator', pp 850ff. These recoveries would boost the company's coffers, and that would benefit the company's creditors. But *Salomon* stood in the way of giving the creditor any *direct* remedy against Ramvrias.)

2. Also see *Re Polly Peck International plc* [1996] 2 All ER 433, where PPI, a holding company at the head of a large group, set up a specially incorporated overseas subsidiary, PPIF, in order to raise funds by a bond issue. All the funds received were on-loaned to PPI, and PPI guaranteed the subsidiary's repayment obligations. PPIF had no separate management or bank account. The court refused to pierce the veil on 'group trading', 'agency' or 'sham' grounds so as to treat PPI as being in reality the borrower of the funds.

Corporate groups: do they warrant special treatment?

These and similar cases decided since *Adams v Cape Industries* **[2.07]** indicate that it is now very unlikely that the *Salomon* principle will be ignored in a group context. On the other hand, as we will see later, ignoring *Salomon* is not always necessary in order to deliver the desired outcome: see 'Connections between the company and other persons', p 75.

Nevertheless, there is increasing interest—although perhaps more in other parts of the world than in the UK—in whether a holding company should be made liable for the debts of an insolvent subsidiary, or the 'enterprise' as a whole for the obligations of one of its members.

The problem is well summarised in the following extract from the judgment of Templeman LJ in *Re Southard & Co Ltd* [1979] 1 WLR 1198 at 1208, CA:

English company law possesses some curious features, which may generate curious results. A parent company may spawn a number of subsidiary companies, all controlled directly or indirectly by the shareholders of the parent company. If one of the subsidiary companies, to change the metaphor, turns out to be the runt of the litter and declines into insolvency to the dismay of its creditors, the parent company and the other subsidiary companies may prosper to the joy of the shareholders without any liability for the debts of the insolvent subsidiary. It is not surprising that, when a subsidiary company collapses, the unsecured creditors wish the finances of the company and its relationship with other members of the group to be narrowly examined, to ensure that no assets of the subsidiary company have leaked away, that no liabilities of the subsidiary company ought to be laid at the door of other members of the group, and that no indemnity from or right of action against any other company, or against any individual, is by some mischance overlooked.

The anxiety of the creditors will be increased where, as in the present case, all the assets of the subsidiary company are claimed by another member of the group in right of a debenture.

Generally speaking, English case law has adhered to the *Salomon* principle in situations such as this and has not developed principles which would allow a court to ignore the separate personality of the companies concerned.[14] This contrasts with attitudes abroad, where factors such as 'domination' and 'undercapitalisation' (or 'thin incorporation') have been relied on to build up a body of rules under which other companies in a group have been held liable to back the obligations of the 'runt of the litter'. In New Zealand and Ireland, the Companies Acts have been amended so as to give the court a discretion to order that one company in a group should make a contribution to the assets of another

---

[14] Of course, in appropriate circumstances the 'members' may be liable on other perfectly orthodox legal grounds: see 'Connections between the company and other persons', p 75.

which is in insolvent liquidation, or to order that the liquidations of two associated companies should proceed jointly, so that their assets and liabilities are pooled.[15] The Cork Committee on Insolvency in its report (Cmnd 8558, 1982) did not suggest that this precedent should be followed in the UK, but did urge that the question be studied further. The Company Law Review (CLR) could have taken this opportunity in its Review, but instead it simply stated that it did not propose any reforms in this area.

By contrast, there are a variety of statutory provisions governing groups, and treating them as a 'group'. For instance, the companies legislation has rules requiring the publication of consolidated accounts (CA 2006 ss 399ff); and the tax laws have rules dealing with such matters as the transfer of assets between member companies of a group (see, eg, Income and Corporation Taxes Act 1988 ss 402ff). Employment legislation, for example in regard to redundancy payments, sometimes treats as continuous employment a succession of jobs with a number of associated companies, or, similarly, a succession of employers following a takeover or reorganisation. In all these statutes, the concepts of 'group' and 'associated company' will be formally defined for the purpose of the particular provision in question.

In the EU, too, there are signs that the veil of incorporation may not be sacrosanct in a group situation. ICI was made to pay fines, even before the UK was a member of the Union, for the breach of EU competition laws by an overseas subsidiary.[16] The Draft Ninth Directive on the Conduct of Groups of Companies would have taken this further, and would in certain circumstances have made a dominant company in a group liable for losses incurred by a dependent company. But this proposal has now been withdrawn.[17]

General recognition that the company *is* a legal person

Having considered the more familiar claims of legal persons—that is, to own property, enter into contracts, run a business and sue and be sued—we can consider a number of more subtle illustrations. It is the *technique* adopted by both statutes and the courts in determining particular aspects of corporate personality which are crucial, not simply the detail of the particular rule under examination.

The fact that a company is a legal person means that the general laws of the land apply to the company, although only so far as is appropriate (eg it is obvious that a company cannot marry, or drive a car,[18] although it can do many other things of legal significance). It also means that the company has a place of residence and a domicile, and can be assigned a legal status for particular purposes (eg, in the next case extract, as an 'enemy alien').

---

[15] At present, this can be done in England only with the approval of the prescribed statutory majorities of the creditors concerned, by a scheme of arrangement under CA 2006 ss 895ff or, in special circumstances, under the 'power to compromise' conferred on liquidators and the court by IA 1986 s 167(1) and Sch 4. For an example of the latter, see *Re Bank of Credit and Commerce International SA (No 3)* [1993] BCLC 1490.

[16] *ICI v EC Commission* (Cases 48, 49, 51–57/69) (the *Dyestuffs* case) [1972] ECR 619, where the Court of Justice of the European Union (CJEU) held that anti-competitive behaviour of a subsidiary company within the EU, acting on the instructions of its parent company outside the EU, was attributable to the parent so as to enforce successfully EU competition rules. In *Provimi Ltd v Roche Products Ltd* [2003] EWHC 961 (Comm), [2003] 2 All ER 683 it was held that because a group does not have legal personality, the Commission must select a specific company within the latter as an addressee of its decision, and be responsible for payment of the penalty.

[17] For further reading on this topic, see T Hadden, *The Control of Corporate Groups* (1983); DD Prentice, 'Groups of Companies: The English Experience' in KJ Hopt (ed), *Groups of Companies in European Laws* (1982), p 99; CM Schmitthoff and F Wooldridge (eds), *Groups of Companies* (1991); K Hofstetter, 'Parent Responsibility for Subsidising Corporations: European Trends' (1990) 30 ICLQ 576; IM Ramsay, 'Holding Company Liable for the Debts of an Insolvent Subsidiary: A Law and Economics Perspective' (1994) 17 *University of New South Wales Law Journal* 520.

[18] *Richmond upon Thames London Borough Council v Pinn & Wheeler Ltd* [1989] RTR 354 (cannot be a lorry driver); *Newstead v Frost* [1980] 1 WLR 135 at 139, HL (cannot be a television entertainer or author).

Note that each of these conclusions will inevitably be based on assessments of relevant activities or decisions made by the company's human agents and '*attributed*' to the company as a legal person. The legal rules which govern this process of attribution are considered in Chapter 3, but the basic question which all these rules seek to answer is 'Whose acts (or intentions or decisions or characteristics) count as the company's acts (or intentions or decisions or characteristics) *for this purpose*?'

Presumption that the law applies to corporate persons as it does to human persons

The Interpretation Act 1978 s 5, and Sch 1, provides that in any Act, unless the contrary intention appears, 'person' includes a body of persons corporate or unincorporated. Those who draft legislation regularly make distinctions between the term 'person' (which includes a corporate body) and 'individual' (which does not). The use of each of these terms, respectively, in the Company Directors Disqualification Act 1986 and the Criminal Justice Act 1993 Pt V, means that a company can be the subject of a disqualification order prohibiting it from acting as a director, but not convicted of insider dealing.

There is a presumption that the word 'person' be construed as including a company, although the final analysis depends on the context.

[2.08] Pharmaceutical Society v London and Provincial Supply Association Ltd (1880) 5 App Cas 857 (House of Lords)

This case predates the Interpretation Act 1978 (above). Consider how the judges worked towards the same ends, and what problems might arise as a result.

The Pharmacy Act 1868 prohibited 'any person' from selling or keeping an open shop for retailing poisons unless such person was qualified and registered as a pharmaceutical chemist. The respondent company was prosecuted for an infringement of the Act. The sale of chemicals by the company was superintended by a registered chemist, who was a salaried employee and also a minority shareholder in the company. The House of Lords held that the company had not infringed the statute.

LORD BLACKBURN: I own I have no great doubt myself . . . that the word 'person' may very well include both a natural person, a human being, and an artificial person, a corporation. I think that in an Act of Parliament, unless there be something to the contrary, probably (but that I should not like to pledge myself to) it ought to be held to include both. I have equally no doubt that in common talk, the language of men not speaking technically, a 'person' does not include an artificial person, that is to say, a corporation. Nobody in common talk if he were asked, Who is the richest person in London, would answer, The London and North-Western Railway Co. The thing is absurd. It is plain that in common conversation and ordinary speech, 'a person' would mean a natural person: in technical language it may mean the artificial person: in which way it is used in any particular Act, must depend upon the context and the subject-matter. I do not think that the presumption that it does include an artificial person, a corporation, if that is the presumption, is at all a strong one. Circumstances, and indeed circumstances of a slight nature in the context, might shew in which way the word is to be construed in an Act of Parliament, whether it is to have the one meaning or the other . . .

But, my Lords, my conclusion, looking at this Act, is that it is clear to my mind that the word 'person' here is so used to show that it does not include a corporation, and that there is no object or intention of the statute which shows that it is requisite to extend the word to a sense which probably those who used it in legislation, were not thinking of at all. I do not think that the legislature was thinking of bodies corporate at all. Beginning with the preamble the Act says, 'Whereas it is expedient for the safety of the public that persons keeping open shop for the retailing, dispensing, or compounding of poisons, and persons known as chemists and druggists, should possess a competent practical knowledge of their business'. Stopping there it is quite plain that those who used that language were not thinking of corporations. A corporation may in one sense, for all substantial purposes of protecting the public, possess a competent knowledge of its business, if it employs competent directors, managers, and so forth. But it cannot possibly have a competent knowledge in itself. The metaphysical entity, the legal 'person', the corporation, cannot possibly have a competent knowledge. Nor, I think, can a corporation be supposed to be a 'person known as a chemist and druggist' . . . A body corporate may keep an open shop, and no mischief is done, if . . . qualified persons perform or superintend the sale . . .

➤ Question

The protective purpose of this Act would be defeated if the Act did not somehow apply to companies operating chemists' shops. It might be obvious that a company cannot be 'qualified and registered as a pharmaceutical chemist'. But we would no longer insist that 'The metaphysical entity, the legal "person", the corporation, cannot possibly have a competent knowledge.' Indeed, precisely the opposite now holds true: see the discussion in Chapter 3 and the very important case of *Meridian Global Funds Management Asia Ltd v Securities Commission* **[3.01]**. How should modern Acts be drafted to provide the necessary protection in the circumstances of the case above?

➤ Note

The preceding case concerned the interpretation of a statute, but the views of Lord Blackburn have also served as a guide in the construction of other documents, for example in *Re Jeffcock's Trust* (1882) 51 LJ Ch 507, where a limited company was held to be a 'person' within the terms of a power to lease conferred by will. The courts have gone so far as to hold that a company is a 'person of full age' within the meaning of the Law of Property Act 1925 (*Re Earl of Carnarvon's Chesterfield Settled Estates* [1927] 1 Ch 138), but have stopped short of holding that a company is capable of 'exercising itself in the duties of piety and true religion' (*Rolloswin Investments Ltd v Chromolit Portugal Cutelarias e Produtos Metálicos SARL* [1970] 1 WLR 912), or of being deemed a rogue and a vagabond (*AG v Walkergate Press Ltd* (1930) 142 LT 408: compare *R v Registrar of Joint Stock Companies, ex p More* **[1.06]**). The Scottish courts have ruled that a company is incapable of shame, and so cannot be guilty of 'shameless conduct': *Dean v John Menzies (Holdings) Ltd* 1981 SLT 50. But Lord Templeman held that a company has a 'conscience' (*Winkworth v Edward Baron Development Co Ltd* **[7.17]**). It also has a 'reputation' and so can sue in defamation: *D and L Caterers Ltd and Jackson v D'Ajou* [1945] KB 364, CA (allegation that company had procured supplies on the black market). It is entitled to protection from invasion of its privacy (*R v Broadcasting Standards Commission, ex p BBC* [2001] 1 BCLC 244, CA (secret filming of transactions in Dixons' shops), but not to compensation for wrongful conviction on a criminal charge (*R v Secretary of State for the Home Department, ex p Atlantic Commercial (UK) Ltd* [1997] BCLC 692)). Interestingly, all these features of a company's legal personality are part of an evolving landscape: contrast the views expressed by Blackstone, 'Limits to the idea of a company as a "person"?', p 62, several hundred years ago.

The Human Rights Act 1998 and companies

Many countries have a constitution or charter by which certain fundamental rights and freedoms are guaranteed, such as freedom of speech and religion, freedom to trade and do business, the privilege against self-incrimination and the right not to have property expropriated without compensation. Whether a company should enjoy such constitutional guarantees is often a question of great difficulty, and it is not surprising that courts in different jurisdictions have given conflicting rulings on what would appear to be much the same issue. The most obvious reason for such a discrepancy is likely to be the language of the relevant legislation: a charter of *human* rights, for example, is less likely to be construed so as to embrace corporate bodies than is a statement of *constitutional* freedoms. Differences in cultural or historical background may also play a part. But even where it is accepted that the freedoms and rights are to be accorded only to human beings, that is not necessarily the end of the matter. A court may be persuaded in some circumstances to look beyond the corporate entity (holding, eg, that interference with the right of a company to publish a newspaper is an infringement of the right to freedom of expression of the individuals concerned).[19] Alternatively, it may accord standing to a company to challenge legislation as unconstitutional even though the company itself is not directly affected by it: thus, in *R v Big M Drug Mart Ltd* (1985) 18 DLR (4th) 321, the Supreme Court of Canada allowed such a challenge by a company, on the ground that the statute in question infringed the guarantee of freedom of religion and conscience in s 2(a) of the Canadian Charter of Rights and Freedoms, irrespective of any question whether a corporation can enjoy or exercise freedom of religion.

The enactment of the Human Rights Act 1998 (HRA 1998) stimulated interest in these issues in the UK. Although the title of the Act, and the Convention behind it, both refer to 'human' rights, some of its provisions expressly confer rights and freedoms on 'legal' (as distinct from 'natural') persons—for example, the right to property, the right to a fair trial in the determination of civil rights and the right to peaceful enjoyment of possessions. The European Court of Human Rights (ECtHR) has held in a number of cases that a body corporate has standing to institute proceedings complaining of a violation of the Convention. As a result of the principle of separate corporate personality, if a company's Convention rights are infringed, no individual member of the entity is a victim of that breach. This means that no member has standing to apply to the ECtHR or bring proceedings under the HRA 1998 in pursuit of the company's claims. The ECtHR has, however, held that a form of derivative claim on behalf of the company would be available where it is not possible for those responsible for the company's litigation to make the application (*Credit and Industrial Bank v Czech Republic* [2003] ECHR 2003-XI).[20]

While it is plain that some parts of the Convention cannot apply to companies (eg the right to life, the prohibition of torture and the right to marry), others can quite readily do so (the right to a fair trial,[21] no retrospective punishment for crimes, the right to freedom of expression[22]). One feature of the decisions of the ECtHR which is rather at odds with the current attitude of the domestic courts in the UK is a much greater willingness to pierce the corporate veil—for example, treating shareholders as the 'victims' of an act aimed at their company.

Nationality, domicile and residence

A company's *nationality* is determined by its place of its registration (ie the place from which it derives its personality), and it retains that nationality throughout its existence: *Kuenigl v Donnersmarck* [1955] 1 QB 515.

---

[19] Note that the company must be party to the proceedings here if the individuals are to have their individual rights protected effectively. Similarly, other company law procedures—even statutory ones—may need to be conducted in particular ways so as not to infringe the human rights of the individuals concerned. See, eg, *Saunders v UK* (1996) 23 EHRR 313, and 'Inspections and subsequent fair trials—criminal and civil cases', p 777.

[20] Also see 'Company claims and the statutory derivative action: CA 2006 ss 260ff', p 671 on derivative actions generally.

[21] Article 6 of the Convention was invoked in *R (Alconbury Developments Ltd) v Secretary of State for the Environment, Transport and the Regions* [2001] UKHL 23, [2003] 2 AC 295.

[22] *R (North Cyprus Tourism Centre Ltd) v Transport for London* [2005] EWHC 1698 (Admin).

A company is also capable of having a *domicile*. This is also the place of its registration, and it too is retained throughout the company's existence.[23] See *Gasque v IRC* [1940] 2 KB 80: 'a company has a domicil—an English domicil if registered in England, and a Scottish domicil if registered in Scotland. The domicil of origin, or the domicil of birth, using with respect to a company a familiar metaphor, clings to it throughout its existence'. Note that the same principles enable an SE (*Societas Europaea*)[24] to move freely within the EU changing its domicile at will. The Commission's plan for a Fourteenth Company Law Directive would enable all EU companies to move within the Union in the same manner.

By contrast, a company's *residence* is determined more flexibly. The concept of a company's 'residence' is primarily of importance in revenue law, but it may also be relevant in other contexts, for example in regard to the place where documents may be served on it.[25]

A company's residence is where it 'really keeps house and does its real business'; its 'real business' is carried on where the central management and control actually abides.[26]

[2.09] De Beers Consolidated Mines Ltd v Howe [1906] AC 455 (House of Lords)

The facts appear from the judgment.

LORD LOREBURN LC: Now, it is easy to ascertain where an individual resides, but when the inquiry relates to a company, which in a natural sense does not reside anywhere, some artificial test must be applied.

Mr Cohen propounded a test which had the merits of simplicity and certitude. He maintained that a company resides where it is registered, and nowhere else. If that be so, the appellant company must succeed, for it is registered in South Africa.

I cannot adopt Mr Cohen's contention. In applying the conception of residence to a company, we ought, I think, to proceed as nearly as we can upon the analogy of an individual. A company cannot eat or sleep, but it can keep house and do business. We ought, therefore, to see where it really keeps house and does business. An individual may be of foreign nationality, and yet reside in the United Kingdom. So may a company. Otherwise it might have its chief seat of management and its centre of trading in England under the protection of English law, and yet escape the appropriate taxation by the simple expedient of being registered abroad and distributing its dividends abroad. The decision of Kelly CB and Huddleston B in the *Calcutta Jute Mills Co Ltd v Nicholson*[27] and the *Cesena Sulphur Co v Nicholson*,[28] now thirty years ago, involved the principle that a company

---

[23] This is the rule in English law and most other legal systems, but in others domicile may be determined by reference to some other factor such as the company's principal place of business. In some jurisdictions a corporate body is not recognised as having a domicile at all. Under the rules of private international law, the law of the domicile regulates questions relating to the validity of the company's incorporation, its dissolution, the effect of a merger, its capacity and the rights and liabilities of its members (including limited liability). It is not possible under UK law for a company to transfer its incorporation and domicile to another jurisdiction, as is the case in many other countries.

[24] Regulation (EC) 2157/2001 allows registration by the companies registrar of any member state of a European public limited-liability company. The Regulation is also known as the Statute for a European Company.

[25] A company which is resident in the UK may not change its residence without the consent of the Treasury (Income and Corporation Taxes Act 1988 s 765(1)). This provision has been held not to be incompatible with the 'freedom of establishment' principle contained in Art 43 of the Treaty of Rome: *R v HM Treasury, ex p Daily Mail and General Trust plc* [1989] QB 446, [1989] 1 All ER 328, CJEU.

[26] Other cases show that the 'central management and control' of a company may in fact be divided, so that its residence is in more than one country: see, eg, *Union Corpn Ltd v IRC* [1952] 1 All ER 646, CA, affd on other grounds [1953] AC 482, HL.

[27] (1876) 1 Ex D 428.

[28] (1876) 1 Ex D 428.

resides for purposes of income tax where its real business is carried on. Those decisions have been acted upon ever since. I regard that as the true rule, and the real business is carried on where the central management and control actually abides....This is a pure question of fact ...

The case stated by the commissioners gives an elaborate explanation of the way in which this company carried on its business. The head office is formally at Kimberley, and the general meetings have always been held there. Also the profits have been made out of diamonds raised in South Africa and sold under annual contracts to a syndicate for delivery in South Africa upon terms of division of profits realised on resale between the company and the syndicate. And the annual contracts contain provisions for regulating the market in order to realise the best profits on resale. Further, some of the directors and life governors live in South Africa, and there are directors' meetings at Kimberley as well as in London. But it is clearly established that the majority of directors and life governors live in England, that the directors' meetings in London are the meetings where the real control is always exercised in practically all the important business of the company except the mining operations. London has always controlled the negotiation of the contracts with the diamond syndicates, has determined policy in the disposal of diamonds and other assets, the working and development of mines, the application of profits, and the appointment of directors. London has also always controlled matters that require to be determined by the majority of all the directors, which include all questions of expenditure except wages, materials, and such-like at the mines, and a limited sum which may he spent by the directors at Kimberley.

The commissioners, after sifting the evidence, arrived at the two following conclusions, viz: (1) That the trade or business of the appellant company constituted one trade or business, and was carried on and exercised by the appellant company within the United Kingdom at their London office. (2) That the head and seat and directing power of the affairs of the appellant company were at the office in London, from whence the chief operations of the company, both in the United Kingdom and elsewhere, were in fact controlled, managed and directed.

These conclusions of fact cannot be impugned, and it follows that this company was resident within the United Kingdom for purposes of income tax, and must be assessed on that footing. I think, therefore, that this appeal fails. . . .

LORD JAMES OF HEREFORD delivered a concurring opinion.

LORDS MACNAGHTEN, ROBERTSON and ATKINSON concurred.

➤ Note

Similarly, in a recent decision of the Supreme Court of Canada, a trustee company was incorporated in Barbados, but the 'trust' was held to be resident, and taxable, in Canada where the main business of the trust was actually conducted by the principal beneficiaries: *Fundy Settlement v Canada*, 2012 SCC 14.

Notice that the current debates on the 'effective' tax rates paid by companies such as Google, Starbucks and Amazon are not illustrations of this approach, but of a quite different feature of modern companies. These multinational companies operate as 'corporate groups', with different companies in the group registered—and resident for tax purposes—in different jurisdictions. The objective with this sort of structure is to ensure that the profitable aspects of the business are located in low-tax jurisdictions.

Notice, too, that the approach adopted in England to these issues is not necessarily adopted elsewhere, and nor is it adopted for all purposes: see 'The market for corporate law: country of incorporation, "seat" and "COMI"', p 13.

Status questions

The twin ideas that a company is a legal person, and that the general law is presumed to apply as far as is possible, are often not enough to answer difficult questions about *how* the law should apply. This is true even when the rules on nationality, residence and domicile are added into the mix. The problems arise under both the general law and statute. In every case, the real difficulty is the tension between treating the company as a separate legal person at law and, by contrast, dealing with the inherent reality that 'behind the corporate veil' lie human individuals with particular characteristics, identities and motivations. This inherent tension plagues a good deal of company law and can be the source of innumerable analytical difficulties if the problem is not addressed transparently. A number of these problems emerge in sharp focus in Chapter 3. The examples below are also illustrations, but in a different context.

The key questions in every case are these: (i) *should* this law (common law or statute) apply to companies at all? And, if it does apply, (ii) whose acts or characteristics, etc, should count as the company's acts or characteristics, etc, *for the purpose of applying this particular law?*[29]

How should a court decide whether a company should be characterised as an 'enemy' in time of war?

The relevant approach is now set out very explicitly in statute (see below), but contrast the dramatically different approaches of the courts before that Act.

Trading with the Enemy Act 1939

2 Definition of enemy

(1) Subject to the provisions of this section, the expression 'enemy' for the purposes of this Act means—
   (a) any State, or Sovereign of a State, at war with His Majesty,
   (b) any individual resident in enemy territory,
   (c) any body of persons (whether corporate or unincorporate) carrying on business in any place, if and so long as the body is controlled by a person who, under this section, is an enemy,
   (d) any body of persons constituted or incorporated in, or under the laws of, a State at war with His Majesty; and
   (e) as respects any business carried on in enemy territory, any individual or body of persons (whether corporate or unincorporate) carrying on that business;
   but does not include any individual by reason only that he is an enemy subject.

(2) The Board of Trade may by order direct that any person specified in the order shall, for the purposes of this Act, be deemed to be, while so specified, an enemy.

[2.10] Daimler Co Ltd v Continental Tyre and Rubber Co (Great Britain) Ltd [1916] 2 AC 307 (House of Lords)

The Continental Tyre company was incorporated in England, but all except one of its shares were held by persons resident in Germany, and all the directors resided in Germany. The secretary, who held the remaining share, resided in England and was a British subject. The issue was whether the company had standing in an English court to sue and recover a debt

---

[29] See the discussion in Chapter 3 and the very important case of *Meridian Global Funds Management Asia Ltd v Securities Commission* **[3.01]**.

when a state of war existed between England and Germany. The company was allowed by the Master to sign summary judgment without proceeding to trial. His decision was affirmed by Scrutton J in chambers and by a greatly enlarged Court of Appeal (Buckley LJ dissenting). [Extracts from the judgments delivered in the Court of Appeal appear at **[2.11]**.] The House of Lords unanimously reversed the order of the Court of Appeal, and directed that the action be struck out as irregular, on the ground that the secretary was not authorised to commence the action; and it held further (by a majority, Lords Shaw of Dunfermline and Parmoor dissenting) that the company, though incorporated in England, was capable of acquiring an enemy character, so that leave to sign summary judgment should not have been given.

LORD PARKER OF WADDINGTON: No one can question that a corporation is a legal person distinct from its corporators; that the relation of a shareholder to a company, which is limited by shares, is not in itself the relation of principal and agent or the reverse; that the assets of the company belong to it and the acts of its servants and agents are its acts, while its shareholders, as such, have no property in the assets and no personal responsibility for those acts. The law on the subject is clearly laid down in . . . *Salomon v A Salomon & Co Ltd* **[2.02]** . . . I do not think, however, that it is a necessary corollary of this reasoning to say that the character of its corporators must be irrelevant to the character of the company; and this is crucial, for the rule against trading with the enemy depends upon enemy character.

A natural person, though an English-born subject of His Majesty, may bear an enemy character and be under liability and disability as such by adhering to His Majesty's enemies. If he gives them active aid, he is a traitor; but he may fall far short of that and still be invested with enemy character. If he has what is known in prize law as a commercial domicil among the King's enemies, his merchandise is good prize at sea, just as if it belonged to a subject of the enemy power. Not only actively, but passively, he may bring himself under the same disability. Voluntary residence among the enemy, however passive or pacific he may be, identifies an English subject with His Majesty's foes. I do not think it necessary to cite authority for these well-known propositions, nor do I doubt that, if they had seemed material to the Court of Appeal, they would have been accepted.

How are such rules to be applied to an artificial person, incorporated by forms of law? As far as active adherence to the enemy goes, there can be no difference, except such as arises from the fact that a company's acts are those of its servants and agents acting within the scope of their authority . . .

In the case of an artificial person what is the analogue to voluntary residence among the King's enemies? Its impersonality can hardly put it in a better position than a natural person and lead to its being unaffected by anything equivalent to residence. It is only by a figure of speech that a company can be said to have a nationality or residence at all. If the place of its incorporation under municipal law fixes its residence, then its residence cannot be changed, which is almost a contradiction in terms, and in the case of a company residence must correspond to the birthplace and country of natural allegiance in the case of a living person, and not to residence or commercial domicil. Nevertheless, enemy character depends on these last. It would seem, therefore, logically to follow that, in transferring the application of the rule against trading with the enemy from natural to artificial persons, something more than the mere place or country of registration or incorporation must be looked at.

My Lords, I think that the analogy is to be found in control, an idea which, if not very familiar in law, is of capital importance and is very well understood in commerce and finance. The acts of a company's organs, its directors, managers, secretary, and so forth, functioning within the scope of their authority, are the company's acts and may invest it definitively with enemy character. It seems to me that similarly the character of those who can make and unmake those officers, dictate their conduct mediately or immediately, prescribe their duties and call them to account, may also be material in a question of the enemy character of the company. If not definite and conclusive, it must at least be prima facie relevant, as raising a presumption that those who are purporting to act in the name of the company are, in fact, under the control of those whom it is their interest to satisfy. Certainly I have found no authority to the contrary. Such a view reconciles the positions of natural and artificial persons in this regard, and the opposite view leads to the paradoxical result that the King's enemies, who chance during war to constitute the entire body of corporators in a company registered in England, thereby pass out of the range of legal vision, and, instead, the corporation, which in itself is incapable of loyalty, or enmity, or residence, or of anything but bare existence in contemplation of law and registration under some system of law, takes their place for almost the most important of all purposes, that of being classed among the King's friends or among his foes in time of war.

What is involved in the decision of the Court of Appeal is that, for all purposes to which the character and not merely the rights and powers of an artificial person are material, the personalities of the natural persons, who are its corporators, are to be ignored. An impassable line is drawn between the one person and the others. When the law is concerned with the artificial person, it is to know nothing of the natural persons who constitute and control it. In questions of property and capacity, of acts done and rights acquired or liabilities assumed thereby, this may be always true. Certainly it is so for the most part. But the character in which property is held, and the character in which the capacity to act is enjoyed and acts are done, are not in *pari materia*. The latter character is a quality of the company itself, and conditions its capacities and its acts. It is not a mere part of its energies or acquisitions, and if that character must be derivable not from the circumstances of its incorporation, which arises once for all, but from qualities of enmity and amity, which are dependent on the chances of peace or war and are attributable only to human beings, I know not from what human beings that character should be derived, in cases where the active conduct of the company's officers has not already decided the matter, if resort is not to be had to the predominant character of its shareholders and corporators. . . .

THE EARL OF HALSBURY LC and LORD ATKINSON delivered concurring opinions.

VISCOUNT MERSEY and LORDS KINNEAR and SUMNER concurred.

LORDS SHAW OF DUNFERMLINE and PARMOOR delivered opinions concurring in the result, but dissenting on this point.

Part of the majority judgment in the Court of Appeal is set out in the following extract. The arguments in favour of recognising or disregarding the corporate entity could hardly be contrasted more sharply. No doubt the factor which most influenced the House of Lords was the paramountcy of the public interest in wartime, and yet their approach is well aligned with modern practice. *If* a company can be an enemy alien (and given the power of companies over the allocation of valuable commercial and domestic resources, it is difficult to suggest it cannot), then characterisation *must* depend on some formal or informal attribute of the company. The House of Lords decided that the formal attribute of 'nationality' was not the relevant test (either for individuals or for companies), and so settled on another test *for the purpose of answering the precise question posed*. For *other* purposes, as the Court of Appeal very properly notes in the next extract, those same concerns need not be material in answering the different question then posed. Appreciating what is going on in these types of analysis is crucial.

[2.11] Continental Tyre and Rubber Co (Great Britain) Ltd v Daimler Co Ltd [1915] 1 KB 893 (Court of Appeal) (subsequently overturned by the House of Lords [2.10])

LORD READING CJ read the judgment of the majority of the court (LORD READING CJ, LORD COZENS-HARDY MR, KENNEDY, PHILLIMORE and PICKFORD LJJ): It cannot be disputed that the plaintiff company is an entity created by statute. It is a company incorporated under the

Companies Acts and therefore is a thing brought into existence by virtue of statutory enactment. At the outbreak of war it was carrying on business in the United Kingdom; it had contracted to supply goods, it delivered them, and until the outbreak of the war it was admittedly entitled to receive payment at the due dates. Has the character of the company changed because on the outbreak of war all the shareholders and directors resided in an enemy country and therefore became alien enemies? Admittedly it was an English company before the war. An English company cannot by reason of these facts cease to be an English company. It remains an English company regardless of the residence of its shareholders or directors either before or after the declaration of war. Indeed it was not argued by Mr Gore-Browne that the company ceased to be an entity created under English law, but it was argued that the law in time of war and in reference to trading with the enemy should sweep aside this 'technicality' as the entity was described and should treat the company not as an English company but as a German company and therefore as an alien enemy. If the creation and existence of the company could be treated as a mere technicality, there would be considerable force in this argument. It is undoubtedly the policy of the law as administered in our courts of justice to regard substance and to disregard form. Justice should not be hindered by mere technicality, but substance must not be treated as form or swept aside as technicality because that course might appear convenient in a particular case. The fallacy of the appellants' contention lies in the suggestion that the entity created by statute is or can be treated during the war as a mere form or technicality by reason of the enemy character of its shareholders and directors. A company formed and registered under the Companies Acts has a real existence with rights and liabilities as a separate legal entity. It is a different person altogether from the subscribers to the memorandum or the shareholders on the register (per Lord Macnaghten in *Salomon v A Salomon & Co Ltd* [2.02]). It cannot be technically an English company and substantially a German company except by the use of inaccurate and misleading language. Once it is validly constituted as an English company it is an artificial creation of the legislature and it retains its existence for all intents and purposes. It is a living thing with a separate existence which cannot be swept aside as a technicality. It is not a mere name or mask or cloak or device to conceal the identity of persons and it is not suggested that the company was formed for any dishonest or fraudulent purpose. It is a legal body clothed with the form prescribed by the legislature . . .

For the appellants' contention to succeed, payment to the company must be treated as payment to the shareholders of the company, but a debt due to a company is not a debt due to all or any of its shareholders: *Salomon v Salomon & Co*. The company and the company alone is the creditor entitled to enforce payment of the debt and empowered to give to the debtor a good and valid discharge. Once this conclusion is reached it follows that payment to the plaintiff company is not payment to the alien enemy shareholders or for their benefit . . .

BUCKLEY LJ delivered a dissenting judgment.

➤ Questions

1. Explain why the personal characteristics of the shareholders were immaterial in *Salomon v A Salomon & Co Ltd* [2.02] but material in *Daimler Co Ltd v Continental Tyre and Rubber Co (Great Britain) Ltd* [2.10].

2. Could a landlord be guilty of an offence under the Equality Act 2010 if he refused to lease premises to a company incorporated in England which was owned and controlled by three Nigerian businessmen?

Note that the selected test must itself be legal. This was famously held not to be the case under the Merchant Shipping Act 1988 and regulations made thereunder: only fishing vessels registered as 'British' were eligible to fish under the quota for the UK fixed by the EU; and vessels owned by a company could be so registered only if 75% of their shareholders fulfilled requirements as to British nationality, residence and domicile. The CJEU in *R v Secretary of State for Transport, ex p Factortame Ltd (No 3)* [1992] QB 680 held that such a restriction was contrary to Art 52 of the EC Treaty, which guarantees freedom of establishment to the nationals of all member states. Consequently, most sections of the Act have now been repealed.

Limits to the idea of a company as a 'person'?

The cases noted previously confirm that the central theoretical and practical feature of company law is that incorporation creates a new and separate legal entity, a 'being' capable of enjoying rights, exercising powers and incurring duties and obligations. It is traditional to describe any subject of rights and duties as a legal 'person'. But it is one thing to attribute *legal* capacities to a company, and quite another to treat it as having *human* characteristics and qualities.[30] Despite an initial hesitation in finding that companies were separate persons, the courts now seem to have pursued the analogy with a physical person almost as far as it is possible to go, ascribing to companies human attributes such as reputation or intention to defraud which would previously have been regarded as unthinkable. For an indication of how far the law has moved, consider the next extract. At least half of its assertions would now be regarded as false.

Blackstone, 'Commentaries on the Laws of England' (1768), Vol 1, p 476

(Blackstone acknowledges that his remarks are based on views expressed by Coke more than a century and a half earlier.) Footnotes in the original are omitted.

> *'Of Corporations'*
>
> There are also certain privileges and disabilities that attend an aggregate corporation, and are not applicable to such as are sole;[31] the reason of them ceasing and of course the law. It must always appear by attorney; for it cannot appear in person, being, as Sir Edward Coke says, invisible, and existing only in intendment and consideration of law. It can neither maintain, or be made defendant to, an action of battery or such like personal injuries; for a corporation can neither beat, nor be beaten, in it's body politic. A corporation cannot commit treason, or felony, or other crime, in it's corporate capacity: though it's members may, in their distinct individual capacities. Neither is it capable of suffering a traitor's or felon's punishment, for it is not liable to corporal penalties, nor to attainder, forfeiture, or corruption of blood. It cannot be executor or administrator, or perform any personal duties; for it cannot take an oath for the due execution of the office. It cannot be seised of lands to the use of another; for such kind of confidence is foreign to the end of it's institution. Neither can it be committed to prison; for it's existence being ideal, no man can apprehend or arrest it. And therefore also it cannot be outlawed; for outlawry always supposes a precedent right of arresting, which has been defeated by the parties absconding, and that also a corporation cannot do: for which reasons the proceedings to compel a corporation to appear to any suit by attorney are always by distress on their lands and goods. Neither can a corporation be excommunicated; for it has no soul, as is gravely observed by Sir Edward Coke: and therefore also

[30] *Collins Steward Ltd v Financial Times Ltd* [2005] EWHC 262 (QB), eg, held that a corporation cannot have hurt feelings.

[31] Where corporate personality is ascribed to a *group* of persons, such as a limited liability company, a chartered body such as a university, or a municipality such as a city or borough, it is referred to as a 'corporation aggregate'. Where the law personifies an *office* occupied by a single person (eg the Crown, the Bishop of Ely), it is customarily called a 'corporation sole'.

it is not liable to be summoned into the ecclesiastical courts upon any account; for those courts act only *pro salute animae*, and their sentences can only be enforced by spiritual censures: a consideration, which, carried to it's full extent, would alone demonstrate the impropriety of these courts interfering in any temporal rights whatsoever.

'Piercing the corporate veil' vs separate legal personality

From the cases considered so far, it is already clear that two important ideas are in competition: the allegedly core and inviolate feature of separate legal personality (and the associated consequence of limited liability of members, as explained below) and the competing claim to 'pierce the corporate veil' (and the associated right to advance claims against the members behind the company). It is this tension and its resolution which is addressed now.

Recall the general rule that if (as is usual) the liability of a company's members is limited 'by shares' or 'by guarantee', then the company's creditors cannot seek satisfaction from the members, even if the company has insufficient funds to pay its own liabilities in full: see 'Companies limited by shares and companies limited by guarantee', p 22. Many of the cases cited previously can be used to illustrate this. Notice in particular that members are *not* made liable to outsiders simply because (as members or shareholders) they controlled the company's activities and thus caused liability to be incurred (see, eg, *Salomon* [2.02] and *Lee's Air Farming* [2.05]). This general point is crucial to understanding this area of the law.

But are there exceptions to this general rule? Are there times where the company's members *can* be called upon, by outsiders, to meet the company's unpaid liabilities? It is not difficult to imagine situations where outsiders might wish to do this. If a profitable holding company has an underfunded subsidiary that cannot meet tort liabilities to hundreds of victims of the subsidiary's negligence, then the victims may want payment from the parent company (ie from the subsidiary's shareholder—see, eg, *Adams v Cape Industries* [2.07]). Can they successfully seek this? The general rule says no, but are there ever any exceptions? Similarly, if a 'one man company' is completely under-resourced and unable to meet its trading debts, but its 'one man owner' is personally wealthy, can the company's creditors ever claim against the owner-shareholder? *Salomon* [2.02] was just such a case, so the general answer is clearly no, but, again, are there exceptions?

This section looks at the exceptions, and at the arguments that have been advanced both successfully and unsuccessfully by outsiders (ie third parties) wishing to pursue such claims. Typically these claims are unsuccessful. Instead, those who adopt the corporate form, or trade with it, are expected to take the rough with the smooth. This was emphasised by Browne-Wilkinson V-C in *Tate Access Floors Inc v Boswell* [1991] Ch 512 at 531 (his focus was on the downside for members, whereas we are concerned with the downside for outsiders):

If people choose to conduct their affairs through the medium of corporations, they are taking advantage of the fact that in law those corporations are separate legal entities, whose property and actions are in law not the property or actions of their incorporators or controlling shareholders. In my judgment controlling shareholders cannot, for all purposes beneficial to them, insist on the separate identity of such corporations but then be heard to say the contrary when discovery [ie disclosure, but by implication any other disadvantage] is sought against such corporations.

The meaning of 'piercing the corporate veil'

This area is considerably more straightforward since the decision of the Supreme Court in *Prest v Petrodel Resources Ltd* **[2.12]**.[32] Before considering that case, one important issue of clarification may be helpful. 'Piercing (or lifting) the corporate veil' (the former term now being more common) refers to the possibility of looking behind the company framework (or behind the company's separate personality) to make the *members* liable, as an exception to the rule that they are normally shielded by the corporate shell (ie they are normally not liable to outsiders at all, either as principals or as agents or in any other guise, *and* are only normally liable to pay the *company* what they agreed to pay by way of share purchase price or guarantee, nothing more).

Before the Supreme Court decision in *Prest v Petrodel Resources Ltd*, cases and commentary used the term 'piercing the corporate veil' rather indiscriminately to describe a wide variety of instances where successful and unsuccessful claims were advanced to make the members liable for corporate failings. As Lord Neuberger PSC put it, at [64]:

> It is ... clear from the cases and academic articles that the law relating to the doctrine is unsatisfactory and confused. Those cases and articles appear to me to suggest that (i) there is not a single instance in this jurisdiction where the doctrine has been invoked properly and successfully, (ii) there is doubt as to whether the doctrine should exist, and (iii) it is impossible to discern any coherent approach, applicable principles, or defined limitations to the doctrine.

After the Supreme Court decision, far greater precision is warranted. The expression 'piercing the corporate veil', and the 'doctrine' of the same name, is now reserved for instances where the court does indeed *ignore* the separate personality of the company, and looks behind the corporate 'veil' to the members. Judicial discretion to ignore the *Salomon* principle in this way is justified on public policy grounds, as explained in *Prest v Petrodel Resources Ltd* **[2.12]**. But although the Supreme Court unanimously agreed that the doctrine exists, their judgments suggest there is not a single illustration of its *necessary* application (see Lord Neuberger, earlier), and that, being a principle of public policy, it should only be relied upon where it is essential.

By contrast, there are a good number of cases where the members are indeed made liable, despite a corporate intermediary standing between the claimant and the members. However, all these cases can be explained on orthodox legal principles (even if the courts before *Prest v Petrodel Resources Ltd* did not explain them this way).

Adopting this approach, various arguments can be run: for example, the members are liable because, exceptionally, their acts are such as to constitute them 'principals' (and the company is merely an agent), or 'beneficiaries' (and the company is merely the trustee of the corporate assets for their benefit), or constructive trustees or 'dishonest assistants' in wrongs committed by the company, or indeed the members themselves are independently liable in tort to the claimants. These and other possibilities are examined later in 'Connections between the company and other persons', p 75.

Finally, this analysis is not to be confused with the possibility of making a company's *directors* liable. It is equally difficult for *outsiders* to sue the company's directors to make

---

[32] For further reading, see WA Day, 'Skirting around the Issue: The Corporate Veil after *Prest v Petrodel*' [2014] LMCLQ 269. For historical accounts, see A Samuels, 'Lifting the Veil' [1964] JBL 107; MA Pickering, 'The Company as a Separate Legal Entity' (1968) 31 MLR 481; CM Schmitthoff, '*Salomon* in the Shadow' [1976] JBL 305; S Ottolenghi, 'From Peeping behind the Corporate Veil to Ignoring it Completely' (1990) 53 MLR 338; Lord Cooke of Thorndon, 'A Real Thing' in *Turning Points of the Common Law* (1996 Hamlyn Lectures, 1997) and 'Corporate Identity' (1998) 16 C & SLJ 160; CH Tham, 'Piercing the Corporate Veil: Searching for Appropriate Choice of Law Rules' [2007] LMCLQ 22. For a comparative perspective (comparing England, the United States, South Africa and Greece), see A Mandaraka-Sheppard, 'New Trends in Piercing the Corporate Veil: The Conservative Versus the Liberal Approaches' (2014) 35 *Business Law Review* 2.

them carry liability for the company's unfulfilled obligations. Third parties must generally sue the company, not its directors. They can sue directors only when one of the agency or trust arguments just aired can be advanced (but this time in the context of the directors, not the members). *But*, unlike the members, the directors' liability is certainly not limited. Directors owe quite significant duties to the company, and the *company* can sue the directors for any wrongs they have committed against it. These recoveries will accrue to the company, and so increase the chance that third parties will be paid. The directors' liability for corporate losses is not strict (ie directors do not guarantee that the company will be a success), but is a liability for wrongs committed against the company, such as negligence and other breaches of duty to the company (see Chapter 7).

The court may 'pierce the corporate veil' (using that expression narrowly) only where a person under an existing legal obligation or subject to an existing legal restriction deliberately evades or frustrates its enforcement by interposing a company under his or her control.

[2.12] Prest v Petrodel Resources Ltd [2013] UKSC 34, [2013] 2 AC 415 (Supreme Court)

In matrimonial proceedings concerning the division of assets said to be worth over £50 million, the appellant wife (W) applied to have certain residential properties transferred to her. The properties were not owned by her husband (H), however, but by the respondent group of companies (X), being companies operated and controlled by H. The trial judge concluded that H was entitled to possession or reversion of the properties, within the Matrimonial Causes Act 1973 s 24(1), and this statute therefore entitled the court to pierce the corporate veil and order H to transfer them to W. The Court of Appeal reversed that decision, holding that there were no legitimate grounds for piercing the corporate veil. The Supreme Court agreed, also holding that the Matrimonial Causes Act 1973 s 24(1) did not provide a distinct power to disregard the corporate veil in matrimonial cases. The court nevertheless found unanimously in favour of W on the basis that the most plausible inference from the little-known facts was that each of the properties was held on a resulting trust by X for H ([45], [47]). There was no reliable evidence to rebut that inference, given the husband's refusal to afford disclosure, and accordingly the seven disputed properties were required to be transferred to W ([49]–[51], [55]). The extracts below concentrate exclusively on the general issue of piercing the corporate veil, although the judgments merit reading in full.

LORD SUMPTION SCJ:

[*The* Salomon *principle*]

8. Subject to very limited exceptions, most of which are statutory, a company is a legal entity distinct from its shareholders. It has rights and liabilities of its own which are distinct from those of its shareholders. Its property is its own, and not that of its shareholders. In *Salomon v A Salomon and Co Ltd* **[2.02]**, the House of Lords held that these principles applied as much to a company that was wholly owned and controlled by one man as to any other company.…

[*Availability of other options*]

16. I should first of all draw attention to the limited sense in which this issue arises at all. 'Piercing the corporate veil' is an expression rather indiscriminately used to describe a number of different things. Properly speaking, it means disregarding the separate personality of the company. There is a range of situations in which the law attributes the acts or property of a company to those who control it, without disregarding its separate legal personality.… But when we speak

of piercing the corporate veil, we are not (or should not be) speaking of any of these situations, but only of those cases which are true exceptions to the rule in *Salomon v A Salomon and Co Ltd* **[2.02]**, i.e. where a person who owns and controls a company is said in certain circumstances to be identified with it in law by virtue of that ownership and control.

[*Existence of general limits to separate legal personality*]

17. Most advanced legal systems recognise corporate legal personality while acknowledging some limits to its logical implications. In civil law jurisdictions, the juridical basis of the exceptions is generally the concept of abuse of rights...which extends not just to the illegal and improper invocation of a right but to its use for some purpose collateral to that for which it exists.

18. English law has no general doctrine of this kind. But it has a variety of specific principles which achieve the same result in some cases. One of these principles is that the law defines the incidents of most legal relationships between persons (natural or artificial) on the fundamental assumption that their dealings are honest. The same legal incidents will not necessarily apply if they are not. The principle was stated in its most absolute form by Denning LJ in a famous dictum in *Lazarus Estates Ltd v Beasley* [1956] 1 QB 702, 712:

> 'No court in this land will allow a person to keep an advantage which he has obtained by fraud. No judgment of a court, no order of a Minister, can be allowed to stand if it has been obtained by fraud. Fraud unravels everything. The court is careful not to find fraud unless it is distinctly pleaded and proved; but once it is proved, it vitiates judgments, contracts and all transactions whatsoever...'

...These decisions (and there are others) illustrate a broader principle governing cases in which the benefit of some apparently absolute legal principle has been obtained by dishonesty. The authorities show that there are limited circumstances in which the law treats the use of a company as a means of evading the law as dishonest for this purpose.

[*English illustrations of 'lifting' or 'piercing' the corporate veil*]

19. The question is heavily burdened by authority, much of it characterised by incautious dicta and inadequate reasoning. [His Lordship then examined those cases in detail.] ...

[*Summary of review of the cases*]

27. In my view, the principle that the court may be justified in piercing the corporate veil if a company's separate legal personality is being abused for the purpose of some relevant wrongdoing is well established in the authorities. It is true that most of the statements of principle in the authorities are obiter, because the corporate veil was not pierced. It is also true that most cases in which the corporate veil was pierced could have been decided on other grounds. But the consensus that there are circumstances in which the court may pierce the corporate veil is impressive. I would not for my part be willing to explain that consensus out of existence. This is because I think that the recognition of a limited power to pierce the corporate veil in carefully defined circumstances is necessary if the law is not to be disarmed in the face of abuse. I also think that provided the limits are recognised and respected, it is consistent with the general approach of English law to the problems raised by the use of legal concepts to defeat mandatory rules of law.

[*Proposed analysis*]

28. The difficulty is to identify what is a relevant wrongdoing. References to a 'facade' or 'sham' beg too many questions to provide a satisfactory answer. It seems to me that two distinct principles lie behind these protean terms, and that much confusion has been caused by failing to distinguish between them. They can conveniently be called *the concealment principle and the evasion principle*. [emphasis added] The concealment principle is legally banal and does not involve piercing the corporate veil at all. It is that the interposition of a company

or perhaps several companies so as to conceal the identity of the real actors will not deter the courts from identifying them, assuming that their identity is legally relevant. In these cases the court is not disregarding the 'facade', but only looking behind it to discover the facts which the corporate structure is concealing. The evasion principle is different. It is that the court may disregard the corporate veil if there is a legal right against the person in control of it which exists independently of the company's involvement, and a company is interposed so that the separate legal personality of the company will defeat the right or frustrate its enforcement. Many cases will fall into both categories, but in some circumstances the difference between them may be critical. This may be illustrated by reference to those cases in which the court has been thought, rightly or wrongly, to have pierced the corporate veil. [His Lordship then proceeded to examine these cases.]

[Conclusion on the broader principle in 'piercing the corporate veil']

34. These considerations reflect the broader principle that the corporate veil may be pierced only to prevent the abuse of corporate legal personality. It may be an abuse of the separate legal personality of a company to use it to evade the law or to frustrate its enforcement. It is not an abuse to cause a legal liability to be incurred by the company in the first place. It is not an abuse to rely upon the fact (if it is a fact) that a liability is not the controller's because it is the company's. On the contrary, that is what incorporation is all about....

35. I conclude that *there is a limited principle of English law* which applies when a person is under an existing legal obligation or liability or subject to an existing legal restriction which he deliberately evades or whose enforcement he deliberately frustrates by interposing a company under his control. [emphasis added] The court may then pierce the corporate veil for the purpose, and only for the purpose, of depriving the company or its controller of the advantage that they would otherwise have obtained by the company's separate legal personality. The principle is properly described as a limited one, because in almost every case where the test is satisfied, the facts will in practice disclose a legal relationship between the company and its controller which will make it unnecessary to pierce the corporate veil. Like Munby J in *Ben Hashem v Al Shayif* [2009] 1 FLR 115 [at [164]], I consider that if it is not necessary to pierce the corporate veil, it is not appropriate to do so, because on that footing there is no public policy imperative which justifies that course....For all of these reasons, the principle has been recognised far more often than it has been applied. But the recognition of a small residual category of cases where the abuse of the corporate veil to evade or frustrate the law can be addressed only by disregarding the legal personality of the company is, I believe, consistent with authority and with long-standing principles of legal policy.

[Application to the facts here: no piercing]

36....The husband has acted improperly in many ways. In the first place, he has misapplied the assets of his companies for his own benefit, but in doing that he was neither concealing nor evading any legal obligation owed to his wife. Nor, more generally, was he concealing or evading the law relating to the distribution of assets of a marriage on its dissolution. It cannot follow that the court should disregard the legal personality of the companies with the same insouciance as he did. Secondly, the husband has made use of the opacity of the Petrodel Group's corporate structure to deny being its owner...but that simply means that the court must ascertain the truth that he has concealed, as it has done. The problem in the present case is that the legal interest in the properties is vested in the companies and not in the husband. They were vested in the companies long before the marriage broke up. Whatever the husband's reasons for organising things in that way, there is no evidence that he was seeking to avoid any obligation which is relevant in these proceedings. The judge found that his purpose was 'wealth protection and the avoidance of tax': para 218. It follows that the piercing of the corporate veil cannot be justified in this case by reference to any general principle of law.

LORD NEUBERGER PSC:

59. I wish…to add a little to what Lord Sumption says on the question of whether, and if so, in what circumstances, the court has power to pierce the corporate veil in the absence of specific statutory authority to do so. [His Lordship then proceeded, agreeing with much of the analysis of Lord Sumption, and also considering the judicial and academic criticisms of 'piercing the corporate veil', before continuing:]

[*Should the doctrine be abolished?*]

79. In these circumstances, I was initially strongly attracted by the argument that we should decide that a supposed doctrine, which is controversial and uncertain, and which, on analysis, appears never to have been invoked successfully and appropriately in its 80 years of supposed existence, should be given its quietus. Such a decision would render the law much clearer than it is now, and in a number of cases it would reduce complications and costs: whenever the doctrine is really needed, it never seems to apply.

80. However, I have reached the conclusion that it would be wrong to discard a doctrine which, while it has been criticised by judges and academics, has been generally assumed to exist in all common law jurisdictions, and represents a potentially valuable judicial tool to undo wrongdoing in some cases, where no other principle is available. Accordingly, provided that it is possible to discern or identify an approach to piercing the corporate veil, which accords with normal legal principles, reflects previous judicial reasoning (so far as it can be discerned and reconciled), and represents a practical solution (which hopefully will avoid the problems summarised in para 75 above), I believe that it would be right to adopt it as a definition of the doctrine. [He then accepted Lord Sumption's formulation.] …

[*But in any event, is this a company-specific doctrine?*]

83. It is only right to acknowledge that this limited doctrine may not, on analysis, be limited to piercing the corporate veil. However, there are three points to be made about that formulation. In so far as it is based on 'fraud unravels everything', as discussed by Lord Sumption in para 18, the formulation simply involves the invocation of a well-established principle, which exists independently of the doctrine. In any event, the formulation is not, on analysis, a statement about piercing the corporate veil at all. Thus, it would presumably apply equally to a person who transfers assets to a spouse or civil partner, rather than to a company. Further, at least in some cases where it may be relied on, it could probably be analysed as being based on agency or trusteeship especially in the light of the words 'under his control'. However, if either or both those points were correct, it would not undermine Lord Sumption's characterisation of the doctrine: it would, if anything, serve to confirm the existence of the doctrine, albeit as an aspect of a more conventional principle. And if the formulation is intended to go wider than the application of 'fraud unravels everything', it seems to me questionable whether it would be right for the court to take the course of arrogating to itself the right to step in and undo transactions, save where there is a well-established and principled ground for doing so. Such a course is, I would have thought, at least normally, a matter for the legislature. Indeed Parliament has decided to legislate to this effect in specified and limited circumstances with protection for third parties, in provisions such as section 37 of the Matrimonial Causes Act 1973 and section 423 of the Insolvency Act 1986.

BARONESS HALE SCJ (with whom LORD WILSON SCJ agreed), LORDS MANCE AND CLARKE SCJJ and LORD WALKER all agreed, adding further comments of their own.

As a result of this case, it might be suggested that the doctrine exists, but has no present or future function, whatever may have been its life in the past. That is confirmed in the next case.

[2.13] Antonio Gramsci Shipping Corpn v Recoletos Ltd
[2013] EWCA Civ 730 (Court of Appeal)

As part of an allegedly fraudulent scheme, a company had entered into a contract containing an exclusive English jurisdiction clause. The issue for decision was whether the corporate veil could be pierced to establish that the company's controller could also be regarded as having consented to the English courts having jurisdiction over a claim against him. Both the trial judge and the Court of Appeal held it could not.

BEATSON LJ (with whom RYDER and LLOYD LJJ agreed):

(vi) The policy-based submission

63. It remains to deal with Mr Rainey [counsel for the claimant]'s policy-based submission…that the court needs to prevent fraudsters sheltering behind the corporate structure of companies in circumstances such as the facts alleged in this case. There is undoubted force in this submission …

64. Mr Rainey's case is that the court can and should pierce the corporate veil where there is a good arguable case that the defendant has set up the puppet company for the purpose of defrauding an innocent party with whom the puppet company contracts in order to avoid being sued in the courts of a member state in which the puppet company has agreed to be sued. . . .

65. The references in Lord Sumption JSC's judgment in *Prest v Prest*, at paras 27, 34 to 'abuse of corporate legal personality' as justifying piercing the corporate veil may appear to give some support to a policy-based approach. But it is clear from the decision of the Supreme Court that, in the present state of English law, the court can only pierce the corporate veil when 'a person is under an existing legal obligation or liability or subject to an existing legal restriction which he deliberately evades or whose enforcement he deliberately frustrates by interposing a company under his control': see paras 35, 60 and 98. Lord Mance and Lord Clarke JJSC, at paras 100 and 103, did not want to foreclose further development of the law, and Baroness Hale of Richmond JSC's approach, at paras 91–92, appears to be to the same effect, but that is where English law stands at present. In the light of the decisions in the *VTB Capital* [2.16] and *Prest* [2.12] cases, the submission that it is possible to pierce the corporate veil in this case to deem Mr Lembergs to have consented to the jurisdiction clause is untenable.

66. As to further development of the law, doing so by classical common law techniques may not be easy. In the *Prest* case Lord Sumption JSC, at para 28, identified two underlying principles which he called 'the concealment principle' and 'the evasion principle'. But Lord Neuberger PSC was of the view, at para 75, that there is a 'lack of any coherent principle in the application of the doctrine' of piercing the corporate veil, and Lord Walker of Gestingthorpe's view, at para 106, was that it is not a doctrine in the sense of a coherent principle or rule of law but a label. Baroness Hale JSC, at para 92, was 'not sure whether it is possible to classify all of the cases in which the courts have been or should be prepared to disregard the separate legal personality of a company neatly into cases of either concealment or evasion'. Absent a principle, further development of the law will be difficult for the courts because development of common law and equity is incremental and often by analogical reasoning.

The current position

The approach adopted here—and the right approach, it is suggested—is that 'piercing the veil' may exist as a matter of law (the Supreme Court has said so), but the Supreme Court has also indicated that the principle cannot be relied upon when other routes to the same ends are available: that is, routes which do *not* ignore the company's separate legal person, but instead rely on particular legal relationships between the corporate person and its members. Interestingly, however, when those other routes are *not* available, it seems—at least empirically—that public policy is also *not* called into play to allow piercing on public policy grounds. So does the principle serve any practical purpose? It appears not.

That view is reinforced by the Supreme Court's own discussion of the older cases illustrating 'concealment' (no piercing involved) and 'evasion' (two cases where the courts themselves expressly based their conclusions on piercing, but where the Supreme Court indicates it was not in fact the only route available, and so, by implication, was not the route which should have been adopted). That discussion appears in the extracts which follow.

Illustrating 'concealment'

[2.14] Prest v Petrodel Resources Ltd [2013] UKSC 34, [2013] 2 AC 415 (Supreme Court)

This extract considers *Gencor ACP Ltd v Dalby* [2000] 2 BCLC 734. Dalby, the director of a public company, had dishonestly diverted assets and business opportunities from this public company to a Virgin Islands company owned and controlled by Dalby himself. An order that the benefits so obtained should be disgorged was made against the offshore company as well as against Dalby personally.

LORD SUMPTION SCJ:

[Contrast a case of 'concealment' only]

31. In *Gencor ACP Ltd v Dalby* [2000] 2 BCLC 734, the plaintiff made a large number of claims against a former director, Mr Dalby, for misappropriating its funds. For present purposes the claim which matters is a claim for an account of a secret profit which Mr Dalby procured to be paid by a third party, Balfour Beatty, to a British Virgin Island company under his control called Burnstead. Rimer J held, at para 26, that Mr Dalby was accountable for the money received by Burnstead, on the ground that the latter was 'in substance little other than Mr Dalby's offshore bank account held in a nominee name', and 'simply...the alter ego through which Mr Dalby enjoyed the profit which he earned in breach of his fiduciary duty to ACP'. Rimer J ordered an account against both Mr Dalby and Burnstead. He considered that he was piercing the corporate veil. But I do not think that he was. His findings about Mr Dalby's relationship with the company and his analysis of the legal consequences show that both Mr Dalby and Burnstead were independently liable to account to ACP, even on the footing that they were distinct legal persons....[He then explained why.]

33. In...the *Gencor* case, the analysis would have been the same if [the nominee company] had been a natural person instead of a company. The evasion principle was not engaged, and indeed could not have been engaged on the facts of either case. This is because [Mr Dalby had not used] the company's separate legal personality to evade a liability that [he] would otherwise have had. [He was liable to account for the secret profit only if the true facts were that the nominee company had received the money *as nominee* for Mr Dalby.] That was proved...The situation was not the same as it had been in *Gilford Motor Co v Horne* [1933] Ch 935 and *Jones v Lipman* [1962] 1 WLR 832 [both cases are considered later, at 'Illustrating "evasion"', p 71], for in these cases the real actors, Mr Horne and Mr Lipman, had a liability which arose independently of the involvement of the company.

Illustrating 'evasion'

[2.15] Prest v Petrodel Resources Ltd [2013] UKSC 34, [2013] 2 AC 415 (Supreme Court)

The relevant facts are indicated in the judgment.

LORD SUMPTION SCJ:

[Revisiting authorities which 'pierced the veil']

29. The first and most famous of them is *Gilford Motor Co Ltd v Horne* [1933] Ch 935. Mr EB Horne had been the managing director of the Gilford Motor Co. His contract of employment precluded him being engaged in any competing business in a specified geographical area for five years after the end of his employment 'either solely or jointly with or as agent for any other person, firm or company'. He left Gilford and carried on a competing business in the specified area, initially in his own name. He then formed a company, JM Horne & Co Ltd, named after his wife, in which she and a business associate were shareholders. The trial judge, Farwell J, found that the company had been set up in this way to enable the business to be carried on under his own control but without incurring liability for breach of the covenant. However the reality, in his view, was that the company was being used as 'the channel through which the defendant Horne was carrying on his business': p 943. In fact, he dismissed the claim on the ground that the restrictive covenant was void. But the Court of Appeal allowed the appeal on that point and granted an injunction against both Mr Horne and the company. As against Mr Horne, the injunction was granted on the concealment principle. Lord Hanworth MR said, at pp 961–962, that the company was a 'mere cloak or sham' because the business was really being carried on by Mr Horne. Because the restrictive covenant prevented Mr Horne from competing with his former employers whether as principal or as agent for another, it did not matter whether the business belonged to him or to JM Horne & Co Ltd provided that he was carrying it on. The only relevance of the interposition of the company was to maintain the pretence that it was being carried on by others. Lord Hanworth MR did not explain why the injunction should issue against the company, but I think it is clear from the judgments of Lawrence and Romer LJJ, at pp 962 and 966, that they were applying the evasion principle. Lawrence LJ, who gave the fullest consideration to the point, based his view entirely on Mr Horne's evasive motive for forming the company. This showed that it was

> 'a mere channel used by the defendant Horne for the purpose of enabling him, for his own benefit, to obtain the advantage of the customers of the plaintiff company, and that therefore the defendant company ought to be restrained as well as the defendant Horne.'

In other words, the company was restrained in order to ensure that Horne was deprived of the benefit which he might otherwise have derived from the separate legal personality of the company…[T]his is properly to be regarded as a decision to pierce the corporate veil. It is fair to say that the point may have been conceded by counsel…It is also true that the court in *Gilford Motor Co Ltd v Horne* [1933] Ch 935 might have justified the injunction against the company on the ground that Mr Horne's knowledge was to be imputed to the company so as to make the latter's conduct unconscionable or tortious, thereby justifying the grant of an equitable remedy against it. But the case is authority for what it decided, not for what it might have decided, and in my view the principle which the Court of Appeal applied was correct. It does not follow that JM Horne & Co Ltd was to be identified with Mr Horne for any other purpose. Mr Horne's personal creditors would not, for example, have been entitled simply by virtue of the facts found by Farwell J, to enforce their claims against the assets of the company.

30. *Jones v Lipman* [1962] 1 WLR 832 was a case of very much the same kind. The facts were that Mr Lipman sold a property to the plaintiffs for £5,250 and then, thinking better of the deal, sold

it to a company called Alamed Ltd for £3,000, in order to make it impossible for the plaintiffs to get specific performance. The judge, Russell J, found that company was wholly owned and controlled by Mr Lipman, who had bought it off the shelf and had procured the property to be conveyed to it 'solely for the purpose of defeating the plaintiffs' rights to specific performance'. About half of the purchase price payable by Alamed was funded by borrowing from a bank, and the rest was left outstanding. The judge decreed specific performance against both Mr Lipman and Alamed Ltd. As against Mr Lipman this was done on the concealment principle. Because Mr Lipman owned and controlled Alamed Ltd, he was in a position specifically to perform his obligation to the plaintiffs by exercising his powers over the company. This did not involve piercing the corporate veil, but only identifying Mr Lipman as the man in control of the company. The company, said Russell J portentously at p 836, was 'a device and a sham, a mask which [Mr Lipman] holds before his face in an attempt to avoid recognition by the eye of equity'. On the other hand, as against Alamed Ltd itself, the decision was justified on the evasion principle, by reference to the Court of Appeal's decision in *Gilford Motor Co Ltd v Horne*. The judge must have thought that in the circumstances the company should be treated as having the same obligation to convey the property to the plaintiff as Mr Lipman had, even though it was not party to the contract of sale. It should be noted that he decreed specific performance against the company notwithstanding that as a result of the transaction, the company's main creditor, namely the bank, was prejudiced by its loss of what appears from the report to have been its sole asset apart from a possible personal claim against Mr Lipman which he may or may not have been in a position to meet. This may be thought hard on the bank, but it is no harder than a finding that the company was not the beneficial owner at all. The bank could have protected itself by taking a charge or registering the contract of sale.

[But contrast the analysis of Lord Neuberger.]

LORD NEUBERGER PSC:

['Piercing' doctrine is not needed to solve the practical problems]

69. On closer analysis of [the cases just discussed], it does not appear to me that the facts and outcomes in the *Gilford Motor* and *Jones* cases provide much direct support for the doctrine. However, the decisions can fairly be said to have rested on the doctrine if one takes the language of the judgments at face value. Further, they indicate that, where a court is of the view (albeit that I think that it was mistaken in those cases) that there is no other method of achieving justice, the doctrine provides a valuable means of doing so. . . .

[He then proceeded to explain why the doctrine was not necessary in deciding these cases, as follows:] . . .

71. In any event, it seems to me that the decision in the *Gilford Motor* case that an injunction should be granted against the company was amply justified on the basis that the company was Horne's agent for the purpose of carrying on the business (just as his wife would have been, if he had used her as the 'cloak'); therefore, if an injunction was justified against Horne, it was justified against the company. There is nothing in the judgments in the *Gilford Motor* case to suggest that any member of the Court of Appeal thought that he was making new law, let alone cutting into the well established and simple principle laid down in *Salomon v A Salomon & Co Ltd* [1897] AC 22. . . .

73. As for *Jones v Lipman* [1962] 1 WLR 832, I am unconvinced that it was necessary for Russell J to invoke the doctrine in order to justify an effective order for specific performance, as sought by the plaintiffs in that case. An order for specific performance would have required Lipman not merely to convey the property in question to the plaintiffs, but to do everything which was reasonably within his power to ensure that the property was so conveyed: see eg *Wroth v Tyler* [1974] Ch 30, 47–51. Lipman and an employee of his solicitors were the sole shareholders and directors of the company, and its sole liability appears to have been a loan of £1,500 to a bank (borrowed to meet half the £3,000 which it paid for the property). In those circumstances, it seems clear that Lipman could have compelled the company to convey the property

to the plaintiffs (on the basis that he would have to account to the company for the purchase price, which would have ensured that the bank was in no way prejudiced). Indeed, I consider that the company could fairly have been described and treated as being Lipman's 'creature', without in any way cutting into the principle established in *Salomon v A Salomon & Co Ltd* [1897] AC 22.

➤ Note

This view of these cases is not novel. Lord Cooke, in his Hamlyn Lectures,[33] said of *Jones v Lipman*:

> Since the company was in the vendor's control, there was no difficulty in granting a decree of specific performance against him. Describing the company as a creation of the vendor, a device, sham and mask, the judge also decreed specific performance directly against it. Those epithets, however, do not appear to have been needed to justify the remedy. No particular difficulty should arise in holding that a company or any other purchaser acquiring property with actual notice that the transaction is a fraud on a prior purchaser takes subject to the latter's equity.

This makes an important point. Courts often say that they are treating the company itself as a sham (as in the remarks by Russell J in *Jones v Lipman* [1962] 1 WLR 832), with the implication that the company's existence is then ignored.[34] Often, however, this is shorthand for finding a reason—and not a special company law reason—for holding that both the company and individual in control should comply with certain obligations. Put another way, the company's separate existence is certainly not ignored: the court orders the company as well as the defendant to comply with the obligations.

➤ Questions

1. It is sometimes suggested that 'piercing the veil' is still needed to explain cases like *Horne* and *Lipman*. In *Horne*, for example, it was Mr Horne who was subject to the restraint of trade clause, no one else, and there was no wrong committed at all unless Horne himself was in breach of this clause. To find Horne in breach when a company was doing the acts which, if done by Horne, would undoubtedly have been a breach of the clause, necessarily involves 'piercing'—or so the argument goes. Is the counter-argument precisely that put by Lord Neuberger: if Horne's wife, or some other individual human person, could in the same circumstances have been restrained from running a competing business, then the legal argument *cannot* be based on 'piercing the veil'; it must be some other argument. Lord Neuberger suggested it was agency. The range of possible options includes (but is perhaps not limited to) those considered in the next section: see 'Connections between the company and other persons', p 75.

2. Consider more carefully Lord Neuberger's suggestion that 'agency' could provide an answer to the *Horne* dilemma. Then comes the very difficult question, *when* will a company be considered to be an agent of its 'controller'? We have seen from *Salomon* [2.02] that mere control, even absolute control, is not enough. Do the cases considered in 'Agency rules and third parties', p 76, provide any clearer guidelines? The question is difficult—but it is undoubtedly a much better 'difficult question' than the unfocused question, 'should the veil be pierced?'

---

[33] Lord Cooke of Thorndon, *Turning Points of the Common Law* (1996 Hamlyn Lectures, 1997), p 17.

[34] Contrast this with a finding that a particular *transaction* is a sham: see the discussion in *Secretary of State for Business, Enterprise and Regulatory Reform v Neufeld* [2009] EWCA Civ 280, [2009] BCC 687, noted in the Note following *Lee's* case [2.05], p 46.

Remedies

One final but important comment is merited on 'piercing the veil'. *If* the corporate veil were to be pierced, what remedies should be available to the outside third party who is then entitled to claim directly against the insider company member? This is not an easy question, although historically it has merited little attention. The reason it is difficult is that, with true 'piercing', the principle underpinning the court's 'piercing' conclusion is at large (see Beatson LJ in *Antonio Gramsci Shipping Corpn v Recoletos Ltd* [2.13], cited earlier). This means that so too is the principle underpinning the remedy which should be awarded. By contrast, matters are much clearer, and correspondingly more certain, when the members are sued under traditional orthodox and general legal principles (eg contract, tort, constructive trust, etc), as discussed later: see 'Connections between the company and other persons', p 75.

No authorities can be cited which are directly on point, but the next case is instructive. It is a Supreme Court decision predating *Prest v Petrodel Resources Ltd*, and for that reason some of the uncertainties it expresses are no longer apt. The extract here focuses solely on the court's discussion of remedies, although even that is compromised, since the court was clearly of the view that 'piercing the veil' was quite inappropriate in any event.

Even if the corporate veil is pierced, the appropriate remedy is not necessarily one which sees the member 'step into the shoes' of the company.

[2.16] VTB Capital plc v Nutritek International Corpn [2013] UKSC 5 (Supreme Court)

The claimant (VTB) entered into a loan facility agreement with Russagroprom LLC (RAP) to fund the latter's acquisition of six Russian dairy plants and three associated companies from the first defendant (Nutritek). Following RAP's subsequent default on the loan, VTB alleged that it entered into the facility agreement in reliance on fraudulent misrepresentations made by Nutritek for which the other defendants were jointly liable. In particular, it claimed that RAP was in fact under the control of the defendants, and that, once the corporate veil was pierced, the defendants could be seen always to have been parties to the two agreements jointly with RAP and the guarantors. VTB could therefore claim damages in contract against the defendants. The Supreme Court, like the trial judge and the Court of Appeal, held that the claimant's contract claim was unsustainable as a matter of law.

> LORD NEUBERGER:
> 132. In so far as VTB invokes the principle of piercing the veil of incorporation, its case involves what, at best for its point of view, may be characterised as an extension to the circumstances where it has traditionally been held that the corporate veil can be pierced. It is an extension because it would lead to the person controlling the company being held liable as if he had been a co-contracting party with the company concerned to a contract where the company was a party and he was not. In other words, unlike virtually all the cases where the court has pierced the corporate veil, VTB is claiming that Mr Malofeev should be treated as if he were, or had been, a co-contracting party with RAP under the two agreements, even though neither Mr Malofeev nor any of the contracting parties (including VTB) intended Mr Malofeev to be a party.
> [After examining the relevant cases:]…[F]ar from there being a strong case for the proposed extension, there is an overwhelming case against it.
> 138. First, it is not suggested by VTB that any of the other contracting parties under the two agreements is not liable. Indeed, as mentioned above, VTB's proposed pleaded case is that Mr Malofeev is 'jointly and severally liable with RAP'. Even accepting that the court can pierce the

corporate veil in some circumstances, the notion of such joint and several liability is inconsistent with the reasoning and decision in *Salomon* **[2.02]**....

139. Subject to some other rule (such as that of undisclosed principal), where B and C are the contracting parties and A is not, there is simply no justification for holding A responsible for B's contractual liabilities to C simply because A controls B and has made misrepresentations about B to induce C to enter into the contract. This could not be said to result in unfairness to C: the law provides redress for C against A, in the form of a cause of action in negligent or fraudulent misrepresentation.

140. In any event, it would be wrong to hold that Mr Malofeev should be treated as if he was a party to an agreement, in circumstances where (i) at the time the agreement was entered into, none of the actual parties to the agreement intended to contract with him, and he did not intend to contract with them, and (ii) thereafter, Mr Malofeev never conducted himself as if, or led any other party to believe, he was liable under the agreement. That that is the right approach seems to me to follow from one of the most fundamental principles on which contractual liabilities and rights are based, namely what an objective reasonable observer would believe was the effect of what the parties to the contract, or alleged contract, communicated to each other by words and actions, as assessed in their context—see e.g. *Smith v Hughes* (1871) LR 6 QB 597, 607.

[Lord Neuberger then continued, dismissing the 'undisclosed principal analogy, denying that RAP was being used as 'a façade concealing the true facts', or (which amounted to much the same thing) that Mr Malofeev was 'abusing the corporate structure'.]

146. The proposed extension is all the more difficult to justify given that it is not needed to enable VTB to seek redress from Mr Malofeev. It is clear that, if VTB establishes that it was induced to enter into the agreements by the fraudulent statements which he is alleged to have made, then Mr Malofeev will be liable to compensate VTB. The measure of damages may be different, but that is not a particularly attractive reason for extending the principle in a new and unprincipled way....

The theoretical problems associated with settling, in a principled way, on appropriate remedies if the corporate veil is pierced, and the implicit approach taken by the Supreme Court to these issues in both this case and *Prest v Petrodel Resources Ltd*, add considerable weight to the view that 'piercing the corporate veil' is no longer a real option. Instead, if outsiders want to look to those standing behind the company, then their claims must be based on alternative, traditional and orthodox legal principles. The potential options are considered in the next section.

Connections between the company and other persons

The cases discussed in this section illustrate orthodox means of establishing (or denying the establishment of) different types of legal relationships between the company and its members, or between members and outside parties. The purpose of establishing such non-corporate relationships is invariably to render the members directly liable to outside parties despite the intermediate corporate vehicle, or, alternatively, to make the company liable when usually only the member would be liable.

After *Prest v Petrodel Resources Ltd*, none of these mechanisms can be referred to as 'piercing the corporate veil': the corporate veil is not ignored; indeed, it is usually essential to the analysis that the company *does* exist, and has a particular relationship with its members (typically its sole shareholder or its holding company).

Control of the company is not enough

Control, even the absolute control that comes with ownership of 100% of the company's shares, is not enough of itself to suggest any legal relationship between the company and its owner-member (other than the company–shareholder relationship), and certainly none which will assist injured outsiders: see *Salomon* **[2.02]**, *Prest v Petrodel Resources* **[2.12]** and *Adams v Cape Industries* **[2.07]**.

Contractual agreements and third parties

Sometimes there is no need to rely on any special relationship between the company and its members. This is because members often contract *directly* with third parties. The members are then of course personally liable on these contracts. For example, parent companies in corporate groups (or individual owners of owner-managed companies) often agree with third parties that they will guarantee the obligations of the subsidiary (or owner-managed company). Indeed, the more undercapitalised the subsidiary, the more likely it is that counterparties such as banks and landlords will require this sort of reassurance, especially if the subsidiary company cannot provide its own security. The effect of such contracts is that the liability of the parent company/owner-manager member for the company's debts is no longer limited (at least in relation to the debts which have been guaranteed), but this is a result of the member's own independent contractual engagements, not any 'veil piercing' or particular corporate law rule.

Note, however, that care is needed in interpreting these contracts to assess what particular liabilities have been undertaken. 'Letters of comfort' are especially suspect: in *Kleinwort Benson Ltd v Malaysia Mining Corpn Bhd* [1989] 1 WLR 379, CA, the 'comfort letter' given by the parent company to the claimant bank was construed as excluding an intention to create legal relations.

Agency rules and third parties

The essence of a principal–agent relationship is not simply that the principal has control over the agent (although that is true), it is that the *purpose* of the P–A relationship is for the agent to do the legwork to deliver legal engagements between the *principal* and the third party, while the agent then drops out of the picture. We will see this in operation in Chapter 3, when directors (as the company's agents) engage with third parties for the purpose of putting the company and the third parties (*not* the directors and third parties) in a contractual relationship.

If a principal/agent argument is to work as a means of enabling third parties to look to the members behind the company, insisting they are liable as the 'principal' in a relationship where the company is merely their 'agent', then special features must exist. Agency can of course be created by express agreement: see *Rainham Chemical Works Ltd v Belvedere Fish Guano Co Ltd* [1921] 2 AC 465, HL. But the issue in most of these cases is, absent such express agreement, when can a court *infer* an agency? That is rare.

Control (typically by the sole shareholder or holding company) is not enough.

[2.17] JH Rayner (Mincing Lane) Ltd v Department of Trade and Industry [1989] Ch 72 (Court of Appeal)

KERR LJ: The crucial point on which the House of Lords overruled the Court of Appeal in that landmark case [of *Salomon* **[2.02]**] was precisely the rejection of the doctrine that agency between a corporation and its members in relation to the corporation's contracts can be inferred from the control exercisable by the members over the corporation or from the fact that the sole objective of the corporation's contracts was to benefit the members. That rejection of the doctrine of agency to impugn the non-liability of the members for the acts of the corporation is the foundation of our modern company law.

Similarly, see *Salomon* [2.02], *Prest v Petrodel Resources* [2.12] and *Adams v Cape Industries* [2.07]. Also see *Ebbw Vale UDC v South Wales Traffic Area Licensing Authority* [1951] 2 KB 366, CA, at 370 (Cohen LJ).

The evidence of the agency relationship must be 'overwhelming'.

[2.18] Bank of Montreal v Westgrowth Petroleums Ltd 1992 ABCA 94, (1992) 2 Alta LR (3d) 221 (Alberta Court of Appeal)

The claimant sought to use the principal/agent argument to make a parent company liable (as alleged principal) on a contract entered into by its wholly owned subsidiary (as alleged agent) where the directors and senior officers of the two companies were identical, meetings of the two boards of directors were held concurrently, audits were concurrent, the parent funded the subsidiary on generous terms and provided management services seemingly at no cost, and most of the dealings concerning the contract in issue were with the parent company personnel. Despite all this, no express or implied agency relationship was found.

> CÔTÉ, JA (for the court):
>
> 6. In this case, we have a written contract which clearly says it is with one party, [the subsidiary]. In order to find that (in some way by agency or otherwise) it isn't really with [the subsidiary], it's really with [the parent], one would need pretty clear—possibly overwhelming—evidence of agency or something else. The evidence which has been pointed out to us is not of that nature. It is clear that it was [the subsidiary] which executed the contract in question. The Bank of Montreal sues only as assignee. The only assignment which we see is an assignment which purports only to be an assignment of a contract with [the subsidiary].
>
> 7. Leaving aside the legalities, there is a point of common sense. [English courts are unlikely to adopt such reasoning!] If the real intention of the parties (for example, through agency) were to have the ultimate party which really is liable as [the parent], then what the parties did would not make any sense. The parties deliberately switched things over and deliberately took [the parent's mistakenly inserted] name off the draft contract and deliberately signed the contract in the name of [the subsidiary]. They must have had some reason for doing that.

➤ Note

It is common for a contract to provide that the purchaser can nominate some third party nominee to take legal title to the property on completion of the sale. This does not of itself suggest that the legal personalities of either can be ignored, or that there is an agency relationship, trust relationship or partnership between the nominator and nominee, even if both are in the same group of companies: see *Attorney-General v Equiticorp Industries Group Ltd* [1996] 1 NZLR 528.

An agency relationship between a company and its shareholders or controllers may, exceptionally, be inferred from the facts. But the likelihood is low. Usually there is simply insufficient evidence of what is seen as necessary consent to such an important legal arrangement: see *Abbar v Saudi Economic & Development Co (SEDCO) Real Estate Ltd* [2013] EWHC 1414 (Ch), where David Richards J found that no agency could be established on the facts, and emphasised, at [178], that 'there is lacking the essential element of consent to the relationship of principal and agent which is necessary to a finding that the relationship has been established'.

One instance of such a finding of agency on the facts is, perhaps, *Smith, Stone & Knight Ltd v Birmingham Corpn* [1939] 4 All ER 116,[35] where Atkinson J allowed a holding company to claim compensation as if it were an owner-occupier, on the ground that its subsidiary (which occupied the land in question) was merely its agent for the purpose of carrying on its business. This decision is, however, in marked contrast to *Gramophone and Typewriter Co Ltd v Stanley* [2.06] and to many other cases involving parent companies and their subsidiaries, and has been the subject of some criticism: see, for example, MA Pickering, 'The Company as a Separate Legal Entity' (1968) 31 MLR 481 at 494; and Toulson J in *Yukong Lines Ltd of Korea v Rendsburg Investments Corpn of Liberia (No 2)* [1998] 1 WLR 294. Post *Prest v Petrodel Resources Ltd*, an analysis delivering the same conclusions would require a good deal more support.

Property law and third parties

The most typical concerns in this area are, first, with possible trust relationships between the company and its members, secondly, with possible unjust enrichment claims against members and, thirdly, with the scope of freezing orders. The relevant cases demonstrate very starkly the property and control consequences of separate legal personality.

Property held on trust

A trust relationship, with the company as trustee and the members as beneficiaries, may, exceptionally, be found to exist as a matter of fact. This does not depend on any special company law rule, but the conclusion can be advantageous to outsiders seeking remedies.

For example, in *Prest v Petrodel Resources Ltd* [2.12], the court concluded that certain houses (or the purchase money for their acquisition) had been transferred by the husband to his company for no consideration. The company therefore held the houses on resulting trust for the husband on normal equitable principles. This conclusion mattered, because *if* the husband was entitled to 'possession or reversion' of the houses within the terms of the Matrimonial Causes Act 1973 s 24(1), then the court had jurisdiction to order the husband to transfer them to the wife as part of the divorce settlement, which the court did. By contrast, if the houses had been legally and beneficially owned by the company, and the husband had merely owned the shares in the company—as is typically the case—then such an order could not have been made.[36]

This was the problem in *Ben Hashem v Al Shayif* [2008] EWHC 2380 (Fam), [2009] 1 FLR 115, where, as in *Prest v Petrodel Resources*, the husband displayed no impropriety in using a corporate vehicle to invest in property, and in any event he owned only 30% of the shares in the relevant company. The court rejected an argument that the remaining shares were held on trust for him. It thus followed that the court could not make an order against either the husband or the interposed company ordering the transfer to the wife of the two apartments owned by the company.

Property relationships are not the exclusive domain of family cases, however. In *Pennyfeathers Ltd v Pennyfeathers Property Co Ltd* [2013] EWHC 3530 (Ch), it was held by Rose J that there was no need to pierce the corporate veil to deliver a remedy for directors'

---

[35] Also see *Re FG (Films) Ltd* [1953] 1 WLR 483 (Ch), where the relationship was characterised as agency, but only in a throwaway line.

[36] The husband could of course have been ordered to transfer his *shares* to his wife, but his chain of ownership was obscure, and the companies were controlled in Nigeria, so the practical advantage to the wife was thought to be minimal.

clear breaches of fiduciary duty in diverting a corporate opportunity away from the company they directed. This was notwithstanding that the opportunity had been diverted to an interposed company rather than taken personally by the disloyal directors, and, moreover, that the wrongdoing directors did not own shares in, and were not directors of, the interposed company; instead, the shares in that company were owned by a trust of which the directors were the only beneficiaries. Rose J used the terminology of 'concealment' and 'evasion' in finding remedies against both the directors and the interposed company (see [116]–[119]). However, the straightforward analysis does not, it seems, depend on this at all (no detail was spelt out in the judgment). In particular, there is no need for recourse to 'concealment' or 'evasion', and most fiduciary disgorgement cases make no such claims. Here the defaulting directors were liable to disgorge their disloyal gains, whether owned legally or beneficially (see Chapter 7, 'Duty to avoid conflicts of interest: CA 2006 s 175', p 385). In addition, the interposed company took its own interest in the diverted opportunity subject to the equitable rights of the company to whom the directors owed their fiduciary duties. Here, the interposed company could not claim to be protected as a bona fide purchaser for value without notice: the facts on their face suggest full knowledge that the opportunity was diverted disloyally. Accordingly, the interposed company would also be liable to the claimant company for benefits knowingly received contrary to the claimant company's interests (see Chapter 7, 'Secondary liability (liability of third parties associated with directors' wrongs)', p 468).

Unjust enrichment

Similar care is needed in considering claims for restitutionary remedies in unjust enrichment. In *MacDonald Dickens & Macklin v Costello* [2011] EWCA Civ 930, [2012] QB 244, the claimant builders entered into a contract with the defendant company for the construction of houses on land which was owned by the company's directors and shareholders (the first and second defendants). When the company failed to meet its liabilities, the claimants sued the directors and shareholders in unjust enrichment. The claim failed. Although these parties had been enriched, the enrichment was not unjust—it was the result of a perfectly proper contractual arrangement between the claimant and the company, and to hold otherwise would undermine the law of contract.

Freezing orders and restraint orders

In certain circumstances the court will order the 'freezing' of a person's assets. Such freezing orders (formerly referred to as *Mareva* injunctions) are granted when the court perceives there is risk that defendants will move assets out of the jurisdiction, or otherwise spirit them away, and then be unable to meet the likely liability under a current or pending action in court. The court also has power to make a 'restraint order' under the Criminal Justice Act 1988 s 77, preventing a person from dealing with assets which are liable to be confiscated as the proceeds of crime.

A number of the earlier cases[37] held that such orders could extend to cover assets which were not owned by these defendants but were owned by companies which they controlled. The modern approach is both stricter and far more compelling. In *Lakatamia Shipping Co Ltd v Su* [2014] EWCA Civ 636, [2015] 1 WLR 291, for example, the relevant freezing order prohibited the defendant from 'disposing of, dealing with or diminishing the value of any of [his] assets'. The Court of Appeal held that this order did not directly prevent the defendants' wholly owned company dealing in *its* assets, but that any disposal of the company's assets other than in its ordinary course of business *would* fall foul of the

---

[37] Eg *International Credit and Investment Co (Overseas) Ltd v Adham* [1998] BCLC 134; *Re H (Restraint Order: Realisable Property)* [1996] 2 BCLC 500.

freezing order as this could well diminish the value of the defendant's own assets, namely his shareholding in the company.

Similarly, in *Group Seven Ltd v Allied Investment Corpn Ltd* [2013] EWHC 1509 (Ch), [2014] 1 WLR 735, Hildyard J held that a debt owed to the defendant's solely owned company fell outside an asset 'which [the defendant] has the power, directly or indirectly, to dispose of or deal with as if it were his own' (as per the freezing order). In reaching this conclusion, the judge highlighted an important feature of the way in which companies act (whether controlled by a sole shareholder or not) (see [64]–[70]): such companies are not given 'directions' by their controllers (typically the directors, but perhaps the sole shareholder); these controllers' acts *are* the company's acts for such purposes.

These two cases—one addressing property ideas, the other power and control—nicely illustrate the ramifications of separate legal personality. Had the judges reached contrary conclusions, they would have been undermining the very foundations of corporate law as seen earlier in *Salomon* **[2.02]**, *Macaura* **[2.03]** and *Lee v Lee's Air Farming* **[2.05]**.

Tort law and third parties

As we saw earlier with contract, sometimes there is no need to discover any special relationship between the company and its members to make those members liable to external third parties. The general law itself may provide for a direct relationship between the insider 'members' (typically a parent company within a corporate group) and the outsider third parties, thus enabling those outsiders to make claims directly against the members.

There are statutes which adopt this approach. This is typically the case in competition law, for example, which, for obvious reasons, focuses on 'undertakings' or 'economic units' rather than on each of the individual elements in a large corporate group: *Shell International Chemical Co Ltd v Commission* (Case T-11/89) [1992] ECR II-757, para 311.

Tort law too is amenable to such claims. The insider—typically the parent company—may simply be *directly* liable to the injured claimant on ordinary tort principles. This direct approach is seen to good effect in *Chandler v Cape plc* [2012] EWCA Civ 525, CA (part of the ongoing *Cape* litigation encountered in **[2.07]**). Here the court applied orthodox negligence principles to hold that a parent company owed a duty of care to the employee of a (now dissolved) subsidiary company. In delivering the judgment of the court, Arden LJ 'emphatically reject[ed] any suggestion that this court is in any way concerned with what is usually referred to as lifting the corporate veil' [69]. Instead, she approached the question purely from the tortious angle of 'assumption of responsibility'.

Chandler was subsequently followed, but distinguished on the facts, in the Court of Appeal's decision in *Thompson v Renwick Group plc* [2014] EWCA Civ 635, CA, in which it was held that the evidence fell far short of what was required for the imposition of a duty of care.

These modern examples stand in stark contrast to older cases which typically reach their desired ends by unnecessary resort to 'piercing the corporate veil'. *Jennings v Crown Prosecution Service* [2008] UKHL 29, [2008] AC 1046 may illustrate the point. There the court pierced the veil to convict an employee of conspiracy to defraud and prevent him from disposing of property obtained by fraud. The fraud consisted of persuading people to pay fees to a company for the arrangement of loans, knowing that no loans would ever be made. But piercing the veil was not necessary to reach these ends. The employee was the company's agent. Where an agent's acts constitute a crime or a tort (here, deceit), it is no defence for the agent to say the acts were committed on behalf of someone else.[38] It would not matter whether the agent acted for a human or a corporate principal.

---

[38] *Standard Chartered Bank v Pakistan National Shipping Corpn (No 2)* [2002] UKHL 43, [2003] 1 AC 959, HL; *Stone & Rolls Ltd (In Liquidation) v Moore Stephens (A Firm)* [2009] UKHL 39, [2009] 1 AC 1391, HL **[3.33]**.

Statutory rules and third parties

Statutory rules could of course render members (or directors) directly liable to outside parties if the company itself fails those outsiders in some regard. But the power of the *Salomon* principle means that 'clear and unequivocal language' would be needed: *Dimbleby & Sons Ltd v National Union of Journalists* [1984] 1 WLR 427, HL, at 435 (Lord Diplock).

More typically, statutes are focused on making the companies themselves liable to outsiders, or—more rarely—enabling companies to sue their insiders.

The first of these approaches was seen in operation in *Daimler Co Ltd v Continental Tyre and Rubber* [2.10], a case concerned with 'enemy aliens'. Recall that the court there used certain nominated characteristics of the company's members to determine a characteristic of the company, being its 'enemy alien' status. We can now note that this approach does not involve either 'veil piercing' or reliance on general (non-company-specific) legal rules. It is simply the court (or, where relevant, a statute) defining the rule of attribution which will determine how, for the purposes of the particular legal context, a given rule will apply to the company. These attribution rules are dealt with in detail in Chapter 3.

By contrast, some statutes are again unconcerned with the injured outsiders, but instead ensure that the *company* has claims against its insiders. This does not 'pierce the veil' at all, and indeed is a purely bilateral issue between company and insider, although any damages award paid to the company will enhance the company's ability to meet its liabilities to the injured outsiders. The CA 2006, for example, makes directors and other officers liable to the company for company wrongs (see Chapter 7). Similarly, the insolvency legislation contains a number of sections providing for directors (and others) to be personally liable to the company. So too the Company Directors Disqualification Act 1986 (CDDA 1986).

Summary

Since the separate personality of companies is fundamental to the structure of company law, there are a wide variety of illustrations of the impact of the doctrine. The cases noted in this chapter are primarily directed at illuminating the essence of separate corporate personality and illustrating the exceptional circumstances in which the company's members may be liable for the company's failings. But it is important not to leave this area without appreciating that the normal rule is that the company is its own person, and this feature has a fundamental impact on engagements between the company and third parties.

By way of illustration, later in this book we consider the company and its engagements with its promoters (those who set up the company), its directors and its auditors. All these parties owe their duties to the *company*, not to the individuals concerned with the company, unless there are special circumstances giving rise to separate duties: see 'Promoters and their dealings with the company', pp 498ff; 'Directors' duties are owed to the company', pp 336ff; 'Auditors and their relationship with the company', pp 481ff.

Equally, when the *company* acts, the procedures it must adopt so that the actions of human agents (directors, members, employees, etc) count as the actions of the company are determined by the company's constitution (assisted by certain statutory and common law rules designed to protect third parties in their dealings with the company): see 'Agency and authority in corporate contracting', pp 93ff.

All these matters are dealt with later, but mentioned here by way of reinforcing the key point of this chapter, which is that companies are separate legal entities.

▨ Further reading

ARMOUR, J, 'Corporate Personality and Assumption of Responsibility' [1999] LMCLQ 246.

LORD COOKE OF THORNDON, 'A Real Thing' in *Turning Points of the Common Law* (1996 Hamlyn Lectures, 1997).

DAY, W, 'Skirting Around the Issue: The Corporate Veil after *Prest v Petrodel*' [2014] LMCLQ 269.

EASTERBROOK, FH and FISCHEL, DR, *The Economic Structure of Corporate Law* (1991), ch 2 'Limited Liability'.

FLANNIGAN, R, 'The Economic Structure of the Firm' (1995) 33 *Osgoode Hall Law Journal* 105.

FREEDMAN, J, 'Limited Liability: Large Company Theory and Small Firms' (2000) 63 MLR 317.

HANSMANN, H and KRAAKMAN, RH, 'The Essential Role of Organizational Law' (2000) 110 *Yale Law Journal* 387 at 387–404.

HANSMANN, H and KRAAKMAN, RH, 'Toward Unlimited Liability for Corporate Torts' (1991) 100 *Yale Law Journal* 1879.

HICKS, A, 'Corporate Form: Questioning the Unsung Hero' [1997] JBL 306.

IRELAND, P, 'Triumph of the Company Legal Form 1856–1914' in J Adams (ed), *Essays for Clive Schmitthoff* (1983), p 29.

SEALY, LS, 'Perception and Policy in Company Law Reform' in D Feldman and F Meisel (eds), *Corporate and Commercial Law* (1996), pp 11–29.

WOLFF, W, 'On the Nature of Legal Persons' (1938) 54 LQR 494.

3

CORPORATE ACTIVITY
AND LEGAL LIABILITY

Introduction

The previous chapter considered what it means to say that a company is a legal person. This chapter looks at how the company *acts* as a legal person: in particular, how it enters into binding contracts, commits torts and crimes, makes gifts, sues and is sued.

Two issues are immediately obvious, and a third should be acknowledged. First, and most obviously, a company can only act because some human agent acts: the company cannot, literally, act 'itself', either physically or mentally. If the company is to act as its own legal person, then it is necessary to hold that the physical or mental acts of a particular human person will 'count as' the physical or mental acts of the company. Notice, too, that the legal rules on what 'counts' are unlikely to be exactly the same legal rules as those which operate between two human individuals—that would be far too restrictive— although of course these rules, too, could be used.[1] So the first question to be addressed must necessarily focus on this: *whose* acts will count as the company's acts *for the particular legal purposes in issue*? It does not take a lawyer to recognise that a shop assistant's acts will be sufficient to conclude a contract between the supermarket and a customer purchasing groceries, but a senior director's acts will likely be needed for the company's purchase of a new retail site. Notice that this conclusion is reached by paying attention not only to 'whose acts will count' but also to the crucial rider 'for this legal purpose'.

The second issue is also an obvious one, and closely related to the first. It recognises the tension between corporate insiders and outsiders in this analysis. The company's insiders are keen to see that the company's assets are not misapplied; the company's outsiders are keen to see that they have legal rights against the company. When the company's directors or other agents misbehave, can the company simply deny that such unauthorised acts 'count as the acts of the company'?[2] If the company *can* deny attribution in these circumstances, then the legal risk of underperforming agents is shifted to the outsiders. If it

---

[1] This point emerges rather sharply in the section on 'Directors' authority and breach of directors' duties', p 124.
[2] See 'Denying attribution', p 164, on the attribution of acts of unauthorised agents.

cannot, then the risk is borne internally. It may seem obvious that the company is typically better placed to internalise the risk (it selects the agents, and it can insure itself against harm), and that commercial activity will be enhanced if the outsiders are protected. This serves to remind us that it is not merely a question of deciding *'whose'* acts will count, but also *'which'* acts will count as the company's acts *for the particular legal purpose in issue*. Yet even this expanded question can sometimes be difficult. The possibility that a company can sometimes deny attribution of the acts, knowledge or intentions of its human agents has produced some of the most difficult litigation in this area in the past decade, and is examined towards the end of this chapter: see 'Denying attribution', p 164.

The legal terminology associated with the questions just discussed is 'attribution': 'Which acts (or intentions, knowledge, etc) of which person will be *attributed* to the company for the particular legal purposes in issue?' This question is key. And it remains the key question regardless of the particular legal purpose in issue. The purposes can vary widely, from discovering whether the company has bound itself in contract or has committed a tort or a crime. If the relevant human person is found, and his or her acts, knowledge or intentions are attributed to the company, then the result is that the *company* has acted in this way: this *is* how a company acts, or knows or intends. And if those actions, etc, are sufficient to generate legal consequences, then the *company itself* is liable accordingly: that is, the company is 'directly' or 'personally' bound in contract or guilty of a crime.

As an aside, note that, by quite separate legal analysis, a company may be held *vicariously liable* for certain torts and crimes committed by its employees and agents (and for which those employees and agents, individually, are personally liable). But this conclusion does not depend on any special company law rule. The question in every case is, rather, whether it is appropriate, on public policy grounds, to hold the company liable for a wrong it has not committed personally,[3] but which its employees or agents have committed. If the difference between personal and vicarious liability is put succinctly, in the former case the company itself has committed the wrong; in the latter it is merely held liable for a wrong that someone else has committed.[4]

Finally, perhaps the least obvious issue in this area but clearly a crucial one, is the question: 'Is this legal rule intended to apply to companies *at all*?' Logically, this is the first question which must be asked in contemplating corporate rights and liabilities. Sometimes the answer is easy; sometimes quite difficult. The logic of enabling corporate commercial activity suggests that companies should be equipped to enter into contracts, and should be subject to the rules on negligence, misrepresentation and fraud. In short, companies *should* be subjects of all this law. This is all done by attribution. By contrast, it is equally easy to see that companies cannot marry. They should not be subjects of these laws. But should a company be 'personally' or 'directly' liable for dangerous driving? If attribution works for fraud, should it not be equally easy to find 'the person' whose dangerous driving should be attributed to the company to make the company personally liable here too? Oddly, the question is rarely raised in such contexts. Instead, this form of liability is typically dealt with by holding the company vicariously liable, not directly liable. This perhaps permits added flexibility; it allows the public policy angle to be brought into play to protect the company whenever it would seem inappropriate to hold the company liable for a wrong *'it has not committed'*. But the italicised words assume a particular conclusion which may be questionable.[5] The problem has been brought into stark relief in one class

---

[3] Notice that on given facts it is perfectly possible to find the company liable personally (via attribution) *and* vicariously (according to the rules on vicarious liability), but the legal reasoning delivering those ends is quite different.

[4] This is the orthodox view, but is now controversial again: see R Stevens, *Torts and Rights* (2007), viewing vicarious liability as a rule of attribution of *acts* between individuals, not merely liability.

[5] See further at 'Tort liability', p 136.

of modern tort claims. This is where companies run children's homes and the children are abused by the corporate managers and staff. The individuals are of course liable for their personal wrongs. But public sentiment weighs in favour of holding the company liable too. The usual rules of vicarious liability would often fail to deliver these ends. Attribution would. But the route chosen by modern cases is not attribution. Instead, it is to find a new tort, a 'non-delegable duty of care', owed by the company to the children. This can be applied without recourse to attribution because it simply imposes strict liability on the company for protecting the children in their care from these sorts of harms. But it is worth considering whether attribution could have delivered some of the same ends more easily and more appropriately.[6]

This sets the scene for thinking about corporate liability in contract, tort and crime. The next section is crucial, and underpins all that follows. It considers in detail the generic technique of corporate attribution. It addresses the issue of whether a particular rule applies to companies at all, and then, if it does, how we should decide 'Which acts (knowledge, intentions, etc) of which people should count as the acts (knowledge, intentions, etc) of the company for the particular legal purposes in issue?' This question is typically abbreviated to 'Whose acts count as the company's acts for this purpose?', but the detail of the expanded version must not be lost sight of.

Rules of attribution: how does a company act?

The most significant contribution to answering the question, '*Whose* acts count as the company's acts *for this purpose*?', comes from the next case. Notice the approach. The outcome in the case turned on what the company 'knew'. To answer that question it was necessary to decide *whose* knowledge was to count as the company's knowledge in this particular context. The Privy Council held that the relevant person was an individual some way down the corporate hierarchy: that is, for the particular purposes in issue, corporate knowledge did not necessarily depend on what was known at the top of the hierarchy by the people who constituted 'the directing mind and will' of the company (ie typically the company's sole owner/manager[7] or board of directors). Deciding whose knowledge counted was based on construction of the particular statutory provision in issue, and cannot be generalised to other contexts. The case is important for laying out the proper analytical steps, not for its factual conclusions.

Identifying the relevant person for the purposes of attribution in a given context.

[3.01] Meridian Global Funds Management Asia Ltd v Securities Commission [1995] 2 AC 500 (Privy Council)

The New Zealand Securities Amendment Act 1988 required a person who became a 'substantial security holder' in a listed company to give notice to the authorities 'as soon as the person knows, or ought to know' that he has become such a holder. The issue was

---

[6] The 'new' duty has one alleged advantage over attribution, if such it is: it means that the company is liable even if the harm is caused by outside contractors, even contractors chosen and supervised with all due care. But the justice of this is surely questionable. Equally, if strangers come onto the school premises and cause such harm, despite proper school security and supervision, surely the 'non-delegable duty of care' would not suggest corporate liability?

[7] Eg Mr Salomon in *Salomon v A Salomon & Co Ltd* [2.02].

whether Meridian 'knew' that it had become such a holder. Its board of directors (regarded as the company's 'directing mind and will') did not know. Indeed, the shareholding had only been acquired because two senior investment managers, Koo and Ng, acting within their authority but for improper purposes of their own, had bought the relevant shares in Meridian's name. The Privy Council held that the relevant person for the purpose of the attribution rules in this statutory context was Koo, as the agent primarily involved in the transaction; it was not necessary that the person (or people) who constituted 'the directing mind and will' of the company also knew.

The opinion of their Lordships was delivered by LORD HOFFMANN:... The phrase 'directing mind and will' comes of course from the celebrated speech of Viscount Haldane LC in *Lennard's Carrying Co Ltd v Asiatic Petroleum Co Ltd* **[3.21]**. But their Lordships think that there has been some misunderstanding of the true principle upon which that case was decided. It may be helpful to start by stating the nature of the problem in a case like this and then come back to *Lennard's* case later.

Any proposition about a company necessarily involves a reference to a set of rules. A company exists because there is a rule (usually in a statute) which says that a *persona ficta* shall be deemed to exist and to have certain of the powers, rights and duties of a natural person. But there would be little sense in deeming such a *persona ficta* to exist unless there were also rules to tell one what acts were to count as acts of the company. It is therefore a necessary part of corporate personality that there should be rules by which acts are attributed to the company. These may be called 'the rules of attribution'.

[Identifying whose acts will generally count]

The company's primary rules of attribution will generally be found in its constitution, typically the articles of association, and will say things such as 'for the purpose of appointing members of the board, a majority vote of the shareholders shall be a decision of the company' or 'the decisions of the board in managing the company's business shall be the decisions of the company'. There are also primary rules of attribution which are not expressly stated in the articles but implied by company law, such as 'the unanimous decision of all the shareholders in a solvent company about anything which the company under its memorandum of association has power to do shall be the decision of the company': see *Multinational Gas and Petrochemical Co v Multinational Gas and Petrochemical Services Ltd* **[7.43]**.

These primary rules of attribution are obviously not enough to enable a company to go out into the world and do business. Not every act on behalf of the company could be expected to be the subject of a resolution of the board or a unanimous decision of the shareholders. The company therefore builds upon the primary rules of attribution by using general rules of attribution which are equally available to natural persons, namely, the principles of agency. It will appoint servants and agents whose acts, by a combination of the general principles of agency and the company's primary rules of attribution, count as the acts of the company. And having done so, it will also make itself subject to the general rules by which liability for the acts of others can be attributed to natural persons, such as estoppel or ostensible authority in contract and vicarious liability in tort.[8]

[Does the law which is in issue apply to companies at all?]

It is worth pausing at this stage to make what may seem an obvious point. Any statement about what a company has or has not done, or can or cannot do, is necessarily a reference to the rules of attribution (primary and general) as they apply to that company. Judges sometimes say that

---

8 Note that these rules (on estoppel, ostensible authority and vicarious liability) are separate from the corporate attribution rules: ie they are rules which apply to companies, but not rules which identify 'whose acts count...etc'.

a company 'as such' cannot do anything; it must act by servants or agents. This may seem an unexceptionable, even banal remark. And of course the meaning is usually perfectly clear. But a reference to a company 'as such' might suggest that there is something out there called the company of which one can meaningfully say that it can or cannot do something. There is in fact no such thing as the company as such, no *Ding an sich*, only the applicable rules. To say that a company cannot do something means only that there is no one whose doing of that act would, under the applicable rules of attribution, count as an act of the company.

The company's primary rules of attribution together with the general principles of agency, vicarious liability and so forth are usually sufficient to enable one to determine its rights and obligations. In exceptional cases, however, they will not provide an answer. This will be the case when a rule of law, either expressly or by implication, excludes attribution on the basis of the general principles of agency or vicarious liability. For example, a rule may be stated in language primarily applicable to a natural person and require some act or state of mind on the part of that person 'himself', as opposed to his servants or agents. This is generally true of rules of the criminal law, which ordinarily impose liability only for the actus reus and *mens rea* of the defendant himself. How is such a rule to be applied to a company?

One possibility is that the court may come to the conclusion that the rule was not intended to apply to companies at all; for example, a law which created an offence for which the only penalty was community service.

[But if the law in issue does apply to companies, then how do we decide whose acts, etc, will count as the company's acts, etc?]

Another possibility is that the court might interpret the law as meaning that it could apply to a company only on the basis of its primary rules of attribution, ie if the act giving rise to liability was specifically authorised by a resolution of the board or a unanimous agreement of the shareholders. But there will be many cases in which neither of these solutions is satisfactory; in which the court considers that the law was intended to apply to companies and that, although it excludes ordinary vicarious liability, insistence on the primary rules of attribution would in practice defeat that intention. In such a case, the court must fashion a special rule of attribution for the particular substantive rule. This is always a matter of interpretation: given that it was intended to apply to a company, how was it intended to apply? Whose act (or knowledge, or state of mind) was *for this purpose* intended to count as the act etc of the company? One finds the answer to this question by applying the usual canons of interpretation, taking into account the language of the rule (if it is a statute) and its content and policy.

The fact that the rule of attribution is a matter of interpretation or construction of the relevant substantive rule is shown by the contrast between two decisions of the House of Lords, *Tesco Supermarkets Ltd v Nattrass* **[3.25]** and *Director General of Fair Trading v Pioneer Concrete (UK) Ltd*.[9] In the *Tesco* case the question involved the construction of [s 24(1) of] the Trade Descriptions Act 1968.

[His Lordship summarised the facts and issues in that case, and continued:] The House of Lords held that the precautions taken by the board were sufficient for the purposes of section 24(1) to count as precautions taken by the company and that the manager's negligence was not attributable to the company. It did so by examining the purpose of section 24(1) in providing a defence to what would otherwise have been an absolute offence: it was intended to give effect to 'a policy of consumer protection which does have a rational and moral justification'. This led to the conclusion that the acts and defaults of the manager were not intended to be attributed to the company . . .

On the other hand, in *Director General of Fair Trading v Pioneer Concrete (UK) Ltd*, a restrictive arrangement in breach of an undertaking by a company to the Restrictive Practices Court was made by executives of the company acting within the scope of their employment. The board knew

[9] [1995] 1 AC 456, HL.

nothing of the arrangement; it had in fact given instructions to the company's employees that they were not to make such arrangements. But the House of Lords held that for the purposes of deciding whether the company was in contempt, the act and state of mind of an employee who entered into an arrangement in the course of his employment should be attributed to the company. This attribution rule was derived from a construction of the undertaking against the background of the Restrictive Trade Practices Act 1976: such undertakings by corporations would be worth little if the company could avoid liability for what its employees had actually done on the ground that the board did not know about it...

Against this background of general principle, their Lordships can return to Viscount Haldane LC. In *Lennard's Carrying Co Ltd v Asiatic Petroleum Co Ltd* **[3.21]** the substantive provision for which an attribution rule had to be devised was section 502 of the Merchant Shipping Act 1894, which provided a shipowner with a defence to a claim for the loss of cargo put on board his ship if he could show that the casualty happened 'without his actual fault or privity'. The cargo had been destroyed by a fire caused by the unseaworthy condition of the ship's boilers. The language of section 502 excludes vicarious liability; it is clear that in the case of an individual owner, only his own fault or privity can defeat the statutory protection. How is this rule to be applied to a company? Viscount Haldane LC rejected the possibility that it did not apply to companies at all or (which would have come to the same thing) that it required fault or privity attributable under the company's primary rules. Instead, guided by the language and purpose of the section, he looked for the person whose functions in the company, in relation to the cause of the casualty, were the same as those to be expected of the individual shipowner to whom the language primarily applied. Who in the company was responsible for monitoring the condition of the ship, receiving the reports of the master and ship's agents, authorising repairs etc.? This person was Mr Lennard, whom Viscount Haldane LC described as the *'directing mind and will'* of the company. It was therefore his fault or privity which section 502 attributed to the company...But this anthropomorphism, by the very power of the image, distracts attention from the purpose for which Viscount Haldane L.C. said...he was using the notion of directing mind and will, namely to apply the attribution rule derived from section 502 to the particular defendant in the case...

Once it is appreciated that the question is one of construction rather than metaphysics [ie a general doctrine for companies which requires recourse to the 'directing mind and will' in all such circumstances], the answer in this case seems to their Lordships to be...straightforward.

[Application of these ideas on attribution to the facts in issue]

The policy of section 20 of the Securities Amendment Act 1988 is to compel, in fast-moving markets, the immediate disclosure of the identity of persons who become substantial security holders in public issuers. Notice must be given as soon as that person knows that he has become a substantial security holder. In the case of a corporate security holder, what rule should be implied as to the person whose knowledge for this purpose is to count as the knowledge of the company? Surely the person who, with the authority of the company, acquired the relevant interest. Otherwise the policy of the Act would be defeated. Companies would be able to allow employees to acquire interests on their behalf which made them substantial security holders but would not have to report them until the board or someone else in senior management got to know about it. This could put a premium on the board paying as little attention as possible to what its investment managers were doing. Their Lordships would therefore hold that upon the true construction of section 20(4)(e), the company knows that it has become a substantial security holder when that is known to the person who had authority to do the deal. It is then obliged to give notice under section 20(3). The fact that Koo did the deal for a corrupt purpose and did not give such notice because he did not want his employers to find out cannot in their Lordships' view affect the attribution of knowledge and the consequent duty to notify.

It was therefore not necessary in this case to inquire into whether Koo could have been described in some more general sense as the 'directing mind and will' of the company.

[The conclusion on the attribution rule is context specific: it is the attribution rule 'for this purpose']

But their Lordships would wish to guard themselves against being understood to mean that whenever a servant of a company has authority to do an act on its behalf, knowledge of that act will for all purposes be attributed to the company. It is a question of construction in each case as to whether the particular rule requires that the knowledge that an act has been done, or the state of mind with which it was done, should be attributed to the company. Sometimes, as in *Director General of Fair Trading v Pioneer Concrete (UK) Ltd* and this case, it will be appropriate. Likewise in a case in which a company was required to make a return for revenue purposes and the statute made it an offence to make a false return with intent to deceive, the Divisional Court held that the mens rea of the servant authorised to discharge the duty to make the return should be attributed to the company: see *Moore v I Bresler Ltd*.[10] On the other hand, the fact that a company's employee is authorised to drive a lorry does not in itself lead to the conclusion that if he kills someone by reckless driving, the company will be guilty of manslaughter. There is no inconsistency. Each is an example of an attribution rule for a particular purpose, tailored as it always must be to the terms and policies of the substantive rule.

➤ Notes

1. In *Deutsche Genossenschaftsbank v Burnhope* [1995] 1 WLR 1580, HL, the legal provision in issue did not apply to a company at all, so the attribution question was never reached. The plaintiff bank was insured against direct financial losses suffered by reason of property lost through 'theft...or false pretences, committed by persons present on the premises' of the bank. The House of Lords held that, on a natural reading, this referred to situations where the thief or fraudster, being a natural person, was physically present on the bank's premises and committed the crime himself. It therefore did not cover a £9 million fraud by one of the bank's corporate customers, even though one step in the fraud involved an innocent employee of the corporate customer attending at the bank's premises to receive the relevant securities taken in the fraud.[11]

2. In *R v St Regis Paper Co Ltd* [2011] EWCA Crim 2527, CA, the relevant criminal provision did apply to companies, so the appropriate attribution rule needed to be identified. The case concerned the Pollution Prevention and Control (England and Wales) Regulations 2000. The company (the owner and operator of mills which manufactured paper and board from waste paper) had pleaded guilty to a number of strict liability offences, but denied liability for intentional falsification of environmental records. The court examined the regulations, and held that criminal liability for this offence could only be imposed if the company's 'directing mind and will' met the required *mens rea* for the actions ([12]): that is, for this purpose, the 'person' whose acts and intentions would count as the acts and intentions of the company was the company's 'directing mind and will'. Here, an employee's intentional falsification of environmental records could not be attributed to the defendant company.

3. Recall Lord Hoffmann's view that a company's 'directing mind and will' is not a term of art, but merely a catching (and, it is suggested, enormously distracting) turn of phrase which is often attached to a particular person within the corporate structure for the purposes of identifying someone whose acts, etc, will be attributed to the company *for the purposes in question*. In *El Ajou v Dollar Land Holdings Ltd* **[3.26]**, the court recognised that different

---

[10] [1944] 2 All ER 515, DC.
[11] This principle has been applied by the Court of Appeal in *Jafari-Fini v Skillglass Ltd* [2007] EWCA Civ 261 and in the Privy Council by Lord Hoffmann in *Lebon v Aqua Salt Co Ltd* [2009] UKPC 2, PC.

people could be the company's 'directing mind and will' for different purposes:[12] in this case the chairman met the criteria; on other occasions it would be the CEO or other individuals within the company. The case is considered further at 'What does a company know?', p 160.

In short, the 'rules of attribution' indicate whose acts, or knowledge or intentions, will count as the company's acts or knowledge or intentions in the particular circumstances in issue. The 'primary rules of attribution' as set out in the Model Articles arts 3 and 4 (for both limited and public companies), provide as follows:

Directors' general authority

3. Subject to the articles, the directors are responsible for the management of the company's business, for which purpose they may exercise all the powers of the company.

Members' reserve power

4. (1) The members may, by special resolution, direct the directors to take, or refrain from taking, specified action.

(2) No such special resolution invalidates anything which the directors have done before the passing of the resolution.

A company may choose its own 'primary attribution' rules, but these model provisions are common. In addition, if permitted by the company's constitution, the board may delegate its powers. See, for example, Model Articles arts 5 and 6. If the board then delegates in a manner permitted by the articles, the delegate(s) will have actual authority to bind the company as long as their actions are within the scope of the delegation.

Contractual liability

General issues

The issue to be addressed here is whether a contract between the company and an outsider is binding. The company and the outsider will only be able to enforce the contract (or be sued on it) if the contract is binding. The Companies Act 2006 (CA 2006) s 43 provides that a company can enter into a contract either in writing under its common seal, or through an authorised agent acting on behalf of the company.

A company is a legal person, and the principles which determine the validity of contracts between legal persons are already familiar. In the corporate context it is especially important to note that a contract is valid and binding only if:[13]

(i)   contracting parties have the *capacity* to contract (or are deemed or presumed to have that capacity); and

(ii) agents effecting the transaction on behalf of the parties have the *authority (real or apparent)* to do so (or are deemed or presumed to have that authority).

Notice that the first question relates to the *company*, and the second to its *directors* (or other agents). The first question now creates few problems (although it used to create enormous ones); the second is often critical.

---

[12] See p 699 (Rose LJ) and p 706 (Hoffmann LJ).
[13] Note the longer list of requirements for a valid contract at 'The framework for assessing effective contractual engagement', p 91.

As will become apparent from what follows, the first question, on corporate capacity, has lost much of its significance in recent years. This is for two reasons: (i) most companies (other than charities) no longer expressly limit their activities (and thus their capacity) by specifying 'objects' in their articles; and (ii) statutory provisions now protect third parties from the effect of any remaining constitutional restrictions. The result is that commercial companies now generally possess either actual or deemed *capacity* to do a great number of things.

Insofar as the second question, on agency, is concerned, even if the company does have the capacity to enter into a particular type of contract (or is deemed to have the necessary capacity), this does not mean that anyone and everyone can decide that the company *will* commit itself. For example, a national petroleum company certainly has the capacity to sell to customers, but not everyone (not even every company employee) can decide that the company *will* sell to a particular customer or enter into a transaction above certain value limits. Only those employees (or company *agents*) with *authority* to make a sale can commit the company in this way.

The framework for assessing effective contractual engagement

When all the various rules are put together, it will be seen that a contract between the company and an outsider will be binding if:

(i)   the company has the *capacity* to enter into the contract, *or* that capacity can be as-sumed (using CA 2006 s 39(1)); *and*

(ii) the director (or other agent transacting the deal) has the necessary *authority*: that is, has *either actual authority* to transact the deal, *or* can be *deemed* to have that authority using CA 2006 s 40, *or* has *ostensible authority*. And if the impediment to successfully demonstrating the particular form of authority is an issue of internal company procedure, then the *indoor management rule* allows the third party to assume that the internal procedures are regular;[14] *and*

(iii) the necessary *formalities* have been complied with (writing, etc) (*or* can be deemed to have been complied with because of the rules in CA 2006); *and*

(iv) the *usual contractual requirements* of offer, acceptance, consideration, etc are met. (These are not company-specific rules and are not considered here.)

The authority issue is now key, but we look at each issue in turn. However, seeing the structure of the analysis from the outset assists. If the necessary elements are made out—and that is done most simply by asking and answering the relevant questions in the order indicated here—then there will be a binding contract between the company and the third party and each side can enforce its contractual rights.

For completeness, three further points should be noted. First, under the normal rules of agency, the acts of an unauthorised agent (ie an agent without actual authority, statutorily deemed authority or common law ostensible authority) will not bind the company (the principal) to the third party in contract. The contract will be void. But if the unauthorised agent has dealt with the third party explicitly as agent, then the principal (the company) may choose to *ratify* the unauthorised transaction, effectively adopting it and render-ing it binding on the third party.[15] Secondly, and alternatively, if the unauthorised agent

---

[14] More accurately, this rule allowed outsiders to presume (in the absence of facts putting the outsider on inquiry) that there had been compliance with all matters of internal (non-public) management and procedure required by the articles (or other internal rules) for the proper exercise of any power.

[15] Note, however, that if the agency is undisclosed (so the third party does not appreciate that the intended counterparty is the company), then the company cannot ratify the unauthorised transaction: *Keighley Maxsted & Co v Durant* [1901] AC 240, HL. By contrast, an authorised agent can effect binding contracts between the principal and the third party whether or not the agency is disclosed.

has dealt with the third party explicitly as agent and the company does *not* ratify, then the third party can sue the *agent* for breach of warranty of authority. Finally, even if the contract is void, its terms may nevertheless have been carried out, and assets transferred (and effectively transferred) between company and intended counterparty. In these circumstances each party has the right to recover the assets it has mistakenly transferred (mistakenly in the assumption that there was a contractual obligation to transfer).[16]

Capacity: what is a company legally set up to do?

A company's capacity may be constrained by provisions in its articles. For example, a charitable company must expressly limit its activities (its *'objects'*) to charitable purposes (CA 2006 s 31(4)), and will likely refine these further to include only particular types of charitable activities in a nominated field. Commercial companies can do the same, although they have less reason, and no obligation, to be so restrictive (CA 2006 s 31(1)). These legal limitations in the company's constitutional documents limit the company's *capacity*—although now to little external effect.

Historically, purported contractual dealings outside such nominated objects were void. Neither party could enforce the contract, and any benefits transferred were subject to restitutionary claims aimed at restoring the parties to their pre-contractual positions.[17] This created great disincentives for outsiders dealing with the company, and could wreak unfair and unexpected consequences on transacting parties. The advantage, if there was one, was for the members: they could be sure (if the directors acted properly) that their investments were confined to selected types of ventures.

In the end, the commercial disadvantages and unfairness to outsiders were seen as a price too high to pay for members' security, and the legislature stepped in with statutory provisions protecting third parties.[18] These provisions do not go so far as to provide that every company actually *has* the capacity to do anything, but they prevent the validity of any act being called into question on the ground of lack of capacity arising from anything in the company's constitution (CA 2006 s 39(1)—extracted below). This is just as beneficial for outsiders, but preserves the right of the company to sue its insiders (directors or other agents) for their breaches of the company's constitution (ie for acting outside the powers given to the directors: CA 2006 s 171, or beyond their agency contract with the company), and recover damages for the loss caused to the company (eg arising from the prohibited transaction). Such breaches have also been used as a justification for imposing disqualification orders on directors (*Re Samuel Sherman plc* [1991] 1 WLR 1070). And a member who is alerted early enough has a right to seek an injunction to prevent the company from entering into what would have been an *ultra vires* transaction.

These internal reasons make it necessary to pay attention to (and to construe very carefully) a company's objects clause (if it has one), particularly in the context of directors' duties when it is necessary to know the proper scope of the directors' activities.[19] But the

---

[16] *Westdeutsche Landesbank Girozentrale v Islington LBC* [1996] AC 669, HL; *Guinness plc v Saunders* **[5.01]**; *Clark v Cutland* [2003] EWCA Civ 810, CA.

[17] See the leading case of *Ashbury Railway Carriage & Iron Co Ltd v Riche* [1875] LR 7 HL 653, HL, which confirmed both that an *ultra vires* act of a company was void and that it could not be validated even by a unanimous ratification.

[18] Generally, see CA 2006 s 39. For charities, see the special rules at CA 2006 ss 31(4), 42. And the old-style 'harsh' *ultra vires* rules continue to apply to companies not registered under CA 2006: see especially *Hazell v Hammersmith and Fulham London Borough Council* [1992] 2 AC 1, HL; and *Westdeutsche Landesbank Girozentrale v Islington LBC* [1996] AC 669, HL, where the swaps contracts entered into by the borough councils were held to be *ultra vires* and therefore void.

[19] Although, as we shall see later, still further deeming rules favouring third parties (CA 2006 s 40(1)—note the good faith limitation) mean that this question is often most important in a company's claims against its defaulting directors (for breach of CA 2006 s 171—acting within powers), rather than for its impact on third parties in relation to the contract in issue.

old cases on construction, decided in the context of the tough *ultra vires* rule, are unlikely to govern modern construction exercises and have been omitted here.

Remember that objects clauses are contained in the company's articles (if they are included at all), and unless the provisions are entrenched, the articles can be changed by special resolution (ss 21 and 22, and see 'Alteration of the articles', p 228); the necessary special resolutions can, it would seem, be passed informally (see ss 29, 281, 283, and 'Informal decision-making—the *"Duomatic"* principle', p 214).

Finally, note that any constitutional restrictions on a company's capacity have no effect in shielding companies from liability in tort and crime, and did not do so even when the *ultra vires* doctrine was at its peak: see the later discussion of these issues.

Companies Act 2006 s 39

39 A company's capacity

(1) The validity of an act done by a company shall not be called into question on the ground of lack of capacity by reason of anything in the company's constitution.

(2) This section has effect subject to section 42 (companies that are charities).

Agency and authority in corporate contracting

Overview of agency principles

Agency law is part of the general common law: private individuals can use agents, as can companies. There are inevitably three parties involved. In the contracting context, the goal is to bind the *principal* (the company) in contract to the *third party* using the efforts of the *agent* (who is probably a company director or company employee). Agency law holds that the principal is only bound by the legal relationship if the agent acted 'with authority'.

In the simplest cases, agents will be acting properly, doing what they are specifically engaged to do: the agent will have *actual authority*. The various ways in which an agent can be given actual authority are considered later, but if the agent has such authority when settling the contract, then the company and the third party will be bound.

Problems arise when the agent does not have actual authority. There are then three potential escape routes, each giving the agent a form of *deemed authority* despite lack of actual authority. If none applies, then the intended contract will be void. First, if the agent has acted in breach of some constitutional limitation (typically an objects clause in the company's articles), then CA 2006 s 40 may deem the agent to have the necessary authority notwithstanding the facts. We might say that the agent has '*deemed authority* under the statute'. Secondly, if someone within the company represents that the agent *has* the necessary authority, then the common law may prevent the company denying that the agent does indeed have the authority so represented: this is a rule based on estoppel, and the agent is then said to have *ostensible (or apparent) authority* (ie purported or professed authority). Finally, if the impediment to successfully demonstrating actual authority is an issue of internal company procedure, then the *indoor management rule* may allow third parties to assume that the necessary internal procedures have been properly carried out. If these deeming provisions apply, then the purported contract between the company and the third party is binding. All these forms of deemed authority come with a good number of technical restrictions on their application, as is to be expected when the starting point is that the agent lacks actual authority to do the deal.

Each category of actual or deemed authority is considered in the sections which follow. Specific attention is then given to a number of remaining problems, and to a number of different rules which apply when the contracting counterparty is a company director rather than a stranger to the company.

Agency and actual authority—who is 'actually' allowed to act for the company?

The actual authority of the agent is determined by looking solely at the principal–agent relationship: what authority has the principal actually given the agent? The third party is irrelevant to this determination. See *Freeman and Lockyer v Buckhurst Park Properties (Mangal) Ltd* **[3.10]**, Diplock LJ:

> An 'actual' authority is a legal relationship between principal and agent created by a consensual agreement to which they alone are parties. Its scope is to be ascertained by applying ordinary principles of construction of contracts, including any proper implications from the express words used, the usages of the trade, or the course of business between the parties. To this agreement the contractor is a stranger; he may be totally ignorant of the existence of any authority on the part of the agent. Nevertheless, if the agent does enter into a contract pursuant to the 'actual' authority, it does create contractual rights and liabilities between the principal and the contractor…

The agent's actual authority is usually derived directly from the company's constitutional documents (the articles), or from an express or implied delegation of authority to the agent. The person delegating much have actual authority to do the act, *and* to delegate the doing of it to others.

If the board of directors, or someone authorised by the board, effects the transaction for the company, there are few problems. The articles typically give the board (not an individual director) the authority to manage the business of the company (see Model Articles, extracted at 'Rules of attribution: how does a company act?', p 90). These are of course subject to any limitations imposed by the company's own articles, incusing any objects clause. Such general authority is also typically accompanied by the authority to delegate to others (see, eg, Model Articles arts 5 and 6).

Delegation of actual authority by the company to the agent can be express (so the agent has '*express actual authority*') or implied (so the agent has '*implied actual authority*')—but it is nevertheless *actual* authority in both cases. Delegation may be implied by appointing a person to a particular role in the company; the assumption is then that the individual has implied actual authority to do all the things necessary to fulfil that role, subject to any express restrictions noted by the appointing parties.[20] Alternatively, delegation can be implied by 'a course of dealing'. Both are illustrated in the extracts which follow.

1. Implied actual authority from appointment to a specific role in the company

The issue of 'implied actual authority' by appointment to a specific role can often get tangled with 'ostensible authority' (see the later discussion), because of the confusing use in quite different contexts of the term 'usual authority':

In the context of *implied actual authority* (as with all actual authority), the question is exclusively one between the principal and agent. The implication of 'usual authority' in this relationship enables some very efficient contractual gap-filling: in any appointment to a recognised role within the company, the appointment itself impliedly confers on the agent all the 'usual authority' typically associated with the role. For example, appointment of a person as the CEO of a company carries with it the power to run the company. If refinements are needed (and almost inevitably they are), then this 'implied' delegation of authority may be expressly narrowed when the delegation is made. The agent's *implied actual authority* is then limited accordingly: as between principal and agent, neither side could suggest their contract had an implied term which contradicted the express terms. But, that aside, the

---

[20] The cases sometimes say that the agent has '*usual*' authority to do what the job requires, but see later for the potential confusion.

implication of 'usual authority' which follows on an appointment to a specific role effectively and efficiently specifies a great deal of detail in the principal/agent contract.

By contrast, in the context of *ostensible authority* (considered later), the issue is one exclusively between the principal and the third party. The question is whether the principal has 'held out' the agent as a 'CEO' (or as CFO, or some other corporate role), and thereby impliedly represented that this agent has all the 'usual authority' typically associated with this specified role (eg as CEO/MD, CFO, etc). Again, if the principal expressly limits the represented role when dealing with the third party, the scope of the agent's 'represented' or 'ostensible' authority is commensurately limited (but such explicit limitation tends to be rare).

'Implied actual authority' from appointment as a managing director—recognising the inevitable need to consider the particular terms and context of the appointment.

[3.02] Smith v Butler [2012] EWCA Civ 314 (Court of Appeal)

The primary issue in this appeal was whether a managing director (B) had implied or usual power to suspend the company's executive chairman (S) in the absence of an express delegation of powers by the board. The issue arose in the context of a dispute in a two man company, where B (who owned 31.2% of the shares) alleged that S was defrauding the company, and S (who owned 68.8% of the shares) threatened to use his majority voting power to sack B.

ARDEN LJ (RIMER AND RYDER LJJ concurring):

The primary issue: the powers of a managing director

15. We are not in this case concerned with the more usual question whether a third party dealing with a managing director is entitled to assume that [the managing director] has power to do what he did.... This appeal...is concerned with the question of what powers the managing director *actually had*. There is surprisingly little authority on that point. The powers of a managing director are not, of course, statutorily defined. The parties could have defined Mr Butler's powers when he was appointed. However, they did not do so. In *Hely-Hutchinson v Brayhead* **[3.04]** at 560, Roskill J, whose decision was affirmed by this court, comprising unusually Lord Denning MR, Lord Wilberforce and Lord Pearson, went so far as to state that the question of the implied authority of a managing director was one of 'considerable difficulty', as well as being 'one upon which there appears to be little or no relevant authority'....

25. In my judgment...the inquiry should proceed...from the provisions of [the company's] articles setting out the powers of the board to appoint a managing director. [These give the board the power to appoint a managing director and to delegate any of their powers to the managing director.]...

27. In this case, however, there is no express delegation of any specific powers by the board to Mr Butler. Mr Butler simply has a contract of employment appointing him as a managing director....On the other hand, it was clearly intended that some powers should be implicitly delegated to him....

28. [Counsel's] proposition is that, in principle, the implied powers of a managing director are those that would ordinarily be exercisable by a managing director in his position. In my judgment, [counsel's] proposition is correct. In *Hely-Hutchinson v Brayhead* **[3.04]** at 583, Lord Denning MR held that the board of directors, on appointing a managing director, 'thereby impliedly authorise him to do all such things as fall within the usual scope of that office.'...Another way of putting that point is that the managing director's powers extend to carrying out those functions on which

he did not need to obtain the specific directions of the board. This is simply the default position. It is, therefore, subject to the company's articles and anything that the parties have expressly agreed. In essence, the issue is one of interpreting the contract of appointment or employment in the light of all the relevant background, and asking what that contract would reasonably be understood to have meant (*Attorney General of Belize v Belize Telecom Ltd* [2009] 1 WLR 1485, PC, and see my judgment in *Stena Line v Merchant Navy Ratings Pension Fund Trustees Ltd* [2010] EWCA Civ 543 at 36–41).

29. On this basis, as might be expected, the test of what is within the implied actual authority of a managing director coincides with the test of what is within the ostensible authority of a managing director: see *Freeman & Lockyer v Buckhurst Park Properties (Mangal) Ltd* **[3.10]**.

30. The holder of the office of managing director might today more usually be called a chief executive officer in (at least) a public company. He or she has generally to work on the basis that his appointment does not supplant that of the role of the board and that he will have to refer back to the board for authority on matters on which the board has not clearly laid out the company's strategy. He or she would thus be expected to work within the strategy the board had actually set.

31. In this case, however, it was clear that the strategy of the board was that Mr Smith should be executive chairman. Therefore, his suspension was clearly a matter for the board, and not for Mr Butler acting alone. To my mind it is inconceivable that Mr Butler did not need the instructions of the board on the question of the suspension of the chairman of the board. The fact that Mr Smith has special rights as a director and shareholder under the quorum provisions in the Company's articles reinforces this conclusion, but my conclusion does not rest on those provisions.

32. I do not accept the submission that my conclusion renders Mr Butler powerless to act even if Mr Smith controlled the board and could prevent any investigation into the claims against himself contrary to the best interests of the Company. Mr Butler is a shareholder himself and has the right to seek relief from unfairly prejudicial conduct by the majority shareholder under section 994 of the 2006 Act. Indeed that is the course which he has now taken. . . .

33. Alternatively, Mr Butler could have brought a statutory derivative action against Mr Smith in accordance with Part 11 of the 2006 Act. Those provisions could be used even if it was necessary to obtain urgent relief. . . .

➤ Question

Is it possible to think in terms of the 'usual' authority of a managing director? Is it not likely that the terms of appointment of managing directors will vary from case to case? (See *Harold Holdsworth & Co (Wakefield) Ltd v Caddies* [1955] 1 WLR 352, HL.)

➤ Note

Sometimes it is difficult to determine what 'usual authority' can be assumed to be associated with any particular role. This is important because an agent will not have implied actual authority derived from appointment to a particular role if that role does not usually include the authority so claimed. This was the case in *British Bank of the Middle East v Sun Life Assurance Co of Canada (UK) Ltd* [1983] BCLC 78, HL, where it was held that a branch manager of a multinational insurance company had no 'usual' authority to represent to a bank that a subordinate employee had actual authority to execute undertakings to pay moneys to the bank. The evidence of general practice was that all such undertakings were typically executed by insurance companies at their head office.

The secretary of a company has usual authority to bind the company in matters concerned with administration.

[3.03] Panorama Developments (Guildford) Ltd v Fidelis Furnishing Fabrics Ltd [1971] 2 QB 711 (Court of Appeal)

Bayne, as the company secretary of the defendant, Fidelis Furnishings, hired cars from the plaintiff, ostensibly for the company's business; but in fact he fraudulently used them for his own purposes. The company was held bound by the contracts to pay the hire charges. The judgments refer primarily to ostensible authority, but see the questions which follow this extract.

LORD DENNING MR: [Counsel] says that the company is not bound by the letters which were signed by Mr Bayne as 'Company Secretary'. He says that, on the authorities, a company secretary fulfils a very humble role: and that he has no authority to make any contracts or representations on behalf of the company. He refers to *Barnett v South London Tramways Co*[21] where Lord Esher MR said: 'A secretary is a mere servant; his position is that he is to do what he is told, and no person can assume that he has any authority to represent anything at all . . .' Those words were approved by Lord Macnaghten in *George Whitechurch Ltd v Cavanagh*.[22] They are supported by the decision in *Ruben v Great Fingall Consolidated* **[11.13]**. They are referred to in some of the textbooks as authoritative.

But times have changed. A company secretary is a much more important person nowadays than he was in 1887. He is an officer of the company with extensive duties and responsibilities. This appears not only in the modern Companies Act, but also by the role which he plays in the day-to-day business of companies. He is no longer a mere clerk. He regularly makes representations on behalf of the company and enters into contracts on its behalf which come within the day-to-day running of the company's business. So much so that he may be regarded as held out as having the authority to do such things on behalf of the company. He is certainly entitled to sign contracts connected with the administrative side of a company's affairs, such as employing staff and ordering cars, and so forth. All such matters now come within the ostensible authority of a company's secretary.

Accordingly I agree with the judge that Mr R L Bayne, as company secretary, had ostensible authority to enter into contracts for the hire of these cars, and therefore, the company must pay for them. Mr Bayne was a fraud. But it was the company which put him in the position in which he, as company secretary, was able to commit the frauds. So the defendants are liable. I would dismiss the appeal, accordingly.

SALMON LJ: I think there can be no doubt that the secretary is the chief administrative officer of the company. As regards matters concerned with administration, in my judgment, the secretary has ostensible authority to sign contracts on behalf of the company. If a company is ordering cars so that its servants may go and meet foreign customers at airports, nothing, to my mind, is more natural than that the company should hire those cars through its secretary. The hiring is part of his administrative functions. Whether the secretary would have any authority to sign a contract relating to the commercial management of the company, for example, a contract for the sale or purchase of goods in which the company deals, does not arise for decision in the present case and I do not propose to express any concluded opinion upon the point; but contracts such as the present fall within the ambit of administration and I entertain no doubt that the secretary has ostensible power to sign on behalf of the company . . .

MEGAW LJ concurred.

---

[21]   (1887) 18 QBD 815, CA.
[22]   [1902] AC 117.

➤ Question

The judgments refer primarily to ostensible authority. Would the same analysis be apt in considering Bayne's implied *actual* authority (subject of course to any express limitations when Bayne was appointed)? Does it make any difference to Bayne's actual authority that he was defrauding his company? (On this last question, see 'Directors' authority and breach of directors' duties', p 124.)

2. Implied actual authority from a course of dealing

The leading case on implying actual authority from a course of dealing.

[3.04] Hely-Hutchinson v Brayhead Ltd [1968] 1 QB 549 (Chancery Division and Court of Appeal)

Richards was chairman and chief executive or '*de facto* managing director' of the defendant company. He often committed the company to contracts on his own initiative and only disclosed the matter to the board subsequently. The board acquiesced in this practice. The plaintiff (referred to in the judgment as Lord Suirdale) was chairman and managing director of another company, 'Perdio', which it was planned should eventually be merged with the defendant. As part of an agreement to put more money into Perdio, Lord Suirdale (who had been made a director of the defendant company) was given letters, signed by Richards, committing Brayhead Ltd to guarantee repayment of the loans and indemnify Lord Suirdale against certain losses. When sued on these undertakings, Brayhead Ltd alleged that Richards had had no authority to make the contract. Roskill J held that Richards had *ostensible* authority to bind his company; the Court of Appeal affirmed his decision, but on the ground that he had *actual* authority. Roskill J's judgment is cited for its setting out of the relevant facts.

ROSKILL J: The set-up in Brayhead is easy to envisage. It was an industrial holding company with a large number of subsidiaries. Its directors were in the main working directors, each in charge of a section of the holding company's subsidiaries. One would look after electronics, another engineering, and so on. They would all come back to Mr Richards for advice and—which is more important—decisions from time to time on matters concerning their own particular group. The final decision—and the final decision most especially on any matter concerning finance—was Mr Richards' and nobody else's. Sometimes, I dare say, the directors persuaded him to take or to refrain from taking a particular step; no doubt, like any wise chief executive, he sought and obtained advice before he made up his mind; but in all these cases the final decision, I am quite satisfied, rested with him and with nobody else.

If one goes through the minutes and documents which have been put before me, one can see repeated examples of Mr Richards acting in this way. Sometimes, of course, the matter would come back to the board for formal ratification after he had committed Brayhead perhaps technically without express authority. On other occasions, of which there are a number of examples in the minutes, he plainly committed Brayhead and then, as it were, reported the matter afterwards...I have no doubt that the board knew that he was doing this sort of thing all the time, and that whenever he thought it was necessary he assumed, or purported to assume, authority to bind Brayhead and that the board allowed him to do it and acquiesced in his doing it. That is not to say, to use Mr Finer's phrase yesterday, that all the directors were 'Yes men'; I am sure they were nothing of the kind. Mr Richards knew they were nothing of the kind. Mr Richards was a forceful personality; he knew his own mind. I think he quite clearly was allowed by Brayhead to hold himself out as having ostensible or apparent authority to enter into commitments of the kind which he entered into or purported to enter into, when he signed C 23 and C 26....

[The Court of Appeal affirmed the decision of Roskill J, but on the ground that Richards had actual authority.]

LORD DENNING MR: I need not consider at length the law on the authority of an agent, actual, apparent or ostensible. That has been done in the judgments of this court in *Freeman and Lockyer v Buckhurst Park Properties (Mangal) Ltd* **[3.10]**. It is there shown that actual authority may be expressed or implied. It is *express* when it is given by express words, such as when a board of directors pass a resolution which authorises two of their number to sign cheques. It is implied when it is inferred from the conduct of the parties and the circumstances of the case, such as when the board of directors appoint one of their number to be a managing director. They thereby impliedly authorise him to do all such things as fall within the usual scope of that office. Actual authority, express or implied, is binding as between the company and the agent, and also as between the company and others, whether they are within the company or outside it.

Ostensible or apparent authority is the authority of an agent as it *appears* to others. It often coincides with actual authority. Thus, when the board appoint one of their number to be managing director, they invest him not only with implied authority, but also with ostensible authority to do all such things as fall within the usual scope of that office. Other people who see him acting as managing director are entitled to assume that he has the usual authority of a managing director. But sometimes ostensible authority exceeds actual authority. For instance, when the board appoint the managing director, they may expressly limit his authority by saying he is not to order goods worth more than £500 without the sanction of the board. In that case his *actual* authority is subject to the £500 limitation, but his *ostensible* authority includes all the usual authority of a managing director. The company is bound by his ostensible authority in his dealings with those who do not know of the limitation....

Apply these principles here. It is plain that Mr Richards had no express authority to enter into these two contracts on behalf of the company: nor had he any such authority implied from the nature of his office. He had been duly appointed chairman of the company but that office in itself did not carry with it authority to enter into these contracts without the sanction of the board....The judge held that Mr Richards had ostensible or apparent authority to make the contract, but I think his findings carry with it the necessary inference that he had also actual authority, such authority being implied from the circumstance that the board by their conduct over many months had acquiesced in his acting as their chief executive and committing Brayhead Ltd to contracts without the necessity of sanction from the board.

LORDS WILBERFORCE and PEARSON delivered concurring judgments.

> Notes

1. The legal subtleties in dealing with these common facts are important. The purported contract was between a company and one of its own new directors. The agent was the company's chairman and chief executive officer or '*de facto* managing director'. The trial judge held that the agent had ostensible authority. However, this finding was unsustainable: the contracting counter-party, as a director, should have known that any alleged representation of the agent's unlimited general authority (merely because of the title 'CEO', etc) was false. Equally there was no implied actual authority merely from the job appointment, since that came with restrictions necessitating board approval. But on the particular facts—and only provable by detailed resort to them—there was implied actual authority from a course of dealing. Thus the contract was saved.

2. In *Freeman & Lockyer v Buckhurst Park Properties (Mangal) Ltd* **[3.10]**, Diplock LJ commented:

> I accept that such actual authority could have been conferred by the board without a formal resolution recorded in the minutes…But to confer actual authority would have required not merely the silent acquiescence of the individual members of the board, but the communication by words or conduct of their respective consents to one another and to [the agent]. [And in the circumstances he declined to hold that such authority had been impliedly delegated.]

By way of concluding comment to this section on actual authority, remember that cases deal exclusively with problems which arise when things go wrong. Mostly, however, contractual dealings with companies run smoothly and agents act within the scope of their authorised roles. But *Guinness plc v Saunders* **[5.01]** provides a dramatic illustration of how easy it is to assume everything is on course, only to discover after the event that the agent lacked authority to bind the company. Here, it was a subcommittee of the board of directors that lacked actual authority to negotiate a remuneration package with a director. The contract was therefore void, and the agreed remuneration had to be repaid to the company.

Deemed authority I: statutory deeming provisions to avoid constitutional limitations on directors' authority—CA 2006 s 40

CA 2006 s 40 protects most third parties where there are restrictions on the power of the company's agents inserted in the company's constitution, although such restrictions are no longer particularly common. (Note, however, that s 41 effectively limits this protection to outsiders—see 'Transactions involving directors', p 122.)

The relevant provision is contained in the following extract. It must be read carefully. It allows 'a person' 'dealing with' the company (defined in s 40(2)) 'in good faith' (with provisions on this in s 40(2)(b)) to deem the power of the 'directors'[23] (not other agents) to bind the company, or authorise others to do so, to be free of any 'limitation under the company's constitution' (defined more widely than limitations in the articles (see s 40(3)).

This provision continues the protection delivered in s 39, which deems the company's capacity not to be limited by constitutional restrictions. Here the provision deems the directors' authority not to be subject to constitutional restrictions, provided the third party acts in good faith (widely defined). This prevents what would otherwise have been a vicious circle: having removed the impediment to outsiders arising from corporate objects and their impact on corporate capacity (the old *ultra vires* rule), they would simply reappear in another guise, with the same effect, because of their impact on agents' authority. So, again, the legislature has intervened. If the Act applies, then the directors (or their authorised delegates) will have authority deemed not to be limited by the constitutional provisions, and the underlying contract may then be binding.

As an aside, notice that CA 2006 s 40 has *external* impact only: it protects outsiders. As between the company and its agent, the agent's actual authority cannot extend to the doing of anything that is not permitted by the company's constitution (eg a company that may only perform charitable works, or only publish English monographs). Such a company remains free to sue its agents who exceed their actual authority (see CA 2006 s 171), recovering from them compensation for any consequential losses their actions have caused to the company.

---

[23] The predecessor provision in CA 1985 s 35A referred to the 'board of directors', which gave it limited application in practice. Presumably this change is intended to widen the application of the provision, although views on this differ, and the Hansard debates on the Bill do not illuminate.

Companies Act 2006 s 40

40 Power of directors to bind the company

(1) In favour of a person dealing with a company in good faith, the power of the directors to bind the company, or authorise others to do so, is deemed to be free of any limitation under the company's constitution.

(2) For this purpose—
   (a) a person 'deals with' a company if he is a party to any transaction or other act to which the company is a party,
   (b) a person dealing with a company—
      (i)   is not bound to enquire as to any limitation on the powers of the directors to bind the company or authorise others to do so,
      (ii) is presumed to have acted in good faith unless the contrary is proved, and
      (iii) is not to be regarded as acting in bad faith by reason only of his knowing that an act is beyond the powers of the directors under the company's constitution.

(3) The references above to limitations on the directors' powers under the company's constitution include limitations deriving—
   (a) from a resolution of the company or of any class of shareholders, or
   (b) from any agreement between the members of the company or of any class of shareholders.

(4) This section does not affect any right of a member of the company to bring proceedings to restrain the doing of an action that is beyond the powers of the directors.
   But no such proceedings lie in respect of an act to be done in fulfilment of a legal obligation arising from a previous act of the company.

(5) This section does not affect any liability incurred by the directors, or any other person, by reason of the directors' exceeding their powers.

(6) This section has effect subject to—
   section 41 (transactions with directors or their associates), and
   section 42 (companies that are charities).

The meaning of some of the expressions in CA 2006 s 40 is controversial, and is considered in the following extracts. There are instances where the dissenting views appear more compelling than the majority's. Given the language of the statute and its admitted policy objectives, which interpretations appear most principled?

1. Meaning of 'a person' in CA 2006 s 40

The term is used quite generally in s 40, although the underlying policy might suggest the section was not intended to protect directors (although see their separate treatment in s 41). In the next case, the Court of Appeal (Robert Walker LJ dissenting) held that—at least on the rather special facts in issue—directors were not protected. For the reasons given by Robert Walker LJ, his dissenting view seems more compelling.

'A person' may not include a director.

[3.05] Smith v Henniker-Major and Co [2002] EWCA Civ 762, [2003] Ch 182 (Court of Appeal)

The question in this case was whether a director/chairman of a company could rely on CA 1985 s 35A [now CA 2006 s 40] to validate a resolution passed at the meeting, attended only by himself, to assign to himself certain causes of action of the company. The chairman believed he had power under the company's articles to act alone, but in fact the 'meeting' was inquorate since the articles provided that the quorum for a board meeting was two. The Court of Appeal divided on the issue. Robert Walker LJ thought the chairman could rely on s 35A to validate what had happened whereas Schiemann and Carnwath LJJ thought he could not.

ROBERT WALKER LJ (dissenting on this point):

46. Mr Mabb [counsel for Smith] relied mainly on the following points in arguing that 'person' in section 35A(1), although necessarily excluding the company (which could not deal with itself) did not exclude a director of the company. (i) The contrary reading would be inconsistent with section 322A of the Companies Act 1985 [CA 2006 s 41], a provision introduced as part of the same set of amendments made by the Companies Act 1989, which must have been intended to have a coherent scheme. (ii) The natural meaning of 'person' is wide and the court should be slow to find an unexpressed limitation in what are quite detailed statutory provisions. (iii) That point was reinforced by doubt as to what limitation ought to be read in, if there were to be any interference with the statutory text. (iv) All or most leading textbooks take the view that section 35A(1) is not restricted in this way....

48. Mr Mabb submitted that these provisions, and those of section 35A(6)...made plain that the two sections were intended to coexist and interact in such a way that a director who acted in good faith but in a transaction to which he himself (or an associate) was a party, and which was beyond the board's powers, got through the first filter of section 35A but was caught by the second filter of section 322A, with the result that the transaction was voidable, not void....

50. I have found Mr Mabb's submissions more persuasive, and especially his reliance on section 35A(6). The two sections do cross-refer, and the terms of the cross-reference in section 35A(6) are to my mind striking....

CARNWATH LJ:

109. I accept that the section does not distinguish between insiders and outsiders. It applies to any 'person dealing with the company'. These words are wide enough to include a director of the company. There is nothing in law to prevent a director from being 'a person dealing' with his own company. If there were any doubt in section 35A itself, it seems implicit in section 322A that a director may be such a person. On the other hand, it is impossible to read that section as giving any comfort to directors seeking to rely on section 35A. Rather it adds a further level of defence for the company against its own directors and connected persons, by making transactions voidable in the circumstances defined; but this is expressly stated not to exclude any other rule by which the transaction may be avoided, and not to affect the operation of section 35A in relation to any other party: see section 322A(4)(7).

110. I would prefer, however, to express no view about the position of directors in other circumstances. The facts here were quite exceptional. Mr Smith was not simply a director dealing with the company, and having some incidental involvement in the decision. As chairman of the company, it was his duty to ensure that the constitution was properly applied; yet he was personally responsible for the error by which he purported to turn himself into a one-man board. We have to assume good faith, but that means no more than that we have to assume that he made an honest mistake. It does not make it any less a mistake, or one for which he is any less responsible. I do not see how he can rely on his own error to turn his own decision, which had no validity of any kind under the company's constitution, into a decision of 'the board'. I see nothing in section 35A, however purposefully interpreted, to give it that magical effect.

SCHIEMANN LJ delivered a separate judgment agreeing with Carnwath LJ.

➤ Note

This issue may seem arcane in relation to directors, but it may be important: if the director cannot rely on s 40, then the contract is *void*; by contrast, if the director can rely on s 40, but the company then has rights under s 41, the contract is *voidable* (see later at 'Transactions involving directors', p 122).

'A person' may not include a shareholder.

[3.06] EIC Services Ltd v Phipps [2004] EWCA Civ 1069 (Court of Appeal)

The Court of Appeal held that shareholder receiving a bonus share was not 'a person dealing with a company' within the meaning of CA 1985 s 35A(1), and so the share issue was void as it had not been effectively authorised by E's members, overruling Neuberger J in the court below. For another aspect of this decision, see **[3.08]**.

PETER GIBSON LJ:

34. For section 35A(1) to validate the bonus issue it was necessary to find that the shareholders receiving the shares were persons dealing with the company in good faith and that the reasons why the bonus issue would otherwise have been invalid were limitations under the company's constitution on the power of the board of directors to bind the company. The judge [Neuberger J] held that a shareholder of a company receiving shares (whether or not bonus shares) from the company is 'a person dealing with the company' within the scope of section 35A(1). He considered that, as a matter of ordinary language, such a shareholder would be within the ambit of those words, and he said that, in the absence of a powerful reason to the contrary, it is inappropriate to treat naturally wide words in a statute as subject to an implied limitation. The judge also referred to the decision of this court in *Smith v Henniker-Major & Co* **[3.05]** and found that the reasoning of each member of this court appeared, if anything, to support his conclusion. He also found that section 322A of the 1985 Act indirectly supported his conclusions. That section sets out circumstances in which section 35A cannot be relied on. Those circumstances are limited to transactions between a company and a director of it or of its holding company or a person connected with the directors or a company with whom such a director is associated. Finally the judge expressed the view that the present case plainly fell within the policy behind section 35A as expressed by Carnwath LJ in *Smith* **[3.05]**, at para 108:

'The general policy seems to be that, if a document is put forward as a decision of the board by someone appearing to act on behalf of the company, in circumstances where there is no reason to doubt its authenticity, a person dealing with the company in good faith should be able to take it at face value.'

35. I have to say that my immediate reaction to the question whether a shareholder receiving bonus shares is 'a person dealing with the company' is not the same as that of the judge....

37....[A]lthough 'third parties' [the term used in the Directive which led to this statutory provision] is not defined, to my mind it is tolerably clear from the Directive itself that third parties do not include members of the company...In the context of a company, the term 'third parties' naturally refers to persons other than the company and its members....

38. As for the other reasons given by the judge as to why section 35A applied, I am not able to derive assistance for the present case from the court's judgment in *Smith*. The issues in that case were entirely different...Nor, in my view, does section 322A assist. It does not follow from the fact that the legislature has dealt specifically with transactions between a director and a company that an inference can be drawn about the applicability of section 35A to shareholders who in that capacity deal with the company.

➤ Question

Is this reasoning persuasive? In particular, if Parliament did not intend shareholders to be protected by CA 1985 s 35A/CA 2006 s 40, why did it not expressly qualify the protection applying to them, as it did for directors in CA 1985 s 322A/CA 2006 s 41?

2. Meaning of 'a dealing with the company' in CA 2006 s 40

Minimum requirements to constitute 'a dealing with the company'.

[3.07] Smith v Henniker-Major and Co [2002] EWCA Civ 762, [2003] Ch 182 (Court of Appeal)

For the facts and another aspect of this decision, see **[3.05]** earlier.

ROBERT WALKER LJ:

41. In my judgment the irreducible minimum, if section 35A is to be engaged, is a genuine decision taken by a person or persons who can on substantial grounds claim to be the board of directors acting as such, even if the proceedings of the board are marred by procedural irregularities of a more or less serious character. This is not a precise test and it would have to be worked out on a case by case basis. But the essential distinction is between nullity (or non-event) and procedural irregularity.

42. That was ultimately, as I see it, the ground on which Sir Nicolas Browne-Wilkinson V-C based his decision on the second issue in *TCB Ltd v Gray*:[24]

'The evidence clearly established that no such meeting of the directors of Link ever took place. But in fact all the directors of Link individually had decided to grant the debenture, although not at a meeting at which they were all present.'

So the absence of a properly-convened meeting, or a signed written resolution, was treated as an irregularity. . . .

43. If an outsider had been negotiating in good faith with the company, believing that the draft contract was to be approved at a board meeting, Mr Smith's [the chairman's] one-man meeting on 12 August 1998 would in my view have passed the test and attracted protection under section 35A. Mr Smith was a duly appointed director of SPDL. He sent a notice of the proposed board meeting to the only other director. He attended the meeting and took decisions, recorded in the minutes which he prepared. His written evidence is that he believed that he was entitled to take that decision on his own, and he signed the assignment of 14 August 1998 in that belief. Had he produced the minutes to a third party acting in good faith, both parties would have been bound by any resulting agreement. . . .

53. I would add that Carnwath LJ (from whom I differ only with misgivings) has referred to the speech of Lord Simonds in *Morris v Kanssen* [1946] AC 459, 475–476. That was a case in which a director and his accomplice conspired together to concoct false minutes of a board meeting which had never taken place (and at which, as it was fraudulently claimed, the accomplice had been appointed as a director). The most surprising thing about the case is that it reached the House of Lords. In the passage which Carnwath LJ has referred to, Lord Simonds was dealing with general principles of agency and with the general presumption of regularity of transactions. I do not find it of much help in construing section 35A of the 1985 Act. Indeed another passage in the speech of Lord Simonds, at p 471—'There is, as it appears to me, a vital distinction between (a) an appointment in which there is a defect or, in other words, a defective appointment, and (b) no appointment at all'—appears to me to give some slight support to the view which I have expressed in paragraph 41 above. I readily acknowledge that it is not a wholly satisfactory

---

[24] [1986] Ch 621, affd on other grounds [1987] Ch 458, CA.

test but I can see no alternative short of what I would regard as an unduly restrictive reading of section 35A.

CARNWATH LJ:

104. The problem is to identify the 'irreducible minimum' needed to bring section 35A into play. Literal interpretation does not help....

105. I do not, with respect to Robert Walker LJ, think that this problem can be solved by the suggested distinction between 'nullity' and 'procedural irregularity'. Such distinctions have not proved workable in administrative law...and I do not think they are workable here. The problem is illustrated by this case. By what criterion is it to be said that Mr Smith's decision to constitute himself as a board of the company is to be treated as a mere procedural irregularity, rather than a nullity? He had no more authority to take a decision in the name of the company than the office-boy. To an outsider, of course, such a document, emanating from the chairman, could reasonably have been assumed to have more validity than a similar document signed by the office-boy. Yet, viewed under the company's constitution, the decision had no validity of any kind; it was a 'nullity'....

108. ... A purposive approach to the section suggests a low threshold. The general policy seems to be that, if a document is put forward as a decision of the board by someone appearing to act on behalf of the company, in circumstances where there is no reason to doubt its authenticity, a person dealing with the company in good faith should be able to take it at face value...In principle, where the person in question is a third party in the ordinary sense, a wide interpretation is wholly appropriate.

An issue of bonus shares may not involve 'a dealing with the company'.

[3.08] EIC Services Ltd v Phipps [2004] EWCA Civ 1069 (Court of Appeal)

For the facts and another aspect of this decision, see **[3.06]** earlier.

PETER GIBSON LJ:

35. ... Having regard to the nature of a bonus issue...and the fact that it is an internal arrangement with no diminution or increase in the assets or liabilities of the company, with no change in the proportionate shareholdings and with no action required from any shareholders (see *Whittome v Whittome (No 1)* 1994 SLT 114, 124, per Lord Osborne), I do not think that the shareholder is a person dealing with the company as a matter of ordinary language. The section contemplates a bilateral transaction between the company and the person dealing with the company, or an act to which both are parties, such as will bind the company only if the section applies and it will not apply if the person deals with the company other than in good faith. It would be very surprising if a bonus issue made by a single resolution applicable to all shareholders were to be rendered by the section binding in part but void in part, depending on the circumstances of the individual shareholders. Nor do I agree with the judge that it matters not whether the shareholder receives a bonus issue or pays for his new shares. If a shareholder receives shares otherwise than by way of a bonus issue (for example, by a rights issue requiring payment of new consideration), then he would have to deal with the company, and the question would be whether a shareholder is within the intended reach of the section.

3. Meaning of 'good faith' in CA 2006 s 40

Re-read s 40(2)(b)—it excludes many matters which might normally be said to suggest bad faith.

Meaning of 'good faith' in CA 2006 s 40.

[3.09] Barclays Bank Ltd v TOSG Trust Fund Ltd [1984] BCLC 1 (Chancery Division)

The facts are immaterial.

> NOURSE J: [Counsel for the defendants] said that even if the assignment agreement was *ultra vires* the trust fund nevertheless, in favour of the agency, it is deemed, by virtue of s 9(1) of the European Communities Act 1972 to have been intra vires, on the ground that at all material times the agency acted in 'good faith', that is to say that it genuinely and honestly believed that it was within the trust fund's corporate powers to enter into the assignment agreement. Counsel for the plaintiffs, on the other hand, says that before s 9(1) can apply the agency must have acted not only genuinely and honestly, but in circumstances where it neither knew nor ought to have known the lack of vires. That means, he says, that the agency must have acted not only genuinely and honestly, but reasonably as well...
>
> My view of that question is this. In the case of a transaction decided on by the directors s 9(1) has abolished the rule that a person who deals with a company is automatically affected with constructive notice of its objects clause. But, by retaining the requirement of good faith, it nevertheless ensures that a defence based on absence of notice shall not be available to someone who had not acted genuinely and honestly in his dealings with the company. Notice and good faith, although two separate beings, are often inseparable. There is a most valuable account of their liaison in the speech of Lord Wilberforce in the recent case of *Midland Bank Trust Co v Green*.[25] What it comes to is that a person who deals with a company in circumstances where he ought anyway to know that the company has no power to enter into the transaction will not necessarily act in good faith. Sometimes, perhaps often, he will not. And a fortiori where he actually knows. Next, a person who acts in good faith will sometimes, perhaps often, act in a manner which can also be described as being reasonable. But I emphatically refute the suggestion, if such it is, that reasonableness is a necessary ingredient of good faith. That would require the introduction of an objective standard into a subjective concept and it would be contrary to everything which the law has always understood of that concept. In my judgment a person acts in good faith if he acts genuinely and honestly in the circumstances of the case. Beyond that it is neither possible nor desirable to attempt an examination of the circumstances in which s 9(1) may or may not apply.
>
> [The decision of Nourse J was reversed on another point: [1984] 1 All ER 628, CA; affd [1984] AC 626, HL; but no comment was made about this passage in any of the judgments on appeal.]

➤ Note

Despite the breadth of the good faith provisions, note the specificity of s 40(2)(b)(i): it does not protect against the need to make inquiries about matters other than constitutional limitations on the power of directors. In *Wrexham Association Football Club Ltd v Crucialmove Ltd* [2006] EWCA Civ 237, CA, the court held that CA 1985 s 35A [CA 2006 s 40] does not protect a person who failed to inquire about matters in circumstances in which he should have done so (eg where the third party does not deal with the entire board of directors, but needs to establish whether the board has authorised the dealing—note that this was in the context of CA 1985 s 35A, which protects dealings with the 'board of directors', not simply the 'directors' as in CA 2006 s 40). However, given the approach to good faith in other contexts, it is questionable whether mere constructive notice would be sufficient to establish lack of good faith. In the context of ostensible authority, see Lord Neuberger NPJ in the Hong Kong Court of Final Appeal in *Thanakharn Kasikorn Thai Chamkat (Mahachon) v*

---

[25] [1981] AC 513 at 528 and 529, HL.

Akai Holdings Ltd (In Liquidation) **[3.11]** preferring absence of good faith to be found only when it would be 'dishonest or irrational' not to inquire further. Similarly, in *LNOC Ltd v Watford Association Football Club Ltd* [2013] EWHC 3615 (Comm), his Honour Judge Mackie QC also preferred the 'dishonest or irrational' approach (as per Lord Neuberger) to the 'question of constructive notice or matters which might have caused a reasonable man to ask some questions' in interpreting the 'good faith' requirement in CA 2006 s 44(5) (dealing with the execution of documents).

4. Meaning of 'directors' and 'limitation under the constitution' in CA 2006 s 40

CA 2006 s 40 was considered by Master Bowles in *Bass Jarrington Ltd v The Royal Bank of Scotland plc, HQ Chester Ltd* (unreported, 2014 WL 6633457). This was a summary judgment application in which it was contended by the claimant, inter alia, that the transactions in question had been entered into without actual authority and that it was not open for the defendant to rely on any ostensible authority or to invoke s 40. It was held, *obiter*, that s 40 operates only where the directors are acting as a board, or under delegated authority from the board. No authority was cited.[26] Similarly, also *obiter*, it was held that s 40 did not protect third parties from breaches of directors' duties: according to Master Bowles, the need to observe their fiduciary (or equivalent statutory) duties 'is not…a limitation imposed, or arising from a company's constitution, but, rather, a limitation arising from the fiduciary status of the directors and/or from the statutory obligations imposed upon directors'.

Deemed authority II: common law intervention in the absence of actual authority—relying on ostensible (or apparent) authority

To the extent that statute does not help with providing deemed authority, company law is thrown back on common law agency doctrine, with certain modifications peculiar to company law: these are the rules on *ostensible (or apparent) authority* and the '*indoor management rule*' (see 'Deemed authority…indoor management rule', p 116).

Ostensible authority arises from the relationship between the *principal* and the *third party*. The agent is irrelevant to the analysis. The agent's ostensible authority is the authority he is represented as having in an effective representation by the principal to the third party.

Again, some care is needed. To be an effective representation by the company (the principal) to the third party, the person acting for the company in making the representation must have the necessary (*actual*) authority to make it (it is not possible to 'build ostensible authority on ostensible authority').

And again, a representation can be implied. The appointment of a person to a particular role can constitute a representation to outsiders that the person has all the authority that usually goes with that role. A managing director can usually do certain things, as can a marketing director or the company's secretary. So 'usual' authority rears its head again.[27] But notice this time that the appointment serves as a representation *to the third party*. The ostensible authority it will support is only the particular usual authority carried by the representation.

Although the third party's bona fides are not relevant when the agent has actual authority to transact for the company,[28] they are certainly relevant when the third party wishes to rely on ostensible authority: then the third party must be able to assert that there was reliance on the representation, and that it was reasonable. The *locus classicus* for all these principles is Diplock LJ's judgment in *Freeman & Lockyer v Buckhurst Park Properties (Mangal) Ltd* **[3.10]**.

---

[26] See fn 23 earlier.

[27] See earlier at 'Implied actual authority from appointment to a specific role in the company', p 94.

[28] Although, of course, the normal contract rules apply if the third party has induced the company, via its agent, to enter into the contract because of the third party's fraud, misrepresentation, etc.

Two further points need to be made for completeness. First, no authority of any sort is generated by mere assertion by the *agent* to the third party that the agent is authorised, no matter how credible the assertion (ie agents cannot 'self-authorise'). Secondly, the deeming provisions permitted by CA 2006 s 40 (relating to corporate capacity constraints) and the indoor management rule (relating to internal procedural matters) can be relied upon to expand the assertion by the third party of the agent's actual or ostensible authority.

Actual and ostensible authority contrasted.

[3.10] Freeman and Lockyer v Buckhurst Park Properties (Mangal) Ltd [1964] 2 QB 480 (Court of Appeal)

Two men had formed the defendant company to buy and resell a large estate. Kapoor was a property developer; Hoon had contributed half of the capital but played no active part in the company's business. Kapoor, Hoon and a nominee of each were appointed the four directors of the company, and under the articles all four were needed to constitute a quorum. Hoon spent much time abroad, leaving all the day-to-day management of the company's affairs to Kapoor. After an initial plan for the immediate resale of the land had fallen through, Kapoor decided to develop the estate and engaged the plaintiffs, a firm of architects and surveyors, to apply for planning permission. The company later refused to pay the plaintiffs' fees on the ground that Kapoor had had no authority to engage them. The county court judge held that the company was bound. The Court of Appeal affirmed his decision on the basis that the agent had ostensible authority.

DIPLOCK LJ: The county court judge made the following findings of fact: (1) that the plaintiffs intended to contract with Kapoor as agent for the company, and not on his own account; (2) that the board of the company intended that Kapoor should do what he could to obtain the best possible price for the estate; (3) that Kapoor, although never appointed as managing director, had throughout been acting as such in employing agents and taking other steps to find a purchaser; (4) that Kapoor was so acting was well known to the board...

This branch of the law has developed pragmatically rather than logically...But it is possible (and for the determination of this appeal I think it is desirable) to restate it upon a rational basis.

It is necessary at the outset to distinguish between an 'actual' authority of an agent on the one hand, and an 'apparent' or 'ostensible' authority on the other. Actual authority and apparent authority are quite independent of one another. Generally they co-exist and coincide, but either may exist without the other and their respective scopes may be different. As I shall endeavour to show, it is upon the apparent authority of the agent that the contractor normally relies in the ordinary course of business when entering into contracts.

An 'actual' authority is a legal relationship between principal and agent created by a consensual agreement to which they alone are parties. Its scope is to be ascertained by applying ordinary principles of construction of contracts, including any proper implications from the express words used, the usages of the trade, or the course of business between the parties. To this agreement the contractor is a stranger; he may be totally ignorant of the existence of any authority on the part of the agent. Nevertheless, if the agent does enter into a contract pursuant to the 'actual' authority, it does create contractual rights and liabilities between the principal and the contractor...

An 'apparent' or 'ostensible' authority, on the other hand, is a legal relationship between the principal and the contractor created by a representation, made by the principal to the contractor, intended to be and in fact acted upon by the contractor of a kind within the scope of the 'apparent' authority, so as to render the principal liable to perform any obligations imposed upon him by such contract. To the relationship so created the agent is a stranger. He need not be (although he generally is) aware of the existence of the representation but he must not purport to make the agreement as principal himself. The representation, when acted upon by the contractor by entering into a contract with the agent, operates as an estoppel, preventing the principal from asserting that he is not bound by the contract. It is irrelevant whether the agent had actual authority to enter into the contract.

In ordinary business dealings the contractor at the time of entering into the contract can in the nature of things hardly ever rely on the 'actual' authority of the agent. His information as to the authority must be derived either from the principal or from the agent or from both, for they alone know what the agent's actual authority is. All that the contractor can know is what they tell him, which may or may not be true. In the ultimate analysis he relies either upon the representation of the principal, that is, apparent authority, or upon the representation of the agent, that is, warranty of authority.[29]

The representation which creates 'apparent' authority may take a variety of forms of which the commonest is representation by conduct, that is, by permitting the agent to act in some way in the conduct of the principal's business with other persons. By so doing the principal represents to anyone who becomes aware that the agent is so acting that the agent has authority to enter on behalf of the principal into contracts with other persons of the kind which an agent so acting in the conduct of his principal's business has usually 'actual' authority to enter into.

In applying the law as I have endeavoured to summarise it to the case where the principal is not a natural person, but a fictitious person, namely, a corporation, two further factors arising from the legal characteristics of a corporation have to be borne in mind. The first is that the capacity of a corporation is limited by its constitution, that is, in the case of a company incorporated under the Companies Act, by its memorandum and articles of association; the second is that a corporation cannot do any act, and that includes making a representation, except through its agent. [Diplock LJ then discussed aspects of the *ultra vires* and constructive notice doctrines (now, of course, repealed), and continued:]

The second characteristic of a corporation, namely, that unlike a natural person it can only make a representation through an agent, has the consequence that in order to create an estoppel between the corporation and the contractor, the representation as to the authority of the agent which creates his 'apparent' authority must be made by some person or persons who have 'actual' authority from the corporation to make the representation. Such 'actual' authority may be conferred by the constitution of the corporation itself, as, for example, in the case of a company, upon the board of directors, or it may be conferred by those who under its constitution have powers of management upon some other person to whom the constitution permits them to delegate authority to make representations of this kind. If follows that where the agent upon whose 'apparent' authority the contractor relies has no 'actual' authority from the corporation to enter into a particular kind of contract with the contractor on behalf of the corporation, the contractor cannot rely upon the agent's own representation as to his actual authority. He can rely only upon a representation by a person or persons who have actual authority to manage or conduct that part of the business of the corporation to which the contract relates.

The commonest form of representation by a principal creating an 'apparent' authority of an agent is by conduct, namely, by permitting the agent to act in the management or conduct of the principal's business. Thus, if in the case of a company the board of directors who have 'actual' authority under the memorandum and articles of association to manage the company's business permit the agent to act in the management or conduct of the company's business, they thereby represent to all persons dealing with such agent that he has authority to enter on behalf of the corporation into contracts of a

---

[29] Or, perhaps more accurately, the third party *hopes* that the agent's appearance or assertions of authority are true, and takes the risk that they are. If proof is needed after the event, the third party will first try to show that the agent did indeed have actual authority, even though the third party had no firm proof of that at the time of contracting. As Diplock LJ says, the third party 'may be totally ignorant of the existence of any authority on the part of the agent. Nevertheless, if the agent does enter into a contract pursuant to the "actual" authority, it does create contractual rights and liabilities between the principal and the contractor'.

kind which an agent authorised to do acts of the kind which he is in fact permitted to do usually enters into in the ordinary course of such business. The making of such a representation is itself an act of management of the company's business. Prima facie it falls within the 'actual' authority of the board of directors, and unless the memorandum or articles of the company either make such a contract ultra vires the company or prohibit the delegation of such authority to the agent,[30] the company is estopped from denying to anyone who has entered into a contract with the agent in reliance upon such 'apparent' authority that the agent had authority to contract on behalf of the company.

If the foregoing analysis of the relevant law is correct, it can be summarised by stating four conditions which must be fulfilled to entitle a contractor to enforce against a company a contract entered into on behalf of the company by an agent who had no actual authority to do so. It must be shown:

(1) that a representation that the agent had authority to enter on behalf of the company into a contract of the kind sought to be enforced was made to the contractor.

(2) that such representation was made by a person or persons who had 'actual' authority to manage the business of the company either generally or in respect of those matters to which the contract relates;

(3) that he (the contractor) was induced by such representation to enter into the contract, that is, that he in fact relied upon it; and

(4) that under its memorandum or articles of association the company was not deprived of the capacity either to enter into a contract of the kind sought or be enforced or to delegate authority to enter into a contract of that kind to the agent.[31]

The confusion which, I venture to think, has sometimes crept into the cases is in my view due to a failure to distinguish between these four separate conditions, and in particular to keep steadfastly in mind (a) that the only 'actual' authority which is relevant is that of the persons making the representation relied upon, and (b) that the memorandum and articles of association of the company are always relevant (whether they are in fact known to the contractor or not) to the questions (i) whether condition (2) is fulfilled, and (ii) whether condition (4) is fulfilled and (but only if they are in fact known to the contractor) may be relevant (iii) as part of the representation on which the contractor relied.

In each of the relevant cases the representation relied upon as creating the 'apparent' authority of the agent was by conduct in permitting the agent to act in the management and conduct of part of the business of the company. Except in *Mahony v East Holford Mining Co Ltd* (1875) LR 7 HL 869, it was the conduct of the board of directors in so permitting the agent to act that was relied upon. As they had, in each case, by the articles of association of the company full 'actual' authority to manage its business, they had 'actual' authority to make representations in connection with the management of its business, including representations as to who were agents authorised to enter into contracts on the company's behalf. The agent himself had no 'actual' authority to enter into the contract because the formalities prescribed by the articles for conferring it upon him had not been complied with.... In *Mahony's* case no board of directors or secretary had in fact been appointed, and it was the conduct of those who, under the constitution of the company, were entitled to appoint them which was relied upon as a representation that certain persons were directors and secretary. Since they had 'actual' authority to appoint these officers, they had 'actual' authority to make representations as to who the officers were. In both these cases the constitution of the company, whether it had been seen by the contractor or not, was relevant in order to determine whether the persons whose representations by conduct were relied upon as creating the 'apparent' authority of the agent had 'actual' authority to make the representations on behalf

---

30 These remarks must now be read in the light of CA 2006 s 40.

31 This fourth requirement will not now be relevant, in the light of the reforms now embodied in CA 2006 ss 39 and 40, except in the case where the 'contractor' cannot bring himself within the latter section, eg because he was not dealing in good faith.

of the company. In *Mahony's* case, if the persons in question were not persons who would normally be supposed to have such authority by someone who did not know the constitution of the company, it may well be that he contractor would not succeed in proving condition (3), namely, that he relied upon the representations made by those persons, unless he proved that he did in fact know the constitution of the company...

The cases where the contractor's claim failed, namely *Houghton & Co v Nothard, Lowe & Wills Ltd* [[1927] 1 KB 246, CA], *Kreditbank Cassel GmbH v Schenkers Ltd* [[1927] 1 KB 826] and the *Rama Corpn* case[32], were all cases where the contract sought to be enforced was not one which a person occupying the position in relation to the company's business which the contractor knew that the agent occupied, would normally be authorised to enter into on behalf of the company. The conduct of the board of directors in permitting the agent to occupy that position, upon the which the contractor relied, thus did not of itself amount to a representation that the agent had authority to enter into the contract sought to be enforced, that is, condition (1) was not fulfilled. The contractor, however, in each of these three cases sought to rely upon a provision of the articles giving to the board power to delegate wide authority to the agent as entitling him to treat the conduct of the board as a representation that the agent had had delegated to him wider powers than those usually exercised by persons occupying the position in relation to the company's business which the agent was in fact permitted by the board to occupy. Since this would involve proving that the representation on which he in fact relied as inducing him to enter into the contract comprised the articles of association of the company as well as the conduct of the board, it would be necessary for him to establish first that he knew the contents of the articles (that is, that condition (3) was fulfilled in respect of any representation contained in the articles) and secondly that the conduct of the board in the light of that knowledge would be understood by a reasonable man as a representation that the agent had authority to enter into the contract sought to be enforced, that is that condition (1) was fulfilled. The need to establish both these things was pointed out by Sargant LJ in *Houghton's* case in a judgment which was concurred in by Atkin LJ; but his observations, as I read them, are directed only to a case where the contract sought to be enforced is not a contract of a kind which a person occupying the position which the agent was permitted by the board to occupy would normally be authorised to enter into on behalf of the company...

In the present case the findings of fact by the county court judge are sufficient to satisfy the four conditions, and thus to establish that Kapoor had 'apparent' authority to enter into contracts on behalf of the company for their services in connection with the sale of the company's property, including the obtaining of development permission with respect to its use. The judge found that the board knew that Kapoor had throughout been acting as managing director in employing agents and taking other steps to find a purchaser. They permitted him to do so, and by such conduct represented that he had authority to enter into contracts of a kind which a managing director or an executive director responsible for finding a purchaser would in the normal course be authorised to enter into on behalf of the company. Condition (1) was thus fulfilled. The articles of association conferred full powers of management on the board. Condition (2) was thus fulfilled. The plaintiffs, finding Kapoor acting in relation to the company's property as he was authorised by the board to act, were induced to believe that he was authorised by the company to enter into contracts on behalf of the company for their services in connection with the sale of the company's property, including the obtaining of development permission with respect to its use. Condition (3) was thus fulfilled. The articles of association, which contained powers for the board to delegate any of the functions of management to a managing director or to a single director, did not deprive the company of capacity to delegate authority to Kapoor, a director, to enter into contracts of that kind on behalf of the company. Condition (4) was thus fulfilled.

I think the judgment was right, and would dismiss the appeal.

WILLMER and PEARSON LJJ delivered concurring judgments.

---

[32] *Rama Corpn Ltd v Proved Tin and General Investments Ltd* [1952] 2 QB 147, [1952] 1 All ER 554, concerning a contract negotiated by a single non-executive director.

➤ Questions

1. Is it easy to distinguish between implied actual authority and ostensible authority? What is the crucial question in each case? (These are quite different.)

2. If Richards had implied actual authority to make the contract in *Hely-Hutchinson v Brayhead Ltd* **[3.04]**, should not the trial judge in *Freeman and Lockyer* **[3.10]** have made a similar finding about Kapoor?

Each of the essential elements of ostensible authority must be addressed in more detail.

1. The representation

The representation can be of any form: express (oral or written); implied from a course of conduct (eg permitting someone to manage the company) or implied from the dealings of the parties (eg the company has conducted business through the person held out before).

It can be a representation based on a person's job title, or on a course of dealing plus acquiescence by the principal: *Armagas Ltd v Mundogas SA* [1986] AC 717, 777, per Lord Keith. But the fact that the articles would permit a delegation of authority is not, of itself, a representation by the company to the third party that authority has been delegated: see *JC Houghton and Co v Nothard, Lowe and Wills Ltd* [1927] 1 KB 246, discussed by Diplock LJ in *Freeman & Lockyer* **[3.10]**.

Sometimes it is necessary to consider how long the representation lasts. In *AMB Generali Holding AG v Manches* [2005] EWCA Civ 1237, the court held that although a company that has endowed one of its members with ostensible authority (eg by virtue of an appointment to a given position) may withdraw that authority by sacking the 'agent', third parties may continue to rely upon the initial representation unless and until the withdrawal of authority is communicated to them specifically.

Representations cannot be built simply on someone's apparent use of authority. In *National Guild of Removers and Storers Ltd v Milner (t/a Intransit Removals and Storage)* [2014] EWHC 670 (IPEC), a case concerning purported trademark infringement, it was alleged by the claimant that its trademark had been published in a directory as advertisement of the respondent's business, and that the publishers of the directory, having acted as the respondent's agent, rendered the respondent liable, as principal, for the infringement of the claimant's trademark and copyright and for passing off. In this case the publishers were not acting as the respondent's agent in any way: the respondent had plainly not given the publishers actual authority to use the subject name or logo; and the argument based on ostensible authority was rejected on the ground that there was neither knowledge nor representation on the part of the respondent that the publishers were to have any such authority.

2. The authority of the representor

This must be made by some person or persons with *actual* authority to make the representation, or representations of that type. A person's lack of authority to enter into the transaction in question also implies that she herself cannot make the representation that she does have such authority: see the section on 'Bars on "self-authorising agents"', p 116. If this were not the law, then limitations on authority would be very easily circumvented: see *British Bank of the Middle East v Sun Life Assurance of Canada (UK) Ltd* [1983] BCLC 78, noted by Collier [1984] CLJ 26.

3. Reliance—no notice of the agent's want of actual authority and causal links

Since ostensible authority is an estoppel-based doctrine, reliance is important. Reliance must be reasonable, and it must be causative. The authorities suggest the hurdles are low.

Freeman & Lockyer [3.10] makes it clear that it is not possible to rely on a representation of the agent's ostensible authority if the person transacting with the company 'knows' that the act is beyond the actual authority of that agent.

As well as actual knowledge of the absence of authority, or suspicion about it (see *Akai* [3.11]), remember that a person has constructive notice of those documents required to be and actually filed at Companies House (eg the company's constitution). This is the 'constructive notice' rule established in *Ernest v Nichols* (1857) 6 HL Cas 401. If a limitation on the authority of the individuals purporting to deal on behalf of the company could be seen from these documents, then the outsider will not be able to rely on their ostensible authority. This is subject to two vitally important exceptions which seriously limit the impact of this much-criticised rule. The first is what has already been said earlier on s 40: recall that s 40(2)(b)(i) means there is no automatic (*Ernest v Nichols*) constructive notice of limitations on the powers of the directors to bind the company, or to authorise others to do so. The second is what is said later on the 'indoor management rule', at 'Deemed authority...indoor management rule', p 116.

Furthermore, the representation must induce the subsequent transaction. Sometimes, this requirement is expressed as a requirement of 'detriment' or 'change of position', but query whether any negative consequences must be shown. The better view is that of Diplock LJ in *Freeman & Lockyer v Buckhurst Park Properties (Mangal) Ltd* [3.10], that mere entry into the contract is sufficient: 'The representation, *when acted upon by the contractor by entering into a contract with the agent*, operates as an estoppel, preventing the principal from asserting that he is not bound by the contract' (emphasis added). In *Criterion Properties plc v Stratford UK Properties LLC* [2004] UKHL 28, [2004] 1 WLR 1846, HL, at [31], Lord Scott said this:

> 31. ...If a person dealing with an agent knows that the agent does not have actual authority to conclude the contract or transaction in question, the person cannot rely on apparent authority. Apparent authority can only be relied on by someone who does not know that the agent has no actual authority. And if a person dealing with an agent knows or has reason to believe that the contract or transaction is contrary to the commercial interests of the agent's principal, it is likely to be very difficult for the person to assert with any credibility that he believed the agent did have actual authority. Lack of such a belief would be fatal to a claim that the agent had apparent authority.

Reliance on ostensible authority is not reasonable where the third party's belief was dishonest or irrational (which includes turning a blind eye and being reckless); presumption of factual reliance following a finding of ostensible authority.

[3.11] Thanakharn Kasikorn Thai Chamkat (Mahachon) v Akai Holdings Ltd (In Liquidation) FACV 9/2010 (Hong Kong Court of Final Appeal)

The transaction in issue was referred to as the 'Switch Transaction'. Mr Ting (T) was the CEO of Akai Holdings Ltd (Akai). Akai and Singer Co NV (S) shared the same parent company. The Switch Transaction was entered into by T purportedly on behalf of Akai: it committed Akai to borrowing US$30 million from the Thai Farmers Bank (the Bank) in order to pay off the liability owed by S to the Bank; this loan was secured by a pledge of shares in one of Akai's subsidiaries. On its face this transaction was detrimental to Akai and advantageous to S (a company in which T had an interest) and the Bank. The liquidators of Akai sued the Bank, essentially on the ground that it must have realised, or ought to have realised, that T had no authority to commit Akai to the Switch Transaction. Prior to entering into the Switch Transaction, the Bank had received, inter alia, a document purporting to be the minutes of an Executive Committee meeting of Akai, as signed by T. This document was later found to have been dishonestly prepared by T, or at least on his instructions; no such meeting ever took place on that day.

The court agreed with the parties' concession that T could have no *actual* authority, given that the transaction was contrary to the interests of Akai (see 'Directors' authority and breach of directors' duties', p 124). After analysis of earlier cases, Lord Neuberger NPJ held that it was next to inconceivable that an agent could self-authorise in order to provide himself with ostensible authority—that part of the judgment is not extracted here, but see 'Bars on "self-authorising agents"', p 116. It followed that here T did not have ostensible (or 'apparent') authority to commit Akai to the Switch Transaction. Finally, Lord Neuberger also held that even if T did have ostensible authority, the Bank could not reasonably have relied on such authority, as that would have been 'simply irrational'. This last issue is the subject of the extract which follows, although the entire judgment repays close reading.

LORD NEUBERGER NPJ (with whose judgment other members of the court agreed):

46. In this case, the Bank's argument in a nutshell is (a) that, by holding him out as its executive chairman and chief executive officer, Akai clothed Mr Ting with apparent [ie ostensible] authority to commit it to the Switch Transaction, and (b) that, when the Bank entered into the transaction, it justifiably relied on his authority to enter into the transaction on Akai's behalf. Stone J accepted both those propositions, but they were both rejected by the Court of Appeal. In this court, Akai challenges both of those propositions....

The [necessary] state of mind of the person alleging apparent authority

49. For the Bank, Mr Jonathan Sumption QC ('Mr Sumption') (who appeared with Mr Eugene Fung) contended that, unless the Bank had actual knowledge of Mr Ting's lack of authority or its belief that Mr Ting had authority was dishonest or irrational, then the Bank's state of mind will suffice for the purpose of establishing apparent authority. Mr Sumption also accepted that, if the Bank was reckless in its belief, or if it was guilty of turning a blind eye, that would not do either, on the basis that recklessness and blind-eye ignorance amount to irrationality or dishonesty in this context. Mr Leslie Kosmin QC ('Mr Kosmin') (who appeared for Akai with Ms Linda Chan) argued that this set too low a standard on the Bank as a third party seeking to establish apparent authority, and that apparent authority could not be relied on if the Bank had failed to make the inquiries that a reasonable person would have made in the circumstances to verify the authority of Mr Ting.

50. I have some doubts as to the extent to which there would, in practice, be much difference in outcome between the application of the rival tests....

51. Approaching the issue by reference to both practicality and principle, I would prefer the Bank's submission. In terms of practicality, at least when it comes to normal commercial transactions, the application of the concept of constructive notice, which is what Akai's approach effectively involves, has been deprecated...

52. In a commercial context, absent dishonesty or irrationality, a person should be entitled to rely on what he is told: this may occasionally produce harsh results, but it enables people engaged in business to know where they stand. As to principle, apparent authority is essentially a species of estoppel by representation (see per Diplock LJ in *Freeman & Lockyer* **[3.10]**, 503... [He then discussed various cases on making inquiries.]

55. Millett J took the clear view that constructive notice did not involve 'the proper approach' in a normal commercial case, on the basis that '[u]nless and until they are alerted to the possibility of wrongdoing, [account officers] proceed, and are entitled to proceed, on the assumption that they are dealing with honest men'. He continued by saying that they were entitled to do so until 'the facts...[make] it imperative for [them] to seek an explanation, because in the absence

of an explanation it was obvious that the transaction was probably improper'—*Macmillan Inc v. Bishopsgate Investment Trust plc* [1995] 1 WLR 978, 1014G–H.

56. It is true that there are judicial dicta which appear at first sight to provide some support for Akai's case on this issue, but, on closer analysis, I do not consider that they are in point.

[He then also considered case law based on the rule in *Turquand's* case (see 'Deemed authority... *Turquand's* case', p 116), before distinguishing that from the requisite state of mind in cases of apparent authority.]

62. I conclude that it is open to the Bank to rely on Mr Ting's apparent authority (if he had such authority) unless the Bank's belief in that connection was dishonest or irrational (which includes turning a blind eye and being reckless)....

Evidence of reliance

72. Given that apparent authority is a species of estoppel by representation, it follows that, as Diplock LJ said in his third proposition in *Freeman & Lockyer* **[3.10]**, 506, the third party must establish that it relied on the apparent authority of the alleged agent before it can succeed in establishing its case. The issue which divides the parties is the quality of the evidence which the third party has to lead to establish reliance. Inevitably, that is a fact-sensitive issue, but I detected a suggestion in Akai's case that it is positively necessary for a third party to establish that he positively relied on the apparent authority in every case....

75. In my view, once a third party has established that the alleged agent had apparent authority, i.e. that the principal held out the alleged agent as having authority to bind the principal, and that the third party has entered into a contract with the alleged agent on behalf of the principal, then, in the absence of any evidence or indication to the contrary, it would be an unusual case where reliance was not presumed.

➤ Note

Akai was cited with approval by the English Court of Appeal in *Paul Quinn v CC Automotive Group Ltd t/a Carcraft* [2010] EWCA Civ 1412. This case concerned the fraud perpetrated by a deceitful employee of a car dealing company and the question was which of the two innocent parties (ie the car purchaser or the company/employer) were to bear the loss. Gross LJ (with whom Sullivan and Mummery LJJ agreed) had this to say about the relatively low standard required of a third party's 'reasonable' belief in the agent's ostensible (or apparent) authority:

23.... There can be no reliance on such a representation [as to an employee's authority in respect of a certain transaction] if the third party did not have an honest belief in the employee's authority; so too, if the third party turns a 'blind eye' to suspicions as to the apparent authority of the employee... However, the touchstone is honest belief and, possibly, 'irrationality'—a point conceded in *Akai* and upon which it is unnecessary to express any concluded view. However and consistent with principle in the field of misrepresentation, the question of the 'reasonableness' of the third party's belief is neither here nor there.... The observations of Lord Neuberger in *Akai*, at [52] and the sources there referred to, are to the same effect. To my mind, an analysis founded on reliance and belief leaves little room for any consideration of whether the third party was 'put on enquiry'. If there is proper scope for such consideration, it would seem to arise as an aspect of whether the third party turned a 'blind eye' to his suspicions as to the employee's apparent authority; possibly too, there could be debate as to whether the third party was put on enquiry if the employee was acting outside of the usual authority of a person holding the position he holds... But on no view can it be said that the third party is put on enquiry because of mere unreasonableness in failing to see through the employee's deceit; *a fortiori*, if the transaction is within the class of acts that an employee in the position of the rogue is usually authorised to do.

4. Bars on 'self-authorising agents'

As noted earlier, where the purported agent has no actual authority to make the contract for the company, she also has no actual authority to represent that she has such authority: see *Freeman & Lockyer* [3.10]; and *Crabtree Vickers Pty Ltd v Australian Direct Mail Advertising & Addressing Co Pty Ltd* (1957) 33 CLR 72, HCA.

However, the facts must be treated carefully: even an agent without actual or ostensible authority to conclude a deal may nevertheless have actual or ostensible authority to represent that the transaction has been approved at a higher level in the company's management. In *First Energy (UK) Ltd v Hungarian International Bank Ltd* [1993] BCLC 1409, CA, the senior manager in charge of the Manchester branch of the defendant bank had no actual authority to sanction a credit facility for the plaintiff (as the plaintiff knew). However, he had signed a letter to the plaintiff offering to provide it with finance. He had no actual authority to sign this letter, either. But, by virtue of his position, he was held to have ostensible authority (and surely actual authority) to communicate such an offer on behalf of the bank—that is, to inform the plaintiff that head office approval had been given for the offer to be made. As a result, the court held that the bank was bound by contract to provide the credit facility.[33] Also see *Kelly v Fraser* [2012] UKPC 25 (on trustees, not directors, but the principles are the same).

Deemed authority III: common law intervention in the absence of actual authority—the residual role of the 'indoor management rule' or 'the rule in *Turquand's* case'

Before the protection for outsiders contracting with the agents of company was clearly formulated in terms of agency (ie before *Freeman & Lockyer* [3.10]), outsiders had (and still have) the benefit of the rule in *Turquand's* case (*Royal British Bank v Turquand* (1856) 6 E & B 327).

The rule has been encapsulated as follows, in *Mahony v East Holyford Mining Co Ltd* (1875) LR 7 HL 869, 894, by Lord Hatherley:

> [W]hen there are persons conducting the affairs of the company in a manner which appears to be perfectly consonant with the articles of association, then those so dealing with them, externally, are not to be affected by any irregularities which may take place in the internal management of the company. They are entitled to presume that that of which only they can have knowledge, namely, the external acts, are rightly done, when those external acts purport to be performed in the mode in which they ought to be performed.... Of course, the case is open to any observation arising from gross negligence or fraud.

Or more simply still in *Morris v Kanssen* [1946] AC 459, 474, by Lord Simonds:

> [P]ersons contracting with a company and dealing in good faith may assume that acts within its constitution and powers have been properly and duly performed and are not bound to inquire whether acts of internal management have been regular.

Most of these cases are surely now covered by CA 2006 s 40 and its rules on good faith and constructive notice. If there are any gaps which the rule in *Turquand's* case could fill, they seem to be these. First, the problem is not always what the constitution says, but rather whether it has been complied with. A person dealing with a company is always subjected to uncertainty as to whether its officers have been properly appointed, its resolutions duly

---

[33] Whether this is the necessary consequence of what was surely only a false and misleading representation that an offer had been approved is doubted. The more appropriate remedy would seem to be reliance losses arising from the false representation, not making good the representation itself.

passed, etc. The outsider simply has to take it for granted that the internal affairs *have* been regularly conducted (and, for that matter, must accept that the company's internal affairs are none of his business). *Turquand's* rule can assist here. Secondly, it may be necessary to fall back on the common law rule for the protection of someone who is not 'dealing with' a company (s 40), as in the Australian case *Australian Capital Television Pty Ltd v Minister of Transport and Communications* (1989) 7 ACLC 525, where the *Turquand* rule was applied in the context of an application to a government minister for a broadcasting licence.

Despite these examples, it is conceded that the occasions on which the indoor management rule will be pleaded are likely to be rare since:

(i) CA 2006 s 40 largely eliminates the need to raise the rule by way of rejoinder to a contention that the person was affected by the constructive notice doctrine.

(ii) In any case, since the decision in *Freeman & Lockyer v Buckhurst Park Properties (Mangal) Ltd* **[3.10]**, it is common to use arguments based on ostensible authority rather than rely on the internal management rule to resolve questions in this area.

(iii) Furthermore, there are now a considerable number of statutory provisions designed to protect third parties against possible internal irregularities in a company's decision-making. See, for example, CA 2006 ss 40, 41, 44, 775. The more of these provisions there are, and the more widely they are drafted, the less is the need for the common law rule.

One final comment on the *Turquand* rule is necessary. It is plain from *Rolled Steel Products (Holdings) Ltd v British Steel Corpn* [1986] Ch 246, CA, that a person who knows or has notice of the irregularity in question or has been put on inquiry will be barred from relying on the rule. This 'put on inquiry' qualification seems to render the rule stricter than the 'reliance rule' for ostensible authority. In *Akai* **[3.11]**, Lord Neuberger specifically distinguished the position in 'agency' cases from those involving the indoor management rule. In arriving at his view that the belief in an agent's purported apparent authority need not be reasonable (but cannot be dishonest or irrational), his Lordship reasoned as follows:

> 61. Whether or not the indoor management rule is part of the law of agency or companies is a category issue which is of no consequence at least for present purposes. The essential point, to my mind, is that it was developed for good practical reasons to mitigate the harsh consequences of the principle (now thankfully historic) that a person dealing with a company was deemed to know the contents of its memorandum and articles. It is therefore unsurprising that the courts developed the principle that one could only rely on the rule if one took reasonable steps to ascertain the relevant facts. There is no obvious reason why the same principle should apply to cases of apparent authority.

➤ Notes

1. The presumption of regularity cannot be relied on by 'insiders', that is, persons who by virtue of their position in the company are in a position to know whether or not the internal regulations have been observed: *Howard v Patent Ivory Manufacturing Co* (1888) 38 Ch D 156 (Chancery Division); *Morris v Kanssen* [1946] AC 459. By contrast, therefore, the lower court was remarkably indulgent in *Hely-Hutchinson v Brayhead Ltd* **[3.04]** in treating as an 'outsider' for the purpose of the rule a person who was a director of a company, though not acting as such in the transaction in question.

2. The presumption of regularity has been held not to apply in the case of forgery: *Ruben v Great Fingall Consolidated* **[11.13]**. But contrast *Lovett v Carson Country Homes* **[3.15]**, where CA 2006 s 44(5) was deemed to apply despite an outright forgery.

1. The interaction between the indoor management rule and agency rules

The 'indoor management' rule, or rule in *Royal British Bank v Turquand*, appears in its simplest form in relation to such questions as the due execution of documents, the passing of authorising resolutions and the regularity of elections and appointments. In all these cases, if nothing has occurred which is evidently contrary to the provisions of the company's constitution, the outsider may assume the regularity of all matters internal to the company and its organisation.

Where, however, the issue is whether a single person has, or is deemed to have, authority to represent the company as its representative or agent, these questions of indoor management may become confused with other questions arising from the ordinary laws of agency. The position may be illustrated by various examples. If a person has been appointed to the office of secretary or managing director and acts as such, but there was some technical defect in the procedure by which he or she was appointed, the indoor management rule will apply so as to protect an outsider dealing with the agent. On the other hand, when a person has been appointed as the company's agent either specially, to act in a particular transaction, or generally (eg to manage a branch office), the questions whether he has exceeded the authority conferred upon him and, if so, whether the company as principal is nevertheless bound vis-à-vis a third party, are matters which ought to be determined by the ordinary rules of agency.

A more complex problem arises when a person holding *some* office in the company (commonly a director) purports to act on behalf of the company in a matter which is not within the scope of such an officer's usual activities, but *would* be within the normal functions of another office to which he might have been appointed—for example, a managing director. Such a person may, depending on the evidence, be regarded as either (i) a managing director defectively appointed, (ii) a person held out by the company[34] as a managing director although never appointed as such or (iii) an officer of limited powers who has without authority simply exceeded those powers. On the first view, the matter is one governed by the indoor management rule;[35] on the second, by the rules of agency;[36] and in either case the third party with whom he deals will be protected. On the third view, the company will not be bound whichever set of rules is applied. It is perhaps not surprising that the cases sometimes fail to keep the *Turquand* and the agency principles distinct.

Many of the older cases seem to have been argued and decided primarily on the basis of the indoor management rule, but they should all now be reconsidered in the light of the judgments in *Freeman & Lockyer v Buckhurst Park Properties (Mangal) Ltd* **[3.10]**, where the problems raised in cases of this nature were reformulated as issues of agency.

Examples

For illustrations of the courts' analyses of ostensible authority, revisit *Freeman & Lockyer* **[3.10]**; *Panorama Developments (Guildford) Ltd v Fidelis Furnishing Fabrics Ltd* **[3.03]**; and *Hopkins v TL Dallas Group Ltd* **[3.13]**.

---

[34] The agent may be 'held out' by the company's documents, or by the board or other duly constituted authority, or there may be circumstances which estop the board or other organ of the company from denying that he is a managing director.

[35] It has been held that, in order to succeed under this head, the third party must have actual knowledge of the article conferring the power to delegate: see *Houghton & Co v Northard Lowe & Wills Ltd* [1927] 1 KB 246, CA.

[36] In this case, knowledge of the existence of a power to delegate is unnecessary.

Establishing an agent's ostensible authority to conclude a deal or, alternatively, to convey the information that a deal has been concluded.

[3.12] PEC Ltd v Asia Golden Rice Co Ltd [2014] EWHC 1583 (Commercial Court)

The issue was whether the claimants, PEC Ltd (PEC), had entered into an arbitration agreement with the respondents, Asia Golden Rice Co Ltd (AGR), as part of a contract to buy rice. AGR's case was that a Mr Jain (of PJS) had made an oral agreement committing PEC to buy the rice from them, and that the contract was confirmed by a written agreement by a Mr Kumar, then Chief General Manager (CGM) at PEC. (PJS is an unincorporated Indian rice trader, who started to do business with PEC in 2002, and is one of the independent traders who conduct their business with access to credit of letter facilities and other financial services provided to Indian businesses by PEC in their public capacity.) PEC's case is that neither Mr Jain nor Mr Kumar had authority to enter into the Purchase Agreement, and therefore they were not bound by any arbitration agreement. The judge held that Kumar had neither express nor implied actual authority to enter into the contract, and Jain therefore had no delegated actual authority from Kumar, and nor did he have apparent (ostensible) authority either to enter into the agreement or to convey PEC's acceptance of the agreement. The extract below deals only with the issue of Jain's ostensible authority.

ANDREW SMITH J:

63. I therefore conclude that Mr Ravi Kumar was not authorised by PEC to make the Purchase Agreement. It also follows that he did not have the power to authorise Mr Jain to make it. I must therefore consider whether PEC were bound by any agreement that Mr Jain made? As I have said, AGR did not advance any other argument that PEC conferred actual authority on Mr Jain. The question is whether he had apparent authority, and I consider it first on the basis that, as AGR contend, it is governed by English law. In order to show apparent authority, AGR have to establish that PEC or someone authorised by PEC made a representation (by words or conduct) that Mr Jain had the requisite authority, and that they acted on that representation. (The law is unclear as to whether they have to show that they acted to their detriment. They might well not: see *Chitty on Contracts* (31st Ed, 2012) para 31-057, and pace *Kelly v Fraser*, [2012] UKPC 25 para 18. But nothing turns on that.)…

68. AGR's case here is pleaded in two ways: (i) that, by their conduct in concluding contracts, PEC held Mr Jain out as their agent to negotiate and to conclude 'contracts'; and (ii) that, by their acquiescence in the earlier contracts, PEC clothed Mr Jain with authority to negotiate and conclude [the particular contracts in issue]. In his submissions Mr Collett [counsel for AGR] also relied…on the fact that PEC were apparently content to deal with AGR with regard to contracts and amendments to them (for example, amendments as to prices, shipping periods and destinations of the cargoes) through Mr Jain in particular and PJS more generally. Accordingly, he submitted, a third party in the position of AGR would reasonably have understood, and AGR did understand, that Mr Jain had authority to conclude contracts on PEC's behalf.

69. It is not enough that AGR understood this to be the position and that they were reasonable to do so. The first question is whether PEC so presented Mr Jain by their words or conduct (including their silence or omissions), and here all that matters is what was done by someone who had actual or apparent authority to speak or act for PEC. Moreover, it is nothing to the point that PEC presented Mr Jain as having authority to conduct negotiations: the question is whether he was presented as having authority to conclude contracts, and more specifically a contract such as the Purchase Agreement. I accept that by a consistent and regular course of dealing in which they fulfilled contracts made in their name by a putative agent a principal could be taken to have represented to counterparties that the agent had authority to commit him to such contracts. However, given the courts' reluctance to infer a representation of this kind, I am persuaded by Mr Brindle

[counsel for PEC] that no such inference is to be drawn in this case.... [T]he fact that PEC had on occasion in the past fulfilled contracts that had been made by Mr Jain purportedly on their behalf is not enough on the facts of this case to amount to a representation that Mr Jain had authority to conclude contracts for them. PEC's conduct is readily, and to my mind more readily, explicable as a reflecting their decisions to ratify particular contracts made by Mr Jain in their name....

70. However, there is another answer to this argument, similar to that about Mr Ravi Kumar's implied [actual] authority. If held out at all, 'The authority will be that which the agent reasonably appeared to have to the third party, taking into account the manifestations of the principal, the implied authority normally applicable to the circumstances or to the person in the agent's position, or both': *Chitty on Contracts*, cit sup, para 31-057. This raises the immediate question, what contracts did PEC hold Mr Jain out as being authorised to make? At its highest, PEC might be said to have represented that Mr Jain had authority to enter into purchase contracts that were comparable to those in which he had previously been involved. Th[is] Purchase Agreement, however, was on a different scale from the previous ones: the quantity of rice and the price were far greater.

71. This is enough to reject the argument that Mr Jain had apparent authority to conclude contracts for PEC. But there is another point: the previous contracts made by Mr Jain were concluded after oral agreement in principle about the main terms of the deal, and when Mr Jain met Ms Patcharin in Bangkok to sign the contracts. Accordingly the previous pattern of dealing was significantly different from the circumstances of th[is] Purchase Agreement. There had been no course of dealing that might represent (or even indicate) that Mr Jain had authority to make a contract on the telephone without discussion with PEC....

72. Accordingly, I reject AGR's case that Mr Jain had apparent authority to make the Purchase Agreement even assuming (i) that AGR acted in reliance on some representation by PEC of Mr Jain's authority, and (ii) that Mr Jain's apparent authority is governed by English and not Indian law. I state my conclusions only briefly about these questions.

73. The question whether AGR could have proved reliance on any representation that PEC made about Mr Jain's authority raises questions (i) whether AGR (through Ms Patcharin) believed that Mr Jain was authorised by PEC to make the Purchase Agreement orally, and (ii) whether they relied on the belief. If this is proved, it does not matter in English law that her belief was unreasonable, so long as it was not dishonest or irrational: see paras 51 et seq of Lord Neuberger's judgment in *Thanakharn v Akai*, **[3.11]**, a case in the Court of Final Appeal in Hong Kong stating the law of Hong Kong, but based on an analysis of English (and Australian) authorities. Ms Patcharin's evidence to the Tribunal was that she believed that Mr Jain had authority because of previous dealings ('I was sure that Mr Pawan Jain had the authority because so far the contract was executed, so far, so good'), and I accept that. I also accept that AGR acted on that belief, and (if necessary) that they did so to their detriment. It suffices for this purpose in cases of apparent authority that the third party simply did not take an alternative available course of action, and generally suffices that he entered into a contract in reliance on his belief that the agent was authorised: *Bowstead & Reynolds on Agency* (19th Ed, 2010) para 8-026. There is no reason not to adopt the general approach in this case. Believing that they had a contract with PEC, AGR pressed for it to be carried out and, no doubt, did not seek to sell the rice elsewhere...

77. AGR have another arrow in their quiver: their argument that, even if Mr Ravi Kumar signed the written agreement without authority, Mr Jain had apparent authority to communicate to AGR that the contract was duly made by PEC: that is to say, apparent authority to convey to AGR the acceptance by PEC of AGR's written contract. Notionally a principal can confer on an agent authority to communicate acceptance of a contract notwithstanding the agent does not himself have authority to make it: see *Kelly v Fraser*, (cit sup) at para 15. A familiar example is that of the company secretary with authority to convey board decisions, but in *First Energy (UK) Ltd v Hungarian International Bank Ltd*, [1993] 2 Lloyd's LR 194 the manager in charge of a bank's office was held to have such authority. However, the court's reluctance to infer such authority

from previous dealings was explained by Goff LJ in *Armagas Ltd v Mundogas SA*, [1986] AC 717, 732:

> '... it does not follow from the mere fact that an agent has on previous occasions been entrusted by his principal with the task of communicating to a third party his principal's approval to certain transactions, that the principal has thereby represented that the agent has authority to communicate such approval in relation to future transactions, with the effect that the principal will be bound by such communication.'

He also described (at p. 731A) as 'a most surprising conclusion' the judge's finding that an agent without apparent authority to contract had apparent authority to say that he had obtained actual authority to do so. He observed (at p.731B) 'As a matter of common sense, this is most unlikely to be the law', and in the House of Lords (loc cit at p.779F) Lord Keith agreed. In the Court of Appeal in the *First Energy (UK) Ltd* case Steyn LJ recognised that Lord Keith had given 'valuable guidance, which Judges at every level will want to consider carefully when the occasion arises, but it does not amount to a rule or principle of law' (loc cit at 202). In concluding that nevertheless in that case the manager had apparent authority to convey an offer by the bank, he observed, '... Lord Keith's observations about specific as opposed to general authority are not relevant to the case before us. The issue in the present case relates to the existence of a general apparent authority arising from the position in which [the bank] had placed [the manager]'.

78. As I see it, AGR's contention is closer to one of specific authority: that PEC held Mr Jain out as having authority to convey that they accepted the written Purchase Agreement not because they appointed him to a position in which he would be expected to do so, but because of the specific role that they had allowed him to adopt when dealing with AGR. The guidance of Goff LJ and Lord Keith is fully applicable. I cannot accept that PEC presented Mr Jain as having such authority. They presented him as the route for conducting negotiations with a view to AGR and PEC concluding contracts or amending concluded contracts and also for carrying out contracts after they had been made, but that is different from presenting him as the route for communicating contractual offers or acceptances. He had not done that in the past: he had himself signed contracts at meetings in Bangkok that were presented to him by AGR at the meetings.

79. I reject the argument that Mr Jain had authority to convey PEC's acceptance of the Purchase Agreement...

➤ Notes

1. The special undertaking to be executed by 'duly authorised representatives' in *British Bank of the Middle East* was distinguished by his Honour Judge Mackie QC in *Playboy Club London Ltd v Banca Nazionale Del Lavoro SPA* [2014] EWHC 2613 (QB), which concerned a routine bank reference that certified that a customer of the Playboy Club was trustworthy and able to meet commitments of up to $1.6 million in any one week (when the account actually had a nil balance). In considering the bank's liability towards the Playboy Club, the judge made the following observation as to the extent of apparent authority possessed by a member of the bank's staff (Ms Guidetti) who had been vested with the title of 'business development':

> 37. In my judgment the Club is right. The facts of *British Bank of the Middle East* involved a special undertaking to be executed by 'duly authorised representatives' and the posing of explicit questions about this. They are very different from those involved in a routine bank reference. Bank employees have a wider variety of titles than they used to both in this country and abroad. 'Business Development' may cover a variety of levels of responsibility but they all connote

a degree of executive as opposed to routine activity. The request was sent by NatWest to Ms Guidetti addressed to the manager. The Club could reasonably expect this lady to pass the request up the chain if that was necessary and, when replying herself, to have obtained the appropriate level of clearance. The fact that Ms Guidetti replied caused no surprise to Mr Rothwell, a highly experienced chartered accountant. There was nothing unorthodox or informal about the approach for or giving of the reference. Bank references are a routine feature of international trade. It is something of a surprise to learn that the Bank's witness was unaware of them. The fact that the standard Club form is addressed to 'the manager' was no reason for it to be cautious when it saw a reply from an employee apparently responsible for its account. Whether put as apparent authority or vicarious liability the Bank is responsible for this reference which it issued through a conventional channel in circumstances which would not have put a third party on enquiry…

2. In *LNOC Ltd v Watford Association Football Club Ltd* [2013] EWHC 3615 (Comm), his Honour Judge Mackie QC rejected the football club's defences to a claim for the recovery of an unpaid debt (based on the suggestion that the club's then *de facto* managing director and ultimate owner had no actual or, alternatively, apparent authority to enter into the transactions in question, as the lender knew or should have known). The judge found against the club on both defences, and concluded, at [99], as follows, '[T]he Club is free to delegate wide ranging authority to a managing director but it has to take the consequences of doing so. The Club, acting through the de facto managing director it appointed, borrowed money but has not paid it back. It should now do so. The Defences of lack of actual or apparent authority fail as does the Counterclaim.'

Transactions involving directors

Transactions between the company and its own directors are something of an exception to all these general rules. This will be obvious in considering later all the duties owed by directors to their companies: see Chapter 7. But for now, note CA 2006 s 41. It is an important qualification to the general rules in this chapter. It qualifies the impact of the presumptions permitted by CA 2006 s 40 where the dealing is with the directors of the company or its holding company, or any persons connected with these directors. Effectively, these 'insiders' are irrebuttably presumed to know the true state of affairs, and the contract between the company and such people is not void (as it would have been before these statutory interventions), but it is voidable at the election of the company, and the remedies available to the company in these 'insider' circumstances are wider than those available at common law, and are set out in s 41 which follows.

Companies Act 2006 s 41

41 Constitutional limitations: transactions involving directors or their associates

(1) This section applies to a transaction if or to the extent that its validity depends on section 40 (power of directors deemed to be free of limitations under company's constitution in favour of person dealing with company in good faith).

Nothing in this section shall be read as excluding the operation of any other enactment or rule of law by virtue of which the transaction may be called in question or any liability to the company may arise.

(2) Where—

(a) a company enters into such a transaction, and

(b) the parties to the transaction include—

    (i) a director of the company or of its holding company, or

    (ii) a person connected with any such director,

the transaction is voidable at the instance of the company.

(3) Whether or not it is avoided, any such party to the transaction as is mentioned in subsection (2)(b)(i) or (ii), and any director of the company who authorised the transaction, is liable—

    (a) to account to the company for any gain he has made directly or indirectly by the transaction, and

    (b) to indemnify the company for any loss or damage resulting from the transaction.

(4) The transaction ceases to be voidable if—

    (a) restitution of any money or other asset which was the subject matter of the transaction is no longer possible, or

    (b) the company is indemnified for any loss or damage resulting from the transaction, or

    (c) rights acquired bona fide for value and without actual notice of the directors' exceeding their powers by a person who is not party to the transaction would be affected by the avoidance, or

    (d) the transaction is affirmed by the company.

(5) A person other than a director of the company is not liable under subsection (3) if he shows that at the time the transaction was entered into he did not know that the directors were exceeding their powers.

(6) Nothing in the preceding provisions of this section affects the rights of any party to the transaction not within subsection (2)(b)(i) or (ii).

But the court may, on the application of the company or any such party, make an order affirming, severing or setting aside the transaction on such terms as appear to the court to be just.

(7) In this section—

    (a) 'transaction' includes any act; and

    (b) the reference to a person connected with a director has the same meaning as in Part 10 (company directors).

➤ Questions

1. If the facts of *Guinness v Saunders* **[5.01]** were to recur, would CA 2006 s 41 be applicable?

2. What is the impact of the saving provision in s 41(1) that preserves the operation of other rules of law that may call into question the validity of the transaction?

Ratification by the company of unauthorised transactions

If none of these deeming provisions assist, remember that acts which are beyond the actual authority of the agent can be ratified by the appropriate organ of the company (this needs some thought) if *it* has the necessary authority to enter into the contract. *New Fairmouth Resorts Ltd v International Hotels Jamaica Ltd* [2013] UKPC 11 provides a nice illustration: the agent had no actual or ostensible authority to enter into the transaction, but the company ratified the deal, thus curing any original want of authority.

Formalities

Unless the context suggests otherwise, the same formalities apply to contracts made by companies as to contracts made by individuals, although how that is achieved requires some special corporate rules. The present position for companies incorporated under the Companies Acts is set out in CA 2006 ss 43–52. The use of a seal is now optional (s 43(1)), and a company may make a contract with no more formality than is required in the case of an individual (s 43(2)).[37] Where the law requires the use of a document and the company's seal is not used, the document is validly executed if signed by two directors or by a director and a secretary (where the company has a secretary) (s 44(2)(a)). Section 44(2)(b) also adds the option of signature by one director in the presence of a witness who attests that signature. This is especially needed for private companies with a single director. Section 44 also contains a number of provisions to protect third parties: these are considered later at 'The problem of forged documents', p 126.

Particular problems in this area

1. Directors' authority and breach of directors' duties

If a director looks to have actual authority to do something, but then uses that authority for improper purposes, does that extinguish the director's *actual* authority? Does it necessarily nullify ostensible authority? What issues are important in answering these questions?

To take a simple example, suppose a director has express actual authority to enter into contracts under £10,000 on behalf of the company,[38] and enters into such a contract, but for improper purposes or in breach of fiduciary duty. Is the contract valid and binding on the company, being within the authority of the agent, but voidable by the company as against third parties who are not bona fide purchasers for value without notice of the company's equitable rights? Or, alternatively, is the contract void, being outside the actual authority of the agent (who can have no actual authority to act in breach of duty), unless the third party can rely on the ostensible authority of the agent to enter into such engagements? Put like this, it is evident that the practical outcome is likely to be the same on either analysis, although importantly the onus of proof lies in different places, and that can be important in practice.

An agent has no actual authority to act in breach of duty (dicta).

[3.13] Hopkins v TL Dallas Group Ltd [2004] EWHC 1379 (Chancery Division)

The question in this case was whether a deputy managing director had actual or ostensible authority to sign a letter on behalf of his company committing the company to pay a sum of £994,000 to a third party. Lightman J held that the director had no actual authority, either because the 'usual' authority of such a deputy managing director did not extend to agreeing to such exceptionally onerous undertakings, or (as is of special interest here) because a director's actual authority could never extend to acting for improper purposes or in breach of fiduciary duty (as was the case here). Further, on the facts here, the third party could not rely on the agent's ostensible authority, since the third party had actual knowledge or was at least on notice that the transactions were both abnormal and suspicious and therefore required confirmation of their propriety and regularity from the company's managing director.

> LIGHTMAN J:... Before I look at the facts I should say a word on the relevant law. The authority of an agent is 'actual (express or implied) where it results from a manifestation of consent that he should represent or act for the principal expressly or impliedly made by the principal to the agent himself': *Bowstead & Reynolds on Agency* 17th ed ('Bowstead') Article 22(1). This authority extends to doing 'whatever is necessary for, or ordinarily incidental to, the effective execution of

---

[37] Few contracts now require writing, but see, eg, contracts for the sale of land (Law of Property (Miscellaneous Provisions) Act 1989 s 2(1)) and contracts for the disposition of an equitable interest in any property (LPA 1925 s 53(1)(c)).

[38] Note that the scope of the director's actual authority can raise difficult questions of construction. See, eg, *Reckitt v Barnett, Pembroke & Slater Ltd* [1929] AC 176, HL, where a power to draw cheques 'without restriction' was construed as limited to drawing cheques related to the conduct of the principal's affairs.

his actual authority': Bowstead Article 27. The authority may in appropriate circumstances extend to raising funds and giving security for borrowings for the purpose of fulfilling the functions and duties assigned to him. Where a board of directors appoint one of the members to an executive position 'they impliedly authorise him to do all such things as fall within the usual scope of that office' (*Hely-Hutchinson v Brayhead Ltd* **[3.04]**, at 583).

The grant of actual authority to an agent will not normally include authority to act for the agent's benefit rather than that of his principal and therefore, without agreement, the scope of actual authority will not include this. The grant of actual authority should be implied as being subject to a condition that it is to be exercised honestly and on behalf of the principal: *Lysaght Bros & Co Ltd v Falk* (1905) 2 CLR 421. It follows that, if an act is carried out by an agent which is not in the interests of his principal, for example signing onerous unconditional undertakings, then the act will not be within the scope of the express or implied grant of actual authority. As a result there cannot be actual authority: 'the agent is simply not authorised to act contrary to his principal's interests: and hence that an act contrary to those interests is outside his actual authority. The transaction is therefore void unless the third party can rely on the doctrine of apparent authority' (Bowstead para 8-218).

In the case of *Macmillan Inc v Bishopgate Trust (No 3)* [1995] 1 WLR 978, Millet [sic] J (as he then was) stated that 'English law...recognises the distinction between want of authority and abuse of authority' (at 984). He then went on to approve the statement that 'an act of an agent within the scope of his actual or apparent authority does not cease to bind his principal merely because the agent was acting fraudulently and in furtherance of his own interests'. Bowstead suggests that this statement of the law should be limited to apparent authority i.e. that acting fraudulently or in furtherance of own interests will by its very nature nullify actual authority, but not apparent authority. I respectfully agree.

➤ Note

Hopkins was distinguished by his Honour Judge Mackie QC in *LNOC Ltd v Watford Association Football Club Ltd* [2013] EWHC 3615 (Comm), on the basis that *LNOC* (unlike *Hopkins*) was a case in which there was no evidence to suggest that the director in question was pursuing his own personal interests at the expense of the club. Thus, in those circumstances, mere negligence on his part will not suffice to vitiate the transaction, and the test remains subjective, namely whether the director (not the court) honestly believes the transaction to be in the company's best interests.

➤ Question

The approach in *Hopkins* **[3.13]** was also the approach implicitly adopted by Lord Neuberger in *Akai* **[3.11]**, accepting the concession that Mr Ting had no actual authority. This approach does not distinguish between agents acting in excess of their delegated authority or in abuse of it: in either case, it is said, the agent lacks actual authority. It ought to follow that in all these cases, unless the third party can rely on ostensible authority, the contract between the company and the third party will be void. But in the largest category of just these types of cases—cases where the contract is between the company and one of its directors, being a person unable to rely on ostensible authority—these contracts are void if the contract is in excess of the agent's authority;[39] otherwise they are voidable only, not void. This is the explicit and uncontroversial common law approach: see p 430. Notably, it is also the statutory approach even for excess of authority (where the common law would hold the contract to be void): see CA 2006 s 41. What does this say about the analysis in *Hopkins* **[3.13]**? Is there perhaps a confusion between recognising that, as between principal and agent, both excess and abuse of authority are breaches of duty by the

---

[39] See *Guinness plc v Saunders* **[5.01]**.

agent[40] for which the principal is entitled to a compensatory remedy. On the other hand, as between principal and third party, an agent who has authority but is abusing it is still (as per *Meridian Global* **[3.01]**) the person whose acts count as the acts of the company for the purpose, for example, of contracting to the value of less than £10,000 (to return to the illustration posed at the outset), even though this same agent would not be such a person if the contract were instead for £11,000. Contrast the approach in *Hopkins* **[3.13]** with that adopted by Arden LJ in the next extract.

[3.14] Clark v Cutland [2003] EWCA Civ 810, [2004] 1 WLR 783 (Court of Appeal)

The facts are immaterial.

> ARDEN LJ:
>
> 26. There seems to me to be a basic inconsistency between [counsel's] submission that the payments to the pension fund trustees were void and his main submission. His submission on this point seems to me to accept that the contributions were misapplications of the company's assets. However that may be, [the company's articles provided that] directors were not entitled to any remuneration unless it was authorised by the company in general meeting. The judge held that there was no such authorisation in the present case. It follows that the payments of pension contributions to the pension fund trustees were without legal effect and not merely voidable: see *Guinness plc v Saunders* **[5.01]**, 693, per Lord Templeman, with whom Lord Keith of Kinkel, Lord Brandon of Oakbrook and Lord Griffiths agreed, and at pp 698–702, per Lord Goff of Chieveley, with whom Lord Griffiths also agreed.
>
> 27. If those payments had merely been made by Mr Cutland in breach of his duty to the company, and he had not also made them without the authority of the company, Mr Stockill's submission that the payments were voidable would have been correct. However, where an agent carries out a transaction without authority, the consequence is (as I have stated) that the transaction is without legal effect. This consequence is more serious in law than that which attaches to a transaction which is voidable since the right to rescind a voidable transaction can be lost. Because the sanction attaching to an unauthorised transaction is more serious, it must supersede the sanction of voidability that would otherwise attach in the present case.

2. The problem of forged documents

Section 44 is protective: a 'purchaser' taking under a document in good faith and for valuable consideration is given very wide statutory protection by s 44(5), wide enough, it would appear, to include a document which is an outright forgery: see *Lovett v Carson Country Homes* **[3.15]**.

Companies Act 2006 s 44

> (2) A document is validly executed by a company if it is signed on behalf of the company—
>   (a) by two authorised signatories, or
>   (b) by a director of the company in the presence of a witness who attests the signature....
>
> (5) In favour of a purchaser a document shall be deemed to have been duly executed by a company if it purports to be signed in accordance with subsection (2).

---

[40] And in that sense are not allowed, or not authorised, or 'without authority'.

A 'purchaser' means a purchaser in good faith for valuable consideration and includes a lessee, mortgagee or other person who for valuable consideration acquires an interest in property.

In *Williams v Redcard Ltd* [2011] EWCA Civ 466, CA, it was held that use of the words 'by or on behalf of' were not necessary to invoke s 44(4); it sufficed that 'the reasonable reader would understand that the signatures of the natural persons are signatures both on their own account and on behalf of the company' [11].

And in *LNOC Ltd v Watford Association Football Club Ltd* [2013] EWHC 3615 (Comm), his Honour Judge Mackie QC adopted the 'dishonest or irrational' formulation from *Akai* **[3.11]** for the purposes of interpreting the 'good faith' requirement in s 44(5).

A forgery is not inevitably a nullity. The normal rules of agency apply to determine whether the company is bound by a forged document.[41]

[3.15] Lovett v Carson Country Homes [2009] EWHC 1143 (Chancery Division)

Administrators were appointed to Carson Country Homes (CCH) by Barclays Bank pursuant to powers conferred under a debenture between CCH and the bank. Carter, a director and shareholder of CCH, asserted that his signature on the debenture was forged by Jewson, also a director and shareholder of CCH. Jewson's own signature was genuine. Carter claimed that the debenture was a nullity, and the administrators were therefore not validly appointed. The judge found that Carter's signature was indeed a forgery, and that Jewson had no actual authority to apply Carter's signature in this way. (Apparently there was a practice of this, sometimes authorised or at least ratified by Carter after the event.) He further decided that Carter and Jewson were 'authorised signatories' for the purposes of CA 2006 s 44, and that the bank was a 'purchaser'. He then had to decide whether the document 'purported' to be signed properly (CA 2006 s 44(2) and (5)).

DAVIS J:

79. . . . [T]he word 'purports' is on its face a wide word which is not defined in the section. In my view, such a word operates to refer to the impression a document conveys. Indeed, it is self-evidently focusing on what appears to be the case rather than on what actually is the case. As it seems to me, if one were to pose as a matter of impression the question here 'Does the debenture purport to be signed on behalf of CCH by two authorised signatories?' the answer would be in the affirmative.

80. It was not disputed before me that such a statutory provision would operate to validate (in favour, of course, only of a purchaser) a document which has, for example, been erroneously signed by someone styled a director when, in fact, that person is not a director. Clearly, for example, it could potentially overcome in favour of a purchaser any defect by reference to the internal management rule. But on the face of the wording there is no such restriction simply as to those kinds of case, and the wording, unless glossed, would at first sight seem to be (in favour of a purchaser) capable of validating also a document where there has been fraud or forgery if the document purports to be signed in accordance with subsection (2). Nor would such a conclusion be without purpose or sense: for notoriously where fraud or forgery is concerned in a company context the innocent suffer: the shareholders and creditors on the one hand if the transaction is held binding; the innocent third party purchaser on the other hand if it is not. To favour the latter, provided and crucially he acts in good faith and is not put on inquiry as to wrongdoing, is

---

[41] This case concerns debentures rather than shares, but the issues are general.

not unprincipled. Indeed, it means that the company has to take the consequence of employing a dishonest director or servant and it is for the company to look for redress from that individual.

Forgery

81. Mr Hill-Smith [counsel], however, submitted that the subsection does not operate to validate documents which are forgeries. At the heart of Mr Hill-Smith's argument is the proposition that a forgery is a nullity. Indeed, as a general rule, a person whose signature on a document has been forged is entitled to say, 'This is not my document'. Mr Hill-Smith goes on to say that there is, as it were, nothing which can be deemed to be 'duly executed' for the purposes of section 44(5). Mr Hill-Smith submitted that this was established by authority. It is to be noted, however, that all counsel before me were agreed that there was no direct authority for this proposition for the actual purposes of section 44(5) itself or its immediate statutory predecessor . . .

85. In *Ruben* **[11.13]**, it has to be said, the facts were very strong. . . .

89. The decision and approach in *Ruben* **[11.13]** has, as it seems to me, to be set in the context of the subsequent well-known decision of the House of Lords in *Lloyd v Grace, Smith & Company* [1912] AC 722 to which, indeed, Lord Loreburn and Lord Macnaghten were themselves party. But whilst aspects of the comments of Lord Davey in his speech in *Ruben* were expressly disapproved in *Lloyd v Grace, Smith*, the decision itself was not . . . Since that time, it seems to be the case that by and large *Ruben* has, nevertheless, been represented as setting out the general position that a forgery is a nullity which cannot be validated, albeit there may be circumstances in which a party may be estopped from disputing the validity of a forged document . . . A particularly extreme version of the purported application of the decision in *Ruben* can be found in the case of *South London Greyhound Racecourses Ltd v Wake* [1931] Ch 496. There, even though the signatures of director and secretary on the certificate were valid and they had affixed the seal, and even though they had done so in order to defer proceedings threatened against the company, it was held that the fact that the board had not authorised the affixing of the seal rendered the certificate a forgery and a nullity: a decision which to my mind is very hard to sustain.

90. No doubt a forged corporate document is a nullity in the sense that no one has actual authority on the part of a company to issue a forged document. But as the exception of estoppel shows, that does not mean that the forged document can in no circumstances have any effect whatsoever: just because circumstances can arise whereby the company may be estopped from disputing its validity. But once one accepts that, then, in my opinion, that immediately opens up the prospect that such a document cannot be sidelined as a nullity for all purposes in the case of apparent authority. Indeed, the principles of apparent authority are a broad reflection of the general principles of estoppel. That that may be so is borne out by *Ruben* itself in my view: for, admittedly in somewhat grudging terms, *Shaw* was not formally disapproved as a decision but instead was distinguished as being capable on its facts as connoting that the secretary was held out as having authority to warrant the genuineness of a certificate. . . .

91. Thus *Ruben* was to be distinguished, not in point of principle, of course, but in point of fact. In *Ruben* there was no ostensible authority vested in the secretary. . . .

92. The position is also dealt with in *Gore Browne on Companies* in its latest edition in chapter 8, paragraph 28, where amongst other things this is said:

'There is authority from the House of Lords for the proposition that forgery as such is a nullity and cannot bind the company. On the other hand, if an organ or official of the company with the authority to bind the company held out the person who committed the forgery as having authority to execute the document in question, the company may be estopped from denying the validity of the forgery . . .'

93. The paragraph then turns to deal with the case of *Ruben* and then this is said:

'Indeed, it is difficult to see why even forgery as in *Ruben's* case must be treated as being governed by a special rule. So far as actual authority is concerned, a forgery is clearly a nullity. However, whether or not it binds the company should depend on general *Turquand* principles [see 'Deemed authority...indoor management rule', p 116]. It is clear that under general agency law forgeries are not treated differently from other fraudulent acts which may be binding on the principal if the agent acts within his ostensible authority. In particular, the company secretary may have a wide authority to represent that minutes and other documents are valid.'

94. In my view, that approach is the correct approach and gives the answer to the present case on the facts, finding as I do that the Bank was a bona fide purchaser for valuable consideration. The question of the authority, both actual and ostensible, of a company secretary has unquestionably moved on since the days of *Ruben*, as a number of authorities show. Moreover, there may well be cases where an officer or employee of a company can in any event be authorised actually or ostensibly by the company to warrant that procedures have been properly complied with and that documents are genuine. Indeed, the realities of modern commerce can sometimes require as much. An example can be found in the Court of Appeal decision in *First Energy (UK) Ltd v Hungarian International Bank Ltd* [1993] 2 Lloyd's Rep 194.

95. Moreover, in general agreement with the comments in *Gore Browne*, I can see no reason in principle why some special approach should be grafted on in the case of forgery by reciting the mantra that a forgery is a nullity which is not to be grafted on in the case of fraud. After all, while not all frauds involve forgeries, all forgeries in their own way involve a fraud. No officer or servant has actual authority to commit a fraud any more than he has actual authority to commit a forgery. But it is clear ever since the decision in *Lloyd v Grace, Smith* that a principal may in appropriate circumstances be bound by the fraudulent acts of his agent in circumstances where there is ostensible authority. True it is that in contractual terms fraud may make a contract voidable, not void, but the general point still remains that something which is done with authority, actual or apparent, is capable of binding the principal. Indeed, were that not so, I do not see how the House of Lords in *Ruben* could have approached the case of *Shaw* as they did or made the comments that they made on authority. . . .

96. On the facts here, Mr Jewson was both director and secretary of CCH, as well as a shareholder in CCH both directly and indirectly through SGJ. But more than that, through the years of the company's incorporation, and by consent of Mr Carter, he and he alone had had on behalf of CCH all dealings with the Bank. This was not merely a self-appointed role on his part; this was the way he and Mr Carter, the other director, had on behalf of CCH agreed that things should be done. As Mr Jewson said and I accept, Mr Carter left all the Bank dealings and documentation to him and was happy for him to look after it all. The Bank itself had no reason to think otherwise. In matters of documentation, therefore, it was to Mr Jewson on behalf of the directors of CCH that Barclays Bank looked in its dealings with CCH, and Mr Carter had throughout been content that that should be so. Further, as I have said, on a significant number of occasions—not just with a separate bank, Denizbank, but also with the Bank itself—Mr Carter had been content to leave it to Mr Jewson to communicate the appropriate signed formal documents to the Bank when Mr Carter must have known that two signatories were required and that he himself had not signed and when he knew that Mr Jewson had been wont to sign bank documents using Mr Carter's purported signature. In such circumstances, I conclude that Mr Jewson had been clothed by CCH with ostensible authority to warrant to the Bank that all formalities relating to approval and execution of the debenture and guarantee had been duly complied with and that the signatures could be relied upon as genuine.

97. Having so concluded on the facts, it seems to me that on any view of section 44 the debenture must be taken to be valid vis-à-vis the Bank. Indeed, Mr Hill-Smith himself accepted in the course of argument that section 44 can at least be taken as reflecting the common law principles; and so would extend (in favour of a purchaser) to a document purporting to be signed by the two directors in circumstances of apparent authority on the part of Mr Jewson.

3. An amendment of the company's articles will not excuse a breach of contract

A company cannot, by altering its articles, justify a breach of contract.

[3.16] Baily v British Equitable Assurance Co [1904] 1 Ch 374 (Court of Appeal)

The claimant, who was not a member of the defendant company, had taken out a life policy with the company. The company's by-laws provided that profits from such policies should be distributed to policyholders without deduction. In 1903 it was proposed to register the company under the Companies Act, with articles of association altering the by-laws so as to authorise the transfer of a percentage of such profits to a reserve fund. The plaintiff claimed a declaration that his policy was not affected by the altered articles. Kekewich J and the Court of Appeal granted the declaration.[42]

> The judgment of the Court of Appeal (VAUGHAN WILLIAMS, STIRLING and COZENS-HARDY LJJ) was read by COZENS-HARDY LJ: It is...contended that, as the company was registered under s 209 of the Companies Act 1862,[43] it thereby acquired power by special resolution to alter...all or any of the by-laws, and that the plaintiff is seeking to restrain the company from altering by-law no 4 in exercise of this statutory power. And it is said that, apart from the statute, the deed of settlement itself contained a power to alter the by-law, of which power the plaintiff had notice. We cannot assent to this argument. As between the members of a company and the company, no doubt this proposition is to some extent true. The rights of a shareholder in respect of his shares, except so far as may be protected by the memorandum of association, are by statute made liable to be altered by special resolution: see *Allen v Gold Reefs of West Africa Ltd* **[4.22]**.
>
> But the case of a contract between an outsider and the company is entirely different, and even a shareholder must be regarded as an outsider in so far as he contracts with the company otherwise than in respect of his shares. It would be dangerous to hold that in a contract of loan or a contract of service or a contract of insurance validly entered into by a company there is any greater power of variation of the rights and liabilities of the parties than would exist if, instead of the company, the contracting party had been an individual. A company cannot, by altering its articles, justify a breach of contract...
>
> In the present case there was a contract for value between the plaintiff and the company, relating to the future profits of a particular branch of the company's business, and the company ought not to be allowed, by special resolution or otherwise, to break that contract. The appeal must be dismissed.

➤ Note

A contract may, of course, be construed as incorporating the terms of the articles whatever they may be and however they may be varied from time to time, just as a person joining a club is taken to agree that he will abide by the club's rules as they may be formulated at any given time. An alteration of the articles would then not be a breach of contract by the company at all (unless it were held to violate an implied term that the company would not alter its articles *mala fide* or unreasonably). *Baily*'s case went to the House of Lords, where the decision of the Court of Appeal was reversed on the basis of such a construction.[44]

---

[42] This decision was reversed by the House of Lords on the basis of a different construction of the policy: *British Equitable Assurance Co Ltd v Baily* [1906] AC 35, HL. But the validity of the passage cited was not disputed by the House of Lords; and, indeed, Lord Macnaghten expressly approved it.

[43] This section directed the compulsory re-registration of certain companies under the 1862 Act.

[44] See *British Equitable Assurance Co Ltd v Baily* [1906] AC 35, HL. Also see *Shuttleworth v Cox Bros & Co (Maidenhead) Ltd* **[6.06]**. A similar distinction was made in *Equitable Life Assurance Society v Hyman* **[4.03]**: should the contract containing the 'guarantee' be read as subject to the discretionary power conferred by the article in question, or would an exercise of the discretion that was inconsistent with the guarantee be a breach of contract?

Summary of corporate contracting

This learning on corporate contracting can be summarised as follows. If the person making the contract for the company has actual authority, the contract will bind the company. The agent will not be in breach of his duties.

If there is no actual authority, but the contract is binding by operation of the law's deeming provisions (eg by reason of s 40, or ostensible authority, or the indoor management rule) then the contract is fully binding. However, the company might sue its delinquent director (agent) for breach of duty, and/or breach of service contract (if there is one). The company might also terminate any such service contract for repudiatory breach. Commonly, such contracts, when terminated, require the director to resign his office. Even if it does not, the company can remove the director from office under CA 2006 ss 168–169.

If the company is not bound, it might still sue the director for breach of duty/service contract, and seek to get rid of him. The disappointed outsider might, if it is financially worthwhile, sue the director for breach of warranty of authority.

And in determining whether a particular purported contract is indeed binding on the company, revisit 'The framework for assessing effective contractual engagement', p 91. The steps are as follows:

(i)   Does the company have actual or deemed capacity? The answer will inevitably be yes for a CA 2006-registered company: see s 31, and s 39 if needs be.

(ii) Does the agent have actual authority (express or implied)? Has that authority been abused? Does that fact deny the existence of actual authority? If actual authority exists, the contract is binding—the analysis can stop here.

(iii) If the agent has no actual authority, does s 40 remedy the defect and make the contract binding (but note s 41)? If yes, the contract is binding—the analysis can stop here. (But the director can be sued by the company for breach of duty: s 171.)

(iv) If the above do not apply, then is there ostensible authority? (Recall the prerequisites: a representation, by someone with actual authority, reasonable and factual reliance.) If ostensible authority makes the contract binding—the analysis can stop here. (But the director can be sued by the company for breach of duty: s 171.)

(v)   If the above do not apply, then does 'the rule in *Turquand's* case' (the 'indoor management rule') assist? Is reliance reasonable? If yes, the contract is binding—the analysis can stop here. (But consider who, if anyone, might be sued by the company for breach of duty.)

(vi) If the above do not apply, then has the company ratified the deal? (The requirements are considered in Chapter 7.) If yes, the contract is binding—the analysis can stop here.

(vii) If the above do not apply, then the contract is *not* binding. If assets have been transferred under the purported contract, then there will be claims in unjust enrichment for their recovery. The third party may also consider suing the agent for breach of warranty of authority.

➤ Question

Has the law got the balance right (ie the commercial convenience of those dealing with companies versus the need to protect the company from unscrupulous agents)?

Pre-incorporation contracts

Before leaving the issue of corporate contracting, one further practical matter deserves mention. It is quite common for negotiations about a contract to take place, and for a contract (or what purports to be a contract) to be made, when one of the parties to this 'contract' is a company which has not yet been formed. Sometimes, the fact that the company has not been incorporated may be known to all concerned and may even be stated in the contract; on the other hand, there may have been some misunderstanding or even a misrepresentation about its existence. Since a 'non-entity' cannot have legal rights or duties ascribed to it, such situations can potentially give rise to all sorts of legal problems. Some of these are resolved by CA 2006 s 51, see following, but not all.

As an illustration, in *Cramaso LLP v Viscount Reidhaven's Trustees* [2014] AC 1093, the Supreme Court considered an analogous question in the case of a limited liability partnership which had yet to be formed at the time of making an alleged misrepresentation; it was held by Lord Reed (with whom Lords Mance, Clarke, Carnwath and Toulson agreed) that the representation may be treated by law as 'having a continuing effect' [21] and that 'in principle, an inference can be drawn from the parties' conduct that they proceeded with the negotiation and conclusion of the contract on the basis that the accuracy of the representation continued to be asserted by the representor, implicitly if not expressly, after the identity of the prospective contracting party had changed' [25].

➤ Questions

1. What business reasons might cause people to make a pre-incorporation contract, rather than form the company first and then conclude the deal?

2. How far would it help to solve the problems to use a ready-made company (Note 8 following Companies Act 2006 s 51, p 135; Note 2 following *HA Stephenson & Son Ltd v Gillanders, Arbuthnot & Co* [1.08], p 31)?

Companies Act 2006 s 51

51 Pre-incorporation contracts, deeds and obligations

A contract that purports to be made by or on behalf of a company at a time when the company has not been formed has effect, subject to any agreement to the contrary, as one made with the person purporting to act for the company or as agent for it, and he is personally liable on the contract accordingly.

. . .

➤ Notes

1. This provision (like its predecessors, CA 1985 s 36C and European Communities Act 1972 s 9(2)) was introduced to implement Art 7 of the First EU Company Law Directive. The aim was to eliminate many of the problems apparent from earlier common law precedents. For example, it seemed that if the purported contract was, on its face, *with* a non-existent company, there could be no contract at all with the company (as it did not exist) and no binding obligations on the promoters (as that was not intended), so third parties were left without a remedy under the contract:[45] *Newborne v Sensolid (Great Britain) Ltd* [1954] 1 QB 45, CA 2006. On the other hand, this rule did not protect promoters who acted as principals (clearly), nor, it seemed, promoters who explicitly acted as agents on behalf of their proposed company: see *Kelner v Baxter* (1866) LR 2 CP 174 (Court of Common Pleas), where the promoters were held liable *on the contract* (ie as parties to it).

The contrasting conclusions in these two cases led to some fine distinctions being made by commentators, and to arguments about whether the issue was one of form or substance.

---

[45] It is a separate question whether these third parties might sue the promoters in damages for breach of warranty of authority: see Note 2.

In *Phonogram Ltd v Lane* [1982] QB 938, Oliver LJ suggested that the distinction was based on the intention of the parties at the time the contract was formed:[46]

> The question I think in each case is what is the real intent as revealed by the contract? Does the contract purport to be one which is directly between the supposed principal and the other party, or does it purport to be one between the agent himself—albeit acting for a supposed principal—and the other party? In other words, what we have to look at is whether the agent intended himself to be a party to the contract.

This was cited with approval by Dillon LJ in *Cotronic (UK) Ltd v Dezonie* [1991] BCC 200 at 205, on facts which lay outside CA 2006 s 51 and its predecessors. In those circumstances, all these cases remain relevant.

2. On the other hand, where CA 2006 s 51 applies, many of the difficulties have been settled, for all practical purposes, by the interpretation put on what is now CA 2006 s 51 by the Court of Appeal in *Phonogram Ltd v Lane* [1982] QB 938. In particular, CA 2006 s 51 expressly renders the agent personally liable on the contract, 'subject to any agreement to the contrary'. Lord Denning MR said:

> The words 'subject to any agreement to the contrary' mean—as Shaw LJ suggested in the course of the argument—'unless otherwise agreed'. If there was an express agreement that the man who was signing was not to be liable, the section would not apply. But, unless there is a clear exclusion of personal liability, [CA 2006 s 51] should be given its full effect. It means that in all cases such as the present, where a person purports to contract on behalf of a company not yet formed, then however he expresses his signature he himself is personally liable on the contract.

3. Recently, in *Hepburn v Revenue and Customs Commissioners* [2013] UKFTT 445, First-tier Tribunal (Tax Chamber), the appellant had agreed to provide consultancy services to a company through the medium of a limited company which had yet to be formed at the time of the agreement. The services were performed and the fees were paid to solicitors, who held the same for the benefit of the limited company until it was eventually formed. The question for the appeal was whether the fees (which had been recognised and taxed as profits in the limited company's accounts) fell to be taxed again as the appellant's income. Insofar as CA 1986 s 36C [CA 2006 s 51] was concerned, it was held that the 'subject to any agreement to the contrary' proviso would be applicable, because although the appellant, on the face of the agreement, was personally liable in accordance with CA 1986 s 36C, there was never any intention on anyone's part that the appellant should become personally entitled to any part of the fees as an individual. The common intention, on the contrary, was that it should be paid to the limited company, in which the appellant was to hold a majority interest.

4. The predecessors to CA 2006 s 51 were criticised because, it was said, they focused largely on the liability of the 'agent' and were, at best, ambiguous on the question of what *rights*, if any, were conferred on this person. Those doubts have been largely resolved by the decision in *Braymist Ltd v Wise Finance Co Ltd* [2002] EWCA Civ 127, [2002] Ch 273, CA, which held that the provision not only confers liabilities on the agent, but also rights of enforcement. In *Hepburn v Revenue and Customs Commissioners* [2013] UKFTT 445, First-tier Tribunal (Tax Chamber), CA 1985 s 36C was described by Judge J Gordon Reid QC as a 'statutory novation of rights and liabilities'.

---

[46] [1982] QB 938 at 945.

This broad interpretation of CA 2006 s 51 leaves the underlying contract subject to all the normal rules of contract. In particular, if a misrepresentation about the identity of the counterparty to the contract (ie the identity of the purported company) induced the other party to enter into the contract, to its detriment, then the other party is entitled to rescind the contract. In *Braymist Ltd v Wise Finance Co Ltd*, the court held that the identity of the vendor (whether it was Braymist or the firm of solicitors) was immaterial to the purchaser, and so the solicitors (the agents who had signed the contract) could enforce the contract of sale.

5. The cases cited previously do not decide the alternative question of whether an agent who has *not* contracted personally might be liable to the opposite party in damages for breach of warranty of authority on the principle of *Collen v Wright*.[47] Parker J at first instance in *Newborne*'s case[48] appears to have doubted this 'because the principal is not in existence', but this begs the question: there are strong *obiter dicta* to the contrary in the Australian case of *Black v Smallwood*;[49] and the well-known case of *McRae v Commonwealth Disposals Commission*[50] plainly establishes that a person may impliedly warrant that what is non-existent exists.

6. A company cannot, by adoption or ratification, obtain the benefit of a contract purportedly made on its behalf before it came into existence. A new contract must be made after its incorporation in the same terms as the old one: *Natal Land Co & Colonization Ltd v Pauline Colliery and Development Syndicate Ltd* [1904] AC 120, PC. CA 2006 retains this rule, in that the contract must be novated; it cannot be ratified. It cannot be ratified, because, at the time the contract was made, the company itself could not have validly entered into the agreement—the company did not exist, and so could have no agents, and cannot now attempt retrospectively to authorise purported agents. Novation may be express or implied.

The Jenkins Committee in its Report (Cmnd 1749, 1962, paras 44, 54(b)) considered the law unsatisfactory and anomalous, and recommended that 'a company should be enabled unilaterally to adopt contracts which purport to be made on its behalf or in its name prior to incorporation, and thereby become a party thereto to the same extent as if the contract had been made after incorporation . . .'. Many Commonwealth countries have enacted provisions which follow the lines of this recommendation, and a similar reform was projected for the UK in the abortive Companies Bill of 1973, but this proposal was not revived when the First EU Directive was implemented; and so the *Natal Land* case is still good law.

7. The traditional doctrine of privity of contract (which states that a contract cannot confer benefits or impose obligations upon someone who is not a party) could be seen as a further obstacle to allowing a company to enforce a pre-incorporation contract. The doctrine has now, in part, been abrogated by the Contracts (Rights of Third Parties) Act 1999, following a recommendation of the Law Commission (Law Com No 242, 1996). This Act allows a person who is not a party to a contract to enforce a term, in certain circumstances, provided that that person is sufficiently identified; and s 1(3) expressly states that the person need not be in existence when the contract is entered into. The Law Commission in its report (paras 8.9–8.16) acknowledged that any change made to the privity doctrine might have some impact on pre-incorporation contracts, but took the view that any considered reform of the latter topic should be dealt with separately as a matter of company law. Of course, since the 1999 Act is concerned only with the

---

[47] (1857) 8 E & B 647.
[48] [1954] 1 QB 45 at 47.
[49] [1966] ALR 744.
[50] (1950) 84 CLR 377.

enforcement of *rights* by a third party, and not with the imposing of obligations, there is no way in which that Act could be invoked in order to make a company a party in the full sense to a pre-incorporation contract. However, there is scope for its application in a more limited sense—that is, where such a contract includes a term which expressly or purportedly confers a benefit on the unformed company. This could extend to the parties agreeing (for a consideration) that the company, when formed, should have the option of entering into a contract on predetermined terms.

8. As already noted, it is very common for those wishing to incorporate a business to acquire a ready-made company for the purpose, possibly changing its name if the existing name is not thought suitable. In *Oshkosh B'Gosh Inc v Dan Marbel Inc Ltd* [1989] BCLC 507, CA, Mr Craze bought a company named E Ltd 'off the shelf' and later changed its name to DM Ltd. Before the change of name was registered the company, acting through Craze, bought goods from the plaintiff. In an action to make Craze personally liable it was held that s 9(2) of the European Communities Act 1972 [CA 2006 s 51] could not be applied because the company had been formed (albeit under another name) at the time when the contract was made: the issue of an amended certificate of incorporation under CA 1985 s 28(6) [CA 2006 s 80(3)] did not imply that the company had been re-formed or re-incorporated. Again, in *Badgerhill Properties Ltd v Cottrell* [1991] BCLC 805, CA 1985 s 36C [CA 2006 s 51] was held to be inapplicable where the company was in existence but had been described by an incorrect name; a similar result was reached in *Manufacturing Excellence Ltd v Hemming (t/a Hemming-Mann Ltd)* [2013] EWHC 2825 (QB), regarding contractual restraint of trade provisions. In contrast, in *Cotronic (UK) Ltd v Dezonie* [1991] BCLC 721, CA, a defendant escaped personal liability under CA 1985 s 36C for a different reason. He made a contract in 1986 in the name of W Ltd in ignorance of the fact that W Ltd had been struck off the register under CA 1985 s 652 [CA 2006 s 1000] in 1981 and had ceased to exist. A new company, also named W Ltd, was incorporated in 1989 to continue the business. The court held that he could not be made liable under s 36C because he had purported to make the contract on behalf of the old company and not the new one, which no one had thought about forming in 1986.

➤ Questions

1. Could any or all of the difficulties revealed by the *Natal Land* case have been met by Mrs de Carrey *assigning* her right to the lease to the company after it had been formed?

2. It is possible to create a valid trust for the benefit of an unborn child. Could the problems revealed by the *Natal Land* case have been surmounted by having someone enter into an agreement as trustee, rather than as agent, for the yet to be formed company?

Corporate gifts

Problems of some complexity may arise when a company makes a gift, such as a donation to a charity or a political party, or when it enters into a transaction which, although perhaps not strictly gratuitous, has an altruistic character—such as guaranteeing someone else's bank overdraft. Agreements to pay remuneration to a company's staff or officers may also be open to challenge (or, at least, arouse suspicion); and, *a fortiori*, the payment of bonuses and pensions in recognition of past services may also be called into question as being unauthorised or unmerited.

The cases show that the courts have, over the years, viewed such payments with no great enthusiasm, and sometimes with outright hostility. The reasons for this are varied. Creditors, of course, stand to be prejudiced if corporate assets are given away. Naturally, therefore, the courts will be alert to the potential need to intervene indirectly on their behalf (eg in a suit brought by a liquidator) and to seek to upset such transactions, especially in cases where the company has become insolvent not long after the gifts were made.

Perhaps the strongest factor influencing the judges, more especially in the Victorian period, has been the difficulty of reconciling notions of altruism with the capitalist ethos. It seems to have been accepted practically without question until only a decade or two ago that the sole purpose of any company was to make the greatest possible profits for its members. A corporate gift which diminishes profits violates this philosophy, unless it can be justified on the ground that it is likely to bring a greater benefit in the longer term. Nowadays, there is greater support for the view that 'responsible' companies ought not to neglect 'wider' interests such as those of their employees, clients and customers, the community, the environment, and so on. However, the 'members' money' attitude can still influence questions such as the propriety of corporate gifts to charity or donations to political parties: why, it is asked, should company directors, or even majority members, decide where this benevolence is to be bestowed, when there are likely to be other members who would choose to do something quite different with their share of the money if it were paid out to them?

The decision in *Re Horsley & Weight Ltd* **[4.31]** confirms that the making of gratuitous payments can be construed as a corporate object if the company's old-style memorandum was framed in sufficiently explicit terms. But where that authority is not clear (or where it might be abused), the courts can challenge the disposition by recourse to the rules on directors' authority and abuse of their powers, the 'maintenance of capital' rules ('Controls over a company's distribution of capital', pp 533ff), the statutory 'wrongful trading' provision, etc, in order to counter the perceived misapplication of corporate assets.

Note that CA 2006 s 366 now prohibits companies from making political donations or incurring political expenditure unless the transaction or the expenditure is authorised by the members of the company. Certain exemptions are specified, with various conditions and ceiling amounts specified.

Unanticipated problems can also arise where the company receives a gift. Unless the intention of the donor is very clear, the 'gift' may presumed to be held on resulting trust for the donor: see *Prest v Petrodel Resources Ltd* **[2.01]**.

Tort liability

There are two routes to finding a company liable in tort. The company may be *primarily* liable for committing the tort, just as any natural person might be, and the usual consequences will follow. To establish such primary liability it is essential to identify the person (or persons) whose acts will count as the acts of the company (as in the *Meridian Global* case **[3.01]**, using Lord Hoffmann's attribution rules), and then to establish that those acts are sufficient to attract liability in tort.

The second route to fixing a company with liability in tort is to find the company *vicariously liable* for the tort. In this case, it is essential to find some individual who is primarily liable for the tort (and who might be sued personally by the claimant). Once that is done, it is then necessary to explain why the company is vicariously liable for that person's acts or omissions. Employers and principals are typically held to be vicariously liable for the acts of their employees or agents in the conduct of their employment or agency (but not for their acts outside this context, of course, although this is a difficult line to draw—see *Dubai Aluminium Company v Salaam* [**3.18**]). Vicarious liability has been described as 'a loss distribution device based on the grounds of social and economic policy'.[51] Liability attaches to the company not because it is regarded as having committed the tort, but because it has created the risk that the tort would be committed,[52] and so, for example, because of the close connection between the nature of the employment and the particular tort and looking at the matter in the round, it is just and reasonable to hold the employer liable.[53] It follows that the company's capacity to commit the tort is irrelevant.[54] Where vicarious liability is established, the individual and the company are jointly liable to the victim for the tort.[55]

One of the problems in this area is whether the individual who 'acts for the company' and whose acts attract *primary* liability in tort on the company, should also be primarily liable *personally* for the same tort (since the facts will usually, but not always, enable that to be established). If this is always the case, then the corporate form is not quite the insulating device in tort that it is in contract (where an agent acting for the company can fasten liability on the company while avoiding any personal obligations under the contract that is negotiated). For a potential resolution of the issues, see *Williams v Natural Life Health Foods* [**3.19**] and *Standard Chartered Bank v Pakistan National Shipping Corpn (No 2)* [**3.20**].

The following cases illustrate the operation of these rules.

A company may be primarily liable in tort, even for acts that it is not authorised or permitted to undertake.

[3.17] Campbell v Paddington Corpn [1911] 1 KB 869
(King's Bench Divisional Court)

The plaintiff occupied premises in Edgware Road of which the balcony and front rooms could be let to persons wishing to view public processions. She had agreed to let a balcony to Mr Albert Ginger to watch the funeral procession of King Edward VII, but had to release him from the contract when the defendant corporation unlawfully erected a stand in the street outside, which blocked the view. In the county court, she was awarded £90 damages. The Corporation's appeal to the Divisional Court was dismissed.

AVORY J: Three objections are taken to this verdict. First, it is said that the defendants, the mayor, aldermen and councillors of the metropolitan borough of Paddington, being a corporation, are not liable because the borough council had no legal right to do what they did, and therefore the corporation cannot be sued. This stand was erected in pursuance of a formal resolution of the borough council. To say that, because the borough council has no legal right to erect it, therefore the corporation cannot be sued, is to say that no corporation can ever be sued for any tort or wrong. The only way in which this corporation can act is by its council, and the resolution of the council is the authentic act of the corporation. If the view of the defendants were correct no company could ever be sued if the directors of the company after resolution did an act which the company by its memorandum of association had no power to do. That would be absurd. The first objection therefore fails, and the defendants are liable to be sued...

---

[51] Lord Millett in *Dubai Aluminium Co Ltd v Salaam* [2002] UKHL 48, [2003] 2 AC 366 at [107].

[52] Lord Nicholls in *Dubai Aluminium Co Ltd v Salaam* [2002] UKHL 48, [2003] 2 AC 366 at [21].

[53] Lord Steyn in *Bernard v AG of Jamaica* [2004] UKPC 47 at [18].

[54] Eg a company may be vicariously liable for an employee's defamatory libel, even though the company itself could not have acted with the necessary malice: *Citizens' Life Assurance Co Ltd v Brown* [1904] AC 423.

[55] *Lister v Romford Ice & Cold Storage Co Ltd* [1957] AC 555, HL.

[The second and third objections are not material.]

LUSH J:... [W]here the wrongful act is done without the express authority of the corporation, an authority from the corporation to do it cannot be implied if the act is outside the statutory powers of the corporation. That principle has no application to a case where the corporation has resolved to do and has, in the only way in which it can do any act, actually done the thing which is unlawful and which causes the damage complained of.

➤ Notes

1. Also see *Director General of Fair Trading v Pioneer Concrete (UK) Ltd* [1995] 1 AC 456, referred to in *Meridian Global* [3.01]; and more recently, *Back Office Ltd v Percival* [2013] EWHC 1385 (QB).

2. *Campbell's* case concerns the primary liability of a company in tort. The principle established by the case extends to acts which are unlawful, as well as to acts which, prior to the coming into force of CA 2006 and its predecessors in Companies Act 1989 (CA 1989), would have been beyond a company's capacity under the *ultra vires* doctrine ('Capacity: what is a company legally set up to do?', p 92). The point is that the company's primary liability in tort cannot be limited to those things that the company is authorised to do. The issue, rather, is whether the acts of the company's human agents count as acts of the company (under the *Meridian Global* [3.01] test), and then whether those acts constitute a tort. It follows that a company may sometimes be held primarily liable for a tort even when none of its human actors commits the same tort. For example, in *WB Anderson and Sons Ltd v Rhodes (Liverpool) Ltd* [1967] 2 All ER 850, Rhodes was held liable for negligent misrepresentation. The Rhodes employee who made the representation was not negligent, as he could only have known the true facts (on a buyer's creditworthiness) if either Rhodes' manager or its bookkeeper had told him, but they negligently did not. They, on the other hand, could not be liable for negligent misrepresentation because they had not made any representations. Nevertheless, Rhodes itself was liable for the tort.[56] (Is this appropriate, and why?)

A company is often, although not invariably, vicariously liable for the torts of its agents and employees even when the acts constituting those torts are unauthorised or even illegal.

[3.18] Dubai Aluminium Company Ltd v Salaam [2002] UKHL 48, [2003] 2 AC 366 (House of Lords)

The facts appear in Lord Nicholls's opinion. This case concerned the Amhurst partnership, 'the firm', not a company, but the general principles remain relevant.

LORD NICHOLLS:

19. Vicarious liability is concerned with the responsibility of the firm [or a company] to other persons for wrongful acts done by a partner [or company agent or employee] while acting in the ordinary course of the partnership [or company] business or with the authority of his co-partners. At first sight this might seem something of a contradiction in terms. Partners do not usually agree with each other to commit wrongful acts. Partners are not normally authorised to engage in wrongful conduct. Indeed, if vicarious liability of a firm for acts done by a partner acting in the ordinary course of the business of the firm were confined to acts authorised in every particular, the reach of vicarious liability would be short indeed. Especially would this be so with dishonesty and other intentional wrongdoing, as distinct from negligence. Similarly restricted would be the

---

[56] And perhaps could have sued its own employees in negligence, for the loss caused.

vicarious responsibility of employers for wrongful acts done by employees in the course of their employment. Like considerations apply to vicarious liability for employees.

20. Take the present case. The essence of the claim advanced by Dubai Aluminium against Mr Amhurst is that he and Mr Salaam engaged in a criminal conspiracy to defraud Dubai Aluminium. Mr Amhurst drafted the consultancy agreement and other agreements in furtherance of this conspiracy. Needless to say, Mr Amhurst had no authority from his partners to conduct himself in this manner. Nor is there any question of conduct of this nature being part of the ordinary course of the business of the Amhurst firm. Mr Amhurst had authority to draft commercial agreements. He had no authority to draft a commercial agreement for the dishonest purpose of furthering a criminal conspiracy.

21. However, this latter fact does not of itself mean that the firm is exempt from liability for his wrongful conduct. Whether an act or omission was done in the ordinary course of a firm's business cannot be decided simply by considering whether the partner was authorised by his co-partners to do the very act he did. The reason for this lies in the legal policy underlying vicarious liability. The underlying legal policy is based on the recognition that carrying on a business enterprise necessarily involves risks to others. It involves the risk that others will be harmed by wrongful acts committed by the agents through whom the business is carried on. When those risks ripen into loss, it is just that the business should be responsible for compensating the person who has been wronged.

22. This policy reason dictates that liability for agents should not be strictly confined to acts done with the employer's authority. Negligence can be expected to occur from time to time. Everyone makes mistakes at times. Additionally, it is a fact of life, and therefore to be expected by those who carry on businesses, that sometimes their agents may exceed the bounds of their authority or even defy express instructions. It is fair to allocate risk of losses thus arising to the businesses rather than leave those wronged with the sole remedy, of doubtful value, against the individual employee who committed the wrong. To this end, the law has given the concept of 'ordinary course of employment' an extended scope.

23 If, then, authority is not the touchstone, what is? Lord Denning MR once said that on this question the cases are baffling: see *Morris v C W Martin & Sons Ltd* [1966] 1 QB 716, 724. Perhaps the best general answer is that the wrongful conduct must be so closely connected with acts the partner or employee was authorised to do that, for the purpose of the liability of the firm or the employer to third parties, the wrongful conduct *may fairly and properly be regarded* as done by the partner while acting in the ordinary course of the firm's business or the employee's employment. Lord Millett said as much in *Lister v Hesley Hall Ltd* [2002] 1 AC 215, 245. So did Lord Steyn, at pp 223–224 and 230....

24. In these formulations the phrases 'may fairly and properly be regarded', 'can be said' and 'can fairly be regarded' betoken a value judgment by the court. The conclusion is a conclusion of law, based on primary facts, rather than a simple question of fact.

25. This 'close connection' test focuses attention in the right direction. But it affords no guidance on the type or degree of connection which will normally be regarded as sufficiently close to prompt the legal conclusion that the risk of the wrongful act occurring, and any loss flowing from the wrongful act, should fall on the firm or employer rather than the third party who was wronged. It provides no clear assistance on when, to use Professor Fleming's phraseology, an incident is to be regarded as sufficiently work-related, as distinct from personal: see Fleming, *The Law of Torts*, 9th ed (1998), p 427. Again, the well known dictum of Lord Dunedin in *Plumb v Cobden Flour Mills Co Ltd* [1914] AC 62, 67, draws a distinction between prohibitions which limit the sphere of employment and those which only deal with conduct within the sphere of employment. This leaves open how to recognise the one from the other.

26. This lack of precision is inevitable, given the infinite range of circumstances where the issue arises. The crucial feature or features, either producing or negativing vicarious liability, vary widely from one case or type of case to the next. Essentially the court makes an evaluative judgment in each case, having regard to all the circumstances and, importantly, having regard also to the assistance provided by previous court decisions. In this field the latter form of assistance is particularly valuable.

27. So I turn to authority, noting that the present appeal concerns dishonest conduct. Historically the courts have been less ready to find vicarious liability in cases of employee dishonesty than in cases of negligence....

30. I turn, then, to cases such as the present where there is no question of reliance or 'holding out', or of the employer having assumed a direct responsibility to the wronged person. Take a case where an employee does an act of a type for which he is employed but, perhaps through a misplaced excess of zeal, he does so dishonestly. He seeks to promote his employer's interests, in the sphere in which he is employed, but using dishonest means. Not surprisingly, the courts have held that in such a case the employer may be liable to the injured third party just as much as in a case where the employee acted negligently. Whether done negligently or dishonestly the wrongful act comprised a wrongful and unauthorised mode of doing an act authorised by the employer, in the oft repeated language of the 'Salmond' formulation: see Salmond, *Law of Torts*, 1st ed (1907), p 83....

32. The limits of this broad principle should be noted. A distinction is to be drawn between cases...where the employee was engaged, however misguidedly, in furthering his employer's business, and cases where the employee is engaged solely in pursuing his own interests: on a 'frolic of his own', in the language of the time-honoured catch phrase. In the former type of case the employee, while seeking to promote his employer's interests, does an act of a kind he is authorised to do. Then it may well be appropriate to attribute responsibility for his act to the employer, even though the manner of performance was not authorised or, indeed, was prohibited. The matter stands differently when the employee is engaged only in furthering his own interests, as distinct from those of his employer....Then the mere fact that the act was of a kind the employee was authorised to do will not, of itself, fasten liability on the employer. In the absence of 'holding out' and reliance, there is no reason in principle why it should. Nor would this accord with authority. To attribute vicarious liability to the employer in such a case of dishonesty would be contrary to the familiar line of 'driver' cases, where an employer has been held not liable for the negligent driving of an employee who was employed as a driver but at the time of the accident was engaged in driving his employer's vehicle on a frolic of his own.

➤ Question

The analysis in the preceding case was based entirely on vicarious liability, but could the company equally well have been found primarily liable for the deceit on the basis of the attribution rules in *Meridian Global* **[3.01]**? This was certainly the conclusion in *Stone & Rolls* **[3.33]**.

➤ Note

It is essential, if the company is to be held vicariously liable for a tort, that someone within the company is found primarily liable for the same tort. Contrast this with the requirements where the company itself is held primarily liable. Then the individuals within the company may or may not also be primarily liable. All depends on the facts. This is the issue in the two cases which follow.

The company may be personally (or primarily or directly) liable for a tort in circumstances where the agent is not personally liable, and so vicarious liability is not an alternative finding.

[3.19] Williams v Natural Life Health Foods Ltd [1998] 1 WLR 830 (House of Lords)

Williams and his partner approached the defendant company with a view to obtaining a franchise from it to run a health food shop in Rugby. They were given a brochure and, later, detailed financial projections for the scheme. Encouraged by these, they entered into a franchise agreement. The project was a failure. The advice they had been given was negligent, and although the company would have been held liable for their loss, it had been dissolved. The plaintiffs therefore sought to have the company's managing director and principal shareholder, Mistlin, held personally liable. Mistlin's expertise had been highlighted in the brochure, and he had played a prominent part in producing the projections, but he had played no part in negotiation of the franchise agreement with them. They succeeded at first instance, and by a majority in the Court of Appeal, but this ruling was reversed by the House of Lords.

LORD STEYN:... What matters is not that the liability of the shareholders of a company is limited but that a company is a separate entity, distinct from its directors, servants or other agents. The trader who incorporates a company to which he transfers his business creates a legal person on whose behalf he may afterwards act as director. For present purposes, his position is the same as if he had sold his business to another individual and agreed to act on his behalf. Thus the issue in this case is not peculiar to companies. Whether the principal is a company or a natural person, someone acting on his behalf may incur personal liability in tort as well as imposing vicarious or attributed liability upon his principal. But in order to establish personal liability under the principle of *Hedley Byrne* [[1964] AC 465, HL], which requires the existence of a special relationship between plaintiff and tortfeasor, it is not sufficient that there should have been a special relationship with the principal. There must have been an assumption of responsibility such as to create a special relationship with the director or employee himself....

The touchstone of liability is not the state of mind of the defendant. An objective test means that the primary focus must be on things said or done by the defendant or on his behalf in dealings with the plaintiff. Obviously, the impact of what a defendant says or does must be judged in the light of the relevant contextual scene. Subject to this qualification, the primary focus must be on exchanges (in which term I include statements and conduct) which cross the line between the defendant and the plaintiff. Sometimes such an issue arises in a simple bilateral relationship. In the present case a triangular position is under consideration: the prospective franchisees, the franchisor company, and the director. In such a case where the personal liability of the director is in question, the internal arrangements between a director and his company cannot be the foundation of a director's personal liability in tort. The inquiry must be whether the director, or anybody on his behalf, conveyed directly or indirectly to the prospective franchisees that the director assumed personal responsibility towards the prospective franchisees....

... [I]t is important to make clear that a director of a contracting company may only be held liable where it is established by evidence that he assumed personal liability and that there was the necessary reliance....

Mr Mistlin owned and controlled the company. The company held itself out as having the expertise to provide reliable advice to franchisees. The brochure made clear that this expertise derived from Mr Mistlin's experience in the operation of the Salisbury shop. In my view these circumstances were insufficient to make Mr Mistlin personally liable to the plaintiffs. Stripped to essentials, the reasons of Langley J [the trial judge], the reasons of the majority in the Court of Appeal and the arguments of counsel for the plaintiffs can be considered under two headings. First, it is said that the terms of the brochure, and in particular its description of the role of Mr Mistlin, are sufficient to amount to an assumption of responsibility by Mr Mistlin. In his dissenting judgment [in the Court of Appeal] Sir Patrick Russell rightly pointed out that in a small one-man company 'the managing director will almost inevitably be the one possessed of qualities essential to the functioning of the company'. By itself this factor does not convey that the managing director is willing to be personally answerable to the customers of the company. Secondly, great emphasis was placed on the fact that it was made clear to the franchisees that Mr Mistlin's expertise derived from his experience in running the Salisbury shop for his own account. Hirst

LJ summarised the point by saying that 'the relevant knowledge and experience was entirely his qua Mr Mistlin, and not his qua director'. The point will simply not bear the weight put on it. Postulate a food expert who over ten years gains experience in advising customers on his own account. Then he incorporates his business as a company and he so advises his customers. Surely, it cannot be right to say that in the new situation his earlier experience on his own account is indicative of an assumption of personal responsibility towards his customers. In the present case there were no personal dealings between Mr Mistlin and the plaintiffs. There were no exchanges or conduct crossing the line which could have conveyed to the plaintiffs that Mr Mistlin was willing to assume personal responsibility to them. Contrary to the submissions of counsel for the plaintiffs, I am also satisfied that there was not even evidence that the plaintiffs believed that Mr Mistlin was undertaking personal responsibility to them. Certainly, there was nothing in the circumstances to show that the plaintiffs could reasonably have looked to Mr Mistlin for indemnification of any loss. For these reasons I would reject the principal argument of counsel for the plaintiffs....

LORDS GOFF OF CHIEVELEY, HOFFMANN, CLYDE and HUTTON concurred.

➤ Note

Note that this conclusion is critically dependent on the particular tort in issue. Here the claim was for negligent misrepresentation (as in *Hedley Byrne*). *This* tort is only committed by defendants who have assumed responsibility for the statements made: Mr Mistlin had not assumed such personal responsibility, although his company had. By contrast, torts such as deceit do not have the same limiting requirements before an individual or a company can be made personally liable. The next extract demonstrates this.

[3.20] Standard Chartered Bank v Pakistan National Shipping Corporation (No 2) [2000] 1 Lloyd's Rep 218 (Court of Appeal), overruled in [2002] UKHL 43, [2003] 1 AC 959 (House of Lords)

Mr Mehra, the managing director of Oakprime Ltd, knowingly made a false statement to Standard Chartered Bank (SCB) that enabled Oakprime Ltd to obtain payment under a letter of credit. To do this he persuaded the ship owners, Pakistan National Shipping Corporation (PNSC), to backdate a bill of lading. SCB did not know that the bill was falsely dated. When SCB sought payment from the bank that had issued the letter of credit, it refused because of discrepancies in the documents. SCB sued PNSC, Oakprime Ltd and Mr Mehra for deceit. It was successful against all three at first instance. PNSC and Mr Mehra appealed, and, in the Court of Appeal, Mr Mehra was successful. SCB successfully appealed. The House of Lords considered a number of issues. The only one of interest here is whether Mr Mehra was personally liable in deceit, or whether the deceit was only that of Oakprime Ltd. The judgments of the Court of Appeal are extracted here, even though overruled, as the comparison clarifies the analysis adopted in the House of Lords.

ALDOUS LJ [*Note this analysis is now overruled by the House of Lords.*]:

88. Since *Salomon v Salomon & Co Ltd* **[2.02]**, companies have been recognised as separate legal entities to their shareholders, their directors and their employees. Leaving aside certain cases, not applicable in this case, where it has been held permissible to lift the corporate veil e.g. where the company is a mere facade, directors or employees acting as such will only be liable for tortious acts committed during the course of their employment in three circumstances.

89. First, if a director or an employee himself commits the tort he will be liable. An example is the lorry driver who is involved in an accident in the course of his employment. Although

Mr Mehra was the person who was responsible for making the misrepresentations, he did not commit the deceit himself. For reasons I have already stated the representations were made by Oakprime and not by him. Further, SCB relied upon them as representations by Oakprime and not as representations by Mr Mehra.

90. The second way that a director or an employee will become liable is a branch of the first. A director or an employee may, when carrying out his duties for the company, assume a personal liability. An example where personal liability was assumed was *Fairline Shipping Corporation v Adamson* [1975] QB 180. A different conclusion was reached in *Trevor Ivory Ltd v Anderson* [1997] 2 NZLR 517. What amounts to such an assumption will depend upon the facts of the particular case. Guidance as to how to decide whether such an assumption took place can be obtained from *Williams v Natural Life Ltd* **[3.19]**. . . . [He then described the facts and cited Lord Steyn, including the passages extracted previously.]

91. In those quoted passages, Lord Steyn had in mind that the cause of action relied on was negligence. However the principles stated are applicable to other torts, in particular to deceit. There must be an assumption of responsibility such as to create a special relationship by the plaintiff with the director or employee himself. Whether that exists is to be judged objectively with the primary focus on things said and done by the director or employee. It is necessary to enquire whether the director conveyed directly or indirectly to the plaintiff that he assumed a personal responsibility towards the plaintiff.

92. In the present case, Mr Mehra, by his actions or statements never led SCB to believe he was assuming personal responsibility for the misrepresentations. SCB believed they were dealing with Oakprime. It follows that Mr Mehra cannot be held liable on this ground.

93. The third ground of liability arises when the director does not carry out the tortious act himself nor does he assume liability for it, but he procures and induces another, the company, to commit the tort.

94. A person who procures and induces another to commit a tort becomes a joint tortfeasor (see *Unilever plc v Gillette (UK) Ltd* [1989] RPC 583 and *Molnlycke AB v Procter & Gamble* [1992] RPC 583. There is no reason why a director of a company should be in any different position to a third party and therefore it is possible that a director can be capable of becoming a joint tortfeasor by procuring and inducing the company, for which he works, to carry out a tortious act. However there are good reasons to conclude that the carrying out of duties of a director would never be sufficient to make a director liable. That was the view of the Court of Appeal in *C. Evans v Spritebrand Ltd* [1985] 1 WLR 317. . . .

98. It was also alleged that Mr Mehra had been guilty of conspiracy. As I understand the allegation, the unlawful act relied was the deceit practised by Oakprime on SCB. That was an act carried out by Oakprime but not with Mr Mehra who acted in his capacity as employee and director.

99. . . . I would allow the appeal by Mr Mehra. . .

EVANS LJ delivered a concurring judgment.

WARD LJ concurred with both.

[The decision of the Court of Appeal was overturned on appeal to the House of Lords.]

LORD HOFFMANN:

20. My Lords, I come next to the question of whether Mr Mehra was liable for his deceit. To put the question in this way may seem tendentious but I do not think that it is unfair. Mr Mehra says, and the Court of Appeal accepted, that he committed no deceit because he made the representation on behalf of Oakprime and it was relied upon as a representation by Oakprime. That is true but seems to me irrelevant. Mr Mehra made a fraudulent misrepresentation intending SCB to rely upon it and SCB did rely upon it. The fact that by virtue of the law of agency his representation and the knowledge with which he made it would also be attributed to Oakprime would be of interest in an action against Oakprime. But that cannot detract from the fact that they were his representation and his knowledge. He was the only human being involved in making the representation to SCB (apart from administrative assistance like someone to type the letter

and carry the papers round to the bank). It is true that SCB relied upon Mr Mehra's representation being attributable to Oakprime because it was the beneficiary under the credit. But they also relied upon it being Mr Mehra's representation, because otherwise there could have been no representation and no attribution.

21. The Court of Appeal appear to have based their conclusion upon the decision of your Lordships' House in *Williams v Natural Life Health Foods Ltd* **[3.19]**. That was an action for damages for negligent misrepresentation. My noble and learned friend, Lord Steyn, pointed out that in such a case liability depended upon an assumption of responsibility by the defendant. As Lord Devlin said in *Hedley Byrne & Co Ltd v Heller & Partners Ltd* [1964] AC 465, 530, the basis of liability is analogous to contract. And just as an agent can contract on behalf of another without incurring personal liability, so an agent can assume responsibility on behalf of another for the purposes of the *Hedley Byrne* rule without assuming personal responsibility. Their Lordships decided that on the facts of the case, the agent had not assumed any personal responsibility.

22. This reasoning cannot in my opinion apply to liability for fraud. No one can escape liability for his fraud by saying: 'I wish to make it clear that I am committing this fraud on behalf of someone else and I am not to be personally liable.' Evans LJ [2000] 1 Lloyd's Rep 218, 230 framed the question as being 'whether the director may be held liable for the company's tort'. But Mr Mehra was not being sued for the company's tort. He was being sued for his own tort and all the elements of that tort were proved against him. Having put the question in the way he did, Evans LJ answered it by saying that the fact that Mr Mehra was a director did not in itself make him liable. That of course is true. He is liable not because he was a director but because he committed a fraud.

23. Both Evans and Aldous LJJ treated the *Williams* case **[3.19]** as being based upon the separate legal personality of a company. Aldous LJ [see earlier] referred to *Salomon v A Salomon & Co Ltd* **[2.02]**. But my noble and learned friend, Lord Steyn, made it clear that the decision had nothing to do with company law. It was an application of the law of principal and agent to the requirement of assumption of responsibility under the *Hedley Byrne* principle. Lord Steyn said it would have made no difference if Mr Williams's principal had been a natural person. So one may test the matter by asking whether, if Mr Mehra had been acting as manager for the owner of the business who lived in the south of France and had made a fraudulent representation within the scope of his employment, he could escape personal liability by saying that it must have been perfectly clear that he was not being fraudulent on his own behalf but exclusively on behalf of his employer.

24. I would therefore allow the appeal against Mr Mehra...

LORDS MUSTILL, SLYNN AND HOBHOUSE concurred.

LORD RODGER delivered a concurring opinion.

> Notes

1. In *Barclay Pharmaceutical Ltd, AAH Pharmaceuticals Ltd, AAH Ltd v Waypharm LP* [2012] EWHC 306 (Comm), therefore, the court rejected the tortfeasor's argument that the only liability rested on the company and that he, as controller, had no separate personal liability. Citing the *dicta* of Lord Hoffmann and Lord Rodger from this decision, Gloster J held that 'a director making fraudulent misrepresentations on behalf of a company cannot escape personal liability for his fraud' [239] and the controller was found personally liable for the tort of causing loss by unlawful means. Indeed, if necessary, Gloster J 'would also hold the tortfeasor liable for inducing his company's breach of an agreement...because of his direct personal involvement and responsibility for the fraudulent presentations made' [245].

2. Applying *Williams v Natural Life* **[3.19]** and *Standard Chartered Bank* **[3.20]**, Norris J drew a clear distinction between three situations in which a (sole) director may become

personally liable alongside the company's liabilities in *JMW Motors Co Ltd v Beverly Hills Group Ltd* [2013] EWHC 4623 (QB). The claimants brought claims for breach of contract and in deceit against the company (D1) and its sole shareholder and director (D2). The defence of illegality failed; and both defendants were held liable in deceit. As to the latter, the learned judge reasoned as follows:

> 25. Mr French [counsel for the claimants] pressed Mr Mulhall [D2] in cross-examination with the proposition that AWI [D1] was really the alter ego of Mr Mulhall himself, he being its sole share-holder and director. In my judgment, the fact that this is a one man company is not of itself enough to make the sole director and shareholder personally liable for the company's acts and defaults. There are, I think, three distinct situations to be identified. First, where the question is one of con-tract, the relationship between the company and its sole director, vis-à-vis third parties, depends on whether the sole director, as agent for the company, has made himself personally responsible for the company's liabilities. It is, of course, perfectly possible for a sole director to make himself per-sonally responsible for the acts and omissions of his company in the same way that it is perfectly possible for any agent to make himself personally liable for the acts and defaults of his principal. But you would have to find something expressed in the contract (or more rarely, implied) for that conclusion to follow. The second situation is negligence and similar torts. There it depends upon whether the sole director has assumed responsibility on behalf of the company, i.e. he has in some sense gone beyond acting as any ordinary director would have acted by doing something which demonstrates a personal involvement or a personal assumption of responsibility. These examples were canvassed in *Williams* **[3.19]**. The third case is the case of fraud or deceit. There the general rule is that no distinction is to be drawn between the company and its sole director or shareholder. In other words, the individual agent of the company cannot say 'I was being fraudulent on the com-pany's behalf, but I was not myself being fraudulent. I was deceiving as agent for the company, but I was not really deceiving myself.' The law is considered in *Standard Chartered* **[3.20]**.

3. In *Foster v Action Aviation Ltd* [2014] EWCA Civ 1368, CA, it was held that a claim against a director (or, in this case, the chairman) of a company for misrepresentation always had its problems because 'in a company context representations by directors are almost always considered to be made on behalf of their companies. It failed for example in *Williams v Natural Life* **[3.19]** because the claimant could not show that any responsibility assumed by the director had created a special relationship between the claimant and that director. If a company is already actively present behind a director who negotiates a deal that will be very difficult to prove; the same must usually be true if the intention is that a contract will be made with the company of which the director is a director' [34] (per Longmore LJ, with whom Gloster and Underhill LJJ concurred). This issue was not fully dealt with by the Court of Appeal, however, as this was not the way the case was opened (or closed) in the court below and the Court of Appeal refused to allow the claimant to withdraw concessions at the appellate stage.

➤ Questions

1. Explain the basis of the different outcomes for the individuals in *Williams v Natural Life* **[3.19]** and *Standard Chartered* **[3.20]**. Is this explanation also consistent with the rules that apply in respect of contractual liability (see earlier) and criminal liability (see the following section)?

2. What are the advantages and disadvantages of this series of decisions on tort liability for those dealing with companies (especially small companies) and those involved in managing such companies?

3. Are these decisions defensible on policy grounds? And on doctrinal grounds?

4. Is there now any need for vicarious liability in the context of companies, or is it always possible to find the company primarily liable in tort by applying an appropriate rule of attribution (as described in *Meridian* **[3.01]**)? Put another way, can a company always be found *primarily* liable for fraud, negligent misstatement, negligent driving, and so on, because the acts of a relevant individual count as the acts of the company for the relevant purpose?

Criminal liability

Some crimes have a mental element. To find the company liable for those, it is necessary to attribute the relevant mental element of one person (or corporate organ) within the company to the company itself. This is most usually done by identifying the 'directing mind and will of the company' (Lord Reid in *Tesco Supermarkets Ltd v Nattrass* **[3.25]**). This rule, however, suffers from the defect that finding such a personal representative is only likely in very small companies, not in large ones. The rather unfair consequence is that it is much easier to find small companies liable in crime than large ones. Sometimes the problem can be overcome by using Lord Hoffmann's 'attribution rules' to find the person whose mental element *for these purposes* (ie for the purposes of the act constituting *this* crime) is to count as the mental element of the company (*Meridian Global* **[3.01]**). Note, however, that identifying a person whose criminal intent will count as the criminal intent of the company is difficult: the idea of limiting it to the person identified as 'the company's directing mind and will' has intuitive appeal in these circumstances, whatever the flaws in that terminology noted by Lord Hoffmann in *Meridian Global* **[3.01]** itself.

It is not possible to make the company *vicariously liable* for crimes with a mental element: this would, in effect, be making the company criminally liable for all the criminal intents of anyone associated with the company. On the other hand, where there is no mental element to the crime (ie so that the commission or omission of the act automatically attracts liability), then vicarious liability is possible. This is the usual rule in relation to offences relating to health and safety or environmental protection, for example. The *Tesco Supermarkets* case **[3.25]** is a case in point.

Alternatively, liability may be imposed if appropriate standards of care are not in place. The Bribery Act 2010 came into force on 1 July 2011, and repealed all existing statutory and common law offences relating to bribery and replaced them with four new offences, including a new 'corporate' offence under s 7 (the failure of commercial organisations to prevent bribery), which will apply where a corporation fails to prevent the payment of bribes by any person (whether an employee, agent or other third party) who is performing services on its behalf. The company's only defence is, pursuant to s 7(2), to show that it has in place 'adequate procedures' to prevent such bribery. In accordance with s 9 of the Act, the Secretary of State for Justice has published *The Bribery Act 2010 Guidance*,[57] which sets out six principles accompanied by case studies to assist companies in understanding the 'adequate procedures' requirement: proportionate procedures, top-level commitment, risk assessment, due diligence, communication and monitoring and review.

Since its inception, the Act has received mixed reception. On one hand, it has been praised as being 'clear and accessible', with the guidance representing a 'useful framework for

---

[57] www.gov.uk/government/publications/bribery-act-2010-guidance.

compliance with the Act'.[58] On the other hand, it has also been described as a 'toothless wonder',[59] containing obvious areas of uncertainty within its terms.[60]

Finally, there is the problem of corporate killing. This issue came to public prominence with a series of corporate disasters which made it clear that it is difficult to find a large company liable for manslaughter, even when the business has been operated with inadequate regard to the health and safety of the public. Again, the problem was that it is often impossible to find one individual with the necessary criminal failings who can be identified with the company, and courts had rejected the use of aggregation to find the company liable by aggregating the failings of a series of individuals that, in total, add up to a corporate failing that might attract criminal liability (as is sometimes done in establishing vicarious liability in tort). See *Attorney General's Reference (No 2 of 1999)* [2000] QB 796.[61] Eventually, Parliament enacted the Corporate Manslaughter and Corporate Homicide Act 2007. It establishes the offence of corporate manslaughter that is committed by a company if the way in which its activities are managed or organised by its senior management causes the death of a person *and* amounts to a gross breach of the relevant duty of care the company owed to the person. The company, if guilty, will be subject to a fine and perhaps to other appropriate orders.

Corporate Manslaughter and Corporate Homicide Act 2007 ss 1 and 18

1 The offence

(1) An organisation to which this section applies is guilty of an offence if the way in which its activities are managed or organised—
   (a) causes a person's death, and
   (b) amounts to a gross breach of a relevant duty of care owed by the organisation to the deceased.

(2) The organisations to which this section applies are—
   (a) a corporation;
   (b) a department or other body listed in Schedule 1;
   (c) a police force;
   (d) a partnership, or a trade union or employers' association, that is an employer.

(3) An organisation is guilty of an offence under this section only if the way in which its activities are managed or organised by its senior management is a substantial element in the breach referred to in subsection (1).

(4) For the purposes of this Act—
   (a) 'relevant duty of care' has the meaning given by section 2, read with sections 3 to 7;
   (b) a breach of a duty of care by an organisation is a 'gross' breach if the conduct alleged to amount to a breach of that duty falls far below what can reasonably be expected of the organisation in the circumstances;
   (c) 'senior management', in relation to an organisation, means the persons who play significant roles in—

---

[58] S Gentle, 'The Bribery Act 2010: Part 2: The Corporate Offence' [2011] Crim LR 101.

[59] D Aaronberg and N Higgins, 'All Hail the Bribery Act—The Toothless Wonder!' [2011] Arch Rev 5.

[60] C Wells, 'Who's Afraid of the Bribery Act 2010' [2012] JBL 420.

[61] The case arose out of the Southall train disaster, when two trains collided at high speed and seven people were killed, but the charges of manslaughter resulted in acquittals on the direction of the judge, for want of evidence to bring home either an *actus reus* or a *mens rea* to a 'directing mind and will'. The Court of Appeal confirmed that this was the correct approach in law.

(i)   the making of decisions about how the whole or a substantial part of its activities are to be managed or organised, or

(ii) the actual managing or organising of the whole or a substantial part of those activities.

(5) The offence under this section is called—

(a) corporate manslaughter, in so far as it is an offence under the law of England and Wales or Northern Ireland;

(b) corporate homicide, in so far as it is an offence under the law of Scotland.

(6) An organisation that is guilty of corporate manslaughter or corporate homicide is liable on conviction on indictment to a fine.

(7) The offence of corporate homicide is indictable only in the High Court of Justiciary.

18 No individual liability

(1) An individual cannot be guilty of aiding, abetting, counselling or procuring the commission of an offence of corporate manslaughter.

(1A) An individual cannot be guilty of an offence under Part 2 of the Serious Crime Act 2007 (encouraging or assisting crime) by reference to an offence of corporate manslaughter. [subs (1A) applies only in England and Wales.]

(2) An individual cannot be guilty of aiding, abetting, counselling or procuring, or being [p]art and part in, the commission of an offence of corporate homicide.

Cotswold Geotechnical Holdings Ltd became the first company to be convicted of corporate manslaughter under the Act in 2011. The case concerned the death of an employee who had entered a pit during the course of soil investigation work; the pit, which was entirely unsupported, collapsed and killed him. The court convicted the company, finding such gross breach of duty as falling within the ambit of the Act. On appeal, the Court of Appeal affirmed the verdict of the Crown Court: *R v Cotswold Geotechnical Holdings Ltd* [2011] EWCA Crim 1337. The fine imposed was less than the statutory minimum on the basis that otherwise the company would have been bankrupted (£385k rather than £500k). This case concerned a one man company, which might have been found liable for the crime in any event, given the common law 'directing mind' analysis.[62]

➤ Questions

1. What are the essential elements of the offence of corporate manslaughter?

2. Does the Act make it easier to convict companies of the offence? What sorts of actions, and by whom, might be sufficient to attract liability?

3. What liability in crime or tort might be attached to individual managers?

Establishing corporate mental states, *mens rea* and criminal liability

The following extracted cases illustrate the process the courts were required to adopt prior to the Corporate Manslaughter and Corporate Homicide Act 2007. These cases remain relevant in contexts outside the crime of manslaughter.

---

[62] For a recent critique of the 2007 Act, see MS Tariq, 'A 2013 Look at the Corporate Killer' (2014) 35 *Company Lawyer* 17.

The mental state of a person who is 'the directing mind and will' of a company may be attributed to the company itself.

[3.21] Lennard's Carrying Co Ltd v Asiatic Petroleum Co Ltd [1915] AC 705 (House of Lords)

The appellant company Lennard's Carrying Co Ltd owned a ship, the *Edward Dawson*, which (together with her cargo which belonged to the respondents) was destroyed at sea as a result of a fire caused by the defective condition of her boilers. The appellant company as owner would have been exonerated from liability by the terms of the Merchant Shipping Act 1894 s 502 (now repealed), if it could show that the loss happened without its 'actual fault or privity'. The House of Lords held that the concepts of fault and privity were capable in law of being attributed to a corporate body, but that on the facts the appellant had failed to show that it came within the exception.

VISCOUNT HALDANE LC: The appellants are a limited company and the ship was managed by another limited company, Messrs J M Lennard & Sons, and Mr J M Lennard, who seems to be the active director in J M Lennard & Sons, was also a director of the appellant company, Lennard's Carrying Company Limited. My Lords, in that state of things what is the question of law which arises? I think that it is impossible in the face of the findings of the learned judge, and of the evidence, to contend successfully that Mr J M Lennard has shown that he did not know or can excuse himself for not having known of the defects which manifested themselves in the condition of the ship, amounting to unseaworthiness. Mr Lennard is the person who is registered in the ship's register and is designated as the person to whom the management of the vessel was entrusted. He appears to have been the active spirit in the joint stock company which managed this ship for the appellants; and under the circumstances the question is whether the company can invoke the protection of s 502 of the Merchant Shipping Act to relieve it from the liability which the respondents seek to impose on it...

Now, my Lords, did what happened take place without the actual fault or privity of the owners of the ship who were the appellants? My Lords, a corporation is an abstraction. It has no mind of its own any more than it has a body of its own; its active and directing will must consequently be sought in the person of somebody who for some purposes may be called an agent, but who is really the directing mind and will of the corporation, the very ego and centre of the personality of the corporation. That person may be under the direction of the shareholders in general meeting; that person may be the board of directors itself, or it may be, and in some companies it is so, that that person has an authority co-ordinate with the board of directors given to him under the articles of association, and is appointed by the general meeting of the company, and can only be removed by the general meeting of the company. My Lords, whatever is not known about Mr Lennard's position, this is known for certain, Mr Lennard took the active part in the management of this ship on behalf of the owners, and Mr Lennard, as I have said, was registered as the person designated for this purpose in the ship's register. Mr Lennard therefore was the natural person to come on behalf of the owners and give full evidence not only about the events of which I have spoken, and which related to the seaworthiness of the ship, but about his own position and as to whether or not he was the life and soul of the company. For if Mr Lennard was the directing mind of the company, then his action must, unless a corporation is not to be liable at all, have been an action which was the action of the company itself within the meaning of s 502. It has not been contended at the Bar, and it could not have been successfully contended, that s 502 is so worded as to exempt a corporation altogether which happens to be the owner of a ship, merely because it happens to be a corporation. It must be upon the true construction of that section in such a case as the present one that the fault or privity is the fault or privity of somebody who is not merely a servant or agent for whom the company is liable upon the footing *respondeat superior*, but somebody for whom the company is liable because his action is the very action of the company itself. It is not enough that the fault should be the fault of a servant in order to exonerate the owner, the fault must also be one which is not the fault of the owner, or a fault to which the owner is privy; and I take the view that when anybody sets up that section to excuse himself from the normal consequences of the maxim *respondeat superior* the burden lies upon him to do so.

Well, my Lords, in that state of the law it is obvious to me that Mr Lennard ought to have gone into the box and relieved the company of the presumption which arises against it that his action was the company's action. But Mr Lennard did not go into the box to rebut the presumption of liability and we have no satisfactory evidence as to what the constitution of the company was or as to what Mr Lennard's position was…Under the circumstances I think that the company and Mr Lennard have not discharged the burden of proof which was upon them, and that it must be taken that the unseaworthiness, which I hold to have been established as existing at the commencement of the voyage from Novorossick, was an unseaworthiness which did not exist without the actual fault or privity of the owning company.

LORD DUNEDIN delivered a concurring opinion.

LORDS ATKINSON, PARKER OF WADDINGTON and PARMOOR concurred.

➤ Questions

1. Was Mr Lennard 'the directing mind and will' of JM Lennard & Sons, or of Lennard's Carrying Co Ltd, or of both? Was this question important?

2. How far do you think that the decision in the *Lennard*'s case depended upon the fact that the onus of proof under the statute was on the appellants, who were required to prove a negative? Who would have won the case if the onus of proof had been on the respondents?

3. Recall Lord Hoffmann's criticisms of the phrase 'directing mind and will' in *Meridian Global* [3.01]. What traps did he identify?

[3.22] HL Bolton (Engineering) Ltd v TJ Graham & Sons Ltd [1957] 1 QB 159 (Court of Appeal)

In this case a corporate landlord was held capable of 'intending' (through its managing directors) to occupy premises for its own use.

DENNING LJ: [The] question is whether the landlords have proved the necessary intention to occupy the holding for their own purpose. This point arises because the landlords are a limited company. Mr Albery says that there was no meeting of any board of directors to express the landlords' intention, and that therefore the landlords—the company—cannot say that it has the necessary intention.

[His Lordship stated the material facts on this part of the case and continued:] [The] judge has found that this company, through its managers, intend to occupy the premises for their own purposes. Mr Albery contests this finding, and he has referred us to cases decided in the last century; but I must say that the law on this matter and the approach to it have developed very considerably since then. A company may in many ways be likened to a human body. It has a brain and nerve centre which controls what it does. It also has hands which hold the tools and act in accordance with directions from the centre. Some of the people in the company are mere servants and agents who are nothing more than hands to do the work and cannot be said to represent the mind or will. Others are directors and managers who represent the directing mind and will of the company, and control what it does. The state of mind of these managers is the state of mind of the company and is treated by the law as such. So you will find that in cases where the law requires personal fault as a condition of liability in tort, the fault of the manager will be the personal

fault of the company. [His Lordship referred to *Lennard's Carrying Co Ltd v Asiatic Petroleum Co Ltd* **[3.21]** and *R v ICR Haulage Ltd* **[3.24]** and continued:] So here, the intention of the company can be derived from the intention of its officers and agents. Whether their intention is the company's intention depends on the nature of the matter under consideration, the relative position of the officer or agent and the other relevant facts and circumstances of the case. Approaching the matter in that way, I think that although there was no board meeting, nevertheless, having regard to the standing of these directors in control of the business of the company, having regard to the other facts and circumstances which we know, whereby plans had been prepared and much work done, the judge was entitled to infer that the intention of the company was to occupy the holding for their own purposes. I am of opinion, therefore, that the judge's decision on this point was right...

HODSON and MORRIS LJJ concurred.

➤ Note

Although the 'directing mind and will' is the most common criterion for attribution, there have been cases in which a person who was not part of the directing mind and will of a company was identified with it. To hold otherwise, would allow those persons who are the actual directing mind of the company to insulate the latter from liability by delegating their functions. See *Director General of Fair Trading v Pioneer Concrete (UK) Ltd* [1995] 1 AC 456 and *Re Bank of Credit and Commerce International SA (No 15)* [2005] EWCA Civ 693, [2005] 2 BCLC 328.

A company is capable of having an intent to deceive.

[3.23] DPP v Kent and Sussex Contractors Ltd [1944] KB 146 (King's Bench Divisional Court)

The company was charged with offences under the petrol rationing regulations involving (i) making use of a false document with intent to deceive, and (ii) making a statement which was known to be false in a material particular. The justices held that the company could not in law be guilty of these offences since there was implicit in them an act of will or state of mind which could not be imputed to a body corporate, and dismissed the informations. The prosecutor appealed by way of case stated to the Divisional Court, which ruled that a company was capable of committing the offences in question, it being sufficient that the particular officer responsible (in this case the transport manager) had the required intention or knowledge.

VISCOUNT CALDECOTE CJ: This special case raises the question whether a limited company, being a body corporate, can in law be guilty of the offences charged against the respondents, or whether a company is incapable of any act of will or state of mind such as that laid in the information. Mr Carey Evans submits that a company can only be held to be responsible in respect of the intention or knowledge of its agents, the officers of the company, to the same extent as a private individual is responsible for the acts of his agent, and, therefore, that the respondent company cannot be held to form the intention or to have the knowledge necessary to constitute the offences charged. He has not disputed the abstract proposition that a company can have knowledge and can form an intention to do an act. A company cannot be found guilty of certain criminal offences, such as treason or other offences for which it is provided that death or imprisonment is the only punishment, but there are a number of criminal offences of which a company can be convicted...

In the present case the first charge against the company was of doing something with intent to deceive, and the second was that of making a statement which the company knew to be false in a material particular. Once the ingredients of the offences are stated in that way it is unnecessary, in my view, to inquire whether it is proved that the company's officers acted on its behalf. The officers are the company for this purpose. Mr Carey Evans stoutly maintained the position that a company cannot have a mens rea, and that a mens rea cannot be imputed to it even if and when its agents have been known to have one, but the question of mens rea seems to me to be quite irrelevant in the present case. The offences created by the regulation are those of doing something with intent to deceive or of making a statement known to be false in a material particular. There was ample evidence, on the facts as stated in the special case, that the company, by the only people who could act or speak or think for it had done both these things, and I can see nothing in any of the authorities to which we have been referred which requires us to say that a company is incapable of being found guilty of the offences with which the respondent company was charged. The case must go back to the justices with an intimation of our opinion to this effect, and for their determination on the facts.

HALLETT and MACNAGHTEN JJ delivered concurring judgments.

➤ Question

Was it true to say that 'the question of *mens rea* seems to be quite irrelevant in the present case'? If it had been thought relevant, would the decision have been the same?

A company can be indicted for a common law conspiracy to defraud.

[3.24] R v ICR Haulage Ltd [1944] KB 551 (Court of Criminal Appeal)

The company was convicted with others at Maidstone Assizes on an indictment charging a common law conspiracy to defraud. The conviction was upheld on appeal.

The judgment of the Court of Criminal Appeal (HUMPHREYS, CROOM-JOHNSON and STABLE JJ) was read by STABLE J: The question before us is whether a limited company can be indicted for a conspiracy to defraud...

It was conceded by counsel for the company that a limited company can be indicted for some criminal offences, and it was conceded by counsel for the Crown that there were some criminal offences for which a limited company cannot be indicted. The controversy centred round the question where and on what principle the line must be drawn and on which side of the line an indictment such as the present one falls. Counsel for the company contended that the true principle was that an indictment against a limited company for any offence involving as an essential ingredient 'mens rea' in the restricted sense of a dishonest or criminal mind, must be bad for the reason that a company, not being a natural person, cannot have a mind honest or otherwise, and that, consequently, though in certain circumstances it is civilly liable for the fraud of its officers, agents or servants, it is immune from criminal process. Counsel for the Crown contended that a limited company, like any other entity recognised by the law, can as a general rule be indicted for its criminal acts which from the very necessity of the case must be performed by human agency and which in given circumstances become the acts of the company, and that for this purpose there was no distinction between an intention or other function of the mind and any other form of activity.

The offences for which a limited company cannot be indicted are, it was argued, exceptions to the general rule arising from the limitations which must inevitably attach to an artificial entity, such as a company. Included in these exceptions are the cases in which, from its very nature, the offence cannot be committed by a corporation, as, for example, perjury, an offence which cannot

be vicariously committed, or bigamy, an offence which a limited company, not being a natural person, cannot commit vicariously or otherwise. A further exception, but for a different reason, comprises offences of which murder is an example, where the only punishment the court can impose is corporal, the basis on which this exception rests being that the court will not stultify itself by embarking on a trial in which, if a verdict of Guilty is returned, no effective order by way of sentence can be made. In our judgment these contentions of the Crown are substantially sound, and the existence of these exceptions, and it may be that there are others, is by no means inconsistent with the general rule...

[His Lordship referred to the authorities, including *DPP v Kent and Sussex Contractors Ltd* **[3.23]** and *Pharmaceutical Society v London and Provincial Supply Association* **[2.08]**, and continued:] In our judgment, both on principle and in accordance with the balance of authority, the present indictment was properly laid against the company, and the learned commissioner rightly refused to quash. We are not deciding that in every case where an agent of a limited company acting in its business commits a crime the company is automatically to be held criminally responsible. Our decision only goes to the invalidity of the indictment on the face of it, an objection which is taken before any evidence is led and irrespective of the facts of the particular case. [Whether] in any particular case there is evidence to go to a jury that the criminal act of an agent, including his state of mind, intention, knowledge or belief is the act of the company, and, in cases where the presiding judge so rules, whether the jury are satisfied that it has been proved, must depend on the nature of the charge, the relative position of the officer or agent, and the other relevant facts and circumstances of the case.[63] It was because we were satisfied on the hearing of this appeal that the facts proved were amply sufficient to justify a finding that the acts of the managing director were the acts of the company and the fraud of that person was the fraud of the company, that we upheld the conviction against the company, and, indeed, on the appeal to this court no argument was advanced that the facts proved would not warrant a conviction of the company assuming that the conviction of the managing director was upheld and that the indictment was good in law.

➤ Questions

1. Contrast the reasoning in these cases with the categorical statement of Blackstone ('Limits to the idea of a company as a "person"?', p 62): 'A corporation cannot commit treason, or felony, or other crime, in it's corporate capacity . . .' Is it possible to account for the change? Why do you think that it was not until as late as 1944 that the breakthrough in making companies liable for crimes involving *mens rea* was made?

2. What indications are there in the judgments that the decisions of the court in *Kent and Sussex Contractors* and *ICR Haulage* were based on *policy* considerations?

➤ Notes

1. The two cases just cited, and *Moore v I Bresler Ltd* [1944] 2 All ER 515, all of which were decided in the same year, established that a company may be guilty of a criminal offence, including an offence involving *mens rea*. (The doctrine of *ultra vires* might have been seen as an obstacle to imposing liability, but it does not seem to have been raised in any of the key cases—presumably because it had long been regarded as irrelevant to the corresponding question in tort: *Campbell v Paddington Corpn* **[3.17]**.)

2. Once this step was taken in 1944, it then became necessary to determine which officers, agents or servants of a company could be identified with the company itself for the

---

63 This sentence was criticised as being too widely stated by Lord Reid in *Tesco Supermarkets Ltd v Nattrass* **[3.25]**.

purpose of ascribing to it a criminal or similar intention. In *Moore v I Bresler Ltd* (Note 1), the secretary of the company and a branch sales manager were so regarded; in *DPP v Kent and Sussex Contractors Ltd* **[3.23]** and in *The Lady Gwendolen* [1965] P 294, CA, the only officer concerned was the transport manager; and in *National Coal Board v Gamble* [1959] 1 QB 11 it appears to have been assumed that a weighbridgeman's knowledge and intention could be attributed to the Coal Board, although the contrary view was taken on the same point in *John Henshall (Quarries) Ltd v Harvey* [1965] 2 QB 233. It is perhaps significant that *Lennard's Carrying* case (and the 'directing mind and will' test of identification) was not mentioned in the judgments (nor even, apparently, by counsel) in any of the criminal law cases referred to earlier—although the link between the two was soon made by contemporary textbooks.

3. In the following case extract, *Tesco Supermarkets* **[3.25]**, the House of Lords took the opportunity to review the question. The *Lennard*'s test of identification was central to their reasoning. However, their decision relies on a stratification of managerial functions which in the case of many companies may be far from obvious. It may well beg the question to describe a transport manager as a 'superior officer' and the manager of a large retail shop as a 'subordinate'. In other contexts, the courts have not been so willing to see a significant difference between running a company's affairs and running part only of those affairs: see *Harold Holdsworth & Co (Wakefield) Ltd v Caddies* [1955] 1 WLR 352, HL.

4. The problems with strict insistence on a 'directing mind and will' test of identification in a criminal context soon emerged. The catalyst, no doubt, was the decision in the *Pioneer Concrete* case (in the Note following *HL Bolton (Engineering) Ltd v TJ Graham & Sons Ltd* **[3.22]**, p 151), where the issue was whether the companies concerned could be held to be in contempt of court through the acts of employees who were of no more than middle-management status. The leading statement of the law is now the Privy Council's opinion, delivered by Lord Hoffmann, in *Meridian Global Funds Management Asia Ltd v Securities Commission* **[3.01]**. On the basis of this, it is now clear that there is no single test of identification but rather a range of 'rules of attribution' which vary from case to case; and *Tesco Supermarkets* may be seen as a decision reached in the special context of the Trade Descriptions Act 1968 rather than a pronouncement of general application to criminal law cases across the board.

The mental state of one who occupies a subordinate position in the company will not necessarily be ascribed to the company itself.[64]

[3.25] Tesco Supermarkets Ltd v Nattrass [1972] AC 153 (House of Lords)

Tesco was charged with an offence under the Trade Descriptions Act 1968, that is, selling a packet of washing powder for 3s 11d (19½p), when it had been advertised at 2s 11d (14½p). An assistant at the company's Northwich branch, Miss Rogers, had restocked the shelves with normally priced packets after supplies of 'special offer' packets bearing a lower price had temporarily run out. She had not informed the branch manager, Mr Clements, of this, while he for his part had failed to detect the discrepancy between the 'special offer' posters and the price of the powder on the shelves. Mr Clements was in complete charge of this store and its 60 employees.

---

[64] The House of Lords in this case adopted the 'directing mind and will' approach, and, consequently, concluded that subordinates would never count as the 'directing mind'. The conclusion would not now be so clear-cut. See *Meridian Global Funds Management Asia Ltd v Securities Commission* **[3.01]**. In this case, Lord Hoffmann stated that it would be a mistake to seize upon the phrase 'directing mind and will' and use that as the sole criterion for determining whose thoughts and/or actions will be attributed to a company. The question should be 'whose act was...intended to count as the act of the company?'

Under s 24(1) of the Trade Descriptions Act, it is a defence for the accused to prove that the commission of the offence was due to the act or default of another person, and that the accused has taken all reasonable precautions and exercised all due diligence to avoid the commission of the offence. In quashing the conviction of Tesco, which had been upheld by the Divisional Court, the House of Lords ruled that for the purpose of the company's criminal liability, the branch manager did not represent its 'directing mind and will', but was merely a subordinate. It followed that the company could plead that the manager's acts were those of 'another person' within the terms of the statutory defence; and that it had discharged the burden of proving that it had taken all reasonable precautions and exercised all due diligence by showing that its managers had been issued with proper instructions.

LORD REID: Where a limited company is the employer difficult questions do arise in a wide variety of circumstances in deciding which of its officers or servants is to be identified with the company so that his guilt is the guilt of the company.

I must start by considering the nature of the personality which by a fiction the law attributes to a corporation. A living person has a mind which can have knowledge or intention or be negligent and he has hands to carry out his intentions. A corporation has none of these: it must act through living persons, though not always one or the same person. Then the person who acts is not speaking or acting for the company. He is acting as the company and his mind which directs his acts is the mind of the company. There is no question of the company being vicariously liable. He is not acting as a servant, representative, agent or delegate. He is an embodiment of the company or, one could say, he hears and speaks through the persona of the company, within his appropriate sphere, and his mind is the mind of the company. If it is a guilty mind then that guilt is the guilt of the company. It must be a question of law whether, once the facts have been ascertained, a person in doing particular things is to be regarded as the company or merely as the company's servant or agent. In that case any liability of the company can only be a statutory or vicarious liability.

In *Lennard's Carrying Co Ltd v Asiatic Petroleum Co Ltd* **[3.21]** the question was whether damage had occurred without the 'actual fault or privity' of the owner of a ship. The owners were a company. The fault was that of the registered managing owner who managed the ship on behalf of the owners and it was held that the company could not dissociate itself from him so as to say that there was no actual fault or privity on the part of the company...

Reference is frequently made to the judgment of Denning LJ in *HL Bolton (Engineering) Co Ltd v TJ Graham & Sons* **[3.22]**. [His Lordship quoted part of the judgment, which is cited earlier at **[3.22]**, and continued:] In that case the directors of the company only met once a year: they left the management of the business to others, and it was the intention of those managers which was imputed to the company. I think that was right. There have been attempts to apply Lord Denning's words to all servants of a company whose work is brain work, or who exercise some managerial discretion under the direction of superior officers of the company. I do not think that Lord Denning intended to refer to them. He only referred to those who 'represent the directing mind and will of the company, and control what it does'.

I think that is right for this reason. Normally the board of directors, the managing director and perhaps other superior officers of a company carry out the functions of management and speak and act as the company. Their subordinates do not. They carry out orders from above and it can make no difference that they are given some measure of discretion. But the board of directors may delegate some part of their functions of management, giving to their delegate full discretion to act independently of instructions from them. I see no difficulty in holding that they have thereby put such a delegate in their place so that within the scope of the delegation he can act as the company. It may not always be easy to draw the line but there are cases in which the line must be drawn. *Lennard*'s case was one of them.

In some cases the phrase alter ego has been used. I think it is misleading. When dealing with a company the word alter is I think misleading. The person who speaks and acts as the company is not alter. He is identified with the company. And when dealing with an individual no other individual can be his alter ego. The other individual can be a servant, agent, delegate or representative but I know of neither principle nor authority which warrants the confusion (in the literal or original sense) of two separate individuals...

In the next two cases a company was accused and it was held liable for the fault of a superior officer. In *DPP v Kent and Sussex Contractors Ltd* **[3.23]** he was the transport manager. In *R v ICR Haulage Ltd* **[3.24]** it was held that a company can be guilty of common law conspiracy. The act of the managing director was held to be the act of the company. I think that a passage in the judgment is too widely stated:

> '[Whether] in any particular case there is evidence to go to a jury that the criminal act of an agent, including his state of mind, intention, knowledge or belief is the act of the company, and, in cases where the presiding judge so rules, whether the jury are satisfied that it has been proved, must depend on the nature of the charge, the relative position of the officer or agent, and the other relevant facts and circumstances of the case.'

... I think that the true view is that the judge must direct the jury that if they find certain facts proved then as a matter of law they must find that the criminal act of the officer, servant or agent including his state of mind, intention, knowledge or belief is the act of the company. I have already dealt with the considerations to be applied in deciding when such a person can and when he cannot be identified with the company. I do not see how the nature of the charge can make any difference. If the guilty man was in law identifiable with the company then whether his offence was serious or venial his act was the act of the company but if he was not so identifiable then no act of his, serious or otherwise, was the act of the company itself...

[His Lordship discussed a number of other cases and concluded:] The Divisional Court decided this case on a theory of delegation. In that they were following some earlier authorities. But they gave far too wide a meaning to delegation. I have said that a board of directors can delegate part of their functions of management so as to make their delegate an embodiment of the company within the sphere of the delegation. But here the board never delegated any part of their functions. They set up a chain of command through regional and district supervisors, but they remained in control. The shop managers had to obey their general directions and also take orders from their superiors. The acts or omissions of shop managers were not acts of the company itself.

In my judgment the appellants established the statutory defence. I would therefore allow this appeal.

LORD MORRIS OF BORTH-Y-GEST, VISCOUNT DILHORNE and LORDS PEARSON and DIPLOCK delivered concurring opinions.

➤ Notes

1. As noted previously, some of the observations and assumptions in these cases need to be reconsidered in the light of the Privy Council's ruling in *Meridian Global Funds Management Asia Ltd v Securities Commission* **[3.01]**. In that case Lord Hoffmann, giving the opinion of the Judicial Committee, said that when the question arises of attributing the act or state of mind of an individual to a company, different rules should be invoked in different circumstances, depending upon the rule of law which is being applied. It would follow that the cases on the Merchant Shipping Acts, such as *Lennard's Carrying Co Ltd v Asiatic Petroleum Co Ltd* **[3.21]** and *The Lady Gwendolen* [1965] P 294, CA, should not be considered under the same rubric as those involving the question of *mens rea*, and

possibly also that the criteria for imputing a mental state in intentional crimes, such as conspiracy to defraud, and in crimes not involving intention, such as manslaughter, may not be the same (although Lord Reid in the *Tesco Supermarkets* case **[3.25]**: 'I do not see how the nature of the charge can make any difference', seems not to support this view).

2. A company cannot commit conspiracy with the one person who is solely responsible for its acts: *R v McDonnell* [1966] 1 QB 233 (Bristol Assizes).

➤ Questions

1. Lord Diplock in *Tesco Supermarkets Ltd v Nattrass* **[3.25]** said ([1972] AC 153 at 199–200):

> My Lords, a corporation incorporated under the Companies Act 1948 owes its corporate personality and its powers to its constitution, the memorandum and articles of association. The obvious and the only place to look to discover by what natural persons its powers are exercisable, is in its constitution. The articles of association, if they follow Table A [the Model Articles], provide that the business of the company shall be managed by the directors and that they may 'exercise all such powers of the company' as are not required by the Act to be exercised in general meeting. Table A also vests in the directors the right to entrust and confer upon a managing director any of the powers of the company which are exercisable by them. So it may also be necessary to ascertain whether the directors have taken any action under this provision or any other similar provision providing for the coordinate exercise of the powers of the company by executive directors or by committees of directors and other persons, such as are frequently included in the articles of association of companies in which the regulations contained in Table A are modified or excluded in whole or in part.
>
> In my view, therefore, the question: what natural persons are to be treated in law as being the company for the purpose of acts done in the course of its business, including the taking of precautions and the exercise of due diligence to avoid the commission of a criminal offence, is to be found by identifying those natural persons who by the memorandum and articles of association or as a result of action taken by the directors, or by the company in general meeting pursuant to the articles, are entrusted with the exercise of the powers of the company.

Is this the same test as Lord Reid's? What do you consider that Lord Diplock meant by 'the powers of the company'? Who in the Tesco organisation was 'entrusted' with the exercise of the relevant power, and what was this power?

2. Could the state of mind of the secretary of a company ever be attributed to the company? (See the *Panorama* case **[3.03]**, and consider what might be said of the role in a company's articles.)

3. Does Lord Reid's analysis allow for the possibility that a company could have more than one individual, acting independently, 'speaking and acting as the company' at the same time? Should it?

4. If a corporate body is to be convicted on the basis of a confession, whose confession is necessary?

5. Half of the shares in Black & White Ltd are owned by Black and half by White, and they are its only directors. Can Black, White and the company be indicted for a conspiracy on the basis of acts of Black and White? Can Black and the company be indicted for a conspiracy on the basis of acts of Black at a time when White was away on holiday?

6. It has been held that a person in total control of a one man company is capable of stealing the property of the company (*Re Attorney General's Reference (No 2 of 1982)* [1984] QB 624, CA): see 'What does a company know?', p 158. Is this decision consistent with *R v McDonnell*? Is this a *de facto* example of the court piercing the corporate veil? Or is it a perfectly proper application of the rules of attribution?

➤ Note

The *policy* of making corporate bodies liable to criminal prosecution in addition to or instead of those officers or agents who are personally at fault has been questioned by writers.[65] If both are proceeded against, and the officers are substantial members, they are doubly punished; if the company only is prosecuted and the wrongdoers have no stake in it, the fine will, in effect, be levied wholly on innocent members or customers, while if it is barely solvent, its creditors will suffer. Commentators have suggested that sanctions other than fines might be imposed, ranging all the way from 'naming and shaming' the company to ordering its dissolution. Note also a recent consultation initiated by the Ministry of Justice for the implementation of Deferred Prosecution Agreements (DPAs) in the UK, a tool which has been extensively used in the United States, and which enables companies to enter into agreements with prosecutors. This mechanism, akin to the tool of 'plea bargaining' as existing in standard criminal cases, will bypass prosecution in consideration for a large sum of money being paid in the form of, for instance, financial penalty and reparation to victims.[66]

What does a company know?

The question whether and in what circumstances knowledge should be attributed to a company or other corporate body is one of considerable complexity. The leading case is undoubtedly *Meridian Global Funds Management Asia Ltd v Securities Commission* [3.01], and that case should be revisited and considered in this specific context. But the circumstances in which a company's knowledge is important are very varied. It may be part of the cause of action against the company; it may be material in deciding whether the company has consented to certain proposals or other activities; it may be material in deciding whether a contract (eg an insurance contract) or a statute (eg as in *Meridian Global* itself) has been breached.

Clearly, information which has been given to a corporate organ acting within its sphere of responsibility (eg a document laid before the directors at a board meeting or the members at a general meeting) has been brought home to the company.

This would also be true of information communicated to a person who is the company's 'directing mind and will' if there is an individual whose relationship to the company can be so described (but see the 'Questions' later at p 162). Thus, in *El Ajou v Dollar Land Holdings Ltd* [3.26] the question was whether DLH had received money with knowledge that it was the proceeds of fraud. The knowledge of its chairman, Ferdman, was attributed to DLH because it was held that for all purposes relevant to the transaction (although not *all* purposes) he was its 'directing mind and will'.[67]

In any area of activity where the members or the directors are competent to act by informal unanimous agreement, knowledge of a matter communicated to all those concerned could readily be attributed to the corporate body.

It is where the knowledge is that of one or more individuals only, whether officers, agents or employees of the company, who do not come into one of these categories, that the question becomes more difficult. See the analysis provided by Hoffmann LJ in *El Ajou v Dollar Land Holdings Ltd* [3.26].

[65] For further reading, see C Wells, *Corporations and Criminal Responsibility* (2nd edn, 2001); GR Sullivan, 'The Attribution of Culpability to Limited Companies' [1996] CLJ 515; CMV Clarkson, 'Kicking Corporate Bodies and Damning their Souls' (1996) 59 MLR 557.
[66] https://consult.justice.gov.uk/digital-communications/deferred-prosecution-agreements.
[67] Importantly, the court recognised that different people could be the company's 'directing mind and will' for different purposes (see p 699 (Rose LJ) and p 706 (Hoffmann LJ)). This is precisely what would be expected from a proper and careful application of the attribution rules as set out in *Meridian Global* [3.01].

In *JC Houghton & Co v Nothard, Lowe & Wills* [1927] 1 KB, CA, the court was concerned with the question whether the knowledge of a single director should be imputed to the company. Viscount Sumner in the House of Lords was of the view that:

> where knowledge may lead to a modification of the company's rights according as it is or is not followed by action, the knowledge which is relevant is that of the directors themselves, since it is their board that deals with the company's rights...What a director knows or ought in the course of his duty to know may be the knowledge of the company, for it may be deemed to have been duly used so as to lead to action which a fully informed corporation would proceed to take on the strength of it.

Also see *Lebon v Aqua Salt Co Ltd* [2009] UKPC 2, PC, where the knowledge of a person who was a promoter, director and substantial shareholder was attributed to the company, so as to put the company in bad faith, even though the information had not been communicated to the other directors.

Two exceptions are recognised to this rule relating to the knowledge of an agent.

The first is where the knowledge is received by him in a private capacity, in circumstances where he is under no obligation to communicate it to his principal—in Viscount Sumner's words, not 'in the course of his duty'. In *Re David Payne & Co Ltd* [1904] 2 Ch 608, CA, money was lent by a company which the borrower intended to use for an improper purpose. One of the lending company's directors was aware of this fact, but because he had received the information privately his knowledge was not attributed to the company. Whether this rule survives today could be debated. It perhaps depends on how 'improper' the borrower's purposes are, and whether the lending company would be in breach of some law in lending to support them. In those circumstances it is difficult to see that the director would not be in breach of duty in failing to pass on information received.[68] See too the suggestion in *Bhullar v Bhullar* [7.29] by Jonathan Parker LJ, [41], that the directors in that case had 'one capacity and one capacity only', denying them a private sphere of operation. This is subject to the second exception, noted immediately below.

The second exception is made where the 'agent' is himself a wrongdoer, as was the case in *Houghton's* case itself. Viscount Sumner went on to say:

> It has long been recognised that it would be contrary to justice and common sense to treat the knowledge of such persons as that of the company, as if one were to assume that they would make a clean breast of their delinquency.

This emerges from the broader '*Hampshire Land* principle', articulated in *Re Hampshire Land Co* [3.28]. The reasoning on this point was applied in *Belmont Finance Corpn Ltd v Williams Furniture Ltd* [10.10] and in *Heron International Ltd v Grade* [1983] BCLC 244, CA. It was also part of the basis of the decision in *Re Attorney General's Reference (No 2 of 1982)* [3.31],[69] where the question was whether a person in total control of a one man company could in law steal its property.

In many of these cases the company is seeking to deny attribution to it of the knowledge of its wrongdoing directors. The interaction of the rules of attribution and director wrongdoing is complex: see the separate discussion, 'Denying attribution', p 164, noting especially the second category of cases discussed there.

---

[68] This is true even though the director may not have been in breach for failing to discover the information, if that had been the case.

[69] See GJ Virgo, 'Stealing from the Small Family Business' [1991] CLJ 464; DW Elliot, 'Directors' Thefts and Dishonesty' [1991] Crim LR 732.

Meanwhile, there are a number of further issues of particular relevance to successfully attributing knowledge to a company.

Knowledge attribution rules generally.

Revisit *Meridian Global Funds Management Asia Ltd v Securities Commission* **[3.01]**.

Knowledge attribution rules and agency.

[3.26] El Ajou v Dollar Land Holdings Ltd [1993] EWCA Civ 4 (Court of Appeal)

The question in issue was whether the knowledge of one director could be treated as the knowledge of the company. The plaintiff was one of many victims of a massive share fraud carried out in Amsterdam by three Canadians, and he claimed to be able to trace some of the proceeds of the fraud from Amsterdam through intermediate resting places in Geneva, Gibraltar, Panama and Geneva (again) to London, where they were invested in a joint venture to carry out a property development project in Battersea in conjunction with the first defendant, Dollar Land Holdings plc (DLH). The plaintiff sought to recover from DLH, alleging that DLH's chairman, Mr Ferdman, possessed the necessary knowledge attributable to DLH that the funds represented the proceeds of fraud.

The court held unanimously that the plaintiff's claim succeeded on the basis that Ferdman was DLH's 'directing mind and will', but it also held unanimously that the same conclusion could not be reached on 'agency' arguments. This conclusion has been doubted (see the Note immediately below), but nevertheless Hoffmann LJ's analysis repays consideration.

HOFFMANN LJ [having discussed other aspects of the case, continued]:

(3) Knowledge

…There are two ways in which Mr Ferdman's knowledge can be attributed to DLH. The first is that as agent of DLH his knowledge can be imputed to the company. The second is that for this purpose he *was* DLH and his knowledge was its knowledge [this is the 'directing mind and will' argument]. [The trial judge, Millett J, had rejected both.]

(a) The agency theory

The circumstances in which the knowledge of an agent is imputed to the principal can vary a great deal and care is needed in analysing the cases. They fall into a number of categories which are not always sufficiently clearly distinguished. I shall mention three such categories because they each include cases on which Mr Beloff [counsel for El Ajou] placed undifferentiated reliance. In fact, however, they depend upon distinct principles which have no application in this case.

(i) Agent's knowledge affecting performance or terms of authorised contract

First, there are cases in which an agent is authorised to enter into a transaction in which his own knowledge is material [and the agent himself is bound, personally, in that regard, in the same way as is the principal]. So for example, an insurance policy may be avoided on account of the broker's failure to disclose material facts within his knowledge, even though he did not obtain that knowledge in his capacity as agent for the insured.…

(ii) Principal's duty to investigate or make disclosure

Secondly, there are cases in which the principal has a duty to investigate or to make disclosure. The duty to investigate may arise in many circumstances...[eg] the duty of a purchaser of land to investigate the title. Or there may be something about a transaction by which the principal is "put on inquiry". If the principal employs an agent to discharge such a duty, the knowledge of the agent will be imputed to him. (There is an exception...in cases in which the agent commits a fraud against the principal. [This includes the *Hampshire Land* **[3.28]** line of cases.]) Likewise in cases in which the principal is under a duty to make disclosure (for example, to an insurer) he may have to disclose not only facts of which he knows but also material facts of which he could expect to have been told by his agents....

None of these cases are relevant because in receiving the traceable assets, DLH had no duty to investigate or make disclosure. There was nothing to put it on inquiry.

(iii) Agent authorised to receive communications

Thirdly, there are cases in which the agent has actual or ostensible authority to receive communications, whether informative (such as the state of health of an insured...) or performative (such as a notice to quit...) on behalf of the principal. In such cases, communication to the agent is communication to the principal. These cases also have no application here. Mr Ferdman did not receive information about the frauds in his capacity as agent for DLH. He found it out while acting for the Canadians.

(iv) Agent's duty to principal irrelevant

What it therefore comes to is that Mr Ferdman, an agent of DLH, had private knowledge of facts into which DLH had no duty to inquire. Mr Beloff said that Mr Ferdman nevertheless owed DLH a duty to disclose those facts. He then submits that because he had such a duty, DLH must be treated as if he had discharged it.

I am inclined to agree that Mr Ferdman did owe a duty, both as broker employed by DLH to find an investor and as chairman of the board, to inform DLH that the Yulara money was the proceeds of fraud....

But Mr Beloff's submission that DLH must be treated as if the duty had been discharged raises an important point of principle. In my judgment the submission is wrong. The fact that an agent owed a duty to his principal to communicate information may permit a court to infer as a fact that he actually did so. But this is a rebuttable inference of fact and in the present case the judge found that Mr Ferdman did not disclose what he knew to anyone else acting on behalf of DLH. In some of the cases in the third of the categories I have mentioned, the fact that an agent with authority to receive a communication had a duty to pass the communication on to his principal is mentioned as a reason why the principal should be treated as having received it. I think, however, that the true basis of these cases is that communication to the agent is treated, by reason of his authority to receive it, as communication to the principal. I know of no authority for the proposition that in the absence of any duty on the part of the principal to investigate, information which was received by an agent otherwise than as agent can be imputed to the principal simply on the ground that the agent owed to his principal a duty to disclose it.

On the contrary, I agree with the judge [Millett J below] that *Young v. David Payne & Co Ltd* [1904] 2 Ch 608 611 is authority against such a proposition. In that case the Exploring Land and Minerals Co Ltd lent £6,000 to David Payne & Co Ltd for 30 days on the security of a debenture. One Kolckmann, a stockbroker who was concerned in an ambitious and somewhat dubious scheme of flotation involving David Payne & Co Ltd, was also a director of the Exploring Land company. In his capacity as stockbroker he knew that the money would not be applied to any authorised purpose of the company but diverted to the use of its controlling shareholder. He actually signed the cheque by which the money was advanced. David Payne & Co. Ltd went into liquidation and the liquidator challenged the validity of the debenture on the ground that Kolckmann's knowledge of the ultra vires purposes for which the money would be used should be imputed to the Exploring Land company.

Buckley J appears to have assumed that, as a director of the Exploring Land company, Kolckmann owed a duty to disclose what he knew about the real purposes for which the money would be used. But he regarded this as insufficient to enable that knowledge to be imputed to the company. He said at p. 611 (my emphasis):

> "I understand the law to be this: that if a communication be made to his agent *which it would be his duty to hand on to his principals*...and if the agent has an interest which would lead him not to disclose to his principals the information that he has thus obtained, and in point of fact he does not communicate it, you are not to impute to his principals knowledge by reason of the fact that their agent knew something which it was not in his interest to disclose and which he did not disclose."

It is true that in the Court of Appeal, both Vaughan-Williams L.J. and Romer L.J. said that Kolckmann owed no duty to impart his knowledge to the Exploring Land company Thus Romer L.J. said:

> 'I take it that in such a transaction the lending company was not bound to inquire as to the application of the money at all by the borrowing company. That being so, it appears to me that knowledge independently acquired by a director in his personal capacity in respect to a matter which was irrelevant so far as concerned the lending company is knowledge which cannot be imputed to the company, for it was knowledge of something which did not really concern the lending company as a matter of law. Therefore, you cannot imply a duty on the part of the director to have told these facts to the lending company, or a duty on the part of the lending company to have inquired into that question...'

It is however clear from the process of reasoning that what Romer L.J. means is that in the absence of a duty to inquire, there was no duty of disclosure on the part of the director on which an outsider could rely for the purpose of imputing his knowledge to the company. I do not think that it would have affected his conclusion if the director had for some other reason (e.g. some internal company rule) owed a duty of disclosure with which he did not in fact comply. I agree with Buckley J that this would have been irrelevant. It follows that in my judgment Millett J was right to hold that Mr Ferdman's position as agent or broker does not enable his knowledge to be imputed to DLH.

➤ Note

Lords Toulson and Hodge in *Bilta v Nazir* **[3.29]**, at [197], noted that there is 'force in the suggestion by the editors of *Bowstead & Reynolds on Agency* (at para 8.214) that the rules of agency could have resulted in imputation of knowledge in [the *El Ajou*] case'.

➤ Questions

1. In Hoffmann LJ's analysis, a lot hangs on his concluding analysis of *David Payne & Co Ltd* [1904] 2 Ch 608. He suggests that an agent's duty to hand over information is irrelevant, unless the company also has a duty to inquire about the information. If both are present, then the company will be taken to have the relevant knowledge even if the agent does not actually pass it on. (*Meridian Global* **[3.01]** may be a nice illustration.) But *are* there instances where the director has a duty to hand over information, but the

company does not have a duty to inquire? What protective purpose would such a duty serve?[70]

2. In *El Ajou* **[3.26]** the court held unanimously that Mr Ferdman was the company's 'directing mind and will', and so the company had the relevant knowledge on this basis, even though not on the 'agency argument' (although see the comment in the previous Note). Is there any difference at all between Hoffmann LJ's 'imputation of knowledge on the basis of agency' (his categories (i)–(iii)) in *El Ajou* **[3.26]**, and Lord Hoffmann's 'attribution rules' (ie 'whose knowledge counts as the company's knowledge *for this purpose?*') in *Meridian Global* **[3.01]**? If there is no difference, then the latter is certainly simpler and more clearly focused on the problem.

3. Some individuals within a company have roles which are expressly focused on receiving and delivering information. On what basis might it be said that information communicated to a company secretary, as the officer charged with general authority in the administrative affairs of the company (see the *Panorama* case **[3.03]**), will almost invariably be deemed to be known to the company?

Aggregating the knowledge of different people is not usually possible.

[3.27] Orr v Milton Keynes Council [2011] EWCA Civ 62 (Court of Appeal)

Orr had been employed by Milton Keynes Council as a part-time youth worker. He was summarily dismissed by his manager, for gross misconduct. Orr unsuccessfully argued that, as a matter of law, his manager's knowledge that the manager had provoked the altercation was imputed to the council, and the failure by the person conducting the disciplinary proceedings on behalf of the council to take that information into account meant that the local authority's decision to dismiss had not been reasonable within the Employment Rights Act 1996.

MOORE-BICK LJ:

58. . . . Parliament cannot have assumed that in a large organisation every allegation of misconduct or other grounds of dismissal against any employee would be investigated by the person or body that represents it at the highest level, who would himself then decide whether to exercise the power of dismissal. . . . The answer to the question 'Whose knowledge or state of mind was *for this purpose* intended to count as the knowledge or state of mind of the employer?' will be 'The person who was deputed to carry out the employer's functions under section 98'.

59. In the present case that person was Mr Cove [the person conducting the investigation]. The submission that the knowledge of Mr Madden [the manager] is to be treated as the knowledge of the council and as such is to be imputed to Mr Cove is in my view unsound. In the first place, it is doubtful whether in circumstances of this kind an employee's knowledge of his own wrongdoing is to be imputed to his employer: see *In re Hampshire Land Co* **[3.28]** in which an officer's knowledge of his own wrongdoing was not attributable to the company. More importantly, however, to impute to Mr Cove knowledge of Mr Madden's behaviour that he could not reasonably have acquired through the appropriate disciplinary procedure in order to enable Mr Orr to treat as unreasonable and therefore unfair a decision that was in all respects reasonable would be to impose on the council as the employer a more onerous duty than that for which s 98 provides.

---

[70] The only instance of such a duty seems to be the controversial suggestion that directors have a duty to disclose their own disloyal breaches to their company, thus enabling the company to sue them for disgorgement of their disloyal gains: see 'Duty to disclose own misconduct?', p 361 and **[7.13]**.

60. Sedley LJ [dissenting] suggests that the person deputed to carry out the investigation on behalf of the employer must be taken to know any relevant facts which the employer actually knows, which include not only matters known to the chief executive but also any relevant facts known to any person within the organisation who in some way represents the employer in its relations with the employee. However, in my view it would be contrary to the language of the statute to hold that the employer had acted unreasonably and unfairly if in fact he had done all that could reasonably be expected of him and had made a decision that was reasonable in all the circumstances. That is why it is important to identify whose state of mind is intended to count as that of the employer for this purpose. To impute to that person knowledge held by others is to reverse the principles of attribution formulated in *Meridian Global Funds Management Asia Ltd* **[3.01]** and to place the whole exercise on an artificial footing. The obligation to carry out a reasonable investigation as the basis of providing satisfactory grounds for thinking that there has been conduct justifying dismissal necessarily directs attention to the quality of the investigation and the resulting state of mind of the person who represents the employer for that purpose. If the investigation was as thorough as could reasonably have been expected, it will support a reasonable belief in the findings, whether or not some piece of information has fallen through the net. There is no justification for imputing to that person knowledge that he did not have and which (*ex hypothesi*) he could not reasonably have obtained. Moreover, the principle cannot logically be restricted to a person in the position of Mr Madden; if sound, it must apply to all employees above a certain level of seniority, though in principle it should apply to any employee who is in possession of information that relates to the organisation's affairs and which it is material for his superiors to know. To impute Mr Madden's knowledge to Mr Cove, therefore, is tantamount to treating Mr Cove as having acquired all the relevant information in the organisation's possession. That is not what section 98(4) or the authorities require.

This case cites *Re Hampshire Land* **[3.28]**, a case which has attracted a surprising degree of attention in the past few years: see the extract and subsequent discussion in the next section, 'The general rule and the historical 'fraud exception'…', p 165.

Denying attribution

In the closing stages of this chapter it is necessary to return to a difficult issue which was raised in the opening pages: see 'Introduction', p 83. The question is when, if ever, can a company *deny* that the acts (or knowledge or intention) of one of its seemingly relevant agents will count as the acts (or knowledge or intention) of the company?

The situations in which this issue merits discussion are threefold: first, when the company denies that these acts of a particular agent can be attributed *at all*; secondly, when the company denies that these acts can be attributed *in these circumstances*, even though it concedes they can be attributed in other circumstances; and, finally, when the company concedes that attribution applies, but denies the legal consequences of it in the particular circumstances in issue. One or two cases from each category will illuminate the issues in play. Keeping the categories analytically distinct is useful.

Certain acts should not be attributed to the company at all

This category of denial of attribution can be dealt with briefly. Its starting assertion is that the acts or knowledge of a particular person simply do not count as the company's acts or knowledge.

We have seen this argument advanced where an agent who is negotiating a contract has *no* authority to act. Revisit the cases considered in the section 'Agency and authority in corporate contracting', p 93, noting especially *Freeman and Lockyer v Buckhurst Park Properties (Mangal) Ltd* [3.10]. Recall too the important debate in this context about *scope* of authority and *abuse* of authority, and whether it is true to say that agents have *no* authority to act (for the purposes of attribution) even though acting within the permitted scope of their designated authority, but in abuse of it: see '1. Directors' authority and breach of directors' duties', p 124.

Note that this argument (ie the company suggesting 'this is not my act') is far less successful in tort cases. Then it is frequently no answer to attribution for the company to insist that the relevant agent was not authorised to act in the improper ways he has done.

We have also seen this denial of attribution argument advanced in the context of an agent's knowledge: revisit *El Ajou* [3.26] and see *Re Hampshire Land* [3.28].

This category of case is important, but relatively straightforward.

Certain acts, knowledge or intentions should not be attributed in these particular circumstances

The starting point in this category is necessarily historical, even though the history has been overtaken by recent decisions in the Supreme Court. *Re Hampshire Land* [3.28] stands for the principle that where one person is an officer (not necessarily a director) of two companies, any personal knowledge of the officer is not necessarily the knowledge of both the companies. Knowledge acquired as an officer of one company will only be imputed to the other where a duty is imposed on the officer to communicate that knowledge to the other company, and a duty is imposed on the same officer to receive the notice for the other company (notice the *El Ajou* [3.26] approach). Moreover, if the common officer has been guilty of fraud, or even irregularity, the court will not draw the inference that the officer has fulfilled these duties.

This first aspect would now be regarded as a straightforward application of the attribution rules: whose knowledge counts as the knowledge of the company for this purpose? Does it include the knowledge of the person with a dual role? On this basis this first aspect falls squarely into the previous category of cases where the company simply denies that this *is* the person whose knowledge counts as the company's knowledge. The second aspect—the rule of exception for wrongdoing agents—is more controversial. It falls into this present second category, where the company concedes that sometimes this person's knowledge of the issue will be attributed to the company, but not, it suggests, for this *particular* purpose. It then becomes important to identify which particular purposes require more care in handling the attribution rules. Consider the case itself before we turn to modern approaches.

The general rule and the historical 'fraud exception': when is it appropriate for the knowledge of a director to be attributed to the director's companies?

[3.28] In Re Hampshire Land Co [1896] 2 Ch 743 (Chancery Division)

The directors of a company were empowered to borrow money on its behalf, but not beyond a certain limit without the consent of a general meeting. A general meeting gave the required consent, but the notices summoning the meeting were irregular, in that they did not specify that borrowing beyond the limit was to be authorised by the meeting. The money was borrowed from a society the secretary of which was also the secretary of the company, and he knew of the irregularity. The court held that the knowledge of the secretary could not be imputed to the society, and that the money lent could therefore be proved in the winding up of the company.

VAUGHAN WILLIAMS J: The question really is, whether the shareholders in the building society or the shareholders in the company ought to bear any loss that would result from the resolution authorizing the directors of the company to borrow this money. So far as the shareholders of both the two corporations are concerned, they are innocent people.

It must be taken that in fact a resolution was passed by the shareholders of the company authorizing the borrowing of the £30,000 [but] no notice was given to them that this special business was intended to be proposed to the meeting [and the directors] had no authority in the absence of a properly passed resolution to borrow this money. But in that state of things, the money having been lent by the society and received by the company, the question which I have stated arises. It is not disputed that the authority of *Royal British Bank v. Turquand* is such that the society had a right to assume in a case like this that all these essentials of internal management had been carried out by the borrowing company, and that it is only in case the law imputes to the society knowledge of these irregularities that the society is not to rank upon the estate of the Hampshire Land Company as a creditor for the amount lent.

The question, therefore, is this: Is it right to impute this knowledge to the society? It is said that it is right, because Mr. Wills was the common officer of both the society and the company, and was aware of these irregularities; and I think it must be taken that he was aware of them. Then it is said that his knowledge as the officer of the company is equally his knowledge as the officer of the society, and that therefore I ought to impute this knowledge to the society. I do not agree. Both Mr. Bramwell Davis and Mr. Jenkins [counsel] shrank from saying that wherever there is a common officer of two societies, the knowledge of such officer personally is to be imputed to both the societies employing him. In fact it was quite impossible, having regard to...[and various authorities were then cited]. But the moment you have done that you have to ask yourself this: Where is the line to be drawn, or what is the test to be applied in order to say whether or not in each case the knowledge of the common officer is the knowledge of each company employing him? It seems to me that, broadly,...the knowledge which has been acquired by the officer of one company will not be imputed to the other company, unless the common officer had some duty imposed upon him to communicate that knowledge to the other company, and had some duty imposed on him by the company which is alleged to be affected by the notice to receive the notice....It seems to me that that is not at all the case here....The case is very much more like the one which both Mr. Bramwell Davis and Mr. Jenkins had to admit was an exception to the general rule that they sought to lay down, for they admitted that if Wills had been guilty of a fraud, the personal knowledge of Wills of the fraud that he had committed upon the company would not have been knowledge of the society of the facts constituting that fraud; because common sense at once leads one to the conclusion that it would be impossible to infer that the duty, either of giving or receiving notice, will be fulfilled where the common agent is himself guilty of fraud. It seems to me that if you assume here that Mr. Wills was guilty of irregularity—a breach of duty in respect of these transactions—the same inference is to be drawn as if he had been guilty of fraud. I do not know, I am sure, whether he was guilty of actual fraud; but whether his conduct amounted to fraud or to breach of duty, I decline to hold that his knowledge of his own fraud or of his own breach of duty is, under the circumstances, the knowledge of the company....

On this rather slender authority a whole industry was built, based on the 'fraud exception' to attribution. The language of 'fraud exception' is now decried, but over the past few years as courts and commentators worked out the proper underpinnings of this approach, some suggested that the 'fraud exception' could be applied quite generally to deny the attribution to companies of the knowledge (and perhaps even the acts) of wrongdoing directors (now accepted as too broad); some that it could only be relied upon to deny attribution when the company was the 'victim' of the wrongdoing rather than the 'villain' (and the 'primary' victim, not the 'secondary' one) (now regarded as unhelpful); still others suggested the rule could only be applied 'defensively' (not accurate); and still others suggested the rule did not exist at all: P Watts, 'Imputed Knowledge in Agency Law—Excising the Fraud Exception' (2001) 117 LQR 300, 319–320.

Thankfully the Supreme Court has brought much-needed clarity to the area in *Bilta (UK) Ltd (In Liquidation) v Nazir* [3.29], assisted by Lord Walker's leading judgment in the Hong Kong Court of Final Appeal's decision in *Moulin Global Eyecare* [3.30]. A precise formulation is still not possible, but—with luck—we are moving to the position where there is *no* special 'Hampshire Land principle' or 'fraud exception' or even 'breach of duty exception' (Lord Sumption's preferred terminology in *Bilta v Nazir* [3.29] at [71]). Instead, the attribution question (whether dealing with attribution of knowledge or otherwise) should be capable of being answered by straightforward application of the analysis advanced in *Meridian Global* [3.01]. The question which invariably has to be answered is 'Which acts (or knowledge or intentions) of which people should count as the company's acts (or knowledge or intentions) for this particular legal purpose?' That question depends far more on the particular legal claim in issue, and who is suing and being sued, than on whether one of the corporate directors has committed a wrong. In most cases they will have, and that is what will have given rise to the litigation. In the particular context—that is, *for the particular legal purpose in issue*—it should be clear whether the wrongdoing director's acts, knowledge or intentions should be attributed to the company or not. The answer will sometimes be yes, sometimes no.

Expressing exactly that sentiment, note the comments of Lords Toulson and Hodge JJSC at [180] of *Bilta v Nazir* [3.29]:

> It has become common to speak of 'the *Hampshire Land* principle' or the 'fraud exception' as the exception to an otherwise general rule that attribution occurs. It is our view that 'the fraud exception' is not confined to fraud but is simply an instance of a wider principle that whether an act or a state of mind is to be attributed to a company depends on the context in which the question arises. 'The fraud exception', applied to prevent an agent from pleading his own breach of duty in order to bar his principal's claim against him, is the classic example of non-attribution. But it is not the only one.

A simple example illustrates this. Suppose a company's fraudulent directors use their corporate vehicle to defraud a third party of £100 million, and the directors themselves then abscond with the funds. In a claim by the third party against the company, the directors' frauds *will* be attributed to the company: the directors' acts and fraudulent intentions will count as the company's acts and intentions, and the company will be 'directly' or 'personally' liable to the third party for the losses suffered by the third party as a result of the frauds.[71] By contrast, if the company sues its own fraudulent directors, seeking to recover from them the losses their activities have caused to the company, the directors' acts will *not* be attributed to the company in any way which might enable the defendant directors to insist that the company is a joint tortfeasor, or has consented to the directors' frauds, or is illegitimately attempting to recover for its own wrongs.

The illustrations of these effective denials of attribution are elaborated in the following extracts.

In every question of attribution, context and purpose are key: that is, for the purpose of this particular legal claim, whose acts, etc, are to count as the acts, etc, of the company?

[3.29] Bilta (UK) Ltd v Nazir [2015] UKSC 23, [2015] 2 WLR 1168 (Supreme Court)

The case concerned a VAT carousel fraud based on trading in carbon credits. It was inherent in the fraud that Bilta would always be insolvent and unable to pay the output VAT to HMRC (in excess of £38 million), while its directors and associated third parties would

---

[71] The fraudulent directors will also be personally liable to the third party in deceit.

reap corresponding benefits. When Bilta (through its provisional liquidator) sued its directors and these third parties, the defendants sought to strike out the claim on the basis of the illegality defence (*ex turpi causa*). This would deny the company the right to recover benefits based on its own wrongdoing. The strike-out application was unanimously dismissed by the Supreme Court (upholding the decisions of Sir Andrew Morritt C and the Court of Appeal) on the basis that in these particular circumstances—that is, when Bilta was suing its own directors and their co-conspirators, but not necessarily in other circumstances—the wrongdoing of Bilta's directors could not be attributed to Bilta, and so the illegality defence could not apply.

Given this conclusion, the true nature of the illegality defence did not need to be settled. The two main judgments in the case (Lord Sumption, and Lords Toulson and Hodge) took different views on this; Lord Neuberger thought it needed urgent resolution by a seven- or nine-member panel of the Supreme Court. The issue is important, but not part of 'core company law'.

The extract below focuses solely on attribution (sometimes adopting Lords Neuberger and Mance's summaries of the main judgments). This case merits reading in full, but what follows identifies the key points in the court's approach to attribution, and denial of attribution.

LORD NEUBERGER PSC (with whom LORD CLARKE and LORD CARNWATH JJSC agreed):

Attribution

7. So far as attribution is concerned, it appears to me that [the judgments of Lord Sumption and of Lords Toulson and Hodge both] reach the conclusion which may, I think be stated in the following proposition. Where a company has been the victim of wrong-doing by its directors, or of which its directors had notice, then the wrong-doing, or knowledge, of the directors cannot be attributed to the company as a defence to a claim brought against the directors by the company's liquidator, in the name of the company and/or on behalf of its creditors, for the loss suffered by the company as a result of the wrong-doing, even where the directors were the only directors and shareholders of the company, and even though the wrong-doing or knowledge of the directors may be attributed to the company in many other types of proceedings....

9. Particularly given the full discussion [in those judgments], I do not think that it would be sensible for me to say much more on the topic. However, I would suggest that the expression 'the fraud exception' be abandoned, as it is certainly not limited to cases of fraud—...Indeed, it seems to me that it is not so much an exception to a general rule as part of a general rule. There are judicial observations which tend to support the notion that it is, as Lord Sumption says...based on public policy—or common sense, rationality and justice...However, I agree with Lord Mance's analysis...that the question is simply an open one: whether or not it is appropriate to attribute an action by, or a state of mind of, a company director or agent to the company or the agent's principal in relation to a particular claim against the company or the principal must depend on the nature and factual context of the claim in question....

The role of statutory policy in this case

18. As well as dismissing this appeal on the attribution issue on the same grounds as Lord Sumption, Lords Toulson and Hodge would also dismiss the appeal on the grounds of statutory policy. They suggest that it would make a nonsense of the statutory duty contained in section 172(3) of the Companies Act 2006... if directors against whom a claim was brought under that provision could rely on the *ex turpi causa* or illegality defence [and by that simple step thereby avoid all their statutory responsibilities]...

19. I agree with Lords Toulson and Hodge that this argument cannot be correct...[quoting and applying the '*for this purpose*' test laid down by Lord Hoffmann in *Meridian Global Funds Management Asia Ltd v Securities Commission* **[3.01]**].

LORD MANCE JSC:

35. The present appeal raises the question whether a company can pursue its directors and sole shareholder for breaches of duty towards the company depriving it of its assets. Lord Toulson and Lord Hodge consider that the straightforward answer to the question is that that it would deprive the duties which the shareholder-directors owed Bilta of all content, if the defence of illegality were open to the appellants. But they consider that, if analysed in terms of attribution, the case is not one where the shareholder-directors' acts and state of mind can or should be attributed to Bilta....

36. Lord Sumption in contrast sees the case as turning on rules of attribution, which he views as applying 'regardless of the nature of the claim or the parties involved'...But he qualifies the effect of his analysis by reference to a policy-based 'breach of duty exception' which covers the present case in order 'to avoid, injustice and absurdity'...Later in his judgment however...he modifies this approach by describing it as no more than a 'valuable tool of analysis.'

37. In common, as I see it, with Lords Neuberger, Toulson and Hodge...I do not think it appropriate to analyse the present case as one of prima facie attribution, which is then negatived under a breach of duty exception. As Lord Sumption's judgment demonstrates, it would, however, make no difference to the outcome in this case, if the matter were to be so analysed, though the plethora of difficult authority to which such an analysis has given rise, far from proving its value, argues for what is to my mind a simpler and more principled analysis.

38. One way or another, it is certainly unjust and absurd to suggest that the answer to a claim for breach of a director's (or any employee's) duty could lie in attributing to the company the very misconduct by which the director or employee has damaged it. A company has its own separate legal personality and interests. Duties are owed to it by those officers who constitute its directing mind and will, similarly to the way in which they are owed by other more ordinary employees or agents....

39. Rules of attribution are as relevant to individuals as to companies. An individual may him- or herself do the relevant act or possess the relevant state of mind. Equally there are many contexts in which an individual will be attributed with the actions or state of mind of another, whether an agent or, in some circumstances, an independent contractor. But in relation to companies there is the particular problem that a company is an artificial construct, and can only act through natural persons. It has no actual mind, despite the law's persistent anthropomorphism...

41. As Lord Hoffmann made clear in *Meridian Global*, the key to any question of attribution is ultimately always to be found in considerations of context and purpose. The question is: whose act or knowledge or state of mind is *for the purpose* of the relevant rule to count as the act, knowledge or state of mind of the company?...

42. Where the relevant rule consists in the duties owed by an officer to the company which he or she serves, then, whether such duties are statutory or common law, the acts, knowledge and states of mind of the company must necessarily be separated from those of its officer. The purpose of the rule itself means that the company cannot be identified with its officers. It is self-evidently impossible that the officer should be able to argue that the company either committed or knew about the breach of duty, simply because the officer committed or knew about it. This is so even though the officer is the directing mind and will of the company. The same clearly also applies even if the officer is also the sole shareholder of a company in or facing insolvency. Any other conclusion would ignore the separate legal identity of the company, empty the concept of duty of content and enable the company's affairs to be conducted in fraud of creditors.

43. At the same time, however, if the officer's breach of duty has led to the company incurring loss in the form of payments to or liability towards third parties, the company must be able as part of its cause of action against its officer to rely on the fact that, in that respect, its officer's acts

and state of mind were and are attributable to the company, causing it to make such payments or incur such liability. In other words, it can rely on attribution for one purpose, but disclaim attribution for another. The rules of attribution for the purpose of establishing or negating vicarious liability to third parties differ, necessarily, from the rules governing the direct relationship inter se of the principal and agent....

LORD SUMPTION JSC:

64. The sole question on this part of the appeal is therefore...whether the dishonesty which engages the illegality defence is to be attributed to Bilta for the specific purpose of defeating its claim against the directors and their alleged co-conspirators. The question is whether the defence is available to defeat an action by a company against the human agent who caused it to act dishonestly for damages representing the losses flowing from that dishonesty. The Chancellor of the High Court and Court of Appeal both held that it was not. While there are dicta in the judgments below, especially in the Court of Appeal, which range wider than is really necessary, their essential reason was the same, namely that the agent was not entitled to attribute his own dishonesty to the company for the purpose of giving himself immunity from the ordinary legal consequences of his breach of duty....

Attribution

66.... [T]he illegality defence applies to companies as it applies to natural persons. This is the combined effect of the company's legal personality and of the attribution to companies of the state of mind of those agents who for the relevant purpose can be said to think for it. But the principles can only apply to companies in modified form, for they are complex associations of natural persons with different interests, different legal relationships with the company and different degrees of involvement in its affairs. A natural person and his agent are autonomous in fact as well as in law. A company is autonomous in law but not in fact. Its decisions are determined by its human agents, who may use that power for unlawful purposes. This gives rise to problems which do not arise in the case of principals who are natural persons.... [Lord Sumption then considered the relevant authorities and noted the important difference between 'primary'/'direct' liability and 'vicarious' liability.]

The exception: breach of the agent's duty to the company

71. Bilta's answer to this, which was accepted by both the judge and the Court of Appeal, is that the dishonesty of Mr Chopra and Mr Nazir is not to be attributed to Bilta, because in an action for breach of duty against the directors there cannot be attributed to the company a fraud which is being practised against it by its agent, even if it is being practised by a person whose acts and state of mind would be attributable to it in other contexts. It is common ground that there is such a principle. It is commonly referred to as the fraud exception, but it is not limited to fraud. It applies in certain circumstances to prevent the attribution to a principal of his agent's knowledge of his own breach of duty even when the breach falls short of dishonesty. In the context of the illegality defence, which is mainly concerned with dishonest or criminal acts, this exception from normal rules of attribution will normally arise when it is sought to attribute to a principal knowledge of his agent's fraud or crime but that is not inherent in the underlying principle. I shall call it the 'breach of duty exception'....

Application to claims by the company against the defaulting agent

86.... The fundamental point made by the Court of Appeal in this case and the Court of Final Appeal in *Moulin* **[3.30]** is that, while the basic rules of attribution may apply regardless of the nature of the claim or the parties involved, the breach of duty exception does not. I agree with this. It reflects the fact that the rules of attribution are derived from the law of agency, whereas the fraud exception, like the illegality defence which it qualifies, is a rule of public policy. Viewed as a question of public policy, there is a fundamental difference between the case of an agent relying on his own dishonest performance of his agency to defeat a claim by his principal for his breach of duty; and that of a third party who is not privy to the fraud but is sued for negligently failing to prevent the principal from committing it.

87. There are three situations in which the question of attribution may arise. First, a third party may sue the company for a wrong such as fraud which involves a mental element. Secondly, the company may sue either its directors for the breach of duty involved in causing it to commit that fraud, or third parties acting in concert with them, or (as in the present case) both. Third, the company may sue a third party who was not involved in the directors' breach of duty for an indemnity against its consequences.

88. In the first situation, the illegality defence does not arise. The company has no claim which could be barred, but is responding to a claim by the third party....

89 A claim by a company against its directors, on the other hand, is the paradigm case for the application of the breach of duty exception. An agent owes fiduciary duties to his principal, which in the case of a director are statutory. It would be a remarkable paradox if the mere breach of those duties by doing an illegal act adverse to the company's interest was enough to make the duty unenforceable at the suit of the company to whom it is owed. The reason why it is wrong is that the theory which identifies the state of mind of the company with that of its controlling directors cannot apply when the issue is whether those directors are liable to the company. The duty of which they are in breach exists for the protection of the company against the directors. The nature of the issue is therefore itself such as to prevent identification. In that situation it is in reality the dishonest directors who are relying on their own dishonesty to found a defence. The company's culpability is wholly derived from them, which is the very matter of which complaint is made. [Lord Sumption then discussed various cases, including *Attorney-General's Reference (No 2 of 1982)* [3.31] and *Belmont Finance Ltd v Williams Furniture Ltd* [10.10].]

91. The position is different where the company is suing a third party who was not involved in the directors' breach of duty for an indemnity against its consequences. In the first place, the defendant in that case, although presumably in breach of his own distinct duty, is not seeking to attribute his own wrong or state of mind to the company or to rely on his breach of duty to avoid liability. Secondly, as between the company and the outside world, there is no principled reason not to identify it with its directing mind in the ordinary way. For a person, whether natural or corporate, who is culpable of fraud to say to an innocent but negligent outsider that he should have stopped him in his dishonest enterprise is as clear a case for the application of the illegality defence as one could have. *Stone & Rolls* [3.33] was a case of just this kind....[72]

92. The technique of applying the general rules of agency and then an exception for cases directly founded on a breach of duty to the company is a valuable tool of analysis, but it is no more than that. Another way of putting the same point is to treat it as illustrating the broader point made by Lord Hoffmann in *Meridian Global* [3.01] that the attribution of legal responsibility for the act of an agent depends on the purpose for which attribution is relevant. Where the purpose of attribution is to apportion responsibility between a company and its agents so as to determine their rights and liabilities to each other, the result will not necessarily be the same as it is in a case where the purpose is to apportion responsibility between the company and a third party....

LORD TOULSON AND LORD HODGE JJSC:

[This joint judgment reiterated the importance of context in attribution. It reviewed the authorities and described the different contexts in which the issues were important. Only small parts are extracted here.]

Attribution

180.... While there is a role in our law for the concept of the directing mind and will of a company, it is important to analyse that role and in particular to avoid the dangers of ascribing human attributes to a non-natural person such as a company....

---

[72] This depends entirely on the fact that the company is suing to recover for a loss derived from its own wrongdoing. In the *Stone & Rolls* context that seems doubtful, although it was the analysis unanimously adopted by the House of Lords. See S Worthington, 'Corporate Attribution and Agency: Back to Basics' (forthcoming).

202.... [A] finding that a person is for a specific purpose the 'directing mind and will' of a company, when it is not merely descriptive, is the product of a process of attribution in which the court seeks to identify the purpose of the statutory or common law rule or contractual provision which might require such attribution in order to give effect to that purpose. Similarly, when the question of attribution arises in the context of an agency relationship, the nature of the principal's or other party's claim is highly material... Even when the primary rules of attribution apply, where the transaction is approved by the board of directors and completed under company seal... the court will not attribute to a company its directors' or employees' knowledge of their own wrongdoing to defeat the company's claim against them and their associates....

207.... [W]here the company claims against a third party, whether or not there is attribution of the director's or employee's act or state of mind depends on the nature of the claim. For example, if the company were claiming under an insurance policy, the knowledge of the board or a director or employee or agent could readily be attributed to the company in accordance with the normal rules of agency if there had been a failure to disclose a material fact. But if the claim by the company, for example for conspiracy, dishonest assistance or knowing receipt, arose from the involvement of a third party as an accessory to a breach of fiduciary duty by a director, there is no good policy reason to attribute to the company the act or the state of mind of the director who was in breach of his fiduciary duty. If the company chose not to sue the director who was in breach of his duty, the third party defendant could seek a contribution from him or her under the Civil Liability (Contribution) Act 1978. We have set out above why we consider that the defence of illegality is not available to a company's directors or their associates who are involved in a conspiracy against the company or otherwise act as accessories to the directors' breach of duty. Equally, there is no basis for attributing knowledge of such behaviour to the company to found an estoppel....

Attribution and the 'fraud exception' in Hong Kong.

[3.30]   Moulin Global Eyecare Trading (In Liquidation) v The Commissioner of Inland Revenue FACV5/2013 (Hong Kong Court of Final Appeal)

The company, via its liquidator, sought to recover around $98 million in overpaid tax, with the twist being that this had been deliberately and fraudulently overpaid so as to create a false impression of profitability. The company unsuccessfully sought to deny attribution of the knowledge of its fraudulent directors in its claim against the CIR to recover the overpayments. The extracts below focus on the general discussion of attribution.

LORD WALKER OF GESTINGTHORPE NPJ (with whom CHIEF JUSTICE MA, RIBEIRO PJ and BOKHARY NPJ agreed; TANG PJ dissented in part):

Attribution: the older authorities

61. Attribution means, in this context, the process of legal reasoning by which the conduct or state of mind of one or more natural persons (that is, human beings) is treated as that of a non-natural person (that is, a company) for the purpose of determining the company's legal liability or rights in civil proceedings (in particular, its liability or rights in contract, in tort or for unjust enrichment) or its criminal liability. In approaching the topic of attribution it is necessary to recognize that there is a problem of terminology in the word 'agent'. A natural person may choose whether or not to appoint an agent to act in the management of his property or the conduct of his business affairs. In principle it is his choice, although there are of course

some activities calling for special professional skills in which the appointment of an agent is strongly advisable, or even mandatory. A company, on the other hand, never has a choice. As English company law developed during the nineteenth century, eminent judges repeatedly emphasised that a company, as a *persona ficta*, a legal construct with no real personality, can act only by its agents....

67. The rather belated recognition of this important qualification of the 'directing mind and will' concept considerably reduces its apparent force. Except in the case of very small companies with very simple activities, there will not be a single individual in a company who satisfies the test for all purposes. After *Meridian* some legal scholars conjectured that the concept might disappear from company law, and it might be better if it had disappeared, as it tends to obscure the underlying importance of the basic principles of agency. To refer instead to 'the relevant responsible director or employee', or some such expression, would be less arresting but a good deal more accurate...

The fraud exception: the principle and the early cases

80. The existence of the fraud exception [the *Hampshire Land* principle] is not in doubt, but there has been a good deal of debate (both in decided cases and among legal scholars) as to its proper scope and limits. The situation to which it most squarely applies (and some would say, the only situation to which it should properly be applied) is where a director or senior employee of a company seeks to rely on his own knowledge of his own fraud against the company as a defence to a claim by the company against him (or accomplices of his) for compensation for the loss inflicted by his fraud. The injustice and absurdity of such a defence is obvious, and for more than a century judges have had no hesitation in rejecting it....

85. One of the issues in this appeal is whether the fraud exception can apply in circumstances where the primary rules of attribution are in play...[noting that *Belmont Finance Corpn Ltd v Williams Furniture Ltd (No 2)* **[10.10]** demonstrates that it can.]

Attribution and the fraud exception: conclusions

106. The decision of the Court of Appeal in [*Bilta (UK) Ltd (In Liquidation) v Nazir (No 2)* [2013] EWCA Civ 968, [2014] Ch 52, CA—note that the Supreme Court decision had not then been handed down] has achieved a welcome clarification of the law in this area. The general effect of the authorities discussed above can in my view be summarized in some short propositions.

(1) Questions of attribution are always sensitive to the factual situation in which they arise, and the language and legislative purpose of any relevant statutory provisions...

(2) The 'directing mind and will' concept in *Lennard* **[3.21]**, although still often referred to in judgments, has been greatly attenuated by recognition of the importance of the factual and legislative context...It might be better if it were to fade away as a general concept.

(3) In some cases acts of directors and employees will be attributed to the corporate employer without their state of mind being so attributed...

(4) The underlying rationale of the fraud exception is to avoid the injustice and absurdity of directors or employees relying on their own awareness of their own wrongdoing as a defence to a claim against them by their own corporate employer...

(5) The exception applies even if the wrongdoing consists of a transaction formally approved by the whole board of directors, and completed under the company seal: *Belmont No 2* at p 398. In other words the exception can apply even when the primary rules of attribution are in play.

(6) But the exception does not apply to protect a company where the issue is whether the company is liable to a third party for the dishonest conduct of a director or employee...

(7) The supposed distinction between primary and secondary victims, although sometimes a useful analytical tool, is ultimately much less important than the distinction between third party claims against a company for loss to the third party caused by the misconduct of a director or employee, and claims by a company against its director or employee (or an accomplice) for loss to the company caused by the misconduct of that director or employee...

(8) In cases concerned with insurance the terms of the policy are likely to be decisive, especially where a company has obtained cover against the risk of breach of duty, including fraud, by directors or employees... [citing cases where internal fraud] was the 'very thing' from which the insurance cover was intended to protect the company.

(9) The fraud exception does not appear to have been even raised as a defence, still less successfully relied on, in a claim by a company against its auditors for failure to detect internal fraud... with the sole exception of the extreme 'one-man' company case of *Stone & Rolls* **[3.33]** (see that case at paras 175 and 176). Again, internal fraud was the 'very thing' from which the auditors had a duty to protect the company.

(10) Criminal law cases are of little assistance in determining issues of attribution in civil law cases, because of the reluctance of the court, especially in the earlier cases, to treat offences as carrying strict liability... but *Tesco No 2* **[3.25]** and *Safeway* **[3.34]** show the more modern approach.

Conclusions on attribution

131.... [T]he true purpose and limits of the fraud exception have become much clearer. The gradual accretion of learning about primary and secondary victims, with or without additional refinements such as 'targeting' or 'vehicle of fraud', can be seen as having missed the point. The crucial distinction depends on the nature of the proceedings in which the issue of attribution arises. On one side there are... the liability cases, such as *El Ajou, Meridian*,... In them a company is being sued by a third party (which may be an official body) because the company is responsible for dishonest conduct on the part of one or more of its directors or employees. Here the fraud exception does not apply, even if the company is in some sense a victim. On the other side are what may be called the redress cases, such as *Gluckstein v Barnes, Belmont*,... and *Bilta* itself. In cases of this sort a company is seeking to make its own delinquent director or employee (probably by then an ex-director or ex-employee), or an accomplice of such a person, accountable for the loss that the company has suffered. That is the situation in which the fraud exception applies, because it would be absurd and unjust to permit a fraudulent director or employee to be able to use his own serious breach of duty to his corporate employer as a defence. [There then followed a nice analysis of several cases—including *Stone & Rolls* **[3.33]**—which do not fit easily into either of these two categories.]

134.... An essential part of the scheme of the IRO [Inland Revenue Ordinance] is that the Commissioner should be able to make assessments on the basis of the taxpayer's returns. It would frustrate this statutory purpose if the fraud exception were to intrude into this scheme. The fraud exception must be limited to its proper, limited role, that is of barring an unmeritorious defence in claims by corporate employers against dishonest directors or employees, or accomplices who have conspired with them.

135. The liquidators cannot therefore rely on the proviso to section 64(1) of the IRO, because [the company] was not prevented from lodging an objection within time; it chose not to do so. Nor can the liquidators rely on section 70A, because [the company] must be taken as having known that its returns were false, and... a deliberate lie is not an 'error' for the purposes of that section.

136. The Commissioner's decision was not flawed. I would dismiss the appeal...

> ➤ Notes

1. It is interesting and instructive to note that Mr Justice Tang PJ was largely in agreement with Lord Walker on the principles to be applied, but reached precisely the opposite conclusion on the facts:

> 29. I turn to consider the facts of the present case.... I proceed on the basis of that tax has been overpaid as a result of the fraud of MGET's [the company's] management. In other words, more tax than properly chargeable had been paid. This results in hardship and is unjust. Precisely, the object and purpose of s 70A to relieve. Of course, whether there was an error depends on whether the fraudulent knowledge of MGET's management should be attributed to MGET. In this context I note that if profits had been overstated due to the negligence or ineptitude of its management or its auditors, s 70A would apply. Looked at with common sense, it is difficult to see why a company whose management was negligent or inept should be better off than one where innocent shareholders had suffered at the hands of fraudulent management. Negligence and ineptitude are more common than fraud and would probably have a greater impact on revenue....
>
> 31. The liability of the Commissioner is statutory and depends on the language of s 70A. I have said this is not a liability or redress claim. The issue is not whether MGET is liable to the Commissioner for the dishonesty of MGET's management. The Commissioner is innocent and we are not concerned with any claim for redress. We are concerned with a statutory scheme under which tax paid in excess of what is properly chargeable may be refunded. The Commissioner is concerned with the proper administration of the scheme. He bears the primary responsibility to decide whether an application satisfies the requirement of the scheme. It is in this very unusual context that the court has to consider the application of the fraud exception. I believe the plain object and purpose of s 70A supply the answer. Has MGET paid more tax than was properly chargeable? If the liquidators could prove that the profits had indeed been inflated, the answer must be yes. Do justice and common sense tell one that they should not have a refund? No, given the purpose of s 70A, I believe justice and common sense require the application of the fraud exception. Subject to the 6 years time limit, the Commissioner has no good policy reason to wish to keep tax paid in excess of what was properly chargeable.

2. The law described in these cases is relevant in a wide variety of circumstances: see, for example, *Goldtrail Travel Ltd v Aydin* [2014] EWHC 1587 (Ch) and *UBS AG (London Branch) v Kommunale Wasserwerke Leipzig GmbH* [2014] EWHC 3615 (Comm) (denying attribution of a director's knowledge when that would have amounted to the company's knowledge of and consent to his own conflict of duty and interest).

Denying attribution where knowledge might amount to conspiracy or consent.

[3.31] Attorney-General's Reference (No 2 of 1982) [1984] QB 624 (Court of Appeal)

The question referred to the court by Attorney-General was whether a sole director and shareholder, or two such persons acting in concert, was capable of stealing from the company. The question arose from thefts of millions of pounds of assets from a number of companies owned and controlled by the two defendants. All the elements of the theft could be made out, but debate centred on whether the company must necessarily be taken to have consented to the appropriation of its assets by the defendants. The court held it must not.

KERR LJ for the court:… In particular, it was submitted that…[t]he defendants were the sole will and directing mind of the company. The company was therefore bound to consent to all to which they themselves consented.… [The trial judge—overruled here by the Court of Appeal—had held that:]

> '…*Salomon v. A. Salomon & Co. Ltd.* **[2.02]** is authority for saying that if all shareholders know of fraud on the company, there is no fraud. When X and Y wrote the cheques as directors, can it be said they did so without the consent of the company?…[T]hey are the company, and therefore they cannot steal from it. They gave consent to the writing of the cheques and the drawing of the money, and therefore, in my view, there is in law no theft.…'

In our view the judge clearly erred in taking this course.… [N]either *Salomon v. A. Salomon & Co. Ltd.* **[2.02]** nor the *Multinational Gas* **[7.43]** case were concerned with allegations that the shareholders and directors had acted illegally or dishonestly in relation to the company. Where this is alleged the position is different, as illustrated by the decision of the civil division of this court in *Belmont Finance Corporation Ltd. v. Williams Furniture Ltd.* **[10.10]**. [Kerr LJ discussed the case and concluded with this citation from it:]

> '… if the allegations in the statement of claim are made good, the directors of the plaintiff company must then have known that the transaction was an illegal transaction. But in my view such knowledge should not be imputed to the company, for the essence of the arrangement was to deprive the company improperly of a large part of its assets. As I have said, the company was a victim of the conspiracy. I think it would be irrational to treat the directors, who were allegedly parties to the conspiracy, notionally as having transmitted this knowledge to the company; and indeed it is a well recognised exception from the general rule that a principal is affected by notice received by his agent that, if the agent is acting in fraud of his principal and the matter of which he has notice is relevant to the fraud, that knowledge is not to be imputed to the principal. So in my opinion the plaintiff company should not be regarded as a party to the conspiracy, on the ground of lack of the necessary guilty knowledge.'

So far as the authorities in the realm of the civil law are concerned, this decision directly contradicts the basis of the defendants' argument in the present case. There can be no reason, in our view, why the position in the criminal law should be any different.… The essence of the defendants' argument is the alleged identity, in all respects, and for every purpose, between the defendants and the company. It is said, in effect, that their acts are necessarily the company's acts; that their will, knowledge, and belief are those of the company, and that their consent necessarily implies consent by the company. But how then can the company be regarded as 'the other' for the purposes of this [statutory provision on theft]? One merely has to read its wording to see that it cannot be given any sensible meaning in a context such as the present, where the mind and will of the defendants are also treated in law as the mind and will of 'the other.' It is for this reason that in such cases there can be no conspiracy between the directors and shareholders on the one hand and the company on the other…

These cases confirm that although the acts, knowledge and intentions of a sole director and shareholder (ie the 'directing mind and will' of the company) will be attributed to the company in almost all contexts—both the primary and general rules of attribution indicate this—there is at least one where they will not: where the company sues its wrongdoing director, the director cannot insist that *her* acts, knowledge or intentions will be attributed to the company *so as to make out the argument* that the company has consented to her wrong. This is equally true of directors with less all-embracing powers.

Summary

The rule which has finally emerged—it is suggested—might be put like this: a wrongdoer can never argue that *her* knowledge and intentions can be attributed to the company so as to provide *her* with either a claim against the company or a defence to its claim against her which she would not otherwise have. This seems to encompass the exceptions to attribution which all the cases in this section are focused on.

This rule can be illustrated by a simple contrast. The amalgam of facts is familiar. When a company's sole director enters into contracts on behalf of the company which deliberately defraud banks, this director's acts *will* count as the company's acts for the purpose of making the company itself liable to the banks for the fraud.[73] But when the company then sues this director for the losses his fraudulent activities have brought on the company, the director will *not* be able to insist that his company is complicit in the wrong, or has consented to his behaviour, or is abusing the court system by trying to recover for its own wrongs,[74] or is barred by the illegality defence,[75] and so deny the company any recovery and insulate the director from redress.

Despite attribution, the usual legal consequences should not prevail in these circumstances

Even when the rules of attribution render a company liable for certain wrongs, the company may be protected from the usual legal consequences when sued by the corporate insider whose own wrongs were the sole cause of the company's liability.

[3.32] Brumder v Motornet Service and Repairs Ltd [2013] EWCA Civ 195, [2013] 1 WLR 2783 (Court of Appeal)

The claimant, B, was the sole director and shareholder of the defendant company, which specialised in servicing vehicles and putting them through MOT inspections. B was injured at work, and brought a claim for damages for personal injury against the company. The trial judge held that statutory regulations imposed strict liability on the company to ensure that work equipment was 'maintained in an efficient state, in efficient working order and in good repair'. The company's failure to do this had caused the injury, so the company was strictly liable. But the claimant, he held, was entirely responsible for this corporate breach, and so was 100% contributorily negligent. On appeal, the Court of Appeal held that the finding of '100% contributory negligence' was wrong in principle, but reached the same conclusion as the trial judge on different grounds, as described below.

BEATSON LJ:

1. The question which falls for decision in this appeal is whether the sole director and shareholder of a company who suffers personal injuries as a result of the breach by the company of an absolute statutory obligation to maintain equipment in efficient working order can bring a claim against the company even though he was in breach of his obligations to the company to exercise reasonable care to enable the company to fulfil that obligation, and the company could only do so vicariously through him....

8. The key question is whether this case falls directly or by analogy within the principle and defence identified in *Ginty v Belmont Building Supplies Ltd* [1959] 1 All ER 414 by Pearson J, and

---

[73] Of course, the director will also be personally liable to the banks: all the elements of a claim in deceit can be made out against him, and he cannot evade the legal consequences by suggesting he was acting 'only' as the company's CEO. See *Standard Chartered Bank v Pakistan National Shipping Corpn (No 2)* **[3.20]**.

[74] See the next extracted case.

[75] See 'Attribution and illegality: companies and the *ex turpi causa* principle', p 180.

considered with approval by the House of Lords in *Boyle v Kodak Ltd* [1969] 1 WLR 661, 666F, 669, 670F, 671 and 672E, to which I will return. At this stage it suffices to refer to the statement of Lord Reid in *Boyle v Kodak Ltd* summarising the effect of the authorities. He stated, at p 667:

> 'once the [claimant] has established that there was a breach of an enactment which made the employer absolutely liable, and that that breach caused the accident, he need do no more. But it is then open to the employer to set up a defence that, in fact, he was not in any way in fault, but that the [claimant] employee was alone to blame.'

If that defence applies either directly or analogically in the circumstances of this case, that is the end of the matter and the appeal must be dismissed. If it does not, the question is whether any part of the claimant's damage resulted from his own fault, and, if so, the extent to which the claimant's damages should be reduced under the 1945 Act [ie Law Reform (Contributory Negligence) Act 1945 s 1(1)]....

34. Mr Coleman [counsel for the claimant], however, submitted that, on the facts of the present case, the principle in *Boyle v Kodak Ltd* could not be applied. [He suggested three reasons: the regulations were ones of strict liability, so fault was not in issue; the claimant was not himself the alter ego of the company and somehow subject to the regulations himself, and thus is breach of them; and in any event the problem with the machinery was not one which he would have discovered even with due care, so he was not at fault.]

37. [Beatson LJ considered that whether these three reasons were material depended on the principles which underpinned the defence.]...A number of explanations and justifications were considered by Pearson J in *Ginty v Belmont Building Supplies Ltd* [1959] 1 All ER 414. He rejected, at p 425, the theory that the performance of the employer's statutory duty had been delegated to the employee, and indicated that he considered that it was unsound to explain the defence as founded on the principle *ex turpi causa non oritur actio* (no action may be founded on illegal or immoral conduct).

38. Pearson J identified three explanations which he considered justified the defence. The first is the common law principle that a person cannot derive any advantage from his own wrong which, in this context, meant that a person cannot by his own wrongful act impose on his employer the liability to pay damages to him.

39. The second, which Pearson J considered is closely allied to the first, is the effect of a claimant's own negligence at common law; that is before the passing of the 1945 Act. At common law, if an accident was caused wholly or in part by a person's own negligence he was barred from recovering anything. Pearson J stated that, on the facts of *Ginty's* case, the accident was caused wholly by one wrongful act which constituted, in one aspect, a breach of obligation by the employee, and in another aspect a breach of obligation by his employer. Although one could say that the accident was wholly caused by the fault of the employee, one could also say that the accident was wholly caused by the fault of the employer. That, he considered, took such a case outside the scope of the 1945 Act and required the consideration of common law principles to see what the position is. He stated: 'if one does that, the common law principle is still valid to this extent, that, if the accident is wholly caused by the [claimant's] own fault, he is disentitled to recover.'

40. The third justification is the need to avoid circuity of action...Pearson J described circuity as existing where the employee is entitled to recover damages for breach of the statutory obligation against the employer but the employer is entitled to recover an equal sum in damages from the employee for (in that case) breach of contract. He stated that 'if that were the position, the litigation would go round in a circle, and for that reason there is, in my view, a valid plea of circuity of action'.

41. *Ginty's* case and *Boyle v Kodak Ltd* concerned an employee claimant, and not a claimant who was the employer company's director, let alone its sole director and shareholder. In the circumstances of the present case, moreover, as the corporate first defendant who is sued can only

act through its sole director, the claimant, there is no question of the director/claimant disobeying the company's instruction. The fact is that the director's acts and omissions constitute the company's breach of its duty under the Regulations. Can the *Ginty/Boyle v Kodak Ltd* defence apply in this situation, and, if it can, how is it to be explained?

42. The policy reasons for the absolute duty on employers in the Regulations are to relieve injured employees from the need to show fault, and therefore to protect them, as the weaker party in the relationship, and to encourage high standards of compliance by those responsible for the performance of the company's duty…. That does not apply to a director/claimant who is the only person through whom the company can act. Those considerations are strong pointers to the defence applying in the case of a director/claimant in the circumstances of this case….

44. [He continued, noting that the absolute nature of the company's duty under the regulations did not deny the defence, but…] [i]f a director/claimant is not in breach of a relevant duty to the defendant company, I do not consider that the company can invoke the *Ginty/Boyle v Kodak Ltd* defence. But, what if he is in breach of a relevant duty to the defendant company?

[He considered the relevant duty to be the claimant's duty to the company to exercise reasonable care, skill and diligence in relation to the first defendant's statutory obligations, including those under the 1998 Regulations, being a duty reiterated in CA 2006 s 174(2)(a), and that the claimant was in breach of this duty.]

48. The consequence of this is that the claimant is a wrongdoer and falls within the first of Pearson J's explanations or justifications for the defence; the common law principle that a person cannot derive any advantage from his own wrong. The common sense proposition in Lord Diplock's speech in *Boyle v Kodak Ltd* [1969] 1 WLR 661 that 'to say "You are liable to me for my own wrongdoing" is neither good morals nor good law' appears to me to be applicable where the director/claimant has paid no attention whatsoever to health and safety issues, and in the judge's words (at para 59) had 'abrogated his responsibilities as owner and director' of the company. I do not consider that it lies in the mouth of a claimant who is the defendant's sole director and shareholder, and through whom the company must act, to assert that the company has not proved that it has done all it could to ensure compliance when it is only through the claimant director's acts that the company can act….

50. Unless there is a particular policy reason which precludes the company from suing the director, the employer would be entitled to recover damages against the director in the sum which the director was supposedly entitled to recover against the employer. In *Safeway Stores Ltd v Twigger* **[3.34]** this court held that the policy of the Competition Act 1998 to impose a personal sanction on a firm which could not be passed on to individuals precluded the company seeking an indemnity from directors whose actions caused the company to be subjected to a regulatory sanction under the Act.

51. There is in my judgment no such precluding policy in the situation before us and no reason for protecting a director who, like the claimant in this case, has made no efforts in respect of the company's health and safety duties, in a situation where it is only that person who is able to act on behalf of the company. Whether or not there could be a valid plea of circuity of action, and whether or not this situation is provided for by provisions for set-off and counterclaim, in this situation, if the director/claimant was entitled to sue, it would not be inaccurate to describe the litigation, as Pearson J did in the passage set out at para 40, as going 'round in a circle'….

56. For these reasons I have concluded that the first defendant was entitled to rely on the *Ginty/Boyle v Kodak Ltd* defence….

LONGMORE LJ delivered a concurring judgment, and SIR ALAN WARD agreed.

➤ Question

This judgement, at [37], suggests this defence is distinct from the illegality defence. Lord Walker in *Stone & Rolls* **[3.33]** at [186] agrees, noting that 'The *ex turpi causa* rule is distinct from the general principle that a claimant should not obtain a personal profit from his own wrong, although the two often overlap.' What *are* the differences?

Attribution and illegality: companies and the *ex turpi causa* principle

This whole chapter concerns companies and their legal claims. This section deals with the illegality defence in the corporate context. In *Stone & Rolls* [**3.33**], Lord Phillips said that '*ex turpi causa* is a principle that prevents a claimant from using the court to obtain benefits from his own illegal conduct'. As a consequence, courts will not enforce illegal contracts, nor assist claimants to recover benefits from their own wrongdoing.

Quite when the illegality defence will operate is uncertain (recall the comments in *Bilta v Nazir* [**3.29**]), but in the corporate context the prior issue is typically whether the company *is* suing on its own wrongdoing, and that is determined by rules of attribution (recall that *Bilta v Nazir* failed at this step). Only if the company *is* held to be suing on its own wrongdoing will it then be appropriate to consider whether the illegality defence bars the claim.

In this section two controversial cases are noted: *Stone & Rolls* [**3.33**] and *Safeway v Twigger* [**3.34**]. In both cases the illegality defence was held to bar the companies' claims, being claims against its auditors in the first case, and against its directors and employees in the second. The authority of both cases is weakened by comments made in *Bilta v Nazir* [**3.29**], although neither case was overruled and there seemed to be at least partial support for the results, if not the reasoning. In the circumstances, the approach here is merely to note the facts and outcomes, and the comments made by the Supreme Court in *Bilta v Nazir* [**3.29**].

Claims by a company against its defaulting directors: relevance of the illegality defence.

Revisit *Bilta v Nazir* [**3.29**]: the Supreme Court held that the directors' own wrongs could not be attributed to the company in the context of the company's claims against those directors and their co-conspirators for the very same wrongs. This meant that the company was *not* suing on its own wrongdoing, and the illegality defence (whatever its scope) could not be in issue.

Frauds perpetrated by a 'one man company'—claims against its auditors: relevance of the illegality defence.

[3.33] Stone & Rolls Ltd (In Liquidation) v Moore Stephens (A Firm) [2009] UKHL 39, [2009] 1 AC 1391 (House of Lords)

The issue before the court was deceptively simple. A one man company had perpetrated frauds on a number of banks to the tune of almost £100 million. The company's auditors had not detected the fraud. Neither the company nor the fraudster could meet the company's liabilities to the banks. Assuming the auditors *were* negligent, could the company (through its liquidator) sue the auditors for the losses the company had suffered because the frauds had not been detected? By a 3:2 majority, the House of Lords held that it could *not*.

The reasons of the majority express different subtleties, but, broadly, they accepted that: (i) the company was a wrongdoer (ie the fraudster's fraud *was* the company's fraud, and the *Hampshire Land* exception did not apply[76]); (ii) as a principle of public policy, a wrongdoer

---

[76] This conclusion may have misconceived the precise wrong in issue in the litigation: see S Worthington, 'Corporate Attribution and Agency: Back to Basics' (forthcoming).

cannot recover in a cause of action based on its own wrongdoing (ie the *ex turpi causa* principle); and (iii) in the proposed action by the company against its auditors, the 'wrongdoers' *would* recover for their own wrong—because, at least in a one man company, the company was exclusively identified with its shareholders (a claim which seems to deny the doctrine in *Salomon* [2.02]). The majority explicitly confined their conclusions to a 'one man'/'sole actor' company.

The same conclusion might also have been reached quite independently (although the analysis was not so explicitly segregated in *Stone & Rolls*) on the basis that the auditors were in any event not liable in these circumstances, either because no duty was owed or alternatively because no loss was caused on the given facts. This too seems doubtful on the facts: see the extracts at [8.05].

The majority judgments focused predominantly on the application of the *Hampshire Land* principle, but their analysis on that issue has been overtaken by *Bilta v Nazir* [3.29], and on the duty of auditors. Perhaps in all of this, however, too little attention was paid to the company as a separate legal person (there was instead an assumed equivalence between the 'one man' and the 'one man company'), and to the fact that the recoveries would benefit the company's creditors not its sole fraudulent shareholder. As an illustration, consider the extract below.

> LORD BROWN OF EATON-UNDER-HEYWOOD:
>
> 197. . . . As Mr Sumption [counsel for the successful auditors] put it, uncontentiously, at the beginning of his printed case:
>
> > '[Mr Stojevic, the fraudster and the "one man" behind the "one man company"] was as completely identified with the company as it is possible for a human agent to be. He had sole control over the company's every act. He was the company's sole beneficial owner. There were no independent or innocent directors whom Mr Stojevic had to deceive to make the fraud happen. There were no innocent shareholders relying upon the auditors to monitor the management. There were no employees.'
>
> 198. How in these circumstances there is any room for the application of the *Hampshire Land* principle...I cannot for the life of me see....
>
> 199. In the present case Mr Stojevic and S & R [Stone & Rolls, his company] were in effect one and the same person....
>
> LORD MANCE (dissenting):
>
> 206. . . . I consider that the key to a proper resolution of this appeal is to bear firmly in mind: (a) the separate legal identities of a company and its shareholders; (b) the common law and contractual duties which it is common ground that auditors owe...

➤ Notes

The most important matters to take from *Stone & Rolls* are limited to those expressly accepted by the Supreme Court in *Bilta v Nazir* [3.29], where the case was reviewed. The following comments are important:

1. The Supreme Court in *Bilta v Nazir* [3.29] effectively shelved *Stone & Rolls* for most purposes other than its specific conclusion on the facts. As Lord Neuberger (with whom Lord Clarke and Lord Carnwath agreed) put it:

> 30. Subject to these points [extracted below], the time has come in my view for us to hold that the decision in *Stone & Rolls* should, as Lord Denning MR graphically put it in relation to another case in *In re King, decd* [1963] Ch 459, 483, be put "on one side in a pile and marked 'not to be

looked at again' ". Without disrespect to the thinking and research that went into the reasoning of the five Law Lords in that case, and although persuasive points and observations may be found from each of the individual opinions, it is not in the interests of the future clarity of the law for it to be treated as authoritative or of assistance save as already indicated.

2. The 'save as already indicated' reference was to the following points, again from Lord Neuberger (with whom Lord Clarke and Lord Carnwath agreed):

24.... [S]ubject to what I say in the next four paragraphs, I am of the view that, so far as it is to be regarded as strictly binding authority, *Stone & Rolls* is best treated as a case which solely decided that…on the facts of the particular case, the illegality defence succeeded and that the claim should be struck out.

25. But it would be unsatisfactory for us to leave the case without attempting to provide some further guidance as to its effect, in so far as we fairly can. For that purpose I welcome Lord Sumption JSC's enumeration of the three propositions which he suggests in his para 80 can be derived from *Stone & Rolls*. [Those were that (i) the illegality defence was available against a company only where the company was directly, as opposed to vicariously, responsible; (ii) even where the company's 'directing mind and will' had committed the wrong, it was critical to the application of the illegality defence that the company was a 'one-man company', that is, a company in which there were no innocent directors or shareholders; and (iii) in these circumstances even a third party (eg the auditors here) could raise the illegality defence, at any rate where it was not itself involved in the dishonesty.] With the exception of the first, I agree with what he says about them, although even the second and third propositions are supported by only three of the judgments at least one of which is by no means in harmony with the other two….

28. However, I note that Lord Mance suggests that it should be an open question whether the third proposition would apply to preclude a claim against auditors where, at the relevant audit date, the company concerned was in or near insolvency. While it appears that the third proposition, as extracted from three judgments in *Stone & Rolls*, would so apply, I have come to the conclusion that, on this appeal at least, we should not purport definitively to confirm that it has that effect….

29. I cannot agree that the first proposition identified by Lord Sumption JSC, namely that the illegality defence is only available where the company is directly, as opposed to vicariously, responsible for the illegality, can be derived from *Stone & Rolls* (whether or not the proposition is correct in law, which I would leave entirely open, although I see its attraction)…

3. Lord Mance similarly disagreed with Lord Sumption's first proposition, agreed with the second, and preferred to leave the third open (see [46]–[50]).

4. Finally, Lords Toulson and Hodge concluded that '*Stone & Rolls* should be regarded as a case which has no majority *ratio decidendi*. It stands as authority for the point which it decided, namely that on the facts of that case no claim lay against the auditors, but nothing more' [154]. They thought the decision was based on the 'fundamental proposition' that the auditors owed no duty for the benefit of those for whose benefit the claim was brought; hence, the claim should be struck out: see [136]–[154].

➤ Questions

1. If fraudulent directors controlled a widely held company (ie one with a number of independent shareholders), then the unanimous view in *Stone & Rolls* is that the pipeline

fraud against the banks would still be the company's fraud (so the banks could sue the company), but the illegality defence would *not* bar the company's claim against its auditors. Does this difference in outcome for 'one man' and 'widely held' companies make sense?

2. Does this public benefit role of auditors suggest that the outcome favoured by the minority in *Stone & Rolls* (permitting claims against the auditors) is preferable as a matter of policy?

3. Does the decision in *Stone & Rolls* fail to distinguish between how the company *acts* (or thinks or knows) and what the company *is*?

Claims by a company against its defaulting directors: attribution, public policy and the illegality defence.

[3.34] Safeway Stores Ltd v Twigger [2010] EWCA Civ 1472 (Court of Appeal)

Safeway was held liable for competition law breaches and required to pay a penalty to the Office of Fair Trading (OFT). When the company sought to recover from the responsible directors/employees, these defendants successfully raised the illegality defence. The court agreed that the *Hampshire Land* principle did not protect the company so as to permit its claim (reversing Flaux J). That might now seem directly contrary to *Bilta v Nazir* **[3.29]** (but see its cautious approval of *Safeway*, cited in the following Note). Consider the reasoning.

> LONGMORE LJ (with whom LLOYD LJ agreed in a short separate judgment):
> 29. …Once it is appreciated that the claimant companies are (personally and not vicariously) liable to pay the penalties exigible under the 1998 [Competition] Act those companies cannot invoke the *Hampshire Land* principle to say that they were not 'truly' liable. The principle gives them no defence to the OFT's claim for the penalties; they are personally liable to pay those penalties and it would be inconsistent with that liability for them to be able to recover those penalties in the civil courts from the defendants. The statutory scheme has attributed responsibility to the claimant companies and the *Hampshire Land* exception to the ordinary rule of attribution can have no import on the application of the *ex turpi maxim*.
> 30. This is not a decision which requires any resolution of fact but is a pure matter of law.
> PILL LJ:
> 44. The policy of the 1998 [Competition] Act is to protect the public and to do so by imposing obligations on the undertaking specifically. The policy of the statute would be undermined if undertakings were able to pass on the liability to their employees or the employees' D & O (directors and officers) insurers. Only if the undertaking itself bears the responsibilities and meets the consequences of their non-observance are the public protected. A deterrent effect is contemplated and the obligation to provide effective preventive measures is upon the undertaking itself.

➤ Question

Note the practical effect of this conclusion. The defaulting directors and employees escape personal liability, despite their breaches of duty, and the costs of the company's penalty therefore fall on the innocent shareholders and customers. Is this good policy?

➤ Note

The conclusions in *Safeway* must be read in the light of subsequent comments by the Supreme Court in *Bilta v Nazir* [3.29], where the case was briefly reviewed. The following comments are important:

> LORD NEUBERGER PSC (with whom LORD CLARKE and LORD CARNWATH JJSC agreed):
>
> 31.... Lord Sumption has accurately summarised the effect of the decision in his para 83. Lords Toulson and Hodge deal with it a little more fully and much more critically in their paras 157–162. I would take a great deal of persuading that the Court of Appeal did not arrive at the correct conclusion in that case. However, I do not believe that it would be right on this appeal to express a concluded opinion as to whether the case was rightly decided, and, if so, whether the reasoning of the majority or of Pill LJ was correct. It is unnecessary to reach any such conclusion and the points were not argued in detail before us: indeed, they were hardly addressed at all.
>
> LORD SUMPTION JSC:
>
> 83.... Safeway was not a one-man company [as in *Stone & Rolls*], but the statutory scheme had the peculiarity, which was critical to the reasoning of the Court of Appeal, that the offence was not capable of being committed by the individuals directly responsible. The Act imposed the prohibition and the resulting penalty only on the company. It was held that this required the attribution of the infringement to the company and its non-attribution to the defendants. On that ground, it was held that to apply the breach of duty exception so as to allow recovery of the penalty from the defendants would be inconsistent with the statutory scheme.[77] The decision is not authority for any proposition applying more generally.
>
> LORDS TOULSON and LORDS HODGE JJSC:
>
> 161. Unless there are special circumstances, the innocent shareholders should not be made to suffer twice. The reasoning in *Safeway*, if taken to its logical conclusion, would also mean that the company could not lawfully dismiss the errant employees or directors; for to rely on their misconduct would be to rely on its own misconduct...
>
> 162. Reference to public policy takes us to the only basis on which we consider that the decision of the Court of Appeal in Safeway may have been justified. Pill LJ considered that the policy of the Competition Act 1998 would be undermined if undertakings were able to pass on their liability to their employees. That may have been a sound reason for striking out Safeway's claims, and we express no view as to the merits of the decision. We accept that there may be circumstances where the nature of a statutory code, and the need to ensure its effectiveness, may provide a policy reason for not permitting a company to pursue a claim of the kind brought in Safeway.

Litigation: procedural issues

Conduct of litigation

Blackstone ('Limits to the idea of a company as a "person"?', p 62) quoted Sir Edward Coke as authority for the view that a company must always appear in court by attorney, 'for it cannot appear in person, being invisible, and existing only in intendment and consideration of the law'. The courts have for many centuries strenuously insisted on this rule, both in civil and in criminal cases, and it has only been by statute that inroads have been

---

[77] Although the company's claim is perhaps better described differently, as a claim against its directors and employees for their personal wrongdoing, causing loss to the company, with that loss assessed as including the company's consequential liability to a penalty.

made into it—and then mainly in relation to lower courts such as the magistrates' courts. So we have the paradox that the law is happy to identify a company with the individual who is its 'directing mind and will' for the purpose of making it criminally liable, while at the same time it will refuse to allow the company to appear before it in the person of the same individual. This remains the basic rule: in *RH Tomlinssons (Trowbridge) Ltd v Secretary of State for the Environment* [1999] 2 BCLC 760, CA, it was solemnly affirmed by the Court of Appeal. However, the Civil Procedure Rules, which came into effect on 26 April 1999, allow a company (with the leave of the court) to appear by an *employee* and, by implication, to appear 'in person' in other ways, so that the rule has now been superseded for civil cases in the county courts and the High Court.

Service of documents

Companies Act 2006 s 1139: Service of documents on company

A document may be served on a company registered under this Act by leaving it at, or sending it by post to, the company's registered office.

Further reading

CAMPBELL, N and ARMOUR, J, 'Demystifying the Corporate Liability of Civil Agents' [2003] CLJ 290.

CLARKSON, CMV, 'Kicking Corporate Bodies and Damning Their Souls' (1996) 59 MLR 557.

CRAIG, R, 'Thou Shall Do No Murder: A Discussion Paper on the Corporate Manslaughter and Corporate Homicide Act 2007' [2009] 30 *Company Lawyer* 17.

DOBSON, A, 'Shifting Sands: Multiple Counts in Prosecutions for Corporate Manslaughter' [2012] Crim LR 200.

FERRAN, E, 'Corporate Attribution and the Directing Mind and Will' (2011) 127 LQR 239.

FISSE, B and BRAITHWAITE, J, 'The Allocation of Responsibility for Corporate Crime: Individualism, Collectivism and Accountability' (1988) 11 *Sydney Law Review* 468.

GOODE, R, 'Corporate Conspiracy: Problems of *Mens Rea* and the Parties to the Agreement' (1975) 2 *Dalhousie Law Journal* 121.

GRANTHAM, R and RICKETT, C, 'Directors' "Tortious" Liability: Contract, Tort or Company Law?' (1999) 62 MLR 133.

GREEN, NN, 'Security of Transactions after *Phonogram*' (1984) 47 MLR 671.

GRIFFITHS, A, 'Agents without Principals: Pre-incorporation Contracts and Section 36C of the Companies Act 1985' (1993) 13 *Legal Studies* 241.

LEE, I, 'Corporate Criminal Responsibility as Team Member Responsibility' (2011) 31 OJLS 755.

LIM, E, 'Attribution in Company Law' (2014) 77 MLR 794.

MANCE, J, '*Ex Turpi Causa*—When Latin Avoids Liability' (2014) 18 Edin LR 175.

ORMEROD, D and TAYLOR, R, 'The Corporate Manslaughter and Corporate Homicide Act 2007: Legislative Comment' [2008] Crim LR 589.

PAYNE, J, 'Corporate Attribution and the Lessons of Meridian' in PS Davies and J Pila (eds), *The Jurisprudence of Lord Hoffmann* (2015).

SEALY, LS, 'The Corporate Ego and Agency Untwined' [1995] CLJ 507.

STEVENS, R, 'Vicarious Liability or Vicarious Action' (2007) 123 LQR 30.

SUMPTION, J, 'Reflections on the Law of Illegality' (2012) 20 RLR 1.

TWIGG-FLESNER, C, 'Sections 35A and 322A Revisited: Who is a "Person Dealing with a Company"?' (2005) 26 *Company Lawyer* 195.

VIRGO, G, 'Stealing from the Small Family Business' [1991] CLJ 464.

WATTS, P, 'Some Wear and Tear on *Armagas v Mundogas*: The Tension between Having and Wanting in the Law of Agency' [2015] LMCLQ 36.

WATTS, P, 'Corrupt Company Controllers, their Companies and their Companies' Creditors: Dealing with Pleas of *Ex Turpi Causa* [2014] JBL 161.

WATTS, P, 'Principals' Tortious Liability for Agents' Negligent Statements—Is "Authority" Necessary?' (2012) 128 LQR 260.

WATTS, P, 'Imputed Knowledge in Agency Law—Excising the Fraud Exception' (2001) 117 LQR 300.

WEDDERBURN, KW, *Ultra Vires* in Modern Company Law' (1983) 46 MLR 204.

WELLS, C, 'Corporate Liability and Consumer Protection: *Tesco v Nattrass* Revisited' (1994) 57 MLR 817.

WILLIAMS, G, 'Vicarious Liability: Tort of the Master or of the Servant?' (1956) 72 LQR 522.

WORTHINGTON, S, 'Corporate Attribution and Agency: Back to Basics' (2017) 133 LQR (forthcoming).

4

SHAREHOLDERS AS AN ORGAN OF THE COMPANY

General issues

In Chapter 2 we saw how the law recognises a company as a person in its own right, capable of having rights, owning property, making contracts, accepting or incurring obligations, committing wrongs and conducting litigation. Chapter 3 then addressed the practical matter of the way in which this artificial legal person functions: how its corporate will is manifested, its decisions taken and its acts performed. Plainly, a company cannot do anything except through human beings who are its members and officers and, vicariously, through its employees and agents.

In neither of these earlier chapters was much attention given to the role of the shareholders, or, more generally, the members of the company.[1] Yet both the Companies Act 2006 (CA 2006) and individual companies' constitutions assume a limited, but nonetheless significant, role for the company's members (as defined in CA 2006 s 112).[2] The Act gives members certain rights and reserves to them certain important decisions, to the exclusion of the company's directors. This is usually done when there is a substantial risk associated with leaving power in the hands of the directors. So members, not directors, must approve certain types of contracts between the company and its directors.[3] In addition, members have the right to decide upon changes to the constitution of their company[4] and to the rights attached to their shares.[5] Some of these statutory rules are mandatory; others can be strengthened or relaxed by the company's own articles. In addition, the members have the right to remove directors,[6] and, when wrongs have been committed against the company

---

[1] Indeed, this chapter might have been better entitled 'Members as an Organ of the Company', since not every company is limited by shares: see CA 2006 s 112.

[2] And every company must keep a register of members: CA 2006 ss 113ff.

[3] CA 2006 ss 182–231, see 'Special rules on notice requirements and members' approval for certain transactions: CA 2006 ss 182–231', pp 462ff.

[4] CA 2006 s 21, see 'Alteration of the articles', pp 228ff.

[5] CA 2006 ss 626–640, see 'Variation of class rights', pp 587ff.

[6] CA 2006 s 168, see 'Removal of directors', pp 300ff.

but the directors (perhaps through self-interest) are not inclined to pursue the claims, the members can sometimes pursue these claims and obtain a remedy for the company.[7]

Beyond this, the members' additional rights of control are derived from the company's constitution itself. This is the agreement that divides a company's power between the directors and the members. As noted earlier (see 'Constitutional documents: articles of association and the company's objects', p 26), the principal constitutional document (and the one on which this chapter focuses) is the company's *articles*: see CA 2006 ss 17 and 18. This sets the constitutional framework for the company. Companies are free to draft their own articles, but CA 2006 provides default sets of Model Articles for different types of companies. These Model Articles will automatically apply to companies that do not register their own articles, and will in any event apply to the extent that any registered articles do not exclude or modify the relevant Model Articles (CA 2006 s 20).

Taking the Model Articles for private companies limited by shares[8] as typical for small companies, we see they contain details about meetings of members, appointment and termination of directors and their duties and proceedings, delegation of power, issues of shares and payment of dividends, and the use of the company's seal. The overriding assumption in these Model Articles is that the directors, not the members, will manage the business of the company (subject of course to any exceptions in CA 2006, and also see *Barron v Potter* [4.08]).

Despite this rather unequal power split, the members and the directors constitute the two 'organs' of the company. The term signifies their constitutional authority to act *as* the company rather than merely to represent the company as its agent under an authority derived from some superior corporate source. Put another way, this is simply an attribution rule of the sort described by Lord Hoffmann in *Meridian Global* [3.01].

These two organs share between them the most important corporate functions, and (except in the case of the single member company, the wholly owned subsidiary or the company with only one director) each organ normally, historically, acted by decisions (resolutions) taken at meetings. The organ constituted by the members is called '*the general meeting*' and by the directors '*the board of directors*' or '*the board*'. This terminology recognised that a *meeting* was the focus of corporate decision-making by these organs.

Historically, too, members' meetings were typically well attended, with vigorous debate and meaningful voting. Nowadays, the 'meetings' of very small companies are perfunctory affairs, if held at all. And attendance at the meetings of large companies is commonly unrepresentative,[9] and the 'business' a routine rubber-stamping of the directors' proposals. CA 2006 and the Model Articles recognise this, and make explicit concessions which expand the normal concept of a meeting or provide for alternative decision-making strategies (see 'Formal decision-making by members', p 202). But old concepts die hard: both the courts and the legislative reformers have striven to preserve some vestiges of the democratic ideal in their attitude to corporate governance, even when it seems to be plain on all sides that the struggle is a relatively hopeless one.

This chapter considers the members' rights and duties under CA 2006 and the company's constitution. It considers the problems in dividing power between the company's members and directors and the consequences of that division, the rules of interpretation which apply to constitutional documents, the practical exercise of the decision-making powers given to members and the legal constraints on that exercise. Finally, it considers

---

[7] CA 2006 ss 260–264, see 'Company claims and the statutory derivative action: CA 2006 ss 260ff', pp 671ff.

[8] See the Companies (Model Articles) Regulations 2008 Sch 1, which prescribes the Model Articles for private companies limited by shares. Schedules 2 and 3 prescribe the Model Articles for private companies limited by guarantee and for public companies respectively.

[9] The small shareholders are often geographically dispersed and see no benefit in making the effort to attend; and the large institutional shareholders generally have sufficient access to the board and other parts of the corporate operation that these avenues, not a general meeting, provide their preferred way of influencing decisions.

the enforcement of the constitution by the members, and their potential use of shareholders' agreements to achieve what they cannot achieve via the articles.

Lurking beneath all of this discussion, however, is a growing recognition that the real power and influence behind companies may come not from it directors, or even its members, but from other—more hidden—sources entirely. In later chapters we consider the role of 'shadow directors' and other 'people with significant control' (see 'Shadow directors: s 251', p 329; and 'Register of "people with significant control": the PSC Register', pp 753ff, respectively).

Dividing corporate power between members and directors

The previous introduction, however brief, shows clearly that the constitutions of modern companies, with the backing of the law, have put the power to run the company's business in the hands of the directors, and have left the members a very minor role. Typically this extends to amendment of the constitution, declaration of a dividend, election or re-election of directors and appointment of auditors—and even in these matters there may be little for them to do except rubber-stamp the recommendations of the directors.

In other words, the role of the member has become more and more that of a passive investor (no doubt partly from choice, but also from apathy and a sense of impotence), while power has progressively come to be concentrated in the hands of the directors, especially the executive directors. The larger and more widely dispersed the membership or shareholding of the company, the more marked this difference between 'ownership' and 'control' usually is. (This trend has in part been reversed by the growth of the institutional members such as the pension funds, unit trusts and insurance companies and, more recently, buy-out funds,[10] although that too has created its own set of problems.)

This commonly described split between 'ownership' and 'control' has generated an enormous literature on the resulting agency problems: how can the members (the owners) ensure that the executives (the controllers) manage the company as they would want? On the other hand, moving too far in the other direction would entail the loss of other benefits. Concentrating management in the hands of the board is not only efficient, it also allows for the employment of dedicated experts to manage the business.

Reformers, motivated both by idealistic notions of 'shareholder democracy' as an end in itself, and also by a sense that directors do have too much power over 'other people's money', which is at times abused ('the unacceptable face of capitalism'), have lobbied for new legislation that consciously seeks to put a larger share of real control into the hands of the members. Since the time of the 1948 Act, and with increasing vigour since then, member approval has been required for certain decisions (see 'General issues', p 202, for illustrations). The procedures for these member-authorisations are sometimes quite rigidly prescribed, and the consequences of failing to observe the formalities very severe. The costs of compliance, both in money and in time, can prove a heavy price to pay for the theoretical gain. By contrast, in many North American jurisdictions reformers have accepted the case for a reduction in member-consents in the interests of business efficiency.

In some European companies codes, by contrast, and most notably in that of Germany, the problems associated with the concentration of power in the hands of the board of

---

[10] See '"Voice" in decision-making', p 213.

directors have been tackled in another way. In these systems, there is provision for a 'two-tier' management structure, consisting of a managerial (or executive) board and a supervisory board, the former having charge of matters of day-to-day management and the latter being responsible for the control of the executive board and, in particular, having the power of appointment and removal of its personnel. These supervisory boards in Germany also play an important role in ensuring worker participation in management, or 'co-determination'. In most German public companies, one-third of the members of the supervisory board must be elected by the company's employees, while the other two-thirds are elected by the members.

The Draft Fifth EU Company Law Directive, in its original form (9 October 1972), contained proposals for the adoption of this model for public companies by all the member states of the EU. If implemented in the UK, such a change would have introduced a further 'organ' into the hierarchy of corporate management, and would have called for a basic reconsideration of the principles laid down in the cases on which we currently rely. However, the move was resisted by various governments, and a compromise in relation to SEs (*Societas Europaea*) allowing the British to retain their own system, was eventually reached.[11]

In the UK, concern for employees' interests has been limited to some very modest provisions in the Companies Acts, such as CA 2006 s 172 (directors to have regard to interests of employees in their duty to promote the success of the company), and CA 2006 s 247 and Insolvency Act 1986 (IA 1986) s 187 (power to make over assets to employees on a cessation of business or in a liquidation). The directors' annual report must give certain information about its employment policies and employee involvement, and there are inducements in the tax legislation to establish employee share-ownership schemes, which have now become relatively common.

All of this only serves to show that, in the *constitutional* split of power, the directors reign supreme. This chapter looks at what few, but sometimes crucial, collective and personal rights the members do have under the constitution, and how they must exercise those rights. There is little by way of provision for general control over the directors here. That is left to mechanisms discussed in Chapters 5 and 6.

Orthodox constitutional division of powers

The division of powers between the members in general meeting and the board of directors is discretionary, and determined by the company's articles (subject, of course, to any mandatory provisions of CA 2006). The relevant Model Articles for private companies from the 2006 and the 1985 Acts are set out in the following extract,[12] the latter primarily because it is relevant in many of the cases extracted later. These are illustrative of the general approach within such companies (and, as noted earlier, apply by default if alternative articles have not been registered: CA 2006 s 20).

---

[11] By this compromise, the Statute for a European Company allows an SE to adopt either a one-tier or a two-tier board structure (Regulation (EC) 2157/2001, Arts 38–51). The former is the equivalent of the British company system and the board in this case is called the administrative organ. In the two-tier system there is a management and a supervisory organ. The functions of each of these organs have been prescribed in the Act. Under Directive 2001/86/EC, the form of employee involvement in an SE is to be determined by negotiation between the management or administrative organs of the existing companies and representatives of their companies' employees.

[12] The Companies (Model Articles) Regulations 2008 apply to all new companies incorporated under CA 2006 on or after 1 October 2009. Companies incorporated earlier than this are subject to CA 1985 Table A articles (as modified at different times): see www.companieshouse.gov.uk/about/tableA/index.shtml.

Companies Act 2006 Model Articles for Private Companies Limited by Shares

3. Directors' general authority

Subject to the articles, the directors are responsible for the management of the company's business, for which purpose they may exercise all the powers of the company.

4. Shareholders' reserve power

(1) The shareholders may, by special resolution, direct the directors to take, or refrain from taking, specified action.

(2) No such special resolution invalidates anything which the directors have done before the passing of the resolution.

Companies (Tables A to F) (Amendment) Regulations (SI 2008/739)

Table A

70 Subject to the provisions of the Act, the memorandum and the articles and to any directions given by special resolution, the business of the company shall be managed by the directors who may exercise all the powers of the company. No alteration of the memorandum or articles and no such direction shall invalidate any prior act of the directors which would have been valid if that alteration had not been made or that direction had not been given. The powers given by this regulation shall not be limited by any special power given to the directors by the articles and a meeting of directors at which a quorum is present may exercise all powers exercisable by the directors.

Articles and the rules governing their interpretation

If the articles, as the company's primary constitutional document, define the division of powers between the members and the directors, then it is important to know how their terms are interpreted. Orthodox rules of contractual interpretation generally apply, since the articles constitute a contract between the company and its members,[13] but the following cases illustrate particular problems and limitations. It emerges that the articles constitute a rather unusual type of contract. (This is even more apparent when the personal rights arising under this contract are considered: see 'Members' personal rights', pp 261ff.)

The court has no jurisdiction to rectify the articles of association.

[4.01] Scott v Frank F Scott (London) Ltd [1940] Ch 794 (Court of Appeal)

The facts appear from the judgment.

The judgment of the Court of Appeal (SCOTT, CLAUSON and LUXMOORE LJJ) was delivered by LUXMOORE LJ: The...question which falls to be considered is whether the defendants are entitled to have the articles of association rectified in the manner claimed by them. Bennett J

[13] CA 2006 s 33, see 'Members' personal rights', pp 261ff.

[at first instance] said he was prepared to hold that the articles of association as registered were not in accordance with the intention of the three brothers who were the only signatories of the memorandum and articles of association, and down to the date of Frank Stanley Scott's death the only shareholders therein. Bennett J, however, held that the court has no jurisdiction to rectify articles of association of a company, although they do not accord with what is proven to have been the concurrent intention of all the signatories therein at the moment of signature. We are in complete agreement with this decision. It seems to us that there is no room in the case of a company incorporated under the appropriate statute or statutes for the application to either the memorandum[14] or articles of association of the principles upon which a court of equity permits rectification of documents whether *inter partes* or not...

The articles cannot be supplemented by additional terms implied from extrinsic circumstances.

[4.02] Bratton Seymour Service Co Ltd v Oxborough [1992] BCLC 693 (Court of Appeal)

The company was set up to manage the commercial aspects of a development consisting of a number of flats, the shares being held by the flat owners. The question for the court was whether it was possible to imply into the company's articles a term that the members should make contributions for the upkeep of the garden, swimming pool and other communal amenity areas of the development. The Court of Appeal held that no such term could be implied.

STEYN LJ:... Section 14(1) of the Companies Act 1985 [now see CA 2006 s 33] provides that 'the memorandum and articles, when registered, bind the company and its members to the same extent as if they respectively had been signed and sealed by each member'. By virtue of s 14 the articles of association become, upon registration, a contract between a company and members. It is, however, a statutory contract of a special nature with its own distinctive features. It derives its binding force not from a bargain struck between parties but from the terms of the statute. It is binding only insofar as it affects the rights and obligations between the company and the members acting in their capacity as members. If it contains provisions conferring rights and obligations on outsiders, then those provisions do not bite as part of the contract between the company and the members, even if the outsider is coincidentally a member. Similarly, if the provisions are not truly referable to the rights and obligations of members as such it does not operate as a contract. Moreover, the contract can be altered by a special resolution without the consent of all the contracting parties. It is also, unlike an ordinary contract, not defeasible on the grounds of misrepresentation, common law mistake, mistake in equity, undue influence or duress. Moreover... it cannot be rectified on the grounds of mistake.

Turning now to the present case, the question is whether the implied term of requiring members to contribute to maintenance of the amenities can be implied not on the basis of any language to be found in the articles, but on the basis of extrinsic circumstances. The question

---

[14] Recall that CA 2006 abolishes the company's memorandum, in this old-style form, and s 28 provides that the provisions of any existing company memorandum which are not required to be in the new-style memorandum will be treated as provisions of the articles, amendable by special resolution. The 'new-style memorandum of association' (s 8) is a statement of intent in prescribed form authenticated by the subscribers to the new company.

is, is it notionally ever possible to imply a term in such circumstances? I will readily accept that the law should not adopt a black-letter approach. It is possible to imply a term purely from the language of the document itself: a purely constructional implication is not precluded. But it is quite another matter to seek to imply a term into articles of association from extrinsic circumstances.

Here, the company puts forward an implication to be derived not from the language of the articles of association but purely from extrinsic circumstances. That, in my judgment, is a type of implication which, as a matter of law, can never succeed in the case of articles of association. After all, if it were permitted, it would involve the position that the different implications would notionally be possible between the company and different subscribers. Just as the company or an individual member cannot seek to defeat the statutory contract by reason of special circumstances such as misrepresentation, mistake, undue influence and duress and is furthermore not permitted to seek a rectification, neither the company nor any member can seek to add to or to subtract from the terms of the articles by way of implying a term derived from extrinsic surrounding circumstances. If it were permitted in this case, it would be equally permissible over the spectrum of company law cases. The consequence would be prejudicial to third parties, namely potential shareholders who are entitled to look to and rely on the articles of association as registered. Despite Mr Asprey's lucid and incisive argument, I take the view that on this ground alone the implication cannot succeed.

DILLON LJ and SIR CHRISTOPHER SLADE delivered concurring judgments.

➤ Notes

1. As long as the article in question is clear and unambiguous, and is not 'commercially absurd' or 'does not flout common sense', the court will not interfere. The hurdle is high. In *Sugarman v CJS Investments LLP* [2014] EWCA Civ 1239, the Court of Appeal would not interfere with the literal interpretation of voting rights in the articles of association of a housing management company which gave each member of the company only one vote regardless of the number of shares held. Members owned one share for every flat they leased. This voting provision therefore meant that a member with one flat had the same voting power as a member with 66 flats.

2. Similarly, when determining the meaning of an amendment of the articles of association, the courts will not consider the effect which the alteration was intended to have, or circumstances in which the alteration was made, but the court will however add words to avoid absurdity, or imply a term which is strictly necessary proceeding from the express words of the articles viewed objectively in their commercial setting. *Re Coroin Ltd* [2011] EWHC 3466 (Ch) is an illustration. The court was prepared to admit some extrinsic background for the purpose of construing the articles in question. David Richards J held that it would be 'somewhat artificial to construe the articles in isolation from the shareholders' agreement (see 'Shareholders' agreements', pp 256ff) and from the background admissible to the construction of that agreement. Nor would it conflict with the reasons for the usual exclusionary rule to take account of the shareholders' agreement and its background' [69]. Key to this approach were the facts that the articles were adopted pursuant to the shareholders' agreement; both documents were negotiated by and were intended to govern relations between the initial investors as members of the company; and the agreement was clearly intended to bind all present *and future* shareholders of the company (although the judge held it unnecessary to reach a final conclusion on this last point for the purpose of determining the issues in dispute). This decision was subsequently affirmed by the Court of Appeal: [2012] BCC 575 per Lloyd, Rimer and Tomlinson LJJ.

'Implied terms' in the articles.

[4.03] Equitable Life Assurance Society v Hyman [2002] 1 AC 408 (House of Lords)

The relevant article (art 65) gave the directors a wide discretionary power to pay bonuses on its members' life assurance policies, and in exercise of this power the directors had paid some policyholders a larger bonus than others. This was contrary to 'guarantees' which had been given when certain of the members took out their policies. Lord Steyn said that the articles should be read as containing an implied term that the directors would not exercise their discretion 'in a manner which deprived the guarantees of any substantial value'.

LORD STEYN: It is necessary to distinguish between the processes of interpretation and implication. The purpose of interpretation is to assign to the language of the text the most appropriate meaning which the words can legitimately bear. The language of article 65(1) contains no relevant express restriction on the powers of the directors. It is impossible to assign to the language of article 65(1) by construction a restriction precluding the directors from overriding GARs ['guaranteed annuity rate' policies]. To this extent I would uphold the submissions made on behalf of the Society. The critical question is whether a relevant restriction may be implied into article 65(1). It is certainly not a case in which a term can be implied by law in the sense of incidents impliedly annexed to particular forms of contracts. Such standardised implied terms operate as general default rules: see *Scally v Southern Health and Social Services Board* [1992] 1 AC 294. If a term is to be implied, it could only be a term implied from the language of article 65 read in its particular commercial setting. Such implied terms operate as ad hoc gap fillers. In *Luxor (Eastbourne) Ltd v Cooper* [1941] AC 108, 137 Lord Wright explained this distinction as follows:

> 'The expression "implied term" is used in different senses. Sometimes it denotes some term which does not depend on the actual intention of the parties but on a rule of law, such as the terms, warranties or conditions which, if not expressly excluded, the law imports, as for instance under the Sale of Goods Act and the Marine Insurance Act...But a case like the present is different because what it is sought to imply is based on an intention imputed to the parties from their actual circumstances.'

It is only an individualised term of the second kind which can arguably arise in the present case. Such a term may be imputed to parties: it is not critically dependent on proof of an actual intention of the parties. The process 'is one of construction of the agreement as a whole in its commercial setting': *Banque Bruxelles Lambert SA v Eagle Star Insurance Co Ltd* [1997] AC 191, 212E, per Lord Hoffmann. This principle is sparingly and cautiously used and may never be employed to imply a term in conflict with the express terms of the text. The legal test for the implication of such a term is a standard of strict necessity. This is how I must approach the question whether a term is to be implied into article 65(1) which precludes the directors from adopting a principle which has the effect of overriding or undermining the GARs.

The inquiry is entirely constructional in nature: proceeding from the express terms of article 65, viewed against its objective setting, the question is whether the implication is strictly necessary. My Lords, as counsel for the GAR policyholders observed, final bonuses are not bounty. They are a significant part of the consideration for the premiums paid. And the directors' discretions as to the amount and distribution of bonuses are conferred for the benefit of policyholders. In this context the self-evident commercial object of the inclusion of guaranteed rates in the policy is to protect the policyholder against a fall in market annuity rates by ensuring that if the fall occurs he will be better off than he would have been with market rates. The choice is given to the GAR policyholder and not to the Society. It cannot be seriously doubted that the provision for guaranteed annuity rates was a good selling point in the marketing by the Society of the GAR policies. It is also obvious that it would have been a significant attraction for purchasers of GAR policies. The Society points out that no special charge was made for the inclusion in the policy of GAR provisions. So be it. This factor does not alter the reasonable expectations of the parties. The supposition of the parties must be presumed to have been that the directors would not exercise their discretion in conflict with contractual rights. These are the circumstances in which the directors of the Society resolved upon a differential policy which was designed to deprive the relevant guarantees of any substantial value. In my judgment an implication precluding the use of the directors' discretion in this way is strictly necessary. The implication is essential to give effect to the reasonable expectations of the parties. The stringent test applicable to the implication of terms is satisfied.

➤ Questions

1. Why did this case need to be decided as a matter of contractual interpretation of the articles, rather than a matter of (improper) exercise of discretion by the directors?

2. Lord Steyn clearly had in mind the distinction between 'constructional' implied terms and ones derived from extrinsic circumstances which he had put forward in *Bratton Seymour* (to which he did not refer). Is it clear from these two cases how the line is to be drawn? Also see *Attorney General of Belize v Belize Telecom Ltd* [2009] UKPC 10, [2009] BCC 433, PC (in the following Note 3).

➤ Notes

1. If the understanding between the founding members as to the basis on which a company is to be incorporated differs from the constitutional arrangements of the company when formed, this may be a reason for winding up the company on the 'just and equitable' ground (IA 1986 s 122, see 'Compulsory winding up on the "just and equitable" ground', pp 840ff). And a member whose 'legitimate expectations' are disappointed, even though they are not formally recorded as constitutional provisions or terms, may also be granted discretionary relief under CA 2006 s 994, on the ground of 'unfairly prejudicial' conduct: see 'Unfairly prejudicial conduct of the company's affairs', pp 715ff.

2. In Australia, on facts similar to *Scott v Frank F Scott (London) Ltd* **[4.01]**, the court has refused rectification but indicated that if new proceedings were brought it would be willing to give a remedy in the nature of specific performance ordering the defendant members to vote in favour of a special resolution to remedy the defect: *Simon v HPM Industries Pty Ltd* (1989) 15 ACLR 427, SC (NSW); *Re Freehouse Pty Ltd* (1997) 26 ACSR 662, SC (Vic).

3. Note the following observations by Lord Hoffmann about the process of implication in *Attorney General of Belize v Belize Telecom Ltd* [2009] UKPC 10 (PC) (where the issue concerned the rights attaching to a 'Special Share' held by the government in a privatised telecommunications company):

16. Before discussing in greater detail the reasoning of the Court of Appeal, the Board will make some general observations about the process of implication. The court has no power to improve upon the instrument which it is called upon to construe, whether it be a contract, a statute or articles of association. It cannot introduce terms to make it fairer or more reasonable. It is concerned only to discover what the instrument means. However, that meaning is not necessarily or always what the authors or parties to the document would have intended. It is the meaning which the instrument would convey to a reasonable person having all the background knowledge

which would reasonably be available to the audience to whom the instrument is addressed: see *Investors Compensation Scheme Ltd v West Bromwich Building Society* [1998] 1 WLR 896, 912–913. It is this objective meaning which is conventionally called the intention of the parties, or the intention of Parliament, or the intention of whatever person or body was or is deemed to have been the author of the instrument.

17. The question of implication arises when the instrument does not expressly provide for what is to happen when some event occurs. The most usual inference in such a case is that nothing is to happen. If the parties had intended something to happen, the instrument would have said so. Otherwise, the express provisions of the instrument are to continue to operate undisturbed. If the event has caused loss to one or other of the parties, the loss lies where it falls.

18. In some cases, however, the reasonable addressee would understand the instrument to mean something else. He would consider that the only meaning consistent with the other provisions of the instrument, read against the relevant background, is that something is to happen. The event in question is to affect the rights of the parties. The instrument may not have expressly said so, but this is what it must mean. In such a case, it is said that the court implies a term as to what will happen if the event in question occurs. But the implication of the term is not an addition to the instrument. It only spells out what the instrument means.

4. In *Cream Holdings Ltd v Stuart Davenport* [2010] EWHC 3096 (Ch), the defendant was removed as a director and, pursuant to the articles, the removal brought about the deemed service of a transfer notice in respect of his shareholding (ie deeming his intention to sell his shareholding). The articles then provided procedures for the valuation and transfer of the shares, including the appointment of a third party valuer where the parties could not agree. The defendant obstructed these procedures, and the court held that terms should be implied into the procedures imposing an obligation to cooperate and a requirement not to withhold consent unreasonably to the nominated appointment. These implied terms were 'necessary [. . . and] represent the minimum machinery necessary to make these articles work' [58]. The Court of Appeal (judgment given by Patten LJ, with whom Mummery and Burnton LJJ agreed) affirmed the judge's decision, holding that the implication was an 'obvious and necessary means of giving effect to the contract' [37]: [2012] 1 BCLC 365, CA.

Practical consequences of the constitutional allocation of powers

The division of powers between the members in general meeting and the board of directors, as determined by the company's articles, has important—and sometimes counter-intuitive—practical consequences for both organs. The next few cases are illustrative.

Where the articles limit the powers of the company in general meeting, such articles cannot be disregarded even by a majority sufficiently large to alter the articles. A formal alteration must be made and then acted upon.

[4.04] Imperial Hydropathic Hotel Co, Blackpool v Hampson
(1882) 23 Ch D 1 (Court of Appeal)

The articles provided that the directors were to hold office for a period of three years and to retire by rotation. At a general meeting specially summoned for this and other purposes, resolutions were carried for the removal of two directors (who were not due for retirement under the articles) and the election of others in their place. The company in this action claimed a declaration that the directors had been validly removed. It was held that the articles could not be disregarded in this way.[15]

> COTTON LJ: There is nothing in the Act or in the articles which directly enables a general meeting to remove directors; but the way it is put is this—that there is power in these articles, as there is power in the Act, by a meeting duly called to pass a resolution altering the articles; and it is said that here there was a resolution which would have been effectual to alter the articles that these directors whom the articles did not authorise to be removed should be removed. Now in my opinion it is an entire fallacy to say that because there is power to alter the regulations, you can by a resolution which might alter the regulations, do that which is contrary to the regulations as they stand in a particular and individual case. It is in no way altering the regulations. The alteration of the regulations would be by introducing a provision, not that some particular director be discharged from being a director, but that directors be capable of being removed by the vote of a general meeting. It is a very different thing to pass a general rule applicable to every one who comes within it, and to pass a resolution against a particular individual, which would be a *privilegium* and not a law. Now here there was no attempt to pass any resolution at this meeting which would affect any director, except those who are aimed at by the resolution, no alteration of the regulations was to bind the company to those regulations as altered; and assuming, as I do for the present purpose, as the second meeting seems to have been regular according to the notice, that everything was regularly done, what was done cannot be treated in my opinion as an alteration first of the regulations, and then under that altered regulation as a removal of the directors...
> JESSEL MR and BOWEN LJ delivered concurring judgments.

Also see *Boschoek Pty Co Ltd v Fuke* [**4.32**].

Where the general management of the company is vested in the directors, the members have no power by ordinary resolution to give directions to the board or to overrule its business decisions.

[4.05] Automatic Self-Cleansing Filter Syndicate Co Ltd v Cuninghame [1906] 2 Ch 34 (Court of Appeal)

Article 96 of the company's articles of association vested in the directors 'the management of the business and the control of the company' in terms similar to the 1985 Table A, art 70; and art 91(1) specifically empowered them to sell any property of the company on such terms and conditions as they might think fit. At a general meeting a resolution was passed directing the board to sell the company's undertaking to a new company formed for the purpose, but the directors disapproved of the proposed terms and declined to carry out the sale. It was held that the shareholders had no say in the matter, which was for the board alone to decide.

> COLLINS MR: This is an appeal from a decision of Warrington J, who has been asked by the plaintiffs, Mr McDiarmid and the company, for a declaration that the defendants, as directors of the company, are bound to carry into effect a resolution passed at a meeting of the shareholders in the company on 16 January...

---

[15] But now see CA 2006 s 168, which gives the general meeting power to remove the directors by ordinary resolution notwithstanding the terms of the articles: see 'Removal of directors', p 300.

The point arises in this way. At a meeting of the company a resolution was passed by a majority—I was going to say a bare majority, but it was a majority—in favour of a sale to a purchaser, and the directors, honestly believing, as Warrington J thought, that it was most undesirable in the interests of the company that that agreement should be carried into effect, refused to affix the seal of the company to it, or to assist in carrying out a resolution which they disapproved of; and the question is whether under the memorandum and articles of association here the directors are bound to accept, in substitution of their own view, the view contained in the resolution of the company. Warrington J held that the majority could not impose that obligation upon the directors, and that on the true construction of the articles the directors were the persons authorised by the articles to effect this sale, and that unless the other powers given by the memorandum were invoked by a special resolution, it was impossible for a mere majority at a meeting to override the views of the directors. That depends, as Warrington J put it, upon the construction of the articles. [His Lordship read the relevant articles and continued:] Therefore in the matters referred to in article 97(1) the view of the directors as to the fitness of the matter is made the standard; and furthermore, by article 96 they are given in express terms the full powers which the company has, except so far as they 'are not hereby or by statute expressly directed or required to be exercised or done by the company', so that the directors have absolute power to do all things other than those that are expressly required to be done by the company; and then comes the limitation on their general authority—'subject to such regulations as may from time to time be made by extraordinary resolution'. Therefore, if it is desired to alter the powers of the directors, that must be done not by a resolution carried by a majority at an ordinary meeting of the company, but by an extraordinary resolution. In these circumstances it seems to me that it is not competent for the majority of the shareholders at an ordinary meeting to affect or alter the mandate originally given to the directors, by the articles of association. It has been suggested that this is a mere question of principal and agent, and that it would be an absurd thing if a principal in appointing an agent should in effect appoint a dictator who is to manage him instead of his managing the agent. I think that that analogy does not strictly apply to this case. No doubt for some purposes directors are agents. For whom are they agents? You have, no doubt, in theory and law one entity, the company, which might be a principal, but you have to go behind that when you look to the particular position of directors. It is by the consensus of all the individuals in the company that these directors become agents and hold their rights as agents. It is not fair to say that a majority at a meeting is for the purposes of this case the principal so as to alter the mandate of the agent. The minority also must be taken into account. There are provisions by which the minority may be overborne, but that can only done by special machinery in the shape of special resolutions. Short of that the mandate which must be obeyed is not that of the majority—it is that of the whole entity made up of all the shareholders. If the mandate of the directors is to be altered, it can only be under the machinery of the memorandum and articles themselves. I do not think I need to say more…

COZENS-HARDY LJ delivered a concurring judgment.

> Notes

1. The decision in *Cuninghame*'s case marked the beginning of a departure from the traditional nineteenth-century view which regarded the members in general meeting as constituting 'the company' and the directors as their delegates or agents.

2. There is nothing in the law which would prevent a company from having a provision in its articles which gave supervisory powers in the widest terms to its members, or allowed them to override the director's decisions—indeed, Model Articles art 4 is such a provision (but a special resolution is needed).

3. In defining the power of the directors, the articles typically refer to 'the company's business' or some similar expression. The ruling in *Cuninghame*'s case does not apply to

decisions outside the company's business and its management. In *Re Emmadart Ltd* [1979] Ch 540, it was held that directors had no power under such an article to resolve to put their company into liquidation (although a failure to give notice to the members of the proposed appointment of administrators was merely a remediable defect, and would not render the appointment null and void: *Re Eiffel Steel Works Ltd* [2015] EWHC 511 (Ch)).

The articles need to be read carefully to determine which organ is authorised to act.

[4.06] Quin & Axtens Ltd v Salmon [1909] AC 442 (House of Lords)

The company's two managing directors, Salmon and Axtens, held between them the bulk of the company's ordinary shares. Article 75 of the articles provided that the business of the company should be managed by the directors, who might exercise all the powers of the company 'subject to such regulations (being not inconsistent with the provisions of the articles) as may be prescribed by the company in general meeting'. Article 80 stated that no resolution of a meeting of the directors having for its object (*inter alia*) the acquisition or letting of certain premises should be valid if either Salmon or Axtens dissented. The directors resolved to acquire and to let various properties, but Salmon dissented. An extraordinary general meeting was then held at which the members by a majority passed similar resolutions. The House of Lords, upholding the decision of the Court of Appeal, held that the members' resolutions were inconsistent with the articles and granted an injunction restraining the company from acting on them.

> LORD LOREBURN LC: My Lords, I do not see any solid ground for complaint against the judgment of the Court of Appeal.
>
>   The bargain made between the shareholders is contained in articles 75 and 80 of the articles of association, and it amounts for the purpose in hand to this, that the directors should manage the business; and the company, therefore, are not to manage the business unless there is provision to that effect. Further the directors cannot manage it in a particular way—that is to say, they cannot do certain things if Mr Salmon or Mr Axtens objects. Now I cannot agree with Mr Upjohn in his contention that the failure of the directors upon the objection of Mr Salmon to grant these leases of itself remitted the matter to the discretion of the company in general meeting. They could still manage the business, but not altogether in the way they desired...
>
>   LORDS MACNAGHTEN, JAMES OF HEREFORD and SHAW OF DUNFERMLINE concurred.

The shareholders cannot overrule the directors' legitimate business decisions.

[4.07] John Shaw & Sons (Salford) Ltd v Shaw [1935] 2 KB 113 (Court of Appeal)

As part of the settlement of a dispute concerning sums owing to the plaintiff company by Peter, John and Percy Shaw (three brothers who were shareholders in, and directors of, the plaintiff company), the articles were altered so as to hand over all control of the financial affairs of the company and the management of its business to three independent persons known as 'permanent directors'. Two of the brothers, however, later failed to accept certain other provisions of the settlement, and as a result it was resolved at a meeting of the permanent directors that the present action should be instituted against them. But before the hearing of the suit the shareholders held an extraordinary meeting, at which a resolution was passed directing the board to discontinue the action forthwith. Du Parcq J disregarded the shareholders' resolution and gave judgment for the plaintiff company. The defendants appealed.

GREER LJ: [This] cause of action, whether likely to succeed or not, was one in respect of which the permanent directors were, in my opinion, empowered to commence and carry on.

I am therefore of opinion that the learned judge was right in refusing to dismiss the action on the plea that it was commenced without the authority of the plaintiff company. I think the judge was also right in refusing to give effect to the resolution of the meeting of the shareholders requiring the chairman to instruct the company's solicitors not to proceed further with the action. A company is an entity distinct alike from its shareholders and its directors. Some of its powers may, according to its articles, be exercised by directors, certain other powers may be reserved for the shareholders in general meeting. If powers of management are vested in the directors, they and they alone can exercise these powers. The only way in which the general body of the shareholders can control the exercise of powers vested by the articles in the directors is by altering their articles, or if opportunity arises under the articles, by refusing to re-elect the directors of whose actions they disapprove.[16] They cannot themselves usurp the powers which by the articles are vested in the directors any more than the directors can usurp the powers vested by the articles in the general body of shareholders...

[ROCHE LJ agreed, for other reasons, that the action had been competently brought, while SLESSER LJ, again for other reasons, thought that it had not. But he agreed, or 'inclined to the view', that the shareholders could not interfere with a power conferred by the articles on the permanent directors, except by altering the articles. The court unanimously held, however, that the defendants were entitled to succeed on the substantive issue of the case, and allowed the appeal.]

> ## Note

These cases may be taken to have established that, where the directors in pursuance of a power conferred upon them have instituted litigation in the company's name, the members in general meeting may not interfere and direct that the proceedings be discontinued. But in the converse case, where the majority of members have instituted or consented to the institution of proceedings in the company's name, and the *directors* object to their being continued, the law is less clear. Certainly if the directors are themselves defendants or if the allegation is that they are party to a wrong against the company, the rule in *Foss v Harbottle* **[13.01]** appears to allow the majority members the ultimate say and even, where the directors are themselves majority members, to permit a minority member to bring a derivative action.

The company in general meeting may act if there is no board competent or able (eg because of deadlock) to exercise the powers conferred upon it.

[4.08] Barron v Potter [1914] 1 Ch 895 (Chancery Division)

The two directors of the company were not on speaking terms, so that effective board meetings could not be held. The plaintiff, Canon Barron, had requisitioned a members' meeting at which additional directors had purportedly been appointed. The defendant objected that the power to make such appointments was vested by the company's articles in the directors. It was held that, in view of the deadlock, the power in question reverted to the general meeting, and so the appointments were valid.

WARRINGTON LJ [having held that no proper board meeting had been held, continued]: The question then arises, Was the resolution passed at the general meeting of the company a valid appointment? The argument against the validity of the appointment is that the articles of association of the company gave to the board of directors the power of appointing additional directors, that the

---

[16] The members can now also remove the directors by ordinary resolution, by provisions first introduced into CA 1948: now see CA 2006 s 168.

company has accordingly surrendered the power, and that the directors alone can exercise it. It is true that the general point was so decided by Eve J in *Blair Open Hearth Furnace Co v Reigart*[17] and I am not concerned to say that in ordinary cases where there is a board ready and willing to act it would be competent for the company to override the power conferred on the directors by the articles except by way of special resolution for the purpose of altering the articles. But the case which I have to deal with is a different one. For practical purposes there is no board of directors at all. The only directors are two persons, one of whom refuses to act with the other, and the question is, What is to be done under these circumstances? On this point I think that I can usefully refer to the judgment of the Court of Appeal in *Isle of Wight Rly Co v Tahourdin* [(1883) 25 Ch D 320, CA], not for the sake of the decision, which depended on the fact that it was a case under the Companies Clauses Consolidation Act 1845, but for the sake of the observations of Cotton and Fry LJJ upon the effect of a deadlock such as arose in the present case. Cotton LJ says: 'Then it is said that there is no power in the meeting of shareholders to elect new directors, for that under the 89th section the power[18] would be in the remaining directors. The remaining directors would no doubt have that power if there was a quorum left. But suppose the meeting were to remove so many directors that a quorum was not left, what then follows? It has been argued that in that case, there being no board which could act, there would be no power of filling up the board so as to enable it to work. In my opinion that is utterly wrong. A power is given by the 89th section to the remaining directors "if they think proper so to do" to elect persons to fill up the vacancies. I do not see how it is possible for a non-existent body to think proper to fill up vacancies. In such a case a general meeting duly summoned for the purpose must have power to elect a new board so as not to let the business of the company be at a deadlock . . .'. Those observations express a principle which seems to me to be as applicable to the case of a limited company incorporated under the Companies (Consolidation) Act 1908 as to a case falling under the Companies Clauses Consolidation Act 1845, and moreover to be a principle founded on plain common sense. If directors having certain powers are unable or unwilling to exercise them—are in fact a non-existent body for the purpose—there must be some power in the company to do itself that which under other circumstances would be otherwise done. The directors in the present case being unwilling to appoint additional directors under the power conferred on them by the articles, in my opinion, the company in general meeting has power to make the appointment . . .

➤ Note

A similar decision was reached in *Foster v Foster* [1916] 1 Ch 532, where there was a dispute over which of two directors should be appointed managing director, there being three directors in all. Although the power to appoint was conferred by the company's articles upon the directors, another article forbade a director from voting in respect of any contract in which he was interested. It was therefore not possible to carry any motion, in view of the disqualification of one director and the opposition of another. Peterson J held that in these circumstances competence to deal with the matter reverted from the board to the general meeting.

➤ Question

Suppose a situation the reverse of that in *Barron v Potter* [**4.08**], where the members cannot act but there is a board of directors capable of functioning. Could the directors exercise

---

[17] (1913) 108 LT 665.
[18] Section 89 of the Act enabled the remaining directors to fill up interim vacancies on the board: compare the 2006 Model Articles.

powers reserved by the articles to the general meeting? If not, what could be done to re-solve matters?

Formal decision-making by members

Various practical issues are important in the mechanics of the exercise of power by the members. How are decisions taken? Must there be a meeting? What counts as a majority? How is this assessed if not all members vote or attend a meeting? What exactly are 'meet-ings'? Is a meeting needed if everyone agrees? Are ordinary and special resolutions man-aged differently in these respects? Many of the answers can be found in the Act; some are provided in a company's articles. The analysis and following cases illustrate some of the issues, although by no means all.

General issues

A century or more ago, the companies legislation assumed that all members' decisions would be taken in formal meetings. These are called *'general meetings'* if all the mem-bers are entitled to attend, or *'class meetings'* if only one class of members is entitled to attend. This style of decision-making is still assumed to be the preferred mode for public companies (CA 2006 s 281). By contrast, CA 2006 assumes that written resolutions will be the normal mode[19] for private companies (CA 2006 ss 281, 288–300), with the limited exception that a meeting is essential if the resolution is to remove directors (ss 281(2) and 168) or auditors (ss 281(2) and 510).

In addition to these formal statutory rules, the informal common law rule is that the *unanimous* decision of the members is effective as their decision, whether or not they meet together or write it down. This rule applies to both public and private companies (see s 281(4)(a), and *Attorney General v Davy* **[4.09]**).

There follows, in outline, a description of the first two formal modes of decision-making by the members (written resolutions and meetings). The third mode (unanimous assent) is covered in the next section (see 'Informal decision-making—the *"Duomatic"* principle', pp 214ff).

In addition to these formal and informal procedural rules, there are important legal constraints on the *way* in which members can exercise their votes in making decisions. These rules are considered in detail at 'Limitations on the free exercise of members' voting rights', pp 222ff.

Voting majorities: ordinary and special resolutions

Most corporate decisions can be taken by simple majority (ie a majority of not less than 50%: CA 2006 ss 281(3) and 282), with each member having one vote per share unless the articles specify otherwise (s 284).[20] Such resolutions are called *'ordinary resolutions'*. On matters where there are added risks, either to the company or its members, CA 2006 may make a special majority essential (ie a majority of not less than 75%). These resolutions are called *'special resolutions'*: CA 2006 s 283. They are required for decisions to amend the company's articles (s 21(1)), to disapply members' pre-emption rights when shares are issued (ss 569–571), to reduce share capital (s 641(1)), to redeem the company's own shares

---

[19] Of course, meetings are still possible: CA 2006 s 281. But the written resolution procedure cannot be ex-cluded by the articles for many types of decisions: CA 2006 s 300.

[20] This follows the very general common law rule about all decision-making in *AG v Davy* **[4.09]**.

(s 716(1)), to resolve that the company be wound up voluntarily (IA 1986 s 84(1)), and so on. Indeed, when there is a particular risk that the minority may be treated unfairly, even though a special resolution has been passed, the dissenting minority may be given the additional protection of a right to request judicial review (eg ss 633 (variation of class rights), 721 (redemption of company's own shares)).

A company's articles cannot override the mandatory provisions of CA 2006, but they can often legitimately specify an even larger majority, or unanimity, for particular decisions.

As might be expected, ordinary and special majorities are assessed differently depending upon whether decisions are made by written resolution or at a meeting (ss 282 and 283). Decisions taken by written resolution must be passed by the required percentage of *all* members with voting rights. Decisions taken at a meeting need only be passed by the appropriate percentage *of those present and voting* either on a show of hands,[21] or by a poll (whether in person, by proxy or in advance (s 322A)). Clearly the outcome on a show of hands can be vastly different from the outcome on a poll. Individuals cannot automatically demand a poll; the demand has to be more representative of the views of the members. A poll can be demanded by a member or group of members meeting the minimum representative conditions set out in s 321(2), unless the company's own articles make more generous provisions (see Model Articles for private companies, art 44(2), and for public companies, art 36(2)). Some requirements for special resolutions in CA 2006 also specify more generous rules for calling for a poll.

Even if the rules are silent, at common law a corporate body may act by a majority vote given at a meeting of members duly summoned.

[4.09] Attorney General v Davy (1741) 2 Atk 212 (Lord Chancellor)

The facts as given in the report were as follows:

> King Edward VI by charter incorporated twelve persons, by name, to elect a chaplain for the church of Kirton, in Lincolnshire. By another clause three of the twelve were to choose a chaplain to officiate in the church of Sandford, within the parish of Kirton, but with the consent and approbation of the major part of the inhabitants of Sandford.
>
> Upon a late vacancy, two of the three chose a chaplain, with the consent of the major part of the inhabitants of Sandford; the third dissented. The question was whether this was a good choice.
>
> LORD HARDWICKE LC: It cannot be disputed that wherever a certain number are incorporated, a major part of them may do any corporate act; so if all are summoned, and part appear, a major part of those that appear may do a corporate act, though nothing be mentioned in the charter of the major part.
>
> This is the common construction of charters, and I am of opinion that the three are a corporation for the purpose they are appointed, and the choice too was confirmed, and consequently not necessary that all the three should join; . . . it is not necessary that every corporate act should be under the seal of the corporation, nor did this need the corporation seal.

Who can propose a written resolution?

As noted earlier, written resolutions provide an alternative to formal meetings for decision-making. In private companies only, written resolutions can be proposed by the directors

---

[21] Where, clearly, the number of shares held by each voter is unknown.

(ss 288(3)(a) and 291), or by members holding 5% of the voting rights or some lower percentage if so specified in the articles (ss 288(3)(b) and 292(5)). There are clear rules for circulating written resolutions (ss 290–295) and agreeing them (ss 296–297). Public companies cannot use this statutory procedure.

What are the essentials of a 'meeting'?

To constitute a meeting, there must prima facie be more than one person present.

Although see Notes 1 and 2, following the extract, indicating exceptions for single member companies.

[4.10] Sharp v Dawes (1876) 2 QBD 26 (Court of Appeal)

A meeting of a company governed by the Stannaries Acts[22] was summoned for the purpose, inter alia, of making a call (ie a demand from the company that members pay further unpaid amounts on their shares). It was attended by only one member, Silversides, and the secretary (who was not a member). The proceedings were conducted formally, as recounted in a notice sent to all members. The call was in due course made, and one member, Dawes, refused to pay it. It was held that the meeting was a nullity and the call was invalid.

> LORD COLERIDGE CJ: This is an attempt to enforce against the defendant a call purporting to have been made under s 10 of the Stannaries Act 1869. Of course it cannot be enforced unless it was duly made within the Act. Now, the Act says that a call may be made at a meeting of a company with special notice, and we must ascertain what within the meaning of the Act is a meeting, and whether one person alone can constitute such a meeting. It is said that the requirements of the Act are satisfied by a single shareholder going to the place appointed and professing to pass resolutions...[The] word 'meeting' prima facie means a coming together of more than one person. It is, of course, possible to show that the word 'meeting' has a meaning different from the ordinary meaning, but there is nothing here to show this to be the case. It appears therefore to me that this call was not made at a meeting of the company within the meaning of the Act.
>
> MELLISH LJ: In this case, no doubt, a meeting was duly summoned, but only one shareholder attended. It is clear that, according to the ordinary use of English language, a meeting could no more be constituted by one person than a meeting could have been constituted if no shareholder at all had attended. No business could be done at such a meeting, and the call is invalid.
>
> BRETT and AMPHLETT JJA concurred.

➤ Notes

1. CA 2006 s 318(1) now provides that in the case of a company limited by shares or guarantee and having only one member, one qualifying person present at a meeting is a quorum. In any other case, two qualifying people must be present (provided they do not both represent the same member). To be a qualifying person under this section, one must be a member in person, a corporate representative or appointed by proxy (s 318(3)). Section 324 extends the right to appoint proxies to members of all companies.

2. The single member company having a one-person 'meeting' presents evidentiary problems which CA 2006 s 357 attempts to meet by requiring the decision to take the form of a written resolution, or the single member to provide the company with a written record

---

[22] These tin-mining companies were unincorporated and governed by special statutes.

of the decision. Failure to comply with this requirement is punishable by a fine, but non-compliance does not affect the validity of the decision itself.

3. Some amusement can occasionally be found in all this procedural detail. *Neptune (Vehicle Washing Equipment) Ltd v Fitzgerald* [1995] BCLC 352 shows that a literal approach to statutory provisions can lead to absurdity bordering on farce. The case concerned the rule laid down by CA 1985 s 317 (now CA 2006 s 177), which imposed on directors a duty to declare any personal interests in contracts or proposed contracts with the company 'at a meeting of the directors of the company'. The company in question had only one director. Lightman J said (at pp 818–819, 359–360):

> . . . a sole director cannot evade compliance with s 317 by considering or committing the company to a contract in which he is interested otherwise than at a director's meeting or by delegating the decision-making to others.
>
> In the context of legislation which specifically authorises sole directorships and where Table A provides for a committee of one, the legislature cannot have intended by use of the word 'meeting' in s 317 to exclude from its ambit and the achievement of the statutory object sole directors, and I so hold. This conclusion is reinforced by the consideration that the concept of the holding of a director's meeting in case of a sole directorship is familiar to company lawyers.
>
> Two different situations may arise. The sole director may hold a meeting attended by himself alone or he may hold a meeting attended by someone else, normally the company secretary. When holding the meeting on his own, he must still make the declaration to himself and have the statutory pause for thought, though it may be that the declaration does not have to be out loud, and he must record that he made the declaration in the minutes. The court may well find it difficult to accept that the declaration has been made if it is not so recorded. If the meeting is attended by anyone else, the declaration must be made out loud and in the hearing of those attending, and again should be recorded. In this case, if it is proved that the declaration was made, the fact that the minutes do not record the making of the declaration will not preclude proof of its making. In either situation the language of the section must be given full effect: there must be a declaration of the interest.

4. CA 2006 s 177 now replaces Companies Act 1986 (CA 1986) s 317, but fails to solve this problem, it seems. There is a specific rule (a writing requirement) where a sole director makes a declaration at a directors' meeting if the company is required to have more than one director; and s 177 itself provides that a declaration need not be made 'to the extent that the other directors are already aware of the interest'. The Company Law Review (CLR) had proposed that sole directors be required to make a declaration to the company's *members* prior to entering into a transaction in which they had a personal interest. This would have been ridiculous, and thankfully there is no such requirement in CA 2006.

5. The court is given power to order meetings pursuant to CA 2006 s 306 (see *Union Music Ltd v Watson* **[4.13]**). Section 306(4) specifically provides that 'such directions may include a direction that one member of the company present at the meeting be deemed to constitute a quorum'. See also *Wheeler v Ross* [2011] EWHC 2527 (Ch) and *Smith v Butler* **[3.02]**.

Being together in the same physical location is not essential.

[4.11] Byng v London Life Association Ltd [1990] Ch 170 (Court of Appeal)

[Another part of this decision is extracted at **[4.12]**.] More members turned up to attend a meeting than could be accommodated in the cinema which had been notified as the venue. Overflow rooms with audio-visual links had been arranged, but these facilities did not work; and, in any case, some people could not get in and had to stay outside in the foyer. The Court of Appeal held, inter alia, that: (i) the assembly in the cinema was a 'meeting' which was capable of being adjourned to another place, even though (since many members who wished to attend were excluded) it was not capable of proceeding to business; and (ii) that it was not essential to a meeting that all members should be present in one room or face to face, provided that proper audio-visual links were in place which would enable everyone present to see and hear what was going on and participate in the proceedings.

> BROWNE-WILKINSON V-C: The rationale behind the requirement for meetings in the Companies Act 1985 is that the members shall be able to attend in person so as to debate and vote on matters affecting the company. Until recently this could only be achieved by everyone being physically present in the same room face to face. Given modern technological advances, the same result can now be achieved without all the members coming face to face: without being physically in the same room they can be electronically in each other's presence so as to hear and be heard and to see and be seen. The fact that such a meeting could not have been foreseen at the time the first statutory requirements for meetings were laid down, does not require us to hold that such a meeting is not within the meaning of the word 'meeting' in the Act of 1985....
>
> I have no doubt therefore that in cases where the original venue proves inadequate to accommodate all those wishing to attend, valid general meetings of a company can be properly held using overflow rooms provided, first, that all due steps are taken to direct to the overflow rooms those unable to get into the main meeting and, second, that there are adequate audio-visual links to enable those in all the rooms to see and hear what is going on in the other rooms. Were the law otherwise, with the present tendency towards companies with very large numbers of shareholders and corresponding uncertainty as to how many shareholders will attend meetings, the organisation of such meetings might prove to be impossible.

> ➤ Questions

Do you think that it is essential for a valid meeting being held by electronic link-up that the participants should be able to: (i) *see* as well as to hear each other or (ii) intervene or participate, verbally, in any discussion taking place at meeting?

In what ways could the law be further changed so as to facilitate the use of modern (and developing) technology, in regard to communication with members, meetings held at several locations, electronic voting, etc? The 2010 amendments to the Insolvency Rules are instructive.

The role of the chairman

It is the chairman's function at a general meeting to preserve order, see that proceedings are properly conducted and ensure that the sense of the meeting is properly ascertained. The chairman has no power to take into his or her own hands decisions that the meeting itself is competent to make: *National Dwelling Society v Sykes* [1894] 3 Ch 159. If the meeting is not competent to act, the next case indicates what the chairman is to do.

[4.12] Byng v London Life Association Ltd [1990] Ch 170 (Court of Appeal)

[See **[4.11]** for another extract from this case.] An extraordinary general meeting of the company had been summoned for 12 noon at Cinema 1, The Barbican Centre, London. Because of an unexpectedly large turnout of some 800 members, this venue was too small.

At 12.45 pm Dawson, the chairman, acting on his own initiative and without following the procedure prescribed by art 18 of the company's articles, announced that he was adjourning the meeting to 2.30 pm at the Café Royal, about one mile away. Only 600 people could attend this adjourned meeting, at which certain resolutions were passed. Byng and others sought declarations that these resolutions were invalid. The Court of Appeal upheld their contentions, ruling that although the chairman had a common law power to adjourn the meeting in circumstances such as these where the views of the members could not be ascertained, and despite the fact that he had acted throughout on advice and in good faith, he had failed in his duty to take into account all relevant considerations, such as the fact that members who were unable to attend the afternoon meeting could not arrange proxies in the time available, with the consequence that the adjourned meeting would not be representative.

BROWNE-WILKINSON V-C: In my judgment, were it not for article 18, Mr Dawson would at common law have had power to adjourn the meeting at the cinema since the inadequacy of the space available rendered it impossible for all those entitled to attend to take part in the debate and to vote. A motion for adjournment could not be put to the meeting as many who would be entitled to vote on the motion were excluded. Therefore, at common law it would have been the chairman's duty to regulate the proceedings so as to give all persons entitled a reasonable opportunity of debating and voting. This would have required him either to abandon the meeting or to adjourn it to a time and place where the members could have a reasonable opportunity to debate or vote. I see no reason to hold that in all circumstances the meeting must be abandoned: in my judgment the chairman can, in a suitable case, merely adjourn such meeting.

What then is the effect of article 18 which expressly confers on the chairman power to adjourn but only with the consent of a quorate meeting? Mr Potts submits that the chairman's power to adjourn having been expressly laid down and expressly circumscribed, there is no room for the chairman to have any implied power at common law...

Like the judge, I reject this submission. In my judgment article 18 regulates the chairman's powers of adjournment to the extent that its machinery is effective to cover the contingencies which occur. Therefore if the circumstances are such that it is possible to discover whether or not the meeting agrees to an adjournment, article 18 lays down a comprehensive code. But if the circumstances are such that the wishes of the meeting cannot be validly ascertained, why should article 18 be read as impairing the fundamental common law duty of the chairman to regulate proceedings so as to enable those entitled to be present and to vote to be heard and to vote?...Say that there was a disturbance in a meeting which precluded the taking of any vote on a motion to adjourn. Would this mean that the meeting had to be abandoned even though a short adjournment would have enabled peace to be restored and the meeting resumed? Again, say that in the present case the adjoining Barbican theatre had been available...so that a short adjournment to the theatre would have enabled an effective meeting of all members wishing to attend to be held that morning. Can it really be the law that because a valid resolution for such an adjournment could not be passed in the cinema (many members entitled to vote being excluded from the cinema) no such adjournment could take place?

I do not find that any principle of construction requires me to hold that an express provision regulating adjournment when the views of the meeting can be ascertained necessarily precludes the existence of implied powers when consent of the meeting cannot be obtained...Accordingly, I reach the conclusion that in any circumstances where there is a meeting at which the views of the majority cannot be validly ascertained, the chairman has a residual common law power to adjourn 'so as to give all persons entitled a reasonable opportunity of voting' and, I would add, speaking at the meeting...

Since such power is only exercisable for the purpose of giving the members a proper opportunity to debate and vote on the resolution, there must in my judgment be very special circumstances to justify a decision to adjourn the meeting to a time and place where, to the knowledge of the chairman, it could not be attended by a number of the members who had taken the trouble to attend the original meeting and could not even lodge a proxy vote. To overlook this factor is to leave out of account a matter of central importance. True it is that those who were available for the afternoon meeting would have been inconvenienced by an adjournment to another date or the convening of a wholly new meeting since they would either have to have attended at the fresh meeting or to have lodged proxies. But in my judgment this could not out-weigh the central point that the form of the adjournment was such as undoubtedly to preclude certain members from taking any part in the meeting either by way of debate or by way of vote...

Accordingly, although Mr Dawson acted in complete good faith, his decision to adjourn to the Café Royal on the same date was not one which, in my judgment, he could reasonably have reached if he had properly apprehended the restricted nature and purposes of his powers. Therefore in my judgment his decision was invalid...

MUSTILL and WOOLF LJJ delivered concurring judgments.

Who can call a meeting?

Clearly the expense in calling and conducting a meeting is far greater than in calling for a written resolution, or in calling for a resolution to be proposed at a meeting that is already scheduled (see 'Who can propose a resolution (or circulate a statement) at a meeting?', p 211). Nevertheless, the directors can call a general meeting (s 302), and members hold-ing 5% of the voting capital or voting rights can require the directors to call a meeting (ss 303 and 304), or can do so themselves if the directors refuse (s 305). But the directors are not obliged to act on such a requisition if its object is something that the general meeting is not competent to decide, for example to give direction to the board on matters of busi-ness policy (see 'Dividing corporate power between members and directors', p 189): *Rose v McGivern* [1998] 2 BCLC 593. Finally, the court may call a meeting if these other means are impracticable (s 306).

The statutory conditions attached to all these rights to call meetings merit close atten-tion. This is especially so because if notice of a meeting is issued by someone who does not have authority to issue such notices, then the notice is void, and any decisions taken at the meeting will also be void (although the court will not intervene if it is clear that the same decisions would have been reached had the correct procedure been followed: *Browne v La Trinidad* (1887) 37 Ch D 1; *Boschoek Proprietary Co Ltd v Fuke* [**4.32**]).

Power of the court to order meetings: CA 2006 s 306.

[4.13] Union Music Ltd v Watson [2003] EWCA Civ 180
(Court of Appeal)

This case concerned Russell Watson (W), the internationally famous opera singer. U applied under CA 1985 s 371 for an order for a general meeting of Arias (A), a company of which U was the majority shareholder (51%) and one of its directors. W was the only other shareholder and director. A shareholders' agreement provided that shareholders should exercise their voting rights so that A could not hold any meeting or transact any business at a meeting unless all shareholders or their representatives were present. A disagreement arose between W and U. W threatened not to attend any meetings. This created a deadlock. No business could be transacted, and no new directors could be ap-pointed to deal with business without a shareholders' meeting. The trial judge refused the application. The Court of Appeal allowed the appeal, agreeing that s 371 did not allow the court to override entrenched or class rights, or to break the deadlock between two equal shareholders, but the instant case involved no such rights and the shareholdings were not equal.

PETER GIBSON LJ:... I venture to make a few preliminary observations about s 371. It is a procedural section plainly intended to enable company business which needs to be conducted at a general meeting of the company to be so conducted. No doubt the thinking behind it is that a company should be allowed to get on with managing its affairs, and that should not be frustrated by the impracticability of calling or conducting a general meeting in the manner prescribed by the articles and the Act....

... But the power confers on the court a discretion and, like all discretions, it must be exercised properly having regard to the relevant circumstances. The authorities provide examples of cases where the power has been exercised and where it has not. The fact that there are quorum provisions in Table A requiring two members' attendance will not in itself be sufficient to prevent the court making an order under s 371, where the applicant is seeking a proper order such as the appointment of a director, something which a majority shareholder would have the right to procure in ordinary circumstances....

... I can see no sufficient reason why the order should not be made so that the deadlock in the board can be broken. Of course, I acknowledge that that means that the majority shareholder will have his way by the appointment of a director of its choice, save where the parties have agreed to complete equality. One side or the other has to prevail, and I cannot see that the contractual provisions in the agreement provide a sufficient reason why the power should not be exercised. Companies should have effective boards able to take decisions. I would therefore be prepared to make an order for the calling of a meeting to consider the question of the appointment of a further director and to allow the voting on that, even though only one member is present at that meeting.... [He then considered whether this would unacceptably affect either shareholders' entrenched rights (there were none) or class rights (no, they were of the same class), or permit a 50% shareholder to override the wishes of the other 50% shareholder (not relevant on the facts here). He then continued:] What the parties had contracted for [by way of shareholders' agreement], I accept, was that if Mr Watson chose not to attend or be represented at a general meeting, then there could be no general meeting.

Clause 6.1.18 [of the shareholders' agreement], however, seems to me more in the nature of a quorum provision than a provision for a class right, which it plainly was not, or a substantive right....

There is no doubt that if, as one would expect, Union exercises its voting rights at a meeting not attended by Mr Watson or his proxy, it would be doing so in contravention of cl 6.1.18. For the reasons which I have already given, I do not see that as being an insuperable obstacle in the way of the court making an order under s 371. The court should consider whether the company is in a position to manage its affairs properly. It ought also to take into account the ordinary right of a majority shareholder to remove or appoint a director in exercise of his majority voting power. A meeting would be limited to the single act of enabling the appointment of a new director to be considered and voted on. Taking the view that I do that cl 6.1.18 is in the nature of a quorum provision rather than a provision confirming a substantive right, it seems to me that the judge was wrong to rely on that provision to refuse to order the meeting.

I would add that I also disagree with the judge's view that Union had chosen the wrong means in view of the possibilities of a derivative action or a s 459 petition [CA 2006 s 994]. I see no reason why a shareholder in the position of Union should not utilise the simple means afforded by s 371 rather than incur the greater difficulties and expense of the other possibilities....

[He therefore proposed to make an order for the calling of a meeting to consider the question of the appointment of a further director and to allow the voting on that, even though only one member would be present at that meeting.]

BUXTON LJ delivered a concurring judgment.

MORLAND J concurred with both.

➤ Notes

1. Where it is 'impracticable' to call a general meeting of the company in the ordinary way, the court may direct that a meeting may be called or conducted in any way that it thinks fit (CA 2006 s 306). See, for example, *Hussain v Wycombe Islamic Mission and Mosque Trust Ltd* [2011] EWHC 971 (Ch). In particular, it may direct that one person shall be deemed to constitute a quorum at a meeting—a power which is commonly invoked where the number of members has fallen to one.

2. In *Re British Union for the Abolition of Vivisection* [1995] 2 BCLC 1, the court held that the section could be applied where previous attempts at holding a general meeting had been frustrated by a disruptive minority, leading to breaches of the peace and intervention by the police. It was ordered that the meeting should be held with only an executive committee attending in person, the bulk of the membership voting by postal ballot.

3. In *Wheeler & Another v Ross & Others* [2011] EWHC 2527 (Ch), Arnold J made an order under s 306 for a meeting to be conducted, in the light of the complete breakdown of mutual trust and confidence between the majority shareholder and the minority shareholder. A s 306 order would overcome the problem of the extraordinary general meeting not being quorate if the minority shareholder chose not to attend the meeting.

4. The Court of Appeal in *Smith v Butler* **[3.02]** held that a trial judge's decision to grant a s 306 order was a discretionary judgement and that the court would therefore not interfere on appeal unless the decision was clearly wrong or some material factor was wrongly taken into or left out of account.

5. However, the s 306 machinery may not be used to override class rights, or rights entrenched in a shareholders' agreement: see *Harman v BML Group Ltd* [1994] 1 WLR 893, CA; or to resolve a deadlock where the company's own constitution contains no provision to cope with such a situation: *Ross v Telford* [1998] 1 BCLC 82, CA (both cases dealing with the predecessor, CA 1985 s 371). *Union Music Ltd v Watson* **[4.13]** and, more recently, *Wheeler & Another v Ross & Others* [2011] EWHC 2527 (Ch), explain the limits of these restrictions and the potential usefulness of the court's power.

➤ Question

In *Wheeler & Another v Ross & Others* [2011] EWHC 2527 (Ch), Arnold J clarified that the s 306 power 'will enable Mr Wheeler to enforce his rights as majority shareholder. It will not extinguish Mrs Ross' rights as the minority shareholder' [31]. Does this accurately reflect the practical reality?

What sort of notice must be given if a meeting is proposed?

In every case when meetings are called, there are strict rules on giving timely (s 307) and appropriate (s 311) notice to all those entitled to attend (ss 307–317).[23] See especially s 310 on who is entitled to notice. CA 2006 s 301 makes the validity of any resolution passed at the meeting depend on proper notice being given (also see *Musselwhite v CH Musselwhite and Son Ltd* [1962] Ch 964).

CA 2006 s 311 requires the notice of a general meeting to state the time and date of the meeting, as well as the location where it is to take place. Subject to any provisions in the company's articles, the notice must also state the general nature of the business to be dealt with. In the case of a listed company, an explanatory circular must also be sent out if any business other than ordinary business is to be discussed or decided at a general meeting

---

[23] Certain resolutions require special notice: see, eg, CA 2006 ss 168, 511 and 515.

(Listing Rules r 13.8.8R(1)). What constitutes ordinary business is to be decided by each company.[24]

If the notice convening a meeting is not sufficiently full and specific to enable the members receiving it to decide whether or not they ought in their own interest to attend, then any resolutions passed at such meetings may be held invalid: see, for example, *Speechley v Allott* [2014] EWCA Civ 230 where the appointment of the president and treasurer were held invalid on these grounds.

In calling a meeting and in advising members about proposed resolutions, directors must exercise their powers only for the purposes for which they were conferred (s 171, and see 'Duty to act within powers: CA 2006 s 171', pp 341ff, and *Dawson International plc v Coats Patons plc* [15.17]).

Note, however, that notice requirements, as with other formalities required under the Companies Act, may be waived in accordance with the *Duomatic* principle [4.15]: *Schofield v Schofield* [2011] EWCA Civ 154, Note 2 following *Re Duomatic* [4.15], p 217. This, of course, applies only if the notice requirement is inserted for the protection of the shareholders generally: in those circumstances, the shareholders can waive that protection. By contrast, the requirements laid out in CA 2006 ss 168 and 169 are inserted for the protection of the impugned director, and cannot be waived by any shareholder majority.

Who can propose a resolution (or circulate a statement) at a meeting?

Clearly the directors can propose resolutions, but so too can a sufficiently large group of members of a public company (not a private one—they can use the written resolution procedure): the group must hold 5% of the total relevant voting rights, or must comprise at least 100 members with an average paid up share value of £100 each (ss 338 and 338A). Notice must be given in the same manner as notice of a meeting (s 339), and the members making the request must carry the cost unless the company resolves otherwise (s 340).

Similarly, a sufficiently large group of members (this time of any type of company) may require the company to circulate a statement before a meeting, being a statement that concerns either a proposed resolution or some other business that is to be dealt with at the meeting (s 314). The group of members who may do this is defined in the same way (s 314), their statement must be no more than 1,000 words (s 314), the notice sent out must generally comply with all the requirements for notice of the meeting (ss 315 and 317) and the members making the request must carry the cost unless the company resolves otherwise (s 314).

Also see s 338A, allowing a specified group of members of a traded company (the group defined in the same way as noted earlier) to request the company to include other matters in the business to be dealt with at the annual general meeting.

Are members' meetings compulsory?

When companies first became part of the landscape, it was considered important to conduct regular meetings of members to enable them to hold the directors to account. By the mid-nineteenth century, these were less frequent, but an '*annual general meeting*' was compulsory. (Other general meetings which were not these ordinary or annual meetings

---

[24] Section 311 has been amended by SI 2009/1632 and now includes ss 311(2), 311(3) and 311A. These changes relate to the general meetings of traded companies only and deal with the contents of notice of meeting, and publication in advance of a meeting of a traded company.

were called 'extraordinary general meetings', although this term is now no longer used in CA 2006.) Public companies are still required to hold annual meetings linked to their reporting cycle (s 336(1)). This annual meeting and the required 'accounts meeting' (for laying the company's reports and accounts before the members, s 437) are usually combined, and the same meeting will usually also deal with resignations and appointments of directors.[25] Private companies, by contrast, need not hold annual general meetings at all.

How must meetings be conducted?

If members are to be bound by the decisions taken at meetings (whether they are present or not), then they must be given proper notice of the meeting (see earlier, so that they can decide whether or not to attend), and the meeting must be properly conducted: there must be a quorum, and the voting must be properly conducted.

The underlying reason for holding meetings was always said to be to allow members to attend in person so as to debate and vote on matters affecting the company (*Byng v London Life Association Ltd* [4.12]). Over the years, however, the perceived need to be together in the same venue has waned, and now the Model Articles provide for meetings where not all members are in the same place (private companies, art 37; public companies, art 29).

The quorum for a meeting is two, unless the company is a one man company (in which case it is one, see Note 1 following *Sharp v Dawes* [4.10], p 204), or unless the articles specify otherwise (s 318). The meeting can elect a chairman, unless the articles provide otherwise (s 319)—they usually do, the chairman usually being a person selected by the directors. Neither CA 2006 nor the Model Articles give the chairman the casting vote. Indeed, CA 2006 s 282 does not permit a members' ordinary resolution to be passed by means of a casting vote, even though this used to be a common provision in private company articles. This outcome seems to have been unintended, and regulations now validate provisions for casting votes, although only if they were in the company's articles before 1 October 2007 (SI 2007/3495, art 2(6) and Sch 5, para 2(1) and (5)).

Voting at a meeting can be by show of hands or by poll (see earlier), and in person or by proxy (ss 324–330 and Model Articles art 45 (private companies) and art 38 (public companies), as the articles require. In *Speechley v Allott* [2014] EWCA Civ 230, CA, the failure to hold a ballot was deemed sufficiently serious to render the election of the president and treasurer ineffective.

A proxy must vote in accordance with any instructions given by the member by whom the proxy is appointed (s 324A). Also see s 323, allowing corporate shareholders to appoint human representatives.

CA 2006 adopts a policy of enfranchising indirect investors, and now allows members (such as corporate trustees) to appoint more than one proxy for a meeting (so as properly to represent the different indirect or beneficial owners), and allows proxies to vote and speak at meetings notwithstanding anything in the company's articles (CA 2006 ss 324ff).

Even more changes have been introduced recently. Note in particular the provisions concerning advance voting on a poll (s 322A), electronic meetings and voting (s 360A), and a wide variety of provisions concerning traded companies (ss 307, 311, 319, 327, 333, 334, 336, 337, 338, 340, 341, 360A and 360B).

The outcome of the meeting must be formally recorded (ss 355–359).

---

[25] Public companies must also convene a general meeting if half or more of the company's capital has been lost: CA 2006 s 656.

'Voice' in decision-making

Even with large numbers of members, proper democracy is difficult.

[4.14] Re Dorman Long & Co Ltd [1934] Ch 635 (Chancery Division)

These remarks were made in reference to a scheme of arrangement under CA 1985 ss 425–427, but are applicable generally.

> MAUGHAM J: It may be observed that when the Joint Stock Companies Arrangement Act 1870 was passed, in the majority of cases all the persons concerned with an arrangement could go to the meeting, listen to what was said and vote for or against the arrangement according to the views which they were persuaded to take. In these days, in many of the cases that come before me, only a fraction of the persons who are concerned can get into the room where the meeting is proposed to be held, and in the great majority of cases, the proxies given to the directors before the meeting begins have in effect settled the question of the voting once for all. It is perhaps not unfair to say that in nearly every big case not more than 5 per cent of the interests involved[26] are present in person at the meeting. It is for that reason that the court takes the view that it is essential to see that the explanatory circulars sent out by the board of the company are perfectly fair and, as far as possible, give all the information reasonably necessary to enable the recipients to determine how to vote. I am assuming, of course, that following the usual procedure, explanatory circulars are sent out, because, I may observe, there is nothing in the Act to render them essential. In a sense, in all these cases, the dice are loaded in favour of the views of the directors: the notices and circulars are sent out at the cost of the company, the board have had plenty of time to prepare the circulars and all the facts of the case are known the them, proxy forms are made out in favour of certain named directors and, although it is true that the word 'for' or 'against' may be inserted in the modern proxy form, the recipients of the circulars very often are in doubt as to whether the persons named as proxies are bound to put in votes by proxy with which they are not in agreement. If we contrast with that position the position of a [member of a] class of objectors...he has a minimum of information, his personal interest in the matter may be exceedingly small, probably he knows few persons in the same position as himself and [the procedural, financial and timing barriers to effective action are high].

➤ Note

In this context, see the reforms introduced by the UK Corporate Governance and Stewardship Codes (Chapter 5), and also note the common law limitations on the free exercise by shareholders of their votes ('Limitations on the free exercise of members' voting rights', pp 222ff).

Reform of the law relating to general meetings

Both the CLR and an earlier Department of Trade and Industry (DTI) consultation document raised issues relating to the general meeting (especially the annual general meeting (AGM)) and members' resolutions. Their principal concerns (and the CA 2006 reactions) were these:

(i)   Many shares are now held by nominees. What steps can, or should, be taken to see that the beneficial (ie the 'real') owners of the shares receive information from the company, and possibly also be permitted to attend meetings, to vote, etc? See CA 2006 ss 145–153.

---

[26] The CLR suggests that the figure today is probably nearer to 1%.

(ii)   Should institutional investors be required to disclose what shares they own and in what capacity, and how they have voted? See the UK Stewardship Code for current best practice ('Regulation of institutional investors by the UK Stewardship Code', p 280).

(iii)   Given that AGMs of public companies are usually only attended by a very small percentage of members, that those who do attend are often quite unrepresentative, and that everything may well have been settled by proxies well in advance of the meeting, it seems clear that the AGM no longer serves its original democratic function as an occasion for general debate and decision-making on matters of company policy. Alternatively, any discussion may well be hijacked by 'campaigners' who have bought a few shares in order to gain publicity for their own separate agendas. Should the traditional AGM therefore be abolished? Is there a better replacement? Should some restrictions be put on the rights of institutional and 'campaigning' shareholders to speak? See CA 2006 ss 324–331, and ss 318–323 and 360B.

(iv)   Should the law be changed so as to oblige companies to circulate members' resolutions without charge? What are the advantages and disadvantages? See CA 2006 ss 292–295, especially s 294; ss 314–317, especially s 316; and ss 338–340B, especially ss 340, 340B.

Informal decision-making—the *'Duomatic'* principle

Members may make decisions formally, by written resolutions (for private companies) or by vote in general meeting, as we have seen. As well, informal assent is possible. In principle, the informal procedures described later apply to both private and public companies. In practice, however, they are only ever likely to be relevant to private companies. The informal unanimous assent rule provides that a formal general meeting or written resolution is unnecessary if all the members entitled to vote on the matter informally assent to the transaction. It does not matter if the members' assent is conveyed simultaneously at a meeting or is given at different times.[27]

A company is bound in a matter intra vires *by the unanimous but informal agreement of its voting members.*

[4.15] Re Duomatic Ltd [1969] 2 Ch 365 (Chancery Division)

The liquidator of Duomatic claimed repayment of remuneration from one of the company's directors, Mr Elvins, on the ground that the payments were not formally authorised by the company in general meeting.

BUCKLEY J: It is common ground that none of the sums which I have mentioned were authorised by any resolution of the company in general meeting, nor were they authorised by any resolution of any formally constituted board meeting; but it is said on behalf of Mr. Elvins that the payments were made with the full knowledge and consent of all the holders of voting shares in the company at the relevant times, and he contends that in those circumstances the absence of a formal resolution by the company in duly convened meeting of the company is irrelevant. Alternatively, he relies on [the equivalent of CA 2006 s 1157 (power of the court to grant relief)]....

---

[27] J Ellis, 'Unanimous Consent of Shareholders: A Principle Without Form?' [2011] *Company Lawyer* 260.

In support of the first part of his argument Mr. McCulloch has relied on two authorities. The first was *In re Express Engineering Works, Ltd.* [1920] 1 Ch. 466 where five persons formed a private company in which they were the sole shareholders, and they sold to it for £15,000, which was in fact secured by debentures of the company, property which they had acquired for £7,000 a few days before. The contract for sale to the company and the issue of debentures was carried out at a meeting of the five individuals, who thereupon appointed themselves directors of the company. That meeting was described in the books of the company as a board meeting. The articles forbade any director to vote in respect of any contract or arrangement in which he might be interested; and in a winding up of the company the liquidator claimed that the issue of the debentures was invalid. In the Court of Appeal it was held, there being no suggestion of fraud, that the company was bound in a matter intra vires by the unanimous agreement of its members. Lord Sterndale M.R. in his judgment, at p. 469, referred to the earlier decision of the Court of Appeal in *In re George Newman & Co. Ltd.* [1895] 1 Ch. 674 and cited a passage from the judgment of Lindley L.J. in that case, at p. 686,[28] and went on himself to say that there were two differences between *Newman's* case and *Express Engineering Works*, first, the transaction in *Newman's* case was ultra vires, and, secondly, there never was a meeting of the corporators. Lord Sterndale M.R. in *In re Express Engineering Works Ltd.* [1920] 1 Ch. 466, 470, went on:

'In the present case these five persons were all the corporators of the company and they did all meet, and did all agree that these debentures should be issued. Therefore it seems that the case came within the meaning of what was said by Lord Davey in *Salomon v. Salomon & Co. Ltd.* [1897] A.C. 22,' and he quotes from Lord Davey. Lord Sterndale M.R. goes on: 'It is true that a different question was there under discussion, but I am of opinion that this case falls within what Lord Davey said. It was said here that the meeting was a directors' meeting, but it might well be considered a general meeting of the company, for although it was referred to in the minutes as a board meeting, yet if the five persons present had said, "We will now constitute this a general meeting," it would have been within their powers to do so, and it appears to me that that was in fact what they did.'

Warrington L.J. said, at p. 470:

'It was competent to them'—that is, the five corporators of the company—'to waive all formalities as regards notice of meetings, etc., and to resolve themselves into a meeting of shareholders and unanimously pass the resolution in question. Inasmuch as they could not in one capacity effectually do what was required but could do it in another, it is to be assumed that as business men they would act in the capacity in which they had power to act. In my judgment they must be held to have acted as shareholders and not as directors, and the transaction must be treated as good as if every formality had been carried out.'

Younger L.J. said, at p. 471:

'I agree with the view that when all the shareholders of a company are present at a meeting that becomes a general meeting and there is no necessity for any further formality to be observed to make it so. In my opinion the true view is that if you have all the shareholders present, then all the requirements in connection with a meeting of the company are observed, and every competent resolution passed for which no further formality is required by statute becomes binding on the company.'

---

[28] The paragraph cited was: 'It may be true, and probably is true, that a meeting, if held, would have done anything which Mr George Newman desired; but this is pure speculation, and the liquidator, as representing the company in its corporate capacity, is entitled to insist upon and to have the benefit of the fact that even if a general meeting could have sanctioned what was done, such sanction was never obtained. Individual assents given separately may preclude those who give them from complaining of what they have sanctioned; but for the purpose of binding a company in its corporate capacity individual assents given separately are not equivalent to the assent of a meeting.'

In that case there were no non-voting shares, but Mr. McCulloch contends that the presence of the non-voting shares in the present case does not matter. If he can establish that those who were entitled to attend and vote at general meetings of the company in fact agreed to all or any of these payments, then he says that that is tantamount to a resolution passed at a general meeting of the company, and that the agreement of those persons is binding on the company in the same way as a resolution of a general meeting is binding on the company.

In *Parker and Cooper Ltd. v. Reading* [1926] Ch. 975, the second case relied upon by Mr. McCulloch, the directors of a company had created a debenture and proceedings were commenced to establish that the debenture and the resolution which authorised its issue and the appointment of a certain receiver under it were invalid. Astbury J. referred to *In re Express Engineering Works Ltd.* [1920] 1 Ch. 466 and to *In re George Newman & Co. Ltd.* [1895] 1 Ch. 674 and himself expressed this view [1926] Ch. 975, at p. 984:

> 'Now the view I take of both these decisions is that where the transaction is intra vires and honest, and especially if it is for the benefit of the company, it cannot be upset if the assent of all the corporators is given to it. I do not think it matters in the least whether that assent is given at different times or simultaneously.'

Thus, the effect of his judgment was to carry the position a little further than it had been carried in *In re Express Engineering Works Ltd.* [1920] 1 Ch. 466, for Astbury J. expressed the view that it was immaterial that the assent of the corporators was obtained at different times, and that it was not necessary that there should be a meeting of them all at which they gave their consent to the particular transaction sought to be upheld. *In Parker & Cooper Ltd. v. Reading* [1926] Ch. 975, as in *In re Express Engineering Works Ltd.* [1920] 1 Ch. 466, no question arose about the position of any shareholders whose shares conferred no right of attending or voting at general meetings of the company.

. . . Mr. Wright, for the liquidator, has contended that where there has been no formal meeting of the company and reliance is placed upon the informal consent of the shareholders the cases indicate that it is necessary to establish that all shareholders have consented. He argues that as the preference shareholder is not shown to have consented in the present case, that require-ment is not satisfied, and that the assent of those shareholders—that is to say, Mr. Elvins and Mr. East—who knew about these matters, and who did approve the figures relating to them in the accounts for the year ending April 30, 1963, is of no significance. It seems to me that if it had occurred to Mr. Elvins and Mr. East, at the time when they were considering the accounts, to take the formal step of constituting themselves a general meeting of the company and pass-ing a formal resolution approving the payment of directors' salaries, that it would have made the position of the directors who received the remuneration, Mr. Elvins and Mr. Hanly, secure, and nobody could thereafter have disputed their right to retain their remuneration. The fact that they did not take that formal step but that they nevertheless did apply their minds to the question of whether the drawings by Mr. Elvins and Mr. Hanly should be approved as being on account of remuneration payable to them as directors, seems to lead to the conclusion that I ought to regard their consent as being tantamount to a resolution of a general meeting of the company. In other words, I proceed upon the basis that where it can be shown that all shareholders who have a right to attend and vote at a general meeting of the company assent to some matter which a general meeting of the company could carry into effect, that assent is as binding as a resolution in general meeting would be. The preference shareholder, having shares which conferred upon him no right to receive notice of or to attend and vote at a general meeting of the company, could be in no worse position if the matter were dealt with informally by agreement between all the shareholders having voting rights than he would be if the shareholders met together in a duly constituted general meeting.

Also see *Re Halt Garage (1964) Ltd* **[5.03]**; *Re Horsley & Weight Ltd* **[4.31]**, CA; *Multinational Gas and Petrochemical Co v Multinational Gas and Petrochemical Services Ltd* **[7.43]**.

➤ Notes

1. Curiously, the *Duomatic* case has received greater recognition than it probably deserves, in that practising lawyers now commonly refer to the rule established by *Express Engineering* and later cases (all cited in *Duomatic*) as '*the Duomatic principle*', overlooking the fact that the principle had been established many decades earlier. Also see P Watts (2006) 122 LQR 15. The '*Duomatic*' principle has been extended to, for instance, decision-making in club committees: *Speechley v Allott* [2014] EWCA Civ 230, CA.

2. What type of informal consent is sufficient to trigger the application of the *Duomatic* principle remains topical. In *Schofield v Schofield* [2011] EWCA Civ 103, CA, Neil Schofield (representing the corporate holder of 99.9% of the shares in the company) unsuccessfully argued that he and Lee (his son and the owner of the remaining share) had agreed, informally, to treat as valid and effective a meeting which was called without the 14 days' notice required by CA 2006 ss 305(4) and 307(1), and at which (amongst other matters) Lee was dismissed as director and Neil was appointed sole director. The judgment of the Court of Appeal was delivered by Etherton LJ, and included this statement of the law:

> 32. What all the authorities show is that the Appellant must establish an agreement by Lee to treat the meeting as valid and effective, notwithstanding the lack of the required period of notice. Lee's agreement could be express or by implication, verbal or by conduct, given at the time or later, but nothing short of unqualified agreement, objectively established, will suffice. The need for an objective assessment was well put by Newey J in the recent case of *Rolfe v Rolfe* [2010] EWHC 244 (Ch) at [41], as follows:
>
> > '. . . I do not accept that a shareholder's mere internal decision can of itself constitute assent for *Duomatic* purposes. I was not referred to any authority in which it had been decided that a mere internal decision would suffice. Further, for a mere internal decision, unaccompanied by outward manifestation or acquiescence, to be enough would, as it seems to me, give rise to unacceptable uncertainty and, potentially, provide opportunities for abuse. A company may change hands or enter into an insolvency procedure; in either event, it is desirable that past decisions should be objectively verifiable. In my judgment, there must be material from which an observer could discern or (as in the case of acquiescence) infer assent. The law applies an objective test in other contexts: for example, when determining whether a contract has been formed. An objective approach must, I think, also have a role with the *Duomatic* principle.'
>
> 33. It is perfectly plain that objectively [on due assessment of the facts] there never was unqualified agreement by Lee to the validity of the meeting or the Company's business which was purportedly transacted during the course of it.

3. In *Hussain v Wycombe Islamic Mission and Mosque Trust Ltd* [2011] EWHC 971 (Ch), the question was whether the *Duomatic* principle could serve to validate the adoption of a revised constitution for the company, given that no meeting of the five original subscribers (whom the court found to be its only members) ever took place, and one of those subscribers (Mr Chouglay) had written a letter setting out his objections. HHJ David Cooke held that notwithstanding this letter, Mr Chouglay could be taken to have agreed to the adoption of the new constitution because:

> 37. Mr Chouglay clearly must have known following the submission of his letter that the constitution was nevertheless regarded as having been adopted. He must have known of the elections that were held the same year, in reliance upon the terms of that constitution. And yet there is no evidence that he took any steps to protest or object, or to pursue his view that affairs would be better conducted without elections. Given the significance of this event in relation

to the affairs of the mosques, the only inference that can be drawn from this silence, it seems to me, is that Mr Chouglay accepted that the Constitution had been adopted and the changes that it set out to make had become effective, notwithstanding his personal reservations about some of them. This inference from his conduct supports the hearsay evidence given by Mr Hussain and Mr Rashid, and I therefore find that Mr Chouglay also assented to the adoption of the 2001 constitution. It thus in my judgment became binding on the company by operation of the *Duomatic* principle.

➤ Questions

1. Before the adoption of the new constitution, what if Mr Chouglay had simply kept silent? Would silence have been a clearer indication of his objection than a courteous letter setting out his 'suggestions'?

2. Compare HHJ David Cooke's treatment of Mr Chouglay's silence following the adoption of the new constitution and the Court of Appeal's approach towards Lee's silence (and, indeed, Lee had attended the invalidly called meeting and voted on resolutions at the meeting). Is the court's general approach consistent? Also see *Re Bailey, Hay & Co Ltd* [1971] 1 WLR 1357.

3. Some companies include provision in their articles for members to pass resolutions informally without a meeting. Could such a provision state that a written resolution with a simple or 75% majority would be valid even if the detailed statutory procedure were not followed?

The principle can apply to shareholders' agreements.

[4.16] Euro Brokers Holdings Ltd v Monecor (London) Ltd
[2003] EWCA Civ 105 (Court of Appeal)

The facts are immaterial.

MUMMERY LJ: [He described the varied circumstances in which the principle applies:]...I see nothing in the circumstances of the present case to exclude the *Duomatic* principle. It is a sound and sensible principle of company law allowing the members of the company to reach an agreement without the need for strict compliance with formal procedures, where they exist only for the benefit of those who have agreed not comply with them. What matters is the unanimous assent of those who ultimately exercise power over the affairs of the company through their right to attend and vote at a general meeting. It does not matter whether the formal procedures in question are stipulated for in the articles of association, in the Companies Acts or in a separate contract between the members of the company concerned. What matters is that all the members have reached an agreement. If they have, they cannot be heard to say that they are not bound by it because the formal procedure was not followed. The position is treated in the same way as if the agreed formal procedure had been followed. The particular context for the application of the principle in this case is that cl 11(2) of the shareholders' agreement requires the notice to be issued by the board. That is a formal corporate procedure. It is irrelevant that the requirement is in a separate agreement entered into by the shareholders in EBFL, rather than in the articles. The shareholders entered into that agreement for the very same purpose as the contract between them constituted by the articles, namely to regulate the relationship between the shareholders in the governance of EBFL. As Neuberger J said in *Re Torvale Group Ltd* [1999] 2 BCLC 605 at 617:

'The articles constitute a contract, and if the parties to that contract, or if the parties for whom the benefit of a particular term has been included in that contract, are happy unanimously to waive or vary the prescribed procedure for a particular purpose, then...it seems to me that there is no good reason why it should not be capable of applying.'

I fail to see why the agreement of the only two shareholders in EBFL to meet a call for capital without the need for a notice issued by the board of EBFL should not be as binding on them as if the call were made pursuant to a notice issued by the board, which would have happened had there been communication between the directors appointed by the members at a formal meeting and resolution of a properly constituted board. When the members of EBFL decided to respond to the capital call it did not matter to them that it had been communicated by Mr Pask rather than by the board.

[But see Note 7 in Further notes following the next extract, p 222.]

➤ Note

Also see *Franbar Holdings Ltd v Casualty Plus Ltd* [2010] EWHC 1164 (Ch), affirmed by the Court of Appeal in [2011] EWCA Civ 60 **[13.08]**.

An informal, unanimous agreement between members may be effective as an extraordinary or special resolution.

[4.17] Cane v Jones [1980] 1 WLR 1451 (Chancery Division)

In 1946, two brothers, Percy and Harold Jones, formed a company to run the family business. Each was a director and the shareholding was divided equally between members of Percy's family and members of Harold's family. The articles gave the chairman a casting vote at both directors' and shareholders' meetings; but Harold's daughter Gillian (the plaintiff, Mrs Cane) claimed that an agreement had been made between all the shareholders in 1967 which provided (inter alia) that the chairman should cease to be entitled to use his casting vote, so that Percy (who was currently chairman) did not have a decisive vote in the company's affairs. The court held that this was so, and that the informal agreement had had the same effect as a special resolution altering the articles. It was immaterial that the statutory obligation to register such resolutions had not been complied with.

MICHAEL WHEELER QC (sitting as a deputy judge of the High Court):... [T]he [*Duomatic*] principle is, I think, conveniently summarised in a short passage in the judgment in that case of Buckley J where he says, **[4.15]** at 373:

'... I proceed upon the basis that where it can be shown that all shareholders who have a right to attend and vote at a general meeting of the company assent to some matter which a general meeting of the company could carry into effect, that assent is as binding as a resolution in general meeting would be.'

Applying that principle to the present case, Mr Weaver says that the agreement of all the shareholders embodied in the 1967 agreement had the effect, so far as requisite, of overriding the articles. In other words, it operated to deprive the chairman for the time being of the right to use his casting vote...

For the first and third defendant, Mr Potts...answers...that on its true interpretation in relation to a special or extraordinary resolution the *Duomatic* principle only applies if there has been (i) a resolution, and (ii) a meeting; and that here he says, with some truth, there was neither a resolution nor a meeting of the four shareholders...

[This argument]—namely that there must be a 'resolution' and a 'meeting'—does not appear to have been raised in any of the...reported cases which were convened with special or extraordinary resolutions. But it is not an argument to which I would readily accede because in my judgment it would create a wholly artificial and unnecessary distinction between those powers which can, and those which cannot, be validly exercised by all the corporators acting together.

For my part I venture to differ from Mr Potts on the first limb of his argument, namely that articles can *only* be altered by special resolution. In my judgment, s 10 of the Act is merely laying down a procedure whereby *some only* of the shareholders can validly alter the articles: and if, as I believe to be the case, it is a basic principle of company law that all the corporators, acting together, can do anything which is intra vires the company, then I see nothing in s 10 to undermine this principle...

Some light is also, I think, thrown on the problem by s 143(4) of the Act of 1948 [CA 2006 s 29(1)]. Section 143 deals with the forwarding to the Registrar of Companies of copies of every resolution or agreement to which the section applies; and sub-s (4) reads:

'This section shall apply to—(a) special resolutions; (b) extraordinary resolutions; (c) resolutions which have been agreed to by all the members of a company, but which, if not so agreed to, would not have been effective for their purpose unless, as the case may be, they had been passed as special resolutions or as extraordinary resolutions...'

Paragraph (c) thus appears to recognise that you can have a resolution, at least, which has been agreed to by all the members and is as effective as a special or extraordinary resolution would have been...

I should add in passing that a copy of the 1967 agreement was never, as far as I am aware, sent to the Registrar of Companies for registration. It may be that there is a gap in the registration requirements of s 143. But be that as it may, the fact that the 1967 agreement was drafted as an agreement and not as a resolution, and that the four signatories did not sign in each other's presence does not in my view prevent that agreement overriding *pro tanto*—and so far as necessary—the articles of the company; in my judgment Mr Potts' first argument fails and...the chairman of the company has no casting vote at board or general meetings...

> ➤ Notes

1. The contention of counsel that the agreement of 1967 had the effect 'so far as requisite' of 'overriding' the articles, exposes the central weakness of the ruling in this case. There can be little doubt that the 1967 agreement was, essentially, nothing more than a shareholder agreement which (because of the doctrine of privity) could be enforced only by the immediate parties. The plaintiff was not such a party, having inherited her shares at a later date. It is difficult to reconcile the lax view taken of the importance of formalities in this case with the stricter approach of *Scott v Frank F Scott (London) Ltd* **[4.01]** and the *Bratton Seymour* case **[4.02]**.

2. This case was followed in *Re Home Treat Ltd* [1991] BCLC 705, in what was clearly a very indulgent ruling. The company, which was in administration, had carried on the business of a nursing home for many years without having power to do so under its objects clause. The administrator wished to continue to run the business with a view to selling it as a going concern. Harman J held that, since the company's only members had agreed to the change of activity, it must be deemed to have changed its memorandum under CA 1985 s 4. It is

inconceivable that such a view would have prevailed a generation ago (see, eg, the ruling of the judge's father in *Re Introductions Ltd* [1970] Ch 199, CA). Also see Note 7 in the following Further notes, p 222.

3. Now see CA 2006, which predictably provides that the articles may be amended by special resolution (s 21), but then includes in s 29(1), in terms that may well accommodate these cases, the resolutions and agreements that must be sent to the registrar (s 30). The implication is that these arrangements will serve to amend the articles.

➤ Questions

1. Did the judge in *Cane v Jones* rule that the agreement *was* a special resolution, or only that it was as good as one?

2. Suppose that Thomas, a stranger, bought out all Percy's family's shares and was appointed chairman, without any knowledge of the events of 1967. Would he have a casting vote? Could he rely on the equivalent of CA 2006 s 33 to enforce the 'articles'?

➤ Further notes

Some glosses may be added to this line of cases.

1. The *Duomatic* principle does not apply if the shareholders do not understand and appreciate the transaction or issue to which they are allegedly assenting: *Vinton v Revenue and Customs Commissioners* [2008] STC (SCD) 592.

2. The *Duomatic* principle not only applies to decisions which formally require special and extraordinary resolutions (*Cane v Jones* **[4.17]**), but also to decisions formally required to be taken by a group or class of shareholders (*Re Torvale Group Ltd* [1999] 2 BCLC 605), and to decisions by members to ratify breaches of directors' duties (*Progress Property Co Ltd v Moore* [2008] EWHC 2577 (Ch), and see **[10.15]**). (On this last matter, see 'Members decisions concerning directors' breaches', pp 247ff.)

3. In contrast with the rule for informal written resolutions introduced by CA 2006 s 288 (see 'What are the essentials of a "meeting"?', p 204), the informal consent of the members must be unanimous. See *Re D'Jan* **[7.22]**, where the principal shareholder held 99% of the shares and his wife 1%. He could not argue that there had been a unanimous informal members' resolution (ratifying his negligence), because, although his wife was likely to have supported him, the issue was never in fact raised.

4. Where a person holds some shares for himself and other shares as a trustee or executor, his assent will prima facie apply only in relation to his own shares, and not the shares he holds on trust for a beneficial owner, unless he intends or purports to be making a decision in relation to those shares: *Rolfe v Rolfe* [2010] EWHC 244 (Ch).

5. The *Duomatic* principle was extended in *Shahar v Tsitsekkos* [2004] EWHC 2659 (Ch) so that the agreement of the beneficial owner of the shares is effective where the trustee can be compelled to vote in accordance with the beneficial owner's wishes. Note the limitation in *Rolfe v Rolfe* [2010] EWHC 244 (Ch), namely that if shares are held for more than one beneficial owner jointly, then the assent of *one* of a number of these owners will not suffice.

6. There are limits to the application of the principle, although these remain unclear. In *Re New Cedos Engineering Co Ltd* [1994] 1 BCLC 797, it was emphasised that the *Duomatic* principle cannot be invoked in order to enable something to be done informally which those concerned would not be competent to do, formally, at a general meeting (or, presumably, in some other specified formal manner). In *New Cedos* the number of registered

members had been reduced to one, so that no 'meeting' complying with the company's articles could effectively be held. It was ruled that nothing done informally by this sole member was equivalent to a decision of the members reached at a meeting. (The rules on meetings have now changed: see 'What are the essentials of a "meeting"?', pp 204ff.)

7. Contrast that case with the decision in *Wright v Atlas Wright (Europe) Ltd* [1999] 2 BCLC 301, CA. A service contract had been entered into between the company and Wright (the former managing director of the company) appointing him a consultant for life at an annual fee. The formalities then prescribed by CA 1985 s 319 had not been followed, but the company's sole member was fully informed of the arrangement and had signed an agreement recording it. The court held that, since the purpose of s 319 was the protection of the company's members, they could override any formal (including statutory) requirements regarding the passing of resolutions at general meetings notwithstanding the absolute terms in the statute. However, the court added that where there was some other underlying intention of a statutory provision, such as the protection of creditors or, perhaps, future members, this would not be so; and so it was possible to distinguish the earlier decision in *Re RW Peak (Kings Lynn) Ltd* [1998] 1 BCLC 193, in which Lindsay J had held that unanimous members' consent, given informally, was not sufficient to bypass the statutory procedure for a repurchase of shares prescribed by CA 1985 s 164.

8. More recently, in *Madoff Securities International Ltd v Raven* [2013] EWHC 3147 (Comm), Mr Justice Popplewell applied *New Cedos* and *Wright* to hold that payments to directors had been ratified by the informal unanimous approval of the voting shareholders, and therefore could not be recovered by the liquidators. He reached this conclusion on the basis of the *Duomatic* principle, having first satisfied himself that the circumstances were such that the shareholders could indeed ratify these payments (see the discussion of the case in Chapter 7, *Madoff Securities International Ltd v Raven* **[7.24]**).

9. After earlier uncertainty, it is now established that there is a similar rule applying to directors' resolutions (see 'Acting as a board of directors: meetings and decisions', p 299).

Limitations on the free exercise of members' voting rights

General issues

The general meeting operates by majority rule. Sometimes decisions are taken by ordinary resolution; in more serious cases (such as changing the company's constitution), they are taken by special resolution. In either case, the dissenting minority will have changes forced upon them to which they have not agreed. This would not happen under normal contract rules. On the other hand, members know, when they take up shares, that their rights are subject to 'majority rule'. In these circumstances, what protections does the law offer to dissenting members against having their rights overridden by the majority? There are very few routes for redress, but the members may be able to complain that, in the circumstances:

(i)   the impugned resolution is ineffective, as an objectionable exercise of power by the members. This ground of complaint relies on equitable control over the exercise by members of their voting rights. These controls, to the extent that they exist, appear to be enforced with more vigour in some circumstances (eg alteration of the articles and class rights) than in others, and to impose weak constraints in any event (see 'Members' personal rights', pp 261ff);

(ii) the company should be wound up on the 'just and equitable' ground: IA 1986 s 122(1)(g) (see 'Compulsory winding up on the "just and equitable" ground', pp 840ff);

(iii) the court should order a remedy (eg compulsory buy-out of the complainant's shares) to combat the unfair prejudice inflicted by the majority (CA 2006 s 994) (see 'Unfairly prejudicial conduct of the company's affairs', pp 715ff).

Only the first is dealt with in this chapter. The principles emerge from the cases.

A member's vote is a property right which, prima facie, may be exercised in the member's own interest and as he or she thinks fit. A member voting as such is under no fiduciary duty to the company, and this is true also of a director when voting as a member.

[4.18] Northern Counties Securities Ltd v Jackson & Steeple Ltd [1974] 1 WLR 1133 (Chancery Division)

The defendant company had given an undertaking to the court to use its best endeavours to obtain a Stock Exchange quotation for its shares, and to allot a certain number of these shares to the plaintiffs. It was necessary, under stock exchange rules, for the consent of the defendant company in general meeting to be obtained to the issue of shares. After the company had for more than a year failed to take any steps to comply with its undertaking, the plaintiffs moved for orders against the company and its directors: (i) that they should summon the required meeting; (ii) that they should send a circular to members calculated to induce them to vote in favour of the resolution, and warning them that the defeat of the resolution would amount to a contempt of court; and (iii) restraining the directors, as members, from voting against the resolution. The court granted orders that the meeting be summoned and that a circular be sent inviting the members to support the resolution, but ruled that neither the members generally nor the directors voting as members would be in contempt of court if they opposed the resolution.

WALTON LJ: Mr Price [counsel for the plaintiffs] argued that, in effect, there are two separate sets of persons in whom authority to activate the company itself resides. Quoting the well known passages from Viscount Haldane LC in *Lennard's Carrying Co Ltd v Asiatic Petroleum Co Ltd* **[3.21]** he submitted that the company as such was only a juristic figment of the imagination, lacking both a body to be kicked and a soul to be damned. From this it followed that there must be some one or more human persons who did, as matter of fact, act on behalf of the company, and whose acts therefore must, for all practical purposes, be the acts of the company itself. The first of such bodies was clearly the board of directors, to whom under most forms of articles...the management of the business of the company is expressly delegated. Therefore, their acts are the defendant company's acts; and if they do not, in the present instance, cause the defendant company to comply with the undertakings given by it to the court, they are themselves liable for contempt of court. And this, he says, is well recognised: see RSC, Ord 45, r 5(1), whereunder disobedience by a corporation to an injunction may result directly in the issue of a writ of sequestration against any director thereof. It is of course clear that for this purpose there is no distinction between an undertaking and an injunction: see note 45/5/3 in *The Supreme Court Practice* (1973).

This is, indeed, all well established law, with which Mr Instone [counsel for the directors] did not quarrel, and which indeed his first proposition asserted. But, continues Mr Price, this is only half of the story. There are some matters in relation to which the directors are not competent to act on behalf of the company, the relevant authority being 'the company in general meeting', that is to say, a meeting of the members. Thus in respect of all matters within the competence—at any rate those within the exclusive competence—of a meeting of the members, the acts of the members are the acts of the company, in precisely the same way as the acts of the directors are the acts of the company. Ergo, for any shareholder to vote against a resolution to issue the shares here in question to the plaintiffs would be a contempt of court, as it would be a step taken by him knowingly which would prevent the defendant company from fulfilling its undertaking to the court. Mr Price admitted that he could find no authority which directly assisted his argument, but equally confidently asserted that there was no authority which precluded it.

Mr Instone indicted Mr Price's argument as being based upon 'a nominalistic fallacy'. His precise proposition was formulated as follows: 'Whilst directors have special responsibilities as executive agents of the defendant company to ensure that the company does not commit a contempt of court, a shareholder, when the position has been put before the shareholders generally, who chooses to vote against such approval will not himself be in contempt of court.'...

In my judgment, these submissions of Mr Instone are correct. I think that in a nutshell, the distinction is this: when a director votes as a director for or against any particular resolution in a directors' meeting, he is voting as a person under a fiduciary duty to the company for the proposition that the company should take a certain course of action. When a shareholder is voting for or against a particular resolution he is voting as a person owing no fiduciary duty to the company and who is exercising his own right of property, to vote as he thinks fit. The fact that the result of the voting at the meeting (or at a subsequent poll) will bind the company cannot affect the position that, in voting, he is voting simply in exercise of his own property rights.

Perhaps another (and simpler) way of putting the matter is that a director is an agent, who casts his vote to decide in what manner his principal shall act through the collective agency of the board of directors; a shareholder who casts his vote in general meeting is not casting it as an agent of the company in any shape or form. His act therefore, in voting as he pleases, cannot in any way be regarded as an act of the company...

I now come to paragraph 4 of the notice of motion, which seeks an order restraining the individual respondents [ie the directors] and each of them from voting against the resolution. Mr Price says that, as the executive agents of the defendant company, they are bound to recommend to its shareholders that they vote in favour of the resolution to issue the shares, and hence, at the least, they cannot themselves vote against it, for they would thereby be assisting the defendant company to do that which it is their duty to secure does not happen. If, as executive officers of the defendant company, they are bound to procure a certain result if at all possible, how can they, as individuals, seek to frustrate that result?

I regret, however, that I am unable to accede to Mr Price's arguments in this respect...I think that a director who has fulfilled his duty as a director of a company, by causing it to comply with an undertaking binding upon it is nevertheless free, as an individual shareholder, to enjoy the same unfettered and unrestricted right of voting at general meeting of the members of the company as he would have if he were not also a director...

See also *Pender v Lushington* [13.23]; *North-West Transportation Co Ltd v Beatty* [4.34]; *Burland v Earle* [1902] AC 83, PC; and *Peters' American Delicacy Co Ltd v Heath* [4.26].

> ➤ Notes

1. *Halton International Inc (Holdings) Sarl v Guernroy Ltd* [2005] EWHC 1968 (Ch) reinforces this finding. The defendant, a member of the company, was given the power to exercise the votes of all other members for the purpose of raising fresh capital in any way he saw fit. The defendant member passed a resolution suspending the pre-emption rights of the other members which were inserted in the company articles, thereby increasing his voting rights in the selection of investors. The court held that the voting agreement did not give rise to any fiduciary duties on the part of the acting member. His actions were authorised by the agreement and were therefore upheld.

2. Similarly, in *McKillen v Misland (Cyprus) Investments Ltd & Ors* [2012] EWHC 521 (Ch), the court rejected an attempt to interpret a shareholders' agreement in a way which would impose fiduciary duties on shareholders.

3. The rule that a member owes no duties to the company and can exercise his rights entirely as he pleases, without regard to the effect of doing so upon the company, is not confined to the right to vote. In *Stothers v William Steward (Holdings) Ltd* [1994] 2 BCLC 266 it was applied to the right of a member (subject, of course, to any provision in the articles) to transfer his shares to a person of his choice. But where the articles do make special provision, the outcome may be different: see *Cream Holdings Ltd v Stuart Davenport* [2010] EWHC 3096 (Ch), in Note 4 following *Equitable Life Assurance Society v Hyman* **[4.03]**, p 196, as has been affirmed by the Court of Appeal in [2012] 1 BCLC 365.

4. By contrast, and quite exceptionally, the courts have on rare occasions been prepared to order that a member's votes should be cast, or at least not cast, in a certain way—in effect, to restrain him from acting perversely.

In *Standard Chartered Bank Ltd v Walker* [1992] 1 WLR 561, a member with a minority holding of shares was ordered not to vote against a restructuring agreement where the consequence of his doing so would have been that the company would collapse and his shares (which had been charged to the company's banks) would become worthless.

Similarly, in *Theseus Exploration NL v Mining & Associated Industries Ltd* [1973] Qd R 81 an injunction was granted against majority members restraining them from voting to remove the existing directors and replace them with a board intent on a policy of destructive asset-stripping.

More recently, in a case before the Companies Court of the Hong Kong Court of First Instance, Harris J granted an injunction to restrain the defendant shareholders from voting against a restructuring proposal which, if exercised, would 'result in the destruction of the economic value of other shareholders' shares for no rational reason' [33]: *Sunlink International Holdings Ltd v Wong* [2010] 5 HKLRD 653, HCA 1527/2010. It has been suggested, however, that the 'no rational basis' test in this case is too general, and requires further refinement and clarification by a higher court when the opportunity arises: WMF Wong, 'Can Shareholders Vote Irrationally?' (2011) 127 LQR 522.

➤ Question

How, if at all, can these cases be seen as consistent with cases that seem to impose restrictions on members when voting to alter the articles, or members when voting to alter class rights (see 'Alteration of the articles', pp 228ff and 'Variation of class rights', pp 588ff)?

A contract by a member to vote in a particular way, or as directed by another person, is binding and may be enforced by a mandatory injunction[29]

[4.19] Puddephatt v Leith [1916] 1 Ch 200 (Chancery Division)

The plaintiff had mortgaged shares in the company to the defendant and transferred them into his name. By a contemporaneous letter, the defendant had undertaken to vote the shares as directed by the plaintiff. The court ordered him to comply with the undertaking.

SARGENT J [after stating the facts and holding that the undertaking to vote in accordance with the plaintiff's wishes contained in the letter constituted a collateral agreement binding on the

---

[29] Contrast the position as regards directors, see 'General issues', p 326.

defendant, continued]: In my opinion, therefore, the right of the plaintiff is clear, and the only remaining question is whether she is entitled to a mandatory injunction to enforce her right. It is not disputed that she is entitled to a prohibitive injunction, and in my opinion she is also entitled to a mandatory injunction. Prima facie this court is bound...to give effect to a clear right by way of a mandatory injunction. There are no doubt certain exceptions from this rule, as in the case of a contract of service, because in such cases, it is impossible for the court to make its order effective, but...in the present case, in as much as there is one definite thing to be done, about the mode of doing which there can be no possible doubt, I am of opinion that I ought to grant not only the prohibitive but also the mandatory injunction claimed by the plaintiff, and I make an order accordingly.

➤ Notes

1. The specific undertaking given in this case displaced the normal rule that a mortgagee of shares may exercise the voting rights in respect of those shares free of any dictation from the mortgagor: *Siemens Bros & Co Ltd v Burns* [1918] 2 Ch 324, CA; *Stablewood Properties Ltd v Virdi* [2010] EWCA Civ 865, CA. Similarly, an *unpaid* vendor of shares who remains on the share register retains the voting rights free from dictation by the purchaser (*Musselwhite v CH Musselwhite & Son Ltd* [1962] Ch 964), although (at least where the contract is specifically enforceable) these rights may be inhibited by a fiduciary obligation to have regard to the purchaser's interests (*Michaels v Harley House (Marylebone) Ltd* [2000] Ch 104, CA). But once the purchaser has paid the full price, the vendor holds the shares as a bare trustee (*Hawks v McArthur* **[11.17]**), and must vote the shares as directed by the purchaser (*Re Piccadilly Radio plc* [1989] BCLC 683).

2. This case concerned a single shareholder. A contract between several shareholders, agreeing to coordinate their votes, or delegating to one the power to cast votes for all—commonly known as 'voting trust'—is lawful. It is more widely used in the United States than in the UK, and can be a powerful tool either to concentrate control behind the management, or to use as a countervailing force against it.[30]

A decision carried by the votes of majority members may be set aside if it is 'oppressive' of the minority.

[4.20] Clemens v Clemens Bros Ltd [1976] 2 All ER 268 (Chancery Division)

The plaintiff held 45% and her aunt ('Miss Clemens') 55% of the shares in the defendant company. The company's articles gave existing members a pre-emptive right if another member wished to transfer his shares. The plaintiff therefore had an expectation of total control of the company after her aunt's death, and 'negative control' (ie the power to block a special resolution) in the aunt's lifetime. The aunt and four non-shareholders were the directors. The directors proposed that the company's capital should be increased by issuing 200 ordinary shares to each of these four directors, and 850 ordinary shares to an employees' trust; and resolutions to this effect were passed by the aunt's votes at a general meeting. Although it was claimed that the object of the resolutions was in the company's interests (namely, to give the directors and employees a stake in the company) the court took the view that the real object was to deprive the plaintiff of her degree of control, and the resolutions were set aside.

---

[30] Of course, such a contract between shareholders may regulate other matters besides voting. See the discussion of shareholders' agreements, 'Shareholders' agreements', pp 256ff.

FOSTER J: For the plaintiff it was submitted that the proposed resolutions were oppressive, since they resulted in her losing her right to veto a special or extraordinary resolution and greatly watered down her existing right to purchase Miss Clemens' shares under article 6. For the defendants it was submitted that if the two shareholders both honestly hold differing opinions, the view of the majority must prevail and that the shareholders in general meeting are entitled to consider their own interests and vote in any way they honestly believe proper in the interests of the company.

There are many cases which have discussed a director's position. A director must not only act within his powers but must also exercise them bona fide in what he believes to be the interests of the company. The directors have a fiduciary duty, but is there any similar, restraint on shareholders exercising their powers as members at general meetings? [His Lordship read extracts from the judgments in a number of cases, including *Greenhalgh v Arderne Cinemas* **[4.27]**,[31] and continued:]

I think that one thing which emerges from the cases to which I have referred is that in such a case as the present Miss Clemens is not entitled to exercise her majority vote in whatever way she pleases. The difficulty is in finding a principle, and obviously expressions such as 'bona fide for the benefit of the company as a whole', fraud on a 'minority' and 'oppressive' do not assist in formulating a principle.

I have come to the conclusion that it would be unwise to try to produce a principle, since the circumstances of each case are infinitely varied. It would not, I think, assist to say more than that in my judgment Miss Clemens is not entitled as of right to exercise her votes as an ordinary shareholder in any way she pleases. To use the phrase of Lord Wilberforce,[32] that right is 'subject...to equitable considerations...which may make it unjust...to exercise [it] in a particular way'. Are there then any such considerations in this case?

I do not doubt that Miss Clemens is in favour of the resolutions and knows and understands their purport and effect; nor do I doubt that she genuinely would like to see the other directors have shares in the company and to see a trust set up for long service employees. But I cannot escape the conclusion that the resolutions have been framed so as to put into the hands of Miss Clemens and her fellow directors complete control of the company and to deprive the plaintiff of her existing rights as a shareholder with more than 25% of the votes and greatly reduce her [preemptive] rights...They are specifically and carefully designed to ensure not only that the plaintiff can never get control of the company but to deprive her of what has been called her negative control. Whether I say that these proposals are oppressive to the plaintiff or that no one could honestly believe they are for her benefit matters not. A court of equity will in my judgment regard these considerations as sufficient to prevent the consequences arising from Miss Clemens using her legal right to vote in the way that she has and it would be right for a court of equity to prevent such consequences taking effect.

➤ Note

This case may have reached a just result on the merits (although that has been doubted, for there was a long history of non-cooperation by the niece), but the judge's use of the authorities contrasts with earlier approaches. The citation of *Greenhalgh* **[4.27]** draws on a line of decisions concerned with special resolutions for the alteration of articles, which had never before been applied to other types of resolution. Further, having read the passage from *Greenhalgh*'s case in which Evershed MR suggested the test of the 'individual hypothetical shareholder', Foster J commented: 'If that is right, the question in the instant case must be posed thus: did Miss Clemens, when voting for the resolutions, honestly

---

[31] See the Note at the conclusion of this extract.
[32] *Ebrahimi v Westbourne Galleries Ltd* **[16.13]**.

believe that those resolutions, when passed, would be for the benefit of the plaintiff?' It might equally be observed that the plaintiff was no more a hypothetical shareholder than Miss Clemens herself; and if the test had been understood in this sense in *Greenhalgh*'s case itself, the decision must surely have gone in Greenhalgh's favour. These cases show how unhelpful the 'hypothetical shareholder' test is, especially in regard to small companies. And, in quoting Lord Wilberforce, the judge is again borrowing, this time from the winding-up cases, a borrowing which might be seen as contrary to the ruling in *Bentley-Stevens v Jones* [1974] 1 WLR 639.

➤ Questions

1. Did Foster J consider that a member in the position of Miss Clemens was under a duty to (i) the company, or (ii) her fellow-shareholder? If so, what was the nature of this duty? If not, what was the rule or principle which he was applying?

2. If the aunt did owe such a duty, did the niece owe the company, or her fellow-shareholder, any corresponding duty?

3. Can the *Clemens* and *Greenhalgh* **[4.27]** cases be reconciled?

Alteration of the articles

CA 2006 s 21: alteration of articles

Provisions in the company's articles can be amended by special resolution (s 21), unless they have been entrenched under s 22.[33] Section 22 allows the articles to contain a *'provision for entrenchment'* nominating specified provisions of the articles that can be amended or deleted only if conditions or procedures more stringent than a special resolution are met. Note that CA 2006 s 22(2) has not been brought into force (see 'History', p 27).

If such a provision for entrenchment was contained in the company's old-style memorandum, it will automatically be treated as part of the company's articles under the new legislation (s 28(2)), so the entrenchment will be preserved. Notice of the existence, amendment or deletion of provisions of entrenchment must be given to the Companies House (s 23, and s 13 for the 'form of compliance').

CA 2006 s 25 retains the principle that a member of a company is not bound by any alteration made to the articles after he or she becomes a member if the alteration has the effect of increasing liability to the company or imposing a requirement to take more shares in the company. A member may, however, give written consent to such an alteration and, in that case, will be bound by it.

Earlier case law thus remains relevant.

Predecessor provisions

Until CA 2006 came into force, companies were required to have both a *memorandum and articles*. There were different statutory rules for altering each of them. The alteration of a company's objects, contained in the memorandum, required a special resolution, and the court became involved only if the holders of 15% or more of the issued share capital of any class made an objection by applying to the court within 21 days. The court then had an absolute discretion to confirm or disallow the alteration.

---

[33] There is no power in CA 2006 to alter the new-style memorandum (the s 8 'memorandum of association'), but then it does not contain elements that members would need or want to change. Under art 28(1), the provisions of existing companies contained in old-style memoranda which are not of the kind mentioned in CA 2006 s 8, will automatically be treated as provisions of the company's articles of association and the rules considered later will apply.

By contrast, the Acts had always allowed the articles to be altered by special resolution, with no statutory constraints except for the protection given by CA 1985 s 125 in relation to variation of 'class rights'.[34] (See 'Variation of class rights', pp 247ff.)

With these bald requirements set by statute, judges have been left with the task of formulating more specific rules controlling the power of majority members to alter articles. Unfortunately the principles that have emerged are anything but clear. As a rule, the courts have been content to fall back on such broad general phrases as 'bona fide for the benefit of the company as a whole', apparently without appreciating that these expressions mask rather than explain the decisions they are making. The difficulty posed by the juxtaposition of the 'benefit of the company' test with the basic concept of the member's vote as a property right is all too rarely faced in the judgments (with the notable exception of *Peters' American Delicacy Co Ltd v Heath* **[4.26]**). If it had been, the cases that follow might have yielded more intelligible principles.

A contract by a company not to alter its articles will not be enforced by injunction.

[4.21] Punt v Symons & Co Ltd [1903] 2 Ch 506 (Chancery Division)

By arts 95 and 97 of the defendant company's articles GG Symons, as governing director, was given the power to appoint and remove directors, and after his death the same power was exercisable by his executors. The company had also agreed in a separate contract, relating to the purchase of Symons's business, that it would not alter these articles. After the death of Symons, friction arose between his executors and the directors, which led to a proposal from the directors to rescind the articles in question by special resolution. The executors moved for an injunction.[35]

> BYRNE J: The first point taken is that passing the resolution would be a breach of the contract which was entered into with the testator; and that the plaintiffs as executors are entitled to enforce the terms of the agreement by restraining any alteration of the articles. I think the answer to this argument is—that the company cannot contract itself out of the right to alter its articles, though it cannot, by altering its articles, [avoid liability for[36]] a breach of contract. It is well established as between a company and a shareholder, the right not depending upon a special contract outside the articles, that this is the case. It has not been, so far as I know, the precise subject of reported decision as between a contractor and a company where the contract is independent of and outside the articles...[His Lordship referred to *Allen v Gold Reefs of West Africa* **[4.22]** and to an unreported decision, *Re Ladies' Dress Association Ltd*, in which a contract not to alter any article was not enforced. He continued:] That appears, so far as I can judge, to be a decision upon the point now before me. Whether that be so or not, I am prepared to hold that in the circumstances of the present case the contract could not operate to prevent the article being altered under the provisions of s 50 of the Companies Act 1862 [CA 2006 s 21], whatever the result of that alteration may be.

See also *Baily v British Equitable Assurance Co* **[3.16]** and *Southern Foundries (1926) Ltd v Shirlaw* **[6.04]**.

---

[34] Note also CA 1985 s 16, which renders ineffective any alteration which increases the liability of a member or obliges him to take more shares—unless he agrees in writing to be bound by the alteration.

[35] They succeeded on another ground, viz that the directors had improperly issued new shares to 'pack' the shareholders' meeting: see **[4.22]**.

[36] See Chapter 3, 'An amendment of the company's articles will not excuse a breach of contract', p 130.

➤ Notes

1. The opinion expressed in this case is supported by the emphatic *obiter dictum* of Lord Porter in *Southern Foundries (1926) Ltd v Shirlaw* **[6.04]**. It is therefore to be preferred, it is submitted, to the contrary view of Sargant J in *British Murac Syndicate Ltd v Alperton Rubber Ltd* [1915] 2 Ch 186, which was based on the mistaken view that *Punt's* case had been overruled by *Baily v British Equitable Assurance Co* **[3.16]**.

2. However, it does not follow that a contractual undertaking by a company that its articles will not be altered might not be enforced in other ways. Lord Porter clearly thought that, if a company *acted upon* its altered articles in a way which was in breach of an existing contract, a remedy in damages would lie. In principle, this must be correct; and further, in principle also, an injunction might in such circumstances be granted, in the discretion of the court, restraining the company from acting upon its altered articles.

3. As Byrne J notes, it was already a well-established rule that a company could not restrict the right to alter its articles by a provision in the articles themselves. This was decided by Jessel MR in *Walker v London Tramways Co* (1879) 12 Ch D 705, where he held that a provision in the company's articles declaring that certain articles were 'essential' and unalterable was ineffective.

4. This ruling is but one illustration of a more general principle that a company cannot bargain away its right to exercise the powers conferred upon it by statute. The extent to which there is such a rule, and (assuming that there is) whether there ought to be such a rule, was a matter of considerable debate, following the decision in *Russell v Northern Bank Development Corpn Ltd* **[4.35]** (see Sealy [1992] CLJ 437). There is clear authority establishing that a company cannot contract not to alter its articles (*Punt's* case, Note 1) nor contract not to alter its capital (*Russell*). This principle would surely also extend to such matters as contracting not to go into liquidation or to petition for a winding-up order. But it is easy to demonstrate that there may be good commercial reasons why a company might wish to bind itself not to do at least some of these things—for instance, a bank lending money to a company may make it a condition of the loan that the company will not reduce its capital—and, indeed, this has been done in practice for many years. So, following the ruling in *Russell*, there has been pressure for Parliament to change the law so as to make contractual undertakings given in such circumstances binding. The case for retaining a general principle of this kind is greatly weakened by the fact that there are many alternative ways of doing indirectly what cannot at present be achieved directly—for example, by a shareholder agreement ('Shareholders' agreements', p 256), by attaching 'class rights' to certain shares (see the *Cumbrian Newspapers* case **[11.05]**, by entrenching the rights which it is sought to protect in the old-style memorandum (see CA 1985 s 17(2)(b)) or, now, in the articles (see CA 2006 s 22), or by the use of 'weighted' voting rights (see *Bushell v Faith* **[6.02]**). And, in the example of the bank loan, the bank could stipulate that the money would become immediately repayable if the company should summon a general meeting to consider a proposed resolution to reduce capital.

5. Finally, note that all these limitations apply to the *company* limiting its statutory rights. The shareholders, by contrast, can agree amongst themselves via a shareholder agreement, not to alter the company's articles, or not to do any manner of other things. But would a shareholder agreement not to alter the company's articles ever be *specifically enforced*, or would it only give rise to damages for breach? (See 'Shareholders' agreements', pp 256ff.)

➤ Question

In *Walker v London Tramways* Co (see earlier), Jessel MR did not give a reasoned judgment but simply asserted that no company could contract itself out of CA 1962 s 50 (the equivalent of CA 2006 s 21). What reasoning do you think that he might have used, and would you agree?

The power to alter a company's articles must be exercised 'bona fide for the benefit of the company as a whole'. An alteration so made is valid and binding on the members and may affect their existing rights as members. It may, however, amount to a breach of an independent contract.

[4.22] Allen v Gold Reefs of West Africa Ltd [1900] 1 Ch 656 (Court of Appeal)

Article 29 of the company's articles of association gave it 'a first and paramount lien' for debts owing by a member to the company 'upon all shares (not being fully paid) held by such members'. The company altered this article by deleting the words 'not being fully paid'. Only one shareholder, Zuccani (who had died insolvent), was affected by this alteration: he had had fully paid shares allotted to him when the company was formed, and had later acquired other shares, that were not fully paid, on which calls were overdue. His executors challenged the company's right to claim a lien on his fully paid shares pursuant to the altered article. Kekewich J held that the company could not enforce its lien. The Court of Appeal reversed this decision, and upheld the alteration.

LINDLEY MR: The articles of a company prescribe the regulations binding on its members: Companies Act 1862, s 14 [CA 2006 s 21]. They have the effect of a contract (see s 16 [CA 2006 s 33]); but the exact nature of this contract is even now very difficult to define. Be its nature what it may, the company is empowered by the statute to alter the regulations contained in its articles from time to time by special resolutions (ss 50 and 51 [CA 2006 ss 21, 283]); and any regulation or article purporting to deprive the company of this power is invalid on the ground that it is contrary to the statute: *Walker v London Tramways Co.*[37]

The power thus conferred on companies to alter the regulations contained in their articles is limited only by the provisions contained in the statute and the conditions contained in the company's memorandum of association. Wide, however, as the language of s 50 is, the power conferred by it must, like all other powers, be exercised subject to those general principles of law and equity which are applicable to all powers conferred on majorities and enabling them to bind minorities. It must be exercised, not only in the manner required by law, but also bona fide for the benefit of the company as a whole, and it must not be exceeded. These conditions are always implied, and are seldom, if ever, expressed. But if they are complied with I can discover no ground for judicially putting any other restrictions on the power conferred by the section than those contained in it. How shares shall be transferred, and whether the company shall have any lien on them, are clearly matters of regulation properly prescribed by a company's articles of association. This is shown by Table A in the Schedule to the Companies Act...Speaking, therefore, generally, and without reference to any particular case, the section clearly authorises a limited company, formulated with articles which confer no lien on fully paid-up shares, and which allow them to be transferred without any fetter, to alter those articles by special resolution, and to impose a lien and restrictions on the registry of transfers of those shares by members indebted to the company.

But then comes the question whether this can be done so as to impose a lien or restriction in respect of a debt contracted before and existing at the time when the articles are altered. Again, speaking generally, I am of opinion that the articles can be so altered, and that, if they are altered

---

[37] (1879) 12 Ch D 705. [See also *Punt v Symons & Co Ltd* **[4.21]**.]

bona fide for the benefit of the company, they will be valid and binding as altered on the existing holders of paid-up shares, whether such holders are indebted or not indebted to the company when the alteration is made. But, as it will be seen presently, it does not by any means follow that the altered article may not be inapplicable to some particular fully paid-up shareholder. He may have special rights against the company, which do not invalidate the resolution to alter the articles, but which may exempt him from the operation of the articles as altered.

But, although the regulations contained in a company's articles of association are revocable by special resolution, a special contract may be made with the company in the terms of or embodying one or more of the articles, and the question will then arise whether an alteration of the articles so embodied is consistent or inconsistent with the real bargain between the parties. A company cannot break its contracts by altering its articles,[38] but, when dealing with contracts referring to revocable articles, and especially with contracts between a member of the company and the company respecting his shares, care must be taken not to assume that the contract involves as one of its terms an article which is not to be altered.

It is easy to imagine cases in which even a member of a company may acquire by contract or otherwise special rights against the company, which exclude him from the operation of a subsequently altered article. Such a case arose in *Swabey v Port Darwin Gold Mining* **[6.03]** where it was held that directors, who had earned fees payable under a company's articles, could not be deprived of them by a subsequent alteration of the articles, which reduced the fees payable to directors.

I take it to be clear that an application for an allotment of shares on the terms of the company's articles does not exclude the power to alter them nor the application of them, when altered, to the shares so applied for and allotted. To exclude that power or the application of an altered article to particular shares, some clear and distinct agreement for that exclusion must be shown, or some circumstances must be proved conferring a legal or equitable right on the shareholders to be treated by the company differently from the other shareholders.

This brings me to the last question which has to be considered, namely, whether there is in this case any contract or other circumstance which excludes the application of the altered article to Zuccani's fully paid-up vendor's shares. [His Lordship ruled that there was no such special circumstance, and continued:]

The fact that Zuccani's executors were the only persons practically affected at the time by the alterations made in the articles excites suspicion as to the bona fides of the company. But, although the executors were the only persons who were actually affected at the time, that was because Zuccani was the only holder of paid-up shares who at the time was in arrear of calls. The altered articles applied to all holders of fully paid shares, and made no distinction between them. The directors cannot be charged with bad faith.

After carefully considering the whole case, and endeavouring in vain to discover grounds for holding that there was some special bargain differentiating Zuccani's shares from others, I have come to the conclusion that the appeal from the decision of the learned judge, so far as it relates to the lien created by the altered articles, must be allowed...

ROMER LJ delivered a concurring judgment.

VAUGHAN WILLIAMS LJ dissented.

[4.23] Sidebottom v Kershaw, Leese & Co Ltd [1920] 1 Ch 154 (Court of Appeal)

The defendant company had altered its articles by introducing a provision which gave the directors power to buy out, at a fair price, the shareholding of any member who competed

---

[38] Later cases (eg **[4.23]** and **[4.25]**) make it plain that this sentence should be understood to mean 'a company *cannot justify* a breach of contract by pleading the valid alteration of its articles', and not 'a company *cannot alter* its articles if to do so would break an existing contract'.

with the company's business. The plaintiffs, who were minority shareholders and who carried on a competing business, unsuccessfully challenged the validity of the alteration.

LORD STERNDALE MR: In my opinion, the whole of this case comes down to rather a narrow question of fact, which is this: When the directors of this company introduced this alteration giving power to buy up the shares of members who were in competing businesses did they do it bona fide for the benefit of the company or not? It seems to me quite clear that it may be very much to the benefit of the company to get rid of members who are in competing business...I think there can be no doubt that a member of a competing business or an owner of a competing business who is a member of the company has a much better chance of knowing what is going on in the business of the company, and of thereby helping his own competition with it, than if he were a non-member; and looking at it broadly, I cannot have any doubt that in a small private company like this the exclusion of members who are carrying on a competing business may very well be of great benefit to the company. That seems to me to be precisely a point which ought to be decided by the voices of the business men who understand the business and understand the nature of competition, and whether such a position is or is not for the benefit of the company. I think, looking at the alteration broadly, that it is for the benefit of the company that they should not be obliged to have amongst them as members persons who are competing with them in business, and who may get knowledge from their membership which would enable them to compete better.

That brings me to the last point. It is said that that might be so were it not for the fact that the directors and the secretary have said, 'This is directed against Mr Bodden', and therefore it is not done bona fide for the benefit of the company, but it is done to get rid of Mr Bodden.[39] If it were directed against Mr Bodden for any malicious motive I should agree with that—the thing would cease to be bona fide at once; but these alterations are not as a rule made without some circumstances having arisen to bring the necessity of the alteration to the minds of the directors. I do not read this as meaning anything more than this: 'It was the position of Mr Bodden that made us appreciate the detriment that there might be to the company in having members competing with them in their business, and we passed this, and our intention was, if it became necessary, to use it in the case of Mr Bodden; that is what we had in our minds at the time; but we also had in our minds that Mr Bodden is not the only person who might compete, and therefore we passed this general article in order to enable us to apply it in any case where it was for the good of the company that it should be applied.' It is a question of fact. I come to the conclusion of fact to which I think the Vice-Chancellor came, that the directors were acting perfectly bona fide, that they were passing the resolution for the benefit of the company; but that no doubt the occasion of their passing it was because they realised in the person of Mr Bodden that it was a bad thing to have members who were competing with them...

For these reasons I think this is a valid article. I think the alteration was within the competence of the company, and therefore this appeal must be allowed with costs here and below.

WARRINGTON LJ and EVE J delivered concurring judgments.

[4.24] Citco Banking Corpn NV v Pusser's Ltd [2007] UKPC 13 (Privy Council)

Before the events in issue in this appeal, the company had share capital of $4.4 million divided into 4.4 million class A shares of $1 each, of which 1,673,217 shares (and warrants for another 248,000) had been issued. Each class A share or warrant carried one vote. At an extraordinary general meeting, the company by special resolution amended its articles

---

[39] Bodden was not, in fact, a plaintiff.

of association to create 200,000 class B shares, each carrying 50 votes. It also resolved that 200,000 of the class A shares held by the chairman of the company, Mr Charles S Tobias, be converted into class B shares. The resolutions were carried by 1,125,665 votes to 183,000, the dissenting shares all being held by Citco. Citco alleged that the resolutions were invalid because they were passed in the interests of Mr Tobias, to give him indisputable control, and not bona fide in the interests of the company. The trial judge agreed; the Court of Appeal reversed his decision and held the resolutions valid. The Privy Council upheld this finding.

LORD HOFFMANN delivered the judgment of the Privy Council:

12. Section 89 of the Act [broadly equivalent to CA 2006 s 21] contains no qualification of the power of a 75% majority to amend the articles of association. But the courts have always treated the power as subject to implied limitations. The problem has been to say where the line should be drawn. [He then examined the authorities, including *Allen v Gold Reefs of West Africa Ltd* **[4.22]**, *Dafen Tinplate Co Ltd v Llanelly Steel Co (1907) Ltd* **[4.25]**, *Shuttleworth v Cox Bros and Co (Maidenhead) Ltd* **[6.06]**, and continued:]

17. These were cases in which the amendment operated to the particular disadvantage of a minority of shareholders: Mr Zuccani's estate in *Allen's* case and the director whose removal was proposed in *Shuttleworth's* case. But the same principle must apply when an amendment which the shareholders bona fide consider to be for the benefit of the company as a whole also operates to the particular advantage of some shareholders. This is illustrated by *Rights & Issues Investment Trust Ltd v Stylo Shoes Ltd* **[4.29]**, . . .

18. These principles, together with the proposition that the burden of proof is upon the person who challenges the validity of the amendment (see *Peters' American Delicacy Company Ltd v Heath* **[4.26]**, per Latham CJ at p 482) appear to their Lordships to be clearly settled and sufficient for the purpose of deciding this case. It must however be acknowledged that the test of 'bona fide for the benefit of the company as a whole' will not enable one to decide all cases in which amendments of the articles operate to the disadvantage of some shareholder or group of shareholders. Such amendments are sometimes only for the purpose of regulating the rights of shareholders in matters in which the company as a corporate entity has no interest, such as the distribution of dividends or capital or the power to dispose of shares. In the Australian case of *Peters' American Delicacy Company*, to which reference has been made, the amendment provided that shareholders should thenceforth receive dividends rateably according to the amounts paid up on their shares rather than, as previously, according to the number of shares (fully or partly paid) which they held. It was, as Dixon J pointed out (at p 512), 'inappropriate, if not meaningless' to ask whether the shareholders had considered the amendment to be in the interests of the company as a whole. Some other test of validity is required. In *Greenhalgh v Arderne Cinemas Ltd* **[4.27]**, where the amendment was to remove a pre-emption clause to facilitate a sale of control to a third party, Sir Raymond Evershed MR tried to preserve the application of the traditional test by saying that in such cases 'the company as a whole' did not mean the company as a corporate entity but 'the corporators as a general body' and that it was necessary to ask whether the amendment was, in the honest opinion of those who voted in favour, for the benefit of a hypothetical member. Some commentators have not found this approach entirely illuminating but for the purposes of this appeal it is not necessary to discuss such cases any further. In this case, as in the *Stylo Shoes* case, it would have been perfectly rational to ask whether the vesting of voting control in Mr Tobias was in the interests of the company as a whole. . . .

21. Their Lordships therefore return to the present appeal. . . .

24. The Court of Appeal, reversing the judge, said (at paragraph 16) that where he went wrong in principle was 'when he attempted to step into the commercial arena'. Their Lordships take this to mean that the judge fell into the same error as Peterson J in *Dafen*

Tinplate Company Ltd v Llanelly Steel Company (1907) Ltd **[4.25]**, namely that he took it upon himself to decide whether the amendment was for the benefit of the company. The Court of Appeal said that he should instead have applied the test laid down in *Shuttleworth's* case, namely, whether reasonable shareholders could have considered that the amendment was for the benefit of the company. The Court of Appeal considered that it would have been reasonable for shareholders to have accepted in good faith the arguments put forward by Mr Tobias as to why the amendment would be in the interests of the company. The only shareholder who gave evidence at the trial was Mr de Vos, who said that he had thought the amendments were in the best interests of the company as a whole. It was not necessary for Mr Tobias and the company to prove to the judge that the arguments were justified by the facts.

25. Their Lordships consider that this reasoning is correct. Mr Todd QC, who appeared for Citco, said that in a case in which one shareholder gained a personal advantage by the amendment, as Mr Tobias did in this case, it was necessary to show that even without his votes, the amendment would have been passed. In *Rights & Issues Investment Trust Ltd v Stylo Shoes Ltd* **[4.29]**, Pennycuick J laid some stress upon the fact that the resolution had been passed at a separate meeting of ordinary shareholders at which the holders of management shares did not vote. In this case there was, prior to the amendment, only one class of shares, but Mr Todd said that it was necessary to show that the resolution would have passed even without the votes controlled by Mr Tobias.

26. Their Lordships do not think that the *Stylo Shoes* case decided that in a case like this, shareholders who particularly stand to gain from the amendment should not vote. As Evershed MR said in *Greenhalgh v Arderne Cinemas Ltd* **[4.27]**, 291:

'It is...not necessary to require that persons voting for a special resolution should, so to speak, dissociate themselves altogether from their own prospects...'

27. If Mr Tobias bona fide considered that the amendment was in the interests of the company as a whole, and there has been no attack on his bona fides, their Lordships do not see why he should not vote. This is only one aspect of the general principle that shareholders are free to exercise their votes in their own interests. As Lord Davey said in *Burland v Earle*,[40] 94:

'Unless otherwise provided by the regulations of the company, a shareholder is not debarred from voting or using his voting power to carry a resolution by the circumstance of his having a particular interest in the subject-matter of the vote.'

28. In any case, it appears to their Lordships that even the test proposed by Mr Todd was satisfied. The only evidence as to the number of shares controlled by Mr Tobias was that of Mr de Vos, who said that it amounted to 28% of the issued share capital. He was cross-examined on this point, with counsel for Citco seeking to establish that Mr Tobias actually controlled very few shares, but stuck to 28%. He did also say that Mr Tobias was indirectly able to exercise the votes of 51% of the share capital, but this was consistent with the additional votes being simply those of supporters who had decided to entrust Mr Tobias with their proxies. Of the 28%, Mr Tobias did not vote the 62,439 shares registered in his own name. If he had not voted the 460,245 shares registered in the names of his wife and Piccadilly Properties Ltd, which made up the rest of the 28%, the votes cast in favour of the resolution would have been 665,420 out of a total of 848,420. This would still have been 78%.

29. Their Lordships will therefore humbly advise Her Majesty that the appeal should be dismissed with costs.

---

[40] [1902] AC 83, PC.

➤ Notes

1. The CLR took the view that the principle that a decision to change a company's articles must be taken bona fide for the benefit of the company as a whole was well established and should be retained. This was also the view adopted in *Citco* **[4.24]**.

2. It is rather curious that in both *Allen* **[4.22]** and *Sidebottom* **[4.23]** there are references to the good faith of the *directors*, when it is plain from the rest of the judgments that it is the bona fides of the majority members who pass the special resolution that is crucial. Of course, it would be easy to imagine a situation where the directors have an improper motive in introducing the proposal for change, and simply carry the opinion of the majority along with them. This may be what is being alluded to in the two cases. In fact, the directors in *Sidebottom*'s case held over half of the company's issued shares, and the majority in favour of the resolution was overwhelming.

➤ Question

Lord Hoffmann, at [18] of the *Citco* judgment **[4.24]**, took the view that 'some other test' is needed where the proposed alteration concerns the 'rights of shareholders in matters in which the company as a corporate entity has no interest', since there it would be inappropriate 'to ask whether the shareholders had considered the alteration to be in the interests of the company as a whole'. What tests might meet this need? Where the company *has* an interest, the court accepts a *subjective* 'bona fide for the benefit of the company as a whole' test (subject to being persuaded of the bona fides). Where the company has *no* interest, and where there must inevitably be winners and losers as between different groups of shareholders, must the test necessarily be *objective* if the court is not simply to cede all power to the majority voter? See the next case cited.

In the case next cited, Peterson J favoured an objective test of what was 'for the benefit of the company'. This view was disapproved in *Shuttleworth v Cox Bros & Co Ltd* **[6.06]** (and in *Citco* **[4.24]**, it seems) but, in the opinion of some writers, this has been to some extent revived by the reformulated test suggested in *Greenhalgh v Arderne Cinemas Ltd* **[4.27]**, which seemed to find favour in *Citco*. But also see the recent Court of Appeal judgment in *Re Charterhouse Capital Ltd* **[4.28]** in which the Chancellor of the High Court (with whom Lewison and McCombe LJJ agreed) preferred 'to express the test as one which depends on the type of vitiating factors described by Latham CJ and Dixon J in *Peters' American Delicacy Co* rather than in terms of the benefit to the "corporators as a general body" or a "hypothetical member" as in Evershed MR's judgment in *Greenhalgh*' [96].

[4.25] Dafen Tinplate Co Ltd v Llanelly Steel Co (1907) Ltd
[1920] 2 Ch 124 (Chancery Division)

The defendant company altered its articles so as to introduce a power enabling the majority of the shareholders to require any member (with one named exception) to transfer his shares at a fair value to an approved transferee. The plaintiff company had transferred its custom as a purchaser of steel from the defendants to a rival company. It held shares in the defendant company and opposed the alteration. Peterson J upheld its objection, because, in his own view, the alteration was wider than necessary.

PETERSON J: In *Sidebottom*'s case **[4.23]** the Court of Appeal sanctioned an alteration of the articles of association which enabled the directors to require a shareholder who carried on a competing business, or was a director of a company carrying on a competing business, to transfer his shares, and it did so on the ground that the alteration was for the benefit of the company as a whole. It has been suggested that the only question in such a case as this is whether the shareholders bona fide or honestly believed that that alteration was for the benefit of the company. But this is not, in my view, the true meaning of the words of Lindley MR or of the judgment in *Sidebottom*'s case. The question is whether in fact the alteration is genuinely for the benefit of the company...

The question of fact then which I have to consider is whether the alteration of the articles which enables the majority of the shareholders to compel any shareholder to transfer his shares, can properly be said to be for the benefit of the company. It may be for the benefit of the majority of the shareholders to acquire the shares of the minority, but how can it be said to be for the benefit of the company that any shareholder, against whom no charge of acting to the detriment of the company can be urged, and who is in every respect a desirable member of the company, and for whose expropriation there is no reason except the will of the majority, should be forced to transfer his shares to the majority or to anyone else? Such a provision might in some circumstances be very prejudicial to the company's interest. For instance, on an issue of new capital, the knowledge that he might be expropriated as soon as his capital was on the point of producing profitable results might well exercise a deterrent influence on a man who was invited to take shares in the company... In my view it cannot be said that a power on the part of the majority to expropriate any shareholder they may think proper at their will and pleasure is for the benefit of the company as a whole. To say that such an unrestricted and unlimited power of expropriation is for the benefit of the company appears to me to be confusing the interests of the majority with the benefit of the company as a whole. In my opinion the power which, in this case, has been conferred upon the majority of the shareholders by the alteration of the articles of association in this case is too wide and is not such a power as can be assumed by the majority. The power of compulsory acquisition by the majority of shares which the owner does not desire to sell is not lightly to be assumed whenever it pleases the majority to do so. The shareholder is entitled to say *non haec in foedera veni*; and while on the authorities as they stand at present it is possible to alter the articles in such a way as to confer this power, if it can be shown that the power is for the benefit of the company as a whole, I am of opinion that such a power cannot be supported if it is not established that the power is bona fide or genuinely for the company's benefit...

[4.26] Peters' American Delicacy Co Ltd v Heath (1939) 61 CLR 457 (High Court of Australia)

As a result of an oversight by the draftsman, the company's articles of association contained inconsistent provisions governing the distribution of profits. Profits distributed as *dividends* were payable in proportion to the amounts paid up on shares, but distributions of *capitalised* profits ('bonus shares') were to be in proportion to the nominal value of shares held. The issued capital consisted of 511,000 fully paid and 169,000 partly paid shares.

At a general meeting the articles were altered by special resolution so that the distribution of capitalised profits was to be made on the same basis as cash dividends, that is, in proportion to the amounts paid up on shares. Some holders of partly paid shares objected, and their objection was upheld at first instance; but on appeal the High Court ruled that the alteration was valid.[41]

RICH J: Company law confers a power of alteration on a general meeting of shareholders requiring for any positive alteration a three-fourths majority. There is no other body to whom the question can be submitted. No rights given by articles of association can prevail against a three-fourths

---

[41] See the Note following this case.

majority and it is well understood that all are subject to it. It is true that the power of alteration must be exercised bona fide with a view to the advancement of the company considered as a whole and not with a view to the advancement of the interests of a majority of voters or of a section of the company only...But in deciding what is for the interest of the company and what is bona fide, the constitution of the company, the condition and effect of the various articles of association and the extent to which rights are conferred upon different classes of shareholders are relevant and important...Where the very problem which arises contains as inherent in itself all the elements of a conflict of interests between classes of shareholders these authorities do not mean that the power of alteration is paralysed, they mean only that the purpose of bringing forward the resolution must not be simply the enrichment of the majority at the expense of the minority. The resolution in the present case was brought forward to solve a difficulty and make possible a capitalisation. It can hardly be supposed that the only solution of such a difficulty which can be lawfully adopted is that which gives the minority an advantage at the expense of the majority. In my opinion the case presents nothing but an ordinary example of an honest attempt on the part of the directors to clear up a difficulty by securing an alteration of the articles not unjust to any class of shareholders, but at the same time conserving the interests of the shareholders who form the great majority of the company...

In my opinion the appeal should be allowed.

DIXON J: Primarily a share in a company is a piece of property conferring rights in relation to distribution of income and of capital. In many respects the proprietary rights are defined by the articles of association, and it is easy to see that a power of alteration might be used for the aggrandisement of a majority at the expense of a minority. For example, if there were no check upon the use of the power, it is conceivable that a three-fourths majority might adopt an article by which the shares which they alone held would participate, to the exclusion of other shares, in the surplus assets in winding up or even in distributions of profit by way of dividend. Again, authority might be obtained under an alteration so as to convert the assets or operations of a company into a source of profit not of the company but of persons forming part of or favoured by the majority. It has seemed incredible that alterations of such a nature could be made by the exercise of the power. But reliance upon the general doctrine that powers shall be exercised bona fide and for no bye or sinister purpose brings its own difficulties. The power of alteration is not fiduciary. The shareholders are not trustees for one another, and, unlike directors, they occupy no fiduciary position and are under no fiduciary duties. They vote in respect of their shares, which are property, and the right to vote is attached to the share itself as an incident of property to be enjoyed and exercised for the owner's personal advantage. No doubt the exercise of the right affects the interests of others too, and it may be that an analogy may be found in other powers which though given to protect the donee's own interests affect the property rights of others, as, for instance, does a mortgagee's power of sale. Some such analogy probably gave rise to the suggestion made in Buckley on *The Companies Acts* that the limitation on the power is that the alteration must not be such as to sacrifice the interests of the minority to those of a majority without any reasonable prospect of advantage to the company as a whole...

Apart altogether from altering articles of association, the voting strength of a majority of shareholders may be used in matters of management and administration to obtain for themselves advantages which otherwise would enure for the benefit of all the members of the company, and in some circumstances such an attempt on the part of the majority to secure advantages to the prejudice of the minority conflicts with ordinary notions of fair dealing and honesty. Often when this is done the thing attempted will be found by its nature to fall outside the power of the members in general meeting and even outside the corporate powers of the company. But this is not necessarily the case, and a thing not of its own nature ultra vires may be invalidated by the effect which it produces or is intended to produce in benefiting some shareholders at the expense of others or individuals at the expense of the company...

An example of a misuse of power on the part of shareholders constituting a majority in the administration of a company's affairs is the unjustifiable refusal to allow an action to be maintained in the name of the company to redress a wrong to it by one of themselves[42]...

In these formulations of general principle there is an assumption that vested in the company or in the minority of shareholders, as the case may be, is an independent title to property, to rights or to remedies, and the ground of the court's intervention is that by the course adopted by the majority, the company or the minority will be deprived of the enjoyment of that to which they are so entitled. The conduct of the majority is then given some dyslogistic description such as 'fraudulent', 'abuse of powers' or 'oppression'. A chief purpose of articles of association is to regulate the rights of shareholders inter se, and their relations to the profits and surplus assets of the company are governed by the provisions of the articles. A power to alter articles of association is necessarily a power to alter the rights of shareholders inter se, including their mutual rights in respect of profits and surplus assets. It is therefore evident that some difficulty must arise in applying to resolutions for the alteration of articles a statement of principle which assumes the independent existence of rights which should not be impaired or destroyed. Prima facie rights altogether dependent upon articles of association are not enduring and indefeasible but are liable to modification or destruction; that is, if and when it is resolved by a three-fourths majority that the articles should be altered. To attempt to distinguish between alterations which deserve the epithet fraudulent or oppressive or unjust and those deserving no moral censure without explaining the considerations upon which the distinction depends, is to leave the whole question to general notions of fairness and propriety... To base the application of these descriptions to a particular resolution upon the fact that it involves a modification or defeasance of rights of a valuable or important nature, is in effect to go back to the discarded distinction between articles affecting the constitution and those affecting the administration of the company or to a distinction very like it. To base the application of the epithets upon the circumstance that the majority obtain a benefit by the change seems to involve some departure from the principle that the vote attached to a share is an incident of property which may be used as the shareholder's interests may dictate...

The chief reason for denying an unlimited effect to widely expressed powers such as that of altering a company's articles is the fear or knowledge that an apparently regular exercise of the power may in truth be but a means of securing some personal or particular gain, whether pecuniary or otherwise, which does not fairly arise out of the subjects dealt with by the power and is outside and even inconsistent with the contemplated objects of the power. It is to exclude the purpose of securing such ulterior special and particular advantages that Lord Lindley used the phrase 'bona fide for the benefit of the company as a whole'. The reference to 'benefit as a whole' is but a very general expression negativing purposes foreign to the company's operations, affairs and organisations. But unfortunately, as appears from the foregoing discussion, the use of the phrase has tended to cause misapprehension. If the challenged alteration relates to an article which does or may affect an individual, as, for instance, a director appointed for life or a shareholder whom it is desired to expropriate, or to an article affecting the mutual rights and liabilities inter se of shareholders or different classes or descriptions of shareholders, the very subject-matter involves a conflict of interests and advantages. To say that the shareholders forming the majority must consider the advantage of the company as a whole in relation to such a question seems inappropriate, if not meaningless, and at all events starts an impossible inquiry. The 'company as a whole' is a corporate entity consisting of all the shareholders. If the proposal put forward is for a revision of any of the articles regulating the rights inter se of shareholders or classes of shareholders, the primary question must be how conflicting interests are to be adjusted, and the adjustment is left by law to the determination of those whose interests conflict, subject, however, to the condition that the existing provision can be altered only by a three-fourths majority. Whether the matter be voting rights, the basis of distributing profits, the basis of dividing surplus

---

42 See 'The old common law rule in *Foss v Harbottle*', pp 669ff.

assets on a winding-up, preferential rights in relation to profits or to surplus assets, or any other question affecting mutual interests, it is apparent that though the subject-matter is among the most conspicuous of those governed by articles and therefore of those to which the statutory power is directed, yet it involves little if anything more than the redetermination of the rights and interests of those to whom the power is committed. No one supposes that in voting each shareholder is to assume an inhuman altruism and consider only the intangible notion of the benefit of the vague abstraction called by Lord Robertson in *Baily*'s case **[3.16]** 'the company as an institution'. An investigation of the thoughts and motives of each shareholder voting with the majority would be an impossible proceeding . . . [When] the very question to be determined is a conflict of interests, unless the subject-matter is held outside the power, the purpose of the resolution, as distinguished from the motives of the individuals, often must be to resolve the conflict in favour of one and against the other interest.

In my opinion it was within the scope and purpose of the power of alteration for a three-fourths majority to decide the basis of distributing shares issued for the purpose of capitalising accumulated profits or profits arising from the sale of goodwill, and in voting for the resolution shareholders were not bound to disregard their own interests. I am far from saying that the resolution for the alteration of the articles would have been bad if the existing articles had been uniform and clear in requiring that, however the 'capitalisation' was effected, the basis of distribution should be the number of shares respectively subscribed for by members. But the facts of the case were that by one method, the older indirect method, a capitalisation might have been effected which would mean a distribution according to capital paid up. Doubts were felt about the propriety of adopting this course, and doubts were agitated as to the meaning of the article providing for the direct method. If there were no capitalisation, the accumulated profits would not be distributed in proportion with capital subscribed. In these circumstances the holders of partly paid shares had no 'right' to receive the profits in proportion with capital paid up. As the articles stood they were entitled only to receive shares in that proportion if and when issued by way of direct capitalisation. That event would never be likely to occur; for the holders of fully paid shares were perfectly entitled to prevent it and would no doubt do so. In these circumstances it appears to me that the resolution involved no oppression, no appropriation of an unjust or reprehensible nature and did not imply any purpose outside the scope of the power . . .

LATHAM CJ delivered a concurring judgment.

McTIERNAN J concurred.

➤ Note

This is a powerfully reasoned case, and seems to have carried the day in Australia despite the decision in *Gambotto v WPC Ltd* (1995) 182 CLR 432, where the High Court ruled that the 'bona fide for the benefit of the company as a whole' test should be replaced by a test which asks whether the alteration or proposed alteration is 'beyond any purpose contemplated by the articles or oppressive as that expression is understood in the law relating to corporations' ([25] and [26]). The latter case was concerned with an alteration of the articles which gave the company rights to buy out minority shareholders compulsorily, and the judgment is often said to be limited to the special case of alterations conferring expulsion or expropriation rights. This is despite the fact that the court went out of its way to disown the English line of authority in general terms.

This new test, if such it is, is clearly one which is almost entirely, if not wholly, objective; and one which will allow the court to play a much more interventionist role. A test based on 'proper purposes' has already gone some way towards displacing one based on 'bona fides' for the purpose of reviewing directors' discretionary decisions: see 'Duty to act for proper purposes: s 171(b)', pp 342ff. However, it seems unlikely that *Gambotto* will ever be followed in the UK (and see the Privy Council confirmation of this in the *Citco* case [**4.24**]). The CLR considered the possibility and drew attention to the fact that in *Gambotto* the alteration of articles was undoubtedly of benefit to the company as a whole (it stood to gain tax advantages), and the minority were to be fully compensated. It considered that there is no case for displacing the 'bona fide in the best interests of the company as a whole' test with some other concept to deal specially with expropriation cases.

➤ Question

Is it consistent to say that the power to alter articles 'shall be exercised *bona fide* and for no bye or sinister purpose' and (in the next sentence) 'the power of alteration is not fiduciary'? See *Merchant Navy Ratings Pension Fund Trustees Ltd v Stena Line Ltd* [2015] EWHC 448 (Ch), [228]–[229].

[4.27] Greenhalgh v Arderne Cinemas Ltd [1951] Ch 286 (Court of Appeal)

The articles of the defendant (a private company) provided that existing members should have pre-emptive rights if a member wished to sell his shares.[43] Mallard, the managing director, had negotiated with an outsider, Sol Sheckman, for the sale to Sheckman of a controlling interest in the company at 6s [30p] per share. Mallard had procured the passing of a special resolution to give effect to this agreement. In effect this negated the pre-emptive rights of the existing members. One of the latter, Greenhalgh, claimed a declaration that the resolutions were invalid as a fraud on the minority.[44] The Court of Appeal, affirming Roxburgh J, refused a declaration.

EVERSHED MR: The burden [of that case is] that the resolution was not passed bona fide and in the interests of the company as a whole, and there are, as Mr Jennings has urged, two distinct approaches.

The first line of attack is this, and it is one to which, he complains, Roxburgh J paid no regard: this is a special resolution, and, on authority, Mr. Jennings says, the validity of a special resolution depends upon the fact that those who passed it did so in good faith and for the benefit of the company as a whole. The cases to which Mr. Jennings referred are *Sidebottom v Kershaw, Leese & Co Ld.* [**4.23**], Peterson J's decision in *Dafen Tinplate Co Ld. v Llanelly Steel Co (1907) Ld.* [**4.25**] and, finally, *Shuttleworth v Cox Bros & Co (Maidenhead) Ld.* [**6.06**]. Certain principles, I think, can be safely stated as emerging from those authorities. In the first place, I think it is now plain that "bona fide for the benefit of the company as a whole" means not two things but one thing. It means that the shareholder must proceed upon what, in his honest opinion, is for the benefit of the company as a whole. The second thing is that the phrase "the company as a whole" does not (at any rate in such a case as the present) mean the company as a commercial entity, distinct from the corporators: it means the corporators as a general body. That is to say, the case may be taken of an individual hypothetical member and it may be asked whether what is proposed is, in the honest opinion of those who voted in its favour, for that person's benefit.

I think that the matter can, in practice, be more accurately and precisely stated by looking at the converse and by saying that a special resolution of this kind would be liable to be impeached if the effect of it were to discriminate between the majority shareholders and the minority shareholders, so as to give to the former an advantage of which the latter were deprived. When the cases are examined in which the resolution has been successfully attacked, it is on that ground.

---

[43] This was the last of many actions between the parties. The parties were involved in seven actions, five of which went to the Court of Appeal; Greenhalgh lost all but the first (LCB Gower, *Modern Company Law* (4th edn, 1979), pp 624–626). See further *Greenhalgh v Arderne Cinemas Ltd* [**11.09**].

[44] For the meaning of this phrase, see 'Exceptions to the rule in *Foss v Harbottle*', pp 670ff.

It is therefore not necessary to require that persons voting for a special resolution should, so to speak, dissociate themselves altogether from their own prospects and consider whether what is thought to be for the benefit of the company as a going concern. If, as commonly happens, an outside person makes an offer to buy all the shares, prima facie, if the corporators think it a fair offer and vote in favour of the resolution, it is no ground for impeaching the resolution that they are considering their own position as individuals.

Accepting that, as I think he did, Mr. Jennings said, in effect, that there are still grounds for impeaching this resolution: first, because it goes further than was necessary to give effect to the particular sale of the shares; and, secondly, because it prejudiced the plaintiff and minority share-holders in that it deprived them of the right which, under the subsisting articles, they would have of buying the shares of the majority if the latter desired to dispose of them.

What Mr. Jennings objects to in the resolution is that if a resolution is passed altering the articles merely for the purpose of giving effect to a particular transaction, then it is quite sufficient (and it is usually done) to limit it to that transaction. But this resolution provides that anybody who wants at any time to sell his shares can now go direct to an outsider, pro-vided that there is an ordinary resolution of the company approving the proposed transferee. Accordingly, if it is one of the majority who is selling, he will get the necessary resolution. This change in the articles, so to speak, franks the shares for holders of majority interests but makes it more difficult for a minority shareholder, because the majority will probably look with disfavour upon his choice. But, after all, this is merely a relaxation of the very stringent restrictions on transfer in the existing article, and it is to be borne in mind that the directors, as the articles stood, could always refuse to register a transfer. A minority shareholder, there-fore, who produced an outsider was always liable to be met by the directors (who presum-ably act according to the majority view) saying, "We are sorry, but we will not have this man in." . . .

As to the second point, I felt at one time sympathy for the plaintiff's argument, because, after all, as the articles stood he could have said: "Before you go selling to the purchaser you have to offer your shares to the existing shareholders, and that will enable me, if I feel so disposed, to buy, in effect, the whole of the shareholding of the Arderne company." I think that the answer is that when a man comes into a company, he is not entitled to assume that the articles will always remain in a particular form; and that, so long as the proposed alteration does not unfairly discriminate in the way which I have indicated, it is not an objection, provided that the resolution is passed bona fide, that the right to tender for the majority holding of shares would be lost by the lifting of the restriction. I do not think that it can be said that that is such a discrimination as falls within the scope of the principle which I have stated. . .

ASQUITH and JENKINS LJJ concurred.

> Notes

1. See also *Clemens v Clemens Bros Ltd* **[4.20]**, where the issue before the court was simi-lar, although no alteration of the articles was involved; the court, although purporting to apply the same principles, reached the opposite conclusion.

2. It is worth noting that all[45] the events complained of in the sorry history of Mr Greenhalgh and his company took place before there was any statutory provision allowing the court to grant relief to a minority shareholder on the ground of 'oppression' (CA 1948 s 210) or 'unfairly prejudicial' conduct (CA 1985 s 459, CA 2006 s 994): see 'Unfairly prejudicial conduct of the company's affairs', pp 715ff. Given the long history of the 'salami tactics' by which Mr Greenhalgh's stake in the company was systematically eroded, he might well

---

[45] In the case of the last in the round of the many resolutions, just *one day* before CA 1948 s 210 came into force! Did the controllers of Arderne Cinemas Ltd have 'the foresight of a Hebrew prophet'?

have succeeded in an application for relief under these provisions—although there is a possibility that they will be construed more restrictively following the ruling of the House of Lords in *O'Neill v Phillips* **[13.34]**.

3. *Greenhalgh v Arderne Cinemas Ltd* is a very difficult judgment. We can put some of the problems which it raises in the form of questions, but it is not possible to give any confident answer to most of them.

➤ Questions

1. The first test posed by Lord Evershed seems to be a subjective one: the shareholders' bona fide opinion is determinative. In the next paragraph, with talk of discrimination, the test is apparently an objective one. Are the two passages consistent with each other, or is the court having the best of both worlds? Could this second limb provide 'some other test' which was seen as necessary by Lord Hoffmann in *Citco* **[4.24]**?

2. Is it possible to reconcile 'the corporators as a general body' (distinct from 'the company as a commercial entity') and 'the company as a going concern'? What weight do you think should be given to the phrase 'at any rate in such a case as the present'? Are Lord Evershed's remarks intended to be confined to special resolutions, or to special resolutions altering articles, or to apply generally to all resolutions?

3. A claimant does not go to court unless he has a grievance. Would it not be true to say that in all the *unsuccessful* cases in which an alteration has been challenged, as well as the successful ones, the minorities were complaining of discrimination?

4. Whom should the court identify as 'the individual hypothetical member' in a case such as *Clemens v Clemens Bros Ltd* **[4.20]**, where the only two actual shareholders have fallen out?

[4.28] Re Charterhouse Capital Ltd [2015] EWCA Civ 536 (Court of Appeal)

The amendment of a company's articles to permit the shares of a minority shareholder to be compulsorily acquired under a takeover offer was held to be consistent with the terms of a shareholders' agreement, not to involve any unfairly prejudicial conduct within the Companies Act 2006 s 994 and not to be open to challenge on other grounds—the last is of interest here. Affirming the judgment of Mrs Justice Asplin, the Court of Appeal held that the amendment was no more than a 'tidying up exercise' which had been consistent with the initial bargain of the founding members, which included the appellant himself. In the absence of any finding of bad faith or improper motive, or irrationality, there was no basis for the challenge to the validity of the amendment.

SIR TERENCE ETHERTON C (with whom LEWISON and McCOMBE LJJ agreed):
[After summarising the background and the findings reached by the learned judge in the court below:]
90. It is common ground that an alteration to a company's articles, even if passed by the requisite majority of shareholders, may be challenged as invalid in certain circumstances. We were taken to a number of cases which consider the conditions for an effective challenge. They included *Allen v Gold Reefs* **[4.22]**, *Sidebottom v Kershaw Leese* **[4.23]**, *Shuttleworth v Cox* **[6.06]**, *Peters' American Delicacy* **[4.26]**, *Greenhalgh* **[4.27]**, *Citco* **[4.24]**, and *Assenagon Asset Management SA v Irish Bank Resolution Corpn Ltd* [2012] EWHC 2090 (Ch). It is not necessary to set out the facts of those cases. I would extract from them the following principles:

(1) The limitations on the exercise of the power to amend a company's articles arise because, as in the case of all powers, the manner of their exercise is constrained by the

purpose of the power and because the framers of the power of a majority to bind a minority will not, in the absence of clear words, have intended the power to be completely without limitation. These principles may be characterised as principles of law and equity or as implied terms: *Allen* at 671; *Assenagon* at 278–280.

(2) A power to amend will be validly exercised if it is exercised in good faith in the interests of the company: *Sidebottom* at 163.

(3) It is for the shareholders, and not the court, to say whether an alteration of the articles is for the benefit of the company but it will not be for the benefit of the company if no reasonable person would consider it to be such: *Shuttleworth* at 18–19, 23–24, 26–27; *Peters' American Delicacy Co* at 488.

(4) The view of shareholders acting in good faith that a proposed alteration of the articles is for the benefit of the company, and which cannot be said to be a view which no reasonable person could hold, is not impugned by the fact that one or more of the shareholders was actually acting under some mistake of fact or lack of knowledge or understanding: *Peters' American Delicacy Co* at 491. In other words, the court will not investigate the quality of the subjective views of such shareholders.

(5) The mere fact that the amendment adversely affects, and even if it is intended adversely to affect, one or more minority shareholders and benefit others does not, of itself, invalidate the amendment if the amendment is made in good faith in the interests of the company: *Sidebottom* at 161, 163–167, 170–173; *Shuttleworth*; *Citco* at 490, 493; *Peters' American Delicacy Co* at 480, 486.

(6) A power to amend will also be validly exercised, even though the amendment is not for the benefit of the company because it relates to a matter in which the company as an entity has no interest but rather is only for the benefit of shareholders as such or some of them, provided that the amendment does not amount to oppression of the minority or is otherwise unjust or is outside the scope of the power: *Peters' American Delicacy Co* at 481, 504, 513, 515; *Assenagon*.

(7) The burden is on the person impugning the validity of the amendment of the articles to satisfy the court that there are grounds for doing so: *Citco* at 491; *Peters' American Delicacy Co* at 482.

...

92. Principle (6) above requires some further explanation. In *Greenhalgh*, the articles of the company contained a pre-emption provision in favour of shareholders. The second defendant, who held a majority of the shares, wished to sell them to the first defendant. At an extraordinary meeting of the company a special resolution was passed amending the articles so as to provide that any member authorised by ordinary resolution could transfer shares to any person named in the resolution and the directors would be bound to register the transfer. That resolution was followed by an ordinary resolution sanctioning the transfer by the second defendant to the purchaser. The plaintiff, a minority shareholder, commenced proceedings claiming a declaration that the resolutions were void and of no effect, and a declaration that the transfer under the resolutions should be set aside. The claim was dismissed as was the appeal from the trial judge. Evershed MR said (at 291) that the expression 'bona fide for the benefit of the company as a whole' did not mean, in such a case as the one in issue, 'the company as a commercial entity, distinct from the corporators'. He said it means the corporators as a general body...

[His Lordship then cited from *Greenhalgh*, *Citco* and *Peters' American Delicacy Co*, before continuing as follows:]

96. In the case of an amendment in which the company as an entity has no interest (which, as it happens, is not the present case) I would prefer to express the test as one which depends on the type of vitiating factors described by Latham CJ and Dixon J in *Peters' American Delicacy Co* rather than in terms of the benefit to the 'corporators as a general body' or a 'hypothetical

member' as in Evershed MR's judgment in *Greenhalgh*. That is the reason why I have expressed paragraph 90(6) as I have.

97. In the light of those principles, I can see no basis for Mr Arbuthnott's challenge to the validity of the amendments to the Articles. The Judge found that there was no evidence of bad faith or improper motive. There can be no possible challenge to that finding.

98. The amendments to the Articles were in substance, as the Judge said, a 'tidying up exercise'...

100. On the face of it those changes—making the Articles clearer and more consistent and facilitating the transfer and registration of shares compulsorily acquired—were for the benefit of the Company even if they also benefited the shareholders as such.

101. The Judge also found that the respondent shareholders considered that they were acting in the best interests of the Company as a whole because they were concerned to resolve the alignment issue in order to secure the Company's future.

...

104. ... The outcome of unfair prejudice petitions invariably turns on disputes of fact, and these proceedings, which resulted in a 27 day trial, are no different. Mr Chivers' submissions which I have briefly summarised amount in reality to an attempt on appeal to re-run the trial. The burden is on Mr Arbuthnott to establish the invalidity of the decision of the majority shareholders to amend the Articles. The Judge, in the light of all the evidence, found no evidence of lack of good faith or improper motive, rejected Mr Arbuthnott's case that the amendment of the Articles was targeted purely at Mr Arbuthnott and intended as an expropriation, and accepted the evidence of Mr Bonnyman and others that they were concerned to resolve the alignment issue in order to secure the Company's future and considered accordingly that they were acting in the best interests of the Company as a whole....

105. On the issue of whether or not a reasonable person could have reached the same conclusion, the Judge concluded, in the light of the evidence, that the lack of alignment would be an impediment to raising a new fund and was a serious issue affecting the Business bearing in mind the number of shareholders who had retired or were about to retire from active management and the fact that Charterhouse was a sequential funds business.... [noting other reasons]...

108. The test is not whether all reasonable people would have agreed that the amendment was in the best interests of the company. It is sufficient that a reasonable person could have thought it was in the company's best interests. It is for Mr Arbuthnott to satisfy the court that no reasonable person would have thought that. In the light of the Judge's findings of fact and her correct decision that the amendment did not introduce any major change from clause 7.2 of the Shareholders' Agreement and the unamended Articles, I cannot see any basis for saying that he has satisfied that requirement.

[4.29] Rights and Issues Investment Trust Ltd v Stylo Shoes Ltd
[1965] Ch 250 (Chancery Division)

The defendant company passed special resolutions increasing the issued share capital and doubling the voting rights of the management shares. The purpose was to preserve the voting strength of the existing 'management shares' notwithstanding the new issue. The resolutions were carried by a large majority at a general meeting of the company and approved by a class meeting of the ordinary shareholders;[46] the holders of management shares did not vote on either occasion. The court ruled that the resolution altering the voting rights was valid.

---

[46] On 'class meetings', see 'Variation of class rights', pp 587ff.

PENNYCUICK J: I am not persuaded that there has been here any discrimination against or op-pression of the holders of the ordinary shares. What has happened is that the members of this company, other than the holders of the management shares, have come to the conclusion that it is for the benefit of this company that the present basis of control through the management shares should continue to subsist notwithstanding that the management shares will hencefor-ward represent a smaller proportion of the issued capital than heretofore. That, it seems to me, is a decision on a matter of business policy to which they could properly come and it does not seem to me a matter in which the court can interfere. So far as I am aware there is no principle under which the members of a company acting in accordance with the Companies Act and the constitution of the particular company and subject to any necessary consent on the part of a class affected, cannot, if they are so minded, alter the relative voting powers attached to various classes of shares. Of course, any resolution for the alteration of voting rights must be passed in good faith for the benefit of the company as a whole, but, where it is so, I know of no ground on which such an alteration would be objectionable and no authority has been cited to that effect. So here this alteration in voting powers has been resolved upon by a great majority of those members of the company who have themselves nothing to gain by it so far as their personal interest is concerned and who, so far as one knows, are actuated only by consideration of what is for the benefit of the company as a whole. I cannot see any ground on which that can be said to be oppressive....

➤ Notes

1. It is apparent from such cases as *North-West Transportation Co Ltd v Beatty* **[4.34]** and *Northern Counties Securities Ltd v Jackson & Steeple Ltd* **[4.18]** that the holders of the man-agement shares were under no legal obligation to abstain from voting. Their self-denying act was, however, a very effective piece of window-dressing. In contrast with the rule which normally governs the acts of *directors*, there seems to be no *general* common law rule that a vote by an interested shareholder renders a decision invalid, or even raises a presumption of *mala fides*. The only situation in which it is clearly improper to exercise the voting rights attached to shares (fraud apart) is where the validity of the shares concerned is at stake, when to allow the vote would be to beg the very question in issue: see *Hogg v Cramphorn Ltd* **[7.08]** and *Bamford v Bamford* in Note 1 of Further notes following *Pender v Lushington* **[13.23]**, p 704.

2. It has from time to time been suggested that it would be a desirable change in the law to allow some issues to be resolved by submitting them to the votes of 'independent' mem-bers only. But this would be very difficult to enforce (consider, eg, relatives, nominees, trustees and friends of 'interested' members), and it would deprive those with most at stake from a meaningful say in their company's affairs.

3. Denying 'interested' members a vote is easier, and there are, indeed, one or two special situations where the holders of 'interested' shares are disfranchised by statute (CA 2006 s 239 is the most obvious one, but also ss 695, 717), and by the Listing Rules in regard to transactions between a listed company and a 'related party', such as a substantial share-holder or director.

4. In *Smith v Croft (No 2)* **[13.19]**, Knox J held that it was proper for the court, in decid-ing whether to allow a minority shareholder's action to be brought as an exception to the Rule in *Foss v Harbottle* ('The old common law rule in *Foss v Harbottle*', pp 669ff), to have regard to the views of 'independent' shareholders, that is, those who were not involved in the proposed litigation as defendants or as persons closely connected with them. The judg-ment (and that of the Court of Appeal in *Prudential Assurance Co Ltd v Newman Industries Ltd (No 2)* **[13.25]** on which it is based) comes very close to suggesting that this issue is to

be resolved by summoning a general meeting, perhaps under the direction of the court, at which the defendants and those in their camp should be disenfranchised. This was something that the Court of Appeal had said that it had no power to do in *Mason v Harris* (1879) 11 Ch D 97, but it appears to have become an accepted part of modern thinking—and, indeed, has now been adopted as a statutory rule in many contexts (eg the ratification of breaches of directors' duties: 'Members' decisions concerning directors' breaches', pp 247ff and 'Ratification of acts of directors: CA 2006 s 239', pp 454ff).

> Question

Given these authorities, what legal rule or principle restricts shareholders' freedom to vote as they wish for a change in their company's articles? Does the rule or principle have wider general application?[47] Should it?

Variation of class rights

See 'Variation of class rights', pp 587ff, and the cases extracted there.

Members' decisions concerning directors' breaches

Breaches of duty by directors are not always inimical to the company's interests. Consider *Regal (Hastings) v Gulliver* **[7.26]** or *Brady v Brady* **[10.08]**. If the company's directors *propose* to engage in an activity that is beyond their powers, or in breach of their duties to the company, but is nevertheless an activity that the majority of the members wish the company to pursue, the members may:[48]

(i)   take the decision themselves to commit the company to the activity (but see *Barron v Potter* **[4.08]**, on the members' limited power to manage the company's business in this way);

(ii) authorise the directors to engage in the activity (again, the members need to have the necessary power to authorise the directors to proceed).

More commonly, however, the members will only discover the directors' breach after the event. If they nevertheless support the directors' activity, they may:

(i)   ratify (or, more accurately, affirm) the *impugned transaction*, if that is necessary for its validity;

(ii) ratify (waive or forgive) the *breach*, so that the directors are secure in the commitment that the company will not sue them at a later date for the wrongdoing: this might be especially important if the company is taken over and a new board is put in place, or the company becomes insolvent and a liquidator is appointed, so that the members who now express support for the directors are no longer in a position to deliver their promises.

Each of these options seems to have slightly different requirements attached to it. The cases that follow expose some of the rules. In addition, CA 2006 enacts new requirements.

---

[47] See, eg, *Assenagon Asset Management SA v Irish Bank Resolution Corp Ltd (formerly Anglo Irish Bank Corp Ltd)* [2012] EWHC 2090 (Ch) (Briggs J); and *Redwood Master Fund Ltd v TD Bank Europe Ltd* [2002] EWHC 2703 (Ch), both cases concerning analogous limits on creditors' voting powers where the majority has power to bind the minority. But contrast *Azevedo v Imcopa Importação, Exportação E Indústria De Olèos Ltda, Imcopa International SA, Imcopa International Cayman Ltd* [2013] EWCA Civ 364.

[48] See S Worthington, 'Corporate Governance: Remedying and Ratifying Directors' Breaches' (2000) 116 LQR 638.

These authorisation and ratification decisions warrant such detailed scrutiny because of the acknowledged risk that defaulting directors, in their role as members, often have the power to obtain or at least influence company decisions that may permit them to get away with unacceptable wrongdoing.

CA 2006 s 180: consent, approval or authorisation by members

CA 2006 s 180 is a general section covering each of: *authorisation* by the directors, according to the terms of the Act, of what would otherwise be a conflict of interest for one of their board members; *approval* by the members of transactions required by statute to have such approval; and, finally, preservation of the general law on *authorisation by the company* of anything that would otherwise be a breach of duty by the directors. This last option is the one under review in this section.

CA 2006 s 239: ratification of acts of directors

CA 2006 s 239 preserves the current law on ratification of acts of directors, but with one significant change. Any decision by a company to ratify conduct by a director amounting to negligence, default, breach of duty or breach of trust in relation to the company must be taken by the members, but *without* reliance on the votes in favour by the director (as member) or any connected person. Section 252 defines what is meant by a person being 'connected' with a director. For the purposes of this section it may also include fellow directors (s 252(5)(d)).

If the ratification decision is taken at a meeting, those members whose votes are to be disregarded may still attend the meeting, take part in the meeting and count towards the quorum for the meeting (if their membership gives them the right to do so) (s 239(4)).

The company in general meeting may by ordinary resolution ratify an act of the directors which is within the capacity of the company but beyond the authority or competence of the directors.[49]

[4.30] Grant v United Kingdom Switchback Railways Co
[1888] 40 Ch D 135 (Court of Appeal)

Article 100 of the articles of association of Thompson's Patent Gravity Switchback Railways Co (the second defendant) disqualified any director from voting at a board meeting in relation to any contract in which he was interested. The directors of this company agreed to sell the company's undertaking to the United Kingdom Co (the first defendant) despite the fact that they were the promoters of the purchasing company. [The remaining facts appear from the judgment.]

> COTTON LJ: This is an appeal from a decision of Mr Justice Chitty refusing an injunction to restrain Thompson's Company and the United Kingdom Company from carrying into effect a contract for the sale of part of the undertaking of the former company to the latter. The ground of the application was that the directors of Thompson's Company had no authority to enter into the contract, as the articles prohibited a director from voting upon a contract in which he was interested, and here all the directors but one were interested. An application for an injunction was made in the Long Vacation, and ordered to stand over till the Michaelmas Sittings, the companies undertaking not to act upon the agreement in the meantime, but being left at liberty to call meetings of their shareholders with reference to the agreement. A general meeting of the shareholders of Thompson's Company was accordingly held, and passed a resolution approving

---

[49] But note the impact CA 2006 s 239 would now have on the ratification decision itself.

and adopting the agreement, and authorising the directors to carry it into effect. Mr Justice Chitty under these circumstances refused an injunction, and the plaintiff has appealed.

It was argued for the appellant that the directors could not, being interested, make a contract which would bind their company, and that a general meeting could not, by a mere ordinary resolution, affirm that contract, for this would be an alteration of the articles, which could only be effected by a special resolution. This is a mistake. The ratifying of a particular contract which had been entered into by the directors without authority, and so making it an act of the company, is quite a different thing from altering the articles. To give the directors power to do things in future which articles did not authorise them to do would be an alteration of the articles, but it is no alteration of the articles to ratify a contract which has been made with authority.

It was urged that the contract was a nullity, and could not be ratified. That is not the case. There was a contract entered into on behalf of the company, though it was one which could not be enforced against the company. Article 100 prevented the directors from binding the company by the contract, but there was nothing in it to prevent the company from entering into such a contract. Two passages in *Irvine v Union Bank of Australia*[50] were referred to. Being in the same judgment, they must be taken together, and they appear to me to express what I have said—that power to do future acts cannot be given to directors without altering the articles, but that a ratification of an unauthorised act of the directors only requires the sanction of an ordinary resolution of a general meeting, if the act is within the powers of the company.

LINDLEY and BOWEN LJJ delivered concurring judgments.

[4.31] Re Horsley & Weight Ltd [1982] Ch 442 (Court of Appeal)

The company's memorandum included among its objects, by clause 3(o): 'to grant pensions to employees and ex-employees and directors and ex-directors . . .' The respondent, Mr Stephen Horsley, had served the company as a director and worked for it as an estimator for many years. The other directors were Mr Campbell-Dick and Mr Frank Horsley (who were the only two members of the company at the material time) and their two wives. Just before the respondent was due to retire from active work at the age of 65, Mr Campbell-Dick and Mr Frank Horsley, purporting to act on behalf of the company, took out a retirement pension policy for his benefit at a cost of over £10,000. The company went into liquidation a year later and in these proceedings the liquidator attacked the validity of the pension payment.

BUCKLEY LJ: I now turn to the second head of Mr Evans-Lombe's argument, viz that the purchase of the pension was effected by Mr Campbell-Dick and Mr Frank Horsley without the authority of the board of directors or of the company in general meeting, and was an act of misfeasance which was not validated as against the company's creditors by virtue of the fact that Mr Campbell-Dick and Mr Frank Horsley were the only shareholders. Ignoring for the moment that Mr Campbell-Dick and Mr Frank Horsley were the only shareholders, the transaction in question was indeed carried out by them without the sanction of any board resolution, whether antecedent, contemporary or by way of subsequent ratification. It was an unauthorised act which they were, as two only of the company's five directors, incompetent to carry out on the company's behalf. It therefore cannot stand unless it has in some way been ratified. The question is whether the fact that Mr Campbell-Dick and Mr Frank Horsley were the only shareholders of the company has the effect of validating the transaction.

Mr Evans-Lombe has submitted that there is a general duty incumbent on directors of a company, whether properly described as owed to creditors or not, to preserve the company's capital

50 (1877) 2 App Cas 366, PC.

fund (which he identifies as those assets which are not distributable by way of dividends) and not to dispose of it otherwise than for the benefit or intended benefit of the company. He submits that creditors dealing with the company are entitled to assume that directors will observe that duty; and that creditors although they are not entitled to interfere in the day-to-day management of a company which is not in liquidation, are entitled through a liquidator to seek redress in respect of a breach of the duty. Consequently, Mr Evans-Lombe submits, the members of the company cannot, even unanimously, deprive the creditors of any remedy so available to them.

On this part of the case Mr Evans-Lombe mainly relies upon *Re Exchange Banking Co, Flitcroft's Case* **[10.13]**...The facts of that case were very different from those of the present case and the principles applicable were, in my opinion, also different. A company cannot legally repay contributed capital to the contributors otherwise than by way of an authorised reduction of capital. Nothing of that kind occurred in the present case. There is nothing in the statute or in the general law which prevents a company or its directors expending contributed capital in doing anything which is an authorised object of the company. In the present case the cost of effecting the pension policy was, in my view, incurred in the course of carrying out an express object of the company.

It is a misapprehension to suppose that the directors of a company owe a duty to the company's creditors to keep the contributed capital of the company intact. The company's creditors are entitled to assume that the company will not in any way repay any paid-up share capital to the shareholders except by means of a duly authorised reduction of capital. They are entitled to assume that the company's directors will conduct its affairs in such a manner that no such unauthorised repayment will take place. It may be somewhat loosely said that the directors owe an indirect duty to the creditors not to permit any unlawful reduction of capital to occur, but I would regard it as more accurate to say that the directors owe a duty to the company in this respect and that, if the company is put into liquidation when paid-up capital has been improperly repaid, the liquidator owes a duty to the creditors to enforce any right to repayment which is available to the company. On the other hand, a company and its directors acting on its behalf, can quite properly expend contributed capital for any purpose which is intra vires the company. As I have already indicated, the purchase of the pension policy was, in my view, intra vires the company. It was not, however, within the powers of Mr Campbell-Dick and Mr Frank Horsley acting not as members of the board of directors but as individual directors. Unless the act was effectually ratified it cannot bind the company. They were, however, the only two shareholders. A company is bound in a matter which is intra vires the company by the unanimous agreement of its members (per Lord Davey in *Salomon v A Salomon & Co Ltd* **[2.02]**; and see *Re Express Engineering Works Ltd* [1920] 1 Ch 466 (CA) even where that agreement is given informally: *Parker & Cooper Ltd v Reading*.[51] That both Mr Campbell-Dick and Mr Frank Horsley assented to the transaction in question in the present case is beyond dispute. They both initialled the proposal form and they both signed the cheques for the premiums. Their good faith has not been impugned, nor, in my view, does the evidence support any suggestion that in effecting the policy they did not honestly apply their minds to the question whether it was a fair and proper thing for the company to do in the light of the company's financial state as known to them at the time. In my judgment, their assent made the transaction binding on the company and unassailable by the liquidator...

CUMMING-BRUCE and TEMPLEMAN LJJ delivered concurring judgments, in the course of which they made the following comments:

CUMMING-BRUCE LJ: On these facts it is unnecessary to decide whether, had misfeasance by the directors been proved, it was open to them in their capacity as shareholders to ratify their own negligence and so to prejudice the claims of creditors. It would surprise me to find that the law is to be so understood.

---

[51] [1926] Ch 975.

TEMPLEMAN LJ: If, however, there had been evidence and a finding of misfeasance and it appeared that the payment of £10,000 in the event reduced the fund available for creditors by that sum, or by a substantial proportion of that sum, I am not satisfied that the directors convicted of such misfeasance, albeit with no fraudulent intent or action, could excuse themselves because two of them held all the issued shares in the company and as shareholders ratified their own gross negligence as directors which inflicted loss on creditors. I should be sorry to find the scope of s 333 [IA 1986 s 212] so restricted and need not do so on this occasion. [This final qualification is crucial, and remains so.]

An ordinary resolution of members which purports to ratify an irregular act of the directors is ineffective if it itself contravenes the articles.

[4.32] Boschoek Pty Ltd v Fuke [1906] 1 Ch 148 (Chancery Division)

The directors had purported to appoint Fuke managing director at a remuneration of £700 per annum notwithstanding that he did not hold 'in his own right' the number of qualification shares prescribed by the articles and that the maximum remuneration of the whole board was fixed by the articles at £500. The company later confirmed the appointment by resolutions passed unanimously at a general meeting; but the court ruled that the resolutions were invalid.

SWINFEN EADY J: The . . . ground on which the plaintiff company has objected to the validity of the . . . resolutions passed at this meeting is that they could only have been properly passed after the articles had been altered by special resolution. The company in general meeting could not appoint, and could not ratify, as from December 1901, the appointment of Fuke as managing director at £700 per annum as he had not the necessary qualification, and the maximum remuneration of the whole board was fixed by the articles at £500. The articles, until altered, bound the shareholders in general meeting as much as the board. The present case is unlike that of *Irvine v Union Bank of Australia*,[52] to which reference was made, as in that case the limitation of the power of borrowing and mortgaging was merely a limitation of the authority of the directors, and not a limitation of the general powers of the company. It was argued that the acts of the directors in excess of their authority might be ratified by the company and rendered binding, and that contention succeeded. Articles must first be altered by special resolution before the altered articles can be acted upon: *Imperial Hydropathic Hotel Co, Blackpool v Hampson* **[4.04]**.

A general meeting may ratify an act of the directors which is voidable as an irregular exercise of their powers.

[4.33] Bamford v Bamford [1970] Ch 212 (Court of Appeal)

The directors of Bamfords Ltd (referred to in the judgment as 'the company') issued 500,000 shares at par to FH Burgess Ltd, one of the principal distributors of the company's products. They did so in exercise of a power vested in them by the articles, but (so the plaintiffs alleged) improperly, being primarily for the purpose of forestalling a takeover bid by JC Bamford (Excavators) Ltd. When the validity of the allotment was challenged by the issue of a writ, the directors convened a members' meeting at which the allotment was ratified and approved. (The newly issued shares were not voted.[53]) The Court of Appeal

---

[52] (1877) 2 App Cas 366, PC.
[53] Compare *Hogg v Cramphorn* **[7.11]**, and see the reference to that case in Note 1 following *Rights and Issues Investment Trust Ltd v Stylo Shoes Ltd* **[4.29]**, p 246.

held as a preliminary point of law, on the assumption that the facts alleged were true, that such a ratification would be effective.

HARMAN LJ:... [This] is a tolerably plain case. It is trite law, I had thought, that if directors do acts, as they do every day, especially in private companies, which, perhaps because there is no quorum, or because their appointment was defective, or because sometimes there are no directors properly appointed at all, or because they are actuated by improper motives, they go on doing for years, carrying on the business of the company in the way in which, if properly constituted, they should carry it on, and then they find that everything has been so to speak wrongly done because it was not done by a proper board, such directors can, by making a full and frank disclosure and calling together the general body of the shareholders, obtain absolution and forgiveness of their sins; and provided the acts are not ultra vires the company as a whole everything will go on as if it had been done all right from the beginning. I cannot believe that this is not a commonplace of company law. It is done every day. Of course, if the majority of the general meeting will not forgive and approve, the directors must pay for it.

[His Lordship referred to *Regal (Hastings) Ltd v Gulliver* **[7.26]** and continued:] So it seems to me here that these directors, on the assumptions which we have to make, made this allotment in breach of their duty—mala fide, as it is said. They made it with an eye primarily on the exigencies of the takeover war and not with a single eye to the benefit of the company, and, therefore, it is a bad allotment. But it is an allotment. There is no doubt that the directors had power to allot these shares. There is no doubt that they did allot them. There is no doubt that the allottees are on the register and are for all purposes members of the company. The only question is whether the allotment, having been made, as one must assume, in bad faith, is voidable and can be avoided at the instance of the company—at their instance only and of no one else, because the wrong, if wrong it be, is a wrong done to the company. If that be right, the company, which had the right to recall the allotment, has also the right to approve of it and forgive it; and I see no difficulty at all in supposing that the ratification by the decision of December 15 in the general meeting of the company was a perfectly good 'whitewash' of that which up to that time was a voidable transaction. And that is the end of the matter....

RUSSELL LJ delivered a concurring judgment.

KARMINSKI LJ concurred.

For another part of the decision, see Note 1 in Further Notes following *Pender v Lushington* **[13.23]**.

[4.34] North-West Transportation Co Ltd v Beatty [1887] 12 App Cas 589 (Privy Council)

The facts appear from the judgment.

The opinion of their Lordships was delivered by SIR RICHARD BAGGALLAY: The plaintiff, Henry Beatty, is a shareholder in the North-West Transportation Company Limited, and he sues on behalf of himself and all other shareholders in the company, except those who are defendants. The defendants are the company and five shareholders, who, at the commencement of the action, were the directors of the company. The claim in the action is to set aside a sale made to the company by James Hughes Beatty, one of the directors, of a steamer called the *United Empire*, of which, previously to such sale, he was sole owner.

The general principles applicable to cases of this kind are well established. Unless some provision to the contrary is to be found in the charter or other instrument by which the company is incorporated, the resolution of a majority of the shareholders, duly convened, upon any question with which the company is legally competent to deal, is binding upon the minority, and consequently upon the company, and every shareholder has a perfect right to vote upon any such question, although he may have a personal interest in the subject-matter opposed to, or different from, the general or particular interests of the company.

On the other hand, a director of a company is precluded from dealing, on behalf of the company, with himself, and from entering into engagements in which he has a personal interest conflicting, or which possibly may conflict, with the interests of those whom he is bound by fiduciary duty to protect; and this rule is as applicable to the case of one of several directors as to a managing or sole director. Any such dealing or engagement may, however, be affirmed or adopted by the company, provided such affirmance or adoption is not brought about by unfair or improper means, and is not illegal or fraudulent or oppressive towards those shareholders who oppose it.

The material facts of the case are not now in dispute . . .

It is proved by uncontradicted evidence, and is indeed now substantially admitted, that at the date of the purchase the acquisition of another steamer to supply the place of the *Asia* was essential to the efficient conduct of the company's business; that the *United Empire* was well adapted for that purpose; that it was not within the power of the company to acquire any other steamer equally well adapted for its business; and that the price agreed to be paid for the steamer was not excessive or unreasonable . . .

It is clear upon the authorities that the contract entered into by the directors on 10 February could not have been enforced against the company at the instance of the defendant JH Beatty, but it is equally clear that it was within the competency of the shareholders at the meeting of the 16th to adopt or reject it. In form and in terms they adopted it by a majority of votes, and the vote of the majority must prevail, unless the adoption was brought about by unfair or improper means.

The only unfairness or impropriety which, consistently with the admitted and established facts, could be suggested, arises out of the fact that the defendant JH Beatty possessed a voting power as a shareholder which enabled him, and those who thought with him, to adopt the bye-law, and thereby either to ratify and adopt a voidable contract, into which he, as a director, and his co-directors had entered, or to make a similar contract, which latter seems to have been what was intended to be done by the resolution passed on 7 February.

It may be quite right that, in such a case, the opposing minority should be able, in a suit like this, to challenge the transaction, and to show that it is an improper one, and to be freed from the objection that a suit with such an object can only be maintained by the company itself.

But the constitution of the company enabled the defendant JH Beatty to acquire this voting power; there was no limit upon the number of shares which a shareholder might hold, and for every share so held he was entitled to a vote; the charter itself recognised the defendant as a holder of 200 shares, one-third of the aggregate number; he had a perfect right to acquire further shares, and to exercise his voting power in such a manner as to secure the election of directors whose views upon policy agreed with his own, and to support those views at any shareholders' meeting; the acquisition of the *United Empire* was a pure question of policy, as to which it might be expected that there would be differences of opinion, and upon which the voice of the majority ought to prevail; to reject the votes of the defendant upon the question of the adoption of the bye-law would be to give effect to the views of the minority, and to disregard those of the majority.

See also *Burland v Earle* [1902] AC 83, PC.

➤ Question

This case has been understood for well over a century as one of the leading authorities for the principle that a general meeting may ratify an act of the directors which is voidable as an irregular exercise of their powers, on the basis that here the *directors* had entered into a contract which was voidable because of Beatty's undisclosed personal interest, but was rescued from invalidity because the contract was *ratified* by the members' resolution—a resolution on which, it was held, Beatty was not debarred from voting. A number of Sir Richard Baggallay's remarks are consistent with this view of the matter (eg his reference to a 'contract entered into by the directors on 10 February'). Later commentators have gone further, interpreting the case as one where there was a breach of duty by Beatty which he was able to whitewash by the use of his own votes. The CLR adopts this approach, taking *North-West Transportation v Beatty* as illustrating the case of a *wrongdoing* director voting in his capacity as a shareholder to ratify the transaction. It proposed by way of an amendment to the law that the member in question should be disenfranchised and the resolution should only be capable of being carried by a majority of disinterested shareholders (see CA 2006 s 239). A close examination of the facts, and of the arguments of counsel, however, suggests that the whole point of the proposed 'bye-law' was to put the proposal that the company should buy the ship *before the members* for them to decide.

Is there any material difference between the constraints that operate on the exercise of powers by members to affirm a voidable transaction, to waive a breach of duty, or to take a corporate decision *ab initio*? If there is a difference, how can an observer decide what the members are trying to vote on?

[See also *Burland v Earle* [1902] AC 83, PC, and the *Multinational Gas* case **[7.43]**.]

➤ Notes

1. The principle established by these cases is subject to the limitation recognised in such cases as *Cook v Deeks* **[7.25]** and *Menier v Hooper's Telegraph Works* (1874) 9 Ch App 350, CA: the power to ratify cannot validate acts of fraud or expropriation, or, perhaps more specifically, that directors guilty of such acts cannot, in their capacity as members, ratify or condone their own wrongdoing. This rigorous approach has been extended to ratification of directors' negligence where that negligence also leads to personal benefit (*Daniels v Daniels* [1978] Ch 406, see Notes 2 and 3 following *Franbar Holdings Ltd v Patel* **[13.13]**, p 688).

2. But even that simple statement has its difficulties. On one measure, a company's claim against its defaulting directors *is* a 'corporate asset'. Accordingly, for the members to agree to waive the right, or give it away, amounts to much the same thing as 'giving away' a corporate opportunity as in *Cook v Deeks* **[7.25]**. That is something the members in general meeting could not do, at least where the resolution was carried by the votes of the wrongdoers. Yet examples abound of just this sort of ratification, where directors control the general meeting and are permitted to vote in favour of resolutions that allow them to keep the benefits of contracts with the company (*North-West Transportation Co Ltd v Beatty* **[4.34]**), or escape claims for compensation for negligence (*Pavlides v Jensen* [1956] Ch 565).

3. Two further points are material. First, there must be a members' decision to ratify: as *Re D'Jan of London Ltd* **[7.22]** shows, it is not enough that the decision of the general meeting would certainly have gone in favour of the errant director (here, the director owned 99% of the shares and his wife 1%). Secondly, as a company approaches insolvency, the shareholders lose their right to vote to distribute corporate assets to particular individuals to the detriment of the claims of the company's creditors (*Kinsela v Russell Kinsela Pty Ltd* **[7.16]**).

4. On the effect of a ratification or approval in relation to directors' duties, also see *Multinational Gas and Petrochemical Co Ltd v Multinational Gas and Petrochemical Services Ltd* **[7.43]** and *Madoff Securities International Ltd v Raven* **[7.24]**.

Summary of limitations on members' voting

On one analysis, these cases appear to establish a general rule that members are free to use the votes attached to their shares as they think fit and that they may, if they so wish, use them to advance their own interests. This proposition is certainly true of most business and policy decisions, such as whether to make a purchase or whom to appoint as a director. However, there are a number of particular and important limitations on members' freedom to vote as they choose, some of which are well recognised and others of more questionable standing. It is not easy to unite these exceptions by any common theme, although it is probably significant that they belong mostly in the area of intra-corporate disputes,[54] where one group of members is complaining that the others have used their more powerful voting strength to gain an unfair advantage.

Some of these special situations are:

(i) Majority members may not use their votes to appropriate to themselves property which belongs to the company or to condone their own fraud (*Cook v Deeks* **[7.25]**; *Menier v Hooper's Telegraph Works* (1974) 9 Ch App 350, CA).

(ii) Where there is a resolution on an issue which affects the rights of members *inter se*, such as an alteration of the articles or a variation of class rights, the majority must act 'bona fide in the interests of the company (or class) as a whole' (*Allen v Gold Reefs of West Africa Ltd* **[4.22]**; *British America Nickel Corpn Ltd v O'Brien* **[11.06]**).

(iii) Where it is sought to bring an action against persons who have allegedly committed wrongs against the company, the alleged wrongdoers may not use their votes to stop the action being brought (historically, an exception to the rule in *Foss v Harbottle* **[12.01]**; and also see 'Ratification of acts of directors: CA 2006 s 239', pp 454ff).

(iv) There are certain *statutory* remedies which may be sought by members who are disadvantaged as a result of some act of the majority, even though what is complained of is within the legal power of the majority. The most popular of these statutory remedies are relief against 'unfairly prejudicial' conduct (on predecessor provisions, see the influential *Scottish Co-operative Wholesale Society Ltd v Meyer* **[13.31]**, and, more generally, see 'Unfairly prejudicial conduct of the company's affairs', pp 715ff), and winding up on the 'just and equitable' ground (*Ebrahimi v Westbourne Galleries Ltd* **[16.13]**).

(v) *Clemens v Clemens Bros Ltd* **[4.20]** and *Re Halt Garage (1964) Ltd* **[5.03]** appear to impose vaguer limitations on the members' voting powers: first, that votes must not be used 'oppressively', and, secondly, that they must be used for 'genuine' purposes. Neither limitation is supported by weighty authority; and nor is either strong enough to make any significant inroad into the line of cases which lay down the general rule.

It would be wrong to deduce from any of the exceptional situations listed here that a member is thereby placed under a *duty* to vote against his own interests, in the altruistic way disowned by Dixon J in the *Peters' American Delicacy* case **[4.26]**, although this is a trap into which judges do occasionally fall (*Re Holders Investment Trust Ltd* **[10.04]**). The realistic choice faced by controlling members wishing to avoid having their role in the general meeting decision questioned may well be between abandoning or modifying the proposal, on the one hand, and, on the other, taking a calculated risk and pressing ahead in the knowledge that the burden of proof on any minority members seeking to challenge a decision has traditionally been a difficult one to discharge. However, the body of case law under CA 2006 s 994 (the 'unfair prejudice' section, previously CA 1985 s 459: see 'Unfairly prejudicial conduct of the company's affairs', pp 715ff), and cases such as *Clemens v Clemens Bros Ltd* **[4.20]**, suggest that the balance may be tipping towards minority members—or may already have done so.

---

[54] Although not exclusively. See, eg *Re Halt Garage* **[5.03]**, noted further later.

Some of the debate in this area (both judicial and extra-judicial) confuses the demands of fiduciary duties and the demands of public law or equitable rules on 'proper purposes'. Because shareholders are not constrained by the former, so the argument goes, they cannot be constrained by the latter (indeed, to some the latter are regarded simply as a subset of the former). It is true that shareholders are not constrained by fiduciary duties: unlike directors, they do not have to deny their own interests and favour those of the company or other shareholders (see 'Duty to avoid conflicts of interest: CA 2006 s 175', pp 385ff).[55] But it is not clear why they should not be subject to the same limitations that routinely apply elsewhere to those given a power to exercise—in those other cases it is not controversial that, to be valid, the power must be exercised bona fide and for proper purposes.

➤ Question

Should members exercising their majority power be constrained to vote both bona fide and for proper purposes?[56]

Shareholders' agreements

The company's constitution may be supplemented by a *shareholders' agreement*—a contract, usually of a quite formal kind, entered into by the shareholders either at the time of the company's formation or at some subsequent time (eg when a family company, in need of extra capital to finance an expansion of its business, invites an outsider to join the company as an additional shareholder).[57]

To be fully effective as a constitutional document, it is necessary that all of the members for the time being should be made parties to the agreement, and so the use of a shareholders' agreement in this way is practicable only if the membership is not too large. Shareholders' agreements are also possible between only some of the members, but for different objectives and with different impact. Historically, the company itself was sometimes also joined as a party, but there are dangers in doing so if there is any risk that it will be held to have fettered its statutory powers (see *Russell v Northern Bank Development Corpn Ltd* **[4.35]**).[58]

The shareholders' agreement is used, almost as a matter of routine, to supplement the constitutional documents of smaller companies in Canada and the United States, and its importance has been recognised by legislation in those jurisdictions. In the UK, there is no legislative recognition, but its use is now standard practice for very many purposes, for example in small owner-managed companies, in joint ventures, management buy-outs and in loan-related securities required by lenders.

---

[55] Although, on special facts, a court could always find the shareholder's relationship to be fiduciary. Then, fiduciary duties will be owed, but this will be *because* of the relationship in question, not *because* the person is a shareholder.

[56] See S Worthington, 'Corporate Governance: Remedying and Ratifying Directors' Breaches' (2000) 116 LQR 638.

[57] See PD Finn, 'Shareholder Agreements' (1978) 6 *Australian Business Law Review* 97.

[58] Even if the company is not a party to the agreement, it may be able to rely on it as a defence: in *Snelling v John G Snelling Ltd* [1973] QB 87, the shareholders had lent money to the company and had agreed with each other that none of them would require the company to repay their loans while certain other funding arrangements were in place. The court refused to allow one of the shareholders to sue for repayment in breach of this agreement. (Is this defensible?)

A shareholders' agreement might typically contain provisions that each of the shareholders should be entitled to appoint a director, that no shareholder should vote in support of an alteration of the company's articles or its capital unless all the members agreed to it, and that except in specified circumstances a shareholder would not require the repayment of money which he or she had lent to the company.

The main advantage of a shareholders' agreement is that normal contractual rules apply, so, unlike the articles of association or the rules governing a company's capital structure, its terms cannot be altered by a majority vote (see 'Alteration of the articles', pp 228ff). Further, contractual obligations are in principle enforceable as of right, and, where appropriate, by injunction. By contrast, most company law remedies are discretionary, and a member who has only a minority shareholding may have no standing to take a complaint to the court. In addition, being normal contracts, shareholders' agreements are not constrained by the odd medley of rules governing enforcement of the articles by individual members (where the courts have added a gloss to the statutory rules so that enforcement must be *qua* member, not in some other capacity, and must concern matters that go beyond mere internal irregularities; see 'Personal claims by members', pp 700ff). On a practical level, unlike the articles of association which is a public document available for inspection by members of the public, a shareholders' agreement offers enhanced privacy which is more fitting for dealing with such matters as directors' remuneration, dividend policy and other sensitive internal management matters. Finally, as per contract law principles, a shareholders' agreement may be set aside where one party entered into the agreement under duress: *Antonio v Antonio* [2010] EWHC 1199 (QB).

On the other hand, there are disadvantages, the main one being that under the rules of privity of contract a shareholders' agreement is binding only on its immediate parties and not on anyone who later takes a transfer of shares or joins the company as a new member. (The Contracts (Rights of Third Parties) Act 1999 is unlikely to be relevant in this context, since it is concerned only with rights and not obligations.) This is often cured by joining subsequent transferees as parties to an existing shareholders' agreement by requiring the newcomer to execute a 'Deed of Adherence'.

Judges have been known to *imply* a shareholders' agreement and give effect to it (eg in *Pennell Securities Ltd v Venida Investments Ltd* (25 July 1974, noted Burridge (1981) 44 MLR 40)), and the terms of a shareholders' agreement will carry much weight in proceedings brought by a minority shareholder for relief against 'unfairly prejudicial' conduct (recall *Re Charterhouse Capital Ltd* **[4.28]**, and see 'Unfairly prejudicial conduct of the company's affairs', pp 715ff) or for a winding-up order on the 'just and equitable' ground ('Compulsory winding up on the "just and equitable" ground', pp 840ff). Note, however, *Sikorski v Sikorski* [2012] EWHC 1613 (Ch), in which the court held that a breach of an agreement between shareholders would not *ipso facto* constitute 'unfair prejudice'; it still falls upon the petitioner to establish that their interests have been unfairly prejudiced.

For examples of the use (and limitations on the use) of shareholders' agreements, see *Russell v Northern Bank Development Corpn Ltd* **[4.35]**; *Puddephatt v Leith* **[4.19]**; *Euro Brokers Holdings Ltd v Monecor (London) Ltd* **[4.16]**; *Punt v Symons & Co Ltd* **[4.21]** (noting that this agreement was with the *company*, but the judgments allow for inferences to be made about the potentially different treatment of shareholders' agreements). See also *Westcoast (Holdings) Ltd (formerly Kelido Ltd) v Wharf Land Subsidiary (No 1) Ltd* [2012] EWCA Civ 1003, CA, in which the court highlighted the importance of accurate and precise drafting.

A company may not bind itself not to exercise the power conferred on it by statute, but an agreement by members that they will not support such a resolution is binding.

[4.35] Russell v Northern Bank Development Corpn Ltd [1992] 1 WLR 588 (House of Lords)

A company (referred to in the report as TBL) was set up in 1979 as the parent company in a group of brick-making companies based in Northern Ireland. It had five shareholders: the respondent bank, which held 120 shares, and four executives (including Russell), who each held 20 shares. Soon after the incorporation of TBL, an agreement was entered into between the five shareholders and the company which provided (inter alia) that no further share capital would be created or issued without the consent of each of the parties. In 1988 the board of directors proposed to make an increase of capital to £4 million by a rights issue. Russell objected to this and was successful in obtaining a declaration that the agreement was binding on his fellow shareholders (although not on the company itself).

> LORD JAUNCEY OF TULLICHETTLE:... The issue between the parties in this House was whether art 3 of the agreement constituted an unlawful and invalid fetter on the statutory power of TBL to increase its share capital or whether it was no more than an agreement between the shareholders as to their manner of voting in a given situation. Both parties accepted the long-established principle that 'a company cannot forgo its right to alter its articles' (*Southern Foundries (1926) Ltd v Shirlaw* [6.04], per Lord Porter), a principle that was earlier stated in *Allen v Gold Reefs of West Africa Ltd* [4.22] per Lindley MR:
>
> > '... the company is empowered by the statute to alter the regulations contained in its articles from time to time by special resolutions ..., and any regulation or article purporting to deprive the company of this power is invalid on the ground that it is contrary to the statute...'
>
> [The judges in the courts below] both considered that this principle applied also to the right of a company to alter its memorandum and I agree that this must be the case. Mr McCartney QC for the appellant advanced a number of arguments to the effect that the agreement in no way contravened the above principle inasmuch as it was merely an agreement between shareholders outside the scope of company legislation which in no way fettered the statutory power of TBL to alter its memorandum and articles. Mr Girvan QC, on the other hand, submitted that the agreement was not only a voting arrangement between shareholders inter se but was tantamount to an article of association which constituted a restriction on the power of TBL to alter its share capital.
>
> My Lords, while a provision in a company's articles which restricts its statutory power to alter those articles is invalid an agreement dehors the articles between shareholders as to how they shall exercise their voting rights on a resolution to alter the articles is not necessarily so. In *Welton v Saffery*,[59] which concerned an ultra vires provision in the articles of association authorising the company to issue shares at a discount, Lord Davey said:
>
> > 'Of course, individual shareholders may deal with their own interests by contract in such way as they may think fit. But such contracts, whether made by all or some only of the shareholders, would create personal obligations, or an *exceptio personalis* against themselves only, and would not become a regulation of the company, or be binding on the transferees of the parties to it, or upon new or non-assenting shareholders....'

---

[59] [1897] AC 299 at 331.

I understand Lord Davey there to be accepting that shareholders may lawfully agree inter se to exercise their voting rights in a manner which, if it were dictated by the articles, and were thereby binding on the company, would be unlawful.

I turn to examine the agreement in more detail.... Clause 3 at least so far as shareholders are concerned constitutes an agreement collateral to the provisions of [the company's articles] and is...neither in substitution for nor in conflict with [them].

However it must be remembered that the agreement was executed not only by the shareholders but also by TBL. In *Bushell v Faith* **[6.02]** one of the articles of a private company provided that in the event of a resolution being proposed at a general meeting of the company for the removal of a director any share held by him should carry three votes per share. The issued capital of the company was equally divided between three persons and an attempt by two shareholders to remove the third from the office of director failed because his 300 votes outnumbered the 200 of the two other shareholders. It was held that the article in question was not invalidated by [the equivalent of CA 2006 s 168] which empowered a company by ordinary resolution to remove a director. Russell LJ said, at pp. 447–448:

> 'Mr. Dillon argued...that a company cannot by its articles or otherwise deprive itself of the power by special resolution to alter its articles or any of them. But the point is the same one. An article purporting to do this is ineffective. But a provision as to voting rights which has the effect of making a special resolution incapable of being passed, if a particular shareholder or group of shareholders exercises his or their voting rights against a proposed alteration, is not such a provision. An article in terms providing that no alteration shall be made without the consent of X is contrary to [the Act] and ineffective. But the provision as to voting rights that I have mentioned is wholly different, and it does not serve to say that it can have the same result.'

Both parties sought to derive comfort from this dictum. Mr McCartney [counsel for the claimant] relied on it as demonstrating that a provision as to the exercise of voting rights, even although it had the effect of preventing a resolution being passed, was nevertheless valid. Mr Girvan [counsel for the defendant] argued that the effect of clause 3 was the same as that of an article containing a provision that 'no alteration should be made without the consent of X.'

I do not doubt that if clause 3 had been embodied in the articles of association so as to be binding on all persons who were or might become shareholders in TBL it would have been invalid but it was, of course, not so embodied. To my mind the significant part of this dictum for the purposes of this appeal is the words 'articles or otherwise' occurring in the first sentence thereof. These words appear to recognise that it is not only fetters on the power to alter articles of association imposed by the statutory framework of a company which are obnoxious.

Turning back to clause 3 of the agreement it appears to me that its purpose was twofold. The shareholders agreed only to exercise their voting powers in relation to the creation or issue of shares in TBL if they and TBL agreed in writing. This agreement is purely personal to the shareholders who executed it and as I have already remarked does not purport to bind future shareholders. It is, in my view, just such a private agreement as was envisaged by Lord Davey in *Welton v Saffery*. TBL on the other hand agreed that its capital would not be increased without the consent of each of the shareholders. This was a clear undertaking by TBL in a formal agreement not to exercise its statutory powers for a period which could, certainly on one view of construction, last for as long as any one of the parties to the agreement remained a shareholder and long after the control of TBL had passed to shareholders who were not party to the agreement. As such an undertaking it is, in my view, as obnoxious as if it had been contained in the articles of association and therefore is unenforceable as being contrary to the provisions of art 131 of the Companies (Northern Ireland) Order 1986 [CA 2006 s 617]. TBL's undertaking is, however, independent of and severable from that of the shareholders and there is no reason why the latter should not be enforceable by the shareholders inter se as a personal agreement which in no way fetters TBL in the exercise of its statutory powers. I would therefore allow the appeal.

It only remains to consider the relief which would be afforded to the plaintiff. He stated in evidence that he had no objection to the proposed resolutions in themselves but that he wished to establish the validity of clause 3... In these circumstances it would be inappropriate to grant him the injunction sought in his writ [which was an injunction to prevent the defendants 'considering and/or voting' on the proposed resolutions]. In my view the proper order would be a declaration as to the validity of clause 3 of the agreement as between the shareholders. No argument was addressed to your Lordships as to the form of such a declaration and accordingly the case must be remitted back to the Court of Appeal to make the appropriate order in the light of such submissions as counsel may think fit....

LORDS GRIFFITHS, LOWRY, MUSTILL and SLYNN OF HADLEY concurred.

➤ Questions

1. Lord Jauncey said that the company could not fetter the exercise of its statutory powers. Which powers are these? Which powers are outside this classification, and could they be fettered?

2. If the company cannot fetter the exercise of *its* powers, *who*, precisely, has to be left free to act, since a company can only act by human agents?

3. The contractual clause binding the company in *Russell v Northern Bank Development Corpn Ltd* was held to be 'unenforceable'. Does this mean it was void (as against the company)? What, if anything, is the difference? Also see the Notes following *Punt v Symons & Co Ltd* [4.21], p 230.

4. By contrast, the contractual clause binding the shareholders in *Russell v Northern Bank Development Corpn Ltd* was enforceable. The House of Lords declined to order an injunction in the circumstances. Would the court *ever* order an injunction to restrain a breach by shareholders, or would it only ever order damages on breach? If it would order an injunction, what impact would this have on fettering the company's exercise of its statutory powers? If it would not order an injunction, what is the value of a shareholders' agreement?

A shareholders' agreement may alter the orthodox corporate law rules that govern amendments to the company's constitution and enforcement of directors' duties.

Read *Wilkinson v West Coast Capital* [7.32].

The shareholders' agreement in *Wilkinson* provided that certain corporate actions could only be pursued with the consent of more than 65% of the shareholders (Clause 5), and that each shareholder should use all reasonable and proper means to promote the interests of the company (Clause 7). Warren J held that Clause 7 must be read subject to Clause 5, and that, therefore, Clause 5 enabled controlling shareholders who were also directors to use their vote to decide that the company should not pursue a new business opportunity, with the result that the opportunity would not then be regarded as a 'corporate opportunity', and so pursuit of it by the directors would not constitute a breach of the conflicts rule (see *Bhullar v Bhullar* [7.29]). A minority shareholder unsuccessfully sought a remedy under the unfair prejudice provisions of the Act (CA 1985 s 459; now see CA 2006 s 994). Also see *Breckland Group Holdings Ltd v London & Suffolk Properties Ltd* [1989] BCLC 100 (Ch).

➤ Note

This decision confirms that shareholders exercising their rights under a shareholders' agreement can use their votes as they wish. Applying general contract law principles, such a conclusion is unsurprising. However, in the context of this case, the finding ensured that the directors (as controlling shareholders) could effectively determine changes to the company's business objects without the constraints inherent in cases such as *Allen v Gold Reefs* **[4.22]**, and could ensure that they were not caught by the fiduciary conflicts rule in pursuing new corporate opportunities.[60]

➤ Questions

1. There are good commercial reasons for shareholders' agreements in this form, allowing the shareholders to limit the future business direction of the company. But if this right is unqualified, what protection exists for the dissenting minority? (Here, the dissenting minority was unsuccessful in claiming 'unfair prejudice'—CA 2006 s 994.) Is the response simply that the minority should not have submitted themselves to the terms of the shareholders' agreement?

2. Should *all* exercises of majority power—that is, *all* cases where a majority can compel a dissenting minority to conform to a decision that they have not consented to—be constrained by the (fairly minimal) requirements that the power should be exercised in good faith (a subjective test) and for proper purposes (an objective test)? In this case, there would then be serious assessment of whether the directors voted as they did in good faith and for proper purposes (see this issue assessed at 'Limitations on the free exercise of members' voting rights', pp 222ff, and at 'Duty to promote the success of the company: CA 2006 s 172', pp 355ff, and at 'Duty to act within powers: CA 2007 s 171', pp 341ff). Would the *practical* effect of this be the unacceptable conclusion that the majority appeared to owe onerous *fiduciary* duties in that they, of all the people in the world, would be the only people who could not pursue any attractive new ventures that might be of interest to their company? *Is* this the practical effect?

3. In this case, Clause 5 provided that 'unless the shareholders holding in excess of 65% of the issued shares otherwise agree in writing the shareholders shall exercise their power in relation to the company so as to ensure that...the company does not acquire or invest in another company or business or incorporate any subsidiary'. This effectively gave *both* groups an individual veto over any further ventures. Does this formulation suggest that the (proper) purposes for which this power might be exercised include preventing the company pursuing an opportunity *so that* (ie for the *purpose* of allowing) the vetoing group can pursue the venture on their own?

4. Could the exercise of powers under shareholders' agreements *ever* fall foul of CA 2006 s 994?

Members' personal rights

It might seem strange to be looking at members' individual and personal rights in a chapter devoted to the collective rights of members as an organ of the company. But the role

---

[60] Note that the directors' freedom on this front was limited: any new ventures that were within the *existing* objects of the company would be caught by the conflicts rule; but the conflicts rule generally stretches its tentacles beyond the defined existing business plans, and here any broadening of the company's activities could be constrained under the shareholders' agreement.

of the members as such an organ is defined in the articles, and the members may need to enforce the rights granted there in order to exercise the constitutional powers they see as theirs. Of course, members may also seek to make claims under the articles to obtain purely personal remedies for wrongs allegedly done to them in breach of specific provisions in the articles. These latter claims generally have nothing to do with the exercise of members' constitutional rights. Whether the same approach is warranted in both types of case is a moot point.

The articles constitute a contract binding on the company and each of the company's members (CA 2006 s 33). It follows, therefore, that the articles will be interpreted according to general rules of contractual interpretation, although recall the constraints noted earlier at 'Articles and the rules governing their interpretation', p 191. It might also seem to follow that the shareholders, as members, have personal rights under this contract and can sue the company, or other members, to enforce those rights. Two impediments lie in the face of such claims:

(i)   The courts have imposed an enormously restrictive interpretation on the types of rights that are protected under the contract, reading into the statutory provision limitations that, prima facie, are nowhere suggested. So, a member must sue 'as member',[61] and 'mere irregularities' cannot be remedied.[62]

(ii) In addition, where the same facts give rise to a potential claim by the *company* against the wrongdoers, the member's claim may be disallowed because his or her losses are merely '*reflected losses*' that will be remedied once the company recovers its losses. This rule is applied as a substantive rule, not merely a procedural rule that (very properly) denies double recovery.[63]

Companies Act 2006 s 33: Effect of company's constitution

(1) The provisions of a company's constitution bind the company and its members to the same extent as if there were covenants on the part of the company and of each member to observe those provisions....

Companies Act 1985 s 14: Effect of memorandum and articles

(1) Subject to the provisions of this Act, the memorandum and articles, when registered, bind the company and its members to the same extent as if they respectively had been signed and sealed by each member, and contained covenants on the part of each member to observe all the provisions of the memorandum and of the articles....

Despite the seemingly clear words, this provision has been an endless source of varying interpretations and conflicting analyses. The least of the problems with the 1985 Act was whether the company was a party to the contract. CA 2006 makes it clear that it is. But, beyond that, the words in the new provision largely duplicate its predecessor, so the same uncertainties seem destined to plague this area. The following extracts are all likely to remain relevant.

---

[61] See the *Hickman* **[4.38]** and *Eley* **[4.37]** cases.

[62] See *Pender v Lushington* **[13.23]** and *MacDougall v Gardiner* **[13.24]**, and see also the Notes and Further notes following *Pender v Lushington* **[13.23]**, pp 703ff.

[63] See *Johnson v Gore, Wood & Co* **[13.26]** and *Giles v Rhind* **[13.27]**, and 'The "no reflective loss" principle', pp 706ff.

Any member has the right[64] to enforce observance of the terms of the constitution, by virtue of the contractual effect given to the constitution by CA 2006 s 33.

[4.36] Wood v Odessa Waterworks Co (1889) 42 Ch D 636
(Chancery Division)

The articles empowered the directors, with the sanction of a general meeting of members, to declare a dividend 'to be paid' to the shareholders. The company passed an ordinary resolution proposing to pay no dividend but instead to give the shareholders debenture-bonds (in effect, obliging them to lend back to the company the money which could have been paid as dividends, for anything up to 30 years). Wood, a shareholder, sought an injunction to restrain the company from acting on the resolution. It was held that the proposal was inconsistent with the articles, and the injunction was accordingly granted.

STIRLING J: It was not disputed that profits available for the payment of a dividend by the company had been actually earned...Neither was it disputed that the company had power to create a charge on the assets of the company, or to raise money by means of such a charge, or to apply the money so raised in payment of a dividend. The question, simply, is whether it is within the power of a majority of the shareholders to insist against the will of a minority that the profits which have been actually earned shall be divided, not by the payment of cash, but by the issue of debenture-bonds of the company bearing interest at £5 per cent and repayable at par by an annual drawing extending over thirty years. It is to be inferred from the terms in which the bonds are offered for subscription that the company cannot issue them in the open market except at a discount of at least £10 per cent. Now the rights of the shareholders in respect of a division of the profits of the company are governed by the provisions in the articles of association. By s 16 of the Companies Act 1862 [CA 2006 s 33] the articles of association 'bind the company and the members thereof to the same extent as if each member had subscribed his name and affixed his seal thereto, and there were in such articles contained a covenant on the part of himself, his heirs, executors, and administrators, to conform to all the regulations contained in such articles, subject to the provisions of this Act'. Section 50 of the Act [CA 2006 s 21] provides the means for altering the regulations of the company contained in the articles of association by passing a special resolution, but no such resolution has in this case been passed or attempted to be passed; and the question is, whether this is a matter as to which the majority of the shareholders can bind those shareholders who dissent. The articles of association constitute a contract not merely between the shareholders and the company, but between each individual shareholder and every other; and the question which I have just stated must in my opinion be answered in the negative if there be in the articles a contract between the shareholders as to a division of profits, and the provisions of that contract have not been followed...That then brings me to consider whether that which is proposed to be done in the present case is in accordance with the articles of association of the company. Those articles provide...that the directors may, with the sanction of a general meeting, declare a dividend to be paid to the shareholders. Prima facie that means to be paid in cash. The debenture-bonds proposed to be issued are not payments in cash; they are merely agreements or promises to pay: and if the contention of the company prevails a shareholder will be compelled to accept in lieu of cash a debt of the company payable at some uncertain future period. In my opinion that contention ought not to prevail...

[64] See the following Notes and also the discussion following *Hickman*'s case [4.38], pp 267ff.

Where the rights of an individual member have been infringed, personal action to enforce such rights individual loss is possible, even though the conduct complained of may also constitute a wrong to the company itself.

See *Pender v Lushington* **[13.23]**. However, any claim for loss or damage is likely to face the '*reflective loss*' arguments discussed at 'The "no reflective loss" principle', pp 706ff.

The articles do not constitute a contract between the company and someone who is not a member.

[4.37] Eley v Positive Government Security Life Assurance Co Ltd (1876) 1 Ex D 88 (Court of Appeal)

Article 118 of the company's articles provided: 'Mr William Eley, of No 27, New Broad Street, in the City of London, shall be the solicitor to the company, and shall transact all the legal business of the company, including parliamentary business, for the usual and accustomed fees and charges, and shall not be removed from his office except for misconduct.' Eley, the plaintiff, who had himself drafted the company's documents for registration, and who became a member several months after its incorporation, sued the company for breach of contract in not employing him as its solicitor. In the Exchequer Division, it was held that the articles did not create any contract between Eley and the company. Eley appealed, but the Court of Appeal affirmed the decision.

> LORD CAIRNS LC: This case was first rested on the 118th article. Articles of association, as is well known, follow the memorandum, which states the objects of the company, while the articles state the arrangement between the members. They are an agreement *inter socios*, and in that view, if the introductory words are applied to article 118, it becomes a covenant between the parties to it that they will employ the plaintiff. Now, so far as that is concerned, it is res inter alios acta, the plaintiff is no party to it. No doubt he thought that by inserting it he was making his employment safe as against the company; but his relying on that view of the law does not alter the legal effect of the articles. This article is either a stipulation which would bind the members, or else a mandate to the directors. In either case it is a matter between the directors and shareholders, and not between them and the plaintiff....
> LORD COLERIDGE CJ and MELLISH LJ concurred.

➤ Notes

1. The judgments do not deal with the question whether it was relevant that Eley did take shares in the company at a later stage and so would then have become entitled to enforce whatever rights his membership conferred on him.

2. This case is commonly cited as authority for the proposition that the articles could confer rights on Eley only in his capacity as a member and not as the company's solicitor. But this reasoning forms no part of the *ratio decidendi*, and was first put forward in *Hickman*'s case **[4.38]**.

3. The Contracts (Rights of Third Parties) Act 1999 abrogates in part the traditional doctrine of privity of contract, by providing that a term in a contract which purports to confer a benefit on a person who is not a party to it may in stated circumstances be enforced by that person. Theoretically, this provision might now have enabled a person in the position of Mr Eley to enforce a term such as art 118, but s 6(2) of the 1999 Act expressly excludes the CA 2006 s 33 contract from its scope.

The effect of s 33 is to bind the company itself, as well as the members, by the terms of the articles. But the contract which s 33 creates affects the members only in their capacity as members, and not in any special or personal capacity (eg as director).

[4.38] Hickman v Kent or Romney Marsh Sheep-Breeders' Association [1915] 1 Ch 881 (Chancery Division)

The defendant association was incorporated as a non-profit-making company. Article 49 of its articles of association provided that disputes between the association and any of its members should be referred to arbitration. Hickman, a member, brought this action complaining of various irregularities in the affairs of the association, including the refusal to register his sheep in its published flock book, and a threat to expel him from membership. The association was granted a stay of proceedings on the ground that the statutory provision corresponding to the present s 33 made art 49 an agreement to arbitrate, enforceable as between the association and a member.

ASTBURY J: This is a summons by the defendants to stay proceedings in the action pursuant to s 4 of the Arbitration Act 1889 [now Arbitration Act 1996 s 9]. The action is against the defendant association and their secretary Chapman, and the plaintiff, who became a member in 1905, claims certain injunctions and a declaration and other relief in respect of matters arising out of and relating solely to the affairs of the association. In substance he claims to enforce his rights under the association's articles...[After stating the objects of the association and reading art 49 as to arbitration, his Lordship continued:] This is a common form of article in private companies, and the objects of this association being what they are, it and its members might be seriously prejudiced by a public trial of their disputes, and if this summons fails, as the plaintiff contends that it should, these arbitration clauses in articles are of very little, if any, value.

It is clear on the authorities that if there is a submission to arbitration within the meaning of the Arbitration Act 1889, there is a prima facie duty cast upon the court to act upon such an agreement...

In the present case the defendants contend, first, that article 49, dealing as it does with the members of the association, in their capacity of members only, constitutes a submission within the meaning of the Arbitration Act, or, secondly, that the contract contained in the plaintiff's application for membership and the association's acceptance of it amounts to such a submission. The plaintiff contests both these propositions, and independently of the particular dispute in this case, the arguments, especially upon the first of these contentions, have raised questions of far-reaching importance.

I will first deal with the question as to the effect of article 49. [His Lordship read s 14(1) of the 1908 Act (equivalent to the present CA 2006 s 33), and referred to the long-standing dispute among leading textbook writers as to its precise effect. He continued:]

The principal authorities in support of the view that the articles do not constitute a contract between the company and its members are *Pritchard's Case*,[65] *Melhado v Porto Alegre Rly Co*,[66] *Eley v Positive Life Assurance Co* **[4.37]** and *Browne v La Trinidad*.[67]

In *Pritchard's* case the articles of association of a mining company provided that the company should immediately after incorporation enter into an agreement with De Thierry the vendor for the purchase of the mine for £2,000 and 3,200 fully paid shares. The articles were signed by the vendor and six other persons, and the directors allotted the 3,200 shares to the vendor or his nominees, but no further agreement was made with him. It was held, affirming the decision of

---

[65] (1873) 8 Ch App 956.
[66] (1874) LR 9 CP 503.
[67] (1887) 37 Ch D 1, CA.

Wickens V-C, that the articles of association did not constitute a contract in writing between the vendor and the company within s 25 of the Companies Act 1867, and that the shares could not therefore be considered as fully paid.[68] Mellish LJ in giving judgment said: 'I am of opinion that the articles of association cannot be considered as a contract in writing between De Thierry and the company for the sale of the mine to them. It may, no doubt, be the case, if no other contract was entered into, and if De Thierry signed these articles and they were acted upon, that a court of equity would hold that as between him and the company—from their acting upon it—there was a binding contract; but in themselves the articles of association are simply a contract as between the shareholders inter se in respect of their rights as shareholders. They are the deeds of partnership by which the shareholders agree inter se.'

[The discussion of *Melhado v Porto Alegre Rly Co* and *Eley v Positive Life Assurance Co* is omitted.] In *Browne v La Trinidad* before the formation of the company an agreement was entered into between B and a person as trustee for the intended company, by which it was stipulated (inter alia) that B should be a director and should not be removable till after 1888. The sixth clause of the articles provided that the directors should adopt and carry into effect the agreement with or without modification, and that subject to such modification (if any) the provisions of the agreement should be construed as part of the articles. The agreement was acted upon, but no contract adopting it was entered into between the plaintiff and the company. It was held that treating the agreement as embodied in the articles, still there was no contract between B and the company that he should not be removed from being a director, the articles being only a contract between the members inter se, and not between the company and B...Lindley LJ said: 'Having regard to the construction put upon [s 33] in the case of *Eley v Positive Live Assurance Co* and subsequent cases, it must be taken as settled that the contract upon which he relies is not a contract upon which he can maintain any action, either on the common law side or the equity side. There might have been some difficulty in arriving at that conclusion if it had not been for the authorities, because it happens that this gentleman has had shares allotted to him, and is therefore a member of the company. Having regard to the terms of [s 33], there would be some force, or at all events some plausibility, in the argument that, being a member, the contract which is referred to in the articles has become binding between the company and him. Of course that argument is open to this difficulty that there could be no contract between him and the company until the shares were allotted to him, and it would be remarkable that, upon the shares being allotted to him, a contract between him and the company, as to a matter not connected with the holding of shares, should arise.'

Now in these four cases the article relied upon purported to give specific contractual rights to persons in some capacity other than that of shareholder, and in none of them were members seeking to enforce or protect rights given to them as members, in common with the other corporators. The actual decisions amount to this. An outsider to whom rights purport to be given by the articles in his capacity as such outsider, whether he is or subsequently becomes a member, cannot sue on those articles treating them as contracts between himself and the company to enforce those rights. Those rights are not part of the general regulations of the company applicable alike to all shareholders and can only exist by virtue of some contract between such person and the company, and the subsequent allotment of shares to an outsider in whose favour such an article is inserted does not enable him to sue the company on such an article to enforce rights which are res inter alios acta and not part of the general rights of the corporators as such...

The wording of [s 33] is difficult to construe or understand. A company cannot in the ordinary course be bound otherwise than by statute or contract and it is in this section that its obligation must be found. As far as the members are concerned, the section does not say with whom they are to be deemed to have covenanted, but the section cannot mean that the company is not to

---

[68] This section required the registration in advance of all contracts for the issue of shares for a consideration other than cash.

be bound when it says it is to be bound, as if, etc, nor can the section mean that the members are to be under no obligation to the company under the articles in which their rights and duties as corporators are to be found. Much of the difficulty is removed if the company be regarded, as the framers of the section may very well have so regarded it, as being treated in law as a party to its own memorandum and articles.

It seems clear from other authorities that a company is entitled as against its members to enforce and restrain breaches of its regulations. See, for example, *MacDougall v Gardiner* **[13.24]**, *Pender v Lushington* **[13.23]** and *Imperial Hydropathic Hotel Co, Blackpool v Hampson* **[4.04]**. In the last case Bowen LJ said: 'The articles of association, by [s 33], are to bind all the company and all the shareholders as much as if they had put their seals to them.'

It is also clear from many authorities that shareholders as against their company can enforce and restrain breaches of its regulations, and in many of these cases judicial expressions of opinion appear, which, in my judgment, it is impossible to disregard.

[His Lordship referred to a number of other cases, including *Wood v Odessa Waterworks Co* **[4.36]** and *Salmon v Quin & Axtens Ltd*.[69] He continued:]

In all these last mentioned cases the respective articles sought to be enforced related to the rights and obligations of the members generally as such and not to rights of the character dealt with in the four authorities first above referred to.

It is difficult to reconcile these two classes of decisions and the judicial opinions therein expressed, but I think this much is clear, first, that no article can constitute a contract between the company and a third person; secondly, that no right merely purporting to be given by an article to a person, whether a member or not, in a capacity other than that of a member, as, for instance, as solicitor, promoter, director, can be enforced against the company; and, thirdly, that articles regulating the rights and obligations of the members generally as such do create rights and obligations between them and the company respectively. . . .

In the present case, the plaintiff's action is, in substance, to enforce his rights as a member under the articles against the association. Article 49 is a general article applying to all the members as such, and, apart from technicalities, it would seem reasonable that the plaintiff ought not to be allowed in the absence of any evidence filed by him to proceed with an action to enforce his rights under the articles, seeing that the action is a breach of his obligation under article 49 to submit his disputes with the association to arbitration. . . .

It is apparent that for a considerable period before *Hickman*'s case there had been uncertainty about the scope and effect of the statutory provision which is now CA 2006 s 33. The controversy centred on three related questions:

(i)   Who were the parties to the 'statutory contract'—the members and the company, or just the members?

(ii)   Were the members deemed to have covenanted with each other, or with the company, or both?

(iii) Could one member sue another directly on the contract, or could the member enforce the statutory rights only through the company?

These questions have been conclusively resolved in the 2006 Act, which makes explicit mention of both the company and its members and provides that the contract may contain rights which are directly enforceable by one member against another, although on the question of one member enforcing rights against another, much may depend on what it is exactly that the right purports to confer.

---

[69] [1909] 1 Ch 311, CA, affd **[4.06]**.

But in his attempts to reconcile the decisions—or at least the results reached—in the earlier cases, it has to be conceded that Astbury J paid little regard to the actual *ratio decidendi* of some of them, and added a gloss to CA 1908 s 14(1) which appears to contradict its express wording ('*all* the provisions of the memorandum and articles of association').[70] It is really quite remarkable that so shaky a first-instance decision was tacitly accepted for the greater part of a century in relation to CA 1908 s 14(1) and CA 1985 s 14, and endorsed without any discussion by the Court of Appeal in *Beattie v E & F Beattie Ltd* [1938] Ch 708. In that case the defendant, a director, also sought to invoke an arbitration clause contained in the articles, when he was sued by his company for the return of certain sums which it was alleged had been improperly paid to him. The court ruled that since he was being sued in his capacity as a *director* and not that as a *member*, he could not rely on the 'statutory contract'.

Hickman's case may have laid some earlier controversies to rest, but it has generated several new ones of its own. *First*, there are a number of cases which it is not easy to reconcile with the '*qua* member' rule: for example, *Pulbrook v Richmond Consolidated Mining Co* **[6.01]**, *Imperial Hydropathic Hotel Co, Blackpool v Hampson* **[4.04]**, *Quin & Axtens Ltd v Salmon* **[4.06]**. In each of these, rights more in the nature of management-rights than member-rights were enforced.

Secondly, there is an inherent conflict in the two propositions which may be deduced from the cases: (i) that any member has a right to have the provisions of the corporate constitution duly observed; and (ii) that s 33 cannot be relied on to enforce the rights of a non-member, or the 'outsider-rights' of one who is a member (but also a director, solicitor, etc), which the articles purportedly confer.

Some commentators (eg Lord Wedderburn [1957] CLJ 194 at 212) have sought to resolve the problem by saying that a member can sue under s 33 to enforce his right to have all the provisions of the corporate constitution observed, even where this would have the consequence of indirectly enforcing 'outsider-rights', so long as he *sues* in his capacity as a member. So, for instance, a disinterested member of the Positive Life company could have sued for an injunction to restrain the company from employing any solicitor other than the constitutionally appointed Mr Eley, and by the same argument Mr Eley himself, suing *qua* member, could have obtained similar relief.

Others would argue that a solution to the conflict lies in a narrowing of proposition (i), above, to say that it is not *every* provision of the articles that can be enforced by a member, but only those which are of a 'constitutional' character. (This requires us to beg the question, for example, by saying that the stipulation that Mr Eley should be the solicitor was not part of the corporate constitution but peripheral to it.) More specifically, GD Goldberg (1972) 35 MLR 362,[71] would confine the members' statutory contractual right to that of having the company's affairs conducted by the particular *organ* of the company which is specified as the appropriate body in the Act or in the articles of association. GN Prentice (1980) 1 Co Law 179, considers that it is necessary to go further, and ask whether the provision in question affects the power of the company to *function*: only then can a member sue to enforce a non-member right.

None of these arguments is really convincing, however far they may go towards reconciling the inconsistent decisions. Each of them involves writing even more by way of gloss into CA 1985 s 14 (now CA 2006 s 33) than Astbury J did, and reading more into some of the judgments than the judges themselves said. Section 14 (and now s 33) was enacted to cover a gap which was thought to have been created when the memorandum and articles replaced the deed of settlement in 1856, and in particular to ensure that a company

---

[70] R Gregory (1981) 44 MLR 526 argues that for these reasons the decision in *Hickman*'s case is insupportable, and that it should be reconsidered despite its long acceptance.
[71] Reaffirmed in (1985) 48 MLR 158.

could enforce a member's liability to pay calls. Its relevance in today's conditions may be regarded as questionable, for it perpetuates the notion that the only 'constituents' of a company are its members (ignoring the claims of employees, management and other 'stakeholders' whose interests in the company and its constituents are arguably quite as significant), and it also puts the relationship between members and company into a contractual straitjacket—a characteristically nineteenth-century approach to many difficult legal questions—which is far from appropriate. (It is also evident that the 'contract' created by s 33 departs radically in a number of respects from the contract of classic tradition: see below.)

A similar gloss was put by the courts on CA 1948 s 210, the early precursor of CA 2006 s 994 (the 'unfair prejudice' provision, see 'Unfairly prejudicial conduct of the company's affairs', pp 715ff): a member bringing a complaint to the court under that section had to show that the conduct in question affected him *qua* member. CA 2006 s 994, and CA 1985 s 459 before it, has been reworded so as to meet many of the criticisms which were levelled at s 210, but no attempt was made to deal with this point. The judges have accordingly been obliged to construe the new section in the same way; but (at least in cases where the company is a 'quasi-partnership') some flexibility has been achieved by giving a fairly broad meaning to the concept of a 'membership' interest. In *Ebrahimi v Westbourne Galleries Ltd* [16.13], the House of Lords did not feel constrained to put the same restriction on the statutory provision which allows a member to petition to have the company wound up.

Thirdly, it is not possible to say that every 'right' which the memorandum or articles purport to confer on a member is enforceable in an absolute sense.[72] The statutory contract which these documents are deemed to create is very different from the classical stereotype, such as a contract for the sale of goods. It is a 'relational' contract,[73] intended to establish a framework for an ongoing set of relationships, rather than one containing a discrete set of obligations which, once performed, will come to an end. Relational contracts necessarily embody an underlying element of 'give and take', rather than outright right and wrong. Moreover, many constitutional irregularities are curable by a majority resolution of the members, or even capable of being condoned by acquiescence or inertia. In *MacDougall v Gardiner* [13.24], for instance, a member's undoubted right to call for a poll was denied him, but the court declined to come to his aid because the matter could be put right (if anyone wanted to) by the company's own internal mechanisms. Even irregularities which the majority have no power to condone may be defeated by the procedural rule known as *Foss v Harbottle* [13.01], under which the member may find that he has no access to the court unless he can carry the majority along with him [13.19]. Any claim that s 33 gives a member a 'right' to have the terms of the constitution observed is defective unless it acknowledges that the right is qualified in these senses.

One member may sue another on the contract created by the articles without joining the company as a party.

[4.39] Rayfield v Hands [1960] Ch 1 (Chancery Division)

Article 11 of the articles of association of Field-Davis Ltd provided: 'Every member who intends to transfer shares shall inform the directors who will take the said shares equally between them at a fair value . . .' Rayfield, a member, sought to compel the defendants, the

---

[72] See RR Drury, 'The Relative Nature of the Shareholder's Right to Enforce the Company Contract' [1986] CLJ 219.

[73] On relational contracts, see IA Macneil, 'Contracts: Adjustment of Long-Term Economic Relations under Classical, Neo-Classical and Relational Contract Law' (1978) 72 *North Western UL Rev* 854.

three directors of the company, to purchase his shares in accordance with this provision. The court declared that they were bound to do so.

VAISEY J dealt first with a question of construction, and continued: The next and most difficult point taken by the defendants, as to which it would appear that there is no very clear judicial authority, is that article 11, as part of the company's articles of association, does not do what it looks like doing, that is, to create a contractual relationship between the plaintiff as shareholder and vendor and the defendants as directors and purchasers. This depends on s 20(1) of the Companies Act 1948 [CA 2006 s 33]. [His Lordship read the section and passages from various textbooks. He continued:]

Now the question arises at the outset whether the terms of article 11 relate to the rights of members inter se (that being the expression found in so many of the cases), or whether the relationship is between a member as such and directors as such. I may dispose of this point very briefly by saying that, in my judgment, the relationship here is between the plaintiff as a member and the defendants not as directors but as members.

In *Re Leicester Club and County Racecourse Co*,[74] Pearson J, referring to the directors of a company, said that they 'continue members of the company, and I prefer to call them working members of the company,' and on the same page he also said: 'directors cannot divest themselves of their character of members of the company. From first to last...they are doing their work in the capacity of members, and working members of the company . . .'. I am of opinion, therefore, that this is in words a contract or quasi-contract between members, and not between members and directors.

I have now to deal with the point for which there is considerable support in the cases, that the notional signing and sealing of the articles creates a contractual relation between the company on the one hand and the corporators (members) on the other, so that no relief can be obtained in the absence of company as a party to the suit. The defendants' case in so far as it is based on this point seems to be met by two recent decisions of the Court of Appeal. I refer first to *Smith and Snipes Hall Farm Ltd v River Douglas Catchment Board*,[75] and to the judgment of Denning LJ in that case, which was a case of a covenant made, not by or with but for the benefit of the plaintiffs, and thereby enabling them to sue without the intervention of the covenantee. Section 56 of the Law of Property Act 1925 was referred to in terms which it is not necessary for me to repeat here. This same principle is further exemplified by the case of *Drive Yourself Hire Co (London) Ltd v Strutt*,[76] see especially the judgment of Denning LJ as there reported.[77] The case of the plaintiff may also be said to rest upon the well-known decision of *Carlill v Carbolic Smoke Ball Co*,[78] to which I need not refer except to say that it seems to me to be relevant here. To the like effect is *Clarke v Earl of Dunraven*,[79] upon which the plaintiff here also relied...

[His Lordship discussed a number of other cases, including *Hickman*'s case **[4.38]** and continued:]

The conclusion to which I have come may not be of so general an application as to extend to the articles of association of every company, for it is, I think, material to remember that this private company is one of that class of companies which bears a close analogy to a partnership; see the well-known passages in *Re Yenidje Tobacco Co*.[80]

Nobody, I suppose, would doubt that a partnership deed might validly and properly provide for the acquisition of the share of one partner by another partner on terms identical with those of article 11 in the present case. I do not intend to decide more in the present case than is necessary

---

[74] (1885) 30 Ch D 629 at 633.

[75] [1949] 2 KB 500, CA.

[76] [1954] 1 QB 250, CA.

[77] Lord Denning's *dicta* in these cases were disapproved in *Beswick v Beswick* [1968] AC 58, HL. But it is arguable that the decision in *Beswick*'s case as a whole gives some support to the reasoning of Vaisey J here.

[78] [1893] 1 QB 256, CA.

[79] [1897] AC 59, HL.

[80] [1916] 2 Ch 426, CA.

to support my conclusion, though it may be that the principles upon which my conclusion is founded are of more general application than might be supposed from some of the authorities on the point.

I will make an appropriate declaration of the plaintiff's rights, or will order the defendants to give effect to them, and if necessary there must be an inquiry to ascertain the fair value of the shares...

➤ Notes

1. The judge in this case circumvented the difficulty raised by *Hickman*'s case **[4.38]** and *Beattie v E & F Beattie Ltd* (see discussion following *Hickman v Kent or Romney Marsh Sheep-Breeders' Association* **[4.38]**, pp 267ff) by the blunt assertion that the article affected the directors 'not as directors but as members'. In the case before him, the directors did happen to be members, and were, in fact, required by the company's articles to hold shares. But in many companies this is not so. The judgment as a whole rather too readily assumes that directors are bound to be members—something that was more likely to be true a century ago when the *Leicester Racecourse* case was decided than it is today.

2. In *Newtherapeutics Ltd v Katz* [1991] Ch 226, Knox J held that the appointment of a person to the office of director did not of itself establish a contractual relationship between him and the company. He might, and commonly would, also enter into a contract (eg of employment) with the company; but merely as office-holder such rights and duties as he had were not based on any contract, express or implied. Vaisey J's reference to *Carlill v Carbolic Smoke Ball Co* and *Clarke v Earl of Dunraven* would not appear to be compatible with this ruling.

➤ Question

CA 2006 s 33 substantially re-enacts its predecessor, CA 1985 s 14. This is despite the fact that both the Law Commissions (*Shareholder Remedies*, Law Com No 246, 1997) and the CLR considered possible amendments to CA 1985 s 14, particularly with a view to defining by statute which rights are 'membership' rights (as distinct from rights which are better seen as vested in the company itself), and are accordingly rights which members can enforce in their personal capacity. Both bodies initially toyed with, but eventually rejected, the idea of setting out in the legislation a non-exhaustive list of such 'personal' rights (eg to attend and vote at meetings and to receive dividends). The CLR also considered whether it would be preferable to declare *all* obligations imposed by the constitution to be enforceable by individual members (subject to an exception where the complaint is trivial or where to pursue it would be pointless), unless the contrary is provided in the constitution. What are the advantages and disadvantages of each approach?

▨ Further reading

AHERN D AND MAHER K, 'The Continuing Evolution of Proxy Representation' [2011] JBL 125.

BAINBRIDGE, S, 'Director Primacy and Shareholder Disempowerment' (2006) 119 *Harvard Law Review* 1735.

BEBCHUK, L, 'The Case for Increasing Shareholder Power' (2005) 118 *Harvard Law Review* 833.

CHEUNG, R, 'The Use of Statutory Unanimous Shareholder Agreements and Entrenched Articles in Reserving Minority Shareholders' Rights: A Comparative Analysis' (2008) 29 *Company Lawyer* 234.

DRURY, RR, 'The Relative Nature of the Shareholder's Right to Enforce the Company Contract' [1986] CLJ 219.

FERRAN, E, 'The Decision of the House of Lords in *Russell v Northern Bank Development Corporation Limited*' [1994] CLJ 343.

FINN, PD, 'Shareholder Agreements' (1978) 6 *Australian Business Law Review* 97.

GODDARD, R, 'The *Re Duomatic* Principle and Sections 320–322 of the Companies Act 1985' [2004] JBL 121.

GOLDBERG, GD, 'The Controversy of the Section 20 Contract Revisited' (1985) 48 MLR 158.

GOLDBERG, GD, 'The Enforcement of Outsider Rights under Section 20(1) of the Companies Act 1948' (1972) 35 MLR 363.

GOWER, LCB, 'The Contractual Effect of Articles of Association' (1958) 21 MLR 401.

GRANTHAM, R, 'The Doctrinal Basis of the Rights of Company Shareholders' [1998] CLJ 554.

HANNIGAN, B, 'Altering the Articles to Provide for Compulsory Transfer—Dragging Minority Shareholders to a Reluctant Exit' [2007] JBL 471.

MARSDEN, A, 'Does a Shareholders' Agreement Require Filing with the Registrar of Companies?' (1994) 15 *Company Lawyer* 19.

PRENTICE, D, 'The Enforcement of Outsider Rights' (1980) 1 *Company Lawyer* 179.

RILEY, CA, 'The Not-So-Dynamic Quality of Corporate Law: A UK Perspective on Hansmann's "Corporation and Contract"' (2010) 21 *King's Law Journal* 469.

RIXON, FG, 'Competing Interests and Conflicting Principles: An Examination of the Power of Alteration of Articles of Association' (1986) 49 MLR 446.

SEALY, LS, '"Bona Fides" and "Proper Purposes" in Corporate Decisions' [1989] *Monash University Law Review* 16.

SEALY, LS, 'Equitable and Other Fetters on the Shareholder's Freedom to Vote' in NE Eastham and B Krivy (eds), *The Cambridge Lectures 1981* (1981).

WEDDERBURN, KW, 'Shareholders Rights and the Rule in *Foss v Harbottle*' [1957] CLJ 194 and [1958] CLJ 93.

WORTHINGTON, S, 'Corporate Governance: Remedying and Ratifying Directors' Breaches' (2000) 116 LQR 638.

XUEREB, PG, 'Voting Rights: A Comparative Review' (1987) 8 *Company Lawyer* 16.

XUEREB, PG, 'Remedies for Abuse of Majority Power' (1986) 7 *Company Lawyer* 53.

XUEREB, PG, 'The Limitation on the Exercise of Majority Power' (1985) 6 *Company Lawyer* 199.

5

CORPORATE GOVERNANCE

General issues

The company is an artificial legal person, and can only act through its human representatives. We saw in the last chapter that a company's constitution typically divides management power between the board of directors and the general meeting. Members cannot instruct the directors on how to exercise the powers assigned to the directors (see 'Orthodox constitutional division of powers', pp 190ff). Indeed, many members of medium to large companies (but not small ones) are attracted to the corporate form precisely because it provides investment opportunities without management responsibilities (the famous 'separation of ownership and control'). Instead, management is conducted by the directors.

The 'agency problems' associated with this are obvious: the directors may use their extensive powers for their own benefit rather than for the benefit of the passive member investors. What mechanisms are typically put in place to manage this problem? As it turns out, there are relatively few imposed by law. The detailed construction and implementation of risk management and reward strategies is left largely to individual companies to work out for themselves. This does not always deliver satisfactory results. The few legal rules relating to the appointment, tenure and remuneration of directors allow those who control a company considerable scope to look after their own interests, generally without any serious risk of being successfully challenged by the minority.[1] Even where the directors do not hold the majority of voting shares, the passive attitude of most members towards company general meetings and corporate decisions means that directors can often ensure they are re-elected when their terms expire, that their service contracts contain advantageous provisions and that directors' fees, salaries and perks are set at an attractive level. Of these, the level of directors' remuneration often comes in for attack and unfavourable comment. The 2008 financial crisis focused public attention on these issues, especially in the context of banks, and many popular risk–reward strategies have come in for serious criticism.

Some of this has been carefully researched. In 2011, Professor John Kay was commissioned by the Secretary of State for Business, Innovation and Skills to 'examine investment in UK equity markets and its impact on the long-term performance and governance of

---

[1] It is important to be aware of the differences between executive and non-executive directors (see 'Balance of executive and non-executive directors', p 277); appointed, *de facto* and shadow directors (see 'Directors' general duties are also owed by *de facto* and shadow directors', pp 328ff); alternate directors and nominee directors. These different categories are not mutually exclusive.

UK quoted companies'. Professor Kay's findings were published in an Interim Report in February 2012, and a Final Report in July 2012.

In his Final Report, Professor Kay identified what he perceived as the major shortcomings in the status quo, before setting out a series of recommendations of good practice. He highlighted the palpable lack of trust and confidence generated by the current focus on the short-term interests of financial agents to the detriment of the long-term interests of the underlying beneficiaries/investors. An October 2014 report on the implementation of the recommendations made in the Kay Review concluded that 'good progress' had been made.[2] These include the government's reforms on corporate narrative reporting, revisions to 'soft law' regimes (see the following section) such as the Corporate Governance Code and the Stewardship Code, and a series of guidance notes published by the Financial Reporting Council (FRC). A list of further work to be undertaken by the government was said to demonstrate 'the Government's continued focus on ensuring that public equity markets support the long-term success of UK companies which is vital to future economic prosperity'.

While the Kay Review is one of the more recent initiatives to review and make recommendations for improving the effectiveness of corporate governance, it is certainly not the first. The development of this type of soft law began as a private initiative, in response to falling public confidence in standards of corporate governance in major public companies, including public concern about levels of directors' remuneration. Little has changed, it seems. The 'Cadbury Committee' was set up in 1991 jointly by the Stock Exchange, the FRC (see later) and the accountancy profession under the chairmanship of Sir Adrian Cadbury. The Committee's remit was to consider the subject of 'corporate governance', particularly its financial aspects. It published its report in December 1992, and, while it did not propose changes in the law, it proposed the adoption on a voluntary basis by larger (listed) companies of a code of best practice which addressed many of these matters of public concern. These best practice principles became known as the 'Cadbury Code'.

The Cadbury Committee spawned various successor committees seeking to improve upon its work. The most important were those delivering the Greenbury (1995), Hampel (1998) and Higgs and Smith (2003) Reports. The Hampel Committee not only reviewed the Cadbury Code, but also undertook a consolidation exercise, producing a new 'Combined Code' in 1998.[3] This code dealt more generally with matters of corporate governance, incorporating rules of best practice from both the Cadbury and Greenbury Committees' recommendations. This Combined Code became the responsibility of the FRC and has been further revised over the years, resulting in the renamed version, the UK Corporate Governance Code, the most recent version of which is dated April 2016, and has applied to listed companies for accounting periods beginning on or after 17 June 2016.[4] This provides some commendable 'soft law' rules, although only for listed companies (regardless, however, of their place of incorporation).

It is noteworthy that the European Commission, too, is introducing reforms to existing rules in order to 'tackle corporate governance shortcomings'.[5] The process began in April 2014, when the Commission issued a package to revise the Shareholder Rights Directive,[6] as well as a recommendation on the quality of corporate governance reporting ('comply or explain').[7] The former will, amongst others, introduce a 'say on pay' similar to the

---

[2] www.gov.uk/government/uploads/system/uploads/attachment_data/file/367070/bis-14-1157-implementation-of-the-kay-review-progress-report.pdf.

[3] These predecessor Codes are all available at www.ecgi.org/codes/all_codes.php#United%20Kingdom.

[4] www.frc.org.uk/Our-Work/Publications/Corporate-Governance/Final-Draft-UK-Corporate-Governance-Code-2016.pdf (draft version).

[5] www.europarl.europa.eu/news/en/news-room/20150703IPR73902/Corporate-governance-MEPs-vote-to-enforce-tax-transparency.

[6] http://europa.eu/rapid/press-release_IP-14-396_en.htm.

[7] See the UK response on progress in implementing recommendations: www.frc.org.uk/News-and-Events/FRC-Press/Press/2015/July/UK-responds-to-European-Commission-s-Recommendatio.aspx.

mandatory vote every three years under the UK regime. As of July 2015, the text, as amended by Parliament, has been approved by MEPs, but the first reading remains open, subject to further negotiation on the terms of the final agreement.[8]

FRC and the UK Corporate Governance Code for listed companies

In the UK, the FRC is the independent regulator responsible for promoting high-quality corporate governance and reporting. It has responsibility for the UK Corporate Governance Code (the Code). This Code describes 'best practice' corporate governance for large public companies. It is not enshrined in legislation, but is 'soft law'—that is, there is no legal compulsion to obey. Nevertheless, even without statutory backing, it is in practice virtually obligatory for listed companies to adhere to it in most respects. The Stock Exchange has appended the Code to the Stock Exchange Listing Rules, and requires every listed company to include in its annual report a statement of whether it has applied the principles of the Code, how it has applied them and, to the extent that it has not applied them, the reasons why it has not. This approach is now routinely described as a 'comply or explain' regulatory regime, and has been adopted in many other jurisdictions around the world to address corporate governance issues.

This 'comply or explain' procedure has been subjected to ongoing review both domestically and on an international level in order to improve its utility.[9] In the latest of the reviews of the Code, in January 2016, the FRC published 'Developments in Corporate Governance and Stewardship in 2015' (the '2015 Review')[10] which evaluates successes and failures to date, and paves the way for further amendments. The process of 'comply or explain' is one of the key areas for improvement, particularly in terms of the quality of 'explanations' given where there is a departure from the Code. This is said to be necessary to enable shareholders to assess whether they are content with the governance arrangements that the company has put in place.

The UK Corporate Governance Code (like its predecessors) is different from legislation in two ways. First, it is not the product of a parliamentary process, but of a series of committees representing business and financial interests, and now an independent regulatory body. These have all elaborated the Code in recent years. Secondly, the Code is binding only on listed companies (by virtue of a provision in the Listing Rules) but, even then, only on a 'comply or explain' basis (see earlier): Listing Rules r 9.8.6(5) and (6).[11]

More generally, reviews of the Code bring to the fore the wider question: to what extent are these non-binding codes effective and to be preferred to hard law? Baroness Hogg, previous Chairman of the FRC, noted in the similar review dated December 2011[12] some

---

[8] www.europarl.europa.eu/news/en/news-room/20150703IPR73902/Corporate-governance-MEPs-vote-to-enforce-tax-transparency.

[9] The European Commission has established a European Corporate Governance Institute to encourage the coordination of national corporate governance codes: see www.ecgi.org/. See the key findings of the 16th Corporate Governance Conference (13 May 2015: www.ecgi.org/presidency/riga2015/key_findings.pdf. In the light of concerns raised on a European level in relation to the effectiveness of the 'comply or explain' mechanism, the FRC published a guideline providing an explanation and defence of the procedure: www.frc.org.uk/Our-Work/Publications/FRC-Board/Report-of-discussions-between-companies-and-invest.aspx.

[10] www.frc.org.uk/Our-Work/Publications/Corporate-Governance/Developments-in-Corporate-Governance-and-Stewa-%281%29.pdf (January 2016).

[11] Available at: www.handbook.fca.org.uk/handbook/LR./ (under 'Listing, Prospectus and Disclosure').

[12] www.frc.org.uk/Our-Work/Publications/Corporate-Governance/Developments-in-Corporate-Governance-2011-The-impa.aspx.

European pressure for additional *legal* limitations on the powers of boards and general meetings (rather than the more flexible 'comply or explain' codes of best practice). However, the FRC remains opposed to this approach, especially given the economic consequences any change might bring in deterring investment in the UK, and with it the flow of equity capital which is so necessary for economic growth. In the 2015 Review, Sir Winfried Bischoff, the incumbent Chairman of the FRC, highlighted the need to breed and maintain a proper culture in companies. This is particularly so in the realm of risk management and in maintaining a consistent corporate culture even when the company is under pressure and experiencing change.

Preference for this style of regulation—that is, best practice statements and guidance rather than detailed regulation—also finds support in the Final Report of the Kay Review. Establishing trust and respect within markets is seen as more likely if financial agents and market participants voluntarily impose such standards on each other, with those who do not comply coming under peer scrutiny, and peer-imposed withdrawal of employment and reward. The Kay Review therefore sets out Good Practice Statements for company directors, asset managers and asset holders. The intention is that these should be endorsed by the regulators and used to supplement and influence the development of the UK Corporate Governance Code and Stewardship Code, but not be reduced to prescriptive legislation or regulation.

Regulation of listed companies by the UK Corporate Governance Code

The UK Corporate Governance Code addresses various aspects of board structure and internal management, and indicates *best practice* for improved standards of corporate governance for listed companies.[13]

Qualities of boards and board members

The Code does not suggest (even on a 'comply or explain' basis) that directors of listed companies ought to have particular qualifications. It does, however, suggest in Main Principle B.1 and its Supporting Principles that the board should have the appropriate balance of skills, experience, independence and knowledge of the company, and be neither too large nor too small to function effectively. Principle B.1.2 also suggests that smaller companies[14] have at least two independent non-executive directors, and that all other companies have at least half the board, excluding the chairman, comprising non-executive directors determined by the board to be independent. Principle B.1.1 defines 'independent' by reference to seven factors (including such matters as family ties, business and previous employment relationships, and so on).

The Code recommends the use of Nomination Committees to make recommendations to the board on all new board appointments. This committee should be chaired by the chairman of the board or by a non-executive director, and should have a majority of non-executive directors (NEDs) as members. The composition of the committee should be identified in the company's annual report. The 2015 Review also emphasises the need for succession planning, making effective use of the Nomination Committee.

The Code also states that every director should receive training on the first occasion that he or she is appointed to the board of a listed company, and subsequently as necessary. The extent of training and by whom it should be given is left open.

---

[13] See P Davies, 'Post-Enron Developments in the United Kingdom' in G Ferrarini et al (eds), *Reforming Company and Takeover Law in Europe* (2004), p 183.

[14] A smaller company is one that is not included in the FTSE 350 throughout the year immediately prior to the reporting year.

Separation of the roles of chairman and managing director

The Code takes the view that the posts of chief executive officer (CEO) or managing director (where the CEO is also a director) and chairman of the board should not normally be held by the same person, and that there should be a clear and written division of responsibilities that will ensure a balance of power and authority with no one individual having unfettered powers of discretion. If the company nevertheless decides that one person should hold both posts, this should be publicly justified. The 2015 Review noted that thirteen companies in the FTSE 350 (ie under 3%) had a single individual occupying both positions, eight of which were temporary arrangements. However, in the majority of the remaining cases, where the arrangements were 'open-ended' or for a longer term, no evidence of obvious rationale or mitigating arrangements was provided.

In addition to the CEO and Chairman, a third person should be identified, a 'senior independent director' (by implication a NED), to whom the concerns of the NEDs can be conveyed.

Although the Higgs Report recommended a blanket prohibition on the CEO (or managing director) of a company subsequently being appointed chairman, the current Code takes a more lenient line and permits a former managing director to become chairman after advance consultation with the company's major members and appropriate explanation subsequently.

Even though it is only listed companies that are under any formal obligations concerning the Code, the failure to have analogous safeguards in place in a relatively small company drew unfavourable comments from Arden J in *Re Macro (Ipswich) Ltd* **[13.30]**.

Balance of executive and non-executive directors

There is a substantial practical difference between the office of a director remunerated, if at all, by the payment of directors' fees (*a non-executive director*) and that of a person who, in addition to serving as a director, holds a management or executive position within the company, whether on a full-time or part-time basis, and is paid a salary in respect of this employment (*an executive director*).

The law generally treats both categories of director similarly as a matter of principle, but the difference between an executive director and a NED can be very important in practice. For instance, an executive director is likely to have greater authority to represent the company in its dealings with third parties; to be more difficult to remove because of entitlements to substantial compensation for loss of office; to be subjected to higher standards of skill and care in the discharge of his or her duties; and, as a working 'insider', to have better access to market sensitive and other information and much greater knowledge of the company's affairs than a NED.[15]

New significance has been accorded to the role of the NED in the Code, following the recommendations of each of the contributing committees to the Code. The current Code now prescribes that half the number of board members should be independent NEDs in the case of FTSE 350 companies; that board committees should be dominated by independent NEDs (with the exception of the remuneration committee, which should be constituted exclusively by NEDs), and that these committees should take on more responsibilities; that NEDs should be appointed from a wider range of possible candidates; and that a NED's tenure on the board can in theory run longer than nine years, subject to both a re-election process every one to three years depending on the size of the company and a thorough review of any decision to re-elect a NED beyond the six-year mark. According to the current Code, NEDs will no longer qualify as 'independent' if they have held their position for

---

[15] Although see *Re Langreen Ltd (In Liquidation)*, Ch D (Companies Ct) (Registrar Derrett) 21/10/2011, LTL 26/10/2011, Document No AC0130205, where, on the facts, the executives and non-executives were indistinguishable.

longer than nine years. The 2015 Review suggests that a number of companies previously non-compliant with the Code in this regard have now become compliant. For the rest, however, although explanations continue to improve, the Review urges better provision of information on the appropriateness of the composition of the board, including any mitigating actions in place to ensure a sufficient degree of independence.

Given these best practice rules, concerns are now emerging as to whether the pool of NEDs is adequate to meet the demand for quality people to take on the role, especially from the perspective of smaller companies, which find it especially difficult to attract suitable candidates. The 2011 Review accepted that there was some evidence to support this perception, and recognised that the problem was exacerbated in the economic climate at the time which placed increased demands on the time and expertise of NEDs. Nevertheless, the FRC reaffirmed its Code policy that companies of all sizes are to look beyond the 'usual suspects' when sourcing candidates to fill non-executive positions. The 2015 Review reiterates the need for better succession planning in order to source the right mix of skills and experience needed, for both executive and non-executive directors.

For financial institutions, the earlier Financial Services Authority (FSA)[16] had also provided draft Guidance on the role of NEDs.[17] The Guidance comes from a 'retail conduct risk perspective', and therefore encourages NEDs to challenge whether, for example, appropriate risk policies are in place, and whether the board is able to take appropriate action in response to problems when they arise.

Directors' remuneration

The Code makes various recommendations related to remuneration of directors. It suggests that companies should have a formal and transparent policy on executive remuneration, as well as a remuneration committee consisting wholly of NEDs charged with responsibility for fixing the remuneration packages of individual directors. No director should be involved in deciding his or her own remuneration. Decisions on the remuneration of executive directors should be taken by a remuneration committee made up exclusively of NEDs (para D.2.1). The remuneration of NEDs should be set by the board itself unless the articles require this remuneration to be determined by the members (para D.2.3).

Every company's annual report should contain a statement of its remuneration policy, and details of the remuneration of each individual director. The Turnbull (1999) and Higgs (2003) Reports were especially influential in strengthening the role of NEDs in the management of the company.

Despite these developments, directors' salary and benefits packages continue to attract unfavourable attention: awards that are thought to be excessive (especially if they are out of step with the performance of the company or individual in question) draw weighty criticism from the media and in Parliament. Further efforts in recent years have focused on increasing the transparency of decisions concerning directors' remuneration, including a series of fresh reforms implemented in October 2013, complemented by changes made to the Code (see later).

Nomination committees

The Code, Main Principle B.2, states that 'There should be a formal, rigorous and transparent procedure for the appointment of new directors to the board'. A listed company's board should establish a nomination committee to make recommendations to the board on all

---

[16] From 1 April 2013, this responsibility was taken over by the Financial Conduct Authority (FCA). This is the date on which the FSA was abolished, and its functions split between the Prudential Regulatory Authority and the FCA, with the Bank of England having an expanded role: see Financial Services Act 2012.

[17] www.fsa.gov.uk/pages/Library/Policy/guidance_consultations/2011/11_30.shtml.

new appointments (para B.2.1). A majority of the members of the nomination committee should be independent NEDs, and the chair should be either the chair of the board or an independent NED.

Code provision B.7.1 requires all directors of listed companies to submit themselves for re-election at least every three years (annually for directors of FTSE 350 companies), and sufficient biographical detail should be supplied on a person submitted for election so as to enable members to take an informed decision on the election. The rules make specific reference to the need to refresh the board and maintain the independence of NEDs. Notwithstanding the controversy surrounding the annual election recommendation, the 2011 Review referred to data which showed that 80% of FTSE 350 companies put all directors up for re-election in 2011, in contrast to only 10% in 2010. That figure might be expected to rise further given companies' increasing willingness to submit themselves to 'comply or explain' regimes rather than face strict legislative regulation.

Gender diversity

In recent years, there has been heightened concern for a more diverse board culture, with current attention focused on increasing the representation of women on boards. In 2010, Lord Davies of Abersoch was commissioned to review the current situation. His report, published in February 2011,[18] presents the business case for gender diversity on boards: namely, improving performance; accessing the widest talent pool; being more responsive to the market; and achieving better corporate governance. Davies urges that it is in the interests of businesses (and shareholders) to encourage gender diversity, and, although he rejects the use of 'quotas' for the time being, he sets out recommendations designed to achieve 25% female representation on boards by 2015.

Two of these recommendations have been incorporated in the UK Corporate Governance Code and applied to financial years beginning on or after 1 October 2012. The first requires the board to describe the board's policy, objectives and progress on developing gender diversity (Principle B.2.4). The second requires board evaluation to include consideration of the balance of skills, experience, independence and knowledge of the company on the board, its diversity, including gender, how the board works together as a unit and other factors relevant to its effectiveness (Principle B.6).[19]

In the October 2015 update on the progress that had been made to achieve gender diversity, Lord Davies reported that women's representation on the FTSE 100 had more than doubled to 26% in less than five years (although primarily as NEDs rather than as executive directors).[20] The UK now stands in sixth place in the international ranking (with those ahead generally having imposed quotas by way of legislation). Further recommendations were made to continue this progress, still on a voluntary basis, focusing on higher targets and a greater number of Chairs rather than ordinary members of the board, with attention given to developing diversity in the executive layer in companies so that the qualified cohort of board members grows. An independent steering body was also proposed in order to maintain momentum through to the next steps.

The European Commission is also on the bandwagon, and has launched its own consultation and investigation on gender imbalance as a cross-EU issue. In October 2013, the European Parliament voted overwhelmingly (459 for, 148 against and 81 abstentions) in support of the Commission's proposal which would set a minimum objective of having

---

[18] The 'Davies Report' at: www.bis.gov.uk/assets/biscore/business-law/docs/w/11-745-women-on-boards.pdf.

[19] See the FRC Feedback Statement on gender diversity at: www.frc.org.uk/Our-Work/Publications/Corporate-Governance/Feedback-Statement-Gender-Diversity-on-Boards.aspx.

[20] www.gov.uk/government/uploads/system/uploads/attachment_data/file/482059/BIS-15-585-women-on-boards-davies-review-5-year-summary-october-2015.pdf.

40% women in non-executive board-member positions in listed companies in Europe by 2020.[21] These proposals need Council approval before they become law.[22]

➤ Questions

1. In *Equitable Life Assurance Society v Bowley* [2003] EWHC 2263 (Comm) at [41], Langley J suggested that 'a company may reasonably, at the least, look to NEDs for independence of judgment *and supervision of the executive management*' (emphasis added). Companies do not appoint NEDs without good reason; they are usually chosen for their specific expertise, experience or business connections. NEDs who provide these services can expect to be paid reasonably well for their contributions, but of course this means that they may become financially dependent on the company to a greater or lesser extent. Is it realistic to expect NEDs to be 'independent', and to supervise executive management? Equally, is it realistic to expect companies to appoint and pay fees to individuals who have little to offer apart from independence and a policing role?

2. How is a line to be drawn between achieving gender diversity and avoiding positive discrimination?

Regulation of institutional investors by the UK Stewardship Code

One phenomenon which had remained largely overlooked until recently was the rise in the number of shares—particularly shares in listed public companies—held by 'institutional' shareholders such as pension funds, insurance companies, unit trusts and mutual funds.[23] The percentage of their holdings overall has grown from about a quarter in the 1960s to about two-thirds in more recent years, and in some companies may be as high as 80% or more, although in some spheres it is now declining.

These bodies hold the long-term savings of millions of citizens, and are managed by specialist professionals who, on the one hand, are in competition with each other but, on the other, are bound by the very nature of their function not to take unwarranted risks with the funds for which they are responsible. Views differ on the extent to which these institutions and their professionals should be expected, or even required, to monitor the performance of those charged with the management of the companies held in their portfolios. Plainly, these large members are in a position to wield considerable influence both in the affairs of a particular company (most notably in a takeover situation) and in the development of general standards of corporate governance.

The 2010 version of the UK Corporate Governance Code declared that institutional shareholders 'have a responsibility to make considered use of their votes', and that they 'should enter into a dialogue with companies based on the mutual understanding of objectives'.[24] But this is not a panacea, and is omitted from the current Code. Early on, the Company Law Review drew attention to the likely risk of conflicts of interest inherent in the position of a fund manager: suppose, for instance, that the same institution is both an investor in a company and trustee of its pension fund, or involved with both bidder and target in a takeover bid.

---

[21] http://europa.eu/rapid/press-release_IP-13-943_en.htm.

[22] In a most recent draft Directive (dated 24 September 2015), it is proposed that women should hold at least 40% of non-executive director positions, and at least 33% of all director positions: http://data.consilium.europa.eu/doc/document/ST-12358-2015-INIT/en/pdf.

[23] See J Farrar and M Russell, 'The Impact of Institutional Investment on Company Law' (1984) 5 *Company Lawyer* 107; PL Davies, 'Institutional Investors in the United Kingdom' in T Baums et al (eds), *Institutional Investors and Corporate Governance* (1994); and John C Coffee Jr, 'Institutional Investors as Corporate Monitors: Are Takeovers Obsolete?' in JH Farrar (ed), *Takeovers, Institutional Investors and the Modernization of Corporate Laws* (1993).

[24] UK Corporate Governance Code 2010, Sch C, Principles 3 and 1 respectively: frc.org.uk/Our-Work/Publications/Corporate-Governance/The-UK-Corporate-Governance-Code.aspx.

These concerns therefore provided the context in which the Institutional Shareholders' Committee (ISC), the representative forum of the institutional shareholding community in the UK, published its 'Code on the Responsibilities of Institutional Investors' in 2009. These good practice principles were geared at 'enhancing the quality of engagement' between institutional investors and their investee companies, thus providing better stewardship services for investors. This Code became the 2010 UK Stewardship Code on its adoption by the FRC.

At the outset, and unlike the UK Corporate Governance Code, it should be noticed that the Stewardship Code is optional, in the sense that institutional shareholders are free to choose whether or not to sign up and engage. However, once they do sign up, their fund managers or agents are responsible for ensuring compliance and, like the UK Corporate Governance Code, the Stewardship Code operates on a 'comply or explain' basis. The FSA introduced in December 2010 under Conduct of Business Rule 22.3 the requirement that stakeholder firms are to disclose the extent of their commitment to the Code; and where they do not commit to the Code, they are requires to outline their 'alternative investment strategy'. This requirement does not deny the Code's voluntary nature.

Client and beneficiary-primacy

Depending on the chosen investor structure, institutional shareholders/investors act for or represent 'clients' or 'beneficiaries'. The Stewardship Code puts the interests of these clients and beneficiaries centre stage. Principle 2 reiterates the institutional investor's duty to act in the interests of all clients and/or beneficiaries when they exercise their powers. This duty is analogous to that imposed on directors (see Chapter 7), who are required by Companies Act 2006 (CA 2006) s 172 to act to promote the success of the company. In both cases, the requirement seeks to ensure that the agents in question do not seek to further their own interests and, in the process, sacrifice the interests of those they are supposed to protect. Principle 2 therefore requires institutional investors to formulate and disclose publicly a clear 'robust' policy to manage any potential conflicts of interest.

To the same ends, Principle 5 requires institutional shareholders to act collectively with other investors where appropriate. Put this way, shareholder value (for the clients/beneficiaries) is to be promoted, even if its achievement comes at the price of commercially sensitive collaboration with actual of potential competitors.

Enhanced interaction with investee companies

Principle 1 requires institutional shareholders to disclose their policy on discharging their stewardship responsibilities. The Guidance indicates that such disclosure should include information as to how investee companies will be monitored by the institutions, and suggests that active dialogue with the board of an investee company may be necessary.

Principle 3 strengthens this idea of monitoring, including appraising investee board and committee structures (especially in the light of any departures from the UK Corporate Governance Code), and elaborates on the need for and nature of any regular and active dialogue with the boards.

Enhanced publicity

A consistent feature of the Code is that institutional investors are not only expected to formulate clear policies for discharging their duties, but are also obliged to disclose these policies and report publicly on their implementation.

Review and amendment

In April 2012, the FRC published a consultation document[25] on proposed revisions to the Stewardship Code (the '2012 Revision'). Critics had complained that the concept of

---

[25] www.frc.org.uk/getattachment/fa05e79c-22c6-4f8f-b5b3-2ab55ec41113/Consultation-Document-Revisions-to-the-UK-Stewards.aspx.

'stewardship' was too vague, and that the Code provided a 'one-size-fits-all' solution which was inappropriate for all types of institutional investors.

The 2012 Revision was designed to address these fundamental issues, as well as more specific or technical issues which had emerged. The changes proposed included clarification of the aim and definition of stewardship; of the varying responsibilities of different types of institutional investors; and (practically) of how the Code was expected to be implemented. This consultation resulted in a number of changes to the Code,[26] but whether they go far enough to meet the challenges posed remains to be seen.

In the 2014 Review, the FRC reported that although the trends were in the right direction, not all signatories were adhering to their commitment to the Stewardship Code. For the future, attention needed to be given to improving implementation, using collected evidence to demonstrate the benefits of stewardship and thus to stimulate demand from asset owners for their fund managers to comply. More attention, too, was needed to ensure a greater degree of engagement between investors and the companies in which they invest.

Narrative reporting reforms

In a further move to combat short-termism, and supplementing changes made to the Corporate Governance Code and the Stewardship Code, the Department for Business, Innovation and Skills introduced detailed narrative reporting regulations in the form of the Companies Act 2006 (Strategic Report and Directors' Report) Regulations 2013, which came into force on 1 October 2013. In essence, the new regulations require certain companies to prepare a strategic report as part of their annual report.

The revised format annual reports are made up of two key documents: a concise 'high level' Strategic Report, replacing the business review and containing 'strategic, headline information', with some extra content for quoted companies concerning the business model, human rights and diversity; and a more detailed Annual Directors' Statement to be made available on company websites. The FRC published an early Staff Guidance Note which contained a succinct summary of the key facts on the changes introduced by the regulations,[27] and this has now been supplemented by a more detailed Guidance on the Strategic Report, published by the FRC (at the request of the government) in June 2014.[28]

Role of the company secretary

Most of the attention and debate surrounding corporate roles is focused on directors and shareholders, but the role of company secretaries should be noted. A public company must have a company secretary (CA 2006 s 271); a private company need not, although the functions must then be carried out by the directors (s 270). CA 2006 s 273 imposes a duty on

---

[26] See FRC Feedback Statement (September 2012) at www.frc.org.uk/Our-Work/Publications/Corporate-Governance/Feedback-Statement-UK-Stewardship-Code-September-2.pdf.

[27] www.frc.org.uk/Our-Work/Publications/Accounting-and-Reporting-Policy/FRC-Staff-Guidance-Note-Strategic-Report-Regulatio.pdf.

[28] https://frc.org.uk/Our-Work/Publications/Accounting-and-Reporting-Policy/Feedback-Statement-Guidance-on-the-Strategic-Repor.pdf. See also a Feedback Statement and as well as more general updates on the FRC's work on the Strategic Report: www.frc.org.uk/Our-Work/Codes-Standards/Accounting-and-Reporting-Policy/Clear-and-Concise-Reporting/Guidance-on-the-Strategic-Report.aspx.

the directors of a public company to take all reasonable steps to ensure that their company secretary is appropriately qualified, and then lists the appropriate qualifications.

The role of company secretary has evolved into one of increasing responsibility and influence within the management structure: for an early recognition of this evolution, see *Panorama Developments (Guildford) Ltd v Fidelis Furnishing Fabrics Ltd* **[3.03]**.[29] For premium listed companies, now see the UK Corporate Governance Code provisions. Supporting Principle B.5 states:

> [B.5] Under the direction of the chairman, the company secretary's responsibilities include ensuring good information flows within the board and its committees and between senior management and non-executive directors, as well as facilitating induction and assisting with professional development as required.
>
> [B.5.2] All directors should have access to the advice and services of the company secretary, who is responsible to the board for ensuring that board procedures are complied with. Both the appointment and removal of the company secretary should be a matter for the board as a whole.

A report by the All Party Parliamentary Corporate Governance Group (APPCGG) at the House of Commons dated May 2012, entitled 'Elevating the Role of the Company Secretary', presented the findings from a study of company secretaries of 'FTSE All Share' companies. These findings show that the scope of the company secretary's role varies considerably between companies, but none of the profiles seem adequately described by the term 'secretary', which is consistently seen as problematic. The most commonly suggested alternative is 'Corporate Governance Director', which goes some way towards reflecting the growing importance of the role in the realm of corporate governance.

➤ Question

Compare the approach in *Panorama Developments (Guildford) Ltd v Fidelis Furnishing Fabrics Ltd* **[3.03]** with the *dicta* of Lord Macnaghten from more than 100 years ago, in *Ruben v Great Fingall Consolidated* **[11.13]**, in which his lordship described the role of the secretary as a 'mere servant'. What factors may have contributed to this substantial change of attitude?

Directors' service contracts

In practical terms, directors could be made virtually irremovable by negotiating for service contracts with very long terms, so that companies could then only get rid of the directors by paying prohibitive sums as compensation. A board of directors acting in collusion could see to it that every member of the board was protected in this way.

To avoid this risk, the legislation now provides that no service contract may be made to run for more than two years without the prior authorisation of the members (CA 2006 ss 188–189).[30] Without this approval, the relevant terms are void and a term is deemed to

---

[29] This case recognises that the secretary may have administrative duties as secretary, which do not involve managing or carrying on the business of the company, but, equally, may in other capacities or contexts have roles which are very much part of corporate management. Similarly, see *Re Maidstone Building Provisions Ltd* [1971] 1 WLR 1085.

[30] For companies with a Stock Exchange listing, the Code sets a standard of terms of one year or less.

be included in the contract allowing the company to terminate the contract at any time on reasonable notice. The rule applies to both contracts of service and contracts for services (s 227), and also to engagements with shadow directors (s 223(1)(a)).

In addition, all directors' service contracts must be open for inspection by the members (ss 227–230), and every company must give, in a note to its annual accounts, information about aggregate directors' remuneration (s 412). (A small company can omit this information from the accounts it files at Companies House.) All unquoted/unlisted companies must give statistical information, but are not required to identify payments to each director by name.

Remuneration of directors

Directors have no prima facie entitlement to remuneration.[31] Provision for payment is therefore usually made in the articles, and the appropriate decision-making process is as determined there. CA 2006 ss 188 and 189 (noted earlier) limit the company's power to determine its own procedures, and ss 227–230 impose disclosure obligations. Beyond these restrictions, the company is free to determine its own practices. *What* is paid by way of remuneration is, however, constrained by various common law and statutory rules described later.

Binding contracts to provide remuneration

It is crucial for directors that there *is* clear constitutional authority for any agreements that are made, and that the proper procedures have been followed. Without these, the purported arrangements are void (see *Guinness plc v Saunders* [5.01]) and directors are not entitled as of right to any remuneration, whether upon a *quantum meruit*, 'equitable allowance', or otherwise. Indeed, if a person is not a director, he or she will fare better in obtaining payment for any services rendered (see *Craven-Ellis v Canons Ltd* [5.02]).

The power to pay directors' remuneration must be strictly observed.

[5.01] Guinness plc v Saunders [1990] 2 AC 663 (House of Lords)

In January 1986, the board of Guinness appointed a committee of three directors, Saunders, Roux and Ward, to handle the day-to-day decisions in connection with a takeover bid which Guinness had made for another company, Distillers. The bid was ultimately successful. Ward had been paid a fee of £5.2 million for his part in the bid, which he said had been agreed by the committee. The company's articles empowered the board of Guinness to fix the remuneration of individual directors, and contained several provisions allowing it to delegate various of its functions. The House of Lords declined to construe the articles in a way that invested the committee with power to pay remuneration to one of its own members, and ordered Ward to repay the £5.2 million.

> LORD TEMPLEMAN: . . . Mr Ward admits receipt of £5.2m from Guinness and pleads an agreement by Guinness that he should be paid this sum for his advice and services in connection with the bid. Mr Ward admits that payment was not authorised by the board of directors of Guinness. The articles of association of Guinness provide:

---

[31] *Hutton v West Cork Railway Co* (1883) 23 Ch D 654, 672; *Guinness plc v Saunders* [5.01].

Remuneration of directors.

90. The board shall fix the annual remuneration of the directors provided that without the consent of the company in general meeting such remuneration (excluding any special remuneration payable under article 91 and article 92) shall not exceed the sum of £100,000 per annum . . .

91. The board may, in addition to the remuneration authorised in article 90, grant special remuneration to any director who serves on any committee or who devotes special attention to the business of the company or who otherwise performs services which in the opinion of the board are outside the scope of the ordinary duties of a director. Such special remuneration may be made payable to such director in addition to or in substitution for his ordinary remuneration as a director, and may be made payable by a lump sum or by way of salary, or commission or participation in profits, or by any or all of those modes or otherwise as the board may determine.

Articles 90 and 91 of the articles of association of Guinness depart from the Table A articles recommended by statute, which reserve to a company in general meeting the right to determine the remuneration of the directors of the company.[32] But by article 90 the annual remuneration which the directors may award themselves is limited and by article 91 special remuneration for an individual director can only be authorised by the board. A committee, which may consist of only two or, as in the present case, three members, however honest and conscientious, cannot assess impartially the value of its work or the value of the contribution of its individual members. A director may, as a condition of accepting appointment to a committee, or after he has accepted appointment, seek the agreement of the board to authorise payment for special work envisaged or carried out. The shareholders of Guinness run the risk that the board may be too generous to an individual director at the expense of the shareholders but the shareholders have, by article 91, chosen to run this risk and can protect themselves by the number, quality and impartiality of the members of the board who will consider whether an individual director deserves special reward. Under article 91 the shareholders of Guinness do not run the risk that a committee may value its own work and the contribution of its own members. Article 91 authorises the board, and only the board, to grant special remuneration to a director who serves on a committee.

It was submitted that article 2 alters the plain meaning of article 91. In article 2 there are a number of definitions each of which is expressed to apply 'if not inconsistent with the subject or context'. The expression 'the board' is defined as 'The directors of the company for the time being (or a quorum of such directors assembled at a meeting of directors duly convened) or any committee authorised by the board to act on its behalf.'

The result of applying the article 2 definition to article 91, it is said, is that a committee may grant special remuneration to any director who serves on a committee or devotes special attention to the business of the company or who otherwise performs services which in the opinion of the committee are outside the scope of the ordinary duties of a director. In my opinion the subject and context of article 91 are inconsistent with the expression 'the board' in article 91 meaning anything except the board. Article 91 draws a contrast between the board and a committee of the board. The board is expressly authorised to grant special remuneration to *any* director who serves on *any* committee. It cannot have been intended that any committee should be able to grant special remuneration to any director, whether a member of the committee or not. The board must compare the work of an individual director with the ordinary duties of a director. The board must decide whether special remuneration shall be paid in addition to or in substitution for the annual remuneration determined by the board under article 90. These decisions could only be made by the board surveying the work and remuneration of each and every director. Article 91 also provides for the board to decide whether special remuneration should take the form of participation

[32] The 2006 Model Articles for private and public companies now reserve this decision to the directors, subject to the requirements of the Act, and any other terms in the articles.

in profits; the article could not intend that a committee should be able to determine whether profits should accrue to the shareholders' fund or be paid out to an individual director. The remuneration of directors concerns all the members of the board and all the shareholders of Guinness. Article 2 does not operate to produce a result which is inconsistent with the language, the subject and the context of article 91. Only the board possessed power to award £5.2m to Mr Ward . . .

[Lord Templeman ruled further that: (i) none of Guinness's other articles conferred a power on the committee to pay Ward remuneration; (ii) Ward was not entitled to sue Guinness for professional services rendered as a solicitor; (iii) Saunders, as chairman, had no actual or ostensible authority to agree that Ward should be paid the sum; and (iv) that since the articles made express provision for the way in which directors should be remunerated, Ward had no claim by way of *quantum meruit*.]

LORD GOFF OF CHIEVELEY delivered a concurring opinion.

LORDS KEITH OF KINKEL, BRANDON OF OAKBROOK and GRIFFITHS concurred.

If the director's appointment is void, remuneration on a quantum meruit *basis may be possible.*

[5.02] Craven-Ellis v Canons Ltd [1936] 2 KB 403 (Court of Appeal)

The facts appear from the judgment.

GREER LJ: The signatories to the memorandum and articles, being entitled to elect the first directors, nominated Mr Phillip du Cros, the plaintiff, and Mr A W Wheeler as the first directors on 15 August 1928, and on 23 August the directors co-opted Sir Arthur de Cros as a director. Under the articles these directors could act without qualification for two months, but after that time they became incapable of acting as directors as none of them had acquired the necessary qualification. The only issued shares of the company were in the two signatories to the memorandum, but there is little room for doubt that these gentlemen were nominees of the du Cros'. Be this as it may it is clear that on the expiration of the two months, the directors having no qualification ceased to be directors, and were unable to bind the company except as de facto directors by agreements with outsiders or with shareholders . . . On 14 April 1931 an agreement was executed under the seal of the company, purporting to be between the company and the plaintiff, stating the terms on which he was to act by resolution of the unqualified directors. The plaintiff in this action sought to recover from the defendant company the remuneration set out in the agreement, and as an alternative, sought to recover for his services on a *quantum meruit*. Until the company purported to put an end to his engagement he continued to perform all the services mentioned in the agreement.

The company, having had the full benefit of these activities, decline to pay either under the agreement or on the basis of a *quantum meruit*. Their defence to the action is a purely technical defence, and if it succeeds the Messrs du Cros as the principal shareholders in the company, and the company, would be in the position of having accepted valuable services and refusing, for purely technical reasons, to pay for them.

As regards the services rendered between 31 December 1930 and 14 April 1931, there is, in my judgment, no defence to the claim. These services were rendered by the plaintiff not as managing director or as a director, but as an estate agent, and there was no contract in existence which could present any obstacle to a claim based on a *quantum meruit* for services rendered and accepted.

As regards the plaintiff's services after the date of the contract, I think the plaintiff is also entitled to succeed. The contract, having been made by directors who had no authority to make it with one of themselves who had notice of their want of authority, was not binding on either party.

It was, in fact, a nullity, and presents no obstacle to the implied promise to pay on a *quantum meruit* basis which arises from the performance of the services and the implied acceptance of the same by the company . . .

I accordingly think that the defendants must pay on the basis of a *quantum meruit* not only for the services rendered after 31 December 1930, and before the date of the invalid agreement, but also for the services after that date. I think the appeal should be allowed, and judgment given for such a sum as shall be found to be due on the basis of a *quantum meruit* in respect of all services rendered by the plaintiff to the company until he was dismissed . . .

GREENE LJ delivered a concurring judgment.

TALBOT J concurred.

➤ Questions

1. On the purported contract with the company the plaintiff, as an 'insider', was deemed to have constructive notice both of the supposed directors' want of competence and of his own ineligibility for appointment as the managing director, because he was not a director. In the light of *Hely-Hutchinson v Brayhead Ltd* **[3.04]**, would he now be considered an 'insider'? In any event, would the protections available to third parties contracting with the company (see 'Deemed authority I: statutory deeming provisions to avoid constitutional limitations on directors' authority—CA 2006 s 40', pp 100ff and CA 2006 s 161) provide any assistance where the company has no board of directors?

2. On the *quantum meruit* claim, the judgment rests in part upon the assumption that 'the company' accepted the plaintiff's services. Which organ or agent of the company could in the circumstances be deemed to have done so? (There were some outside members.)

3. Why was this reasoning not acceptable in the context of a validly appointed director in *Guinness plc v Saunders*?

4. In *Re Richmond Gate Property Co Ltd* [1965] 1 WLR 335, Plowman J held that a managing director was not entitled to remuneration on a *quantum meruit* basis, because the articles of the company provided that a managing director was to receive 'such remuneration . . . as the directors may determine', and the company had gone into liquidation without any consideration of the matter by the directors. The existence of an express arrangement about remuneration, the judge held, ruled out any possibility of an alternative claim based on a *quantum meruit*. The case depends in part on a misunderstanding of *Craven Ellis v Canons Ltd*, and may be open to criticism on other grounds also, so that its authority is questionable. After *Guinness plc v Saunders*, how would a court decide this case? (And in case it is thought that *Richmond Gate Property* lacks current force, it was applied recently in *Diamandis v Wills* [2015] EWHC 312 (Ch) to deny a *quantum meruit*/unjust enrichment claim, on the basis that it was bound to fail in law, as 'there can be no claim for restitution where a subsisting contract between the parties allocates the risk between them' [83], and see [83]–[85].)

Common law rules on setting directors' remuneration

It is permissible to pay directors remuneration when the company has made no profits, and even when the company is not solvent (subject to any other misfeasance this may involve). The amount of remuneration is for the members (or other authorised body) to fix, and need not necessarily be determined by the market value of those services. But an award of remuneration must be 'genuine' and not a 'disguised gift' or an unlawful return of capital to a member, as illustrated by the next case.

An award of remuneration must be 'genuine'.

[5.03] Re Halt Garage (1964) Ltd [1982] 3 All ER 1016 (Chancery Division)

Mr and Mrs Charlesworth were the only directors and members of the company, and initially they had both worked in the business, drawing sums as directors' remuneration under express powers in the memorandum and articles. In 1967 Mrs Charlesworth became ill and ceased to take an active part in the business, but she remained a director and continued to draw remuneration at a reduced rate. From 1968 onwards, the company became unprofitable, and in 1971 it went into insolvent liquidation. The liquidator claimed that Mrs Charlesworth had no right to be paid after she had given up work, and also that Mr Charlesworth had been paid more than the market value of his services, and sought restitution of the sums allegedly overpaid. The payments to Mr Charlesworth were upheld, even those made after the company had ceased to be profitable. But Mrs Charlesworth was obliged to refund that part of the money paid to her which the judge held was not a 'genuine award of remuneration' but a 'disguised gift out of capital'.

> OLIVER J: Now there is no presumption that directors' remuneration is payable only out of divisible profits . . .
>
> Counsel for the liquidator does not go to the extent, in fact, of suggesting that when a company has fallen on bad times the directors must either close the business down immediately or go on trying to pull it round for nothing . . . What I think counsel's submission comes to is this, that while the company has divisible profits remuneration may be paid on any scale which the shareholders are prepared to sanction within the limits of available profits, but that, as soon as there cease to be divisible profits, it can only lawfully be paid on a scale which the court, applying some objective standard of benefit to the company, considers to be reasonable. But assuming that the sum is bona fide voted to be paid as remuneration, it seems to me that the amount, whether it be mean or generous, must be a matter of management for the company to determine in accordance with its constitution which expressly authorises payment for directors' services. Shareholders are required to be honest but, as counsel for the respondent suggests, there is no requirement that they must be wise and it is not for the court to manage the company.
>
> Counsel for the liquidator submits, however, that if this is right it leads to the bizarre result that a meeting of stupid or deranged but perfectly honest shareholders can, like Bowen LJ's lunatic director,[33] vote to themselves, qua directors, some perfectly outlandish sum by way of remuneration and that in a subsequent winding up the liquidator can do nothing to recover it. It seems to me that the answer to this lies in the objective test which the court necessarily applies. It assumes human beings to be rational and to apply ordinary standards. In the postulated circumstances of a wholly unreasonable payment, that might, no doubt, be prima facie evidence of fraud, but it might also be evidence that what purported to be remuneration was not remuneration at all but a dressed-up gift to a shareholder out of capital . . .
>
> This, as it seems to me, is the real question in a case such as the present. The real test must, I think, be whether the transaction in question was a genuine exercise of the power. The motive is more important than the label. Those who deal with a limited company do so on the basis that its affairs will be conducted in accordance with its constitution, one of the express incidents of which is that the directors may be paid remuneration. Subject to that, they are entitled to have the capital kept intact. They have to accept the shareholders' assessment of the scale of the remuneration, but they are entitled to assume that, whether liberal or illiberal, what is paid is genuinely remuneration and that the power is not used as a cloak for making payments out of capital to the shareholders as such . . .

[33] In *Hutton v West Cork Rly Co* (1883) 23 Ch D 654, 671.

[His Lordship referred to Mrs Charlesworth's illness, and continued:] The fact is that, however valuable and exacting may have been the services which Mrs Charlesworth had rendered in the past, her continued directorship contributed nothing to the company's future, beyond the fact that she was and remained responsible as a director and was able to make up the necessary quorum for directors' meetings (of which remarkably few took place if the minutes are any accurate guide).

On the other hand, it is said that the Companies Act 1948 imposes on every company incorporated under its provisions an obligation to have a director and it contemplates that those who assume the responsibilities of office, whether they carry them out well or ill, may be paid for that service in such way and in such measure as the company's regulations prescribe or permit. Here the company's constitution conferred on it in express terms a power to award to a director a reward or remuneration for the bare fact of holding office, and that power the company purported to exercise. If it be legitimate for the company to award some remuneration, however nominal, to Mrs Charlesworth for acting as a director and taking on herself, for good or ill, the responsibilities which that office entails, at what point, counsel for the respondents asks, does it become beyond the company's power to do that which its constitution permits it to do and how can the court take on itself the discretion as to *quantum* which is vested in the shareholders, there being, *ex concessis*, no *mala fides*? I have not found the point an easy one, but on the view that I take of the law the argument of counsel for the respondents is very difficult to meet *if* the payments made really were within the express power conferred by the company's constitution.

But of course what the company's articles authorise is the fixing of 'remuneration', which I take to mean a reward for services rendered or to be rendered; and, whatever the terms of the resolutions passed and however described in the accounts of the company's books, the real question seems to me to be whether the payments really were 'directors' remuneration' or whether they were gratuitous distributions to a shareholder out of capital dressed up as remuneration.

I do not think that it can be said that a director of a company cannot be rewarded as such merely because he is not active in the company's business. The mere holding of office involves responsibility even in the absence of any substantial activity, and it is indeed in part to the mere holding of office that Mrs Charlesworth owes her position as a respondent in these proceedings. I can see nothing as a matter of construction of the article to disentitle the company, if the shareholders so resolve, from paying a reward attributable to the mere holding of the office of director, for being, as it were, a name on the notepaper and attending such meetings or signing such documents as are from time to time required. The director assumes the responsibility on the footing that he will receive whatever recompense the company in general meeting may think appropriate. In this case, however, counsel for the liquidator is entitled to submit that the sums paid to Mrs Charlesworth were so out of proportion to any possible value attributable to her holding of office that the court is entitled to treat them as not being genuine payments of remuneration at all but as dressed-up dividends out of capital . . .

[His Lordship considered the evidence, and ruled that only £10 out of the £30 per week which had been paid to Mrs Charlesworth while she was ill was genuinely 'remuneration'. He ordered her to repay the balance.]

➤ Questions

1. Mrs Charlesworth was a member. Could Oliver J have reached the same conclusion if she had not held shares?

2. Earlier in his judgment, Oliver J said:

> It is commonplace in private family companies, where there are substantial profits available for distribution by way of dividend, for the shareholder directors to distribute those profits by way of directors' remuneration rather than by way of dividend, because the latter course has certain fiscal disadvantages. But such a distribution may, and frequently does, bear very little relation to the true market value of the services rendered by the directors . . . Yet it is very difficult to see why the payment of directors' remuneration, on whatever scale the company in general meeting chooses, out of funds which could perfectly well be distributed by way of dividend, should be open to attack merely because the shareholders, in their own interests, choose to attach to it the label of directors' remuneration . . .

Does this mean that different rules apply if a company has undistributed profits?

3. Could Mrs Charlesworth have kept the payments if:

   (i) the company had been solvent at the time they were made?

   (ii) the members had believed that the company was solvent, when in fact it was not?

4. This case indicates there are limits to the power of shareholders to decide freely on matters of remuneration. Does the decision, in effect, suggest that shareholders must act 'bona fide and for proper purposes' in exercising their powers? (See 'Summary of limitations on members' voting', pp 254ff.) Could this common law approach impact on the shareholders' vote proposed under the new legislative reforms in relation to directors' remuneration (see later)?

5. If the power to decide remuneration lies with the directors (see the Model Articles art 19 (private companies) and art 23 (public companies)), are the constraints on decision-making the same, or greater? Who *should* the power be given to?

6. Could a failure to ensure that the board fixes salaries that are affordable by the company show a director's unfitness and be a ground for a disqualification order under the Company Directors Disqualification Act 1986?

7. Could a directors' (or majority members') decision to award 'excessive' remuneration be open to challenge as a 'fraud on the minority' (see 'Exceptions to the rule in *Foss v Harbottle*', pp 670ff and consider whether it now has a statutory equivalent) or 'unfair prejudice' (see 'Unfairly prejudicial conduct of the company's affairs', pp 715ff)?

▶ Notes

1. In *Barclays Bank plc v British & Commonwealth Holdings plc* [1996] 1 BCLC at 9 Harman J said that he found the decision in *Halt Garage* difficult to accept because, in his view, it is not possible for a resolution to be held valid in part and unlawful as to the rest: the irregularity should have led to a finding that it was void *in toto*. (The Court of Appeal ([1996] 1 BCLC 1 at 26ff) did not refer to this point.) What would this have meant for the liquidator's claim?

2. The payments to Mrs Charlesworth might now be caught by Insolvency Act 1986 (IA 1986) s 238 (as a 'transaction at an undervalue', subject to the time limits fixed by that section). In an appropriate case, IA 1986 s 423 might also be applicable (this has no time limits but requires proof of an intention to put assets beyond the reach of the company's creditors). See 'The conduct of the liquidation', pp 851ff. Would they be caught by IA 1986 s 214 (wrongful trading)?

3. The reasoning of Oliver J was followed by Hoffmann J in *Aveling Barford Ltd v Perion Ltd* **[10.14]** to strike down as not 'genuine' and as an unauthorised return of capital a sale of land made at an undervalue by a company to another company controlled by its principal member. Can these cases be seen as part of an emerging new doctrine which may be invoked where corporate assets are wrongfully depleted for the benefit of insiders? Is the doctrine, if there is one, even wider than this? Does this support an 'arm's length approach' as emerging from *Progress Property Co Ltd v Moore* **[10.15]**.

Statutory rules on setting directors' remuneration

In the wake of the global financial crisis, the general public has been vocal in expressing concern, and sometimes outrage, that alarmingly high levels of directors' remuneration often bear no relationship to the laggardly performance of their listed companies, and certainly cannot be justified when employee wages are being cut or frozen.

In response to this sentiment, in June 2012 the government announced 'the most comprehensive reform' in relation to directors' remuneration. The proposed measures have now been introduced through the Enterprise and Regulatory Reform Act 2013, which came into force on 1 October 2013. In other words, these changes now exist in the form of binding law, not merely 'best practice'.

The proposed reforms were geared towards giving shareholders of quoted companies a direct voice on pay policies and on the structure and implementation of exit payments. In conjunction with these objectives, the reforms will also facilitate better access to information related to directors' remuneration.

At the heart of these changes is the proposal for a binding shareholders' vote on directors' pay in the case of quoted companies (CA 2006 ss 439 and 439A). Each year (or at a minimum every three years), the shareholders must be given an opportunity to vote on the company's *policy* on directors' remuneration. Before the vote, shareholders must have access to a policy report compiled by the board which sets out the key elements of pay with supporting information, and compares these figures with the company's overall strategy or objectives, and indicates the principles or factors which formed the basis for the pay policy (CA 2006 s 422A). The policy report must also specify the impact on directors' pay if the company's performance is above, on or below target. A majority vote in favour of the policy is required before the policy is adopted.

The required content of the new directors' remuneration report is stipulated in the Large and Medium-sized Companies and Groups (Accounts and Reports) (Amendment) Regulations 2013, which also came into force on 1 October 2013. There are two parts to the report, namely a remuneration policy, as well as an implementation report (on how the company intends to implement the approved directors' remuneration policy in the upcoming financial year).

Shareholders must also be given an 'advisory vote on implementation', that is, in relation to directors' remuneration actually paid in accordance with the policy adopted by the annual vote. If the vote fails, then the policy will return to the binding vote for re-approval in the subsequent year. This will ensure that the company's remuneration policy does not become a toothless document, but is in fact directly linked to the level of remuneration paid to directors.

Finally, 'exit pay' for any departing directors must also feature in the policy report and the corresponding votes mentioned earlier. This will ensure that directors do not receive substantial exit packages on leaving the company, which (unfortunately) seems to have been the case in recent years despite poor performance of companies and the markets in general. CA 2006 s 226C (as part of ss 226A–F) prohibits any payment for loss of office unless (i) the payment is consistent with the most recently approved directors'

remuneration policy, or (ii) the payment is approved by resolution of the members of the company.

To add support to these legislative changes, revisions were made to the Code in September 2014. More specifically, Main Principle D.1 was amended to refer to the objective of promoting the long-term success of the company in the design of executive remuneration. The supporting provisions were also changed to make clear that 'paying more than is necessary' should be avoided, and that schemes of performance-related remuneration should enable the company to recover sums paid or withhold the payment of any sum, in the appropriate circumstances (which are also to be specified).

Other related changes to the Code were also introduced.[34] For example, if a vote reveals a significant dissenting minority, then the company should publish a public statement setting out how it will address such shareholder concerns (Principle E.2.2), thus holding directors to public account.

These reforms are further supported by changes to narrative reporting, namely the production of strategic reports by companies (see 'Narrative reporting reforms', p 282). These will encapsulate a section on directors' pay, so that cross-references can be made between the key information contained in the report and the policy document on which the shareholders will vote.

Finally, it is noteworthy that the FCA has in place four Remuneration Codes tailored to different types of firm, including Deposit Taker and Investment firms (19A), Alternative Investment Fund Managers (19B), BIPRU Investment firms (19C) and Dual-regulated firms (19D). These Codes are directed at enhancing awareness of risk and ensuring that risk is better managed and better aligned with individual reward.[35]

In a research paper dated March 2015,[36] the Department for Business, Innovation and Skills concluded that most companies in a sample complied with the majority of the requirements in the new regulations, save however as to the disclosure requirements relating to the details of pension entitlements, information on payments to past directors, information on payments for loss of office, and future salary policy, in which there were more notable levels of non-compliance.

➤ Questions

1. Are these changes too interventionist? Is the government placing too many limits on companies' freedom to set their own goals and policies, including how much they pay their directors?

2. What problems may arise when so much emphasis is placed on shareholder control? Is it realistic to expect shareholders, especially those with small shareholdings in many different companies, to play such an active role in monitoring directors? How should shareholder control measures be structured so as not to defeat the purpose of centralised management in the first place?

3. Is it congruent with the idea of 'enlightened shareholder value' that only shareholders get a vote on such matters as directors' remuneration? Should other stakeholders, for example the employees, also receive a vote? What practical disadvantages are likely to emerge if that is the case?

---

[34] www.frc.org.uk/Our-Work/Publications/Corporate-Governance/Feedback-Statement-Revisions-to-the-UK-Corporate-G.pdf.
[35] www.the-fca.org.uk/remuneration.
[36] www.gov.uk/government/uploads/system/uploads/attachment_data/file/409714/bis-15-168-Directors-reforms-how-companies-and-shareholders-are-responding.pdf.

Further reading

ARSALIDOU, D, 'The Regulation of Executive Pay and Economic Theory' [2011] JBL 431.

BAINBRIDGE, SM, 'Why a Board? Group Decisionmaking in Corporate Governance' (2002) 55 *Vanderbilt Law Review* 41.

BERLE Jr, AA and MEANS, GC, *The Modern Corporation and Private Property* (1932).

CHEFFINS, BR, 'The Undermining of UK Corporate Governance(?)' (2013) 33 OJLS 503.

CHEFFINS, BR, 'The Stewardship Code's Achilles' Heel' (2010) 73 MLR 1004.

CHEFFINS, BR and THOMAS, RS, 'Should Shareholders Have a Greater Say Over Executive Pay? Learning from the US Experience' (2001) 1 *Journal of Corporate Law Studies* 277.

CHOUDHURY, B, 'New Rationales for Women on Boards' (2014) 34 OJLS 511.

DAVIES, PL, 'Post-Enron Developments in the United Kingdom' in G Ferrarini et al (eds), *Reforming Company and Takeover Law in Europe* (2004), p 183.

FAMA, EF and JENSEN, MC, 'Separation of Ownership and Control' (1983) 26 J Law and Econ 301.

HIGGS, D, 'Review of the Role and Effectiveness of Non-Executive Directors' (2003) available at: http://webarchive.nationalarchives.gov.uk/20090609003228/http://www.berr.gov.uk/files/file23012.pdf.

JENSON, MC and MECKLING, WH, 'Theory of the Firm: Managerial Behavior, Agency Costs and Ownership Structure' (1976) 3 J Fin Econ 305.

KAY, J, 'The Kay Review of UK Equity Markets and Long-Term Decision Making', Final Report (July 2012), available at: www.gov.uk/government/uploads/system/uploads/attachment_data/file/253454/bis-12-917-kay-review-of-equity-markets-final-report.pdf.

KEAY, A, 'Assessing Accountability of Boards under the UK Corporate Governance Code' [2015] JBL 551.

KEAY, A, 'Comply or Explain in Corporate Governance Codes: In Need of Greater Regulatory Oversight?' (2014) 34 *Legal Studies* 279.

REISBERG, A, 'The UK Stewardship Code: On the Road to Nowhere?' (2015) 15 JCLS 217.

RILEY, CA, 'The Case for Non-Governing Directors in Not-For-Profit Companies' (2010) 10 *Journal of Corporate Law Studies* 119.

SAPPIDEEN, R, 'Ownership of the Large Corporation: Why Clothe the Emperor?' (1996–7) 7 King's College LJ 27.

WATSON, S, 'How the Company Became an Entity: A New Understanding of Corporate Law' [2015] JBL 120.

WATSON, S, 'The Significance of the Source of the Powers of Boards of Directors in UK Company Law' [2011] JBL 597.

WEST, L, 'Challenging the "Golden Goodbye"' [2009] JBL 447.

WHEELER, S, 'Non-Executive Directors and Corporate Governance' (2009) 60 *Northern Ireland Law Quarterly* 51.

6

THE BOARD OF DIRECTORS AS AN ORGAN OF THE COMPANY

Introduction

In the previous chapter we considered the scope of corporate governance as a means of mitigating the 'agency problems' arising from centralised management. In this chapter we continue with this general theme, but now focus attention on the mechanics of the board of directors, namely the appointment, removal and disqualification of directors, as well as their functioning as a board. The next chapter will then consider the functioning of directors as *individuals*, and will review the duties owed by directors under common law and Companies Act 2006 (CA 2006).

The relatively few legal rules relating to the appointment, tenure and remuneration of directors allow those who control a company considerable scope to look after their own interests, generally without any serious risk of being successfully challenged by the minority.[1] Even where the directors do not hold the majority of voting shares, the passive attitude of most members towards company general meetings and corporate decisions means that directors can often ensure they are re-elected when their terms expire, that their service contracts contain advantageous provisions and that directors' fees, salaries and perks are set at an attractive level.

Some of the external regulatory controls include:

(i) **Controls over the appointment and dismissal of directors**: CA 2006 gives members certain guaranteed rights, by far the most important being the absolute right to dismiss directors by ordinary resolution (s 168), although even this can be rendered ineffective by defensive voting arrangements. CA 2006 does little to impose eligibility criteria on potential directors.

---

[1] It is important to be aware of the differences between executive and non-executive directors (see 'Balance of executive and non-executive directors', p 277); appointed (*de jure*), *de facto* and shadow directors; alternate directors and nominee directors—all of whom owe directors' duties. These different categories are not mutually exclusive.

(ii) **Controls over the particular division of powers between the board of directors and the members**: see 'Dividing corporate powers between members and directors', pp 189ff for the general issues, including the rule that changes to the constitution are reserved to the members (s 21), and at 'Permitted reductions of capital', pp 534ff and 'Variation of class rights', pp 587ff for particular examples in the context of capital reductions and class rights.

(iii) **Legal duties imposing minimum standards on directors' performance of their management functions**: see Chapter 7 on directors' duties.

(iv) **Controls over the structure and composition of the board of directors and its subcommittees**: CA 2006 imposes few requirements, but public listed companies are subject to the 'comply or explain' regulations in the Code.

(v) **Public disclosure of information about the company's directors and their activities**: CA 2006 provides for public registers of directors, annual accounts, directors' reports, etc, subject to certain exemptions for smaller companies.

(vi) **Service contracts and remuneration packages**: CA 2006 provides for disclosure to, and members' approval of, most of these arrangements.

(vii) **Disqualification of unfit directors, with criminal sanctions and banning for defined periods**: see Company Directors Disqualification Act 1986 (CDDA 1986) and the many changes to that Act introduced by the Small Business, Enterprise and Employment Act 2015 (SBEEA 2015), 'Directors' disqualification', pp 309ff.

Appointment of directors

Apart from providing that a public company must have at least two directors and a private company at least one (CA 2006 s 154), and stipulating that vacancies on the board of a public company shall not normally be filled by a single resolution appointing a number of candidates *en bloc* (s 160), the Act has little to say about the appointment of directors; and so the matter is left to the articles of the particular company.

Currently, while a company must have at least one natural person acting as a director it can also appoint corporate bodies as directors (CA 2006 s 155(1)). SBEEA 2015 s 87 (currently proposed to be introduced in October 2016) would repeal CA 2006 s 155 and make provisions in new ss 156A–C barring appointment of corporate directors; empowering the Secretary of State to provide by regulations for exceptions to that rule; and providing for a 12-month transitional period for existing corporate directors who are not excepted under these new regulations.

On eligibility, CA 2006 allows persons over the age of 70 to act as directors of public companies without members' approval, and establishes a new *minimum* age qualification for all directors of 16 (s 157).

A company's articles typically provide that the first directors will be appointed by the subscribers to the memorandum and that thereafter directors will be elected by the members in general meeting[2] and that a proportion, such as one-third, should retire every year but be eligible for re-election. Casual vacancies are usually filled by co-option by the remaining directors. In small companies, by contrast, the directors will very likely be appointed on a permanent basis by the articles themselves, as in *Lee's Air Farming Ltd* **[2.05]**.

---

[2] CA 2006 Model Articles for Private Companies art 17, provides for appointment by *either* the general meeting or the board of directors. There is the same provision for public companies (Model Articles art 20), but if the appointment is made by the directors it is subject to confirmation by the members (art 21).

In the absence of any provision in the articles, the general meeting has inherent power to appoint directors by ordinary resolution.[3] If the articles give exclusive power of appointment to a specific person or group (eg the board of directors or the vendor of a business), then the power of appointment of the general meeting is displaced, although the general meeting does have the power to change the articles.

The power of the majority to appoint directors must 'be exercised for the benefit of the company as a whole and not to secure some ulterior advantage' (see *Re HR Harmer Ltd* in the Note following *Scottish Co-operative Wholesale Society Ltd v Meyer* [13.31], p 732). This seems to require the general meeting to act for proper purposes.[4] Also see 'Limitations on the free exercise of members' voting rights', pp 222ff.

A company's articles may legitimately confer the right to appoint the directors (or one or more of them) on a third party, such as a majority member, or the sole trader whose business was incorporated. This power may be given directly, or attached to a special class of shares (on classes of shares, see 'Classes of shares and class rights', pp 581ff).

If the articles do not provide for such a right in third parties, then its creation by contract may be difficult. When the members alone have the right to appoint, then the directors cannot by agreement with a stranger give the latter a power to appoint a director. Where both groups have power to appoint directors, then one group (or a subset of that group) cannot by contract usurp the powers of the other. In any event, the members have the ultimate right to dismiss any directors of whom they disapprove by ordinary resolution, and without cause (CA 2006 s 168, see 'Removal of directors', pp 300ff).

The appointment of a person as a director of a company does not take effect unless the person properly agrees to the appointment.[5] If someone has been appointed, but is wrongly prevented from acting, there is authority suggesting that the director (or any member) may bring an action to enforce the right to act: *Pulbrook v Richmond Consolidated Mining Co* [6.01]). Where someone who has not been properly appointed is acting as a director, a member may sue to restrain continuing activity. Any acts already undertaken, however, are likely to be effective as against third parties (see CA 2006 s 161 and 'Defective appointments and the validity of acts of directors: CA 2006 s 161', p 298).

The appointment of *managing directors* and other *executive directors* is usually a question for the board.[6] Of course, to be eligible the appointee must be a director, appointed by the customary constitutional process; and if removed as a director for any reason, the appointee will typically automatically lose his management or executive office as well (see 'Removal of directors', pp 300ff).

While properly appointed, directors can insist on their right to act.

[6.01] Pulbrook v Richmond Consolidated Mining Co (1878) 9 Ch D 610 (Chancery Division)

A director was required by the company's articles, by way of qualification for the post, to hold 'as registered member in his own right' shares to the nominal amount of £500.

---

[3] *Worcester Corsetry Ltd v Witting* [1936] Ch 640.

[4] In *Theseus Exploration NL v Mining and Associated Industries Ltd* [1973] Qd R 81, the court issued an interim injunction to prevent members of the company electing certain persons as directors, because there was sufficient evidence that those persons intended to use the company's assets solely for the benefit of the majority member.

[5] It is now the company which notifies Companies House of this consent. The Registrar of Companies will send a notice (and other details on being a director) to the new director. The new director may request removal from the register if he or she did not consent to act (SBEEA 2015 ss 101 and 102, inserting s 1079B and amending s 1095 of CA 2006).

[6] Recall that the functions of a managing director are not set by law: *Harold Holdsworth & Co (Wakefield) Ltd v Caddies* [1955] 1 WLR 352, HL.

Pulbrook had granted an equitable mortgage over his qualification shares, and delivered to the mortgagee an unregistered transfer. The directors, on learning of this, refused to allow him to sit on the board. Jessel MR held: (i) that he still held the shares 'in his own right'; and (ii) that he had suffered an individual wrong for redress of which he could sue in his own name.[7]

> JESSEL MR: In this case a man is necessarily a shareholder in order to be a director, and as a director he is entitled to fees and remuneration for his services, and it might be a question whether he would be entitled to the fees if he did not attend meetings of the board. He has been excluded. Now, it appears to me that this is an individual wrong, or a wrong that has been done to an individual. It is a deprivation of his legal rights for which the directors are personally and individually liable. He has a right by the constitution of the company to take a part in its management, to be present, and to vote at the meetings of the board of directors. He has a perfect right to know what is going on at these meetings. It may affect his individual interest as a shareholder as well as his liability as a director, because it has been sometimes held that even a director who does not attend board meetings is bound to know what is done in his absence.
>
> Besides that, he is in the position of a shareholder, or a managing partner in the affairs of the company, and he has a right to remain managing partner, and to receive remuneration for his service. It appears to me that for the injury or wrong done to him by preventing him from attending board meetings by force, he has a right to sue. He has what is commonly called a right of action, and those decisions which say that, where a wrong is done to the company by the exclusion of a director from board meetings, the company may sue and must sue for that wrong, do not apply to the case of wrong done simply to an individual. There may be cases where, by preventing a director from exercising his functions in addition to its being a wrong done to the individual, a wrong is also done to the company, and there the company have a right to complain. But in a case of an individual wrong, another shareholder cannot on behalf of himself and others, not being the individuals to whom the wrong is done, maintain an action for that wrong. That being so, in my opinion, the plaintiff in this case has a right of action.
>
> [His Lordship then ruled that he still held the qualification shares 'in his own right', and so had been properly elected a director. He accordingly granted an injunction.]

➤ Notes

1. It is probably impossible to square all the remarks in this judgment either with the *ratio decidendi* of *Hickman*'s case **[4.38]** or with the view (commonly associated with Lord Wedderburn: see his article in [1957] CLJ 194 at 212) that every member of a company has a right to have the provisions of the corporate constitution observed. (On these questions, see further 'Members' personal rights', pp 261ff and 'General issues', pp 664ff.) The difficulties can be highlighted by supposing that in this case the company's articles did not require a director to hold shares, and that the excluded director held none.

2. Also, on the issue of whether this director held shares 'in his own right', making him a member of the company, note the different outcome in *Enviroco Ltd v Farstad Supply A/S* [2011] UKSC 16, where the shareholder had granted a *legal* mortgage over its shares, so the mortgagee became the registered owner. In these circumstances the mortgagor was no longer a 'member' of the company (CA 1985 ss 736, 736A(6) and (7); now see CA 2006 s 1159 and Sch 6), and so, in this case, there was no longer a parent/subsidiary relationship, and the 'subsidiary' was no longer protected by a contractual indemnity clause which covered the parent and its affiliates.

---

[7] See the discussion at 'Members' personal rights', pp 261ff.

Eligibility for appointment as a director

The age restrictions imposed by CA 2006 have been mentioned (see 'Appointment of directors', p 295). The general law also prevents bankrupts and certain classes of individuals from acting as directors, and a company's own articles can impose further restrictions.

But, in addition, a significant aspect of the control of companies in the general public interest lies in the prohibition of certain people (as a class, or specifically) from acting as company directors. Under the CDDA 1986, the courts may make disqualification orders against individuals or the Secretary of State may accept undertakings in lieu of such orders (see 'Directors' disqualification', pp 309ff).

Further restrictions (subject to some limited exceptions) have been imposed by the Insolvency Act 1986 (IA 1986) s 216 to prevent the *phoenix syndrome*. The goal is to prevent directors (including shadow directors, see 'Shadow directors: s 251', pp 329ff) of companies that have gone into insolvent liquidation from being directors (or in any way promoting, managing or being involved in a company or unincorporated business, whether or not as directors) that uses the same or substantially the same registered business or trading name as that used by the insolvent company during the 12 months preceding insolvency. Breach of this restriction is an offence punishable by fine or imprisonment (IA 1986 s 216). In addition, the individual may be personally liable for the debts and liabilities incurred by the company during the period that he or she is involved in its management (IA 1986 s 217). Liability is strict and ignorance is no defence.

Defective appointments and the validity of acts of directors: CA 2006 s 161

Despite all the preceding rules on appointment of directors, the acts undertaken by those acting as directors are generally valid even if the appointment is flawed: see the very strong wording of CA 2006 s 161. This means that third parties dealing with the company are generally protected,[8] and the company's remedy is to take action, if appropriate, against those responsible for the appointments and those acting improperly as directors.

CA 2006 s 161 supplements the protective provisions discussed earlier in the context of corporate contracting (see 'Deemed authority I: statutory deeming provisions to avoid constitutional limitations on directors' authority—CA 2006 s 40', pp 100ff). There are likely to be two limitations on s 161 coverage. First, these third parties are protected only if they act in good faith. Section 161 is silent on the issue, but *any* corporate transaction is voidable at the option of the company if the third party knew the director was acting beyond authority. This was also the approach in the identically worded CA 1985 provision.

Secondly, despite the breadth of the wording in CA 2006 s 161, cases on the CA 1985 provision require that there must, at some stage, have been a *purported* appointment of the person to the role of director. As Lord Simonds put it in *Morris v Kanssen*:[9]

> There is, as it appears to me, a vital distinction between (a) an appointment in which there is a defect or, in other words, a defective appointment, and (b) no appointment at all. In the first case it is implied that some act is done which purports to be an appointment but is by reason of some

---

[8] Indeed, s 161 applies even if the third party is aware of a dispute concerning the appointment or election of directors: *Abdelmamoud v The Egyptian Association in Great Britain Ltd* [2015] EWHC 1013 (Ch).

[9] [1946] AC 459.

> defect inadequate for the purpose; in the second case, there is not a defect, there is no act at all. The section does not say that the acts of a person acting as director shall be valid notwithstanding that it is afterwards discovered that he was not appointed a director.

Publicity and the appointment of directors: CA 2006 ss 162 and 167

Under CA 2006, the company must: (i) register particulars about its directors with the registrar at Companies House (s 167); (ii) keep its own register of directors (ss 162–164); and (iii) keep its own register of directors' residential addresses (s 165). (Public companies must also keep a register of secretaries: ss 275, 277–279.)

It is not clear why companies still need to maintain their own registers of directors, open for inspection by members for no fee and to others for a fee, when most people searching the records prefer the anonymity of Companies House.

The separate register of residential addresses (not open for inspection) is a 2006 change, introduced because directors' addresses need no longer be filed at Companies House. Indeed, CA 2006 now contains several provisions protecting the privacy of directors' residential addresses (see ss 240–246). The change reflects a growing concern for the safety of directors and their families, especially after some of the tactics used by campaigners, particularly against directors of companies involved in the use of animals in biomedical research.

The company and its defaulting officers (including shadow directors, see 'Shadow directors: s 251', pp 329ff) are liable to fines on conviction for any failure to comply with these provisions.

Additional publicity is required about directors of public companies, especially details of salary, qualifications and experience, that appear in annual reports for the company.

Acting as a board of directors: meetings and decisions

Absent special provisions, the general rule is that a board is expected to act by majority resolution on decisions taken at board meetings. After some early doubts, it was established that the informal and *unanimous* agreement of the directors is, for all ordinary purposes (but not for all purposes—see 'Removal of directors', p 300), equivalent to a resolution passed at a duly convened meeting: see *Runciman v Walter Runciman plc* [1992] BCLC 1084 at 1092; *Base Metal Trading Ltd v Shamurin* [2004] EWCA Civ 1316, CA. (Recall that the same rule applies to members, see *Cane v Jones* [4.17].)

In practice, most companies have articles containing specific provisions for various forms of decision-making, so overriding the general law on meetings and unanimous assent. The articles typically allow for 'meetings' to take place without all the directors being in the same place, so long as they can communicate with each other, and it does not matter how that is done (see Model Articles art 10 (private companies) and art 9 (public companies)). The articles may also allow directors to record their consent in writing (see Model Articles art 8 (private companies) and arts 17 and 18 (public companies) on consent to a *unanimous* decision only; indeed, the Model Articles for private companies go further, and allow for unanimous decisions regardless of how the directors communicate their common assent to each other (art 8)). Generally the votes of interested directors will not count towards the necessary majority (art 14 (private companies) and art 16 (public companies)).

As already noted, if the articles do not make the necessary provisions, the general law rule that unanimous informal decisions of the directors are binding may need to be relied upon. However, in *Guinness plc v Saunders* **[5.01]**[10] the Court of Appeal declined to accept that a *statutory* requirement of disclosure to a 'meeting of directors' (CA 1985 s 317(1) in that case; now see CA 2006 s 177) could be deemed to have been complied with simply because every individual member of the board knew of the matter. Fox LJ said ([1988] 1 WLR 863 at 868) that disclosure to 'a meeting of the directors of the company' is 'a wholly different thing from knowledge of individuals and involves the opportunity for positive consideration of the matter by the board as a body'. And yet CA 2006 s 177(6)(b) itself provides that a director need not declare an interest if, or to the extent that, the other directors are already aware of it. (For further discussion, see 'Duty to exercise independent judgement: CA 2006 s 173', pp 373ff.)

In addition, it is well established that a meeting cannot be held informally against the will of a dissenting director (*Barron v Potter* [1914] 1 Ch 895).

Removal of directors

Both CA 2006 and a company's articles provide mechanisms for the termination of appointments of directors. The trigger may be dissatisfaction with the director's performance; but, equally, it may simply be part of the company's process of management renewal, as with directors' retirement by rotation.[11] The court may also force the termination of a director's appointment (see 'Directors' disqualification', pp 309ff). In addition, a director may simply resign.

Here, forced removal by the members or by the board is considered; voluntary retirement and resignation are not.

Removal by the members

CA 2006 ss 168–169 provide wide powers for the removal of directors, by ordinary resolution, before the expiration of the director's period of office and notwithstanding anything in any agreement between the company and the director (s 168(1)).[12] Special formalities (including special notice) must be observed and a director is guaranteed certain protections (eg the right to protest his or her removal).

The statutory requirement for a meeting is mandatory. The *Duomatic* principle (**[4.15]**) of effective unanimous informal assent or informed acquiescence without a meeting is not appropriate in this context. This is because the formal procedure is designed to protect the impugned directors, not the voting members, and so it can only be waived by those directors. See *Re New Cedos Engineering Co Ltd* [1994] 1 BCLC 797; *Wright v Atlas Wright (Europe) Ltd* [1999] 2 BCLC 301 at 314–315.

---

[10] The House of Lords affirmed the decision of the Court of Appeal on grounds that did not raise this question.

[11] Eg for public companies, see Model Articles art 21; there is no equivalent in the Model Articles for private companies.

[12] The predecessor section, CA 1985 s 303, also indicated that the right was 'notwithstanding anything in the articles', but, since the Act overrides the articles, this was seen as unnecessary.

CA 2006 s 168 does not derogate from any other powers that might exist apart from this section (s 169(5)(b)). This means that all articles, including those that provide for dismissal of directors without the special protections inherent in s 168, remain valid (eg see later, on dismissal by the board). Nor does the section deprive the director of any compensation or damages payable in respect of the termination of the appointment as director or of any appointment terminating with that as director (s 168(5)(a)).

The intended impact of CA 2006 s 168 can sometimes be neutered, however. It is possible, although only in private companies, to put in place weighted voting rights that can make it impossible for the ordinary members to use the powers in s 168: see *Bushell v Faith* [6.02]. Such weighted voting is inappropriate in public companies, and impossible in listed companies (the London Stock Exchange would refuse listing).

Special voting rights may protect directors against removal under CA 2006 s 168.

[6.02] Bushell v Faith [1970] AC 1099 (House of Lords)

Bush Court (Southgate) Ltd had capital of £300 in £1 shares, with 100 shares held by Faith and each of his sisters, Mrs Bushell and Dr Bayne. Article 9 of the articles of association provided: 'In the event of a resolution being proposed at any general meeting of the company for the removal from office of any director, any shares held by that director shall on a poll in respect of such resolution carry the right to three votes per share . . .' Faith was thus able to record 300 votes and outvote his sisters, who recorded 200 votes between them, by demanding a poll on a motion to remove him from office. Ungoed-Thomas J held that art 9 was invalid because it infringed the Companies Act 1948 (CA 1948) s 184 (the equivalent of CA 2006 s 168), but his decision was reversed on appeal. The House of Lords (Lord Morris of Borth-y-Gest dissenting) upheld the effectiveness of the article.

LORD DONOVAN: My Lords, the issue here is the true construction of s 184 of the Companies Act 1948 [CA 2006 s 168] and I approach it with no conception of what the legislature wanted to achieve by the section other than such as can reasonably be deducted from its language.

Clearly it was intended to alter the method by which a director of a company could be removed while still in office. It enacts that this can be done by the company by ordinary resolution. Furthermore, it may be achieved notwithstanding anything in the company's articles, or in any agreement between the company and the director.

Accordingly any case (and one knows there were many) where the articles prescribed that a director should be removable during his period of office only by a special resolution or an extraordinary resolution, each of which necessitated inter alia a three to one majority of those present and voting at the meeting, is overridden by s 184. A simple majority of the votes will now suffice; an ordinary resolution being, in my opinion, a resolution capable of being carried by such a majority. Similarly any agreement, whether evidenced by the articles or otherwise, that a director shall be a director for life or for some fixed period is now also overreached.

The field over which s 184 operates is thus extensive for it includes, admittedly, all companies with a quotation on the Stock Exchange.

It is now contended, however, that it does something more; namely that it provides in effect that when the ordinary resolution proposing the removal of the director is put to the meeting each shareholder present shall have one vote per share and no more: and that any provision in the articles providing that any shareholder shall, in relation to *this* resolution, have 'weighted' votes attached to his shares, is also nullified by s 184. A provision for such 'weighting' of votes which applies generally, that is, as part of the normal pattern of voting, is accepted by the appellant as unobjectionable: but an article such as the one here under consideration which is special to a resolution seeking the removal of a director falls foul of s 184 and is overridden by it.

Why should this be? The section does not say so, as it easily could. And those who drafted it and enacted it certainly would have included among their numbers many who were familiar with the phenomenon of articles of association carrying 'weighted votes'. It must therefore have been plain at the outset that unless special provision were made, the mere direction that an ordinary resolution would do in order to remove a director would leave the section at risk of being made inoperative in the way that has been done here. Yet no such provision was made, and in this Parliament followed its practice of leaving to companies and their shareholders liberty to allocate voting rights as they pleased . . . .

LORDS REID and UPJOHN delivered concurring opinions.

LORD GUEST concurred.

LORD MORRIS OF BORTH-Y-GEST (dissenting): Some shares may . . . carry a greater voting power than others. On a resolution to remove a director shares will therefore carry the voting power that they possess. But this does not, in my view, warrant a device such as article 9 introduces. Its unconcealed effect is to make a director irremovable. If the question is posed whether the shares of the respondent possess any added voting weight the answer must be that they possess none whatsoever beyond, if valid, an ad hoc weight for the special purpose of circumventing s 184. If article 9 were writ large it would set out that a director is not to be removed against his will and that in order to achieve this and to thwart the express provisions of s 184 the voting power of any director threatened with removal is to be deemed to be greater than it actually is. The learned judge thought that to sanction this would be to make a mockery of the law. I think so also.

➤ Notes

1. As Lord Donovan observes, companies with a listing on the Stock Exchange may not circumvent CA 2006 s 168 by provisions in their articles, for this is forbidden by the Listing Rules. *De facto*, therefore, we have one regime for listed companies and another for all other companies.

2. One important consequence of CA 2006 s 168 is that a member or group of members together holding more than half of the shares in a company may remove the board and replace it with directors of their own choice.[13] For this reason, a takeover bid is usually made conditional upon acceptances being received which will take the bidder's holding to at least 51% of the voting shares.

3. 'Weighted voting' is not the only technique by which a director may be made irremovable, or virtually so. The draftsman of the company's articles in *Bushell v Faith* could have achieved much the same position if its shares had been divided into three classes (eg 100 'A' shares, 100 'B' shares and 100 'C' shares) and it was provided that each class of share should carry the exclusive right to appoint one director. Each member would then have had the protection of the rules relating to class rights (see 'Variation of class rights', pp 587ff). Alternatively, the three members could have entered into a shareholders' agreement which guaranteed each of them a permanent seat on the board: see *Russell v Northern Development Corpn Ltd* [4.35], in which the precedent of *Bushell v Faith* was of considerable weight.

4. Where there are no mitigating class rights, a majority shareholder is entitled to exercise his or her voting rights to appoint and remove directors. In support of that, the court may grant an order under CA 2006 s 306 (see Chapter 4) convening a general meeting in circumstances where the majority shareholder's voting entitlement is being neutered by the minority shareholder's refusal to attend meetings, thus denying a quorum: *Smith v Butler* [3.02].

---

[13] Although note the practical impediment of having to give special notice, and hold a meeting: see 'Removal of directors', pp 300ff.

➤ Questions

1. The members can use CA 2006 s 168 to dismiss a director 'without cause' (ie even if the director is performing perfectly properly and effectively). Why should the members have this right? Are there any disadvantages?

2. In *Russell v Northern Development Corpn Ltd* [4.35], the *company* could not bind itself by contract in a way that made it impossible for the company to alter its capital as permitted by the Act. Presumably a *company* could not bind itself in a way that made exercise of the rights in CA 2006 s 168 impossible. And yet in both these instances the company's rights can only be exercised by the members in general meeting. Given this, do shareholders' agreements and weighted voting rights make a mockery of the Act, or is the appropriate analysis a little more subtle?

Dismissal by the board

Articles often provide that the office of director is to be vacated if all the other members of the board make a written request for the director's resignation, although the Model Articles (both private and public) make no such provision.

Like all powers held by directors, exercise of this power is subject to the directors' duties to act for proper purposes, in good faith to promote the success of the company, and in a way that does not involve unacceptable conflicts of interest (see Chapter 5). But, subject to that limitation, the courts appear loath to allow this power to be further limited unless by explicit agreement: *Dear v Jackson* [2013] EWCA Civ 89.

➤ Question

An early suggestion (since dropped) for Model Articles for Private Companies gave power to the directors to terminate the appointment of one of their number only 'with cause'. Why should the dismissal power of the board of directors be more limited than that of members in general meeting?

Directors acting after their office is vacated

If directors continue to act after their office is vacated, for whatever reason, their acts will generally continue to bind the company: see CA 2006 s 161(1)(c) and s 161 generally. Also see 'Agency and authority in corporate contracting', pp 93ff, on a company's dealings with third parties.

Rights of directors on termination of appointment

Compensation claims for loss of office

Recall that directors have no entitlement to remuneration and generally no claim to any kind of tenure unless specifically provided for by contract. Even then, they cannot specifically enforce their rights to remain in office; they can only claim damages for breach.[14]

---

[14] The removal of a director may sometimes justify the making of a winding-up order on the 'just and equitable' ground, at least in a small company (see 'Compulsory winding up on the "just and equitable" ground', pp 840ff), or, alternatively, amount to 'unfairly prejudicial' conduct within CA 2006 s 994 (see 'Unfairly prejudicial conduct of the company's affairs', pp 715ff).

If there is a contract between the director and the company, then dismissal from office under CA 2006 s 168 may be a breach of that contract by the company. This will be the case if the contract is for a fixed period which has not expired, or if the director is entitled to a period of notice. Alternatively (or in addition), dismissal of a person from the office of director may breach a second contract between the director and the company if the director can perform the second contract only by being a director. For example, a contract between the managing director and his company may depend upon the person continuing to be a director of the company.

The company will then be liable in damages,[15] and the damages payments may be large. This is why provision is made to ensure that members can discover the terms of their directors' contracts of service (CA 2006 ss 228–229), and why long-term contracts are subject to approval by the members (s 188).[16] The following case extracts all concern arguments that termination of a directorship was *not* a breach of contract between the company and the director.

A contract that incorporates the provisions of a company's articles is subject to the articles being altered in the usual way, although an alteration cannot have retrospective effect.

[6.03] Swabey v Port Darwin Gold Mining Co (1889) 1 Meg 385 (Court of Appeal)

The articles provided that the directors were to be remunerated at the rate of £200 per annum. In July 1888 the company passed a special resolution altering the articles so that directors were thereafter to receive £5 per month. Swabey, a director, thereupon resigned office and claimed three months' accrued fees at the old rate. Stephen J rejected his claim, but he was successful in the Court of Appeal.

> LORD ESHER MR: The articles do not themselves form a contract, but from them you get the terms upon which the directors are serving. It would be absurd to hold that one of the parties to a contract could alter it as to service already performed under it. The company has power to alter the articles, but the directors would be entitled to their salary at the rate originally stated in the articles up to the time the articles were altered.
>
> LORD HALSBURY LC delivered a concurring judgment.
>
> LINDLEY LJ concurred.

It may be a breach of contract for a company to alter its articles or to act upon a power created by altering its articles.

[6.04] Southern Foundries (1926) Ltd v Shirlaw [1940] AC 701 (House of Lords)

In 1933, the respondent was by a written agreement appointed managing director of the appellant company ('Southern') for ten years. In 1936, after Southern had been taken over by Federated Foundries Ltd ('Federated'), Southern altered its articles so as to include,

---

[15] CA 2006 s 168 does not deprive the director of any compensation or damages payable in respect of termination of the appointment as director or of any appointment terminating with that as director (s 168(5)(a)).

[16] Although note that the director is subject to the usual common law duty to mitigate his or her damages by seeking substitute employment, ie the director is not automatically entitled to be 'paid out' to the end of the contractual term.

inter alia, a new art 8 which empowered Federated by a written instrument to remove any director of Southern. In 1937 Federated exercised this power and removed the respondent from his directorship. He sued Southern for breach of contract and Federated for wrongly procuring the breach of contract. He was awarded £12,000 damages against both defendants (a substantial sum at the time, hence the appeals), and the award was upheld by the Court of Appeal (Sir Wilfrid Greene MR dissenting), and by the House of Lords (Viscount Maugham and Lord Romer dissenting).

LORD ATKIN: My Lords, the question in this case is whether the appellant company have broken their contract with the respondent made in December 1933 that he should hold the office of managing director for ten years. The breach alleged is that under the articles adopted by the company, after the agreement, the respondent was removed from the position of director of the company by the Federated Foundries Ltd. There can be no doubt that the office of managing director could only be held by a director, and that upon the holder of the office of managing director ceasing for any cause to be a director the office would be ipso facto vacated. Under the articles in existence at the date of the agreement, by article 89 the office of a director could be vacated on the happening of six various events, bankruptcy, lunacy, etc, including the giving by the director of one month's notice to resign; while by article 105 the company by extraordinary resolution could remove him from his office. I feel no doubt that the true construction of the agreement is that the company agreed to employ the respondent and the respondent agreed to serve the company as managing director for the period of ten years. It was by the constitution of the company a condition of holding such office that the holder should continue to be a director: and such continuance depended upon the terms of the articles regulating the office of director. It was not disputed, and I take it to be clear law, that the company's articles so regulating the office of director could be altered from time to time: and therefore the continuance in office of the managing director under the agreement depended upon the provisions of the articles from time to time. Thus the contract of employment for the term of ten years was dependent upon the managing director continuing to be a director. This continuance of the directorship was a concurrent condition. The arrangement between the parties appears to me to be exactly described by the words of Cockburn CJ in *Stirling v Maitland*:[17] 'If a party enters into an arrangement which can only take effect by the continuance of an existing state of circumstances'; and in such a state of things the Lord Chief Justice said: 'I look on the law to be that . . . there is an implied engagement on his part that he shall do nothing of his own motion to put an end to that state of circumstances under which alone the arrangement can be operative.' That proposition in my opinion is well-established law. Personally I should not so much base the law on an implied term, as on a positive rule of the law of contract that conduct of either promiser or promisee which can be said to amount to himself 'of his own motion' bringing about the impossibility of performance is in itself a breach. If A promises to marry B and before performance of that contract marries C, A is not sued for breach of an implied contract not to marry anyone else, but for breach of his contract to marry B. I think it follows that if either the company of its own motion removed the respondent from the office of director under article 105, or if the respondent caused his office of director to be vacated by giving one month's notice of resignation under article 89, either of them would have committed a breach of the agreement in question . . .

The question that remains is whether if the removal by the company would have been a breach by the company, the removal under the altered articles by the Federated Foundries Ltd was a breach by the company. In this matter the Master of the Rolls agreed with the other members of the Court of Appeal; but all the members of this House are not agreed. My Lords, it is obvious that the question is not as simple as in the case just considered of the removal

[17] (1864) 5 B & S 840 at 852.

being by the Southern Foundries Ltd; but I venture respectfully to think that the result must be the same. The office of director involves contractual arrangements between the director and the company. If the company removes the director it puts an end to the contract: and indeed the contract relations cannot be determined unless by events stipulated for in the contract, by operation of law, or by the will of the two parties. The altered article 8 which gives power to the Federated Foundries Ltd to remove from office any director of the company is, when analysed, a power to the Federated to terminate a contract between the Southern and its director. It is an act which binds the Southern as against its promisee; and if a wrong to the respondent if done by the Southern it surely must be a wrong to the respondent if done by the Federated who derive their power to do the act from the Southern only. If a landlord gives power to a tenant to discharge the landlord's servants, gardener or gamekeeper, it is the master, the landlord, who is bound by the consequences of that discharge whether rightful, or whether wrongful, and so involving the payment of damages . . . The action of the Federated was, I think I may say avowedly, taken for the sole purpose of bringing the managing director's agreement to an end. I do not think that it could be said that the Southern committed any breach by adopting the new articles. But when the Federated acted upon the power conferred upon them in the new articles they bound the Southern if they acted in such a way that action by the Southern on the same articles would be a breach. It is not a question of agency but of acting under powers conferred by contract to interfere with a contract between the party granting the power and a third person . . .

LORD PORTER: The general principle therefore may, I think, be thus stated. A company cannot be precluded from altering its articles thereby giving itself power to act upon the provisions of the altered articles—but so to act may nevertheless be a breach of the contract if it is contrary to a stipulation in a contract validly made before the alteration.

Nor can an injunction be granted to prevent the adoption of the new articles and in that sense they are binding on all and sundry, but for the company to act upon them will none the less render it liable in damages if such action is contrary to the previous engagements of the company. If, therefore, the altered articles had provided for the dismissal without notice of a managing director previously appointed, the dismissal would be intra vires the company but would nevertheless expose the company to an action for damages if the appointment had been for a term of (say) ten years and he were dismissed in less . . .

LORD WRIGHT delivered a concurring opinion.

VISCOUNT MAUGHAM and LORD ROMER dissented.

➤ Notes

1. A *managing director* is often both the chief executive officer (CEO) of a company and a director who works full time for the company for a salary. The functions of a managing director are not fixed by law, but depend upon the particular terms of the appointment: *Harold Holdsworth & Co (Wakefield) Ltd v Caddies* [1955] 1 WLR 352, HL. Under the articles of most companies, a managing director will automatically lose office on ceasing for any reason to be a director. In larger companies, there may be more than one managing, or executive, director, but there will only be one CEO. See *Smith v Butler* **[3.02]**, where the powers and authority of managing directors are discussed.

2. The *Shirlaw* case was followed by Diplock J in *Shindler v Northern Raincoat Co Ltd* [1960] 1 WLR 1038, where the managing director had a written service agreement appointing him for ten years. By contrast, in the case next cited, the appointment was an informal one, and the only source from which the terms of the contract could be determined was the articles themselves. There was therefore no breach of contract when the company exercised a power of removal which was expressly contained in the articles.

Reasonable notice rules.

[6.05] Read v Astoria Garage (Streatham) Ltd [1952] Ch 637
(Court of Appeal)

The defendant company's articles included art 68 of Table A of the 1929 Act, which provided that the directors might appoint a managing director for such term and at such remuneration as they might think fit: '. . . but his appointment shall be subject to determination *ipso facto* if he ceases from any cause to be a director, or if the company in general meeting resolve that his tenure of the office of managing director . . . be determined'. Read was appointed managing director at a salary of £7 per week by a resolution of the board. Seventeen years later the board, with the approval of the company in general meeting, gave him notice terminating his employment. It was held that he had no claim for wrongful dismissal.

> JENKINS LJ: There is no record anywhere of any terms on which the plaintiff was appointed managing director beyond the minute of resolution no 4 which was passed at the first meeting of the directors by which the plaintiff was appointed managing director at a salary of £7 a week from 1 February 1932, and the articles of association of the company. The company's articles adopted Table A, with certain modifications. Amongst the articles of Table A adopted was article no 68. [His Lordship read the article.]
>
> It is argued by Mr Harold Brown for the plaintiff that, notwithstanding the provisions of article 68, there was a contract between the plaintiff and the defendant company in the nature of a contract of general hiring—a plain contract of employment, one of the terms of which was the plaintiff's employment should not be determined by the defendant company except by reasonable notice. The judge came to the conclusion that the terms of the plaintiff's appointment were not such as to entitle him to any notice in the event of the company choosing under article 68 to resolve in general meeting that his tenure of office as managing director be determined, and, in my judgment, the judge was clearly right . . .
>
> The directors purported by a resolution of the board to appoint him managing director. In my view, it is really clear beyond argument that the directors must be taken to have been making that appointment with reference to the provisions of article 68 of Table A—it was only under that article that they could make the appointment. Accordingly, in my view, the resolution, containing as it did no other special terms beyond the fixing of the remuneration of £7 a week, and containing nothing whatever amplifying, or inconsistent with, the provisions of article 68, must be taken to have been an appointment of the plaintiff as managing director on the terms of article 68, and accordingly it was an appointment upon terms, inter alia, that it should be subject to termination if the company in general meeting resolved that the plaintiff's tenure of the office of managing director be determined . . .
>
> MORRIS LJ concurred.

➤ Notes

1. In *Nelson v James & Sons Ltd* [1914] 2 KB 770, CA, Nelson had been appointed managing director of the company by a written agreement 'for so long as he shall remain a director of the company and retain his qualification and shall efficiently perform the duties of the said office'. The board revoked his appointment. It did not allege any breach of the terms of the agreement but purported to rely upon a provision in the articles authorising them to do so. The company argued that in any agreement entered into by the directors for the appointment of a managing director, a term must be implied giving them the right to revoke such appointment. It was held, however, that no term could be incorporated by implication

from the articles into this contract so as to override its express terms, and that Nelson's dismissal was unjustified. He was awarded £15,000 damages.

2. In *Read v Astoria Garage*, the director might have sought to rely on an implied term or an estoppel that required the company to give him reasonable notice of termination, but recall the failure of such arguments in *Baird Textile Holdings Ltd v Marks & Spencer plc* [2001] EWCA Civ 274, after M&S terminated a long-standing arrangement with Baird for the supply of goods.

Complaint that alteration of the articles is invalid as an objectionable exercise of power by the members.

[6.06] Shuttleworth v Cox Bros & Co (Maidenhead) Ltd [1927] 2 KB 9 (Court of Appeal)

The plaintiff had been removed from the position of 'permanent' director, to which he had been appointed by the articles, in the circumstances described by Atkin LJ in his judgment. This followed the discovery of irregularities in the accounts between him and the company. He claimed his dismissal was wrongful. The Court of Appeal, affirming Avory J, upheld the validity of the company's action.

ATKIN LJ: The plaintiff was a director of the defendant company from May 1921, when the company was incorporated, until 1926. Up to 1924 he was a director on the terms of article 18, which provided that he and others should be the first directors of the company, that they should be permanent directors, and that each of them should be entitled to hold office so long as he should live, unless he should become disqualified from any of the causes specified in article 22. At that time article 22 provided that the office of director should be vacated in any of the events specified in the six clauses of the article. In 1924 the company passed an altered article by a special resolution . . . adding to the six clauses of article 22 a seventh clause: 'If he shall be requested in writing by all the other directors to resign his office.' Some ten or eleven months after article 22 was altered he was requested in writing to resign his office. He claims in this action that the clause added to the article is invalid, and that he still remains a director . . .

[The] contract that they shall be permanent directors at a salary is contained in the articles only . . . In these circumstances the proper inference appears to be that there was a contract that the plaintiff should be a permanent director, but a contract . . . which could be altered by a special resolution of the company in accordance with the provisions of the Companies Act; and inasmuch as the contract contemplated the permanent office being vacated in one of six contingencies, it is not inconsistent with the contract that the article should be altered so as to add a seventh contingency. In other words, it is a contract made upon the terms of an alterable article, and therefore neither of the contracting parties can complain if the article is altered. Consequently I cannot find that there has been any breach of contract in making the alteration.

The only other question is whether the article is upon general principles objectionable as being not honestly made within the powers of the company. Here the limits to the power of the company to alter its articles have to be considered. Certain limits there are, and they have been laid down in several cases, notably by Lindley MR in *Allen v Gold Reefs of West Africa Ltd* **[4.22]** . . . There in a reasoned and lucid judgment the Master of the Rolls uses the phrase 'bona fide for the benefit of the company'. But neither this court nor any court should consider itself fettered by the form of words, as if it were a phrase in an Act of Parliament which must be accepted and construed as it stands. We must study what its real meaning is by the light of the principles which were being laid down by the Master of the Rolls when he used the phrase . . . The only question is whether or not the shareholders, in considering whether they shall alter articles, honestly intend to exercise their powers for the benefit of the company. If they do then, subject to one or two reservations which have been explained, the alteration must stand. It is not a matter of law for the court whether or not a particular alteration is for the benefit of the company; nor is it the business of a judge to review the decision of every company in the country on these questions. And even if the question were not for the shareholders themselves, but for some other body, it must be a question of fact. In this case there is a finding of fact by the jury that the alteration was for the benefit of the company; but I do not decide the case on that ground. In my view the question is solely for the shareholders acting in good faith. The circumstances may be such as to lead to one conclusion only, that the majority of the shareholders are acting so oppressively that they cannot be acting in good faith; or, to put it in another way, it may be that their decision must be one which could [not] be taken by persons acting in good faith with a view to the benefit of the company. But these are matters outside and apart from the question, does this or that tribunal consider, in the light of events which have happened, that the alteration was or was not for the benefit of the company? With great respect to a very learned judge I cannot agree with the judgment of Peterson J to the contrary on this point.[18] In my view the passage which has been cited from the judgment of Lord Sterndale MR in *Sidebottom's* case **[4.23]** makes it clear that in his view the ultimate decision is to be the decision of the majority of the shareholders . . .

BANKES and SCRUTTON LJJ delivered concurring judgments.

➤ Question

In what circumstances might it be possible for directors to advance this sort of argument successfully? (See 'Removal of directors', pp 300ff.)

Other payments for loss of office

Any *voluntary or non-contractual* termination payment must be approved by the members (CA 2006 ss 215–222). CA 2006 s 222 specifies the remedies for breach of this requirement subject to limited exceptions. The remedies are: any such payment to the director is held on trust for the company; and any director who authorised such payment is jointly and severally liable to indemnify the company for any loss resulting from the payment. For the avoidance of doubt, these rules do not apply to any bona fide payment by way of damages for breach of contract, or by way of pension in respect of past services, or any payment required to be made by virtue of the terms of the director's contract.

Directors' disqualification

Outline of the statutory jurisdiction

Acting to protect the public interest, the Secretary of State for Business, Innovation and Skills may apply to the courts to have certain individuals disqualified from acting as directors (*Re Sevenoaks Stationers (Retail) Ltd* **[6.08]**).[19] A related but subsidiary goal is to raise the standards of honesty and diligence in corporate management (*Re Barings plc* [1998] BCC 583 at 590).

The courts have wide statutory powers to order that directors of companies that have gone into insolvent liquidation, or people who have committed serious or persistent

---

[18] In *Dafen Tinplate Co Ltd v Llanelly Steel Co (1907) Ltd* **[4.25]**.
[19] Or may direct the Official Receiver to make the application, if it comes under CDDA 1986 s 6.

breaches of company law, shall be banned for a period of time from being directors of a company or being concerned (directly or indirectly) in their management, except with the leave of the court. The legislation on disqualification is consolidated in CDDA 1986.[20]

Under this Act, the court *must* make a disqualification order against a person who is deemed 'unfit' to manage a company (CDDA 1986 s 6 and ss 9Aff), being a person who has:

(i)   been a director of a company that has become insolvent and who is found 'unfit' to be concerned in the management of a company (s 6), or similarly been found 'unfit' after a statutory investigation into the affairs of a company (s 8); or

(ii) been a director of a company that has breached competition law and who is found 'unfit' to be concerned in the management of a company (s 9A);

and may make a disqualification order in other circumstances (CDDA 1986 ss 1–5A, 10ff), including against someone who has:

(iii) been convicted of an indictable offence in connection with the formation or management of a company (s 2);

(iv) been persistently in breach of his or her obligations under the Companies Act, for example to file returns (ss 3, 5);

(v)   been guilty of fraud or fraudulent trading revealed in a winding up (s 4);

(vi) been guilty of fraudulent or wrongful trading as defined in IA 1986 ss 213–214 (s 10).

The SBEEA 2015 introduced several amendments to CDDA 1986 with a view to strengthening the directors' disqualification regime. These broaden the matters which must be taken into account: a new CDDA 1986 s 12C requires a number of factors listed in CDDA 1986 Sch 1 to be considered in every case where a mandatory or discretionary disqualification order is made or an undertaking accepted. These factors also apply to shadow directors, and now cover conduct in relation to both domestic and overseas companies. The factors include the frequency and extent to which the person was responsible for the causes of the company either becoming insolvent or contravening applicable legislative or other requirements; the nature and extent of any actual or potential loss or harm caused by the person's conduct; and any misfeasance or breach of any fiduciary or other duty by the director and its frequency.

Other amendments introduced by SBEEA 2015 extend the power of the Secretary of State or the official receiver to request information directly from any person (not just an insolvency office-holder as previously) in relation to a person's conduct as a director of a company that has been insolvent; permit an extension of the time period for bringing proceedings from two years to three years (for post-commencement insolvencies); and—very significantly—introduce the possibility of compensation orders against disqualified directors.

In addition, in the event that a director is disqualified on the ground of unfitness, the court may also impose a disqualification order against the person 'instructing' such director if it is satisfied that the director acted in accordance with the person's directions or instructions (SBEEA 2015 s 105, inserting a new s 8ZA into CDDA 1986).[21]

Amongst the various grounds of disqualification, CDDA 1986 ss 6, 8 and 9A are of particular interest because of the statutory concept of 'unfitness', which is elaborated in CDDA 1986 Sch 1. These provisions amplify the directors' traditional common law duties of care

---

[20] See A Walters, 'Directors' Duties: Impact of the CDDA' (2000) 21 *Company Lawyer* 110.

[21] Note that this is wider than the definition of a 'shadow director', with whose instructions the *board* must customarily comply.

and skill; indeed, this is a 'growth area' in which new standards of conduct are being set and a greater awareness of the responsibilities of directors is being fostered.[22]

The Insolvency Service is charged with the task of enforcing this branch of the law. Whenever a company goes into receivership, administration or insolvent liquidation, a report on the conduct of every director has to be made to the Secretary of State for Business, Innovation and Skills by the insolvency practitioner concerned (see 'Investigating and reporting the affairs of the company', pp 870ff). Disqualifications are currently being made at the rate of about 1,200 per annum. A *disqualification order* may ban the person from being a director or being concerned in the management of a company for up to 15 years in the more serious cases (eg fraudulent trading) and up to five years in other cases (eg persistent failure to file returns with the registrar). The registrar maintains a register of the names of those against whom disqualification orders have been made (CDDA 1986 s 18). Under the new regime, the Secretary of State may also apply to the court for a compensation order against a disqualified director if his conduct has caused loss to one or more creditors of the insolvent company (SBEEA 2015 s 110, inserting new ss15A–C into CDDA 1986).

When CDDA 1986 was introduced, it made no provision for directors to admit that their conduct justified a finding of 'unfitness' and, in effect, plead guilty to the charge brought against them. As a result, every case carried the burden and expense of a contested trial, and the resulting workloads inevitably led to delays.[23] Now disqualification can be imposed without any court hearing at all. The Act was amended in 2000 and 2015 respectively to allow the Secretary of State to accept *disqualification undertakings* from directors (or persons instructing unfit directors) that for specified periods they will not do any of the things normally prohibited by a disqualification order. Such undertakings have consequences identical in all material respects to disqualification orders (see CDDA 1986 ss 1A, 7(2A) and 8(2A)). In the past few years almost all disqualifications are a result of undertakings rather than court orders, and reporting of new cases is now rare.

Note that, despite a disqualification order or undertaking, the court has a discretion to allow the director to act as a director in specific circumstances that make his or her input essential (CDDA 1986 ss 1(1) and 1A(1)): see *Secretary of State for Trade and Industry v Swan (No 2)* **[6.11]**.

An enormous number of disqualification cases used to be heard and reported in this area. Those cited in the following extracts provide an illustration. Two are particularly significant. In the early decision of *Re Sevenoaks Stationers (Retail) Ltd* **[6.08]**, the Court of Appeal laid down guidelines for the exercise of this jurisdiction. And *Re Barings plc (No 5)* **[6.12]** probably remains the best example of the significant role that disqualification cases played in the development of the law on directors' duties of care, skill and diligence.

Human rights issues have arisen. In *Saunders v UK* (see 'Inspections and subsequent fair trials—criminal and civil cases', p 777), the European Court of Human Rights decided it was an infringement of human rights for statements obtained under compulsion (in company investigations) to be used as evidence in criminal prosecutions of the individual in question. Such usage is no longer allowed. Nevertheless, these statements are regularly relied on in disqualification proceedings, and both the European Court of Human Rights and UK courts have ruled that, since the nature of these proceedings is essentially civil

---

[22] Especially when the possible liability of directors for wrongful trading (*Re Produce Marketing Consortium Ltd (No 2)* **[16.16]**) is also taken into account.

[23] This difficulty was initially overcome by judicial ingenuity: under what was known as the '*Carecraft*' procedure (named after *Re Carecraft Construction Co Ltd* [1993] 4 All ER 499), if a director was willing to concede that a finding of unfitness was appropriate, and also agree that a period of disqualification within a certain range (say, four to six years) was merited, the court could proceed on the basis of an agreed statement of facts and dispose of the case without a full hearing. This procedure remains available, but in practice it has been overtaken by the improved statutory provisions.

and regulatory, not criminal, no violation of human rights is involved: see *DC, HS and AD v UK* [2000] BCLC 710 and *Re Westminster Property Management Ltd* [2000] 2 BCLC 396, CA.

Finally, the court has warned against case preparation practices by the Secretary of State which risk unfairness and oppression of both witnesses and defendant directors: see the statement of Peter Smith J following the discontinuance of proceedings in *Secretary of State v Fowler* (formerly known as *Home Retail v Farepak*), 21 June 2012.[24]

Jurisdiction to disqualify for 'unfitness' under CDDA ss 6 and 8

CDDA 1986 ss 6 and 8 compared.

[6.07] Re JA Chapman and Co Ltd [2003] EWHC 532 (Ch) (Chancery Division)

> PETER SMITH J: The application is made under section 8 CDDA 86 following a report from inspectors following an investigation under section 447 of the Companies Act 1985 [this is still in force]. In the case of an application under section 8 CDDA 86 the Court has a discretionary power of disqualification against a person where it is satisfied that his conduct in relation to the company makes him unfit to be concerned in the management of a company.
>
> This contrasts with the applications that are normally made under section 6 CDDA 86, where the Court is under an obligation to make a disqualification order against a person where such unfitness is satisfied.
>
> There are a number of differences between the two sections. First, as I have said under the power of disqualification under section 8 the Court retains a discretionary power not to disqualify even if the Defendant's conduct is unfit. That must be read in the light of the observations of Lloyd J in *re Atlantic Computers plc* [Ch, 15 June 1998] where he observed that it would be unusual for the Court to use its discretion in this way. Second, under section 8 there is no minimum period of disqualification whereas under section 6 there is a minimum of 2 years. Third there is no limitation period for proceedings under section 8. Fourth, there is no requirement for the company to become insolvent for an application under section 8. Fifth, the application under section 8 must be made by the Secretary of State. The Official Receiver cannot apply and finally, the County Court has no jurisdiction under section 8.
>
> Nevertheless, there are a number of similarities. I have already observed the test is the same as to unfitness. Second, it is established that the disqualification periods (if any) set out under section 6 in *re Sevenoaks Stationers (Retail) Ltd* **[6.08]** are to be applied to the period of disqualification under section 8 see *re Samuel Sherman plc* [1991] 1 WLR 1070.

➤ Note

Although there is a two/three-year period[25] for proceedings to be brought without leave under s 6 (CDDA 1986 s 7(2)), this is not strictly a limitation period: *Instant Access Properties Ltd* [2011] EWHC 3022 (Ch). There, Floyd J held that 'after the period has expired a defendant director does not acquire an immunity from suit. All that occurs is that the Secretary of State needs to surmount an additional hurdle' [8]. The court therefore embarked on a

---

[24] www.judiciary.gov.uk/judgments/farepak-judges-statement.

[25] Two years for insolvencies before 1 October 2015; three years now (SBEEA 2015 s 108(1), amending CDDA 1986 s 7(2)).

balancing exercise, eventually concluding that the public interest in bringing the case outside the two-year period (in view of the gravity of the allegations and their prospect of success) outweighed the purported prejudice caused by the delay.

Guidelines for exercise of the jurisdiction.

[6.08] Re Sevenoaks Stationers (Retail) Ltd [1991] Ch 164 (Court of Appeal)

Cruddas, a chartered accountant, was a director of five companies which had become insolvent with a total net deficiency of £600,000. The defaults proved against him in respect of one or more of the companies included: failing to keep proper accounting records; failing to ensure that annual returns were filed and that annual accounts were prepared and audited; causing the companies to incur debts when he ought to have known that they were in severe financial difficulties; causing them to trade while insolvent; and failing to pay Crown debts in respect of PAYE and NIC contributions and VAT. The Court of Appeal upheld the judge's finding that he was 'unfit to be concerned in the management of a company' (CDDA 1986 s 6). A disqualification order for five years was imposed.

> DILLON LJ: . . . [This] appeal has an importance beyond its own facts, since it is the first appeal against a disqualification order which has come to this court . . .
>
> I would for my part endorse the division of the potential 15 year disqualification period into three brackets, which was put forward by Mr Keenan for the official receiver to Harman J in the present case and has been put forward by Mr Charles for the official receiver in other cases, viz: (i) the top bracket of disqualification for periods over 10 years should be reserved for particularly serious cases. These may include cases where a director who has already had one period of disqualification imposed on him falls to be disqualified yet again. (ii) The minimum bracket of two to five years' disqualification should be applied where, though disqualification is mandatory, the case is, relatively, not very serious. (iii) The middle bracket of disqualification for from six to 10 years should apply for serious cases which do not merit the top bracket.
>
> I will come back to the appropriate bracket and period of disqualification when I have considered the facts and other issues.
>
> [His Lordship discussed the facts, and continued:]
>
> It is beyond dispute that the purpose of s 6 is to protect the public, and in particular potential creditors of companies, from losing money through companies becoming insolvent when the directors of those companies are people unfit to be concerned in the management of a company. The test laid down in s 6—apart from the requirement that the person concerned is or has been a director of a company which has become insolvent—is whether the person's conduct as a director of the company or companies in question 'makes him unfit to be concerned in the management of a company'. These are ordinary words of the English language and they should be simple to apply in most cases. It is important to hold to those words in each case.
>
> The judges of the Chancery Division have, understandably, attempted in certain cases to give guidance to what does or does not make a person unfit to be concerned in the management of a company. Thus in *Re Lo-Line Electric Motors Ltd*,[26] Sir Nicolas Browne-Wilkinson V-C said:
>
>> 'Ordinary commercial misjudgment is in itself not sufficient to justify disqualification. In the normal case, the conduct complained of must display a lack of commercial probity, although I have no doubt in an extreme case of gross negligence or total incompetence disqualification could be appropriate.'

---

[26] [1988] Ch 477 at 486.

Then he said that the director in question

'has been shown to have behaved in a commercially culpable manner in trading through limited companies when he knew them to be insolvent and in using the unpaid Crown debts to finance such trading.'

Such statements may be helpful in identifying particular circumstances in which a person would clearly be unfit.

This is not a case in which it was alleged that Mr Cruddas had, in the colloquial phrase, 'ripped off' the public and pocketed the proceeds. On the contrary, and as the judge found, he had lost a lot of his own money . . . There was evidence that Mr Cruddas had remortgaged his home to raise money to pay creditors of the companies, and he claimed to have lost from £200,000 to £250,000 of his own money.

I turn next to the question of Crown debts. As to this the judge said:[27]

'In the circumstances I am faced with admitted deficiencies of a most serious character, including in particular Crown debts in total of an order of £120,000 which were left outstanding . . . It is, in my judgment, a badge of commercial immorality to cause moneys which have been taken under force of law from third parties (PAYE deductions, after all, are taken under compulsion of law from wages which are owed to employees; VAT is taken under compulsion of law from members of the public who purchase goods as an addition to the price of the goods) to be not paid over to the Crown.'

There have been differing views expressed by Chancery judges about the significance of Crown debts on a disqualification application and the phrase has tended to become something of a ritual incantation. In some earlier cases, Harman J regarded such Crown debts as 'quasi-trust moneys'. That view has not however been followed by other judges, and the official receiver does not seek to resurrect it. A different view was expressed by Hoffmann J in *Re Dawson Print Group Ltd*,[28] where he said, in a passage with which I entirely agree:

'. . . but the fact is that, no doubt for good reasons, the Exchequer and the Commissioners of Customs and Excise have chosen to appoint traders to be tax collectors on their behalf with the attendant risk. That risk is, to some extent, compensated by the preference which they have on insolvency. There is, as yet, no obligation on traders to keep such moneys in a separate account, as there might be if they were really trust moneys. They are simply a debt owed by the company to the revenue or the Commissioner of Customs and Excise. I cannot accept that failure to pay these debts is regarded in the commercial world generally as such a breach of commercial morality that it requires in itself a conclusion that the directors concerned are unfit to be involved in the management of the company.'

The official receiver cannot, in my judgment, automatically treat non-payment of any Crown debt as evidence of unfitness of the directors. It is necessary to look more closely in each case to see what the significance, if any, of the non-payment of the Crown debt is.

Mr Cruddas made a deliberate decision to pay only those creditors who pressed for payment. The obvious result was that the . . . companies traded, when in fact insolvent and known to be in difficulties, at the expense of those creditors who, like the Crown, happened not to be pressing for payment. Such conduct on the part of a director can well, in my judgment, be relied on as a ground for saying that he is unfit to be concerned in the management

---

[27] [1990] BCLC 668 at 671.
[28] [1987] BCLC 601.

of a company. But what is relevant in the Crown's position is not that the debt was a debt which arose from a compulsory deduction from employees' wages or a compulsory payment of VAT, but that the Crown was not pressing for payment, and the director was taking unfair advantage of that forbearance on the part of the Crown, and, instead of providing adequate working capital, was trading at the Crown's expense while the companies were in jeopardy. It would be equally unfair to trade in that way and in such circumstances at the expense of creditors other than the Crown . . .

[His Lordship reviewed the various defaults which had been established against the respondent, and fixed a disqualification period of five years.]

BUTLER-SLOSS and STAUGHTON LJJ concurred.

➤ Notes

1. Applications under the CDDA 1986 are normally brought by the Secretary of State for Business, Innovation and Skills or the official receiver against individuals who are or have been company directors. The jurisdiction is broader than that, however. In *Asegaai Consultants Ltd* [2012] EWHC 1899 (Ch), a successful application was brought by the company's liquidator against his predecessor liquidator (who had never been a director of any of the companies in question) for disqualification as a director and insolvency practitioner. Newey J held that the liquidator had standing: he did not need a financial interest in a disqualification order being made, since applications are essentially for the protection of the public and not for private advantage; moreover, there was no suspicion that the liquidator had an improper ulterior motive, and the application was fully supported by the company's only legitimate creditor and the Secretary of State.

2. In the same case, Newey J also considered the appropriate way of cumulating relatively minor breaches in order to satisfy the test laid down in s 6:

Were a serious breach of duty established, the Court could surely take other, less important breaches into account when deciding what, if any, order to make under section 4. A number of relatively minor breaches of duty could also, taken together, be thought serious enough to warrant a disqualification order [24].

3. It is clear that s 6 extends to *de facto* directors. The paramount purpose of disqualification is to protect the public from unscrupulous corporate management. It would frustrate a primary objective of the CDDA if a person who actually was responsible for such management could escape disqualification by the simple expedient of never formally being appointed as a director: *Re UKLI Ltd* [2013] EWHC 680 (Ch) at [24].

4. A 15-year term was granted in *Secretary of State for Business, Innovation and Skills v Whyte* [2014] CSOH 148 by the Scottish Court of Session (Outer House). In applying *Sevenoaks Stationers* **[6.08]**, Lord Tyre opted for 'as long a period of disqualification as I am statutorily empowered to do', for the 'present case consists of a combination of dishonesty, disregard for the interests of the companies to which he owed duties and of the creditors of those companies, use of Crown debts to finance trade, misappropriation of company funds . . . for private purposes, and wilful breach of a director's administrative duties', and described their effect as 'quite out of the ordinary'; it was also relevant that the respondent had previously undergone a lengthy period of disqualification [13].

5. In *Secretary of State for Business, Innovation and Skills v Warry* [2014] EWHC 1381 (Ch), Judge Hodge QC laid down some guidance on the approach to the disqualification of directors involved in 'MTIC fraud' ('missing trader intra-community VAT fraud'). Because the persistence, prevalence and loss to the HMRC is potentially so great, at least the minimum tariff should be imposed (two to five years); where the director ought to have known but did not,[29] then the period should be in the middle bracket (five to ten years), but towards the top half unless there were extenuating circumstances; and where the director was knowingly involved (including wilfully turning a blind eye) or played a significant role, the highest bracket (over ten years) should be imposed. Although Judge Hodge QC was applying his mind to this specific type of fraud, his discussion sheds further light on the guidance in *Sevenoaks Stationers* **[6.08]**.

Summary of the law and its application.

[6.09] Secretary of State for Trade and Industry v Swan [2005] EWHC 603 (Chancery Division)

The Secretary of State applied for disqualification orders against former directors (S and N) of a parent company and certain other companies within the group. S was both the chairman and chief executive of the parent company and N was a non-executive director. The group had practised 'cheque kiting',[30] which fell within the control of the finance director. As a result of the cheque-kiting practice, an indebtedness statement sent to shareholders showed misleading figures. Other irregularities were alleged. The judge held that it was not established that S had actual knowledge of the cheque kiting, but his failure properly to inquire into the reason for the cheques (for sums completely out of line with the company's normal scale of transaction) before signing them had permitted the group's cheque-kiting policy to continue, and was a serious dereliction of his duty as a director, although only within the lowest of the three categories specified in *Re Sevenoaks Stationers (Retail) Ltd* **[6.08]**. In the circumstances, bearing in mind the purpose of the Act, and that the cheque-kiting policy had not caused any person any loss or played a role in the insolvency of the company, the appropriate period of disqualification was four years. Equally, there was no cogent evidence that N had known of the cheque-kiting policy, but he had failed to react appropriately to serious allegations of financial and accounting irregularities, made to him against the finance director. If he had investigated, the cheque kiting would have come to light. This lapse in judgement was serious, precisely when decisive action was required of a non-executive director. In all the circumstances, N was disqualified for three years.

ETHERTON J:

76. The burden of proving unfitness [under CDDA 1986 s 6] lies on the SoS [Secretary of State]. Although the standard of proof is the civil standard, that is to say on the balance of probabilities, the seriousness of the allegation is reflected in the need for evidence of appropriate cogency to discharge the burden of proof: *Re Living Images Ltd* [1996] 1 BCLC 348, 355–356; *Re H* [1996] AC 563, 586–587 (Lord Nicholls).

---

[29] Ie no actual knowledge and no wilfully shutting eyes to the obvious.

[30] Cheque kiting can take a number of different forms. At the heart of the process is the utilisation by the kiter of the period taken by the bank to clear a cheque so as to obtain a fictional increase in the balance of the payee's account before the cheque is cleared and its amount is deducted from the payer's account. It can therefore be used as a means to generate fictitious funds which may then be misappropriated or used to cover short-term cash-flow problems, or simply to create the false impression of a healthier bank balance or cash-flow than would otherwise be the case.

77. The determination of unfitness under s.6 is a two-stage process. First, the SoS must establish as facts, to the requisite standard of proof, the matters on which the allegation of unfitness is based. Second, the court must be satisfied that the conduct alleged is sufficiently serious to warrant disqualification.

78. In determining whether past conduct leads to the conclusion of 'unfitness' the court is entitled to consider any relevant contemporary extenuating circumstances.

79. The question is whether, viewed cumulatively and taking into account any extenuating circumstances, the director's conduct in relation to the company has fallen below the standards of probity and competence appropriate for persons fit to be directors of companies: *Re Grayan Building Services Ltd* [1995] Ch. 241, 253 (Hoffmann LJ).

80. So far as incompetence is concerned, the authorities indicate that a high level of incompetence is required to satisfy s.6 of the Act. In *Re Barings plc (No.5)* [1999] 1 BCLC 433 at pp. 483–484 Jonathan Parker J said:

'Where, as in the instant case, the Secretary of State's case is based solely on allegations of incompetence (no dishonesty of any sort being alleged against any of the respondents), the burden is on the Secretary of State to satisfy the court that the conduct complained of demonstrates incompetence of a high degree. Various expressions have been used by the courts in this connection, including "total incompetence" (see *Re Lo-Line Electric Motors Ltd* [1998] BCLC 325 at 337, [1988] Ch 477 at 486 per Browne-Wilkinson V-C), incompetence "in a very marked degree" (see *Re Sevenoaks Stationers (Retail) Ltd* **[6.08]** [1991] Ch 164 at 184 per Dillon LJ) and "really gross incompetence" (see *Re Dawson Print Group Ltd* [1987] BCLC 601 per Hoffmann J). Whatever words one chooses to use, the substantive point is that the burden on the Secretary of State in establishing unfitness based on incompetence is a heavy one. The reason for that is the serious nature of a disqualification order, including the fact that (subject to the court giving leave under section 17 of the Act) the order will prevent the respondent being concerned in the management of any company.'

81. On appeal from the decision of Jonathan Parker J, Morritt LJ, giving the judgment of the Court of Appeal, said at [2000] 1 BCLC 523, 534:

'. . . the judge made a number of observations on the proper construction and application of the Act to which we refer, not because we disagree with the judge, but because we wish to emphasise the propositions to which he referred. . . . Third, where the allegation is incompetence without dishonesty it is to be demonstrated to a high degree . . . This follows from the nature of the penalty. Nevertheless the degree of incompetence should not be exaggerated given the ability of the court to grant leave, as envisaged by the disqualification order as defined in s.1, notwithstanding the making of such an order'.

82. If the court finds the allegations of unfitness proved to the requisite standard and degree, then the court must, under s.6, disqualify the director for a period of two years at least.

83. The fact that the director may be unlikely to offend again may be relevant to the length of the period of disqualification, but not to whether or not he should be disqualified: *Re Landhurst Leasing plc* [1999] 1 BCLC 286, 344h–345b.

84. The disqualification is mandatory in order to protect the parties, raise standards and to act as a deterrent. Hoffman[n] LJ expressed the position as follows in *Re Grayan Building Services Ltd* at p.253H–254D:

'Parliament has decided that it is occasionally necessary to disqualify a company director to encourage the others. Or as Sir Donald Nicholls V.-C. said in *In re Swift 736 Ltd.* [1993] BCLC 896, 899:

"Those who make use of limited liability must do so with a proper sense of responsibility. The directors' disqualification procedure is an important sanction introduced by Parliament to raise standards in this regard."

> If this should be thought too harsh a view, it must be remembered that a disqualified director can always apply for leave under section 17 and the question of whether he has shown himself unlikely to offend again will obviously be highly material to whether he is granted leave or not. It may also be relevant by way of mitigation on the length of disqualification . . .'

It follows that I agree with the approach of Vinelott J in *In re Pamstock Ltd* [1994] 1 BCLC 716 when he said that it was his duty to disqualify a director whose conduct 'fell short of the standard of conduct which is today expected of a director of a company which enjoys the privilege of limited liability' even though he did so with regret because, he said, at p. 737:

> 'The respondent seemed to me (so far as I can judge from the evidence before me) to be a man who today is capable of discharging his duties as a director honestly and diligently.'

But the court is required to disqualify a director whose conduct has made him unfit, as the judge said:

> 'even though the misconduct may have occurred some years ago and even though the court may be satisfied that the respondent has since shown himself of capable of behaving responsibly.'

85. Lord Woolf MR summarised the policy behind the legislation as follows in *Re Blackspur Group plc* [1998] 1 WLR 422 CA at p. 426:

> 'The purpose of the Act of 1986 is the protection of the public, by means of prohibitory remedial action, by anticipated deterrent effect on further misconduct and by encouragement of higher standards of honesty and diligence in corporate management, from those who are unfit to be concerned in the management of a company.'

86. The relevant period of disqualification is in the discretion of the judge, to be exercised in accordance with the relevant principles set down in *Re Sevenoaks Stationers (Retail) Ltd* **[6.08]** (particularly serious cases: 11–15 years; serious cases which do not merit the top bracket: 6–10 years; relatively, not very serious cases: 2–5 years).

It is no defence to disqualification proceedings that the company's creditors would be, or could have been, paid in full.

[6.10] Official Receiver v Jupe [2011] 1 BCLC 191 (Nottingham County Court)

When faced with disqualification proceedings brought by the Official Receiver, Jupe, the director, alleged that the liquidator had sold the company's land at a gross undervalue, and that, had it been sold at its true value, all the company's creditors would have been paid in full. Judge Mithani QC, without hearing argument, held that he would have rejected such a defence.

JUDGE MITHANI QC:

21. It is clear that a company becoming insolvent within the meaning of s 6 of the Company Directors Disqualification Act 1986 is simply the gateway to the bringing of disqualification proceedings against a defendant under s 6. Once that gateway is passed, the fact that the creditors of the company have, or might be, paid in full will not, ordinarily, amount to a defence to the proceedings, although the court might take that fact into account in coming to its overall assessment about whether unfitness is established. This is because in all but a few cases—for example where the allegation of misconduct relates to the failure of a defendant to co-operate

with the office holder—the misconduct complained of will relate to the manner in which a direc-tor has conducted the affairs of a company prior to the company having become insolvent within the meaning of s 6(1)(a). Accordingly, any return made to creditors will have little bearing upon that. A substantial or significant return to creditors might, in an appropriate case, if unfitness is established, be a mitigating factor resulting in the imposition of a lesser period of disqualification against a defendant but will seldom amount to a defence to a claim for a disqualification order under s 6. It follows that even if there had been evidence to the effect that the liquidator had sold Normanton's land at an undervalue—and there is none in the present case—that could provide no defence to the defendant to the claim for the disqualification order in the present circumstances.

Permitting disqualified directors to act

Applicable principles when the court is asked to give a disqualified director leave to act.

[6.11] Secretary of State for Trade and Industry v Swan (No 2) [2005] EWHC 2479 (Chancery Division)

The facts are outlined in **[6.09]**.

ETHERTON J:

10. There is no dispute as to the relevant principles. The court has a general discretion and, in deciding how exercise it, must balance various different factors, including the need or legitimate interest of the applicant to be a director, the importance of protecting the public from the conduct that led to the Disqualification Order, and also that the purposes of a disqualification are not only to protect the public but to act as a deterrent and to raise standards: see *Re Grayon Building Services Ltd.* [1995] Ch. 241, 253H–254D (Hoffmann L.J.) and *Re Blackspur Group plc* [1998] 1 WLR 422, 426 (Lord Woolf M.R.).

11. In *Re Barings (No.4)* [1999] 1 BCLC 262, Sir Richard Scott V.-C. said at p.269B–D:

'It seems to me that the importance of protecting the public from the conduct that led to the disqualification order and the need that the applicant should be able to act as a director of a particular company must be kept in balance with one another. The court in considering whether or not to grant leave should, in particular, pay attention to the nature of the defects in company management that led to the disqualification order and ask itself whether, if leave were granted, a situation might arise in which there would be a risk of recurrence of those defects.'

12. In *Re Dawes & Henderson (Agencies) Ltd. (No 2)* [1999] 2 BCLC 317, 326A–D, Sir Richard Scott V.-C. said:

'The discretion given to the court under the 1986 Act to grant leave to an individual against whom a disqualification order has been made, enabling him during the currency of the dis-qualification order to act as a director of a particular company, is a discretion unfettered by any statutory condition or criterion. It would in my view be wrong for the court to create any such fetters or conditions. The reason why it would be wrong is that no one, when sitting in a particular case to give judgment, can foresee the infinite variety of circumstances that might apply in future cases not before the court. Where Parliament has given the courts an unfettered discretion, I do not think it is for the courts to reduce the ambit of that discre-tion. But in exercising the statutory discretion courts must, of course, not take into account any irrelevant factors. The emphasis given in a judgment in a particular case on particular

> circumstances in that case is not necessarily a guide to the weight to be attributed to similar circumstances in a different case. Anything I say in this case about the circumstances that seem to me of weight in this case must be read subject to that warning.'

➤ Note

To this may be added the comments of Jonathan Parker J in *Re Barings plc (No 5)* **[6.12]** which usefully explain the relevance of Sch 1 [now substantially amended] in considering 'unfitness' (at 486):

> Although in considering the question of unfitness the court had to have regard (among other things) to 'any misfeasance or breach of any fiduciary or other duty' by the respondent in relation to the company, it was not a prerequisite of a finding of unfitness that the respondent should have been guilty of misfeasance or breach of duty in relation to the company. Unfitness might be demonstrated by conduct which did not involve a breach of any statutory or common law duty: for example, trading at the risk of creditors might be the basis of a finding of unfitness even though it might not amount to wrongful trading under s 214 of the Insolvency Act 1986. Nor would it necessarily be an answer to a charge of unfitness founded on allegations of incompetence that the errors which the respondent made could be characterised as errors of judgment rather than as negligent mistakes. It was possible to envisage a case where a respondent had shown himself so completely lacking in judgment as to justify a finding of unfitness, notwithstanding that he had not been guilty of misfeasance or breach of duty. Conversely the fact that a respondent might have been guilty of misfeasance or breach of duty did not necessarily mean that he was unfit. Schedule 1 made it clear that there were a number of matters to which the court was required to have regard in considering the question of unfitness, in addition to misfeasance and breach of duty.

2. In determining whether to grant leave to act, the court will also take into account the efficacy of the conditions to be imposed on the disqualified director. In *Re Clenaware Systems Ltd* [2013] EWHC 2514 (Ch), the applicant was granted leave to act as a director for one of the companies where the court was satisfied that the risk of harm to the public could be minimised by imposing additional conditions.

Cross-fertilisation: CDDA and directors' general duties

Use of the disqualification jurisdiction to refine the law on directors' duty of care to include appropriate oversight.

[6.12] Re Barings plc (No 5) [1999] 1 BCLC 433 (Chancery Division and Court of Appeal)

The Barings Group, a long-established banking organisation of unquestionable standing, collapsed in 1995 owing to unauthorised trading activities carried out by a single trader, Leeson, in Singapore, which resulted in massive losses. In these proceedings disqualification orders were sought against three of its former directors who were based in London. Their honesty and integrity were not challenged, but it was alleged that they had been guilty of serious failures of management in relation to Leeson's activities, thereby demonstrating such a high degree of incompetence as to justify their disqualification. More specifically: they had left Leeson in sole control of both the dealing and settlement offices in Singapore, ignoring an internal audit recommendation that the roles be separated; they had met Leeson's requests for funding on a huge scale without proper inquiry; and they had not instituted appropriate internal management controls. Jonathan Parker J, at first instance, held that the case for disqualification had been made, and his ruling was upheld on appeal.

JONATHAN PARKER J: '[E]ach individual director owes duties to the company to inform himself about its affairs and to join with his co-directors in supervising and controlling them' (see *Re Westmid Packing Services Ltd* [1998] 2 BCLC 646 at 653, [1998] 2 All ER 124 at 130 per Lord Woolf MR, giving the judgment of the Court of Appeal). Later in the judgment Lord Woolf MR said:

> 'It is of the greatest importance that any individual who undertakes the statutory and fiduciary obligations of being a company director should realise that these are inescapable personal responsibilities.'

This does not mean, of course, that directors cannot delegate. Subject to the articles of association of the company, a board of directors may delegate specific tasks and functions. Indeed, some degree of delegation is almost always essential if the company's business is to be carried on efficiently: to that extent there is a clear public interest in delegation by those charged with the responsibility for the management of a business . . .

But just as the duty of an individual director as formulated by the Court of Appeal in *Re Westmid Packing Services Ltd* does not mean that he may not delegate, neither does it mean that, having delegated a particular function, he is no longer under any duty in relation to the discharge of that function, notwithstanding that the person to whom the function has been delegated may appear both trustworthy and capable of discharging the function . . .

It is not in dispute in the instant case that where delegation has taken place the board (and the individual directors) will remain responsible for the delegated function or functions and will retain a residual duty of supervision and control . . . The precise extent of the ritual duty will depend on the facts of each particular case, as will the question whether it has been breached. These are matters which are in dispute in the instant case. It is the Secretary of State's case (denied by the respondents) that each of the respondents was incompetent in failing to discharge his individual duties as a director . . .

Where there is an issue as to the extent of a director's duties and responsibilities in any particular case, the level of reward which he is entitled to receive or which he may reasonably have expected to receive from the company may be a relevant factor in resolving that issue. It is not that the fitness or otherwise of a respondent depends on how much he is paid. The point is that the higher the level of reward, the greater the responsibilities which may reasonably be expected (prima facie, at least) to go with it. As Sir Richard Scott V-C said when making a disqualification order in respect of Mr Maclean (see *Re Barings plc, Secretary of State for Trade and Industry v Baker* [1998] BCLC 583 at 586):

> '[Counsel for the respondent] made the point that if an efficient system is in place, or if the individual in question has good reason for believing there to be an efficient system in place, the delegation within the system of functions to be discharged in accordance with the system by others cannot be the subject of serious criticism if, in the event, the persons to whom responsibilities are delegated fail properly to discharge their duties. That may be so up to a point in theory, but the higher the office within an organisation that is held by an individual, the greater the responsibilities that fall upon him. It is right that that should be so, because status within an organisation carries with it commensurate rewards. These rewards are matched by the weight of responsibilities that the office carries with it, and those responsibilities require diligent attention from time to time to the question whether

the system that has been put in place and over which the individual is presiding is operating efficiently, and whether individuals to whom duties, in accordance with the system, have been delegated are discharging those duties efficiently.'

In summary, the following general propositions can, in my judgment, be derived from the authorities to which I was referred in relation to the duties of directors:

(i)   Directors have, both collectively and individually, a continuing duty to acquire and maintain a sufficient knowledge and understanding of the company's business to enable them properly to discharge their duties as directors.

(ii) Whilst directors are entitled (subject to the articles of association of the company) to delegate particular functions to those below them in the management chain, and to trust their competence and integrity to a reasonable extent, the exercise of the power of delegation does not absolve a director from the duty to supervise the discharge of the delegated functions.

(iii) No rule of universal application can be formulated as to the duty referred to in (ii) above. The extent of the duty, and the question whether it has been discharged, must depend on the facts of each particular case, including the director's role in the management of the company.

[An appeal by one of the directors was dismissed: [2000] 1 BCLC 523.]

Individual directors must ensure they remain adequately informed.

[6.13] Re Landhurst Leasing plc [1999] 1 BCLC 286 (Chancery Division)

The company, which was in the leasing finance business, had had a meteoric rise followed by a calamitous collapse. Its principal directors, Ball and Ashworth, had been sentenced to terms of imprisonment for offences of corruption and dishonesty. The present disqualification proceedings were brought against three minor players, formerly employees of the company, who had been made directors at a relatively late stage in the company's history. Despite the fact that control of the business remained very much in the hands of Ball and Ashworth and that their roles in the company's affairs continued, as before, to be essentially that of employees, it was held that the respondents could not accept office as directors without assuming corresponding responsibilities, and that it was no answer to a charge of misconduct that they had left to others matters for which the board as a whole had to accept responsibility. Disqualification orders were made against two of the three respondents.

HART J: . . . [T]he Court of Appeal in *Re Westmid Packing Services Ltd, Secretary of State for Trade and Industry v Griffiths* [1998] 2 BCLC 646 at 653, [1998] 2 All ER 124 at 130 accepted as correct the following propositions:

'. . . the collegiate or collective responsibility of the board of directors of a company is of fundamental importance to corporate governance under English company law. That collegiate or collective responsibility must however be based on individual responsibility. Each individual director owes duties to the company to inform himself about its affairs and to join with his co-directors in supervising and controlling them. A proper degree of delegation and division of responsibility is of course permissible, and often necessary, but total abrogating of responsibility is not. A board of directors must not permit one individual to dominate them and use them, as Mr Griffiths plainly did in this case. Mr Davis commented that the appellants' contention (in their affidavits) that Mr Griffiths was the person who must carry the whole blame was itself a depressing failure, even then, to acknowledge the nature of a director's responsibility. There is a good deal of force in that point.'

Closely allied to the difficulty of distinguishing the responsibilities and conduct of the individual directors from that of the board as a whole is the question of the extent to which an individual director may trust his or her colleagues. The judgment of Romer J in *Re City Equitable Fire Insurance Co Ltd* [7.21] is usually taken as authority for the general proposition that a director may rely on his co-directors to the extent that (a) the matter in question lies with their sphere of responsibility given the way in which the particular business is organised and (b) that there exist no grounds for suspicion that that reliance may be misplaced. But even where there are no reasons to think the reliance is misplaced, a director may still be in breach of duty if he leaves to others matters for which the board as a whole must take responsibility . . .

[Dealing with the case against one of the respondents, his Lordship continued:] A director in the position of Mr Illidge from September 1991 onwards was necessarily in a difficult position, arriving in the post as he did at a time when it must have been already known to the chairman and the managing directors that the company was about to face possibly terminal difficulties and that knowledge was not being fully shared with him. In setting a standard against which his conduct must be judged for the purposes of the 1986 Act a balance must be struck between the need on the one hand not to deter honest and competent employees (as it is accepted he was) from accepting board appointment in such circumstances and the desirability on the other of reinforcing the hands of those accepting such office by emphasising that their duties require them to act with independence and courage. I have not found striking that balance easy in Mr Illidge's case. I have borne in mind the comparatively short time during which he was a director. I have also borne in mind that, where I have found him to be open to criticism, it is very doubtful whether had he acted differently the course which events ultimately took would have been significantly altered. What has caused me difficulty is deciding whether or not the cumulative effect of the omissions for which I have criticised him compel a conclusion that his conduct did not meet the standards which today are expected of a company director. That conduct appears to me to reveal a pattern . . . of acquiescence in Mr Ball's suppression of information to the auditors and to the board. I do not accept the case he now seeks to make that he was in fact at all times reassured by what Mr Ball told him. I think he well appreciated that a potentially parlous situation had developed, and was conscious that Mr Ball was not sharing that information with the non-executive directors. I consider that this situation obtained for a sufficiently long period during his directorship for it to have been a serious failure on his part not at some stage to take steps to see that the matter was raised at board level. While I have considerable sympathy for him in the position in which he found himself, I have regretfully come to the conclusion that the conduct was such as to require me to disqualify him. My regret is due to the fact that I have little doubt that in any normal context he is a man who is perfectly fit to be concerned in the management of a company.

[His Lordship made a similar finding against a second respondent, Dyer, but held that the case against a third respondent had not been made out.]

Disqualification orders and the disqualification period

Factors to be considered in assessing the disqualification period.

[6.14] Secretary of State for Trade and Industry v Carr [2006] EWHC 2110 (Chancery Division)

C, a director of a public listed company, settled a substantial compensation claim by F against that company for US$18 million. Then, according to the Secretary of State, C participated in false accounting processes which were intended to hide the company's real financial position from creditors, members and possible investors, making possible a more positive financial outlook than was warranted. Although C had been acquitted of criminal charges relating to some of the conduct which was the subject of the application under CDDA 1986 s 8, he was nevertheless disqualified for 9½ years.

DAVID RICHARDS J: . . . The allegations which I have held to be established amount to deliberate and dishonest conduct on the part of Mr Carr in the performance of his duties as a director of a listed company. They were not isolated acts but amounted to a sustained attempt over an extended period to conceal and misrepresent the true position as regards the claim by Ford and its settlement by the company. Both were highly material in the context of the group. It involved concealing information which, as I find, he knew should be disclosed to the board, the auditors, the Stock Exchange, and others and should be disclosed in the accounts. It further involved the use of false accounting treatments, leading to the approval and publication of accounts which he knew to be false, achieved only by misleading the auditors as to the true position. Similarly improper conduct is shown by the treatment of the Rover payment.

These are, in my judgment, very serious matters, which make a substantial period of disqualification inevitable. The top bracket of disqualification for 10 to 15 years is invoked in particularly serious cases, of which in my view this is one. My starting point is that the period of disqualification in this case should be in that bracket, subject to any counter-balancing circumstances.

Submissions were made to me on behalf of Mr Carr as to matters which I should take into account in fixing the period of disqualification. There are some to which I attach no weight. First, I attach no weight to the fact that Mr Carr lost the value of his shareholding, which over a period had cost him approximately £2 million, exceeding, as was submitted, the total value of his remuneration over his period of employment. All other shareholders also lost the value of their shares, but they were deprived by Mr Carr's conduct of the timely provision of highly material information to which they were entitled. If the group had been able to survive, the concealment of the Ford claim and settlement might well have benefited him in terms of the value of his shareholding. Mr Carr's personal financial loss does not lessen the seriousness of his conduct or the need to protect the public. At most, it can be said that he did not make money from his misconduct.

Secondly, attention was drawn on Mr Carr's behalf to the periods of disqualification for those former directors who had given undertakings at the date of the hearing. I do not regard these periods, which range from 3 to 6½ years, as providing any useful guidance. Their misconduct, as summarised in the schedules to their undertakings, is not comparable in terms of the duration, scope or, save in some instances, seriousness of the case against Mr Carr. I have not seen Mr Jeffrey's undertaking or the schedule of allegations to which he has admitted. Mr Carr was not only himself closely involved in the matters which I have established against him, but he was also, as chief executive, senior to Mr Jeffrey.

There are other factors which, to a greater or lesser extent, I do take into account. First, while not agreeing to give an undertaking, his decision not to defend the application has saved time and expense for the court, the Secretary of State and witnesses. I should however note that this is not motivated by any apparent recognition of wrongdoing on Mr Carr's part, and it is in the circumstances a factor of only very slight significance. Secondly, there is no evidence or suggestion of other misconduct and he had previously enjoyed a successful career. Thirdly, and significantly, following his resignation from the company and its collapse in December 1999, both of which were well-publicised, he has had no significant management responsibilities. The disqualification proceedings did not commence until August 2004, following delivery of the Inspectors' report in January 2003. I should also take account of the period since the hearing of this application. Fourthly, before the issue of the disqualification proceedings, the Secretary of State was prepared to accept an undertaking for a period of 9 years.

In all the circumstances, I consider that a period of disqualification for 9½ years is appropriate.

➤ Note

There are innumerable cases providing further illustration of the types of factors the court will consider in the context of directors' disqualification orders: these include the specific role and degree of involvement of the director in the alleged wrongs; lack of cooperation with regulators; and the director's conduct during the disqualification proceedings themselves.

◾ Further reading

KEAY, A, 'Company Directors Behaving Poorly: Disciplinary Options for Shareholders' [2007] JBL 656 (on CA 2006 s 168).

McCONVILL, J and HOLLAND, E, '"Pre-Nuptial Agreements" for Removing Directors in Australia—Are They a Valid Part of the Marriage between Shareholders and the Board?' [2006] JBL 204.

McGLYNN, CMS, 'The Constitution of the Company: Mandatory Statutory Provisions v Private Agreements' (1994) 15 *Company Lawyer* 301.

NOONAN, C and WATSON, S, 'Examining Company Directors through the Lens of De Facto Directorship' [2008] JBL 587 (on s 161).

OGILVY, DC, 'Payments in Lieu of Notice and Shareholder Approval' (2007) 82 *Employment Law Bulletin* 3.

WALTERS, A, 'Directors' Duties: Impact of the CDDA' (2000) 21 *Company Lawyer* 110.

WEST, L, 'Challenging the "Golden Goodbye"' [2009] JBL 447.

WILLIAMS, R, 'Disqualifying Directors: A Remedy Worse than the Disease' (2007) 7 *Journal of Corporate Law Studies* 213.

7

DIRECTORS' DUTIES

General issues

Directors normally have exclusive power to manage the business of the company. The advantage of a board of directors is both concentrated expertise, relative independence from the company's various stakeholders (eg members or shareholders, and executive management) and the efficiency of centralised decision-making. The disadvantage, however, is that the directors may manage the company in their own interests rather than in the interests of those they are supposed to serve. There are several ways of addressing this risk.

One option is to give more power to the members. Clearly it would not help to have the members make all the company's decisions. However, in earlier chapters we saw that certain crucial decisions are reserved to the members and that they have the power to remove the directors by ordinary resolution, with all the benefits that this implies by way of implicit or explicit threat to underperforming directors. Another option is to insist on certain governance arrangements within the board of directors and certain procedures in the decision-making process itself. Again, in Chapter 5 we saw that the UK Corporate Governance Code for public listed companies sets out rules of best practice for the composition of the board and its various subcommittees. In addition, adequate disclosure to those likely to be most affected by the activities of the directors is always helpful. That, too, is required by the Companies Act 2006 (CA 2006) Pt 15 (requirements for accounts

and directors' reports, including the forward-looking *'business review')*[1] and, for larger companies, Pt 16 (requirement for audited accounts).

All of these regimes are directed at creating incentives (or threats) to improve directors' performance. But the third option for dealing with the various agency problems arising from centralised decision-making is the one most familiar to lawyers: legal duties are imposed on directors which set limits within which they must exercise their powers. These legal duties are the subject of this chapter.

Historically, these duties were developed by the courts of equity, largely by analogy with the rules applying to trustees (the roles have fundamental similarities, but also certain important differences[2]). One of the most significant changes introduced by CA 2006 Pt 10 is to codify these common law and equitable duties applying to directors.

Overview of codified directors' duties (the 'general' duties)

Codification was recommended by the Law Commissions,[3] and the Company Law Review (CLR) published a draft code in its Final Report,[4] along with extensive commentary.[5] The primary reason for recommending codification was to make the relevant rules clear and accessible—for both directors and those affected by their decisions. CA 2006 s 170 sets out the scope and nature of the codified general duties, and these then follow in successive sections, being:

- three duties dealing with the exercise of directors' powers:
  - (i) duty to act within powers (s 171);
  - (ii) duty to promote the success of the company (s 172);
  - (iii) duty to exercise independent judgement (s 173);
- one duty dealing with skill and competence/negligence:
  - (iv) duty to exercise reasonable care, skill and diligence (s 174);
- three duties dealing with fiduciary loyalty and proscribing self-interest:
  - (v) duty to avoid conflicts of interest (s 175);
  - (vi) duty not to accept benefits from third parties (s 176); and
  - (vii) duty to declare an interest in a proposed or existing transaction or arrangement (ss 177 and 182).

Each of these duties is dealt with in detail in this chapter. This codification supersedes the older case law. But those cases remain relevant to the interpretation of the new statutory provisions where those codified duties are formulated in a way that quite faithfully reflects the older case law (but not otherwise, of course). The rules set out in the Act are deliberately expressed at a sufficiently high level of generality so as to be capable of judicial development within their terms, and the Act itself provides a novel mechanism for applying and interpreting a statute: it *requires* the courts to have regard to the existing

---

[1] There are few if any cases on the directors' obligations to make disclosure in this way, but reformers have certainly seen the importance of disclosure, and CA 2006 makes specific provisions which bear concentrated attention: see CA 2006 Pt 15 on accounts and reports, and especially ss 415ff on the content of the directors' report.

[2] Trustees must conserve property, while directors must take business risks. Trustees must act unanimously, or seek the court's guidance; but directors may act by a quorum, and must accept the principle of majority rule. See further LS Sealy, 'The Director as Trustee' [1967] CLJ 83.

[3] *Company Directors: Regulating Conflicts of Interest and Formulating a Statement of Duties* (Law Com No 261, 1999), Pt 4.

[4] *Modern Company Law for a Competitive Economy: Final Report* (2001), Vol 1, Annex C.

[5] See S Worthington, 'Reforming Directors' Duties' (2001) 64 MLR 439, published before the CLR produced its Final Report.

interpretation and continuing development of the common law rules and equitable principles on which the statutory statement is based when interpreting and applying the statutory statement (s 170(3) and (4)). This approach is not normally allowed in interpreting the words of a statute.

The remedies for breach have not been codified. The common law and equitable rules are simply imported into the Act (s 178): an overview is provided in this chapter. On the other hand, the rules that allow certain activities which might otherwise constitute breaches to be *authorised* (before the event) or *ratified* (afterwards) have been codified. A new ban on implicated directors voting as shareholders in ratifying resolutions (ss 180 and 239) has been included: the need for such a rule is obvious, and the common law had struggled with the issue.

Finally, these duties are mandatory. CA 2006 s 232(1) provides: 'Any provision that purports to exempt a director of a company (to any extent) from any liability that would otherwise attach to him in connection with any negligence, default, breach of duty or breach of trust in relation to the company is void.' It is irrelevant whether the provision is contained in the articles or in a separate contract. Section 232 merits reading in full for the few qualifications it does permit.

Other duties owed by directors

In working through this chapter, do not forget that directors are subject to many other rules and regulations. CA 2006 itself imposes substantial disclosure obligations, noted earlier, and there are various rules that apply when directors seek funding for the company (see Chapters 9, 11 and 12), or make use of the company's capital and profits (see Chapter 10). Breach of these rules may attract criminal sanctions, as well as civil ones.

The Insolvency Act 1986 (IA 1986) also empowers the court to review directors' conduct in the period leading up to insolvency, and to penalise directors who have failed to operate according to the statutory standards (see Chapter 16).

In addition, if a company goes into insolvent liquidation or administration, or an administrative receiver is appointed, or in other defined circumstances, a director whose conduct makes him 'unfit to be concerned in the management of a company' may be disqualified under the Company Directors Disqualification Act 1986 (CDDA 1986) (see 'Directors' disqualification', pp 309ff).

All these rules have had their own impact in developing the law on directors' duties. So too has CA 2006 s 994, which provides shareholders with relief for 'unfairly prejudicial conduct' (which includes conduct by directors—and others—which need not be in breach of any legal duty): see 'Unfairly prejudicial conduct of the company's affairs', pp 715ff.

Finally, in all this discussion of the duties owed by directors to their *companies*, do not forget that directors may occasionally be found personally liable to third parties who have dealt with the company. Recall *Williams v Natural Life Health Foods Ltd* **[3.19]** (where the claim for negligent misstatement was unsuccessful) and *Standard Chartered Bank v Pakistan National Shipping Corpn (No 2)* **[3.20]** (where the claim in deceit was successful).

Directors' general duties are also owed by *de facto* and shadow directors

Section 250 defines 'director' as including 'any person occupying the position of director, by whatever name called'. This means these general duties apply equally to *de facto*

directors.[6] And notice s 170(2), which applies *some* of the statutory duties to former directors: see 'Statutory changes to the equitable rules', p 387.

The position with *shadow directors* (defined in the following section) is qualified: s 170(5) provides that 'The general duties apply to a shadow director of a company where and to the extent that they are capable of so applying.' This requires potentially difficult questions to be answered, on which there is no current judicial analysis.[7]

These provisions—which expand the reach of the general duties—make it necessary to ask whether an individual who has significant management input is, by virtue of that, either a *de facto* or a shadow director, even though not a *de jure* director, and is therefore subject to the general statutory duties imposed on directors.

Shadow directors: s 251

A 'shadow director' is defined as 'a person in accordance with whose directions or instructions the directors of a company are accustomed to act'. The court in *Ultraframe (UK) Ltd v Fielding* **[7.49]** interpreted this as meaning that at least a consistent majority of the directors must be accustomed to act in that way. If only a minority of the company's directors are accustomed so to act, it is not enough to make the person a shadow director (*Lord v Sinai Securities Ltd* [2004] EWHC 1764 (Ch)).

Section 251 contains two important categories of exclusion. First, s 251(2) excludes professional persons on whose advice the directors act, or persons who give directions or instructions to directors in the exercise of a function conferred by legislation or in their capacity as a minister. Secondly, s 251(3) provides that a 'body corporate is not to be regarded as a shadow director of any of its subsidiary companies...by reason only that the directors of the subsidiary are accustomed to act in accordance with its directions or instructions.' An individual with a substantial shareholding is not given the same protection, for obvious policy reasons.

On one reading, the definition of a 'shadow director' precludes a person from being both a shadow director and a *de facto* director (see *Re Hydrodam (Corby) Ltd* **[7.01]**), but this is not explicit in the section.

Distinguishing de facto and shadow directors.

[7.01] Re Hydrodam (Corby) Ltd [1994] 2 BCLC 180 (Chancery Division)

> MILLETT J: I would interpose at this point by observing that in my judgment an allegation that a defendant acted as de facto or shadow director, without distinguishing between the two, is embarrassing. It suggests—and counsel's submissions to me support the inference—that the liquidator takes the view that de facto or shadow directors are very similar, that their roles overlap, and that it may not be possible to determine in any given case whether a particular person was a de facto or a shadow director. I do not accept that at all. The terms do not overlap. They are alternatives, and in most and perhaps all cases are mutually exclusive.

---

[6] Note the difference between showing that a person is a *de facto* director, or that he or she can be classed as a fiduciary under the normal equitable rules for identifying fiduciary relationships (on the latter, see *Ranson v Customer Systems plc* **[7.04]**). Also see *Canadian Aero Services Ltd v O'Malley* (1973) 40 DLR (3d) 371 at 381.

[7] This provision only took effect in October 2015, and its predecessor was considerably less clear: it provided that shadow directors were subject to the statutory duties 'to the same extent that, before the Act, they were subject to the corresponding common law rules and equitable principles'. A difficult decision was thus left to the courts, with some taking very restrictive views: see, eg, *Ultraframe (UK) Ltd v Fielding* **[7.49]**; contrast *Vivendi SA v Richards* [2013] EWHC 3006 (Ch), [2013] BCC 771 at [143] per Newey J; and see also D Prentice and J Payne, 'Directors' Fiduciary Duties' (2006) 122 LQR 122.

A de facto director is a person who assumes to act as a director. He is held out as a director by the company, and claims and purports to be a director, although never actually or validly appointed as such. To establish that a person was a de facto director of a company it is necessary to plead and prove that he undertook functions in relation to the company which could properly be discharged only by a director. It is not sufficient to show that he was concerned in the management of the company's affairs or undertook tasks in relation to its business which can properly be performed by a manager below board level. . . .

A shadow director, by contrast, does not claim or purport to act as a director. On the contrary, he claims not to be a director. He lurks in the shadows, sheltering behind others who, he claims, are the only directors of the company to the exclusion of himself. He is not held out as a director by the company. To establish that a defendant is a shadow director of a company it is necessary to allege and prove: (1) who are the directors of the company, whether de facto or de jure; (2) that the defendant directed those directors how to act in relation to the company or that he was one of the persons who did so; (3) that those directors acted in accordance with such directions; and (4) that they were accustomed so to act. What is needed is, first, a board of directors claiming and purporting to act as such; and, secondly, a pattern of behaviour in which the board did not exercise any discretion or judgment of its own, but acted in accordance with the directions of others.

➤ Notes

1. In *Kaytech International* [1999] 2 BCLC 351, Robert Walker LJ suggested, tentatively, that on given facts it may not be so clear whether the influence is 'open' or 'concealed'. Also see *Holland* **[7.02]**, in the extract immediately following.

2. In *Secretary of State for Trade and Industry v Deverell* [2001] Ch 340, CA, Morritt LJ noted that although a shadow director must exercise 'real influence in the corporate affairs of the company', it was 'not necessary that such influence should be exercised over the whole field of its corporate activities.'

3. In appropriate cases, a holding company (and possibly also its directors), a consultant called into assist in a corporate rescue and a company's bank could be held to be 'shadow directors', subject to the protections in s 251(2)–(3). But for this to be the case, the whole board has to act in accordance with the shadow director's instructions or directions.

4. In *Ultraframe (UK) Ltd v Fielding* **[7.49]** it was held that the fact that the directors of a company are obliged to conduct it in accordance with requirements laid down by a major lender or customer for the protection of that person's interests does not necessarily make that person a shadow director.

5. The leading judicial analysis of the concept of shadow director is to be found in the judgment of Morritt LJ in *Secretary of State for Trade and Industry v Deverell* [2001] Ch 300, CA. In particular, Morritt LJ stressed that its interpretation may depend on the statutory context (eg a stricter construction may be more appropriate in a criminal or quasi-criminal provision); that the purpose of the legislation is to identify those with 'real influence' in the corporate affairs of the company, or part of them; that advice (other than professional advice) is capable of coming within the phrase 'directions or instructions'; and that it is not necessary that the board should be reduced to a subservient role or surrender its discretion.

De facto directors

The issue of who might be made liable as a director is clearly of general importance, but it held particular significance in the context of corporate directors. This was because

'company A' might well appoint an undercapitalised corporate director, 'company B', as one of its directors.[8] In a very practical sense, this corporate director could only take decisions according to the deliberations and activities of its *own* human directors (D). If D was wealthy, and clearly 'pulling the strings', could company A sue D as a *de facto* or shadow director of company A? This problem will soon be moot, since corporate directors are to be abolished (see Small Business, Enterprise and Employment Act 2015 (SBEEA 2015) s 87, currently proposed to be introduced in October 2016).[9] But short extracts are included here because the context highlights rather dramatically the difficult lines which have to be drawn in deciding whether someone should be classed as a director of some sort.

In *Re Hydrodam*, Millett J added some further observations as to what is required before the director of a corporate director can be classified as *de facto* director of the company:

> Attendance of board meetings and voting, with others, may in certain limited circumstances expose a director to personal liability to the company of which he is a director or its creditors. But it does not, without more, constitute him a director of any company of which his company is a director.

As to what that 'something more' may entail, and the difficulties which can arise in applying the test, see the next case.

Whether the director of a corporate director of company A is himself a *de facto* director of company A depends upon whether he does more than merely discharge his duties as director of the corporate director.

[7.02] Revenue and Customs Commissioners v Holland [2010] UKSC 51, [2010] 1 WLR 2793 (Supreme Court)

A complex corporate structure was created to minimise the tax liabilities of contractors. This involved the setting up of 42 subsidiary companies within a corporate structure. The scheme failed, with the result that all 42 companies went into insolvency owing substantial unpaid tax which, in the circumstances, would not be recouped from the companies themselves. Each company had only one under-capitalised corporate director,[10] so an action against the companies' defaulting directors would not enhance recoveries. HMRC therefore brought proceedings against Mr Holland. He was the *de jure* director of the corporate director of each of the 42 insolvent companies, and HMRC alleged he was also the *de facto* director of each of the 42 companies, so was liable as a defaulting director for his role in contributing to the losses sustained by those companies. By a narrow majority (Lords Hope, Collins, and Saville, with Lords Walker and Clarke dissenting), the Supreme Court held that Mr Holland was only a *de jure* director of the corporate director, and not also a *de facto* director of the 42 companies.

---

[8] Recall this could not be a sole director: every company is currently required to have at least one director who is a natural person, CA 2006 s 155.

[9] This would repeal CA 2006 s 155 and make provisions in new ss 156A–C barring appointment of corporate directors; empowering the Secretary of State to provide by regulations for exceptions to that rule; and providing for a 12-month transitional period for existing corporate directors who are not excepted under these new regulations.

[10] This is no longer lawful: see CA 2006 s 155(1), which requires a company to have at least one director who is a natural person, and corporate directorship itself is soon to be prohibited: see fn 9.

LORD HOPE:

39. ...[Recalling Millett J's reasoning in *Hydrodam*, and asking what the 'something more' was, continued:] As Millett J said in *Re Hydrodam (Corby) Ltd* **[7.01]**...those who assume to act as directors and who thereby exercise the powers and discharge the functions of a director, whether validly appointed or not, must accept the responsibilities of the office. So one must look at what the person actually did to see whether he assumed those responsibilities in relation to the subject company.

40. The problem that is presented by this case, however, is that Mr Holland was doing no more than discharging his duties as the director of the corporate director of the composite companies. Everything that he did was done under that umbrella. Mr Green QC for HMRC was unable to point to anything that he did which could not be said to have been done by him in his capacity as a director of the corporate director. When asked what it was that lay outside his performance of that role, he said that it was simply the quality of his acts. He did everything. He was the decision maker, and he was the person who gave effect to those decisions. In *Hydrodam* **[7.01]** at p 184 Millett J rejected the proposition that, where a body corporate is a director of a company, whether it be de jure, de facto or shadow director, its own directors must ipso facto be shadow directors of the subject company. He said that attendance at board meetings and voting with others did not, without more, constitute him a director of any company of which his company is a director. That would not be a fair description of what Mr Holland did in this case. But in a later paragraph on p 184 Millett J said this:

> 'It is possible (although it is not so alleged) that the directors of Eagle Trust as a collective body gave directions to the directors of the company and that the directors of the company were accustomed to act in accordance with such directions. But if they did give such directions as directors of Eagle Trust, acting as the board of Eagle Trust, they did so as agents for Eagle Trust (or more accurately as the appropriate organ of Eagle Trust) and the result is to constitute Eagle Trust, but not themselves, shadow directors of the company.'

This passage indicates that the 'without more' requirement that Millett J had in mind would not be satisfied by evidence that the individual director of the body corporate was actually giving instructions in that capacity to the subject company and the subject company was accustomed to act in accordance with those directions. That would not be enough to prove that the individual director assumed a role in the management of the subject company which imposed responsibility on him for misuse of the subject company's assets. . . .

42. [After referring to *Salomon v A Salomon & Co Ltd* **[2.02]**]...Those who act as directors of a corporate director are entitled to know what it is that they can and cannot do when they are procuring acts by the corporate director.... I think that the guiding principle can be expressed in this way, unless and until Parliament provides otherwise. So long as the relevant acts are done by the individual entirely within the ambit of the discharge of his duties and responsibilities as a director of the corporate director, it is to that capacity that his acts must be attributed.

43. It is, of course, right to bear in mind the interests of the creditors. Their protection lies in the remedies that are available for breach of the fiduciary duty that rests on the shoulder of every director. But the essential point, which Millett J was at pains to stress in *Hydrodam*, is that for a creditor of the subject company to obtain those remedies the individual must be shown to have been a director, not just of the corporate director but of the subject company too.... it has not been shown that Mr Holland was acting as de facto director of the composite companies so as to make him responsible for the misuse of their assets.

LORD WALKER (dissenting):

101. I am unable to agree with the reasoning and conclusions of the majority on the first issue in this appeal. The court's decision will, I fear, make it easier for risk-averse individuals to use artificial corporate structures in order to insulate themselves against responsibility to an insolvent company's unsecured creditors. . . .

114. Mr Holland was . . . the founder and guiding spirit of the whole Paycheck empire. With the concurrence of his wife (whose responsibilities were no more than secretarial) he was the only active director of both Paycheck Directors and Paycheck Secretarial; he was the original holder of all the A shares which carried voting control of the composite companies, and he was the only active director of the corporate trustee which held the A shares under settlements which he had created. He took the decision (after receiving the advice of leading counsel at the consultation on 18 August 2004) that composite companies should continue trading, and should continue to pay dividends without reserving for higher rate corporation tax.

115. If those facts did not amount to the 'something more' referred to in the authorities, it is hard to imagine circumstances that would do so. The repeated assertion that everything that Mr Holland did was done in his capacity as a director of Paycheck Directors, and was within his authority as a director of that company, is no doubt not 'pure sham' but it is, in my view, the most arid formalism. In my view Mr Holland was acting both as a de jure director of Paycheck Directors and as a de facto director of the composite companies. A de facto director is not formally invested with office, but if what he actually does amounts to taking all important decisions affecting the relevant company, and seeing that they are carried out, he is acting as a director of that company. It makes no difference that he is also acting as the only active de jure director of a corporate director of the company. . . .

> Questions

1. There are powerful arguments on both sides in this case. The case would never have arisen if it were not possible to have single corporate directors, and single (human) directors of corporate directors. Given that neither is (or will soon) be possible, are the arguments now purely academic?

2. The majority was concerned not to ride roughshod over the separate entity doctrine; the minority was concerned to impose appropriate liability (as the CA 2006 requires) on individuals who assume the role of *de facto* directors. Which analysis is more persuasive? Is it material that the legislation at the time explicitly permitted 'one man companies' and corporate directors? Does the difference between the majority and the minority turn on a matter of legal principle (per Lord Collins at [53]) or simply on matters of fact?

3. Note that it was not possible to pursue Mr Holland personally *unless* he was a *de facto* or shadow director. As such a director of the 42 companies, he would have been strictly liable for paying out assets when there were no distributable profits (see Chapter 10). But solely as a *de jure* director of the corporate director, this was not the wrong he had committed; his only potential liability was in negligence to the corporate director for advising it to recommend this course of action to the 42 companies, but he had taken legal advice on this.

4. Both Lord Walker and Lord Clarke were of the view that a person can be a shadow director *and* a *de facto* director simultaneously. Also see Robert Walker LJ in *Re Kayteck International plc* [1999] 2 BCLC 351 at 424. Is this conceptually possible? How does this square with Millett J's comments in *Re Hydrodam* [7.01]?

[7.03] Smithton Ltd v Naggar [2014] EWCA Civ 939 (Court of Appeal)

The facts are immaterial.

ARDEN LJ:

31. [On whether someone is a director at all.] The Companies Act definition does not elucidate that matter. Provisionally it seems to me that that term is to be tested against the usual split of powers between shareholders and directors under [the articles], ie on the basis that the powers of management of the company's business are delegated to the directors and the shareholders cannot intervene except by special resolution. On that basis it means a person who either alone or with others has ultimate control of the management of any part of the company's business. In the usual case, in my judgment, it would not include a purely negative role of giving or receiving permission for some business activity.

32. The role of a de facto or shadow director need not extend over the whole range of a company's activities: see *In re Mea Corpn Ltd* [2007] 1 BCLC 618; *Secretary of State for Trade and Industry v Deverell* [2001] Ch 340. A person may be both a shadow director and a de facto director at the same time: *In re Mea Corpn.*

Practical points: what makes a person a de facto director?

33. Lord Collins JSC [in *Holland* **[7.02]**] sensibly held that there was no one definitive test for a de facto director. The question is whether he was part of the corporate governance system of the company and whether he assumed the status and function of a director so as to make himself responsible as if he were a director. However, a number of points arise out of *Holland's* case and the previous cases which are of general practical importance in determining who is a de facto director. I note these points in the following paragraphs.

34. The concepts of shadow director and de facto are different but there is some overlap.

35. A person may be de facto director even if there was no invalid appointment. The question is whether he has assumed responsibility to act as a director.

36. To answer that question, the court may have to determine in what capacity the director was acting (as in *Holland's* case).

37. The court will in general also have to determine the corporate governance structure of the company so as to decide in relation to the company's business whether the defendant's acts were directorial in nature.

38. The court is required to look at what the director actually did and not any job title actually given to him.

39. A defendant does not avoid liability if he shows that he in good faith thought he was not acting as a director. The question whether or not he acted as a director is to be determined objectively and irrespective of the defendant's motivation or belief.

40. The court must look at the cumulative effect of the activities relied on. The court should look at all the circumstances 'in the round' (per Jonathan Parker J in *Secretary of State for Trade and Industry v Jones* [1999] BCC 336).

41. It is also important to look at the acts in their context. A single act might lead to liability in an exceptional case.

42. Relevant factors include: (i) whether the company considered him to be a director and held him out as such; (ii) whether third parties considered that he was a director.

43. The fact that a person is consulted about directorial decisions or his approval does not in general make him a director because he is not making the decision.

44. Acts outside the period when he is said to have been a de facto director may throw light on whether he was a de facto director in the relevant period.

45. In my judgment, the question whether a director is a de facto or shadow director is a question of fact and degree.

Also see *Secretary of State for Business, Innovation and Skills v Chohan* [2013] EWHC 680 (Ch) (Hildyard J) and *Vivendi SA v Richards* [2013] EWHC 3006 (Ch) (Newey J).

People who are not typically directors

When senior managers or employees act to the detriment of their companies, the argument is often advanced that they too are *de facto* or shadow directors. This then attracts all the statutory rules applying to such directors—proof that these people fall into this category has been addressed already. Alternatively, the claim is made that these people, even if not directors, are nevertheless in a fiduciary relationship with their company. The argument is typically motivated by the possibility of seeking disgorgement of profits, rather than the often less attractive remedy of compensation for breach of contract or for some tort. The next case shows how difficult the argument is.

Employees do not, as such, owe fiduciary duties to their employers, although such duties may sometimes be found on the facts. This rule can be crucial in considering the role of senior managers in a company.

[7.04] Ranson v Customer Systems plc [2012] EWCA Civ 841
(Court of Appeal)

An employee started a competing business. His previous employer (CS) alleged breach of fiduciary duties. The trial judge found that Ranson had breached his duties when he failed to inform CS of an opportunity obtained for his own company; when he canvassed for work in competition with CS while still a CS employee; and when he copied details of CS's business contacts, invoices, time sheets and order confirmations for use by his own company. The Court of Appeal (Pill, Lloyd and Lewison LJJ) disagreed, and allowed the appeal.

LEWISON LJ:

20. It is, at the outset, necessary to distinguish between directors of a company and employees of a company. . . .

21. The appointment of a person as a company director does not make that person an employee of the company. A director is the holder of an office. Nor does appointment as a company director of itself bring into existence any contract between the director and the company. Many directors will have contracts of service running in parallel with their status as officers of the company. But they are distinct legal relationships.

22. Whereas a company director will stand in a fiduciary relationship to the company, an employee will not, merely by reason of his role as an employee, assume fiduciary obligations to his employer.

23. In addition as Lord Browne-Wilkinson pointed out in *Henderson v Merrett Syndicates Ltd* [1995] 2 AC 145, 206:

'The phrase "fiduciary duties" is a dangerous one, giving rise to a mistaken assumption that all fiduciaries owe the same duties in all circumstances. That is not the case.'

24. Since fiduciary obligations are not 'one size fits all' it is, in my judgment, dangerous to reason by analogy from cases about company directors to cases about employees. The former cases (obviously enough) proceed on the basis that the director, while in office, owes a wide-ranging and single minded duty of loyalty to the company. In the case of a company director there is no question but that the director owes fiduciary duties to the company. The cases explore the

extent to which, consistently with those duties, a director may prepare for business life after the end of his directorship. But in the case of an employee there is an anterior question: does the employee owe fiduciary (as opposed to contractual) duties at all? . . .

59. In his analysis of the law the judge directed himself by reference to a number of cases dealing with breaches of fiduciary duties by company directors. In my judgment this was an approach liable to lead to confusion. Thus in paragraph 76 of his judgment the judge said that 'Mr Ranson's position is here not materially distinct from that of the director defendant in Towers.' But in my judgment there was a highly material difference: Mr Ranson was not a director; he was only an employee.

60. In addition, in his analysis of the law the judge did not refer to the terms of Mr Ranson's contract of employment. In paragraph 77 of his judgment the judge said that he was 'satisfied that the situation with Mr Clothier was one in which fiduciary duties arose'. Mr Stafford submitted that the judge had, in effect, approached the question from the wrong end. He had started with the facts; finding inferentially that Mr Ranson was in a position where there was a conflict between his interests and those of CS, and had reasoned backwards to find from that conflict the existence of a fiduciary duty on the part of Mr Ranson. Having decided that fiduciary duties arose as a result of 'the situation with Mr Clothier' the judge reasoned that Mr Ranson was 'thereby in breach of his contractual duty of loyalty'. There is undoubted force in these submissions.

61. In my judgment, therefore, the judge's analysis got off on the wrong foot.

PILL and LLOYD LJJ concurred.

Persons connected with a director: s 252

It is important to bear in mind that statutory rules on directors' duties may affect individuals other than the directors. A person is 'connected with' a director for the purposes, at least, of Pt 10 of the Act and much of the insolvency legislation, in the circumstances laid down by CA 2006 s 252. The people connected with a director are (defined exclusively): members of the director's family, other companies with which the director is 'connected' (ie in which he has, with his 'connected persons', at least a 20% stake), any trustee of a family trust and any partners.

These statutory provisions do not, of course, affect matters at common law (but then the common law has some healthy rules of its own to cope with problems of this sort: see, eg, *Gilford Motor Co Ltd v Horne* [1933] Ch 935 and *Selangor United Rubber Estates Ltd v Cradock* [10.11]).

Directors' duties are owed to the company

The statement that directors' duties 'are owed by a director of a company to the company' (s 170(1)) may seem to state the obvious. But debates have raged over the issue for more than a century. The problem has two strands. First, historically, companies were viewed as associations of individuals: the language used was plural (a company reaching a decision would be described as 'they decided', where now we would say 'it decided'); and the directors were seen as mere agents of the shareholders and subject to their direction.[11] In this environment it might seem natural to say the directors owed their fiduciary duties

---

[11] Contrast 'dividing corporate power between members and directors', p 189.

to the shareholders, since they *were* 'the company'. That notion is now dead, impelled by *Salomon* **[2.02]**: directors owe their duties to the company, *not* to the shareholders individually (unless the facts are rather special: see the extracts following). But that still left the second strand of the problem. In performing their duties, looking to the interests of 'the company', exactly *who* should the directors have in mind? The label 'the company' does not provide an answer.

Until fairly recently, it would not have occurred to anyone to doubt that in this context, too, 'the company' meant 'the shareholders collectively' or 'the shareholders present and future', for no other interest group was recognised as having any stake in the corporate enterprise. So, for example, in cases like *Hutton v West Cork Rly Co* and *Parke v Daily News Ltd* (1988) 23 Ch D 654), generosity to employees was held to be lawful only if it could be justified by reference to the long-term interests of the shareholders.

But for the past 30 years or more this view was increasingly under attack, seen as inappropriate in conceptualising 'the company', and increasingly as out of keeping with contemporary values. It is now accepted that the claims of other interest groups—commonly referred to as 'stakeholders'—such as the company's workforce and its customers and suppliers, deserve recognition as much as those of the passive investors in the enterprise. Indeed, it is possible to go even further, and see the 'responsible company' (and its directors) as necessarily having regard to wider considerations, such as the community, the environment, charitable and other good causes and even the national interest. These conceptions are intended to go well beyond merely requiring a company to obey the law: employment laws, insolvency laws, environmental laws, and so on. On the other hand, it is probably true that there are limits to what company law can achieve in this difficult area. For instance, if directors are expected to have regard to the (often conflicting) claims of many different stakeholders, there is a real sense in which their decisions are effectively unreviewable by any judicial or other process: any decision can be justified as appropriate for *some* group of stakeholders.[12]

The change in approach is described as a change from a narrow *pro-shareholder* approach to a wider-ranging *pro-stakeholder* ('*pluralist*') approach. In CA 2006, the final approach—after much debate—was to retain a predominantly shareholder-oriented approach, but framed in an 'inclusive' way, so that, in assessing what might be likely to promote success of the company for the members' benefit, directors should take into account the interests of stakeholders (and wider interests, such as the environment) insofar as they believed, in good faith, that these factors were relevant. (The CLR called this approach '*enlightened shareholder value*'.) CA 2006 s 172, imposing on directors a duty to promote the success of the company, adopts the enlightened shareholder value approach.

Claims that directors owe duties to particular individuals

The corollary of what has just been said, is that directors do *not* generally owe their duties to anyone other than the company.[13] Nevertheless, that has not prevented shareholders, employees, creditors and other third parties from attempting to sue directors, claiming

---

[12] See LS Sealy, 'Directors' "Wider" Responsibilities—Problems Conceptual, Practical and Procedural' (1987) 13 *Monash University Law Review* 164; also the well-known debate between AA Berle, Jr and E Merrick Dodd, Jr in (1931) 44 *Harvard Law Review* 1049, (1932) 45 *Harvard Law Review* 1145, 1365 and (1942) 9 *University of Chicago Law Review* 538, and JL Weiner, 'The Berle–Dodd Dialogue on the Nature of Corporations' (1964) 64 *Columbia Law Review* 1458; and, for a detailed exploration of the 'stakeholder', JE Parkinson, *Corporate Power and Responsibility* (1993). On the stakeholder debate generally, see FH Easterbrook and DR Fischel, *Economic Structure of Corporate Law* (1991), ch 1; G Kelly and J Parkinson, 'The Conceptual Foundations of the Company: A Pluralist Approach' [1998] *Company Financial and Insolvency Law Review* 174; A Alcock, 'The Case against the Concept of Stakeholders' (1996) 17 *Company Lawyer* 177; Lady Justice Arden, 'Regulating the Conduct of Directors' (2010) 1 *Journal of Corporate Law Studies* 1.

[13] See the very limited exception illustrated by *Coleman v Myers* **[7.06]**.

remedies for the wrongs allegedly committed by directors against them personally.[14] These claimants would often (but not always) have no trouble establishing a legitimate claim against the company, but if the company is insolvent, then directors with deep pockets become attractive targets.

Duties to shareholders?

Directors do not normally owe fiduciary duties to individual members or shareholders.

[7.05] Percival v Wright [1902] 2 Ch 421 (Chancery Division)

The plaintiffs offered to sell their shares, and the defendants (the chairman and two other directors) agreed to buy them at £12.50 per share. After completion of the transfers, the plaintiffs discovered that at the time the board had been negotiating with an outsider for the sale to him of the company's whole undertaking at a price which represented well over £12.50 per share, but this information had not been disclosed to the plaintiffs. In fact, the takeover negotiations ultimately proved abortive. The plaintiffs claimed that the directors stood in a fiduciary relationship towards them as shareholders, and sought to avoid the transfers on the grounds of non-disclosure; but the court held that there was no fiduciary relationship between directors and the shareholders individually.

SWINFEN EADY J: It was strenuously urged [but with no authority able to be cited] that, though incorporation affected the relations of the shareholders to the external world, the company thereby becoming a distinct entity, the position of the shareholders inter se was not affected, and was the same as that of partners or shareholders in an unincorporated company. I am unable to adopt that view. I am therefore of opinion that the purchasing directors were under no obligation to disclose to their vendor shareholders the negotiations which ultimately proved abortive. The contrary view would place directors in a most invidious position, as they could not buy or sell shares without disclosing negotiations, a premature disclosure of which might well be against the best interests of the company. I am of opinion that directors are not in that position.

There is no question of unfair dealing in this case. The directors did not approach the shareholders with the view of obtaining their shares. The shareholders approached the directors, and named the price at which they were desirous of selling. The plaintiffs' case wholly fails, and must be dismissed with costs.

Also see *Peskin v Anderson* [2001] 1 BCLC 372, CA, especially [27]–[37] and [53]–[59] (Mummery LJ).

➤ Notes

1. Directors are subject to 'insider dealing' rules, see 'Insider dealing', p 768. As the rules then stood, this transaction would not have been caught, since the shareholders made the offer to sell at a nominated price and the directors merely accepted. Would modern 'insider dealing' rules change the outcome? Should they?

2. Although fiduciary duties are rarely owed to shareholders, and therefore shareholders cannot bring a personal claim[15] against a director for breach of fiduciary duty, it should be noted that 'non-compliance by shareholders *cum* directors with their duties will generally

---

[14] Note, however, that shareholders can sometimes pursue 'derivative claims' to enforce wrongs done *to the company*, not to the shareholders personally. And shareholders also have distinctive personal rights, and avenues for pursuing them. See Chapter 13.

[15] As distinct from a derivative claim: see Chapter 13.

indicate that unfair prejudice has occurred': *Maidment v Attwood* [2012] EWCA Civ 998 at [22], CA; and may also constitute a breach of the statutory contract (CA 2006 s 33, see 'Members' personal rights', p 261).[16]

3. In *Sharp v Blank* [2015] EWHC 3220 (Ch), as part of a series of summary judgments concerning Lloyds Banking Group's acquisition of Halifax Bank of Scotland plc in early 2009, Nugee J reviewed the case law and summarised the relevant principle as follows, [12]:

> although a director of a company can owe fiduciary duties to the company's shareholders, he does not do so by the mere fact of being a director, but only where there is on the facts of the particular case a 'special relationship' between the director and the shareholders. It seems to me to follow that this special relationship must be something over and above the usual relationship that any director of a company has with its shareholders. It is not enough that the director, as a director, has more knowledge of the company's affairs than the shareholders have: since they direct and control the company's affairs this will almost inevitably be the case. Nor is it enough that the actions of the directors will have the potential to affect the shareholders – again this will always, or almost always, be the case. On the decided cases the sort of relationship that has given rise to a fiduciary duty has been where there has been some personal relationship or particular dealing or transaction between them

Here there was nothing more, and Nugee J therefore held that, in giving advice and information to shareholders to enable them to vote at a forthcoming EGM, they were subject only to a 'duty to give advice and information in clear and readily comprehensible terms' [15].

Exceptionally, directors may owe fiduciary duties to individual members or shareholders, for example when they undertake to act as the members' or shareholders' agents.

[7.06] Coleman v Myers [1977] 2 NZLR 225 (New Zealand Court of Appeal)

The defendants were directors of a family company. The first defendant made a takeover offer to all the other shareholders and ultimately succeeded in acquiring total control of the company. The plaintiffs were minority shareholders who had reluctantly agreed to sell when the first defendant invoked statutory powers of compulsory purchase under a section equivalent to CA 2006 s 979. They then brought an action against the defendants alleging, inter alia, breaches of fiduciary duty owed by the defendants as directors to the plaintiffs as shareholders. Mahon J at first instance considered that *Percival v Wright* [7.05] had been wrongly decided, although he found in favour of the defendants on other grounds. On appeal, the New Zealand Court of Appeal did not regard *Percival v Wright* as having been wrong on its own particular facts, but did hold that a fiduciary relationship had existed between the directors and the shareholders in the special circumstances of *Coleman*'s case: the company was a private company with shares held largely by members of the one family; the other members of the family had habitually looked to the defendants for business advice; and information affecting the true value of the shares had been withheld from the other family shareholders by the defendants. The defendants were accordingly held liable to compensate the plaintiffs.

---

[16] Although note that the courts will not imply terms which simply create a parallel set of duties owed by the directors to individual shareholders: *Towcester Racecourse Co Ltd v The Racecourse Association Ltd* [2003] 1 BCLC 260.

In the course of his judgment, WOODHOUSE J, referring to *Percival v Wright*, said: In my opinion it is not the law that anybody holding the office of director of a limited liability company is for that reason alone to be released from what otherwise would be regarded as a fiduciary responsibility owed to those in the position of shareholders of the same company. Certainly their status as directors did not protect the defendants in a Canadian case which finally made its way to the Privy Council: see *Allen v Hyatt*.[17] The decision in that case turned upon the point that the directors of the company had put themselves in a fiduciary relationship with some of their shareholders because they had undertaken to sell shares of the shareholders in an agency capacity. But there is nothing in the decision to suggest that in the case of a director the fiduciary relationship can arise only in an agency situation. On the other hand, the mere status of company director should not produce that sort of responsibility to a shareholder and in my opinion it does not do so. The existence of such a relationship must depend, in my opinion, upon all the facts of the particular case . . .

As I have indicated it is my opinion that the standard of conduct required from a director in relation to dealings with a shareholder will differ depending upon all the surrounding circumstances and the nature of the responsibility which in a real and practical sense the director has assumed towards the shareholders. In the one case there may be a need to provide an explicit warning and a great deal of information concerning the proposed transaction. In another there may be no need to speak at all. There will be intermediate situations. It is, however, an area of the law where the courts can and should find some practical means of giving effect to sensible and fair principles of commercial morality in the cases that come before them; and while it may not be possible to lay down any general test as to when the fiduciary duty will arise for a company director or to prescribe the exact conduct which will always discharge it when it does, there are nevertheless some factors that will usually have an influence upon a decision one way or the other. They include, I think, dependence upon information and advice, the existence of a relationship of confidence, the significance of some particular transaction for the parties and, of course, the extent of any positive action taken by or on behalf of the director or directors to promote it. In the present case each one of those matters had more than ordinary significance and when they are taken together they leave me in no doubt that each of the two directors did owe a fiduciary duty to the individual shareholders.

Duties to creditors?

There are *obiter dicta* in a number of cases to the effect that directors owe a duty to have regard to the interests of *creditors* of their company. Sometimes this is put more loosely as a duty *owed to* the creditors.[18] The former is accurate, although of little relevance when the company is solvent (and in any event should have the added rider that the duty is owed to the company, not to its creditors); the latter is inaccurate. The difference turns on who can enforce this 'duty', and the short answer is that the creditors cannot enforce any claim against the directors; their only claim is against the company: see, for example, *Re Halt Garage (1964) Ltd* **[5.03]**; *Re Horsley & Weight Ltd* **[4.31]**; the *Multinational Gas* case **[7.43]**; *Kuwait Asia Bank EC v National Mutual Life Nominees Ltd* **[7.48]**; and *Yukong Line Ltd of Korea v Rendsburg Investments Corpn of Liberia* **[7.18]**.

---

[17] (1914) 30 TLR 444, PC.

[18] There is an extensive literature on this topic. See, eg, LS Sealy, 'Directors' "Wider" Responsibilities—Problems Conceptual, Practical and Procedural' (1987) 13 *Monash University Law Review* 164; S Worthington, 'Directors' Duties, Creditors' Rights and Shareholder Intervention' (1991) 18 *Melbourne University Law Review* 121; R Grantham, 'The Judicial Extension of Directors' Duties to Creditors' [1991] JBL 1; PL Davies, 'Directors' Creditor-Regarding Duties' (2006) 7 *European Business Organization Law Review* 301; A Keay, 'Directors' Duties and Creditors' Interests' (2014) 130 LQR 443.

Even the notion that directors owe a duty to have regard to the interests of creditors of their company needs some elaboration: see 'The interests of creditors', p 367.

Duties to employees?

Similar instrumental concerns have motivated disgruntled employees to seek recourse directly against the company's directors rather than against their corporate employer, but with equal lack of success. Although s 172(1)(b) requires directors to 'have regard...to the interests of the company's employees', this is a duty owed to the company (s 170), not to the employees themselves: see 'The interests of employees', p 372.

Scope and nature of directors' general duties: CA 2006 s 170

The next sections of this chapter examine, in turn, each of the general duties imposed by CA 2006 Pt 10, ss 170ff. The provisions themselves are not generally repeated in the text. It is essential, therefore, to have a copy of the Act close at hand.

Section 170 restates the fundamental principle that directors' duties are owed to the company (see earlier). This means that only the company can bring actions for a breach of these duties. Such actions may be initiated on behalf of the company by the board of directors, a liquidator, etc, or by means of a derivative action (see 'Company claims and the statutory derivative action: CA 2006 ss 260ff', pp 671ff.

In addition, the duties in ss 175 (conflicts of interest) and 176 (benefits from third parties) *may* continue after a person has ceased to be a director, but they apply only 'to the extent stated' in s 170(2), and 'subject to any necessary adaptation', indicating that the courts may be flexible. Existing case law is likely to remain relevant, but the provision itself provides some clarification: see *Industrial Development Consultants Ltd v Cooley* [1972] 1 WLR 443; *CMS Dolphin Ltd v Simonet* **[7.35]**.

Importantly, s 170(3) explains that these general statutory duties replace the common law rules and equitable principles from which they are derived. Actions against directors will have to be based on breach of some statutory provision, not breach of related common law rules and equitable principles. But s 170(4) then provides a new way of interpreting and applying the statute. It requires the court to have regard to the existing interpretation and the continuing development of the common law rules and equitable principles on which the statutory statement is based. This is not normally allowed as a means of statutory interpretation.

The practical effect of this is that reference will have to be made to the statutory statement of duties, but in order to understand and apply these duties the surrounding case law must also be read. Practitioners and judges will therefore continue to be required to refer back to the cases.

Duty to act within powers: CA 2006 s 171

Section 171 requires directors to (a) act in accordance with the company's constitution (as defined in s 257, which is wider than s 17), and (b) only exercise powers for the purposes for which they are conferred. Notice the two steps: 'Does the director have the power?' Has it been abused?

Duty to act in accordance with the company's 'constitution': s 171(a)

Determining whether a director *has* the power to act, or, alternatively, is in breach of this duty is principally a matter of construing the 'constitution' and any personal contracts between company and director, and then deciding whether, on the facts, the director's acts are in breach of the imposed prescriptions. There is nothing especially 'corporate' about the applicable rules, and they are not considered further, despite their important in practice.

We have already seen, in Chapter 3, that these are also the rules which determine, in part, the 'actual authority' of the directors to bind the company in contract: see 'Agency and actual authority', p 94.

Because many of the cases considered in the next section (on s 171(b) and the requirement to act for proper purposes) deal with share issues motivated by improper purposes, it is timely to note here that there are an increasing number of modern constitutional restrictions on directors' powers to issue shares. See in particular CA 2006 ss 551(1), 561–577.[19] These provisions deny the directors the power to issue shares in certain circumstances.

Duty to act for proper purposes: s 171(b)

Section 171(b) is more difficult. It codifies the *proper purposes doctrine* as it applies to directors, thus putting to rest a number of earlier debates about whether such a duty existed. The controversy arose because the precursor omnibus equitable duty to 'act *bona fide* in what they [ie the directors] consider—not what a court may consider—is in the interests of the company, and not for any collateral purpose' (*Re Smith and Fawcett Ltd* [11.10]) was variously seen as imposing either one duty (bona fides only) or two (bona fides and proper purposes). The latter view prevails in CA 2006, which separates the two limbs, with the proper purposes aspect appearing here in s 171, and the 'interests of the company', reformulated as the 'duty to promote the success of the company', appearing in s 172.

This separation makes it plain that directors might act in complete good faith, but nevertheless find themselves in breach of the requirement to act for proper purposes.[20] In addition, as will be seen from the following extracts, the good faith duty is assessed subjectively, but the proper purposes duty objectively.[21] Any objective element in the assessment of breach gives the courts far greater opportunity to intervene in corporate management decisions.

Note too the positive formulation of the proper purposes obligation in s 171(b) (a director 'must . . . exercise powers for . . . [proper] purposes') as opposed to the negative version in *Smith and Fawcett* (must not act for any collateral purpose). This aligns the duty more closely with the common law version that is familiar in public and administrative law (*Associated Provincial Picture Houses Ltd v Wednesbury Corporation* [1948] 1 KB 223, Lord Greene MR), although whether this has any intended practical significance is doubted.

Nominee directors in particular are at risk of breaching this duty: they may be tempted to use their powers improperly to advance the interests of their nominator, not the interests

---

[19] See also General Principle 3 and Rule 21, City Code on Takeovers and Mergers, in relation to pre-bid frustration by directors of public companies.

[20] See LS Sealy, '"Bona Fides" and "Proper Purposes" in Corporate Decisions' (1989) 15 *Monash University Law Review* 265; S Worthington, 'Corporate Governance: Remedying and Ratifying Directors' Breaches' (2000) 116 LQR 638.

[21] Ie the permissible 'proper purposes' for which a power may be exercised are assessed objectively by the court, as a matter of law; it is irrelevant that the directors, subjectively, thought that particular purposes were 'proper'. On the other hand, the purposes which actually motivated the director are a question of fact, based on the director's subjective motivations. But see *Eclairs Group Ltd v JKX Oil & Gas plc* [7.11], [15] (Lord Sumption), although perhaps referring only to determining the question of fact.

of the company itself (see *Scottish Co-operative Wholesale Society Ltd v Meyer* **[13.31]**; *Kuwait Asia Bank EC v National Mutual Life Nominees Ltd* **[7.48]**).

Another illustration of the most common allegations of improper purpose concern the directors' power to allot shares, especially in response to a hostile takeover bid—this is the issue in the next four cases. The fifth and final case is the crucial 2015 decision of the Supreme Court in *Eclairs Group Ltd v JKX Oil & Gas plc* **[7.11]**.

As all these cases make plain, two issues of law and one of fact present difficulties: first, defining the 'proper' purposes for which a power may be exercised; secondly, if, as is common, a power has been exercised for both proper and improper purposes (ie for 'mixed purposes'), what test determines whether the exercise itself is flawed; and, finally, proving reliably which purposes actually motivated directors and to what extent.

These cases also make plain the path of reasoning: in all the following cases the judges first established that the directors *had* the powers which they purported to exercise (ie there would have been no breach of s 171(a)); and then considered whether they were abusing them (ie s 171(b)). This is because it is far easier to prove an excess of power than an abuse of it. As a further illustration of this point, see the recent 3:2 decision of the Supreme Court in *Braganza v BP Shipping Ltd* [2015] UKSC 17, concerning the 'unreasonableness' of a company's decision, as employer, as to the likely cause of an employee's death.[22]

➤ Question

The first four cases extracted below predated the codification of directors' duties in CA 2006 (indeed, two come from Australia, and predated their different statutory enactment). This means the duty is often articulated less precisely. Yet CA 2006 s 170(4) requires these common law cases to be considered in interpreting s 171(b). Consider the following for each of the four cases: How was the directors' duty described? Would such a duty apply generally, beyond the context of issues of shares by directors? Was the test of breach of duty objective or subjective? What remedy was awarded by the court? Would the outcome have been different if the law had been as prescribed in CA 2006 s 171?

The power to issue shares—improper use to alter voting majorities.

[7.07] Punt v Symons & Co Ltd [1903] 2 Ch 506 (Chancery Division)

[For the facts and another part of the decision, see **[4.21]**.] In order to secure the passing of a special resolution, the directors had issued new shares to five additional members. This was held to be an abuse of their powers.

> BYRNE J: I am quite satisfied that the meaning, object and intention of the issue of these shares was to enable the shareholders holding the smaller amount of shares to control the holders of a very considerable majority. A power of the kind exercised by the directors in this case, is one which must be exercised for the benefit of the company: primarily it is given them for the purpose of enabling them to raise capital when required for the purposes of the company. There may be occasions when the directors may fairly and properly issue shares in the case of a company constituted like the present for other reasons. For instance, it would not be at all an unreasonable

---

[22] No extracts are included here since the case makes no special reference to corporate law issues. Nevertheless, the case is interesting for its discussion of the non-statutory constraints on the exercise of powers in private law, with the court drawing analogies with the public law concept of *Wednesbury* unreasonableness (Lord Greene MR in *Associated Provincial Picture Houses Ltd v Wednesbury Corpn* [1948] 1 KB 223, 233–234, CA): see especially paras 18, 19, 24, 29–30, 52–53, 102–103.

thing to create a sufficient number of shareholders to enable statutory powers to be exercised; but when I find a limited issue of shares to persons who are obviously meant and intended to secure the necessary statutory majority in a particular interest, I do not think that it is fair and bona fide exercise of the power . . .

I propose to grant an injunction . . .

[7.08] Hogg v Cramphorn Ltd [1967] Ch 254 (Chancery Division)

The directors of the defendant company, acting in good faith, had issued 5,707 shares with special voting rights to the trustees of a scheme set up for the benefit of the company's employees, in an attempt (which proved successful) to forestall a takeover bid by one Baxter. This was held to be an improper use of the directors' power to issue shares, but to be capable of ratification by the shareholders in general meeting.

BUCKLEY J: It is not, in my judgment, open to the directors in such a case to say, 'We genuinely believe that what we seek to prevent the majority from doing will harm the company and therefore our act in arming ourselves or our party with sufficient shares to outvote the majority is a conscientious exercise of our powers under the articles, which should not be interfered with'.

Such a belief, even if well founded, would be irrelevant. A majority of shareholders in general meeting is entitled to pursue what course it chooses within the company's powers, however wrong-headed it may appear to others, providing the majority do not unfairly oppress other members of the company. These considerations lead me to the conclusion that the issue of the 5,707 shares, with the special voting rights which the directors purported to attach to them, could not be justified by the view that the directors genuinely believed that it would benefit the company if they could command a majority of the votes in general meetings . . . The power to issue shares was a fiduciary power and if, as I think, it was exercised for an improper motive, the issue of these shares is liable to be set aside. . . .

[His Lordship then went on to hold that the shareholders by majority could have ratified a *proposed* defective exercise of power by the directors.] It follows that a majority in a general meeting of the company at which no votes were cast in respect of the 5,707 shares could [equally, after the event] ratify the issue of those shares. Before setting the allotment and issue of the 5,707 shares aside, therefore, I propose to allow the company an opportunity to decide in general meeting whether it approves or disapproves of the issue of these shares to the trustees. Mr Goulding will undertake on behalf of the trustees not to vote at such a meeting in respect of the 5,707 shares . . .

[The action of the directors was ratified by the members at the subsequent meeting. Compare *Bamford v Bamford* **[4.33]**.]

[7.09] Howard Smith Ltd v Ampol Petroleum Ltd [1974] AC 821 (Privy Council)

Until the *Eclairs* case **[7.11]**, this was regarded as the leading case on abuse of power by directors (and note that even it is a Privy Council case). Rival takeover offers for all the issued shares in RW Miller (Holdings) Ltd had been made by Howard Smith Ltd and Ampol Ltd. Since Ampol, with an associated company ('Bulkships'), already owned 55% of Millers' shares, there was no prospect that Howard Smith's offer would succeed; but a majority of Millers' directors favoured this offer, both because its terms were more generous and because of fears as to the future of Millers if it were to pass into Ampol's control. Millers' directors resolved to issue some $10 million worth of new shares to Howard Smith.

This served the dual purposes of providing Millers with much needed capital to finance the completion of two tankers, and of converting the Ampol-Bulkships holding into a minority one, so that the Howard Smith offer was likely to succeed. In these proceedings, Ampol challenged the validity of the share issue. At first instance, Street J found that, while Millers' directors were not motivated by any consideration of self-interest or desire to retain control, their primary purpose was not to satisfy Millers' admitted need for capital but to destroy the majority holding of Ampol and Bulkships. He rejected as 'unreal and unconvincing' the directors' own statements to the contrary in the witness-box, and set aside the allotment. The Privy Council upheld his decision.

The opinion of their Lordships was delivered by LORD WILBERFORCE: The directors, in deciding to issue shares…acted under [a power in the company's articles of association]…. Thus, and this is not disputed, the issue was clearly intra vires the directors. But, intra vires though the issue may have been, the directors' power under this article is a fiduciary power: and it remains the case that an exercise of such a power, though formally valid, may be attacked on the ground that it was not exercised for the purpose for which it was granted. It is at this point that the contentions of the parties diverge. The extreme argument on one side is that, for validity, what is required is bona fide exercise of the power in the interests of the company; that once it is found that the directors were not motivated by self-interest—ie by a desire to retain their control of the company or their positions on the board—the matter is concluded in their favour and that the court will not inquire into the validity of their reasons for making the issue. All decided cases, it was submitted, where an exercise of such a power as this has been found invalid, are cases where directors are found to have acted through self-interest of this kind.

On the other side, the main argument is that the purpose for which the power is conferred is to enable capital to be raised for the company, and that once it is found that the issue was not made for that purpose, invalidity follows.

It is fair to say that under the pressure of argument intermediate positions were taken by both sides, but in the main the arguments followed the polarisation which has been stated.

In their Lordships' opinion neither of the extreme positions can be maintained. It can be accepted, as one would only expect, that the majority of cases in which issues of shares are challenged in the courts are cases in which the vitiating element is the self-interest of the directors, or at least the purpose of the directors to preserve their own control of the management…

Further it is correct to say that where the self-interest of the directors is involved, they will not be permitted to assert that their action was bona fide thought to be, or was, in the interest of the company; pleas to this effect have invariably been rejected…

But it does not follow from this, as the appellants assert, that the absence of any element of self-interest is enough to make an issue valid. Self-interest is only one, though no doubt the commonest, instance of improper motive: and, before one can say that a fiduciary power has been exercised for the purpose for which it was conferred, a wider investigation may have to be made … On the other hand, taking the respondents' contention, it is, in their Lordships' opinion, too narrow an approach to say that the only valid purpose for which shares may be issued is to raise capital for the company. The discretion is not in terms limited in this way: the law should not impose such a limitation on directors' powers. To define in advance exact limits beyond which directors must not pass is, in their Lordships' view, impossible. This clearly cannot be done by enumeration, since the variety of situations facing directors of different types of company in different situations cannot be anticipated. No more, in their Lordships' view, can this be done by the use of a phrase—such as 'bona fide in the interest of the company as a whole', or 'for some corporate purpose'. Such phrases, if they do anything more than restate the general principle applicable to fiduciary powers, at best serve, negatively, to exclude from the area of validity cases where the directors are acting sectionally, or partially: ie improperly favouring one section of the shareholders against another …

In their Lordships' opinion it is necessary to start with a consideration of the power whose exercise is in question, in this case a power to issue shares. Having ascertained, on a fair view, the nature of this power, and having defined as can best be done in the light of modern conditions the, or some, limits within which it may be exercised, it is then necessary for the court, if a particular exercise of it is challenged, to examine the substantial purpose for which it was exercised, and to reach a conclusion whether that purpose was proper or not. In doing so it will necessarily give credit to the bona fide opinion of the directors, if such is found to exist, and will respect their judgment as to matters of management; having done this, the ultimate conclusion has to be as to the side of a fairly broad line on which the case falls.

The main stream of authority, in their Lordships' opinion, supports this approach. In *Punt v Symons & Co Ltd* **[7.07]** Byrne J expressly accepts that there may be reasons other than to raise capital for which shares may be issued. In the High Court case of *Harlowe's Nominees Pty Ltd v Woodside (Lakes Entrance) Oil Co NL*,[23] an issue of shares was made to a large oil company in order, as was found, to secure the financial stability of the company. This was upheld as being within the power although it had the effect of defeating the attempt of the plaintiff to secure control by buying up the company's shares . . . [Reference was also made to *Teck Corpn Ltd v Miller*.[24]]

By contrast to the cases of *Harlowe* and *Teck*, the present case, on the evidence, does not, on the findings of the trial judge, involve any considerations of management, within the proper sphere of the directors. The purpose found by the judge is simply and solely to dilute the majority voting power held by Ampol and Bulkships so as to enable a then minority of shareholders to sell their shares more advantageously. So far as authority goes, an issue of shares purely for the purpose of creating voting power has repeatedly been condemned . . . [I]t must be unconstitutional for directors to use their fiduciary powers over the shares in the company purely for the purpose of destroying an existing majority, or creating a new majority which did not previously exist. To do so is to interfere with that element of the company's constitution which is separate from and set against [the directors'] powers. If there is added, moreover, to this immediate purpose, an ulterior purpose to enable an offer for shares to proceed which the existing majority was in a position to block, the departure from the legitimate use of the fiduciary power becomes not less, but all the greater . . . Directors are of course entitled to offer advice, and bound to supply information, relevant to the making of such a decision, but to use their fiduciary power solely for the purpose of shifting the power to decide to whom and at what price shares are to be sold cannot be related to any purpose for which the power over the share capital was conferred upon them. That this is the position in law was in effect recognised by the majority directors themselves when they attempted to justify the issue as made primarily in order to obtain much needed capital for the company. And once this primary purpose was rejected, as it was by Street J, there is nothing legitimate left as a basis for their action, except honest behaviour. That is not, itself, enough.

Their Lordships therefore agree entirely with the conclusion of Street J that the power to issue and allot shares was improperly exercised by the issue of shares to Howard Smith.

Issue of bonus shares—a more difficult question.

[7.10] Mills v Mills (1938) 60 CLR 150 (High Court of Australia)

The plaintiff, Ainslie Mills, and his uncle, Neilson Mills (the defendant), were two of the directors and the largest shareholders of a family company. Neilson Mills (who was managing director) held mostly ordinary shares (with one vote each), and Ainslie

---

[23] (1968) 121 CLR 483, Aust HCt.
[24] (1972) 33 DLR (3d) 288.

Mills mostly preference shares (with three votes each). A resolution was passed by a majority of the directors, including Neilson Mills, by which accumulated profits were capitalised and distributed to the ordinary shareholders in the form of fully paid bonus shares. Such profits would have gone to the ordinary shareholders had the same sums been paid as dividends rather than bonus shares. This resolution greatly strengthened the voting power of the ordinary shareholders (and in particular of Neilson Mills) and diminished the rights of the preference shareholders to share in assets in a winding up. However, it did not encroach upon the rights to dividends of either preference or ordinary shareholders. Lowe J found that the majority of directors had acted honestly in what they believed to be the best interests of the company, and he held that the fact that Neilson Mills stood to gain from their decision did not invalidate it. This view was upheld by the High Court.

> LATHAM CJ:...Directors are required to act not only in matters which affect the relations of the company to persons who are not members of the company but also in relation to matters which affect the rights of shareholders inter se. Where there are preference and ordinary shares a particular decision may be of such a character that it must necessarily affect adversely the interests of one class of shareholders and benefit the interests of another class. In such a case it is difficult to apply the test of acting in the interests of the company. The question which arises is sometimes not a question of the interests of the company at all, but a question of what is fair as between different classes of shareholders. Where such a case arises some other test than that of 'the interests of the company' must be applied, and the test must be applied with knowledge of the fact already mentioned that the law permits directors, and by virtue of provisions in articles of association often requires them, to hold shares, ordinary or preference, as the case may be. A director who holds one or both classes of such shares is not, in my opinion, required by the law to live in an unreal region of detached altruism and to act in a vague mood of ideal abstraction from obvious facts which must be presented to the mind of any honest and intelligent man when he exercises his powers as a director. It would be setting up an impossible standard to hold that, if an action of a director were affected in any degree by the fact that he was a preference or ordinary shareholder, his action was invalid and should be set aside ...
>
> DIXON J: When the law makes the object, view or purpose of a man, or of a body of men, the test of validity of their acts, it necessarily opens up the possibility of an almost infinite analysis of the fears and desires, proximate and remote, which, in truth, form the compound motives usually animating human conduct. But logically possible as such an analysis may seem, it would be impracticable to adopt it as a means of determining the validity of the resolutions arrived at by a body of directors, resolutions which otherwise are ostensibly within their powers. The application of the general equitable principle to the acts of directors managing the affairs of a company cannot be as nice as it is in the case of a trustee exercising a special power of appointment. It must, as it seems to me, take the substantial object, the accomplishment of which formed the real ground of the board's action. If this is within the scope of the power, then the power has been validly exercised. But if, except for some ulterior and illegitimate object, the power would not have been exercised, that which has been attempted as an ostensible exercise of the power will be void,[25] notwithstanding that the directors may incidentally bring about a result which is within the purpose of the power and which they consider desirable ...
>
> RICH and STARKE JJ delivered concurring judgments.
>
> EVATT J concurred.

---

[25] More accurately, voidable: see *Bamford v Bamford* **[4.33]**.

➤ Questions

1. How are the 'proper purposes' for the exercise of any given power determined? Can directors be confident they are acting for 'proper purposes'?

2. Is *Mills v Mills* a 'proper purposes' case or a 'bona fide/good faith in the interests of the company' case? Does it matter? Why is it especially difficult to answer either question when the decision in issue is whether profits will be distributed by way of bonus share issue (which will affect voting majorities) rather than cash (which will have no impact)? Is the requirement to identify, objectively, 'the proper purpose(s)' a significant practical impediment to reliable use of the proper purposes doctrine?

3. Was the judge in *Re Halt Garage (1964) Ltd* **[5.03]** applying a 'proper purposes' test when he examined the 'genuineness' of the payment of the directors' remuneration? If so, why did he not think that a similar payment made out of undistributed profits was wrong? If not, was he applying merely a 'bona fides' test?

4. Do these takeover cases miss the real issue by focusing on the scope of the power exercised by the directors on the particular occasion? Would it be more satisfactory to build on the basis of such cases as *John Shaw & Sons (Salford) Ltd v Shaw* **[4.07]**, where the separate roles of the different constitutional organs are recognised, and to say that the real issue is which organ should have control of this decision? If it were seen to be the members, then the sanction of a members' vote would be required in all such cases, not simply under the guise of ratifying an ill-purposed act of the directors, but because the decision involved a matter which was not within the directors' sphere of action. This point was recognised, but was not made the *ratio decidendi*, in the speech of Lord Wilberforce in *Howard Smith*, earlier. It is also in keeping with CA 2006 s 551(1), which allows directors to allot shares only where authorised under the company's articles or by resolution of the company (see 'Limiting access to shares: directors' allotment rights and shareholders' pre-emption rights', pp 514ff).

5. When, if ever, might it be proper for the directors to use their powers to ensure that they retain control? Could it ever be their *duty* to do so?

6. A quite different approach to the problem is mooted in *Criterion Properties plc v Stratford Properties LLC* [2004] UKHL 28, [2004] 1 WLR 1846, HL. The former managing director of the claimant company had caused it to enter into a contract which left it with a 'poison pill' in the form of a right by an outsider to demand a potentially crippling payment if control of the company should change hands or if the managing director or chairman should leave office. Lord Scott pointed out that the payment would have to be made even if the directors resigned voluntarily or there was a wholly beneficial takeover, and questioned whether the managing director had *authority* (real or apparent) to make the contract (see 'Agency and authority in corporate contracting', pp 93ff). On this approach, what remedies are available to the various affected parties, and how do these differ from the remedies available on an approach that relies on proper purposes? Is this approach defensible?

7. Where the directors are motivated by more than one purpose, the decision in *Howard Smith* indicates that regard is to be held to their *primary* purpose in deciding whether the court will intervene. However, in *Whitehouse v Carlton Hotel Pty Ltd* (1987) 162 CLR 285, the High Court of Australia appeared to favour a narrower 'but for' interpretation. The majority (Mason, Deane and Dawson JJ) in a joint judgment said (at p 721):

> In this court, the preponderant view has tended to be that the allotment will be invalidated only if the impermissible purpose or a combination of impermissible purposes can be seen to have been

dominant—'the substantial object' (per Williams ACJ, Fullagar and Kitto JJ, *Ngurli Ltd v McCann*[26] quoting Dixon J in *Mills v Mills* **[7.10]** and see *Harlowe's Nominees*); 'the moving cause' (per Latham CJ, *Mills v Mills*). The cases in which that view has been indicated have not, however, required a determination of the question whether the impermissible purpose must be *the* substantial object or moving cause or whether it may suffice to invalidate the allotment that it be one of a number of such objects or causes. As a matter of logic and principle, the preferable view would seem to be that, regardless of whether the impermissible purpose was the dominant one or but one of a number of significantly contributing causes, the allotment will be invalidated if the impermissible purpose was causative in the sense that, but for its presence, 'the power would not have been exercised' per Dixon J, *Mills v Mills*.

What difference, if any, would the different tests make in these cases? (If they truly are different: Lord Sumption in *Eclairs Group Ltd v JKX Oil & Gas plc* **[7.11]** suggests they are the same; Lord Mance is perhaps not persuaded. See the extract which follows.)

Improper purposes more generally—use of statutory or constitutional power.

[7.11] Eclairs Group Ltd v JKX Oil & Gas plc [2015] UKSC 71 (Supreme Court)

The board of directors of JKX had power[27] to disenfranchise shareholders who failed to respond to requests for information about their interests in the company's shares. It was not disputed that the power to disenfranchise had been exercised so as to disentitle certain shareholders from voting at the AGM, thereby securing the passage of certain resolutions, rather than for the purpose of enforcing the company's demand for information. At first instance, Mann J held this to be an improper purpose, so the purported restrictions on voting were held ineffective. The Court of Appeal allowed the appeal (Longmore LJ and Sir Robin Jacob, with Briggs LJ dissenting). They distinguished previous cases on the basis that the purported 'victim' here was a 'victim of his own choice, not a victim of any improper use of a power of the board of directors' since it was his choice how to respond to the questions properly raised [136]. Moreover, the majority held that restrictive purposes which had not been expressed in the statute or the articles could not be 'implied', and in any event a proper purpose test would essentially frustrate the purpose or utility of the provisions in question. The Supreme Court disagreed, indicating unanimously that the proper purpose doctrine had a central role to play in controlling the exercise of power by directors.

The decision is less powerful than it might have been, however. A majority (Lords Clarke, Mance and Neuberger) declined to commit to the general principles set out by Lord Sumption (Lord Hodge agreeing). The parties had argued the case on the basis that *if* the proper purposes doctrine applied in this context, then the directors were in breach. This meant that the scope of the rule and its application where there were mixed purposes for a decision were not the subject of oral argument before the court, although written submissions had been received. That means that only the minority agree with paras 14–24 below, while all agree with paras 30–44. (For further detail, see Worthington [2016] CLJ 202.)

---

[26] (1953) 90 CLR 425 at 445, Aust HCt.
[27] Under Part 22 of CA 2006 and the company's articles.

LORD SUMPTION: (with whom LORD HODGE agreed):

Introduction

1. This appeal is about an alleged 'corporate raid'....

2. One of the tools available to a public company seeking to resist the covert acquisition of control by raiders is a statutory disclosure notice calling for information about persons interested in its shares. There are statutory provisions empowering the court to restrict the exercise of rights attaching to shares if those interested in them fail to comply with a disclosure notice. But it is common for the articles of a public company to empower the board to impose such restrictions. The questions at issue on this appeal affect companies which have adopted powers of this kind in their articles. They are, in bald summary, what are the proper purposes for which the board may restrict the exercise of rights attaching to shares, and in what circumstances can the restrictions be challenged on the ground that they were imposed for a collateral purpose?...

The proper purpose rule

14. Part 10, Chapter 2 of the Companies Act 2006 codified for the first time the general duties of directors. The proper purpose rule is stated in section 171(b) of the 2006 Act, which provides that a director of a company must 'only exercise powers for the purposes for which they are conferred'. The rule thus stated substantially corresponds to the equitable rule which had for many years been applied to the exercise of discretionary powers by trustees....

15. The proper purpose rule has its origin in the equitable doctrine which is known, rather inappropriately, as the doctrine of 'fraud on a power'....

The principle has nothing to do with fraud. As Lord Parker of Waddington observed in delivering the advice of the Privy Council in *Vatcher v Paull* [1915] AC 372, 378, it

> 'does not necessarily denote any conduct on the part of the appointor amounting to fraud in the common law meaning of the term or any conduct which could be properly termed dishonest or immoral. It merely means that the power has been exercised for a purpose, or with an intention, beyond the scope of or not justified by the instrument creating the power.'

The important point for present purposes is that the proper purpose rule is not concerned with excess of power by doing an act which is beyond the scope of the instrument creating it as a matter of construction or implication. It is concerned with abuse of power, by doing acts which are within its scope but done for an improper reason. It follows that the test is necessarily subjective. 'Where the question is one of abuse of powers,' said Viscount Finlay in *Hindle v John Cotton Ltd* (1919) 56 Sc LR 625, 630, 'the state of mind of those who acted, and the motive on which they acted, are all important'.

16. A company director differs from an express trustee in having no title to the company's assets. But he is unquestionably a fiduciary and has always been treated as a trustee for the company of his powers. Their exercise is limited to the purpose for which they were conferred. One of the commonest applications of the principle in company law is to prevent the use of the directors' powers for the purpose of influencing the outcome of a general meeting. This is not only an abuse of a power for a collateral purpose. It also offends the constitutional distribution of powers between the different organs of the company, because it involves the use of the board's powers to control or influence a decision which the company's constitution assigns to the general body of shareholders.... [He considered *Hogg v Cramphorn Ltd* **[7.08]**.]

[Mixed purposes—the test?]

17. In all of these cases, either there was no dispute about the directors' purpose or else the only purpose which could plausibly be ascribed to them was an improper one. But what if there are multiple purposes, all influential in different degrees but some proper and others not? An analogy with public law might suggest that a decision which has been materially influenced by a

legally irrelevant consideration should generally be set aside, even if legally relevant considerations were more significant: *R(FDA) v Secretary of State for Work and Pensions* [2013] 1 WLR 444, at paras 67–69 (per Lord Neuberger of Abbotsbury MR). In some contexts, such as rescission for deceit or breach of the rules relating to self-dealing, equity is at least as exacting. But the proper purpose rule, at any rate as applied in company law, has developed in a different direction. Save perhaps in cases where the decision was influenced by dishonest considerations or by the personal interest of the decision-maker, the directors' decision will be set aside only if the primary or dominant purpose for which it was made was improper. To some extent this is a pragmatic response to the range of a director's functions and the conflicts which are sometimes inseparable from his position. The main reason, however, is a principled concern of courts of equity not just to uphold the integrity of the decision-making process, but to limit its intervention in the conduct of a company's affairs to cases in which an injustice has resulted from the directors' having taken irrelevant considerations into account.... [He then considered *Mills v Mills* **[7.10]**, citing Dixon J on the difficulties associated with too rigorous an application of the public law test.]

19.   Once one accepts the need to compare the relative significance of different considerations which influenced the directors, the question inevitably arises what is the 'primary' or 'dominant' purpose, and how is it to be identified. One possibility is that it is the 'weightiest' purpose, ie the one about which the directors felt most strongly. The other is that it is the purpose which caused the decision to be made as it was. Of course, the two things are connected. The ordinary inference is that the 'weightiest' purpose (in this sense) will also have been causative, and that minor purposes will not have been. In most cases the two tests will in practice lead to the same result. But that will not always be so and, as will be seen, it is not necessarily the case here.

20.   The first test seems to me to be difficult to justify, for reasons of both practicality and principle. The practical difficulty was pointed out by Dixon J [in *Mills v Mills* **[7.10]**] in the passage which I have quoted. It would involve a forensic enquiry into the relative intensity of the directors' feelings about the various considerations that influenced them. A director may have been influenced by a number of factors, but if they all point in the same direction he will have had no reason at the time to arrange them in order of importance. The attempt to do so later in the course of the dispute is likely to be both artificial and defensive. Moreover, a realistic appreciation of the directors' position will show that it is liable to lead to the wrong answer. Directors of companies cannot be expected to maintain an unworldly ignorance of the consequences of their acts or a lofty indifference to their implications. A director may be perfectly conscious of the collateral advantages of the course of action that he proposes, while appreciating that they are not legitimate reasons for adopting it. He may even enthusiastically welcome them. It does not follow without more that the pursuit of those advantages was his purpose in supporting the decision. All of these problems are aggravated where there are several directors, each with his own point of view.

21.   The fundamental point, however, is one of principle. The statutory duty of the directors is to exercise their powers 'only' for the purposes for which they are conferred. That duty is broken if they allow themselves to be influence by *any* improper purpose. If equity nevertheless allows the decision to stand in some cases, it is not because it condones a minor improper purpose where it would condemn a major one. It is because the law distinguishes between some consequences of a breach of duty and others. The only rational basis for such a distinction is that some improprieties may not have resulted in an injustice to the interests which equity seeks to protect. Here, we are necessarily in the realm of causation. The question is which considerations led the directors to act as they did.... One has to focus on the improper purpose and ask whether the decision would have been made if the directors had not been moved by it. If the answer is that without the improper purpose(s) the decision impugned would never have been made, then it would be irrational to allow it to stand simply because the directors had other, proper considerations in mind as well, to which perhaps they attached greater importance. This was the point

made by Dixon J in the passage immediately following the one which I have cited from his judgment in *Mills v Mills* **[7.10]**

> 'But if, except for some ulterior and illegitimate object, the power would not have been exercised, that which has been attempted as an ostensible exercise of the power will be void, notwithstanding that the directors may incidentally bring about a result which is within the purpose of the power and which they consider desirable.'

Correspondingly, if there were proper reasons for exercising the power and it would still have been exercised for those reasons even in the absence of improper ones, it is difficult to see why justice should require the decision to be set aside.

22. Dixon J's formulation has proved influential in the courts of Australia. As the majority (Mason, Deane and Dawson JJ) pointed out in the High Court of Australia in *Whitehouse v Carlton [Hotel Pty Ltd]* (1987) 162 CLR 285, 294:

> 'As a matter of logic and principle, the preferable view would seem to be that, regardless of whether the impermissible purpose was the dominant one or but one of a number of significantly contributing causes, the allotment will be invalidated if the impermissible purpose was causative in the sense that, but for its presence, "the power would not have been exercised".'

I think that this is right. It is consistent with the rationale of the proper purpose rule. It also corresponds to the view which courts of equity have always taken about the exercise of powers of appointment by trustees ...

23. The leading modern case is *Howard Smith Ltd v Ampol Petroleum Ltd* **[7.09]** ...

Lord Wilberforce did not express the point in terms of causation, but it is I think clear that by the 'substantial or primary purpose', he meant the purpose which accounted for the board's decision. He approved the judge's adoption of Dixon J's test (pp 831–832), and went on to adopt an analysis of the facts based on that test. Although the directors were influenced by the company's need for capital, the decisive factor in *Howard Smith Ltd v Ampol Petroleum Ltd* was that but for their desire to convert the majority shareholders into a minority, the directors would not have sought to raise capital by means of a share issue, nor at that point of time.

[He then discussed the decisions in the lower courts, and continued:]

29. In a formidable dissent, Briggs LJ set out the rationale for the proper purpose test and the authorities for its application to the exercise of discretionary powers by companies. He accepted the view of Mann J that the purpose of article 42 was to encourage or coerce the provision of information which had been requested under section 793, with the rider that it was also to prevent the accrual of any unfair advantage to any person as a result of the failure to comply with such a request. Even with that limited expansion, on the judge's findings of fact the directors' decision to impose restrictions under article 42 was improper, and there were no satisfactory reasons why the rule should not be applied to the draconian powers conferred by article 42 of JKX's articles. He added (para 122):

> 'Furthermore, I consider it important that the court should uphold the proper purpose principle in relation to the exercise of fiduciary powers by directors, all the more so where the power is capable of affecting, or interfering with, the constitutional balance between shareholders and directors, and between particular groups of shareholders. The temptation on directors, anxious to protect their company from what they regard as the adverse consequences of a course of action proposed by shareholders, to interfere in that way, whether by the issue of shares to their supporters, or by disenfranchisement of their opponents' shares, may be very hard to resist, unless the consequences of improprieties of that kind are clearly laid down and adhered to by the court.'

[How to determine the 'proper' purposes for which a power can be exercised]

The proper purpose of article 42

30. The submission of Mr Swainston QC, who appeared for the company, was that where the purpose of a power was not expressed by the instrument creating it, there was no limitation on its exercise save such as could be implied on the principles which would justify the implication of a term. In particular, the implication would have to be necessary to its efficacy. In my view, this submission misunderstands the way in which purpose comes into questions of this kind.... that is not the basis of the proper purpose rule. The rule is not a term of the contract and does not necessarily depend on any limitation on the scope of the power as a matter of construction. The proper purpose rule is a principle by which equity controls the exercise of a fiduciary's powers in respects which are not, or not necessarily, determined by the instrument. Ascertaining the purpose of a power where the instrument is silent depends on an inference from the mischief of the provision conferring it, which is itself deduced from its express terms, from an analysis of their effect, and from the court's understanding of the business context.

31. The purpose of a power conferred by a company's articles is rarely expressed in the instrument itself. It was not expressed in the instrument in any of the leading cases about the application of the proper purpose rule to the powers of directors which I have summarised. But it is usually obvious from its context and effect why a power has been conferred, and so it is with article 42....

32. ... In my view article 42 [the article in issue here] has three closely related purposes. The first is to induce the shareholder to comply with a disclosure notice.... Secondly, the article is intended to protect the company and its shareholders against having to make decisions about their respective interests in ignorance of relevant information.... Thirdly, the restrictions have a punitive purpose. They are imposed as sanctions on account of the failure or refusal of the addressee of a disclosure notice to provide the information for as long as it persists, on the footing that a person interested in shares who has not complied with obligations attaching to that status should not be entitled to the benefits attaching to the shares.... These three purposes are all directly related to the non-provision of information requisitioned by a disclosure notice. None of them extends to influencing the outcome of resolutions at a general meeting. That may well be a consequence of a restriction notice. But it is no part of its proper purpose. It is not itself a legitimate weapon of defence against a corporate raider, which the board is at liberty to take up independently of its interest in getting the information....

33. ... However difficult it may be to draw in practice, there is in principle a clear line between protecting the company and its shareholders against the consequences of non-provision of the information, and seeking to manipulate the fate of particular shareholders' resolutions or to alter the balance of forces at the company's general meetings. The latter are no part of the purpose of article 42. They are matters for the shareholders, not for the board....

Does the proper purpose rule apply?

[This is by way of explanation of the flaws the Supreme Court perceived in the Court of Appeal's view that the proper purpose rule should not apply at all in this context.]

35. At this stage, two preliminary observations are called for.

36. The first is that the imposition of restrictions under article 42 is a serious interference with financial and constitutional rights which exist for the benefit of the shareholder and not the company....

37. The second preliminary observation concerns the role of the proper purpose rule in the governance of companies. The rule that the fiduciary powers of directors may be exercised only for the purposes for which they were conferred is one of the main means by which equity enforces the proper conduct of directors. It is also fundamental to the constitutional distinction

between the respective domains of the board and the shareholders. These considerations are particularly important when the company is in play between competing groups seeking to control or influence its affairs.... Of all the situations in which directors may be called upon to exercise fiduciary powers with incidental implications for the balance of forces among shareholders, a battle for control of the company is probably the one in which the proper purpose rule has the most valuable part to play....

39. That brings me to the majority's first and, I think, main reason, which was that the power to impose restrictions under article 42 was not a 'unilateral' power. The addressees of the disclosure notices had only to answer the questions fully and truthfully to bring the restrictions to an end. I reject this also. The short and principled objection to it was given by Briggs LJ. The limitation of the power to its proper purpose derives from its fiduciary character. If its exercise would otherwise be an abuse, it cannot be an answer to say that the person against whom it is directed had only himself to blame. Moreover, the majority's proposition assumes that that person is the only one whose interests are adversely affected. But that is not right. Other shareholders who agreed with them would be deprived of their support....

[And since the rule applied, the parties had effectively conceded that the directors were then in breach of it.]

LORD CLARKE:

46. I initially intended simply to agree with Lord Sumption's judgment. Like Lord Mance (and Lord Neuberger), I agree with Lord Sumption that the appeal should be allowed for the reasons given in his paras 27 to 43. I am inclined to agree with the other views expressed by Lord Sumption but there does seem to me to be force in Lord Mance's reservation that not all the points were the subject of full argument and consideration below. In these circumstances I would prefer to defer reaching a final conclusion on the other points identified by Lord Mance until they arise for decision and have been the subject of such argument.

LORD MANCE (with whom LORD NEUBERGER agreed):

47. ... I also agree with his reasons for allowing this appeal in paras 30 to 44.

48. I have read with interest the discussion of the proper purpose rule in paras 14 to 24....

49. ... Eclairs submitted that any issue as to whether a 'but for' test should be applied should in these circumstances [ie given the basis on which the case had been argued before the Supreme Court] await a case where it arose squarely. Eclairs and Glengary each supplied a copy of its submissions to the judge at the trial in 2013, which had suggested a two-pronged alternative analysis, according to which the notices would be set aside if a court concluded either that (a) the principal purpose was to ensure the passing of the resolutions or (b) even if that was not the principal purpose, the notices would not have been issued but for the wish to ensure the passing of the resolutions.... [He then expressed a number of reservations, not detailed here, and added:]

53. ... I do not for my part think that the interpretation which Lord Sumption puts in para 24 on Lord Wilberforce's speech in *Howard Smith Ltd v Ampol Petroleum Ltd* [1974] AC 821 is necessarily or clearly what Lord Wilberforce meant. Equally, the passage already quoted from Dixon J's judgment in *Mills v Mills* appears to me far from conclusive, while its later explanation in the High Court in *Whitehouse v Carlton [Hotel Pty Ltd]* (1987) 162 CLR 285, 294 (quoted by Lord Sumption at para 22) is, at least arguably, consistent with 'but for' causation being viewed either as the only test or as affording an extended basis for the grant of relief, even where the principal purpose was legitimate, as Eclairs and Glengary submitted to the judge. In these circumstances, although I have sympathy with Lord Sumption's view that 'but for' causation offers a single, simple test, which it might be possible or even preferable to substitute for references to the principal or primary purpose, I am not persuaded that we can or should safely undertake what all parties consider would be 'a new development' of company law, without having heard argument.

➤ Questions

1. *Is* the proper purpose test subjective? (See Lord Sumption, at [15].) In what sense? Clearly it is not subjective in the same sense as the director's duty to act in what the director bona fide considers to be the interests of the company (see s 172, following), where it is irrelevant that the court does not regard the decision as in the interests of the company. Here it clearly matters that the court regards the director's purposes as 'proper'.

2. What test *should* be applied to determine whether a decision offends s 171(b) when the decision has been taken for 'mixed purposes'? Do the cited authorities support a 'principal purposes' or a 'but for' test? What risk is the proposal advanced by the shareholders, as described by Lord Mance at [49], seeking to avoid? How would directors offer credible proof that a 'principal purpose' was not also a 'but for' purpose?

3. Is there an explicitly recognised parallel concept of 'proper purposes', as a test separate from that of bona fides, in *members'* decision-making? Should there be, given the generality of the rule as expressed in *Eclairs Group Ltd v JKX Oil & Gas plc* [7.11]?[28]

For a possible modern illustration, see *Burry & Knight Ltd v Knight* [2014] EWCA Civ 604, where the Court of Appeal had to decide whether a member's request to inspect the register of members was made for improper purposes, thus entitling the company to an order that it need not comply with this or any future requests: see CA 2006 ss 116–117, noting that although the applicant must state the purpose of the request, there is no indication in the section of which purposes are 'proper'.

Also revisit *Re Halt Garage (1964) Ltd* [5.03]; *Gambotto v WPC Ltd* (1995) 182 CLR 432, Aust HCt (see 'Note', p 240); *Kinsela v Russell Kinsela* [7.16], the cases on alteration of the company's constitution ('Alteration of the articles', pp 228ff), variations of class rights ('Variation of class rights', pp 587ff), and ratification of directors' wrongdoing ('Members' decisions concerning directors' breaches', pp 247ff, and 'Subsequent ratification by the company', p 398, 'Ratification of acts of directors: CA 2006 s 239', pp 454ff). In the context of ratification, note especially CA 2006 s 239(3) and (4).

Duty to promote the success of the company: CA 2006 s 172

As noted earlier, this section codifies the common law rule on bona fides in *Re Smith and Fawcett Ltd* [11.10]: the directors have a duty to 'act *bona fide* in what they consider—not what a court may consider—is in the interests of the company, and not for any collateral purpose'. This duty has always depended on two factors. First, the director's good faith: this is necessarily assessed subjectively, subject to one rider noted later, and is notoriously difficult to prove except in the most extreme cases (see 'The director's "good faith"', p 356). And secondly, the meaning of 'the interests of the company' (at common law) or 'the success of the company' (in s 172): the more widely the latter is defined, the less likely it is that directors will be in breach of the duty (see 'The success of the company for the benefit of its members as a whole', p 356). These two factors mean the section

---

[28] See P Finn, *Fiduciary Obligations* (1977), p 73, contending that members' decisions should be subject to a similar test to those of the directors; also S Worthington, advocating a proper purposes test (but not accompanied by fiduciary duties of loyalty) for all members' decisions: 'Corporate Governance: Remedying and Ratifying Directors' Breaches' (2000) 116 LQR 638.

is likely to be something of a toothless tiger. Indeed, its function may instead be one of defining clearly the context in which breaches of other duties (to act for proper purposes, without conflicts, etc) can be judged.[29] That function is important, of course. So too the ability to catch clear cases of directors acting in bad faith. But this duty ought to be one of the easiest for directors to obey.

Nevertheless, when codification of directors' duties was mooted, this section was regarded as one of the more important and controversial provisions in the Act, and took up much of the discussion through the various stages of the Companies Bill that produced CA 2006. Its approach purports to end the debate over the meaning of 'the company' (see 'Directors' duties are owed to the company', p 336). Whether it achieves that is debatable. The section also explicitly favours a long-term, rather than short-term, outlook in corporate decision-making (see s 172(1)(a)).[30]

The crucial elements of s 172

Section 172(1) enshrines a number of important elements:

The director's 'good faith'

The essential principle is that it is for *directors* to make decisions, in good faith, as to how to promote the success of the company for the benefit of the members as a whole. This test repeats the common law rule from which it is derived (*Re Smith and Fawcett Ltd* [11.10]). A court will not inquire whether, objectively, the decision was actually the best decision for the company (*Howard Smith Ltd v Ampol Petroleum Ltd* [7.09]; *Regentcrest plc v Cohen* [7.12] at [105]), nor whether the director's honestly held belief was a reasonable one (*Smith v Fawcett; Regentcrest plc v Cohen*).

On the other hand, where it is alleged that directors lacked good faith, it will be especially hard for directors to defend themselves if the court considers that *no* reasonable director could have believed that the decision taken was in the interests of the company. This is a high hurdle for finding a decision to be flawed. The test is most likely to be met when the director's decision is self-interested.

The same test is obviously necessary where the directors gave no consideration at all to the question of the company's interests. In *Re HLC Environmental Projects Ltd* [7.19], Deputy High Court Judge John Randall QC suggested that in such circumstances 'the proper test is objective, namely whether an intelligent and honest man in the position of a director of the company concerned could, in the circumstances, have reasonably believed that the transaction was for the benefit of the company...' Note the use of 'could' rather than 'would': this is the same test as in the previous paragraph, but put in positive form. See also *Item Software (UK) Ltd v Fassihi* [7.13].

Where the directors have simply not considered the matters in s 172(1), the question of whether it might be possible to switch from assertions of a breach of s 172 to assertions of a breach of s 171(b) (ie failure to act for proper purposes—here, failing to take into account material considerations) is not clear. What should the answer be?

'The success of the company for the benefit of its members as a whole'

Section 172(1) relates the success of the company to the interests of its members as a whole,[31] (although note s 172(2)), and then adds a long list of issues to which the directors *must* have regard. The practical consequences of this formulation can be difficult.

---

[29] And the wider the scope of permitted endeavour in s 172, the less likely is there to be a breach of the other sections where the scope and purpose of the endeavour is relevant. See *Merchant Navy Ratings* case [2015] EWHC 448 (Ch), [228]-[229].

[30] On this, see the 2012 Kay Review, noted at 'General issues', p 273.

[31] This approach was advocated by the CLR, *Modern Company Law for a Competitive Economy: Developing the Framework* (URN 00/656) (2000), para 3.51.

Moreover, given the detail in the statute, older cases should either be ignored or treated with due caution.

The specification that the director's duty is to promote the success of the company for the benefit of its members as a whole (and thus, implicitly, not for the benefit of other stakeholders or constituencies) rejects the 'pluralist approach' and adopts the 'enlightened shareholder value' recommendations of the Law Commissions and CLR.[32] One important reason for this choice was said to be that the pluralist view risks leaving directors accountable to no one, since there is no clear yardstick for judging their performance.[33] Whether the position is really any different under the current formulation seems debatable.

'Success' is a slippery concept. It needs to be determined on a company-by-company basis (note s 172(2)). At its simplest, success may often mean the long-term increase in financial value of the company, but even this has its difficulties. It is not clear, for example, whether the directors should favour increased dividend rates, increased market price for the shares or some other manifestation of the long-term growth and stability of the company. In the end, it is for the directors to interpret the company's objectives and make practical decisions about how best to achieve them.

The duty is owed to the company alone. This means that only the company—and not the members, or any other stakeholders named in s 172—can sue.

The primacy of the company seems significant. If the interests of the company as a separate entity are in conflict with the interests of the members as a whole, or at least some of them, it would appear that the interests of the company should be preferred (*Mutual Life Assurance Co of New York v Rank Organisation Ltd* [1985] BCLC 11 at 21 (Goulding J); *Re BSB Holdings Ltd (No 2)* [1996] 1 BCLC 155 at 251 (Arden J)).

The formulation 'for the benefit of its members as a whole' suggests that deliberately promoting sectional shareholder interests would be a breach of the duty to promote the success of the company, yet incidental sectional shareholder benefits are often inevitable (see *Mills v Mills* **[7.10]**).[34]

Moreover, in paying attention to the long list of issues to which the directors *must* have regard, it will often be the case that members' interests are disadvantaged (at least in the short term), while the sectional interests of other stakeholders are favoured, all in the cause of advancing 'the success of the company'.

It is difficult to resist the conclusion that a straightforward commitment to 'the success of the company' (as its own legal person) might have been simpler. The 'members as a whole' could then have been relegated to the list of issues to which the directors should have regard. It seems not much would have been lost in stating the law in this way, and greater clarity would have been achieved both for directors and for potential litigants. The same reluctance to a straightforward commitment to regarding the company as a separate legal person was seen in Chapter 2.

A defence rather than duty?

Although the 'enlightened shareholder value' approach was designed to avoid the problems of director accountability inherent in the 'pluralist approach', it is not clear that this ambition is achieved (see the earlier comments). Section 172(1) sets out proper considerations for director decision-making, but these considerations will allow directors to justify almost any bona fide approach to delivering the success of the company. Where directors

---

[32] See the White Paper, *Company Law Reform* (Cm 6456, 2005), para 3.3; CLR, *Modern Company Law for a Competitive Economy: A Strategic Framework* (1999), para 5.

[33] Committee on Corporate Governance, *Final Report*, para 1.17.

[34] By contrast, most decisions will differentiate between different classes of stakeholders: eg, more money for dividends means less for wages or customer price reductions, etc.

have made a good faith business judgement to favour employees' interests[35] over short-term financial gain, for example in order to promote the success of the company for the benefits of its members as a whole, then this legitimate decision cannot be challenged (see *Re Welfab Engineers Ltd* (1990) BCLC 833). Similarly, directors are not compelled to make decisions according to the wider interests of community and the environment, and they are protected from reproach if they choose to do so. Is there *any* decision the directors might take which would self-evidently fall outside the requirements of s 172(1)?

This idea that directors could simply use the section defensively was evident during the legislative process leading to enactment of s 172. Concerns were expressed that the section would require directors to keep a 'paper trail' of all business judgements made, and that the section would lead to an increase in litigation. Both were denied. The government insisted that the section did not introduce a 'tick-box culture' requiring directors to consider each factor one by one,[36] since the list of factors was non-exhaustive and intended to illustrate elements of the wider principle behind making good faith business judgements to promote the success of the company for the long-term benefit of members as a whole. And there was said to be little risk of increased litigation, since the class of potential litigants is limited, and it will also often be difficult to identify any loss.[37] All this merely adds to the sense that s 172 has a greater role in defining the context for operation of the other general duty provisions than in delivering significant duties or remedies itself.

Illustrations of the duty to act in good faith for the success of the company

Good faith is judged subjectively.

[7.12] Regentcrest plc v Cohen [2001] BCC 494 (Chancery Division)

Richardson (the second defendant) had agreed on behalf of his company, Regentcrest, to waive the company's entitlement to claw back a sum from a third party. When Regentcrest went into liquidation, its liquidators (on behalf of the company) sued Richardson for breach of duty, alleging that he had disposed of the clawback asset for negligible consideration and for an improper purpose. Richardson successfully argued that he had agreed to the waiver for a valid commercial reason and had honestly believed that he was acting in the best interest of the company and in accordance with his duties as a director.

> JONATHAN PARKER J:
>
> 96. . . . [T]he only live claim is a claim against Mr Don Richardson for having agreed to the waiver of the clawback claim. . . .
>
> 101. . . . [T]he central issue in the case is whether, when he voted in favour of the first resolution [to waive the clawback], Mr Don Richardson honestly believed that he was acting in the best

---

[35] In the context of s 172(1)(b), also see the power to make provision for employees on cessation or transfer of business (s 247): s 247(2) states that this latter power 'is exercisable notwithstanding the general duty imposed by s 172'.

[36] On the other hand, see s 414C (contents of strategic report: business review, previously part of the director's report, CA 2006 s 417, repealed in 2013), especially s 414C(1).

[37] The class of potential litigants is limited to the board, a majority of members, a minority of members under Pt 11 and liquidators acting on behalf of an insolvent company. It is only during a takeover that a board or a majority of members is likely to bring an action against a director; in most cases there are far better remedies available against directors, eg removal of the director. Further, a derivative action under Pt 11 is extremely difficult to advance against the wishes of the majority of members. In reality, it is only during takeovers and liquidation proceedings that the section is likely to be utilised. Moreover, an action will only be useful where there is a loss to the company: a breach of the duty to promote the success of the company is unlikely, alone, to give rise to significant calculable financial loss.

interest of Regentcrest. If he did not honestly hold that belief, then . . . it follows that he must have breached his fiduciary duty to Regentcrest and must accordingly be liable to Regentcrest for any resulting loss. As to the quantification of that loss, it is common ground that the loss is equal to the value of the clawback claim as at 5 September 1990. Plainly, the value of the clawback claim cannot exceed its face value of £1.5M, but equally clearly it may, depending on a number of factors including the ability of the vendors to satisfy any judgment and the existence of any defences to the claim, be less than its face value. . . .

120. The duty imposed on directors to act *bona fide* in the interests of the company is a subjective one . . . The question is not whether, viewed objectively by the court, the particular act or omission which is challenged was in fact in the interests of the company; still less is the question whether the court, had it been in the position of the director at the relevant time, might have acted differently. Rather, the question is whether the director honestly believed that his act or omission was in the interests of the company. The issue is as to the director's state of mind. No doubt, where it is clear that the act or omission under challenge resulted in substantial detriment to the company, the director will have a harder task persuading the court that he honestly believed it to be in the company's interest; but that does not detract from the subjective nature of the test.

121. As Lord Greene put it in *Re Smith and Fawcett, Ltd* **[11.10]**:

'The principles to be applied in cases where the articles of a company confer a discretion on directors . . . are, for present purposes, free from doubt. *They must exercise their discretion bona fide in what they consider—not what a court may consider—is in the interests of the company, and not for any collateral purpose.*' (Emphasis supplied.)

122. To similar effect is the following passage from the judgment of Millett LJ in *Bristol & West Building Society v. Mothew* [1998] Ch 1 at 18:

'The various obligations of a fiduciary merely reflect different aspects of his core duties of loyalty and fidelity. Breach of fiduciary obligation, therefore, connotes disloyalty or infidelity. Mere incompetence is not enough. A servant who loyally does his incompetent best for his master is not unfaithful and is not guilty of a breach of fiduciary duty.'

123. The position is different where a power conferred on a director is used for a collateral purpose. In such circumstances it matters not whether the director honestly believed that in exercising the power as he did he was acting in the interests of the company; the power having been exercised for an improper purpose, its exercise will be liable to be set aside (see, e.g., *Hogg v. Cramphorn Ltd* **[7.08]**). However, it has not been contended that that principle applies in the instant case. . . .

146. Three main reasons [for the waiver] were identified by the Richardson brothers in evidence. First, the need to retain the services of Mr Scott and Mr Farley, with the concomitant benefit of their knowledge and experience in seeking to realise the various properties in the Regentcrest Group's property portfolio, and (in the case of Mr Cohen) the desirability of retaining his services in relation to the Altrincham Site, about which he was thought to have a good deal of useful local knowledge; secondly, the need to preserve a united board in the face of pressure from the banks and other creditors; thirdly, the fact that it was (to put it at its lowest) questionable to what extent the vendors would be able to satisfy any judgment; and fourthly the fact that the vendors had made it clear (through Mr Farley) that they would not submit to judgment on the clawback claim but would defend the claim on whatever grounds might be open to them—in other words, they were not going to go quietly.

147. In assessing the 'commerciality' of the reasons put forward by the Richardson brothers I have to eschew hindsight and to place myself so far as possible in their shoes as at 5 September 1990. . . .

158. In the result, therefore, I have no hesitation in accepting the evidence of each of the Richardson brothers as to his reasons for agreeing to the waiver of the clawback claim, and I find that in voting in favour of the resolution for waiver each of them honestly believed that he was acting in the best interests of Regentcrest.

159. It follows that the claim of breach of fiduciary duty on the part of Mr Don Richardson fails.

The Damages Issue

160. In the light of my conclusions on the breach of the duty issue, the damages issue does not arise. However, for the sake of completeness I will address it shortly. I do so on the assumption, contrary to the conclusion which I have expressed above, that Mr Don Richardson was in breach of his fiduciary duty to Regentcrest in voting in favour of the resolution for waiver of the clawback claim.

161. It is common ground that the correct measure of damage is the value of the clawback claim as at 5 September 1990, and that that value is to be assessed on an objective basis. Thus, the court is not limited to such knowledge as the Richardson brothers had at that date as to the vendors' means.

162. I turn, then, to the evidence as to the vendors' means. . . .

174. In the circumstances as disclosed by the evidence (which is admittedly incomplete), I conclude that as at September 1990 (a) there was no sensible prospect of recovering more than 20 per cent at the most of the face value of the clawback claim, (b) there was a real risk, given the vendors' expressed intention to contest the claim so far as possible, that the total sum recovered under a judgment might not cover the costs of obtaining it, and (c) subject to that, it was a matter of speculation how much might be recovered. . . .

175. Doing the best I can on the basis of the above conclusions, I assess the value of the clawback claim as at September 1990 at £50,000. . . .

176. In the result, for the reasons already given, the action must be dismissed.

➤ Notes

1. Also see *Extrasure Travel Insurances Ltd v Scattergood* [2003] 1 BCLC 598, [138] (Mr Jonathan Crow):

> [A] director's duty is to do what he honestly believes to be in the company's best interests. The fact that his alleged belief was unreasonable may provide evidence that it was not in fact honestly held at the time: but if, having considered all the evidence, it appears that the director did honestly believe that he was acting in the best interests of the company, then he is not in breach of his fiduciary duty merely because that belief appears to the trial judge to be unreasonable, or because his actions happen, in the event, to cause injury to the company.

2. The onus of proof of lack of good faith lies on the company (or its liquidator) asserting the claim against its directors. As Jonathan Parker J notes, however, the greater the detriment to the company from the directors' actions, the harder it will be for the directors to defend themselves against allegations of absence of good faith. If, in the face of the company's assertions, the directors mount a credible rationale for their actions, ones that indicate it is plausible that directors in the circumstances could think the chosen course of action was in good faith in the interests of the company, then they will escape liability, subject to the court testing the credibility of these assertions.

► Questions

1. Does a subjective rule of good faith catch only those directors whose behaviour is patently fraudulent or grossly negligent? Could, and should, a higher standard be imposed? (See the discussions of subjective/objective tests in the context of the director's duty of care ('The subjective/objective test', pp 378ff) and 'dishonest assistance' by third parties in a director's breach of duty ('Required knowledge for secondary liability', pp 469ff).

2. See *Charterbridge Corpn Ltd v Lloyds Bank Ltd* [1970] Ch 62. There, the directors of a company within a corporate group did not expressly consider the benefits to *their* company of a proposed course of action, as distinct from the benefits to the corporate group. When, if ever, could such directors be found guilty of breach of the duty in CA 2006 s 172? Does a subjective test of good faith mean that the directors must give explicit consideration to the issue of whether their actions are in good faith in the interests of the company?

Duty to disclose own misconduct?

The controversial finding in *Item Software (UK) Ltd v Fassihi* **[7.13]** at [44] (a case predating CA 2006) may be embraced by the terms of s 172. *Fassihi* suggests that a director who acts in breach of his fiduciary duty is under a further duty to disclose the breach to the company if disclosure is required by the general equitable duty to act bona fide in what the director considers to be the interests of the company. The parallels with the statutory duty in s 172(1) are obvious. It is difficult to see when it would not be in the company's interest to know of a breach of duty, and on that basis any breach of duty will always involve a further breach in failing to disclose. The further breach may be sufficient to warrant a director's loss of employment benefits (eg termination rights, share options, pension benefits), and may provide justification for summary dismissal (*Tesco Stores Ltd v Pook* [2003] EWHC 823 (Ch); *Fulham Football Club (1987) Ltd v Tigana* [2004] EWHC 2585 (QB)). On the other hand, this aspect of the *Fassihi* decision represents a radical extension of the traditional equitable duties owed by directors, and the approach mandated in s 170(4) to these statutory rules may argue against its acceptance.

Less controversially, a director also has always been under an equitable duty to disclose breaches of duty committed by fellow directors if this is what the director, acting bona fide, considers to be in the best interests of the company (*British Midland Tool Ltd v Midland International Tooling Ltd* [2003] EWHC 466 (Ch), [2003] 2 BCLC 523). Again, the analogy with the statutory duty in s 172(1) is apparent. Also see *Brandeaux Advisers (UK) Ltd v Chadwick* [2010] EWHC 3241 (QB), referred to later.

The duty to act bona fide in the interests of the company includes the duty to disclose misconduct by the director to the company.

[7.13] Item Software (UK) Ltd v Fassihi [2004] EWCA Civ 1244 (Court of Appeal)

Fassihi was both a director and employee of Item Software (IS), a distributor of products for Isograph. The company tried to renegotiate its distribution agreement with Isograph on more favourable terms. During negotiations, Fassihi put to Isograph the idea of establishing a new company to take over the distribution agreement. At the same time, he encouraged IS to take an aggressive stance in its negotiations with Isograph. Perhaps predictably, negotiations between IS and Isograph broke down because Isograph refused to accept IS's terms. Isograph terminated the distribution agreement with IS and entered into a new agreement with Fassihi's own company. IS dismissed Fassihi when it learned of this and commenced proceedings against Fassihi, alleging that his actions amounted to a breach of his duty as both a director and an employee to act bona fide in the interests of the company (ie IS). It was also alleged that this duty was breached by Fassihi's failure to disclose his misconduct to the company.

> ARDEN LJ: . . . [I]t seems to me that the logical place to start in relation to the disclosure issue is to consider the position of Mr Fassihi as a director since the duties of a director are in general higher than those imposed by law on an employee. This is because a director is not simply a senior manager of [a] company. He is a fiduciary and with his fellow directors he is responsible for the success of the company's business.
>
> Merely to call a person a fiduciary is only the beginning of the analysis. It is necessary to identify the respects in which he is a fiduciary and the duties which follow. . . .
>
> For my part, I do not consider that it is correct to infer from the cases to which I have referred that a fiduciary owes a separate and independent duty to disclose his own misconduct to his principal or more generally information of relevance and concern to it. So to hold would lead to a proliferation of duties and arguments about their breadth. I prefer to base my conclusion in this case on the fundamental duty to which a director is subject, that is the duty to act in what he in good faith considers to be the best interests of his company. This duty of loyalty is the 'time-honoured' rule: per Goulding J in *Mutual Life Insurance Co of New York v Rank Organisation Ltd* [1985] BCLC 11, 21. The duty is expressed in these very general terms, but that is one of its strengths: it focuses on principle not on the particular words which judges or the legislature have used in any particular case or context. It is dynamic and capable of application in cases where it has not previously been applied but the principle or rationale of the rule applies. It reflects the flexible quality of the doctrines of equity. As Lord Templeman once put it 'Equity is not a computer. Equity operates on conscience . . .' (*Winkworth v Edward Baron Development Co Ltd* [1986] 1 WLR 1512, 1516.)
>
> Professor Robert C Clark *Corporate Law* (1986), pp 34 and 141, has described the fundamental nature of the duty of the loyalty in these terms:
>
>> 'The most general formulation of corporate law's attempted solution to the problem of managerial accountability is the *fiduciary duty of loyalty*: the corporation's directors . . . owe a duty of undivided loyalty to their corporations, and they may not so use corporate assets, or deal with the corporation, as to benefit themselves at the expense of the corporation and its shareholders. *The overwhelming majority of particular rules, doctrines, and cases in corporate law are simply an explication of this duty or of the procedural rules and institutional arrangements involved in implementing it.* The history of corporate law is largely the history of the development of operational content for the duty of loyalty. Even many cases that appear to be about dull formalities or rules of the road in fact involve disputes arising out of alleged managerial disloyalty . . . Most importantly, this general fiduciary duty of loyalty is a residual concept that can include factual situations that no one has foreseen and categorised. The general duty permits, and in fact has led to, a continuous evolution in corporate law.'

Although Professor Clark was writing about the duty of loyalty in the United States, his observations seem to me to express qualities of the duty of loyalty applying equally to the law of England and Wales.

The only reason that I can see that it could be said that the duty of loyalty does not require a fiduciary to disclose his own misconduct is that it has never been applied to this situation before. As I have explained, that is not a good objection to the application of the fiduciary principle. . . .

. . . Furthermore, on the facts of this case, there is no basis on which Mr Fassihi could reasonably have come to the conclusion that it was not in the interests of Item to know of his breach of duty. In my judgment, he could not fulfil his duty of loyalty in this case except by telling Item about his setting up of RAMS, and his plan to acquire the Isograph contract for himself. . . .

Both counsel have addressed the court on the policy reasons for holding that Mr Fassihi was in breach of his duty of loyalty in this case. These are relevant questions. If the approach of the law were overly intrusive, legitimate entrepreneurial activity would be discouraged and this would not be a beneficial outcome. But that is not in my judgment the result of holding that a duty of loyalty applies in the present case. This is because, on well established principles of law, Mr Fassihi's setting up of a new company to which the business of Item would be diverted was not a legitimate entrepreneurial activity. In addition, the effect of my decision in this case (if the majority of the court is of the same opinion) is not to make any substantive extension of the duties of directors, such as would be involved for example if the courts held that a director of one company could not accept a directorship of another company. . . .

A conclusion that a director owes no obligation to disclose his improper actions would be also inefficient in economic terms. It would mean that the company has to expend resources in investigating his conduct and that the enforcement of a liability to compensate the company for misconduct depends on the happenchance of the company finding out about the impropriety. To this it may be said that the law ought not to hold that the duty of loyalty involves a positive duty to disclose because it is unlikely that the consciously misbehaving director will comply with it: this indeed is the rationale for the fraud exception (in *Re Hampshire Land Co*[38]) referred to above.

My answer to that is two wrongs do not make a right: the fact that a director is unlikely to comply with a duty is not a logically sustainable reason for not imposing it if it is otherwise appropriate. As the facts of this case demonstrate, the consequence of non-disclosure may be that the company makes erroneous business decisions because it lacks essential information. A legal rule which condones this, in my judgment, condones inefficient outcomes. Moreover, there is a constant dilemma in company law as to the manner in which the shareholders of a company can monitor those who manage its business on their behalf. The duty upheld above helps to ameliorate these problems (often called agency problems) by encouraging the provision of information on which proper decision-making can take place. In many companies, an agency problem exists not only between shareholders and directors but between the board and executive or managing directors. There is an oversight duty owed by the board in respect of executives by virtue of their duty of care. (The precise extent of the duty depends on the facts of the case: *Re Barings plc (No.5)* **[6.12]**.) The duty of loyalty as applied by me above supports the board in the performance of this duty and is thus efficient for that reason also. Accordingly, in so far as my conclusion on this issue involves a new application of the duty of loyalty, it is supported for policy reasons. For all these reasons, in my judgment, the appeal against the judge's judgment on the disclosure issue must be dismissed.

HOLMAN J delivered a concurring judgment.

MUMMERY LJ concurred.

Also see *Industrial Development Consultants Ltd v Cooley* as explained in *Bhullar v Bhullar* **[7.29]**.

➤ Note

At first instance, [2003] EWHC 3116 (Ch), N Strauss QC Deputy Judge came to the same conclusion that Mr Fassihi's misconduct gave rise to a 'super added' duty of disclosure. However, the learned judge came to that conclusion not as a matter of fiduciary duty, but on a contractual basis:

52. . . . [T]here was a separate and independent aspect of his duties which required him to disclose the facts. He was involved in the negotiations between Item and Isograph and his contractual obligations of fidelity and care required him to disclose important information known to him

---

[38] [1896] 2 Ch 743.

which was relevant to those negotiations. If he had learned that a rival distributor had been trying to sabotage the negotiations with Isograph, it would have been his duty to tell Mr. Dehghani; the fact that it was himself cannot relieve him of the duty. That it would have been in Item's interest to know of the misconduct in order to deal with Mr. Fassihi would not have justified the imposition of a duty; what justifies it is its relevance to the ongoing negotiations with Isograph. This therefore seems to me to be a case in which a duty of disclosure was owed.

Citing this part of the first instance judgment, Jack J in *Brandeaux Advisers (UK) Ltd v Chadwick* [2010] EWHC 3241 (QB) expressed the view that 'it might be said that it was unnecessary in *Item Software* for the Court of Appeal to have developed the law as it did' [47]. Nevertheless, since *Item Software* was binding on him, he held that a breach had been committed: the director had taken her company's confidential information and, had there been proper disclosure, she would have been dismissed by the company. He then held, however, that no loss had been shown by the company: 'the company had the benefit of her work, and I should take its value as the salary the company had agreed to pay' [56].

Where it is deemed to be in the interests of the company, the duty to disclose may include the disclosure of information other than misconduct, and may entail disclosing such information to individuals other than the board, for example the shareholders.

[7.14] GHLM Trading Ltd v Maroo [2012] EWHC 61 (Chancery Division)

GHLM Trading Ltd sued its former directors, Mr and Mrs Maroo, for breach of directors' duties, and also alleged that the directors had committed a further breach by failing to disclose their misconduct. This latter allegation was not upheld, since it had not been pleaded or proved adequately, so Newey J's comments on the law are by way of *dicta* only.

NEWEY J:

192. Recent authority establishes that it can be incumbent on a director to reveal his own wrongdoing. [Then citing *Item Software* **[7.13]**, and noting that Arden LJ had not proposed a separate and independent duty to disclose misconduct (her [41]), but that the good faith duty might mean that disclosure was required (her [41] and [44]).]

193. As was mentioned in *Brandeaux Advisers (UK) Ltd v Chadwick* [2010] EWHC 3241 (QB) (at paragraph 47), *Item Software (UK) Ltd v Fassihi* is a somewhat controversial decision. Arguably, it breaks new ground in treating a fiduciary duty as prescriptive rather than merely proscriptive. Its result can perhaps now be justified also by reference to section 172 of the Companies Act 2006, which came into force on 1 October 2007. The duty to promote the success of a company which that provision imposes can be said to be expressed in prescriptive terms (a director '*must* act in the way he considers, in good faith, would be most likely to promote the success of the company . . .'—emphasis added). Be that as it may, *Item Software (UK) Ltd v Fassihi* is clearly binding on me. I therefore proceed on the basis that a director's duty of good faith can potentially require him to disclose misconduct.

194. Two points of relevance seem to me to flow from the Court of Appeal's analysis in *Item Software (UK) Ltd v Fassihi*. The first derives from the fact that the duty of good faith focuses on a fiduciary's subjective intentions. Thus, in *Regentcrest plc v Cohen* **[7.12]** Jonathan Parker J explained . . . [at [120], see **[7.12]**] . . .

Accordingly, a company complaining of a director's failure to disclose a matter must, I think, establish that the fiduciary subjectively concluded that disclosure was in his company's interests or, at least, that the director would have so concluded had he been acting in good faith.

195. The second point is that it can be incumbent on a fiduciary to disclose matters other than wrongdoing. The 'single and overriding touchstone' being the duty of a director to act in what he considers in good faith to be in the best interests of the company (to quote from Etherton J in *Shepherds Investments Ltd v Walters* [2006] EWHC 836 (Ch), [2007] 2 BCLC 202, at paragraph 132), there is no reason to restrict the disclosure that can be necessary to misconduct. Were a director subjectively to consider that it was in the company's interests for something other than misconduct to be disclosed, he would, it appears, commit a breach of his duty of good faith if he failed to do so. . . .

198. [Turning to the question of the person to whom disclosure should be made.] Since the 'touchstone' is the duty of a director to act in what he considers in good faith to be in the best interests of the company, the focus must be on what the relevant director in fact believed to be in the company's interests or would have believed to be in the company's interests had he been acting in good faith. If a director subjectively concluded that it was in the company's interests for a matter to be disclosed to a person who was not a member of the board (or if he would have so concluded had he been acting in good faith), it would, it appears, be incumbent on him to ensure that such disclosure was made.

199. On the other hand, a director's duty of good faith is owed to his company, not to share-holders. The question is therefore as to what the director thought (or would have thought) was in the *company's* interests. That disclosure might have been in a *shareholder's* interests will not matter as such.

200. It is perhaps also relevant in this context that [GHLM's articles provide] that, subject to exceptions, 'the business of the company shall be managed by the directors'. In a normal case, therefore, disclosure to the board should suffice. [Counsel] pointed out that, where the two members of a board are involved in wrongdoing [as here], disclosure by one director to the other would not be likely to achieve anything. However, I do not think a director in such a case would necessarily be bound to inform shareholders. Supposing that he had a change of heart and was acting in good faith in the company's interests, he could potentially conclude that what the company's interests required was a change of course by the board or, if the wrongdoing were in the past, that nothing need be done. There could even be cases in which directors could legitimately take the view that it would be contrary to their companies' interests for shareholders to be given information. It is necessary, I think, to look at the particular facts of individual cases.

➤ Questions

1. Is there any indication in the cases of how the necessary balancing of the different interests of stakeholders or other constituencies is to be carried out?

2. Perhaps the real issue in *Fassihi* **[7.13]** is one of remedies. A director's contract may provide that he or she is to be dismissed for any breach of duty, and may add further options in favour of the company. This is not in issue. But in *Fassihi* the company was not seeking the traditional remedy of an account of *profits* from Fassihi for the profits he had made from his own new company (under the conflicts of interest rule, see 'Duty to avoid conflicts of interest: CA 2006 s 175', pp 385ff). It was seeking compensation for the *losses* it had suffered in losing its own contract. (And on recovery of losses, see 'Proving causative loss in negligence cases', p 385 and 'Equitable compensation', p 431.) Were these losses caused by a failure to 'act in good faith in the interests of the company'? If so, what does a 'failure to disclose' add? What losses are caused by a failure to disclose?

3. Is the duty as proposed by Arden LJ the same as the duty described by Newey J? Are the issues further clarified in *Maroo* by the discussion of disclosure to the board?

Regard for other stakeholders?

Both section 172(1) and s 170 make it clear that directors' duties are owed to the company, and the duty imposed on directors to consider the interests of persons other than the company (eg employees, suppliers, customers, the community) does not mean that directors owe any duty directly to these people. That being so, when can the company complain that these stakeholder interests have not been appropriately considered? (And, significantly, when might the company be motivated to do so?)

The interests of members

Recall 'Duties to shareholders?', p 338. This strict approach was specifically reiterated in the context of s 172 in the next case.

[7.15] Arbuthnott v Bonnyman [2015] EWCA Civ 536 (Court of Appeal)

SIR TERENCE ETHERTON (with whom LEWISON and McCOMBE LJJ agreed) explained the duties of directors in relation to takeover offers:

50. The duty in section 172 is owed to the company. In the context of a takeover offer, it is not owed to the current individual shareholders with respect to the disposal of their shares: *Dawson International Plc v Coats Patons Plc* **[15.17]**. The primary role of directors is to ensure that the offer and any competing offers are put to the members so that they can decide for themselves whether to accept or reject the best bid available: *Heron International Ltd v Lord Grade* [1983] BCLC 244. As Hoffmann J said in *In Re a Company* **[15.16]** in the context of two rival bids for the shares of a private company, of which the lower bid was by a company set up for the purpose by directors of the target company:

'I do not think that fairness can require more of the directors than to give the shareholders sufficient information and advice to enable them to reach a properly informed decision and to refrain from giving misleading advice or exercising their fiduciary powers in a way which would prevent or inhibit shareholders form choosing to take the better price...'

51. In their capacity as shareholders, the members, whether or not also directors, are usually entitled to vote their shares in their own self-interest. As was said in *Re Astec (BSR) Plc* [1998] 2 BCLC 556 at 584–585:

'The starting point is the proposition that in general the right of a shareholder to vote his shares is a right of property which the shareholder is free to exercise in what he regards as his own best interests. He is not obliged to cast his vote in what others may regard as the best interests of the company as an entity in its own right.'

➤ Question

Also see *Mills v Mills* **[7.10]**, in which it was recognised that in matters affecting the relative rights of different categories of members or shareholders, where no considerations of the paramount interest of the company as a corporate body arise, the directors owe a duty to act fairly as between the different classes of shareholders. Is the duty which is described in this way still a duty owed by the directors to the *company*, or is it some sort of duty owed to the shareholders?

The interests of creditors

Creditors are not specifically mentioned in s 172(1), but it is their interests which are most commonly litigated. The stakeholders mentioned specifically may of course be creditors. But s 172(3) crucially makes the entirety of s 172 subject to any 'other enactment or rule of law requiring directors, in certain circumstances, to consider or act in the interests of creditors of the company'. The relevant rules are found in the Insolvency Act 1986 s 214 (wrongful trading) (see 'Re Produce Marketing [16.16]', pp 860–864) and at common law (see the extracts which follow). The complaint is typically brought by a liquidator, suing on behalf of the insolvent company but for the practical benefit of the unpaid creditors, alleging that creditors' interests have not been properly considered.

The directors are required to act in a way which ensures the success of the company. It follows that directors must act to ensure that the company can pay its creditors and that it will not be wound up on insolvency. Both the common law and statute adhere to this approach. While the company is solvent, the directors can properly take calculated risks (with both the directors and creditors knowing that these made lead to the company's insolvency), and can drive a hard a bargain with their creditors.

The picture is different when a company is insolvent, or nearly so. Both the common law and the law of insolvency (IA 1986 ss 214, 246ZB, and see, in relation to 'wrongful trading', *Re Produce Marketing Consortium Ltd (No 2)* [16.16]) then require directors to have regard to the interests of the company's creditors—not because any duty directly owed to the creditors has come into being,[39] but because it is the creditors' position in the company's liquidation which will be affected by the directors' acts. Note that the directors' duty is one owed only to the company, as confirmed by the *Yukong* case [7.18]: if the directors are in breach, they will be sued through a liquidator acting on behalf of the company (or an administrator or, perhaps, a receiver), although any remedies obtained by the company will undoubtedly be of practical benefit to the creditors.

Judicial statements that directors are obliged to have regard to the interests of their company's creditors will be found invariably to have been made in the context just described. See the following cases. In the next extract, note especially the effect on the shareholders when they take corporate decisions, as well as on the directors.

Directors' 'duties' to creditors—or merely a company's duties to creditors?

[7.16] Kinsela v Russell Kinsela Pty Ltd (1986) 10 ACLR 395 (New South Wales Court of Appeal)

STREET CJ: The learned judge at first instance held, as I have noted, that he was bound by authority to hold that the approval by all the shareholders validated an action which would otherwise be beyond the powers of the directors provided that there had been a full and frank disclosure to the shareholders of all the circumstances relevant to the proposed transaction . . .

The authorities to which His Honour submitted, notwithstanding the generality of their enunciations of principle, were not intended to, and do not, apply in a situation in which the interests of the company as a whole involve the rights of creditors as distinct from the rights of shareholders. In a solvent company the proprietary interests of the shareholders entitle them as a general body to be regarded as the company when questions of the duty of directors arise. If, as a general body, they authorise or ratify a particular action of the directors, there can be no challenge to the

---

[39] *Dicta* to this effect in *Nicholson v Permakraft (NZ) Ltd* [1985] 1 NZLR 242 at 249, per Cooke J are, it is submitted, too wide.

validity of what the directors have done. But where a company is insolvent the interests of the creditors intrude. They become prospectively entitled, through the mechanism of liquidation, to displace the power of the shareholders and directors to deal with the company's assets. It is in a practical sense their assets and not the shareholders' assets that, through the medium of the company, are under the management of the directors pending their liquidation, return to solvency, or the imposition of some alternative administration . . .

It is, to my mind, legally and logically acceptable to recognise that, where directors are involved in a breach of their duty to the company affecting the interests of shareholders, then shareholders can either authorise that breach in prospect or ratify it in retrospect. Where, however, the interests at risk are those of creditors I see no reason in law or in logic to recognise that the shareholders can authorise the breach. Once it is accepted, as in my view it must be, that the directors' duty to a company as a whole extends in an insolvency context to not prejudicing the interests of creditors . . . the shareholders do not have the power or authority to absolve the directors from that breach.

➤ Note

This case clearly has relevance for issues of ratification, discussed at 'Ratification of acts of directors: CA 2006 s 239', pp 454ff.

A company's duties to creditors?

[7.17] Winkworth v Edward Baron Development Co Ltd [1986] 1 WLR 1512 (House of Lords)

LORD TEMPLEMAN: [A] company owes a duty to its creditors, present and future. The company is not bound to pay off every debt as soon as it is incurred, and the company is not obliged to avoid all ventures which involve an element of risk, but the company owes a duty to its creditors to keep its property inviolate and available for the repayment of its debts. The conscience of the company, as well as its management, is confided to its directors. A duty is owed by the directors to the company and to the creditors of the company to ensure that the affairs of the company are properly administered and that its property is not dissipated or exploited for the benefit of the directors themselves to the prejudice of the creditors.

[7.18] Yukong Line Ltd of Korea v Rendsburg Investments Corporation of Liberia (No 2) [1998] 1 WLR 294 (Queen's Bench)

The facts are immaterial.

TOULSON J: To remove the funds in Rendsburg's bank account when it had a probable liability to Yukong far in excess of its assets involved a clear breach of that fiduciary duty: *West Mercia Safetywear Ltd. v. Dodd* [1988] B.C.L.C. 250. . . .

The critical questions are whether Mr. Yamvrias's [the director's] breach of duty was actionable at the suit of Yukong [the creditor] . . .

In *West Mercia Safetywear Ltd. v. Dodd*, at pp. 252–253, Dillon L.J. [after citing with approval the statement of principle by Street C.J. in *Kinsela v. Russell Kinsela Pty. Ltd.* (see **[7.16]**)] continued:

'Prima facie the relief to be granted where money of the company has been misapplied by a director for his own ends is an order that he repay that money with interest...[But the relevant 1948 statutory provision provides that] [t]he court has a discretion over the matter of relief, and it is permissible for the delinquent director to submit that the wind should be tempered because, for instance, full repayment would produce a windfall to third parties, or, alternatively, because it would involve money going round in a circle or passing through the hands of someone else whose position is equally tainted.'

The relevant provisions [to the same effect] are now contained in section 212 of the Insolvency Act 1986.

Where a director, or person having the management, of an insolvent company acts in breach of his duty to the company by causing assets of the company to be transferred in disregard of the interests of its creditor or creditors, under English law he is answerable through the scheme which Parliament has provided. In my judgment he does not owe a direct fiduciary duty towards an individual creditor, nor is an individual creditor entitled to sue for breach of the fiduciary duty owed by the director to the company. [And so Yukong (the creditor) had no direct claim; only the liquidator, pursuing the company's claims, could sue the defaulting director.]

A director who prefers one creditor to another may be in breach of the duty to act in the interests of the creditors as a whole.

[7.19] Re HLC Environmental Projects Ltd [2013] EWHC 2876 (Ch) (Chancery Division)

Liquidators brought misfeasance proceedings (under IA 1986 s 212) against the company's director in relation to payments he had caused the company to make to one of its creditors at a time when the company had insufficient assets to pay all its creditors in full. The liquidators argued that such payments were in breach of the director's duty to act bona fide in the best interests of the company, and—specifically—to consider the interests of the company's creditors, urging that their interests had not been considered at all. John Randall QC considered the duty, and the appropriate assessment of breach where no consideration at all had been afforded.

JOHN RANDALL QC: [After discussing the subjective test [ie bona fide in what the *director* considers to be the interests of the company] elucidated by Jonathan Park J (as he then was) in *Re Regentcrest Plc v Cohen* **[7.12]**, he continued:]

92. However, this general principle of subjectivity is subject to three qualifications of potential relevance in this case:

(a) Where the duty extends to consideration of the interests of creditors, their interests must be considered as 'paramount' when taken into account in the directors' exercise of discretion...

(b) As Miss Leahy [counsel] submitted, the subjective test only applies where there is evidence of actual consideration of the best interests of the company. Where there is no such evidence, the proper test is objective, namely whether an intelligent and honest man in the position of a director of the company concerned could, in the circumstances, have reasonably believed that the transaction was for the benefit of the company (*Charterbridge Corp Ltd v Lloyds Bank Ltd*[40] at 74E–F, (*obiter*), *per* Pennycuick J.; *Extrasure Travel Insurances Ltd v Scattergood* [2003] 1 B.C.L.C. 598 at [138] *per* Mr Jonathan Crow[41]).

[40] [1970] Ch 62.
[41] See the citation earlier at 'Notes', p 360.

(c) Building on (b), I consider that it also follows that where a very material interest, such as that of a large creditor (in a company of doubtful solvency, where creditors' interests must be taken into account), is unreasonably (i.e. without objective justification) overlooked and not taken into account, the objective test must equally be applied. Failing to take into account a material factor is something which goes to the validity of the directors' decision-making process. This is not the court substituting its own judgment on the relevant facts (with the inevitable element of hindsight) for that of the directors made at the time; rather it is the court making an (objective) judgment taking into account all the relevant facts known or which ought to have been known at the time, the directors not having made such a judgment in the first place. I reject the respondent's contrary submission of law.

93. Therefore, whilst I accept the respondent's submission that the general principle of subjectivity applies to directors' consideration of the interests of creditors as well as to their consideration of the interests of the company, that has no application to a situation [where no consideration at all was given to the interests of one of the company's major creditors]....

106. I find that the substantial purpose for which the respondent caused these payments to be made was to assist Engenharia [another creditor], and that the decision to make them was made without giving any consideration to the best interests of the company's creditors as a whole, nor specifically those of its contingent creditor FRIE Grupo, despite the company having (and the respondent knowing it to have) substantial creditors, substantial net current liabilities and overall net liabilities, no live projects or revenue stream, and no realistic prospect of gaining any. The respondent was in effect choosing which creditors to pay, and which to leave exposed to a real risk of being left unpaid. An intelligent and honest man in the respondent's position could not, in the circumstances, have reasonably believed that making the Engenharia payments was for the benefit of the company, nor of its creditors as a whole. I am not persuaded on the evidence that making the Engenharia payments was a necessary step to enable the company to collect [certain benefits or avoid forfeiting them]. Breach of both the common law duties relied on by the applicants [duty to act bona fide in the best interests of the company and its creditors and duty to exercise powers for the purpose for which they were conferred] is therefore made out. [And in considering the *quantum*, the order was made subject to the '*West Mercia* proviso' which recognises the possibility of reducing the sum prima facie due (being the sum misapplied): see Toulson J's citation of this rule in *Yukong* [7.18].]

➤ Questions

1. Compare this common law duty not to prefer one creditor over others with the statutory prohibition against the giving of preference to a creditor (IA 1986 s 239). What are the differences? Which approach is preferable?

2. The director in this case argued that since the repayments reduced a genuine liability of a company, the company had *ex hypothesi* not suffered any loss. This argument was rejected on the basis that a defaulting fiduciary is liable to restore to the company the sums which he has caused to be misapplied, and the court is not concerned with loss or damage to the company. Why is this rule at common law and in IA 1986 s 214, despite its apparent conflict with the usual rules on equitable compensation? (Think carefully about the problem which the remedy seeks to address: that will indicate that the 'apparent conflict' with *Target Holdings* and *AIB* is not real.) (See *Target Holdings Ltd v Redferns* [1996] AC 421, HL; and *AIB Group (UK) Plc v Mark Redler & Co Solicitors* [2014] UKSC 58, SC, and the discussion on 'Equitable compensation' at p 431.)

➤ Note

Note the monumental decision in *Westpac Banking Corporation v The Bell Group Ltd (In Liquidation) (No 3)* [2012] WASCA 157, a judgment of the Court of Appeal of the Supreme Court of Western Australia. This litigation ranks as the largest, longest and most expensive legal proceedings in Australian history, and, although special leave to appeal to the High Court was granted, the case then settled. The Court of Appeal's judgment is 1,027 pages long; the trial judge's 2,643 pages. The court found that the directors' implementation of a scheme to prioritise the interests of certain banks when the corporate group was on the verge of insolvency had prejudiced the different companies' respective ability to meet the claims of other creditors. Accordingly, it was held that the directors had breached their duties to act in the best interests of the companies.[42] The court saw this duty as resting on an essentially subjective test of bona fides, although noting that the mere assertion of honest belief on the part of the directors would not inevitably suffice to excuse their liability (similarly, see *Re HLC Environmental Projects Ltd* **[7.19]**). Indeed, the court may have been prepared to be even more interventionist:

DRUMMOND AJA:

2046. Owen J [the trial judge in this case] was correct, in my opinion, . . . that when a company is in an insolvency context the interests of creditors are not in all circumstances paramount, to the exclusion of other interests including that of the shareholders. His conclusion . . . was that directors could not properly commit their company to a transaction if the circumstances were such that 'the only reasonable conclusion to draw, once the interests of creditors have been taken into account, is that a contemplated transaction will be so prejudicial to creditors that it could not be in the interests of the company as a whole'. I would prefer to say that if the circumstances of the particular case are such that there is a real risk that the creditors of a company in an insolvency context would suffer significant prejudice if the directors undertook a certain course of action, that is sufficient to show that the contemplated course of action is not in the interests of the company.

2047. Changes in the organisation of large corporations that occurred during the 20th century and changes in ideas about the proper role of corporations in society, particularly large and powerful ones, by those controlling them and by the public may explain the change from judicial restraint to increased intervention in corporate decision-making that is described by Sealy [LS Sealy, ' "Bona Fides" and "Proper Purposes" in Corporate Decisions' (1989) 15 *Monash University Law Review* 265, 265–266].

2048. As to the first matter, when owners controlled their companies, a laissez faire attitude to directors' conduct on the part of the courts was understandable and acceptable: there was a coincidence of interest in companies' activities between their owners and controllers. But with the development during the 20th century of large economically significant corporations, and the consequent wide dispersion of ownership, control passed to management whose interests do not always coincide with the shareholders, hence a need for legal intervention to protect shareholder interests . . .

2049. As to the second matter, the quite recent development of the rule requiring directors of insolvent companies to take into account the interests of creditors is a significant departure from earlier judicial attitudes which left corporate decision-making largely to management provided only that it acted honestly in what it believed to be the interests of the

---

[42] Although the litigation was not, in the end, against the directors for these breaches, but against the banks for 'knowing assistance' in the directors' breaches (in the UK, 'dishonest assistance'). In 2009, Owen J found against the banks, and awarded A$1.56 billion in equitable compensation. The Court of Appeal, by a 2:1 majority (Lee AJA and Drummond AJA, Carr AJA dissenting), upheld this award, increased by additional interest, damages and costs.

company. Further, it has become common in recent decades for directors, particularly those running large public corporations, to speak of the need to take into account a wide range of interests in addition to that of shareholders in order to better advance the company's business. Parliament in the UK has followed up on these kinds of aspirational statements by corporate boards. Section 172 the *Companies Act 2006* (UK) now requires a director of a company, in acting in the way he considers, in good faith, to be most likely to promote the success of the company for the benefit of its members as a whole, to have regard, not only to the interests of creditors, but also to various other interests including those of the company's employees, suppliers, customers and the impact of the company's operations on the community and the environment. . . .

2051. The impacts of corporate decision-making on a wider range of interests than shareholders are now being given more recognition. The need to ensure protection of those interests also I think serves to explain why modern company courts have become more interventionist, in reviewing the activities of directors than was traditionally the case.

➤ Questions

1. In the *Westpac* case, the court was considering the common law duty imposed on directors to act bona fide in the interests of the company and for proper purposes. Is there a difference between the formulations of the 'bona fides' element of these duties as advanced by Owen J and Drummond AJA? Does English law go so far, even with the benefit of CA 2006 s 172?

2. In the same way that directors may be said to be under a duty to have regard to the interests of creditors, do shareholders have a similar duty? (See *Re Halt Garage (1964) Ltd* **[5.03]**, and contrast the *Kuwait Asia Bank* case **[7.48]**.)

The interests of employees

CA 1985 s 309(1) (the predecessor of CA 2006 s 172(1)(b)[43]) provided that 'the matters to which the directors of a company are to have regard in the performance of their functions include the interests of the company's employees in general, as well as the interests of its members'. Much of the interest in this provision centred on the question of enforcement— the statute gave employees no rights to sue the directors personally. But on the nature of the duty imposed, it is plain from the wording that the directors are not merely *permitted* to consider the employees' interest but *bound* to do so; but the borderline between 'may' and 'must' in this context is probably meaningless, for there is no requirement that the interests of the employees should be *preferred* to those of the members. Additionally, there will be many cases in which a decision adverse to the employees will be justifiable by reference to the benefits of long-term profitability and thus the interests of the members. However, this is an argument that can cut both ways: a decision that is unpopular with the members or shareholders or adverse to their interest may also be defended because in reaching it the directors took account of its effect on the company's employees. In *Re Welfab Engineers Ltd* [1990] BCLC 833, the company's liquidator alleged that the company's directors, faced with insolvency, had improperly sold the company's business for less than its full value. But Hoffmann J held them not liable because the purchaser was prepared to take on the company's workforce and work in progress, whereas another, higher, offer which they might have been able to accept was for the company's freehold premises alone, and would have led to all the employees being made redundant.

---

[43] See Lord Wedderburn, 'Employees, Partnership and Company Law' (2002) 31 ILJ 99.

➤ Questions

1. What difference does an enactment such as CA 1985 s 309(1) or CA 2006 s 172(1)(b) make in theory or in practice to company law?

2. The CLR described CA 1985 s 309 as 'ambiguous and unsatisfactory', but its repeal as 'neither desirable nor politically sustainable'. Has CA 2006 s 172(1)(b) resolved the issues?

Duty to exercise independent judgement: CA 2006 s 173

Directors must exercise independent judgement (traditionally expressed as 'directors must not fetter their discretion'). The modern formulation is more illuminating than its traditional expression. This duty to exercise independent judgement is not breached if the director merely takes advice, or acts in accordance with an agreement duly entered into by the company (even one that restricts the future exercise of discretion by its directors: see CA 2006 s 173(2)(a) and **[7.20]**), or acts in a way permitted by the company's constitution. And, even though this is not made explicit in s 173, nor does the duty prevent directors from delegating their functions, provided the exercise of any power to delegate is in accordance with the company's constitution.

The duty applies equally to nominee directors, who cannot blindly follow the judgement of those who appointed them (this allegation is perhaps the most common complaint under this head of duty), although they may rely on their advice provided they make the judgement their own: *Scottish Co-operative Wholesale Society Ltd v Meyer* **[13.31]**; *Kuwait Asia Bank EC v National Mutual Life Nominees Ltd* **[7.48]**.

Legitimate fetters on directors' discretion through contracts with outsiders.

[7.20] Fulham Football Club Ltd v Cabra Estates plc [1994] 1 BCLC 363 (Court of Appeal)

In return for a substantial payment, Fulham Football Club (FFC) and its directors contracted with the landlords of the football ground which they held on lease that they would not oppose any future application to the planning authorities which the landlords might make for the development of the ground. The directors later wished to go back on this undertaking, and pleaded (amongst other things) that it was an unlawful fetter on their ability to act in the best interests of the company at any relevant time in the future, and was therefore void. The Court of Appeal rejected the argument.

> The judgment of the court (NEILL, BALCOMBE and STEYN LJJ) was delivered by NEILL LJ: It is trite law that directors are under a duty to act bona fide in the interests of their company. However, it does not follow from that proposition that directors can never make a contract by which they bind themselves to the future exercise of their powers in a particular manner, even though the contract taken as a whole is manifestly for the benefit of the company. Such a rule could well prevent companies from entering into contracts which were commercially beneficial to them.
>
> The true rule was stated by the High Court of Australia in *Thorby v Goldberg* (1964) 112 CLR 597. . . . [Kitto J dealt with the argument that any fetter on a director's exercise of discretion is void for illegality in the following terms, at pp 605–606:]

'The argument for illegality postulates that since the discretionary powers of directors are fiduciary, in the sense that every exercise of them is required to be in good faith for the benefit of the company as a whole, an agreement is contrary to the policy of the law and void if thereby the directors of a company purport to fetter their discretions in advance . . . There may be more answers than one to the argument, but I content myself with one. There are many kinds of transactions in which the proper time for the exercise of the directors' discretion is the time of the negotiation of a contract, and not the time at which the contract is to be performed. A sale of land is a familiar example. Where all the members of a company desire to enter as a group into a transaction such as that in the present case, the transaction being one which requires action by the board of directors for its effectuation, it seems to me that the proper time for the directors to decide whether their proposed action will be in the interests of the company as a whole is the time when the transaction is being entered into, and not the time when their action under it is required. If at the former time they are bona fide of opinion that it is in the interests of the company that the transaction should be entered into and carried into effect, I see no reason in law why they should not bind themselves to do whatever under the transaction is to be done by the board. In my opinion the defendants' contention that the agreement is void for illegality should be rejected.'

. . . In the present case the undertakings given by the directors were part of the contractual arrangements made on 28 January 1990 which conferred substantial benefits on the company. In those circumstances it cannot be said that the directors improperly fettered the future exercise of their discretion, nor is there any scope for the implication of any such term as is suggested by the plaintiffs.

➤ Note

The position of nominee directors is particularly difficult in this context. The nominator clearly expects its appointed director to look after its interests, and yet the director's duties are expressly owed to the whole *company*, not to the specific nominator. In *Scottish Co-operative Wholesale Society Ltd v Meyer* **[13.31]**, the difficult and special position of a 'nominee director' is discussed in detail.[44] That case confirms the view that a nominated director must *not* put the principal's (ie the nominator's) interest above those of the company, and indicates that members of the company may be able to invoke CA 2006 s 994 if this happens.

But in Australia and New Zealand there are cases which suggest that this may be too narrow a view. The whole object of having a director appointed to represent a special interest may have been the furtherance of some ulterior corporate good, and in such circumstances it may be justifiable to put that interest first. Thus in *Levin v Clark* [1962] NSWR 686, directors nominated to the board to represent the interests of a secured creditor were held not to be in breach of any fiduciary duties to the company when they acted to enforce the security: the company, by accepting the credit on the terms in question, had waived its right to have the unqualified loyalty of those directors.

Again, in *Berlei Hestia (NZ) Ltd v Fernyhough* [1980] 2 NZLR 150 at 165–166, Mahon J (without deciding the point) adverted to the possibility that the normal fiduciary duties might be modified where a company had been set up as a joint venture between two or

---

[44] On nominee directors, see E Boros, 'The Duties of Nominee and Multiple Directors' (1989) 10 *Company Lawyer* 211 and (1990) 11 *Company Lawyer* 6; and P Crutchfield, 'Nominee Directors: The Law and Commercial Reality' (1991) 12 *Company Lawyer* 136.

more participants on the understanding that each of them would be separately represented on its board by nominee directors.

But in the UK this approach remains unacceptable. See, for example, a recent case where the joint venture nature of a company was held not to abrogate the duties each director owed to it: *Gwembe Valley Development Co Ltd v Koshy (No 3)* **[7.41]**.

➤ Questions

1. If a company's constitution provides for the election of employee representatives to the board, is there a case for adopting the reasoning in *Levin v Clark*?

2. Directors sometimes confer upon a 'management company' all their powers of management, pursuant to a 'management agreement' (eg *Lee Panavision Ltd v Lee Lighting Ltd* [1992] BCLC 22, CA). Does such an arrangement infringe the principle of 'independent judgement'? To be effective, must such an arrangement have the shareholders' approval? Would such approval make any difference (eg if new shareholders joined the company)?

3. If this sort of 'management company' arrangement is put in place, what, if any, duties would the directors continue to owe to the company? Consider the following excerpt from the recent judgment of *Weavering Macro Fixed Income Fund Ltd (In Liquidation) v Peterson* FSD 113 of 2010 (Grand Court of the Cayman Islands):[45]

> 10. Directors have a duty to exercise an independent judgment . . . In the context of open ended investment funds, investment management, administration and accounting funds are invariably delegated to contracted professional service providers, but the exercise by the directors of their power of delegation in this way does not absolve them from the duty to supervise the delegated functions. This means that they must do more than react to whatever problems may be brought to their attention by the other professional service providers. They must apply their minds and exercise an independent judgment, in the ordinary course of business, in respect of all the matters falling within the scope of their supervisory responsibilities . . . They are not entitled to assume the posture of automatons, as these Directors did, by signing whatever documents are put in front of them by the investment manager without making enquiry or applying their minds to the matter in issue, on the assumption that the other service providers have all performed their respective roles (actual or perceived) and therefore do not need to be supervised in any way whatsoever.

Duty to exercise reasonable care, skill and diligence: CA 2006 s 174

Historically, it was widely asserted in the UK that the common law did not require directors to exhibit a greater degree of skill than may reasonably be expected from a person with their knowledge and experience (a subjective test).[46] This test allowed inherently

---

[45] Reversed by the Court of Appeal on findings of fact: *Weavering Macro Fixed Income Fund Ltd (In Liquidation) v Peterson* CICA 10 of 2011.

[46] The qualification is warranted, because Australian courts may be said to have led the way in developing the law on directors' negligence (see, eg, *Daniels v Anderson* at Note 2 in '"Reasonable" directors: keeping informed and delegating responsibilities', p 380), and yet have done so on the basis that their statutory provisions largely restate the common law, including the common law as stated by Romer J in *Re City Equitable Fire Insurance Co* **[7.21]**.

poor directors to escape liability for company losses, even when most reasonable people would have regarded their decisions as negligent. In the absence of legislative intervention, the courts had to act to raise standards. Their approach was to suggest that the common law standard was not so low as often suggested, and indeed that it mirrored the tests laid down in IA 1986 s 214, which includes both an objective and a subjective assessment of a director's conduct (see Hoffmann LJ leading this move in, eg, *Re D'Jan of London Ltd* **[7.22]**). The current law, in CA 2006 s 174, is modelled on this IA 1986 section. It provides that a director owes a duty to the company to exercise the same standard of care, skill and diligence that would be exercised by a reasonably diligent person with:

(i)   the general knowledge, skill and experience that may reasonably be expected of a person carrying out the same functions as the director in relation to that company (*an objective test*); and

(ii) the general knowledge, skill and experience that the director actually has (*a subjective test*).

The CA 2006 provision thus codified the approach increasingly found in the more recent case law, and marked an end to the subjective test identified from *Re City Equitable Fire Insurance Co Ltd* **[7.21]**. The statutory approach adopts as the minimum standard that objectively expected of a person in the directors' position; that standard may then be raised by the subjective element of the test if the particular director has any special knowledge, skill and experience.

The Act does not indicate whether this duty is to be modelled (as per s 170(3) and (4)) on the common law or the equitable duty of care (if there is a difference between the two[47]), but it is expressly not fiduciary (see CA 2006 s 178). The duty is owed to the company (s 170), not to the members. Members, for example, have no right to expect a reasonable standard of general management from the company's managing director: management quality is one of the normal risks of investing (*Re Elgindata Ltd* [1991] BCLC 959).

As well as liability to the company, breach of this duty may show unfitness to be concerned in the management of the company and so lead to disqualification under the Company Directors Disqualification Act 1986 s 6 (see 'Directors' disqualification', pp 309ff).

The old subjective test

The extent of the duty of care and skill and assessment of its breach.

[7.21] Re City Equitable Fire Insurance Co Ltd [1925] Ch 407 (Chancery Division)

The company had lost £1,200,000 (a fantastic amount at the time), owing partly to the failure of certain investments but mainly to the frauds of the chairman of directors, Bevan, 'a daring and unprincipled scoundrel'. In this action the liquidator sought to make the other directors liable for the losses on the ground of negligence.[48] The action failed because of a provision in the articles which exempted the directors from liability apart from losses caused by 'their own wilful neglect or default'.[49] The decision of Romer J remains important as a summary of the old 'subjective-only' duties of care and skill. It also indicates

---

[47] There are arguments that the common law and equitable rules are different, and, perhaps more forcefully, that they are not: see fn 53.

[48] The action also sought to make the auditors liable, and on these issues went to the Court of Appeal; but the auditors too were held, having acted honestly, to be exonerated by the special provision in the company's articles.

[49] Such articles are now invalidated by statute: see CA 2006 ss 232 and 532, although auditors can limit their liability (ss 534–536): see 'Auditors' liability', pp 484ff.

some of the potential problems in applying an objective test, and defining the outlook of a 'reasonable director'.

ROMER J: It has sometimes been said that directors are trustees. If this means no more than that directors in the performance of their duties stand in a fiduciary relationship to the company, the statement is true enough. But if the statement is meant to be an indication by way of analogy of what those duties are, it appears to me to be wholly misleading. I can see but little resemblance between the duties of a director and the duties of a trustee of a will or of a marriage settlement. It is indeed impossible to describe the duty of directors in general terms, whether by way of analogy or otherwise. The position of a director of a company carrying on a small retail business is very different from that of a director of a railway company. The duties of a bank director may differ widely from those of an insurance director, and the duties of a director of one insurance company may differ from those of a director of another. In one company, for instance, matters may normally be attended to by the manager or other members of the staff that in another company are attended to by the directors themselves. The larger the business carried on by the company the more numerous, and the more important, the matters that must of necessity be left to the managers, the accountants and the rest of the staff. The manner in which the work of the company is to be distributed between the board of directors and the staff is in truth a business matter to be decided on business lines . . .

In order, therefore, to ascertain the duties that a person appointed to the board of an established company undertakes to perform, it is necessary to consider not only the nature of the company's business, but also the manner in which the work of the company is in fact distributed between the directors and the other officials of the company, provided always that this distribution is a reasonable one in the circumstances, and is not inconsistent with any express provisions of the articles of association. In discharging the duties of his position thus ascertained a director must, of course, act honestly; but he must also exercise some degree of both skill and diligence. To the question of what is the particular degree of skill and diligence required of him, the authorities do not, I think, give any very clear answer. It has been laid down that so long as a director acts honestly he cannot be made responsible in damages unless guilty of gross or culpable negligence in a business sense. But as pointed out by Neville J in *Re Brazilian Rubber Plantations and Estates Ltd*,[50] one cannot say whether a man has been guilty of negligence, gross or otherwise, unless one can determine what is the extent of the duty which he is alleged to have neglected . . . The care that he is bound to take has been described by Neville J . . . as 'reasonable care' to be measured by the care an ordinary man might be expected to take in the circumstances on his own behalf . . .

There are, in addition, one or two other general propositions that seem to be warranted by the reported cases: (1) A director need not exhibit in the performance of his duties a greater degree of skill than may reasonably be expected from a person of his knowledge and experience. [But contrast CA 2006 s 174.] A director of a life insurance company, for instance, does not guarantee that he has the skill of an actuary or of a physician . . . It is perhaps only another way of stating the same proposition to say that directors are not liable for mere errors of judgment. (2) A director is not bound to give continuous attention to the affairs of his company . . . [Romer J continued in words seemingly applicable only to non-executive directors, and even then requiring less of them than would now be expected.] (3) In respect of all duties that, having regard to the exigencies of business, and the articles of association, may properly be left to some other official, a director is, in the absence of grounds for suspicion, justified in trusting that official to perform such duties honestly . . . [again, continuing in words that reflect perhaps more lenient views of the oversight that would now be seen as necessary.]

[50] [1911] 1 Ch 425.

➤ Questions

1. *Does* Romer J apply a subjective test in this case, or an objective one? The orthodox view is that it is the former, but see A Hicks, 'Directors' Liability for Management Errors' (1994) 110 LQR 390 and A Walters, 'Directors' Duties: The Impact of CDDA 1986' (2000) 21 *Company Lawyer* 110.

2. Would a subjective duty alone work satisfactorily? See C Riley, 'The Case for an Onerous but Subjective Duty of Care' (1999) 63 MLR 697.

The subjective/objective test

A simple common law illustration of the issues: standards of care and skill, breach, damages and potential relief from liability granted either by the members (ratification) or by the court (CA 2006 s 1157).

[7.22] Re D'Jan of London Ltd [1994] 1 BCLC 561 (Chancery Division)

The facts appear from the judgment.

> HOFFMANN LJ (sitting as a judge of the Chancery Division): This is a summons under s 212 of the Insolvency Act 1986 by a liquidator against a former officer of the company. . . . The liquidator alleges [and Hoffmann LJ subsequently agreed] that the respondent Mr D'Jan was negligent in completing and signing a proposal form [which contained material errors] for fire insurance with Guardian Royal Exchange Assurance plc. As a result, the insurers repudiated liability for a fire at the company's premises in Cornwall which had destroyed stock said to be worth some £174,000. The company is insolvent, having a deficiency as regards unsecured creditors of about £500,000. The liquidator therefore brings these proceedings for the benefit of the unsecured creditors . . .
>
> [D'Jan trusted his insurance broker to complete the form correctly.] Nevertheless I think that in failing even to read the form, Mr D'Jan was negligent. Mr Russen [counsel for D'Jan] said that the standard of care which directors owe to their companies is not very exacting and signing forms without reading them is something a busy director might reasonably do. I accept that in real life, this often happens. But that does not mean that it is not negligent. People often take risks in circumstances in which it was not necessary or reasonable to do so. If the risk materialises, they may have to pay a penalty. I do not say that a director must always read the whole of every document which he signs. If he signs an agreement running to 60 pages of turgid legal prose on the assurance of his solicitor that it accurately reflects the board's instructions, he may well be excused from reading it all himself. But this was an extremely simple document asking a few questions which Mr D'Jan was the best person to answer. By signing the form, he accepted that he was the person who should take responsibility for its contents. In my view, the duty of care owed by a director at common law is accurately stated in s 214(4) of the Insolvency Act 1986. [He then set out the subjective and objective limbs, now largely replicated in CA 2006 s 174, which is itself noted earlier] . . .
>
> Both on the objective test and, having seen Mr D'Jan, on the subjective test, I think that he did not show reasonable diligence when he signed the form. He was therefore in breach of his duty to the company.
>
> Mr Russen said that nevertheless the company could not complain of the breach of duty because it is a principle of company law that an act authorised by all the shareholders is in law the act of the company: see *Multinational Gas and Petrochemical Co v Multinational Gas and Petrochemical Services Ltd* **[7.43]**. Mr D'Jan held 99 of the 100 issued ordinary shares and Mrs D'Jan held the other. Mr D'Jan must be taken to have authorised the wrong answer in the proposal because he signed it himself. As for Mrs D'Jan, she had never been known to object

to anything which her husband did in the management of the company. If she had known about the way he signed the form and it was too late to put the matter right the chances are that she would also have approved. She could hardly have brought a derivative action to sue her husband for negligence because he could have procured the passing of a resolution absolving himself from liability.

The difficulty is that unlike the *Multinational* case, in which the action alleged to be negligent was specifically mandated by the shareholders, neither Mr nor Mrs D'Jan gave any thought to the way in which the proposal had been filled in. Mr D'Jan did not realise that he had given a wrong answer until the insurance company repudiated. By that time the company was in liquidation. In my judgment the *Multinational* principle requires that the shareholders should have, whether formally or informally, mandated or ratified the act in question. It is not enough that they probably would have ratified if they had known or thought about it before the liquidation removed their power to do so.[51]

It follows that Mr D'Jan is in principle liable to compensate the company for his breach of duty. But s 727 of the Companies Act 1985 [equivalent to CA 2006 s 1157] gives the court a discretionary power to relieve a director wholly or in part from liability for breaches of duty, including negligence, if the court considers that he acted honestly and reasonably and ought fairly to be excused. It may seem odd that a person found to have been guilty of negligence, which involves failing to take reasonable care, can ever satisfy a court that he acted reasonably. Nevertheless, the section clearly contemplates that he may do so and it follows that conduct may be reasonable for the purposes of s 727 despite amounting to lack of reasonable care at common law.

In my judgment, although Mr D'Jan's 99% holding of shares is not sufficient to sustain a *Multinational* defence, it is relevant to the exercise of the discretion under s 727. It may be reasonable to take a risk in relation to your own money which would be unreasonable in relation to someone else's. And although for the purposes of the law of negligence the company is a separate entity [to] which Mr D'Jan owes a duty of care which cannot vary according to the number of shares he owns, I think that the economic realities of the case can be taken into account in exercising the discretion under s 727. His breach of duty in failing to read the form before signing was not gross. It was the kind of thing which could happen to any busy man, although, as I have said, this is not enough to excuse it. But I think it is also relevant that in 1986, with the company solvent and indeed prosperous, the only persons whose interests he was foreseeably putting at risk by not reading the form were himself and his wife. Mr D'Jan certainly acted honestly. For the purposes of s 727 I think he acted reasonably and I think he ought fairly to be excused for some, though not all, of the liability which he would otherwise have incurred.

[His Lordship accordingly gave judgment against D'Jan for an amount limited to the sum which he remained entitled to claim as an unsecured creditor of the company.]

➤ Questions

1. Why was this case not brought under IA 1986 s 214? (Look closely at the conditions that must be met for the liquidator to bring such a claim.)

2. *Could* the company have authorised the breach before the event (however unlikely that scenario)? *Could* the shareholders have ratified the breach afterwards? See *Kinsela v Russell Kinsela Pty Ltd* [7.16], *Daniels v Daniels* [1978] Ch 406 and *Pavlides v Jensen* [1956] Ch 565. Also see CA 2006 ss 180 and 239 for the current provisions.

3. Was the application of CA 1985 s 727 (CA 2006 s 1157) sensible in the circumstances?

---

[51] Also see *Rolfe v Rolfe* [2010] EWHC 244 (Ch), extracted at Note 2 following *Re Duomatic* [4.15], p 217, on the application of the *Duomatic* principle where there is a single shareholder.

'Reasonable' directors: keeping informed and delegating responsibilities

How do the courts decide on the qualities of a 'reasonable director'? The problem here is that companies range from the very large to the very small, and that even within the same company the roles of different directors may vary considerably: some may be highly qualified and bring wide commercial experience to their post, and work for the company full time for a substantial salary; while others may serve as non-executive directors and be required only to attend monthly or quarterly board meetings. Yet others may be appointed to bring expertise of a technical nature—as engineers or scientists, for instance—without any background in business. And, of course, the law allows those who form a small family company or a one person company to appoint themselves directors regardless of their abilities and circumstances. The subjective standards brought to the role will certainly be different, but so too are the objective standards of a 'reasonable director' in the circumstances. So it is not altogether surprising that the search for an objective standard has proven, and likely will continue to prove, elusive.[52]

The following details provide further elaboration, but Lord Woolf MR put it this way in *Re Westmid Packing Services Ltd, Secretary of State for Trade and Industry v Griffiths* [1998] 2 BCLC 646:

> The collegiate or collective responsibility of the board of directors of a company is of fundamental importance to corporate governance under English company law. That collegiate or collective responsibility must however be based on individual responsibility. Each individual director owes duties to the company to inform himself about its affairs and to join with his co-directors in supervising or controlling them.... A proper degree of delegation and division of responsibility is of course permissible, and often necessary, but total abrogation of responsibility is not. A board of directors must not permit one individual to dominate them and use them.

➤ Notes

1. Re-read *Re Barings plc (No 5)* **[6.12]** and *Re Landhurst Leasing plc* **[6.13]** (both disqualification proceedings).

2. Similar developments in directors' duties of care have taken place in Australia. In *Daniels v Anderson* (1995) 16 ACSR 607, NSWCA (commonly known as the *AWA* case), the court signalled what was then a new approach, and made a number of emphatic statements: that it is no longer appropriate to judge directors' conduct by the subjective tests applied in the older cases; that (by analogy with cases under the Australian insolvent trading legislation) ignorance should not be regarded as a defence to proceedings brought against directors; and that more is required of directors than supine indifference.[53] It was alleged (by the auditors) that the chief executive and several non-executive directors of AWA were liable in negligence for their failure to prevent the massive foreign exchange trading losses caused by one of their employees. In the event, only the chief executive was held to have acted negligently. The same duty of care was owed by both types of director but, in the circumstances, the non-executive directors were entitled to assume (contrary

---

[52] And for public companies, note the best practice guidelines in the UK Corporate Governance Code.

[53] The controversial opinion of the majority of the court in this case, that directors' liability could be founded in the tort of negligence rather than as a breach of purely equitable obligations, is now academic in the UK, given the introduction of a statutory rule in s 174. The controversy persists in other forms, however: see the Questions following *Medforth v Blake* **[16.06]**.

to the fact) that they had been given a comprehensive account of the company's problems, especially given their publicly expressed concerns and frequent requests for detailed information and considered action. AWA's chief executive, on the other hand, was deemed to have acted negligently: knowing nothing himself about foreign exchange trading, he had delegated the function to someone relatively inexperienced and had allowed this person to operate without ensuring that appropriate management controls were in place; the obvious problems this was likely to cause were compounded because this was a novel venture for AWA and so its managers lacked experience in the area; moreover, when the problems eventually came to light, the chief executive failed to obtain all the information necessary to take remedial action, failed to delegate the rescue operation to someone sufficiently experienced and failed to give the entire matter the degree of personal attention, energy and detailed supervision that its obvious seriousness demanded in order to achieve a successful resolution. One practical consequence of application of an objective test is that directors are increasingly focused on ensuring that management systems, processes and procedures are adequately developed, documented and applied—and that their application is assured by systematic measurement, reporting and audit processes.

3. Directors cannot escape liability for negligence simply by avoiding undertaking any activities in their director's role. In *Dorchester Finance Co Ltd v Stebbing* (1977), reported [1989] BCLC 498, a money-lending company had three directors, Stebbing, Parsons and Hamilton. Stebbing worked full time for the company; the other two paid very little attention to it and visited its premises only rarely. They signed blank cheques at Stebbing's request, and he used these to make loans that were illegal and accordingly irrecoverable. No board meetings were held. All three directors were held liable to make good the company's losses. Foster J laid some stress on the fact that the two non-executive directors were experienced in accountancy; but it appears that this was not crucial to his decision. He said:

> For a chartered accountant and an experienced accountant to put forward the proposition that a non-executive director has no duties to perform I find quite alarming. It would be an argument which, if put forward by a director with no accountancy experience, would involve total disregard of many sections of the Companies Act 1948 . . . The signing of blank cheques by Hamilton and Parsons was in my judgment negligent, as it allowed Stebbing to do as he pleased. Apart from that, they not only failed to exhibit the necessary skill and care in the performance of their duties as directors, but also failed to perform any duty at all as directors of Dorchester. In the Companies Act 1948 the duties of a director whether executive or not are the same.

4. For the suggestion that directors have a duty to take positive action and keep themselves informed, see *Re Barings plc (No 5)* **[6.12]** (a disqualification case), and its references to *Re Westmid Packing Services Ltd* [1998] 2 All ER 124. More recently, see *Lexi Holdings plc (In Administration) v Luqman* [2009] EWCA Civ 117, [2009] BCC 716, CA, where the court held two sisters liable as directors for the consequences of failing to exercise active oversight of the company's affairs which would have ended their brother's dishonest dealings. He, as managing director, had stolen almost £60 million that banks had lent the company for use in its business. Because of their negligence, the sisters were held liable (jointly with their brother) for the stolen money. Similarly, see *Weavering Capital (UK) Ltd (In Liquidation) v Peterson* [2012] EWHC 1480 (Ch), affd [2013] EWCA Civ 71, where the court held both the husband (the only active director) and his wife (also a director) liable for losses resulting from a fraudulent scheme involving swap agreements and misrepresentations to investors. The wife's argument that she had only a 'confined area of responsibility' was rejected. The court held that her conduct fell short of what was expected of a reasonable director of a

hedge fund management company in her position, with her experience, actual knowledge and intelligence, and she simply failed to acquire a sufficient knowledge of the business to discharge such duties [173]–[174]. *Should* it be possible to be a director, but one who does not participate in the company's governance?[54]

5. For the extent to which directors can, without being negligent, rely on other officials and employees, see: *Re Barings plc (No 5)* **[6.12]** (a disqualification case). Also see *Madoff Securities International Ltd v Raven* **[7.24]**, where Popplewell J held that two directors had legitimately deferred to the views of a fellow director with greater experience.

6. In deciding whether a director's acts fall short in discharging his duty to exercise due care, skill and diligence, courts may seek evidence of best or normal practice in the business in which the company operates, especially if the breach of duty concerns the precise way in which the business is run: *Abbey Forwarding Ltd (In Liquidation) v Hone* [2010] EWHC 2029 (Ch) (finding then that the directors were not liable); *ASIC v Rich* [2003] NSWSC 85 (where the judge referred to the Higgs Review, noted at 'Separation of the roles of chairman and managing director ', p 277).

7. By way of exception, note CA 2006 s 463, which exempts directors from liability for negligent misstatements in or omissions from the directors' report and remuneration report, imposing liability only on the basis of knowledge or recklessness.

Directors' obligations to keep informed, pay due attention, and ensure their board is appropriately competent.

[7.23] Australian Securities and Investments Commission v Healey [2011] FCA 717 (Federal Court of Australia)

The case concerned the collapse of the Centro group, and the allegation of negligence related to a failure by the directors to disclose in annual reports sums amounting to almost $4 billion in short-term liabilities.[55]

> MIDDLETON J:
>
> 8. . . . The directors are intelligent, experienced and conscientious people. There has been no suggestion that each director did not honestly carry out his responsibilities as a director. However, . . . the directors failed to take all reasonable steps required of them, and acted in the performance of their duties as directors without exercising the degree of care and diligence the law requires of them . . .
>
> 10. This proceeding is not about a mere technical oversight. The information not disclosed was a matter of significance to the assessment of the risks facing [two companies in the group]. Giving that information to shareholders and, for a listed company, the market, is one of the fundamental purposes of the requirements of the Act that financial statements and reports must be prepared and published . . .
>
> 11. The significant matters not disclosed were well known to the directors, or if not well known to them, were matters that should have been well known to them.
>
> 12. In the light of the significance of the matters that they knew, they could not have, nor should they have, certified the truth and fairness of the financial statements, and published the

---

[54] CA Riley, 'The Case for Non-Governing Directors in Not-For-Profit Companies' (2010) 10(1) *Journal of Corporate Law Studies* 119. See also SM Bainbridge, 'Why a Board? Group Decisionmaking in Corporate Governance' (2002) 55 *Vanderbilt Law Review* 1.

[55] See J Lowry, 'The Irreducible Core of the Duty of Care, Skill and Diligence of Company Directors' (2012) 75 MLR 249.

annual reports in the absence of the disclosure of those significant matters. If they had understood and applied their minds to the financial statements and recognised the importance of their task, each director would have questioned each of the matters not disclosed. Each director, in reviewing financial statements, needed to enquire further into the matters revealed by those statements.

13. The central question in the proceeding has been whether directors of substantial publicly listed entities are required to apply their own minds to, and carry out a careful review of, the proposed financial statements and the proposed directors' report, to determine that the information they contain is consistent with the director's knowledge of the company's affairs, and that they do not omit material matters known to them or material matters that should be known to them.

14. A director is an essential component of corporate governance. Each director is placed at the apex of the structure of direction and management of a company. The higher the office that is held by a person, the greater the responsibility that falls upon him or her. The role of a director is significant as their actions may have a profound effect on the community, and not just shareholders, employees and creditors.

15. This proceeding involves taking responsibility for documents effectively signed-off by, approved, or adopted by the directors. What is required is that such documents, before they are adopted by the directors, be read, understood and focused upon by each director with the knowledge each director has or should have by virtue of his or her position as a director. I do not consider this requirement overburdens a director, or as argued before me, would cause the boardrooms of Australia to empty overnight. Directors are generally well remunerated and hold positions of prestige, and the office of director will continue to attract competent, diligence and intelligent people.

16. The case law indicates that there is a core, irreducible requirement of directors to be involved in the management of the company and to take all reasonable steps to be in a position to guide and monitor. There is a responsibility to read, understand and focus upon the contents of those reports which the law imposes a responsibility upon each director to approve or adopt.

17. All directors must carefully read and understand financial statements before they form the opinions which are to be expressed in the declaration required by s 295(4). Such a reading and understanding would require the director to consider whether the financial statements were consistent with his or her own knowledge of the company's financial position. This accumulated knowledge arises from a number of responsibilities a director has in carrying out the role and function of a director. These include the following: a director should acquire at least a rudimentary understanding of the business of the corporation and become familiar with the fundamentals of the business in which the corporation is engaged; a director should keep informed about the activities of the corporation; whilst not required to have a detailed awareness of day-to-day activities, a director should monitor the corporate affairs and policies; a director should maintain familiarity with the financial status of the corporation by a regular review and understanding of financial statements; a director, whilst not an auditor, should still have a questioning mind.

18. A board should be established which enjoys the varied wisdom, experience and expertise of persons drawn from different commercial backgrounds. Even so, a director, whatever his or her background, has a duty greater than that of simply representing a particular field of experience or expertise. A director is not relieved of the duty to pay attention to the company's affairs which might reasonably be expected to attract inquiry, even outside the area of the director's expertise.

. . .

20. Nothing I decide in this case should indicate that directors are required to have infinite knowledge or ability. Directors are entitled to delegate to others the preparation of books and accounts and the carrying on of the day-to-day affairs of the company. What each director is expected to do is to take a diligent and intelligent interest in the information available to him or her,

to understand that information, and apply an enquiring mind to the responsibilities placed upon him or her. Such a responsibility arises in this proceeding in adopting and approving the financial statements. Because of their nature and importance, the directors must understand and focus upon the content of financial statements, and if necessary, make further enquiries if matters revealed in these financial statements call for such enquiries.

21. No less is required by the objective duty of skill, competence and diligence in the understanding of the financial statements that are to be disclosed to the public as adopted and approved by the directors.

Legitimate reliance on other directors.

[7.24] Madoff Securities International Ltd v Raven [2013] EWHC 3147 (Commercial Court)

POPPLEWELL J:

193. In fulfilling this personal fiduciary responsibility, a director is entitled to rely upon the judgment, information and advice of a fellow director whose integrity skill and competence he has no reason to suspect: see *Dovey v Cory* [1901] AC 477 at 486, 492. Moreover, corporate management often requires the exercise of judgement on which opinions may legitimately differ, and requires some give and take. A board of directors may reach a decision as to the commercial wisdom of a particular transaction by a majority. A minority director is not thereby in breach of his duty, or obliged to resign and to refuse to be party to the implementation of the decision. Part of his duty as a director acting in the interests of the company is to listen to the views of his fellow directors and to take account of them. He may legitimately defer to those views where he is persuaded that his fellow directors' views are advanced in what they perceive to be the best interests of the company, even if he is not himself persuaded. A director is not in breach of his core duty to act in what he considers in good faith to be the interests of a company merely because if left to himself he would do things differently.

194. Where a director fails to address his mind to the question whether a transaction is in the interests of the company, he is not thereby, and without more, liable for the consequences of the transaction. In such circumstances the Court will ask whether an honest and intelligent man in the position of a director of the company concerned could, in the whole of the existing circumstances, have reasonably believed that the transaction was for the benefit of the company: *Charterbridge Corp Ltd v Lloyds Bank Ltd* [1970] Ch 62 at 74E–F. If so, the director will be treated as if that was his state of mind....

220. (3) Directors bring different experience and expertise to the joint exercise of corporate management. Whilst each is required to exercise his independent judgment, he may legitimately defer to the views of those with greater experience or expertise than him. Where there is a director who has a record and reputation for outstanding skill and experience in the company's business activity, his fellow directors are entitled to accord a high degree of deference and trust to his views as to what is in the company's best interests. It would be unfair and unrealistic to expect Mr Flax, or any of the other directors, to have done anything other than attach great weight to the views of Bernard Madoff in deciding what was in the interests of MSIL. To take the view, as Mr Flax to some extent did, that Bernard Madoff knew best, was not a dereliction of the duty to exercise independent judgment. It was a legitimate recognition that Bernard Madoff's high standing in the financial world reflected a level of skill and experience which did indeed equip him to know what was best for the company, and put him in a much better position to make that judgment than Mr Flax or any other director.

[Note, however, that two other directors were found to have breached their duty to exercise reasonable skill and care by failing to address their minds to the question whether the payments were in the interests of the company.]

➤ Question

What legal principle emerges from a combined understanding of *Healey* and *Madoff*?

Proving causative loss in negligence cases

Not only is proof of breach difficult in this area. The cases against directors are also hampered by problems in proving a causative loss. Typically, the facts are similar to those of *City Equitable* **[7.21]**: a rogue, reasonably trusted by all, at the centre of the action, his frauds deceiving even the auditors; and a board of directors, many of them non-executive, meeting only at intervals and justifiably delegating many functions to committees or subordinate officers. On such facts, it is sometimes virtually impossible to hold that the acts (or, more likely, the omissions) of those directors who were not directly involved in the wrongdoing were the *cause* of the company's loss.

For example, in *Cohen v Selby* [2001] 1 BCLC 176, CA, a father-and-son jewellery company was run by the father, who was a *de facto* director only, not formally appointed. His son, a student, was a director, but took no part in the company's affairs. Uninsured jewellery worth £395,000 was stolen while the father travelled with it. The father was held fully liable for the loss. The son escaped personal liability for negligence because it was considered not unreasonable for him to have trusted his father, an experienced businessman, and also because there was insufficient causal link between his conduct and the company's loss (although he was nevertheless disqualified (in separate proceedings) for three years). Similarly, see *Re Denham & Co* (1883) 25 Ch D 752, where the director had asked questions about potential fraud, but had been given so much information that he was none the wiser for his investigations.

These difficulties perhaps explain why the law on directors' negligence is now being driven not by these breach of duty cases, but primarily by the cases on director disqualification (with some input also from cases under CA 2006 s 994 and its predecessors (unfairly prejudicial conduct) and IA 1986 s 214 (wrongful trading)). All these statutory routes now also permit orders for compensation to be made against the directors (with CDDA 1986 ss 15A–C being added by SBEEA 2015).

Duty to avoid conflicts of interest: CA 2006 s 175

Context—three sections dealing with fiduciary loyalty: CA 2006 ss 175–177

Section 175 is only the first of three general sections, appearing in succession, that address the true fiduciary duties of loyalty owed by directors to their companies (also see CA 2006 Pt 10, Ch 4 on specific transactions between directors and the company and Pt 14 on political donations and expenditure).[56] These earlier equitable rules were stated simply

---

[56] Also see R Nolan, 'Directors' Self-Interested Dealings: Liabilities and Remedies' [1999] *Company Financial and Insolvency Law Review* 235; J Lowry and R Edmunds, 'The Corporate Opportunity Doctrine: The Shifting Boundaries of the Duties and its Remedies' (1998) 61 MLR 515; D Kershaw, 'Lost in Translation: Corporate Opportunities in Comparative Perspective' (2005) 25 *Oxford Journal of Legal Studies* 603.

and comprehensively as the overlapping 'no conflict' and 'no profit/no misuse of position' rules—as, for example, in *Bray v Ford*, cited later. In CA 2006, the equitable rules have been differently divided, into three distinct (ie non-overlapping) statutory provisions.

Section 175 imposes a duty to avoid situations where there is a conflict between the director's interests and those of the company,[57] and in particular not to exploit any property, information or opportunity (presumably only where such property, information or opportunity 'belongs' to the company, a restriction which is sometimes difficult to assess in relation to opportunities). This section thus replaces part of the equitable 'no conflict' and 'no profit' rule, although *only* as it applies to conflicts of interest arising from the director's appropriation for himself of the company's property or information, or to conflicts of interest arising from the director's dealings with third parties. Other aspects of the equitable 'no conflict' and 'no profit' rules appear in separate sections, dealing with 'third party benefits' (s 176) (typically bribes and secret commissions), and with the conflicts that inevitably exist in transactions between directors and their own companies (ss 175(3), 177 and 182).

This area of directors' duties (ss 175–177, and the earlier equitable rules) has probably generated more case law than any of the others, and what follows is merely an illustrative selection. The cases that predate CA 2006 not only apply the equitable concepts of the no conflict and no profit rules; they also apply the equitable rules on authorisation and ratification. These have been profoundly affected by CA 2006 (ss 175, 177, 180 and 239), so care is needed in using the cases even as persuasive authorities. On the other hand, s 178 preserves the common law and equitable rules as to remedies, so here these cases remain applicable (s 178).

In addressing the legal uncertainties implicit in s 175 ('the conflicts rules'), the approach is as follows. The first three sections look in turn at statements of the earlier equitable rule; the changes introduced by s 175; and several classical illustrations of the jurisdiction in issue. The next two sections then deal with the controversial issues of what does not and what does count as a conflicting corporate opportunity. The penultimate section deals with remedies. The final section deals briefly with conflicts of duty and duty (see s 175(7)).

The earlier equitable principles

Before considering the wording of the duty as codified under s 175, it is useful to begin with an understanding of the orthodox position prior to the CA 2006 codification. Two early judicial statements of the no conflict rule are invariably cited, even in modern cases. The first is from Lord Cranworth LC, in *Aberdeen Rly Co v Blaikie Bros* (there is a longer extract at [7.37]):

> . . . it is a rule of universal application that no one having such duties [fiduciary duties as an agent] to discharge shall be allowed to enter into engagements in which he has or can have a personal interest conflicting or which possibly may conflict with the interests of those whom he is bound to protect.

The second is from Lord Herschell in *Bray v Ford* [1896] AC 44 at 51:

> It is an inflexible rule of the court of equity that a person in a fiduciary position, such as the plaintiff's, is not, unless otherwise expressly provided, entitled to make a profit; he is not allowed to put himself in a position where his interest and duty conflict. It does not appear to me that this rule is, as has been said, founded upon principles of morality. I regard it rather as based on the

---

[57] And then notes in s 175(7) that any reference to a conflict of interest includes conflicts of interest and duty and conflicts of duty and duty.

consideration that, human nature being what it is, there is danger, in such circumstances, of the person holding a fiduciary position being swayed by interest rather than by duty, and thus prejudicing those whom he was bound to protect. It has, therefore, been deemed expedient to lay down this positive rule. But I am satisfied that it might be departed from in many cases, without any breach of morality, without any wrong being inflicted, and without any consciousness of wrong-doing. Indeed, it is obvious that it might sometimes be to the advantage of the beneficiaries that their trustee should act for them professionally rather than a stranger, even though the trustee were paid for his services.

Also see *Aberdeen Railway Co v Blaikie Bros* **[7.37]**.

Statutory changes to the equitable rules

The general rule set out in s 175 is a reformulation of a particular part of the general equitable rule. Note that it comprehends both actual and potential conflicts. The codification effects a number of important changes to the law:

(i)   The exclusion of conflicts of interest arising in relation to transactions or arrangements *with* the company (s 175(3)), and their separate treatment elsewhere, as noted earlier, is perhaps statutory acknowledgement that companies' articles routinely permit their directors to have interests in company transactions, provided they are declared. CA 2006 now follows this model: these transactions will merely have to be declared to the other directors (see s 176 and CA 2006 Pt 10, Ch 3), unless the transaction is a substantial transaction requiring the approval of members (as defined in CA 2006 Pt 10, Ch 4).

(ii)   The three statutory duties in ss 175–177 replace the equitable no conflict and no profit rules. To the extent (if any) that the statutory no conflict rule and third party benefits rule fails to cover the no profit rule, the new statutory regime deviates from existing equitable rules.[58]

(iii)   The statutory duty in s 175 substantially modifies the equitable rules with regard to prior authorisation of conflicts of interest (see s 175(4)(b), (5) and (6)).

(iv)   The statutory duty covers both conflicts of interest and duty and conflicts of duties (see s 175(7)). The precise implications and remedial consequences of this bundling may need further working out.

(v)   Section 170(2) makes it clear that a person who ceases to be a director will continue to be subject to the duty to avoid conflicts of interest as regards the exploitation of any property, information or opportunity of which he became aware at a time when he was a director. This will come into play, for example, in situations where a director exploits an opportunity *after* he resigns from the directorship.

Illustrations of the 'conflicts' rule

Boardman v Phipps [1966] UKHL 2 is the landmark English trusts law case on the conflicts rule. Although not extracted here (not being a company case), its statement of principles

---

[58]   Sometimes the no profit/misuse of position rule is regarded as part of the no conflict rule: see, eg, *Bray v Ford* [1896] AC 44 at 51–52, and *Boardman v Phipps* [1967] 2 AC 46 at 123. But other cases have regarded the two rules as distinct, although overlapping, so that a breach of the no profit rule cannot always be readily analysed as a conflict of duty and interest: see, eg, *Regal (Hastings) Ltd v Gulliver* **[7.26]**. To the extent the latter view is correct, there is now a gap, since s 176(4) makes it clear that there must be both profit and conflict.

remains relevant: see Note 1 following *Peso Silver Mines* **[7.28]**. Several other cases provide classical illustrations of the conflicts rule in the corporate context.

Taking corporate opportunities for personal benefit—constructive trust remedies.

[7.25] Cook v Deeks [1916] 1 AC 554 (Privy Council)

Three of the four directors of the Toronto Construction Company (Deeks, Deeks and Hinds—the three defendants) resolved to break their business relations with the fourth director, Cook (the plaintiff). The company had built up considerable goodwill with the Canadian Pacific Railway Company as a result of the satisfactory performance of a series of construction contracts, each of which had been negotiated with the railway company's representative by one of the defendants. The last of these contracts, the Shore Line contract, was negotiated in the same way, but when the arrangements were completed, the defendants took the contract in their own names and not that of the company. Cook claimed that the company was entitled to the benefit of the contract, and that a shareholders' resolution (which the defendants had carried by their own votes) purporting to confirm (ie ratify) that the company claimed no interest in the contract was ineffective. The Privy Council upheld both contentions, reversing the decisions of the courts in Ontario in favour of the defendants.

The opinion of their Lordships was delivered by LORD BUCKMASTER, who stated the facts, and continued: Two questions of law arise out of this long history of fact. The first is whether, apart altogether from the subsequent resolutions, the company would have been at liberty to claim from the three defendants the benefit of the contract which they had obtained from the Canadian Pacific Railway Company; and the second, which only arises if the first be answered in the affirmative, whether in such event the majority of the shareholders of the company constituted by the three defendants could ratify and approve of what was done and thereby release all claim against the directors.

It is the latter question to which the Appellate Division of the Supreme Court of Ontario have given most consideration, but the former needs to be carefully examined in order to ascertain the circumstances upon which the latter question depends.

It cannot be properly answered by considering the abstract relationship of directors and companies; the real matter for determination is what, in the special circumstances of this case, was the relationship that existed between Messrs Deeks and Hinds and the company that they controlled. Now it appears plain that the entire management of the company, so far as obtaining and executing contracts in the east was concerned, was in their hands, and indeed, it was in part this fact which was one of the causes of their disagreement with the plaintiff. The way they used this position is perfectly plain. They accelerated the work on the expiring contract of the company in order to stand well with the Canadian Pacific Railway when the next contract should be offered, and although Mr McLean [Manager of the Toronto Construction Co] was told that the acceleration was to enable the company to get the new contract, yet they never allowed the company to have any chances whatever of acquiring the benefit, and avoided letting their co-director have any knowledge of the matter. Their Lordships think that the statement of the trial judge upon this point is well founded when he said that 'it is hard to resist the inference that Mr Hinds was careful to avoid anything which would waken Mr Cook from his fancied security', and again, that 'the sole and only object on the part of the defendants was to get rid of a business associate whom they deemed, and I think rightly deemed, unsatisfactory from a business standpoint'. In other words, they intentionally concealed all circumstances relating to their negotiations until a point had been reached when the whole arrangement had been concluded in their own favour and there was no longer any real chance that there could be any interference with their plans. This means that while entrusted with the conduct of the affairs of the company they deliberately designed to exclude, and used their influence and position to exclude, the company whose interest it was their first duty to protect . . .

It is quite right to point out the importance of avoiding the establishment of rules as to directors' duties which would impose upon them burdens so heavy and responsibilities so great that men of good position would hesitate to accept the office. But, on the other hand, men who assume the complete control of a company's business must remember that they are not at liberty to sacrifice the interests which they are bound to protect, and, while ostensibly acting for the company, divert in their own favour business which should properly belong to the company they represent.

Their Lordships think that, in the circumstances, the defendants TR Hinds and GS and GM Deeks were guilty of a distinct breach of duty in the course they took to secure the contract, and that they cannot retain the benefit of such contract for themselves, but must be regarded as holding it on behalf of the company.

There remains the more difficult consideration of whether this position can be made regular by resolutions of the company controlled by the votes of these three defendants. The Supreme Court have given this matter the most careful consideration, but their Lordships are unable to agree with the conclusion which they reached.

In their Lordships' opinion the Supreme Court has insufficiently recognised the distinction between two classes of case and has applied the principles applicable to the case of a director selling to his company property which was in equity as well as at law his own, and which he could dispose of as he thought fit,[59] to the case of the director dealing with property which, though his own at law, in equity belonged to his company. The cases of *North-West Transportation Co v Beatty* [4.34] and *Burland v Earle*,[60] both belonged to the former class. In each, directors had sold to the company property in which the company had no interest at law or in equity. If the company claimed any interest by reason of the transaction, it could only be by affirming the sale, in which case such sale, though initially voidable, would be validated by subsequent ratification. If the company refused to affirm the sale the transaction would be set aside and the parties restored to their former position, the directors getting the property and the company receiving back the purchase price. There would be no middle course. The company could not insist on retaining the property while paying less than the price agreed. This would be for the court to make a new contract between the parties.[61] It would be quite another thing if the director had originally acquired the property which he sold to his company under circumstances which made it in equity the property of the company. The distinction to which their Lordships have drawn attention is expressly recognised by Lord Davey in *Burland v Earle* and is the foundation of the judgment in *North-West Transportation Co v Beatty* [4.34], and is clearly explained in the case of *Jacobus Marler Estates Ltd v Marler*[62] . . .

If, as their Lordships find on the facts, the contract in question was entered into under such circumstances that the directors could not retain the benefit of it for themselves, then it belonged in equity to the company and ought to have been dealt with as an asset of the company. Even supposing it be not ultra vires of a company to make a present to its directors, it appears quite certain that directors holding a majority of votes would not be permitted to make a present to themselves. This would be to allow a majority to oppress the minority. To such circumstances the cases of *North-West Transportation Co v Beatty* [4.34] and *Burland v Earle* have no application. In the same way, if directors have acquired for themselves property or rights which they must be

---

[59] These cases are now dealt with by CA 2006 s 177, requiring only notification to the directors *before* the transaction takes place, but where there *is* a breach, it seems the statutory ratification rules in s 239 apply equally; the equitable difference has been abolished.

[60] [1902] AC 83, PC.

[61] Cf the discussion on promoters, 'Promoters and their dealings with the company', pp 498ff.

[62] (1913) 85 LJPC 167n.

regarded as holding on behalf of the company, a resolution that the rights of the company should be disregarded in the matter would amount to forfeiting the interest and property of the minority of shareholders in favour of the majority, and that by the votes of those who are interested in securing the property for themselves. Such use of voting power has never been sanctioned by the court, and, indeed, was expressly disapproved in the case of *Menier v Hooper's Telegraph Works*.[63]

If their Lordships took the view that, in the circumstances of this case, the directors had exercised a discretion or decided on a matter of policy (the view which appears to have been entertained by the Supreme Court) different results would ensue, but this is not a conclusion which their Lordships are able to accept. It follows that the defendants must account to the Toronto Company for the profits which they have made out of the transaction . . .

Also see *Item Software (UK) Ltd v Fassihi* **[7.13]**.

➤ Note

The ratification rules set out in cases such as *North-West Transportation Co Ltd v Beatty* **[4.34]** (which allowed the interested director to vote in shareholder meetings to approve or ratify the offending transaction, even if the vote was only carried by the director's shares) have been abrogated by statute: CA 2006 s 239. There is now no difference between the procedures that must be followed to ratify the various different directors' duties. Note that s 239(7) does not affect any other rules of law imposing additional requirements or rendering acts incapable of being ratified by the company.

➤ Questions

1. Would the position have been any different if the defendants had told Cook beforehand of their plans? Or if the matter had been put to a members' meeting in advance, and the defendants had used their majority votes to carry a resolution giving them a 'clearance' to proceed independently of the company? Now see s 175(4)–(6), permitting advance authorisation by the directors: what would have happened in this case?

2. Can you suggest circumstances in which the directors might be said to have 'exercised a discretion or decided on a matter of policy', with the result that the defendants could have had the benefit of the Shore Line contract for themselves?

3. Did the Privy Council regard this breach as 'unratifiable' (ie by any constituency, however independent)? Should it be, or has CA 2006 s 239 adopted appropriate safeguards? Does CA 2006 s 239(7) itself incorporate the notion of 'unratifiable' breaches?

Irrelevant that company cannot or would not pursue the opportunity

Taking corporate opportunities for personal benefit when they cannot be exploited by the company—personal restitutionary remedies.

[7.26] Regal (Hastings) Ltd v Gulliver [1942] 1 All ER 378, [1967] 2 AC 134n (House of Lords)

The appellant company ('Regal') owned a cinema in Hastings, and the directors decided to acquire two others in the same area and sell all three to an outsider as a going concern.

---

[63] (1874) 9 Ch App 350.

For this purpose, they formed a subsidiary company, Hastings Amalgamated Cinemas Ltd ('Amalgamated') to lease the other two cinemas. The landlord of the cinemas insisted on either a personal guarantee of the rent from the directors or that the paid-up capital of Amalgamated be increased to £5,000. Regal was unable to pay for more than 2,000 £1 shares in Amalgamated from its own resources, and so the directors, not wishing to give the requested guarantees, agreed to take up the other 3,000 shares between themselves. In the event, four directors took 500 shares each personally, the chairman Gulliver found outside subscribers for 500, and the remaining 500 were offered by the board to Garton, the company's solicitor. Some three weeks later, the proposal for a sale of the actual cinemas was abandoned, and was replaced by an agreement to sell to the purchasers all the shares in the two companies. As a result, the directors and others who had subscribed for the 3,000 shares in Amalgamated made a profit of £2 16s 1d [£2.80] per share. Regal, now under the control of the purchasers, then issued a writ claiming reimbursement of this profit from the four directors and Gulliver and Garton. The action was based alternatively in negligence, misfeasance and money had and received. Before the House of Lords, only the last of these claims was argued, and the four directors (but not Gulliver or Garton) were held severally liable to account.

LORD RUSSELL OF KILLOWEN: . . . We have to consider the question of the respondents' liability on the footing that, in taking up these shares in Amalgamated, they acted with bona fides, intending to act in the interest of Regal.

Nevertheless, they may be liable to account for the profits which they have made, if, while standing in a fiduciary relationship to Regal, they have by reason and in course of that fiduciary relationship made a profit . . .

. . . The rule of equity which insists on those, who by use of a fiduciary position make a profit, being liable to account for that profit, in no way depends on fraud, or absence of bona fides; or upon such questions or considerations as whether the profit would or should otherwise have gone to the plaintiff, or whether the profiteer was under a duty to obtain the source of the profit for the plaintiff, or whether he took a risk or acted as he did for the benefit of the plaintiff, or whether the plaintiff has in fact been damaged or benefited by his action. The liability arises from the mere fact of a profit having, in the stated circumstances, been made. The profiteer, however honest and well-intentioned, cannot escape the risk of being called upon to account.

The leading case of *Keech v Sandford*[64] is an illustration of the strictness of this rule of equity in this regard, and of how far the rule is independent of these outside considerations. A lease of the profits of a market had been devised to a trustee for the benefit of an infant. A renewal on behalf of the infant was refused. It was absolutely unobtainable. The trustee, finding that it was impossible to get a renewal for the benefit of the infant, took a lease for his own benefit. Though his duty to obtain it for the infant was incapable of performance, nevertheless he was ordered to assign the lease to the infant, upon the bare ground that, if a trustee on the refusal to renew might have a lease for himself, few renewals would be made for the benefit of *cestuis que trust*. Lord King LC said, at p 62: 'This may seem hard, that the trustee is the only person of all mankind who might not have the lease: but it is very proper that the rule should be strictly pursued, and not in the least relaxed . . .' . . .

Let me now consider whether the essential matters, which the plaintiff must prove, have been established in the present case. As to the profit being in fact made there can be no doubt. The shares were acquired at par and were sold three weeks later at a profit of £2 16s 1d [£2.80] per share. Did such of the first five respondents as acquired these very profitable shares acquire them by reason and in course of their office of directors of Regal? In my opinion, when the facts are examined and appreciated, the answer can only be that they did . . .

[64] (1726) Sel Cas Ch 61.

It now remains to consider whether in acting as directors of Regal they stood in a fiduciary relationship to that company. Directors of a limited company are the creatures of statute and occupy a position peculiar to themselves. In some respects they resemble trustees, in others they do not. In some respects they resemble agents, in others they do not. In some respects they resemble managing partners, in others they do not. [His Lordship considered a number of the authorities and continued:]

In the result, I am of the opinion that the directors standing in a fiduciary relationship to Regal in regard to the exercise of their powers as directors, and having obtained these shares by reason and only by reason of the fact that they were directors of Regal and in the course of the execution of that office, are accountable for the profits which they have made out of them. The equitable rule laid down in *Keech v Sandford* and . . . similar authorities applies to them in full force. It was contended that these cases were distinguishable by reason of the fact that it was impossible for Regal to get the shares owing to lack of funds, and that the directors in taking the shares were really acting as members of the public. I cannot accept this argument. It was impossible for the *cestui que trust* in *Keech v Sandford* to obtain the lease, nevertheless the trustee was accountable. The suggestion that the directors were applying simply as members of the public is a travesty of the facts. They could, had they wished, have protected themselves by a resolution (either antecedent or subsequent) of the Regal shareholders in general meeting. In default of such approval, the liability to account must remain. The result is that, in my opinion, each of the respondents Bobby, Griffiths, Bassett and Bentley is liable to account for the profit which he made on the sale of his 500 shares in Amalgamated.

The case of the respondent Gulliver, however, requires some further consideration, for he has raised a separate and distinct answer to the claim. He says: 'I never promised to subscribe for shares in Amalgamated. I never did so subscribe. I only promised to find others who would be willing to subscribe. I only found others who did subscribe. The shares were theirs. They were never mine. They received the profit. I received none of it.' If these are the true facts, his answer seems complete. The evidence in my opinion establishes his contention . . . As regards Gulliver, this appeal should, in my opinion be dismissed . . .

There remains to consider the case of Garton. He stands on a different footing from the other respondents in that he was not a director of Regal. He was Regal's legal adviser; but, in my opinion, he has a short but effective answer to the plaintiffs' claim. He was requested by the Regal directors to apply for 500 shares. They arranged that they themselves should each be responsible for £500 of the Amalgamated capital, and they appealed, by their chairman, to Garton to subscribe the balance of £500 which was required to make up the £3,000. In law his action, which has resulted in a profit, was taken at the request of Regal, and I know of no principle or authority which would justify a decision that a solicitor must account for profit resulting from a transaction which he has entered into on his own behalf, not merely with the consent, but at the request of his client.

My Lords, in my opinion the right way in which to deal with this appeal is (i) to dismiss the appeal as against the respondents Gulliver and Garton with costs, (ii) to allow it with costs as against the other four respondents, and (iii) to enter judgment as against each of these four respondents for a sum of £1,402 1*s* 8*d* [£1,402.08] with interest at 4% . . .

LORD PORTER: My Lords, I am conscious of certain possibilities which are involved in the conclusion which all your Lordships have reached. The action is brought by the Regal company. Technically, of course, the fact that an unlooked for advantage may be gained by the shareholders of that company is immaterial to the question at issue. The company and its shareholders are separate entities. One cannot help remembering, however, that in fact the shares have been purchased by a financial group who were willing to acquire those of Regal and Amalgamated at a certain price. As a result of your Lordships' decision that group will, I think, receive in one hand part of the sum which has been paid by the other. For the shares in Amalgamated they paid £3 16s 1d [£3.80] per share, yet part of that sum may be returned to the group, though not necessarily to the individual shareholders, by reason of the enhancement in value of the shares in Regal—an enhancement brought about as a result of the receipt by the company of the profit made by some of its former directors on the sale of Amalgamated shares. This, it seems, may be an unexpected windfall, but whether it be so or not, the principle that a person occupying a fiduciary relationship shall not make a profit by reason thereof is of such vital importance that the possible consequence in the present case is in fact as it is in law an immaterial consideration.

VISCOUNT SANKEY and LORDS MACMILLAN and WRIGHT delivered concurring opinions.

➤ Questions

1. In an editorial note to the All ER report of this case, it is stated: 'As their Lordships point out, no question as to the right to retain this profit could have arisen if the respondents had taken the precaution of obtaining the approval of the appellant company in general meeting, and this would have been a mere matter of form, since they doubtless controlled the voting.' Now see s 175(4)–(6). Applying these statutory rules, the matter could not have been authorised by the board of directors prior to the transaction. How might the directors have protected themselves, prior to the deal, in these circumstances?

2. Although there is superficially a close resemblance between this case and *Cook v Deeks* **[7.25]**, it is most difficult to attempt to reconcile them on points of detail, and especially to deal satisfactorily with the question of post-breach ratification. In *Regal, could* such a breach have been ratified (the question is academic, because the transfer of shares makes a vote in favour most unlikely in practical terms)? Would it have mattered whether the directors of *Regal* had voted as shareholders on a resolution to ratify their acts?

[7.27] Towers v Premier Waste Management Ltd [2012] BCC 72 (Court of Appeal)

Mr Towers, a director of a waste disposal and treatment company, accepted a personal loan of plant and equipment without charge from an existing client, Mr Ford, and failed to disclose such dealing to the board. He was found to have breached the duties of loyalty he owed to the company. Although this was a pre-CA 2006 case, reference was made to the directors' duties as codified in CA 2006 as 'it is unrealistic to ignore the terms in which the general statutory duties have been framed for post-2006 Act cases.'

MUMMERY LJ for the court (MUMMERY, WILSON and ETHERTON LJJ):

Scope of duty

47. The emphasis in Mr Quiney's [counsel for Mr Towers] submissions was that Mr Towers did not make a significant profit from plant and equipment in poor condition that would have been of no value to the Company and that there was no evidence that Mr Towers would have gone out into the market to hire equipment at commercial rates. It was not established that he had obtained a valuable benefit.

48. In my judgment, the submissions miss the point. The applicable duties are of a director's loyalty to the Company and the duty to observe the no conflict principle, which embrace a duty not to make a secret profit for himself. The no conflict duty extends to preventing Mr Towers from disloyally depriving the Company of the ability to consider whether or not it objected to the diversion of an opportunity offered by one of its customers away from itself to the director personally . . .

Breach of duty

51. The 'commercially sensible' defences set up by Mr Quiney to the breach of the undivided loyalty duty also miss the point: the strict loyalty and no conflict duties were breached by Mr Towers. The absence of evidence that the Company would have taken the opportunity, or has in fact suffered any loss, or that Mr Towers or Mr Ford had any corrupt motive or that, if there had been no free loan, Mr Towers would have hired that sort of equipment in the market; the fact that the value of the benefit to Mr Towers was small and that Mr Ford received no benefit from it; the fact that Mr Rafter [a subordinate of Mr Towers in the company] and not Mr Towers dealt directly with Mr Ford and was the prime mover: none of those matters supported the contention that there was no breach of the duty of loyalty or the no conflict duty.

➤ Question

Given that the director here did not pay for the benefit received, would the case now be analysed as a conflicts case (CA 2006 s 175) or as a third party benefits case (CA 2006 s 176)? What difference (if any) does the classification make to proof of breach, authorisation, ratification and remedies?

Which conflicts does CA 2006 s 175 catch?

What counts as a 'conflict'?

Conflicts of interest are easy (or relatively easy) to assess when the conflict involves a defaulting director making unauthorised personal use of the company's tangible or intangible property. Familiar trust law authorities govern the breach and its consequences, even though directors do not hold the company's assets on trust: see especially *Foskett v McKeown* [2001] 1 AC 102, HL.

The assessment is more difficult when the director makes unauthorised personal use of information.[65] And more difficult still where the conflict (or alleged conflict) involves directors taking opportunities for themselves that might have been pursued by their companies. Many of the cases in this area involve directors pursuing lucrative commercial interests on their own behalf, or on behalf of other companies with which they are associated. *Cook v Deeks* **[7.25]** is a classic and dramatic illustration, where three directors plotted to acquire a contract for their own company rather than for the company they were supposed to be representing.

But it cannot be the case that directors have no 'private self', and that no commercial venture is open to them in their private capacity once they assume the role of director. Taken to extremes, this would prevent personal ownership or investment, and offend many of the aspects of autonomy we take for granted. The difficult task is therefore to draw the line between opportunities that can be pursued privately and without censure, and those that are regarded as 'corporate opportunities' where pursuit should, and will, attract legal sanctions. This is the focus of the extracts which follow, with many of them illustrating the difficulties in drawing this line satisfactorily.

---

[65] The problem is easily addressed if the use also involves a breach of confidence (either equitable or contractual), which it often does. But outside that arena, the line which needs to be drawn is typically between use of the director's own slowly acquired general know-how, skill and experience (not actionable, subject to breach of confidence constraints) and use of information to start up a competing business (in which case the general proscriptions in s 175 apply as they would without the added use of corporate information, or breach of confidence rules will assist).

Earlier cases on the equitable rule vary in their approach, some taking a narrow view of which opportunities are caught,[66] and some a wider view.[67] It is noticeable that later cases predominantly take a wider view—that is, adverse to the director's private capacity. This could be seen as further encouraged by s 175, which bars any conflicts with the *interests* of the company, not merely with the director's *duties* to the company (as in the equitable formulation in *Bray v Ford* [1896] AC 44 at 51–52).

Section 175(2) repeats the equitable rule that it is immaterial whether the company could take advantage of the property, information or opportunity exploited by the defaulting director. This must also indicate that this element is immaterial in deciding whether a situation can reasonably be regarded as likely to give rise to a conflict of interest (s 175(4)(a)). This accords with the equitable rule (see *Keech v Sandford* (1726) Sel Cas Ch 61; *Regal (Hastings) Ltd v Gulliver* [7.26]).

What does not count as a conflict?

1. No possibility of a conflict

Section 175(4)(a) indicates the duty is not infringed if the situation cannot reasonably be regarded as likely to give rise to a conflict of interest. Some situations will fall very clearly into this category. These *may* include cases where the company's articles contain exemption clauses preventing a conflict of interest arising in the first place. But not all these clauses are valid; the question is left to the common law: see s 232 (provisions protecting directors from liability).

But the next case is controversial: it deals with the difficult question of whether an opportunity, once declined by the company (on a properly informed and bona fide basis), may then be taken up by one of the directors on his own account, without any notification to or approval by the other directors or the shareholders. There are no UK cases adopting this approach, and indeed *Bhullar v Bhullar* [7.29] might be seen as going against it.

Situations that 'cannot reasonably be regarded as likely to give rise to a conflict'.

[7.28] Peso Silver Mines Ltd v Cropper [1966] SCR 673, 1966 CanLII 75, (1966) 58 DLR (2d) 1 (Supreme Court of Canada)

The board of directors of the appellant company Peso was approached by an outsider named Dickson, who wished to sell to it 126 prospecting claims near to the company's own mining territories. The proposal was rejected by the company after bona fide consideration by the board. Later, a syndicate was formed by Dr Aho, the company's geologist, to purchase Dickson's claims. The syndicate included Cropper, a director of Peso. A company called Cross Bow Mines Ltd was incorporated by the syndicate for the purpose. Cropper had taken part in the earlier decision of Peso's board to reject Dickson's proposal. Control of Peso later passed to a company referred to as 'Charter', which caused this action to be brought, claiming that Cropper was accountable to the company for the Cross Bow shares which he had thus obtained. The Supreme Court of Canada decided that he held them on his own behalf and was not bound to account.[68]

---

[66] See *Balston Ltd v Headline Filters Ltd* [1990] FSR 385 at 412; *Industrial Development Consultants Ltd v Cooley* (noted in *Bhullar v Bhullar* [7.29], p 401); and see too the partnership case of *Aas v Benham* [7.30].

[67] See especially *Bhullar v Bhullar* [7.29]; and *Allied Business and Financial Consultants Ltd v Shanahan* (also known as *O'Donnell v Shanahan*) [7.31].

[68] See S Beck, 'The Saga of *Peso Silver Mines*: Corporate Opportunity Reconsidered' (1971) 49 *Canadian Bar Review* 80; and, by the same author, 'The Quickening of the Fiduciary Obligation' (1975) 53 *Canadian Bar Review* 771.

The judgment of the court (CARTWRIGHT, MARTLAND, JUDSON, RITCHIE and HALL JJ) was delivered by CARTWRIGHT J: On the facts of the case at bar I find it impossible to say that the respondent obtained the interests he holds in Cross Bow and Mayo by reason of the fact that he was a director of the appellant and in the course of the execution of that office. [This is the *Regal Hastings* **[7.26]** test.]

When Dickson, at Dr Aho's suggestion, offered his claims to the appellant it was the duty of the respondent as director to take part in the decision of the board as to whether that offer should be accepted or rejected. At that point he stood in a fiduciary relationship to the appellant. There are affirmative findings of fact that he and his co-directors acted in good faith, solely in the interests of the appellant and with sound business reasons in rejecting the offer. There is no suggestion in the evidence that the offer to the appellant was accompanied by any confidential information unavailable to any prospective purchaser or that the respondent as director had access to any such information by reason of his office. When, later, Dr Aho approached the appellant it was not in his capacity as a director of the appellant, but as an individual member of the public whom Dr Aho was seeking to interest as a co-adventurer.

The judgments in the *Regal* case **[7.26]** in the Court of Appeal are not reported but counsel were good enough to furnish us with copies. In the course of his reasons Lord Greene M.R. said:

'To say that the Company was entitled to claim the benefit of those shares would involve this proposition: Where a Board of Directors considers an investment which is offered to their Company and bona fide comes to the conclusion that it is not an investment which their Company ought to make, any Director, after that Resolution is come to and bona fide come to, who chooses to put up the money for that investment himself must be treated as having done it on behalf of the Company, so that the Company can claim any profit that results to him from it. That is a proposition for which no particle of authority was cited; and goes, as it seems to me, far beyond anything that has ever been suggested as to the duty of directors, agents, or persons in a position of that kind.'

In the House of Lords, Lord Russell of Killowen concluded his reasons, at p. 391, with the following paragraph:

'One final observation I desire to make. In his judgment Lord Greene MR stated that a decision adverse to the directors in the present case involved the proposition that, if directors bona fide decide not to invest their Company's funds in some proposed investment, a director who thereafter embarks his own money therein is accountable for any profits which he may derive therefrom. As to this, I can only say that to my mind the facts of this hypothetical case bear but little resemblance to the story with which we have had to deal.'

I agree with Bull J.A.[69] when after quoting the two above passages he says: 'As Greene M.R. was found to be in error in his decision, I would think that the above comment by Lord Russell on the hypothetical case would be superfluous unless it was intended to be a reservation that he had no quarrel with the proposition enunciated by the Master of the Rolls, but only that the facts of the case before him did not fall within it.'

As Bull J.A. goes on to point out, the same view appears to have been entertained by Lord Denning M.R. in *Phipps v Boardman*.[70]

If the members of the House of Lords in *Regal* had been of the view that in the hypothetical case stated by Lord Greene the director would have been liable to account to the company, the elaborate examination of the facts contained in the speech of Lord Russell of Killowen would have been unnecessary.

---

69   Bull JA was one of the majority judges in the court below (British Columbia Court of Appeal (1965) 56 DLR (2d) 117.)

70   [1965] Ch 992, affd by the House of Lords [1967] 2 AC 46: see Note 1.

The facts of the case at bar appear to me in all material respects identical with those in the hypothetical case stated by Lord Greene and I share the view which he expressed that in such circumstances the director is under no liability. I agree with the conclusion of the learned trial judge and of the majority in the Court of Appeal that the action fails . . .

➤ Notes

1. *Boardman v Phipps* [1967] 2 AC 46, HL, referred to in the extract, was not a company law case, but is of interest as an application of the principle of *Regal (Hastings) Ltd v Gulliver* **[7.26]**. B, a solicitor, and P, acting together as agents for the trustees of an estate, attended the annual general meeting of a company in which the estate had a minority holding of shares. Later, they obtained information about share prices from that company. They formed the opinion that the company could be made more profitable and, acting honestly and without concealment (but not having first obtained the 'informed consent' of all the trustees), used their own money to bid for and eventually to acquire a controlling interest in it. The estate itself could not have made the bid without the trustees committing a breach of trust, and in any case it had no funds available for the purpose. Ultimately, they succeeded in making considerable profits for both themselves and the estate from capital distributions on their respective holdings of shares. By a 3:2 majority, the House of Lords held that they must account to the trust for the profit which they had made from their own investment: the profit had been made by reason of their fiduciary position as agents and by reason of the opportunity and the knowledge which had come to them while acting in that capacity. The remedy was proprietary (the order granted by Wilberforce J was reinstated). However, the House of Lords did think it proper to decree that the defendants should be paid 'on a liberal scale' for their work and skill.

2. In *Thermascan Ltd v Norman* [2011] BCC 535 (Ch), David Donaldson QC held that, once the contractual basis for a restraint not to compete with the company has lapsed, the restraint does not persist under CA 2006 s 175. In this case, the company provided services to customers using infrared technology, in particular for surveying commercial buildings to reveal hotspots caused by electrical faults. A former director launched his own business to offer thermal imaging surveys and was successful in canvassing orders from the claimant company's former clients. It was held that these possible new surveys more than eight months later cannot 'properly be described as a business opportunity in the course of maturing' [19] as at the director's resignation. Although it is not necessary to demonstrate that formal negotiations were underway; the learned judge found it hard to see how a claim can succeed without it being demonstrated that there had been at least some form of significant discussion of the potential business at the time of resignation.

➤ Questions

1. Can the decision in the *Peso Silver Mines* case be reconciled with *Boardman v Phipps* (earlier), *Aberdeen Rly Co v Blaikie Bros* **[7.37]** and the passage from *Keech v Sandford* quoted in *Regal (Hastings) Ltd v Gulliver* **[7.26]**?

2. Is *Peso Silver Mines* likely to be embraced in the UK, even with the introduction of s 175(4)(a)? Should it be?

2. Prior authorisation by the directors

Section 175(4)(b) states that the duty is not infringed if the matter has been given prior authorisation by the directors, and s 175(5) describes how and when such authorisation may be given. Section 175(5) distinguishes between private and public companies. Authorisation may be given by the directors of a private company so long as the constitution does not contain any provision to the contrary; and by the directors of a public company only if the constitution contains a provision enabling such approval.

Section 175(6) states the minimum procedural requirements for an authorisation to be effective. In particular, it provides that the director in question and any other interested director is not to be counted for quorum requirements nor for voting numbers. It follows that this route could not have been used on the facts in *Regal (Hastings)* [7.26] or *Cook v Deeks* [7.25]. In the same vein, the court in *Goldtrail Travel Ltd v Aydin* [2014] EWHC 1587 (Ch) indicated that a sole director is unable to take advantage of s 175(4) as his vote is to be disregarded pursuant to s 175(6).

The provision overrides any more lenient approaches to disapplying the conflicts rules that might be set out in a company's articles (the words used are 'The authorisation is effective only if...'). On the other hand, it keeps in place any additional restrictions derived from the company's constitution or from the common law (since the section does *not* provide that 'if those requirements are met the authorisation is effective').[71] For example, the common law indicates that any authorisation must be 'informed authorisation' in order to be effective.

3. Subsequent ratification by the company

A breach of the duty to avoid conflicts may be ratified by the company, typically by a majority of members in general meeting, although the statutory rules on this (see s 180(4)(a) (consent, approval and authorisation by members)) effect several important changes when compared with the common law (eg *North-West Transportation Co Ltd v Beatty* [4.34]). Ratification may be useful where the board has either failed or refused to authorise a conflict of interest.

Which 'opportunities' are caught by the conflicts rule?

1. Scope issues

As indicated earlier, the most difficult task in dealing with the no conflict rule is to draw the line between opportunities that can be pursued by directors in their private capacity, without censure, and those that are regarded as 'corporate opportunities', where pursuit will be a breach of duty which attracts legal liability.

Some cases take an exceptionally wide view of the opportunities that are caught—anything that could possibly be of interest to the company, even if pursuit is legally or practically impossible, is deemed a 'corporate opportunity'. *Regal (Hastings)* [7.26] and *Boardman v Phipps* (even though not a company case) are sometimes put in this class (although both might well also be caught by narrower rules). *Bhullar v Bhullar* [7.29] is in this class.

But too wide a view is generally seen as unrealistic, even when the goal is to secure the highest possible standards of loyalty. Inevitably, therefore, some means of narrowing the range of prohibited opportunities have been sought. An intermediate approach confines 'corporate opportunities' to those that lie within the company's own *scope of business*. Pursuit of these opportunities involves a conflict with the company's interests, and so constitutes a breach of duty; but outside this category there is no breach. (But see the rejection of this approach in *Allied Business and Financial Consultants Ltd v Shanahan* (also known as *O'Donnell v Shanahan*) [7.31].)

A still tighter definition of 'corporate opportunities', and one that gives even greater freedom to directors to pursue their own personal interests, is the '*maturing business opportunity*' test. Only opportunities that are real and maturing business opportunities for

---

[71] Lord Goldsmith, HL GC Day 4, Hansard HL 678, 9/2/06, col 326.

the company (as in *Cook v Deeks* **[7.25]**) are prohibited; other opportunities are open to the director to pursue in a private capacity. But again see *Allied Business and Financial Consultants Ltd v Shanahan* (also known as *O'Donnell v Shanahan*) **[7.31]**.

Conflicts arise even when the company is not pursuing the opportunities in question, and they are presented to the directors in their private capacity.

[7.29] Bhullar v Bhullar [2003] EWCA Civ 424 (Court of Appeal)

Two brothers, M and S, founded and equally controlled a family company (BBL), later dividing their respective shareholdings among their wives and sons. By May 1998, family relations had broken down to the point where negotiations to split the company's assets and business between the M family and the S family had taken place but were not successful. Around this time, M and one of his sons told S and his sons, I and J (the appellants), at a board meeting, that they did not wish any more properties to be purchased by the company, which S and his sons accepted in principle. In June 1999, I and J learned that the property next door to one of the company's existing properties was for sale, and purchased it in the name of Silvercrest, a company controlled by them. The M family issued a petition under CA 1985 s 459 (now see CA 2006 s 994, the 'unfair prejudice' provision) seeking relief on this basis or on the basis of breach of fiduciary duty. The judge held that I and J were in breach of their fiduciary duty in purchasing the property for their own benefit. As a consequence, he held that Silvercrest held the property on trust for the company and ordered the appellants to compel Silvercrest to transfer the property to the company at cost, and to account for any other profits. I and J appealed, arguing that a director was under no duty to offer to the company business opportunities which came to him privately, notwithstanding that the company might be in a position to exploit such opportunities. The Court of Appeal upheld the judgment of the lower court, with Jonathan Parker LJ delivering the leading judgment.

JONATHAN PARKER LJ:

27. I agree with Mr Berragan [counsel for I] that the concept of a conflict between fiduciary duty and personal interest presupposes an existing fiduciary duty. But it does not follow that it is a prerequisite of the accountability of a fiduciary that there should have been some improper dealing with property 'belonging' to the party to whom the fiduciary duty is owed, that is to say with trust property. The relevant rule, which Lord Cranworth LC in *Aberdeen Railway Co v. Blaikie* described as being "of universal application", and which Lord Herschell in *Bray v. Ford* [1896] AC 44 at 51, described as 'inflexible', is that (to use Lord Cranworth's formulation [in *Aberdeen Railway Co v Blaikie*]) no fiduciary 'shall be allowed to enter into engagements in which he has, or can have, a personal interest conflicting, or which may possibly conflict, with the interests of those whom he is bound to protect'.

28. In a case such as the present, where a fiduciary has exploited a commercial opportunity for his own benefit, the relevant question, in my judgment, is not whether the party to whom the duty is owed (the Company, in the instant case) had some kind of beneficial interest in the opportunity: in my judgment that would be too formalistic and restrictive an approach. Rather, the question is simply whether the fiduciary's exploitation of the opportunity is such as to attract the application of the rule. As Lord Upjohn made clear in *Phipps v. Boardman*, flexibility of application is of the essence of the rule. Thus, at *ibid.* p.123 he said:

'Rules of equity have to be applied to such a great diversity of circumstances that they can be stated only in the most general terms and applied with particular attention to the exact circumstances of each case.'

Later in his speech (at p.125) Lord Upjohn gave this warning against attempting to reformulate the rule by reference to the facts of particular cases:

'The whole of the law is laid down in the fundamental principle exemplified in Lord Cranworth's statement [in *Aberdeen Railway Co v Blaikie*]. But it is applicable…to such a diversity of different cases that the observations of judges…must be regarded as applicable only to the particular facts of the particular case in question and not regarded as a new and slightly different formulation of the legal principle so well settled.'

29. To my mind that warning is particularly apt in the instant case . . .

30. As it seems to me, the rule is essentially a simple one, albeit that it may in some cases be difficult to apply. The only qualification which is required to Lord Cranworth's formulation of it is that which was supplied by Lord Upjohn in *Phipps v. Boardman*, where he said this (at p. 124):

'The phrase "possibly may conflict" requires consideration. In my view it means that the reasonable man looking at the relevant facts and circumstances of the particular case would think that there was a real sensible possibility of conflict; not that you could imagine some situation arising which might, in some conceivable possibility in events not contemplated as real sensible possibilities by any reasonable person, result in conflict.' …

36. In so far as reference to authority is of assistance in applying the rule to the facts of any particular case, the authority which (of those cited to us) is nearest on its facts to those of the instant case is the decision of Roskill J in *Industrial Development Consultants Ltd v. Cooley*. In that case, a commercial opportunity was offered to the defendant, who was at the time the managing director of the plaintiff company, in his private capacity. The defendant subsequently obtained his release by the company in order to exploit that opportunity for his own benefit. Had the company known that he had been offered that opportunity, it would not have agreed to release him. He was held accountable for the benefits he had received by exploiting the opportunity. The opportunity was not one which the company could itself have exploited.

37. Roskill J, after quoting extensively from Lord Upjohn's speech in *Phipps v. Boardman*, observed (plainly correctly, if I may respectfully say so) that although Lord Upjohn dissented (with Viscount Dilhorne) in the result, there was no difference between any of their Lordships as to the applicable principles, but only as to the application of those principles to the facts of the case. Turning to the facts, Roskill J said this (at p.451):

'The first matter that has to be considered is whether or not the defendant was in a fiduciary relationship with his principals, the plaintiffs. [Counsel for the defendant] argued that he was not because he received this information which was communicated to him privately. With respect, I think that argument is wrong. The defendant had one capacity and one capacity only in which he was carrying on business at that time. That capacity was as managing director of the plaintiffs. Information which came to him while he was managing director and which was of concern to the plaintiffs and was relevant for the plaintiffs to know, was information which it was his duty to pass on to the plaintiffs because between himself and the plaintiffs a fiduciary relationship existed . . .' . . .

39. He went on to stress the rigidity with which the rule had since been applied. As confirmation of this, he cited the following well-known passage from the judgment of James LJ in *Parker v. McKenna*:

'I do not think it is necessary, but it appears to me very important, that we should concur in laying down again and again the general principle that in this court no agent in the course of his agency, in the matter of his agency, can be allowed to make any profit without the knowledge and consent of his principal; that that rule is an inflexible rule, and must be applied inexorably by this court, which is not entitled, in my judgment, to receive evidence, or suggestion, or argument as to whether the principal did or did not suffer any injury in fact by reason of the dealing of the agent; for the safety of mankind requires that no agent shall be able to put his principal in the danger of such an inquiry as that.'

40. I turn, then, to the facts of the instant case.

41. Like the defendant in *Industrial Development Consultants Ltd v. Cooley*, the appellants in the instant case had, at the material time, one capacity and one capacity only in which they were carrying on business, namely as directors of the Company. In that capacity, they were in a fiduciary relationship with the Company. At the material time, the Company was still trading, albeit that negotiations (ultimately unsuccessful) for a division of its assets and business were on foot. As Inderjit accepted in cross-examination, it would have been 'worthwhile' for the company to have acquired the Property. Although the reasons why it would have been 'worthwhile' were not explored in evidence, it seems obvious that the opportunity to acquire the Property would have been commercially attractive to the Company, given its proximity to Springbank Works. Whether the Company could or would have taken that opportunity, had it been made aware of it, is not to the point: the existence of the opportunity was information which it was relevant for the Company to know, and it follows that the appellants were under a duty to communicate it to the Company. The anxiety which the appellants plainly felt as to the propriety of purchasing the Property through Silvercrest without first disclosing their intentions to their co-directors—anxiety which led Inderjit to seek legal advice from the Company's solicitor—is, in my view, eloquent of the existence of a possible conflict of duty and interest.

42. I therefore agree with the judge when he said . . . that 'reasonable men looking at the facts would think there was a real sensible possibility of conflict'.

BROOKE and SCHIEMANN LJJ concurred.

This case is noted, D Prentice and J Payne, 'The Corporate Opportunity Doctrine' (2004) 120 LQR 198.

➤ Question

Should it have made any difference that the claimants themselves had insisted, and it seemed a board meeting had agreed, that the company should *not* purchase more property? If I and J had purchased the property for the *company* in these circumstances, would they have been in breach of their s 171 duty, and liable to compensate the company for losses? If the answer is yes, is the outcome in *Bhullar* justified?

➤ Note

Bhullar and many other cases like it make it clear that disputes can easily arise when a director learns of an opportunity and then pursues it on his or her own account rather than for the benefit of the company. Yet it is surely not the case that a director must pursue every opportunity for the company's benefit alone, and not for personal gain. What seemed to be a useful 'scope of business' test was articulated over a century ago by Lindley LJ in the case next extracted.

Outside the corporate context, a 'scope of business' test is used to limit the range of potential conflicts of interest.

[7.30] Aas v Benham [1891] 2 Ch 244 (Court of Appeal)

The facts are immaterial, other than to note that the case concerned a partnership, not a company. See how the case was therefore distinguished in [7.31].

LINDLEY LJ: As regards the use by a partner of information obtained by him in the course of the transaction of partnership business, or by reason of his connection with the firm, the principle is that if he avails himself of it for any purpose which is within the scope of the partnership business, or of any competing business, the profits of which belong to the firm, he must account to the firm for any benefits which he may have derived from such information, but there is no principle or authority which entitles a firm to benefits derived by a partner from the use of information for purposes which are wholly without the scope of the firm's business, nor does the language of Lord Justice Cotton in *Dean v. MacDowell* [8 Ch D 345] warrant any such notion. By "information which the partnership is entitled to" is meant information which can be used for the purposes of the partnership. It is not the source of the information, but the use to which it is applied, which is important in such matters. To hold that a partner can never derive any personal benefit from information which he obtains as a partner would be manifestly absurd. Suppose a partner to become, in the course of carrying on his business, well acquainted with a particular branch of science or trade, and suppose him to write and publish a book on the subject, could the firm claim the profits thereby obtained? Obviously not, unless, by publishing the book, he in fact competed with the firm in their own line of business.

[Lindley LJ had earlier distinguished these 'corporate opportunities' cases from cases where the fiduciary used the principal's assets for personal advantage, or competed directly with the principal in the same line of business. On those matters, he said:]

It is clear law that every partner must account to the firm for every benefit derived by him without the consent of his co-partners from any transaction concerning the partnership or from any use by him of the partnership property, name or business connection . . . It is equally clear law that if a partner without the consent of his co-partners carries on business of the same nature as, and competing with that of the firm, he must account for and pay over to the firm all profits made by him in that business . . . *Dean v. MacDowell* [8 Ch D 345] shews that a partner is not bound to account to his co-partners for profits made by him in carrying on a separate business of his own, unless the case can be brought within one or other of the two principles to which I have alluded, even if he carries on such separate business contrary to one of the partnership articles.

➤ Note

If the principles in *Aas v Benham* applied in the corporate context, then any use of the company's own assets for the director's personal gain would constitute a conflict, but the director's pursuit of corporate opportunities would not unless those opportunities were within the scope of the company's own business. However, the next extract, **[7.31]**, suggests that this 'scope of business' test is not applicable in the context of directors, whatever its merits might seem as a matter of principle.

No 'scope of business' test for corporate opportunities?

[7.31] Allied Business and Financial Consultants Ltd v Shanahan (also known as O'Donnell v Shanahan) [2009] EWCA Civ 751 (Court of Appeal)

The extract which follows is a long one, but the principles it describes are important. The judgment also provides a useful summary of older precedents. O, S and L were shareholders and directors of C, which provided clients with financial advice and assistance. S and L were also involved in property investment and development on their own account through their own company, K. O, in an action under CA 1985 s 459 [CA 2006 s 994], claimed that S and L's conduct of C's affairs had unfairly prejudiced her interests as a member, and, in particular, that S and L's acquisition of an investment property through K was in breach of S and L's duties as directors of C; and that the acquisition should have been channelled through C, as S and L had come across the opportunity to purchase it in the course of C's business when one of C's clients dropped out of the purchase opportunity himself. At first instance, and relying on *Aas v Benham* **[7.30]**, the judge held that the equitable no conflict and no profit rules [CA 2006 s 175 was not then in force] had not been breached because the acquisition fell outside the 'scope of business' of C. The Court of Appeal allowed the appeal, and held that *Aas v Benham* was of no relevance in considering the extent and application of the no conflict and no profit rules so far as they applied to fiduciaries such as trustees and directors.

RIMER LJ:

52. Subject to the *Aas v. Benham* 'scope of business' point, to which I will come, I would regard this as a plain case in which Mr Shanahan and Mr Leonard had (without the company's informed consent) adopted for their private benefit a business opportunity that came to them in their capacities as directors of the company with the consequence that they would in principle be accountable to the company for any profit derived from it. The prime mover of the two in the Aria House matter [the property purchase in issue] as a whole was Mr Shanahan, but neither the judge nor the argument before us drew any distinction between the roles of the two respondents.

53. Mr Sulaiman's engagement of the company [C] (acting by Mr Shanahan) to find a purchaser of Aria House was the company's first venture into estate agency. That shows that by 1999 the categories of its activities were not closed. All that Mr Shanahan then learnt about Aria House and its virtue as an investment opportunity derived from information he obtained as a director of the company in seeking such a purchaser: in particular, the Matthews & Goodman report, the interest of the banks and Jacobsens' work. It may be that Mr Shanahan and the company owed duties of confidence to Mr Walsh with regard to the use of this information, and Mr Walsh might legitimately have complained about its appropriation by others. But as between Mr Shanahan and the company, the latter had the better right to its use than the former because it was information obtained by Mr Shanahan in the course of acting as a director of the company. When Mr Walsh withdrew from the purchase, it was this information that Mr Shanahan used in acting on behalf of the company in seeking a substitute purchaser; and when the opportunity arose for the respondents to participate personally in the purchase, it was this information that they used in making their decision.

54. In my judgment, this was obviously a case in which, once that opportunity arose, the respondents could not properly make use of the information they had so obtained in deciding to take up the opportunity for their own benefit. That was because they had obtained the information in the course of acting as directors of the company; and the opportunity also came to them in such course. As I shall explain, I consider that the opportunity led the respondents straight into a breach of 'no conflict' rule. But quite apart from this, it was one that they ought obviously to have made known to the company. In practice, that meant that they needed to discuss it with Ms O'Donnell. If the company was not interested in taking up the opportunity, its members could consent to its being taken up by the respondents personally. As the respondents did not offer the opportunity to the company, but took it up personally, they engaged in a transaction that rendered them liable to account under the 'no profit' rule.

55. The authorities relating to trustees' and directors' duties to account for profit earned in consequence of a breach of the 'no profit' rule are legion, they all appear to me to point to the same conclusion and none appears to qualify the liability to account by reference to whether the impugned transaction was (in the case of an alleged breach by a director) within or without the scope of the company's business. The principle of accountability by directors in breach of the rule derives from the strict rule affecting trustees, the leading case in the latter field being *Keech v. Sandford* Sel. Cas. Ch. 61. In that case it had been *impossible* for the trustee to obtain a renewal of the trust's lease for the beneficiary, but the trustee was nevertheless held accountable for then renewing it for himself. It may be thought odd that a strict principle of that nature, which

fathered the like principle of accountability applicable to directors, can enable a director to answer a claim under the 'no profit' rule by asserting that the impugned transaction was unimpeachable because it was not the kind of transaction the company ordinarily engaged in. That is to ignore the point that the rationale of the 'no conflict' and 'no profit' rules is to underpin the fiduciary's duty of undivided loyalty to his beneficiary. If an opportunity comes to him in his capacity as a fiduciary, his principal is entitled to know about it. The director cannot be left to make the decision as to whether he is allowed to help himself to its benefit.

56. The authorities relating to directors' accountability not only do not support the 'scope of business' exception in relation to the 'no profit' rule, they are contrary to it. They show that the principle is a rigorous one. In *Parker v. McKenna* (1874) 10 Ch. App. 96, the directors of a bank acquired for themselves, and made a profit on, certain shares the subject of a new issue that were not taken up by the bank's shareholders. Lord Cairns LC said, at 118:

> 'The Court will not inquire, and is not in a position to ascertain, whether the bank has or has not lost by the acts of the directors. All that the Court has to do is to examine whether a profit has been made by an agent, without the knowledge of his principal, in the course and execution of his agency, and the Court finds, in my opinion, that these agents in the course of their agency have made a profit, and for that profit they must, in my opinion, account to their principal.'

James LJ said, at 124:

> '. . . it appears to me very important, that we should concur in laying down again and again the general principle that in this Court no agent in the course of his agency, in the matter of his agency, can be allowed to make any profit without the knowledge of his principal; that that rule is an inflexible rule, and must be applied inexorably by this Court, which is not entitled, in my judgment, to receive evidence, or suggestion, or argument, as to whether the principal did or did not suffer any injury in fact by reason of the dealing of the agent; for the safety of mankind requires that no agent shall be able to put his principal to the danger of such an inquiry as that.'

57. According to James LJ, therefore, nothing less than the 'safety of mankind' depends on the rigorous application of the 'no profit' rule. How, it might be asked, is it consistent with that for the profiteer to claim, as do the respondents, that the company would not have taken advantage of the acquisition opportunity because it was outside the scope of its business? In *Furs Ltd v. Tomkies* (1936) 54 CLR 583, Rich, Dixon and Evatt JJ affirmed in their joint judgment in the High Court of Australia, at 592:

> '. . . the inflexible rule that, except under the authority of a provision in the articles of association, no director shall obtain for himself a profit by means of a transaction in which he is concerned on behalf of the company unless all material facts are disclosed to the shareholders and by resolution a general meeting approves his doing so or all the shareholders acquiesce.[72] An undisclosed profit which a director derives from the execution of his fiduciary duties belongs in equity to the company. It is no answer to the application of the rule that the profit is of a kind which the company itself could not have obtained, or that no loss is caused to the company by the gain of the director. It is a principle resting upon the impossibility of allowing the conflict of duty and interest which is involved in the pursuit of private advantage in the course of dealing in a fiduciary capacity with the affairs of the company . . .'

[72] Note that this assertion relates to transactions *between* the company and its director (see CA 2006 ss 177 and 182), not to contracts between the director and third parties, and it is only the latter where the scope issue in relation to 'corporate opportunities' arises.

58. The like rigorous approach is also to be found in the speeches in the House of Lords in *Regal (Hastings) Ltd v. Gulliver* **[7.26]** . . .

59. In the same case, at 153E, Lord Macmillan posed the relevant issue as being one of fact:

'The plaintiff company has to establish two things: (i) that what the directors did was so related to the affairs of the company that it can properly be said to have been done in the course of their management and in utilisation of their opportunities and special knowledge as directors; and (ii) that what they did resulted in a profit to themselves.'

And Lord Wright said, at 154F:

'What the respondents did, it was said, caused no damage to the appellant and involved no neglect of the appellant's interests or similar breach of duty. However, I think the answer to this reasoning is that, both in law and equity, it has been held that, if a person in a fiduciary relationship makes a secret profit out of the relationship, the court will not inquire whether the other person is damnified or has lost a profit which would otherwise he would have got. The fact is in itself a fundamental breach of the fiduciary relationship.'

60. Those statements, of high authority, appear to me to exclude the making of the 'scope of business' inquiry that the judge made in this case. Once he had found, as he did, that the opportunity to buy Aria House came to the respondents' attention in their capacity as directors of the company acting on the company's business and using information they also obtained in the course of so acting, that was the end of the point. In principle, subject to any defences that might be available (acquiescence, for example), the respondents would have been liable to account to the company for any profit they made by their purchase. Their proper course was to obtain the company's informed consent to their private venture. They did not do that.

61. What of *Aas v. Benham* **[7.30]**? That was a decision of a strong court, binding upon us, and showing that, in the context of a commercial partnership, the strict duties of accountability in accordance with the principles of, for example, *Parker v. McKenna* and *Regal (Hastings) Ltd v. Gulliver* will not apply in a case in which partnership information has been used by the defendant partner for the purpose of a separate business of a nature beyond the scope of the partnership business.

62. *Aas v. Benham* was not cited in *Regal (Hastings) Ltd v. Gulliver*, but it was cited in *Boardman and Another v. Phipps* [1967] AC 46, a case involving a successful claim against the appellants that they were accountable to a trust on the basis that, as agents of the trustees, they had obtained information that they then used to buy shares for themselves. The appellants argued (inter alia) that their case was akin to *Aas v. Benham* in that the purchase of the shares was 'wholly outside the scope of any agency undertaken for the trustees' ([1967] AC 46, at 66C). The test was said to be whether the information could have been used by the principal for the purpose for which it was used by the agent; and if the answer was no, the information was not the principal's property ([1967] AC 46, at 71A). The counter-argument was that *Aas v. Benham* was 'distinguishable as being a very special case for a partner is only in a fiduciary position in relation to matters within the ambit of the partnership business.' ([1967] AC 46, at 70A). . . . [Then followed an interesting assessment of the treatment of *Aas v Benham* by the House of Lords in *Boardman v Phipps*.]

67. Coming to my conclusions on the 'no profit' case, in my judgment the answer to the reliance placed by the judge and (before us) by Mr Mallin [counsel] on *Aas v. Benham* is that it is of no relevance in considering the extent and application of the 'no profit' and 'no conflict' rules so far as they apply to fiduciaries such as trustees and directors. By way of an introduction to the reason why, it is helpful to consider Lord Browne-Wilkinson's observations in *Henderson and Others v. Merrett Syndicates Ltd and Others* [1995] 2 AC 145, at 206:

'The phrase "fiduciary duties" is a dangerous one, giving rise to a mistaken assumption that all fiduciaries owe the same duties in all circumstances. That is not the case. Although, so far as I am aware, every fiduciary is under a duty not to make a profit from his position (unless such profit is authorised), the fiduciary duties owed, for example, by an express trustee are not the same as those owed by an agent. Moreover, and more relevantly, the extent and nature of the fiduciary duties owed in any particular case fall to be determined by reference to any underlying contractual relationship between the parties. Thus, in the case of an agent employed under a contract, the scope of the fiduciary duties is determined by the terms of the underlying contract.'

68. The point about *Aas v. Benham* is that it concerned the fiduciary duties owed by a partner whose duties were circumscribed by the contract of partnership. The extent of Mr Benham's fiduciary duties was determined by the nature of the partnership business, which was expressly limited by the terms of the partnership agreement. The consequence was that if he used partnership information for any purpose that fell within the scope of the partnership business, he was required by the fiduciary obligations to which the contract subjected him to account to the firm for any profits so made; but his fiduciary obligations did not require him similarly to account to the firm for any profits made by the use of such information for a purpose that was beyond the scope of the business of the partnership. To those familiar with the wider obligations of accountability to which trustees and directors are subject, the decision in *Aas v. Benham* may at first sight appear to reflect a surprisingly narrow approach. But the explanation is that a trustee's and director's fiduciary duties are not similarly circumscribed by the terms of a contract. That distinction was squarely recognised by Lord Hodson in *Boardman v. Phipps*, and also, I consider, by Lord Guest. The explanation for the decision in *Aas v. Benham* was correctly summarised in the respondents' submission to the House of Lords that I have earlier cited ([1967] AC 46, at 70A).

69. By contrast with Mr Benham's position, directors of companies occupy what Lord Hodson in *Boardman v. Phipps* called a 'general trusteeship or fiduciary position'. By that he was referring to those occupying a position whose fiduciary obligations are not circumscribed by contract. In his argument for the appellants in *Boardman v. Phipps*, Mr Arthur Bagnall QC, in distinguishing the appellants' case from that of the directors in *Regal (Hastings) Ltd v. Gulliver*, submitted that the directors 'were at all times directors of the company and therefore they were in a fiduciary capacity which was unlimited' ([1967] AC 46, 65G). Submissions do not always reflect the law so much as what the advocate might wish the law to be. But I would regard it as correct to characterise the nature of a director's fiduciary duties as being so unlimited and as akin to a 'general trusteeship'. In my judgment, the decision in *Aas v. Benham* provides no assistance in determining the nature and reach of the 'no profit' rule so far as it applies to trustees and directors. In particular, in the present case, the scope of the company's business was in no manner relevantly circumscribed by its constitution: it was fully open to it to engage in property investment if the directors so chose. The resolution of Ms McDonnell's claim in the present case was and is not assisted by reference to *Aas v. Benham*. The relevant authorities are those relating to the fiduciary duties of directors, of which *Regal (Hastings) Ltd v. Gulliver* is the leading one.

70. The statements of principle in the authorities about directors' fiduciary duties make it clear that any inquiry as to whether the company could, would or might have taken up the opportunity itself is irrelevant; so also, therefore, must be a 'scope of business' inquiry. The point is that the existence of the opportunity is one that it is relevant for the company to know and of which the director has a duty to inform it. It is not for the director to make his own decision that the company will not be interested and to proceed, without more, to appropriate the opportunity for himself. His duty is one of undivided loyalty and this is one manifestation of how that duty is required to be discharged.

71. This was a case in which, in the course of acting as directors on behalf of the company in an estate agency capacity, the respondents obtained information relating to the virtue of Aria

House as an investment and were given the opportunity of personally sharing in the opportunity of purchasing it. It may have been improbable that the company could or would want or be able to take up the opportunity itself. But the opportunity was there for the company to consider and, if so advised, to reject and it was no answer to the claimed breach of the 'no profit' rule that property investment was something that the company did not do. Nor, until Mr Sulaiman telephoned Mr Shanahan, did the company do estate agency work. There was no bright line marking off what it did and did not do.

72. In my judgment the judge came to the wrong conclusion on the 'no profit' rule. I consider that, in principle, the respondents' acquisition of their interest in Aria House exposed them to a claim for an account of profits by the company. . . .

AIKENS and WALLER LJJ concurred.

➤ Questions

This is a significant case on 'corporate opportunities', so it is important to understand the analysis.[73]

1. What is the rationale for applying *Aas v Benham* to fiduciaries who are partners, but not to fiduciaries who are trustees or company directors? Does it make sense in practice, given their different (or similar) roles?

2. Could the Court of Appeal have reached the same conclusion by *applying Aas v Benham*, but holding that on the facts the opportunity was within the 'scope of business' of C, since C's business was not well defined? What practical difference would this have made for future cases? Even if the company's business was not well defined, did it seem likely to venture into property *purchase*, or just into advising a wider range of clients, including vendors and purchasers, and assisting in their transactions (see [53])?

3. Is every company with wide objects, or with no specified objects (see 'Capacity: what is a company legally set up to do?', pp 92ff), or with an undefined business plan, at an advantage in claiming the loyalty of its directors as a result of this decision?

4. Whatever the width of the objects of a company, *should* the no conflicts rule catch corporate opportunities that it 'may have been improbable that the company could or would want or be able to take up' (para [71] in the extract)? Given that the equitable rule is not breached unless there is a 'real, sensible possibility of conflict' (Lord Upjohn in *Boardman v Phipps*), is the conclusion in this case justified? What impact, if any, would CA 2006 s 175(4)(a) have had on this decision?

5. The decision relies heavily on *Keech v Sanford*. There, the trust property was a lease, and the trustee was not allowed to take a renewal of the lease for his own personal benefit even though the lease could not be renewed for the benefit of the trust. But does the analysis in that case go the extra step, and suggest that the trustee could not have taken the personal benefit of *any* lease without first obtaining the approval of the beneficiary? What is the difference between the conflict in the former situation and in the latter?

6. It is much easier to assess breaches of the no conflict rule where the director uses corporate property (whether real property, personal property or intellectual property) to achieve his or her ends. Where the director uses information, as in this case, the assessment is much more difficult. Why?

---

[73] See D Prentice and J Payne, 'The Corporate Opportunity Doctrine' (2004) 120 LQR 198.

*A shareholders' agreement giving shareholder-directors control over
the direction of the company may enable those directors to deny that
a new venture could be classed as a 'corporate opportunity'.*

[7.32] Wilkinson v West Coast Capital [2005] EWHC 3009 (Chancery Division)

[Also see on this case the Note and Questions at the end of the section entitled 'Shareholders' agreements', p 260.] This is a rather odd case. A claim was made by one shareholder against others in unfair prejudice [now CA 2006 s 994], alleging breach of fiduciary duty. This was notwithstanding that the 'corporate opportunity' in question was subsequently sold at a loss, meaning there were no profits which could be disgorged to the company, nor any losses which could be claimed by the company under other heads of duty. This of itself would not prevent an unfair prejudice claim, but some wrong or infringement of legitimate expectations must be shown, and was not here.

W held 40% of the shares in N; X and G held the remaining 60%. X and G also owned and controlled a separate company, Y, which they used to purchase a third company, B. B was subsequently sold at a loss. W asserted that the opportunity to acquire B was a corporate opportunity belonging to N, and that the directors of N were therefore in breach of their fiduciary duties in causing it to be purchased by Y. The complicating factor was a shareholders' agreement which provided that certain actions by N (including this purchase) required the consent of more than 65% of shareholders, and that each shareholder should use all reasonable and proper means to promote the interests of N. It was held that the latter obligation was subject to the former restriction on the company's scope of activity, and that X and G were not required to vote in favour of the purchase. W's claim for a remedy for unfair prejudice under CA 1985 s 459 [now CA 2006 s 994] was unsuccessful.

WARREN J:

272. Mr McCaughran [counsel for the defendants] identifies Mr Wilkinson's main complaint this way: The directors of NGS obtained information about Birthdays, and the opportunity to acquire Birthdays, in the course of carrying out their role as directors of NGS; that because of this, the directors were not free to take up the opportunity to acquire Birthdays themselves; and that they were in breach of duty in doing so. However, I think that the complaint goes wider than that: even if the directors learnt of the opportunity, and of the relevant information to permit them to formulate their offer, quite independently of their capacity as directors of NGS, nonetheless they were in a position of conflict in relation to the acquisition of Birthdays and should not have acquired it for themselves.

273. In considering that complaint, Mr McCaughran says, correctly I think, that one must have regard not only to the scope of the directors' duties, but also to the related question of the scope of NGS's business. In that context, he relies on the decision of the Court of Appeal in *Aas v Benham* **[7.30]**, the decision of the Privy Council in *Trimble v Goldberg* [1906] AC 493 and on certain passages of the judgments in *Boardman v Phipps*.

274. *Aas v Benham* was a partnership case [citing the extract at **[7.30]**] . . . Mr McCaughran submits that exactly the same approach should be applied in the case of a company and the duties owed to it by a director . . .

281. So *Aas v Benham* is an illustration of the importance of defining the scope of the duty before being able to decide whether a person is in breach of it and in particular whether the 'no conflict' rule or the 'no profit' rule applies . . .

284. [Mr McCaughran] also says that there is nothing in the company law authorities 'which in any way detracts from the principle in *Aas v Benham*'. I am not sure that there is anything which warrants the epithet 'principle' which can be derived from *Aas v Benham* . . . The case possibly

establishes, or re-affirms, a negative proposition *viz* that there is no principle which entitles a firm to benefits derived from the use of information for purposes which are wholly outside the scope of the firm's activities.

285. In applying that negative principle, one must act with care because the firm's activities may not be limited by the formal partnership agreement . . .

295. Mr McCaughran submits that what these cases [all the usual orthodox authorities] show is only that, *once a conflict has been established*, a director who makes a profit, is accountable for the profit. They do not establish accountability where no conflict is established. Of course, a fiduciary can only be made to account for a profit if he has made a profit. That goes to remedy. At this stage, however, I am more concerned with whether there has been any breach of duty—at a time when it cannot be known whether a profit will in fact be made. Mr McCaughran accepts that, once a conflict has arisen and a profit has been made, it is no defence for the director to allege that the company could not *as a matter of fact* have acquired the opportunity itself, for example because the company could not afford to pursue the opportunity (as in *Regal (Hastings) Ltd v Gulliver*) or because the third party would not have wanted to deal with the company (as in *Industrial Development Consultants Ltd v Cooley*). But he submits that none of the cases is concerned with the situation where, as in *Aas v Benham* there was a legal impediment to the company taking up the opportunity; he says that, where there is a legal impediment of this sort, there is no relevant conflict of interest. On the facts in the present case there was, he submits, a legal impediment to the acquisition of Birthdays by NGS and therefore no relevant conflict of interest in the acquisition by WCC and Mr Gorman . . .

297. However, what I think is important in the present case is not so much the effect of a legal impediment on the duty of directors generally; but rather the impact of the director himself being able, in a non-fiduciary capacity, to prevent the company of which he is a director from obtaining the benefit of the opportunity. I doubt very much that a legal impediment requiring shareholder consent to certain matters impacts to any great extent on the duties of a director who is not a shareholder. It does not follow from the fact that a particular acquisition requires shareholder consent that a director is freed from any duty which would otherwise arise to bring an opportunity of acquisition to the attention of the board and the shareholders. In contrast, the ability of a shareholder, who also happens to be a director, to block certain action on the part of the company may be of great importance in the context of his duties to account under the 'no conflict' and 'no profit' rules.

298. Let me take an example. Consider a company (call it X) carrying on a particular business. Suppose X has three equal shareholders A, B and C, each of whom is a director; and suppose that it has one additional, non-shareholder, director D. Suppose that the Memorandum and Articles of Association restrict X's business to its current business but so that activities can be diversified (either directly or through a corporate acquisition) with the consent of 66% of the shareholders.

299. Suppose, then, that an opportunity to acquire a company (call it Y) whose business is outside the scope of X's existing business becomes generally known. There would be nothing, I think, to prevent A and B acquiring Y for themselves even if the board of X considered that it would be a good thing for X to acquire Y. In these circumstances, there is of course a conflict between the personal interests of A and B on the one hand and their duties, as directors, to X on the other hand. But it is not a conflict to which the 'no conflicts' rule has any application because A and B are entitled, as shareholders, to block the acquisition by X. There is, I consider, no duty on them to use their votes as shareholders to approve the acquisition (and this is so, in my judgment, even though it may be in the interests of X to make it and even though they are directors). There is no risk (such as that which caused concern in *Keech v Sandford*) which needs to be guarded against and no occasion for the intervention of equity. There is no question of the application of the 'no profits' rule either since the opportunity is, in the example, generally known.

300. The position would be the same, I consider, if the opportunity had come to the attention of A and B other than in their capacities as directors. It would be open, I think, for them to keep that opportunity for themselves. At most, detecting a possible advantage to X in acquiring Y, it may be their duty, acting in the interests of X, to bring the opportunity to the attention of the board. But having done that, they could not be compelled to agree to the actual acquisition by X of Y. Being able, acting perfectly properly, to block such an acquisition, there is, as before, no relevant conflict of interest; and, in this case, there would clearly be no use of a corporate opportunity were A and B to acquire Y for themselves. I ignore the possibility of intervention by a court [of] equity if Y would be in competition with X. But that is not the present case, where the businesses of TGS and Birthdays were so different to make it unrealistic to think that they were competitors.

301. Now suppose that the opportunity has, instead, come to the notice of X and its board in circumstances where that opportunity is clearly that of X exclusively (*eg* because the owner of Y approaches D in his capacity as a director with an offer to sell to X). The board and the shareholders decide that it might be in the interests of X to effect the acquisition of Y because its business, whilst outside the scope of its own business, presents synergies with that business. Actual acquisition of Y will require the consent of A, B and C once the merits of the acquisition have been investigated. Suppose that the vendor of Y provides confidential information to the board to enable X to make an offer. At this stage, there is a 'maturing business opportunity' which belongs to X and if D were to attempt to divert it, both the 'no conflict' rule and the 'no profit' rule would apply if he in fact acquired the target business/company and made a profit. It would not be open to D to claim, as against X or A, B and C, that the scope of X's business, and therefore his duty, was restricted by the scope of X's current business and that he could therefore obtain Y for himself. Nor would he escape the rules if X were unable to make the acquisition because it could not raise the finance: the case would fall squarely within the principles established in *Regal (Hastings) Ltd v Gulliver*.

302. Next suppose that the board, having looked carefully at the potential acquisition, decides, for commercial reasons, not to proceed. It is a very difficult question whether this would take D out of either or both the 'no conflict' and 'no profit' rules. *Aas v Benham* certainly does not provide an answer. That D can do so with the informed consent of the company in general meeting is clear; that he cannot do so without it is not clear.

303. Whatever the position of D, however, the position of any two of the other shareholders, say A and B, acting together may be different. As before, where the opportunity is generally known, there is, I consider, no duty on them to use their votes as shareholders to approve the acquisition; they remain able to block it. Further, for the reasons already given in the example where the opportunity is generally known, I do not consider that there is any scope for the application of the 'no conflicts' rule. The question then is whether there is any scope of the application of the 'no profits' rule when the opportunity is confidential to X. Can A and B, who are both directors and shareholders and who, together as shareholders, can block the acquisition be permitted to take advantage of the opportunity themselves? That is not an easy question to answer; and I prefer to leave it unanswered since, as will be seen, I do not consider that, on the facts, it arises in that stark form.

304. Applying these principles to the present case, there has, in my judgment, been no breach by Mr Gorman or Mr McMahon (or indeed by Sir Tom even if he is a *de facto* director) of the 'no conflicts' rule. On my findings of fact, there was no agreement that NGS should acquire Birthdays so that they were, as shareholders, able to block the acquisition. There is no question, on my findings, of the board being able to proceed with the acquisition in the face of the provisions of the Shareholders Agreement to which NGS itself was a party. In any event, Mr Gorman and Mr McMahon could not be criticised if, acting as board members, they had voted against NGS acquiring Birthdays in order to respect the provisions of [the] Shareholders Agreement which, as between 100% of the shareholders and NGS itself, were stated to take precedence over the

unamended Articles. There is no 'omission' for the purposes of section 459 in the board failing to acquire Birthdays for NGS.

305. There is more difficulty with the 'no profit' rule. It is, of course, the position that the confidentiality agreement was given by Mr Gorman on behalf of TGS (so that, strictly speaking, the information provided by Birthdays in reliance on that confidentiality agreement was provided to TGS rather than NGS but no point has been taken about that). Moreover, a considerable amount of work in the evaluation of the Birthdays business was carried out by NGS personnel in NGS time and, initially at least, at NGS expense. In these circumstances, WCC and Mr Gorman were able to make the successful bid only by use of the information provided to TGS and work done by NGS personnel.

306. However, this is not a case where the original opportunity came to NGS. The possibility of acquiring Birthdays did not come to the notice of Mr Gorman because he was a director of NGS/TGS or because of the trial sales of TGS products in Birthdays' shops. It came to his notice because he knew Mr Boland and spoke to him about the opportunity. Nor did the possibility of the acquisition come to the notice of Mr McMahon because he was a director of NGS/TGS or to Sir Tom because of his connection with NGS/TGS. They learned of the possibility through a combination of their network of information in the business world and Mr Gorman. Perhaps it would not have been an opportunity which would have interested them if they had not been connected with NGS; and it was clearly an opportunity which they thought could have been of value to NGS, otherwise they would not have been considering an acquisition through NGS. But that does not alter the fact that they did not become aware of the opportunity as directors (or in Sir Tom's case as a *de facto* director if he is one). . . .

310. That, however, is not an answer to the question whether the 'no profit' rule applies: see the passage from the speech of Lord Russell in *Boardman v Phipps* quoted by Lewison J in paragraph 1321 of *Ultraframe* . . .

312. Had a profit been made out of Birthdays, this would be a real issue: were NGS bringing an action to make Mr Gorman—and possibly Mr McMahon (and even Sir Tom if he was a *de facto* director)—account for the profit made, then there are powerful arguments that he (or they) should do so. However, the fact is that Birthdays was sold at a loss and there is no profit to account for. Further, NGS has suffered no detriment as a result of the acquisition by New Gifts: NGS was unable to acquire Birthdays itself and, as I have already found, it would not have acquired Birthdays even if WCC and Mr Gorman had been advised that they could not themselves acquire it . . .

316. It might have been argued, had Birthdays been sold at a profit, that the directors were in breach of their duties in not suing New Gifts for an account of such profit; and that such a breach would have been unfairly prejudicial conduct. But that argument does not begin to get off the ground on the facts . . .

➤ Questions

1. Does this judgment adopt the 'scope of business' test (from *Aas v Benham* **[7.30]**) or some other test of 'corporate opportunity'?

2. If the company's constitution (ie its objects or its articles) do not permit the company to pursue the venture in question, then its pursuit for personal benefit by the directors is surely not in breach of their duty to avoid conflicts. Is this the key to the *Wilkinson v West Coast Capital* **[7.32]** decision? Put another way, if the company *could not* pursue the opportunity *unless* the directors, as shareholders, exercised their vote to expand the scope of the business of the company, then the law would not compel the directors to vote to do so, and therefore the opportunity would never be classed as a 'corporate opportunity'.

3. But is the opposite true? That is, if the company *could* do any deal, could the controlling director-shareholders use their powers under a shareholders' agreement to block the pursuit by their company of a venture that was otherwise allowed and within the scope of business of the company, so that they could then take the benefits personally?

4. Is the conclusion the same if the directors hold sufficient shares to *be able* to change the company's objects so that pursuit by the company is not permitted, even if those votes have not yet been used to make this change? If the directors tried to make this change at a late stage, after discovering the opportunity but before pursuing it themselves, *could* they use their shareholder votes to this end? (See 'Alteration of the articles', pp 228ff, especially *Allen v Gold Reefs* [4.22].)

5. Is it important to the analysis in this case that the company is a party to the shareholders' agreement?

6. Towards the end of the judgment, there is a suggestion (*obiter*) that although the no conflict rule is not breached, the no profit rule might nevertheless be breached (but was not here because no profits had been generated). Is this logical? If sale of the new venture *had* generated a profit, what would the outcome have been on this approach? Is that justified, notwithstanding that the directors' entry into the new venture involved no conflict (according to the earlier part of the judgment)? Now see s 176(4) on benefits from third parties, which is thought to cover the old 'no profits' rule, but which does not seem apt on the facts here, which surely remain to be judged under s 175.

7. Is it material that the company might have suffered a *loss* because it could not take up the new venture (although here it did not, because the new venture was eventually sold at a loss)? Which breaches of directors' duties allow recovery of the company's losses, and which allow recovery of the profits generated by the defaulting director?

2. Resigning to take up a corporate opportunity

The issue for this section is whether a director who resigns is then free to take up what would otherwise have been a corporate opportunity. The answer is clearly no: s 170(2) indicates that s 175 is to apply to some extent (this is not elaborated) to directors who are no longer in office.[74]

This was also the case under the older equitable rules, including a relatively recent and rare appeal to the Court of Appeal: *Foster Bryant Surveying Ltd v Bryant, Savernake Property Consultants Ltd* [7.33]. This case and two others are extracted later, and a number of earlier authorities summarised here, but note that all these cases predate CA 2006, which may deliver different conclusions on the same facts.

In *Canadian Aero Service Ltd v O'Malley* (1973) 40 DLR (3d) 371, the president and the executive vice-president of the plaintiff company ('Canaero') were negotiating for a large aerial surveying and mapping contract with the government of Guyana, to be financed by the external aid programme of the Canadian government. Instead of securing the contract for Canaero, they resigned their managerial posts and formed their own company ('Terra'), to which they successfully diverted the contract. The Supreme Court of Canada held that their fiduciary duty had survived their resignation and that that duty was enforceable against Terra as well as the individual defendants. The remedy took the form of an award of damages for breach of duty, rather than an account of profits. All three features are noteworthy. Key factors in this case were that: (i) the defendants had diverted for their own benefit a 'maturing business opportunity' which their company was actively pursuing; (ii) they were participants in the negotiations on behalf of the company; (iii) their resignation

---

[74] Even in the normal case, the common law rule is that the remedy for pursuit of the corporate opportunity while the director was in office may include profits gained after retirement, since those profits are causally connected to the breach: *Foster Bryant Surveying Ltd v Bryant, Savernake Property Consultants Ltd* [7.33].

had been 'prompted or influenced' by a wish to acquire the opportunity for themselves; and (iv) it was their position with the company rather than a 'fresh initiative' which led them to the opportunity which they later required.

These elements were all present in *Industrial Development Consultants Ltd v Cooley* [1972] 1 WLR 443, where Cooley, an architect, was managing director of the plaintiff company, which was in business as building and development consultants. As the company's representative, he took part in negotiations with officers of the Eastern Gas Board, endeavouring to secure contracts for the company to build four large depots; but these negotiations were unsuccessful because the Gas Board would not engage a firm of consultants (as distinct from a private architect). Shortly afterwards, the work was offered to Cooley in his private capacity. Cooley obtained a release from his employment (by falsely representing that he was in ill health), and was later given the contract by the Gas Board. Roskill J held that he was accountable to the company for the whole of his benefits under the contract or, alternatively, liable in damages for breach of his service contract. The amount awardable under the second head would, however, have been relatively small—it was put by the judge at 'a 10% chance'—because the likelihood that the company might itself have secured the contract was so remote.

Note that in these two cases the issue was relatively straightforward because the officers in question had an express mandate from the board to negotiate for the acquisition of the particular contract on behalf of their company; and there was also no question of ratification.

In contrast with *Canaero* and *Cooley*, Umunna, the director in *Island Export Finance Ltd v Umunna* [1986] BCLC 460, was allowed to keep the profits he had derived from contracts he obtained after he had resigned as the managing director of his company, IEF. These contracts to supply postal boxes to the Cameroons postal authorities were of the same kind, and made with the same party, as an earlier contract which he had secured for IEF while working as its managing director. But Hutchinson J accepted evidence that IEF was not actively seeking further orders either when Umunna resigned or when he later obtained the contracts; that the resignation was for unrelated reasons; and that Umunna had not made improper use of any confidential information.

So which opportunities are caught? In *Balston Ltd v Headline Filters Ltd* [1990] FSR 385, Head, an employee and director of Balston who had worked for it for 17 years, gave notice terminating his employment and resigned his directorship. He had already agreed to lease premises where he intended to set up his own business, but he said in evidence that he had not then decided what that business was to be. Shortly afterwards one of Balston's customers telephoned Head after being notified by Balston that it would continue to supply him with a particular kind of filter tube for only a limited further period. As a result of this call, Head commenced business making the filter tubes and supplied them to the customer. Falconer J held that it was not a breach of fiduciary duty for a director to form an intention to set up business in competition with his company after his directorship had ceased, and that there was no maturing business opportunity in which the company had a 'specific interest' which Head had improperly diverted to himself.

These cases illustrate the difficulties in reaching predictable conclusions in different situations. As Rix LJ expressed it in *Foster Bryant Surveying Ltd v Bryant, Savernake Property Consultants Ltd* **[7.33]**:

> At one extreme (*In Plus Group v. Pyke* **[7.36]**) the defendant is director in name only. At the other extreme, the director has planned his resignation having in mind the destruction of his company or at least the exploitation of its property in the form of business opportunities in which he is currently involved (*ID, Canaero, Simonet, British Midland Tool*). In the middle are

more nuanced cases which go both ways: in *Shepherds Investments v. Walters* **[7.34]** the combination of disloyalty, active promotion of the planned business, and exploitation of a business opportunity, all while the directors remained in office, brought liability; in *Umunna, Balston,* and *Framlington,* however, where the resignations were unaccompanied by disloyalty, there was no liability.

Resigning and moving on to new work without breaching the conflicts rule.

[7.33] Foster Bryant Surveying Ltd v Bryant, Savernake Property Consultants Ltd [2007] EWCA Civ 200 (Court of Appeal)

Bryant, a director, was effectively forced out of the company by his business partner and co-director, Foster, who was the majority shareholder in the company. Bryant resigned, although not in order to take work or clients from the company. Nevertheless, during his notice period, the company's major client (Alliance) pressed Bryant to continue working for Alliance after his departure from the company. Bryant agreed, and took up what was essentially an employee's role, but through a new company of his own. This company was formed a few days before Bryant's resignation took effect, and, when it took effect, he started to work for the client. Previously, Alliance had channelled all its work exclusively to the company, under an exclusivity contract which had expired without renewal a few weeks before the resignation took effect. However, Alliance, in its own interests, wanted the personal services of Bryant and Foster, not anyone else, and was determined to split the work, or to use other suppliers. Bryant was found not to have breached his fiduciary duty.

RIX LJ:

8. At trial it was common ground between the parties that the synthesis of principles expounded by Mr Livesey QC, sitting as a deputy judge of the High Court, in *Hunter Kane Limited v. Watkins* [2002] EWHC 186 (Ch) [which Mr Livesey had himself taken largely from the judgment of Lawrence Collins J in *CMS Dolphin Ltd v Simonet*] accurately stated the law . . . Mr Livesey said:

'1. A director, while acting as such, has a fiduciary relationship with his Company. That is he has an obligation to deal towards it with loyalty, good faith and avoidance of the conflict of duty and self-interest.

2. A requirement to avoid a conflict of duty and self-interest means that a director is precluded from obtaining for himself, either secretly or without the informed approval of the Company, any property or business advantage either belonging to the Company or for which it has been negotiating, especially where the director or officer is a participant in the negotiations.

3. A director's power to resign from office is not a fiduciary power. He is entitled to resign even if his resignation might have a disastrous effect on the business or reputation of the Company.

4. A fiduciary relationship does not continue after the determination of the relationship which gives rise to it. After the relationship is determined the director is in general not under the continuing obligations which are the feature of the fiduciary relationship. [But now see CA 2006 s 170(2).]

5. Acts done by the directors while the contract of employment subsists but which are preparatory to competition after it terminates are not necessarily in themselves a breach of the implied term as to loyalty and fidelity.

6. Directors, no less than employees, acquire a general fund of skill, knowledge and expertise in the course of their work, which is plainly in the public interest that they should be

free to exploit it in a new position. After ceasing the relationship by resignation or otherwise a director is in general (and subject of course to any terms of the contract of employment) not prohibited from using his general fund of skill and knowledge, the 'stock in trade' of the knowledge he has acquired while a director, even including such things as business contacts and personal connections made as a result of his directorship.

7. A director is however precluded from acting in breach of the requirement at 2 above, even after his resignation where the resignation may fairly be said to have been prompted or influenced by a wish to acquire for himself any maturing business opportunities sought by the Company and where it was his position with the Company rather than a fresh initiative that led him to the opportunity which he later acquired.

8. In considering whether an act of a director breaches the preceding principle the factors to take into account will include the factor of position or office held, the nature of the corporate opportunity, its ripeness, its specificness and the director's relation to it, the amount of knowledge possessed, the circumstances in which it was obtained and whether it was special or indeed even private, the factor of time in the continuation of the fiduciary duty where the alleged breach occurs after termination of the relationship with the Company and the circumstances under which the breach was terminated, that is whether by retirement or resignation or discharge.

9. The underlying basis of the liability of a director who exploits after his resignation a maturing business opportunity of the Company is that the opportunity is to be treated as if it were the property of the Company in relation to which the director had fiduciary duties. By seeking t[o] exploit the opportunity after resignation he is appropriating to himself that property. He is just as accountable as a trustee who retires without properly accounting for trust property.

10. It follows that a director will not be in breach of the principle set out as point 7 above where either the Company's hope of obtaining the contract was not a 'maturing business opportunity' and it was not pursuing further business orders nor where the director's resignation was not itself prompted or influenced by a wish to acquire the business for himself.

11. As regards breach of confidence, although while the contract of employment subsists a director or other employee may not use confidential information to the detriment of his employer, after it ceases the director/employee may compete and may use know-how acquired in the course of his employment (as distinct from trade secrets—although the distinction is sometimes difficult to apply in practice).' . . .

48. It may be observed that the factual situation presented by this case falls uneasily between the scenarios dealt with in [earlier] jurisprudence. This is not a case where a director has used corporate property. It is not a case where a director has resigned in order to make use of a corporate opportunity. It is not a case where a director has solicited corporate business in competition with his company. It is not a case where a director has acted in bad faith, deceitfully or clandestinely. It is, however, at any rate arguably, a case where, by agreeing, while still a director, to work for Alliance after he ceased to be a director, Mr Bryant was still obtaining for himself a business opportunity, possibly even existing business, of the company, or putting himself in a position of conflict with the company, before he was free to do so. Moreover, these events happened at a time of transition, after a forced resignation but before the resignation had taken contractual effect, in circumstances where both parties might be said to be in need of protection. It is possibly above all when a director is leaving that a company needs the protection which the law relating to directors' fiduciary duties provides. But it is also when a director is forced out of his own company that he needs the protection that the law allows to someone who has thereafter to earn his living. Many of these considerations are discussed in the jurisprudence, but not in our particular setting. [Then followed a discussion of other authorities, including *Regal Hastings, Boardman v Phipps,*

Industrial Development Consultants v Cooley [1972] 1 WLR 443, *Canadian Aero Service Ltd v O'Malley* (1973) 40 DLR (2d) 371, and continuing:]

57. The defendants [in *Canaero*] were castigated as 'faithless fiduciaries'. It was again irrelevant that the company might not have obtained the contract, for the defendants' liability was [measured by] their gain rather than the company's loss. . . . the decision on the facts appears best encapsulated in the following extract from [Laskin J's] judgment (at 382):

'An examination of the case law . . . shows the pervasiveness of a strict ethic in this area of the law. In my opinion, this ethic disqualifies a director or senior officer from usurping for himself or diverting to another person or company with whom or with which he is associated a maturing business opportunity which the company is actively pursuing; he is also precluded from so acting even after his resignation where the resignation may fairly be said to have been prompted or influenced by a wish to acquire for himself the opportunity sought by the company, *or* where it was his position with the company rather than a fresh initiative that led him to the opportunity which he later acquired.' [Emphasis added[75]] . . .

66. In *CMS Dolphin Ltd v. Simonet* [2001] 2 BCLC 704 the relevant jurisprudence was carefully considered by Lawrence Collins J . . . The director there resigned (without any notice) in order to profit from the claimant company's business. Having made plans in advance of resignation, after his departure he immediately set up in competition, first in partnership and subsequently through a new company. He approached the claimant's staff and clients, to draw them both to him. Before long, the claimant had no staff and no clients. The director was found to be in breach of fiduciary duty and liable to account. By resigning, he had exploited the maturing business opportunities of the claimant, which were to be regarded as its property. The case made by the claimant and accepted by Lawrence Collins J was that the director had been prompted or influenced to resign by a wish to acquire for himself or his company the business opportunities which he had previously obtained or was actively pursuing with the claimant's clients and had now actually diverted to his own profit. . . .

68. [Lawrence Collins J considered the legal principles, concluding:]

'In English law a director's power to resign from office is not a fiduciary power. A director is entitled to resign even if his resignation might have a disastrous effect on the business or reputation of the company. So also in English law, at least in general, a fiduciary obligation does not continue after the determination of the relationship which gives rise to it . . . In my judgment the underlying basis of the liability of a director who exploits after his resignation a maturing business opportunity of the company is that the opportunity is to be treated as if it were property of the company in relation to which the director had fiduciary duties.'

69. In my judgment, Lawrence Collins J was not saying that the fiduciary duty survived the end of the relationship as director, but that the lack of good faith with which the future exploitation was planned while still a director, and the resignation which was part of that dishonest plan, meant that there was already then a breach of fiduciary duty, which resulted in the liability to account for the profits which, albeit subsequently, but causally connected with that earlier fiduciary breach, were obtained from the diversion of the company's business property to the defendant's new enterprise. [He then considered further cases, including the novel facts in *In Plus Group Ltd v Pyke* **[7.36]**, and continued:]

74. Finally, there have been two further cases in which the essence of the finding of a breach of fiduciary duty has consisted in what the directors had done while directors, rather than in post-resignation competition. Thus in *British Midland Tool Ltd v. Midland International Tooling*

---

[75] But note that in *CMS Dolphin Ltd v Simonet* [2001] 2 BCLC 704 at [91], Lawrence Collins J said that Laskin J's 'or' highlighted here was probably meant to be 'and'.

Ltd [2003] EWHC 466 (Ch), . . . the director who merely resigned in order to compete was not in breach, but his three former colleague directors who remained and thereafter conspired with him to poach the claimant's employees were in breach . . . And in *Shepherds Investments Ltd v. Walters* **[7.34]** . . .

76. . . . The jurisprudence which I have considered above demonstrates, I think, that the summary [at [8] above] is perceptive and useful. For my part, however, I would find it difficult accurately to encapsulate the circumstances in which a retiring director may or may not be found to have breached his fiduciary duty. As has been frequently stated, the problem is highly fact sensitive . . .

78. On which side of the line does Mr Bryant fall? . . .

79. Mr Bryant's resignation had no ulterior purpose. In human terms, and even though there was no repudiation of the shareholders' agreement, it was forced on him by Mr Foster's hostile and truculent manner and the sacking of Mrs Bryant [who was an employee of the company]. As soon as he was told that his wife was to be made redundant, Mr Bryant, not unreasonably, reacted by announcing his resignation. At that time his intention was to find employment with a firm of chartered surveyors . . . In this important aspect, Mr Bryant's case has no connection or similarity with, for instance, *Canaero's* 'faithless fiduciaries' . . .

87. All that Mr Bryant did was to agree to be retained by Alliance after his resignation became effective. He did nothing more. His resignation was not planned with an ulterior motive. He did not seek employment, or a retainer, or any business from Alliance. It was offered to him, it might be said pressed upon him . . .

88. Moreover, in considering the claim for loss and damage, the judge was unable to identify any existing projects which had actually been subsequently transferred to Mr Bryant or his new company . . .

93. . . . As for the extent of his fiduciary duties, it seems to me that the judge's realistic findings as to the position within the company after Mr Bryant's resignation makes it very arguable that, so long as he remained honest and neither exploited nor took any property of the company, his duties extended no further than that. To demand more while he is excluded from his role as a director appears to me to be unrealistic and inequitable. As for the innocence of his resignation, although the matter may not be free of doubt, it again seems well arguable on the authorities that it is critically opposed to liability to account, where there is no active competition or exploitation of company property while a defendant remains a director. And as for a reassignment of projects, I have already pointed out that the judge was unable to find that any existing company projects had been reassigned . . .

96. . . . I would dismiss the appeal.

MOSES and BUXTON LJJ delivered concurring judgments.

➤ Questions

1. In the course of his judgment, Buxton LJ made the following point:

as Sedley LJ emphasised in his judgment in *In Plus Group Ltd v Pyke* **[7.36]**, . . . the mere fact that a fiduciary has not sought to place himself in a position where his interest conflicts with his duty does not exonerate him from the obligation to perform that duty. Accordingly, it cannot be in any way conclusive that it was Mrs Watts who offered Mr Bryant the opportunity, indeed pressed it on him, rather than that he resigned in order to be free for that purpose, or asked for the opportunity once he had resigned.

Nevertheless, Buxton LJ held that, in the circumstances, it was not a breach for Bryant to accept the offer. Where is the line drawn?

2. In the course of his judgment, Rix LJ noted the trial judge's conclusions on Bryant's potential liability if he *had* been found in breach of his duties (Rix LJ at para [46]). The trial judge noted that if Bryant had ruled himself out of working for Alliance, the work he might have done would *not* then have gone to his old company, as it had in the past—recall Alliance wanted the personal services of Bryant and Foster—it would have gone elsewhere. The significance of this, so the trial judge thought, was that in *Warman International Ltd v Dwyer* (1995) 182 CLR 544, the High Court of Australia emphasised that the rule requiring a fiduciary to account for profits should not be applied in a manner which makes it a vehicle for unjust enrichment of the claimant. It followed, according to the trial judge, that even if Bryant *had* breached his duty, there were no profits for which he was liable to account. This, however, seems to confuse claims for profits disgorgement from Bryant with claims to recover the company's loss. In assessing profits, it is irrelevant that the company could not itself have generated those profits (*Regal (Hastings); Boardman v Phipps*). *Warman*, by contrast, was concerned to ensure that the *net* profits (emphasising net profits, not gross profits) of the offending venture were assessed fairly, and linked causally to the breach that generated them.

3. Would the outcome have been the same under CA 2006, given ss 170(2) and 175?

Resigning and pursuing competing opportunities in a way that breaches the conflicts rule.

[7.34] Shepherds Investments Ltd v Walters [2006] EWHC 836 (Chancery Division)

This was a claim against former directors (and employees) of Shepherds for various breaches of duty, including setting up a competing business, diversion of a business opportunity and misuse of confidential information. Walters and Hindle were directors and employees of Shepherds (Financial) Ltd ('Financial'). Simmons was a former employee and *de facto* director of Shepherds Investments Ltd ('Investments'). 'Assured' and 'PSL' were the companies through which the individuals carried on their competing business. The individuals were held to have breached their duties, and were therefore liable to account for the profits generated for the period of 'advance start' that their breach had given them, but not liable for damages because no loss was proved to have been caused by the breach.

ETHERTON J:

82. At the heart of these proceedings is the question whether, in taking the steps which they did to establish Assured and PSL prior to their retirement from Financial and Investments, the Individual Defendants acted in breach of their duties to the companies which employed them and of which they were directors. The parties are not agreed on the legal principles and test applicable to determine that central issue....

106. In my judgment it is plain that the necessary starting point of the analysis is that it is the fiduciary duty of a director to act in good faith in the best interests of the company ...

107. It is difficult to see any legitimate basis for the 'trumping' of those duties by 'rules of public policy [aimed at preventing] restraint of trade' as suggested by Falconer J in *Balston* at p.412. There is no reference to any such principle in any of the relevant cases prior to *Balston* ... Hart J in *British Midland Tool* rejected any such principle. . . .

108. What the cases show, and the parties before me agree, is that the precise point at which preparations for the establishment of a competing business by a director become unlawful will turn on the actual facts of any particular case. In each case, the touchstone for what, on the one

hand, is permissible, and what, on the other hand, is impermissible unless consent is obtained from the company or employer after full disclosure, is what, in the case of a director, will be in breach of the fiduciary duties to which I have referred or, in the case of an employee, will be in breach of the obligation of fidelity. It is obvious, for example, that merely making a decision to set up a competing business at some point in the future and discussing such an idea with friends and family would not of themselves be in conflict with the best interests of the company and the employer. The consulting of lawyers and other professionals may, depending on all the circumstances, equally be consistent with a director's fiduciary duties and the employee's obligation of loyalty. At the other end of the spectrum, it is plain that soliciting customers of the company and the employer or the actual carrying on of trade by a competing business would be in breach of the duties of the director and the obligations of the employee. It is the wide range of activity and decision making between the two ends of the spectrum which will be fact sensitive in every case. In that context, Hart J [in *British Midland Tool*] may have been too prescriptive in saying, at paragraph [89] of his judgment, that the director must resign once he has irrevocably formed the intention to engage in the future in a competing business and, without disclosing his intentions to the company, takes any preparatory steps....

127. In the light of all those matters, I am quite clear that from 12 August 2003 not only had the Individual Defendants formed the irrevocable intention to establish a business which they knew would fairly be regarded by Financial and Investments as a competitor to the business carried on by SSF, but they continued to take steps to bring into existence that rival business, contrary to what they knew were the best interests of Financial and Investments, and without the consent of those companies to do so after full disclosure of all material facts, and so in breach of their respective fiduciary duties and their obligation of fidelity. That conflict between the duties owed by the Individual Defendants to Financial (in the case of Mr Walters and Mr Hindle) and Investments (in the case of Mr Simmons), on the one hand, and the personal and private interests of the Individual Defendants, on the other hand, in the promotion of the new and rival business is exemplified by Mr Simmons' acknowledgement, in cross examination, that he found it difficult to promote 'the Shepherds product' when developing the 'new product'.

128. Further, irrespective of whether, by virtue of *Balston* and contrary to my view, there was no obligation to disclose their own individual 'preparatory' activity, I am bound by *British Midland Tool* to hold that each of the Individual Defendants was obliged, by 12 August 2003 at the latest, to disclose to Financial or Investments, as the case may be, the actual and threatened activity of the others to set up the competing business....

129. Finally, on this aspect of the case, I should record for completeness that, even if, contrary to my view, Mr Simmons was a mere employee owing no fiduciary duties to Investments, I nevertheless conclude that his conduct between 12 August 2003 and his resignation on 21 September 2003 was such as to breach his employee's duty of good faith and fidelity . . .

132. . . . As Arden LJ so clearly stated in *Item Software*, in relation to a fiduciary's duty to disclose his own misconduct to his principal, or, more generally, information of relevance and concern to his principal, the single and overriding touchstone is the fundamental duty of a director to act in what he considers in good faith to be in the best interests of the company. There is no separate and independent duty of disclosure. In the context of the director's own acts to promote a competing business, the breach of fiduciary duty is to carry out the impermissible acts of promotion without first disclosing the intention to do them and obtaining permission to do so. . . .

133. . . . [A] director who exploits after his resignation a maturing business opportunity of the company is to be treated as appropriating for himself property of the company in relation to which he had fiduciary duties. He is, accordingly, just as accountable as a trustee who retires without properly accounting for the trust property. In the case of the director, he becomes a constructive trustee of the fruits of his abuse of the company's property ...

146. Investments having established breach of fiduciary duty and breach of the obligation of fidelity by each of the Individual Defendants . . . is, on the face of it, entitled to an inquiry as to damages . . .

150. It is critical that, in order to establish a claim for damages, the loss allegedly suffered by Financial and Investments is linked to the Individual Defendants' unlawful acts rather than the mere fact of loss of senior management personnel and sales people. The Individual Defendants were entitled to resign. In general, there is no legal impediment to a number of employees deciding in concert to leave their employer and set themselves up in competition . . .

➤ Note

These 'competition' cases clearly depend on the fact that the competing opportunity is classed as a 'corporate opportunity', so these cases provide insights into the law on 'maturing business opportunities' and other tests. In this case, Etherton J devoted a good part of his judgment (not extracted here) to the factual assessment of this issue.

➤ Questions

1. Of the four 'key factors' identified in *Canaero* (earlier), which were missing in *Island Exports Finance Ltd v Umunna* and in *Balston Ltd v Headline Filters Ltd* (earlier)? Do the more modern cases such as *Foster Bryant Surveying Ltd v Bryant, Savernake Property Consultants Ltd* **[7.33]**, *Shepherds Investments Ltd v Walters* **[7.34]** and *In Plus Group Ltd v Pyke* **[7.36]** adopt the same set of 'key factors'?

2. Jane is a director of three unrelated investment companies. She is approached in confidence by two young scientists whose company needs a major injection of finance to develop a newly discovered drug. After investigating the project, she forms the view that it is likely to be a highly profitable venture for any one of the three companies. What advice should Jane be given?

3. Do these cases represent the current state of the law, applying CA 2006 ss 170(2), 175 and 239?

4. Now that we have a statutory formulation of the duties, should these cases be brought under CA 2006 s 175 (conflicts of interest) or CA 2006 s 172 (good faith for the success of the company)? Does it matter? Are the remedies different?

Remedies for breach of the conflicts rule

Only one case is extracted here because it illustrates a number of issues and also illustrates the general fact pattern often present in these cases. For the more general discussion of remedies, see 'Remedies for breach of the general duties: s 178', p 431.

Remedial options when defaulting directors pursue corporate opportunities—remedies against the director and against any corporate vehicle used to pursue the opportunity.

[7.35] CMS Dolphin Ltd v Simonet [2001] EWHC 415 (Chancery Division)

Ball and Simonet formed an advertising agency, CMS Dolphin Ltd (CMSD), financed by Ball and run by Simonet. It was permanently underfunded, and tensions grew between Ball and Simonet. On 16 April 1999, Simonet resigned as managing director and set up in business, first under the trade name Millennium, and later as Blue (GB) Ltd (Blue), with Patterson who had previously been chief executive of a company in the WPP group, the well-known international advertising agency. Following Simonet's resignation, all the staff of CMSD left to join Simonet and Patterson, and the principal clients whom Simonet had introduced to CMSD switched their business to Millennium/Blue.

LAWRENCE COLLINS J:

2. The case raises (among other questions) the existence and applicability of the principle . . . that a director is disqualified from usurping for himself or diverting to a company with which he is associated a maturing business opportunity of his company not only while he is still a director, but also even after his resignation, when the resignation may fairly be said to have been prompted or influenced by a wish to acquire for himself the opportunity sought by the company . . .

96. In my judgment the underlying basis of the liability of a director who exploits after his resignation a maturing business opportunity of the company is that the opportunity is to be treated as if it were property of the company in relation to which the director had fiduciary duties. By seeking to exploit the opportunity after resignation he is appropriating for himself that property. He is just as accountable as a trustee who retires without properly accounting for trust property. In the case of the director he becomes a constructive trustee of the fruits of his abuse of the company's property, which he has acquired in circumstances where he knowingly had a conflict of interest, and exploited it by resigning from the company.

Duty to account

97. In many cases, an account of profits will be a more advantageous remedy than equitable compensation, since the actual profits obtained by the director may be higher than the damages for the loss of opportunity suffered by the company, particularly where (as in *Industrial Development Consultants Ltd v. Cooley* and *Canadian Aero Service Ltd. v. O'Malley*) the company had little or no prospect of obtaining the benefit of the opportunity. The fiduciary is liable for the whole of the profit. There are no firm rules for determining which is the relevant profit: see *Hospital Products Ltd. v. United States Surgical Corp.* (1984) 156 C.L.R. 41, at 110, *per* Mason J. Where, as here, the business (to use a neutral term, not distinguishing between Mr Simonet and Blue) is not restricted exclusively to the performance of contracts which were obtained from CMSD, the fiduciary should be accountable for the profits properly attributable to the breach of fiduciary duty, taking into account the expenses connected with those profits and a reasonable allowance for overheads (but not necessarily salary for the wrongdoer), together with a sum to take account of other benefits derived from those contracts. For example, other contracts might not have been won, or profits made on them, without (e.g.) the opportunity or cash flow benefit which flowed from contracts unlawfully obtained. There must, however, be some reasonable connection between the breach of duty and the profits for which the fiduciary is accountable.

Effect of use of corporate vehicle

98. In this case . . . Blue is hopelessly insolvent . . . although it is said to have made profits from the contracts in question. Mr Simonet has personally made no profits, and claims that there is therefore nothing for which he should account. According to CMSD, he remains accountable for the profits. Does it make a difference to the remedy for an account of profits whether the director exploits the opportunity personally, or through a partnership, or through a company controlled by him? In particular, is there a remedy against the director where the profits are made by a company against which there is no effective remedy, because for reasons unconnected with the relevant contracts it is hopelessly insolvent? The question is one of practical importance because the case of an individual trading as such (as distinct from through a corporate vehicle) is rare in purely commercial transactions. In this case the trading was done through the Millennium partnership for about two weeks, and then through Blue . . .

100. Where the business is put into a company which is established by the directors who have wrongfully taken advantage of the corporate opportunity, it was held in *Cook v. Deeks* **[7.25]** that both the directors and the company are liable to account for profits . . .

101. In *Canadian Aero Service Ltd. v. O'Malley* it was clearly no impediment to the liability of the directors to account for profits that the contract was obtained by a company which they had formed to exploit the opportunity . . .

102. Neither *Cook v. Deeks* nor *Canadian Aero Service Ltd. v. O'Malley* was treated a case of piercing or lifting the corporate veil. The directors and their company were each liable to account. Some cases have held the director liable to account on the basis that he was to be identified with the company on a piercing or lifting the corporate veil rationale. [Then followed a discussion of various cases, but this is now overtaken by *Prest v Petrodel Resources Ltd* **[2.01]**.] . . .

103. . . . But I do not think that it is necessary to resort to piercing or lifting the corporate veil, since *Cook v. Deeks* shows clearly (as does *Canadian Aero Service Ltd. v. O'Malley*) that the directors are equally liable with the corporate vehicle formed by them to take unlawful advantage of the business opportunities. The reason is that they have jointly participated in the breach of trust.

104. Nor in my judgment does it make a difference whether the business is taken up by the corporate vehicle directly, or is first taken up by the directors and then transferred to a company . . .

Remedies

140. As regards the allegation of unlawful diversion of the business opportunities of CMSD, CMSD is entitled (at its option) to equitable compensation or an account of profits . . . from Mr Simonet, not only in respect of profits made by him in the short period in which he and Mr Patterson traded as Millennium, but also for the period they traded as Blue. What Mr Simonet diverted was not simply such business as gave rise to profits in the period that Millennium traded. He diverted the benefit of the existing Argos and DFB contracts and the opportunities that were associated with them and with the Reebok connection. CMSD does not seek an account for any period beyond 1999, and there are therefore no difficult issues of connection and causation . . . It is implicit in this exercise that Mr Simonet is entitled to credit for the expenses incurred by Millennium/Blue in earning the profits including a reasonable proportion of overhead, and I will hear argument as to whether that should include salary paid to Mr Simonet and Mr Patterson, and as to whether any other points of principle will arise on the taking of an account . . .

142. . . . If there had been no effective remedy in relation to the allegations of breach of fiduciary duty, I would have held that the breach of the duty of fidelity (which would have involved the acquisition of the Argos, Reebok and DFB accounts) would have justified the remedy of an account of profits and not simply damages. In *Att. Gen. v. Blake* [2000] 3 WLR 625, 639 (H.L.) Lord Nicholls said that one of the exceptional circumstances which would justify a restitutionary remedy for breach of contract was the characterisation of a contractual obligation as fiduciary and a finding that the claimant has a legitimate interest in preventing the profit-making activity of the defendant. This is such a case . . .

➤ Note

Lawrence Collins J suggests that the corporate opportunity (here, the 'maturing business opportunity') is treated as the company's property, and trustee-type remedies follow if the directors misuse that property. Note that not every opportunity is a 'corporate opportunity'; it is still necessary to decide first whether pursuit of *this* venture by the directors is in breach of their duty of loyalty. Remember, too, that in making this assessment it is irrelevant that pursuit of the opportunity by the company itself might have been legally or practically impossible.

➤ Questions

1. The defaulting director has to account for the profits made in breach of his or her duty to avoid conflicts. A constructive trust over the whole business venture, forever, is rarely warranted—this is not the proper measure of the 'profit' that the director has made *from the breach* (but see *Cook v Deeks* **[7.25]**, *Regal (Hastings)* **[7.26]**). If the director accounts in money, the net profits generated by the opportunity are usually demanded for a period of time. Which of the cases extracted earlier take this approach? How is the time period assessed? How are the 'net profits' assessed—in particular, why do some cases allow the directors to claim a salary, and others do not?

2. The orthodox equitable remedy awarded against directors (or other fiduciaries) who engage in conflicts of interest is to strip profits from them, not to award compensation to the company for breach of a 'duty' (now see CA 2006 ss 175 and 178). Breach of the obligation to act bona fide and in the interests of the company, by contrast, attracts the remedy of equitable compensation (now see CA 2006 ss 171, 172 and 178). Does this mean, in practice, that there is always a choice of profits disgorgement or compensation in any case of corporate opportunities? Can the injured company have *both*?

3. When the defaulting director uses a new company to pursue the opportunity, Lawrence Collins J suggested both the director and the company would be liable, either because the corporate veil might be lifted (now doubtful, given *Prest v Petrodel Resources Ltd* **[2.01]**) or because the company had knowingly participated in a breach of duty. Does the choice of legal analysis affect the *quantum* of liability of either the director or the new company? Are the director and the new company each liable for the *same amount* (whether profits disgorgement or compensation)? Is this appropriate? What is the outcome if the new company is a 'real' company with innocent shareholders?

Conflicts of duty and duty

Section 175(7) makes it clear that a conflict of interest includes conflicts of interest and duty and conflicts of duties. The general equitable rule prohibits a fiduciary from entering into a position which gives rise to conflicting fiduciary duties to another person, without the informed consent of both principals (*Clark Boyce v Mouat* [1994] 1 AC 428). The statutory formulation adopts this equitable rule (see *In Plus Group Ltd v Pyke* **[7.36]**), and discards the controversial approach found in various earlier authorities, including *Bell v Lever Bros Ltd* [1932] AC 161, HL, which had suggested that a director of one company may be a director of competing companies unless prohibited by contract, and provided other legal rules were not breached (in respect of confidential information, etc). This treated directors more leniently than employees, was arguably inconsistent with the equitable rule on conflict of duties, and now also with CA 2006. But a conflict is required before there is a breach, and sometimes that can be disputed. The next case is unusual, but airs some of the concerns in this area, and is a rare Court of Appeal authority on a difficult issue.

Since conflicting multiple directorships may now be caught by the duty to avoid conflicts of duty and duty, these appointments will need to be authorised according to the process outlined in s 175(5) and (6).

[7.36] In Plus Group Ltd v Pyke [2002] EWCA Civ 370 (Court of Appeal)

The company, In Plus Group Ltd, was controlled by two men, Pyke and Plank, its only directors and members. When the business relationship between Pyke and Plank deteriorated, Pyke was entirely excluded from the management of the company. He was refused access to financial records, no longer received his monthly payments from the company and his office was relocated without consultation or notice. With neither job nor income, Pyke established a new company and started doing business with Constructive, one of the company's major clients. The claimants argued that this competition with the company amounted to a breach of Pyke's fiduciary duties to it, and they sought an account of Pyke's profits.

BROOKE LJ: . . . There is no completely rigid rule that a director may not be involved in the business of a company which is in competition with another company of which he was a director. [He then considered the controversial cases of *London and Mashonaland Exploration Co Ltd v New Mashonaland Exploration Co Ltd* [1891] WN 165 and *Bell v Lever Bros Ltd* (see earlier), and noted the criticisms of these cases, but continued:], It is unnecessary on the present occasion to resolve this controversy, because the facts of the present case are so unusual . . .

In the present case Mr Pyke, who was a sick man following his stroke, had been effectively expelled from the companies of which he was a director more than six months before any of the events occurred of which the claimants now make complaint. Although he had invested a very large sum of money in the first and second claimants on interest free loan accounts, he was not being permitted to withdraw any of it. At the same time he was being denied any remuneration from the companies. When he entered into business with Constructive in the autumn of 1997 he was not using any of the claimants' property for the purpose of that business. Nor was he making use of any confidential information which had come to him as a director of any of the companies.

In these circumstances I consider that the judge was right when he held that Mr Pyke committed no breach of fiduciary duty in trading with Constructive . . .

SEDLEY LJ [after repeating the conclusions and criticisms of *Mashonaland* and *Bell v Lever Bros*, continued]:

The problem is obvious if one thinks of how shareholders in X Ltd or X plc, or for that matter its creditors, would regard a director who used his boardroom vote, perhaps crucially, in a way which helped a competitor, when the competitor was the director himself or another company of which he was also a director. Whatever the perceived commercial morality of such a situation, I do not consider that it is sanctioned by law. The fiduciary duty of a director to his company is uniform and universal. What vary infinitely are the elements of fact and degree which determine whether the duty has been breached. If Mr Pyke's solicitors' view of the law is as widely held as it seems to be, it needs to be revised. They wrote this:

'The authorities are quite clear that it is no breach of any fiduciary duty to be involved with a business either of the same kind or in competition with the company of which he is a director.'

Counsel have put before us what three of the leading modern textbooks say about this received view of the law. The authors' and editors' views range from the dubious to the sceptical. [He then cited from two of them, and continued:]

Gower's Principles of Modern Company Law [says this]:

'**Competing with the company**. One of the most obvious examples of a situation which might be expected to give rise to a conflict between a director's interests and his duties is where he carries on or is associated with a business competing with that of the company. [After criticising the authorities:]

In arguing that a director who carries on a business which competes with that of his company inevitably places himself in a position where his personal interest will conflict with his duty to the company, it is not being contended that he will necessarily have breached his fiduciary duty; he will not if the company has consented so long as he observes his subjective duty to the company by subordinating his interests to those of the company. Nor is it being suggested that there is anything objectionable in his holding other directorships so long as all the companies have consented if their businesses compete. But in both cases consent is unlikely if he is a full-time executive director or if the extent of the competition is substantial. And even if the consent is given the director is likely to be faced with constant difficulties in avoiding breaches of his subjective duty of good faith to the company or companies concerned. He may be able to subordinate his personal interests to those of a single company but it is less easy to reconcile conflicting duties to more than one company. Nor would a reformed rule be inconsistent with the modern emphasis on a more important role for non-executive directors, who are often executive directors of other companies. Even if executive directors are regarded as a good source of non-executive talent for other companies (which some would question), a reformed rule would simply require executive directors not to become non-executive or competing companies, which they are, in fact, rarely asked to become.'

If one bears in mind the high standard of probity which equity demands of fiduciaries, and the reliance which shareholders and creditors are entitled to place upon it, the *Mashonaland* principle is a very limited one. If, for example, the two Mashonaland Exploration companies had been preparing to tender for the same contract, I doubt whether Lord Mayo's position [he was the common director] would have been tenable, at least in the absence of special arrangements to insulate either company from the conflict of his interests and duties, for I see no reason why the law should assume that any directorship is merely cosmetic. A directorship brings with it not only voting rights and emoluments but responsibilities of stewardship and honesty, and those who cannot discharge them should not become or remain directors.

All the foregoing concerns breach of fiduciary duty. From such a breach, appropriate remedies will follow. But both common sense and equity indicate that it is not necessary to wait for a breach giving rise to a remedy before the possibility of intervention arises . . .

Without the need of any proven breach, the court will set aside a transaction entered into in the shadow of such a conflict. It will also in an appropriate case restrain entry into such a transaction or restrain the director from involving himself in it. The distinction . . . between a director's putting himself into a position of conflict and his being in breach of fiduciary duty is of course legally correct and is relevant to remedies; but it does not mean that a director can cheerfully go to the brink so long as he does not fall over the edge. It means that if he finds himself in a position of conflict he must resolve it openly or extract himself from it . . .

In this situation the room in the present case for absolving Mr Pyke was very limited indeed. . . .

. . . Quite exceptionally, the defendant's duty to the claimants had been reduced to vanishing point by the acts (explicable and even justifiable though they may have been) of his sole fellow director and fellow shareholder Mr Plank. Accepting as I do that the claimants' relationship with Constructive was consistent with successful poaching on Mr Pyke's part, the critical fact is that it was done in a situation in which the dual role which is the necessary predicate of Mr Yell's case is absent. The defendant's role as a director of the claimants was throughout the relevant period entirely nominal, not in the sense in which a non-executive director's position might (probably wrongly) be called nominal but in the concrete sense that he was entirely excluded from all decision-making and all participation in the claimant company's affairs. For all the influence he had, he might as well have resigned.

For the rest, I agree with the judgments of my Lords . . .

JONATHAN PARKER LJ: I agree with the order proposed by Brooke LJ, for the reasons which he has given.

I further agree with him that this is not an appropriate case in which to examine the scope and application of what Sedley LJ refers to as the *Mashonaland* principle . . .

➤ Questions

1. By bundling up conflicts of interest and duty and conflicts of duty and duty in the same provision (s 175), is CA 2006 likely to encourage a hardening of the courts' approach to the latter types of conflicts?

2. Consider the remedies available in breach of duty and duty cases. The defaulting director may of course be required to disgorge any disloyal profits (eg fees from the second directorship). But this is usually not the principal complaint of the disgruntled company: it is more likely to be concerned with the losses it may have suffered from biased advice given to it by its disloyal director (biased because of the director's conflicting loyalties). For *this* breach (of the duty in s 171(b) or perhaps s 172, 173 or 174), the company can recover compensation.

Duty not to accept benefits from third parties: CA 2006 s 176

For directors, this provision reformulates and replaces the equitable principle that fiduciaries must not accept bribes or secret commissions (*Attorney General for Hong Kong v Reid* [1994] 1 AC 324, PC, although that is not a company case).

Several points are worth noting:

(i) To the extent that the pre-statute equitable 'no profits' rule applying to directors was regarded as independent of, rather than a subset of, the 'no conflicts' rule,[76] CA 2006 s 176 denies that approach: the statutory rule is not infringed if acceptance of the benefit cannot reasonably be regarded as likely to give rise to a conflict of interest (s 176(4)). That seems appropriate. These equitable and statutory duties are designed to deliver loyal service from the company's directors—that is, service where the director favours the company's interests, not his own[77]—and to do that by ensuring the director does not profit from disloyalty; the remedy is therefore, appropriately, disgorgement of any benefits disloyally obtained.

(ii) 'Benefits' are not defined in CA 2006. During parliamentary debates on the Bill, the Solicitor-General said: 'In using the word "benefit", we intend the ordinary dictionary meaning of the word. The *Oxford English Dictionary* defines it as "a favourable or helpful factor, circumstance, advantage or profit"' (HC Comm D, 11/7/06, cols 621–622). A benefit may be financial or non-financial, of any shape or size, although s 176(4) ensures that trivial benefits are not caught by the provision, and s 176(3) covers payment of normal salary and benefits.

(iii) The most significant difference between s 175 (no conflict) and this section (s 176, no benefits from third parties) is that there is no provision for authorisation by the board of directors. Of course, the company's articles could (although it is most unlikely) contain specific provisions concerning benefits from third parties (see s 180(4)(b) and s 232(4): provisions protecting directors from liability).

---

[76] See fn 58.

[77] That tension necessarily connotes a conflict between duty to the company and personal interest. Indeed, of all the cases in this area, the only one which arguably does not demonstrate that conflict—ie the director taking for himself what, if taken at all, should have been taken for his company—is, surprisingly, *Attorney General for Hong Kong v Reid* [1994] 1 AC 324, PC. Of course, the prosecutor in that case committed a wrong, and disgorgement was the appropriate remedy, but whether the wrong and the remedy should have been characterised as disloyal *fiduciary* (conflicts) breaches seems debatable.

Alternatively, s 180(4)(a) (consent, approval and authorisation by members) may apply, but see the following Questions. Finally, the members may ratify the receipt under s 239 (ratification of acts of directors): again, see the following Questions.

➤ Questions

1. What 'benefits' received by directors will be assessed under this section rather than under s 175? Both sections require a conflict (ss 175(4) and 176(4)). Both sections require a 'benefit' in the director's hands: this is the benefit which is required to be disgorged on proof of breach. Is the difference that the 'benefits' contemplated under s 175 are all derived from dealings in the company's 'property' (*exceedingly* loosely conceived of, so as to include information and corporate opportunities), whereas the 'benefits' contemplated under s 176 are likely to be derived from disloyal 'services' provided by the director to the third party (bribes or secret commissions to steer deals a particular way, etc)? Clearly not: see the duty and duty cases in s 175(7), which might on that approach be s 176 cases. If the answer is not clear, then should the authorisation mechanisms be the same? Does the answer to this question matter?

2. Section 176 does not provide for board authorisation as a 'whitewashing' procedure. If the board *did* consent (in the manner fully set out in s 175(5)–(6)), could anyone obtain a remedy against the director for breach of duty? Would such authorisation comply with the exceptions in s 180?

3. The authorisation and ratification procedures for members (ss 180 and 239) expressly import any general law restrictions on granting pre-transaction approval or post-event ratification (see ss 180(4)(a) and 239(7)). Does the general law prevent members approving or ratifying a director's receipt of benefits from third parties? Are there any s 175 conflicts that could not be authorised or ratified?

4. If a director as employee of company A accepts bribes from company B, and company A is found guilty under the Bribery Act 2010 s 7, can company A then claim against the director under s 176? Or under any other section? Accordingly, is it reasonable to argue that s 176 will now be more readily used because, with the Bribery Act regime in place, companies are more motivated to investigate and pursue against their directors (who are often employees of the companies) suspected of receiving bribes?

Duty to declare an interest in a proposed or existing transaction or arrangement: CA 2006 ss 177 and 182

Section 177 is the third of the general provisions designed to reformulate and codify the fiduciary duties owed by directors. It deals with conflicts of interest in *proposed* transactions or arrangements *with* the company. Directors with direct or indirect[78] interests in transactions proposed by the company must declare to the other directors the nature and extent of those interests, unless it is an interest, or involves a transaction, of which the director is unaware.

---

[78] Note that this means that the director need not necessarily be a party to the deal for the transaction or arrangement to be subject to this section.

Section 180 then makes it clear that, *subject to the company's constitution*, if directors comply with s 177, the transaction is not liable to be set aside by virtue of the usual equitable rule requiring the consent of the company's members. This is the significant reform introduced by this provision.

Failure to comply with s 177 constitutes a breach of duty, for which the purely civil remedies in s 178 apply. If the company then enters into the impugned transaction, the director is under a new and continuing duty to disclose, expressed in substantially similar terms in s 182 (declaration of interest in existing transaction or arrangement). Breach of s 182 is an offence (s 183).[79] Why the two regimes need to be separated at all, or by three intervening provisions, is not clear. (On s 182, see 'Declarations of interest in existing transactions or arrangements: ss 182–187', pp 462ff.)

Under various subsections in s 177, directors are treated as being aware of matters of which they ought to be aware; declarations must be updated if necessary; the form of disclosure is not prescribed, but may be made at a meeting of directors, by notice in writing, or by general notice. The articles may impose further requirements. Certain exceptions exist; all are reflected in existing common law rules. These apply where there is no reasonable likelihood of a conflict (*Cowan de Groot Properties Ltd v Eagle Trust plc* [1991] BCLC 1045); where the other directors are already aware or ought reasonably to be aware of the interest; and where the interest concerns service contracts which have been, or are to be, considered by a meeting of directors or by a remuneration committee (*Runciman v Walter Runciman plc* [1992] BCLC 1084). A fourth exception, not included in the section but recognised in s 186, is that the director of a company with only one director is not required to make a declaration to himself, although the terms of these arrangements must be set out in writing or recorded in the minutes (s 231).

If a director enters into a transaction or arrangement with the company in breach of s 177 (ie without making the appropriate declaration to the directors), then the transaction is voidable.[80] For the ramifications of this, see the Note following the next extract. The more general issues relating to remedies are discussed at 'General issues', pp 431ff.

For the impact of possible authorisation or ratification by the members, see 'Ratification of acts of directors: CA 2006 s 239', pp 454ff.

Transactions between the company and its directors (or a company with which the directors are associated) are voidable at the option of the company unless approved by the company.

[7.37] Aberdeen Rly Co v Blaikie Bros (1854) 1 Macq 461 (House of Lords)

The respondents, Blaikie Bros, had agreed to manufacture iron chairs for the railway company at £8.50 per ton, and sued to enforce the contract. The railway company pleaded that it was not bound by the contract because, at the time when it was made, the chairman of its board of directors was also managing partner of the respondents. This plea was upheld by the House of Lords.

LORD CRANWORTH LC: This, therefore, brings us to the general question, whether a director of a railway company is or is not precluded from dealing on behalf of the company with himself, or with a firm in which he is a partner.

The directors are a body to whom is delegated the duty of managing the general affairs of the company.

---

[79] So, in practice, retaining the criminal sanctions imposed by the predecessor provision, CA 1985 s 317.
[80] See *Hely-Hutchinson v Brayhead Ltd* [1968] 1 QB 549, CA **[3.04]**; and *Guinness plc v Saunders*, HL **[5.01]**.

A corporate body can only act by agents, and it is of course the duty of those agents so to act as best to promote the interests of the corporation whose affairs they are conducting. Such agents have duties to discharge of a fiduciary nature towards their principal.[81] And it is a rule of universal application that no one, having such duties to discharge, shall be allowed to enter into engagements in which he has, or can have, a personal interest conflicting, or which possibly may conflict, with the interests of those whom he is bound to protect.

So strictly is this principle adhered to that no question is allowed to be raised as to the fairness or unfairness of a contract so entered into.

It obviously is, or may be, impossible to demonstrate how far in any particular case the terms of such a contract have been the best for the interest of the *cestui que trust*, which it was possible to obtain.

It may sometimes happen that the terms on which a trustee has dealt or attempted to deal with the estate or interest of those for whom he is a trustee, have been as good as could have been obtained from any other person—they may even at the time have been better.

But still so inflexible is the rule that no inquiry on that subject is permitted. The English authorities on this head are numerous and uniform.

The principle was acted on by Lord King in *Keech v Sandford*,[82] and by Lord Hardwicke in *Whelpdale v Cookson*,[83] and the whole subject was considered by Lord Eldon on a great variety of occasions . . .

It is true that the questions have generally arisen on agreements for purchases or leases of land, and not, as here, on a contract of a mercantile character. But this can make no difference in principle. The inability to contract depends not on the subject-matter of the agreement, but on the fiduciary character of the contracting party, and I cannot entertain a doubt of its being applicable to the case of a party who is acting as manager of a mercantile or trading business for the benefit of others, no less than to that of an agent or trustee employed in selling or letting land.

Was then Mr Blaikie so acting in the case now before us?—If he was, did he while so acting contract on behalf of those for whom he was acting with himself?

Both these questions must obviously be answered in the affirmative. Mr Blaikie was not only a director, but (if that was necessary) the chairman of the directors. In that character it was his bounden duty to make the best bargains he could for the benefit of the company.

While he filled that character, namely, on 6 February 1846, he entered into a contract on behalf of the company with his own firm, for the purchase of a large quantity of iron chairs at a certain stipulated price. His duty to the company imposed on him the obligation of obtaining these chairs at the lowest possible price.

His personal interest would lead him to an entirely opposite direction, would induce him to fix the price as high as possible. This is the very evil against which the rule in question is directed, and here I see nothing whatever to prevent its application.

I observe that Lord Fullerton seemed to doubt whether the rule would apply where the party whose act or contract is called in question is only one of a body of directors, not a sole trustee or manager.

But, with all deference, this appears to me to make no difference. It was Mr Blaikie's duty to give to his co-directors, and through them to the company, the full benefit of all the knowledge and skill which he could bring to bear on the subject. He was bound to assist them in getting the articles contracted for at the cheapest possible rate. As far as related to the advice he should give

---

[81] *York and North Midland Rly Co v Hudson* (1853) 16 Beav 485.
[82] (1726) Sel Cas Ch 61.
[83] (1747) 1 Ves Sen 9.

them, he put his interest in conflict with his duty, and whether he was the sole director or only one of many, can make no difference in principle.

The same observation applies to the fact that he was not the sole person contracting with the company; he was one of the firm of Blaikie Brothers, with whom the contract was made, and so interested in driving as hard a bargain with the company as he could induce them to make . . .

LORD BROUGHAM delivered a concurring opinion.

> Questions

1. Given the reasons for the strict rule set out in this case, is the approach adopted in CA 2006 s 177 warranted? Will the company get 'the full benefit of all the knowledge and skill which [the director] could bring to bear on the subject'?

2. The traditional equitable rule was that disclosure must be to the members; disclosure to a disinterested quorum of directors was insufficient (unless the articles provided otherwise, which they usually did). This is now amended by s 177. Is the approach in s 177 the more principled one in any event? Directors owe their fiduciary duties to the company, so the *company* must consent to any potential conflicts, and cases such as *John Shaw & Sons (Salford) Ltd v Shaw* [4.07] suggest that where there is a board of directors capable of acting, it and it alone is competent to make business decisions for the company.

> Note

In these cases where the director's breach involves a contract *with* the company, the contract is voidable at the option of the company. It follows that the company will lose its right to rescind, on general contractual principles, if it has affirmed the transaction, or cannot make proper restitution (*restitutio in integrum*), or the rights of a third party would be adversely affected.

On orthodox principles, rescission is the *only* remedy (unless the director has also infringed some other rule that will deliver an alternative), and if rescission is no longer possible for any reason, then the court will not intervene. The cases dealing with promoters, for example *Erlanger v New Sombrero Phosphate Co* [8.06] and *Re Cape Breton Co* (Note 3 following *Gluckstein v Barnes* [8.07], p 504), confirm this. Also see *Cook v Deeks* [7.25]. Even though impugned contracts between the director and the company are an illustration of the 'no conflict' duty, for which directors are typically required to disgorge the profits they have made (holding them on constructive trust for the company, see *FHR European Ventures* [7.39] and *JJ Harrison (Properties) Ltd v Harrison* [7.40]), the courts in these cases say that the director's profit is 'unquantifiable' since that would involve the courts fixing a new contract price for the parties. Given all the other situations in which courts are content to make commercial assessments of value, this seems precious.

And if the courts will not give a 'profits' remedy for breach of the fiduciary duty, few options remain. The company cannot sue the director for breach of the contract, because by definition the contract is either affirmed (not breached) or rescinded (so rendered totally ineffective from the outset). The only option is to avoid (rescind) the contract and seek a personal (monetary) restitutionary remedy; this practice seems to be becoming increasingly acceptable.[84]

---

[84] See J Poole and A Keyser, 'Justifying Partial Rescission in English Law' (2005) 121 LQR 273.

Remedies for breach of the general duties: CA 2006 s 178

The remedies for breach of directors' duties have not been codified, despite the recommendations of the Law Commissions. CA 2006 s 178 preserves the existing civil consequences of breach (or threatened breach) of any of the general duties. If the statutory duty departs from its equitable equivalent, the court will have to identify the equivalent rule and apply the same consequences and remedies. For the avoidance of doubt, s 179 makes the obvious point that more than one of the general duties may apply in any given case.

General issues

Remedial options

The remedial options for breach of the director's general duties may include:

(i)   injunctions and declarations (generally only when the breach is still threatened)—available for breach of any of the general duties;

(ii) common law damages or equitable compensation (whichever is appropriate) where the company has suffered loss—available for breach of ss 171–174;[85]

(iii) personal remedy of disgorgement of profits ('an account of profits') made by the director—available for breach of ss 175 and 176;

(iv) proprietary remedy of disgorgement of profits, requiring restoration of specific property following a declaration that particular assets (being the disloyal profits or their proceeds) are held by the director on constructive trust for the company—available for breach of ss 175 and 176; or

(v)   rescission of a contract (or, alternatively, perhaps 'pecuniary rescission') where the director failed to disclose a conflicting interest in a contract with the company—available for breach of s 177.

Note, however, that claims may be subject to limitation periods (see later) and there are also avenues for relief from liability, either in whole or in part: see especially s 1157 (see 'Relief from liability granted by the court: CA 2006 s 1157', p 460) but note too the avenues internal to the company (see 'Relief from liability', p 452ff).

Several of these remedies deserve specific comment before reading the relevant case extracts.

Equitable compensation

Equitable compensation is awarded to compensate for loss caused by the director's breach of the equitable (and now the analogous statutory) duties to exercise powers within their terms, for proper purposes, bona fide, and independently (ie the equitable equivalents of ss 171–173). Common law damages are awarded for breach of the statutory equivalents of common law duties (the duty to exercise reasonable care and skill, comply with contractual engagements, and perhaps compliance with the terms of the company's constitution—ie ss 171(a) and 174).

The orthodox view is that equitable compensation is not available for breach of 'fiduciary duties' strictly labelled—that is, the equitable no conflict and no profit rules. Common

---

[85] CA 2006 does not spell out whether the remedies for breach of s 174 (duty to exercise reasonable care, skill and diligence) should be assessed on common law or equitable principles. Arguably it is the former, given the exclusion of s 174 in s 178(2). This would lay to rest the debates in that area (*Henderson v Merrett Syndicates Ltd* [1995] 2 AC 145; *Bristol & West Building Society v Mothew* [1998] Ch 1).

assertions to the contrary usually mean only that, on the facts, both fiduciary and other duties have been breached, and disgorgement is available for the former and compensation for the latter (or an election between the two if claiming both would require reliance on in-consistent claims). For example, misuse of the company's property may involve a conflict of duty and interest (for which profits are recoverable) *and* a breach of the duty to act within the authority granted, bona fide and/or for proper purposes (for which equitable compensation is recoverable, even if the director has not made a profit from the misuse[86]): if both are available, the company must elect between these two inconsistent claims.[87] Equally, a self-dealing transaction may also involve an actionable non-disclosure: see *Gwembe Valley Development Co Ltd v Koshy (No 3)* **[7.41]**.[88]

If equitable compensation is available, the loss is measured at the time of the trial and must—as you would expect—be causally related to the breach (*AIB Group (UK) Plc v Mark Redler & Co Solicitors* [2014] UKSC 58, SC;[89] and *Target Holdings Ltd v Redferns* [1996] 1 AC 421, both cases concerning fiduciary obligations of solicitors, not directors).

Disgorgement of profits—personal remedy

This is also called an 'account of profits'.[90] The practical issues in assessing the remedy typically concern precise quantification of the profits to be disgorged, and assessment of any equitable allowance which should be granted to the director.

A director is only liable for profits made *as a result of* the disloyalty. The most detailed explanation of how this line should be drawn comes from the Australian High Court in *Warman International Ltd v Dwyer* (cited extensively in *Murad* **[7.38]**). In addition, direc-tors are liable only for profits made personally, not for profits made by others, unless the latter wider claim can be brought under some other head of liability, for example know-ing receipt, dishonest assistance or partnership law. Where disloyal directors 'hide' their disloyal profits in wholly owned companies rather than receiving them personally, their companies are readily required to disgorge (see *Cook v Deeks* **[7.25]** and Chapter 2). On the more general issues, see especially *Regal (Hastings) Ltd v Gulliver* **[7.26]** and *Ultraframe (UK) Ltd v Fielding* **[7.49]**.

Disloyalty is not always dishonest. *Boardman v Phipps*,[91] although not a company case, is typically cited to illustrate a fiduciary's bona fide concern for the welfare of the trust, despite the court's finding of breach of the conflicts rules. In that case an allowance 'on a liberal scale' was awarded to the defaulting fiduciaries by way of compensation for their efforts in generating the profits which were now required to be disgorged to the beneficiar-ies. Similarly, see *Warman International Ltd v Dwyer* (cited extensively in *Murad* **[7.38]**). By contrast, a far more restrictive approach was taken in *Guinness v Saunders* **[5.01]**, where

---

[86] The two non-company cases which provide the underlying principles for assessment of equitable compensa-tion demonstrate just this scenario: *AIB Group (UK) Plc v Mark Redler & Co Solicitors* [2014] UKSC 58, SC; *Target Holdings Ltd v Redferns* [1996] AC 421, HL. And the non-company cases illustrating the advantages of disgorgement claims in these circumstances is of course *Foskett v McKeown* [2001] 1 AC 102, HL.

[87] *Tang Man Sit v Capacious Investments Ltd* [1996] AC 415, PC.

[88] In this case Mummery LJ did raise, but not answer, the question whether equitable compensation is available if the *only* breach is of the no conflict or no profit rules. It is, however, difficult to think of facts which would give rise to this problem.

[89] See especially [47]–[77] (Lord Toulson JSC) and [90]–[138] (Lord Reed JSC). Also see *Libertarian Investment Ltd v Hall* (2013) 16 HKCFAR 681 (HK Court of Final Appeal), especially [84]–[96] (Ribeiro PJ) and [166]–[175] (Lord Millett NPJ).

[90] 'Account' is simply an equitable remedy requiring the trustee (and perhaps other fiduciaries) to give an account of their dealings with trust property, and on the basis of that information and proof of wrongdoing the trustees will be subjected to remedies (required to account) by restoring trust property, paying compensation or effecting disgorgement of profits as appropriate. Remedies of 'account' thus cover restoration, compensation and disgorgement remedies as appropriate for the particular wrongdoing.

[91] *Boardman v Phipps* [1967] 2 AC 46, HL: see Note 1 following *Peso Silver Mines Ltd (NPL) v Cropper* **[7.28]**, p 397.

no allowance at all was allowed, despite all the work clearly done. Similarly, see *Murad v Al-Saraj* **[7.38]**.

Disgorgement of profits—proprietary remedy

For too long there was both judicial and academic dispute over whether disloyal directors held the profits of their disloyalty on constructive trust for the company, always assuming 'the profits' which had to be disgorged were identifiable as an asset which *could* be held on trust. The answer is now clear—such profits are held on constructive trust: see *FHR European Ventures LLP v Cedar Capital Partners LLC* **[7.39]**; and no difficult distinctions need to be drawn between different types if disloyal gains.

FHR was a 'bribe case'—or, less pejoratively—the fiduciary here had received a secret commission from the vendor while acting as the purchaser's agent. The case was argued on the basis that if the disgorgement remedy in these circumstances was proprietary, then it was proprietary in all cases where disloyal profits could be identified as an asset (or assets) capable of being held on constructive trust. In reaching this conclusion, the Supreme Court approved of the outcome in *A-G for Hong Kong v Reid* [1994] 1 AC 324, PC, and overruled *Lister & Co v Stubbs* (1890) 45 Ch D 1, CA, and *Sinclair Investments (UK) Ltd v Versailles Trade Finance Ltd* [2011] EWCA Civ 347, [2012] Ch 453, CA.

The constructive trust remedy is available in self-dealing transactions (ie where defaulting directors deal with their own companies and the contract is rescinded, see the following section) and in conflicts cases (where directors deal with third parties and take a corporate opportunity: see *Cook v Deeks* **[7.25]**).

In the latter cases (the corporate opportunity cases), however, a personal disgorgement remedy (an account of profits—see earlier) will necessarily be adopted whenever the proprietary disgorgement remedy by way of constructive trust would overcompensate the company given the real extent of the profit arising from the breach (see the discussion in *Murad* **[7.38]** of the approach taken by the Australian High Court in *Warman International Ltd v Dwyer*). Alternatively, the constructive trust remedy can be moderated by permitting 'a liberal allowance' for the fiduciary's input in generating the profit (see *Boardman v Phipps* [1967] 2 AC 46, HL, but contrast *Guinness plc v Saunders* **[5.01]**).

Rescission

There are no company-specific problems in this area, although the law on rescission is not necessarily straightforward. For illustrations of the remedy, see *Cook v Deeks* **[7.25]** explaining the incidence of rescission. Also see the Note following *Aberdeen Rly Co v Blaikie Bros* **[7.37]**, p 430. For an example of its application, see *JJ Harrison (Properties) Ltd v Harrison* **[7.40]**, noting that there the asset bought by the director under the voidable contract with his company was land, which he later sold, so the claim against the director was for this sum (representing the traceable proceeds of the land/the profits he had derived from his unauthorised/disloyal purchase).

Limitation periods

The normal limitation period for breach of directors' duties is six years (whether common law, equitable or specifically fiduciary), unless the Limitation Act 1980 s 21(1) applies (extracted below), in which case there is no limitation. See *JJ Harrison (Properties) Ltd v Harrison* **[7.40]**; and *Gwembe Valley Development Co Ltd v Koshy (No 3)* **[7.41]**) (this case contains a long and informative analysis of limitation periods). For the purpose of this Act, directors are treated as if they were trustees, even though they do not hold assets on trust for the company.

A company may also want to make claims against third parties. In this regard, the scope of Limitation Act 1980 s 21(1) was given detailed scrutiny by the Supreme Court in *Williams v Central Bank of Nigeria* [2014] UKSC 10, [2014] AC 1189. The issues was whether a dishonest assister in a breach of trust and/or a knowing recipient of trust assets falls under the s 21(1)(a) exception so that no limitation period applies. The answer was no: the limitation period is six years. Lord Sumption and Lord Neuberger, giving judgment for the majority, held that the words 'trust' and 'trustee' in s 21(1)(a) bore their orthodox meaning and did not include a constructive trust or a third party who was liable to account in equity because of dishonest assistance or knowing receipt. Further, the words 'party or privy' to a fraud or fraudulent breach of trust within s 21(1)(a) were to be narrowly construed and applied only to claims brought against trustees and not to claims brought against third parties who were involved in the breach of trust. Thus, the six-year limitation period applies to a claim against third parties for dishonest assistance and/or knowing receipt.

Limitation Act 1980 s 21

21 Time limit for actions in respect of trust property

(1) No period of limitation prescribed by this Act shall apply to an action by a beneficiary under a trust, being an action—

(a) in respect of any fraud or fraudulent breach of trust to which the trustee was a party or privy; or

(b) to recover from the trustee trust property or the proceeds of trust property in the possession of the trustee, or previously received by the trustee and converted to his use.

(2) [Omitted as immaterial]

(3) Subject to the preceding provisions of this section, an action by a beneficiary to recover trust property or in respect of any breach of trust, not being an action for which a limitation period is prescribed by any other provision of this Act, shall not be brought after the expiration of six years from the date on which the right of action accrued....

And section 36 preserves, except as indicated specifically in the statute, the cases in which a court of equity would have applied the statutory limitation periods by analogy.

Specific examples

Many of the cases throughout this chapter include a discussion of the relevant remedial issues. See especially *Cook v Deeks* **[7.25]**; *Regal (Hastings) Ltd v Gulliver* **[7.26]**; *In Plus Group Ltd v Pyke* **[7.36]**; *CMS Dolphin Ltd v Simonet* **[7.35]**; *Ultraframe (UK) Ltd v Fielding* **[7.49]**, at [1511]–[1576]; and *Murad v Al-Saraj* **[7.38]**.

Murad v Al-Saraj **[7.38]** repays careful reading. The extract here is one of the longest in this chapter, but illustrates and helps to explain many of the more significant problems in this area, and summarises the relevant earlier precedents. Note, in particular, on disgorgement claims, the irrelevance of the fact that the company could not have made the profit now being claimed from the director or that the company would have given consent if requested; note also the deterrence function, the objective to strip profits and the problems in identifying the relevant profits.

The disgorgement remedy—issues of causation and quantification.

[7.38] Murad v Al-Saraj [2005] EWCA Civ 959 (Court of Appeal)

Westwood (W) was a company owned by Al-Saraj (S). S had proposed to the Murads (M), who were two sisters, that they should together buy a hotel for £4.1 million, S contributing

£500,000 to the purchase price, M contributing £1 million and the balance being borrowed from a bank. M and W entered into an agreement regulating the distribution of the proceeds of sale pro rata according to their initial contributions (ie 1/3:2/3). The hotel was purchased by a company (D) owned by S and M. The hotel was subsequently sold for a profit of £2 million. In proceedings by M the judge held that there had been a fiduciary relationship between S and M in relation to the joint venture to buy the hotel and that S had fraudulently misrepresented that his contribution would be made in cash, when in fact it had been made by setting off obligations owed by the vendor to S. He ordered that S and W should account to M for the entire profit that they had made from the transaction. The appellants submitted that the account of profits should have been limited to the profits obtained by the breach of fiduciary duty on the basis that if the set-off arrangement *had* been disclosed to M they would have agreed to go ahead but with a higher profit share so that S and W should only be liable for the loss incurred by M as a result of the non-disclosure of the set-off arrangement.

ARDEN LJ:

46. . . . The judge gave a remedy of account because there was a fiduciary relationship. For wrongs in the context of such a relationship, an order for an account of profits is a conventional remedy. . . .

54. The argument which Mr Cogley [counsel for S] makes is a powerful one. His case is that, where a fiduciary is made to account, there has to be a link between the profit and his wrongful act. . . .

55. On Mr Cogley's submission, the account ordered by the judge would not be restitutionary or restorative. It would result in unjust enrichment of the Murads. It is (he submits) wrong in principle that the Murads should receive the benefit of any profits which, if there had been full disclosure, they would have been content for Mr Al-Saraj to have. They all along anticipated being co-venturers with him and so expected him to have a share of the profits from the acquisition of Parkside Hotel. Increases in profits not attributable to his wrongful conduct should be excluded from the profits for which he has to account. . . .

56. To test Mr Cogley's argument on the extent of the liability to account, in my judgment it is necessary to go back to first principle. . . . Equity recognises that there are legal wrongs for which damages are not the appropriate remedy . . . a court of equity instead awards an account of profits. . . . the purpose of the account is to strip a defaulting fiduciary of his profit. . . .

59. I would highlight two well-established points about the reach of the equitable remedies: (1) the liability of a fiduciary to account does not depend on whether the person to whom the fiduciary duty was owed could himself have made the profit. (2) when awarding equitable compensation, the court does not apply the common law principles of causation.

60. Proposition (1) is established by numerous authorities . . . [including *Regal (Hastings)* **[7.26]**: 'The liability arises from the mere fact of a profit having, in the stated circumstances, been made.']

61. The position is no different in Australia: see *Warman International Ltd v Dwyer*[92], where the High Court specifically rejected the notion of unjust enrichment:

'It has been suggested that the liability of the fiduciary to account for a profit made in breach of the fiduciary duty should be determined by reference to the concept of unjust enrichment, namely, whether the profit is made at the expense of the person to whom the fiduciary duty is owed, and to the honesty and bona fides of the fiduciary. But the authorities in Australia and England deny that the liability of a fiduciary to account depends upon detriment to the plaintiff or the dishonesty and lack of bona fides of the fiduciary.' (page 557)

---

92 *Warman International Ltd v Dwyer* (1995) 182 CLR 546, Aust HCt.

62. The High Court went on to say that (in a context such as this) the fiduciary will be liable to account (only) 'for a profit or benefit if it was obtained by reason of his taking advantage of [an] opportunity or knowledge derived from his fiduciary position' (page 557). It must of course be the case that no fiduciary is liable for all the profits he ever made from any source. However, it is clear that the High Court contemplated that the relevant profits would be ascertained through the process of the account. The court held: 'Ordinarily a fiduciary will be ordered to render an account of the profits made within the scope and ambit of his duty.' (page 559)

63. The High Court considered the allowances appropriate in that case. It concluded that a distinction should be drawn between the profits made from the use of a specific asset and those generated by a business which the defaulting fiduciary had diverted to himself. In the latter case, an allowance for skill, experience and expenses might have to be made. I return to the question of allowances below.

64. The High Court made it clear that the power to make an allowance for skill and efforts (or some other reason):

'is not to say that the liability of a fiduciary to account should be governed by the doctrine of unjust enrichment, though that doctrine may well have a useful part to play; it is simply to say that the stringent rule requiring a fiduciary to account for profits can be carried to extremes and that in cases outside the realm of specific assets, the liability of the fiduciary should not be transformed into a vehicle for the unjust enrichment of the plaintiff.' (page 561) . . .

67. The fact that the fiduciary can show that that party would not have made a loss is, on the authority of the *Regal* case, an irrelevant consideration so far as an account of profits is concerned. Likewise, it follows in my judgment from the *Regal* case that it is no defence for a fiduciary to say that he would have made the profit even if there had been no breach of fiduciary duty.

68. . . . [L]iability does not depend on fraud or lack of good faith. The existence of a fraudulent intent will, however, be relevant to the question of the allowances to be made on the taking of the account (which subject I consider below). . . .

70. The next issue is that of authorisation or consent to the breach of duty. There was no consent in fact in this case. What is said is that the Murads would have consented to the set off arrangement and reduction in the purchase price for the hotel, if they had been asked. The House of Lords in the *Regal* case recognised that there would have been no liability to account in that case if the directors had been authorised by their company to take the opportunity which they had appropriated for themselves. . . .

71. In my judgment it is not enough for the wrongdoer to show that, if he had not been fraudulent, he could have got the consent of the party to whom he owed the fiduciary duty to allow him to retain the profit. The point is that the profit here was in fact wholly unauthorised at the time it was made and has so remained. To obtain a valid consent, there would have to have been full and frank disclosure by Mr Al-Saraj to the Murads of all relevant matters. It is only actual consent which obviates the liability to account. . . .

77. . . . [F]or the policy reasons, on the taking of an account, the court lays the burden on the defaulting fiduciary to show that the profit is not one for which he should account . . .

78. This principle was applied by the High Court of Australia in the *Warman* case:

'It is for the defendant to establish that it is inequitable to order an account of the entire profits. If the defendant does not establish that that would be so, then the defendant must bear the consequences of mingling the profits attributable to those earned by the defendant's efforts and investment, in the same way that a trustee of a mixed fund bears the onus of distinguishing what is his own.'

79. In the *Warman* case, the defaulting fiduciary was able to show that some of the profit was not attributable to his wrongful act, but to his own skill and effort. The Court limited the account

accordingly. On the facts, the court was satisfied that the period of time for which profits were to be accounted should be limited to two years. I will come back to this point below.

80. The above examination of the rule of equity applied in the *Regal* case is not promising for Mr Cogley's argument. On the contrary, on its most obvious analysis, his argument is clearly inconsistent with it, since the essence of his approach is to seek to limit Mr Al-Saraj's liability to account for profit to the loss suffered by the Murads. As the *Regal* case shows, liability to account for profit in equity does not depend on whether the beneficiary actually suffered any loss. I thus turn to consider whether there is any other way in which Mr Cogley's argument can be analysed in conformity with the principles of equity. . . .

82. ... Moreover, it would not be impossible for a modern court to conclude as a matter of policy that, without losing the deterrent effect of the rule, the harshness of it should be tempered in some circumstances.... though I express no view as to the circumstances in which there should be any relaxation of the rule in this jurisdiction. That sort of question must be left to another court. [And [83] expresses the same idea.]

84. . . . [But that would not be appropriate here, where] Mr Al-Saraj was found to have made a fraudulent misrepresentation to the Murads who had placed their trust in him.... The appropriate remedy is that he should disgorge all the profits, whether of a revenue or capital nature, that he made from inducing the Murads by his fraudulent representations from entering into the Parkside Hotel venture, subject to any allowances permitted by the court on the taking of the account.

85. The imposition of liability to account for secret profits and the placing of the burden of proof on the defaulting trustee are not, however, quite the end of the matter. The kind of account ordered in this case is an account of profits, that is a procedure to ensure the restitution of profits which ought to have been made for the beneficiary and not a procedure for the forfeiture of profits to which the defaulting trustee was always entitled for his own account. That is Mr. Cogley's case and I agree with him on this point. Even when the fiduciary is not fraudulent, the profit obtained from the breach of trust has to be defined . . . equity does not take the view that simply because a profit was made as part of the same transaction the fiduciary must account for it. . . . [See] *Docker v Somes* (1834) 39 ER 1095 at 1099, where Lord Brougham expressed the view that in some circumstances a trustee who had applied considerable skill and labour to trust property which he had misapplied would be awarded a share of the product of his skill and labour:

'Mr. Solicitor General might have taken the case of trust money laid out in purchasing a piece of steel or skein of silk, and these being worked up into goods of the finest fabric, Birmingham trinkets or Brussels lace, where the work exceeds by 10,000 times the material in value. But such instances, in truth, prove nothing; for they are cases not of profits upon stock, but of skilful labour very highly paid; and no reasonable person would ever dream of charging a trustee, whose skill thus bestowed had so enormously augmented the value of the capital, as if he had only obtained from it a profit; although the refinements of the civil law would certainly bear us out, even in charging all gains accruing upon those goods as in the nature of accretions belonging to the true owners of the chattels.'

86. . . . The profit which belongs to the trust has to be disentangled from that which belongs to the defaulting trustee because it is a profit of his business. I have explained above how these difficulties were resolved in the *Warman* case by limiting the account to two years' profits. The problem in the *Warman* case has also faced courts within our own jurisdiction. In *Vyse v Foster* (1872) 9 Ch App 309, one of the partners in a business died but his capital remained in the business and was thus used by the surviving partners. One of the residuary legatees of the deceased partner sought an account of the share of the profits of the business to which she was entitled. . . . This court was prepared in principle to ascertain the share of the profits of the business but when it came down to working out how this was to be done this court decided that the appropriate remedy would be to order repayment of the capital with interest. In his judgment, James LJ held

that the share of profits to which the plaintiff was entitled could not simply be ascertained by working out the proportion of the capital to which she was entitled . . .

87. Does this line of authority help Mr Al-Saraj in this case? I think not. . . .

88. It would, however, be open to Mr Al-Saraj to apply to the court for an allowance for his services and disbursements, as indeed he did. . . .

JONATHAN PARKER LJ:

[He agreed with Arden LJ's conclusions and reasons, but, given their disagreement with Clarke LJ, he added:]

108. It is thus clear on authority, in my judgment, that the 'no conflict' rule is neither compensatory nor restitutionary: rather, it is designed to strip the fiduciary of the unauthorised profits he has made whilst he is in a position of conflict....

110. By contrast...a claim for equitable compensation for breach of trust the court may have regard to what would have happened but for the breach ...

111. I therefore conclude, on the basis of long-standing authority, that Mr Al-Saraj's liability to account extends to the entirety of the profits which he made from the joint venture. As the judge put it (at the hearing on 12 July 2004):

'the general principle is that a fiduciary is obliged by the strict rule of equity to disgorge all the profits that he has made from the transaction, which has involved his breach of duty, . . . it does not matter whether or not the transaction would have been entered into by the beneficiary instead of the fiduciary in its entirety or as to part.'

112. The judge's reference to the transaction 'which has involved his breach of duty' is important, for the fiduciary is liable to account only for profits which he has made 'within the scope and ambit of the duty which conflicts or may conflict with his personal interest' [*Boardman v Phipps* at 127D per Lord Upjohn]. In the instant case, however, the point does not arise, since on the judge's findings all the profits which Mr Al-Saraj made from the joint venture fall within that description.

113. In *Warman International Ltd v. Dwyer* . . . the defendants, in breach of their fiduciary duty to the claimant company, set up a competing business.... [T]he High Court of Australia held the defendants liable to account to the claimant company for the profits made by the new business during its first two years of operation.

114. ... [T]he High Court of Australia continued:

'In the case of a business it may well be inappropriate and inequitable to compel the errant fiduciary to account for the whole of the profit of his conduct of the business or his exploitation of the principal's goodwill over an indefinite period of time. In such a case, it may be appropriate to allow the fiduciary a proportion of the profits, depending on the particular circumstances. That may well be the case when it appears that a significant proportion of an increase in profits has been generated by the skill, efforts, property and resources of the fiduciary, the capital he has introduced and the risks he has taken, so long as they are not risks to which the principal's property has been exposed. Then it may be said that the relevant proportion of the increased profits is not the product or consequence of the plaintiff's property but the product of the fiduciary's skill, efforts, property and resources. That is not to say that the liability of a fiduciary to account should be governed by the doctrine of unjust enrichment, though that doctrine may well have a useful part to play; it is simply to say that the stringent rule requiring a fiduciary to account for profits can be carried to extremes and that in cases outside the realm of specific assets, the liability of a fiduciary should not be transformed into a vehicle for the unjust enrichment of the plaintiff.

It is for the defendant to establish that it is inequitable to order an account of the entire profits. If the defendant does not establish that that would be so, then the defendant must bear the consequences of mingling the profits attributable to the defendant's breach of fiduciary duty and the profits attributable to those earned by the defendant's efforts and investment, in the same way that a trustee of a mixed fund bears the onus of distinguishing what is his own.

Whether it is appropriate to allow an errant fiduciary a proportion of profits or to make an allowance in respect of skill, expertise and other expenses is a matter of judgment which will depend on the facts of the given case. However, as a general rule, in conformity with the principle that a fiduciary must not profit from a breach of fiduciary duty, a court will not apportion profits in the absence of an antecedent arrangement for profit-sharing but will make an allowance for skill, expertise and other expenses.'

115. I do not, for my part, read that passage in the judgment of the High Court of Australia as sanctioning any departure from, or as recognising any qualification to, the 'no conflict' rule. Rather, as I read its judgment, the court is regarding the defendants as trustees who have made a profit from trust property in breach of what I may call the 'no profit' rule, and recognising that given that the property in question is the goodwill of the claimant company's business, there will in all probability come a time when it can safely be said that any future profits of the new business will be attributable not to the goodwill misappropriated from the claimant company when the new business was set up but rather to the defendants' own efforts in carrying on that business.

116. Even if, contrary to my reading of its judgment, the court is applying the 'no conflict' rule as opposed to the 'no profit' rule, the conclusion which it reaches is in my judgment entirely consistent with the 'no conflict' rule in that it is merely recognising that an order for an account of all the profits of the new business over an indefinite period would in all probability include profits which are not tainted in any way by the position of conflict in which the defendants placed themselves: that is to say profits which . . . are not within the scope and ambit of the relevant fiduciary duty and hence not within the scope of the 'no conflict' rule. In *Warman* itself, the court concluded that the appropriate cut off point was the expiry of two years after the commence-ment of the new business.

117. If, contrary to my reading of the court's judgment in *Warman*, the court was (as Clarke LJ concludes that it was) recognising or introducing a qualification to the 'no conflict' rule, then I can only say that, on my reading of the authorities, no such qualification exists as yet in this jurisdiction. . . .

121. All that said, there can be little doubt that the inflexibility of the 'no conflict' rule may, de-pending on the facts of any given case, work harshly so far as the fiduciary is concerned. It may be said with force that that is the inevitable and intended consequence of the deterrent nature of the rule. On the other hand, it may be said that commercial conduct which in 1874 was thought to imperil the safety of mankind may not necessarily be regarded nowadays with the same depth of concern. So, like Arden LJ (see paragraph 82 above), I can envisage the possibility that at some time in the future the House of Lords may consider that the time has come to relax the severity of the 'no conflict' rule to some extent in appropriate cases.

122. In my judgment, however, that day has not yet arrived. Nor, in any event, would I regard the instant case as being an appropriate case for any such relaxation. . . .

CLARKE LJ:

124. With one important exception, I agree with the conclusions reached by Arden LJ. That exception relates to the principles applicable to the taking of an account in a case of this kind. I have reached the conclusion that the principles applicable to the correct approach to the amount of the profits in respect of which an account should be ordered are more flexible than Arden LJ suggests. . . .

138. Whatever the position with regard to equitable compensation, which the Murads do not claim, the cases relevant to the obligation to account for a breach of fiduciary duty provide a strong basis for Arden LJ's conclusion that Mr Al-Saraj should account for the whole of the profit which derived from the joint venture. However, Mr Cogley submits that, notwithstanding the

strong statements of principle in the cases, including those which say that causation is irrelevant and that it is irrelevant what the principal or person to whom the fiduciary duty is owed would have done if full disclosure had been made, some element of causation must be established . . .

162. In all these circumstances I have reached a different conclusion from Arden LJ. I would hold that the finding that the Murads would have entered into this joint venture in any event is relevant to the scope of the account which should be ordered. The judge did not so hold because he regarded the finding as irrelevant because of equity's inflexible rule. In these circumstances, subject to hearing submissions as to the precise scope of the remission, I would remit the matter to the judge in order to give Mr Al-Saraj the opportunity to seek to persuade him that it would be inequitable to order him to account for all the profits of the joint venture, subject only to his expenses and skill. I would therefore allow the appeal to that extent.

> Questions

1. When is an account of profits awarded? When is equitable compensation awarded? How is each quantified?

2. How did Arden and Jonathan Parker LJJ distinguish the approach to quantifying (and cutting back) the recoverable profits in *Warman* from the approach they felt obliged to take on the facts before them? Is their approach more satisfactory than that of Clarke LJ?

3. Do the rules on account of profits need to be relaxed? (See Arden and Clarke LJJ, at [81]–[82] and [121]–[122], in the previous extract.) Also see the comments of Arden LJ in *Geoffrey Maidment v Allan Attwood, Nicola Heard, Tobian Properties Limited* [2012] EWCA Civ 998, CA, an unfair prejudice case, where she cited *Murad* **[7.38]** and noted that 'This is a harsh result. Equity has not developed exceptions to avoid this because there is a strong deterrent element in the imposition of liability for breach of fiduciary duty' [22].

4. In *Murad*, S and W also submitted that the proper claimant in respect of any alleged secret commission paid to S on the acquisition of the hotel was D, but the Court of Appeal did not decide this matter. What is the right answer? In any event, would S and W be allowed to benefit from any successful recovery by D? (The question was remitted to the trial judge for determination in [2006] EWHC 2404 (Ch), but D made no claim to the sum, therefore the sum remained owing to M.)

5. This same strict approach is also applied to assessing the profits which have to be disgorged in actions against third parties who knowingly assist in a fiduciary's breach of fiduciary duty: see Andrew Smith J in *Fiona Trust & Holding Corporation v Privalov* [2011] EWHC 664 (Comm), this decision being one very small part of major litigation concerning fraud and bribery in the Russian shipping industry.

Disloyal profits, if identifiable, are held on constructive trust.

[7.39] FHR European Ventures LLP v Cedar Capital Partners LLC
[2014] UKSC 45, [2015] AC 250 (Supreme Court)

The detailed facts are irrelevant. The case involved a claim by FHR against its agent (Cedar Capital) who took a secret commission of €10 million from the vendor counterparty while negotiating FHR's purchase of a hotel complex. The Supreme Court held that an agent who received a bribe or secret commission in breach of his fiduciary duty to his principal held it on trust for his principal. For the general significance of this, see 'Disgorgement of profits—proprietary remedy', p 433 (And for the endgame, see [2016] EWHC 359 (Ch)).

LORD NEUBERGER PSC for the court:

18. It is fair to say that in the majority of the cases identified...it appears to have been tacitly accepted that the rule applied, so that the plaintiff was entitled not merely to an equitable account in respect of the benefit, but to the beneficial ownership of the benefit....

22. However, there is one decision of the House of Lords[93] which appears to go the other way, and several decisions of the Court of Appeal[94] which do go the other way, in that they hold that, while a principal has a claim for equitable compensation in respect of a bribe or secret commission received by his agent, he has no proprietary interest in it....

28. More recently, in 1993, in *Attorney General for Hong Kong v Reid* [1994] 1 AC 324 [and see the Notes immediately following], the Privy Council concluded that bribes received by a corrupt government legal officer were held on trust for his principal, and so they could be traced into properties which he had acquired in New Zealand. In his judgment on behalf of the Board, Lord Templeman disapproved the reasoning in *Heiron*, and the reasoning and outcome in *Lister*...In *Daraydan Holdings Ltd v Solland International Ltd* [2005] Ch 119, paras 75 et seq, Lawrence Collins J indicated that he would follow *Reid* rather than *Lister*, as did Toulson J in *Fyffes Group Ltd v Templeman* [2000] 2 Lloyd's Rep 643, 668–672. But in *Sinclair Investments (UK) Ltd v Versailles Trade Finance Ltd* [2012] Ch 453, in a judgment given by Lord Neuberger of Abbotsbury MR, the Court of Appeal decided that it should follow [the *Lister* line of cases] for a number of reasons set out in paras 77ff, although it accepted that this court might follow the approach in *Reid*. In this case, Simon J considered that he was bound by *Sinclair*, whereas the Court of Appeal concluded that they could and should distinguish it.

[After discussing some academic articles, continued:]

Arguments based on principle and practicality

33. The position adopted by the respondents, namely that the rule applies to all unauthorised benefits which an agent receives, is consistent with the fundamental principles of the law of agency. The agent owes a duty of undivided loyalty to the principal, unless the latter has given his informed consent to some less demanding standard of duty. The principal is thus entitled to the entire benefit of the agent's acts in the course of his agency. This principle is wholly unaffected by the fact that the agent may have exceeded his authority. The principal is entitled to the benefit of the agent's unauthorised acts in the course of his agency, in just the same way as, at law, an employer is vicariously liable to bear the burden of an employee's unauthorised breaches of duty in the course of his employment. The agent's duty is accordingly to deliver up to his principal the benefit which he has obtained, and not simply to pay compensation for having obtained it in excess of his authority. The only way that legal effect can be given to an obligation to deliver up specific property to the principal is by treating the principal as specifically entitled to it.

34. On the other hand, there is some force in the notion advanced by the appellant that the rule should not apply to a bribe or secret commission paid to an agent, as such a benefit is different in quality from a secret profit he makes on a transaction on which he is acting for his principal, or a profit he makes from an otherwise proper transaction which he enters into as a result of some knowledge or opportunity he has as a result of his agency. Both types of secret profit can be said to be benefits which the agent should have obtained for the principal, whereas the same cannot be said about a bribe or secret commission which the agent receives from a third party.

35. The respondents' formulation of the rule has the merit of simplicity: any benefit acquired by an agent as a result of his agency and in breach of his fiduciary duty is held on trust for the principal. On the other hand, the appellant's position is more likely to result in uncertainty. Thus,

---

[93] *Tyrrell v Bank of London* (1862) 10 HL Cas 26.

[94] Including *Metropolitan Bank v Heiron* (1880) 5 Ex D 319, CA; and *Lister & Co v Stubbs* (1890) 45 Ch D 1, where the notion that the bribe might be held on trust was thought to be startling, not least because it would give the company priority to the money in the event of the agent's bankruptcy, and would attract claims to traceable proceeds.

there is more than one way in which one can identify the possible exceptions to the normal rule, which results in a bribe or commission being excluded from the rule: see the differences between Professor Goode and Professor Worthington described in paras 10 and 32 above,[95] and the other variations there described…Clarity and simplicity are highly desirable qualities in the law. Subtle distinctions are sometimes inevitable, but in the present case, as mentioned above, there is no plainly right answer, and, accordingly, in the absence of any other good reason, it would seem right to opt for the simple answer.

36. A further advantage of the respondents' position is that it aligns the circumstances in which an agent is obliged to account for any benefit received in breach of his fiduciary duty and those in which his principal can claim the beneficial ownership of the benefit…. The expression equitable accounting can encompass both proprietary and non-proprietary claims. However, if equity considers that in all cases where an agent acquires a benefit in breach of his fiduciary duty to his principal, he must account for that benefit to his principal, it could be said to be somewhat inconsistent for equity also to hold that only in some such cases could the principal claim the benefit as his own property. The observation of Lord Russell in *Regal (Hastings)* [1967] 2 AC 134 quoted in para 6 above, and those of Jonathan Parker LJ in *Bhullar* [2003] 2 BCLC 241 quoted in para 14 above would seem to apply equally to the question of whether a principal should have a proprietary interest in a bribe or secret commission as to the question of whether he should be entitled to an account in respect thereof.

37. The notion that the rule should not apply to a bribe or secret commission received by an agent because it could not have been received by, or on behalf of, the principal seems unattractive. The whole reason that the agent should not have accepted the bribe or commission is that it puts him in conflict with his duty to his principal. Further, in terms of elementary economics, there must be a strong possibility that the bribe has disadvantaged the principal. Take the facts of this case: if the vendor was prepared to sell for €211.5m, on the basis that it was paying a secret commission of €10m, it must be quite likely that, in the absence of such commission, the vendor would have been prepared to sell for less than €211.5m, possibly €201.5m. While Simon J was not prepared to make such an assumption without further evidence, it accords with common sense that it should often, even normally, be correct; indeed, in some cases, it has been assumed by judges that the price payable for the transaction in which the agent was acting was influenced pro rata to account for the bribe: see eg *Fawcett* 1 Russ & M 132, 136.

38. The artificiality and difficulties to which the appellant's case can give rise may be well illustrated by reference to the facts in *Eden* 23 QBD 368 and in *Whaley Bridge* 5 QBD 109. In *Eden*, the promoter gave 200 shares to a director of the company when there were outstanding issues between the promoter and the company. The Court of Appeal held that the director held the shares on trust for the company. As Finn J said in *Grimaldi v Chameleon Mining NL (No 2)* (2012) 287 ALR 22, para 570, the effect of that decision, if *Heiron* and *Lister* were rightly decided, would appear to be that where a bribe is paid to an agent, the principal has a proprietary interest in the bribe if it consists of shares but not if it consists of money, which would be a serious anomaly.

---

[95] Professor Goode took the view that no proprietary interest arises where an agent obtains a benefit in breach of his duty unless the benefit either (i) flows from an asset which was (a) beneficially owned by the principal, or (b) intended for the principal, or (ii) was derived from an activity of the agent which, if he chose to undertake it, he was under an equitable duty to undertake for the principal: 'Proprietary Restitutionary Claims' in WR Cornish (ed), *Restitution: Past, Present and Future* (1998), p 69 and see more recently (2011) 127 LQR 493. He would be critical of *FHR*. Professor Worthington advanced a slightly different test. She suggested that proprietary claims arise where benefits are (i) derived from the principal's property, or (ii) derived from opportunities in the scope of the agent's endeavours on behalf of the principal, but not (iii) benefits derived from opportunities outside the scope of those endeavours: 'Fiduciary Duties and Proprietary Remedies: Addressing the Failure of Equitable Formulae' [2013] CLJ 720. On that basis all disgorgement remedies in the cases under discussion (including *FHR*) would be proprietary other than in the influential case of *Reid*!

39. In *Whaley Bridge*, a director of a company who negotiated a purchase by the company for £20,000 of a property was promised but did not receive £3,000 out of the £20,000 from the vendor. The outcome according to Bowen J was that the vendor was liable to the company for the £3,000, because the company was entitled to treat the contract between the vendor and the director as made by the director on behalf of the company. Bowen J held that it 'could not be successfully denied' that if the £3,000 had been paid to the director he would have held it on trust for the company. Mr Collings suggested that the decision was correct because, unlike in this case, the director and vendor had agreed that the £3,000 would come out of the £20,000 paid by the company. Not only is there no trace of such reasoning in Bowen J's judgment, but it would be artificial, impractical and absurd if the issue whether a principal had a proprietary interest in a bribe to his agent depended on the mechanism agreed between the briber and the agent for payment of the bribe.

40. The notion that an agent should not hold a bribe or commission on trust because he could not have acquired it on behalf of his principal is somewhat inconsistent with the long-standing decision in *Keech* [noted in *Regal (Hastings)* **[7.26]**], the decision in *Phipps* approved by the House of Lords, and the Privy Council decision in *Bowes* 11 Moo PC 463. In each of those three cases, a person acquired property as a result of his fiduciary or quasi-fiduciary position, in circumstances in which the principal could not have acquired it: yet the court held that the property concerned was held on trust for the beneficiary. In *Keech*, the beneficiary could not acquire the new lease because the landlord was not prepared to let to him, and because he was an infant; in *Boardman*, the trust could not acquire the shares because they were not authorised investments; in *Bowes*, the city corporation would scarcely have been interested in buying the loan notes which it had just issued to raise money.

41. The respondents are also able to point to a paradox if the appellant is right and a principal has no proprietary right to his agent's bribe or secret commission. If the principal has a proprietary right, then he is better off, and the agent is worse off, than if the principal merely has a claim for equitable compensation. It would be curious, as Mr Collings frankly conceded, if a principal whose agent wrongly receives a bribe or secret commission is worse off than a principal whose agent obtains a benefit in far less opprobrious circumstances, eg the benefit obtained by the trustees' agents in *Boardman*. Yet that is the effect if the rule does not apply to bribes or secret commissions.

42. Wider policy considerations also support the respondents' case that bribes and secret commissions received by an agent should be treated as the property of his principal, rather than merely giving rise to a claim for equitable compensation. As Lord Templeman said giving the decision of the Privy Council in *Attorney General for Hong Kong v Reid* [1994] 1 AC 324, 330H, 'bribery is an evil practice which threatens the foundations of any civilised society'. Secret commissions are also objectionable as they inevitably tend to undermine trust in the commercial world. That has always been true, but concern about bribery and corruption generally has never been greater than it is now: see for instance, internationally, the OECD Convention on Combating Bribery of Foreign Public Officials in International Business Transactions 1999 and the United Nations Convention against Corruption 2003, and, nationally, the Bribery Acts 2010 and 2012. Accordingly, one would expect the law to be particularly stringent in relation to a claim against an agent who has received a bribe or secret commission.

43. On the other hand, a point frequently emphasised by those who seek to justify restricting the ambit of the rule is that the wide application for which the respondents contend will tend to prejudice the agent's unsecured creditors, as it will serve to reduce the estate of the agent if he becomes insolvent. This was seen as a good reason in *Sinclair* [2012] Ch 453, para 83 for not following *Reid*. While the point has considerable force in some contexts, it appears to us to have limited force in the context of a bribe or secret commission. In the first place, the proceeds of a bribe or secret commission consists of property which should not be in the agent's estate at all,

as Lawrence Collins J pointed out in *Daraydan* [2005] Ch 119, para 78 (although it is fair to add that insolvent estates not infrequently include assets which would not be there if the insolvent had honoured his obligations). Secondly, as discussed in para 37 above, at any rate in many cases, the bribe or commission will very often have reduced the benefit from the relevant transaction which the principal will have obtained, and therefore can fairly be said to be his property.

44. None the less, the appellant's argument based on potential prejudice to the agent's unsecured creditors has some force, but it is, as we see it, balanced by the fact that it appears to be just that a principal whose agent has obtained a bribe or secret commission should be able to trace the proceeds of the bribe or commission into other assets and to follow them into the hands of knowing recipients (as in *Reid*). Yet, as Mr Collings rightly accepts, tracing or following in equity would not be possible, at least as the law is currently understood, unless the person seeking to trace or follow can claim a proprietary interest. Common law tracing is, of course, possible without a proprietary interest, but it is much more limited than equitable tracing. Lindley LJ in *Lister* 45 Ch D 1, 15 appears to have found it offensive that a principal should be entitled to trace a bribe, but he did not explain why, and we prefer the reaction of Lord Templeman in *Reid*, namely that a principal ought to have the right to trace and to follow a bribe or secret commission.

45. Finally, on this aspect, it appears that other common law jurisdictions have adopted the view that the rule applies to all benefits which are obtained by a fiduciary in breach of his duties. In the High Court of Australia, Deane J said in *Chan v Zacharia* (1984) 154 CLR 178, 199 that any benefit obtained

> 'in circumstances where a conflict…existed…or…by reason of his fiduciary position or of opportunity or knowledge resulting from it…is held by the fiduciary as constructive trustee.'

More recently, the Full Federal Court of Australia has decided not to follow *Sinclair*: see *Grimaldi* 287 ALR 22, where the decision in *Reid* was preferred: see the discussion at paras 569–584. Although the Australian courts recognise the remedial constructive trust, that was only one of the reasons for not following Sinclair. As Finn J who gave the judgment of the court said, at para 582 (after describing *Heiron* and *Lister* as imposing 'an anomalous limitation…on the reach of *Keech v Sandford*', at para 569), 'Australian law' in this connection 'matches that of New Zealand…, Singapore, United States jurisdictions…and Canada'. As overseas countries secede from the jurisdiction of the Privy Council, it is inevitable that inconsistencies in the common law will develop between different jurisdictions. However, it seems to us highly desirable for all those jurisdictions to learn from each other, and at least to lean in favour of harmonising the development of the common law round the world.

[Their Lordships thus concluded that the considerations of practicality and principle support the respondents' case, namely that a bribe or secret commission accepted by an agent is held on trust for his principal. The appeal was dismissed.]

➤ Notes

1. The Supreme Court in *FHR* explained why parties are often keen to prove entitlement to a proprietary remedy:

> First, if the agent becomes insolvent, a proprietary claim would effectively give the principal priority over the agent's unsecured creditors, whereas the principal would rank *pari passu*, ie equally, with other unsecured creditors if he only has a claim for compensation. Secondly, if the principal has a proprietary claim to the bribe or commission, he can trace and follow it in equity, whereas (unless we develop the law of equitable tracing beyond its current boundaries) a principal with a right only to equitable compensation would have no such equitable right to trace or follow.

2. Lord Templeman in *Attorney General for Hong Kong v Reid* [1994] 1 AC 324, PC, explained why the disgorgement remedy was proprietary:

> As soon as the bribe was received it should have been paid or transferred *instanter* to the person who suffered from the breach of duty. Equity considers as done that which ought to have been done. As soon as the bribe was received, whether in cash or in kind, the false fiduciary held the bribe on a constructive trust for the person injured. Two objections have been raised to this analysis. First it is said that if the fiduciary is in equity a debtor to the person injured, he cannot also be a trustee of the bribe. But there is no reason why equity should not provide two remedies, so long as they do not result in double recovery. If the property representing the bribe exceeds the original bribe in value, the fiduciary cannot retain the benefit of the increase in value which he obtained solely as a result of his breach of duty. Secondly, it is said that if the false fiduciary holds property representing the bribe in trust for the person injured, and if the false fiduciary is or becomes insolvent, the unsecured creditors of the false fiduciary will be deprived of their right to share in the proceeds of that property. But the unsecured creditors cannot be in a better position than their debtor. The authorities show that property acquired by a trustee innocently but in breach of trust and the property from time to time representing the same belong in equity to the *cestui que trust* and not to the trustee personally whether he is solvent or insolvent. Property acquired by a trustee as a result of a criminal breach of trust and the property from time to time representing the same must also belong in equity to his *cestui que trust* and not to the trustee whether he is solvent or insolvent.

3. Reference was made by the Supreme Court to the recent rejection of *Sinclair* by the Australian Full Federal Court in *Grimaldi v Chameleon Mining NL (No 2)* [2012] FCAFC 6. In that case, Finn J refused to follow *Sinclair*, but nevertheless did not award a constructive trust notwithstanding that this was a case where the claimant's funds had been diverted in part-payment (an exceptionally tiny part) of the purchase price of a mining venture. According to Finn J at [584]:

> . . . First, to accept that money bribes can be captured by a constructive trust does not mean that they necessarily will be in all circumstances. As is well accepted, a constructive trust ought not to be imposed if there are other orders capable of doing full justice . . . Such could be the case, for example, where a bribed fiduciary, having profitably invested the bribe, is then bankrupted and, apart from the investment, is hopelessly insolvent. In such a case a lien on that property may well be sufficient to achieve 'practical justice' in the circumstances. This said, a constructive trust is likely to be awarded as of course where the bribe still exists in its original, or in a traceable, form, and no third party issue arises.

4. For academic debate on this issue, see Gummow (2015) 131 LQR 21; Conaglen [2014] CLJ 490; and on the earlier decisions: Hayton (2011) 127 LQR 487; Goode (2011) 127 LQR 493; Lord Millett [2012] CLJ 583; and Smith [2013] CLJ 206.

➤ Questions

1. The disgorgement remedy is proprietary, but why is it proprietary? And when is it not proprietary?

2. In the Court of Appeal in *FHR European Ventures LLP* [2013] EWCA Civ 17, [2014] Ch 1, Pill LJ said, at [64]: 'At bottom, this is a question of public policy. There would be a case for deciding that whenever, as in the present case, the agent payee is a wrongdoer, the law,

applying equitable principles, should grant a proprietary remedy to the principal. A principal shall stand in his agent's shoes.' What, if anything, is the flaw in that logic? In what circumstances would/should it apply?

Directors and limitation periods—disgorgement claims.

[7.40] JJ Harrison (Properties) Ltd v Harrison [2001] EWCA Civ 1467 (Court of Appeal)

H, a director of HP, acquired land from HP without making the necessary disclosures. He then argued that the claim against him was statute barred. The Court of Appeal held that HP's claim fell within s 21(1)(b) of the Limitation Act 1980—that is, an action 'to recover trust property or the proceeds of trust property previously received by the trustee and converted to his use'—and therefore was not statute barred. It also ordered an account of profits on the value of the land (now resold).

CHADWICK LJ:

The constructive trust issue

25. I start with four propositions which may be regarded as beyond argument: (i) that a company incorporated under the Companies Acts is not trustee of its own property; it is both legal and beneficial owner of that property; (ii) that the property of a company so incorporated cannot lawfully be disposed of other than in accordance with the provisions of its memorandum and articles of association; (iii) that the powers to dispose of the company's property, conferred upon the directors by the articles of association, must be exercised by the directors for the purposes, and in the interests, of the company; and (iv) that, in that sense, the directors owe fiduciary duties to the company in relation to those powers and a breach of those duties is treated as a breach of trust. . . .

26. It follows from the principle that directors who dispose of the company's property in breach of their fiduciary duties are treated as having committed a breach of trust that a person who receives that property with knowledge of the breach of duty is treated as holding it upon trust for the company. He is said to be a constructive trustee of the property. . . .

27. It follows, also, from the principle that directors who dispose of the company's property in breach of their fiduciary duties are treated as having committed a breach of trust that, a director who is, himself, the recipient of the property holds it upon a trust for the company. He, also, is described as a constructive trustee. But, as Millett LJ explained in *Paragon Finance plc v Thakerar & Co* [1999] 1 All ER 400, at pp 408g–409g, his trusteeship is different in character from that of the stranger....

29. ... His obligations as a trustee in relation to that property do not arise out of the transaction by which he obtained it for himself. The true analysis is that his obligations as a trustee in relation to that property predate the transaction by which it was conveyed to him. The conveyance of the property to himself by the exercise of his powers in breach of trust does not release him from those obligations. He is trustee of the property because it has become vested in him; but his obligations to deal with the property as a trustee arise out of his pre-existing duties as a director; not out of the circumstances in which the property was conveyed.

30. In the present case the deputy judge found that . . . Mr Harrison acted in breach of his fiduciary duties as a director in failing to ensure that the land was sold at its full value . . . Not only did Mr Harrison fail to make a proper disclosure of his interest; his existing duties as a director required him to ensure that the development land was not conveyed at all until the company had received and considered advice as to its value in the light of the change in planning potential. In

those circumstances it seems to me impossible to reach a conclusion that Mr Harrison did not hold the development land as a constructive trustee ...

49. On the basis that Mr Harrison held the development land as trustee for the company, the remedy sought by the cross-appeal is an order that he account for the value of the land as at 23 December 1988—that being the date of the sale of the barn.

50. ...He should be entitled to bring to the credit of that account [the sum] which he paid for the development land and the cost of any works which led to an enhancement in the value of that [land]. It is pertinent to have in mind that the costs of pursuing planning applications has already been borne by the company.

LAWS LJ and SIR ANTHONY EVANS concurred.

Profits disgorgement and equitable compensation—rules on disclosure that will exempt the breach, quantification of profits and compensation, and effect of the Limitation Act 1980 s 21(1)(a).

[7.41] Gwembe Valley Development Co Ltd v Koshy
[2003] EWCA Civ 1048 (Court of Appeal)

The essential facts appear in the judgment. K was the managing director of the joint venture company G. He dishonestly caused G to enter into loan transactions with K and L from which K and L made substantial undisclosed profits. K was liable to disgorge his profits. He had no defence based on limitation periods or on disclosure and consent, nor any claim to have the assessment of profits reduced on some basis.

MUMMERY LJ for the court (MUMMERY, HALE and CARNWATH LJJ):

Core issues

1. Despite the thickets of company law, contract, fiduciary law, limitation of actions and equitable remedies, which have grown around this case, the central questions for decision can be stated quite concisely: ... did the managing director of a joint venture company deliberately and dishonestly fail to disclose his personal interest in transactions with the company and, if so, is he liable to account to the company for all, or for only part of, the unauthorised profits made by him; alternatively, did that failure to disclose his interest render him liable to compensate the company for its losses in the joint venture? . . .

19. The essential point in all the claims against Mr Koshy is that he was at the same time both the managing director of GVDC, in which the majority interest was held by Lasco, and a director and the controlling shareholder of Lasco . . .

26. ... [The effect of the loan transactions] was that Mr Koshy and Lasco could treat GVDC as liable to pay $US 5.8m on demand. Mr Koshy later procured GVDC to repay to Lasco substantial sums in respect of that purported debt. It was claimed that an award of equitable compensation should be made to restore GVDC to the position it was in prior to the pipeline loan transactions . . .

Basis of liability

43. Rimer J concluded that Mr Koshy was liable to account to GVDC for profits made by him from the pipeline loan transactions . . . Mr Koshy's liability arose in two ways: (1) Under the 'no profit rule' i.e. the rule of equity that a company director may not make an unauthorised (secret) profit from his fiduciary position . . .; (2) Dishonest breaches of fiduciary duty i.e. dishonestly using his position as managing director of GVDC to procure, in his own interests rather than in the interests of the company, GVDC to enter into the pipeline loan transactions, while deliberately not

disclosing to the other directors and to the shareholders of GVDC his controlling interest in Lasco and the scale of Lasco's, and his, intended profit from the transactions ... The judge found that the non-disclosure was deliberate, that it was part of Mr Koshy's dishonest scheme to benefit himself and that it involved the misapplication of GVDC's assets.

The no profit rule

44. The relevant principle was forcefully expressed and elegantly explained in the joint judgment of Rich, Dixon and Evatt JJ in the High Court of Australia in *Furs Ltd v. Tomkies* (1936) 54 CLR 583 at 592 as:

> '... the inflexible rule that, except under the authority of a provision in the articles of association, no director shall obtain for himself a profit by means of a transaction in which he is concerned on behalf of the company unless all the material facts are disclosed to the shareholders and by resolution a general meeting approves of his doing so or all the shareholders acquiesce. An undisclosed profit which a director so derives from the execution of his fiduciary duties belongs in equity to the company. It is no answer to the application of the rule that the profit is of a kind which the company itself could not have obtained, or that no loss is caused to the company by the gain of the director. It is a principle resting upon the impossibility of allowing the conflict of duty and interest which is involved in the pursuit of private advantage in the course of dealing in a fiduciary capacity with the affairs of the company. If, when it is his duty to safeguard and further the interests of the company, he uses the occasion as a means of profit to himself, he raises an opposition between the duty he has undertaken and his own self interest, beyond which it is neither wise nor practicable for the law to look for a criterion of liability. The consequences of such a conflict are not discoverable. Both justice and policy are against their investigation.'

45. That is the same equitable doctrine of accountability for unauthorised profits as was applied by the House of Lords in *Regal (Hastings) Ltd v. Gulliver* **[7.26]** ...

Exemption under the articles through disclosure

46. Mr Koshy denied that he was under any duty to account to GVDC under the strict 'no profit rule' [because (a)] ... he was expressly exempted by Article 89 of the Articles of Association of GVDC from the strict duty to account to the company for the profits made from the pipeline loan transactions, even if he had made no disclosure to the board of his personal interest in the transactions or of his profits; and that (b) the disclosure in fact made by him was sufficient for that purpose and under the general law ...

51. We are unable to accept this submission. It is necessary to read Article 89 in its proper context and, in particular, in conjunction with [and effectively subject to] Article 88, which requires a formal declaration of interest to be made by a director at a meeting of the board of the company ...

Implied modification of fiduciary duty

55. Mr Koshy's second ground of appeal under this head also emphasised the special joint venture character of GVDC. It was submitted that none of the members of the board of GVDC would expect other members of the board to disclose their principal's profits from transactions with GVDC. The board was made up of representatives of the investors ... It was not intended to be an independent board. The directors did not owe fiduciary obligations to GVDC in respect of transactions between the principals they represented and GVDC. In particular, it was argued that the directors of GVDC were well aware that Mr Koshy had a conflict of interest and was making a personal profit. It was to be implied from all the circumstances that the fiduciary's duty of disclosure of interests in relation to transactions with the company was excluded.

56. This argument should be rejected. It has no valid factual or legal basis ...

Disclosure under the general law

64. Rimer J held that Mr Koshy failed to make sufficient disclosure in order to avoid liability to account under the general law for breach of fiduciary duty, as distinct from being exempted from the duty to account by making formal disclosure of his interest under the Articles.

65. The requirement of the general law is that, although disclosure does not have to be made formally to the board, a company director must make *full* disclosure to all the shareholders of all the material facts. The shareholders in the company, to which he owes the fiduciary duty not to make an unauthorised profit from his position, must approve of, or acquiesce in, his profit. Disclosure requirements are not confined to the nature of the director's interest: they extend to disclosure of its extent, including the source and scale of the profit made from his position, so as to ensure that the shareholders are 'fully informed of the real state of things,' as Lord Radcliffe said in *Gray v. New Augarita Porcupine Mines* [1952] 3 DLR 1 at 14.

66. Rimer J held that Mr Koshy, on whom the onus of proving full disclosure to shareholders lay, fell short of the requirements of the general law . . .

Dishonest breach of fiduciary duty

70. Rimer J found that Mr Koshy had pursued a fraudulent scheme of deliberate conceal-ment from GVDC . . . The non-disclosure of his profits from the pipeline loan transactions was, he found, deliberate and dishonest. That was a grave finding of fact. It is particularly relevant to Mr Koshy's limitation defences to an account of profits . . .

Fiduciary duties and limitation—summary

111. . . . [I]n our view, it is possible to simplify the court's task when considering the application of the 1980 [Limitation] Act to claims against fiduciaries. The starting assumption should be that a six year limitation period will apply—under one or other provision of the Act, applied directly or by analogy—unless it is specifically excluded by the Act or established case-law. Personal claims against fiduciaries will normally be subject to limits by analogy with claims in tort or contract (1980 Act s 2, 5 . . .). By contrast, claims for breach of fiduciary duty, in the special sense explained in *Mothew*, will normally be covered by section 21. The six-year time-limit under section 21(3), will apply, directly or by analogy, unless excluded by subsection 21(1)(a) (fraud) or (b) (Class 1 trust)[.]

[And then the court concluded that these principles were applicable to a director in Mr Koshy's position; that he was therefore in principle subject to a six-year time-limit under section 21(3) unless that was excluded; that it could not be excluded under s 21(1)(b); and so could only be ex-cluded under s 21(1)(a), and that depended on establishing fraud. Continuing with that issue, they held that the question to be decided was, at [121]: 'was Mr Koshy guilty of simple non-disclosure or of deliberate and dishonest concealment?']

Conclusions on dishonesty

135. In the end, the issue [is] a very narrow one. The main point of the case against Mr Koshy was not his failure to disclose his interest in Lasco. If that had been the critical factor, it would, in our view, have been difficult to sustain a case of dishonesty . . . Nor was it the fact that Lasco was making *some* profit, which, as the judge found, was known to the directors. The essential point was, as the judge said, that the profit was not just substantial, but 'massive'. That made it something which was 'obviously' in GVDC's interests to know before committing itself to the Lasco agreements. As he said, the fact that the other directors may have been at fault in not making more diligent inquiries, and might even have accepted the position if they had known the full truth, does not exonerate Mr Koshy. The judge, having heard him in evidence and cross-examination, and after a painstakingly fair analysis of the evidence in this very complex case, was satisfied that the reason for non-disclosure was dishonest. In our view, this is not a conclusion with which this court can or should interfere . . .

Scope of the account

136. In our judgment, Rimer J was wrong in limiting the scope of the account as he did. [In addition] no part of the claim against Mr Koshy for an account of profits for dishonest breach of fiduciary duty was statute barred.

137. The point is not, as Mr Page [counsel] contended, whether the loan transactions are void or voidable, or whether they were rescinded or not, or whether the property in the sums repaid passed out of the beneficial ownership of GVDC and became the property of Lasco, or even whether Lasco received the sums as trust property. The point is that Mr Koshy was not, as a fiduciary vis a vis GVDC, entitled to retain for his personal benefit any of the unauthorised profits dishonestly made from transactions between him and the company. If he received those profits directly in the form of payments to him or indirectly by, for example, the consequent increase in the value of his shareholding in Lasco, he cannot be heard to say, as against the beneficiary company, that he was entitled to retain any of the profits for himself.

138. The judge failed to follow through the consequences of his finding of dishonesty on the part of Mr Koshy when he declined to order an account against him of *all* the profits obtained by him from the pipeline loan transactions. It is true that Mr Koshy received profits of the pipeline loan transactions indirectly via Lasco rather than directly from GVDC, but, in our judgment, that fact does not affect the application of the doctrine that the profits made by him, as a result of his dishonest breach of fiduciary duty, belong in equity to GVDC. Mr Koshy is accordingly liable to account to GVDC in respect of all profits made by him . . .

Laches and acquiescence

140. The defence of laches is not available. As already explained no period of limitation is specified by the 1980 Act in respect of the cause of action for dishonest breach of fiduciary duty. The effect of s 21(1)(a) is that either as a result of direct application, or of analogy, there is no period of limitation applicable to that cause of action . . .

Equitable Compensation

142. A company director may be held personally liable to pay equitable compensation to a company where, as a result of a breach of fiduciary duty on his part, the company has suffered loss. The paradigm case is the application of the company's property, without authority, for a purpose which is in the interests of the directors, but is not in the interests of the company. In such cases the measure of compensation is the value of the company's property which has been misapplied. The director may be held liable for the company's loss, even though he has not himself received any of the misapplied property. (In cases in which he has actually received property of the company, as a result of a breach of fiduciary duty on his part, the company is more likely to seek to establish liability as a constructive trustee)....

144. ...We agree that causation has no part to play in determining whether there has been non-compliance by the director with the fiduciary-dealing rules. Non-disclosure is non-compliance. If there has been non-compliance, the company is entitled to seek rescission of the transaction and an account of profits made by the director. In order to establish breach of the rules the company does not have to prove that it would not have entered into the transaction, if there had been compliance by the director with the fiduciary-dealing rules and he had made disclosure of his interest in the transaction. As was said by Lord Thankerton in the Privy Council in *Brickenden v. London Loan & Savings Co* (1934) 3 DLR 465 at 469:

'When a party, holding a fiduciary relationship, commits a breach of his duty by non-disclosure of material facts, which his constituent is entitled to know in connection with the transaction, he cannot be heard to maintain that disclosure would not have altered the decision to proceed with the transaction, because the constituent's action would be solely determined by some other factor, such as the valuation by another party of the property proposed to be mortgaged. Once the Court has determined that the non-disclosed facts were material, speculation as to what course the constituent, on disclosure would have taken is not relevant.'

145. The strictness of the rule of equity that a fiduciary should not profit from the trust and confidence placed in him in respect of the management of the property and affairs of another is such that the transaction should not be allowed to stand, if it is still possible to rescind it, and that the director, who has failed to disclose his interest in the transaction, should not be allowed to retain the unauthorised gains that he has made from the transaction. In considering whether the transaction should be rescinded for non-disclosure or whether the director should account for unauthorised profits, what would have happened, if the required disclosure had been made, is irrelevant....

147. However, when determining whether any compensation, and, if so, how much compensation, should be paid for loss claimed to have been caused by actionable non-disclosure [here, Mr Koshy's], the court is not precluded by authority or by principle from considering what would have happened if the material facts had been disclosed. If the commission of the wrong has not caused loss to the company, why should the company be entitled to elect to recover compensation, as distinct from rescinding the transaction and stripping the director of the unauthorised profits made by him? There is no sufficient causal link between the non-disclosure of an interest by Mr Koshy and the loss suffered by GVDC, if it is probable that, even if he had made the required disclosure of his interest in the transaction, GVDC would nevertheless have entered into it. In our judgment, a director is not legally responsible for loss, which the company would probably have suffered, even if the director had complied with the fiduciary-dealing rules on disclosure of interests. . . .

Conclusion

159. In our judgment, Rimer J was entitled to refuse to order equitable compensation on the factual basis that he was not satisfied that loss had been caused to GVDC as a result of the breaches of duty by Mr Koshy. The crux of Mr Koshy's wrongdoing was non-disclosure of his personal interest in the pipeline loan transactions and the unauthorised profit made by him from the transactions. The appropriate remedy for non-disclosure is to make him account to GVDC for that profit. It is not appropriate, if GVDC so elected, to require him to compensate GVDC for loss suffered in the venture when the probabilities are, as the judge, on the evidence, found them to be, that disclosure by Mr Koshy of his interest would have made no difference to what GVDC would have done.

160. We accordingly dismiss GVDC's appeal on the equitable compensation point . . .

➤ Questions

1. Why, if at all, was it material that Koshy's behaviour was fraudulent?

2. Why was the claimant pursuing both an account of profits and equitable compensation? Could *both* be recovered? Is one generally preferable to the other?

3. Can equitable compensation be claimed in corporate opportunity cases (ie cases not involving the defaulting director contracting with the company) or only in self-dealing cases (ie cases where the impugned transaction is a contract between the defaulting director and his or her company)? Can equitable compensation be claimed in *all* self-dealing cases?

Relief from liability

The available options

Directors may be relieved from liability for a breach of duty to the company in four ways:

(i)   prior consent, approval or authorisation by the directors where that is permitted (see ss 175, 177);

(ii) prior consent, approval or authorisation by the company: CA 2006 s 180;

(iii) ratification by the company: CA 2006 s 239; or

(iv) by the court: CA 2006 s 1157.

The first has been considered already; the latter three are considered in the sections which follow. It is clear that any attempt to contract out of liability will be void: CA 2006 ss 232–238.

Consent, approval or authorisation by the company: CA 2006 s 180

Section 180 records the ways in which directors can avoid liability for breaches of their general statutory duties by making the appropriate declaration or obtaining the appropriate consent, approval or authorisation from either the directors or the company, typically through the company's members (and indeed the section is headed 'Consent, approval or authorisation by members').

Recall that a director may already have exemptions from liability because he or she has board of directors' authorisation for dealings with outsiders (s 175) or has made a declaration to the directors about dealings with the company (s 177). Section 180(1) indicates that these mechanisms replace the equitable rule which requires the members, not the directors, to authorise these types of breaches of duty. This is subject to any contrary enactment (eg CA 2006 Pt 10, Ch 4), or any provision in the company's constitution imposing additional demands.

Section 180(4) is the crucial subsection. It retains the equitable and common law rules which allow *companies* to authorise (in *advance*—note the wording of s 180(4)(a)) what would otherwise be a breach of duty by the directors, and to make provision in their articles for dealing with conflicts of interest in specific ways.

Equitable rules for authorisation by the company

The equitable rules indicate that authorisation must be given by the members, not the directors (*Furs Ltd v Tomkies* (1936) 54 CLR 583, 590, 599), unless perhaps the members and directors are the same persons (*Queensland Mines Ltd v Hudson* (1978) 18 ALR 1, PC, see Note 2 following *Multinational Gas* **[7.43]**, p 458).

Consent is effective only if it is proper and fully informed (*Kaye v Croydon Tramways Co* [1898] 1 Ch 358; *Knight v Frost* [1999] 1 BCLC 364). This means that the decision of the members must not be a fraud on the creditors (*Re Halt Garage (1964) Ltd* **[5.03]**) or (it seems) a fraud on the minority or an abuse of power (*North West Transportation Co Ltd v Beatty* **[4.34]**. This last aspect is controversial (*Burland v Earle* [1902] AC 83, PC; *Cook v Deeks* **[7.25]**; *Prudential Assurance Co Ltd v Newman Industries Ltd (No 2)* **[13.25]**; and *Smith v Croft (No 2)* **[13.19]**).

It is sometimes alleged that authorisation or ratification of negligence is more controversial, but arguably the same rules apply—companies, like other individuals, can waive the duty of care and forgive past acts of negligence. Moreover, *every* waiver of forgiveness of director's liability is effectively an agreement to give up a valuable corporate asset: it is not so only in negligence cases. However, see *Pavlides v Jensen* [1956] Ch 565; *Daniels v Daniels* [1978] Ch 406 (for both these cases, see Notes 2 and 3 following *Franbar Holdings Ltd v Patel* **[13.13]**, p 688); *Re Horsley and Weight Ltd* **[4.31]**; and *Multinational Gas and Petrochemical Co v Multinational Gas and Petrochemical Services Ltd* **[7.43]**).

Explicit authorisation or acquiescence, and full disclosure requirements.

[7.42] Sharma v Sharma [2013] EWCA Civ 1287 (Court of Appeal)

The sole director of a family company running dental practices was not in breach of her fiduciary or statutory duty (s 175) by acquiring certain dental practices for her own benefit. She had made full disclosure of all material facts to the shareholders at an informal meeting. One had authorised the acquisition and the others had silently acquiesced (so it was held).

JACKSON LJ (with whom McCOMBE and FLOYD LJJ agreed):

43. The significance of *Boardman*[96] for present purposes is…it establishes that the beneficiary's consent does not absolve the fiduciary from liability, unless he has disclosed all material facts.…

45. The principle which emerges from *Duomatic* **[4.15]** is that if payments are made by a company with the full knowledge and consent of all the shareholders, then those payments are duly authorised as if there had been a formal resolution to that effect at a general meeting.

46. In *Re Home Treat Ltd* [1991] B.C.C. 165 Harman J. held that acquiescence by the shareholders of a company with knowledge of what was being done was as good as actual consent. The company in that case had two shareholders, one of whom remained silent when the objects of the company were being changed. Harman J. held that his silence was as good as acquiescence.

47. These principles are also applicable when the question is whether the shareholders of a company have authorised a director to do that which would otherwise be a breach of fiduciary duty. In such a situation, however, the court is scrupulous to ensure that the director has made full disclosure of all relevant facts to the shareholders: see *Gwembe Valley Development Co Ltd (in rec.) v Koshy (No.3)* **[7.41]** at [64]–[66]. Although the shareholders must be made aware of the relevant facts, it is not necessary that they understand the legal characterisation of those facts, namely that they would constitute a breach of fiduciary duty: see *Knight v Frost* [1999] B.C.C. 819 at 828.

48. In *EIC Services Ltd v Phipps* [2003] EWHC 1507 (Ch); [2003] B.C.C. 931 [which later went to the Court of Appeal, but not on this issue: see **[3.06]** and **[3.08]**] one of the issues was whether the issue and allotment of bonus shares had been effectively authorised by the members of the company, as required by [the articles]. The 13 shareholders had been told of the projected bonus issue and its general effect, but there was no question of their consent being sought or given. Neuberger J. held that the shareholders had not thereby consented to the bonus issue. He formulated the principle as follows at [133]:

'If a director of a company informs shareholders of an intended action (or a past action) on the part of the directors, in circumstances in which neither the directors nor the shareholders are aware that the consent of the shareholders is required to that action, I do not think it is right, at least without more, to conclude that the shareholders have assented to that action for *Duomatic* purposes. As a matter of both ordinary language and legal concept, it

---

96 *Boardman v Phipps* [1967] 2 AC 46, HL.

does not seem to me that, in such circumstances, it could be said that the shareholders have "assent[ed]" to that action. The shareholders have simply been told about the action or intended action, on the basis that it is something which can be, and has been or will be, left to the directors to decide on, and no question of "assent" arises.'

49. In that passage the words 'at least without more' may be significant. It is relevant to consider whether the circumstances were such that the shareholders would be expected to voice any objections, even if they were not aware of their legal rights. When a court is considering what, if anything, can be inferred from a party's silence, the factual context is a matter of critical importance. If the surrounding circumstances are such that it would be unconscionable for a party to remain silent at the time and only raise his objections later, then I would have thought that assent can be inferred from silence....

51. Directors' fiduciary duties have recently been codified in s.175 of the 2006 Act. Section 175 came into force on 1 October 2008, a date which fell during the course of the events which are the subject of this litigation. It is common ground between the parties that for present purposes there is no material difference between the statutory duties under s.175 of the 2006 Act and the pre-existing fiduciary duties imposed by equity.

52. Let me now draw the threads together. I must apply the following principles in resolving the issues in the present appeal. In this summary 'statutory duty' means the statutory duty imposed by s.175 of the 2006 Act.

(i) A company director is in breach of his fiduciary or statutory duty if he exploits for his personal gain (a) opportunities which come to his attention through his role as director or (b) any other opportunities which he could and should exploit for the benefit of the company.

(ii) If the shareholders with full knowledge of the relevant facts consent to the director exploiting those opportunities for his own personal gain, then that conduct is not a breach of the fiduciary or statutory duty.

(iii) If the shareholders with full knowledge of the relevant facts acquiesce in the director's proposed conduct, then that may constitute consent. However, consent cannot be inferred from silence unless:

(a) the shareholders know that their consent is required, or

(b) the circumstances are such that it would be unconscionable for the shareholders to remain silent at the time and object after the event.

(iv) For the purposes of propositions (ii) and (iii) full knowledge of the relevant facts does not entail an understanding of their legal incidents. In other words the shareholders need not appreciate that the proposed action would be characterised as a breach of fiduciary or statutory duty.

Ratification of acts of directors: CA 2006 s 239

This important provision settles new statutory minimum requirements for effective ratification. The provision draws on existing equitable rules, but imposes more stringent demands. In addition, to the extent (if any) that the statutory version may still be more lenient than the equitable rules, the latter rules—and rules in any other enactment—remain effective to supplement or enhance the statutory requirements (s 239(7)).

Section 239(1) makes it clear that the provision is designed to afford a mechanism for the company, via its members, to forgive a defaulting director for conduct amounting to negligence, default, breach of duty or breach of trust in relation to the company (ie the provision includes all the wrongs which are the subject of Pt 10, including negligence, and not simply fiduciary wrongs).

Section 239(2) insists that the ratification must be by resolution of the members of the company. This minimum requirement will apply regardless of any more lenient alternative provided by the company's articles, or by existing general law. And s 239(3) and (4) indicate that ratification is effective only if the resolution is passed *without* votes in favour of the resolution by the defaulting director (if a member of the company) and any member connected with him.

This changes the law as expressed in *North-West Transportation Co Ltd v Beatty* **[4.34]**; *Burland v Earle* [1902] AC 83, PC; and *Pavlides v Jensen* [1956] Ch 565 (see Note 3 following *Franbar Holdings Ltd v Patel* **[13.13]**, p 688). Instead, it adopts the approach advocated in *Atwool v Merryweather* (1867) LR 5 Eq 464n; *Cook v Deeks* **[7.25]**; *Hogg v Cramphorn* **[7.08]**; *Bamford v Bamford* **[4.33]**; *Howard Smith Ltd v Ampol Petroleum Ltd* **[7.09]**; *Daniels v Daniels* [1978] Ch 406 (see Note 2 following *Franbar Holdings Ltd v Patel* **[13.13]**, p 688); *Prudential Assurance Co Ltd v Newman Industries Ltd (No 2)* **[13.25]**; and *Smith v Croft (No 2)* **[13.19]**.

➤ Notes and Questions

1. Does CA 2006 s 239 create difficulties for smaller companies? If the majority of shares in a company are held by directors (which is the norm for smaller family-type companies), then their votes will be disregarded for ratification purposes, giving much more power to small shareholders (or, in an insolvency, to a liquidator), who will then have leverage over the owners, which will not necessarily serve the best interests of the company. What if the minority shareholders own, say, only 1% of the company? Should they still have a veto over ratification? What if there are no independent shareholders? On the other hand, it is difficult to see why wrongdoers should be able to vote to forgive themselves.

2. Section 239(6) makes clear that nothing in this clause changes the law on unanimous consent, so the restrictions imposed by this clause as to who may vote on a ratification resolution will not apply when every member votes (informally or otherwise) in favour of the resolution. On unanimous consent, see: *Re Duomatic Ltd* **[4.15]** (need the agreement of every member entitled to vote); *Re D'Jan of London Ltd* **[7.22]** (confirming that all members must actually apply their minds to the question and decide in favour of the proposal).

3. Section 239(6) also makes clear that nothing in the section removes any power of the directors to 'agree not to sue, or to settle or release a claim made by them on behalf of the company'. Does this abrogate the entire section, allowing the directors to override the tough members' ratification rule, and agree themselves to ratify (ie forgive, and agree not to sue) any wrongdoing director? In making such decisions, however, directors would of course continue to be bound by their normal duties, for example to promote the success of the company.

Approval or ratification by the shareholders.

[7.43] Multinational Gas and Petrochemical Co Ltd v Multinational Gas and Petrochemical Services Ltd [1983] Ch 258 (Court of Appeal)

Three international oil companies established a joint venture to deal in liquefied gas. They set up the plaintiff company to carry on the business, and the defendant company 'Services' to manage it and to provide advisory services. The three oil companies were the sole shareholders in both companies and appointed their directors. The plaintiff company went into liquidation owing approximately £114 million, and its liquidator sued its directors and also the defendant company, alleging that they had all been negligent. The Court of Appeal held that the action was not founded on any tort committed within the jurisdiction and so refused leave to serve the proceedings on those defendants who were abroad. But Lawton and Dillon LJJ also accepted an argument that there could be no complaint about commercial decisions, alleged to be negligent, which had been made by the directors with the approval of the three oil companies as shareholders.

LAWTON LJ: No allegation had been made that the plaintiff's directors had acted ultra vires or in bad faith. What was alleged was that when making the decisions which were alleged to have caused the plaintiff loss and giving instructions to Services to put them into effect they had acted in accordance with the directions and behest of the three oil companies. These oil companies were the only shareholders. All the acts complained of became the plaintiff's acts. The plaintiff, although it had a separate existence from its oil company shareholders, existed for the benefit of those shareholders, who, provided they acted intra vires and in good faith, could manage the plaintiff's affairs as they wished. If they wanted to take business risks through the plaintiff which no prudent businessman would take they could lawfully do so. Just as an individual can act like a fool provided he keeps within the law so could the plaintiff, but in its case it was for the shareholders to decide whether the plaintiff should act foolishly. As shareholders they owed no duty to those with whom the plaintiff did business. It was for such persons to assess the hazards of doing business with them. It follows, so it was submitted, that the plaintiff, as a matter of law, cannot now complain about what they did at their shareholders' behest.

This submission was based on . . . a long line of cases starting with *Salomon v A Salomon & Co Ltd* **[2.02]** and ending with the decision of this court in *Re Horsley & Weight Ltd* **[4.31]**. In my judgment these cases establish the following relevant principles of law: first, that the plaintiff was at law a different legal person from the subscribing oil company shareholders and was not their agent (see *Salomon v A Salomon & Co Ltd*). Secondly, that the oil companies as shareholders were not liable to anyone except to the extent and the manner provided by the Companies Act 1948 (see *Salomon v A Salomon & Co Ltd*). Thirdly, that when the oil companies acting together required the plaintiff's directors to make decisions or approve what had already been done, what they did or approved became the plaintiff's acts and were binding on it: see by way of examples *A-G for Canada v Standard Trust Co of New York*,[97] *Re Express Engineering Works Ltd*[98] and *Re Horsley & Weight Ltd*. When approving whatever their nominee directors had done, the oil companies were not, as the plaintiff submitted, relinquishing any causes of action which the plaintiff may have had against its directors. When the oil companies, as shareholders, approved what the plaintiff's directors had done there was no cause of action because at that time there was no damage. What the oil companies were doing was adopting the directors' acts and as shareholders, in agreement with each other, making those acts the plaintiff's acts.

It follows that the plaintiff cannot now complain about what in law were its own acts. Further, I can see no grounds for adjudging that the oil companies as shareholders were under any duty of care to the plaintiff.

DILLON LJ: It is not alleged that the joint venturers or the directors of the plaintiff acted fraudulently or in bad faith in any way or were guilty of fraudulent trading. What is alleged is that they all acted negligently in that they made five speculative decisions in relation to the ships, when they knew or ought to have known that they did not have sufficient information to make sensible business decisions. The decisions which they took in good faith went, it is said, outside the range of reasonable commercial judgment.

The heart of the matter is therefore that certain commercial decisions which were not ultra vires the plaintiff were made honestly, not merely by the directors but by all the shareholders of the plaintiff at a time when the plaintiff was solvent. I do not see how there can be any complaint of that.

[97] [1911] AC 498.
[98] [1920] 1 Ch 46, CA.

An individual trader who is solvent is free to make stupid, but honest, commercial decisions in the conduct of his own business. He owes no duty of care to future creditors. The same applies to a partnership of individuals.

A company, as it seems to me, likewise owes no duty of care to future creditors. The directors indeed stand in a fiduciary relationship to the company, as they are appointed to manage the affairs of the company and they owe fiduciary duties to the company though not to the creditors, present or future,[99] or to individual shareholders. The duties owed by a director include a duty of care, as was recognised by Romer J in *Re City Equitable Fire Insurance Co Ltd* **[7.21]**, though as he pointed out the nature and extent of the duty may depend on the nature of the business of the company and on the particular knowledge and experience of the individual director.

The shareholders, however, owe no duty to the company. Indeed, so long as the company is solvent the shareholders are in substance the company . . .

The well known passage in the speech of Lord Davey in *Salomon v A Salomon & Co Ltd* that the company is bound in a matter intra vires by the unanimous agreement of its members is, in my judgment, apt to cover the present case whether or not Lord Davey had circumstances such as the present case in mind.

If the company is bound by what was done when it was a going concern, then the liquidator is in no better position. He cannot sue the members because they owed no duty to the company as a separate entity and he cannot sue the directors because the decision which he seeks to impugn were made by, and with the full assent of, the members.

MAY LJ (dissenting): It is well established by such authorities as *Salomon v A Salomon & Co Ltd* and the many authorities to like effect to which we were referred that a company is bound, in a matter which is intra vires and not fraudulent, by the unanimous agreement of its members or by an ordinary resolution of a majority of its members. However, I do not think that this line of authority establishes anything more than that a company is bound by the legal results of a transaction so entered into: that is to say, for instance, by the terms of contract which is so approved; or that neither it nor for that matter its liquidator can challenge the legal consequences, such as a transfer of title, of a transaction to which its members have agreed to the extent that I have mentioned.

This, however, is very different from saying that where all the acts of the directors of a company, for instance, Services, have been carried out by them as nominees for, at the behest and with the knowledge of all the members of the company, namely the joint venturers, then forever the company as a separate legal entity is precluded from complaining of the quality of those acts in the absence of fraud or unless they were ultra vires. If we assume for the purposes of this argument that the directors of the plaintiff did commit breaches of the duty of care that they owed that company, as a result of which it suffered damage, then I agree with the submission made by counsel for the plaintiff that the company thereby acquired a cause of action against those directors in negligence. The fact that all the members of the company knew of the acts constituting such breaches, and indeed knew that those acts were in breach of that duty, does not of itself in my opinion prevent them from constituting the tort of negligence against the company or by itself release the directors from liability for it. Of course, in the circumstances of the present case, whilst the joint venturers retained effective control of the company they would be extremely unlikely to complain of the negligence of their nominees. But such restraint on their part could not and did not in my opinion amount to any release by the company of the cause of action which ex hypothesi had become vested in it against its directors. *Salomon's* case and the subsequent authorities make it clear that a limited company is a person separate and distinct from its members, even though a majority of the latter have the power to control its activities so long as it is not put

[99] Dillon LJ qualified this in *West Mercia Safetywear Ltd v Dodd* (1988) 4 BCLC 30, by saying that these remarks only apply to a company which is solvent at the time.

into liquidation and whilst they remain members and a majority. Once, however, the joint venturers ceased to be able to call the tune, either because the company went into liquidation or indeed, though it is not this case, because others took over their interest as members of the company, then I can see no legal reason why the liquidator or the company itself could not sue in respect of the cause of action still vested in it. I agree with counsel's submission that that cause of action was an asset of the company which could not be gratuitously released . . .

➤ Notes

1. All three members of the Court of Appeal in this case referred to the doubts expressed *obiter dicta* by Templeman and Cumming-Bruce LJJ in *Re Horsley & Weight Ltd* [4.31] whether directors holding a majority of shares were competent to ratify their own making of a corporate gift. This is now outlawed by CA 2006 s 239(3) and (4). CA 2006 therefore abrogates the rule in *North West Transportation Co Ltd v Beatty* (1887) 12 App Cas 589, PC, which held that a contract between the director and his company, which was voidable because of the director's undisclosed interest in it, could be ratified by the company in general meeting; and that the interested director could vote as a member in such a meeting, even though he held the majority of votes.

2. In *Queensland Mines Ltd v Hudson* (1978) 18 ALR 1, 52 ALJR 399, PC, the plaintiff company was set up as a joint venture by A Ltd, a company controlled by Hudson, and F Ltd, a company controlled by Korman. Hudson, as managing director of Queensland Mines, was involved in negotiations with the Tasmanian government for licences to mine iron ore. Just before the licences were issued, Korman and his company F Ltd ran into financial difficulties and Korman told Hudson that he had not the financial resources to proceed with the venture. Hudson took the licence in his own name. He later resigned as managing director of Queensland Mines and formed his own new company, which, at considerable risk and expense, exploited the licences and earned profits. The Privy Council held (i) that the opportunity to make the profits had come to Hudson through his position as managing director of Queensland Mines, but (ii) that since the board of that company had known of Hudson's interest at all times (and had resolved a year after the issues of the licences that Queensland Mines 'should not pursue the matter [ie the licences] any further'), Hudson was not accountable for his profit.

➤ Questions

1. What were the members in the *Multinational Gas* case purporting to do: exercise management decision-making power themselves; or authorise the directors in advance of the directors' action in order to enable the directors to pursue activities that would otherwise be in breach of duty; or ratify, after the event, thereby indicating that the company would not sue the defaulting directors for their breaches?

2. If the members were ratifying the wrongdoing (see *Murad v Al-Saraj* [7.38]), would their decision bind a liquidator who was subsequently appointed to the company and inclined to sue the wrongdoers?

3. If the alleged acts of negligence were committed by the directors with the *prior authorisation* of the members, do you consider the reasoning of Lawton LJ or that of May LJ more appropriate?

4. If the alleged acts of negligence were committed by the directors on their own initiative and later approved by the members, do you consider the reasoning of Lawton LJ or that of May LJ more appropriate?

5. In *Queensland Mines*, how could a decision of the board have this effect? Was the board the legitimate organ of the company to make arrangements with Hudson in advance of any breach? Or was the board of directors really also the 'general meeting' in all but name, representing all the corporate joint venturer members, and so able to count in effect as a members' vote at a members' meeting?

Approval or ratification by shareholders is not effective unless the decision is honest, bona fide and in the best interests of the company, including but not limited to instances of prejudice to creditors.

[7.44] Madoff Securities International Ltd v Raven [2011] EWHC 3102 (Commercial Court)

This case was part of the Madoff litigation where a US company (B) had been used for a massive Ponzi scheme fraud orchestrated by Madoff (M). Investors in the scheme had lost about US$19.5 billion. This litigation [or the part of interest here] concerned C, an English company, in which 99% of the shares were held by M and 1% by his brother who acted in accordance with his instructions. C was used to launder money and to make payments of stolen money. C brought proceedings against its directors alleging (amongst other matters) breach of fiduciary duty in relation to the moneys paid out. In response, it was suggested that there was no serious issue to be tried because the directors' acts had been either requested or approved by the shareholders, in the person of M, so that there was no breach of fiduciary duty or any breach had been ratified. The court disagreed.

FLAUX J:

94. Mr Mowschenson's [counsel for the defendants]...submits that, where the acts of directors of a company have been either requested or approved by the shareholders, those acts are the acts of the company and that, as a matter of company law, the company cannot contend that the directors have acted in breach of fiduciary duty. Either there was no breach or any breach has been ratified. Mr Mowschenson contends that the only exception to this principle is if the transaction carried out by the directors at the request of or with the approval of the shareholders is one which is likely to jeopardise the solvency of the company or cause loss to its creditors.

95. [This general principle] is recognised in a number of cases. A summary of the relevant principles of law is set out in . . . *Multinational Gas v Multinational Services* [7.43] . . .

97. The existence of an exception to that principle, where the transaction authorised by the shareholders is one which jeopardises the company's solvency or causes loss to its creditors . . . can be traced to dicta of Cumming-Bruce and Templeman LJ in *Re Horsley & Weight Ltd* [4.31] . . . [He continued, citing other cases referred to at 'The interests of creditors', p 367 on duties to creditors.] . . .

103. Mr Mowschenson submitted that this [solvency] exception...was the limit of any exception to the general principle. In particular, he submitted that there was not some wider exception that the directors' breach of fiduciary duty could not be ratified where the transaction in question was not bona fides or honest.

104. [After making the point that C was completely solvent when the relevant payments were made]...In those circumstances, it was nothing to the point that Mr Madoff, the 99% shareholder of [C], was a fraudster or that the [outgoing] payments...were the proceeds of that fraud . . . It is equally irrelevant that the true nature of the payments was disguised by Mr Madoff . . . The directors' actions in making the payments had been requested or approved by Mr Madoff, so [C] was bound by his consent and could not be heard to complain of breach of fiduciary duty by the directors.

105. Mr Saini [counsel for the claimant] challenged that conclusion. He submitted that there was a wider exception based on grounds of public policy, that the general principle would not apply where the shareholders, in ratifying the directors' acts, were acting dishonestly or using the company as a vehicle for fraud or wrongdoing. That was the case here, since Mr Madoff was using [C] as a money laundering vehicle to disguise and distribute the proceeds of his fraud . . .

106. In support of the submission that the 'doubtful solvency or loss to creditors' exception is not the only exception or is, at least, part of a wider exception, Mr Saini relies upon the judgment of the Vice-Chancellor in *Bowthorpe Holdings* [[2003] 1 BCLC 226] [which itself relies on a number of cases, including Lawton LJ in *Multinational Gas v Multinational Services* **[7.43]**, 268 that the members must act in good faith; and in *Re Duomatic* **[4.15]**, 372 Buckley J cited with approval the view of Astbury J in *Parker and Cooper Ltd v Reading* [1926] Ch 975, 984 that the transaction must be both intra vires and honest.] . . .

108. Mr Mowschenson sought to suggest that even this 'wider' exception was limited to cases where the directors' acts, albeit approved by the shareholders, have caused prejudice to the creditors of the company . . .

109. He questioned the juridical basis of a wider interpretation of the first exception. If the shareholders and directors acted dishonestly, but not in a manner which prejudiced the creditors, then their acts were still those of the company and bound the company, so that the company could not complain. No question of public policy arises in such a situation. It is all simply a question of the internal management of the company. Accordingly, if the Vice-Chancellor was stating some wider exception based on public policy, he was wrong.

110. Although I see the force of Mr Mowschenson's submissions, I am unable to accept them [at least here, on a strike-out action].

111. In my judgment, the wider first exception stated by Sir Andrew Morritt V-C was not intended to be limited to cases where there is prejudice to the creditors. . . .

112. . . . *Bowthorpe Holdings* stands as an authority of a court of concurrent jurisdiction to this court in support of the wider exception for which Mr Saini contends . . . [and]

113. . . . that decision does not stand alone. Whilst I accept that the authorities on this wider exception, both before and after *Bowthorpe Holdings*, are limited, those to which the Vice-Chancellor refers do not suggest that the earlier courts were limiting the exception to instances of prejudice to creditors. Rather, although none of the cases contains full reasoning, the exception recognised seems a much more general one, applicable where the transaction is one which would be a fraud on the company . . . [He referred again to Lawton LJ in the *Multinational Gas* case **[7.43]** and to other cases relied upon by Mr Saini.] . . .

123. . . . One explanation of that exception may be that public policy demands that a transaction which is not honest, bona fide and in the best interests of the company is not binding on the company. However, whatever the precise juridical basis of the wider exception, I consider that the claimants can show a serious issue to be tried that that exception applies here . . .

➤ Question

What is the basis of the 'wider exception'? Is it likely to be the explanation in para [123]? Is it more likely to be concerned with general rules about decision-making by shareholders? (See Question 3, after *Eclairs* **[7.11]**, p 355.)

Relief from liability granted by the court: CA 2006 s 1157

The court has a discretion to grant relief to directors and other officers from liability for breach of duty, similar to that which exists in relation to trustees, if they have 'acted honestly and reasonably and . . . ought fairly to be excused': CA 2006 s 1157.

The court in *Coleman Taymar Ltd v Oakes* [2001] 2 BCLC 749 held that the section could apply to a liability to account for profits, as well as to a liability to pay damages to the company. The discretion was exercised in *Re D'Jan of London Ltd* **[7.22]**, but refused, in a number of well-known cases, for example *Dorchester Finance Co Ltd v Stebbing* (Note 3 at '"Reasonable" directors: keeping informed and delegating responsibilities', p 381), *Guinness plc v Saunders* **[5.01]**, and *Clark v Cutland* [2003] EWCA Civ 810, CA. (Note that in *Re Produce Marketing Consortium Ltd* [1989] 1 WLR 745, Knox J ruled that, as a matter of principle, relief under CA 1985 s 727—now CA 2006 s 1157—could not be granted in favour of a director who is held liable to pay compensation for wrongful trading under IA 1986 s 214: see *Re Produce Marketing Consortium Ltd (No 2)* **[16.16]**.) It is clear that the economic realities of the case are relevant to the court's exercise of its CA 2006 s 1157 discretion.[100]

Two recent Court of Appeal decisions (both of which refused to grant the relief) further illustrate the court's approach under s 1157. In *Towers v Premier Waste Management Ltd* **[7.27]**, the failure to make disclosure was found to be a breach of the director's fiduciary duties; the regurgitation of arguments used to show that there had not been a breach proved similarly ineffective in seeking relief under s 1157. Given the limited additional arguments under this head, the Court of Appeal commended the brevity of the lower court's treatment of this part of the case. T had owed fiduciary duties to P and had acted in breach of those duties in circumstances where there was no mitigating factor and no evidence of injustice or hardship which might be relevant to granting relief in his favour. Just as the absence of any finding of bad faith or actual conflict, the reasonableness of T's reliance on R and the lack of direct contact between T and F, and the absence of quantifiable loss by P or the negligible profit to T, did not justify a finding that there was no breach of duty, so too they did not justify relieving him from the consequences of his breach of duty.

In *Smith v Butler* [2012] EWCA Civ 314, CA, having clarified the ambit of a managing director's powers, and thus finding that the managing director had no authority to exclude the chairman from the company, it was then held that the manager director had no power to cause the company to support his actions by resisting the chairman's applications. As the managing director had already proposed to resist the applications, the company could have avoided any significant expenditure if it had simply filed a defence to the effect that it would abide by any court orders arising from those proceedings. It was this feature of the case which led to Arden LJ's conclusion that no relief under s 1157 should be granted.

More recently in *Re HLC Environmental Projects Ltd* **[7.19],** Deputy High Court Judge John Randall QC set out the principles for the exercise of discretion under s 1157 at [108]:

(a) in order to be relieved of liability a director must establish three things: (i) that he acted honestly, (ii) that he acted reasonably, and (iii) that having regard to all the circumstances he ought fairly to be excused. The first of these is a subjective requirement, the second an objective requirement: *Coleman Taymar Ltd v Oakes* [2001] 2 B.C.LC. 749 per Judge Reid QC at [85];

(b) the burden of establishing honesty and reasonableness lies on the director: *Bairstow v Queens Moat Houses Plc* [2001] EWCA Civ 712; [2002] B.C.C. 91 per Robert Walker L.J. (as he then was) at [58]; and

(c) it is only if both of the first two requirements of honesty and reasonableness are established that the court needs to consider the third requirement, that in all the circumstances the director hought fairly to be excused.

---

[100] See, eg, *Re D'Jan of London Ltd* **[7.22]**; *Green v Walkling* [2007] All ER (D) 299.

Contracting out of liability: CA 2006 ss 232–238

Under CA 2006 s 232, 'Any provision that purports to exempt a director of a company (to any extent) from any liability that would otherwise attach to him in connection with any negligence, default, breach of duty or breach of trust in relation to the company is void.' The rule covers provisions in the articles and in separate contracts (s 232(3)). The early predecessors to this section were introduced as a knee-jerk reaction to the decision in *Re City Equitable Fire Insurance Co Ltd* **[7.21]**.

Specific exceptions are allowed by way of providing the director with insurance, qualifying third party indemnity provisions or qualifying pension scheme indemnity provisions (s 232(2)). A further exception is provided in s 205 (exception for expenditure on defending proceedings etc).

Section 232 retains the unresolved difficulty of its predecessors, however, since s 232(4) provides: 'nothing in the section is to be taken as preventing the company's articles from making such provision as had previously been lawful for dealing with conflicts of interest.' Such provisions in the articles are common, permitting certain activities by directors that would otherwise constitute breaches of the no conflict rule. How these provisions could be regarded as legitimate in the face of the predecessor to s 232 (CA 1985 ss 309A–309C) was troubling.

In *Movitex Ltd v Bulfield* [1988] BCLC 104, Vinelott J attempted to resolve the issue by holding that the rule against self-dealing by a trustee or a director is properly seen as a *disability* or restriction on the conduct of a fiduciary and not a *duty*: articles which exclude or modify the application of this rule did not, therefore, infringe CA 1985 ss 309A–310. It did not help matters much, and the analysis was described in *Gwembe Valley Development Co Ltd v Koshy (No 3)* **[7.41]** as a 'needless complication'. In any event, all this rather unsatisfying mental gymnastics is no longer possible now that the codified rules expressly regard all the rules as 'duties'. Also see R Nicholson, 'Authorising Multiple Directorships in Unrelated Companies: Table A to the Rescue?' (2011) 9 *Journal of International Banking and Finance Law* 534.

Special rules on notice requirements and members' approval for certain transactions: CA 2006 ss 182–231

Declarations of interest in existing transactions or arrangements: ss 182–187

Section 182 provides that if a director enters into a transaction or arrangement with the company without declaring his interest under s 177 (duty to declare interest in proposed transaction or arrangement), he will be under an immediate obligation to declare that interest and failure to do so will constitute a criminal offence (see s 183 (offence of failure to declare interest)). Even in these circumstances, however, it seems that the director is given a reasonable amount of time in which to comply with the duty in s 182 (see subs (4)).

Unlike s 177, s 182(2) makes it clear that directors must use one of the three prescribed methods of declaration. Sections 184–187 elaborate on these, and in particular provide rules for sole directors of companies that ought to have two or more directors, and for shadow directors. Presumably a failure to make a declaration in the prescribed manner will render the declaration either a nullity or incomplete, and a further declaration will be required (s 182(3)); how this requirement will be reconciled with s 182(6)(b), indicating that the duty does not apply if the other directors are already aware of the interest, or ought to be aware of the interest, is unclear. As with s 177, certain interests do not have to be declared.

Unlike the duty to declare an interest in a *proposed* transaction or arrangement (s 177), it is a criminal offence not to comply with the duty to declare an interest in an *existing* transaction or arrangement. The Attorney General, Lord Goldsmith, in Grand Committee explained the rationale behind this:

> because one is here concerned with an existing transaction or arrangement, the failure to declare cannot affect the validity of the transaction or give rise to any other civil consequences. That is to be contrasted with the position where there is a failure to disclose an interest in relation to a proposed transaction where the law can say that as a result of the failure to disclose that interest—and the company then enters into the transaction in ignorance of that—consequences follow. The transaction may be voidable, to be set aside. The company may wish to claim financial redress in one form or another as a result of what has taken place. But, as I say, that is different from a failure to declare an interest in an existing transaction where those considerations probably cannot arise. That is why a criminal offence is created. (HL GC Day 4, Hansard HL 678, 9/2/06, col 338)

This does not appear to be an accurate description of the differences between these two provisions. If a director *complies* with s 177, then the company can decide on a fully informed basis whether to proceed with the proposed transaction or arrangement. Section 180 indicates that this declaration replaces the need for the approval of the company's members under the equitable rules, although any additional requirements imposed by the articles will still have to be met. Assuming these additional requirements (if any) have also been met, the transaction cannot be impugned for breach of s 177 or for breach of the no conflict and no profit rules in relation to transactions with the company. However, note that the deal might nevertheless be a breach of some other general statutory duty, and give rise to an action for a remedy under some other head. The availability of the relevant remedies in those particular circumstances will then need to be assessed in the usual way.

On the other hand, if s 177 is *not* complied with, and the company nevertheless enters into the proposed transaction or arrangement, then the director will be in breach of s 177 and, if the breach continues, will also be in breach of s 182. The equitable remedies for breach of the general statutory duty can be pursued against the defaulting director (and, again, an assessment will have to be made about the availability of various remedies—eg rescission will not be available against a bona fide third party purchaser, but will be available against other parties not protected by this equitable rule, including the director). In addition, the director will also be liable for the criminal offence described in s 183. Put this way, there is no logical divide between the remedies available for breach of ss 177 and 182; indeed, if s 177 is breached, and the proposed arrangement is pursued, s 182 will also be breached so long as the director fails to declare the interest. Section 177 is therefore not a provision designed to *impose* liability on directors, but a provision designed to afford protection to those who comply with it.

In this sense, there is the same relationship between ss 183 and 178 (as influenced by s 180) as there is between CA 1985 s 317 and the equitable consequences of breach of the no conflict and no profit rules (as influenced by any relevant consents given by the members or given in the way allowed by the articles). See *Guinness plc v Saunders* [1990] 2 AC 663, 697 (Lord Goff) **[5.01]**; *Coleman Taymar Ltd v Oakes* [2001] 2 BCLC 749.

Transactions with directors requiring the approval of members

Certain transactions between the company and its directors are deemed sufficiently 'risky' to require members' approval for their validity, rather than the simpler procedure of board approval set out in s 177. The details of the statutory provisions are not addressed here, but the sections repay careful reading. Several categories of transactions are affected:

(i) Directors' long-term service contracts: ss 188–189

See 'Directors' service contracts', pp 283ff.

(ii) Substantial property transactions: ss 190–196

Substantial property transactions (defined in s 191) are permitted, provided they are approved by the members. Failure to obtain the necessary authorisation will not result in any liability for the company (s 190(3)).

An 'arrangement' includes an agreement or understanding that does not have contractual effect (*Re Duckwari plc* [7.45]). Note the exceptions in ss 192–194. The civil consequences are described in s 195. These sections apply equally to shadow directors: s 223(1)(b).

The remedies provided by s 195 enlarge both the types of recovery (including recovery of losses, and not just profits) and the persons against whom recovery is available, when compared with the remedies available in equity for breach of fiduciary duty in entering into transactions involving a conflict of interest. These remedies are not available if the members approve the transaction within a reasonable time (s 196). Also see s 1157 (power of court to grant relief in certain circumstances).

See *Re Duckwari plc* [7.45] (general remedies issues) and *Re Ciro Citterio Menswear plc* [7.46] (no constructive trust before rescission).

(iii) Loans, quasi-loans and credit transactions: ss 197–214

Company loans to directors and connected persons are no longer generally prohibited but are subject to the requirement of member approval, and sometimes also approval of the members of the company's holding company. The sections apply equally to shadow directors (s 223(1)(c)).

The provisions relating to loans apply to all UK-registered companies (with the exception of wholly owned subsidiaries (s 197(5)). The provisions for quasi-loans and credit transactions apply only to public companies and associated companies (ss 198 and 201). See other related restrictions (ss 198–203).

The requirement for members' approval is subject to the exceptions in ss 204–209 inclusive: the exceptions extend to expenditure on company business; expenditure on defending proceedings etc, in connection with regulatory action or investigation; expenditure for minor and business transactions; expenditure for intra-group transactions and expenditure for money-lending companies). Of these, the most general is s 207, which sets the minimum threshold value for transactions requiring the approval of members (£10,000 for loans, etc; £15,000 for credit transactions).

The remedies are set out in s 213, and there is, again, a provision for subsequent affirmation (s 214).

(iv) Payments for loss of office: ss 215–222

See 'Compensation claims for loss of office', pp 303ff.

(v) Directors' service contracts—definition and inspection rights of members: ss 227–230

See 'Directors' service contracts', pp 283ff.

(vi) Contracts not in the ordinary course of business with sole member who is also a director: s 231

Outside the range of Pt 10, directors are subject to a raft of statutory provisions imposing liability for:

(i)   losses of capital, for example through issuing shares without complying with the statutory rules about payment; or for making an improper repurchase of shares out of capital (see 'Redemptions and repurchases of shares', pp 542ff);

(ii) 'insider dealing': see 'Insider dealing', pp 768ff;

(iii) directors are liable to reimburse the company if political donations are made without shareholder authorisation: CA 2006 ss 366ff and see 'Corporate gifts', pp 135ff.

Enhanced range of statutory remedies for these transactions

It is crucial to read the relevant statutory provisions if you want to understand this area.

Statutory remedies for breach of duty may include losses not caused by the breach itself.

[7.45] Re Duckwari plc [1999] Ch 253 (Court of Appeal)

Mr Cooper was a director of Offerventure Ltd and also of Duckwari plc. Offerventure had contracted to buy a property in High Wycombe for development for £495,000 (a fair price). Cooper offered to pass on the property to Duckwari at cost, on terms that he would receive a 50% share of any profits resulting from the development. This offer was accepted by the board of Duckwari, but not approved by its members. After Duckwari had bought the property, there was a fall in the market and the property was eventually sold for £177,970. The Court of Appeal held that Cooper, Duckwari's other directors and Offerventure (as an associated company) were liable under CA 1985 ss 320–322 [now CA 2006 ss 190ff] to indemnify Duckwari for the whole of its loss, including that due to the fall in market value, and not simply for the difference between the price paid for the property and its value at the time of the transaction (which would have been nil).

NOURSE LJ: It is convenient to start with the judge's comparison of the purchase with an unauthorised investment by a trustee. The assets of a company being vested in the company, the directors are not accurately described as trustees of those assets. Nevertheless, they have always been treated as trustees of assets which are in their hands or under their control. The principle is best stated by Lindley LJ in *Re Lands Allotment Co*:[101]

'Although directors are not properly speaking trustees, yet they have always been considered and treated as trustees of money which comes to their hands or which is actually under their control; and ever since joint stock companies were invented directors have been liable to make good moneys which they have misapplied upon the same footing as if they were trustees . . .'

As to what is meant by a misapplication in this context, I adopt as correct the statement in *Gore-Browne on Companies*, 44th edn (1986), p 27/010, para 27.6:

'any disposition of the company's property which by virtue of any provision of the company's constitution or *any statutory provision* or any rule of general law the company or the board is forbidden or incompetent or unauthorised to make, or which is carried out by the

---

[101] [1894] 1 Ch 616, CA.

directors otherwise than in accordance with their duty to act bona fide in the interests of the company and for the proper purposes.' (Emphasis added.)

A statutory provision well known in this context was section 54 of the Companies Act 1948 (now re-enacted, though with substantial amendments, by sections 151 to 158 of the Act of 1985), which prohibited a company from giving financial assistance for the acquisition of its own shares. It has been held that directors who cause the company's funds to be applied in breach of that prohibition are to be treated as trustees of those funds: see, for example, *Belmont Finance Corpn Ltd v Williams Furniture Ltd (No 2)* **[10.10]**. Similarly, by virtue of section 320(1)(b) Duckwari was prohibited from entering into the arrangement with Offerventure pursuant to which it purchased the property unless the arrangement was first approved by a resolution of Duckwari in general meeting. Such approval not having been obtained, the payment of £495,000, together with the other costs of the acquisition, was a misapplication of Duckwari's funds which, had section 320 stood alone, the directors responsible would have been liable to make good as if they were trustees.

The basis on which trustees would have been liable to make good the misapplication is well settled. If a trustee applies trust moneys in the acquisition of an unauthorised investment, he is liable to restore to the trust the amount of the loss incurred on its realisation: see *Knott v Cottee* (1852) 16 Beav 77. He is also liable for interest. Where more than one trustee is responsible for the acquisition their liability is joint and several.

If these rules were to apply to the present case, the directors responsible would prima facie appear to be jointly and severally liable to restore to Duckwari the difference between the gross acquisition cost, £505,923, and the £177,970 which has since been realised on the sale of the property, plus interest, credit being given for the amount of any rents and profits received before completion of the sale.

That would have been the position if section 320 had stood alone, which it does not. A company's remedies for a contravention of that section are spelled out in section 322, in this case in section 322(3)(b). So the question is what loss or damage is comprehended by that provision. The persons who are rendered liable to indemnify Duckwari are not only Mr Cooper and the other directors responsible but also Offerventure, as a person connected with Mr Cooper.

[His Lordship outlined the arguments of counsel and continued:] In considering these rival submissions I return once more to the wording of section 322(3)(b), which provides for an indemnity 'for any loss or damage resulting from the arrangement or transaction.' Plainly those words, if read in isolation, are capable of including a loss incurred by Duckwari on a realisation of the property for less than the cost of its acquisition. Such a loss can fairly be said to result from the purchase, on the ground that if the purchase had not been made the loss would not have been incurred. But the loss can also fairly be said to result from the fall in value of the property. So it is necessary to look at the other provisions of sections 320 and 322 and the general law in order to see whether a loss of the former kind was intended to be included.

I agree with Mr Richards [counsel for the company] that the judge was wrong both in thinking that the general distinction between the decision-making powers of directors and trustees had some relevance to the question and in restricting the mischief addressed by the provisions to acquisitions at an inflated value or disposals at an undervalue. It is obvious that there will be many other circumstances in which it is appropriate for the approval of shareholders to be obtained. In the present case, for example, the shareholders might well have declined to approve the purchase either because it was a new kind of venture or, more pertinently, because Offerventure or Mr Cooper was to take 50 per cent of any profits arising from the development of the property but was not to bear a share of any loss. A one-sided arrangement thus favourable to the director would seem to be an exemplar of the kind of arrangement which was intended to be within the scope of section 320.

Bearing in mind the evident purpose of sections 320 and 322 to give shareholders specific protection in respect of arrangements and transactions which will or may benefit directors to the detriment of the company, I am unable to construe section 322(3)(b) as denying the company a remedy which appears to flow naturally from a combination of section 320(1)(b) and the general law. No doubt it is possible to cite instances where Parliament has been held to take away with one hand what it appears to give with the other. But I cannot conceive that one would be found where the result was to give a narrow effect to provisions plainly intended to afford a protection and equally amenable to being given some wider effect.

This broad approach to section 322(3)(b) is entirely consistent with the provisions of section 322(2)(a) and (3)(a) . . .

It is well recognised that the basis on which a trustee is liable to make good a misapplication of trust moneys is strict and sometimes harsh, especially where, as here, there has been a huge depreciation in the value of the asset acquired. I can understand what I believe to have been the reluctance of the judge to visit Mr Cooper (with whom I include Offerventure) with the consequences of the loss. But the loss has to fall somewhere and, if a proposal to purchase the property had been put to and rejected by the shareholders, it would have lain with Mr Cooper. The approval of the shareholders not having been obtained, it is not unfair that the loss should continue to lie with Mr Cooper rather than Duckwari . . .

PILL and THORPE LJJ concurred.

➤ Question

The general principle here (although not the expanded list of parties against whom claims may be made) is not inconsistent with *Target Holdings* and *AIB*.[102] Why not?

Not every case in which a director receives a loan (or a quasi-loan) results in a constructive trusteeship.

[7.46] Ciro Citterio Menswear plc v Thakrar [2002] EWHC 662 (Ch), [2002] 1 WLR 2217 (Chancery Division)

ANTHONY MANN QC: The principal question in this part of this case is whether an unlawful loan gives rise to constructive trusteeship at any stage. I take as a starting point that a loan to a director is not of itself the sort of transaction that is inevitably a misapplication of company moneys. There is nothing inherently wrong with such a transaction in the abstract. It may or may not be a misapplication on any particular set of facts, but it is not, as such, a breach by a director of his trusteeship of company assets. Statute did not intervene until the Companies Act 1929, when the predecessor of section 330 made its first appearance. The bar was repeated in the Companies Act 1948, but without the civil consequences of the bar being spelt out. It was not until 1985 that statute specified civil consequences.

The civil consequences are specified as being that the loan is voidable. That is of obvious significance to this part of the case. If a loan is voidable, it stands until avoided. That means that property in the money paid under the loan passes to the borrower. In my view that concept is

---

[102] *Target Holdings Ltd v Redferns* [1996] AC 421, HL; *AIB Group (UK) Plc v Mark Redler & Co Solicitors* [2014] UKSC 58, SC.

inimical to the existence of a constructive trusteeship, or any form of tracing claim, at least in the absence of special circumstances. That view is supported by the speech of Lord Goff of Chieveley in *Guinness plc v Saunders* **[5.01]**, 698. Lord Goff was considering a breach by a Guinness director of the disclosure rules in section 317 of the companies Act 1985 [now see CA 2006 s 177]. The consequences of that breach were that the contract in question, under which the director took considerable financial benefits, was voidable, not void. [Recall, importantly, that for other reasons the House of Lords found the contract to be *void*, not merely voidable, but that does not affect the correctness of the analysis advanced here on voidable contracts.] The Court of Appeal had held that the director, therefore, became a constructive trustee of the moneys he had received under that contract and had to pay them back. Lord Goff, with whom Lord Griffiths agreed, held that this part of the analysis could not be sustained. A voidable contract stood until avoided. He considered, at p 698, an argument by counsel for Guinness to the effect that the director

> 'having received the money as constructive trustee, must pay it back. This appears to have formed, in part at least, the basis of the decision of the Court of Appeal. But the insuperable difficulty in the way of this proposition is again that the money was on this approach paid not under a void, but under a voidable, contract. Under such a contract, the property in the money would have vested in Mr Ward (who, I repeat, was ex hypothesi acting in good faith); and Guinness cannot short circuit an unrescinded contract simply by alleging a constructive trust.'

In my view, that reasoning applies in this case. Until any avoidance by the company the loan stood, and there was no constructive trust. In the case of section 330 that conclusion is reinforced by the terms of section 341 [now see CA 2006 s 213]. That sets out the civil consequences, and it seems to me that in the absence of special facts making the loan a breach of fiduciary duty they leave no room for constructive trusteeship. Section 341(2)(a) [CA 2006 s 213(3)(a)] seems to presuppose the absence of constructive trusteeship, because it expressly provides for what would otherwise be one of the consequences of constructive trusteeship, namely an obligation to account for gains made.

Also see *Currencies Direct Ltd v Ellis* [2002] 2 BCLC 821, CA, which addresses the issue of whether payments received by a director from his company should be characterised as loans or remuneration. In *Brown v Button* [2011] EWHC 1034 (Ch) the point was made that the six-year limitation period (see *Gwembe Valley Development Co Ltd v Koshy* **[7.41]**) does not apply to actions to recover illegal loans from directors (now CA 2006 s 213(3)(a)), where the claim is in reality a claim to recover property which a director has obtained from the company in breach of trust; but that the six-year limitation period applies to claims against all the directors rendering them jointly and severally liable to indemnify the company for the losses in relation to such unauthorised loans (now CA 2006 s 213(3)(b)).

Secondary liability (liability of third parties associated with directors' wrongs)

When directors act in breach of their fiduciary duties to the company, third parties may sometimes also be liable to the company for their associated or secondary role in the wrongdoing.[103] The company may be keen to pursue such claims, especially if the

---

[103] Of course, quite separately, the company will have all the usual contract and tort claims against third parties who have committed wrongs against the company. Here, however, we are only examining the issue of third parties whose liability is somehow associated with the directors' wrongdoing.

defaulting director has absconded or is insolvent. The favoured third parties to sue are 'deep pockets', such as banks and law firms. Shareholders, even substantial shareholders, are unlikely to be considered as such third parties unless the evidence overwhelmingly takes them outside the usual role of shareholders (including controlling shareholders): see *Kuwait Asia Bank* **[7.48]**.

Third party liability typically falls under the following heads:

(i)   Personally liable as *'knowing recipients'*, that is, people who 'knowingly' receive the company's property as a result of the director's breach of duty. Since liability is personal, not proprietary, it is irrelevant whether these people still have the property or its proceeds in their possession when the claim is brought. The necessary degree of knowledge to make these people liable remains unsettled (see the unconscionability test, later). These people are liable to the extent of the personal benefit received.

(ii)   Personally liable as *'dishonest accessories'*, that is, people who dishonestly assist or procure the director's breach of duty. These people are liable with the defaulting director, as accessories.[104]

(iii)   Subject to a proprietary claim, having received the company's property without being able to assert the protection of bona fide purchaser for value without knowledge of the company's interests; that is, people who are donees of gifts of the company's property, or who purchase it without the necessary bona fides. These people hold the property on trust for the company.

The following case extracts illustrate the types of claims.

Required knowledge for secondary liability

In *Baden Delvaux & Lecuit v Société Général pour Favoriser le Développement du Commerce et de l'Industrie en France SA* [1983] BCLC 325 at 407, [1993] 1 WLR 509n at 575, Peter Gibson J identified five different kinds of mental state which might be relevant in assessing the knowledge required for the secondary liability, as follows:

(i)   actual knowledge;

(ii)   wilfully shutting one's eyes to the obvious;

(iii)   wilfully and recklessly failing to make such inquiries as an honest and responsible man would make;

(iv)   knowledge of circumstances which would indicate the facts to an honest and reasonable man;

(v)   knowledge of circumstances which would have put an honest and reasonable man on inquiry.

However, in *Bank of Credit and Commerce International (Overseas) Ltd v Chief Akindele* [2000] BCLC 968, the Court of Appeal ruled that it was time to make a clean break, and that there should be a single test of knowledge for *knowing receipt*: was the recipient's state of knowledge such as to make it unconscionable for him to retain the benefit of the receipt? Although the fivefold classification had often been found 'helpful', the new test would 'better enable the courts to give common-sense decisions in the commercial context in which claims in knowing receipt are now frequently made'.

With *'dishonest assistance'* (formerly 'knowing assistance'), there has also been radical change. In the *Royal Brunei Airlines* case (also sometimes referred to simply as *Tan*) **[7.47]**,

---

[104]   See S Elliott and C Mitchell, 'Remedies for Dishonest Assistance' (2004) 67 MLR 16.

it was held that what is relevant is the state of mind of the person who, as an accessory, procures or assists in the breach of trust or other fiduciary obligation. For this purpose it must be shown that the accessory was dishonest.

The test of dishonesty applied by Lord Nicholls in *Tan* was widely assumed to be an objective test: would a reasonable person in the same circumstances have thought the transaction or arrangements dishonest? But in *Twinsectra Ltd v Yardley* [2002] UKHL 12, [2002] 2 AC 164 the majority of the House adopted a double objective–subjective test of dishonesty. Not only must the transaction be dishonest according to reasonable standards of honesty, but the defendant must also appreciate that fact. Lord Hutton gave the leading speech, purporting to apply the *Royal Brunei Airlines* principles of accessory liability, and Lord Hoffmann added that these required 'more than knowledge of the facts which make the conduct wrongful. They require a dishonest state of mind, that is to say, consciousness that one is transgressing ordinary standards of honest behaviour' [20]. Lord Hoffmann went on to clarify: 'I do not suggest that one cannot be dishonest without a full appreciation of the legal analysis of the transaction. A person may dishonestly assist in the commission of a breach of trust without any idea of what a trust means. The necessary dishonest state of mind may be found to exist simply on the fact that he knew perfectly well that he was helping to pay away money to which the recipient was not entitled' [24]. Lord Millett gave a powerful dissent, suggesting the subjective element was inappropriate in civil cases, and wrongly borrowed from the criminal law.

Lord Millett's (and Lord Nicholls's) views now seem to have prevailed. In *Barlow Clowes v Eurotrust International* [2005] UKPC 37, [2006] 1 WLR 1476, Lord Hoffmann delivered the opinion of the Privy Council (which included Lord Nicholls), and explicitly adopted the objective test of honesty: would a reasonable person, knowing what the defendant knew, regard the transaction or arrangement as dishonest? Indeed, the *Barlow Clowes* approach was explicitly endorsed by the Court of Appeal in *Starglade Properties Ltd v Roland Nash* [2010] EWCA Civ 1314:

> There is a single standard of honesty objectively determined by the court. That standard is applied to specific conduct of a specific individual possessing the knowledge and qualities he actually enjoyed [25] . . .
>
> [After considering *Twinsectra* and *Barlow Clowes*:]
>
> There is no suggestion in this case either that the standard of dishonesty is flexible or determined by any one other than by the court on an objective basis having regard to the ingredients of the combined test as explained by Lord Hutton in *Twinsectra* and Lord Hoffmann in *Barlow Clowes*.

Also see *Bank of Ireland (UK) plc v Jaffery* [2012] EWHC 1377 (Ch) and *Vivendi SA v Richards* [2013] EWHC 3006 (Ch), [2013] BCC 771.

'Dishonest assistance'—meaning of dishonesty.

[7.47] Royal Brunei Airlines Sdn Bhd v Tan Kok Ming [1995] 2 AC 378 (Privy Council)

Royal Brunei Airlines appointed Borneo Leisure Travel as its agent to sell passenger and cargo transportation, on written terms which provided that moneys collected by BLT for the sale of such services should be held by it on trust for RBA. BLT became insolvent owing over $335,000 to RBA. The question was whether Tan Kok Ming, who was BLT's managing

director and principal shareholder, was accountable to RBA for this sum as a constructive trustee. In holding that he was, the Privy Council formulated revised rules of liability.

The opinion of the Judicial Committee was delivered by LORD NICHOLLS: The proper role of equity in commercial transactions is a topical question. Increasingly plaintiffs have recourse to equity for an effective remedy when the person in default, typically a company, is insolvent. Plaintiffs seek to obtain relief from others who were involved in the transactions, such as directors of the company, or its bankers, or its legal or other advisers. They seek to fasten fiduciary obligations directly onto the company's officers or agents or advisers, or to have them held personally liable for assisting the company in breaches of trust or fiduciary obligations.

This is such a case. An insolvent travel agent company owed money to an airline. The airline seeks a remedy against the travel agent's principal director and shareholder. Its claim is based on the much-quoted dictum of Lord Selborne LC, sitting in the Court of Appeal in Chancery, in *Barnes v Addy*.[105]

[His Lordship quoted from the judgment in this case and continued:] In the conventional shorthand, the first of these two circumstances in which third parties (non-trustees) may become liable to account in equity is 'knowing receipt', as distinct from the second, where liability arises from 'knowing assistance'. Stated even more shortly, the first limb of Lord Selborne LC's formulation is concerned with the liability of a person as a *recipient* of trust property or its traceable proceeds. The second limb is concerned with what, for want of a better compendious description, can be called the liability of an *accessory* to a trustee's breach of trust. Liability as an accessory is not dependent upon receipt of trust property. It arises even though no trust property has reached the hands of the accessory. It is a form of secondary liability in the sense that it only arises where there has been a breach of trust. In the present case the plaintiff airline relies on the accessory limb. The particular point in issue arises from the expression 'a dishonest and fraudulent design on the part of the trustees'. . . .

In short, the issue on this appeal is whether the breach of trust which is a prerequisite to accessory liability must itself be a dishonest and fraudulent breach of trust by the trustee.

The honest trustee and the dishonest third party

. . . Take the simple example of an honest trustee and a dishonest third party. Take a case where a dishonest solicitor persuades a trustee to apply trust property in a way the trustee honestly believes is permissible but which the solicitor knows full well is a clear breach of trust. The solicitor deliberately conceals this from the trustee. In consequence, the beneficiaries suffer a substantial loss. It cannot be right that in such a case the accessory liability principle would be inapplicable because of the innocence of the trustee. In ordinary parlance, the beneficiaries have been defrauded by the solicitor. If there is to be an accessory liability principle at all, whereby in appropriate circumstances beneficiaries may have direct recourse against a third party, the principle must surely be applicable in such a case, just as much as in a case where both the trustee and the third party have been dishonest. Indeed, if anything, the case for liability of the dishonest third party seems stronger where the trustee is innocent, because in such a case the third party alone was dishonest and that was the cause of the subsequent misapplication of the trust property.

The position would be the same if, instead of *procuring* the breach, the third party dishonestly *assisted* in the breach. Change the facts slightly. A trustee is proposing to make a payment out of the trust fund to a particular person. He honestly believes he is authorised to do so by the terms of the trust deed. He asks a solicitor to carry through the transaction. The solicitor well knows that the proposed payment would be a plain breach of trust. He also well knows that the trustee

mistakenly believes otherwise. Dishonestly he leaves the trustee under his misapprehension and prepares the necessary documentation. Again, if the accessory principle is not to be artificially constricted, it ought to be applicable in such a case.

These examples suggest that what matters is the state of mind of the third party sought to be made liable, not the state of mind of the trustee. The trustee will be liable in any event for the breach of the trust, even if he acted innocently, unless excused by an exemption clause in the trust instrument or relieved by the court. But his state of mind is essentially irrelevant to the question whether the *third party* should be made liable to the beneficiaries for the breach of trust. If the liability of the third party is fault-based, what matters is the nature of his fault, not that of the trustee. In this regard dishonesty on the part of the third party would seem to be a sufficient basis for his liability, irrespective of the state of mind of the trustee who is in breach of trust. It is difficult to see why, if the third party dishonestly assisted in a breach, there should be a further prerequisite to his liability, namely that the trustee also must have been acting dishonestly. The alternative view would mean that the dishonest third party is liable if the trustee is dishonest, but if the trustee did not act dishonestly that of itself would excuse a dishonest third party from liability. That would make no sense.

[His Lordship discussed the authorities further, and continued:]

Drawing the threads together, their Lordships' overall conclusion is that dishonesty is a necessary ingredient of accessory liability. It is also a sufficient ingredient. A liability in equity to make good resulting loss attaches to a person who dishonestly procures or assists in a breach of trust or fiduciary obligation. It is not necessary that, in addition, the trustee or fiduciary was acting dishonestly, although this will usually be so where the third party who is assisting him is acting dishonestly.

[It was held, accordingly, that, even on the assumption that dishonesty could not be imputed to BLT, Tan Kok Ming's own dishonesty rendered him liable. But it was also held that BLT's breach of trust was itself dishonest.]

➤ Question

Compare the *objective* test used in *Tan*, *Barlow Clowes* and *Starglade Properties* with the *Ghosh* test of dishonesty under criminal law. Is there a difference between how 'dishonesty' is interpreted in criminal and civil cases? Should there be such a difference? What about 'quasi-criminal' cases such as fraud?

Substantial shareholders who appoint nominee directors owe no duties to anyone for the way in which the nominee performs as a director. It makes no difference that the nominee director is an employee of the nominating shareholder.

[7.48] Kuwait Asia Bank EC v National Mutual Life Nominees Ltd [1991] 1 AC 187 (Privy Council)

The Kuwait Asia bank owned 40% of the shares in AICS, a New Zealand company which had taken money on deposit from the public. House and August, employees of the bank, were appointed by the bank to be two of the five directors of AICS; the remaining three were nominees of another large shareholder, Kumutoto. The plaintiff company, NMLN, had acted as trustee for the depositors investing in AICS, pursuant to requirements of the New Zealand securities legislation. When AICS went into liquidation, the depositors sued NMLN for breach of its duties as their trustee (these claims were settled), and here NMLN in turn sought contribution from, inter alia (i) House and August and (ii) the bank. NMLN contended that it had relied on certificates of AICS's financial position which

were inaccurate and for which the directors bore collective responsibility. The Judicial Committee held that while a prima facie case existed against House and August, no claim lay against the bank. The bank was not vicariously liable for any breach of duty which might be proved against the two directors whom it had nominated, and this was so even though they were also its employees; and it did not *qua* shareholder owe duties to anybody.

The opinion of the Judicial Committee was delivered by LORD LOWRY: . . . Their Lordships now proceed to consider the causes of action pleaded by the plaintiff against the bank. Two general principles may first be stated. (1) A director does not by reason only of his position as director owe any duty to creditors or to trustees for creditors of the company. (2) A shareholder does not by reason only of his position as shareholder owe any duty to anybody . . .

But although directors are not liable as such to creditors of the company, a director may by agreement or representation assume a special duty to a creditor of the company. A director may accept or assume a duty of care in supplying information to a creditor analogous to the duty described by the House of Lords in *Hedley Byrne & Co Ltd v Heller & Partners Ltd* [[1964] AC 465, HL].

[His Lordship held that there was an arguable case against House and August personally on this ground, and continued:]

As against the bank, the statement of claim pleaded that the bank was liable to contribute to the loss suffered by the plaintiff . . . for all or any of the following reasons: (1) House and August were appointed to the board of directors of AICS by the bank, were employed by the bank and carried out their duties as directors in the course of their employment by the bank. (2) House and August were, as directors of AICS, the agents of the bank which was the principal. (3) As a substantial shareholder . . . the bank owed a duty of care to the plaintiff and to the depositors to ensure that the business of AICS was not conducted negligently or recklessly or in such a manner as to materially disadvantage the interests of those unsecured depositors. (4) House and August were persons occupying a position of directors of AICS who were accustomed to act in accordance with the bank's directions, and therefore the bank was a director of AICS within the meaning of section 2 of the Companies Act 1955 [see the UK equivalent on 'shadow directors'].

As to (1) the power of appointing a director of a company may be exercised by a shareholder or a person who is not a shareholder by virtue of the articles of association of the company, or by virtue of the control of the majority of the voting shares of the company, or by virtue of the agreement or acquiescence of other shareholders. In the present case, the bank and Kumutoto, who together controlled AICS, decided that the bank should nominate two directors. In the absence of fraud or bad faith (which are not alleged here), a shareholder or other person who controls the appointment of a director owes no duty to creditors of the company to take reasonable care to see that directors so appointed discharge their duties as directors with due diligence and competence . . .

The liability of a shareholder would be unlimited if he were accountable to a creditor for the exercise of his power to appoint a director and for the conduct of the director so appointed. It is in the interests of a shareholder to see that directors are wise and that the actions of the company are not foolish; but this concern of the shareholder stems from self-interest, and not from duty . . . It does not make any difference if the directors appointed by a shareholder are employed by the shareholder and are allowed to carry out their duties as directors while in the shareholder's employment. House and August owed three separate duties. They owed in the first place to AICS the duty to perform their duties as directors without gross negligence; . . . They owed a duty to the plaintiff to use reasonable care to see that the certificates complied with the requirements of the trust deed. Finally, they owed a duty to their employer, the bank, to exercise reasonable diligence and skill in the performance of their duties as directors of AICS.

If House and August did not exercise reasonable care to see that the quarterly certificates were accurate, they committed a breach of the duty they owed to the plaintiff and may have committed a breach of the duty they owed to the bank to exercise reasonable diligence and skill. But these duties were separate and distinct and different in scope and nature. The bank was not responsible for a breach of the duties owed by House and August to AICS or to the plaintiff any more than AICS or the plaintiff were responsible for a breach of duty by House and August. If House and August committed a breach of the duty which was imposed on them and other directors of AICS and was owed to the plaintiff under and by virtue of the trust deed they did so as individuals and as directors of AICS and not as employees of the bank; House and August were not parties to the trust deed, nor was the bank. House and August were allowed by the bank to perform their duties to AICS in the bank's time and at the bank's expense. It was in the interest of the bank that House and August should discharge with diligence and skill the duties which they owed to AICS, but these facts do not render the bank liable for breach by House and August of the duty imposed on them by the trust deed. In the performance of their duties as directors and in the performance of their duties imposed by the trust deed, House and August were bound to ignore the interests and wishes of their employer, the bank. They could not plead any instruction from the bank as an excuse for breach of their duties to AICS and the plaintiff. Of course, if the bank exploited its position as employers of House and August to obtain an improper advantage for the bank or to cause harm to the plaintiff then the bank would be liable for its own misconduct. But there is no suggestion that the bank behaved with impropriety . . .

(2) Then it is said that House and August were the agents of the bank. But, as directors of AICS, they were the agents of AICS and not of the bank. As directors of AICS, House and August were agents of AICS for the purposes of the trust deed and, by the express terms of the trust deed, responsibility for the accuracy of the quarterly certificates was assumed by the directors of AICS. House and August accepted responsibility for the quarterly certificates as directors of AICS and not as agents or employees of the bank.

(3) Next it was said that the bank owed a personal duty of care to the plaintiff. For the protection of the depositors the plaintiff stipulated for and obtained by the trust deed a duty of care in the preparation of the quarterly certificates by the directors of AICS. The plaintiff may or may not have known that two of the directors of AICS were employed by the bank and that the bank would allow those two directors to carry out their duties as directors while in the employment of the bank. Any of these circumstances, even if known, could change at any time. The plaintiff may or may not have known that the bank was beneficially interested in 40 per cent of the shares of AICS. That circumstance also could change at any time. The plaintiff did not rely on any of these circumstances . . . An employer who is also a shareholder who nominates a director owes no duty to the company unless the employer interferes with the affairs of the company. A duty does not arise because the employee may be dismissed from his employment by the employer or from his directorship by the shareholder or because the employer does not provide sufficient time or facilities to enable the director to carry out his duties. It will be in the interests of the employer to see that the director discharges his duty to the company but this again stems from self-interest and not from duty on the part of the employer.

[His Lordship ruled, finally, that the bank was not in the position of a 'shadow director'. The proceedings against the bank were accordingly struck out as disclosing no valid cause of action.]

➤ Note

The dismissed alternatives, (1)–(3), while not accepted here, might well be accepted if the facts supported the allegation, but this cases indicates the hurdles would be high.

Remedies associated with secondary liability

Remedies associated with secondary liability.

[7.49] Ultraframe (UK) Ltd v Fielding [2005] EWHC 1638 (Chancery Division)

The facts, so far as necessary, appear from the judgment. Lewison J's judgment is extremely long and thorough: at [1476]ff he describes the two types of secondary liability and how they arise; at [1511]–[1576] he surveys the law on remedies for fiduciary breaches; and at various places, extracted in the following, he addresses the issue of remedies against third parties.

LEWISON J:

1. This is (for the moment) the culmination of a long war of attrition . . . The trial alone, on liability only, occupied 95 days of court time. Both Ultraframe and Burnden are competitors in the market for the manufacture and supply of conservatories, and conservatory roofs in particular . . . The war has been bitterly fought. There have been accusations and counter-accusations of forgery, theft, false accounting, blackmail and arson, not to mention the widespread allegations that many of the principal witnesses are lying. At the heart of the litigation is a dispute about the ownership of businesses in the field of conservatory roof design and manufacture originally developed by Mr Howard Davies . . .

Personal or proprietary liability?

1484. It is important to keep distinct the two forms of secondary liability; because they have different consequences in terms of remedy.

Knowing receipt

1486. Although a claim in knowing receipt is receipt-based, it is not dependent on the recipient having retained the trust property. If he has retained it, or if he has retained property which is an identifiable substitute for the original trust property, then the claimant is entitled simply to assert his proprietary rights in that property.[106] He does this by invoking the principles of following and tracing. If the original recipient has passed on the property or its substitute to another person then, subject to any defence which that other may be entitled to raise, the principles of following or tracing continue to apply to the property or its substitute in the hands of that other. If the recipient has not retained the trust property, and its proceeds are no longer identifiable, then the claimant has a personal remedy against the recipient.

What counts as trust property for the purposes of knowing receipt? . . .

1488. Plainly, property which is vested in the company, both legally and beneficially, before any disposition in breach of fiduciary duty, will count as trust property. This was the case in *JJ Harrison (Properties) Ltd v Harrison* **[7.40]** where a director who had bought land belonging to the company, without disclosing its development potential, was held to have acquired the property as constructive trustee.

1489. But property will also count as the company's property if it is property which the fiduciary has acquired for his own benefit but which, consistently with his fiduciary duties, he ought

---

[106] Unless the recipient is a bona fide purchaser for value.

to have acquired on behalf of the company ... [He cited *Attorney General of Hong Kong v Reid* [1994] 1 AC 324 and *Keech v Sandford* (1726) Sel Cas Ch 61, and continued:]

Dishonest assistance

1495. In *Tan* **[7.47]** Lord Nicholls said (p 387):

'Within defined limits, proprietary rights, whether legal or equitable, endure against third parties who were unaware of their existence. But accessory liability is concerned with the liability of a person who has not received any property. His liability is not property-based. His only sin is that he interfered with the due performance by the trustee of the fiduciary obligations undertaken by the trustee. These are personal obligations. They are, in this respect, analogous to the personal obligations undertaken by the parties to a contract.'

1496. In similar vein Lord Millett said in *Twinsectra* (p 194, dissenting, although not on this point):

'The accessory's liability for having assisted in a breach of trust is quite different. It is fault-based, not receipt-based....the claimant seeks compensation for wrongdoing....Liability is not restricted to the person whose breach of trust or fiduciary duty caused their original diversion....Nor is it limited to those who assist him in the original breach. It extends to everyone who consciously assists in the continuing diversion of the money. Most of the cases have been concerned, not with assisting in the original breach, but in covering it up afterwards by helping to launder the money.' ...

What counts as dishonest assistance?

1509. It is clear that the passive receipt of trust property does not count as assistance: *Brown v Bennett* [1999] BCLC 525, 533. As Morritt LJ said:

'... if there is no causative effect and therefore no assistance given by the person ... on whom it is sought to establish the liability as constructive trustee, for my part I cannot see that the requirements of conscience require any remedy at all.'

1510. Likewise in *Brink's Ltd v Abu-Saleh* Rimer J held that Mrs Elcombe's presence in the car accompanying her husband abroad on money laundering trips did not amount to assistance 'of a nature sufficient to make her an accessory'. She was in the car merely in her capacity as Mr Elcombe's wife ...

Remedies against the knowing recipient

1577. In addition to the proprietary remedy (if it is still available) the claimant has a personal remedy for an account against the knowing recipient. Obviously, the personal remedy depends on establishing knowing receipt, but it does not depend on retention. Indeed it is needed precisely where the recipient has not retained the property. In addition, the personal remedy requires the knowing recipient to account for any benefit he has received or acquired as a result of the knowing receipt. However, a knowing recipient is not, in my judgment, liable to account for a benefit received by someone else. [He then went on to explain that the remedy must be fashioned to ensure that there is no double recovery, and continued:]

Fashioning the account

1579. The ordering of an account is an equitable remedy. It is not discretionary in the true sense. It is granted or withheld on the basis of equitable principles. But one of those principles is that of proportionality. In *Satnam Investments Ltd v Dunlop Heywood* [1999] 3 All ER 652

property agents had acquired confidential information about a potential development site in the course of acting for a client. In breach of duty they disclosed that information to a rival (Morbaine). The question arose whether Morbaine (which had since purchased the site) could be made liable to account for profits. Nourse LJ said:

'What the judge found was that some at least of the information was confidential at the time that it was disclosed, in that its disclosure to a rival developer would or might be detrimental to Satnam. However, even assuming that but for the disclosure Morbaine would not have acquired the Brewery Street site, it does not follow that it would be a proportionate response to hold it liable for an account of profits. All the circumstances must be considered. The information, though confidential, was not of the same degree of confidentiality as the information in the *Spycatcher* case and in *Schering Chemicals Ltd v Falkman Ltd*. All of it was either already available to Morbaine or would have been available to it on reasonable inquiry once, as was inevitable, the news of Satnam's receivership became known. There being no other basis of recovery available, it would in our view be inequitable and contrary to commercial good sense to allow Satnam to recover simply on the basis that there was a degree of confidentiality in the information at the time that it was disclosed to Morbaine.'

[He then considered various cases, including *Warman v Dwyer* (Question 2 following *Foster Bryant Surveying Ltd v Bryant, Savernake Property Consultants Ltd* **[7.33]**, p 418), and *CMS Dolphin v Simonet* **[7.35]**, and continued:]

1588. . . . The governing principles are, in my judgment, these:

i)   The fundamental rule is that a fiduciary must not make an unauthorised profit out of his fiduciary position;

ii)   The fashioning of an account should not be allowed to operate as the unjust enrichment of the claimant;

iii)   The profits for which an account is ordered must bear a reasonable relationship to the breach of duty proved;

iv)   It is important to establish exactly what has been acquired;

v)   Subject to that, the fashioning of the account depends on the facts. In some cases it will be appropriate to order an account limited in time; or limited to profits derived from particular assets or particular customers; or to order an account of all the profits of a business subject to all just allowances for the fiduciary's skill, labour and assumption of business risk. In some cases it may be appropriate to order the making of a payment representing the capital value of the advantage in question, either in place of or in addition to an account of profits. . . .

Remedies against a dishonest assistant

1600. I can see that it makes sense for a dishonest assistant to be jointly and severally liable for any *loss* which the beneficiary suffers as a result of a breach of trust. I can see also that it makes sense for a dishonest assistant to be liable to disgorge any profit which he *himself* has made as a result of assisting in the breach. However, I cannot take the next step to the conclusion that a dishonest assistant is also liable to pay to the beneficiary an amount equal to a profit which he did not make and which has produced no corresponding loss to the beneficiary. . . .

[Applying these various principles to the complicated facts, he then settled detailed orders between the parties, with some matters reserved for later.][107]

---

[107] This approach was explicitly endorsed in *Fiona Trust* [2010] EWHC 3199 (Comm) at [63]–[66].

➤ **Note**

Many of the relevant cases are not especially 'corporate'. For a modern illustration of the general legal and practical difficulties in pursuing these claims against third parties, and the extent to which courts are prepared to assist, see *Relfo Ltd (In Liquidation) v Varsani* [2014] EWCA Civ 360: this was a claim by a liquidator in relation to funds misappropriated by the company's former director; the funds had been used in a series of chain transactions, and the court had to determine whether the initial moneys could be traced along the chain to enable a knowing receipt claim against more distant third parties, or, alternatively, whether a claim in unjust enrichment was equally available given the third party's enrichment as a matter of 'economic reality'.

➤ **Questions**

1. What is the difference between the liability attaching to third parties who are 'knowing recipients' and those who are 'dishonest accessories'?

2. Is it possible to claim (i) constructive trusts, (ii) accounts of profits, (iii) equitable compensation against 'knowing recipients' or 'dishonest accessories'?

3. How, if at all, is liability shared between the defaulting director and the offending third party? Can a claimant recover against both of them?

▨ Further reading

This is the area of corporate law that attracts the most attention from commentators: the volume of literature is enormous, a lot of it very good, but it is clearly necessary to be selective.

General

AUSTIN, RP, 'Moulding the Content of Fiduciary Duties' in AJ Oakley (ed), *Trends in Contemporary Trust Law* (1996), ch 7.

CONAGLEN, M, 'The Nature and Function of Fiduciary Loyalty' (2005) 121 LQR 452.

IRELAND, P, 'Company Law and the Myth of Shareholder Ownership' (1999) 62 MLR 32.

LEE, R, 'Rethinking the Content of the Fiduciary Obligation' [2009] 3 *Conveyancer* 236.

LEEMING, M, 'The Scope of Fiduciary Obligations: How Contract Informs, but Does Not Determine, the Scope of Fiduciary Obligations' (2009) 3 J Eq 181.

SEALY, LS, 'The Director as Trustee' [1967] CLJ 83.

WORTHINGTON, S, 'Reforming Directors' Duties' (2001) 64 MLR 439.

Stakeholder debate

ALCOCK, A, 'The Case against the Concept of Stakeholders' (1996) 17 *Company Lawyer* 177.

BAINBRIDGE, S, 'In Defence of the Shareholder Wealth Maximization Norm: A Reply to Professor Green' (1993) 50 *Washington and Lee Law Review* 1423.

BLAIR, M and STOUT, L, 'A Team Production Theory of Corporate Law' (1999) 85 *Virginia Law Review* 247.

DODD, Jr, EM, 'For Whom are Corporate Managers Trustees?' (1932) 45 *Harvard Law Review* 1145. (The entire debate between AA Berle Jr and Em Dodd Jr appears in (1931) 44 *Harvard Law Review* 1049, (1932) 45 *Harvard Law Review* 1145, 1365 and (1942) 9 *University of Chicago Law Review* 538.)

EASTERBROOK, FH and FISCHEL, DR, *Economic Structure of Corporate Law* (1991), ch 1.

EISENBERG, MA, 'Corporate Law and Social Norms' (1999) 99 *Columbia Law Review* 1253.

KELLY, G and PARKINSON, J, 'The Conceptual Foundations of the Company: A Pluralist Approach' [1998] *Company Financial and Insolvency Law Review* 174.

SEALY, LS, 'Directors' "Wider" Responsibilities— Problems Conceptual, Practical and Procedural' (1987) 13 *Monash University Law Review* 164.

WILLIAMSON, OE, 'Corporate Governance' (1984) 93 *Yale Law Journal* 1197.

Duty to act within powers— proper purposes

KEAY, A, 'Ascertaining the Corporate Objective: An Entity Maximisation and Sustainability Model' (2008) 71 MLR 663.

LIM, E, 'Directors' Duties: Improper Purposes or Implied Terms?' (2014) 34 *Legal Studies* 395.

NOLAN, R, 'Controlling Fiduciary Power' [2009] CLJ 293.

NOLAN, R, 'The Proper Purpose Doctrine and Company Directors' in BAK Rider (ed), *The Realm of Company Law* (1998), ch 1.

SEALY, LS, ' "Bona Fides" and "Proper Purposes" in Corporate Decisions' (1989) 15 *Monash University Law Review* 265.

Duty to act for the success of company— good faith

HAYNE, KM, 'Directors' Duties and a Company's Creditors' (2014) 38 *Melbourne University Law Review* 795.

HO, L and LEE, PW, 'A Director's Duty to Confess: A Matter of Good Faith' [2007] CLJ 348.

KEAY, A, 'Directors' Duties and Creditors' Interests' (2014) 130 LQR 443.

KEAY, A, 'Section 172(1) of the Companies Act 2006: An Interpretation and Assessment' (2007) 28 *Company Lawyer* 106.

LORD WEDDERBURN, 'Employees, Partnership and Company Law' (2002) 31 ILJ 99.

WORTHINGTON, S, 'Directors' Duties, Creditors' Rights and Shareholder Intervention' (1991) 18 *Melbourne University Law Review* 121.

Duty to exercise independent judgement

KEAY, A, 'The Duty of Directors to Exercise Independent Judgment' (2008) 29 *Company Lawyer* 290.

Duty to exercise care and skill

FINCH, V, 'Company Directors: Who Cares about Skill and Care' (1992) 55 MLR 179.

GRIGGS, L and LOWRY, J, 'Finding the Optimum Balance for the Duty of Care Owed by the Non-Executive Director' in F Patfield (ed), *Perspectives on Company Law: 2* (1997), ch 12.

RILEY, C, 'The Company Director's Duty of Care and Skill: The Case for an Onerous but Subjective Duty of Care' (1999) 62 MLR 697.

WORTHINGTON, S, 'The Duty to Monitor: A Modern View of the Director's Duty of Care' in F Patfield (ed), *Perspectives on Company Law: 2* (1997), ch 11.

Duty to avoid conflicts

BECK, S, 'The Quickening of the Fiduciary Obligation' (1975) 53 *Canadian Bar Review* 771.

CONAGLEN, M, 'Equitable Compensation for Breach of the Fiduciary Dealing Rules' (2003) 119 LQR 246.

COOTER, R and FREEDMAN, B, 'The Fiduciary Relationship: Its Economic Character and Legal Consequences' (1991) 66 *New York University Law Review* 1045.

FARRAR, J AND WATSON, S, 'Self-Dealing, Fair Dealing and Related Transactions—History, Policy and Reform?' (2011) 11 *Journal of Corporate Law Studies* 495.

GRANTHAM, R, 'Can Directors Compete with the Company?' (2003) 66 MLR 109.

KERSHAW, D, 'Does it Matter How the Law Thinks About Corporate Opportunities?' (2005) 25 *Legal Studies* 533.

LIM, E, 'Directors' Fiduciary Duties: A New Analytical Framework' (2013) 129 LQR 242.

LOWRY, J and EDMUNDS, R, 'The No Conflict–No Profit Rules and the Corporate Fiduciary: Challenging the Orthodoxy of Absolutism' [2000] JBL 122.

LOWRY, J and EDMUNDS, R, 'The Corporate Opportunity Doctrine: The Shifting Boundaries of the Duties and its Remedies' (1998) 61 MLR 515.

LORD MILLETT, 'Bribes and Secret Commissions Again' [2012] CLJ 583.

NOLAN, R, 'Directors' Self-Interested Dealings: Liabilities and Remedies' [1999] *Company Financial and Insolvency Law Review* 235.

PRENTICE, D and PAYNE, J, 'Director's Fiduciary Duties' (2006) 122 LQR 558.

PRENTICE, D and PAYNE, J, 'The Corporate Opportunity Doctrine' (2004) 120 LQR 198.

WATTS, P, 'The Transition from Director to Competitor' (2007) 123 LQR 21.

Duty to declare interest

MACDONALD, R, 'The Companies Act 2006 and the Directors' Duty to Disclose' [2011] *International Company and Commercial Law Review* 96.

Authorisation, ratification and remedies

ETHERTON, Sir T, 'The Legitimacy of Proprietary Relief' (2014) 2 *Birkbeck Law Review* 59.

NOLAN, R, 'Enacting Civil Remedies in Company Law' (2001) 1 JCLS 245.

PAYNE, J, 'A Re-Examination of Ratification' [1999] CLJ 604.

POOLE, J and KEYSER, A, 'Justifying Partial Rescission in English Law' (2005) 121 LQR 273.

WEDDERBURN, KW, 'Shareholders' Rights and the Rule in *Foss v Harbottle*' [1957] CLJ 194 and [1958] CLJ 93.

WORTHINGTON, S, 'Corporate Governance: Remedying and Ratifying Directors' Breaches' (2000) 116 LQR 638.

Relief from liability

EDMUNDS, R and LOWRY, J, 'The Continuing Value of Relief for Director's Breach of Duty' (2003) 66 MLR 195.

Shadow directors, nominee directors

BOROS, EJ, 'The Duties of Nominee and Multiple Directors' (1989) 10 *Company Lawyer* 211 and (1990) 11 *Company Lawyer* 6.

CRUTCHFIELD, P, 'Nominee Directors: The Law and Commercial Reality' (1991) 12 *Company Lawyer* 136.

Secondary liability

ELLIOTT, S and MITCHELL, C, 'Remedies for Dishonest Assistance' (2004) 67 MLR 16.

GUMMOW, The Hon William, 'Dishonest Assistance and Account of Profits' [2015] CLJ 405.

8

COMPANY AUDITORS AND PROMOTERS

Introduction

The previous chapter considered the liabilities of a company's directors to the company. This chapter fills out that picture. It examines the duties and liabilities of the company's auditors and its promoters. The duties of auditors derive from contract and tort, supplemented by their professional rules. Promoters, too, may owe duties in contract and tort, but their more significant duties are imposed in equity, and map very closely the duties owed by the company's directors.

The issues addressed in this chapter also reinforce the notion of the company as a separate legal person (re-read 'The consequences of separate legal personality', p 42) and the special issues that arise because the artificial legal construct that is a company can only operate through human agents (see Chapters 2 and 3 generally). The problems that arise in this context are especially acute in the context of 'one man companies' and their relationship with the fraudsters who might run them and the auditors and general creditors who might deal with them (see *Stone & Rolls Ltd (In Liquidation) v Moore Stephens* [8.05]). The temptation—which must be resisted—is to blur the distinctions between the company as a separate legal person and the individuals who are the company's agents (especially any fraudulent individuals who act as the company's 'directing mind and will'[1]).

Auditors and their relationship with the company

The company's directors are responsible for the company's statutory accounts and reports. But it has long been accepted that the reliability of these outputs will be enhanced if there is independent third party verification of both the documents and the corporate processes that deliver them. The company audit—conducted by the company's independent external auditor—is intended to provide this verification. All the rules and regulations associated with auditors and their conduct of the audit are designed to increase the value of the audit without imposing too high a cost on either the companies or their auditors.

---

[1] This nomenclature may be evocative, but it should not survive Lord Hoffmann's analysis of the rules of attribution in *Meridian Global* [3.01]: see Lord Walker in *Moulin Global* [3.30], p 173.

General policy and regulatory issues

If the primary function of the audit is to provide independent verification, then auditor competence and independence are essential. The relatively recent collapses of companies such as Enron have highlighted the crucial importance of this issue. The Audit Directive (2006/43/EC), the Statutory Auditors Regulations (SI 2007/3494 and SI 2008/499) and the Companies Act 2006 (CA 2006) Pt 42 provide a regulatory framework in the UK to reinforce the market demands for auditor competence and independence. Public oversight used to be provided by the Professional Oversight Board (a subsidiary of the Financial Reporting Council (FRC)). Since 2 July 2012, following restructuring of the FRC, the Board no longer exists, its previous functions having been transferred to the Conduct Committee and the Conduct Division within the FRC itself. Despite much discussion, there is no blanket ban on the auditors also providing non-audit work to the company, but, especially given how lucrative this work is, there is a clear risk of conflicts of interest. This non-audit remuneration is therefore regulated in the same way as more general conflict situations (see CA 2006 Sch 10).

Secondly, the companies seen to be most at risk (or, more accurately, the companies seen to expose those dealing with them to greatest risks) need to have mandatory audits. Until recently, it was a statutory requirement that *every* company should appoint an auditor or auditors. However, three exceptions are now made (see CA 2006 s 475): for 'small' companies (s 477),[2] for 'dormant companies' (s 480) and for non-profit-making companies subject to public sector audit (s 482). These exemptions are not available to banking, insurance and certain other categories of company. In addition, a statutory audit must be held if members holding 10% or more of the share capital require one (s 476). There are conditions attached to all these provisions, so the Act needs to be read carefully. Of course, although CA 2006 does not require certain companies to undergo an audit, many do, so as to provide external assurance to their members, creditors or investors. With these voluntary audits, the company is free to choose the scale of audit to suit its purposes. The EU has recently followed suit; there are now proposed changes to Arts 43 and 43b, which will lift the auditing requirement for small undertakings.

Thirdly, the choice of individual auditor and the terms of their appointment can also ensure independence. CA 2006 lays down rules for the appointment of auditors (ss 485–494), their functions and duties (ss 495–509), their removal and resignation (ss 510–526; although note s 994(1A)—see the following paragraph) and their liability (ss 532–538). These rules give a degree of power to shareholders and to audit committees, and so go some way to giving further assurance that the appointed auditor is independent of the directors. Equally, giving power to the auditors to compel the company and its officers to comply with requests for information goes some way to enhancing the value of the audit.

The increasing importance of an independent and competent audit function is clearly reflected in the addition of s 994(1A) to the s 994 'unfair prejudice' provisions in CA 2006. Section 994(1A) deems the 'improper' removal[3] of an auditor to be unfairly prejudicial conduct, thus opening up the wide-ranging remedies for unfair prejudice to any disaffected member (on 'unfair prejudice', see 'Unfairly prejudicial conduct of the company's affairs', pp 715ff). This provision therefore effectively qualifies the general rule that auditors may be dismissed at any time by ordinary resolution of the shareholders, subject to the giving of special notice (ss 510 and 511).[4] Section 994(1A) purports to implement

---

[2] And see CA 2006 ss 478–479C.

[3] Ie, on the grounds of divergence of opinions on accounting treatments or audit procedures, or on any other improper grounds (not specified).

[4] Although it seems the removal is effective in the meantime, subject to any court orders under s 996.

Art 37 of the Audit Directive 2006/43, which stipulates that auditors can only be removed for 'proper reasons'.[5]

Finally, imposing personal liability on auditors for failure to live up to the standards expected can also assist in raising the standards of the audit. On the other hand, imposing *too* much liability on auditors can have a chilling effect—good auditors are deterred; indeed, the larger the company, the larger the risk, and so it is these companies especially, companies where audits are especially valuable, that are likely to be left without competent auditors to oversee operations. After years of lobbying by auditors for changes to the law, new provisions have been introduced in CA 2006 ss 534ff that allow companies to agree to cap auditors' liability. The agreement cannot apply to more than one year's audit; it must be authorised by members (s 536 specifies the requirements); and it cannot limit liability to a sum that is less than what is 'fair and reasonable' (although the provisions of the Unfair Contract Terms Act 1977 ss 2(2) and 3(2)(a) do not apply). In the absence of such a power to contractually limit liability, and in the face of provisions such as CA 2006 s 532 making other arrangements void, the auditors had few options open to them to protect themselves against the risk of enormous claims (see *Caparo Industries plc v Dickman* **[8.04]**, and pp 491ff).

The European Commission has also been active in this area. It has adopted a new regulation imposing specific requirements on the statutory audit of Public-Interest Entities (PIE), and made several amendments to the relevant Directive. PIEs are defined as those entities which are of significant public interest because their businesses affect a wide range of stakeholders, so the regulation of their statutory audit might therefore be expected to be most stringent. The Directive amending the Statutory Audit Directive 2006/43/EC (Directive 2014/56/EU) and the Regulation on Statutory Audit (Regulation 537/2014) came into force on 16 July 2014. In that context, PIEs are defined as listed entities, credit institutions, insurance undertakings and entities designated by member states as public-interest entities, for instance undertakings that are of significant public relevance because of the nature of their business, their size or the number of their employees. The reform is designed to achieve several objectives,[6] including: (i) further clarifying the role of the statutory auditor; (ii) reinforcing the independence and professional scepticism of the statutory auditor; (iii) facilitating cross-border provision of statutory audit services in the EU; (iv) contributing to a more dynamic audit market in the EU; and (v) improving the supervision of statutory auditors and the coordination of audit supervision by competent authorities in the EU.

A number of features of the reform merit highlighting. As mentioned earlier, there is currently no blanket ban on auditors also providing non-auditing work to their clients. However, as part of a chapter dealing with 'conflicts of interest', the reforms will prevent the provision of prescribed non-audit services which may compromise auditor independence in performing their 'societal role' in carrying out the statutory audit. Auditors may only continue providing other non-audit services (ie those not prohibited under this Regulation) if their provision has been approved in advance by the audit committee, and the statutory auditor (or audit firm) has satisfied itself that any threats to auditor independence can be reduced to an acceptable level by the application of safeguards (recital (9) of the Preamble to Regulation 537/2014). Even this, however, is subject to the proviso that the total fees for such services calculated over a period of at least three consecutive financial years is limited to a maximum of 70% of the average of the fees paid in the last three

---

[5] It is not clear why the Directive requirement was implemented through an amendment to CA 2006 s 994 rather than an amendment to s 510 (removal of auditors by ordinary resolution), although the decision may avoid some of the difficulties that members typically have in enforcing their statutory and constitutional rights (see 'Members' personal rights', p 261).

[6] http://europa.eu/rapid/press-release_MEMO-14-427_en.htm?locale=en.

consecutive financial years for the statutory audit(s) of the audited entity (and, where applicable, as calculated on a group level) (Art 4(2) of the Regulation).

The composition of the audit committee is also more regulated. Non-executive members should be introduced to audit committees in order to broaden expertise. At least one member of the audit committee must have competence in accounting and/or auditing, and the committee members as a whole must have competence relevant to the sector in which the audited entity is operating (Art 39 of the Directive). The Regulation also introduces various measures for avoiding uninterrupted appointments of the same audit firm. For instance, there is proposed mandatory rotation of audit firms after a maximum ten years (although member states may set a lower maximum duration or, upon satisfaction of certain requirements, longer maximum periods) (Art 17 of the Regulation). These amendments are designed to address directly the problem of the 'threat of familiarity'.

Article 28 of the Directive sets out the scope of the auditor's duties, and indicates that their role is to provide an opinion as to whether the financial statements give a true and fair view. Their role does not, for instance, include providing an assurance on the future viability of the audited entity, nor does it entail an assessment of the efficiency and effectiveness of management (as, indeed, is expressly stated in Art 25a of the Directive). In adopting this approach, these provisions reflect the court's approach in *Re London and General Bank (No 2)* **[8.01]**.

The reforms also introduce measures to govern the way member states regulate their auditors, and the way auditors operate internally. Articles 3(2) and 32 of the Directive now mandate each member state to have a designated competent authority for approving and overseeing statutory auditors and audit firms auditing PIEs.

Overall, the Commission is of the view that auditor self-regulation is not adequate and that auditors should be subjected to a uniform and harmonised framework within the Union, especially in relation to PIEs which often carry out cross-border activities.

The FRC itself also publishes a Guidance on Audit Committees[7] (last updated in September 2012 following a consultation exercise) and a note on Best Practice Guide on Audit Tendering[8] (dated July 2013).

Auditors' liability

A company contemplating an audit invariably enters into a contract with the auditor for the provision of professional services. Then, like anyone who renders professional services for reward, the auditor will owe the company an implied contractual duty of care in the proper performance of the audit.

Auditors may also be liable in tort for negligent misstatement. This liability is potentially to any third parties to whom the auditors owe a duty of care. Here the courts have protected the auditors by adopting very restrictive approaches to the scope of the auditors' duty.

The standard of care to be exercised by auditors is illustrated by the cases beginning with *Re London & General Bank (No 2)* **[8.01]** which are cited later. But these cases (some of which are a century old) give only half the picture, for today it is the accountancy profession itself (through the Accounting Standards Board) which is largely responsible for prescribing norms (through its *Financial Reporting Standards* ('FRSs')), for the preparation of company accounts and the duties of auditors in relation to them. Broadly speaking, auditors are unlikely to be held to be negligent if they have conformed to currently accepted professional practices. On the other hand, if they depart from them, this will be regarded

---

[7] www.frc.org.uk/Our-Work/Publications/Corporate-Governance/Guidance-on-Audit-Committees-September-2012.pdf.
[8] www.frc.org.uk/Our-Work/Publications/Corporate-Governance/Audit-Tenders-Notes-on-best-practice.pdf.

as strong evidence of a breach of duty (*Lloyd Cheyham & Co Ltd v Littlejohn & Co* [1987] BCLC 303).

There can be little doubt that the standard of care required from auditors has progressively risen throughout the past century through the influence of the profession itself. CA 2006 also introduces criminal liability for auditors for knowingly or recklessly causing an auditors' report to include any matter that is misleading, false or deceptive in a material particular: s 507.

A rather more difficult question has been: to whom is the auditor's duty of care owed, for the purposes of civil liability? This has been largely resolved by the decision of the House of Lords in *Caparo Industries plc v Dickman* **[8.04]**, although some aspects of it still require clarification.

The reason why an auditor's duty of care is owed to the company, and not its individual members, appears from the case of *Equitable Life Assurance Society v Ernst and Young* [2003] EWCA Civ 1114: since the contract under which the work of a company's auditors is performed is with the company as a separate person, the auditors owe an implied *contractual duty of care* to the company in and about the manner in which they perform their services. Auditors *also* have general liability in tort for negligent misstatement under which individual members may (but only in exceptionally limited circumstances) be able to claim. The scope of that duty was defined in *Johnson v Gore Wood and Co* [2003] EWCA Civ 1728. It includes anything and everything which the company in general meeting (note the 'corporate purposes' restriction) could be expected to do on the strength of that auditors' report. By contrast, the slender likelihood of individual members being able to sue auditors directly for personal losses they have sustained is explained in compelling terms in *Caparo Industries plc* **[8.04]**.

Finally, there is the vexed issue—at least for the company—of possible limitations on a company's right to sue its auditor for negligence when the auditor fails to detect a fraud that is being perpetrated by the company's own management: see *Stone & Rolls* **[8.05]**.

The following extracts illustrate the issues and the judicial reasoning in resolving them.

Auditors must exercise reasonable care and skill, and must certify to the members or shareholders only what they believe to be true.

[8.01] Re London and General Bank (No 2) [1895] 2 Ch 673
(Court of Appeal)

This was an appeal by Theobald, one of the bank's auditors, from a judgment in which Vaughan Williams J had held him liable to reimburse the company, now in liquidation, for the amount of certain dividends which had been paid out of capital after the shareholders had been presented with a balance sheet which Theobald had certified as correct. The appeal failed, except for a variation in the sum for which he was held liable. The main respect in which the accounts were defective was the entry of certain loans at their face value when it was known that most of the amounts were not realisable. It was held that none of the following matters absolved Theobald from liability: (i) that he had included in his report the words 'The value of the assets as shown on the balance sheet is dependent upon realisation'; (ii) that he had submitted a full report to the *directors* in which the gravity of the company's position was shown in detail; (iii) that the report (to the *directors*) had initially expressed the view that no dividend should be paid, but the chairman later persuaded the auditors to delete the sentence; and (iv) that the chairman had undertaken to explain the true position verbally to the shareholders in general meeting. (In fact, he had done so only in ambiguous terms.)

LINDLEY LJ: It is no part of an auditor's duty to give advice, either to directors or shareholders, as to what they ought to do. An auditor has nothing to do with the prudence or imprudence of making loans with or without security. It is nothing to him whether the business of a company is being conducted prudently or imprudently, profitably or unprofitably. It is nothing to him whether dividends are properly or improperly declared, provided he discharges his own duty to the shareholders. His business is to ascertain and state the true financial position of the company at the time of the audit, and his duty is confined to that. But then comes the question, How is he to ascertain that position? The answer is, By examining the books of the company. But he does not discharge his duty by doing this without inquiry and without taking any trouble to see that the books themselves show the company's true position. He must take reasonable care to ascertain that they do so. Unless he does this his audit would be worse than an idle farce. Assuming the books to be so kept as to show the true position of a company, the auditor has to certify that the balance-sheet presented is correct in that sense. But his first duty is to examine the books, not merely for the purpose of ascertaining what they do show, but also for the purpose of satisfying himself that they show the true financial position of the company . . . An auditor, however, is not bound to do more than exercise reasonable care and skill in making inquiries and investigations. He is not an insurer; he does not guarantee that the books do correctly show the true position of the company's affairs; he does not even guarantee that his balance-sheet is accurate according to the books of the company. If he did, he would be responsible for error on his part, even if he were himself deceived without any want of reasonable care on his part, say, by the fraudulent concealment of a book from him. His obligation is not so onerous as this. Such I take to be the duty of the auditor: he must be honest—ie must not certify what he does not believe to be true, and he must take reasonable care and skill before he believes that what he certifies is true. What is reasonable care in any particular case must depend upon the circumstances of that case. Where there is nothing to excite suspicion very little inquiry will be reasonably sufficient, and in practice I believe businessmen select a few cases at haphazard, see that they are right, and assume that others like them are correct also. Where suspicion is aroused more care is obviously necessary; but, still, an auditor is not bound to exercise more than reasonable care and skill, even in a case of suspicion, and he is perfectly justified in acting on the opinion of an expert where special knowledge is required. Mr Theobald's evidence satisfies me that he took the same view as myself of his duty in investigating the company's books and preparing his balance-sheet. He checked the cash, examined vouchers for payments, saw that the bills and securities entered in the books were held by the bank, took reasonable care to ascertain their value, and in one case obtained a solicitor's opinion on the validity of an equitable charge. I see no trace whatever of any failure by him in the performance of this part of his duty. It is satisfactory to find that the legal standard of duty is not too high for business purposes and is recognised as correct by businessmen. The balance-sheet and certificate of February 1892 (ie for the year 1891) was accompanied by a report to the directors of the bank. Taking the balance-sheet, the certificate and report together, Mr Theobald stated to the directors the true financial position of the bank, and if this report had been laid before the shareholders Mr Theobald would have completely discharged his duty to them. Unfortunately, however, this report was not laid before the shareholders . . .

In this case I have no hesitation in saying that Mr Theobald did fail to discharge his duty to the shareholders in certifying and laying before them the balance-sheet of February 1892 without any reference to the report which he laid before the directors and with no other warning than is conveyed by the words 'The value of the assets as shown on the balance-sheet is dependent upon realisation'. [His Lordship referred to the details of the balance sheet, and to the report made to the directors, including the warning that no dividend should be paid, and continued:] A dividend of 7% was, nevertheless, recommended by the directors, and was resolved upon by the shareholders at a meeting furnished with the balance-sheet and profit and loss account certified by the auditors, and at which meeting the auditors were present, but silent. Not a word was said to inform the shareholders of the true state of affairs. It is idle to say that these ac-counts are so remotely connected with the payment of the dividend as to render the auditors legally irresponsible for such payment. The balance-sheet and account certified by the auditors, and showing a profit available for dividend, were, in my judgment, not the remote but the real operating cause of the resolution for the payment of the dividend which the directors improperly recommended. The auditors' account and certificate gave weight to this recommendation, and rendered it acceptable to the meeting . . .

RIGBY LJ delivered a concurring judgment.

LOPES LJ concurred.

It is not part of the duty of auditors to repeat work already undertaken internally: in the absence of suspicion, auditors may rely on the assurances of a manager or other apparently responsible employee.

[8.02] Re Kingston Cotton Mill Co (No 2) [1896] 2 Ch 279 (Court of Appeal)

The facts appear from the judgment.

LOPES LJ: [In] determining whether any misfeasance or breach of duty has been committed, it is essential to consider what the duties of an auditor are. They are very fully described in *Re London and General Bank* **[8.01]**, to which judgment I was a party. Shortly they may be stated thus: It is the duty of an auditor to bring to bear on the work he has to perform that skill, care and caution which a reasonably competent, careful and cautious auditor would use. What is reasonable skill, care and caution must depend on the particular circumstances of each case. An auditor is not bound to be a detective, or, as was said, to approach his work with suspicion or with a foregone conclusion that there is something wrong. He is a watch-dog, but not a bloodhound. He is justi-fied in believing tried servants of the company in whom confidence is placed by the company. He is entitled to assume that they are honest, and to rely upon their representations, provided he takes reasonable care. If there is anything calculated to excite suspicion he should probe it to the bottom; but in the absence of anything of that kind he is only bound to be reasonably cautious and careful.

In the present case the accounts of the company had been for years falsified by the manag-ing director, Jackson . . . Jackson deliberately overstated the quantities and values of the cotton and yarn in the company's mills. He did this for many years. It was proved that there is a great wastage in converting yarn into cotton, and the fluctuations of the market in the prices of cotton and yarn are exceptionally great. Jackson had been so successful in falsifying the accounts that what he had done was never detected or even suspected by the directors. The auditors adopted the entries of Jackson and inserted them in the balance-sheet as 'per manager's certificate'. It is not suggested but that the auditors acted honestly and honestly believed in the accuracy and reliability of Jackson. But it is said that they ought not to have trusted the figures of Jackson, but should have further investigated the matter. Jackson was a trusted officer of the company in whom the directors had every confidence; there was nothing on the face of the accounts to excite suspicion, and I cannot see how in the circumstances of the case it can be successfully contended that the auditors are wanting in skill, care or caution in not testing Jackson's figures.

It is not the duty of an auditor to take stock; he is not a stock expert, there are many matters in respect of which he must rely on the honesty and accuracy of others. He does not guarantee the discovery of all fraud. I think the auditors were justified in this case in relying on the honesty and accuracy of Jackson, and were not called upon to make further investigation . . .

LINDLEY and KAY LJJ delivered concurring judgments.

➤ Question

How can this approach be reconciled with the 'verification' function of auditors?

An auditor who has been, or ought to have been, put on inquiry is under a duty to make an exhaustive investigation.

[8.03] Re Gerrard & Son Ltd [1968] Ch 455 (Chancery Division)

The company's managing director, Croston, had caused the company's books to be falsified in three ways: (i) by altering the half-yearly stocktaking figures so as to include nonexistent stock; (ii) by altering invoices relating to purchases of stock so that the amounts payable were made to appear just *after*, instead of just *before*, the half-yearly 'cut off' date; and (iii) (the converse of (ii)) by advancing *into* the half-yearly period sums due in respect of goods sold which were in fact invoiced *after* the 'cut-off' date. The auditors ('Kevans') had accepted the explanations given by Croston and his brother-in-law Heyes (now deceased) regarding the altered invoices. The court held that Kevans had been negligent in relation to (ii) and (without any finding in relation to (i) and (iii)) held them liable to the company's liquidator in respect of dividends which the company had wrongly paid on the strength of the false accounts.

PENNYCUICK J: [He noted *Re Kingston Cotton Mill Co (No 2)* **[8.02]** and continued:] This case appears, at any rate at first sight, to be conclusive in favour of Kevans as regards the falsification of the stock taken in isolation. Mr Walton, for the liquidator, pointed out that before 1900 there was no statutory provision corresponding to section 162 of the Companies Act 1948 [CA 2006 s 498]. That is so, but I am not clear that the quality of the auditor's duty has changed in any relevant respect since 1896. Basically that duty has always been to audit the company's accounts with reasonable care and skill. The real ground on which *Re Kingston Cotton Mill Co (No 2)* is, I think, capable of being distinguished is that the standards of reasonable care and skill are, upon the expert evidence, more exacting today than those which prevailed in 1896. I see considerable force in this contention. It must, I think, be open, even in this court, to make a finding that in all the particular circumstances the auditors have been in breach of their duty in relation to stock. On the other hand, if this breach of duty stood alone and the facts were more or less the same as those in *Re Kingston Cotton Mill Co (No 2)*, this court would, I think, be very chary indeed of reaching a conclusion different from that reached by the Court of Appeal in *Re Kingston Cotton Mill Co (No 2)* . . .

I find it impossible to acquit Kevans of negligence as regards purchases of stock before the end of each current period of account and the attribution of the price to the succeeding period of account. I will assume in their favour that Mr Nightingale [a partner in Kevans] was entitled to rely on the assurances of Mr Heyes and Mr Croston until he first came upon the altered invoices, but once these were discovered he was clearly put upon inquiry and I do not think he was then entitled to rest content with the assurances of Mr Croston and Mr Heyes, however implicitly he may have trusted Mr Croston. I find the conclusion inescapable alike on the expert evidence and as a matter of business common sense that at this stage he ought to have taken steps on the lines indicated by Mr Macnamara [an expert witness], that is to say, he should have examined the suppliers' statements and where necessary have communicated with the suppliers. Having ascertained the precise facts so far as it was possible for him to do so, he should then have informed the board. It may be that the board would then have taken some action. But whatever the board did he should in each subsequent audit have made such checks and inquiries as would have ensured that any misattribution in the cut-off procedure was detected. He did not take any of these steps. I am bound to conclude that he failed in his duty.

[His Lordship accordingly held the auditors liable for the amount of the dividends wrongly paid.]

The auditors of a company owe no duty of care either to members of the public who rely on the accounts in deciding whether to invest in the company's shares, or to existing members of the company who may also rely on the accounts for the purpose of decisions in relation to present or future investment in the company.

[8.04] Caparo Industries plc v Dickman [1990] 2 AC 605 (House of Lords)

Touche Ross & Co had audited the 1983–84 accounts of Fidelity plc, a listed company, which showed a pre-tax profit of £1.3 million. Both before and after the publication of these accounts, Caparo bought Fidelity shares in the market, and subsequently it made a takeover bid, as a result of which it acquired all the shares. In these proceedings Caparo alleged that it had paid too much for the shares because the trading figures should have shown a loss of £0.4 million instead of a profit, and claimed damages from the auditors on the ground that they had been negligent in certifying that the accounts showed a true and fair view of Fidelity's financial position. The House of Lords, reversing in part the judgment of the Court of Appeal, held that the auditors owed Caparo no duty of care.

LORD BRIDGE: [He referred to a number of well-known cases, including *Hedley Byrne & Co Ltd v Heller & Partners* [1964] AC 465, HL, and continued:] The salient feature of all these cases is that the defendant giving advice or information was fully aware of the nature of the transaction which the plaintiff had in contemplation, knew that the advice or information would be communicated to him directly or indirectly and knew that it was very likely that the plaintiff would rely on that advice or information in deciding whether or not to engage in the transaction in contemplation. In these circumstances the defendant could clearly be expected, subject always to the effect of any disclaimer of responsibility, specifically to anticipate that the plaintiff would rely on the advice or information given by the defendant for the very purpose for which he did in the event rely on it. So also the plaintiff, subject again to the effect of any disclaimer, would in that situation reasonably suppose that he was entitled to rely on the advice or information communicated to him for the very purpose for which he required it. The situation is entirely different where a statement is put into more or less general circulation and may foreseeably be relied on by strangers to the maker of the statement for any one of a variety of different purposes which the maker of the statement has no specific reason to anticipate. To hold the maker of the statement to be under a duty of care in respect of the accuracy of the statement to all and sundry for any purpose for which they may choose to rely on it is not only to subject him, in the classic words of Cardozo CJ to 'liability in an indeterminate amount for an indeterminate time to an indeterminate class': see *Ultramares Corpn v Touche*;[9] it is also to confer on the world at large a quite unwarranted entitlement to appropriate for their own purposes the benefit of the expert knowledge or professional expertise attributed to the maker of the statement. Hence, looking only at the circumstances of these decided cases where a duty of care in respect of negligent statements has been held to exist, I should expect to find that the 'limit or control mechanism . . . imposed upon the liability of a wrong-doer towards those who have suffered economic damage in consequence of his negligence'[10] rested in the necessity to prove, in this category of the tort of negligence, as an essential ingredient of the 'proximity' between the plaintiff and the defendant, that the defendant knew that his statement would be communicated to the plaintiff, either as an individual or as a member of an identifiable class, specifically in connection with a particular transaction or transactions of a particular kind (eg in a prospectus inviting investment) and that the plaintiff would be very likely to rely on it for the purpose of deciding whether or not to enter upon that transaction or upon a transaction of that kind . . .

---

[9] 174 NE 441 at 444 (1931).
[10] *Candlewood Navigation Corpn Ltd v Mitsui OSK Lines Ltd* [1986] AC 1 at 25, PC.

These considerations amply justify the conclusion that auditors of a public company's accounts owe no duty of care to members of the public at large who rely upon the accounts in deciding to buy shares in the company. If a duty of care were owed so widely, it is difficult to see any reason why it should not equally extend to all who rely on the accounts in relating to other dealings with a company as lenders or merchants extending credit to the company. A claim that such a duty was owed by auditors to a bank lending to a company was emphatically and convincingly rejected by Millett J in *Al Saudi Banque v Clark Pixley*[11] . . .

The main submissions for Caparo are that the necessary nexus of proximity between it and the appellants giving rise to a duty of care stems (1) from the pleaded circumstances indicating the vulnerability of Fidelity to a take-over bid and from the consequent probability that another company, such as Caparo, would rely on the audited accounts in deciding to launch a take-over bid, or (2) from the circumstance that Caparo was already a shareholder in Fidelity when it decided to launch its take-over bid in reliance on the accounts . . .

I should . . . be extremely reluctant to hold that the question whether or not an auditor owes a duty of care to an investor buying shares in a public company depends on the degree of probability that the shares will prove attractive either en bloc to a take-over bidder or piecemeal to individual investors. It would be equally wrong, in my opinion, to hold an auditor under a duty of care to anyone who might lend money to a company by reason only that it was foreseeable as highly probable that the company would borrow money at some time in the year following publication of its audited accounts and that lenders might rely on those accounts in deciding to lend. I am content to assume the high probability of a take-over bid in reliance on the accounts which the proposed amendment of the statement of claim would assert but I do not think it assists *Caparo's* case . . .

[Lord Bridge referred to the statutory provisions dealing with the auditor's report (Companies Act 1985 (CA 1985) ss 253ff), and continued:] No doubt these provisions establish a relationship between the auditors and the shareholders of a company on which the shareholder is entitled to rely for the protection of his interest. But the crucial question concerns the extent of the shareholder's interest which the auditor has a duty to protect. The shareholders of a company have a collective interest in the company's proper management and in so far as a negligent failure of the auditor to report accurately on the state of the company's finances deprives the shareholders of the opportunity to exercise their powers in general meeting to call the directors to book and to ensure that errors in management are corrected, the shareholders ought to be entitled to a remedy. But in practice no problem arises in this regard since the interest of the shareholders in the proper management of the company's affairs is indistinguishable from the interest of the company itself and any loss suffered by the shareholder, eg by the negligent failure of the auditor to discover and expose a misappropriation of funds by a director of the company, will be recouped by a claim against the auditors in the name of the company, not by individual shareholders.

I find it difficult to visualise a situation arising in the real world in which the individual shareholder could claim to have sustained a loss in respect of his existing shareholding referable to the negligence of the auditor which could not be recouped by the company. But on this part of the case your Lordships were much impressed with the argument that such a loss might occur by a negligent undervaluation of the company's assets in the auditor's report relied on by the individual shareholder in deciding to sell his shares at an undervalue. The argument then runs thus. The shareholder, *qua* shareholder, is entitled to rely on the auditor's report as the basis of his investment decision to sell his existing shareholding. There can be no distinction in law between the shareholder's investment decision to sell the shares he has or to buy additional shares. It follows, therefore, that the scope of the duty of care owed to him by the auditor extends to cover any loss sustained consequent on the purchase of additional shares in reliance on the auditor's negligent report.

[11] [1990] Ch 313.

I believe this argument to be fallacious. Assuming without deciding that a claim by a share-holder to recover a loss suffered by selling his shares at an undervalue attributable to an under-valuation of the company's assets in the auditor's report could be sustained at all, it would not be by reason of any reliance by the shareholder on the auditor's report in deciding to sell; the loss would be referable to the depreciatory effect of the report on the market value of the shares before ever the decision of the shareholder to sell was taken. A claim to recoup a loss alleged to flow from the purchase of overvalued shares, on the other hand, can only be sustained on the basis of the purchaser's reliance on the report. The specious equation of 'investment decisions' to sell or to buy as giving rise to parallel claims thus appears to me to be untenable.

LORDS ROSKILL, OLIVER OF AYLMERTON and JAUNCEY OF TULLICHETTLE delivered concurring opinions.

LORD ACKNER concurred.

➤ Notes

1. In *Galoo Ltd v Bright Grahame Murray* [1994] 1 WLR 1360, CA, it was held that, before a claim in the tort of negligence can be maintained by a third party against an auditor, a 'special relationship' must be shown to have existed between them and, in particular, an intention (actual or inferred) on the part of the auditor that the third party should rely on the audit, together with actual reliance by the third party.

2. In the same vein, in *Al Saudi Banque v Clark Pixley* [1990] Ch 313, it was held that a company's auditors owed no duty of care to existing or future creditors who might foresee-ably lend money to the company or continue its existing credit on the faith of its audited accounts.

3. *Caparo Industries plc v Dickman* may, however, be contrasted with *Morgan Crucible Co plc v Hill Samuel & Co Ltd* [1991] Ch 295, CA, where the court declined to rule, as a pre-liminary point of law, that the directors and financial advisers, including the auditors, of the target company in a contested takeover bid owed no duty of care towards the bidder (whose identity was publicly known) in making representations as to the target's position, as a result of which the bidder had allegedly been induced to offer more for the shares than they were worth.[12] This was, of course, only a preliminary ruling. There are several other cases in which a court has declined to strike out in advance an action brought by a party other than the company itself against its auditors—holding, in effect, that the ele-ments going to establish a 'special relationship' could only be ascertained by hearing the evidence at the trial. Not too much can be read into such decisions: it is perhaps significant that there is no report of further proceedings in any of these cases.

4. And there are cases which seem to go much further. In *Barings plc v Coopers & Lybrand (A Firm)* [1997] 1 BCLC 427, CA, it was held that the auditors of a subsidiary owed a duty of care not only to the subsidiary, but also to its parent company. An argument (based primarily on *Prudential Assurance Co Ltd v Newman Industries Ltd (No 2)* **[13.25]**) that any

---

[12] Although, by contrast, see *In Mira Makar v PricewaterhouseCoopers LLP* [2011] EWHC 3835 (Comm), where the court *was* prepared to strike down an application made by the claimant, who was the chief executive director and former director of a company which engaged PricewaterhouseCoopers as its auditor. In the absence of matters pleaded suggesting 'exceptional circumstances of a special relation or any intention on the part of the auditors that a director such as the claimant should rely on the audit' [28]–[29], Teare J found that there was no arguable case for alleging that a duty of care was owed by the auditors to the claimant as the director of the company being audited. See also, recently, in *Barclays Bank plc v Grant Thornton UK LLP* [2015] EWHC 320 (Comm), where the auditing firm anticipated that its non-statutory audit reports would be forwarded by its client to their bank, the court was satisfied that no duty of care could arise, by reason of the existence of an effective and reasonable disclaimer in the auditors' report. Summary judgment was thereby granted on the basis that the particulars of claim had disclosed no reasonable cause of action.

damage caused by the breach of the auditors' duty would be suffered by the subsidiary, and only indirectly by the parent in its capacity as shareholder, was unsuccessful. (Is this finding affected by the cases on 'reflective loss' (see *Foster Bryant Surveying Ltd v Bryant, Savernake Property Consultants Ltd* **[7.33]**)?) In *Bank of Credit and Commerce International (Overseas) Ltd v Price Waterhouse* [1998] BCLC 617, CA, the position was more defensible: the question was whether the parent company's auditors might owe a duty of care to the parent in respect of the affairs of a subsidiary which had been audited separately by another firm. Because the business of all the companies in the group was so close that they were in effect interdependent, the court held that there would need to have been a constant interchange of information between the two firms of auditors, and that in the circumstances such a duty might arise.

5. In recent years, there have been increasing obligations placed on company auditors both by legislation and by extra-statutory measures. Thus, for example, an auditor is required to state whether the directors' report (required by CA 2006 s 415, except companies qualifying as micro-entities under s 384A) is consistent with the accounts (s 496); the Listing Rules stipulate that the auditor must review the company's statement of compliance with the UK Corporate Governance Code. The potential exposure of firms of auditors to liability for very large sums has caused concern in accountancy circles and has been the subject of debate in many countries. One suggestion advanced for some years is that auditors should be allowed to limit their liability by contract: this is now permitted by CA 2006 ss 534ff, subject to certain conditions (see 'General policy and regulatory issues', p 482). The alternatives were unacceptably limited. Auditors could, at least to some extent, cover their position by insurance, but this drives up the cost of the audit. Another solution is offered by the Limited Liability Partnerships Act 2000, which allows the members of auditing firms to limit their liability for losses caused by the negligence of *other* members of the firm. Another possibility suggested during this debate was to amend the law of joint liability in tort, so that (at least in this context) a tortfeasor should not be jointly and severally liable with the others who were at fault for all the loss sustained by the claimant, but only for a proportionate part of the loss corresponding to his share of the liability. In a number of cases decided in Commonwealth countries, auditors have successfully pleaded that their liability should be reduced because of the contributory negligence of the company itself (the acts of the company's directors being attributed to the company for this purpose). Examples include *Daniels v Anderson* (1995) 16 ACSR 607 and *Dairy Containers Ltd v NZI Bank Ltd* [1995] 2 NZLR 30.

6. The UK Corporate Governance Code ('FRC and the UK Corporate Governance Code for listed companies', p 275) requires that, as a matter of good practice, the board of a listed company should establish an *audit committee* of at least three directors, all non-executive (and having a majority of 'independent' non-executive directors (NEDs)), whose duties should include keeping under review the scope and results of the audit and its cost-effectiveness, and the independence and objectivity of its auditors.

The next case is controversial. Its authority is weakened by comments in *Bilta v Nazir* **[3.29]** (see 'Notes', p 181), although all seven Supreme Court justices in that case appeared to support the outcome on its facts, but perhaps for different reasons, and perhaps only when the company was insolvent. That last qualifier rings alarm bells: it suggests that auditors' duties to the company vary depending on the company's solvency. That seems doubtful.[13] The extract which follows focuses on auditor liability; for other aspects, see *Stone & Rolls* **[3.33]**.

---

[13] Although of course their public reporting obligations will vary according to just that factor.

Frauds perpetrated by a 'one man company': the company cannot sue its auditors for negligence in failing to detect the fraud; nature of the auditors' liability.

[8.05] Stone & Rolls Ltd (In Liquidation) v Moore Stephens (A Firm) [2009] UKHL 39, [2009] 1 AC 1391 (House of Lords)

Read the facts of this case and another part of the judgment at **[3.33]**: the conclusion there was that a one man company could not sue its auditors in negligence for failing to detect the fraud of the company's sole agent and owner. This conclusion relied on the application of the rules of attribution, the *Hampshire Land* principle and the *ex turpi causa* principle. The following extracts deal exclusively with the issue of auditor liability. The opinions expressed may be *obiter* (even that is not clear), but repay consideration.

LORD PHILLIPS:

The duties of auditors

19. [T]he starting point for considering the issues raised by this appeal is the duties undertaken by Moore Stephens as auditors....I would summarise the position as follows. The leading authority is *Caparo Industries plc v Dickman* **[8.04]**. The duties of an auditor are founded in contract and the extent of the duties undertaken by contract must be interpreted in the light of the relevant statutory provisions and the relevant auditing standards. The duties are duties of reasonable care in carrying out the audit of the company's accounts. They are owed to the company in the interests of its shareholders. No duty is owed directly to the individual shareholders. This is because the shareholders' interests are protected by the duty owed to the company. No duty is owed to creditors . . . The auditing standards require auditors who have reason to suspect that the directors of a company are behaving fraudulently to draw this to the attention of the proper authority....For present purposes it suffices to note that the duty is unquestionably imposed in the interests of, at least, the shareholders of the company....

68. One fundamental proposition appears to me to underlie the reasoning of Lord Walker and Lord Brown. It is that the duty owed by an auditor to a company is owed for the benefit of the interests of the shareholders of the company but not of the interests of its creditors. It seems to me that here lies the critical difference of opinion between Lord Walker and Lord Brown on the one hand and Lord Mance on the other. Lord Mance considers that the interests that the auditors of a company undertake to protect include the interests of the creditors....

81. I have had difficulty in this case in distinguishing between questions of duty, breach and actionable damage and, indeed, it is questionable whether it is sensible to attempt to distinguish between them. In *Caparo* . . . Lord Oliver [said, at p 651]:

> 'It has to be borne in mind that the duty of care is inseparable from the damage which the plaintiff claims to have suffered from its breach. It is not a duty to take care in the abstract but a duty to avoid causing to the particular plaintiff damage of the particular kind which he has in fact sustained.'

82. These comments were made in relation to duty of care in tort. In *Banque Bruxelles Lambert SA v Eagle Star Insurance Co Ltd (sub nom South Australia Asset Management Corpn v York Montague Ltd)* [1997] AC 191 Lord Hoffmann held that precisely the same reasoning applied to a duty of care in contract....

LORD BROWN OF EATON-UNDER-HEYWOOD:

202. Lord Mance, as I understand his opinion, would find liability here in respect of all such losses as were occasioned by the fraud from the time when the auditors should have uncovered it. But what is this if not 'liability in an indeterminate amount for an indeterminate time to an indeterminate class' of claimants—whoever came to be defrauded by the company in the trading period after the fraud should have been ended to whatever was the extent of their loss. (The

quoted phrase comes, of course, from Cardozo CJ's judgment in *Ultramares Corpn v Touche* (1931) 174 NE 441 . . .) The company, through its liquidator, would be suing to recover on behalf of all those whom it had defrauded. That, indeed, is precisely the nature of this claim. Such an approach seems to me to run diametrically counter to the principles established in *Caparo*. . . .

203. I recognise, of course, that confining the *ex turpi causa* defence, as I would, to one man company frauds means that, where any innocent shareholders are involved, a claim against the auditors may well lie (through the company) at their suit. This, however, would not be an open-ended claim, wholly indeterminate as to its potential scope and extent at the time of the audit, such as that presently brought. Quite how it would fall to be confined is no doubt open to argument. But on one view it might be limited to the innocent shareholders' own loss suffered through the continuing fraud from the time when, following a diligent audit, it should have been uncovered and brought to an end. A claim of that nature would seem to me to accord altogether more readily with the policies and principles generally understood to apply in this context.

LORD MANCE (dissenting):

206. My Lords, the world has sufficient experience of Ponzi schemes operated by individuals owning 'one man' companies for it to be questionable policy to relieve from all responsibility auditors negligently failing in their duty to check and report on such companies' activities. The speeches of my noble and learned friends in the majority have that effect. In my opinion, English law does not require it. . . .

The auditors' liability where the company's directing mind is fraudulent

241. . . . Leaving aside situations in which the directing mind(s) is or are the sole beneficial shareholder(s), it is obvious—although the Court of Appeal's judgment is surprisingly silent on the point—that an auditor cannot, by reference to the maxim *ex turpi causa*, defeat a claim for breach of duty in failing to detect managerial fraud at the company's highest level by attributing to the company the very fraud which the auditor should have detected. It would lame the very concept of an audit—a check on management for the benefit of shareholders—if the higher the level of managerial fraud, the lower the auditor's responsibility. When Lord Bridge noted in *Caparo* that shareholders' remedy in the case of negligent failure by an auditor to discover and expose misappropriation of funds by a director consisted in a claim against the auditors in the name of the company (p 626e), he cannot conceivably have had in mind that it would make all the difference to the availability of such a claim whether the director was or was not the company's directing mind. The fact that a 'very thing' that an auditor undertakes is the exercise of reasonable care in relation to the possibility of financial impropriety at the highest level makes it impossible for the auditor to treat the company itself as personally involved in such fraud, or to invoke the maxim *ex turpi causa* in such a case. Context is once again all . . . Lord Phillips's statement (para 5) that 'common sense' might suggest that S & R's claim should fail because Moore Stephens were victims of deceitfully prepared company accounts must be categorically rejected. It would emasculate audit responsibility and the auditor's well-recognised duty to approach their audit role if not as bloodhounds, then certainly as watchdogs—planning and performing their audit with the 'attitude of professional scepticism' required by paras 27 and 28 of auditing standard SAS 110 in relation to the possibility of fraud as well as of error in management representations and company records and documents.[14]

242. Auditing standards and procedures have changed significantly over the years. But the potential responsibility of auditors for negligent failure to detect accounting deficiencies or managerial fraud—leading the company to sustain further loss connected with such deficiencies or the continuation of such fraud—dates back to the early days of auditing: see, eg, *In re London and General Bank (No 2)* **[8.01]** (liability for a dividend voted by shareholders on the basis of misleading

---

14 See **[3.33]** for the details of this debate.

accounts on which the auditors failed adequately to report) and *In re Thomas Gerrard & Son Ltd*
[8.03] (liability for dividends voted and tax liabilities incurred on the basis of accounts containing
fraudulent inflation of the company's profits by Mr Croston, its managing director and holder of
18,000 of its shares, which the auditors negligently failed to discover and report on). In the latter
case, the auditors argued (somewhat faintly), that Mr Croston knew and was not misled about
the true position and that the payment of the dividends and tax flowed from his or the directors'
actions . . . Pennycuick J gave short shrift to the argument . . . [And to similar effect Lord Mance
also considered *Galoo Ltd v Bright Grahame Murray* [1994] 1 WLR 1360, and *Sasea Finance Ltd
v KPMG (formerly KPMG Peat Marwick McLintock)* [2000] 1 All ER 676, CA, concluding, at [244],
that:] The Court of Appeal [in *Sasea*] cannot have thought such a duty in shareholders' interests
would only exist if senior management *below* the level of the company's directing mind or board
were complicit in the fraud.

245. It is in principle therefore no answer to an auditor who has failed to discover fraud to point
to involvement or knowledge on the part of the company's directing mind. This conclusion is
justified on grounds paralleling those applicable between the company and its directing mind . . .
That is not surprising, since both senior management and auditors owe duties to the company
intended to protect shareholders' interests, and such duties must be enforceable. The two sets
of relationship are essentially complementary, although the duty is in one case primary and in the
other confirmatory. However the present scheme of fraud is categorised, it cannot in the context
of the audit engagement be attributed to the company itself, so as to relieve the auditors from
their duty or prevent the company complaining of its breach. Again, this is so as a matter of general principle having regard to the nature of the roles and duties undertaken....

The auditor's position where some of the shareholders have engaged in fraud

249. Fraud of the company's directing mind is as such, therefore, no bar to a claim by the company against its auditor for loss sustained by the company due to negligent failure to detect such
fraud: paras 241–247 above. It cannot in principle make any difference if (as will very commonly
be the case) the same person owns some shares in the company. As a matter of basic company
law, the company's separate legal personality entitles it to claim, and the situation mentioned
by Lord Hoffmann in the *Meridian* case . . . in which it is legitimate to look behind the veil at the
shareholders, applies only when *all* the shareholders in a solvent company concur in committing
the company to some decision within its memorandum of association.

250. Lord Phillips expresses the view (para 61) that the position 'becomes unclear . . . if some
of the shareholders were complicit in the directing mind and will's misconduct' because of the
possibility of 'the fraudulent shareholders profiting from their dishonesty'. Self-evidently this focuses only on the presently irrelevant situation of a solvent company. But even in a situation
of solvency, I consider that the doubt expressed by Lord Phillips about the company's right of
recovery conflicts with the principle precluding the lifting of the corporate veil. In reality, it would,
if accepted, transform the law regarding auditors' responsibility, since in many cases fraudulent
management own some shares.

251. The concern behind the doubt is that auditors might be liable to the company in amounts
which would then enure to the benefit of guilty shareholders. This is however an insubstantial
spectre, whether or not the company is insolvent. In cases of insolvency . . . there is commonly
no conceivable prospect of any shareholder benefiting by any recovery, however large, made
against a negligent auditor....

252. Nevertheless [even though it does not arise on the facts here], it is appropriate to give
some further consideration to the position of a solvent company...on the remote hypothesis
that...shareholders who had already benefited by or were involved in the wrongdoing might
[obtain a double benefit by sharing in the damages paid by the auditors to the company]....253 The
whole topic was however comprehensively revisited by Giles J in the Supreme Court of New

South Wales in *Segenhoe Ltd v Akins* (1990) 1 ACSR 691 where he held that it did not matter whether the company paying the [illegal dividend mandated because the auditors had negligently overstated profits] was solvent rather than insolvent. In either case the company as a separate entity was out of pocket to the extent of the money paid away. To prevent recovery by the company because the money was paid to shareholders rather than to a third party 'would negate the company's status as a legal entity separate from its shareholders' and in any event, even if the shareholders remained the same, they would not necessarily be paid twice over. Giles J's full reasoning at pp 701–702 repays reading. The only contrary suggestion in any authority appears to consist of a single dictum of Cotton LJ in *In re Exchange Banking Co (Flitcroft's Case)* (1882) 21 Ch D 519 [which he then explained in a way consistent with the analysis being advanced]....

254. I turn now to situations where the loss consists not of dividends paid out to shareholders, but of other payments fraudulently extracted from the company. In these situations, by definition, the only shareholders, who might conceivably benefit twice over if a company were able to recover such losses from wrongdoers such as its directors or auditor, would be shareholders participating in the fraud. Again, the issue would only arise in a case where (unlike the present) the company was solvent or (improbably) would be made so by recovery from its directors or auditor. In my view, English law would find, as some American courts have found, a way of addressing this issue, even though it may be a different way.... I also believe that would be so. The common law is not so barren as to be unable to achieve in this area what Lord Goff of Chieveley once described in another context as 'practical justice'.

255. One approach that could not, with respect, be adopted is that suggested by my noble and learned friend, Lord Brown, in his judgment at para 203. That paragraph ignores separate corporate personality when it refers to 'a claim against the auditors [which] may well lie (through the company) at their [ie innocent shareholders'] suit'. A company (all the more so when in insolvent litigation) sues in its own right, not for or at the suit of its shareholders. I am also aware of no 'policies and principles', generally understood or not, which might limit a company's recovery for a wrong done to it by reference to whatever loss its innocent shareholders might, if the corporate veil were lifted, be said themselves to have suffered. The suggestion that this could be the measure of a company's recovery again ignores the company's separate legal identity and interests. Suppose senior management own 50% of the shares, and are operating a scheme of fraud which the auditor should have detected at the end of year 1, and that fraud costs the company £1m in year 2. Why should it matter whether, but for the £1m abstraction in year 2, shareholders' equity would or would not have increased in value? What if the £1m abstraction imperils the company or renders it insolvent? The company has suffered a loss of £1m, and is entitled to recover this for its own purposes including payment of its debts. The only qualification on full recovery that might, theoretically, exist in a solvent situation (other than those inherent in conventional contractual and tortious principles of causation and remoteness) is one tailored to ensuring that no guilty shareholder actually benefits, and this could be achieved, if it were ever to be a real concern . . .

The auditor's position where all the shareholders have engaged in fraud

256. The issue which is, or should be, critical to this appeal arises where the person(s) responsible for the scheme of fraud own *all* the company's shares. The auditor is there to check on management and report to shareholders. But the shareholders know the true position. In a situation of solvency, the straightforward analysis is that there is nothing to report, no-one to complain and no loss. It might also be questioned whether there is any breach of duty, at least in tort and perhaps also in contract, in failing to report to persons who already know; however, this may overlook the fact that the negligent auditor will by definition not know that the shareholders do know, and it also needs to be considered in the light of the auditor's statutory role and the duties, here largely express, which an auditor undertakes. More pertinently, 'so long as the company is solvent the shareholders are in substance the company' (para 235), and the company cannot therefore say that it was ignorant or misled or suffered loss.

[Lord Mance then considered two cases which illustrated 'the application of this straightforward analysis to companies solvent at the audit date': *Pendleburys Ltd v Ellis Green & Co* (1936) 181 LT 410; and Hobhouse J's decision in *Berg* [2002] Lloyd's Rep PN 41.[15]] ...

262. Moore Stephens argue, and I understand the majority of your Lordships to consider, that this appeal is covered by the same analysis [as found in US cases]. In short, Mr Stojevic was S & R's sole directing mind and its sole beneficial owner; and the company cannot in consequence complain that it succeeded in deceiving Moore Stephens and was in consequence not stopped by others (regulatory or investigating authorities) from pursuing its scheme of fraud. Such a conclusion could be explained in various ways: the auditor's duty did not extend to supplying information which all persons who can represent the company already have; or whistle-blowing on S & R was and is outside the statutory purpose of the audit as between the company and the auditor; or the principle *ex turpi causa* applies. Which way was adopted would be presently immaterial....

267. The decisions in *Caparo* **[8.04]** and *Al Saudi Banque* [1990] Ch 313 establish that auditors' duties are normally limited to the protection of the company's interests for the benefit of its shareholders....

268. Other than in special situations, therefore, auditors owe no direct duties towards third parties. But none of the above cases addresses the present situation of a claim by the *company* against its auditors for failure to pick up a fraudulent scheme rendering it increasingly insolvent. But in *Caparo*, both Lord Bridge and Lord Oliver recognised the company's standing to bring claims for loss which it has suffered by its officers' fraud (see para 214 above); and, further, Lord Oliver described an auditor's duty as being, first of all, 'to protect the company itself from the consequences of undetected errors or, possibly, wrongdoing', before identifying a second duty 'to provide shareholders with reliable intelligence' (para 214 above).

269. In my opinion it is in no way inconsistent with *Caparo* ... to hold auditors responsible to the company they audit in the present circumstances. I underline four points in this connection. First, the concern about indefinite exposure to third parties does not exist in the context of a claim by the company. S & R's claim is to recover its own (not its creditors') loss by reason of the continuing scheme of fraud. Loss to the company is not the same as loss to its creditors, although there may or may not be an overlap. An insolvent company may by fraud raise £1m from bank A which it uses in a Ponzi type scheme to pay off a borrowing from bank B. Bank A is £1m worse off, and bank B £1m better off. But the company itself is no worse off from the continuing fraud. It is liable to pay bank A £1m, but it has benefited by £1m by paying off bank B using bank A's £1m. Of course if (as here) it raises £1m by fraud and pays only £500,000 to bank B and if its directing mind makes off with the other £500,000, then the company is £500,000 worse off due to the continuation of the fraud, but that is and remains its own loss. Secondly, S & R's claim is for precisely the same loss as a company with some shareholders innocent of involvement in top management's fraud would be entitled to claim from negligent auditors who had failed to detect and report the fraud (paras 249–255 above). Thirdly, it cannot be suggested that the care to be expected of Moore Stephens as auditors varied according to whether all of S & R's shares happened to be owned and/or controlled by Mr Stojevic. Their express contractual duty was under auditing standard SAS 110.10 and 110.12 to report to a proper authority without delay where suspected or actual fraud cast doubt on the integrity of directors. This duty in fact exists under SAS 110 irrespective of whether there are or are not independent shareholders of integrity. Auditors would not in any event necessarily have any idea whether any such shareholders exist.

270. Fourthly, quite apart from the express provisions of auditing standard SAS 110, a situation of insolvency introduces new considerations for reasons previously explained. The identity of interest which normally exists between a company and its shareholders ceases, and the duties of auditors, like those of directors, must recognise this. The company as a legal personality

---

[15] Although not Lord Mance's analysis, these cases might be better regarded as cases where there was a provable breach by the auditors, but no causally related loss arising from their negligence.

continues and the auditors' duty continues to be, in Lord Oliver's words in *Caparo* (p 630), 'to protect the company itself from the consequences of undetected errors or, possibly, wrongdoing'.
If, in Hobhouse J's words in *Berg* [2002] Lloyd's Rep PN 41, 55, 'those in charge of the affairs of
a company or in control of it are acting contrary to the principles governing insolvency', then the
auditors can no longer treat them as representing the company, and must take other action—
according to SAS 110 'without informing the directors in advance'....

➤ Questions

1. In *Stone & Rolls*, Lord Walker said, 'Much of the opinion of my noble and learned friend,
Lord Mance, seems to me, with great respect, to be seeking to attenuate by indirect means the
House's decision in *Caparo*, although we are not invited to depart from it.' Is this accurate?

2. What are the doctrinal and policy reasons in favour of and against each of the opposing
viewpoints advanced in the House of Lords?

3. Is it simply impossible in the context of a one man company to maintain purist adherence to the doctrine of separate legal personality? Or do the recent Supreme Court cases
on separate legal personality suggest that Lord Mance's analysis is to be preferred? (See
especially *Prest v Petrodel Resources* **[2.01]** and *Bilta v Nazir* **[3.29]**.)

Promoters and their dealings with the company

The term 'promoter' is not defined in the Companies Act, and such attempts at definition
as have been made by the courts (mainly in the nineteenth century) seem to have been
concerned only to ensure that enough flexibility was retained to catch the next ingenious
rogue which the pre-incorporation period might produce. The best known of these is the
description given by Cockburn CJ in *Twycross v Grant* (1877) 2 CPD 469 at 541: 'one who
undertakes to form a company with reference to a given project, and to set it going, and
who takes the necessary steps to accomplish that purpose'.

There is an enormous body of old case law concerned with the obligations of promoters
towards the companies which they form and the investing public whose capital they seek
to attract. But to all intents and purposes this law has become obsolete. This is due partly
to changes in the practice of marketing securities: it is unusual for a newly formed company to make an initial public issue, and not normally possible to obtain a market listing,
without an established trading record. It is also due to the stringent control of such activities now imposed by statute and by the Listing Rules (which must be complied with in
order to gain access to the Stock Exchange)[16] and the professional codes of issuing houses
and others whose services are nowadays essential. There is thus little need to include extracts from these cases, insofar as they relate to promoters' duties, as such cases are now
mainly of historical interest.

CA 2006, too, pays little specific attention to promoters. The only issue of real concern
is, perhaps predictably, the propriety of any sales of non-cash assets to the company by
its promoters (or those in similar positions). Even here, CA 2006 only concerns itself with
public companies. CA 2006 ss 598–604 require the independent valuation of all non-cash
assets sold to a public company within two years of its formation or re-registration by
persons who were either the subscribers to the memorandum at the time the company was

---

[16] See Chapter 14.

registered as a public company, or were its members at the time it was re-classified and re-registered as a public company. The valuer's report must state that the asset is worth at least the price being paid for it by the company. In addition, the agreement for sale must be approved by an ordinary resolution of the company's members, and a copy of this resolution and the valuation sent to Companies House within 15 days of adoption. Companies House then gives public notice of receipt of the report (ss 1077 and 1078(3)). There are *de minimis* exceptions to these requirements if the asset is worth less than 10% of the nominal value of the company's allotted share capital. In addition, the rules do not apply to any sales in the normal course of the company's business.

Here the focus is simply on illustrations of the promoters' relationships and dealings with the company as a separate legal person. The next two cases have strong parallels with the approach taken to the relationship and dealings between a company and its directors. Shades of this could be seen in the analysis in *Salomon* **[2.02]**.

Promoters are fiduciaries. A contract between the promoter and the company is voidable at the company's option unless the promoter has disclosed all material facts relating to that contract to an independent board, and the company has freely agreed to the terms.

[8.06] Erlanger v New Sombrero Phosphate Co (1878) 3 App Cas 1218 (House of Lords)

A syndicate headed by Erlanger, a Paris banker, acquired for £55,000 the lease of an island in the West Indies with the right to work its phosphate deposits. The syndicate, through Erlanger, then formed the respondent company and named its first directors. Of these, one, the Lord Mayor of London, was independent of the syndicate; two were abroad, and the remainder were mere puppets of Erlanger. The lease was then sold through a nominee to the company for £110,000, the purchase being 'ratified' without inquiry at a meeting of directors eight days after the incorporation of the company. Many members of the public subscribed for shares, but the real circumstances of the sale and purchase were not disclosed to them and were not discovered until eight months later, after the first phosphate shipments had proved a failure. The members then removed the original directors and elected a new board, which brought these proceedings to have the sale rescinded.

LORD CAIRNS LC: In the whole of this proceeding . . . the syndicate, or the house of Erlanger as representing the syndicate, were the promoters of the company, and it is now necessary that I should state to your Lordships in what position I understand the promoters to be placed with reference to the company which they proposed to form. They stand, in my opinion, undoubtedly in a fiduciary position. They have in their hands the creation and moulding of the company; they have the power of defining how, and when, and in what shape, and under what supervision, it shall start into existence and begin to act as a trading corporation. If they are doing all this in order that the company may, as soon as it starts into life, become, through its managing directors, the purchaser of the property of themselves, the promoters, it is, in my opinion, incumbent upon the promoters to take care that in forming the company they provide it with an executive, that is to say, with a board of directors, who shall both be aware that the property which they are asked to buy is the property of the promoters, and who shall be competent and impartial judges as to whether the purchase ought or ought not to be made. I do not say that the owner of the property may not promote and form a joint stock company, and then sell his property to it, but I do say that if he does he is bound to take care that he sells it to the company through the medium of a board of directors who can and do exercise an independent and intelligent judgment on the transaction, and who are not left under the belief that the property belongs, not to the promoter, but to some other person . . .

LORD O'HAGAN: The original purchase of the island of Sombrero was perfectly legitimate—and it was not less so because the object of the purchasers was to sell it again, and to sell it by forming a company which might afford them a profit on the transaction. The law permitted them to take that course, and provided the machinery by which the transfer of their interest might be equitably and beneficially effected for themselves and those with whom they meant to deal. But the privilege given them for promoting such a company for such an object, involved obligations of a very serious kind. It required, in its exercise, the utmost good faith, the completest truthfulness, and a careful regard to the protection of the future shareholders. The power to nominate a directorate is manifestly capable of great abuse, and may involve, in the misuse of it, very evil consequences to multitudes of people who have little capacity to guard themselves. Such a power may or may not have been wisely permitted to exist. I venture to have doubts upon the point. It tempts too much to fraudulent contrivance and mischievous deception; and, at least, it should be watched with jealousy and restrained from employment in such a way as to mislead the ignorant and the unwary. In all such cases the directorate nominated by the promoters should stand between them and the public, with such independence and intelligence, that they may be expected to deal fairly, impartially and with adequate knowledge in the affairs submitted to their control. If they have not those qualities, they are unworthy of trust. They are the betrayers and not the guardians of the company they govern, and their acts should not receive the sanction of a court of justice.

Now, my Lords, for reasons repeatedly given by my noble and learned friends, which I shall not detail again, I think that the promoters in this case failed to remember the exigencies of their fiduciary position, when they appointed directors who were in no way independent of themselves, and who did not sustain the interests of the company with ordinary care and intelligence . . .

Apparently, there was no inquiry as to the enormous advance in the price . . ., no consideration of the state of the property—and no intelligent estimate of its capabilities and prospects. If the directors had been nominated merely to ratify any terms the promoters might dictate, they discharged their function; if it was their duty, as it certainly was, to protect the shareholders, they never seem to have thought of doing it. Their conduct was precisely that which might have been anticipated from the character of their selection, and taking that conduct and character together, I concur in, I believe, the unanimous opinion of your Lordships that such a transaction ought not to be allowed to stand.

The promoters, who so forgot their duty to the company they formed, as to give it a directorate without independence of position or vigilance and caution in caring for its interests, must take the consequences. And this without the necessary imputation of evil purpose or conscious fraud. The fiduciary obligation may be violated though there may be no intention to do injustice. If the protection, proper and needful for a person standing at disadvantage in relation to his guardian or his solicitor, or to the promoters of a company, be withheld, the guardian, the solicitor or the promoters cannot sustain a contract equitably invalidated by the want of it, merely because it may be impossible to prove that he is impeachable with indirect or improper motives . . .

LORDS PENZANCE, HATHERLEY, SELBORNE, BLACKBURN and GORDON delivered concurring opinions.

➤ Notes

1. The principles of fiduciary obligation are rules applied by the courts of equity to impose high standards of selfless conduct upon trustees and others, such as agents and solicitors, who undertake responsibility to look after the interests or handle the property of others. Company promoters, like company directors (see Chapter 7), are subject to these rules. Is it appropriate to put promoters in the same category? (See the following Note.)

2. Newey J cited *Erlanger* in arriving at the view that, by analogy, a shadow director owed fiduciary duties to at least some degree (this was when CA 2006 s 170 was less clear). On

promoters, he said: '[I]f, therefore, an undertaking/assumption is crucial to the existence of fiduciary duties, a promoter's acceptance and use of powers "which so greatly affect the interests of the corporation" must imply an undertaking/assumption of responsibility': *Vivendi SA v Richards* [2013] BCC 771 at [140].

3. It has been accepted at least since *Salomon v A Salomon & Co Ltd* **[2.02]** that, if there is no independent board of directors, the company may be bound by the consent of all the original *members*, provided that a full disclosure is made to them of all material facts. But, as is shown by *Gluckstein v Barnes* **[8.07]** even this will not protect a promoter if the original members themselves are not independent and the scheme as a whole is designed to attract and deceive the investing public at large. (This has obvious parallels with *Cook v Deeks* **[7.25]**.)

Promoters, as fiduciaries, may not make a secret profit while acting in that capacity. Any profits so received must be accounted for to the company.

[8.07] Gluckstein v Barnes [1900] AC 240 (House of Lords)

Gluckstein and three others bought the Olympia exhibition premises in liquidation proceedings for £140,000 and then promoted a company, Olympia Ltd, to which they sold the property for £180,000. There were no independent directors. In a prospectus inviting applications for shares and debentures the £40,000 profit was disclosed, but not a further profit of some £20,000 which they had made by buying securities on the property at a discount and then enforcing them at their face value (though there was a vague reference to 'interim investments'). The company went into liquidation within four years, and the liquidator claimed in this action £6,341, part of the £20,000 received by Gluckstein.

EARL OF HALSBURY LC: My Lords, I am wholly unable to understand any claim that these directors, vendors, syndicate, associates, have to retain this money. I entirely agree with the Master of the Rolls that the essence of this scheme was to form a company. It was essential that this should be done, and that they should be directors of it, who would purchase. The company should have been informed of what was being done and consulted whether they would have allowed this profit. I think the Master of the Rolls is absolutely right in saying that the duty to disclose is imposed by the plainest dictates of common honesty as well as by well-settled principles of common law.

Of the facts there cannot be the least doubt; they are proved by the agreement, now that we know the subject-matter with which that agreement is intended to deal, although the agreement would not disclose what the nature of the transaction was to those who were not acquainted with the ingenious arrangements which were prepared for entrapping the intended victim of these arrangements.

In order to protect themselves, as they supposed, they inserted in the prospectus, qualifying the statement that they had bought the property for £140,000, payable in cash, that they did not sell to the company, and did not intend to sell, any other profits made by the syndicate from interim investments.

Then it is said there is the alternative suggested upon the agreement that the syndicate might sell to a company or to some other purchaser. In the first place, I do not believe they ever intended to sell to anybody else other than a company. An individual purchaser might ask inconvenient questions, and if they or any one of them had stated as an inducement to an individual purchaser that £140,000 was given for the property, when in fact £20,000 less had been given, it is a great error to suppose that the law is not strong enough to reach such a statement; but as I say, I do not believe it was ever intended to get an individual purchaser, even if such an intention would have had any operation. When they did afterwards sell to a company, they took very good care there should be no one who could ask questions. They were to be sellers to themselves as buyers, and it was a necessary provision to the plan that they were to be both sellers and buyers, and as buyers to get the money to pay for the purchase from the pockets of deluded shareholders.

My Lords, I decline to discuss the question of disclosure to the company. It is too absurd to suggest that a disclosure to the parties to this transaction is a disclosure to the company of which these directors were the proper guardians and trustees. They were there by the terms of the agreement to do the work of the syndicate, that is to say, to cheat the shareholders; and this, forsooth, is to be treated as a disclosure to the company, when they were really there to hoodwink the shareholders, and so far from protecting them, were to obtain from them the money, the produce of their nefarious plans.

I do not discuss either the sum sued for, or why Gluckstein alone is sued.

The whole sum has been obtained by a very gross fraud, and all who were parties to it are responsible to make good what they have obtained and withheld from the shareholders.

I move your Lordships that the appeal be dismissed with costs.

LORD MACNAGHTEN: My Lords, Mr Swinfen Eady argued this appeal with his usual ability, but the case is far too clear for argument . . . For my part, I cannot see any ingenuity or any novelty in the trick which Mr Gluckstein and his associates practised on the persons whom they invited to take shares in Olympia Limited. It is the old story. It has been done over and over again.

These gentlemen set about forming a company to pay them a handsome sum for taking off their hands a property which they had contracted to buy with that end in view. They bring the company into existence by means of the usual machinery. They appoint themselves sole guardians and protectors of this creature of theirs, half-fledged and just struggling into life, bound hand and foot while yet unborn by contracts tending to their private advantage, and so fashioned by its makers that it could only act by their hands and only see through their eyes. They issue a prospectus representing that they had agreed to purchase the property for a sum largely in excess of the amount which they had, in fact, to pay. On the faith of this prospectus they collect subscriptions from a confiding and credulous public. And then comes the last act. Secretly, and therefore dishonestly, they put into their own pockets the difference between the real and the pretended price. After a brief career the company is ordered to be wound up. In the course of the liquidation the trick is discovered. Mr Gluckstein is called upon to make good a portion of the sum which he and his associates had mis-appropriated. Why Mr Gluckstein alone was selected for attack I do not know any more than I know why he was only asked to pay back a fraction of the money improperly withdrawn from the coffers of the company.

However that may be, Mr Gluckstein defends his conduct or, rather I should say, resists the demand, on four grounds, which have been gravely argued at the bar. In the first place, he says that he was not in a fiduciary position towards Olympia Limited, before the company was formed. Well, for some purposes he was not. For others he was. A good deal might be said on the point. But to my mind the point is immaterial, for it is not necessary to go back beyond the formation of the company.

In the second place, he says that if he was in a fiduciary position he did in fact make a proper disclosure. With all deference to the learned counsel for the appellant, that seems to me to be absurd. 'Disclosure' is not the most appropriate word to use when a person who plays many parts announces to himself in one character what he has done and is doing in another. To talk of disclosure to the thing called the company, when as yet there were no shareholders, is a mere farce. To the intended shareholders there was no disclosure at all. On them was practised an elaborate system of deception.

The third ground of defence was that the only remedy was rescission. That defence, in the circumstances of the present case, seems to me to be as contrary to common sense as it is to authority. The point was settled more than sixty years ago by the decision in *Hichens v Congreve*[17] and so far as I know, that case has never been questioned.

The last defence of all was that, however much the shareholders may have been wronged, they have bound themselves by a special bargain, sacred under the provisions of the Companies Act 1862,[18] to bear their wrongs in silence. In other words, Mr Gluckstein boldly asserts that he is entitled to use the provisions of an Act of Parliament, which are directed to a very different purpose, as a shield and shelter against the just consequences of his fraud . . .

There are two things in this case which puzzle me much, and I do not suppose that I shall ever understand them. I mention them merely because I should be very sorry if it were thought that in those two matters the House unanimously approved of what has been done. I do not understand why Mr Gluckstein and his associates were not called upon to refund the whole of the money which they misappropriated. What they did with it, whether they put it in their own pockets or distributed it among their confederates, or spent it in charity, seems to me absolutely immaterial. In the next place, I do not understand why Mr Gluckstein was only charged with interest at the rate of 3%. I should have thought it was a case for penal interest.

In these two matters Mr Gluckstein has been in my opinion extremely fortunate. But he complains that he may have a difficulty in recovering from his co-directors their share of the spoil, and he asks that the official liquidator may proceed against his associates before calling upon him to make good the whole amount with which he has been charged. My Lords, there may be occasions in which that would be a proper course to take. But I cannot think that this is a case in which any indulgence ought to be shown to Mr Gluckstein. He may or may not be able to recover a contribution from those who joined with him in defrauding the company. He can bring an action at law if he likes. If he hesitates to take that course or takes it and fails, then his only remedy lies in an appeal to that sense of honour which is popularly supposed to exist among robbers of a humbler type. I agree that the appeal must be dismissed with costs.

LORD ROBERTSON delivered a concurring opinion.

See also *Re Darby, ex p Brougham* [1911] 1 KB 95.

➤ Notes

1. A wide choice of remedies is available against a promoter who has acted in breach of his fiduciary obligations. The company may rescind any contract between the promoter and the newly formed company (see *Erlanger* **[8.06]**, and the following Note 3), or the company may bring proceedings for the restitution of a benefit which the promoter has received from third parties, either in equity on the basis of a constructive trust (see *FHR European Ventures LLP v Cedar Capital Partners LLC* **[7.39]**), or at law as a claim for money had and received. The parties to a secret bargain may also be sued in an action of deceit. Where a promoter has been promised, but has not received, a profit, bribe or other benefit, the company may itself enforce his claim for payment against the promisor, on the ground that he holds the claim as trustee for it: *Whaley Bridge Calico Printing Co v Green* (1879) 5 QBD 109.

2. Where the company does not seem able to avail itself of the remedies noted earlier (most commonly because rescission is barred because *restitutio in integrum* has become impossible), then the courts have often avoided the ensuing injustice by finding the promoter liable in *damages* for deceit (see, eg, *Re Leeds and Hanley Theatres of Varieties Ltd*

---

[17] (1831) 4 Sim 420.
[18] Lord Macnaghten is referring to the fact that the contract to purchase the premises was expressly mentioned in the company's memorandum and articles; the 'bargain' was the 'statutory contract' created by the equivalent of CA 2006 s 33 ('Members' personal rights', p 261).

[1902] 2 Ch 809, CA), or for negligence in allowing the company to purchase at too high a price (see, eg, *Jacobus Marler Estates Ltd v Marler* (1913) 85 LJPC 167n, PC), or under the Misrepresentation Act 1967 (*if* there has been an actionable misrepresentation[19]).[20]

3. Where a promoter has sold to his company property which he did not acquire as a promoter or did not acquire with a view to launching the promotion—for example, property which he inherited some years before—the remedy of rescission of the contract of sale is, of course, available to the company if he did not make a proper disclosure of his interest at the time of the sale. However, if rescission is no longer possible (eg because of supervening third party rights), or if the company elects to affirm the contract, an alternative remedy by way of an account of profits does not lie: *Re Cape Breton Co* (1885) 29 Ch D 795, CA; *Ladywell Mining Co v Brookes* (1887) 35 Ch D 400, CA. This seemingly anomalous rule is commonly explained by saying that the promoter's alleged 'profit' is unquantifiable, and that by giving such a remedy the court would in effect be fixing a new price for the parties.

4. These old rulings on the liability of promoters are significant because there is a close parallel between the fiduciary obligations of promoters and the fiduciary obligations of directors (see Chapter 7), and decisions like *Re Cape Breton Co* may be relevant in the latter context. Compare the rules as they apply to directors, especially where there has been statutory intervention: see 'Deemed authority I: statutory deeming provisions to avoid constitutional limitations on directors' authority—CA 2006 s 40', p 100 (in the context of CA 2006 s 41), and 'Directors' duties are owed to the company', pp 336ff (in the context of directors' statutory duties).

5. A promoter may also be liable to pay compensation to persons who subscribe for shares or other securities on the faith of listing particulars or a prospectus for which he is responsible: see 'Liability for misleading statements and omissions in prospectuses', pp 766ff.

➤ Question

Suppose that the company on facts similar to *Re Cape Breton Co were* to bring an action for equitable compensation[21] against the promoter-vendor, and it is accepted that there is jurisdiction to award such compensation. What issues in regard to (i) causation and (ii) the measure of compensation would arise, and how do you think that they should be resolved?

▨ Further reading

DORALT, W, FLECKNER, A, HOPT, K, KUMPAN, C, STEFFEK, F, ZIMMERMANN, R, HELLGARDT, A and AUGENHOFER, S, 'Auditor Independence at the Crossroads—Regulation and Incentives' (2012) 13 *European Business Organization Law Review* 89.

FERRAN, E, 'Corporate Attribution and the Directing Mind and Will' (2011) 127 LQR 239.

GOLD, J, 'The Liability of Promoters for Secret Profits in English Law' (1943) 5 *University of Toronto Law Journal* 21.

---

[19] Mere non-disclosure of profit is not such a misrepresentation: see *Jacobus Marler Estates Ltd* in *Cook v Deeks* **[7.25]**.

[20] These damages or equitable compensation remedies are *not* awarded for breach of the promoter's *fiduciary* obligation, but for breach of other legal or equitable obligations owed (by the fiduciary promoter) to the company. See *Target Holdings Ltd v Redferns* [1996] AC 421, HL; *AIB Group (UK) Plc v Mark Redler & Co Solicitors* [2014] UKSC 58, SC; and *Knight v Frost* [1999] 1 BCLC 364 at 373. But also see, IE Davidson, 'The Equitable Remedy of Compensation' (1982) 13 *Melbourne University Law Review* 349 and WMC Gummow, 'Compensation for Breach of Fiduciary Duty' in TG Youdan (ed), *Equity Fiduciaries and Trusts* (1989), ch 2, arguing that compensation (not, strictly speaking, damages) was commonly awarded in an earlier period for at least some breaches of fiduciary obligation.

[21] See Note 3.

GROSS, JH, 'Who is a Company Promoter?' (1970) 86 LQR 493.

KERSHAW, D, 'Waiting for Enron: The Unstable Equilibrium of Auditor Independence Regulation' (2006) 33 *Journal of Law and Society* 388.

KERSHAW, D, 'Evading Enron: Taking Principles Too Seriously in Accounting Regulation' (2005) 68 MLR 594.

McCREA, BE, 'Disclosure of Promoters' Secret Profits' (1968) 3 *University of British Columbia Law Review* 183.

MORRIS, PE, 'Contractual Limitations on the Auditor's Liability: An Uneasy Combination of Law and Accounting' (2009) 72 MLR 602.

PATERSON, M, 'Reform of the Law on Auditors' Liability: An Assessment' (2012) 23 *International Company and Commercial Law Review* 55.

WATTS, P, *'Stone & Rolls Ltd (In Liquidation) v Moore Stephens (A Firm)*: Audit Contracts and Turpitude' (2010) 126 LQR 14.

9

THE RAISING OF CAPITAL

Company 'capital' and its importance

'Capital' is a word that can have many meanings. In company law, however, *legal capital* (or simply *'capital'*) may be used in a restricted technical sense. Broadly speaking, it is cash (or, less often, the value of the assets) received by the company from investors who subscribe for the company's shares.[1] The company's capital, in this technical sense, is measured in terms of 'value received' into the company, rather than the current value of the assets themselves, since that will change with the business activities of the company. If the company receives cash in exchange for its shares, for example, the company will use that cash to promote and expand the company's business. If the business is successful, the value of the business will increase; if not, it will decrease.

The value of the company's legal capital is likely to be far less than the total value of the company's assets. Even before the company begins to trade, and certainly once it is up and running, the company is likely to borrow money from banks and from other lending sources. It is also likely to rely on other sources of credit, such as debt funding from suppliers who supply the company with goods and services on deferred payment terms or 'on credit'. None of this large and small scale *'debt funding'* is part of the company's legal capital. Important distinctions exist between the treatment of debt, and the *creditors* who provide those funds,[2] and the treatment of *'equity funding'* (as fundraising by share issues is known) and the *shareholders* who provide those funds. Both sources of funds will be deployed in the company's business, however, and, if the business is successful, will generate additional company assets by way of

---

[1] This is a simplification: as is explained later (see 'Issue of shares at a premium', p 527), the total sum received by the company in exchange for the share may include both a 'capital' sum and a 'premium' sum. Both of these sums are subject to substantially similar restrictions on the possible uses the company may make of them, but the 'company's capital', in the strictest sense, includes only the former sums.

[2] See Chapters 12 and 16.

retained business profits. These profits do not form part of the company's legal capital either. Of course, if the business is unsuccessful and losses are incurred, the total value of the company's assets, and hence its *capital*, may fall below the company's legal capital.

Why is such a sharp distinction drawn between legal capital (or contributions from shareholders) and other assets held by the company? The distinction reflects the special protection provided to creditors by the company's legal capital. This is seen most dramatically when the company is in financial difficulty. Take a simple example. Suppose a company is set up with £100,000 in 'equity funding' contributed by shareholders, and £200,000 in 'debt funding' provided over time by the bank and other creditors. If the business fails, and the company is put into insolvency, then whatever remains of the company's assets will be used to repay the company's creditors, in full if possible, before any of the shareholders are repaid any part of their contribution to funding the company. In other words, the two types of financiers of the company's operation do not share the losses equally. In the example given, suppose the company's remaining assets amount to £150,000. The creditors clearly cannot be repaid in full, but they will share *all* of this sum (obtaining 75p in the pound), and the shareholders will receive nothing. Of course, in practice the situation is usually more complicated. There are invariably different types of creditors (some with security provided by mortgages and charges, others unsecured, and still others given special privileges and priorities by statute), and there may be different classes of shareholders (perhaps with different rights when the company goes into insolvency). And some part of the company's assets will need to be spent simply in the mechanics of sale and distribution to those entitled (the expenses of liquidation and receivership). All of this detail is covered later.[3]

The outlook for the shareholder is not all gloomy, of course. If the company is successful, then the shareholders, not the creditors, will share in the company's profits. The shareholders will receive dividends (distributions based on company profits),[4] and the value of their shares is likely to increase by the value of retained profits and enhanced expectations about future profits (so that if they sell their investment to a third party, they will reap a capital gain). The creditors, on the other hand, are restricted to the scale of return defined by their contract with the company (eg a loan with specified rate of interest, or a sale of goods with a built-in profit margin).

Finally, by way of concluding introductory comment, note that contributions to a company's capital are made only by shareholders purchasing shares *from the company*. When these shareholders then sell their shares to third parties (who will become the new shareholders), they may sell at a price far greater, or far less, than the price initially paid to the company for the share. But this sale price is received *by the shareholders*, and, although it will reflect their personal profit or loss on the investment, it will not alter the company's legal capital.

Many shareholders are motivated by the possibility of realising an increase in total shareholder value comprising capital gain on their share investment and dividends (ie income from the investment), rather than by the attraction of being an 'owner' of a small business (ie by the benefits of management or voting control). Markets, such as the London Stock Exchange, were originally set up and regulated precisely to provide for this possibility. Their importance in attracting investors is well recognised by the increasing efforts put into appropriate regulation.[5]

---

[3] See Chapter 16.
[4] See Chapter 10.
[5] See Chapter 14.

Attracting and protecting shareholders and creditors

The interplay between the rights of shareholders and the rights of creditors is critical to the success of companies as business entities. A company is a separate legal person. It follows that the claims of the company's creditors must be met from the company's assets.[6] The shareholders' capital contributions mitigate the risks to which creditors are exposed. The returns for shareholders are proportionately greater if the company is a success, and proportionately worse if the company is a failure. That is why the cost of equity funding (in terms of *expected* total shareholder return) is generally higher than for debt funding (an *expected* interest entitlement). In addition, if shareholders are to be attracted to this form of investment, then there must be appropriate protections of their rights and appropriate limitations on their obligations. And, unless shareholders are attracted, creditors are unlikely to be forthcoming.

For shareholders, these protections include:

(i)   limitations on the issue of new shares, so that shareholders' interests in the company are not unacceptably diluted (*pre-emption rights* and *limitations on the directors' powers of allotment*) (see 'Limiting access to shares: directors' allotment rights and shareholders' pre-emption rights', pp 514ff);

(ii)   protection against misleading inducements to purchase shares (see 'Offers to the public to purchase shares and remedies for misleading offers', pp 519ff);

(iii) protection of the financial rights attached to shares (including protection of 'class rights') (see Chapter 11);

(iv)   protection of shareholders' established and agreed relationships with the company (via shareholder control over changes to the company's constitution (see Chapter 2), or by personal claims by shareholders against the company or its managers, as permitted by common law (under Companies Act 2006 (CA 2006) s 33) or by statute (eg CA 2006 s 994) (see Chapter 13));

(v)   protection of shareholders' influence over the potential success of the company (via control over the management, and, sometimes, control over the pursuit of claims on behalf of the company) (see Chapters 4, 6 and 13).

Only the first two of these are directly associated with the process of raising capital for the company, and are dealt with in this chapter.

What of the protection provided for company lenders and other creditors? Normal rules of contract law and security law (see Chapters 13 and 16) provide much assistance. Here, however, we are concerned with the special protections associated with the acquisition and treatment of company capital. These protective rules include:

(i)   rules requiring the company to have a certain minimum level of capital before it begins trading ('*minimum capital requirements*') (see 'Minimum capital requirements for company formation', p 514);

---

[6] It is not the same with partnerships, where the partners are personally liable for the debts of the partnership (with limitations on that liability only if the partnership is a Limited Liability Partnership): see 'Companies and other business structures', pp 24ff. Of course, if the company's directors have caused an unwarranted diminution in the company's assets, then the *company, not* the creditors, can sue the directors, and the recoveries will augment the company's assets, and be available for the benefit of the company's creditors (and its shareholders, if the company is solvent): see 'Pursuing claims for maladministration', pp 665ff. If the company is being wound up, different rules determine who may sue, and who may be sued: see 'Statutory framework', pp 811ff.

(ii) rules designed to ensure that the amount of legal capital shown in the company records is in fact received in full by the company (rules relating to *payment for shares*) (see 'Collecting in the company's capital: payment for shares', p 525);

(iii) rules designed to ensure the maintenance of stated levels of legal capital by restricting the freedom of companies to return assets to its shareholders ('*capital maintenance rules*' and '*dividend distribution rules*') (see Chapter 10).

Terminology associated with legal capital

Various terms are commonly used, and need to be understood. These include 'allotment' and 'issue' of shares, and 'authorised' or 'nominal' capital (the terms are interchangeable, and are of less concern now that CA 2006 has abolished the requirement to state this value, although of course it appears in older cases), 'nominal value' or 'par value' (again used interchangeably), 'issued capital' and 'share premiums'.

Formally a share is not *issued* to a shareholder until the investor's name is registered in the company's register of members (CA 2006 s 112(2)). This is when the shareholder acquires the legal title to the share. Until this has been done the person entitled to the shares is neither a member nor their legal owner. Of course, there is an earlier stage, where the company enters into a binding contract with the investor to sell a share in return for payment of the price, and the investor acquires an unconditional right to be included in the company's register of members in respect of the shares; a share is then said to be *allotted* to the investor (CA 2006 s 558).

All companies with shares used to be incorporated with a '*nominal*' or '*authorised*' *capital*, the total amount of which had to be stated in the memorandum (ie the document which, with the articles, provided the company's constitution). This figure had very little practical significance. It merely fixed a ceiling upon the amount of capital the company could raise by the issue of shares without further formalities. For example, a company might be incorporated with an authorised capital of £1 million, indicating that it was entitled to sell £1 million worth of shares to shareholders; in fact it might only issue £500,000 worth of shares, or even only £100,000 worth of shares.[7] Indeed, companies typically plucked large figures out of the air for authorised capital, since the only significance was to set this notional cap on issues, a cap which could in any event be increased by ordinary resolution of the shareholders.

The specified authorised capital was required to be divided into shares of a fixed unit value. In other words, a monetary value had (and still has: CA 2006 s 542[8]) to be attached to the shares. As a consequence, it is common to describe a company's capital as divided into a certain number of '£1' shares, or '10p' shares. We would then say that the '*nominal value*' or '*par value*' of the shares was £1 or 10p respectively.

When the company *allots* or, later on, *issues* some of these shares, it is possible to speak of 'allotted' or 'issued' capital (CA 2006 s 546). The '*issued capital*' (or, in the case of the first shareholders, the '*subscribed capital*') is the sum equivalent to the nominal value or par value of all the shares that have been issued, and the '*paid-up capital*' is so much of the issued capital as is represented by money which the shareholders have in fact paid: there may be an unpaid balance on each share which is not due for payment until a call is made

---

[7] And indeed, as indicated later, a sale of '£100,000 worth of shares' might well net the company more than £100,000.

[8] And note the permission in s 542(3), subject to s 765, to have share capital denominated in different currencies.

(although this is rarely the case now; shares are usually issued fully paid, so the issued capital and paid-up capital are identical). CA 2006 s 547 also defines 'called-up share capital', which is the aggregate of paid-up capital plus capital that has been called up (whether or not paid) plus any defined commitments to pay share capital at a future date, but which has not yet been called up or paid.

So, in *Salomon's* case **[2.02]**, the authorised or nominal capital was £40,000 comprising 40,000 shares of £1 each; the subscribed capital was £7, the total issued capital was £20,007, which was fully paid up, and the debt capital (a loan secured by the debenture) was a further £10,000.

Note that the 'issued capital' is *not* simply the consideration received by the company for the sale of its shares. The calculation is more convoluted. The advantage of this, if there is one, is that it enables a creditor to calculate that if a company has issued 100,000 shares with a nominal value of £1, for example, then the company's issued capital is £100,000, and this sum is subject to all the capital maintenance and other creditor protection rules supplied by company law. In other words, the creditor has an easy basis on which to assess the company's legal capital.

In fact, this easy calculation underestimates the extent to which a creditor is protected. It is perhaps obvious, given the way the nominal value is determined, that it bears no necessary relationship to the price at which the shares may be sold. When the company issues shares, it may well sell its '£1' shares at a *premium* of £0.50 to the nominal value, that is, for £1.50, if that is what the market will bear.[9] The 'legal capital' rules insist that the company cannot sell its shares for *less* than the nominal value (see 'Collecting in the company's capital: payment for shares', p 525). But if it sells its shares for *more* than the nominal value, as in this case, then the £1 (representing the nominal value) received by the company must be allocated to the company's *'capital account'*, and the £0.50 'premium' to the *'share premium account'*. The creditor is then super-protected, because the restrictions on the use of both accounts are reasonably similar, although not identical (see 'Issue of shares at a premium', p 527); in other words, the company does not receive a 'premium' which it is free to use at will, and the creditor receives buffering protection beyond the company's strict legal capital.[10]

CA 2006 specifies the acceptable uses of the share premium account: in line with the recommendations of the Company Law Review (CLR), the section imposes restrictions on the application of the share premium account that go beyond the Companies Act 1985 (CA 1985) rules. Companies are no longer able to use the account to write off preliminary expenses (ie expenses incurred in connection with the company's formation). Apart from two 'exceptions', and two forms of 'relief', the account can only be used as if it was a share capital account. The two exceptions are that the account may be used to write off any expenses incurred, or commission paid, in connection with the particular issue of shares, and also to pay up new shares to be allotted to existing members as fully paid bonus shares (CA 2006 s 610). The two forms of relief are related to mergers and reconstructions, and ensure that undistributed profits are not reallocated to share premium accounts, thus making them undistributable (CA 2006 ss 611 and 612).

---

[9] And (although this has nothing to do with legal capital) when existing shareholders sell their shares to willing purchasers, whether privately or on a recognised market, they will again sell at whatever price the market will bear. This may be more or less than the nominal value of the shares, depending upon the success of the company and the estimated value of an interest in it.

[10] Note that the shareholder does not receive similar benefits: different shareholders may have purchased the same class of shares for different prices (ie paying different premia for shares of the same par value); if the company goes into solvent liquidation (ie there are assets to be returned to shareholders), then all shareholders will receive a return of their capital (ie the nominal capital associated with the share) and share equally in the division of any surplus profits.

As noted earlier, a company no longer needs to register its authorised capital when it is incorporated. Instead, the company must provide the registrar with a statement of capital and initial shareholdings. This statement must contain the following information:

(i) the total number of shares of the company to be taken on formation by the subscribers to the memorandum;

(ii) the aggregate nominal value of those shares;

(iii) for each class of shares: prescribed particulars of the rights attached to those shares, the total number of shares of that class and the aggregate nominal value of shares of that class; and

(iv) the amount to be paid up and the amount (if any) to be unpaid on each share (whether on account of the nominal value of the shares or by way of premium).

One historical point is worth making. It was very common practice in the early days for companies to issue shares on terms that only a small part of the capital—perhaps only 5% or 10% of the nominal value—was to be paid up, and so a very large sum of uncalled capital was left in reserve as a kind of 'guarantee fund' for creditors. Such shares were called *partly paid shares*; and the balance of unpaid capital could generally be *called up* by the company (or its liquidators) upon demand. This could have horrendous consequences for investors in the event of a liquidation (or, worse still, a spate of liquidations, as might occur in a recession) when the shareholder was obliged to pay up the balance of unpaid capital when there was no possibility of recovering any value via increased share value or future dividend. It also coloured much of the thinking in company law matters generally. Nowadays, the whole of the issue price of shares is normally payable on or soon after allotment, and so partly paid shares are not at all common. In some jurisdictions, they have been banned altogether, primarily for the sake of simplifying the law, but perhaps also out of a desire that investors should not be overcommitted with potential liabilities.

➤ Questions

1. When shares in British Telecom plc were sold to the public in 1984, the company was permitted to issue a simplified prospectus, for the benefit of the 'wider' public. This prospectus omitted to state that the nominal value of the shares was 25p. Why might it have been thought appropriate to withhold this information?

2. The issue price of a 25p British Telecom share was £1.30. Were the shares expensive at that price?

3. If a dividend of 10p is paid on a share of nominal value 25p, does this mean that the investor has done well?

4. What protection is provided to creditors by having shares with a nominal value, and capital and share premium accounts, that could not be equally well provided by eliminating the concept of nominal value and simply having a capital account for all the consideration received by a company for issue of its shares? (See DTI, *Completing the Structure* (URN 00/1335, November 2000) para 7.3; also see 'Issue of shares at a discount', p 525, on the inability of companies to issue shares at a discount.)

5. Are the exceptions and reliefs that apply in relation to use of the share premium account in accord with a philosophy that is actually designed to treat in the same way all the consideration received by a company for issue of its shares?

The legal nature of shares

Before investigating the detailed rules relating to legal capital, it is worth giving some attention to the legal nature of a share: what does a shareholder receive in return for providing the company with legal capital?

A share in a partnership reflects the partner's proprietary interest in the partnership assets: the assets are jointly owned by the partners. In the case of a company, it is not the shareholders but the company that owns the corporate assets, and the concept of a share serves somewhat different functions. In the first place, it is a fraction of the capital, denoting the holder's proportionate *financial stake* in the company and defining his or her liability to contribute to its equity funding. Secondly, it is a measure of the holder's interest in the company as *an association of members or shareholders* and the basis of his or her right to become a member and to enjoy the rights of voting, etc, so conferred. And, thirdly, it is a *species of property*, in its own right, a rather complex form of chose in action, which the holder can buy, sell, charge, etc, and in which there can be both legal and beneficial interests.[11] None of this is quite revealed in the definition in CA 2006 s 540.

The terms *'shareholder'* and *'member'* are commonly regarded as interchangeable, but this is not always the case. A company limited by guarantee has members, but it cannot have shareholders, for it has no shares. On the other hand, the holders of bearer shares ('share warrants', CA 2006 s 779—now abolished by s 779(4)) did not become members, since entry in the register of members is necessary for this purpose (s 112). The most common form of company is a company limited by shares, however, and in these companies the members are the shareholders.

Finally, a company can issue classes of shares with different rights attaching to each class (ie shares with different *'class rights'*, see Chapter 11). For example, shares may have different voting rights (recall the weighted voting rights in *Bushell v Faith* **[6.02]**), different rights to dividends or different rights to capital on a return of capital or on winding up (all these rights are explained in Chapters 10 and 11). *'Preference shares'* have a preferred right (as defined in the articles or in the share issue itself) to a specified dividend (if any dividend is declared), and perhaps to a return of capital while the company is operating or on winding up. *'Ordinary shares'* are defined in CA 2006 s 560 as shares *other than* shares that carry a right to participate only up to a specified amount in a distribution of dividends or capital (ie other than preference shares). And *'equity securities'*, also defined in CA 2006 s 560, are ordinary shares *and* rights to subscribe for, or convert securities into, ordinary shares. These definitions are important later, because certain rights, such as pre-emption rights, are given only to equity securities (see 'Limiting access to shares: directors' allotment rights and shareholders' pre-emption rights', pp 514ff).

What is a share?

[9.01] Borland's Trustee v Steel Bros & Co Ltd [1901] 1 Ch 279 (Chancery Division)

The company's articles provided that the shares of a member should in certain events, including bankruptcy, be transferable compulsorily to designated persons at a fair price

---

[11] Where conflict of laws rules must be applied to decide which national law is appropriate to determine questions of title etc in relation to the shares, the accepted rule is that where ownership of the shares is recorded in a register, the appropriate law is that of the place where the register is kept, which is normally (but not always) the country of incorporation; but where the shares are in bearer form the certificates or warrants are regarded as negotiable instruments and the relevant law is that of the place where the documents happen to be (*Re Harvard Securities Ltd* [1997] 2 BCLC 369).

not exceeding the par value.[12] On the bankruptcy of Borland, who held 73 £100 shares, the company gave notice to his trustee in bankruptcy requiring him to transfer the shares in accordance with the articles. The trustee objected that this provision in the articles was void, either on the ground that it was repugnant to absolute ownership, or as tending to perpetuity. The court rejected both contentions.

FARWELL J: It is said, first of all, that such provisions are repugnant to absolute ownership. It is said, further, that they tend to perpetuity. They are likened to the case of a settlor or testator who settles or gives a sum of money subject to executory limitations which are to arise in the future, interpreting the articles as if they provided that if at any time hereafter, during centuries to come, the company should desire the shares of a particular person . . . he must sell them. To my mind that is applying to the company law a principle which is wholly inapplicable thereto. It is the first time that any such suggestion has been made, and it rests, I think, on a misconception of what a share in a company really is. A share, according to the plaintiff's argument, is a sum of money which is dealt with in a particular manner by what are called for the purpose of argument executory limitations. To my mind it is nothing of the sort. A share is the interest of a shareholder in the company measured by a sum of money, for the purpose of liability in the first place, and of interest in the second, but also consisting of a series of mutual covenants entered into by all the shareholders inter se in accordance with s 16 of the Companies Act 1862 [CA 2006 s 33]. The contract contained in the articles of association is one of the original incidents of the share. A share is not a sum of money settled in the way suggested, but is an interest measured by a sum of money and made up of various rights contained in the contract, including the right to a sum of money of a more or less amount . . . [His Lordship then held that the rule against perpetuities had no application to personal contracts such as this, and ruled that the article was valid and enforceable.]

The nature of the 'various rights' enjoyed by a shareholder.

[9.02] White v Shortall [2006] NSWSC 1379 (New South Wales Supreme Court)

CAMPBELL J at [197]–[199]: Some of the rights to sue the company that a shareholder has exist simply by virtue of having the status of shareholder, regardless of the number of shares held. Such rights include rights to receive the information that statute requires shareholders to be given, the right to be given notice of and to attend at certain meetings of the company, and the right to vote at certain company meetings. Other rights that a shareholder has to sue the company are ones that a shareholder has proportionately to the number of shares held—such as the right to a dividend, to a return of capital, or to vote on a poll at the meeting. Some of the rights of a shareholder to sue the company arise by virtue of the contract contained in the company's constitution. Other rights of a shareholder to sue the company—including some very important ones—might arise directly by statute (eg rights to receive accounts and reports, to join in a requisition of a company general meeting, or to appoint a proxy). Other rights that any shareholder has in a company by virtue of the status of being a shareholder can arise from a contract arising separately to the company's constitution (eg if the company in question holds itself out as willing to provide goods or services to a shareholder at a special discounted price).

Some of the rights that attach to shares are themselves inherently assignable, even in circumstances where the shares themselves are not assigned—it is possible to make an equitable assignment of the right to receive dividends from a particular parcel of shares in particular years . . . and

---

[12] See 'Terminology associated with legal capital', p 509, for the meaning of 'par value'.

possible to make an equitable assignment of the right to receive some particular measure of money on a particular type of return of capital. Such assignments can take place only because the rights assigned are themselves treated as property. And the only type of property they could be is choses in action. Thus, some of the rights that a shareholder has by virtue of being a shareholder are themselves items of property that are separate to the item of property that constitutes the share itself.

And it is not only fractional rights in a share that are capable of being seen as separate items of property. For rights of the type where the number of shares provides the measure by reference to which a shareholder's right against the company is calculated, the chose in action can be seen as being the right to sue the company to receive some particular type of benefit. For example, when the holder of 1000 shares in a company sues to recover a dividend that has been declared but is unpaid, there is just one action that the shareholder brings, to recover the dividend—there are not 1000 separate rights to be paid a dividend . . . In that way, the chose in action—the thing that the law regards as a piece of property because it can be sued for—is the single right to be paid the dividend, the measure of which is the number of shares held.

➤ Question

Do the compulsory share redemption provisions in *Borland's Trustee* [9.01] offend the anti-deprivation principle? Would your answer be different if the terms provided for the sale of the deceased's shares at a *discounted* value? See Chapter 16.

Minimum capital requirements for company formation

A *public company* must have a nominal value of allotted share capital which is not less than the statutory 'authorised minimum' amount fixed by CA 2006 s 761. At present, the prescribed authorised minimum is £50,000, or the prescribed euro equivalent (s 763), denominated in sterling or euros, but not both (s 765). At least a quarter of this must be paid up before it begins trading (s 586).

The protection that this minimum delivers to creditors is dubious: the sum is relatively trivial, and is measured at the time the company commences trading, paying little account to what business risks or mishaps may happen as business continues. CA 2006 s 656 requires directors of public companies to call a general meeting to consider what to do if the company's assets fall to half or less than its called-up share capital. The equivalent CA 1985 predecessor to this seemed unimportant in practice: well before that stage some sort of rescue or insolvency procedure was likely to be in place (see Chapter 16).

There is no minimum capital requirement for *private* companies.

Limiting access to shares: directors' allotment rights and shareholders' pre-emption rights

Allotment

There is a risk that directors may use their power of allotment of shares to influence the composition of the company's membership, and in particular to ensure that the majority of members support them and will keep them in office (see 'Duty to act within powers: CA 2006 s 171', pp 341ff on directors' use of power for improper purposes).

CA 2006 ss 549–551 limit this possibility of abuse by providing as a general rule that it is an offence for directors to allot shares (or grant options to subscribe for shares or issue securities convertible into shares) without the authority of the members given either in the articles or by ordinary resolution. This authority must be renewed every five years.

The exceptions relate to: (i) issues of shares to the original subscribers, to an employees' share scheme or to existing holders of rights to acquire or convert their shares (s 549); and (ii) in the case of a private company, issues of shares where the company has only one class of share (s 550), although such a company may restrict its directors' allotment powers by inserting a provision to that effect in the company's articles (s 550(b)).

Since there is now no 'authorised capital' limit, a company's changes to issued capital must be notified to the registrar at Companies House each time a new allotment is made (s 555).

Pre-emption rights governing the issue of new shares

A *pre-emption right* is a right of first refusal given to the shareholders of a company to subscribe for any new shares that the company issues in proportion to their existing shareholdings. In this way, the balance of control between the respective shareholders can be maintained. A pre-emption right may also prevent the 'watering' or dilution in value of existing shares, which will happen if the new shares are issued at a price which is below their true value.

Prior to 1980, shareholders were legally entitled to pre-emption rights only if this was expressly provided for in the company's articles; although it was a requirement under the London Stock Exchange's Listing Rules that equity shares of listed companies should be offered in the first instance on a pro rata basis to existing equity shareholders. Since 1980, UK legislation implementing the Second EU Directive (and extending its provisions to private companies), has provided a statutory pre-emption right. The relevant provisions are in CA 2006 ss 560–577. The statutory right is given to ordinary shareholders (excluding the company itself as holder of treasury shares), and applies only to new issues of 'equity securities' (s 560).[13]

The right is subject to certain *exceptions* (issues of bonus shares or shares as part of an employee share scheme, and issues for non-cash consideration); *exclusions* (by the articles of private companies); *disapplications* (by the articles for private companies with only one class of shares, or generally by special resolution, or by statute for the sale of treasury shares); and *savings* (for other rules and for certain older pre-emption procedures) (see ss 564–577). The wide ambit of these exceptions means that in practice the statutory provisions do not impose a serious restriction on companies that wish not to be bound by them.

Breach of these provisions does not invalidate the new issue, but generally exposes the company and every officer who knowingly authorised or permitted the contravention to compensation claims in favour of those to whom offers should have been made (CA 2006 s 653).

---

[13] Although pre-emption rights are mandatory in the EU, they have been abandoned in the United States. The reasons for pre-emption rights are examined in Paul Myners, *Pre-Emption Rights: Final Report* (URN 05/679) (DTI, 2005). Also see LCB Gower, 'Some Contrasts between British and American Corporation Law' (1956) 69 *Harvard Law Review* 1369.

Pre-emption rights governing the transfer of existing shares

Just as shareholders maintain control over power distributions in a company through pre-emption provisions applying to the issue of new shares, so they also do with transfers of existing shareholdings. Such pre-emption provisions are typically found in the articles or in a shareholder agreement (see 'Constitutional documents: articles of association and the company's objects', p 26, and 'Shareholders' agreements', p 256 for the advantages and disadvantages of these two options). Such restrictions are only possible in private companies, however; shares listed on stock exchanges must be freely transferable.

A pre-emption provision governing the transfer of issued shares was not triggered by a change in ownership of the corporate shareholder of those issued shares.

[9.03] Re Coroin Ltd [2011] EWHC 3466 (Chancery Division)

Coroin Ltd was formed for the purpose of acquiring control of four well-known hotels in London. The original investors were McKillen, the claimant (36.23%), Misland (a company owned by A&A Investments Ltd, itself owned by Peter Green and his family) (24.78%), Quinlan (35.4%) and McLaughlin (3.58%). Their interests were governed by a shareholder agreement which granted pre-emption rights in favour of existing shareholders should any one of the investors wish to sell its interest.

The Barclay brothers (Sir David and Sir Frederick) wished to acquire complete ownership and control of Coroin. They acquired the interests of Quinlan and McLaughlin, but could not reach agreement with Mr McKillen. They did, however, purchase (via a corporate alter ego) the issued shares in Misland from A&A Investments. McKillen held that this acquisition of Misland breached the pre-emption provisions in the shareholder agreement. The court disagreed, holding that a proper construction of the shareholder agreement indicated that the sale of the shares in a corporate shareholder of the company did not trigger the pre-emption provisions.

DAVID RICHARDS J: A principle applicable to pre-emption articles which has been repeated in the authorities is that, as the right to deal freely with a share is an important attribute of ownership and the prima facie right of a shareholder, the existence and extent of any restriction on transfer, such as pre-emption provisions, must be clearly stated: see in re *Smith and Fawcett Ltd* **[11.10]** at 306, *Greenhalgh v Mallard* [1943] 2 All ER 234 at 237 . . . In the case of [a shareholder] agreement, the court's function is to discern objectively the meaning of the provision against the relevant background facts. This fundamental principle applies as much to an ambiguously framed pre-emption provision as it does to any other. If, applying that approach, the court considers that, on the proper construction of the agreement, the right of pre-emption has arisen, the court should not reject it because there is a lack of clarity in the language used.

It is, however, right to say that pre-emption provisions are generally drafted with precision, as befits provisions dealing with property rights. As appears from authorities to which I later refer, commonly used phrases have distinct legal meanings and superficially small variations can have significant legal effects. This is a relevant consideration when construing pre-emption provisions, particularly when as in this case they are complex and have been professionally drafted, using and adapting well-known standard provisions....

Clause 6.1 identifies as the person who may give a transfer notice 'a Shareholder desiring to transfer one or more Shares (or any interest therein)'. Each word of significance in that phrase carries a legal meaning.

First, 'Shareholder' is defined in clause 1.1 as 'any holder of Shares for the time being and shall as the context permits include any beneficial owner of shares for the time being.' A 'holder' of shares is the person registered in the company's register of members as the holder of the shares.

He holds the legal title to the shares. He may or may not own the beneficial interest in the shares, as the second part of the definition recognises. If company A owns the beneficial interest in shares registered in its name, it alone is the beneficial owner of the shares. This remains the case even though company A is wholly-owned by company B or by one individual, in accordance with basic principles of legal personality: *Salomon v A. Salomon & Co Ltd* **[2.02]**, *JH Rayner (Mincing Lane) Ltd v Department of Trade and Industry* [1990] 2 AC 418.

Secondly, what constitutes a 'desire', or an intention, to transfer shares has been considered in a number of authorities: *Lyle & Scott v. Scott's Trustees* [1959] AC 763, *Safeguard Industrial Investments Ltd v. National Westminster Bank Ltd* [1982] 1 WLR 589, *Theakston v. London Trust plc* [1984] BCLC 389.

Thirdly, a 'transfer' of shares means the transfer of the legal title to the shares, by providing a signed stock transfer form or other similar instrument and by registration of the transfer in the register of members: see *Lyle & Scott Ltd v. Scott's Trustees* (*supra*), *Safeguard Industrial Investments Ltd v. National Westminster Bank Ltd* (*supra*), *Scotto v. Petch, Re Sedgefield Steeplechase Co (1927) Ltd* [2001] BCC 889 (CA).

Fourthly, 'any interest therein' means a proprietary, i.e. beneficial, interest in the shares, as opposed to the legal title. These words are included so as to broaden the effect of clause 6.1, which without them would be confined to the legal title. It is nonetheless the language of property, and a precise use of it.

There can, in my judgment, be no dispute that, read on its own, clause 6.1 has no application to the case where company A is the legal and beneficial owner of shares in the company and the issued shares of company A are sold. Such a sale involves no change in company A's legal and beneficial ownership of the underlying shares, nor evidences a desire to transfer those shares or any interest in them.

No doubt for this reason, Mr Miles' submissions do not start with clause 6.1, but with clause 6.17: 'No Share nor any interest therein shall be transferred, sold or otherwise disposed of save as provided in this clause 6.'

He submits that the words 'any interest therein' are, as a matter of language, ambiguous. They may carry their legally accurate meaning of a proprietary interest or they may carry, as Mr Miles submits they do, a broader, commercial meaning which would include the sale of a company owning the shares. [. . . and, after considering the issues . . .]

These unambiguous provisions [6.6, 6.1 and 6.15] resolve any ambiguity which may be said to exist in clause 6.17. The clause must be read as a whole, and the earlier provisions of the clause show that the reference to an interest in shares in clause 6.17 is to the same direct proprietary interests as appear in those provisions.

The various commercial considerations on which Mr Miles relies might, if the parties had so wished, have provided good reasons for including clear provisions to the effect that a disposal of Misland would trigger the pre-emption procedure. The absence of any such provisions in what is a complex clause, providing for many eventualities, itself tells against the suggested construction. It is a reasonable objective assumption that these sophisticated investors in a large commercial venture, and their advisers, did not overlook the possibility of a sale of Misland, particularly in the light of both the definition of 'Shareholder Group' with its special provisions for Misland and the proviso to clause 6.15. The absence of provisions dealing with a sale of a corporate shareholder is, objectively speaking, consistent with a decision by the parties not to include them . . .

For all these reasons, I conclude that the sale of the share capital of Misland in January 2011 was not made contrary to clause 6.17 of the shareholder agreement and did not trigger the other shareholders pre-emption rights. I reach the same conclusion on the articles and do so whether or not reference may be made to background facts . . .

[An appeal to the Court of Appeal by Mr McKillen was subsequently dismissed: [2012] EWCA Civ 179, CA.]

Effect of breach of pre-emption provisions governing the transfer of issued shares.

[9.04] Re Coroin Ltd; McKillen v Misland (Cyprus) Investments Ltd [2013] EWCA Civ 781 (Court of Appeal)

As a further part of the litigation considered in the preceding case, McKillen also argued that the proposed sale of shares in Misland constituted 'unfairly prejudicial' conduct (CA 2006 s 994). This claim too was dismissed, first by David Richards J then by the Court of Appeal here (see 'Meaning of "unfairly prejudicial"', p 721). In delivering his judgment, Rimer LJ began with a discussion of the operation of pre-emption provisions. That is extracted here.

RIMER LJ:

157....[The parties' agreed pre-emption scheme contains a number of interacting provisions which provide] that, apart from permitted transfers (which include a transfer to a mortgagee), all transfers or other dispositions must be made in a manner compliant with the requirements of cl.6: see cl.6.17. There are, however, questions as to the operation of, and inter-relation between, cl.6.1, 6.6 and 6.17.

158. As for cl.6.1, does the provision that 'a Shareholder...desiring to transfer...Shares (or any interest therein)...may at any time give [a transfer notice] to the Company...' mean that such a shareholder *must* give such a notice? I consider that the answer is yes, although it needs a little explanation. Clause 6.1 does not compel the giving of a transfer notice as soon as a proposing transferor forms a desire to transfer any shares. A desire formed on Monday may have evaporated by Friday; and if, in the meantime, no transfer notice has been given, it would be odd if such an ephemeral desire could result in a shareholder being compelled to give a transfer notice when he no longer wishes to transfer his shares at all. On the other hand, I regard it as clear that, once the formation of the desire has moved into the valley of decision intended to be followed by action, the sense of cl.6.1 is that it is a condition of a valid transfer that the shareholder must first give a transfer notice for the purpose of activating the pre-emption provisions. If he does not, any attempt by him to transfer his shares will run into (i) the provisions of cl.6.6, under which the directors are empowered to deem him to have given a transfer notice; and (ii) in default of an exercise by the board of that power, the provisions of cl.6.17. The answer to the 'may' or 'must' question is, therefore, simply that it is a condition of a valid transfer of shares––and of any interest in shares––that the proposing transferor first gives a transfer notice.

159. Clause 6.6 also raises interpretational questions. It provides that, following the occurrence of any such events as are referred to in cl.6.6.1–6.6.3, the directors may 'deem' the relevant shareholder to have given a transfer notice in respect of all his shares. Such events include the case in which the shareholder 'attempts' to deal with, or otherwise dispose of, his shares or an interest therein otherwise than in accordance with the provisions of the shareholders' agreement.

160. Clause 6.6 provides, however, that the directors can only so deem 'within a period of one month after the occurrence of any such event'. The problem here is that it is likely that in many cases the directors will only learn of such occurrence after the expiration of the one-month period: the relevant event might, for example, be a non-compliant share transfer which, with a view to circumventing the cl.6.6 time limit, the parties had deliberately kept secret and of which they had deferred applying for registration. This raises a question as to whether, in the final paragraph of cl.6.6, the quoted words mean what they say, namely that the board's discretionary power is exercisable only within the specified one-month period; or whether there is any basis for a more flexible reading to the effect that the one-month period runs from when the directors first have relevant knowledge.

161. In my view, the words mean what they say. First, as a matter of language, there is no scope for reading them as meaning anything else; and no basis for an inference that something has gone wrong with the drafting. It may perhaps not be a very clever piece of drafting, but it is

not the court's function, by a process of purported interpretation, to improve the scheme that Coroin has chosen to adopt. Second, that interpretation is anyway unlikely to be injurious to the members' pre-emption rights. An attempted transfer, sale or disposition of shares, or of any interest in shares, that is made without prior compliance with cl.6.1 and slips the net of clause 6.6 does not get away scot-free, because the effect of cl.6.17 is to strike down any transfer, sale or disposition 'save as provided by this clause 6'. That means, in my judgment, that no such transaction will be effective between the parties unless it has been preceded by compliance with the pre-emption provisions.

162. As to the practical consequences of an attempted, but non-compliant, share transfer, the board would have no power to register it as it would have been made in breach of the articles. That is shown by the Court of Appeal's decision in *Tett v Phoenix Property and Investment Co Ltd* (1986) 2 B.C.C. 99140 . In *Emily Hunter v THV Hunter*, unreported, 15 January 1934 ('the *Emily Hunter* case', not apparently cited in *Tett's* case (above)), Bennett J. came to a like conclusion in relation to share transfers made in breach of [pre-emption provisions materially identical to those here, but without a restriction on dispositions of an *interest* in shares]. Bennett J. made an order for the rectification of the registration of the transferees so as to restore to the register the name of the purporting transferor.

163. Bennett J.'s decision was upheld by the Court of Appeal [and there was no appeal] to the House of Lords... The *Emily Hunter* case shows that a purported transfer of shares made in defiance of the pre-emption provisions of cl.6 will be ineffective.

164. As for an attempted, but non-compliant, disposition of an *interest* in shares (for example, by a declaration of trust)...Mr Peter Prescott QC, sitting as a deputy High Court judge of the Chancery Division in *Re Claygreen Ltd; Romer-Ormiston v Claygreen Ltd* [2005] EWHC 2032 (Ch); [2006] B.C.C. 440, took that view in relation to [a similar] article that..., at [53]:

'A share in a company should not be thought of as a tangible object, but as a bundle of rights. Those rights have existence in virtue of the company's articles. If Epsom has acquired any rights in the claimant's shares, they must be rights recognised in equity alone, for no legal transfer of the shares has been or could be effected without registration. Now, how can equity recognise or give effect to a transaction in relation to a bundle of rights which, by their very nature, do not admit of that transaction, the parties having had notice thereof?'

I agree.

165. The result is that I consider that, in a case where there has been no prior compliance with the pre-emption provisions, cl.6.17 renders ineffective both a purported transfer of shares and a purported transfer of any proprietary interest in shares. Of course, if, as it should not be, a transfer of shares were in fact to be registered, Coroin might well have to regard the registered owner as a member so long as he remains registered. But the other members would in principle be entitled to ask for the register to be rectified so as to restore the prior position.

➤ Question

This is very protective of existing shareholders and detrimental to third parties purchasing their shares. What justifies such an approach? Is it just 'a matter of property'?

Offers to the public to purchase shares and remedies for misleading offers

When shares are offered to the public, a prospectus must be published and, additionally, when an application is made for listing on a stock exchange either a prospectus or listing particulars must be published. There are special rules about liability for errors or omissions in those documents (see Chapter 14). In practice, however, the professionalisation of the investment industry and the high standards set both by stock exchanges and by investment practitioners themselves mean that the chances of a misleading document getting into circulation in consequence of sharp or sloppy practice have been virtually eliminated.

In what follows, the special rules under the Financial Services and Markets Act 2000 (FSMA 2000) are ignored, and what is described is the general law applicable to those who have been induced by misrepresentation to subscribe for shares in a company. These rules, although of general application, are usually invoked only when the special rules on public offers are inapplicable.

The different remedies available may be summarised as follows:

(i)   as against the company, rescission of the contract and consequent rectification of the share register (for material misrepresentation of *any* kind);

(ii) damages for deceit (for *fraudulent* misrepresentation);[14]

(iii) damages under the Misrepresentation Act 1967 s 2(2) (in lieu of rescission) and also possibly under s 2(1) (for so-called 'negligent' misrepresentation); and

(iv) as against the company, a possible claim in damages for breach of contract, on the basis that the statements in the prospectus or offer have been incorporated as terms of the contract.

Note that no civil remedy lies against the *company* at common law for the *omission* of information required to be included in the listing particulars or prospectus: *Re South of England Natural Gas and Petroleum Co Ltd* [1911] 1 Ch 573.

Misrepresentation

If a person is induced to enter into a contract by false statements of fact made by the other party, then there is a misrepresentation, and the innocent party is entitled to rescind the contract. A number of issues may prevent an allottee of shares from obtaining an appropriate remedy, however. The misrepresentation must have been made by the other party to the contract (ie by the company), be one of fact and have induced the contract.

The misrepresentation must have been made by the company.

[9.05] Lynde v Anglo-Italian Hemp Spinning Company [1896] 1 Ch 178 (Chancery Division)

ROMER J: The first question I desire to deal with is this—Assuming that Mr. Waithman [a promoter] made material misrepresentations to the plaintiff which induced him to apply for the shares, could the plaintiff, on that ground, hold the company liable, and have the contract set aside? It appears to me that, speaking generally, to make a company liable for misrepresentations inducing a contract to take shares from it the shareholder must bring his case within one or other of the following heads:—(1.) Where the misrepresentations are made by the directors or other [of] the general agents of the company entitled to act and acting on its behalf—as, for example, by a prospectus issued by the authority or sanction of the directors of a company inviting

---

[14] The measure of damages is normally the difference between the price that was paid for the shares and their true value at the time of the transaction, together with any consequential loss. Exceptionally (eg where the defendant's fraud has created a false market or was such as to have prevented the victim from realising the shares at that time), a different value may be substituted: *Smith New Court Securities Ltd v Citibank NA* [1997] AC 254, HL.

subscriptions for shares; (2.) Where the misrepresentations are made by a special agent of the company while acting within the scope of his authority—as, for example, by an agent specially authorized to obtain, on behalf of the company, subscriptions for shares. This head of course includes the case of a person constituted agent by subsequent adoption of his acts; (3.) Where the company can be held affected, before the contract is complete, with the knowledge that it is induced by misrepresentations—as, for example, when the directors, on allotting shares, know, in fact, that the application for them has been induced by misrepresentations, even though made without any authority; (4.) Where the contract is made on the basis of certain representations, whether the particulars of those representations were known to the company or not, and it turns out that some of those representations were material and untrue—as, for example, if the directors of a company know when allotting that an application for shares is based on the statements contained in a prospectus, even though that prospectus was issued without authority or even before the company was formed, and even if its contents are not known to the directors.[15]

. . . Now, it appears to me that the plaintiff does not bring his case within any of these heads. Such misrepresentations, if any, as were made to the plaintiff were made by Mr Waithman, one of the two promoters of the company. But the company at the time had two directors entitled to act for it, and Mr Waithman was not a director or general agent of the company. No doubt the promoters had a great deal to do with the company at the time, and their wishes and views may have been highly regarded by the directors. But I see nothing to justify me in coming to the conclusion that the promoters are to be regarded as really constituting the company, or that the directors left everything in their hands, or were what may be called dummies, or left it to the promoters to do whatever they pleased in the affairs of the company. Nor was Mr Waithman, when he made the representations he did make to the plaintiff, authorized to act on behalf of the company in procuring shares or authorized to make any representations on behalf of the company to the plaintiff or others to induce him or them to apply for shares. The fact that Mr Waithman was a promoter of the company did not in itself authorize him to procure shares for the company, or to make representations to the plaintiff on the company's behalf . . . And although the company knew that Waithman was applying to his friends to get them to subscribe for shares, that did not, in my opinion, make him the company's agent, or put the company to inquire as to whether he had made any, and, if any, what, representations to those friends to induce them to subscribe. In most cases directors must be aware that subscriptions for shares are obtained through the intermediary of persons interested in the company, and it would lead to the most astonishing results if that was held sufficient to affect the directors with knowledge of, or to put them upon inquiry as to, the representations, if any, made by those persons to the people applying for the shares. The fact that in the case of this company some applications, including that of the plaintiff, were made on printed forms prepared by the company's solicitor does not, in my opinion, make any real difference. Mr Waithman got his forms by applying to the company's solicitor, because he wanted his friends to make proper applications for shares. No authority was given by the directors to the solicitor to supply Mr Waithman with forms, nor can the directors, by seeing these forms used, be held thereby to have adopted Mr Waithman as their agent in obtaining applications for shares. The directors did not issue any prospectus themselves or try to get applications for shares, and, no doubt, because they thought Waithman and Thomson would get a sufficient number of their friends to take up the necessary number of shares. But this did not, in my opinion, make Waithman and Thomson the special agents of the company to procure subscriptions on its behalf, or authorize them to make any representations on behalf of the company with a view of inducing their friends to subscribe.

---

[15] This is now modified by *Collins v Associated Greyhound Racecourses Ltd* [1930] 1 Ch 1, to require that, to the knowledge of the company or its agents, the contract was made on the basis of particular representations that later turned out to be untrue.

> And, lastly, this is not a case . . . coming at all within the fourth head. The application for shares
> made by the plaintiff was not one made conditional upon, or to the knowledge of the directors
> based upon, any special or other representations made by Waithman. The application was not
> even, to the knowledge of the directors, induced by representations by Waithman, though, even
> if it had been, whether that would in itself have been sufficient to bring the case within my fourth
> head or have entitled the plaintiff to rescind I need not now inquire.
>
> On this ground, therefore, I hold that the action must fail, for in my judgment the plaintiff has
> not shewn any ground upon which I can rescind this contract by reason of misrepresentations, if
> any, made to him which induced him to apply for these shares.
>
> [And, further, on the questions of fact, Romer J also held that the alleged misrepresentations
> were not made out, nor the fact that they had induced the contract.]

➤ Question

The case would now be decided by application of the principles in *Meridian Global* [3.01].
Would the answer be the same?

Loss of the remedy of rescission

The allottee will lose the right to rescission if the parties cannot be returned to their pre-
contractual positions (ie if *restitutio in integrum* is no longer possible; see later), if the contract has been affirmed, if third party rights have intervened or if the allottee has delayed
for too long after discovering the misrepresentation.

***Rescission is not possible after an order for winding up has been made, even if the share
purchase was induced by fraud.***

[9.06] Oakes v Turquand and Harding (1867) LR 2 HL 325 (House of Lords)

Overend, Gurney & Co Ltd was incorporated in July 1865 to take over the long-established
banking business of Overend, Gurney & Co. The prospectus issued to the public concealed
the fact that the business was insolvent and had been carried on at a loss for some years.
Within a year after the incorporation of the company it stopped payment and went into
liquidation. In order to meet the claims of its creditors, large calls were made on the numerous members of the public who had become shareholders. Many of them combined
to form a defence association, which appointed Oakes (an original allottee of shares) and
Peek (who had bought shares in the market) as representatives to conduct test cases on
behalf of all the shareholders. In this case they claimed that their names should be taken
off the list of contributories on the ground that their contracts to take and to purchase
shares, respectively, had been induced by fraud, but it was held that they had lost the right
to rescind.

(In later proceedings (*Peek v Gurney* (1873) LR 6 HL 377) Peek was again unsuccessful,
this time in a claim against the directors. Among the score or so of other reported cases
arising out of the same liquidation, the best known is *Overend, Gurney & Co v Gibb and
Gibb* (1872) LR 5 HL 480, in which the liquidators failed in a claim against the directors,
alleging that they had been negligent in allowing the company to purchase the business.)

> LORD CHELMSFORD LC: It is said that everything which is stated in the prospectus is literally
> true, and so it is. But the objection to it is, not that it does not state the truth as far as it goes, but
> that it conceals most material facts with which the public ought to have been made acquainted,

the very concealment of which gives to the truth which is told the character of falsehood. If the real circumstances of the firm of Overend, Gurney & Co had been disclosed it is not very probable that any company founded upon it would have been formed. Indeed, it was admitted in the course of the argument that if the true position of the affairs of Overend, Gurney & Co had been published it would have entailed the ruin of the old firm, and would have been utterly prohibitory of the formation of the new. To which the only answer which fairly suggests itself is, 'Then no company ought ever to have been attempted, because it was only possible to entice persons to become shareholders by improper concealment of facts' . . .

It is quite clear, therefore, that Oakes might originally have disaffirmed that contract, and divested himself of his shares, and that he never did any act to affirm it, nor was aware of the true state of the firm of Overend, Gurney & Co at the time of the formation of the new company, nor until after the failure . . .

Such was the position of Oakes when the order for winding up the company was made on 22 June 1866. His name being upon the register of shareholders, was placed (as a matter of course) by the liquidators upon the list of contributories . . .

On the part of the creditors, it is said that every person whose name is found upon the register at the time when the order for winding up is made is a shareholder, and liable to contribute towards the payments of the debts of the company to the extent of the sums due upon his shares, unless he can prove that his name was put upon the register without his consent.

Did the appellant then agree to become a member? His counsel answer this question in the negative; because they say that a person who is induced by fraud to enter into an agreement cannot be said to have agreed; the word 'agreed' meaning having entered into a binding agreement. But this is a fallacy. The consent which binds the will and constitutes the agreement is totally different from the motive and inducement which led to the consent. An agreement induced by fraud is certainly, in one sense, not a binding agreement, as it is entirely at the option of the person defrauded whether he will be bound by it or not. In the present case, if the company formed on the basis of the partnership of Overend, Gurney & Co had realised the expectations held out by the prospectus, the appellant would probably have retained his shares, as he would have had an undoubted right to do. But when the order for winding up came, and found him with the shares in his possession, and his name upon the register, the agreement was a subsisting one. How could it then be said that he was not a person who had agreed to become a member? To hold otherwise would be to disregard the long and well-established distinction between void and voidable contracts . . .

[His Lordship then held that the supervening rights of the creditors in a winding up barred the right of a member to avoid the contract on the ground of fraud. He concluded:] It only remains to observe that all that has been said with respect to Oakes applies with greater force to Peek, even if his situation as a purchaser of shares in the market did not preclude him from most of the objections which have been raised in Oakes' case.

LORD CRANWORTH and LORD COLONSAY delivered concurring opinions.

Availability of the remedy of damages

Damages are available instead of rescission, or in addition to rescission for consequential losses: (i) at common law if the misrepresentation was fraudulent (*Derry v Peek* (1889) 14 App Cas 337): see the important and detailed analysis of Lord Steyn in *Smith New Court Securities Ltd Citibank NA* [1997] AC 254; (ii) at common law for negligent misstatement;[16] and (iii) under the Misrepresentation Act 1967, but only between parties to an induced

---

[16] See *Hedley Byrne and Co Ltd v Heller and Partners Ltd* [1964] AC 465; *Caparo Industries plc v Dickman* **[8.04]**, but so far no cases seem to have been brought for misstatements in offers.

contract, for any form of misrepresentation, unless the misrepresentor can prove that he or she had reasonable grounds to believe, and did believe, up to the time the contract was made, that the facts represented were true (s 2(1)).[17]

➤Notes

1. For over a hundred years, the rule laid down in *Houldsworth v City of Glasgow Bank* (1880) 5 App Cas 317, HL, prevented a person who had been induced by fraud to take shares in a company from claiming damages against the company while he or she remained a member. The same principle was applied where damages for breach of contract were sought, based on the contract of shareholding: *Re Addlestone Linoleum Co* (1887) 37 Ch D 191, CA. The juridical basis of this rule was never satisfactorily explained, but it has now been reversed by statute: CA 2006 s 655. There is one statutory exception: CA 2006 s 735 expressly excludes the possibility of a claim in damages when a company has broken an obligation to redeem or repurchase shares (but without prejudice to other remedies, which may include an action for specific performance or an application for relief under s 994 (unfairly prejudicial conduct) (see 'Unfairly prejudicial conduct of the company's affairs', pp 715ff) or for winding up on the 'just and equitable' ground (see 'Compulsory winding up on the "just and equitable" ground', pp 840ff)).

2. In *Peek v Gurney* (1873) LR 6 HL 377, the House of Lords held that a prospectus should be regarded as addressed only to those who might become allottees of shares directly from the company, and that it could not be relied on by someone who had bought shares from another source. FSMA 2000 now imposes civil liability for breach of the listing particulars and prospectus requirements in favour of any person who has acquired securities, and this is defined in terms sufficiently wide to include both original allottees and persons who have purchased shares on the market (see 'Liability for misleading statements and omissions in prospectuses', pp 766ff). In *Possfund Custodian Trustee Ltd v Diamond* [1996] 2 BCLC 665, Lightman J held that, in the light of changes in market practice, a person who had bought shares on the market might nowadays be regarded as someone to whom a prospectus was addressed, particularly if the prospectus made reference to future dealing on that market. (This judgment also contains an excellent summary of the various remedies available to a person deceived by misstatements in a prospectus, and their historical development.)

3. In *Erlson Precision Holdings Ltd (formerly GG132 Ltd) v Hampson Industries plc* [2011] EWHC 1137 (Comm), income and customer forecasts were provided to representatives of the purchaser on behalf of the vendor listed company; these were found to have carried an implied representation of fact, namely that the company had reasonable grounds, or knew of facts, that justified the forecasts. The forecasts turned out to be false, as the second largest of the company's customers had already notified Mr Ward, CEO of the company, of its final decision to terminate its relationship with the company entirely. In holding that the share purchase agreement was induced by a fraudulent misrepresentation as alleged by the claimant, Field J said the following, at [43]:

> If an individual in the position of Mr. Ward, the CEO of a listed company, knows that a forecast has been falsified by events to which he is privy but remains silent intending that the forecast should

---

[17] Under the statute, damages are said to be measured in the same way as for fraud, regardless of the type of misrepresentation: *Royscot Trust Ltd v Rogerson* [1991] 2 QB 297, strongly criticised in R Hooley, 'Damages and the Misrepresentation Act 1967' (1991) 107 LQR 547. Recently, Leggatt J in *Yam Seng Pte Ltd v International Trade Corp Ltd* [2013] EWHC 111 (QB) also criticised *Royscot* but concluded that he was nevertheless bound by the Court of Appeal's decision unless and until it be overruled: see [207] of the decision.

be relied on by persons to whom the forecast is directly communicated, dishonesty on the part of that individual will have been proved without it being necessary distinctly and separately to show a conscious awareness of a duty to correct the statement.

Collecting in the company's capital: payment for shares

Issue of shares at a discount

A company is, in general, forbidden to issue shares[18] at a discount: see CA 2006 s 552 and the following case extracts. But the professional people and institutions who handle new issues must, of course, be remunerated for their services, or compensated for taking the risk of an issue not being fully subscribed for by the public (ie for 'underwriting' the issue). Accordingly, CA 2006 s 553 authorises the payment of commissions and discounts up to a statutory limit (currently 10%), subject to certain safeguards.

A company may not issue shares at a discount.

[9.07] Ooregum Gold Mining Co of India Ltd v Roper [1892] AC 125 (House of Lords)

This action was brought by a holder of ordinary shares to test the validity of an issue of preference shares which had been made by the directors, in accordance with resolutions duly passed by the members, on the basis that each new share of £1 nominal value should be automatically credited with 75p paid, leaving an actual liability of only 25p per share. The transaction was bona fide thought to be the best way of raising further funds for the company, especially since the ordinary shares stood at a great discount. The House of Lords held, however, that it was beyond the power of the company to issue the shares at a discount, and that in consequence the holders were liable for the full nominal amount of the shares.

LORD HALSBURY LC: My Lords, the question in this case has been more or less in debate since 1883, when Chitty J decided that a company limited by shares was not prohibited by law from issuing its shares at a discount. That decision was overruled, though in a different case, by the Court of Appeal in 1888, and it has now come to your Lordships for final determination.

My Lords, the whole structure of a limited company owes its existence to the Act of Parliament, and it is to the Act of Parliament one must refer to see what are its powers, and within what limits it is free to act. Now, confining myself for the moment to the Act of 1862, it makes one of the conditions of the limitation of liability that the memorandum of association shall contain the amount of capital with which the company proposes to be registered, divided into shares of a certain fixed amount. It seems to me that the system thus created by which the shareholder's liability is to be limited by the amount unpaid upon his shares, renders it impossible for the company to depart from that requirement, and by any expedient to arrange with their shareholders that they shall not be liable for the amount unpaid on the shares, although the amount of those shares has been, in accordance with the Act of Parliament, fixed at a certain sum of money. It is manifest that if the company could do so the provision in question would operate nothing.

---

[18] But not debentures: see 'Issue of debentures at a discount', p 527.

I observe in the argument it has been sought to draw a distinction between the nominal capital and the capital which is assumed to be the real capital. I can find no authority for such a distinction. The capital is fixed and certain, and every creditor of the company is entitled to look to that capital as his security.

It may be that such limitations on the power of a company to manage its own affairs may occasionally be inconvenient, and prevent its obtaining money for the purposes of its trading on terms so favourable as it could do if it were more free to act. But, speaking for myself, I recognise the wisdom of enforcing on a company the disclosure of what its real capital is, and not permitting a statement of its affairs to be such as may mislead and deceive those who are either about to become its shareholders or about to give it credit.

I think . . . that the question which your Lordships have to solve is one which may be answered by reference to an inquiry: What is the nature of an agreement to take a share in a limited company? and that that question may be answered by saying, that it is an agreement to become liable to pay to the company the amount for which the share has been created. That agreement is one which the company itself has no authority to alter or qualify, and I am therefore of opinion that, treating the question as unaffected by the Act of 1867, the company were prohibited by law, upon the principle laid down in *Ashbury Co v Riche*,[19] from doing that which is compendiously described as issuing shares at a discount.

LORDS WATSON, HERSCHELL, MACNAGHTEN and MORRIS delivered concurring opinions.

➤ Notes and Questions

1. The position in which this company found itself is not at all uncommon: unprofitable trading had led to a depressed market price for the shares, and the company was seeking an injection of new funds to 'keep head above water' while the directors endeavoured to surmount the immediate financial difficulties and find a way back to profitability.[20] The classical solution of an earlier generation was to issue preference shares, so that those who provided the new capital ranked ahead of the existing shareholders as regards both income and capital rights (see 'Classes of shares and class rights', pp 581ff). The other possible solution—to issue new shares ranking *pari passu* with the existing shares but at a discounted price—is, on the authority of this case, unlawful in England. Does the rule protect the company's creditors? Does it protect the existing shareholders?

2. One way of making such a course of action possible would be for the law to authorise companies to create and issue *no par value* shares—something which is permitted in many jurisdictions and, indeed, compulsory in some. There is, after all, something unreal and simplistic about the concept of a par or nominal value. If the share in question was originally issued at a premium, or in exchange for a non-cash consideration, it may never have been worth its face value; and certainly after the date of its issue its market value is never again likely to bear any relation to the historic figure which was once ascribed to it. If it were lawful for companies to issue shares of no par value, many of the misunderstandings associated with the concept of a nominal value would disappear, and in addition it would be possible for a company to issue shares, ranking *pari passu*, at a price of £1 in January, £1.05 in February and £0.90 in March (depending on what the market would stand), without any implication that there was a par value which was being enhanced by a premium or reduced by a discount. Recommendations have been made at different times for such an innovation to be made in the UK—eg by the Gedge Committee (Cmnd 9112, 1954), the Jenkins

---

[19] [1875] LR 7 HL 653, HL.

[20] As in fact happened in *Ooregum*: soon afterwards, the company struck gold and its ordinary shares rose in value from 12½p to £2.

Committee (Cmnd 1749, 1962, paras 32–34) and the Wilson Committee (Cmnd 7937, 1980, para 735), as well as by professional bodies—but the response from successive governments has been nil. The CLR also considered the possibility of allowing (or even requiring) private companies to issue no-par shares. (This would not be possible for public companies unless the Second EU Directive were to be amended.) In the end, no change was proposed.

3. In more modern company law codes where shares of no par value are permitted, the 'maintenance of capital' rules do not apply (see Chapter 10); but the payment of dividends and other distributions to shareholders, and analogous transactions such as the repurchase by a company of its issued shares, are permitted only if the company is able to satisfy a statutory 'solvency test' at the relevant time. In consequence, attention is focused on the company's current financial position rather than on what may be quite misleading historic costs as shown in the accounts—indeed, the whole business of accounting is made much more straightforward and meaningful.

Issue of debentures at a discount

There is ordinarily no prohibition on the issue of debentures at a discount, because the 'maintenance of capital' principle does not apply to debt capital. A company may find it attractive to create debentures on terms which give the holders the option at some later date of converting the debentures into shares at a predetermined rate of exchange. Such *convertible* debentures may not be issued at a discount on terms that they may be immediately exchanged for shares of an equivalent nominal value, for this would be only an indirect way of achieving an issue of shares at a discount (*Mosely v Koffyfontein Mines Ltd* [1904] 2 Ch 108). The rate at which the exchange of securities is to take place must, to be above challenge, represent a realistic assessment of future trends in the value of money and the market prices in securities.

➤ Questions

1. What might be the attractions of an issue of convertible debentures, rather than a straightforward issue of shares, for (i) the company, (ii) the investor?

2. The basis of conversion set out in the terms of issue of convertible debentures commonly prescribes a declining tariff, for example 75 shares for every £100 of debentures converted after three years, 70 shares per £100 converted after four years, 65 shares per £100 after five years. Why?

Issue of shares at a premium

The rule that shares may not be issued at a discount means that a company which allots a share of nominal value £1 must get £1 and nothing less for it; but there is no corresponding rule which says that the company must get £1 and nothing more for it. If investors can be found who are willing to pay the company £1.20 or £2 or £5 for a share of nominal value £1, the company is free to charge that sum. (Indeed, it may give the company's existing shareholders cause for complaint if a new issue of shares is made at par, for that would reduce (or 'water down') the value of their shareholdings.[21])

The excess received by the company over the nominal value of the shares is called a *premium*, and, as noted earlier, CA 2006 requires such sums to be shown in the company's

---

[21] The directors would not breach any legal duty to the company (see [9.10]), but the existing shareholders might complain of unfairly prejudicial treatment (CA 2006 s 994). The statutory pre-emption rights are designed to help, but do not always apply or meet the problem: see 'Pre-emption rights governing the transfer of existing shares', p 516.

accounts under a separate head, as the 'share premium account'. This ensures that these are treated for almost all purposes as capital in the company's hands and not in any sense as income or profit: see 'Terminology associated with legal capital', pp 509ff.

Shareholders who have paid a premium for their shares have no right to the return of their premium in a winding up: at least in the absence of specific provision in the terms of issue, any surplus remaining after the return of the nominal amount of the shares is distributable on a rateable basis (*Re Driffield Gas Light Co* [1898] 1 Ch 451).

A company is not bound to issue its shares at a premium even though a price above par could be obtained.

[9.08] Hilder v Dexter [1902] AC 474 (House of Lords)

Immediately after its incorporation, the company issued one-sixth of its shares to selected private persons in order to obtain working capital. These shares were issued at par on the terms that the allottees should later have the option to take up further shares at par on a one-for-one basis. Hilder exercised his option at a time when the shares were worth £2 17s 6d [£2.87] per £1 share. Dexter, another shareholder, sought and obtained an injunction restraining Hilder and the company from carrying out the agreement on the ground that such an arrangement was forbidden by s 8(2) of the Act of 1900 [CA 2006 s 582]. The House of Lords reversed this decision and discharged the injunction.

> LORD DAVEY: The advantage which the appellant will derive from the exercise of his option is certainly not a 'discount or allowance', because he will have to pay 20s [100p] in the pound for every share. Nor is it, in my opinion, a commission paid by the company, for the company will not part with any portion of its capital which is received by it intact, or indeed with any moneys belonging to it. But the words relied on are, 'either directly or indirectly', and the argument seems to be that the company, by engaging to allot shares at par to the shareholder at a future date, is applying or using its shares in such a manner as to give him a possible benefit at the expense of the company in this sense, that it foregoes the chance of issuing them at a premium. With regard to the latter point, it may or may not be at the expense of the company. I am not aware of any law which obliges a company to issue its shares above par because they are saleable at a premium in the market. It depends on the circumstances of each case whether it will be prudent or even possible to do so, and it is a question for the directors to decide. But the point which, in my opinion, is alone material for the present purpose is that the benefit to the shareholder from being able to sell his shares at a premium is not obtained by him at the expense of the company's capital . . .
>
> THE EARL OF HALSBURY LC and LORD BRAMPTON delivered concurring opinions.
>
> LORD ROBERTSON concurred.

Shares may be issued at a premium even though not issued for cash.

[9.09] Henry Head & Co Ltd v Ropner Holdings Ltd [1952] Ch 124 (Chancery Division)

The defendant company was formed to acquire by way of amalgamation the shares of two shipping companies, and did so by exchanging the shares in these companies for shares in itself of equivalent nominal value. In this way it acquired assets worth some £7 million in exchange for shares of a nominal value of £1,175,000. The court held that the difference of just over £5 million had rightly been shown in the company's balance sheet as carried to a share premium account.

HARMAN J: The directors have been advised that they are bound to show their accounts in that way, and not only they but the plaintiffs, who are large shareholders, regard that as a very undesirable thing, because it fixes an unfortunate kind of rigidity on the structure of the company, having regard to the fact that an account kept under that name, namely, the Share Premium Account, can only have anything paid out of it by means of a transaction analogous to a reduction of capital. It is, in effect, as if the company had originally been capitalised at approximately £7,000,000 instead of £1,750,000.

The question which I have to determine is whether the defendants were obliged to keep their accounts in that way. That depends purely on s 56 of the Companies Act 1948 [CA 2006 s 610], which is a new departure in legislation and was, it is said, intended to make compulsory that which had long seemed to be desirable, namely, the practice of putting aside as a reserve and treating in the ordinary way as capital cash premiums received on the issue of shares at a premium . . .

Counsel for the plaintiff company asks who would suppose that a common type of transaction of the sort now under consideration was the issue of shares at a premium and says that nobody in the city or in the commercial world would dream of so describing it. It is with a sense of shock at first that one hears that this transaction was the issue of shares at a premium. Everybody, I suppose, who hears those words thinks of a company which, being in a strong trading position, wants further capital and puts forward its shares for the subscription of the public at such a price as the market in those shares justifies, whatever it may be, [£1.50] a £1 share, £5 a £1 share, or any price obtainable; and the [50p] or £4 above the nominal value of a share which it acquires as a result of that transaction is no doubt a premium. That is what is ordinarily meant by the issue of shares at a premium. The first words of sub-s (1) are: 'Where a company issues shares at a premium'. If the words had stopped there, one might have said that the subsection merely refers to cash transactions of that sort, but it goes on to say 'whether for cash or otherwise'.

What 'otherwise' can there be? It must be a consideration other than cash, namely, goods or assets of some physical sort.

> Note

The general principle expressed in this case remains valid, but CA 2006 (and its predecessors) contain relief against the application of the share premium restrictions in the case of certain mergers and reconstructions (ss 611–613), and the Secretary of State has power to make further regulations, either amplifying or restricting the relief so provided (s 614).

Issue of shares in exchange for property

It is not necessary that shares be allotted for cash. It is very common instead for the issue price to be satisfied by the transfer to the company of property, such as a business, previously owned by the allottee: this is what Mr Salomon **[2.02]** did. Or the new shares may be exchanged for shares in another company: see, for example, *Henry Head* **[9.09]**.

Two problems may arise here. If the property taken by the company as consideration is worth *more than* the nominal value of the new shares, then the shares will have been issued at a premium, and this will bring into play the burdensome and restrictive accounting provisions of CA 2006 ss 610ff discussed earlier. If, on the other hand, the property is worth *less than* the nominal value of the shares (as may well have been true in Mr Salomon's case), then in practical terms the shares will have been issued at a discount, contrary to law. Creditors who assume that the shares have been paid for in full may then suffer loss, or at least be exposed to risk, and existing shareholders also may be prejudiced through the 'watering down' of their own investment.

The common law leaves this problem to be settled by the business judgement and integrity of the directors, and courts will normally accept the valuation made at the time of the allotment unless it is shown to have been made dishonestly or falsely or the contract for allotment is itself set aside for fraud (*Re Wragg* **[9.10]**). This means that the rule against issuing shares at a discount can be circumvented fairly easily, for challenges to the board's decisions are rarely mounted, and those that are face the formidable procedural obstacles of *Foss v Harbottle* **[13.01]**: compare the analogous cases of *Pavlides v Jensen* [1956] Ch 565 (sale of assets at alleged undervalue) and *Prudential Assurance Co Ltd v Newman Industries Ltd (No 2)* **[13.25]** (purchase of assets at alleged overvalue). The case for some form of statutory control has always seemed a strong one.

Rules for public companies

Such a step has been taken in regard to *public* companies, as a result of the Second EU Directive (which was implemented in 1980). The relevant provisions are now in CA 2006 ss 584–587 and 593–609. Some forms of consideration for the allotment of shares are banned altogether, for example an undertaking to do work for the company in the future (s 585(1)) and an undertaking of a long-term nature (other than a promise to pay cash) which may take five years or more to perform (s 587(1)). Other forms of 'non-cash' consideration have to be valued by an expert (ss 593–594 and 603), and sometimes a second expert has to certify that the first one is competent (s 1150(2))! Rules of even greater severity are laid down for subscribers to the memorandum (ss 584 and 598–599). In all, it is a very elaborate (and costly) procedure that the Act spells out, in the most finicky detail: a pretty large sledge-hammer to crack a fairly small nut.

It is not so important, here, to explain all the finer points of the statutory procedure. But something must be said about the code of sanctions for a failure to comply—even with these finer points; and these are formidable. The allottee is obliged to pay to the company the nominal value of the shares and any premium, with interest, regardless of any benefit that the company may already have had (so that he or she may in effect have to pay for the shares twice over); and, in addition, a subsequent holder of the shares is jointly and severally liable with the allottee to pay the same amounts, unless the holder is (or has derived title through) a bona fide purchaser for value without (actual) notice: see ss 588 and 605. The only relief that those who are caught by these provisions have against what may be potentially a double liability to pay for their shares is that they have a right to make application to the court and ask for exemption from some or all of the statutory liability (ss 589 and 606: see *Re Bradford Investments plc (No 2)* in the Note following *Re Wragg Ltd* **[9.10]**). In addition to these civil consequences, criminal penalties are imposed upon the company and its officers; and the transactions which infringe the statutory rules, though enforceable by the company against the allottee, are (by implication, and in the case of a contract with a subscriber to the memorandum, expressly) unenforceable or 'void' as against the company.

There is an exception from the valuation requirement in the case of a takeover in which all or part of the consideration for the shares allotted is the exchange of shares in the offeree company (s 594(1)–(3)); and it also does not apply in a merger (s 595).

One last point is worth emphasising: all of these rules apply only to issues by public companies for non-cash consideration; if the consideration is cash, the rules are not relevant. 'Cash' is defined in CA 2006 s 583(3): it includes undertakings to pay in the future, or to release a liability of the company (the latter is useful in debt for equity swaps).

It should be remembered that the rules stated here govern public companies only; private companies continue to be subject to the common law, as declared in the case next cited **[9.10]**.

➤ Questions

1. Fred comes to an arrangement with the directors of XYZ plc that he will subscribe for 200,000 £1 ordinary shares in the company at their par value. He also agrees to sell to XYZ plc a leasehold shop property for a price of £200,000. On 1 April the shares are allotted to

him in exchange for his cheque, payable to the company, for £200,000, and on the same day, the leasehold interest in the shop is transferred to the company in return for the company's cheque, payable to Fred, for £200,000. What legal issues arise?

2. What do you consider is the policy reasoning behind CA 2006 ss 598–599? Suppose that X and Y are the promoters of a public company and intend within a few days of its incorporation to transfer a business to it: is there any need to have regard to ss 598–599 if they take the precaution of ensuring that the memorandum is subscribed only by two clerks in their solicitor's office?

3. Why do you think that the legislation requires a copy of the valuation to be sent to the proposed allottee (s 593(1)(c))? If the valuer's report advises the company that the transferor's property would be a snip at twice the price, can the allottee withdraw from the transaction and negotiate for more? If the valuer negligently overvalues the property, could the allottee sue the valuer in tort?

4. Where there has been an infringement of s 593, could the company and the allottee effectively agree that the latter should be released from liability under s 593(3) without going to court under s 606?

Rules for private companies

Private company share issues for non-cash consideration.

[9.10] Re Wragg Ltd [1897] 1 Ch 796 (Court of Appeal)

This case indicates that a *private* company may buy property at any price it thinks fit, and pay for it in fully paid shares. Unless the transaction itself is impeached (eg on the ground of fraud), the actual value of the consideration received by the company for its shares cannot be inquired into. Wragg and Martin had sold to the company on its incorporation their omnibus and livery-stable business for £46,300, which was paid partly in cash and debentures and partly by the allotment to them of the whole of the company's original capital of £20,000 in fully paid shares. The liquidator of the company later sought to show that the value of the business had been overstated by some £18,000; and he claimed either to be entitled to treat shares representing this amount as unpaid, or alternatively to charge Martin and Wragg as directors with misfeasance in connection with the purchase. Both claims failed.

LINDLEY LJ: . . . That shares cannot be issued at a discount was finally settled in the case of the *Ooregum Gold Mining Co of India v Roper* **[9.07]**, the judgments in which are strongly relied upon by the appellant in this case. It has, however, never yet been decided that a limited company cannot buy property or pay for services at any price it thinks proper, and pay for them in fully paid-up shares. Provided a limited company does so honestly and not colourably, and provided that it has not been so imposed upon as to be entitled to be relieved from its bargain, it appears to be settled by *Pell's* case,[22] and the others to which I have referred, of which *Anderson's* case[23] is the most striking, that agreements by limited companies to pay for property or services in paid-up shares are valid and binding on the companies and their creditors . . .

[If] a company owes a person £100, the company cannot by paying him £200 in shares of that nominal amount discharge him . . . from his obligation as a shareholder to pay up the other £100 in respect of those shares. That would be issuing shares at a discount. The difference between such a transaction and paying for property or services in shares at a price put upon them by a vendor and

[22] (1869) 5 Ch App 11.
[23] (1877) 7 Ch D 75.

agreed to by the company may not always be very apparent in practice. But the two transactions are essentially different, and whilst the one is ultra vires the other is intra vires. It is not law that persons cannot sell property to a limited company for fully paid-up shares and make a profit by the transaction. We must not allow ourselves to be misled by talking of value. The value paid to the company is measured by the price at which the company agrees to buy what it thinks it worth its while to acquire. Whilst the transaction is unimpeached, this is the only value to be considered ...

AL SMITH and RIGBY LJJ delivered concurring judgments.

> Notes

1. The pre-conditions in *Re Wragg* are important: contrast *Tintin Exploration Syndicate v Sandys* (1947) 177 LT 412 (bad faith); *Re White Star Line* [1939] Ch 458 (the consideration was patently not of an equivalent value to the shares).

2. This common law ruling may be contrasted with *Re Bradford Investments plc (No 2)* [1991] BCLC 688, which illustrates the operation of the statutory rules governing the issue of shares by public companies for a non-cash consideration. Here the four members of a partnership had converted a dormant private company into a public company and transferred the business of the partnership to it in consideration of the allotment to them of 1,059,000 fully paid £1 ordinary shares. No valuation of the business was obtained, as required by CA 1985 s 103 [CA 2006 s 593]. Two-and-a-half years later, the company, now under independent management, claimed £1,059,000 from the original partners as the issue price of the shares. The partners applied to the court under s 113 [CA 2006 s 606] to be relieved from liability to pay this sum. In this they were unsuccessful, for s 113 places the onus of proving that value was given on the applicants, and they were unable to satisfy the court that the partnership business had any net value at the time when it was transferred to the company.

> Question

What is the purpose of all these rules regulating the 'price' of shares? Who, if anyone, do they protect?

Further reading

ARMOUR, J, 'Legal Capital: An Outdated Concept?' (2006) 7 *European Business Organization Law Review* 5.

ARMOUR, J, 'Share Capital and Creditor Protection: Efficient Rules for a Modern Company Law?' (2000) 63 MLR 355.

DAEHNERT, A, 'The Minimum Capital Requirement—An Anachronism under Conservation, Parts 1 and 2' [2009] 30 *Company Lawyer* 3 and 34.

FERRAN, E, 'Creditors' Interests and "Core" Company Law' (1999) 20 *Company Lawyer* 314.

GOWER, LCB, 'Some Contrasts between British and American Corporation Law' (1956) 69 *Harvard Law Review* 1369.

MYNERS, P, *Pre-Emption Rights: Final Report* (URN 05/679) (DTI, 2005).

PENNINGTON, R, 'Can Shares in Companies be Defined?' (1989) 10 *Company Lawyer* 140.

POPE, P and PUXTY, A, 'What is Equity?' (1991) 54 MLR 889.

RICKFORD, J, et al, 'Reforming Capital' (2004) 15 *European Business Law Review* 919.

WORTHINGTON, S, 'Shares and Shareholders: Property, Power and Entitlement—Parts I and II' (2001) 22 *Company Lawyer* 258 and 307.

10

DISTRIBUTIONS AND CAPITAL MAINTENANCE

Controls over a company's distribution of capital

The previous chapter illustrated the concern of the law to see that those who take shares in a company do, in fact, contribute the value of their shares in money or money's worth. This fund of such contributions, being the company's legal capital, is intended by law to provide creditor protection, in some senses at the expense of the company's members. The law does not restrict every disposal of the company's assets—companies are free to run their businesses at differing rates of success. However, the ambition of creditor protection would be defeated if, once the funds had been received, companies were completely free to return them to the members, thereby adversely affecting the creditors' overall position vis-à-vis the company.

This chapter examines the rules that are designed to ensure that a company's legal capital is, as far as possible, maintained in the company's hands consistently with all the risks associated with any business venture. In particular, these rules ensure that a company's legal capital is not returned to the members themselves, directly or indirectly, except through some statutory procedure, such as a reduction of capital (Companies Act 2006 (CA 2006) ss 641ff) or a redemption or a repurchase of shares (ss 684ff), which provides proper safeguards for creditors and others who might be prejudiced by the diminution of the company's assets. In this way, the law does its best for the company's creditors who are, generally, denied any direct recourse against the members, or against the directors, whilst at the same time allowing corporate entrepreneurial activity to continue without too much state intervention.

There is, of course, only so much protection that any formal rules of law can give. In addition to the normal business risks mentioned previously, the historic figure representing the issued capital may be eroded in real terms by the effects of inflation. But these are risks which creditors necessarily accept; and UK company law does provide a further measure of protection through the publicity given to company accounts and through the remedial regime provided by the insolvency legislation.

The rules providing for 'maintenance of capital' were formulated in the first place by the courts in the latter part of the nineteenth century. But the Second EU Company Law Directive (77/91/EEC) required the UK to make specific legislative provision for many matters relating to the use of capital and the payment of dividends. The required rules to some extent overlapped with the existing judge-made law, and in other respects went much further. English statutory provisions are now more extensive than the Directive required, in that some of the provisions apply not just to public companies (as the Directive stipulated) but to private companies as well.

English statute law later introduced still further changes, in the form of rules allowing a company to repurchase its own shares.[1] This had been declared unlawful in *Trevor v Whitworth* **[10.05]**, and the common law ban is, indeed, still confirmed as a general rule in CA 2006 s 658. It also made changes to the rules related to the giving by a company of financial assistance towards the purchase of its shares. Much of the earlier case law was superseded as a result. It is not possible here to describe the detail of all the statutory rules—still less to try to explain some of their byzantine obfuscations; all that can be attempted is to summarise them, and to cite some of the relevant judicial pronouncements.

This chapter deals, in turn, with:[2]

(i)   permitted returns of capital implemented by a *reduction of capital* (see 'Permitted reductions of capital', pp 534ff);

(ii) permitted returns of capital implemented by a *repurchase or redemption of shares* (see 'Redemptions and repurchases of shares', pp 542ff);

(iii) prohibitions on a company giving *financial assistance* to others for the purchase of its shares (see 'Financial assistance by a company for the acquisition of its own shares', pp 546ff);

(iv) rules requiring *dividend distributions* to be made out of profits, not capital (see 'Dividend distributions', pp 565ff); and

(v)   impermissible *'disguised' returns of capital* (see 'Disguised returns of capital', pp 572ff).

Permitted reductions of capital

Once a company has raised a particular level of legal capital, can it adjust the amount downwards? If this could happen at will, the rules on legal capital would become meaningless. On the other hand, there may be good reason for adjustments.

If the company has excess capital that it cannot, or prefers not to, use profitably in pursuing its objectives, it may wish to return this to the members rather than expand or diversify the company's business. This involves no risk to the creditors, provided they are satisfied first.

By contrast, if the company has traded unsuccessfully, the value of its existing assets may fall well short of the legal capital. Potential new equity investors may want the value of the company's existing shares to be reduced to reflect the actual value of the company's assets before new investments are made. This is desired so that, if the business is resuscitated, its profits can be paid out to members (including the new members) rather than going to meet the shortfall in undistributable legal capital. Although this type of revaluation does not involve paying any of the company's cash to its shareholders, it does have

---

[1] A limited statutory exception allowing companies to issue redeemable *preference* shares had existed since 1929. Now redeemable shares can be of any class.

[2] Also revisit some of the further reading from Chapter 9: see especially J Armour, 'Share Capital and Creditor Protection: Efficient Rules for a Modern Company Law?' (2000) 63 MLR 355; J Rickford et al, 'Reforming Capital' (2004) 15 *European Business Law Review* 919; J Armour, 'Legal Capital: An Outdated Concept?' (2006) 7 *European Business Organization Law Review* 5; E Ferran, 'Creditors' Interests and "Core" Company Law' (1999) 20 *Company Lawyer* 314; and also E Ferran, 'Financial Assistance: Changing Policy Perceptions but Static Law' [2004] CLJ 225.

a detrimental impact on creditors: the value of the protective 'creditor buffer' is reduced, and the risk to creditors therefore increases.

CA 2006 imposes restraints on a company wishing to reduce its capital. In summary, it can only do so by: (i) special resolution confirmed by the court (CA 2006 ss 641(1)(b), 645–651); or (ii) for private companies, by special resolution supported by a solvency statement by the directors, filed with the registrar, provided that at least one shareholder will remain (ie that the share capital will not be reduced to zero) (CA 2006 ss 641(1)(a), 642–644).[3] This is a major relaxation for private companies, introduced by CA 2006. Under (i), the court must not confirm a reduction unless it is satisfied that affected creditors have consented, been paid or had their debts secured (s 648), and then the court order and the new statement of capital must be registered at Companies House. Creditors may object to the proposed reduction if it involves either a diminution of shareholder liability in respect of unpaid capital, or the payment to any shareholder of paid-up capital (s 646), unless the court thinks that creditors should not be able to object,[4] or should be able to object in an even wider range of circumstances (s 645). Subject to this, a company may reduce its capital in any way, and s 641(4) provides illustrations.

Court approval, in (i), is designed to ensure that the prescribed formalities have been strictly observed (including creditor approval), and that the reduction treats the company's shareholders fairly (see the cases cited later).

The procedure is rarely used by private companies, since they can now repurchase their own shares out of capital (see 'Redemptions and repurchases of shares', p 542), and prefer to use this approach to buy out retiring or deceased members. Public companies may still find the procedure useful on occasion. Note, too, the requirement in s 656 for directors of public companies to call a general meeting if the company's assets fall to half or less of the company's called up capital (see 'Minimum capital requirements for company formation', p 514).

Finally, where the rights of a *class* of shareholders are affected by a reduction, it may be necessary to have regard also to the provisions of CA 2006 s 630 (especially since s 630(6) indicates that references to 'variation' of class rights is taken to include references to 'abrogation'), but the approach of the courts to this topic gives less scope to that section than its draftsman probably appreciated: see **[10.03]** and **[10.01]**).

A company may not bind itself to refuse to exercise the power conferred on it by statute to alter its capital, but an agreement by members that they will not support a resolution to alter capital is binding.

Re-read *Russell v Northern Bank Development Corpn Ltd* **[4.35]**.

➤ Question

Can the first ruling in this case (that a company cannot agree that it will not exercise its statutory power to alter its capital) be readily circumvented by the second (that members may agree by contract, either with each other or with a third party, that they will not vote

---

[3] If the company's articles prohibit reductions of capital, then the company's articles will first have to be altered before this procedure can be followed: see CA 2006 s 641(6) and 'Permitted reductions of capital', p 534ff.

[4] Under s 646(1)(b), a creditor can object by showing a 'real likelihood' that the reduction would result in an inability to discharge the debt when it became due. The creditor has to demonstrate 'a particular present assessment about a future state of affairs'; thus the 'entirely theoretical possibility' of certain pension claims does not suffice: *In re Liberty International plc* [2010] EWHC 1060 (Ch), per Norris J. It follows that if the court is to be persuaded to 'direct otherwise' (s 645(2)(b) and (3))—ie bar the creditors from objecting—then the company will have to show that creditor complaint is unlikely. The *Liberty* test was applied for that purpose in *Re Vodafone Group Plc* [2014] EWHC 1357 (Ch), [32]–[35], [52].

for a change in the company's capital structure)? If so, is the reasoning flawed? Does the answer to this depend upon whether a court would remedy infringements by orders for specific performance or injunction, or only by orders for the payment of damages?

The court's discretion in confirming a reduction of capital.

[10.01] Scottish Insurance Corpn Ltd v Wilsons and Clyde Coal Co Ltd [1949] AC 462 (House of Lords)

The company's business had been nationalised, so that it could no longer earn profits. Its proposal to pay off the preference capital[5] in anticipation of liquidation was opposed, partly because it was believed that this would rob the preference shareholders of a right to participate in 'surplus assets' in a liquidation. The House of Lords rejected this construction of the preference shareholders' rights (see **[11.04]**) and held that the reduction was in any case fair.

LORD SIMONDS: The Companies Act 1929, no more than its predecessors, prescribes what is to guide the court in the exercise of its discretionary jurisdiction to confirm or to refuse to confirm a reduction in capital. But I agree with the learned Lord President [in the court below] that, important though its task is to see that the procedure, by which a reduction is carried through, is formally correct and that creditors are not prejudiced, it has the further duty of satisfying itself that the scheme is fair and equitable between the different classes of shareholders: see, eg, *British and American Trustee and Finance Corpn Ltd v Couper.*[6] But what is fair and equitable must depend upon the circumstances of each case and I propose . . . to consider the elements on which the appellants rely for saying that this reduction is not fair to them.

In the formal case which they have presented to the House the element of unfairness on which the appellants insist is that the reduction deprives them of their right to participate in the surplus assets of the company on liquidation and leaves the ordinary stockholders in sole possession of those assets. But in their argument both in the Court of Session and before your Lordships they have further relied on the fact that they have been deprived of a favourable 7% investment which they cannot hope to replace and might have expected to continue to enjoy. They further contend that the deprivation of these rights, which would in any case have been unmerited hardship, is rendered more unfair because it is likely to be followed at an early date by liquidation of the company or, as it is less accurately expressed, because it is itself only a step in the liquidation of the company.

The first plea makes an assumption, viz that the articles give the preference stockholders the right in a winding up to share in surplus assets, which I for the moment accept but will later examine. Making that assumption, I yet see no validity in the plea. The company has at a stroke been deprived of the enterprise and undertaking which it has built up over many years: it is irrelevant for this purpose that the stroke is delivered by an Act of Parliament which at the same time provides some compensation. Nor can it affect the rights of the parties that the only reason why there is money available for repayment of capital is that the company has no longer an undertaking to carry on. Year by year the 7% preference dividend has been paid; of the balance of the profits some part has been distributed to the ordinary stockholders, the rest has been conserved in the business. If I ask whether year by year the directors were content to recommend, the company in general meeting to vote, a dividend which has left a margin of resources, in order that the preference stockholders might in addition to repayment of the capital share also in surplus assets, I think that directors and company alike would give an emphatic negative. Anyway they would, I think, add that they have always had it in their power, and have it still, by making use of articles

5 See 'Classes of shares and class rights', pp 581ff.
6 [1894] AC 399.

139 or 141, to see that what they had saved for themselves they do not share with others[7] . . .
Reading these articles as a whole with such familiarity with the topic as the years have brought,
I would not hesitate to say, first, that the last thing a preference stockholder would expect to get
(I do not speak here of the legal rights) would be a share of surplus assets, and that such a share
would be a windfall beyond his reasonable expectations and, secondly, that he had at all times the
knowledge, enforced in this case by the unusual reference in article 139 to the payment off of the
preference capital, that at least he ran the risk, if the company's circumstances admitted, of such
a reduction as is now proposed being submitted for confirmation by the court. Whether a man
lends money to a company at 7% or subscribes for its shares carrying a cumulative preferential
dividend at that rate, I do not think that he can complain of unfairness if the company, being in a
position lawfully to do so, proposes to pay him off. No doubt, if the company is content not to do
so, he may get something that he can never have expected but, so long as the company can lawfully repay him, whether it be months or years before a contemplated liquidation, I see no ground
for the court refusing its confirmation. [His Lordship later held that the preference shareholders
had in any case no right to participate in 'surplus assets' in a liquidation: see **[11.04]**.]

VISCOUNT MAUGHAM and LORD NORMAND delivered concurring opinions.

LORD MORTON OF HENRYTON dissented.

*In a reduction of capital, the prima facie rule is that money is to be repaid and losses are
to be borne in the order in which the different classes of shares would rank, as regards
repayment or loss of capital respectively, in a winding up.*

[10.02] Re Chatterley-Whitfield Collieries Ltd [1948] 2 All ER 593 (Court of Appeal)

The company's principal business had been nationalised. It proposed to continue operations on a much smaller scale, for which it would need far less capital. It therefore proposed to reduce its capital by paying off its preference shareholders, leaving the ordinary
shareholders unaffected. This was confirmed by the court as fair, since it was in accordance with the respective rights of the two classes in a winding up.

LORD GREENE MR: [T]he company is faced with the following situation. Its principal business
has gone and it is proposing to embark on certain new activities which may or may not turn
out to be successful. So long as it was possessed of its colliery it clearly required to keep all its
issued capital in the business—there was no question of its having capital surplus to its business
requirements. The reduced form of its activities is, however, such that it has a great deal more
capital than it requires . . .

What is a company in that situation to do? The business answer to this question does not admit
of doubt, particularly where a substantial part of its capital consists of preference shares bearing
a higher rate of dividend than the company is reasonably likely to earn in the future. It will do what
this company seeks to do, ie reduce its capital by paying off as much of its preference capital
as it is able to pay off out of its surplus. A company which satisfies its capital requirements by
issuing preference shares only does so where it is satisfied that the new capital will earn at least
the promised rate of dividend. A company which has issued preference shares carrying a high
rate of dividend and finds its business so curtailed that it has capital surplus to its requirements
and sees the likelihood, or at any rate the possibility, that its preference capital will not, if I may

---

[7] These articles dealt respectively with the paying off of the preference capital out of a reserve fund, and the
distribution of capitalised profits, in the form of bonus shares, to the ordinary shareholders.

use the expression, 'earn its keep', would be guilty of financial ineptitude if it did not take steps to reduce its capital by paying off preference capital so far as the law allowed it to do so. That is mere commonplace in company finance.

There has been a tendency, indeed more than a tendency, to represent a company confronted by this sort of practical question as though it were nothing but an uneasy and warring combination of hostile classes of shareholders. In a sense, no doubt, it is. But it is more than this. The position of the company itself as an economic entity must be considered, and nothing can be more destructive of a company's financial equilibrium than to have to carry the burden of capital which it does not need, bearing a high rate of dividend which it cannot earn. In a company so situated, the ordinary shareholders will be unfairly treated vis-à-vis the preference shareholders, and the company may well fall into the situation when its preference dividends will begin to fall into irretrievable arrears. It is a fallacy to suppose that because ordinary shareholders will benefit, the transaction ought to be vetoed as being unfair to the preference shareholders.

It is a clearly recognised principle that the court, in confirming a reduction by the payment off of capital surplus to a company's needs, will allow, or rather require, that the reduction shall be effected in the first instance by payment off of capital which is entitled to priority in a winding up. Apart from special cases where by agreement between classes the incidence of reduction is arranged in a different manner, this is and has for years been the normal recognised practice of the courts, accepted by the courts and by businessmen as the fair and equitable method of carrying out a reduction by payment off of surplus capital. I know of no case where this method has, apart from agreement, been departed from . . .

In the result, I am of opinion that the present appeal should be allowed and the proposed reduction confirmed, the application being otherwise in order.

ASQUITH LJ delivered a concurring judgment.

EVERSHED LJ dissented.

This decision was affirmed by the House of Lords: *Prudential Assurance Co Ltd v Chatterley-Whitfield Collieries Ltd* [1949] AC 512.

Subject to the Act and the company's articles,*[8] *no separate class meetings are necessary to approve a reduction of capital if priority is given to the different classes in accordance with the terms on which they were issued.

[10.03] Re Saltdean Estate Co Ltd [1968] 1 WLR 1844 (Chancery Division)

The company's preferred shareholders were entitled to participate in the 'balance of profits' in each year after a 10% preferred dividend and an equivalent sum in dividends on the ordinary shares had been paid; but in a winding up they had no right to participate in surplus capital. The ordinary shareholders controlled the voting. The court was asked to confirm a reduction of capital which was to be effected by paying off the preferred shares at 75p per 50p share. The reduction was approved by the court, which ruled that there was no 'variation' of the preferred shareholders' rights which would call for approval by a separate class meeting.

BUCKLEY J: [It] is said that the proposed cancellation of the preferred shares will constitute an abrogation of all the rights attached to those shares which cannot validly be effected without an extraordinary resolution of a class meeting of preferred shareholders under

---

[8] The Act and the articles can impose crucial qualifications—see the following extract.

article 8 of the company's articles. In my judgment, that article has no application to a cancellation of shares on a reduction of capital which is in accord with the rights attached to the shares of the company. Unless this reduction can be shown to be unfair to the preferred shareholders on other grounds, it is in accordance with the right and liability to prior repayment of capital attached to their shares. The liability to prior repayment on a reduction of capital, corresponding to their right to prior return of capital in a winding up is a liability of a kind of which Lord Greene MR [in the *Chatterley-Whitfield* case **[10.02]**] said that anyone has only himself to blame if he does not know it. It is part of the bargain between the shareholders and forms an integral part of the definition or delimitation of the bundle of rights which make up a preferred share. Giving effect to it does not involve the variation or abrogation of any right attached to such a share. Nor, in my judgment, has s 72 of the Companies Act 1948 [CA 2006 s 633], upon which the opponents place some reliance, any application to this case. That section relates to variation of rights attached to shares, not to cancellation of shares . . .

The fact is that every holder of preferred shares of the company has always been at risk that his hope of participating in undrawn or future profits of the company might be frustrated at any time by a liquidation of the company or a reduction of its capital properly resolved upon by a sufficient majority of his fellow members. This vulnerability is, and always has been, a characteristic of the preferred shares. Now that the event has occurred, none of the preferred shareholders can, in my judgment, assert that the resulting state of affairs is unfair to him.

For these reasons the opposition to this petition, in my judgment, fails.

➤ Notes

1. In *House of Fraser plc v ACGE Investments Ltd* [1987] AC 387, HL, the House of Lords endorsed this decision, and approved the following passage from one of the judgments in the court below (1987 SLT 273 at 278):

> In our opinion the proposed cancellation of the preference shares would involve fulfilment or satisfaction of the contractual rights of the shareholders, and would not involve any variation of their rights. Variation of a right presupposes the existence of the right, the variation of the right, and the subsequent continued existence of the right as varied. A different situation obtains where a right is fulfilled and satisfied and thereafter ceases to exist.

2. These rulings do not apply where the company's articles of association expressly provide that the rights attached to a class of shares shall be deemed to be varied by a reduction of the capital paid up on the shares. A separate class meeting must then be held: *Re Northern Engineering Industries plc* [1994] 2 BCLC 704, CA.

➤ Questions

1. How do these decisions relate to the statutory provision in CA 2006 s 630, especially s 630(6) which indicates that references to a 'variation' of class rights is taken to include references to 'abrogation'? (See 'Variation of class rights, pp 587ff, and *Re Northern Engineering Industries plc*, in the previous Note 2.)

2. If the company has a *shortfall* of capital, how should a capital reduction be implemented as between the company's ordinary shareholders (class A), preference shareholders with a preferential right to both a dividend and a return of capital on a winding up (class B) and preference shareholders with only a preferential right to a dividend (class C)?

3. If the company has a *surplus* of capital, how should a capital reduction be implemented as between the company's ordinary shareholders (class A), preference shareholders with a preferential right to both a dividend and a return of capital on a winding up (class B) and preference shareholders with only a preferential right to a dividend (class C)?

A shareholder voting at a class meeting held in connection with a reduction of capital must have regard to the interests of the class of shareholders as a whole.

[10.04] Re Holders Investment Trust Ltd [1971] 1 WLR 583 (Chancery Division)

The company petitioned for confirmation of a reduction of capital, under which it was proposed to cancel its redeemable preference shares and to allot to the holders an equivalent amount of unsecured loan stock.[9] The reduction was approved by both a special resolution of the company and an extraordinary resolution of a separate class meeting of the preference shareholders. At the latter meeting, some 90% of the votes cast were held by certain trustees (referred to in the judgment as 'the supporting trustees') who also held about 52% of the ordinary stocks and shares, and in that respect stood to gain substantially from the reduction. Megarry J held that the vote at the class meeting was ineffectual, because the majority preference shareholders had considered their own interests, without regard to what was best for the preference shareholders as a class.

MEGARRY J: Unopposed petitions by a company for the confirmation of a reduction of capital are a commonplace of the Companies' Court; but an opposed petition such as the one I have before me is a comparative rarity . . .

Put briefly, Mr Drake's opposition to the confirmation of the reduction is twofold. First, he contends that the extraordinary resolution of the preference shareholders was not valid and effectual because the supporting trustees did not exercise their votes in the way that they ought to have done, namely, in the interests of the preference shareholders as a whole. Instead, being owners of much ordinary stock and many shares as well, they voted in such a way as to benefit the totality of the stocks and shares that they held. Secondly, Mr Drake contends that even if the extraordinary resolution was valid, the terms on which the reduction of capital is to be effected are not fair, in particular in that the increase in the rate of interest from 5% to 6% is not an adequate recompense for having the right of repayment or redemption postponed from 31 July 1971, until at earliest 31 October 1985, and at latest some unspecified date in 1990. I may say at the outset that it is common ground that the proposed reduction is not in accordance with the class rights of the preference shareholders . . .

[His Lordship referred to *Carruth v ICI Ltd*,[10] *British America Nickel Corpn Ltd v MJ O'Brien Ltd* **[11.06]** and *Shuttleworth v Cox Bros & Co (Maidenhead) Ltd* **[6.06]** and continued:]

In the *British America* case, Viscount Haldane, in speaking for a strong Board of the Judicial Committee, referred to 'a general principle, which is applicable to all authorities conferred on majorities of classes enabling them to bind minorities; namely, that the power given must be exercised for the purpose of benefiting the class as a whole, and not merely individual members only . . .' The matter may, I think, be put in the way in which Scrutton LJ put it in the *Shuttleworth* case, where the question was the benefit of the company rather than of a particular class of members.

---

[9] A company, in reducing its capital, is not bound to pay off its shareholders in cash: see *ex p Westburn Sugar Refineries Ltd* [1951] AC 625, HL.

[10] [1937] AC 707.

Adapting his language . . . I have to see whether the majority was honestly endeavouring to decide and act for the benefit of the class as a whole, rather than with a view to the interests of some of the class and against that of others . . .

I pause here to point the obvious. Without guidance from those skilled in these matters, many members of a class may fail to realise what they should bear in mind when deciding how to vote at a class meeting. The beneficial owner of shares may well concentrate on his own personal interests: even though he regards the proposal per se as one to be rejected, collateral matters affecting other interests of his may lead him to vote in favour of the resolution. Trustees, too, are under a fiduciary duty to do the best they properly can for their beneficiaries. A proposal which, in isolation, is contrary to the interests of those owning the shares affected may nevertheless be beneficial to the beneficiaries by reason of the improved prospects that the proposal will confer on other shares in the company which the trustees hold on the same trusts: and that, in essence, is what is in issue here . . .

[His Lordship referred to correspondence between the 'supporting trustees' and their professional advisers, and continued:] That exchange of letters seems to me to make it perfectly clear that the advice sought, the advice given, and the advice acted upon, was all on the basis of what was for the benefit of the trusts as a whole, having regard to their large holdings of the equity capital. From the point of view of equity, and disregarding company law, this is a perfectly proper basis; but that is not the question before me. I have to determine whether the supporting trustees voted for the reduction in the bona fide belief that they were acting in the interests of the general body of members of that class. From first to last I can see no evidence that the trustees ever applied their minds to what under company law was the right question, or that they ever had the bona fide belief that is requisite for an effectual sanction of the reduction. Accordingly, in my judgment there has been no effectual sanction for the modification of class rights . . .

[His Lordship considered the evidence, and ruled that the reduction had not been shown to be fair to the preference shareholders. Accordingly, he refused to confirm the reduction.]

> Notes

1. This case was decided at common law, before the enactment of the statutory provisions on class rights which are now to be found in CA 2006 ss 630ff.

2. In this case, it might be said that Megarry J is expecting the majority preference shareholders to show a 'detached altruism' which the court in such cases as *Mills v Mills* **[7.10]** dismissed as unrealistic. See LS Sealy, 'Equitable and Other Fetters on the Shareholder's Freedom to Vote' in NE Eastham and B Krivy (eds), *The Cambridge Lectures 1981*, attacking the rule as wrong. What *is* expected of shareholders? A good number of cases suggest that some restrictions on voting are appropriate. Are such cases all best explained as illustrating judicial review of powers which are subject to equitable 'proper purposes' restrictions (although not, with shareholders, fiduciary loyalty constraints) (see Chapter 14 generally)?

3. The same judgment also set out the parties' respective burdens of proof (at 586):

If there is [effective sanction by the majority], the court will confirm the reduction unless the opposition proves that it is unfair; if there is not, the court will confirm the reduction only if it is proved to be fair. [And so, on finding that there was no effectual sanction in this case, His Lordship held, at 589, that the burden here rested on those supporting the reduction to prove that it was fair.]

4. These prohibitions on return of capital apply equally to disguised returns of capital: see 'Disguised returns of capital', pp 572ff.

Redemptions and repurchases of shares

The general rule in CA 2006 s 658 is that a company is not permitted to acquire its own shares, except in accordance with the Act. Any contravention is an offence committed by the company and by every officer in default, and the purported acquisition of shares is void. This provision confirms the rule established at common law by *Trevor v Whitworth* **[10.05]**, which recognised the issue was not a domestic matter concerned with compliance with the articles, or even a question of *vires* dependent upon the powers set out in the memorandum, but a matter of legality under the Companies Act itself.

In fact, both law and practice in this area have moved well away from the restrictive attitudes embodied in the general rule. This is because the general prohibition is subject to a number of substantial statutory exceptions, the most significant being the various rules permitting companies to *redeem* and to *repurchase* their own shares in defined circumstances. It is now quite common to see listed public companies advertise billion pound on-market and off-market share buy-backs, usually at a discount to the market price. The exercise demonstrates the company's commitment to capital discipline, and the terms maximise the economic value for the remaining shareholders, who benefit from the enhanced value of their shares through increased value and returns attributable to each share. The repurchase is, in effect, a judgement by the company that its shares are undervalued and represent a better investment than any available alternative acquisition of assets or investment in a business opportunity it owns or to which it has access. For different reasons, a company may also wish to repurchase its shares from employees who have shares under an employees' shares scheme: that too is possible. (See 'Repurchase of shares', p 544.)

Any redemption or repurchase effected otherwise than in full compliance with the statutory rules will not displace the general prohibition, however, so the purported transaction will be void. This makes it important to address the technical details of the Act very carefully. The repurchased shares are either cancelled or held by the company as so-called 'treasury shares' until cancelled or subjected to some other permitted disposal (see 'Protection of shareholders', p 545).

General rule: it is illegal for a company to acquire its own shares, except as provided in CA 2006. The common law rule is 'the rule in **Trevor v Whitworth***'.*

[10.05] Trevor v Whitworth (1887) 12 App Cas 409 (House of Lords)

LORD WATSON: . . . One of the main objects contemplated by the legislature, in restricting the power of limited companies to reduce the amount of their capital as set forth in the memorandum, is to protect the interests of the outside public who may become their creditors. In my opinion the effect of these statutory restrictions is to prohibit every transaction between a company and a shareholder, by means of which the money already paid to the company in respect of his shares is returned to him, unless the court has sanctioned the transaction. Paid-up capital may be diminished or lost in the course of the company's trading; that is a result which no legislation can prevent; but persons who deal with, and give credit to a limited company, naturally rely upon the fact that the company is trading with a certain amount of capital already paid, as well as upon the responsibility of its members for the capital remaining at call; and they are entitled to assume that no part of the capital which has been paid into the coffers of the company has been subsequently paid out, except in the legitimate course of its business.

When a share is forfeited or surrendered, the amount which has been paid upon it remains with the company, the shareholder being relieved of liability for future calls, whilst the share itself reverts to the company, bears no dividend, and may be re-issued. When shares are purchased at par, and transferred to the company, the result is very different. The amount paid up on the shares is returned to the shareholder; and in the event of the company continuing to hold the shares (as in the present case) is permanently withdrawn from its trading capital. It appears to me that . . . it is inconsistent with the essential nature of a company that it should become a member of itself. It cannot be registered as a shareholder to the effect of becoming debtor to itself for calls, or of being placed on the list of contributories in its own liquidation . . .

General exceptions to the prohibition in CA 2006 s 658

CA 2006 s 659 provides particular exceptions to the general prohibition in s 658.

These include instances where the company's *fully paid* shares are acquired for no consideration, so there is no detriment to creditors because the company's legal capital is unaffected.

It also includes instances where a court has ordered or approved the acquisition (eg by way of formal reduction of capital (see earlier), or by court order following complaints of unfair prejudice (see 'Unfairly prejudicial conduct of the company's affairs', pp 715ff)), or where the company has acquired its shares by forfeiture or surrender for non-payment of calls.[11]

Shares so acquired by a *public* company or by a nominee on its behalf must normally be cancelled within a maximum period of three years (one year in the case of shares which have been purchased by third parties with direct or indirect financial assistance from the company (see 'Financial assistance by a company for the acquisition of its own shares', pp 546ff)), and the company's share capital reduced accordingly, and pending cancellation or disposal no voting rights may be exercised in respect of those shares (s 662). If this were permitted, the directors of the company would have a voting power disproportionate to their personal stake as shareholders. (We may quite reasonably ask why these rules, including the prohibition on voting, are restricted to public companies.)

Redeemable shares

CA 2006 s 684 permits a company to issue redeemable shares if authorised by its articles (public companies) or if not prohibited by its articles (private companies), and so long as the company also has issued shares that are not redeemable.

CA 2006 ss 685–689 provide rules for the issue and redemption of such shares. Note that:

(i) the terms on which redeemable shares are issued is determined by the directors, provided they are authorised by the articles or by an ordinary resolution (even if this ordinary resolution effects a change to the articles) (s 685);

(ii) shares cannot be redeemed unless they are fully paid (s 686);

(iii) the shares must be paid for in full on redemption, unless the agreement between the company and holder allows for deferred payment (s 686);

[11] There is no return of capital to the member in such cases: the company keeps whatever payments have already been made on the shares, and under the terms of the company's articles the forfeited shares may normally be re-issued to another holder.

(iv)   private companies can redeem shares out of capital (although only subject to the onerous condition in ss 709–723, including a requirement for a directors' statement and an auditor's report, and a right for members and creditors to apply to court for the cancellation of the resolution); public companies must redeem out of distributable profits (see 'Permitted distributions', pp 565ff) or from the proceeds of a new share issue made for the purpose (s 687);

(v)   redeemed shares must then be cancelled, and the company must reduce its issued share capital by the nominal value of the cancelled shares (s 688);

(vi)   to the extent that the redemption is made out of profits, the company must also transfer an amount equivalent to the nominal value of the redeemed shares to a new capital account called the *'capital redemption reserve'*, which can only be reduced by transfer to the share capital account to pay up fully paid bonus shares, or otherwise as if it were part of the paid up share capital (s 733). In effect, this means that the company must have available a surplus equivalent to double the funds needed to effect the repurchase, and one-half has to be set aside and treated as capital thereafter;

(vii)   there are extensive disclosure provisions.

Repurchase of shares

The essential difference between a *repurchase* and a *redemption* is as follows: in the former, the buyer and seller need to agree to the terms and conditions of repurchase at the time of the repurchase; whereas with the latter, the shares will have been issued as redeemable shares, so that the terms and conditions of the reacquisition will be known from the outset. Subject to that essential difference and some recent relaxations over the restrictions on repurchase of shares in predefined circumstances, however, the two transactions are treated by CA 2006 in broadly similar ways.

A company's power to repurchase its own shares is broad: subject to any constraints or prohibitions in the company's articles, a company may repurchase its shares in accordance with the rules set out in CA 2006 ss 690ff.

Again, it is necessary to pay strict attention to the detailed wording of the Act itself, although with the warning that these sections are long-winded and not easy to follow. Note that different rules apply to a purchase by a company of its own shares *off the market* and a purchase by a (public) company of its own shares *on the market*.

The following rules apply to an *off-market* purchase:

(i)   it must be authorised by ordinary resolution (for both private and public companies) (ss 693A, 694, 697 and 700);

(ii)   for public companies, and for the purposes of employees' share schemes (defined in s 1166), this authority can be a 'standing authority', but not operating for longer than five years from the date on which the resolution is passed (ss 693A, 694, 697 and 700);

(iii)   the shareholders whose shares are to be repurchased cannot be counted in the vote (ss 695 and 698).

For an *on-market* purchase an ordinary resolution is required (s 701); the authority granted may be general or specific, and unconditional or conditional, but this authority cannot be granted for longer than five years from the date on which the resolution is passed.

Note, too, that:

(i)   the company's right to repurchase its shares cannot be assigned (s 704);

(ii)   shares cannot be repurchased unless they are fully paid shares (s 691(1));

(iii) the shares must be paid for in full at the time of repurchase, except where a private company is purchasing shares for the purposes of or pursuant to an employees' share scheme (s 691(2) and (3));

(iv) the permitted sources of the purchase funds for repurchases by private and public companies are largely the same as for redemptions (see earlier) (ss 692 and 705), but note a *de minimis* exception: if authorised by its articles, a private company may purchase its own shares out of capital up to the lower of £15,000 or 5% of the company's 'share capital' in any financial year without having to specify that the cash for the repurchase comes from distributable reserves (s 692(1ZA));

(v) when a private company uses capital to fund the purchase, a declaration of solvency is needed (ss 692, 709ff);

(vi) the rules on creation of a capital redemption reserve are the same as for redemptions (see earlier) (s 733);

(vii) the repurchased shares must be cancelled, and the company must reduce its issued share capital by the nominal value of the cancelled shares, *unless* the shares can be held and dealt with as *'treasury shares'*[12] in accordance with ss 724ff (s 706);[13] and

(viii) there are extensive disclosure provisions.

Protection of shareholders

The rules discussed in this section are primarily aimed at protecting creditors while allowing companies to use their resources in an efficient and financially sensible manner. But the rules have built-in protections for both exiting and remaining shareholders that are worth noting:

(i) *Share redemptions*: these work largely on the 'buyer beware' principle, since the exiting shareholder is aware of the exit terms before the shares are purchased, and the ordinary shareholders are assumed to know that the company may issue such shares (either as a general power (private companies), or as expressly permitted in the articles (public companies)).

(ii) *Share repurchases*: agreement to the terms of the repurchase is a matter of choice for the exiting shareholder, who cannot be forced to exit; and the non-exiting ordinary shareholders are protected, either by majority vote plus normal on-market purchase rules, or simply by the protective requirement of an ordinary resolution for off-market repurchases; and in both cases the intending exiting shareholders cannot vote in these general meetings. This is a rare formal protection in the context of shareholder voting.

➤ **Notes**

1. A statutory rule which has some links with these principles is that contained in CA 2006 s 136. This states that a company cannot itself be a member of a company which is its holding company, either directly or through a nominee (s 144).[14] The weakness

---

[12] Treasury shares cannot vote or receive dividends (other than by way of bonus shares); they can be sold (or used to fund a bonus issue or employee share scheme), or may be cancelled (ss 726–731).

[13] Note that in share redemptions, the shares must be cancelled and cannot be held as treasury shares: see 'Redeemable shares', p 543.

[14] There are exceptions for subsidiaries acting as personal representatives or trustees, or as authorised dealers in securities.

of this provision, however, is that it is confined in its operation to 'holding companies' and their subsidiaries as these terms are defined by ss 1159ff. There is nothing in these definitions which stops company A from owning 40% of the shares in company B, which itself has 40% of the shares in company A. If a majority of the board of each of the two companies consists of the same persons, they can usually, in practice, wield unrestricted control of both companies, regardless of the size of their own individual shareholdings.

2. In *Acatos & Hutcheson plc v Watson* [1995] BCC 446 it was held not to be unlawful for a company, A & H plc, to acquire all of the shares in another company, A Ltd, whose only asset was a 29.4% shareholding in A & H plc itself, even though it would not have been legitimate for it to have bought these latter shares directly.

3. Analogous to the acquisition of its own shares by a company is the taking of security over them. This, too, is forbidden by the Act in the case of *public* companies: see s 670, although there are exceptions when (i) the charge is to secure calls on partly paid shares, or (ii) it is an ordinary business dealing by a money-lending company.

➤ Questions

1. In the example given in Note 1, in which A Ltd and B Ltd have cross-shareholdings of 40% in each other, why is it that the board will usually have *de facto* control?

2. Is there any infringement of the principle of maintenance of capital in such a case?

Financial assistance by a company for the acquisition of its own shares

Another statutory rule that has links with the maintenance of capital principle is that contained in CA 2006 s 678, which imposes a prohibition against a *public* company or any of its subsidiaries[15] giving financial assistance to a person directly or indirectly for the purpose of an acquisition of its own shares.[16] Contravention of the prohibition constitutes an offence committed by every officer who is in default, and, more surprisingly, also by the company whose protection the section is intended to promote.

Before the introduction of the 2006 Act, the prohibition applied to all companies, although private companies had their own special 'whitewash' procedures which enabled them to avoid the application of the rule in certain circumstances. The exclusion of private companies from the prohibition means that there is no inhibition, at least from this source,[17] for private company 'management buy-outs' and other 'hiving-down' arrangements, under which a business or part of it is sold off to the existing managers or to similar entrepreneurial figures who wish to become owner-executives of the business but cannot finance the purchase except through the direct or indirect use of the company's own assets as security.

---

[15] But not a subsidiary which is a foreign company: CA 2006 s 1(1), as applied to s 678, and giving effect to *Arab Bank plc v Mercantile Holdings Ltd* [1994] Ch 71 (Millett J).

[16] There is also a prohibition on the provision of financial assistance by a *public* company subsidiary for the acquisition of shares in its *private* holding company (s 689).

[17] Although of course there are other control mechanisms, eg directors' duties ('General issues', pp 326ff), 'wrongful trading' provisions (*Re Produce Marketing Consortium Ltd (No 2)* **[16.16]**), and other CA 2006 and Insolvency Act 1986 (IA 1986) rules.

The general prohibition on the giving of financial assistance by a public company is required by the Second EU Company Law Directive (77/91/EEC). The prohibition in the UK Act extends to post-acquisition assistance (see s 678(3)), although only if the company in which the shares were acquired is a public company at the time that the assistance is given.[18]

'Financial assistance' is defined in s 677, and includes any provision by the public company (or its subsidiaries) of assistance by way of gifts, loans, security arrangements, guarantees and, indeed, any arrangements where the company fulfils its side of a deal but those of the other party remain unfulfilled. There is also a catch-all provision that includes 'any other financial assistance given by the company' where the company has no net assets, or where the net assets of the company are reduced to a material extent.

Examples of the kind of transaction in question are where the public company (or its subsidiary):

(i)   lends money to A to put A in funds so that he can buy shares from an existing member;

(ii) guarantees B's bank overdraft, and on the security of this the bank advances money to B so that she can buy shares in the company;

(iii) lends money to C so that C can repay a loan provided earlier by C's bank which C has already used to buy shares in the company;

(iv) buys an asset from D, on terms that materially reduce the net assets of the company, so that D can use the purchase money she receives to pay for shares in the company that she has agreed to buy.

The same kind of assistance can readily occur in a takeover: the person who seeks to buy all the shares, or a controlling block of shares, in a company may wish to use some of the company's own funds or assets to pay for the shares or provide security for their price.

If, in examples (i) to (iii), the purchaser of the shares repays the money he or she has borrowed, then no harm may be done. However, the risk is that the loan may never be repaid or that the bank may enforce the guarantee against the company after the customer has defaulted so that the company will have lost money which was part of its capital. Indeed, it may have been lost in favour of one of its shareholders so that the 'maintenance of capital' rule is infringed. Similar consequences necessarily follow in (iv) if the asset is not worth what the company has paid D for it. So it is not surprising that a statutory prohibition similar to s 678 has been in the Companies Acts since 1929.

Earlier versions of this provision (before 1981) were both much wider in their terms and notorious for the uncertainty of their language, which seemed to catch many quite innocent transactions. Responsible lending institutions and professional advisers were unwilling to be associated with schemes which might offend against the vague wording of the statute, and so companies were often prevented from taking a course of action which made good business sense and was not morally objectionable. At the same time, the relatively low penalty imposed for the offence was no real deterrent to the unscrupulous.

In 1981, amendments were made which were intended to define more precisely the conduct to be prohibited and introduce general and specific exemptions. These changes are

---

[18] It follows that where a company has re-registered as a private company since the shares were acquired and is a private company at the time the post-acquisition assistance is given, the prohibition will not apply. On the other hand, if at the time the shares were acquired the company was a private company, but at the time the post-acquisition assistance is given it has re-registered as a public company, the prohibition will apply.

all substantially carried forward in CA 2006 ss 677ff (apart from the provisions relating to private companies).[19]

There is a *general exemption* from the prohibition on the giving of financial assistance: such assistance is not prohibited if (i) the principal purpose of the assistance is not for an acquisition of shares, *or* (ii) the assistance is incidental to some other larger purpose of the company, *and* (in either case) the assistance is given in good faith in the interests of the company (ss 678(2) and (4), 679(2) and (4)). There are also a number of types of financial assistance (eg the payment of lawful dividends) that are specifically allowed (s 681), and a number of transactions that are exempted subject to specified conditions (s 682).

The principal cases on the meaning of 'financial assistance' and the application of the general exemptions are all somewhat controversial. The words of the Act must remain the primary source of guidance. The following cases that deal with the civil consequences of an infringement of the statute arose under older versions of the statutory provisions, but may still be regarded as authoritative on the issues cited (although not on the application of the prohibition itself).

The meaning of 'financial assistance'

The test of financial assistance is one of commercial substance and reality.

[10.06] Chaston v SWP Group Ltd [2002] EWCA Civ 1999 (Court of Appeal)

This case was decided under the Companies Act 1985 (CA 1985) provisions. CA 2006 s 678 would not apply, since the target company was a private company, but the Court of Appeal's discussion of the meaning of 'financial assistance' remains relevant.

The company allegedly providing financial assistance was the subsidiary, DRC Polymer Products Ltd (DRC) and its parent was Dunstable Rubber Company Holdings Ltd (DRCH). Chaston (C) was a director and majority shareholder in DRC. SWP wished to acquire the DRC Group by acquiring the shares of the holding company, DRCH, and needed a due diligence report on the Group for its members. Work for this report was done by the accountants, Deloitte and Touche (D&T). C agreed that D&T should invoice DRC for their fees for that work. It was not entirely clear whether DRC committed itself to pay the fees before the invoices were rendered, nor was it clear when the fees were paid by DRC.

The Court of Appeal held that the payment of D&T's fees by the subsidiary, DRC, was within the definition of unacceptable 'financial assistance' in CA 1985 s 152 [now CA 2006 s 677].

> ARDEN LJ: . . . It is clear from the way in which s 151 and s 152 [CA 2006 ss 678 and 677] are drafted that it covers financial assistance in many forms apart from loans (see for example the wide wording of s 152(3)). The general mischief, however, remains the same, namely that the resources of the target company and its subsidiaries should not be used directly or indirectly to assist the purchaser financially to make the acquisition. This may prejudice the interests of the creditors of the target or its group, and the interests of any shareholders who do not accept the offer to acquire their shares or to whom the offer is not made.

---

[19] Note that the prohibition does not have extra-territorial effect, so assistance can be given by an overseas subsidiary for the purchase of shares in its UK holding company: *Arab Bank plc v Mercantile Holdings Ltd* [1994] Ch 71. The fact that such assistance reduces the value of the subsidiary's shares, and so reduces the net assets of the holding company, does not turn the arrangement into financial assistance by the holding company: *AMG Global Nominees (Private) Ltd v Africa Resources Ltd* [2008] EWCA Civ 1278, [2009] 1 BCLC 281.

Thus although s 152 proscribes a number of forms of financial assistance, it does not define the words 'financial assistance'. It is clear from the authorities that what matters is the commercial substance of the transaction: 'The words ["financial assistance"] have no technical meaning and their frame of reference is the language of ordinary commerce' (per Hoffmann J in *Charterhouse v Tempest Diesels* [see later], approved by the Court of Appeal in *Barclays Bank plc v British & Commonwealth Holdings plc* [1996] 1 BCLC 1 at 40). . . .

It is thus apparent that ss 151 to 153 distinguish between various categories of transactions. First, there are the categories of financial assistance listed in s 152(1)(a)(i) to (iii) [CA 2006 s 677(1)(a)–(c)] which are prohibited whether or not there is any diminution in net assets, unless s 153 applies [ie certain exemption provisions noted later]. Second, there is financial assistance of a kind not specifically mentioned in s 152(1)(a)(i) to (iii). This does not contravene s 151 [CA 2006 s 678] provided the company has positive net assets and the reduction in actual net assets is immaterial [CA 2006 s 677(1)(d)]. (Again, I leave to one side the case of companies with no net assets.) Third, there are those which although carried out for the purpose of an acquisition of shares and have financial implications do not constitute financial assistance for the purposes of s 151. This category includes lawful dividends: see s 153(3) [CA 2006 s 681]. Fourth, there are transactions which although they constitute financial assistance within s 152(1)(a) are taken outside the prohibition in s 151 by the principal purpose defences in s 153(1) and (2) [CA 2006 s 678(2) and (4)]. Fifth, there are the transactions exempted by s 153(4), such as the lending of money by a money-lending company in the ordinary course of its business [CA 2006 s 682]. . . .

Here as a commercial matter assistance was clearly given. D&T received payment for their services and both the purchaser and the vendors were relieved of any obligation to pay for this service themselves. Mr Cunningham submits that s 151 should be restricted to assistance given to purchasers, alternatively to assistance given to vendors and purchasers. However, in so far as that point matters in this case there is no mandate in my judgment for reading any such limitation in that section. There is no reason why assistance which is paid to a subsidiary or associated company or other person nominated by one of the parties to the transaction should not be assistance contrary to the section. . . .

Mr Cunningham made a further submission that there was a distinction to be drawn between financial assistance given in advance of a transaction and financial assistance given in the course of a transaction. As to the former, this was not prohibited. On this, he relied on the four cases referred to above. In my judgment, this distinction is not justified by s 151. It prohibits financial assistance given 'directly or indirectly' and those words are sufficiently wide to cover 'pre-transactional' financial assistance. Moreover, s 151(1) provides that a transaction can offend the section even though a person is only 'proposing' to acquire shares. . . .

➤ **Note**

In this case it was irrelevant to the finding of financial assistance that:

(i)   The value of the fees (about £20,000) was trivial in comparison with the total consideration for the acquisition (about £2.55 million).

(ii) The assistance was not provided to the purchaser of the shares. The reality was that the instructions to D&T were given at least in part to enable SWP to conclude a due diligence exercise which was SWP's responsibility and for SWP's benefit and which should therefore have been paid by SWP. By paying for part of that exercise DRC had given financial assistance to SWP.

(iii) There had been no financial detriment to the company being acquired, the financial assistance was not given in advance of or in the course of the takeover, and the payment of the fees had no impact on the share price.

A more commercial approach in defining 'financial assistance'?

[10.07] Anglo Petroleum Ltd v TFB (Mortgages) Ltd [2007] EWCA Civ 456 (Court of Appeal)

The facts are complicated, since the alleged financial assistance involved a series of transactions. Shares in APL had been sold by APL's parent, Repsol, to another company (Kaluna) for £1. At the same time under a compromise agreement Repsol agreed to release APL's indebtedness to Repsol of £30 million and APL agreed to pay Repsol £6 million immediately and £9 million after six months. To secure that debt APL gave Repsol a charge over a number of petrol stations. Under the share purchase agreement, Kaluna guaranteed the performance by APL of its obligations under the compromise agreement and that guarantee was secured by a charge granted by Kaluna to Repsol over the shares in APL. Three months later APL borrowed £15 million from the respondent (TFB) under a credit agreement and used £9 million to effect early repayment of the £9 million owed to Repsol. The charge given by APL to Repsol was released and replaced by a security agreement between APL and TFB relating to the same or substantially the same properties. S had given a guarantee of APL's liabilities under the credit agreement. APL went into receivership and TFB claimed against APL and S. APL claimed against TFB on the ground that the security agreement was in breach of CA 1985 s 151 (CA 2006 ss 677 and 678). Preliminary issues were tried as to whether the credit transactions were accordingly illegal and void. APL argued that, by entering into the compromise agreement and giving the charge to Repsol, APL incurred liabilities and thereby gave financial assistance for the purpose of the acquisition of its shares by Kaluna within the meaning of s 151(1) and that by borrowing money from TFB and using it to discharge the balance of its indebtedness to Repsol, APL gave financial assistance for the purpose of discharging liabilities incurred for the purpose of the acquisition of the shares within the meaning of s 151(2), and that TFB knew the purpose of the loan and was therefore not entitled to enforce it; alternatively, that the guarantee given by Kaluna under the share purchase agreement and the supporting charge over the shares in APL were liabilities incurred by Kaluna for the purposes of its acquisition of the shares in APL, and that APL's repayment of its outstanding indebtedness to Repsol, using money borrowed from TFB, amounted to giving financial assistance for the purpose of discharging Kaluna's outstanding liabilities to Repsol.

TOULSON LJ:

1. This appeal [concerns] the validity of three agreements . . . The three agreements ('the credit transactions') were a Credit Agreement made between Anglo Petroleum Limited ('APL') as borrower and TFB (Mortgages) Limited ('TFB') as lender, a Security Agreement made between the same parties, and a Guarantee given to TFB by Mr Paul Sutton.

2. Three months before the credit transactions, APL's shares had been the subject of an acquisition. It is contended by APL that it gave financial assistance for the acquisition in breach of [CA 1985] s 151 and that this tainted the credit transactions. The judge rejected these contentions. . . .

Validity issues

19. APL advanced two arguments (referred to as Routes 1 and 2) in support of the contention that the credit transactions were illegal and void.

20. The focus of Route 1 was on APL's dealings with Repsol. It was contended that, by entering into the Compromise Agreement and the APL/Repsol charge, APL incurred liabilities and thereby gave financial assistance for the purpose of the acquisition of its shares by Kaluna within the meaning of s 151(1). By borrowing money from TFB and using it to discharge the balance of its indebtedness to Repsol, APL gave financial assistance for the purpose of discharging liabilities incurred for the purpose of the acquisition of the shares within the meaning of s 151(2). TFB knew the purpose of the loan and was therefore not entitled to enforce it. . . .

22. The focus of Route 2 was on Kaluna's dealings with Repsol. It was contended that the guarantee given by Kaluna under the Share Purchase Agreement and the supporting charge over the shares in APL were liabilities incurred by Kaluna for the purposes of its acquisition of the shares in APL, and that APL's repayment of its outstanding indebtedness to Repsol, using money borrowed from TFB, amounted to giving financial assistance for the purpose of discharging Kaluna's outstanding liabilities to Repsol. . . .

24. The essential issues on the appeal are:

(i) Did the payment of £9 million by APL to Repsol (from the TFB loan) in discharge of APL's indebtedness to Repsol constitute the giving of financial assistance within the meaning of s 151, either via Route 1 or via Route 2?

(ii) If so, is TFB prevented by the doctrine of illegality from enforcing the credit transactions? . . .

26. It is understandable that it has not been thought wise for the legislature to lay down a precise definition of financial assistance because of the risk that clever people would devise ways of defeating the purpose of the section while keeping within the letter of the law. However, the absence of a clear definition means that the section can give rise to uncertainties and has the potential to catch transactions which might be considered innocuous. In cases where its application is doubtful, it is important to remember its central purpose, to examine the commercial realities of the transaction and to bear in mind that it is a penal statute.

27. Recognition of the need to examine the commercial realities, rather than search for a legal formula for the meaning of 'financial assistance', comes from the judgment of Hoffmann J in *Charterhouse Investment Trust Limited v Tempest Diesels Limited* [1986] BCLC 1 at 10, cited by Arden LJ in *Chaston* **[10.06]** at para 17:

> 'There are two elements in the commission of an offence under s 54 [the section that preceded s 151]. The first is the giving of financial assistance and the second is that it should have been given "for the purpose of or in connection with", in this case, a purchase of shares . . . There is no definition of giving financial assistance in the section, although some examples are given. The words have no technical meaning and their frame of reference is in my judgment the language of ordinary commerce. One must examine the commercial realities of the transaction and decide whether it can properly be described as the giving of financial assistance by the company, bearing in mind that the section is a penal one and should not be strained to cover transactions which are not fairly within it.'

28. The court would not in any event strain a statute to cover transactions which are not fairly within it, but the fact that the statute is penal provides an additional reason for caution in doubtful cases. . . .

34. There was discussion during the course of the argument about the meaning of the word 'purpose', and the court was referred to the observations of Lord Oliver in *Brady v Brady* **[10.08]**, 779–780, where he drew a distinction between a purpose and a reason for forming a purpose.

35. A purpose requires a mind. The relevant purpose is that of the company or subsidiary, through its relevant officer or officers, in giving the alleged assistance. At stages of his argument Mr Martin came close to eliding purpose and effect, arguing that if a person does an act knowing that it will have a particular consequence it must be his purpose (or at least one of his purposes) in doing the act to produce the consequence. There is no must about it. Whether the consequence was the actor's purpose is a matter for inference from all the circumstances. There may be many situations in life in which a person does a particular act knowing that it will have a particular consequence, but without that consequence being the purpose for which he does the act.

Financial assistance—conclusions

43. . . . Standing back from the minutiae of the arguments, and looking at the transactions attacked by APL from a commercial perspective, I do not consider that they exemplify the mischief against which the section is aimed.

44. Mr Martin's arguments are ingenious and were skilfully deployed, but in my view the commercial reality is that APL and Mr Sutton are seeking to avoid their liabilities to TFB, for what was in essence a straightforward commercial loan, by a strained reading of the statute.

45. I begin with the Compromise Agreement, the nature of which was that APL's liability to Repsol was reduced. I do not consider that it should be characterised as giving financial assistance to the purchaser on account of the fact that it thereby made the company a more attractive acquisition and can thus be said to have smoothed the path to its acquisition. Just because it smoothed the path to the acquisition, it does not follow that it amounted to financial assistance. Nor can the APL/Repsol charge, by which APL gave security to Repsol for its reduced indebtedness, properly be described as financial assistance to the purchaser.

46. As to the purpose of the transactions from APL's viewpoint, the judge fairly described them as 'a bona fide restructuring of APL's indebtedness with a significant reduction in exchange for a security'. Repsol's reason for wanting to restructure APL's indebtedness was in order to sell the shares to Kaluna and to obtain security for the reduced amount of the indebtedness, but that does not make APL's purpose in entering into the restructure that of giving financial assistance to the purchaser.

47. In any event, the liabilities undertaken by APL under the Compromise Agreement did not come within any of the categories identified in s 152 (1) as capable of amounting to financial assistance under s 151. The APL/Repsol charge was ancillary to the Compromise Agreement in that its purpose was to secure APL's obligation under the Compromise Agreement. The giving of security over a company's assets can come within s 152(1)(a)(ii), but the APL/Repsol charge did not in my judgment amount to giving financial assistance within s 151 in the present circumstances where it was merely a means of enforcing an obligation of APL which did not involve the giving of financial assistance.

48. Moving on from the issues under s 151(1) to s 151(2), the next step of Mr Martin's argument presents further difficulty. He accepts that APL's agreement to pay £15 million to Repsol under the Compromise Agreement was not unlawful (because it did not fall within s 152(1)), but he submits that APL's payment of £9 million in discharge of that obligation was unlawful. That is a surprising proposition and goes against the grain of the authorities that the repayment by a company of its lawful indebtedness is not prohibited by s 151. Mr Martin does not dispute the correctness of those authorities, but he seeks to distinguish them by reference to the cost of the borrowing from TFB.

49. I am not persuaded that this [is] a valid ground of distinction. Mr Martin makes the point that the cost of borrowing reduced APL's assets, but I do not see how logically this converts the discharge of the company's indebtedness from a lawful act into the giving of unlawful financial assistance. . . .

51. As to the Security Agreement (between APL and TFB), I agree with the judge's reasoning that 'if it is lawful for a company to repay its own indebtedness and there is a genuine commercial justification it must also equally be lawful [for] the company to assist that repayment by providing security.' . . .

53. Accordingly, I reject the Route 1 argument that APL incurred a liability for the purpose of Kaluna's acquisition of the shares or (which would require a tortuous reading of the statute) that it gave financial assistance for the purpose of discharging such liability by repaying £9 million to Repsol. As to the Route 2 argument, there is no dispute that Kaluna undertook obligations for the purpose of its acquisition of the shares, but I reject the argument that APL by repaying its own indebtedness to Repsol gave financial assistance for the purpose of discharging Kaluna's liabilities. . . . [And see the discussion of illegality, 'Consequences when a transaction breaches the prohibition', pp 558ff.]

85. I would dismiss the appeal.

SMITH and MUMMERY LJJ concurred.

➤ Note

Kaluna could clearly afford to pay £1 for the shares it acquired. The issue of 'financial assistance' arose because of the associated compromise agreement over the £30 million debt that APL owed to Repsol. The wide statutory definition of financial assistance makes these related transactions material (now see CA 2006 s 677).

Further guidance on the meaning of 'financial assistance'

The following cases were all decided under the predecessors to CA 2006 ss 677 and 678, but to the extent that they discuss the meaning of 'financial assistance' they remain relevant to the interpretation of the 2006 Act.[20]

On its terms, *Chaston* **[10.06]** adopts a market-friendly test of financial assistance, looking to the 'commercial substance and reality' of the transaction; but in its application to the facts, the Court of Appeal's approach might lead to the conclusion that many transactions will fall foul of the provisions and will find no relief in the 'principal purpose' test.

Earlier and later cases have adopted a more 'commercial' approach, often finding as a matter of commercial reality that *no* financial assistance has been given. *Chaston* **[10.06]** may well come to be regarded as a high-water mark, much like *Brady* **[10.08]** on the 'principal purpose'/'main purpose' exceptions. See:

(i) *Charterhouse Investment Trust Ltd v Tempest Diesels Ltd* [1986] BCLC 1: this case was decided under the repealed Companies Act 1948 (CA 1948) s 54, and concerned a 'management buy-out' transaction under which Charterhouse hived off a subsidiary company, Tempest, by selling its entire shareholding to one of its managers, Allam. Hoffmann J was asked to decide whether a surrender of tax losses by Tempest to Charterhouse, as part of the transaction, constituted financial assistance. In ruling that it did not, he said:

> . . . There is no definition of giving financial assistance in the section, although some examples are given. The words have no technical meaning and their frame of reference is in my judgment the language of ordinary commerce. One must examine the commercial realities of the transaction and decide whether it can properly be described as the giving of financial assistance by the company, bearing in mind that the section is a penal one and should not be strained to cover transactions which are not fairly within it.

The *Belmont* case **[10.10]** indicates that the sale of an asset by the company at a fair value can properly be described as giving financial assistance if the effect is to provide the purchaser of its shares with the cash needed to pay for them. It does not matter that the company's balance sheet is undisturbed in the sense that the cash paid out is replaced by an asset of equivalent value. In the case of a loan by a company to a creditworthy purchaser of its shares, the balance sheet is equally undisturbed but the loan plainly constitutes giving financial assistance. It follows that if the only or main purpose of such a transaction is to enable the purchaser to buy the shares, the section is contravened. But the *Belmont* case is of limited assistance in deciding whether or not an altogether different transaction amounts to giving financial assistance.

The need to look at the commercial realities means that one cannot consider the surrender letter [relating to the tax losses] in isolation. Although it constituted a collateral contract, it was in truth part of a composite transaction under which

---

[20] In applying those findings to cases concerning acquisitions of shares in *private* companies, however, they have been superseded by CA 2006 s 678.

Tempest both received benefits and assumed burdens. It is necessary to look at this transaction as a whole and decide whether it constituted the giving of financial assistance by Tempest. This must involve a determination of where the net balance of financial advantage lay. I see no contradiction between this view and anything which was said in the *Belmont* case. In *Belmont* the company made cash available to the purchaser. This amounted to giving financial assistance and no less so because it was done without any net transfer of value by the company. On the facts of this case there is no question of cash being provided and the only way in which it can even plausibly be suggested that Tempest gave financial assistance is if it made a net transfer of value which reduced the price Mr Allam would have had to pay for the shares if the transaction as a whole had not taken place.

(ii) *MT Realisations Ltd v Digital Equipment Co Ltd* [2003] EWCA Civ 494, [2003] 2 BCLC 117, CA: the Court of Appeal held that there was no financial assistance in breach of CA 1985 s 151, since the chosen method of arranging the share purchase reflected the commercial realities of the deal, not some disguised form of financial assistance. The claimant, MTR, was a subsidiary in the Digital group of companies, which were suppliers of computer equipment. MTR was loss-making and insolvent. It owed £8 million to another company in the group, repayable on demand. MTI bought all the shares in MTR from Digital for £1, and also bought the £8 million loan for £6.5 million, payable in instalments. The facts are complicated, but the fundamental claim was that when money due to MTR was paid to MTI and then used by MTI to pay the loan instalments to Digital, financial assistance was given for the purchase of MTR's shares. The Court of Appeal rejected the argument on the basis that: (i) it was never claimed that the shares were worth more than £1, or that MTI could not afford £1, so no assistance was needed; (ii) the liability to make the loan repayments was not incurred for the purpose of acquiring the shares; and (iii) when MTR made payments to MTI under the loan agreement, it was only paying a debt which it already owed before any of the acquisition dealings were commenced.

(iii) *Dyment v Boyden* [2004] EWCA Civ 1586, [2005] 1 WLR 792, CA: the applicant and the two respondents entered into partnership to run a residential care home. The real property was owned by the partners in equal shares. The business was operated through a company, and the partners were each directors of the company. The company's registration under the Registered Homes Act 1984 was cancelled by the local authority when one of the respondents was charged with assault. The partnership was then dissolved by an agreement under which the respondents transferred their shares in the company to the applicant who in turn transferred her interest in the property to the respondents, who then granted a 21-year lease of the property to the company at a rental well above the market rate. The applicant contended that payment of the additional rent above the market rate was 'financial assistance' because it had the effect of reducing the company's net assets to a material extent, and since that assistance had been given in relation to a transaction involving the acquisition by the applicant of the respondents' shares, it had therefore been given either directly or indirectly for the purposes of that acquisition, contrary to s 151(1). The Court of Appeal affirmed the finding of the trial judge that the rent insisted on by the respondents was simply not linked to the acquisition of the shares, and not agreed 'for the purpose of' acquiring the shares.

Exceptions to the statutory prohibition

Recall the statutory exceptions noted at 'The meaning of "financial assistance"', p 548. Here the focus is on the 'purpose' exceptions.

Proof by the company that the 'principal purpose' is not the acquisition of shares, or that the acquisition is merely 'an incidental part of a larger purpose' requires proof of something more than an alternative reason why the transaction was entered into.

[10.08] Brady v Brady [1989] AC 755 (House of Lords)

A group of companies run by the Brady brothers, Bob and Jack, had a haulage and drinks business in Barrow-in-Furness. Following differences between the two brothers, it was agreed that they should divide the business in two, Jack taking the haulage side and Bob the drinks side. A complex scheme of reconstruction was drawn up under which drinks business assets were transferred from the principal company ('Brady') to a new company controlled by Bob. Jack (through his company Motoreal) acquired his brother's shares in Brady. This transfer, it was conceded, involved the giving of financial assistance by Brady towards discharging the liability of its holding company ('Motoreal') for the price of shares which Motoreal had purchased in Brady, and so there was a prima facie infringement of CA 1985 s 151 [CA 2006 s 678]. Accordingly, when Jack brought proceedings for specific performance of the agreement, Bob (who had had second thoughts) argued that the transaction was illegal.[21] However, Jack contended that the financial assistance was an incidental part of a larger purpose of the company, namely the resolution of the conflict and deadlock between the brothers which was paralysing its business and threatening to lead to its liquidation, so that the exception set out in s 153(2)(a) [CA 2006 s 678(2)] applied. The House of Lords rejected this argument: the alleged 'larger purpose' was nothing more than the reason why the transaction was entered into. However, it ruled that an order for specific performance should be made because Brady was a solvent private company and could lawfully give financial assistance by following the procedure prescribed by ss 155–158 [abolished by CA 2006, since s 678 no longer applies to private companies].

LORD OLIVER OF AYLMERTON: Where I part company both from the trial judge and from the Court of Appeal is on the question of whether para (a) [of CA 1985 s 153(2), now CA 2006 s 678(2)] can, on any reasonable construction of the subsection, be said to have been satisfied. As O'Connor LJ observed, the section is not altogether easy to construe. It first appeared as part of s 42 of the Companies Act 1981 and it seems likely that it was introduced for the purpose of dispelling any doubts resulting from the query raised in *Belmont Finance Corpn Ltd v Williams Furniture Ltd (No 2)* **[10.10]** whether a transaction entered into partly with a genuine view to the commercial interests of the company and partly with a view to putting a purchaser of shares in the company in funds to complete his purchase was in breach of s 54 of the Companies Act 1948. The ambit of the operation of the section is, however, far from easy to discern, for the word 'purpose' is capable of several different shades of meaning. This much is clear, that para (a) is contemplating two alternative situations. The first envisages a principal and, by implication, a subsidiary purpose [CA 2006 s 678(2)(a)]. The inquiry here is whether the assistance given was principally in order to relieve the purchaser of shares in the company of his indebtedness resulting from the acquisition or whether it was principally for some other purpose—for instance, the acquisition from the purchaser of some asset which the company requires for its business. That is the situation envisaged by Buckley LJ in the course of his judgment in the *Belmont Finance* case as giving rise to doubts. That is not this case, for the purpose of the assistance here was simply and solely to reduce the indebtedness incurred by Motoreal . . . The alternative situation is where it is not suggested that the financial assistance was intended to achieve any other object than the reduction or discharge of the indebtedness but where that result (ie the reduction or

---

[21] It was also claimed that the transfer by Brady of its assets was *ultra vires*. In the Court of Appeal, Nourse LJ accepted this contention; but the House of Lords held that the transfer was within the company's objects.

discharge) is merely incidental to some larger purpose of the company [CA 2006 s 678(2)(b)]. Those last three words are important. What has to be sought is some larger overall corporate purpose in which the resultant reduction or discharge is merely incidental. The trial judge found Brady's larger purpose to be that of freeing itself from the deadlock and enabling it to function independently and this was echoed in the judgment of O'Connor LJ where he observed that the answer 'embraces avoiding liquidation, preserving its goodwill and the advantages of an established business'. Croom-Johnson LJ found the larger purpose in the reorganisation of the whole group. My Lords, I confess that I have not found the concept of a 'larger purpose' easy to grasp, but if the paragraph is to be given any meaning that does not in effect provide a blank cheque for avoiding the effective application of s 151 in every case, the concept must be narrower than that for which the appellants contend.

The matter can, perhaps, most easily be tested by reference to s 153(1)(a) where the same formula is used. Here the words are 'or the giving of the assistance for that purpose' (ie the acquisition of shares) 'is but an incidental part of some larger purpose of the company'. The words 'larger purpose' must here have the same meaning as the same words in sub-s (2)(a). In applying sub-s (1)(a) one has, therefore, to look for some larger purpose in the giving of financial assistance than the mere purpose of the acquisition of the shares and to ask whether the giving of assistance is a mere incident of that purpose. My Lords, 'purpose' is, in some contexts, a word of wide content but in construing it in the context of the fasciculus of sections regulating the provision of finance by a company in connection with the purchase of its own shares there has always to be borne in mind the mischief against which s 151 is aimed. In particular, if the section is not, effectively, to be deprived of any useful application, it is important to distinguish between a purpose and the reason why a purpose is formed. The ultimate reason for forming the purpose of financing an acquisition may, and in most cases probably will, be more important to those making the decision than the immediate transaction itself. But 'larger' is not the same thing as 'more important' nor is 'reason' the same as 'purpose'. If one postulates the case of a bidder for control of a public company financing his bid from the company's own funds—the obvious mischief at which the section is aimed—the immediate purpose which it is sought to achieve is that of completing the purchase and vesting control of the company in the bidder. The reasons why that course is considered desirable may be many and varied. The company may have fallen on hard times so that a change of management is considered necessary to avert disaster. It may merely be thought, and no doubt would be thought by the purchaser and the directors whom he nominates once he has control, that the business of the company will be more profitable under his management than it was heretofore. These may be excellent reasons but they cannot, in my judgment, constitute a 'larger purpose' of which the provision of assistance is merely an incident. The purpose and the only purpose of the financial assistance is and remains that of enabling the shares to be acquired and the financial or commercial advantages flowing from the acquisition, whilst they may form the reason for forming the purpose of providing assistance, are a by-product of it rather than an independent purpose of which the assistance can properly be considered to be an incident. Now of course in the instant case the reason why the reorganisation was conceived in the first place was the damage being occasioned to the company and its shareholders by reason of the management deadlock, and the deadlock was the reason for the decision that the business should be split in two, so that the two branches could be conducted independently. What prompted the particular method adopted for carrying out the split was the commercial desirability of keeping Brady in being as a corporate entity. That involved, in effect, Jack buying out Bob's interest in Brady and it was, presumably, the fact that he did not have free funds to do this from his own resources that dictated that Brady's own assets should be used for the purpose. No doubt the acquisition of control by Jack was considered, at any rate by Jack and Robert [Jack's nephew], who were and are Brady's directors, to be beneficial to Brady. Indeed your Lordships have been told that the business has thrived under independent management. But this is merely the result, and no doubt the intended result, of Jack's assumption of control and however one analyses the transaction the only purpose that can be discerned in the redemption of loan stock is the payment in tangible form of the price payable to enable the Brady shares to be acquired and ultimately vested in Jack or a company controlled by him. The scheme of reorganisation was framed and designed to give Jack and Robert control of Brady for the best of reasons, but to say that the 'larger purpose' of Brady's financial assistance is to be found in the scheme of reorganisation itself is to say only that the larger purpose was the acquisition of the Brady shares on their behalf. For my part, I do not think that a larger purpose can be found in the benefits considered to be likely to flow or the disadvantages considered to be likely to be avoided by the acquisition which it was the purpose of the assistance to facilitate. The acquisition was not a mere incident of the scheme devised to break the deadlock. It was the essence of the scheme itself and the object which the scheme set out to achieve. In my judgment therefore, sub-s (2)(a) of s 153 is not satisfied and if the matter rested there the appeal ought to fail on that ground.

[His Lordship went on to hold that, since the transaction involved a private company, an order for specific performance could be made, the parties being directed to follow the 'whitewash' procedure in CA 1985 ss 155–158.[22]]

LORDS KEITH OF KINKEL, HAVERS, TEMPLEMAN and GRIFFITHS concurred.

➤ Notes

1. This was regarded a very restrictive interpretation of statutory provisions which, it had been widely believed, were intended not only to clarify the former law but also to make it possible for many routine business transactions—some of them of long-standing—to go ahead without the fear that they might be illegal because they incidentally involved a breach of the financial assistance rule. This uncertainty is very costly—it has been estimated that well over £20 million a year is spent on obtaining legal advice in an endeavour to ensure that proposed transactions do not fall foul of 'financial assistance' prohibitions. In consequence, there has been a demand ever since *Brady* for further reform of the law. That has been given, at least to some extent, by CA 2006. *Brady*, being concerned with a private company, would now not be caught by the prohibition at all. But the uncertainty in interpreting the 'purpose' exceptions, as illustrated by *Brady*, unfortunately remains in full. The reason given is that, at least for public companies, the UK must keep in place a provision sufficiently strong to meet the requirements of the Second EU Company Law Directive. In the government's view, none of the proposed changes in the wording of CA 2006 s 678(4)(a) sufficed to meet the Directive's requirements *and* clarify the 'purpose' exception.

2. Note the comments on 'purpose' by Toulson LJ in *Anglo Petroleum Ltd v TFB (Mortgages) Ltd* [10.07].

3. Despite this gloomy assessment of the uncertainties in the application of the section, there are instances where the 'principal purpose' test has been relied upon to exempt transactions from being classed as 'financial assistance' notwithstanding the company's knowledge that its moneys would be used to fund the acquisition of shares in the company or its holding company, although only as part of a larger scheme or purpose: see, for example, *Re Uniq plc* [2011] EWHC 749 (Ch). Here a restructuring scheme was devised to provide a solution to the imminent insolvency threatened by large pension fund deficits. Intergroup transactions provided funds which would be used to purchase shares in the target company and thus provide a necessary injection of capital. In these circumstances, David

---

[22] Given the detailed legal examination that this problem must have been subjected to, it seems remarkable that no one had thought of this option well before the case was concluded in the House of Lords.

Richards J held that 'notwithstanding that it is known and intended that it [the funds] will be used by Newco to pay up the new shares. Even if that could properly be regarded as a purpose of the loans and payment, I would be satisfied that the principal purpose was to obtain the release and that they were made in good faith in the interests of the relevant companies, so falling within [CA 2006] s.678(2).'

4. Recall, too, that the prohibition now applies only to public companies. This was material in *Paros plc v Worldlink Group plc* [2012] EWHC 394 (Comm), where a public company entered into a payment obligation (a 'break fee') which prima facie infringed the prohibition on financial assistance (as described later), but where the obligation would only arise on fulfilment of a condition precedent that the public company be re-registered as a private company. In such circumstances the court held there was no infringement of CA 2006 s 678. Jonathan Hirst QC, sitting as a Deputy High Court judge, held:

> 72. In my judgment, . . . the break fee . . . did amount to the giving of unlawful financial assistance contrary to s.151 [of CA 1985, now see CA 2006 s 678]. It is clear that s.151 applies to cases where a person is proposing to acquire shares in the company, just as much as where he is actually acquiring them. Here Paros was proposing to buy the issued shares in Worldlink. It would clearly have constituted unlawful financial assistance for Worldlink to agree to pay Paros's fees and costs incurred in connection with the acquisition whilst Worldlink was a public company. [Although the] break fee was only payable in the event that the acquisition fell through, [it provided for] Worldlink to bear all ParOS' and its advisers' agreed fees and costs. . . . it was plainly intended to ensure that, if Worldlink withdrew from the negotiations before it was re-registered as a private company, ParOS was certain to recover a minimum contribution towards its expenses. As such the fee was 'smoothing the path to the acquisition of the shares' . . . The break fee was not a mere inducement to enter into the transaction (if relevant) . . . it amounted to 'other financial assistance' and that it materially reduced the net assets of Worldlink, given that they were negative at the time.
>
> 73. On the other hand, the undertaking to pay Paros' fees and costs after it re-registered as a private company does not in my judgment infringe s.151. The commitment was subject to a condition precedent that Worldlink re-registered. Unless and until it did so, there was no obligation to pay ParOS' fees and expenses. If Paros did re-register, the financial assistance would not be caught by s.151 because it does not apply to private companies. I think it is taking s.151 too far to hold that because the conditional promise was given at a time when Worldlink was still a public company, it is unlawful.[23] There is support for this conclusion at the highest level: see *Brady v. Brady* **[10.08]** where the House of Lords granted an order for specific performance of an agreement to give financial assistance where there was a means by which the appellants could perform the contract lawfully by using the 'whitewashing procedure'. The parties were to be presumed to intend that the contract was to be performed in the lawful rather than the unlawful manner: per Lord Oliver of Aylmerton at p. 783D. Here the position is *a fortiori*. The obligation to pay Paros' fees and costs only arose if the company re-registered as a private company, when it would become lawful.

Consequences when a transaction breaches the prohibition

The only statutory sanction for breaching the financial assistance prohibition is that an offence is committed by the company and by every officer of the company who is in default (being an offence that can lead to a prison term): CA 2006 s 680. Note that criminal

---

[23] By contrast, see the comment made earlier in the judgment that assistance is generally considered to be given on the date when the commitment to provide it is entered into, rather than the date on which the money is paid: *Parlett v Guppys (Bridport) Ltd* [1996] BCC 299. This is because the net assets of the company making the commitment are impaired at the date it is given.

liability is imposed on the company itself, even though the provisions are allegedly designed to *protect* the company against disposal of its assets.

In practice the civil consequences are usually even more important, but for a time they seemed more troubling. The difficulty arose from the wording of the section (which has not changed in successive re-enactments): instead of making it illegal for the purchaser to *accept* financial assistance, CA 2006 s 678 makes it illegal *for the company* (or its subsidiary) to *give* financial assistance. This suggested to some judges that the object was not to protect the company, but to punish it, and for a while the consequences of illegality were analysed in that rather counter-intuitive way.[24]

Although older judicial authorities in this area have not been overruled, and are extracted here, it is not at all clear how relevant they remain, at least in some of their detail. This is because the whole area of 'illegality' is in a state of uncertainty following comments in *Bilta v Nazir* **[3.29]** (see especially Lord Neuberger, at [15], p 168). In addition, the specific question of when a company can sue its officers or third parties in such contexts has attracted a good deal of recent judicial attention: see especially *Bilta v Nazir* **[3.29]** and *Moulin Global* (HKCFA) **[3.30]**, both of which emphasise the importance of context in deciding legal outcomes. With that warning, the following cases merit study, but with a critical eye.

A transaction which infringes CA 2006 s 678 is illegal and unenforceable by either party.

[10.09] Re Hill and Tyler Ltd (In Administration) [2004] EWHC 1261 (Ch) (Chancery Division)

The facts are immaterial.

RICHARD SHELDON QC: The argument can be broken down into three questions: (1) Is a contract involving the provision of financial assistance in contravention of s 151 [CA 2006 s 678], even where the whitewash procedure is available but not properly complied with, void and unenforceable as a matter of statutory interpretation of s 151? (2) If not, under the common law, is such a contract illegal as to its formation? (3) If not, is such a contract illegal as to its performance?

I consider first whether every contract which constitutes financial assistance within s 151 is rendered void and unenforceable as a matter of statutory interpretation. In *Chitty on Contracts* (29th edn) paras 16-141 to 16-146 the following is stated (citations omitted):

'Unenforceability by statute . . . arises where a statute itself on its true construction deprives one or both of the parties of their civil remedies under the contract in addition to, or instead of, imposing a penalty upon them. If the statute does so, it is irrelevant whether the parties meant to break the law or not . . .' (para 16-141) 'where the statute is silent as to the civil rights of the parties but penalises the making or performance of the contract, the courts consider whether the Act, on its true construction, is intended to avoid contracts of the class to which the particular contract belongs or whether it merely prohibits the doing of some particular act . . . it is important to note that where a contract or its performance is implicated with breach of statute this does not entail that the contract is avoided. Where the Act does not expressly deprive the plaintiff of his civil remedies under the contract the appropriate question to ask is whether, having regard to the Act and the evils against which it was intended to guard and the circumstances

---

[24] See especially the much criticised case of *Victor Battery Co Ltd v Curry's Ltd* [1946] Ch 242. This case has now been disapproved or not followed in a series of subsequent cases, and is accepted as wrong.

in which the contract was made and to be performed, it would in fact be against public policy to enforce it.' (para 16-145)

'If, on the true construction of the statute, "the contract be rendered illegal, it can make no difference, in point of law, whether the statute which makes it so has in mind the protection of the revenue or any other object. The sole question is whether the statute means to prohibit the contract". If, on the other hand, the object of the statute is the protection of the public from possible injury or fraud, or is the promotion of some object of public policy, the inference is that contracts made in contravention of its provisions are prohibited.' (para 16-146)

Applying these principles, and having regard to the mischief to which s 151 is directed, I consider that contracts which are entered into in breach of s 151 are rendered illegal by that section. The section provides that it is 'not lawful' for a company to give financial assistance directly or indirectly for the purpose of the acquisition of its own shares. It seems to me to follow that contracts which are entered into in contravention of that section are illegal. In consequence, such contracts are void and unenforceable. Although the consequences on an innocent party may be harsh, it is well recognised that the courts will not lend their assistance to transactions which are rendered unlawful by statute.

➤ Notes

1. In *Anglo Petroleum Ltd v TFB (Mortgages) Ltd* **[10.07]**, Toulson LJ made the following comments on illegality:

54. There are different ways in which a statute may give rise to an argument that a contract was illegal in its formation and therefore unenforceable. They are (1) that its formation was prohibited by statute, (2) that it was a contract to do an act prohibited by statute or (3) that . . . it was entered into for the purpose of doing an act prohibited by statute. Mr Martin argued that the Credit Agreement was unlawful on grounds 2 and 3. Since I agree with the judge that the use of the funds borrowed by APL from TFB did not contravene s 151, it is not strictly necessary to decide whether the credit transactions would have been unlawful if the use of the funds had contravened the section. . . . [but, had the transactions been in breach of s 151 . . .]

83. It is hard to see how public policy would be served by invalidating a contract which is not unlawful in its terms and which a reasonable person in the position of TFB would have seen as an ordinary, innocuous commercial transaction. It is also hard to see how public policy would be served by stretching the principle that ignorance of the law is no excuse so as to attribute to the party seeking to enforce the contract an unrealistic knowledge that the other party intended to act illegally. . . .

84. In the present case it was reasonable for TFB to regard the loan as an ordinary commercial loan made in the course of its business. There is no good reason why public policy should have required TFB to investigate whether the proposed use of the loan would amount to a breach of s 151, and the law would be out of touch with reality if it deemed TFB to have knowledge that the proposed use would be a breach. Even if Mr Martin were right in his argument about the effect of the section, this would have been far from obvious to a lawyer, let alone to a party in the position of TFB. Moreover, as Mr Todd pointed out, even if s 151 was potentially engaged, it would not necessarily follow that it would be breached, because if APL had itself been aware of a problem it would have had the possibility of using the whitewash procedure.

85. Even if the use of the funds had involved a breach of s 151, the judge was right to hold that the Credit Agreement, the Security Agreement and the Guarantee were not illegal. The agreements did not necessitate any breach of the law, and it was not the purpose of TFB in

entering into them to procure or assist the commission of conduct which would be a breach of the law. In the circumstances, it would not be just to equate TFB's knowledge of APL's intended use of the loan with knowledge of its alleged illegality, nor would it be just to draw an inference of a shared unlawful design if a reasonable person in the position of TFB would have seen it as an ordinary commercial transaction.

2. An otherwise unenforceable obligation to pay a break fee was rendered enforceable in *Paros plc v Worldlink Group plc* (see Note 4 following *Brady v Brady* **[10.08]**, p 558), per Jonathan Hirst QC:

80. It seems to me that the correct analysis is that illegality renders a contract unenforceable rather than void, if by void is meant that the agreement was never made. It is clear that property can pass under an illegal contract, and in some circumstances a Court will enforce a contract which involves an element of illegality. If the contract was truly void, in the sense that it is to be treated as never having existed, it is difficult to see how that could occur. The distinction between void and unenforceable is in any event narrow. The *Shorter Oxford Dictionary* defines 'void' as 'having no legal force, not binding in law; (legally) invalid, ineffective Freq. in *null and void*'. The essence of a contractual obligation is that it is enforceable. If it is not, then it is ineffective as a contract.

81. In any event, whether the obligation to pay a break fee is to be regarded as at 25 February 2009 as void or unenforceable, or both, should to make no real difference. On 4 March 2009, the parties varied the HoT in a significant way. Their objective intention was clearly that clause 5.1 should apply in full to the arrangement as varied. The break clause ceased to be unlawful under s.151 . It is to be treated as either reinstated or rendered enforceable. There is no longer any reason why the Court needs, as a matter of public policy, to decline to enforce the break fee obligation. After all the parties would have been entirely free to tear up the HoT and to conclude a new contract. It is irrational to say that they could not achieve the same result by varying the HoT.

➤ Question

What *is* the appropriate civil response in these cases? While it is obvious that a court should not *enforce* contracts made in breach of the financial assistance prohibition, should the remedy not be a simple 'unwinding' of the impermissible transfers so made? Contrast the response to the void contract in *Westdeutsche Landesbank Girozentrale v Islington LBC* [1996] AC 669, HL (an unjust enrichment case), where the borough council 'illegally' entered into a swaps contract. Is the 'illegality' here one which ought to be punished further?

Although a company that is party to a transaction which infringes CA 2006 s 678 cannot enforce the illegal contract, it is not prevented by law from suing others who have participated in the wrongdoing, for example in an action for damages for conspiracy.

[10.10] Belmont Finance Corpn Ltd v Williams Furniture Ltd [1979] Ch 250 (Court of Appeal)

It was alleged that four of the defendants, with the connivance of two of the three directors of the plaintiff company, had sold its property worth £60,000 for a price of £500,000 and that the four had then used the money to purchase all the issued shares in the plaintiff. The company claimed damages for conspiracy against the defendants. It was held that the company could sue, despite the fact that it had been itself a party to the transaction which infringed the statute.

> BUCKLEY LJ: In the course of the argument in this court counsel for the first and second defendants conceded that the plaintiff company is entitled in this appeal to succeed on the conspiracy point, unless it is debarred from doing so on the ground that it was a party to the conspiracy, which was the ground that was relied upon by the judge.
>
> The plaintiff company points out that the agreement was resolved on by a board of which the seventh and eighth defendants constituted the majority, and that they were the two directors who countersigned the plaintiff company's seal on the agreement, and that they are sued as two of the conspirators. It is conceded by Mr Miller [counsel] for the plaintiff company that a company may be held to be a participant in a criminal conspiracy, and that the illegality attending a conspiracy cannot relieve the company on the ground that such an agreement may be ultra vires; but he says that to establish a conspiracy to which the company was a party, having as its object the doing of an illegal act, it must be shown that the company must be treated as knowing all the facts relevant to the illegality; he relies on *R v Churchill*[25] . . . But I feel impelled to ask: can the plaintiff company sensibly be regarded as a party to the conspiracy, and in law ought it to be regarded as a party to the conspiracy?
>
> Section 54 of CA 1948 [CA 2006 s 678] is designed for the protection of the relevant company whose shares are dealt with in breach of the section; that was so held in *Wallersteiner v Moir*.[26]
>
> In the present case the object of the alleged conspiracy was to deprive the plaintiff company of over £400,000-worth of its assets, assuming always, of course, that it succeeds in establishing that allegation. The plaintiff company was the party at which the conspiracy was aimed. It seems to me that it would be very strange that it should also be one of the conspirators. The majority of the board which committed the company to carry out the project consisted of two of the alleged conspirators.
>
> The judge said that the plaintiff company was a vital party to the agreement, and it could not be said that the other parties were conspirators but not the plaintiff company. With deference to the judge, who I think probably had very much less reference to authority in the course of the argument before him than we have had in this court, that view seems to me to be too simplistic a view, and not to probe far enough into the true circumstances of the case.
>
> On the footing that the directors of the plaintiff company who were present at the board meeting on 11 October 1963 knew that the sale was at an inflated value, and that such value was inflated for the purpose of enabling the third, fourth, fifth and sixth defendants to buy the share capital of the plaintiff company, those directors must be taken to have known that the transaction was illegal under s 54.
>
> It may emerge at a trial that the facts are not as alleged in the statement of claim, but if the allegations in the statement of claim are made good, the directors of the plaintiff company must then have known that the transaction was an illegal transaction.
>
> But in my view such knowledge should not be imputed to the company, for the essence of the arrangement was to deprive the company improperly of a larger part of its assets. As I have said, the company was a victim of the conspiracy. I think it would be irrational to treat the directors, who were allegedly parties to the conspiracy, notionally as having transmitted this knowledge to the company; and indeed it is a well-recognised exception from the general rule that a principal is affected by notice received by his agent that, if the agent is acting in fraud of his principal and the matter of which he has notice is relevant to the fraud, that knowledge is not to be imputed to the principal.

---

[25] [1967] 2 AC 224 (sub nom *Churchill v Walton*).
[26] [1974] 1 WLR 991.

So in my opinion the plaintiff company should not be regarded as a party to the conspiracy, on the ground of lack of the necessary guilty knowledge.

GOFF LJ: [In] support of what Buckley LJ has said, I would wish to cite two short passages from *Wallersteiner v Moir*; the first passage is in the judgment of Lord Denning MR where he said:

> 'In *Essex Aero Ltd v Cross*,[27] Harman LJ said: "the section was not enacted for the company's protection, but for that of its creditors; . . . the company . . . cannot enforce it." I do not agree. I think the section was passed so as to protect the company from having its assets misused. If it is broken, there is a civil remedy by way of an action for damages.'

Scarman LJ spoke to the same effect and said:

> 'There was, on these facts, a breach of duty by Dr Wallersteiner as a director. The companies were, also, in breach of the section. But the maxim *"potior est conditio defendentis"* is of no avail to Dr Wallersteiner, for the section must have been enacted to protect company funds and the interests of shareholders as well as creditors. I do not agree with the dictum of Harman LJ in *Essex Aero Ltd v Cross* . . . to the effect that the section was enacted not for the company's protection but for that of its creditors.'

ORR LJ delivered a concurring opinion.

A company that is party to a transaction which infringes CA 2006 s 678 may bring an action against its directors and other implicated third parties for recovery of its misapplied property, on the grounds of breach of trust or constructive trust.

[10.11] Selangor United Rubber Estates Ltd v Cradock (No 3) [1968] 1 WLR 1555 (Chancery Division)

The facts are immaterial.

UNGOED-THOMAS J: Does [this] principle, however, prevent an action succeeding for breach of trust in doing what is illegal?

In *Steen v Law*[28] directors of a company, incorporated in New South Wales, lent the company's funds which the directors had to give financial assistance to purchase the company's shares. The liquidator of the company claimed that there had thus been a breach of a New South Wales section, which, so far as material, was in the terms of s 54 [CA 2006 s 678]; and that the directors had thereby committed a breach of their fiduciary duty to the company and should reimburse the company the sums so illegally applied. It was not contended that the directors were absolved from accounting by reason of the illegality of the loan by the company. Such illegality was clearly before the Privy Council and, if available against such a claim, provided a complete answer to it. Yet the point was neither taken by the defendants nor by the Privy Council; and it seems to me for the very good reason that the company was not relying for its claim on the unlawful loan and the relationship of creditor and debtor thereby created, but upon the misapplication by the directors of the company's moneys by way of the unlawful loan. That is the position with regard to the plaintiff company's claim in our case. It was founding its claim, as in our case, not on a wrong done by it as a party to the unlawful loan, but as a wrong done to it by parties owing a fiduciary duty to it. The courts were being invited,

---

[27] [1961] CA Transcript 388.
[28] [1964] AC 287.

as in our case, not to aid illegality but to condemn it. If this were not so, the courts would give redress to companies against directors for misapplication and breach of fiduciary duty which did not involve the company in illegality, but no redress if they were so serious as to involve the company in illegality.

I appreciate that, in the ordinary case of a claim by a beneficiary against a trustee for an illegal breach of trust, the beneficiary is not a party to the illegality; but that, when directors act for a company in an illegal transaction with a stranger, the company is itself a party to that transaction and therefore to the illegality.[29] The company, therefore, could not rely on that transaction as 'the source of civil rights' and, therefore, for example, it could not successfully sue the stranger with regard to rights which it was claimed that the transaction conferred . . . [But in] a claim based on an illegal breach of trust the claimant does not rely on a right conferred or created by that breach. On the contrary, he relies on a right breached by the breach, as the very words 'breach of trust' indicate. It is only on the footing that there is a breach of trust that the defence of illegality becomes relevant. So it is assumed, for present purposes, that there is a breach of trust against the plaintiff company by those who are directors and by those who are claimed to be constructive trustees. The constructive trustees are, it is true, parties with the plaintiff company itself to the transaction which is illegal. The plaintiff company's claim, however, for breach of trust is not made by it as a party to that transaction, or in reliance on any right which that transaction is alleged to confer, but against the directors and constructive trustees for perpetrating that transaction and making the plaintiff company party to it in breach of trust owing to the plaintiff company. The breach of trust includes the making of the plaintiff a party to the illegal transaction. So it seems to me clear on analysis that the plaintiff company is not precluded from relying on breach of trust by a party to an illegal transaction, to which the plaintiff itself is a party, when the breach includes the making of the plaintiff a party to that very transaction. Those who proved to be constructive trustees, sharing the responsibility with the directors for the breach of trust, share the liability too.

The result is that the plaintiff company in this case would not, by reason of illegality, be prevented from being reimbursed money paid by it unlawfully under a transaction to which it is a party. But this does not mean that this would nullify the ordinary operation of illegality with regard to companies and parties outside the company, and not being or treated as being a trustee to it. But it would prevent such operation shielding those whose position or conduct makes them responsible as owing a fiduciary duty or as constructive trustee . . .

➤ Questions

1. In the light of the reasoning in *Belmont* **[10.10]**, will a company ever have the *mens rea* necessary for it to be convicted under CA 2006 ss 678, 680?

2. Tortuous plc lends £5,000 to Smith for the purpose of a purchase by Smith of Tortuous shares. Can it recover £5,000 or any sum from Smith: (i) as repayment of the loan when due; (ii) as damages on the basis of *Belmont*; or (iii) on the ground that Smith is liable to it as a constructive trustee, following *Selangor*?

3. In *Armour Hick Northern Ltd v Armour Trust Ltd* [1980] 1 WLR 1520, A Ltd was a subsidiary of B Ltd. B owed £93,000 to X, the owner of 7,000 shares in B. Y and Z wished to buy these shares, but X was unwilling to sell them unless the debt was first repaid. A accordingly paid off the debt out of its own funds. Y and Z then used their own money to buy the shares. Would there in your opinion be an infringement of CA 1985 s 151 on these

---

[29] See, however, the ruling in the *Belmont* case **[10.10]**.

facts (the 1985 Act being, for relevant purposes, in the same form as CA 2006, but applying also to private companies)?

Dividend distributions

Permitted distributions

Before 1980, there were no general rules in the Companies Acts regulating the distribution of dividends to the members of a company, although there were specific bans on using the share premium account and the capital redemption reserve for this purpose. The only legal constraint was a broad prohibition established by the cases that dividends should not be paid out of 'capital'. Most of these cases were decided in the late Victorian period, and reflected concepts of bookkeeping which were regarded as odd even then by some contemporary critics. In fact, for the greater part of the past century the standards of propriety in relation to distributions have been set by the accountancy profession and not by the law at all; and these standards have increased progressively over time. This continues to be so, even though we now have formal statutory rules about the payment of dividends in CA 2006 ss 829ff. These rules implement in part the Second EU Company Law Directive and also incorporate some recommendations made by the Jenkins Committee in 1962 and the Company Law Review more recently.

The current Act, CA 2006, makes separate rules for private companies, public companies and investment companies (defined in s 833).

The first and primary rule, applicable to all companies, is that a company may not make a '*distribution*' to any of its members except out of profits which are available for that purpose (s 830(1)). 'Distribution' is defined exceptionally widely in s 829, to mean 'every description of distribution of a company's assets to its members, whether in cash or otherwise, subject to [specified] exceptions', being issues of bonus shares, reductions of capital, share redemptions or repurchases, and distributions on winding up.

This rule may be thought to correspond in its effect to the old common law principle laid down in *Re Exchange Banking Co, Flitcroft's Case* **[10.13]**, that dividends could not be paid from 'capital'; but when taken with other sections of the Act its consequences are altogether different from the position at common law. At common law, perhaps because of old accounting practices, only the *current* year's profit and loss account was looked at, and the profits for that particular year reckoned by taking it in isolation; money lost in earlier years of trading, and *a fortiori* capital losses, did not have to be brought into account. And it was not necessary for profits to be realised profits before they were regarded as distributable—although of course, as a practical matter, the company had to have available or be able to raise the cash necessary to pay the dividend when declared. This could lead to some odd results.

Matters are different now, although it is still the case that a company may not make a distribution to any of its members except out of profits which are available for the purpose (CA 2006 s 830(1)). Under Pt 23 of CA 2006, 'profits' available for distribution by a company are 'its accumulated, realised, profits, so far as not previously utilised by distribution or capitalisation, less its accumulated, realised losses, so far as not previously written off in a reduction or reorganisation of capital duly made' (s 830(2)).

The two important features of this formulation are:

(i)   the current year's trading figures cannot be looked at in isolation, but regard must be had to the net overall position of the company, taking into account its *accumulated* surpluses and losses over the years up to date; and

    (ii) the figures used in the calculation of profits must be those for the company's *realised*[30] profits and losses: mere 'revaluation surpluses'—that is, 'paper profits'—cannot be brought into account in reckoning profits.

This approach looks to the company's 'balance sheet surplus': the company's cumulative position, involving past years as well as the current year, has to be considered, and dividends can be paid only if justified by the picture as a whole.

    Special rules apply to *public* companies and to *investment* companies:

    (i) A *public company* must ensure that its net assets (aggregate assets less aggregate liabilities) after the distribution do not fall below the value of its share capital and undistributable reserves,[31] and its 'undistributable reserves' are defined so as to require public companies to allow for any excess of *unrealised* losses over unrealised profits on the capital account—that is, provision must be made for any unrealised revaluation deficit (s 831).

    (ii) An *investment company* (defined in s 833) must draw a distinction between its revenue (trading) profits and its capital profits, and it may make a distribution only out of the accumulated, realised revenue profits (ie not including even realised capital profits, and taking into account realised revenue profits and both realised and unrealised revenue losses), and it may make such a distribution provided that its assets are not thereby reduced to less than one-and-a-half times its aggregate liabilities to creditors (s 832).

Requirement to pay dividends

There is no rule that all profits must be distributed (until, of course, the company is wound up), and there has been no English case in which a shareholder has succeeded in an action brought to compel a company to pay a dividend. Indeed, in *Burland v Earle* [1902] AC 83, the Privy Council made it clear that this was a matter where the court would not interfere. By contrast, in the well-known US case *Dodge v Ford Motor Co* 170 NW 668 (1919), Ford was ordered to pay a substantial dividend to its shareholders when the directors would have preferred to spend the company's trading surplus on increasing the wages and improving the work conditions of its employees, reducing prices to its customers and similar altruistic objects.

    However, in *Re a Company* [1988] 1 WLR 1068, Harman J did not rule out the possibility that failure to pay a dividend might, in a particular case, be a ground for ordering the winding up of a company on the just and equitable ground ('Compulsory winding up on the "just and equitable" ground', p 840) if it had pursued a restrictive dividend policy and denied the shareholders a return on their investment which they were reasonably entitled to expect. In *Re Sam Weller & Sons Ltd* [1990] Ch 682, Peter Gibson J held that such a policy might also justify relief on the ground of 'unfairly prejudicial conduct' (then CA 1985 s 459, now CA 2006 s 994). This section has since been amended so as to put it beyond doubt that the view of Peter Gibson J could be followed where this was justified on the facts (see 'Use of CA 2006 s 994 to protect non-member interests', pp 723ff).

---

[30] The term 'realised' is not defined in the Act (although see s 841), but formal guidance is given by accountancy practice. It is, however, acknowledged that the concepts of realised profits and losses will change over time, reflecting changes in the financial environment, and accountancy guidelines change accordingly.

[31] Given the general rule on available profits in s 830, this requirement seems to add nothing, but it is specifically included in s 831(1) for public companies.

Payment of a dividend

No dividend is payable on a company's shares, even on the preference shares, until the company has 'declared' (or decided to pay) a dividend. Authority to make the decision is usually determined in the articles and the entitlements, as between shareholders, are determined by the class rights attached to the shares. In *Precision Dippings Ltd v Precision Dippings Marketing Ltd* [1986] Ch 447, CA, it was held that the statutory procedure prescribed for the declaration of a dividend (involving, inter alia, an auditors' report on the accounts[32]) was mandatory and that a departure from it could not be rectified by a subsequent resolution of the shareholders.

Once the dividend is payable, it is a debt owed by the company to the member, and is subject to all the usual rules on debts (limitation periods, etc). Unless the articles provide otherwise, distributions must be in cash (*Wood v Odessa Waterworks Co* (1889) 42 Ch D 636).

Distributions in kind

If a distribution in kind is made, then the valuation rules in CA 2006 ss 845–846 apply.

CA 2006 s 845 is intended to remove the doubts that arose after *Aveling Barford* **[10.14]**, which concerned a property sale at a considerable undervalue by a company that had no distributable profits. The contract was held to be void as an unauthorised return of capital. That case left it unclear whether intra-group transfers of assets could be conducted by reference to the asset's book value rather than its market value (which will frequently be higher than the book value, and which would require expensive formal valuation). A transfer at book value may have an element of undervalue, and would therefore constitute a distribution requiring the company to have distributable profits sufficient to cover the difference in value. As a result, companies often abandoned their plans or structured them in more complex ways. CA 2006 s 845 does not disturb the position in the *Aveling Barford* case if the company does not have distributable profits: then the transaction will be an unlawful distribution; it does, however, clarify the position where a company has an appropriate level of available distributable profits, and it then permits asset transfers at book value.

➤ Notes

1. *Clydebank Football Club Ltd v Steedman* 2002 SLT 109: a transaction which is genuinely conceived of and effected as an exchange for value is not a distribution despite being for less than the amount of a professional valuation. Similarly, see the Supreme Court's decision in *Property Progress Co Ltd v Moore* **[10.15]**.

2. With small companies where the business affairs are conducted with little formality, the courts may have to distinguish between payments that can be justified as directors' remuneration and payments that amount to an unauthorised distribution of assets, either because there were no realised profits available or because the statutory procedure has not been followed. See, for example, *Re Halt Garage (1964) Ltd* **[5.03]**. Also see 'Disguised returns of capital', pp 572ff.

Consequences of an unauthorised distribution

There are no criminal consequences. The statutory civil consequences are set out in CA 2006 s 847, which provides that a member who 'knows or has reasonable grounds for

---

[32] A declaration was held to be unlawful on the ground that no accounts had been prepared: *Vardy Properties v Revenue and Customs Commissioners* [2012] UKFTT 564 (TC), [2012] SFTD 1398.

believing' that the distribution contravenes the statutory requirements is obliged to repay the sum (or the value of the asset) received in contravention. This remedy is without prejudice to general remedies available at law. Nevertheless, its usefulness may be rather limited. Except in relation to small private companies, it is unlikely that members will have the necessary knowledge that any distributions are unauthorised. The common law equivalent is similar (see **[10.12]**), although earlier cases suggest the added advantage of a better remedy by way of constructive trust of the distribution (although that now seems doubtful[33]): *Precision Dippings Ltd v Precision Dippings Marketing Ltd* [1986] Ch 447; *Allied Carpets plc v Nethercott* [2001] BCC 81.

Statutory and general law remedies against the members.

[10.12] It's a Wrap (UK) Ltd (In Liquidation) v Gula [2006] EWCA Civ 544 (Court of Appeal)

This case concerned the statutory liability under CA 1985 s 277(1) [CA 2006 s 847] of an insolvent company's directors and shareholders to repay certain dividends that had been paid out in contravention of CA 1985 Pt VIII [CA 2006 ss 630ff].

> ARDEN LJ:
>
> 1. This appeal raises a short point of law. [CA 1985 s 277(1)] provides a statutory remedy against a shareholder for recovery of an unlawful distribution paid to him if he knew or had reasonable grounds to believe that it was made in contravention of the Act. I will call the first kind of knowledge actual knowledge, and the second kind of knowledge constructive knowledge [but see CHADWICK LJ later]. The question that we have to decide is this: if a company brings a claim against a shareholder under this section, is the actual or constructive knowledge that the section requires actual or constructive knowledge of:
>
> (i)   the relevant facts constituting the contravention, or
>
> (ii) those facts and in addition the fact that the Act was contravened?
>
> 2. The deputy judge held . . . that the second of these alternatives was correct. In my judgment, the deputy judge was wrong on this question of law. I reach my conclusions by the following steps:
>
> (A) s 277(1) has to be interpreted in conformity with Art.16 of the second EC directive on company law . . . which it is designed to implement;
>
> (B) Art.16 has to be read in the context of the rules on distributions in Art.15 of the second directive and the general principles of Community law;
>
> (C) the provisions of ss 263–276 of the Act [CA 2006 ss 830ff] are designed to implement Art.15 of the second directive;
>
> (D) on its true interpretation, Art.16 means that a shareholder is liable to return a distribution if he knows or could not have been unaware that it was paid in circumstances which amount to a contravention of the restrictions on distributions in the second directive, whether or not he knew of those restrictions;
>
> (E) accordingly s 277 must be interpreted as meaning that the shareholder cannot claim that he is not liable to return a distribution because he did not know of the restrictions in the Act on the making of distributions. He will be liable if he knew or ought reasonably to have known of the facts which mean that the distribution contravened the requirements of the Act.

---

[33] These proprietary remedies may now be excluded by the analysis adopted in *Westdeutsche Landesbank Girozentrale v Islington London Borough Council* [1996] AC 669, HL.

... As to remedies against shareholders who receive dividends not lawfully made, the general law of the United Kingdom was, arguably at least, not to exactly the same effect as Art.16 .... Liability under the general law attaches where the shareholder knew or ought to have known that the distribution was unlawful. ...

The following are some of the differences between the two types of liability, that is, liability under s 277(1) and liability under the general law. First, s 277(1) only applies where the distribution contravenes the Act, and thus it does not apply where the distribution for instance violates a provision of the general law or the company's constitution. Secondly, there is no defence in s 277(1) for the member who acts on advice. The member is instead left to sue the person who gave him inaccurate advice (if he can). By contrast, under the general law a shareholder may be able to claim that he did not have the requisite knowledge where he acted on advice. As a constructive trustee he would be able to claim that he was entitled in appropriate circumstances to relief under s 61 of the Trustee Act 1925 (see the definition of 'trustee' in s 68(7) of that Act). (I would add, however, that there is no inquiry under the general law into the question whether the shareholder was aware of the law's requirements regarding the payment of dividends.) In sum, the remedy under Art.16 is more absolute and stringent than that available under the general law. That is no doubt because it has been tailor made to facilitate the recovery of unlawful distributions whereas the remedy under the general law is an adaptation of the law of constructive trusteeship. However, the need for some form of actual or constructive knowledge on the part of the shareholder is common to both forms of remedy.

... The underlying rationale for this rule [on distributions] is that capital constitutes the security for creditors. A distribution that is not paid out of profits available for distribution is paid out of the reserves that must remain available for the payment of debts. The claims of shareholders rank behind those of creditors. It is a factor to be borne in mind that any defence given to shareholders who receive a distribution paid in contravention of this Act detracts from the protection available to creditors. One of the objects of the second directive was to give protection to creditors by harmonising restrictions on the profits which may be used for the payment of distributions. ...

SEDLEY LJ delivered a concurring judgment.

CHADWICK LJ delivered a concurring judgment, but differed from Arden LJ on one point (which was not material on the facts): ... I take the view that it is unnecessary, on the facts of this case, to decide what meaning should be given to the words 'has reasonable grounds for believing that'. Those words, plainly, do enable the second (or knowledge) condition in s 277(1) to be established without proof of actual knowledge. But, to my mind, it is by no means self-evident that they are to be equated with 'constructive knowledge' if by that expression is meant knowledge which a person would have but for his negligence. I do not think that the composite phrase 'knows or has reasonable grounds for believing' has the same meaning as 'knows or ought to know'.

General law remedies against the directors: directors who pay dividends improperly are liable to compensate the company personally for the money so paid away (regardless of whether it was paid to the director).

[10.13] Re Exchange Banking Co, Flitcroft's Case (1882) 21 Ch D 519 (Court of Appeal)

At common law, dividends could not be paid from capital. The directors had for several years made it appear that the company had made profits, when in fact it had not, by laying before the shareholders reports and balance sheets in which debts known to be bad were entered as assets. On the faith of these reports, the shareholders had passed resolutions declaring dividends, which the directors had paid. In the winding up of the company the liquidator successfully applied to have the directors who had been responsible on each occasion made accountable to the company for the sums wrongly paid away.

> JESSEL MR: A limited company by its memorandum of association declares that its capital is to be applied for the purposes of the business. It cannot reduce its capital except in the manner and with the safeguards provided by statute, and looking at the Act . . . it clearly is against the intention of the legislature that any portion of the capital should be returned to the shareholders without the statutory conditions being complied with. A limited company cannot in any other way make a return of capital, the sanction of a general meeting can give no validity to such a proceeding, and even the sanction of every shareholder cannot bring within the powers of the company an act which is not within its powers. If, therefore, the shareholders had all been present at the meetings, and had all known the facts, and had all concurred in declaring the dividends, the payment of the dividends would not be actually sanctioned. One reason is this—there is a statement that the capital shall be applied for the purposes of the business, and on the faith of that statement, which is sometimes said to be an implied contract with creditors, people dealing with the company give it credit. The creditor has no debtor but that impalpable thing the corporation, which has no property except the assets of the business. The creditor, therefore, I may say, gives credit to that capital, gives credit to the company on faith of the representation that the capital shall be applied only for the purposes of the business, and he has therefore a right to say that the corporation shall keep its capital and not return it to the shareholders, though it may be a right which he cannot enforce otherwise than by a winding-up order. It follows then that if directors who are quasi trustees for the company improperly pay away the assets to the shareholders, they are liable to replace them. It is no answer to say that the shareholders could not compel them to do so. I am of opinion that the company could in its corporate capacity compel them to do so, even if there were no winding up . . .
>
> COTTON LJ: It was contended that though the directors might be ordered to repay what they had themselves retained, they ought not to be ordered to refund what they had paid to the other shareholders. But directors are in the position of trustees, and are liable not only for what they put into their own pockets, but for what they in breach of trust pay to others . . .
>
> BRETT LJ delivered a concurring judgment.

This liability is in addition to the liability imposed on directors who pay dividends improperly *to themselves*: they will hold these receipts on constructive trust for the company, according to normal fiduciary principles (see *JJ Harrison (Properties) Ltd v Harrison* **[7.40]**).

➤ Notes

1. This obligation to repay illegal dividends is imposed on the directors who authorised the excessive payment regardless of whether the company is solvent or insolvent when it claims repayment. See *Bairstow v Queens Moat Houses plc* [2001] EWCA Civ 712. The Supreme Court, in *Revenue and Customs Commissioners v Holland* **[7.02]**, concluded (although without expressing a definitive view) that this obligation is a form of 'strict liability', subject to the court's discretion to grant relief under CA 1985 s 727 [CA 2006 s 1157]. By contrast, Popplewell J tentatively held the contrary view in *Madoff Securities v Raven* [2013] EWHC 3147 (Comm), at [197]–[200], suggesting that the liability might, in certain circumstances, be fault-based, and citing Lord Walker's judgment in *Progress Property Co Ltd v Moore* (at [32]) **[10.15]** in support (see Question 5 following *Progress Property* **[10.15]**). Does the difference depend on whether the distribution is regarded as in excess of the

director's authority (ie in breach of s 171(a)) or in abuse of it, being an exercise for improper purposes (ie in breach of s 171(b))?

2. In *Allied Carpets Group plc v Nethercott* [2001] BCLC 81 it was held that the object of the remedy is restitution of what was wrongfully paid out by the company, not compensation for the loss the company has suffered. Therefore where the dividend was unlawful because the accounts were erroneous, it is irrelevant that the dividends might have been lawful if the accounts had been drawn up correctly. In *Revenue and Customs Commissioners v Holland* **[7.02]**, Lord Hope held that, while the obligation is restitutionary in nature, it is nonetheless within the trial judge's discretion under IA 1986 s 212 'to limit the award to what was required to make up the deficiency of a particular creditor where the claim was made by a party other than the liquidator'. Thus, 'it was open to the deputy judge to limit the amount that Mr Holland [the defendant] should pay to what HMRC [the only creditor] had lost from his unlawful conduct'. Does IA 1986 s 212 give the court that discretion, or must it depend on CA 2006 s 1157?

3. In *Re Marini Ltd* [2003] EWHC 334 (Ch), [2004] BCLC 172, the court did not accept that, because the dividend had been paid on the advice of the company's accountant, the directors should qualify for relief under CA 1985 s 727 [CA 2006 s 1157]. Although they agreed that the directors had acted reasonably and honestly on their accountant's advice, the honesty of their actions did not allow them to enjoy a benefit at the expense of the company's creditors.

➤ **Questions**

1. According to *Re Exchange Banking Co, Flitcroft's Case* **[10.13]**, the fact that the illegal distribution was approved by the shareholders does not cure the defect, nor does it ratify the directors' acts so as to absolve them from liability. *Could* a shareholder resolution fail to achieve the former goal but succeed on the latter?

2. What knowledge does a *shareholder* need to have, and of what, to be fixed with liability to repay unauthorised distributions?

3. What knowledge does a *director* need to have, and of what, to be fixed with liability to repay unauthorised distributions?

4. Can a director be excused from liability? See *Dovey v Corey* [1901] AC 477 and CA 2006 s 1157. Can a shareholder be excused from liability?

5. Can an auditor be made liable for unauthorised distributions?

Capitalisations and bonus shares

A profitable company that does not distribute all its profits as dividends will accumulate reserves (retained earnings). The shares will in consequence have a market value which is greater than their nominal value. There will be a similar situation when a company's fixed assets appreciate in value as a result of inflation or of a movement in their market value. Suppose, for example, that a company with a nominal capital of 10,000 £1 shares, all issued and fully paid, has accumulated profits of £90,000. Instead of paying out this surplus to its shareholders as dividends it may resolve to 'capitalise' these reserves by issuing a further 90,000 shares, so that nine new shares are allotted to the holder of each existing share, and treating the new shares as fully paid because the £90,000 is appropriated to meet the issue price. No cash changes hands at all. The formal result will be that the reserve has become capital and ceases to be available for distribution as dividend, the company's issued share capital has risen from £10,000 to £100,000, each shareholder now has ten times as many shares as before, and the market value of each share will have fallen back from something like £10 to £1.[34] (Of course, other factors influence the market price of shares, apart from their 'asset backing', but this in simplified terms will be what happens.)

A capitalisation issue is not a 'distribution' of profits or assets for the purposes of the statutory restrictions in CA 2006 ss 829ff (see s 829(2)(a)). It follows that profits which are not distributable (eg because they are unrealised profits) may be capitalised and issued to members as bonus shares provided the articles are so worded as to permit this.[35] Note, however, that in *EIC Services Ltd v Phipps* [2004] EWCA Civ 1069, [2005] 1 WLR 1377, an issue of bonus shares was declared void for mistake because the underlying ordinary shares were totally unpaid and no resolution allowing the issue was ever passed.

➤ Questions

1. What might be the advantages to (i) the company, (ii) its shareholders, of making an issue of bonus shares?

2. Are the shareholders better off in any real sense as a result? Is the expression 'bonus shares' misleading?

Disguised returns of capital

The rules noted previously provide various mechanisms for controlling what are seen as unacceptable disposals of the company's property. However, they do not seem to touch the ability of small companies to pay away their assets to their members in the form of directors' fees or employees' salaries, or, in corporate groups, for subsidiaries to pay large fees to holding companies for 'group services' or other notional (or real) benefits. There is no rule that directors' fees (see **[5.03]**), still less employees' wages or business expenses, must be paid out of profits.

But it is also true, as we saw earlier, that directors cannot make gifts out of the company's assets unless (i) in furtherance of the company's objects, or (ii) out of distributable profits (and even then subject to certain limitations): see 'Corporate gifts', pp 135ff. This rule provides a further avenue for restraining unacceptable distributions of the company's assets, although it catches only the most blatant of abuses.

The possibility of recovery of the company's assets from *third party recipients* is limited. The abolition of the doctrine of *ultra vires* by the Companies Act 1989 deprived the courts of the most potent of their traditional weapons when dealing with allegations that corporate property has been misapplied. With the demise of the *ultra vires* doctrine, the courts needed to have recourse to other rules and remedies in such cases. It may be possible to show that *directors* have behaved unconstitutionally, exceeded their authority, abused their powers or acted in breach of their fiduciary duties, with the consequence that they may be liable to make compensation to the company. In addition (or alternatively) the relevant transaction may be declared void or voidable, and both the directors and any third party who has received corporate assets with knowledge of the circumstances will be liable to reimburse the company (*Selangor United Rubber Estates Ltd v Cradock (No 3)* **[10.11]**). If the third party has dealt in good faith, for value and without notice of the irregularity, however, the company's remedy against that person will, of course, be lost; but very often the person will be an 'insider' or party to the wrong-doing and not able to plead this defence. There is also the possibility that a formal or informal ratification of the irregular act will be alleged to have occurred. But some breaches of directors' duty

---

[34] Bonus issues may also be financed out of the share premium account and capital redemption reserve.

[35] This confirms the position at common law declared by Buckley J in *Dimbula Valley (Ceylon) Co Ltd v Laurie* [1961] Ch 353, but the judge's reasoning (based on the view that such profits were distributable) has not survived the statutory changes of 1980.

are not capable of ratification (*Cook v Deeks* **[7.25]**, *Kinsela v Russell Kinsela Pty Ltd* **[7.16]**); and where the act involves breach of statutory prohibitions (eg a prohibited distribution (s 830) or a breach of the 'financial assistance' prohibition (s 678)), it will not be capable of ratification at all. So the courts are still relatively well equipped to deal with cases of wrongful depletion of corporate assets.

The following cases illustrate a possible approach to these issues, perhaps linked as a matter of underlying principle with the 'maintenance of capital' doctrine. So, in *Re Halt Garage (1964) Ltd* **[5.03]**, Oliver J struck down a payment of remuneration to an inactive director as 'not genuine' and a 'dressed-up return of capital' to her. While the basis of this reasoning is open to question (not least because as a shareholder she held only one £1 share), it has since been adopted and applied by Hoffmann J in *Aveling Barford Ltd v Perion Ltd* **[10.14]**, where again the 'dressed-up return of capital' argument was somewhat shaky because the beneficiary of the asset-stripping, although totally lacking in merit, was not strictly a shareholder. The Supreme Court has perhaps provided much needed clarification in this area in *Progress Property Co Ltd v Moore* **[10.15]**, where the court adopted an 'arm's length approach' in determining whether an undervalue transaction between the company and its member was genuine or not.

Matters are simpler when the company is insolvent or approaching insolvency. There are now a number of statutory provisions which may be invoked when corporate assets have been plundered or imperilled in the run-up to liquidation. These include preferences (IA 1986 s 239), transactions at an undervalue (IA 1986 ss 238 and 423), floating charges subject to avoidance (IA 1986 s 245), fraudulent and wrongful trading (IA 1986 ss 231 and 214) and misfeasance proceedings (IA 1986 s 212).[36] In the light of these statutory developments in the UK, it is unlikely that a new common law remedy will develop based on a duty owed by directors to creditors (see 'Duties to creditors?', pp 340ff).

A sale at an undervalue made by a company to one of its shareholders (or to another company controlled by the shareholder) may be open to challenge on the ground that it is not a genuine sale but a disguised return of capital.

[10.14] Aveling Barford Ltd v Perion Ltd [1989] BCLC 626 (Chancery Division)

Aveling Barford and Perion were both owned and controlled by Lee. Aveling Barford, which was not at the material time insolvent but was not in a position to make any distribution to its shareholders, owned a sports ground which had planning permission for residential development. In October 1986 its directors resolved to sell this property to Perion for £350,000 when they knew that it had recently been valued at £650,000, but no binding contract was entered into at that stage. A later valuation put it at £1.15 million and Perion was subsequently offered £1.4 million. There was some evidence of an agreement reached in January 1987 that a further payment of £400,000 was to be paid to Aveling Barford by Perion if it resold the property within a year for more than £800,000. The property was conveyed to Perion for £350,000 in February 1987 and resold by it for £1.52 million the following August. Aveling Barford was subsequently put into liquidation and successfully sued in this action to have Perion declared a constructive trustee of the proceeds of the sale.

HOFFMANN J: Counsel for the defendants said that even if the 10 January contract was a rewriting of history in the summer of 1987, when it was plain that Perion would be reselling for more

---

[36] See 'The courts' discretion to order a compulsory winding up', pp 850ff.

than £800,000, it was reasonable for the parties retrospectively to affirm the sale at £750,000, which would have been a proper sum to fix as the value in February 1987. I do not agree. If the February sale was, as I think, a breach of duty and liable to be set aside at the time, Dr Lee or Mr Chapman [solicitor to all the parties] on his behalf had no right to confirm it retrospectively as a sale at £750,000 at a time when they knew the value to be over £1,400,000. It was the duty of the directors to set aside the February sale and obtain the full value of the land for Aveling Barford. On any view, therefore, the sale was a breach of fiduciary duty by Dr Lee. Perion, through Dr Lee and Mr Chapman, knew all the facts which made it a breach of duty and was therefore accountable as a constructive trustee.

In the alternative, counsel for the defendant submitted that whether or not the sale to Perion was a breach of fiduciary duty by Dr Lee, it cannot be challenged by the company because it was unanimously approved by the shareholders. This approval was both informal and formal. Informal approval was given at the time of sale by virtue of the fact that Dr Lee owned or controlled the entire issued share capital. Formally, a sale at £750,000 was approved when the 1987 accounts were adopted at the company's annual general meeting. For the purposes of this motion I shall assume that shareholder consent was given in both these ways.

The general rule is that any act which falls within the express or implied powers of a company conferred by its memorandum of association, whether or not a breach of duty on the part of the directors, will be binding on the company if it is approved or subsequently ratified by the shareholders: see *Rolled Steel Products (Holdings) Ltd v British Steel Corpn* [1986] Ch 246, CA. But this rule is subject to exceptions created by the general law and one such exception is that a company cannot without the leave of the court or the adoption of a special procedure return its capital to its shareholders. It follows that a transaction which amounts to an unauthorised return of capital is ultra vires and cannot be validated by shareholder ratification or approval. Whether or not the transaction is a distribution to shareholders does not depend exclusively on what the parties choose to call it. The court looks at the substance rather than the outward appearance. [His Lordship referred to *Re Halt Garage (1964) Ltd* **[5.03]** and an earlier case, *Ridge Securities Ltd v IRC* [1964] 1 All ER 275, [1964] 1 WLR 479, and continued:]

So it seems to me in this case that looking at the matter objectively, the sale to Perion was not a genuine exercise of the company's power under its memorandum to sell its assets. It was a sale at a gross undervalue for the purpose of enabling a profit to be realised by an entity controlled and put forward by its sole beneficial shareholder. This was as much a dressed-up distribution as the payment of excessive interest in *Ridge Securities* or excessive remuneration in *Halt Garage*. The company had at the time no distributable reserves and the sale was therefore ultra vires and incapable of validation by the approval or ratification of the shareholder. The fact that the distribution was to Perion rather than to Dr Lee or his other entities which actually held the shares in Aveling Barford is in my judgment irrelevant . . .

Counsel for the defendants says that this was an act within the terms of the memorandum. It may have been a sale at an undervalue, but it was certainly a sale: a conveyance in exchange for a payment in money. It was not a sham. The terms of the transaction were in no way different from those appearing on the face of the documents. The purpose for which it was done was therefore irrelevant. Counsel submits that the test for the genuineness of the transaction proposed by Oliver J in *Re Halt Garage* admits by the back door all the questions about the motives, state of mind and knowledge of the company's directors which the Court of Appeal appeared to have expelled by the front door in the *Rolled Steel* case.

It is clear however that Slade LJ [in *Rolled Steel*] excepted from his general principle cases which he described as involving a 'fraud on creditors'. As an example of such a case, he cited *Re Halt Garage*. Counsel for the defendants said that frauds on creditors meant transactions entered into when the company was insolvent. In this case Aveling Barford was not at the relevant time insolvent. But I do not think that the phrase was intended to have such a narrow meaning. The rule that capital

> may not be returned to shareholders is a rule for the protection of creditors and the evasion of the rule falls within what I think Slade LJ had in mind when he spoke of a fraud on creditors. There is certainly nothing in his judgment to suggest that he disapproved of the actual decisions in *Re Halt Garage* or *Ridge Securities*. As for the transaction not being a sham, I accept that it was in law a sale. The false dressing it wore was that of a sale at arms' length or at market value. It was the fact that it was known and intended to be a sale at an undervalue which made it an unlawful distribution.
>
> It follows that in my judgment even on the view of the facts most favourable to Perion, it has no arguable defence . . .

➤ Question

In *Re Halt Garage (1964) Ltd* [5.03], referred to earlier, the issued capital of the company was two £1 shares, of which Mrs Charlesworth held one. Was the judge right to describe the overpayment of £20 per week as a disguised 'return of capital' to her?

➤ Notes

1. Although in *Aveling Barford* Hoffmann J several times described the transaction as *ultra vires* (and accordingly unratifiable), his remarks will continue to be valid and relevant despite the abolition of the *ultra vires* doctrine because of his ruling that the transaction was illegal as an unauthorised return of capital.

2. In declining to make a distinction between Lee and his company Perion, was Hoffmann J 'piercing the corporate veil'? How would his conclusion now be explained? (See *Prest v Petrodel Resources Ltd* [2.01].)

3. This case was cited with approval by Harman J in *Barclays Bank plc v British and Commonwealth Holdings plc* [1996] 1 WLR 1. Here B & C plc had issued redeemable preference shares to C and had undertaken to redeem them on a certain date. If B & C plc failed to do so (which would be unavoidable if it had no distributable profits or was insolvent), T Ltd promised to buy the shares from C, and B & C plc promised to indemnify T against the cost of doing so. The arrangement was held to be unlawful. Harman J said (at 17): 'as it seems to me it must . . . be unlawful to make an agreement expressed to impose a liability to make a gratuitous payment, that is, one not for the advancement of a company's business nor made out of distributable profits, at a future date when in the event the company has no distributable profits'.

4. However defensible the *Aveling Barford* decision may be on the merits, it caused concern in commercial circles because it created uncertainty as to when payments by a company to its members in other such circumstances might also infringe ss 829 and 830 of the Act. CA 2006 might usefully have clarified the position and made it clear that the rules apply only to distributions to members in their capacity as members, but this was not done and the uncertainty therefore remains. Alternative protection is provided by other provisions of company law and insolvency law that apply on similar facts.

In determining whether an undervalue transaction constitutes a disguised return of capital, the court will look to the substance, not the form, of the transaction, characterising it as a matter of law, and regardless of its form or the label attached to it by the parties.

[10.15] Progress Property Co Ltd v Moore [2010] UKSC 55 (Supreme Court)

The whole of the issued share capital of company (Y), a subsidiary of the appellant company (P), was sold to the respondent company (M). All three companies were indirectly controlled by the same holding company. The sale price was calculated on the basis of Y's open market value, subtracting liabilities for creditors and a further sum in respect of an indemnity believed to have been given by P for a repairing liability. It transpired that P had no such indemnity liability to be released from and that there was therefore no justification for the reduction in Y's value. P alleged that the transaction had been at a gross undervalue, and was therefore automatically a disguised return of capital. The Supreme Court disagreed, upholding the Court of Appeal and the High Court.

LORD WALKER:

A question of characterisation

24. The essential issue then, is how the sale by PPC [claimant] of its shareholding in YMS [Y Ltd] is to be characterised. That is how it was put by Sir Owen Dixon CJ in *Davis Investments Pty Ltd v Comr of Stamp Duties (New South Wales)* (1958) 100 CLR 392, 406 (a case about a company reorganisation effected at book value in which the High Court of Australia were divided on what was ultimately an issue of construction on a stamp duty statute). The same expression was used by Buxton LJ in *MacPherson v European Strategic Bureau Ltd* [2000] 2 BCLC 683, para 59. The deputy judge did not ask himself (or answer) that precise question. But he did [2008] EWHC 2577 (Ch) at [39]–[41] roundly reject the submission made on behalf of PPC that there is an unlawful return of capital 'whenever the company has entered into a transaction with a shareholder which results in a transfer of value not covered by distributable profits, and regardless of the purpose of the transaction'. A relentlessly objective rule of that sort would be oppressive and unworkable. It would tend to cast doubt on any transaction between a company and a shareholder, even if negotiated at arm's length and in perfect good faith, whenever the company proved, with hindsight, to have got significantly the worse of the transaction.

25. In the Court of Appeal Mummery LJ developed the deputy judge's line of thought into a more rounded conclusion, at para 30:

'In this case the deputy judge noted that it had been accepted by PPC that the sale was entered into in the belief on the part of the director Mr Moore that the agreed price was at market value. In those circumstances there was no knowledge or intention that the shares should be disposed of at an undervalue. There was no reason to doubt the genuineness of the transaction as a commercial sale of the YMS1 shares. This was so, even though it appeared that the sale price was calculated on the basis of the value of the properties that was misunderstood by all concerned.'

26. In seeking to undermine that conclusion Mr Collings QC (for PPC) argued strenuously that an objective approach is called for. The same general line is taken in a recent article by Dr Eva Micheler commenting on the Court of Appeal's decision, 'Disguised Returns of Capital—An Arm's Length Approach' [2010] CLJ 151. This interesting article refers to a number of cases not cited to this court or to the courts below, and argues for what the author calls an arm's length approach.

27. If there were a stark choice between a subjective and an objective approach, the least unsatisfactory choice would be to opt for the latter. But in cases of this sort the court's real task is to inquire into the true purpose and substance of the impugned transaction. That calls for an investigation of all the relevant facts, which sometimes include the state of mind of the human beings who are orchestrating the corporate activity.

28. Sometimes their states of mind are totally irrelevant. A distribution described as a dividend but actually paid out of capital is unlawful, however technical the error and however well-meaning the directors who paid it. The same is true of a payment which is on analysis the equivalent of a dividend, such as the unusual cases (mentioned by Dr Micheler) of *In re Walters' Deed of Guarantee* [1933] Ch 321 (claim by guarantor of preference dividends) and *British and*

Commonwealth Holdings plc v Barclays Bank plc [1996] 1 WLR 1 (claim for damages for contractual breach of scheme for redemption of shares). Where there is a challenge to the propriety of a director's remuneration the test is objective (*In re Halt Garage* **[5.03]**), but probably subject in practice to what has been called, in a recent Scottish case, a 'margin of appreciation': *Clydebank Football Club Ltd v Steedman* 2002 SLT 109, para 76 (discussed further below). If a controlling shareholder simply treats a company as his own property, as the domineering master-builder did in *In re George Newman & Co Ltd* [1895] 1 Ch 674, his state of mind (and that of his fellow directors) is irrelevant. It does not matter whether they were consciously in breach of duty, or just woefully ignorant of their duties. What they do is enough by itself to establish the unlawful character of the transaction.

29. The participants' subjective intentions are however sometimes relevant, and a distribution disguised as an arm's length commercial transaction is the paradigm example. If a company sells to a shareholder at a low value assets which are difficult to value precisely, but which are potentially very valuable, the transaction may call for close scrutiny, and the company's financial position, and the actual motives and intentions of the directors, will be highly relevant. There may be questions to be asked as to whether the company was under financial pressure compelling it to sell at an inopportune time, as to what advice was taken, how the market was tested, and how the terms of the deal were negotiated. If the conclusion is that it was a genuine arm's length transaction then it will stand, even if it may, with hindsight, appear to have been a bad bargain. If it was an improper attempt to extract value by the pretence of an arm's length sale, it will be held unlawful. But either conclusion will depend on a realistic assessment of all the relevant facts, not simply a retrospective valuation exercise in isolation from all other inquiries.

30. Pretence is often a badge of a bad conscience. Any attempt to dress up a transaction as something different from what it is is likely to provoke suspicion. In the *Aveling Barford* case **[10.14]** there were suspicious factors, such as Dr Lee's surprising evidence that he was ignorant of the Humberts' valuation, and the dubious authenticity of the 'overage' document. But in the end the disparity between the valuations and the sale price of the land was sufficient, by itself, to satisfy Hoffmann J that the transaction could not stand.

31. The right approach is in my opinion well illustrated by the careful judgment of Lord Hamilton in *Clydebank Football Club Ltd v Steedman* 2002 SLT 109. It is an example of the problems which can arise with football clubs owned by limited companies, where some small shareholders see the club as essentially a community enterprise, and other more commercially-minded shareholders are concerned with what they see as underused premises ripe for profitable redevelopment. The facts are complicated, and the main issue was on section 320 of the Companies Act 1985 (approval by company in general meeting of acquisition of non-cash asset by director or connected person). But the judge also dealt with a claim under section 263 (unlawful distribution). He held that the sale of the club's derelict ground at Kilbowie Park, and another site originally purchased under an abortive plan for a new ground, was a genuine arm's-length sale even though effected at a price £165,000 less than the value as eventually determined by the court after hearing expert evidence. Lord Hamilton said, at para 76:

'It is also clear, in my view, that a mere arithmetical difference between the consideration given for the asset or assets and the figure or figures at which it or they are in subsequent proceedings valued retrospectively will not of itself mean that there has been a distribution. If the transaction is genuinely conceived of and effected as an exchange for value and the difference ultimately found does not reflect a payment "manifestly beyond any possible justifiable reward for that in respect of which allegedly it is paid", does not give rise to an exchange "at a gross undervalue" and is not otherwise unreasonably large, there will not to any extent be a "dressed up return of capital". In assessing the adequacy of the consideration, a margin of appreciation may properly be allowed.'

The words quoted by Lord Hamilton are from *In re Halt Garage* **[5.03]** and the *Aveling Barford* case **[10.14]**.

32. Lord Hamilton said, at para 79:

'It is plain, in my view, that directors are liable only if it is established that in effecting the unlawful distribution they were in breach of their fiduciary duties (or possibly of contractual obligations, though that does not arise in the present case). Whether or not they were so in breach will involve consideration not only of whether or not the directors knew at the time that what they were doing was unlawful but also of their state of knowledge at that time of the material facts. In reviewing the then authorities Vaughan Williams J in *In re Kingston Cotton Mill Co (No 2)* **[8.02]**, 347: "In no one of [the cases cited] can I find that directors were held liable unless the payments were made with actual knowledge that the funds of the company were being misappropriated or with knowledge of the facts that established the misappropriation." Although this case went to the Court of Appeal, this aspect of the decision was not quarrelled with (see [1896] 2 Ch 279).'

I agree with both those passages.

33. In this case there are concurrent findings that the sale of YMS1 to Moorgarth was a genuine commercial sale. The contrary was not pleaded or put to Mr Moore in cross-examination. I would dismiss this appeal.

LORD MANCE:

42....Like Lord Walker, I would not go so far as Mr McGhee QC for Moorgarth in his submission that the ultimate test is always one of the directors' (subjective) motives in effecting the transaction. The courts will not second-guess companies with regard to the appropriateness or wisdom of the terms of any transaction: see eg *In re Halt Garage* **[5.03]**. But there may come a point at which, looking at all the relevant factors, an agreement cannot be regarded as involving in substance anything other than a return or distribution of capital, whatever the label attached to it by its parties. I do not regard *Aveling Barford Ltd v Perion Ltd* **[10.14]** as inconsistent with this. The facts in that case made it possible to speak of knowledge and intention to sell at an undervalue, but that does not mean that such knowledge or intention are always necessary factors. In the present case, it is however unnecessary in my view to go further into such areas.

Also see *Ilife News & Media Ltd v Revenue and Customs Commissioners* [2012] UKFTT 696, [2014] FSR 6 (First Tier Tribunal (Tax Chamber)). In this case, it was held that licence fees paid in excess of market value were not, in light of all circumstances, unlawful distributions.

➤ Questions

1. What are the principal objectives of the capital maintenance rules—creditor protection against removal of a preferential capital 'buffer', or company/shareholder protection against asset-stripping?

2. Do the current rules provide effective protection, either for creditors or for shareholders?

3. What are the advantages and disadvantages in adopting 'solvency declarations' as a simple hurdle to these types of transactions?

4. The Second EU Company Law Directive (77/91/EEC) was nominated for review as part of the EU Company Law Action Plan announced in May 2003, but until then many of the identified problems will necessarily remain on the statute books. What are the principal problems for which solutions might be found?

5. When might it be appropriate to take into account subjective elements such as the mental state of mind of directors of a company involved in an undervalue transaction?

When and how should this line be drawn so as to prevent inappropriate judicial activism in 'second-guessing companies with regard to the appropriateness or wisdom of the terms of any transaction' (per Lord Mance, *Progress Property Co Ltd v Moore* **[10.15]**)? See also *Madoff Securities v Raven* [2013] EWHC 3147 (Comm), where Popplewell J, citing *Progress Property* **[10.15]** and *Aveling Barford v Perion Ltd* **[10.14]**, summarised the position as follows, at [204]:

> ...Whether a transaction infringes the rule is a question of categorisation or characterisation based on substance, not form. The label attached to the transaction by the parties is not decisive. Sometimes the exercise for the court will be a purely objective one in which the subjective intentions of the directors are irrelevant: for example a distribution described as a dividend, but actually paid out of capital, is unlawful, however technical the error and however well-meaning the directors who caused it to be paid. But where what is impugned purports to be a transaction of a different character to a distribution, such as for example a contract for the purchase of assets or services, the intentions of the parties to the transaction are often highly relevant to the categorisation exercise, being one in which the court is inquiring whether the transaction was in substance that which it purported to be. The question whether the transaction was in substance a disguised distribution of capital may be heavily influenced by whether that was the intention of the parties. In such a case an attempt to dress up a transaction as something different from what it is, is likely to provoke suspicion, and may lead to the conclusion that its true characterisation is a distribution of capital, although not all cases involving some pretence or dressing up will justify that conclusion. As Lord Walker put it at [30] [of *Progress Property*], pretence is often a badge of bad conscience. On the other hand the court will not recategorise an arm's length transaction if the directors intended it to be in substance that which its form purports to be.

Further reading

ARMOUR, J, 'Share Capital and Creditor Protection: Efficient Rules for a Modern Company Law?' (2000) 63 MLR 355.

CLEMENTELLI, F, '(Under)valuing the Rules on Capital Maintenance' [2012] *International Company and Commercial Law Review* 191.

DAVENPORT, B, 'What Did *Russell v Northern Bank Development Corporation Ltd* Decide?' (1993) 109 LQR 533.

FERRAN, E, 'Simplification of European Company Law on Financial Assistance' (2005) 6 *European Business Organisation Law Review* 93.

FERRAN, E, 'Corporate Transactions and Financial Assistance: Shifting Policy Perceptions but Static Law' [2004] CLJ 225.

HO, LC, 'Financial Assistance after *Chaston* and *MT Realisations*: Deepsix and Double Think' [2003] *Journal of International Banking Law and Regulation* 424.

MERCOURIS, S, 'The Prohibition on Financial Assistance: The Case for a Commercially Pragmatic Interpretation' (2014) 35 *Company Lawyer* 321.

MICHELER, E, 'Disguised Returns of Capital—An Arm's Length Approach' [2010] CLJ 151.

NIRANJAN, V and NARAVANE, S, 'A Reassessment of Fundamental Dividend Principles' [2009] *International Company and Commercial Law Review* 88.

PAYNE, J, 'Unjust Enrichment, Trusts and Recipient Liability for Unlawful Dividends' (2003) 119 LQR 583.

PROCTOR, C, 'Financial Assistance: New Proposals and New Perspectives?' (2007) 28 *Company Lawyer* 3.

THAM, CH, 'Unjust Enrichment and Unlawful Dividends: A Step Too Far?' [2005] CLJ 177.

11

SHARES

The nature and classification of shares

Recall the description of a share given at 'The legal nature of shares', p 512, and in *Borland's Trustee v Steel Bros & Co Ltd* **[9.01]**. It indicated that shares are a means of denoting three things: first, the shareholders' *financial stake* in the company (including the shareholders' liability to contribute funds to the company, and rights to capital and income receipts from the company); secondly, their *interest in the company as an association* (including rights as members, especially voting rights and rights conferred by statute and the company's constitution); and, thirdly, their rights as owners of a species of *property* (which is able to be bought, sold, charged, etc, and in which there can be both legal and equitable interests).

This chapter is about the nature of the asset held by shareholders, and the rights that accrue as a result of that ownership.[1] It does not consider the uses that shareholders may make of their voting power in the company or their rights to influence and control the management of the company in other ways. That is discussed at various stages in this book, especially in Chapters 6, 7 and 13. It does, however, look at the initial allocation of financial and voting rights to different classes of shares and the variation of those rights, the rights to transfer shares and the protections associated with that and, finally, the valuation of shares.

In total, these combined privileges and limitations on voting and financial rights raise the question of what it means when we say that the shareholders 'own' the company. The answer is material in differentiating the rights of shareholders from those of creditors, employees and other outsiders, as highlighted in the corporate governance debates associated with this: recall the 'shareholder' and 'stakeholder' views of a company and their impact on corporate governance issues (see 'Directors' duties are owed to the company', pp 336ff).

---

[1] See RR Pennington, 'Can Shares in Companies be Defined?' (1989) 10 *Company Lawyer* 140; S Worthington, 'Shares and Shareholders: Property, Power and Entitlement—Parts I and II' (2001) 22 *Company Lawyer* 258 and 307.

Classes of shares and class rights

'Classes of shares' and 'class rights' are not defined in the Companies Act 2006 (CA 2006), other than in s 629. Nevertheless, the shares in a company may be divided into different classes, either by the company's constitution, or by the terms of the share issue itself. The differing rights usually relate to entitlements to vote, entitlements to dividends and entitlements to a return of capital when the company is wound up. Some classes of shares may fall into a well-known category such as 'preference shares', but even so there is no fixed formula defining such shares: it is a matter of construction of the terms of issue in each case what the rights of the particular class are. In broad terms, however, we may describe some well-known types of shares as follows:

Ordinary shares: this is the basic or residual category. If all the company's shares are issued without differentiation, they will be ordinary shares. If the shares are divided into classes, and the special rights of such classes are set out, the remaining shares will be ordinary shares. Where the class or classes of shares are preference shares, then the ordinary shares are commonly called 'equity' shares; but in CA 2006 this term has a more elaborate definition (see s 548).

Preference shares: these shares will usually be entitled to have dividends paid, at a predetermined rate (eg at a rate of 10% on their nominal value) in priority to any dividend on the ordinary shares. Of course, it is first necessary for the company to have distributable profits, and for a dividend to be declared. However, if these conditions are met, the first claim on the corporate profits in any year will be that of the preference shareholders. The right to a preference dividend may be *cumulative* (in which case arrears of preference dividends not declared in earlier years must be paid, as well as that for the current year, before any dividend is paid to the ordinary shareholders) or *non-cumulative* (when only the current year's preference dividend is payable). Where the preference shares are *participating*, they will be entitled to a further distribution after the ordinary shareholders have received a dividend equivalent to their own 10% (or whatever the rate is). A company may have more than one class of preference shares, ranking one behind the other.

Preference shareholders commonly also have a right to priority over the ordinary shareholders when capital is returned to the members in a winding up. It is quite usual for preference shareholders to have no voting rights at shareholders' meetings, or alternatively to have a vote only if the preference dividend is in arrears.

Deferred shares: these are sometimes called 'founders' shares' reflecting the founders' offer to defer their own entitlements to those of other investors from whom additional capital is sought. They are not common today except as part of tax-saving schemes. As the name implies, deferred shares normally enjoy rights to distributable profit or to return of capital ranking *after* the claims of the preference shareholders (if any) and the ordinary shareholders.

Redeemable shares: these are created on terms that they shall be (or, at the option of the company or of the member, may be) bought back by the company at a future date. The rules governing such shares and their redemption are set out in CA 2006 ss 684ff. Prior to 1981, only preference shares could be issued as redeemable. Although that rule fell away, it is now clear that a company must always have *some* non-redeemable shares (s 684(4)). The rules on the issue of redeemable shares and their redemption were discussed at 'Redemptions and repurchases of shares', pp 542ff.

Non-voting shares: these may be issued where it is sought to restrict control of the company to the holders of the remaining shares. This is quite commonly desired when a family-controlled company looks to outside investors for additional capital (although it may, of course, find that the latter are not prepared to invest on those terms). A capital structure which includes non-voting shares may also be imposed on a company by an outside body, for example as a condition of obtaining a broadcasting licence (see *Heron International Ltd v Lord Grade* [1983] BCLC 244, CA). The Stock Exchange does not encourage listed companies to create non-voting shares, although it does not ban them altogether; they must, however, be clearly designated.

Shares with limited voting rights or enhanced voting rights: these may also be created, even to the extent of giving one shareholder a right of veto in specified circumstances. We have seen examples in *Quin & Axtens Ltd v Salmon* **[4.06]** and *Bushell v Faith* **[6.02]**.[2]

Employees' shares: many companies issue shares to their employees, commonly under an 'employees' share scheme' (defined in CA 2006 s 1166), which carries certain tax advantages. Employees' shares are not usually designated as a separate class of shares by the articles of association, but are issued simply as ordinary shares (or, as the case may be, preference shares, etc) ranking *pari passu* with the other shares of this class. Normally, however, they are subject to special restrictions (eg as to the holder's right of disposal) and would undoubtedly be regarded as a separate class of shares for some legal purposes. Various sections of CA 2006 make special provision for employees' shares, for example s 566 excludes shares that are to be held under an employees' share scheme from the restrictions (but not the benefits) of the usual pre-emptive rights rules.

In addition, of course, classes of shares may be created for other reasons. Thus a 'quasi-partnership' company with three founding shareholders might well have a capital of £300 divided into £100 in 'A' shares, £100 in 'B' shares and £100 in 'C' shares, the shares to rank equally in all respects except that each class should have the right to appoint one of the directors to the board. In this way, the right of each founder to participate in management could be entrenched.

Some common law rules about classes of shares and about the construction of the terms of issue of shares are illustrated by the cases which follow. The question of variation of class rights is discussed in the next section.

A company may alter its articles so as to take power to issue shares ranking in preference to its existing shares. There is no implied condition in a company's articles that all the shares in a company shall be equal.

[11.01] Andrews v Gas Meter Co [1897] 1 Ch 361 (Court of Appeal)

The facts appear from the judgment.

The judgment of the court (LINDLEY, AL SMITH and RIGBY LJJ) was delivered by LINDLEY LJ: The question raised by this appeal is whether certain preference shares issued by a limited company as long ago as 1865 were validly issued or not . . . The company's original capital as stated in its memorandum of association was '£60,000, divided into 600 shares of £100 each, every share being sub-divisible into fifths, with power to increase the capital as provided by the articles of association'. By the articles of association which accompanied the memorandum of association, and were registered with it, power was given to the company to increase the capital (article 27), and it was provided that any new capital should be considered as part of the original capital (article 28). The issue of preference shares was not contemplated or authorised. In 1865 the company desired to acquire additional works, and passed a special resolution . . . altering the articles and authorising the issue of 100 shares of £100 each, fully

---

[2] In *Investment Trust Corpn Ltd v Singapore Traction Co Ltd* [1935] Ch 615, one 'management share' could outvote the remaining 399,999! A device of this kind (normally termed a 'golden share') is sometimes employed to retain government control when a nationalised industry or enterprise is privatised.

paid, and bearing a preferential dividend of £5 per cent per annum. Those shares were accordingly issued to the vendors of the works referred to, and are the shares the validity of which is now in question . . . The learned judge has held that the creation of the preference shares was ultra vires, and that their holders never became and are not now shareholders in the company, and that they have none of the rights of shareholders, whether preference or ordinary . . . The judgment against the validity of the preference shares is based upon the well-known case of *Hutton v Scarborough Cliff Hotel Co Ltd*,[3] which came twice before Kindersley V-C in 1865, and which Kekewich J [the trial judge] very naturally held to be binding on him. Kindersley V-C's first decision was that a limited company which had not issued the whole of its original capital could not issue the unallotted shares as preference shares unless authorised so to do by its memorandum of association or by its articles of association. This decision was affirmed on appeal, and was obviously correct; and would have been correct even if the whole of the original capital had been issued and the preference shares had been new and additional capital. The company, however, afterwards passed a special resolution altering the articles and authorising an issue of preference shares. This raised an entirely different question, and led to the second decision. The Vice-Chancellor granted an injunction restraining the issue of the preference shares, and he held distinctly that the resolution altering the articles was ultra vires. He did so upon the ground, as we understand his judgment, that there was in the memorandum of association a condition that all the shareholders should stand on an equal footing as to the receipt of dividends, and that this condition was one which could not be got rid of by a special resolution altering the articles of association under the powers conferred by ss 50 and 51 of the Act [CA 2006 ss 21 and 283 (changed)]. The judgment of the Vice-Chancellor is a little obscure, because he treats the condition as a condition of the constitution of the company, and he may have meant by that expression either the constitution as fixed by the memorandum of association or the constitution as fixed by the memorandum of association and the original articles. But unless he had meant the constitution of the company as fixed by the memorandum of association his decision is unintelligible; for, so far as the constitution depended on the articles, it clearly could be altered by special resolution under the powers conferred by ss 50 and 51 of the Act . . .

[His Lordship examined a number of cases, and continued:] These decisions turned upon the principle that although by s 8 of the Act [CA 2006 changes these rules; see Chapter 1] the memorandum is to state the amount of the original capital and the number of shares into which it is to be divided, yet in other respects the rights of the shareholders in respect of their shares and the terms on which additional capital may be raised are matters to be regulated by the articles of association rather than by the memorandum, and are, therefore, matters which . . . may be determined by the company from time to time by special resolution pursuant to s 50 of the Act. This view, however, clearly negatives the doctrine that there is a condition in the memorandum of association that all shareholders are to be on an equality unless the memorandum itself shows the contrary. That proposition is, in our opinion, unsound . . .

➤ Note

Although this case established that there is no implied condition in the constitution of a company that all its shares should rank equally, there is nevertheless a presumption (as is shown by the cases which follow) that all shares do enjoy equal rights unless the terms of issue make some express provision to the contrary.

In many jurisdictions of the United States, the principle of equality as between shares was developed much further by the courts, so that shareholders commonly have pre-emptive

---

[3] (1865) 2 Drew & Sm 514 at 521.

rights as regards any new shares issued. This has been achieved in the UK only by legislation; see 'Pre-emption rights governing the issue of new shares', pp 515ff.

Where the terms of issue make no express distinction between the rights of different categories of share in respect of (i) dividend, (ii) the return of capital (and participation in surplus assets in a winding up), or (iii) voting, the rule of construction in each case is that, prima facie, all shareholders rank equally. The fact that a preference in respect of any one of these matters is conferred does not imply any right to preference in some other respect: the presumption of equality is undisturbed.

[11.02] Birch v Cropper (1889) 14 App Cas 525 (House of Lords)

The articles of the Bridgewater Navigation Co Ltd provided that dividends should be paid in proportion to the amounts paid up on the shares. There was no express provision governing the distribution of assets in a winding up. The company had issued 5% preference shares at £10 each which were paid up in full, and ordinary shares of £10 on which £3.50 had been paid. The House of Lords, reversing the Court of Appeal and varying the order of North J, held that in distributing the surplus assets available in the company's liquidation after the return of capital, the paid-up and partly paid shares were to be treated alike; and that the preference shareholders were to participate rateably with the ordinary shareholders in proportion to the nominal amounts of the shares held.

LORD MACNAGHTEN: . . . Every person who becomes a member of a company limited by shares of equal amount becomes entitled to a proportionate part in the capital of the company, and, unless it be otherwise provided by the regulations of the company, entitled, as a necessary consequence, to the same proportionate part in all the property of the company, including its uncalled capital. He is liable in respect of all moneys unpaid on his shares to pay up every call that is duly made upon him. But he does not by such payment acquire any further or other interest in the capital of the company. His share in the capital is just what it was before. His liability to the company is diminished by the amount paid. His contribution is merged in the common fund. And that is all.

When the company is wound up, new rights and liabilities arise. The power of the directors to make calls is at an end; but every present member, so far as his shares are unpaid, is liable to contribute to the assets of the company to an amount sufficient for the payment of its debts and liabilities, the costs of winding up, and such sums as may be required for the adjustment of the rights of the contributories[4] amongst themselves . . .

Amongst the rights to be adjusted, the most important are those which arise when there is a difference between shareholders in the amount of calls paid in respect of their shares. Before winding up no such rights exist; whatever has been paid by the shareholders of one issue in excess of the contributions of their fellow shareholders of a different issue, must have been paid in pursuance of calls duly made or in accordance with the conditions under which the shares were held. While the company is a going concern no capital can be returned to the shareholders, except under the statutory provisions in that behalf. There is therefore during that period no ground for complaint; no room for equities arising out of unequal contributions. In the case of winding up everything is changed. The assets have to be distributed. The rights

---

[4] The term 'contributory' is used in a winding up to refer to members and some former members: see Insolvency Act 1986 (IA 1986) s 79.

arising from unequal contributions on shares of equal amounts must be adjusted, and the property of the company, including its uncalled capital not required to satisfy prior claims, must be applied for that purpose. But when those rights are adjusted, when the capital is equalised, what equity founded on inequality of contribution can possibly remain? The rights and interests of the contributories in the company must then be simply in proportion to their shares . . .

It now only remains to deal with the various claims put forward in the course of the argument.

The ordinary shareholders say that the preference shareholders are entitled to a return of their capital, with 5% interest up to the day of payment, and to nothing more. That is treating them as if they were debenture-holders, liable to be paid off at a moment's notice. Then they say that at the utmost the preference shareholders are only entitled to the capital value of a perpetual annuity of 5% upon the amounts paid up by them. That is treating them as if they were holders of irredeemable debentures. But they are not debenture-holders at all. For some reason or other the company invited them to come in as shareholders, and they must be treated as having all the rights of shareholders, except so far as they renounced those rights on their admission to the company. There was an express bargain made as to their rights in respect of profits arising from the business of the company. But there was no bargain—no provision of any sort—affecting their rights as shareholders in the capital of the company.

Then the preference shareholders say to the ordinary shareholders, 'We have paid up the whole of the amount due on our shares; you have paid but a fraction on yours. The prosperity of a company results from its paid-up capital; distribution must be in proportion to contribution. The surplus assets must be divided in proportion to the amounts paid up on the shares.' That seems to me to be ignoring altogether the elementary principles applicable to joint-stock companies of this description. I think it rather leads to confusion to speak of the assets which are the subject of this application as 'surplus assets' as if they were an accretion or addition to the capital of the company capable of being distinguished from it and open to different considerations. They are part and parcel of the property of the company—part and parcel of the joint stock or common fund—which at the date of the winding up represented the capital of the company. It is through their shares in the capital, and through their shares alone, that members of a company limited by shares become entitled to participate in the property of the company. The shares in this company were all of the same amount. Every contributory who held a preference share at the date of the winding up must have taken that share and must have held it on the terms of paying up all calls duly made upon him in respect thereof. In paying up his share in full he has done no more than he contracted to do; why should he have more than he bargained for? Every contributory who was the holder of an ordinary share at the date of the winding up took his share and held it on similar terms. He has done all he contracted to do; why should he have less than his bargain? When the preference shareholders and the ordinary shareholders are once placed on exactly the same footing in regard to the amounts paid up upon their shares, what is there to alter rights which were the subject of express contract? . . .

Then it is said on behalf of the preference shareholders that the provision for payment of dividends in proportion to the amounts paid up on the shares leads to an inference that the distribution of surplus assets was to be made in the same proportion. I do not think that it leads to any inference of the kind. It is a very common provision nowadays, though it is not what you find in Table A, and it is a very reasonable provision, because during the continuance of the company, and while it is a going concern, it prevents any sense of dissatisfaction on the part of those who have paid more on their shares than their fellow shareholders of a different issue. But when it has come to an end I cannot see how it can be used to regulate or disturb rights with which it had nothing to do even while it was in force . . .

LORDS HERSCHELL and FITZGERALD delivered concurring opinions.

Where the terms of issue do make express provision as to the rights of a class of shares in respect of (i) dividend, (ii) the return of capital (and participation in surplus assets), or (iii) voting, then that provision is presumed to be an exhaustive statement of the rights of the class in that particular respect.

[11.03] Re National Telephone Co [1914] 1 Ch 755 (Chancery Division)

SARGANT J: [It] appears to me that the weight of authority is in favour of the view that, either with regard to dividend or with regard to the rights in a winding up, the express gift or attachment of preferential rights to preference shares, on their creation, is, prima facie, a definition of the whole of their rights in that respect, and negatives any further or other right to which, but for the specified rights, they would have been entitled . . .

[11.04] Scottish Insurance Corpn Ltd v Wilsons and Clyde Coal Co Ltd [1949] AC 462 (House of Lords)

For the facts and another part of the decision, see **[10.01]**.

The rights of the preference shareholders were, so far as is material, defined by articles 159 and 160 of the articles of association as follows:

159. In the event of the company being wound up, the preference shares (first issue) shall rank before the other shares of the company on the property of the company, to the extent of repayment of the amounts called up and paid thereon.

160. In the event of the company being wound up, the preference shares (second issue) shall rank before the ordinary shares but after the said preference shares (first issue) on the property of the company to the extent of repayment of the amounts called up and paid thereon.

LORD SIMONDS: It is clear from the authorities, and would be clear without them, that, subject to any relevant provision of the general law, the rights inter se of preference and ordinary shareholders must depend on the terms of the instrument which contains the bargain that they have made with the company and each other. This means that there is a question of construction to be determined, and undesirable though it may be that fine distinctions should be drawn in commercial documents such as articles of association of a company, your Lordships cannot decide that the articles here under review have a particular meaning, because to somewhat similar articles in such cases as *Re William Metcalfe & Sons Ltd*[5] that meaning has been judicially attributed. Reading the relevant articles, as a whole, I come to the conclusion that articles 159 and 160 are exhaustive of the rights of the preference stockholders in a winding up. The whole tenor of the articles, as I have already pointed out, is to leave the ordinary stockholders masters of the situation. If there are 'surplus assets' it is because the ordinary stockholders have contrived that it should be so, and, though this is not decisive, in determining what the parties meant by their bargain, it is of some weight that it should be in the power of one class so to act that there will or will not be surplus assets . . .

But, apart from those more general considerations, the words of the specifically relevant articles, 'rank before the other shares . . . on the property of the company to the extent of repayment of the amounts called up and paid thereon', appears to me apt to define exhaustively the rights of the preference stockholders in a winding up. Similar words, in *Will v United Lankat Plantations Co Ltd*[6] 'rank, both as regards capital and dividend, in priority to the other shares', were held to define exhaustively the rights of preference shareholders to dividend, and I do not

---

[5] [1933] Ch 142.
[6] [1914] AC 11 at 13.

find in the speeches of Viscount Haldane LC or Earl Loreburn in that case any suggestion that a different result would have followed if the dispute had been in regard to capital. I do not ignore that in the same case in the Court of Appeal[7] the distinction between dividend and capital was expressly made by both Cozens-Hardy MR and Farwell LJ, and that in *Re William Metcalfe & Sons Ltd*, Romer LJ reasserted it. But I share the difficulty, which Lord Keith has expressed in this case, in reconciling the reasoning that lies behind the judgments in *Will's* case and *Re William Metcalfe & Sons Ltd* respectively. [His Lordship accordingly held that the latter decision should be overruled.]

VISCOUNT MAUGHAM and LORD NORMAND delivered concurring opinions.

LORD MORTON OF HENRYTON dissented.

➤ Note

The conclusion reached in the *Scottish Insurance* case naturally made preference shares a less secure form of investment. It was also thought at the time to be harsh on the holders of such shares, for the overruling of *Metcalfe*'s case inevitably depressed the value of shares carrying a high rate of return. To offset the effect of the *Scottish Insurance* decision, many listed companies have since adopted the 'Spens formula', under which the sum to be repaid to preference shareholders on a reduction of capital is geared to the recent market price of the shares.

Variation of class rights

Statutory requirements

If the share capital of a company has been divided into classes,[8] statutory provisions come into play, defining the ability of the company to alter the rights attached to a class of shares. CA 2006 s 630 provides that class rights may only be varied:

(i)   in accordance with the relevant provisions in the company's articles; or

(ii) if no provision is made in the articles, if three-quarters in value of the shares of that class consent in writing, or a special resolution is passed at a separate meeting of the holders of such shares (also see ss 283 and 334).[9]

The company's articles may specify either more *or* less onerous provisions for variation of class rights than the default provisions in the Act.[10] All three sets of model articles of association (for private companies, companies limited by guarantee and public companies) make provision for the issue of shares of different classes, but make no special provisions for variation of class rights. However, if the company *entrenches* the class rights in its articles (ie sets conditions for change that are more demanding than the special resolution

---

[7] [1912] 2 Ch 571.

[8] Note that the CA 2006 provisions on variation of class rights extend the rules to companies without share capital, eg companies limited by guarantee with different classes of members having different voting rights. CA 2006 ss 631, 335 and 635 provide appropriate rules in the same terms as those discussed earlier.

[9] This effects a change to the Companies Act 1985 (CA 1985), which only allowed the company to impose conditions that were *more* onerous than the statute. The company could do this by inserting the conditions into the memorandum, the articles or the terms of the share issue itself: see CA 1985 s 125.

[10] And any provisions inserted in a company's memorandum before CA 2006 will be treated as contained in the company's articles: CA 2006 s 28.

procedure) then that protection cannot be circumvented by changing the rights attached to the class of shares under s 630: see ss 630(3) and 22.

Additional common law requirements

These statutory provisions are reinforced by a rule of common law established in the *British America Nickel* case **[11.06]**. This case establishes the rule that members voting at a class meeting must act 'for the purpose of benefiting the class as a whole'. This obviously has some links with the principle of *Allen v Gold Reefs of West Africa Ltd* **[4.22]**, that members must vote 'bona fide for the benefit of the company as a whole'. That principle has been extended in some later cases (eg *Re Holders Investment Trust Ltd* **[10.04]**). If taken literally, the rule as so interpreted would not permit the class to subordinate its own interests to those of the company as a whole, and class rights could never be varied except to the class-holders' advantage. This surely cannot have been intended. On the other hand, some limitations on the exercise of majority voting power are now a familiar theme from earlier chapters.

Meaning of 'class right'

These statutory provisions apply only if the shareholders have 'class rights',[11] and only if those rights have been 'varied'. Both requirements have caused more debate than might be imagined. Indeed, some textbooks devote considerable attention to the meaning and scope of the term 'class right'. If the preference shareholders have a right under the articles to a 10% preference dividend, that is obviously a 'class right', but if the articles say nothing about the dividend rights of ordinary shareholders in the same company, is their dividend right a 'class right' too? And if nothing is said about voting in regard to either class of shares in their terms of issue, are their voting rights 'class rights'? In the example given following the list of types of shares in 'Classes of shares and class rights', p 582, where the only expressed right is that of appointing a director, are the dividend rights of each class 'class rights'?

In the *Cumbrian Newspapers* case **[11.05]**, Scott J was called on to give the first judicial consideration to the meaning of the terms 'class of shares' and 'class rights'. His conclusion was that they might extend to include cases where rights are enjoyed by a particular member or category of members but no specific shares are designated to which those rights are referable.[12] This is a surprisingly wide interpretation, but has the merit of ensuring that the protection conferred by s 630 will be applied fairly comprehensively.

Defining a 'variation' of class rights

The only light thrown on this issue by the Act itself is in s 630(5) and (6). Section 630(5) states that amendment or insertion of a 'variation of rights' provision in the articles is itself a variation of rights. Section 630(6) deals with the extinction of rights but not the extinction of the share itself: *Re Saltdean Estate Co Ltd* **[10.03]**.

Paradoxically, the judges have not shown themselves anything like so solicitous for the interests of class members in the cases concerned with the interpretation of the term

---

[11] Interestingly, the term is used in the heading to s 630, but not in the section itself, which refers to 'variation of the rights attached to a class of shares'. The 2006 Act then specifies that 'shares are of one class if the rights attached to them are in all respects uniform' (s 629(1)). Another way of putting the question posed in the previous paragraph is to ask whether shares are of a *different* class, for the purpose of s 630, if some of the rights attached to them are different, even if the right being varied is the same for all of them. The assumed answer is no, and the analysis is invariably one that approaches the issue from a 'class rights' perspective, as discussed earlier. CA 1985 s 125 was in the same terms in this respect (although not in others), and this was the conclusion.

[12] This is not covered by the new CA 2006 s 631, which concerns companies without share capital.

'variation'. In many cases it may be possible to make class rights less effective without effecting any technical 'variation' of the rights themselves: this is illustrated by *White v Bristol Aeroplane Co* **[11.08]** and *Greenhalgh v Arderne Cinemas Ltd* **[11.09]**.

Right of dissenting member to object to court

CA 2006 s 633 gives dissenting members of a class, who hold at least 15% of the shares of that class, the right to challenge the variation in court within 21 days. They are thus given access to the court free from the hazards of *Foss v Harbottle* **[13.01]**, but the requirements of 15% and the need to act within 21 days may lead to difficulties, especially in a large company.

Rights enjoyed by a member may be class rights although they are not referable to particular shares.

[11.05] Cumbrian Newspapers Group Ltd v Cumberland and Westmorland Herald Newspaper and Printing Co Ltd [1987] Ch 1 (Chancery Division)

The plaintiff had acquired 10.67% of the ordinary shares in the defendant company ('Cumberland') in 1968 as part of an arrangement designed to concentrate the local newspaper publishing business under one title and to make it difficult for an outsider to acquire control of this paper. The articles of Cumberland were altered so that the plaintiff had (i) rights of pre-emption over the company's other ordinary shares (arts 7 and 9); (ii) rights in respect of unissued shares (art 5); and (iii) the right to appoint a director, so long as it held at least 10% of the shares (art 12). Scott J held that these were class rights enjoyed by the plaintiff which could only be altered pursuant to CA 1985 s 125 [CA 2006 s 630].

SCOTT J: I turn to the critical question: are the plaintiff's rights under articles 5, 7, 9 and 12, rights attached to a class of shares?

Rights or benefits which may be contained in articles can be divided into three different categories. First, there are rights or benefits which are annexed to particular shares. Classic examples of rights of this character are dividend rights and rights to participate in surplus assets on a winding up. If articles provide that particular shares carry particular rights not enjoyed by the holders of other shares, it is easy to conclude that the rights are attached to a class of shares, for the purpose both of s 125 of the Act of 1985 and of article 4 of Table A [1948]. It is common ground that rights falling into this category are rights attached to a class of shares for those purposes. Mr Howarth submitted at first that this category should be restricted to rights that were capable of being enjoyed by the holders for the time being of the shares in question. Such a restriction would exclude rights expressly attached to particular shares issued to some named individual, but expressed to determine upon transfer of the shares by the named individual. *Palmer's Company Precedents*, 17th edn (1956), Pt I, p 818, contains a form for the creation of a life governor's share in a company. Mr Howarth accepted that the rights attached to a share in accordance with this precedent would be rights attached to a class of shares. He accepted, rightly in my judgment, that a provision for defeasance of rights on alienation of the share to which the rights were attached, would not of itself prevent the rights, pre-alienation, from being properly described as rights attached to a class of shares. The plaintiff's rights under articles 5, 7, 9 and 12 cannot, however, be brought within this first category. The rights were not attached to any particular shares. In articles 5, 7 and 9, there is no reference to any current shareholding held by the plaintiff. The rights conferred on the plaintiff under article 12 are dependent on the plaintiff holding at least 10% of the issued ordinary shares in the defendant. But the rights are not attached to any particular shares. Any ordinary shares in the defendant, if sufficient in number and held by the plaintiff, would entitle the plaintiff to exercise the rights.

A second category of rights or benefits which may be contained in articles (although it may be that neither 'rights' nor 'benefits' is an apt description), would cover rights or benefits conferred on individuals not in the capacity of members or shareholders of the company but, for ulterior reasons, connected with the administration of the company's affairs or the conduct of its business. *Eley v Positive Government Security Life Assurance Co Ltd* **[4.37]** was a case where the articles of the defendant company had included a provision that the plaintiff should be the company solicitor. The plaintiff sought to enforce that provision as a contract between himself and the company. He failed. The reasons why he failed are not here relevant, and I cite the case only to draw attention to an article which, on its terms, conferred a benefit on an individual but not in the capacity of member or shareholder of the company. It is, perhaps, obvious that rights or benefits in this category cannot be class rights. They cannot be described as rights attached to a class of shares. The plaintiff in *Eley v Positive Government Security Life Assurance Co Ltd* was not a shareholder at the time the articles were adopted. He became a shareholder some time thereafter. It is easy, therefore, to conclude that the article in question did not confer on him any right or benefit in his capacity as a member of the company. In a case where the individual had been issued with shares in the company at the same time and as part of the same broad arrangement under which the article in question had been adopted, the conclusion might not be so easy. But if, in all the circumstances, the right conclusion was still that the rights or benefits conferred by the article were not conferred on the beneficiary in the capacity of member or shareholder of the company, then the rights could not, in my view, be regarded as class rights. They would not be rights attached to any class of shares . . .

In my judgment, the plaintiff's rights under those articles do not fall within this second category.

That leaves the third category. This category would cover rights or benefits that, although not attached to any particular shares, were nonetheless conferred on the beneficiary in the capacity of member or shareholder of the company. The rights of the plaintiff under articles 5, 7, 9 and 12 fall, in my judgment, into this category. Other examples can be found in reported cases.

In *Bushell v Faith* **[6.02]**, articles of association included a provision that on a resolution at a general meeting for the removal of any director from office, any shares held by that director should carry the right to three votes. The purpose of this provision was to prevent directors being removed from office by a simple majority of the members of the company. The validity of the article was upheld by the Court of Appeal and by the House of Lords; the reasons do not, for present purposes, matter. But the rights conferred by the article in question fall, in my view, firmly in this third category. They were not attached to any particular shares. On the other hand, they were conferred on the director/beneficiaries in their capacity as shareholders. The article created, in effect, two classes of shareholders—namely, shareholders who were for the time being directors, on the one hand, and shareholders who were not for the time being directors, on the other hand.

The present case is, and *Bushell v Faith* was, concerned with rights conferred by articles. The other side of the coin is demonstrated by *Rayfield v Hands* **[4.39]**. That case was concerned with obligations imposed on members by the articles. The articles of the company included an article entitling every member to sell his shares to the directors of the company at a fair valuation. In effect, the members enjoyed 'put' options exercisable against the directors. Vaisey J held that the obligations imposed by the article on the directors for the time being were enforceable against them. He held that the obligations were imposed on the directors in their capacity as members of the company. It follows from his judgment that, as in *Bushell v Faith*, there were in effect two classes of shareholders in the company. There were shareholders who were not for the time being directors, and shareholders who were for the time being directors: the former had rights against the latter which the latter did not enjoy against the former. The two classes were identifiable not by reference to their respective ownership of particular shares, but by reference to the office held by the latter. But the rights of the former, and the obligations of the latter, required their respective ownership of shares in the company. Accordingly, as a matter of classification, the rights in question fall, in my view, into the third category.

In the present case, the rights conferred on the plaintiff under articles 5, 7, 9 and 12 were, as I have held, conferred on the plaintiff as a member or shareholder of the defendant. The rights would not be enforceable by the plaintiff otherwise than as the owner of ordinary shares in the defendants. If the plaintiff were to divest itself of all its ordinary shares in the defendant, it would not then, in my view, be in a position to enforce the rights in the articles. But the rights were not attached to any particular share or shares. Enforcement by the plaintiff of the rights granted under articles 5, 7 and 9, would require no more than ownership by the plaintiff of at least some shares in the defendant. Enforcement by the plaintiff of the rights granted under article 12 require the plaintiff to hold at least 10% of the issued shares in the defendant. But any shares would do. It follows, in my judgment, that the plaintiff's rights under the articles in question fall squarely within this third category.

The question for decision is whether rights in this third category are within the meaning of the phrase in s 125 of the Companies Act 1985 and in article 4 of Table A, rights attached to a class of shares. [His Lordship examined the language and the background of the section and concluded that this was the case.]

> Questions

1. The implications of this case are potentially far-reaching. In the *Bushell v Faith* case, for example, the director's right to deploy super-voting powers on a motion for his dismissal could only be changed by the class rights procedure (s 630, requiring his agreement, as the only member of the relevant class). If the director's right had been classified differently, it could have been changed by the statutory procedure for changing the articles (s 21, requiring a special majority of *all* the shareholders). Which is the preferable outcome? Which outcome was likely to have been contemplated at the time the right was created?

2. Where the rights are not specifically attached to a share issue, how can you tell whether rights are 'class rights' or rights under a shareholders' agreement (see 'Shareholders' agreements', pp 256ff and 'Classes of shares and class rights', pp 581ff)? What practical consequences flow from classifying rights one way or the other? In deciding on the appropriate classification, is it of any significance that in one case a transfer from X to Y of the shares to which the special rights are allegedly attached would not be effective to transfer the special rights to Y—that is, the special rights are personal to X? See *Grays Timber Products Ltd v Commissioners for HM Revenue and Customs* [2010] UKSC 4, SC.

A vote on a resolution to modify class rights must be exercised for the purpose, or dominant purpose, of benefiting the class as a whole.

[11.06] British America Nickel Corpn Ltd v O'Brien [1927] AC 369 (Privy Council)

The company had issued mortgage bonds, secured by a trust deed, which provided (inter alia) that a majority of the bondholders, representing not less than three-fourths in value, might sanction any modification of the rights of the bondholders. A scheme for the reconstruction of the company, which involved a modification of the bondholders' rights, was approved by the requisite majority. However, it was objected that one of the bondholders, without whose vote the proposal would not have been carried, had been induced to give his support by a promise of a large block of ordinary stock. The Privy Council, affirming the decision of the Ontario courts, held that the vote was invalid.

The opinion of their Lordships was delivered by VISCOUNT HALDANE: To give a power to modify the terms on which debentures in a company are secured is not uncommon in practice. The business interests of the company may render such a power expedient, even in the interests of the class of debenture-holders as a whole. The provision is usually made in the form of a power, conferred by the instrument constituting the debenture security, upon the majority of the class of holders. It often enables them to modify, by resolution properly passed, the security itself. The provision of such a power to a majority bears some analogy to such a power as that . . . which enables a majority of the shareholders by special resolution to alter the articles of association. There is, however, a restriction of such powers, when conferred on a majority of a special class in order to enable that majority to bind a minority. They must be exercised subject to a general principle, which is applicable to all authorities conferred on majorities of classes enabling them to bind minorities; namely, that the power given must be exercised for the purpose of benefiting the class as a whole, and not merely individual members only. Subject to this, the power may be unrestricted. It may be free from the general principle in question when the power arises not in connection with a class, but only under a general title which confers the vote as a right of property attaching to a share. The distinction does not arise in this case, and it is not necessary to express an opinion as to its ground. What does arise is the question whether there is such a restriction on the right to vote of a creditor or member of an analogous class on whom is conferred a power to vote for the alteration of the title of a minority of the class to which he himself belongs . . .

[T]heir Lordships do not think that there is any real difficulty in combining the principle that while usually a holder of shares or debentures may vote as his interest directs, he is subject to the further principle that where his vote is conferred on him as a member of a class he must conform to the interest of the class itself when seeking to exercise the power conferred on him in his capacity of being a member. The second principle is a negative one, one which puts a restriction on the completeness of freedom under the first, without excluding such freedom wholly.

The distinction, which may prove a fine one, is well illustrated in the carefully worded judgment of Parker J in *Goodfellow v Nelson Line*.[13] It was there held that while the power conferred by a trust deed on a majority of debenture-holders to bind a minority must be exercised bona fide, and while the court has power to prevent some sorts at least of unfairness or oppression, a debenture-holder may, subject to this, vote in accordance with his individual interests, though these may be peculiar to himself and not shared by the other members of the class. It was true that a secret bargain to secure his vote by special treatment might be treated as bribery, but where the scheme to be voted upon itself provides, as it did in that case, openly for special treatment of a debenture-holder with a special interest, he may vote, inasmuch as the other members of the class had themselves known from the first of the scheme. Their Lordships think that Parker J accurately applied in his judgment the law on this point . . .

Their Lordships are of opinion that judgment was rightly given for the respondents in this appeal . . . [It] is plain, even from his own letters, that before Mr JR Booth would agree to the scheme of 1921 his vote had to be secured by the promise of $2,000,000 ordinary stock of the Nickel Corporation. No doubt he was entitled in giving his vote to consider his own interests. But as that vote had come to him as a member of a class he was bound to exercise it with the interests of the class itself kept in view as dominant. It may be that, as Ferguson JA thought, he and

---

[13] [1912] 2 Ch 324.

those with whom he was negotiating considered the scheme the best way out of the difficulties with which the corporation was beset. But they had something else to consider in the first place. Their duty was to look to the difficulties of the bondholders as a class, and not to give any one of these bond-holders a special personal advantage, not forming part of the scheme to be voted for, in order to induce him to assent . . .

➤ Note

Contrast this case with the facts and outcome in *Azevedo v Imcopa Importacao Ltd* [2015] QB 1, CA (also a case concerning bondholder voting[14]), where 'consent payments' were offered by the company to *all* those voting on the issue, and the consequential passing of the resolution was held to be proper. This was despite the fact that the promised payments were only received by those who did indeed 'consent' and vote in favour of the resolution. The court denied this involved the company 'buying' votes. As Lloyd LJ put it:

> 69. Mr Goldblatt [counsel for the appellants] ... described the votes of the assenting note holders as being 'sold' to the company.... [I]f a vote is cast in the way which the company has proposed and asked for, and has encouraged note holders to think would be in their best interests as well as in those of the company, that is not the 'sale' of a vote even if the company has offered an incentive to fortify the encouragement. Moreover, I see nothing wrong in principle with the idea that a company, which has taken the view that a particular course of action is in its best interests and in those of its creditors and shareholders, but which requires favourable votes from one or more classes, should take part in the process which leads to the relevant resolution being put to the necessary vote. It seems to me that it would be extraordinary to suggest that the company cannot take part in the process. Indeed, in practical terms it must do so. The only issue is whether it is allowed to strengthen its urging and encouragement in favour of a vote by offering an incentive. For my part I find no objection to that in principle under English law, so long as all is open and above board.

➤ Questions

1. What exactly was the problem in *British America Nickel* **[11.06]**? Why was this not a problem in *Azevedo* (see previous Note)? (Also see the Note and Questions following **[11.07]**.)

2. Does the limitation described in *British America Nickel* **[11.06]** require the shareholders to vote in the class meeting *in* the interests of the class (which might require self-denial of a fiduciary nature from individual shareholders whose own self-interest conflicts with the interests of the class), or does it merely require shareholders to vote for proper purposes (which might require shareholders not to use their power to achieve ulterior ends)? Does the requirement that shareholders vote bona fide add anything? How is such a power exercised *mala fide*?

3. You are asked to advise a preference shareholder about a class meeting which is to be held to consider a scheme to replace the preference shares with debentures. There is evidence suggesting that this will be to the disadvantage of the preference shareholders as a class, but that the scheme as a whole will benefit the company. Should the preference shareholder have regard to the interests of the class, or of the company, in deciding how to cast her vote; or is she free to weigh the relative merits of each? (See *Re Holders Investment*

---

[14] The case concerned special majority voting by bondholders rather than shareholders (ie people with 'debt securities' rather than 'equity securities'), to change the terms of their debt contracts, but the equitable restrictions on valid class voting are identical.

Trust Ltd **[10.04]** and *Re Hellenic and General Trust Ltd* **[15.05]**, and contrast *Re Chatterley-Whitfield Collieries Ltd* **[10.02]**.)

4. If all the members of a class are to take account of the same considerations when voting, will a resolution invariably be carried (or lost) by 100% to nil?

[11.07] Assénagon Asset Management SA v Irish Bank Resolution Corpn Ltd (Formerly Anglo Irish Bank Corpn Ltd) [2012] EWHC 2090 (Chancery Division)

This case concerned voting by classes of creditors, not shareholders, but similar rules were held to apply. The claimant was the holder of bonds ('2017 Notes') issued by the bank, which were subordinate to claims by secured and unsecured creditors in the event of insolvency, and ahead only of equity shareholders. Following the global financial crisis, the bank faced a liquidity crisis which resulted in its rescue by the Irish government. Following a series of measures, the government announced in September 2010 that it expected subordinated debt-holders to make a significant contribution towards meeting the costs to the bank in meeting its substantial losses. The bank subsequently adopted a technique known as 'exit consent' in respect of certain series of its notes, including the 2017 Notes. In essence, it was proposed that a holding of 20 cents of new notes (the 'New Notes') would be exchanged for every €1 of the 2017 Notes, that is, an exchange ratio of 0.20. In accepting the exchange proposal, the noteholders would also agree to vote in favour of an extraordinary resolution to vary the terms of the old 2017 Notes so as to enable the bank to redeem any outstanding 2017 Notes at a rate of €0.01 per €1,000, that is, a payment ratio of 0.00001 (the 'Resolution'). The combined effect of the exchange offer and the Resolution led to 92.03% of noteholders offering their notes for exchange and conditionally binding themselves to vote in favour of the Resolution. The Resolution was duly passed, and the bank exercised its newly acquired right to redeem the remaining 2017 Notes at the payment ratio of 0.00001. The claimant received €170 for its €17 million face value of 2017 Notes. The claimant challenged the validity of the exit consent technique as being an abuse by the majority noteholders of their power to bind the minority, albeit at the invitation of the issuer. The court allowed the claim.

> BRIGGS J:
>
> 1. This [claim tests], for the first time, the legality under English law of a technique used by the issuers of corporate bonds which has acquired the label 'exit consent'. The technique may be summarised thus. The issuer wishes to persuade all the holders of a particular bond issue to accept an exchange of their bonds for replacement bonds on different terms. The holders are all invited to offer their bonds for exchange, but on terms that they are required to commit themselves irrevocably to vote at a bondholders' meeting for a resolution amending the terms of the existing bonds so as seriously to damage or, as in the present case substantially destroy, the value of the rights arising from those existing bonds. The resolution is what has become labelled the exit consent.
>
> 2. The exit consent has no adverse effect in itself upon a holder who both offers his bonds for exchange and votes for the resolution. That is either because the issuer nonetheless fails to attract the majority needed to pass the resolution (in which case both the resolution and the proposed exchange do not happen) or simply because, if the requisite majority is obtained, his bonds are exchanged for new bonds and cancelled by the issuer. By contrast, a holder who fails to offer his bonds for exchange and either votes against the resolution or abstains takes the risk, if the resolution is passed, that his bonds will be either devalued by the resolution or, as in this

case, destroyed by being redeemed for a nominal consideration. This is in part because the efficacy of the technique depends upon the deadline for exchange being set before the bondholders' meeting so that, if the resolution is then passed, the dissenting holder gets no *locus poenitentiae* during which to exchange his bonds on the terms offered, and accepted in time, by the majority.

3. It is readily apparent, and not seriously in dispute, that the purpose of the attachment of the exit consent to the exchange proposal is to impose a dissuasive constraint upon bondholders from opposing the exchange, even if they take the view that the proffered new bonds are (ignoring the exit consent) less attractive than the existing bonds. The constraint arises from the risk facing any individual bondholder that a sufficient majority of his fellow holders will participate in the exchange and therefore (as required to do) vote for the resolution. The constraint is variously described in textbooks on both sides of the Atlantic as encouraging, inducing, coercing or even forcing the bondholders to accept the exchange.

4. The technique depends for its persuasive effect upon the difficulties faced by bondholders in organising themselves within the time allowed by the issuer in such a way as to find out before the deadline for accepting the exchange whether there is a sufficient number (usually more than 25% by value) determined to prevent the exchange going ahead by voting against the resolution. They were described in argument as facing a variant of the well-known prisoner's dilemma.

...

84. After some hesitation [and a review of all the relevant authorities], I have concluded that Mr Snowden [counsel for the claimant] arrived eventually at the correct question, which is whether it can be lawful for the majority to lend its aid to the coercion of a minority by voting for a resolution which expropriates the minority's rights under their bonds for a nominal consideration. In my judgment the correct answer to it is in the negative. My reasons derive essentially from my understanding of the purpose of the exit consent technique, as described at the beginning of this judgment. It is not that the issuer positively wishes to obtain securities by expropriation, rather than by the contractual exchange for value which it invites the bondholders to agree. On the contrary, the higher percentage of those accepting, generally the happier the issuer will be. Furthermore, the operation of the exit consent (here the Bank's new right to redeem for a nominal consideration) is not the method by which the issuer seeks to achieve the reconstruction constituted by the replacement of existing securities with new. The exit consent is, quite simply, a coercive threat which the issuer invites the majority to levy against the minority, nothing more or less. Its only function is the intimidation of a potential minority, based upon the fear of any individual member of the class that, by rejecting the exchange and voting against the resolution, he (or it) will be left out in the cold.

85. This form of coercion is in my judgment entirely at variance with the purposes for which majorities in a class are given power to bind minorities, and it is no answer for them to say that it is the issuer which has required or invited them to do so. True it is that, at the moment when any individual member of the class is required (by the imposition of the pre-meeting deadline) to make up his mind, there is at that point in time no defined minority against which the exit consent is aimed. But it is inevitable that there will be a defined (if any) minority by the time when the exit consent is implemented by being voted upon, and its only purpose is to prey upon the apprehension of each member of the class (aggravated by his relative inability to find out the views of his fellow class members in advance) that he will, if he decides to vote against, be part of that expropriated minority if the scheme goes ahead.

➤ Note

Note the way that Briggs J distinguished the facts of this case from *Azevedo v Imcopa Importacao, Exportaacao e Industria de Oleos Ltda* [2012] EWHC 1839 (Comm) (later affd on appeal [2013] EWCA Civ 364: see Note following **[11.06]**):

79. In *Azevedo* the defendant issuer of notes with provisions for alteration by majority substantially similar to those here [offered] fully disclosed monetary inducements (described as consent payments) to all those voting in favour [of issuer-recommended changes designed to facilitate a restructuring of the issuer for the benefit of all its stakeholders] . . .

. . .

81. Hamblen J [the trial judge] rejected the claimant's case, concluding in particular that the open manner in which the inducements had been offered prohibited any characterisation of them as bribery or fraud, following *Goodfellow* and *British America Nickel* [11.06]. He also took comfort from the approval of 'consent payments' of a similar type by the Delaware courts and from academic comment that such payments had been a common feature of debt refinancing in the USA for some time.

82. I accept that there is, at least at first sight, some similarity between the 'consent payments' in the *Azevedo* case and the 'exit consent' technique adopted in the present case. It is just possible to characterise the offer of the New Notes as a financial inducement to vote in favour of the Resolution. Nonetheless I consider that characterisation to be flawed. The reality is the other way round. The Resolution is used as a negative inducement to deter Noteholders from refusing the proffered exchange.

83. More generally the differences between the two cases substantially outweigh their similarities. First and foremost, the resolutions to postpone the interest payments in the *Azevedo* case were the substance of that which the issuer (and in the event the majority of noteholders) wished to achieve, whereas in the present case the substance of the Bank's plan was to substitute New Notes for the Existing Notes by way of a contractual exchange. The Resolution in the present case was no more than a negative inducement to deter Noteholders from refusing the proffered exchange. Secondly it was the issuer in *Azevedo* which proffered the inducement, whereas here it is the majority of the Noteholders which (albeit at the issuer's request) wields the negative inducement constituted by the Resolution. Thirdly the postponements sought by the resolutions in *Azevedo* were plainly capable of being beneficial to noteholders, since they were designed to facilitate a reconstruction of the issuer, beneficial to all its stakeholders. Here the Resolution was designed in substance to destroy rather than to enhance the value of the Notes and was, on its own, of no conceivable benefit to Noteholders. Fourthly, no case of oppression or unfairness was advanced in *Azevedo*, only a case of bribery. Here by contrast the case is centred on alleged oppression, and bribery is not alleged at all.

➤ Questions

These questions are designed to tease out the distinctions in the preceding cases.

1. Does it matter what the inducement is? Is the distinction between *Assénagon* and *Azevedo* proposed by Briggs J (as he then was) persuasive? What *is* the difference between a 'consent payment' and an 'exit consent'? And between those inducements and the inducement in *British America Nickel* [11.06]?

2. Does it matter what benefits are received by those voting in favour and those voting against? In *Assénagon*, if the majority vote had bound *all* the bondholders to accept €0.20 for each €1.00 Note, then would there have been any problem? The bondholders had agreed to majority rule, and a vote for such a proposal would not have been—at least on its face—tainted. By contrast, in *Assénagon* the dissenting minority did not get the deal accepted by the majority, but something far worse. Is *that* the material different between *Assénagon* and *Azevedo*? Or does the benefit received only by those voting in favour in *Azevedo* amount to the same problem?

3. Does it matter *who* votes as the majority, or *why* they vote? Who held the majority of the 2017 Notes at the time of the vote in *Assénagon*? The claimant argued, and Briggs J

agreed (at [64]–[68]), that the exchange contract between the noteholders and the bank was specifically enforceable, and so the noteholders held the 2017 Notes on constructive trust for the bank.[15] Not only did this contradict the terms of the bond issue and its voting rules (and so operate as a distinct basis for reaching the finding that the vote was invalid), but it made proof of improper purposes in the voting process still easier. This is because, if the bond and its associated vote is held on constructive trust for the issuer/the debtor on the bond, then the vote is effectively a vote by the debtor in a decision-making process undertaken by the creditors (the bondholders). The conflict of interest, and the likelihood of a vote for 'improper purposes' is self-evident. But does the 'consent payment' in *Azevedo* create the same 'improper purposes' problem, even though the vote is not 'owned' by the issuer/debtor?

The rights of a class of shareholders are not altered, or even 'affected', by a change in the company's structure (or in the rights attached to other shares) if this change affects merely the enjoyment of such rights.

[11.08] White v Bristol Aeroplane Co [1953] Ch 65 (Court of Appeal)

Article 68 of the defendant company's articles provided that the rights attached to any class of shares might be 'affected, modified, varied, dealt with, or abrogated in any manner' with the sanction of an extraordinary resolution passed at a separate meeting of the members of that class. The plaintiff, on behalf of the preference shareholders, claimed that a proposal to increase the capital of the company by a bonus issue of new shares to the existing shareholders (to both preference and ordinary shareholders) 'affected' the voting rights attached to their shares, and therefore came within the terms of the article cited. The company's view, which was upheld by the Court of Appeal, was that the rights themselves (as distinct from the enjoyment or the effectiveness of those rights) were not 'affected' by the proposal, so that no class meeting was required.

ROMER LJ: The rights attaching to the preference stockholders are those which are conferred by articles 62 and 83; and the only relevant article for present purposes is article 83. Under that article it is provided . . . that on a poll every member present in person or by proxy shall have one vote for every share held by him, or in the case of the preference stock, one vote for every £1 of preference stock held by him. It is suggested that, as a result of the proposed increase of capital, that right of the preference stockholders will in some way be 'affected'; but I cannot see that it will be affected in any way whatever. The position then will be precisely the same as now—namely, that the holder of preference stock will have on a poll one vote for every £1 of preference stock held by him. It is quite true that the block vote, if one may so describe the total voting power of the class, will, or may, have less force behind it, because it will pro tanto be watered down by reason of the increased total voting power of the members of the company; but no particular weight is attached to the vote, by the constitution of the company, as distinct from the right to exercise the vote, and certainly no right is conferred on the preference stock-holders to preserve anything in the nature of an equilibrium between their class and the ordinary stockholders or any other class.

During the course of the discussion I asked Mr Gray [counsel] whether it would not be true to say that the logical result of his argument would be that the rights of ordinary shareholders would be affected by the issue of new ordinary capital on the ground that every one of the considerations on which he was relying would be present in such a case. The votes of the

---

[15] See *Michaels v Harley House (Marylebone) Ltd* [2000] Ch 104, CA.

existing shareholders would be diminished in power; and they would have other people with whom to share the profits, and, on a winding up, to share the capital assets. In answer to that he was constrained, I think rightly, to say that was so. But in my opinion it cannot be said that the rights of ordinary shareholders would be affected by the issue of further ordinary capital; their rights would remain just as they were before, and the only result would be that the class of persons entitled to exercise those rights would be enlarged; and for my part I cannot help thinking that a certain amount of confusion has crept into this case between rights on the one hand, and the result of exercising those rights on the other hand. The rights, as such, are conferred by resolution or by the articles, and they cannot be affected except with the sanction of the members on whom those rights are conferred; but the results of exercising those rights are not the subject of any assurance or guarantee under the constitution of the company, and are not protected in any way. It is the rights and those alone, which are protected, and . . . the rights of the preference stockholders will not, in my judgment, be affected by the proposed resolutions . . .

EVERSHED MR delivered a concurring judgment.

DENNING LJ concurred.

[11.09] Greenhalgh v Arderne Cinemas Ltd [1946] 1 All ER 512 (Court of Appeal)

For later litigation between the same parties, see [4.27]. The company had issued ordinary shares of 10s [50p] each and other ordinary shares of 2s [10p] each (created in 1941), ranking *pari passu* for all purposes. On a poll, every member had one vote for each share held by him, which meant that Greenhalgh, who held the bulk of the 2s shares, could control about 40% of the votes and so block a special resolution. The holders of the 10s shares procured the passing of an ordinary resolution subdividing the 10s shares into five 2s shares, each ranking *pari passu* with the 1941 2s shares. Greenhalgh objected unsuccessfully that the rights attaching to his 2s shares were 'varied' by this manoeuvre.

LORD GREENE MR: Looking at the position of the original 2s ordinary shares, one asks oneself: What are the rights in respect of voting attached to that class within the meaning of article 3 of Table A [of the 1929 Act; there is no equivalent in later Model Articles] which are to be unalterable save with the necessary consents of the holders? The only right of voting which is attached in terms to the shares of that class is the right to have one vote per share pari passu with the other ordinary shares of the company for the time being issued. That right has not been taken away. Of course, if it had been attempted to reduce that voting right, eg by providing or attempting to provide that there should be one vote for every five of such shares, that would have been an interference with the voting rights attached to that class of shares. But nothing of the kind has been done; the right to have one vote per share is left undisturbed . . . I agree, the effect of this resolution is, of course, to alter the position of the 1941 2s shareholders. Instead of Greenhalgh finding himself in a position of control, he finds himself in a position where the control has gone, and to that extent the rights of the 1941 2s shareholders are affected, as a matter of business. As a matter of law, I am quite unable to hold that, as a result of the transaction, the rights are varied; they remain what they always were—a right to have one vote per share pari passu with the ordinary shares for the time being issued which include the new 2s ordinary shares resulting from the subdivision.

In the result, the appeal must be dismissed with costs.

MORTON LJ delivered a concurring judgment.

SOMERVELL LJ concurred.

> Notes

1. See also *Re Saltdean Estate Co Ltd* **[10.03]** and *House of Fraser plc v ACGE Investments Ltd* (Note 1 following *Re Saltdean Estate Co Ltd* **[10.03]**, p 539), where it was held that no variation of rights was involved in the *cancellation* of a class of shares on a reduction of capital, this being consistent with the terms of issue of the shares in question.

2. Note that a determination of 'classes of shares' and 'variation of class rights' is not necessarily the same as a determination of 'classes of members' (or 'classes of creditors') which may be required under CA 2006 for other purposes, such as the approval of schemes of arrangement. In that context, see for example, *Re Hellenic and General Trust Ltd* **[15.05]**, where Templeman J ruled that, for the purposes of a scheme of arrangement under CA 1985 ss 425–427A [CA 2006 ss 895ff], ordinary shares owned by the intending purchaser's subsidiary constituted a different 'class' from ordinary shares owned by outsiders, although the terms of issue of all these shares were identical. This approach, taking account (as it does) of matters peculiar to the holder rather than to the shares themselves, is in strong contrast with that in the two cases last cited. However, it may be justified by reference to the wording of s 425, which refers to classes *of members* rather than classes *of shares* (CA 2006 s 895 is the same). (See the discussion in 'Defining the classes for member or creditor meetings', pp 786ff.)

3. These cases deal with the *rights* of the different classes of shareholder as a matter of formal law. But an act which is within the rights of the controlling shareholders in this sense may nevertheless sometimes justify the grant of relief to minority members under CA 2006 s 994 (see 'Unfairly prejudicial conduct of the company's affairs', pp 715ff) or IA 1986 s 122(1)(g) (see 'Compulsory winding up on the "just and equitable" ground', pp 840ff).

Transfer of shares

This section examines the transfer of shares, but most of the remarks apply also to dealings in other company securities, such as bonds (ie 'debt securities'). A number of general points can be made.

Shares in a company are in principle freely transferable, subject to any restrictions imposed by the company's articles of association (CA 2006 s 544). However, the articles of nearly all (if not all) private companies restrict their members' rights to transfer their shares. This is done to ensure control over the management and direction of the company.

Although a share is a chose in action, the transfer of shares is not governed solely by the ordinary rules of assignment of choses in action. The *legal* title to shares is transferred only by registration of the new holder's name in the company's register of members.[16] Oddly, it is not possible to find any categorical statement to this effect in the Companies Act, although it is perhaps implicit from a reading of ss 112(2) and 540ff. The rule goes back to the days when shares normally had a substantial element of unpaid liability, and the act of registration established beyond argument the contractual bond of the new member to the company, so that his or her liability for calls could be enforced. (There was

---

[16] Bearer shares ('share warrants', CA 2006 s 779) used to be an exception, transferable by delivery, but these types of shares have been abolished (subject to some transitional arrangements): see CA 2006 s 779(4) and Small Business, Enterprise and Employment Act 2015 s 84. In Canada, the transfer of shares is governed by a modern code which comes close to making all share certificates negotiable instruments.

also probably some analogy with the transfer of government stock, where the requirement of registration is statutory.)

CA 2006 s 770 provides that a transfer of shares (or of company debentures[17]) cannot be registered (unless the transfer occurs by operation of law) unless: (i) a proper instrument of transfer has been delivered to the company; (ii) it is an exempt transfer within the Stock Transfer Act 1982; or (iii) it is a transfer undertaken in accordance with CA 2006 Pt 21, Ch 2, dealing with uncertificated transfers.

On ordinary contract law principles, specific performance will be ordered of contracts for the sale of company shares unless there is a ready market for the purchase of substitute shares, when a damage award will suffice (*Re Schwabacher* (1907) 98 LT 127).

Share certificates, uncertificated shares and dematerialised securities

The primary record of the ownership of company shares is the register of members (CA 2006 s 112). Companies may also provide their shareholders with share certificates, which provide evidence of ownership. Until 1996, every sale of shares had to be accompanied by the relevant share certificate. Since 1996, the London Stock Exchange has developed a centralised securities depository, called CREST,[18] which is a computer-based system that records title to shares and enables title to be transferred. When the title to a share is recorded in CREST, no share certificate is issued, and the share is said to be '*uncertificated*' or '*dematerialised*'. At present, only listed companies need to have uncertificated shares. In all other companies, shares are typically certificated.

Transfer of certificated securities

The holder of fully paid certificated shares transfers them by completing and signing a share-transfer form which indicates the name of the company, the details of the shares being transferred (number, nominal value, class), the consideration for the transfer (nil if by way of gift) and the name and address of both the transferor and the transferee.[19]

In the simplest case of a sale of all the shares represented on one share certificate, the transferor sends the completed transfer form, plus the share certificate,[20] to the transferee, who pays the price and the relevant stamp duty, and requests the company to register the transfer. The transfer is recorded by the company in the register of members and a new certificate, made out in the transferee's name, is issued to him. This procedure (prescribed by the Stock Transfer Act 1982) may be used for all fully paid securities even though the company's articles provide otherwise. Further practical steps are added if the transferor wants to sell only part of a holding denominated on one share certificate, or if the transferee wants the shares to be converted to uncertificated securities.

If a share transfer is made as a result of fraudulently forged share certificates, then anyone who suffers loss as a result can sue the fraudster in deceit (see 'Forged and fraudulent transfers', p 604). The same measure of remedy (ie as in deceit) is available against a company that makes a negligent false certification (CA 2006 s 775(3)), and the

---

[17] See Chapter 12.

[18] A great deal of information about CREST (or 'Euroclear UK and Ireland') is given on its website at: www.euroclear.com/dam/PDFs/Settlement/EUI/MA2740-CREST-settlement.pdf and also at: www.euroclear.com/dam/PDFs/Settlement/EUI/Becoming-a-client-EUI.pdf.

[19] 'Blank' transfer forms, sometimes used by shareholders to provide security to lenders, are these transfer forms completed in all the details other than the name of the transferee.

[20] A share certificate is prima facie evidence of title: CA 2006 s 768.

certification is taken to have been made by the company if it was issued and signed by the person authorised to issue certifications (s 775(4)(b)) (see *Balkis Consolidated Co v Tomkinson* **[11.12]**).

Under the Model Articles for private companies, art 25, and the Model Articles for public companies, art 49, a member will be supplied with a replacement for a certificate that is damaged or defaced, or which is said to be lost, stolen or destroyed.

Transfer of uncertificated shares

The rules noted previously apply in the main to shares (or other securities) not traded on a public market. Although the rules could apply in a wider context, most purchasers of publicly traded shares use a different process. For shares traded on a public market, the Listing Rules do not permit any restrictions on transferability; the buyers and sellers deal through the Exchange, via a broker, not face-to-face; and the transfer is effected in uncertificated form, through CREST, on the basis of real-time delivery against payment. This electronic system of transfer reduces costs and risks.

As mentioned earlier, CREST is a computer-based securities transfer settlement system which enables securities to be transferred electronically without a written instrument, and title to be evidenced without a certificate. CREST came into operation in July 1996. It is operated by a company called CRESTCo Ltd, authorised for the purpose by the Financial Conduct Authority under powers delegated by the Treasury. Securities held on CREST are recorded in electronic form and are transferred by means of electronic instructions received from participating members (primarily brokers), subject to elaborate provisions for security. Participation in the CREST scheme is optional, in the sense that a company may choose to have some or all of its securities held in uncertificated form, and there is also an option for any individual holder of the securities to hold his or her securities in one form or the other.

Until 2001, CREST did not itself maintain any register of holders, but merely provided a settlement system, and an instruction to the company to amend its share register accordingly. An entry in the company's register remained evidence of title in the same way as if the entry related to certificated securities. Since 2001, CRESTCo has maintained an Operator register (separate from the company's own register), and registers the transfers immediately they occur. The Operator register is prima facie evidence of the title to uncertificated shares (just as the company's register is for certificated shares).

Restrictions on transfer: directors' approval and pre-emption rights

Listed companies are not permitted to impose restrictions on transfer. Private companies typically do, however. The two provisions most commonly found are: (i) an article giving the directors a discretion to refuse to register any transfer (see Model Articles art 26(5)[21]), and (ii) some form of pre-emptive right for existing members. A transfer of certificated shares is not complete until the transfer is registered in the company's register of members. After paying for the shares and before registration, the transferee only has an equitable interest in the shares.

If the directors are given absolute discretion to refuse to transfer the shares, they must, as directors, exercise this power bona fide and for proper purposes: see 'Duty to act within powers: CA 2006 s 171', pp 341ff, and *Re Smith and Fawcett Ltd* **[11.10]**. CA 2006 s 771(1) requires the directors to consider the matter and either register the transfer or give the

---

[21] Contrast this with art 63(5) of the Model Articles for public companies, which gives a general power of refusal only in relation to partly paid shares, and transfers that do not comply with administrative requirements.

transferee notice of and reasons for refusal as soon as practicable and, in any event, within two months. The reasons for refusal must be such as may reasonably be requested, but need not extend to the minutes of board meetings at which the matter was considered.

If transfers are subject to pre-emption rights (requiring the shares to be offered first to the existing shareholders), then directors must refuse to register transfers to outsiders until this is done. Absent this, the existing shareholders' equitable interest in the shares takes priority over the transferee's equitable interest under the sale: *Tett v Phoenix Property and Investments Co Ltd* [1984] BCLC 599.

Where the articles confer on the directors a discretion to refuse to register a transfer of shares, they must exercise their power bona fide and for proper purposes; but, subject to this qualification, they may be given an absolute discretion.

[11.10] Re Smith and Fawcett Ltd [1942] Ch 304 (Court of Appeal)

Article 10 of the company's articles provided that the directors might in their absolute and uncontrolled discretion refuse to register any transfer of shares. There were only two directors and shareholders, Smith and Fawcett, who held 4,001 shares each. After Fawcett's death, Smith and a co-opted director refused to register a transfer of his shares into the names of his executors, or one of them; but Smith offered instead to register 2,001 shares and to buy the remaining 2,000 shares at a price fixed by himself. The court refused to intervene in the exercise of this discretion without evidence of *mala fides*.

LORD GREENE MR: The principles to be applied in cases where the articles of a company confer a discretion on directors with regard to the acceptance of transfer of shares are, for the present purposes, free from doubt. They must exercise their discretion bona fide in what they consider—not what a court may consider—is in the interests of the company, and not for any collateral purpose. They must have regard to those considerations, and those considerations only, which the articles on their true construction permit them to take into consideration, and in construing the relevant provisions in the articles it is to be borne in mind that one of the normal rights of a shareholder is the right to deal freely with his property and to transfer it to whomsoever he pleases. When it is said, as it has been said more than once, that regard must be had to this last consideration, it means, I apprehend, nothing more than that the shareholder has such a prima facie right, and that right is not to be cut down by uncertain language or doubtful implications. The right, if it is to be cut down, must be cut down with satisfactory clarity. It certainly does not mean that articles, if appropriately framed, cannot be allowed to cut down the right of transfer to any extent which the articles on their true construction permit. Another consideration which must be borne in mind is that this type of article is one which is for the most part confined to private companies. Private companies are in law separate entities just as much as are public companies, but from the business and personal point of view they are much more analogous to partnerships than to public corporations. Accordingly, it is to be expected that in the articles of such a company the control of the directors over the membership may be very strict indeed. There are, or may be, very good business reasons why those who bring such companies into existence should give them a constitution which confers on the directors powers of the widest description.

The language of the article in the present case does not point out any particular matter as being the only matter to which the directors are to pay attention in deciding whether or not they will allow the transfer to be registered. The article does not, for instance, say, as is to be found in some articles, that they may refuse to register any transfer of shares to a person not already a member of the company or to a transferee of whom they do not approve. Where articles are framed with some such limitation on the discretionary power of refusal as I have mentioned in those two examples, it follows on plain principle that if the directors go outside the matters which the articles say are to be the matters and the only matters to which they are to have regard, the directors will have exceeded their powers.

Mr Spens [counsel], in his argument for the plaintiff, maintained that whatever language was used in the articles, the power of the directors to refuse to register a transfer must always be limited to matters personal to the transferee and that there can be no personal objection to the plaintiff becoming a member of the company because the directors are prepared to accept him as the holder of [2,001] of the shares which have come to him as legal personal representative of his father. Mr Spens relies for his proposition on the observations in several authorities, but on examination of those cases it becomes clear that the form of article then before the court by its express language confined the directors to the consideration of the desirability of admitting the proposed transferee to membership on grounds personal to him . . .

There is nothing, in my opinion, in principle or in authority to make it impossible to draft such a wide and comprehensive power to directors to refuse to transfer as to enable them to take into account any matter which they conceive to be in the interests of the company, and thereby to admit or not to admit a particular person and to allow or not to allow a particular transfer for reasons not personal to the transferee but bearing on the general interests of the company as a whole—such matters, for instance, as whether by their passing a particular transfer the transferee would obtain too great a weight in the councils of the company or might even perhaps obtain control. The question, therefore, simply is whether on the true construction of the particular article the directors are limited by anything except their bona fide view as to the interests of the company. In the present case the article is drafted in the widest possible terms, and I decline to write into that clear language any limitation other than a limitation, which is implicit by law, that a fiduciary power of this kind must be exercised bona fide in the interests of the company. Subject to that qualification, an article in this form appears to me to give the directors what it says, namely, an absolute and uncontrolled discretion . . .

LUXMOORE LJ and ASQUITH J concurred.

➤ Notes

1. *Re Smith and Fawcett Ltd* is also a leading case on the general subject of directors' powers and duties: see 'General issues', pp 326ff. Recently, in *Mooney v Keys* [2012] NI Ch 23 (Chancery Division (Northern Ireland)), it was held that 'the court has no power to water down' an absolute discretion conferred by the articles of a company on the directors to decline to register any transfer of any share without assigning a reason ([21]).

2. In *Re Swaledale Cleaners Ltd* [1968] 1 WLR 1710 it was held that the discretionary power of directors to refuse registration of a transfer must be affirmatively exercised. The directors must consider the matter and make a decision not to register within a reasonable time after the transfer has been submitted, failing which the transferee is entitled to registration. In the light of CA 2006 s 771(1), a reasonable time for this purpose is prima facie two months. However, in *Popely v Planarrive Ltd* [1997] 1 BCLC 8 it was held that, so long as the directors had reached a decision not to register a transfer within two months, it was not fatal to the effectiveness of their decision that the applicant had not been informed of it within that period. In *Re New Cedos Engineering Co Ltd* [1994] 1 BCLC 797 the company had no directors during the whole of the two months following the receipt by it of an application to have a transfer of shares registered. It was held, following *Swaledale Cleaners*, that the transferee was entitled to registration.

3. In *Curtis v Pulbrook* [2011] EWHC 167 (Ch), [2011] 1 BCLC 638, a director purported to give shares to his wife and daughter in an attempt to evade his creditors. In respect of

some of these shares, the director had ensured that new share certificates were issued and entries made on the company's register. However, the director had no authority to register a purported share transfer, so no legal title had passed despite the documentation. Other gifts were allegedly by deed of gift, but as nothing more had been done, neither legal nor equitable title passed (*Re Rose* [1952] Ch 499, see 'Equitable interests in shares', p 608). In any event, in these circumstances even if the gifts had been effective, they would have been unwound under IA 1986 s 423(3) (transactions at an undervalue).

Forged and fraudulent transfers

The extracts which follow indicate that even a forged share certificate can have quite significant legal consequences.

A share certificate is prima facie evidence of a person's title. The company is estopped from denying, as against a bona fide purchaser of the shares, that the person named in the certificate is entitled to the shares described there.

[11.11] Re Bahia and San Francisco Rly Co (1868) LR 3 QB 584
(Court of Queen's Bench)

Five shares in the company were owned by Miss Amelia Trittin. Without her knowledge Stocken and Goldner procured a forged transfer of the shares to themselves, and lodged the transfer and Miss Trittin's share certificate with the company for registration. The secretary in due course entered their names on the share register in place of Miss Trittin's, and issued a new share certificate in their names. Relying on this certificate, Burton and Mrs Goodburn, acting in good faith, bought the five shares on the Stock Exchange. After they had been registered as holders of the shares and issued with share certificates, the company was obliged to restore Miss Trittin's name to the share register. This action was brought by Burton and Mrs Goodburn, who claimed to be entitled to equivalent shares in the company, or damages. The court awarded them damages, holding the company estopped by the share certificate from denying the title of Stocken and Goldner.

COCKBURN CJ: I am of opinion that our judgment must be for the claimants. If the facts are rightly understood, the case falls within the principle of *Pickard v Sears*[22] and *Freeman v Cooke*[23] The company are [sic] bound to keep a register of shareholders, and have power to issue certificates certifying that each individual shareholder named therein is a registered shareholder of the particular shares specified. This power of granting certificates is to give the shareholders the opportunity of more easily dealing with their shares in the market, and to afford facilities to them of selling their shares by at once showing a marketable title, and the effect of this facility is to make the shares of greater value. The power of giving certificates is, therefore, for the benefit of the company in general; and it is a declaration by the company to all the world that the person in whose name the certificate is made out, and to whom it is given, is a shareholder in the company, and it is given by the company with the intention that it shall be so used by the person to whom it is given, and acted upon in the sale and transfer of shares. It is stated in this case that the claimants acted bona fide, and did all that is required of purchasers of shares; they paid the value of the shares in money on having a transfer of the shares executed to them, and on the production of the certificates which were handed to them. It turned out that the transferors had in fact no

[22] (1837) 6 Ad & El 469.
[23] (1848) 2 Exch 654.

shares, and that the company ought not to have registered them as shareholders or given them certificates, the transfer to them being a forgery. That brings the case within the principle of the decision in *Pickard v Sears*, as explained by the case of *Freeman v Cooke*, that, if you make a representation with the intention that it shall be acted upon by another, and he does so, you are estopped from denying the truth of what you represent to be the fact.

The only remaining question is, what is the redress to which the claimants are entitled. In whatever form of action they might shape their claim, and there can be no doubt that an action is maintainable, the measure of damages would be the same. They are entitled to be placed in the same position as if the shares, which they purchased owing to the company's representation, had in fact been good shares, and had been transferred to them, and the company had refused to put them on the register, and the measure of damages would be the market price of the shares at that time; if no market price at that time, then a jury would have to say what was a reasonable compensation for the loss of the shares.

BLACKBURN, MELLOR and LUSH JJ delivered concurring judgments.

➤ Notes

1. A similar estoppel operates as regards the amount stated in the certificate to be paid up on the shares: see *Burkinshaw v Nicolls* (1878) 3 App Cas 1004.

2. At the time this case was decided it was particularly important to establish liability on the basis of an estoppel, since there is no privity as between the company and the transferee which would give a remedy in contract, and the notion of a duty of care which would allow a claim to be based in negligence was then a century away. But now that liability in negligence for misrepresentations is well established (*Hedley Byrne & Co Ltd v Heller & Partners Ltd* [1964] AC 465, and, perhaps most pertinently, *Ministry of Housing and Local Government v Sharp* [1970] 2 QB 223), a transferee might well have a remedy on this ground, although of course it would be necessary to prove negligence.

3. Although in *Re Bahia and San Francisco Rly Co* [11.11] the final purchaser could recover damages from the company, the company would have been able to recover damages from the vendor who had presented the company with the forged transfer initially. This would be true even if the presenter of those documents had been unaware of the fraud or forgery (see later, and *Royal Bank of Scotland plc v Sandstone Properties Ltd* [1998] 2 BCLC 429).

➤ Questions

1. Is the protection given by CA 2006 s 588 to transferees of shares that are not fully paid more, or less, extensive than that which they would get under *Burkinshaw v Nicolls* (see Note 2)?

2. Note the ambit of CA 2006 ss 768 and 775. Would this have affected the outcome in this case?

In an appropriate case, the certificate holder may rely on an estoppel.

[11.12] Balkis Consolidated Co v Tomkinson [1893] AC 396 (House of Lords)

Tomkinson, who held a share certificate stating that he was the owner of 1,000 shares in the company, sold the shares on the market to various purchasers. The company refused to register the transfers, on the ground that Powter, who had transferred the shares to Tomkinson, had had no title at the time, and that Powter had procured the issue of Tomkinson's certificate by fraud. Tomkinson bought shares on the market to honour the contracts with his transferees, and sued the company in damages to recoup this expenditure. The House of Lords, affirming the courts below, upheld Tomkinson's claim.

> LORD HERSCHELL LC: After carefully considering the able arguments at the Bar, I have no hesitation in expressing my concurrence in the law laid down by the Court of Queen's Bench in *Re Bahia and San Francisco Rly Co* **[11.11]** . . . The appellants argued, however, and correctly, that the present case is distinguishable from that in the Queen's Bench, inasmuch as it is not the purchasers who are seeking to render the company liable by way of estoppel, but the vendor of the shares, who himself received the certificate from the company. Does that, in the circumstances which your Lordships have to consider, make any difference? If the company must have known, as was said in the *Bahia and San Francisco Rly* case, that persons wanting to purchase shares might act upon the statement of fact contained in the certificate, it must equally have been within the contemplation of the company that a person receiving the certificate from them might on the faith of it enter into a contract to sell the shares. The plaintiff did enter into such a contract, and thereby altered his position by rendering himself liable to the persons with whom he contracted to sell the shares. All the elements necessary to create an estoppel would appear, therefore, to be present . . .
>
> LORDS MACNAGHTEN and FIELD delivered concurring opinions.

➤ Notes

1. There is one exception to the principle illustrated by these cases. Where a certificate is issued which is based on the registration of a forged transfer, no estoppel against the company arises in favour of the person who submitted the transfer for registration. The law takes the view that since this person has at least equally good means as the company of knowing whether the transfer is genuine, it should not be deemed to have made any representation to him: *Simm v Anglo-American Telegraph Co* (1879) 5 QBD 188, CA.

2. Later cases show that the company's position in such a case is even stronger. A person who presents a transfer to a company for registration, whether it is in favour of himself or someone else (eg a broker presenting a transfer on behalf of his or her client) impliedly warrants that it is genuine and, if it is not, may be liable to indemnify the company if it suffers loss by acting on it: *Sheffield Corpn v Barclay* [1905] AC 392, HL; *Yeung Kai Yung v Hong Kong and Shanghai Banking Corpn* [1981] AC 787, PC; *Royal Bank of Scotland plc v Sandstone Properties Ltd* [1998] 2 BCLC 429.

3. These exceptions require qualification in the case of reliance upon an erroneous statement in a share certificate issued by the company. Ordinarily, a person who presents a share transfer for registration is required to indemnify the company against any liability it incurs to other persons as a result of registering the transfer. However, where the person presenting a share certificate for registration relied upon an erroneous statement of ownership on a share certificate, the estoppel raised against the company overrides the company's right to an indemnity (see earlier, and also *Cadbury Schweppes plc v Halifax Share Dealing Ltd* [2006] EWHC 1184 (Ch)).

In some (quite rare) circumstances a forged share certificate is a nullity and does not bind the company.[24]

[11.13] Ruben v Great Fingall Consolidated [1906] AC 439 (House of Lords)

The plaintiffs Ruben and Ladenburg, who were stockbrokers, had procured a loan for one Rowe (the secretary of the defendant company) on the security of a share certificate for

---

[24] But see the Notes following this case extract, and see *Lovett v Carson Country Homes* **[3.15]**.

5,000 shares in the defendant company, to which Rowe had affixed his own signature and the company's seal and had forged the signatures of two directors. The plaintiffs, having reimbursed the mortgagees, claimed damages from the company for failure to register them as owners of the shares. It was held that the company was not estopped by the certificate.

> LORD MACNAGHTEN: My Lords, this case was argued at some length and with much ingenuity by the learned counsel for the appellants. In my opinion there is nothing in it.
>
> Ruben and Ladenburg are the victims of a wicked fraud. No fault has been found with their conduct. But their claim against the respondent company is, I think, simply absurd.
>
> The thing put forward as the foundation of their claim is a piece of paper which purports to be a certificate of shares in the company. This paper is false and fraudulent from beginning to end. The representation of the company's seal which appears upon it, though made by the impression of the real seal of the company, is counterfeit, and no better than a forgery. The signatures of the two directors which purport to authenticate the sealing are forgeries pure and simple. Every statement in the document is a lie. The only thing real about it is the signature of the secretary of the company, who was the sole author and perpetrator of the fraud. No one would suggest that this fraudulent certificate could of itself give rise to any right or bind or affect the company in any way. It is not the company's deed, and there is nothing to prevent the company from saying so.
>
> Then how can the company be bound or affected by it? The directors have never said or done anything to represent or lead to the belief that this thing was the company's deed. Without such a representation there can be no estoppel.
>
> The fact that this fraudulent certificate was concocted in the company's office and was uttered and sent forth by its author from the place of its origin cannot give it an efficacy which it does not intrinsically possess. The secretary of the company, who is a mere servant, may be the proper hand to deliver out certificates which the company issues in due course, but he can have no authority to guarantee the genuineness or validity of a document which is not the deed of the company.
>
> I could have understood a claim on the part of the appellants if it were incumbent on the company to lock up their seal and guard it as a dangerous beast and if it were culpable carelessness on the part of the directors to commit the care of the seal to their secretary or any other official. That is a view which once commended itself to a jury, but it has been disposed of for good and all by the case of *Bank of Ireland v Evans' Charities Trustees*[25] in this House . . .
>
> LORD LOREBURN LC and LORDS DAVEY and JAMES OF HEREFORD delivered concurring opinions.
>
> LORDS ROBERTSON and ATKINSON concurred.

➤ Notes

1. *Ruben*'s case is House of Lords' authority, but is defensible upon only the narrowest possible *ratio decidendi*, as set out at the head of this extract. As has already been observed (*Balkis Consolidated Co v Tomkinson* [11.12]), the company ought to be bound in such circumstances if a person who may be assumed to have authority to do so has put forward the share certificate as genuine. Now that it is recognised that the secretary of a company is not a 'mere servant', but a responsible officer having an important role in administrative matters (see the *Panorama* case [3.03]), it could not be seriously argued that he or she does not have usual authority to guarantee the genuineness of a document such as a share certificate. In the same context, see *Lovett v Carson Country Homes* [3.15], which indicates that a company can be estopped from disputing the validity of a forged document.

---

[25] (1855) 5 HL Cas 389.

2. CA 2006 s 44(5) reads as follows:

> (5) In favour of a purchaser a document shall be deemed to have been duly executed by a company if it purports to be signed in accordance with subsection (2).
>
> A 'purchaser' means a purchaser in good faith for valuable consideration and includes a lessee, mortgagee or other person who for valuable consideration acquires an interest in property.

And subsection (2) reads:

> (2) A document is validly executed by a company if it is signed on behalf of the company—
> (a) by two authorised signatories, or
> (b) by a director of the company in the presence of a witness who attests the signature.

Would *Ruben*'s case **[11.13]** be decided differently today in the light of this provision?

3. In deciding these issues, the modern law, as presented in Chapter 3, has overtaken many of these older cases. And if *Ruben* cannot be distinguished, it would, of course, be open to the Supreme Court to disown its earlier rulings. It is also possible that CA 2006 s 775 modifies the effect of these cases, but the repeated use of the word 'authorised' in s 775(4) leaves some room for doubt, but only if a court can be persuaded to hold that this means 'having *actual* authority' as opposed to having *either* actual or ostensible authority. That seems unlikely.

4. If the transfer takes place within CREST, then different rules apply. The Uncertificated Securities Regulations 2001 (SI 2001/3755) provide that the court may make an order against the CREST operator, although several limitations apply to such orders. The most significant is that if the perpetrator of the forgery is identified, then no compensation order can be made against CREST even where the loss cannot be recovered from the perpetrator. See reg 36.

Equitable interests in shares

Legal title does not pass until the transferee's name is entered into the company's register (or onto the CREST register). Before this registration step is completed, it is often important to know whether the dealings between transferor and transferee have been sufficient to constitute the transferee the owner in equity, even if not at law. This can happen in a number of ways.

First, there is nothing to prevent the transferor declaring a trust of the shares for the benefit of the transferee. No special formalities are required; the declaration may be oral—although writing is usually advisable if only as a means of proof of the three certainties necessary to establish a valid trust. So, in *Shah v Shah* [2010] EWCA Civ 1408, CA, a letter written by the donor (and accompanied by a signed stock transfer form but without the share certificate) was held sufficient to manifest an intention in the donor to dispose of his shares forthwith, and to do so by way of trust in favour of his brother. His brother, as sole beneficiary, would then have been entitled to terminate the trust and call for the transfer of legal title.[26]

---

[26] *Saunders v Vautier* (1841) 4 Beav 115. Also see *Stablewood Properties v Virdi* [2010] EWCA Civ 865 (declaration of conditional trust nevertheless taking effect immediately).

Secondly, if the dealing is a sale which is specifically enforceable[27] and unconditional,[28] then the transferee will become the owner in equity once the price is paid, even before the transfer is registered.[29] The transferor then holds the shares on constructive trust for the transferee, and must account for dividends and vote the shares as the transferee directs.[30] Before then, the transferor remains entitled to protect his or her own interests.[31] This rule applies even if the shares are subject to pre-emption or first refusal rights, although then the transferee's interest can be no greater than the transferor's, that is, subject to the pre-emption rights in question.

Finally, even if the intended transfer is by way of gift, the donee may acquire equitable ownership in advance of the transfer of legal title. In two cases, each coincidentally named *Re Rose*, reported in [1949] Ch 78 and [1952] Ch 499, it was held that where the donor of shares has done everything in his power to divest himself in favour of the donee (eg by delivering to the donee, or to the donee's agent, or to the company, an executed transfer and the relevant share certificate), then the gift is complete in equity despite the absence of registration.[32] This rule applies even where the directors have a discretion to refuse registration of the transfer, although then the transferee's rights are subject to that restriction. By way of illustration, contrast the successful arguments in the *Rose* decisions with the unsuccessful attempt to apply the same arguments in *Zeital v Kaye* [2010] EWCA Civ 159, CA, where there was no written transfer document and the share certificate had gone missing without the transferor applying for a duplicate. Another unsuccessful attempt appears to be found in *Waghorn v Waghorn* (unreported, Chancery Division, 14 June 2013).

The rule in *Re Rose* was extended still further in *Pennington v Waine* [2002] EWCA Civ 227, [2002] 1 WLR 2075, CA, where the court found that equitable title had passed even though the transferor still had functions to perform in transferring legal title. This conclusion is difficult to justify, unless the particular facts entitle the transferee to rely on equitable estoppel, as in *Curtis v Pulbrook* [2011] EWHC 167 (Ch).

Also see *Hawks v McArthur* **[11.17]**, illustrating the problems exemplified in the next section, where there are competing legal and equitable claims to the same parcel of shares.

These problems in determining when equitable interests arise have emerged rather dramatically over the past few decades in the context of dealings in a part only of a shareholder's holding, as in dispositions by way of trust of '50 of my 950 shares' (*Hunter v Moss* [1994] 1 WLR 452, CA) or by way of sale (*Re Harvard Securities Ltd* [1997] 2 BCLC 369 (Ch, Neuberger J).[33] In that context, see the detailed analysis of Campbell J in *White v Shortall* [2006] NSWSC 1379.

---

[27] Sales of shares in public companies, where shares are freely available on the market, are not specifically enforceable; sales of shares in private companies are: *Duncuft v Albrecht* (1841) 12 Sim 189, 59 ER 1104.

[28] See *Re Coroin; McKillen v Misland (Cyprus) Investments Ltd* [2013] EWCA Civ 781, Arden LJ at [39]: 'In my judgment, an interest in shares would not pass under a contract for the sale of shares which is subject to a true condition precedent until the condition precedent is fulfilled . . . Fulfilment of the condition precedent was under the control of [a third party], but that did not, in my judgment, prevent it from being a true condition precedent so far as Mr Quinlan as transferor was concerned [and] (Contrary to Lord Goldsmith's [counsel's] submission, Mr Quinlan could not waive the condition as to the chargee's consent).' Also see [137] (Moore-Bick LJ). And see **[9.03]** and **[9.04]**.

[29] *Michaels v Harley House (Marylebone) Ltd* [2000] Ch 104, CA; *Wood Preservation Ltd v Prior* [1969] 1 WLR 1077, CA.

[30] *Hardoon v Belilios* [1901] AC 118, PC; *Musselwhite v CH Musselwhite & Son Ltd* [1962] Ch 964.

[31] *Hardoon v Belilios* [1901] AC 118, PC; *Musselwhite v CH Musselwhite & Son Ltd* [1962] Ch 964. Also see *Michaels v Harley House (Marylebone) Ltd* [2000] Ch 104, CA; *Stablewood Properties v Virdi* [2010] EWCA Civ 865.

[32] Thus equity provides relief against the old strict rule in *Milroy v Lord* (1862) 4 De GF & J 264 that equity will not assist a volunteer, and that a gift of shares by deed is therefore ineffective.

[33] See S Worthington, 'Sorting Out Ownership Interests in a Bulk: Gifts, Sales and Trusts' [1999] JBL 1.

Competing claims to shares

The problem being addressed here is this: where two parties claim competing interests in the same shares, whose claim should win? The answer depends on the operation of old and well-established priority rules, as illustrated in extracts which follow.

A legal title to shares will prevail over an earlier equitable title; but a transfer of the legal title is not perfected until registration of the transferee as holder of the shares.[34]

[11.14] Shropshire Union Railways and Canal Co v R (1875) LR 7 HL 496 (House of Lords)

Mrs Robson sought a writ of mandamus to compel the directors of the company to register a transfer of stock to her from George Holyoake, in whose name it stood. (Holyoake had given the transfer as security for a loan made by Mrs Robson's late husband.) She failed because Holyoake had only a bare legal title (the beneficial interest being in the defendants themselves) and nothing which had happened had displaced the defendants' earlier equity.

LORD CAIRNS LC: [Undoubtedly] the position of matters was, that the defendants had the whole beneficial interest in the stock . . . Theirs was the equitable title. Holyoake was a person who held merely the legal title and the right to transfer the stock. He was able, if not interfered with, to transfer the stock to any other person, and to give a valid receipt for the purchase-money to any person who had not notice of the beneficial interest of the defendants. On the other hand, any person with whom Holyoake might deal by virtue of his title upon the register, had, or ought to have had, these considerations present to his mind. He ought to have known that although Holyoake's name appeared upon the register as the owner of these shares, and although Holyoake could present to him the certificates of this ownership, still it was perfectly possible either that these shares were the beneficial property of Holyoake himself, or that they were the property of some other person. If he dealt merely by equitable transfer, or equitable assignment with Holyoake, and if it turned out that the beneficial ownership of Holyoake was co-incident and co-extensive with his legal title, well and good; his right would be accordingly, so far as Holyoake was concerned, complete. But, if, on the other hand, it should turn out that Holyoake's beneficial interest was either nil, or was not coextensive with the whole of his apparent legal title, then I say any person dealing with Holyoake, by way of equitable bargain or contract, should have known that he could only obtain a title which was imperfect, and would not bind the real beneficial owner. And, my Lords, he also might have known, and should have known, this, that if he desired to perfect his title, and make it entirely secure, he had the most simple means open to him—he had only to take Holyoake at his word. If Holyoake represented that he was the real owner of these shares, the proposed transferee had only to go with Holyoake, or to go with the authority of Holyoake in his possession, to the company, and to require a transfer of those shares from the name of Holyoake into his own name. If he had obtained that transfer, and the company had made it, no question could have arisen, and no litigation could subsequently have taken place . . .

LORDS HATHERLEY and O'HAGAN delivered concurring opinions.

---

[34] The requirement of registration had more justification in an earlier period when it was common for shares to be only partly paid up, but it makes less sense in the case of the fully paid, listed security, of the present day, where the responsibilities of a shareholder are negligible, the directors have no discretion to refuse registration, and the mechanics of transfer are a matter of pure routine. It is not obvious, eg, why the law should continue to refuse to recognise the possibility of a transfer of the legal title to such shares by, say, a deed of gift.

➤ Note

This rule has some surprising consequences. If the legal owner of shares enters into transactions that purport to deliver equitable ownership interests to each of two innocent purchasers, it is possible for the holder of the later interest to obtain priority over the holder of the prior interest if that registration is secured first, and it does not matter that the registration process was pursued in full knowledge of the earlier equitable interest: *Macmillan Inc v Bishopsgate Investment Trust plc (No 3)* [1995] 1 WLR 978 (Millett J) (affd on different grounds in [1996] 1 WLR 387, CA); and *MCC Proceeds Inc v Lehman Bros International (Europe)* [1998] 4 All ER 675, CA.

Where the equities as between successive transferees of shares are equal, the first in time prevails.

[11.15] Peat v Clayton [1906] 1 Ch 659 (Chancery Division)

Clayton assigned all his property, including the blocks of shares in question, to trustees for the benefit of his creditors, but failed to hand over the share certificates when requested to do so. The trustees then gave notice of the assignment to the company, but took no further steps. (It should be appreciated that the company was not bound to receive this notice: see s 360 of the Act [CA 2006 s 126].) Clayton later sold the shares through Cohen & Co, brokers, on the Stock Exchange, handing over the certificates and transfers duly executed. When the company refused registration, Cohen & Co provided their purchaser with other shares in the company, and then in these proceedings sought to resist a claim brought by the trustees, as plaintiffs, for a declaration that they were entitled to the shares. It was held, however, that the trustees' interest prevailed, being prior in time.

> JOYCE J: As I understand the law, where there are several claimants to shares registered in the name of a third person, the equitable title which is prior in time prevails, unless the claimant under a subsequent equitable title proves that, as between him and the company, he had acquired an absolute and unconditional right to be registered as the owner of the shares before the company received notice of the other claim.[35] In my opinion, therefore, the plaintiffs appear to be entitled to these forty shares in the Randfontein company. But Messrs Cohen claim a lien upon them. If they have any lien, however, it is only equitable, and can only be upon Clayton's interest, which is subject to the right of the plaintiffs under the deed of assignment. Then it was said that the plaintiffs had disentitled themselves by negligence. I see no negligence on the part of the plaintiffs, unless it be, as Messrs Cohen allege, in not adopting the procedure now substituted by Ord 46, r 4, for the old procedure by distringas.[36] I cannot accede to the contention that by reason of the omission to adopt this course the plaintiffs must be postponed. If they had proceeded by distringas the result would have been just the same. It would only have prevented the company from registering the transfer to the purchaser, which in fact they did refuse to do by reason of the notice given to them on 8 November on behalf of the plaintiffs . . .
>
> The result is that the plaintiffs are entitled to a declaration in their favour, and to an order . . . to register them as the holders of the shares.

Also see *Hawks v McArthur* **[11.17]**.

---

[35] In spite of assertions to this effect both here and in other cases, it is generally accepted that nothing short of the registration of the subsequent transferee as legal owner will defeat the prior equity.

[36] This is a 'stop notice': see *Hawks v McArthur* **[11.17]**.

Although a company is not ordinarily bound by notice of a trust or other equitable interest affecting its shares, this rule does not apply when the company itself asserts an interest in the shares in competition with the person who gave notice.

[11.16] Mackereth v Wigan Coal and Iron Co Ltd [1916] 2 Ch 293 (Chancery Division)

Shares in the defendant company which had formerly belonged to James Hodgson, deceased, were registered in the name of the trustees of his estate, one of whom was the son of the deceased, James Hodgson, junior. The company had notice that the registered shareholders held only as trustees. Later James Hodgson, junior, became indebted to the company and the company, purporting to exercise a lien conferred upon it by the articles, impounded certain dividends due on the shares and subsequently sold the shares to reduce the amount of the debt. It was held that this was an infringement of the rights of the beneficiaries of the estate, and that neither s 27 of the Companies Act 1908 [CA 2006 s 126] nor an article in similar terms applied in a case such as this, where the company was itself involved in the transaction.

> PETERSON J: For the company it was argued that under s 27 of the Act of 1908, and the articles of association, no notice of any equitable interest or trust can affect the company in any way, and that, as the notice of the trust in the present case, which the company in fact received, must be treated as non-existent, or at least ineffectual, the lien which is conferred by the articles is operative. The argument leads far; for it would follow that, if a trustee of shares in a company informed the company that he held the shares for the benefit of other persons, and that he had not as against his cestui que trust any power of mortgaging them for his own benefit, he could yet effectually charge them to the company as security for money lent to him by the company . . . In several cases it has been stated in broad terms that a company 'need not take notice in any way of trusts': per Brett MR in *Société Générale de Paris v Tramways Union Co*;[37] or that any notice is absolutely inoperative to affect a company with any notice: per Lord Selborne in the same case in the House of Lords—*Société Générale de Paris v Walker*.[38] These observations had, however, reference to the obligation of the company to register transfers of shares. If the passages in the judgments to which I have referred were intended to be of universal application, they are not in accordance with the judgments of the House of Lords in *Bradford Banking Co Ltd v Briggs, Son & Co Ltd*.[39] The effect of this decision is briefly stated by Stirling LJ in *Rainford v Keith and Blackman Co Ltd*,[40] in these words: 'Where the company in which the shares are held sees fit to deal with the shares for its own benefit, then that company is liable to be affected with notice of the interest of a third party.'
>
> I am therefore of opinion that s 27 of the Act of 1908 and article 9 of the articles of association do not protect a company which, in the face of notice that the shareholder is not the beneficial owner of the shares, makes advances or gives credit to the shareholder . . . The result is that the company in the present case was wrong in asserting a lien against the beneficiaries, and must account for the proceeds of sale of the shares, and for the dividends which it has applied towards the satisfaction of the indebtedness of James Hodgson, junior.

[37] (1884) 14 QBD 424 at 439.
[38] (1885) 11 App Cas 20 at 30.
[39] (1886) 12 App Cas 29.
[40] [1905] 2 Ch 147 at 161.

➤ Note

Although CA 2006 s 126 provides that no notice of any trust affecting shares shall be 'entered on the register of members . . . or be receivable by the registrar',[41] it is possible by using the procedures described as 'stop orders' or 'stop notices' (Charging Orders Act 1979 s 5(2)(a) and (b) respectively, and Civil Procedure Rules 1998 rr 73.11–73.15 and 73.16–73.21 respectively) to prohibit a company from registering any transfer of the shares in question or paying any dividend on them, or, alternatively, to require a company to refrain from doing these things without first sending a notice to the person serving the stop notice and giving him or her a specified time to take action.

➤ Question

To what extent does a stop notice give a person with an equitable interest in shares effective protection? (See *Drayne v McKillen* [2011] EWHC 3326 (QB) in which the court refused an interlocutory application to discharge a stop notice granted in favour of the alleged beneficial owner of the shares in question, where there was a real prospect of demonstrating such an interest.)

A transfer of shares for valuable consideration, even if it is irregular under the company's articles, is effective to transfer an equitable interest to the purchaser which will prevail over another equitable right accruing at a later date, for example a charging order.

[11.17] Hawks v McArthur [1951] 1 All ER 22 (Chancery Division)

The facts appear from the judgment.

> VAISEY J: The plaintiff is the holder of a charging order affecting five hundred ordinary shares of £1 each in a private company called W Lucas & Sons Ltd, which stand in the name of, and were originally the property of, the first defendant, Mr Theodore Hunter McArthur, who has not entered an appearance in these proceedings. He claims that that charging order operates on Mr McArthur's interest in those shares, which, he says, is a complete interest, both legal and equitable. The second and third defendants, Mr Roberts and Mr Fraser, claim that the beneficial interest in the shares in question has passed to them as a result of transfers executed in their favour by Mr McArthur in pursuance of certain agreements entered into between themselves and Mr McArthur prior to the execution of those transfers, and they allege that Mr McArthur had no interest in the shares at the date of the charging order on which the charge could operate . . .
>
> There is, undoubtedly, a basic principle that a charging order only operates to charge the beneficial interest of the person against whom the order is made, and that it is not possible, for instance, to obtain an effective charging order over shares where the person against whom the order is made holds them as a bare trustee. The charging order affects only such interest, and so much of the property affected, as the person whose property is purported to be affected could himself validly charge . . . [His Lordship then observed that the transfers of the shares had been made in total disregard of the requirements of the articles of association, which obliged an intending transferor to give notice to the company so that the other members could exercise rights of pre-emption. He continued:]
>
> The real question in this case, I think, is whether the alleged agreements . . . operated so as to amount in equity to a transfer of the shares held by Mr McArthur, as to 200 of them to Mr Roberts,

---

[41] This wording is probably not quite what might be expected of a provision having the effect described in [11.16].

and as to 300 of them to Mr Fraser, or whether the failure or neglect to follow the code laid down by articles 11, 12 and 13 completely vitiates the whole transaction, so that the transfers are worthless and there has been a total failure of consideration for the moneys which were admittedly paid over by Mr Roberts and Mr Fraser to Mr McArthur. It is suggested on behalf of Mr Roberts and Mr Fraser that, notwithstanding the complete failure to comply with the articles, the transfers and the antecedent agreements which must have been made—for one does not execute a transfer without a previous intention to do so—did, in fact, operate as a sale by Mr McArthur to Mr Roberts and Mr Fraser of, at any rate, the beneficial interest in the shares—otherwise the result would be that Mr Roberts and Mr Fraser paid their money and got nothing for it . . .

Admittedly, Mr McArthur is still the legal owner of the shares. Admittedly, the plaintiff's rights under this charging order are in the nature of equitable rights. And admittedly, the rights of Mr Roberts and Mr Fraser, if they have any rights, are also equitable rights. As I have come to the conclusion that Mr Roberts and Mr Fraser have some rights and that what they did was not a complete nullity, the question is whose rights should prevail. A not irrelevant circumstance is that the equitable rights of Mr Roberts and Mr Fraser precede the equities or quasi-equitable rights under the charging order. In my opinion, the rights of Mr Roberts and Mr Fraser had already accrued at the time the charging order was obtained, and I think, as between the merits (not moral merits, but legal merits) of the plaintiff and the defendants, the rights of the second and third defendants, Mr Roberts and Mr Fraser, must prevail over the claims of the plaintiff . . .

Disclosure of substantial interests in shares

It is often material to know who has controlling interests in a company. For public companies, there are requirements relating to disclosure of substantial interests in shares: see 'Transparency obligations: investigation and notification of major voting shareholdings in certain public companies', pp 759ff.

Valuation of shares

Proper valuation of shares is essential for a number of reasons. Most often it is in pursuit of their sale or their compulsory purchase (where that has been ordered, eg as a result of a successful unfair prejudice claim). (See CA 2006 s 994 and 'Remedies: valuing shares in buy-out orders', pp 741ff.)

In the valuation of shares,[42] *the valuer is entitled to consider the realities of the company's situation, and may, for example, decline to value the company's assets as a going concern if there is no expectation that the business will make profits.*

[11.18] Dean v Prince [1954] Ch 409 (Court of Appeal)

Dean (now deceased), Prince and Cowen had formed a private company in 1938, taking respectively 140, 30 and 30 shares. All three were 'working directors'. The company's

[42] See generally N Easterway, H Booth and K Eamer, *Practical Share Valuation* (4th edn, 1998); A Gregory and A Hicks, 'Valuation of Shares: A Legal and Accounting Conundrum' [1995] JBL 56.

articles provided that on the death of a director his shares should be bought by the surviving directors at a price to be certified as fair by the auditor. On Dean's death in 1951, his holding was valued for the purpose of this article at £7 per share. His widow challenged the valuation in these proceedings, but the Court of Appeal, reversing Harman J, held that the correct principles had been followed by the auditor and upheld his valuation.[43]

DENNING LJ: In this case Harman J has upset the valuation on the ground that the auditor failed to take into account some factors and proceeded on wrong principles. I will take the points in order:

1. *The right to control the company.* Harman J said that the auditor should have taken into account the fact that the 140 shares were a majority holding and would give a purchaser the right to control the company. I do not think that the auditor was bound to take that factor into account. Test it this way: suppose it had been Prince who had died, leaving only 30 shares. Those 30 shares, being a minority holding, would fetch nothing in the open market. But does that mean that the other directors would be entitled to take his shares for nothing? Surely not. No matter which director it was who happened to die, his widow should be entitled to the same price per share, irrespective of whether her husband's holding was large or small. It seems to me that the fair thing to do would be to take the whole 200 shares of the company and see what they were worth, and then pay the widow a sum appropriate to her husband's holding. At any rate if the auditor was of opinion that that was a fair method, no one can say that he was wrong. The right way to see what the whole 200 shares were worth, would be to see what the business itself was worth: and that is what the auditor proceeded to do.

2. *Valuation of the business 'as a going concern'.* Harman J seems to have thought that the auditor should have valued the business as a going concern. I do not think that the auditor was bound to do any such thing. The business was a losing concern which had no goodwill: and it is fairly obvious that, as soon as Mrs Dean had sold the 140 shares to the other two directors—as she was bound to do—she would in all probability call in the moneys owing to herself and to her husband amounting to over £2,000. The judge said that she was not likely to press for the moneys because that would be 'killing the goose that laid the eggs', but he was wrong about this; because as soon as she sold the shares, she would have got rid of the goose and there was no reason why she should not press for the moneys. She was an executrix and the company's position was none too good. It had only £1,200 in the bank to meet a demand for £2,200. In these circumstances the auditor was of opinion that there was a strong probability of the company having to be wound up: and he rejected the going-concern basis. For myself, I should have thought he was clearly right, but at any rate no one can say that his opinion was wrong.

3. *Valuation of the assets of the business.* Once the going-concern basis is rejected, the only possible way of valuing the business is to find out the value of the tangible assets. Harman J thought that the assets should have been valued as a whole in situ. It was quite likely, he said, that 'some one could have been found who would make a bid for the whole thing, lock, stock and barrel'. But the judge seems to have forgotten that no one would buy the assets in situ in this way unless he could also buy the premises; and the company had no saleable interest in the premises. In respect of part of the premises the company had only a monthly tenancy; in respect of the rest the company had only a contract for the purchase of the premises on paying £200 a year for twenty-five years. It had no right to assign this contract; and its interest was liable to be forfeited if it went into liquidation, either compulsory or voluntary; and the probability was, of course, that, if it sold all the assets, it would go into liquidation, and hence lose the premises. The company could, therefore, only sell the assets without the premises. That is how the auditor valued them and no one can say that he was wrong in so doing.

---

[43] This case was overruled in *Veba Oil Supply & Trading GmbH v Petrotrade Inc* [2001] EWCA Civ 1832, although it remains relevant in respect of the valuation of shares. See *Begum v Hossain* [2015] EWCA Civ 717, CA (see Note 7) in which the Court of Appeal applied *Veba Oil* for the distinction between a mistake and a departure from instructions.

4. *Valuation on a 'break-up' basis.* The auditor instructed the valuer, Colonel Riddle, to value the plant and machinery at the break-up value as loose chattels on a sale by auction. Harman J thought that that was a wrong basis because it was equivalent to a forced sale. I would have agreed with the judge if the business had been a profitable concern. The value of the tangible assets would then have been somewhere in the region of £4,000 or £5,000, being either the balance sheet figure of £4,070 or Pressley's figure of £4,835. But the business was not a profitable concern. It was a losing concern: and it is a well-known fact that a losing concern cannot realise the book value of its assets. There is an element to be taken into account which is sometimes spoken of as 'negative goodwill'. It comes about in this way: if a business is making a loss, that shows that its assets, regarded as an entity, are not a good investment. A purchaser will decline, therefore, to buy on that basis. He will only buy on a piecemeal basis, according to what the various assets taken individually are worth: and it is obvious that on a sale of assets piecemeal, the vendor will suffer heavy losses as compared with the book figures. The auditor was therefore quite justified in asking the valuer to value the assets as loose chattels sold at an auction. At any rate, if he honestly formed that opinion, no one can say that he was wrong.

5. *The special purchaser.* Harman J thought that someone could have been found to buy the 140 shares who would use his majority holding to turn out the two directors, and reorganise the factory and put in his own business. In other words, that the shares would have a special attraction for some person (namely, the next-door neighbour) who wanted to put his own business into these premises. I am prepared to concede that the shares might realise an enhanced value on that account: but I do not think that it would be a fair price to ask the directors to pay. They were buying these shares—under a compulsory sale and purchase—on the assumption that they would continue in the business as working directors. It would be unfair to make them pay a price based on the assumption that they would be turned out. If the auditor never took that possibility into account, he cannot be blamed; for he was only asked to certify the fair value of the shares. The only fair value would be to take a hypothetical purchaser who was prepared to carry on the business if it was worth while so to do, or otherwise to put it into liquidation. At any rate if that was the auditor's opinion, no one can say that he was wrong.

I have covered, I think, all the grounds on which Harman J upset the valuation. I do not think they were good grounds. I would, therefore, allow the appeal and uphold the valuation.

EVERSHED MR and WYNN-PARRY J delivered concurring judgments.

➤ Notes

1. In holding that it was proper for the auditor not to take into account the fact that the block of shares carried with it control of the company, Denning LJ was no doubt correct on the particular facts of this case; but his remarks should not be accepted as laying down a general rule. In the court below, Harman J had held that the control factor was of paramount importance. In the Court of Appeal, Evershed MR said that he 'should not himself quarrel' with a rateable apportionment of an assets valuation among all the shares, but his judgment turned essentially on other points; while Wynn-Parry J held that no extra value should be placed on the controlling shares because (i) the article in question referred to the current worth of *the company's* shares, not the deceased director's shares; and (ii) whereas the seller might be parting with control, none of the surviving directors was necessarily *buying* it, since they were more than one in number.

2. It was established by *Short v Treasury Comrs* [1948] AC 534 that where one purchaser is buying control but none of the vendors is itself selling a controlling interest, the extra value should be disregarded. But there are *dicta* in that case which strongly support the view that where a majority shareholding is sold by a single seller to a single buyer, it is proper to value the holding more highly. The same point is made *obiter dicta* in *Re Grierson, Oldham & Adams Ltd* **[15.14]** and *Gold Coast Selection Trust Ltd v Humphrey* [1948] AC 459 at 473.

3. An indication of the value of 'control' in practice can be gained from the following relative figures put by an expert on the value of different holdings in a small private company:[44]

Value of 100% shareholding:			£100,000
"	51%	"	48,000
"	50%	"	35,000
"	20%	"	5,000
"	10%	"	1,000

4. There are other alternatives to assets-based formulae for ascertaining the value of a share. For example, in *Re Macro (Ipswich) Ltd* **[13.30]** Arden J preferred to use a valuation reckoned by grossing up the average dividend yield. This would be appropriate in a case where the company is making steady profits but its assets are difficult to value or are undervalued in its accounts. In *Ng v Crabtree* [2012] EWCA Civ 333, CA, the Court of Appeal accepted the experts' opinion that an earnings-based approach was appropriate in valuing 'a company generating earnings, or a small profitable trading company'. On the facts, therefore, it was appropriate to ignore a debt owed to the company's principal supplier, since valuation was being undertaken on a different basis.

5. Where parties have agreed that company shares should be sold at a value to be determined by an expert valuer, and the valuer has adhered to the instructions, the valuation is binding on the parties and cannot be set aside: *Premier Telecom Communications Group v Webb* [2014] EWCA Civ 994, CA.

6. Instructions can be very specific. In *Hut Group Ltd v Nobahar-Cookson* [2014] EWHC 3842 (QB), the parties agreed that two different methods would be applied to value the shares in question. For the shares subject to the claim, since these shares constituted the *whole of the issued capital*, the shares were valued by reference to adjustments on the company's earnings before interest, tax, depreciation and amortisation (EBITDA). For the shares subject to the counterclaim, which comprised a *minority interest*, a discounted cash flow method was applied.

7. By contrast, where the valuer has not complied with instructions, the valuation can be set aside. See *Begum v Hossain* [2015] EWCA Civ 717, CA, where a settlement agreement provided for expert valuation, with the valuer instructed to value the company's shares on the basis of all records, including 'any handwritten takings' (these being company receipts recorded informally to avoid tax); the court held that adherence to this instruction was mandatory. See too *Swain v Swain Plc* [2015] EWHC 600 (Ch), where the auditors' valuation required to set a 'fair value' was set aside on the basis that the valuation method adopted favoured the buyer over the seller, and (or alternatively) not all material facts had been taken into account.

8. In *Chilukuri v RP Explorer Master Fund* [2013] EWCA Civ 1307, CA, Briggs LJ at [52] held that 'It is axiomatic that in any complicated process of valuation, the valuer must take the relevant aspects of the world as he finds them (unless constrained by his instructions), and that he must, after looking at each element of the process, stand back and ask himself whether his provisional valuation makes commercial or business sense, viewed in the round.' The first instance judge had failed to consider the reality that the minority shareholding being valued was in fact of limited

---

[44] RM Walters [1977] *British Tax Review* 34 at 44.

worth, as it would give the purchaser 'precious little by way of control or influence' (Lewison LJ, [58]).

9. Special considerations arise when the price of a minority holding of shares has to be fixed when the court orders it to be bought by the majority shareholders pursuant to an order under the 'unfairly prejudicial conduct' section (CA 2006 s 994): see 'Remedies: valuing shares in buy-out orders', pp 741ff. This is especially so where the conduct complained of has reduced the value of the shares. Otherwise, of course, the date of the order may be considered the most appropriate date as it 'has the advantage of certainty' and (if the facts support this) seems to be 'most fair' in the light of all circumstances: see *Re KR Hardy Estates Ltd* [2014] EWHC 4001 (Ch) [93]; and see the discussion and analysis of other potential dates at [89]–[93]. Also see *Re Sunrise Radio Ltd* [2013] EWCA Civ 667, CA.

■ Further reading

GREGORY, A and HICKS, A, 'Valuation of Shares: A Legal and Accounting Conundrum' [1995] JBL 56.

PENNINGTON, R, 'Can Shares in Companies be Defined?' (1989) 10 *Company Lawyer* 140.

WORTHINGTON, S, 'Shares and Shareholders: Property, Power and Entitlement—Parts I and II' (2001) 22 *Company Lawyer* 258 and 307.

WORTHINGTON, S, 'Sorting Out Ownership Interests in a Bulk: Gifts, Sales and Trusts' [1999] JBL 1.

12

BORROWING, DEBENTURES AND CHARGES

General issues

Most companies do not operate using only equity funding from shareholders. Borrowing from lenders, and use of credit such as deferred payment for goods and services, provide additional and important methods of financing corporate activity.

The rights of lenders (bank lenders, creditors, debenture holders, etc: see later) depend on the precise terms of their contract with the company. As a general rule, creditors are entitled to an agreed rate of interest (fixed or variable) regardless of the commercial success of the company. Their loan agreements may be secured or unsecured providing different protection to different creditors should the company become insolvent. However, all creditors are paid out, in full if possible, before the shareholders are entitled to any return (see Chapter 16). Shareholders, on the other hand, generally expect to receive a higher total return (dividend plus capital growth of share value) on their equity funding than providers of debt funding. The level of dividend depends on the commercial success of the company and on the discretion of the directors. The rate of share value growth depends upon the company's overall actual and projected success. Debt is commonly considered a cheaper (ie its cost in terms of interest, versus dividend plus share value appreciation) but less flexible form of corporate funding than equity funding.

In this chapter, the focus is on *secured* debt, looking at options that are used by small and large companies alike (with the exception of use of the Financial Collateral Arrangements (No 2) Regulations 2003 (SI 2003/3226) and subsequent amendments, which are beyond the scope of this book[1]). But some general comments are warranted first. Like any other legal person, a company may borrow money, subject to any restrictions in its constitution.[2]

---

[1] See M Bridge, H Beale, L Gullifer and E Lomnicka, *The Law of Security and Title-Based Financing* (2nd edn, 2012) and M Bridge, L Gullifer, G McMeel and S Worthington, *The Law of Personal Property* (2013).

[2] A lender may, however, be protected from the effect of such restrictions by the internal management rules ('Deemed authority:...the "indoor management rule"', pp 116ff), by Companies Act 2006 (CA 2006) ss 39–40, or by a provision in the articles.

There are, however, a number of special features of corporate borrowing that are worth noting.

(i) To raise very large sums of money, a company may wish to attract funds on the investment market, that is, to borrow from very many lenders at once, or in sequence, all on the same terms. The mechanics of such a procedure are not greatly different from those involved in making an issue of shares, and indeed such issues may (but need not) be traded on the Stock Exchange subject to the same rules as equivalent dealings in equity securities (see Notes following, p 621). The investors will become a class of *creditors* of the company rather than *members* of the company; and the *debentures* (or more often *bonds*, in Europe and the United States, and increasingly here) held by each creditor will be *marketable securities*. The theoretical differences between being a creditor and a member are considerable, from a legal point of view, but (at least in the case of a solvent and prosperous company) the practical consequences (including, often, the total returns, ie interest plus capital appreciation) for investors, apart sometimes from tax considerations, may be very similar.

(ii) Where numerous investors advance money to a company in this way, it is usual for their rights to be regulated by a debenture trust deed, under which trustees are appointed to represent the investors as a class vis-à-vis the company. In the trust deed, provision is made for the collective views of investors to be ascertained by votes taken at meetings, with the usual apparatus of proxies, etc. Recall that where creditors vote as a class, the majority is prohibited from voting in ways which oppress the minority, just as shareholders are restrained: see *British America Nickel Corpn Ltd v O'Brien* **[11.06]**; *Assénagon Asset Management SA v Irish Bank Resolution Corporation Ltd (Formerly Anglo Irish Bank Corporation Ltd)* **[11.07]**; cp *Azevedo v Imcopa Importacao Exportaacao e Industria de Oleos Ltda* [2015] QB 1, [2013] EWCA Civ 364, at Note p 595. Two basic arrangements are common. In the first, each investor lends to the company directly, and simultaneously agrees to be bound by the terms of the trust deed in his dealings with the company. In the second (which is the more usual form in modern practice), all the loans are consolidated into one fund and the aggregate sum is advanced to the company by the trustees, who alone stand in a contractual relationship with the company: each investor then subscribes for so much 'debenture stock' or 'loan stock' out of the fund. Creditors can realise their investments strictly according to the terms of the debenture, or, if the debentures are marketable securities, by trading on the market. The ability to trade has advantages for creditors (increased liquidity and potentially higher total returns), and for the company (the loan repayment dates are certain, and not affected by creditors wanting early repayment).

(iii) A company can give security for its obligations, just like any other legal person. Where a company *charges* its property to secure an obligation to a creditor (not necessarily, of course, a borrowing obligation), CA 2006 may require that particulars of the charge be *registered* under the provisions of Pt 25 (ss 859Aff), failing which the security will be for many (but not all) purposes void: see 'Requirement to register charges', pp 627ff.

(iv) A company has the ability, not enjoyed by an individual in English law,[3] to create a '*floating charge*' over assets such as stock-in-trade and book

---

[3] To do so would infringe the Bills of Sale Acts of 1878 and 1882 (which do not apply to companies), and in any event it would be impossible to describe specifically the goods affected where these are to include assets acquired in the future. The Cork Committee recommended that it should be made possible for an individual to

debts,[4] which may fluctuate from time to time, on terms that the company remains free to deal with them in the ordinary course of business: see 'Fixed and floating charges: definitions', pp 632ff.

(v)   When a company makes default in any of its obligations under the document creating a charge, or when the security it has created is in jeopardy, the company's obligation is normally enforced by the appointment by the creditors (or the trustee for such creditors in the case of a debenture trust deed) of a *receiver* to look after the secured creditors' interests: see 'Receivership and administrative receivership', pp 822ff. Alternatively, where the charge is floating, changes to the statutory regime now ensure that *administration*, rather than administrative receivership,[5] is increasingly the norm (see 'Administration', pp 813ff).

(vi) Borrowing transactions secured by a floating charge may raise special questions in a *winding up*: see 'Different protections afforded to fixed and floating charge holders', pp 626ff, indicating the relative disadvantages of floating charges over other forms of security in providing protection to the security holder.

➤ Notes

1. It is apparent from the earlier commentary that an investment in debentures or debenture stock is very similar to an investment in shares: both are known as 'securities' in the corporate sector of the economy, each offering different kinds of risk and different kinds of return. Many companies have their debentures or debenture stock listed for dealing on the Stock Exchange. These securities are transferred in the same way as shares, with companies maintaining registers of debenture holders alongside their registers of members.

2. The form of the prospectus required for debt securities is prescribed in Regulation (EC) 809/2004. This distinguishes between the retail market (intended for the general public) and the wholesale market (intended for professional investors). The distinguishing criterion is the nominal value of the securities: those with a nominal value of less than €50,000 are regarded as intended for the retail market. And by Directive 2003/71/EC (Art 3(2)(c)), no prospectus is required for a public offer of wholesale debt securities (traded on the Professional Securities Market).

3. Under the CA 2006 s 616, companies are no longer able to use their share premium account to write off any expenses incurred, commission paid or discount allowed in respect of an issue of debentures or in providing for the premium payable on a redemption of debentures.

4. Major companies may also raise money by the issue of 'bonds', commonly referred to as 'Eurobonds' or 'international bonds' (a form of bearer security), which are usually denominated in a currency other than sterling and, because they are for large amounts, will

---

create a floating charge for business purposes: see (Cmnd 8558, 1982), para 1569. Also see P Giddins, 'Floating Mortgages by Individuals: Are They Conceptually Possible?' (2011) 3 *Butterworths Journal of International Banking and Financial Law* 125.

[4] The term 'book debts' is well established in English law, although its exact scope is unclear. Broadly speaking, in the present context it is used to describe the sums due to a company for goods sold or services rendered which have been, or are due to be, invoiced but have not yet been paid. There is growing support for the American expression 'receivables', which is more or less equivalent.

[5] A '*receiver*' takes control of all the assets that are subject to the charge. If the charge covers the entirety of the assets and undertaking of the company, or almost so, then the receiver is typically also given power to administer the company's business, and is then called an '*administrative receiver*'. A charge with this breadth is generally necessarily a combination of fixed and floating charges. The ability of such a chargee to appoint an administrative receiver is now curtailed by the Insolvency Act 1986 (IA 1986): see 'Administrative receivership', pp 824ff.

be bought and dealt in by banks and other institutional investors rather than the general public. There are various international markets and securities exchanges for dealings in such bonds.

➤ Questions

1. List some of the points of similarity and difference between shareholders and debenture holders which follow from the fact that a shareholder is a *member*, while a debenture holder is a *creditor*, of the company. Think of:

    (i)   the right to income;

    (ii) application of the 'maintenance of capital' rules;

    (iii) the right to return of capital during the lifetime of the company;

    (iv) the right to return of capital in a liquidation;

    (v) taxation;

    (vi) voting.

2. Some of these points may be varied by the terms of issue of the share or debenture, for example a share *may* carry no vote, a debenture holder *may* be given a vote in some circumstances. Which of the points listed earlier may be varied in this way?

Debentures

Definitions.

Companies Act 2006 s 738

> 738 In the Companies Acts 'debenture' includes debenture stock, bonds and any other securities of a company, whether or not constituting a charge on the assets of the company.

[12.01] Levy v Abercorris Slate and Slab Co (1887) 37 Ch D 260 (Chancery Division)

The facts are immaterial.

> CHITTY J: In my opinion a debenture means a document which either creates a debt or acknowledges it, and any document which fulfils either of these conditions is a 'debenture'. I cannot find any precise legal definition of the term, it is not either in law or commerce a strictly technical term, or what is called a term of art.

➤ Note

In *Fons HF (In Liquidation) v Corporal Ltd* [2014] EWCA Civ 304, [2015] 1 BCLC 320, the Court of Appeal applied Chitty J's *dicta* in *Levy* and gave a wide construction to the word 'debenture' (while also recognising that context mattered, and so the usual principles of contractual interpretation might expand or limit the scope of the word in any given document):

> As a matter of language, the term can apply to any document which creates or acknowledges a debt; [it] does not have to include some form of charge; and can be a single instrument rather than one in a series.

The issue mattered in this case, because Fons had granted security to a bank, the security covering various assets, including 'debentures'. See also the Note to **[12.02]** below.

An instrument may be a debenture although it is not under seal and gives no security to creditors for the company's obligation.

[12.02] British India Steam Navigation Co v IRC (1881) 7 QBD 165 (Queen's Bench Division)

A higher rate of stamp duty applied to 'debentures'. The company had issued instruments described on their face as 'debentures', by which the company undertook to pay the holder £100 on 30 November 1882, and to pay interest half-yearly at 5% per annum. It was argued unsuccessfully that the instruments, not being under seal, came within the definition of a promissory note and so did not attract the higher rate of stamp duty ordinarily payable on debentures.

> LINDLEY LJ: Now, what the correct meaning of 'debenture' is I do not know. I do not find anywhere any precise definition of it. We know that there are various kinds of instruments commonly called debentures. You may have mortgage debentures, which are charges of some kind on property. You may have debentures which are bonds; and, if this instrument were under seal, it would be a debenture of that kind. You may have a debenture which is nothing more than an acknowledgment of indebtedness. And you may have a thing like this, which is something more; it is a statement by two directors that the company will pay a certain sum of money on a given day, and will also pay interest half-yearly at certain times and at a certain place, upon production of certain coupons by the holder of the instrument. I think any of these things which I have referred to may be debentures within the Act.
>
> [His Lordship accordingly held that the instrument was a debenture and liable to be stamped as such.]

➤ Note

The term 'debenture' is capable in law of having a very wide meaning—it is simply a document evidencing a debt of any kind. But both in commercial usage and in the layman's understanding, it is commonly understood to refer to a document evidencing some *secured* obligation, and so the Listing Rules require that any issue of unsecured debentures be specifically denominated 'unsecured', and indeed it is more common for the word to be avoided altogether in this situation and a term such as 'loan stock' or 'loan notes' used instead.

Debentures and debenture stock may be issued in bearer form (ie not requiring registration for legal effect), and may also be created on terms which make them negotiable instruments: *Bechuanaland Exploration Co v London Trading Bank* [1898] 2 QB 658. As regards convertible debentures, see 'Issue of debentures at a discount', p 527.

Secured debt: mortgages, fixed and floating charges

Many companies will need to provide security for the repayment of their funding obligations, and not only obligations by way of loan. Only the largest companies, invariably trading on the London Stock Exchange or some other national equivalent, can avoid this. Since the issue is so common, and so important, the rest of this chapter is devoted to examining the rules relating to corporate security, especially fixed and floating charges. First, though, some definitions of the types of interests used to provide security.

Mortgages

A mortgage is a security interest created by transfer of legal title in the secured asset from the borrower/mortgagor to the lender/mortgagee. The borrower has an *'equity of redemption'*, allowing recovery of legal title once the secured obligation is fulfilled (eg the loan, interest, etc repaid) and, in the meantime, the lender has the right to take possession, and perhaps even to foreclose if permitted by court order, if the borrower defaults.

Historically, purchases of real property were secured by mortgages of this type over the land being bought. Now, however, the legal title to the land is *not* transferred to the lending bank (or other mortgagee), and the bank merely takes a legal *charge* over the property. (Nevertheless, we continue to speak of mortgages over land, and describe buyers as mortgagors and banks as mortgagees.) This charge over land is anomalous only in the sense that it is a *legal* charge, created by statute (Law of Property Act 1925 ss 85–87), whereas the charges discussed in this chapter are all necessarily *equitable*, not legal.

Charges

A *charge* is a security interest created in or over an asset or assets by their owner (the *'chargor'*) in favour of a creditor (the *'chargee'*), by which it is agreed[6] that that property shall be appropriated to the discharge of a debt or other obligation. There is no transfer of title. The chargee's rights are proprietary, but created by contract, and only for real consideration (since this is in equity, a deed for no consideration will not do: see *Re Earl of Lucan* (1890) 45 Ch D 470). The chargee's right may be enforced by the sale of the property, if necessary by court order; but in practice most security documents expressly empower the chargee to sell the property for this purpose without recourse to the court (see Slade J in *Re Bond Worth Ltd* [1980] Ch 228, 250). Legal charges are possible over some forms of property, such as land (see earlier), but not over personalty. The charges discussed in this section are all equitable charges.

Fixed charges

All charges are either fixed or floating. A fixed charge (or 'specific' charge) is a charge created over identified property which restricts the debtor's power to dispose of or otherwise deal with the property without the creditor's consent. It is not necessary that the property should be presently owned by the chargor: future property may be the subject of an agreement to charge, provided that it is sufficiently well described to be identifiable when acquired. The effect of such an agreement, if for value consideration, is that a charge is deemed to come into existence as soon as the property is acquired by the chargor (*Holroyd v Marshall* (1862) 10 HL Cas 191).

---

[6] The charges described in this chapter are all created by agreement between the parties. Charges may also sometimes be created by operation of law (and then are referred to as *equitable liens*, although note that, despite the name, the rights associated with them mirror the non-statutory rights associated with equitable charges, and not the rights associated with contractual liens, which are quite different), but these equitable liens are not relevant for present purposes.

Floating charges

A floating charge also requires the property affected to be identified, in the same sense, but it is of the essence of a floating charge that it contemplates that the chargor will be free to deal with the charged property in the ordinary course of business without reference to the chargee (sometimes called the 'trading power'). The floating charge thus allows a company to give security over assets which are continually turned over or used up and replaced as a matter of routine trading. This is an enormously valuable invention, devised by equity draftsmen in the latter part of the nineteenth century, founded upon the agreement of the parties and owing nothing to legislation—rather like the device of hire-purchase which evolved at about the same time.[7] What successive Companies Acts and Insolvency Acts have done since its creation is to adopt a variety of rules designed to restrict the full power of its impact, which is potentially to sweep up *all* the company's resources (by securing *'the undertaking'* or *'all the assets and undertaking'* of the company) and dedicate them to securing the debt of *one* of the company's creditors,[8] leaving all the others unprotected, unable even to share *pari passu* in the company's resources on a winding up.

The significance of the floating charge lies in the fact that, for many businesses, fluctuating assets such as stock-in-trade, raw materials and book debts may form a significant part of the property of the concern, and may be the only worthwhile security available for an advance. Indeed, the proprietors of an unincorporated business which is in need of finance may find themselves compelled to form a company if they are to raise the loans they are seeking: hence the ability to grant a floating charge can be an important consideration in deciding whether or not to trade in the corporate form. Banks, in particular, have wide experience of the floating charge and encourage its use by their clients.

The nature of a charge.

[12.03] National Provincial Bank v Charnley [1924] 1 KB 431 (Court of Appeal)

The facts are immaterial.

> ATKIN LJ: It is not necessary to give a formal definition of a charge, but I think there can be no doubt that where in a transaction for value both parties evince an intention that property, existing or future, shall be made available as security for the payment of a debt, and that the creditor shall have a present right to have it made available, there is a charge, even though the present legal right which is contemplated can only be enforced at some future date, and though the creditor gets no legal right of property, either absolute or special, or any legal right to possession, but only gets a right to have the security made available by an order of the Court. If those conditions exist I think there is a charge. If, on the other hand, the parties do not intend that there should be a present right to have the security made available, but only that there should be a right in the future by agreement, such as a licence, to seize the goods, there will be no charge . . .

---

[7] A voluminous literature exists on floating charges, covering both practical and theoretical aspects. See especially J Getzler and J Payne (eds), *Company Charges: Spectrum and Beyond* (2006), which also provides reference to much of the earlier literature.

[8] *Re Panama, New Zealand and Australian Royal Mail Co* (1869–70) LR 5 Ch App 318, CA, provided early confirmation that this is possible.

Debenture holders' remedies and the protection afforded by charges

We have not yet examined the approach the courts adopt in determining whether the security the parties have created is effective, and if so whether it is fixed or floating in form. However, in large measure the reason for the efforts in that direction are because a valid security delivers particular protections to the security holder. It is helpful to be aware of what those are before descending into the detail of the analysis required to establish the nature and effectiveness of the security itself.

Any creditor whose debt is unsatisfied may, of course, sue to recover payment, and may also seek to have the company wound up if it fails to meet a statutory demand for payment (IA 1986 ss 122(1)(f) and 123(1)(a): see 'Grounds for compulsory winding up', pp 838ff). But secured creditors also have recourse to their security. Where the charge affects specific property, powers of sale and of entry into possession may be exercised by the secured creditor personally, although usually the creditor will appoint a professional third party as a *receiver*. This may always be done by obtaining a court order; but almost invariably the need to go to court will be obviated by the inclusion in the instrument creating the charge of a clause empowering the creditor itself (or the trustees, where there is a trust deed) to appoint a receiver in the event of default. Note, however, that if the charge is a floating charge secured over the whole or substantially the whole of the company's property, then the holder may no longer appoint an administrative receiver (IA 1986 s 72A), subject to certain limited exceptions in IA 1986 ss 72B–72EA, but must instead appoint an *administrator* who has defined objectives in dealing with the company's assets.

The subject of receivers, including administrative receivers, is discussed further at 'Receivership and administrative receivership', pp 822ff.

If the borrowing company is insolvent (ie unable to pay all its debts in full), then security affords secured creditors priority in repayment of their debts. Basically, the secured assets are used first to fund repayment of the secured debt, and only then are any remaining assets used to repay all or a pro rata part of the debts owed to the unsecured creditors. If a company owes £100,000 to a secured creditor and £100,000 to its unsecured creditors, for example, and its assets are only worth £100,000, then those assets (assuming these are the assets over which security has been taken) will go entirely to repaying the secured debt, and the unsecured creditors will get nothing. In practice, the statutory rules are more sophisticated and more complicated, but this gross generalisation is fundamentally true. The statutory rules are considered in detail in Chapter 16.

Being secured is obviously advantageous, but, in addition, the advantages afforded to holders of fixed charges are substantially greater than those afforded to holders of floating charges, as described next.

Different protections afforded to fixed and floating charge holders

The distinction between fixed and floating charges has important consequences. These charges are treated differently during the term of the security, during receivership and on the insolvency of the debtor. For example, with floating charges (but not with fixed charges):

(i)   the chargor can legitimately deal with floating charge assets in the ordinary course of business (until an event of default that causes the charge to *crystallise*—see 'Crystallisation of floating charges', p 641), so the value of the security may be depleted before the chargee calls on it;

(ii)   prior to the 6 April 2013 amendments, it used to be the case that all floating charges needed to be registered, but not all fixed charges (see CA 2006 s 860 as it was, and now s 859A and 'Requirement to register charges', p 627);

(iii) a floating charge is subordinated to the costs and expenses of administration and liquidation (see IA 1986 Sch B1, paras 70 and 99, and IA 1986 s 176ZA; and 'Administration', pp 813ff and 'Liquidation or winding up', pp 834ff);

(iv)   an administrator can dispose of assets subject to a floating charge without first obtaining court approval (IA 1986 Sch B1, paras 70–71, and 'Powers and duties of the administrator', pp 817ff);

(v)   preferential creditors rank ahead of the floating charge holder in their call on assets subject to the floating charge (IA 1986 ss 40 and 175(2)(b); Sch B1, para 65(2); and Sch 6, paras 8–12: see 'Distribution of assets subject to the receivership', pp 832ff);

(vi)   on insolvency, a statutory proportion of floating charge realisations must be set aside for the unsecured creditors (see IA 1986 s 176A, and 'Distribution of assets subject to the receivership', pp 832ff);

(vii) a floating charge created for no new value in the period immediately leading up to insolvency may be set aside (IA 1986 s 245). No equivalent exists for fixed charges, which can only be set aside if they involve a preference (IA 1986 s 239). See 'The liquidator's ability to "claw back" property—unwinding transactions', p 852.

Requirement to register charges

Statutory requirements

Part 25 of CA 2006 imposes on companies a statutory obligation to register particulars of charges which they have created over their property. Following a long history of failed attempts at reforming the law in this area (see later), the existing rules have finally been modified, although perhaps not greatly, with the aim of delivering a more modern regime which will save time and cost for those using it. The Department of Business, Innovation and Skills suggests the cost savings could be of the order of £22 million per annum.[9] The reforms were made by way of the Companies Act 2006 (Amendment of Part 25) Regulations 2013,[10] which repealed CA 2006 Pt 25, Chs 1 and 2, replacing them with Ch A1, which came into force on 6 April 2013.

This requirement to register charges was first imposed by the Companies Act 1900. Up until the 2013 changes, the approach adopted was to list the types of charges which were required to be registered. Not every category of charge was affected—fixed charges over shares or negotiable instruments, for instance, escaped the net—although the list was always fairly comprehensive, and included all floating charges. Under the new rules, there is no longer a prescribed list. On the contrary, s 859A quite simply states that the section will apply 'where a company creates a charge', subject only to three exceptions set out in s 859A(6). The hope is that this will reduce the uncertainty surrounding which charges must be registered. Section 859B provides parallel provisions for charges given to support a series of debentures. But note that it is only charges *created by the company* which come

---

[9] See Explanatory Notes available at: www.bis.gov.uk/assets/biscore/business-law/docs/e/12-1028-explanatory-notes-draft-regulations-part-25-companies.pdf.

[10] Under CA 2006 ss 894(1) and 1292(1).

within Pt 25: a charge created by operation of law, such as an unpaid vendor's lien over land which is the subject of a contract of sale, is outside the scope of the Act.

For every charge created by a company, CA 2006 s 859A does not make it mandatory for the parties to register the charge (as the previous rules had, with criminal sanctions to back up the rule), but instead compels the registrar to register the charge *if* the parties deliver the appropriate instruments and details to the registrar within the specified time (basically 21 days, but see ss 859E and 859F). Either the company or the charge holder (or 'any person interested in the charge', s 859A(2)) may see to the registration, and would be well advised to do so if there is any risk that the company will default. The change from compulsion to permission may be immaterial, however, as the consequence of failure to register is that the charge is void on precisely the occasions when it is most needed: see 'Effect of failure to register', p 628.

If a company acquires property which is already subject to a charge, particulars of the charge may similarly be delivered for registration (s 859C).

Where the charge (eg a charge over land or a ship) requires registration under other legislation, that does not provide a reason for non-compliance with CA 2006 Pt 25, unless the other Act excludes the application of the CA 2006 provisions (see s 859A(6)).

Certificate of registration

On registration, a certificate is issued which must state the unique reference code allocated to the charge (s 859I(4)). Under s 859I(6), the certificate is 'conclusive evidence that the documents required by the section concerned were delivered to the registrar before the end of the relevant period allowed for delivery.'

This is far more specific than its predecessor, which simply stated that the certificate was 'conclusive evidence that the requirements of this Chapter as to registration have been satisfied'. Earlier cases suggested the force of the certificate—and of the register—was assured even where the certificate was inaccurate (*Re Mechanisations (Eaglescliffe) Ltd* [1966] Ch 20), or the facts on which the certificate was based were untrue (eg where the charge instrument is falsely dated: *Re CL Nye Ltd* [1971] Ch 442), or the charge was registered by mistake (*Ali v Top Marques Car Rental Ltd* [2006] EWHC 109 (Ch)). The effect was that notwithstanding that the details on the register were incorrect, and people inspecting the register would be misled, the certificate would be conclusive proof that the statutory requirements had been met.[11] As a consequence, the *actual* charge as created by the company would be deemed to be duly registered, and would have to be observed by the company's creditors and its liquidator or administrator, notwithstanding creditors who may have been misled as to the company's true position. And because the certificate was conclusive evidence that the requirements had been met, it was impossible to have proceedings for judicial review of the registrar's decision.

Despite all this, the conclusiveness of the certificate was seen as a crucial benefit of the registration system, and a proposed downgrading of it was in large measure the reason for the unpopularity of certain proposed 1989 reforms. The new rules seem to have worked around this.

Effect of failure to register

If particulars are not registered within 21 days of the creation of the charge (a date defined in s 859E, attempting to provide for both English and Scottish securities), or such longer

---

[11] In Hong Kong, a similar statutory provision regarding the certificate has been taken to mean that the certificate is conclusive evidence of due registration, *and* of the accuracy of the creation date on the certificate: *Re Moulin Global Eyecare Holdings Ltd* (2009) 12 HKCFAR 621.

period as allowed by the court (s 859F, see the following section), then CA 2006 s 859H declares the *security* to be void against the liquidator, administrator and any creditor of the company[12] (s 859H(3)), although the personal obligation remains and, indeed, the money secured becomes immediately payable (s 859H(4)).

The nature of this sanction of 'partial voidness' should be noted. First, it is only the *security* that is avoided, not the underlying obligation, which remains good as an unsecured debt. Secondly, the charge is void only as against the persons mentioned and not, for instance, *inter partes*, or against an execution creditor. And the chargee may dispose of the property in exercise of a power of sale and give a good title to the purchaser, even though the charge is 'void'.

Extension of the registration period and rectification of the register

CA 2006 s 859F enables applications to court to extend the 21-day registration period. The court may make whatever orders it sees as just and expedient provided certain pre-conditions are satisfied (s 859F(2)), including that it is just and equitable to grant relief. This replicates predecessor rules, so see *Barclays Bank plc v Stuart Landon Ltd* [2001] EWCA Civ 140, CA, for a discussion of the factors to be considered by the court when dealing with an application for late registration of a charge created by a company which was close to liquidation.

In analogous circumstances, and subject to the same conditions, s 859M enables the court to make an order rectifying the register where there has been an omission or misstatement, and s 859N provides the court with a discretion to replace the instrument or debenture where there has been an omission, mistake or defect.

Registration, priority and constructive notice of registered charges

Registration does not of itself confer priority or give any protection to a charge holder, although of course, as noted previously, non-registration has almost fatal consequences for the security. Instead, priority as between different charges over the same property is determined by the ordinary rules of law. Thus, for example, a legal charge will normally have priority over an equitable charge, a fixed charge over a floating charge (because of their terms) and, as between two equitable charges, the earlier in time will prevail. So, if a company were to create a charge in favour of A on the first of the month, and then give an identical charge over the same property to B on the 10th, registering particulars on the 15th, B (who had searched the register on the 10th and found it clear) could in all innocence believe that he has a first charge, only to discover later that A has a charge which ranks ahead of his own, so long as it has been registered within the statutory 21 days. B is deemed to have notice of the earlier charge provided A files for registration within the statutory 21-day period. (This is referred to in the Company Law Review (CLR) as 'the 21-day invisibility problem'. It could be eliminated if 'notice filing' were introduced, although even then there could be a gap

---

[12] But see *Smith v Bridgend County Borough Council* [2001] UKHL 58, [2002] 1 AC 336 (the appeal of *Cosslett* [12.08]), Lord Hoffmann:

> When a winding-up order is made and a liquidator appointed, there is no divesting of the company's assets. The liquidator acquires no interest, whether beneficially or as trustee. The assets continue to belong to the company but the liquidator is able to exercise the company's right to collect them for the purposes of the liquidation…It must in my opinion follow that when [Companies Act 1985 (CA 1985)] s 395 [now CA 2006 s 874] says that the charge shall be 'void against the liquidator', it means void against a company acting by its liquidator, that is to say, a company in liquidation.

> The same analysis applies to administration.

between the time when a document is delivered to Companies House and the time when it is recorded on the register.)

The doctrine of constructive notice has not been abolished in regard to particulars of charges held by the registrar, and so everyone dealing with a company is deemed to have notice of those particulars which are required by statute to be registered.[13] These are defined in s 859D, and include the date of creation of the charge, the nature of the charge (fixed or floating), the amount secured, short particulars of the property charged, and the persons entitled to the charge, and, by way of change from the earlier rules, whether the charge includes a 'negative pledge' clause (ie a provision by which the company undertakes not to create other charges ranking in priority to or *pari passu* with the charge; see s 859D(2)(c)).

This change in the rules on negative pledges eliminates the problem illustrated in *Siebe Gorman & Co Ltd v Barclays Bank Ltd* [1979] 2 Lloyd's Rep 142, Ch (overruled in *Spectrum* **[12.20]**, but not on this issue). Under the predecessor rules, details of negative pledges were not mandatory, but a practice developed of including such details in the registered particulars. In *Siebe Gorman*, it was held that the constructive notice doctrine did not extend to such additional information, but only to those matters which the Act prescribed, and so a searcher would be taken to know of such a clause only if he had *actual* notice of it. The point always remained controversial, with little persuasive authority or argument.[14]

Section 859L contains provision for entering on the register a 'statement' that the debt secured by a charge has been satisfied or some or all of the property charged has been released from the security. But there is no obligation to register this information under the existing law.

Company's own register of charges

Under the old rules, the company itself was also required to keep a register of charges. Since this register was required to cover every kind of charge, not only those which were registrable, the obligations were potentially very burdensome. They were also largely pointless, since neither the validity of the charge nor any question relating to priority was affected by a failure to observe these requirements, and in practice the related criminal sanctions were never invoked. This may explain why the new rules no longer require companies to keep their own registers, but merely demand that companies keep copies of the full instruments available for inspection (s 859Q).

Further reform of the registration system

The need for some sort of registration system is almost universally accepted, but the present system, which has changed little for over a century, despite the various 2013 changes, has long been thought to be deficient. Almost 25 years ago, changes were made to the Companies Act 1989 that were intended to sweep away the old law and replace it with a completely new regime containing provisions which would reduce the burden on Companies House but at the same time give rather less protection to persons who

---

[13] Although interestingly the final version of the Regulations omits any specific reference to constructive notice. An earlier draft included s 859R, which explicitly provided for deemed constructive notice in relation to 'any matter requiring registration and disclosed on the register', although the provision remained within square brackets with the accompanying explanatory notes issued by BIS inviting further comments on the issue: see www.bis.gov.uk/assets/biscore/business-law/docs/e/12-1028-explanatory-notes-draft-regulations-part-25-companies.pdf.

[14] See *Wilson v Kelland* [1910] 2 Ch 306. Also see J de Lacy, 'Constructive Notice and Company Charge Registration' [2001] *Conveyancer* 122.

relied on the registration system. Those proposed reforms met with such opposition from business and professional circles that the government was dissuaded from bringing the regime into operation. Instead, a consultation process was begun which envisaged retaining the earlier CA 1985 provisions, but introducing some modifications. That idea was subsequently overtaken by the decision to set up the CLR, which published its own consultation document seeking views on possible ways forward. Following that, the Law Commission was asked to examine the whole of the law on the registration, perfection and priority of company charges, and to consider the case for a new registration system. It was also asked to consider whether such a system should be extended to quasi-securities (retention of title agreements, etc), and to securities created by individuals as well as companies.

The Law Commission, looking to have changes included in CA 2006, made various recommendations, including adoption of a notice-filing system (see later) for company charges (see *Company Security Interests* (Law Com No 296, 2005)). The government then issued a further consultation document (*The Registration of Companies' Security Interests (Company Charges): The Economic Impact of the Law Commissions' Proposals*, 2005). This received a rather negative response, and so all the issues were parked, subject to still further discussions and deliberations before any decision could be taken on what ought to be done. The latest 2013 reforms fall far short of counting as movement on this front. Their biggest changes are simply the elimination of the list of registrable charges in favour of making all charges registrable, and also including public notification on the register of negative pledge clauses.

This rocky road to reform might be seen as both surprising and disappointing. Both the Crowther Committee (which was concerned with reform of the law on consumer credit: Cmnd 4596, 1971) and Professor Diamond in his report (*A Review of Security Interests in Property* (1989)) categorically recommended that this country should follow the lead of the United States and Canadian jurisdictions in setting up an entirely new system of registration for all personal property security interests, whether created by individuals or companies, on the model of Art 9 of the American Uniform Commercial Code. This would make a separate regime for company charges unnecessary. The same conclusion was reached independently by reform bodies in other Commonwealth jurisdictions, such as Australia and New Zealand—each of which has now implemented this major change. But, sadly, there seems to be little enthusiasm for any such reform in the UK, despite the most recent consultation responses in its favour.[15]

What is different about these other regimes? Article 9 of the Uniform Commercial Code is at the same time a more comprehensive system and yet a simpler and more flexible one: it governs all transactions which *in effect* create a security, whatever their form (including, eg, hire-purchase agreements and sales on retention of title (*Romalpa* **[12.21]** terms), and works on the principle of 'notice filing'. Priority as between competing registered securities is governed simply by the time of filing of the notice of such security: the security filed first has priority over all that follow. It gives better protection—first, for security holders, in that registration confers priority over others who may claim interests in the same property; secondly, for those intending to take security who, by filing a notice, can cover their position provisionally until the security is completed or the charge attaches; and, thirdly, for those seeking to rely on searches of the register, who can take the record at its face value.

---

[15] Paragraph 28, 'Government response: consultation on registration of charges created by companies and limited liability partnerships' (December 2010); available at: www.gov.uk/government/uploads/system/uploads/attachment_data/file/49949/10-1319-government-response-consultation-registration-of-charges.pdf.

Fixed and floating charges: definitions

The preceding sections described the structure of the regime for company securities. It is now appropriate to look at the nature of the securities themselves. Recall that charges may be over present or future property and can be either fixed or floating. A *fixed* (or 'specific') charge is one which restricts the debtor's power to dispose of or otherwise deal with the specific property charged, without first obtaining the creditor's consent. A *floating* charge, on the other hand, permits the debtor the freedom to deal with the charged property in the ordinary course of business without recourse to the creditor for approval. This liberty to deal with the charged assets continues until the floating charge *crystallises* into a fixed charge. The parties can nominate in the charge document the conditions, or time, at which this will happen. Additionally, the charge will crystallise by operation of law if the debtor company ceases to carry on business for any reason (see 'Crystallisation of floating charges', pp 641ff).

The distinction between fixed and floating charges is completely irrelevant in assessing the rights, as between the company (chargor) and the lender (chargee) arising under the charge; these are determined by the charge document. The distinction is critical solely because various statutory rules relating to validity and priority are worded to apply to one form of security but not the other: see 'Different protections afforded to fixed and floating charge holders', p 626.

Categorisation of a charge as fixed or floating is based on the *substance* of the arrangement between the parties, not on the label they attach to their arrangement.[16] The following cases indicate the process adopted by the courts in making this determination.

[12.04] Agnew v Commissioner of Inland Revenue (Re Brumark Investments Ltd) [2001] UKPC 28, [2001] 2 AC 710 (Privy Council)

The facts and a longer extract appear at **[12.19]**.

> LORD MILLETT: The most celebrated, and certainly the most often cited, description of a floating charge is that given by Romer LJ in *In re Yorkshire Woolcombers Association Ltd* [1903] 2 Ch 284, 295:
>
> > 'I certainly do not intend to attempt to give an exact definition of the term "floating charge", nor am I prepared to say that there will not be a floating charge within the meaning of the Act, which does not contain all the three characteristics that I am about to mention, but I certainly think that if a charge has the three characteristics that I am about to mention it is a floating charge. (1) If it is a charge on a class of assets of a company present and future; (2) if that class is one which, in the ordinary course of the business of the company, would be changing from time to time; and (3) if you find that by the charge it is contemplated that, until some future step is taken by or on behalf of those interested in the charge, the company may carry on its business in the ordinary way as far as concerns the particular class of assets I am dealing with.'

---

[16] Eg *Re Armagh Shoes Ltd* [1984] BCLC 405 per Hutton J, holding that the charge was floating even though stated to be fixed. Although there was no provision for crystallisation, this did not matter: the charge would crystallise on the winding up of the company or the appointment of a receiver (at 408–411, 419). Also see *Re Brightlife Ltd* [1987] Ch 200, 209 per Hoffmann J (see **[12.12]**). There is a vast body of precedent, going back to the earliest Bills of Sale Acts last century, concerned with the question of whether a composite transaction such as a sale and lease-back is what it purports to be or is in reality a concealed form of charge. For contrasting modern illustrations, see *Welsh Development Agency v Export Finance Co Ltd* [1992] BCLC 148, CA (agency with power to sell held genuine) and *Re Curtain Dream plc* [1990] BCLC 925 (purported sale and repurchase held to be a disguised form of security).

This was offered as a description and not a definition. The first two characteristics are typical of a floating charge but they are not distinctive of it, since they are not necessarily inconsistent with a fixed charge. It is the third characteristic which is the hallmark of a floating charge and serves to distinguish it from a fixed charge. Since the existence of a fixed charge would make it impossible for the company to carry on business in the ordinary way without the consent of the charge holder, it follows that its ability to [do] so without such consent is inconsistent with the fixed nature of the charge.

Also see the *Spectrum* decision at **[12.20]**.

[12.05] Illingworth v Houldsworth [1904] AC 355 (House of Lords)

This is the appeal to the House of Lords of the decision in *Re Yorkshire Woolcombers Association*, cited by Lord Millett at **[12.04]**.

> EARL OF HALSBURY LC: In the first place you have that which in a sense I suppose must be an element in the definition of a floating security, that it is something which is to float, not to be put into immediate operation, but such that the company is to be allowed to carry on its business. It contemplates not only that it [the security] should carry with it the book debts [the charged assets] which were then existing, but it contemplates also the possibility of those book debts being extinguished by a payment to the company, and that other book debts should come in and take the place of those that had disappeared. That . . . seems to me to be an essential characteristic of what is properly called a floating security . . .
>
> LORD MACNAGHTEN: I should have thought there was not much difficulty in defining what a floating charge is in contrast to what is called a specific charge. A specific charge, I think, is one that without more fastens on ascertained and definite property or property capable of being ascertained and defined; a floating charge, on the other hand, is ambulatory and shifting in its nature, hovering over and so to speak floating with the property which it is intended to affect until some event occurs or some act is done which causes it to settle and fasten on the subject of the charge within its reach and grasp . . .

[12.06] Evans v British Granite Quarries Ltd [1910] 2 KB 979 (Court of Appeal)

The facts are immaterial.

> BUCKLEY LJ: A floating charge is not a future security; it is a present security which presently affects all the assets of the company expressed to be included in it . . . A floating security is not a specific mortgage of the assets plus a licence to the mortgagor to dispose of them in the course of his business, but it is a floating mortgage applying to every item comprised in the security, but not specifically affecting any item until some act or event occurs or some act on the part of the mortgagee is done which causes it to crystallise into a fixed security . . .

[12.07] Re Bond Worth [1980] Ch 228 (Chancery Division)

The case concerned an unsuccessful attempt to give a supplier of goods the benefit of a retention of title clause (discussed at 'Retention of title agreements', pp 660ff).

> SLADE J: There is, however, one type of charge (and I think one type only) which, by its very nature, leaves a company at liberty to deal with the assets charged in the ordinary course of its

business, without regard to the charge, until stopped by a winding up or by the appointment of a receiver or the happening of some other agreed event. I refer to what is commonly known as a 'floating charge' . . . Such a charge remains unattached to any particular property and leaves the company with a licence to deal with, and even sell, the assets falling within its ambit in the ordinary course of business, as if the charge had not been given, until it is stopped by one or other of the events to which I have referred, when it is said to 'crystallise'; it then becomes effectively fixed to the assets within its scope.

. . . This description of a floating charge shows that it need not extend to all the assets of the company. It may cover assets merely of a specified category or categories . . .

. . . The critical distinction in my judgment is that between a specific charge on the one hand and a floating charge on the other. Vaughan Williams L.J. pointed out in the *Woolcombers* case [1903] 2 Ch. 284 that it is quite inconsistent with the nature of a specific charge, though not of a floating charge, that the mortgagor is at liberty to deal with the relevant property as he pleases. He said, at p 294:

> 'I do not think that for a "specific security" you need have a security of a subject matter which is then in existence. I mean by "then" at the time of the execution of the security; but what you do require to make a specific security is that the security whenever it has once come into existence, and been identified or appropriated as a security, shall never thereafter at the will of the mortgagor cease to be a security. If at the will of the mortgagor he can dispose of it and prevent its being any longer a security, although something else may be substituted more or less for it, that is not a "specific security".'

Floating charges: creation and effect

Creation of floating charges and impact of failure to register

It is possible for a floating charge to arise even though the parties never contemplated that this might be the result of their actions.[17]

[12.08] Re Cosslett (Contractors) Ltd [1998] Ch 495 (Court of Appeal)

This case went on appeal to the House of Lords, but not on this issue: [2002] 1 AC 336.

Cosslett had contracted with the Mid-Glamorgan County Council to carry out land rec-lamation work which involved the washing of large amounts of coal-bearing shale, and for this purpose it brought two coal-washing plants onto the site. A clause in the contract empowered the council, if the company abandoned the work: (i) to use the plants to com-plete the job, or (ii) to sell the plants and use the proceeds towards the satisfaction of any sums due to it from Cosslett. Before the work was completed, the company abandoned the site, leaving the plants behind. The company then went into administration. The council applied to the court for an order requiring the administrator to deliver the plants to it; the company contended that the clause in the contract created a charge which was a floating charge and void because it had not been registered. At first instance, Jonathan Parker J held that there was a charge, but that it was a fixed charge. On appeal, it was held that

---

[17] Unsurprisingly, then, these charges are not registered as permitted under CA 2006 s 859A (or as was required by CA 2006 s 874 or its predecessor, CA 1985 s 395) and so are ineffective to give priority on the chargor's insol-vency: see 'Requirement to register charges', p 627.

although no charge was created by paragraph (a) of the clause in question, a floating charge was created by paragraph (b); but that non-registration of (b) did not stand in the way of the council's right to enforce (a).

MILLETT LJ: . . . There are only four kinds of consensual security known to English law: (i) pledge; (ii) contractual lien; (iii) equitable charge and (iv) mortgage. A pledge and a contractual lien both depend on the delivery of possession to the creditor. The difference between them is that in the case of a pledge the owner delivers possession to the creditor as security, whereas in the case of a lien the creditor retains possession of goods previously delivered to him for some other purpose. Neither a mortgage nor a charge depends on the delivery of possession. The difference between them is that a mortgage involves a transfer of legal or equitable ownership to the creditor, whereas an equitable charge does not.

In the present case the council's rights in relation to the plant and materials are exclusively contractual, and are not attributable to any delivery of possession by the company. When the company brings plant and materials onto the site they remain in the possession of the company to enable it to use them in the completion of the works. There is no question of the company delivering possession at that stage, either by way of security (i.e. as a pledge) or otherwise (i.e. by way of lien). The council comes into possession of the plant and materials when it expels the company from the site leaving the plant and materials behind. But this does not amount to a voluntary delivery of possession by the company to the council. It is rather the exercise by the council of a contractual right to take possession of the plant and materials against the will of the company.

In my judgment, therefore, the council's rights are derived from contract not possession and, in so far as they are conferred by way of security, constitute an equitable charge . . .

Is the charge a fixed or floating charge?

In my judgment the three characteristics of a floating charge which were identified by Romer L.J. in *In re Yorkshire Woolcombers Association Ltd.; Houldsworth v. Yorkshire Woolcombers Association Ltd.* [1903] 2 Ch. 284, 295 are all present. There is no difficulty in regard to the first two characteristics. Plant and materials become subject to the charge as they are brought onto the site and cease to be subject to it as they are removed from the site. Accordingly the charge is a charge on present and future assets of the company which, in the ordinary course of the business of the company, would be changing from time to time. The dispute has centred on the third characteristic. The administrator submits that, until the council takes steps under clause 63(1) to enter upon the site and expel the company therefrom, the company is free to carry on its business in the ordinary way with the plant and materials on the site. The judge accepted the council's submission that this was not so, because of the council's absolute right under clause 53(6) to refuse to permit the company to remove from the site plant and materials immediately required to complete the works, and its qualified right to refuse permission for the removal of plant and materials not immediately required for this purpose provided only that it acts reasonably. I am unable to agree with him.

The judge held that it is of the essence of a floating charge that until the charge crystallises the chargor should retain an unfettered freedom to carry on his business in the ordinary way. He relied for this purpose on two passages, one in the judgment of Vaughan Williams L.J. in the *Yorkshire Woolcombers* case, at p 294, and the other in the judgment of Slade J. in *In re Bond Worth Ltd.* **[12.07]** [1980] Ch. 228, 266. The first passage reads as follows:

'If *at the will of the mortgagor* he can dispose of [the asset] and prevent its being any longer a security, although something else may be substituted more or less for it, that is not a "specific security."' (My emphasis.)

The second passage reads:

> 'It is in my judgment quite incompatible with the existence of an effective trust by way
> of specific charge in equity over specific assets that the *alleged trustee* should be free
> to use them as he pleases for his own business in the course of his own business.'
> (My emphasis.)

But with respect the converse does not follow. The chargor's unfettered freedom to deal with
the assets in the ordinary course of his business free from the charge is obviously inconsistent
with the nature of a fixed charge; but it does not follow that his unfettered freedom to deal with
the charged assets is essential to the existence of a floating charge. It plainly is not, for any well
drawn floating charge prohibits the chargor from creating further charges having priority to the
floating charge; and a prohibition against factoring debts is not sufficient to convert what would
otherwise be a floating charge on book debts into a fixed charge: see in *In re Brightlife Ltd.* **[12.12]**
[1987] Ch. 200, 209, per Hoffmann J.

The essence of a floating charge is that it is a charge, not on any particular asset, but on
a fluctuating body of assets which remain under the management and control of the chargor,
and which the chargor has the right to withdraw from the security despite the existence of the
charge. The essence of a fixed charge is that the charge is on a particular asset or class of assets
which the chargor cannot deal with free from the charge without the consent of the chargee.
The question is not whether the chargor has complete freedom to carry on his business as he
chooses, but whether the chargee is in control of the charged assets. . . .

Accordingly . . . I hold the charge to be a floating charge.

What are the consequences of the want of registration?

Of all the contractual rights which the council enjoys only one, the power of sale, constitutes
a charge of a kind which is registrable under section 395 of the Companies Act 1985 [CA
2006 s 859A]. The section provides that the failure to register a charge makes the charge
(that is to say the registrable charge) void as a security against a liquidator or administrator
of the company [now see CA 2006 s 859H]. The effect of this is to entitle the liquidator or
administrator to deal with the company's assets free from the security created by the charge
in question.

In my judgment, therefore, the failure to register the charge renders the security created by
the power of sale void as against the administrator, but does not affect any other right of the
council which is not a security and which does not require registration. In particular, it does not
invalidate the council's contractual right to retain possession of plant and materials and use them
to complete the works. But after the completion of the works the council's right to continue in
possession [and certainly to sell] is referable to a security which is void against the administrator
and cannot prevail against him . . .

Limitations on the assets which may be made subject to a floating charge

If a company has a proprietary interest in an asset, then it is usually assumed that the asset
can be charged by the company as security for an obligation.

The possible limits to this assumption were tested in the House of Lords. The issue
arose from a practice adopted by banks in attempting to enlarge the security they take
from borrowing customers. Banks typically take fixed and floating charges over all a
customer's fixed assets and stock-in-trade. But what of any sums of money the customer
might have on deposit with the bank? Put in contractual terms, these are sums of money
that the bank owes to the customer. The customer 'owns' a debt owed to it by the bank.

Can the bank take a charge over this asset to secure a loan it might make to its customer? The issue has now been resolved in favour of this form of security, as illustrated by the following extract.

[12.09] Re Bank of Credit and Commerce International SA (No 8) [1998] AC 214 (House of Lords)

The facts are immaterial.

LORD HOFFMANN: The doctrine of conceptual impossibility was first propounded by Millett J in *In re Charge Card Services Ltd.* [1987] Ch 150, 175–176 and affirmed, after more extensive discussion, by the Court of Appeal in this case. It has excited a good deal of heat and controversy in banking circles; the Legal Risk Review Committee, set up in 1991 by the Bank of England to identify areas of obscurity and uncertainty in the law affecting financial markets and propose solutions, said that a very large number of submissions from interested parties expressed disquiet about this ruling. It seems clear that documents purporting to create such charges have been used by banks for many years. The point does not previously appear to have been expressly addressed by any court in this country. Supporters of the doctrine rely on the judgments of Buckley L.J. (in the Court of Appeal) and Viscount Dilhorne and Lord Cross of Chelsea (in the House of Lords) in *Halesowen Presswork Assemblies Ltd. v. Westminster Bank Ltd.* [1971] 1 Q.B. 1; [1972] A.C. 785. The passages in question certainly say that it is a misuse of language to speak of a bank having a lien over its own indebtedness to a customer. But I think that these observations were directed to the use of the word 'lien', which is a right to retain possession, rather than to the question of whether the bank could have any kind of proprietary interest. Opponents of the doctrine rely upon some 19th century cases, of which it can at least be said that the possibility of a charge over a debt owed by the chargee caused no judicial surprise.

The reason given by the Court of Appeal [1996] Ch. 245, 258 was that 'a man cannot have a proprietary interest in a debt or other obligation which he owes another.' In order to test this proposition, I think one needs to identify the normal characteristics of an equitable charge and then ask to what extent they would be inconsistent with a situation in which the property charged consisted of a debt owed by the beneficiary of the charge. [Lord Hoffmann then considered the general attributes of charges, and continued:]

The depositor's right to claim payment of his deposit is a chose in action which the law has always recognised as property. There is no dispute that a charge over such a chose in action can validly be granted to a third party. In which respects would the fact that the beneficiary of the charge was the debtor himself be inconsistent with the transaction having some or all of the various features which I have enumerated? The method by which the property would be realised would differ slightly: instead of the beneficiary of the charge having to claim payment from the debtor, the realisation would take the form of a book entry. In no other respect, as it seems to me, would the transaction have any consequences different from those which would attach to a charge given to a third party. It would be a proprietary interest in the sense that, subject to questions of registration and purchaser for value without notice, it would be binding upon assignees and a liquidator or trustee in bankruptcy. The depositor would retain an equity of redemption and all the rights which that implies. There would be no merger of interests because the depositor would retain title to the deposit subject only to the bank's charge. The creation of the charge would be consensual and not require any formal assignment or vesting of title in the bank. If all these features can exist despite the fact that the beneficiary of the charge is the debtor, I cannot see why it cannot properly be said that the debtor has a proprietary interest by way of charge over the debt.

The Court of Appeal said that the bank could obtain effective security in other ways . . . All this is true. It may well be that the security provided in these ways will in most cases be just as good as that provided by a proprietary interest. But that seems to me no reason for preventing banks and their customers from creating charges over deposits if, for reasons of their own, they want to do so. The submissions to the Legal Risk Review Committee made it clear that they do . . .

Since the decision in *In re Charge Card Services Ltd.* [1987] Ch. 150 statutes have been passed in several offshore banking jurisdictions to reverse its effect . . . The striking feature about all these provisions is that none of them amend or repeal any rule of common law which would be inconsistent with the existence of a charge over a debt owed by the chargee. They simply say that such a charge can be granted. If the trick can be done as easily as this, it is hard to see where the conceptual impossibility is to be found.

In a case in which there is no threat to the consistency of the law or objection of public policy, I think that the courts should be very slow to declare a practice of the commercial community to be conceptually impossible. Rules of law must obviously be consistent and not self-contradictory; thus in *Rye v. Rye* [1962] A.C. 496, 505, Viscount Simonds demonstrated that the notion of a person granting a lease to himself was inconsistent with every feature of a lease, both as a contract and as an estate in land. But the law is fashioned to suit the practicalities of life and legal concepts like 'proprietary interest' and 'charge' are no more than labels given to clusters of related and self-consistent rules of law. Such concepts do not have a life of their own from which the rules are inexorably derived. It follows that in my view the letter was effective to do what it purported to do, namely to create a charge over the deposit in favour of B.C.C.I. . . .

➤ Questions

1. Is the analysis persuasive?

2. Is such a charge registrable? Lord Hoffmann, in **[12.09]**, suggested the asset was not a 'book debt', but the 2013 amendments have abolished the list of registrable securities, and CA 2006 s 859A simply refers to charges created by a company. On the other hand, there is no longer any *obligation* to register under the amended 2013 rules. Is it advisable to register such a charge in any event?

Dealings with assets subject to a floating charge

A vital feature of the floating charge is that, until the company defaults in its obligations, the charge authorises the company to deal with the charged assets in the ordinary course of business. It follows that, in the absence of specific provisions to the contrary in the charge document itself, the company may not only use, sell and buy such property during the currency of a floating charge, but may also create mortgages and fixed charges ranking in priority to the floating charge itself.

Permitting the company to continue buying and selling the charged assets is usually necessary to ensure the viability of the company's business, but specific constraints are generally inserted by way of what is commonly termed a 'negative pledge clause' or 're-strictive clause', to forbid the creation of later charges. These negative pledge clauses form part of the registrable particulars of a charge (s 859D(2)(c)), and so any subsequent debenture holder will have constructive notice of the restrictions, and its claim will not take priority.

In practice, and by way of further protection, floating charges generally provide for auto-matic crystallisation into a fixed charge in the event that the chargor attempts in any way to create a mortgage or fixed charge over any of the company's assets or undertaking the subject of the floating charge. (See [12.12].)

A floating charge is also vulnerable to set-offs and other claims arising in favour of unsecured creditors while the company's power to trade continues.

This freedom to deal with the assets continues until the floating charge 'crystallises'. (We must ignore the mixed metaphor, which has been hallowed by a century's use.) On crystallisation, the charge becomes a fixed charge attaching to the company's assets at that point of time, and the company's freedom to trade and to incur cross-claims ceases; but until then, the security is subject to all the risks to which the assets may be exposed in the ordinary course of business.

A fixed charge (and other subsequent interests) may be created having priority over an earlier floating charge.

[12.10] Re Castell and Brown Ltd [1898] 1 Ch 315 (Chancery Division)

In 1885, the company issued a series of debentures secured by a floating charge over all of its assets. The title deeds of various properties, which had been left in the possession of the company, were later deposited with the company's bank to secure an overdraft. The bank's charge was held to have priority over the earlier floating charge debentures.[18]

> ROMER J: In the first place, I cannot hold that there was any negligence on the part of the bank. When making its advances to Castell & Brown Ltd (which I will hereafter call the company), it found the company in possession of the deeds in question, and apparently able, as unincumbered owner, to charge the property.
>
> The company purported as such unincumbered owner to give a charge to the bank, and I think the bank was, under the circumstances, entitled to rely upon obtaining a charge free from incumbrance. It is suggested on behalf of the debenture-holders that the bank ought to have made some special inquiries of the company. But it is not suggested that the bank wilfully abstained from making inquiries, and as the bank had no reason to suppose that the company was not fully able to give a valid first charge, and found the company in possession of the deeds, which showed no incumbrance, I think the bank was not bound to make any special enquiry . . .
>
> And I now look to see how it was that the company retained possession of the deeds notwithstanding the issue of the debentures. The reason appears to me obvious. The debentures were only intended to give what is called a floating charge, that is to say, it was intended, notwithstanding the debentures, that the company should have power, so long as it was a going concern, to deal with its property as absolute owner. And I infer it was on this account that the company was allowed to, and did, retain possession of the deeds. In other words, the debenture-holders, notwithstanding their charge, and indeed by its very terms, authorised their mortgagor, the company, to deal with its property as if it had not been incumbered, and left with their mortgagor the deeds in order to enable the company to act as owner.

---

[18] The debentures contained a provision that the company was not at liberty to create any mortgage or charge having priority to the floating charge, but the bank had no knowledge or notice of this 'negative pledge' provision, and so was held not to have been affected by it. Contrast the current rules: see 'Registration, priority and constructive notice of registered charges', p 629.

➤ **Notes**

1. This decision gives rise to the following related conclusions:

    (i) Can a company which has given a floating charge over its assets to A later give a fixed charge to B over part of those assets, having priority? Answer—yes: *Re Castell and Brown Ltd* **[12.10]**. It is immaterial whether B's charge is legal or equitable, or whether B has notice of A's charge.[19]

    (ii) Can a company which has given a floating charge over its assets to A later give a fixed charge to B over all of those assets, having priority? Answer (it seems)—yes; but if the class of assets affected is extensive the second transaction may not be 'in the ordinary course of business' and may therefore be outside the terms of the express or implied trading power. What impact will this have on third parties? Is knowledge relevant?

    (iii) Can a company which has given a floating charge over its assets to A later give a *floating* charge to B over the *same* assets, having priority? Held—no, in *Re Benjamin Cope & Sons Ltd* [1914] 1 Ch 800: the equities being equal, the first in time prevails.

    (iv) Can a company which has given a floating charge over its assets to A later give a floating charge to B over part of those assets, having priority? Held—yes, in *Re Automatic Bottle Makers Ltd* [1926] Ch 412, CA, where the first charge expressly empowered the company to do so. Where no such power is reserved, commentators generally agree that the first charge, being first in time, should have priority.

2. Where a company has created more than one charge over the same property, it is open to the charge holders to agree to vary the order of priority which would otherwise apply, and it is not necessary to obtain the company's consent: *Cheah Theam Swee v Equiticorp Finance Group Ltd* [1992] 1 AC 472, PC.

A floating charge does not operate as an assignment to the debenture holder of the company's book debts and other choses in action. Until the charge has crystallised, the company's unsecured creditors may set off debts due by the company against sums which they owe to it.

[12.11] Biggerstaff v Rowatt's Wharf Ltd [1896] 2 Ch 93 (Court of Appeal)

The respondent company had, to the knowledge of Harvey Brand & Co, issued debentures secured by a floating charge. A receiver was appointed, who took possession on 30 October 1894. On this date Harvey Brand & Co owed the respondent a liquidated sum for rent, while Harvey Brand & Co had a cross-claim against it for the price of 4,000 barrels at 3*s* 6*d* [17½p] each. Harvey Brand & Co was held entitled to set off its claim, on the ground that there had been no assignment of the respondent company's property to the debenture holders prior to the appointment of the receiver, so that Harvey Brand & Co had the earlier equity.

---

[19] Although if there is a negative pledge clause, B will now have constructive notice of it, and A's charge will prevail: see 'Registration, priority and constructive notice of registered charges', p 629.

LOPES LJ: In the present case I think that Harvey, Brand & Co could sue for money had and received . . . There is a total failure of consideration as regards the barrels not delivered, and the demand is a liquidated demand which can be set off against the rent.

But it is said that there is no right of set-off against an assignee of a chose in action where the person claiming the set-off had notice of the assignment when the debt due to him was contracted. That is quite true in ordinary cases; but a debenture differs from an ordinary assignment. If this doctrine were applied to debentures, no creditor of a company could ever get the benefit of a set-off where debentures had been issued. Now, it is the essence of a floating security that it allows the company to carry on business in its ordinary way until a receiver is appointed; and it would paralyse the business of companies to give to the issuing of debentures the effect now contended for. I am of opinion, therefore, that the set-off must be allowed . . .

KAY LJ: It is true that as against an assignee there can be no set-off of a debt accrued after the person claiming set-off has notice of the assignment. But does that apply to debentures such as these? Counsel hesitated to go so far as that, but said that there was no right of set-off, as no action had been brought in which it could have been asserted before 30 October 1894. I think that is not so. I think that if at the time of the assignment there was an inchoate right to set-off it can be asserted after the assignment, for the assignment is subject to the rights then in existence. The question is whether the assignment took place at the issue of the debentures or at the appointment of a receiver. The debentures contain provisions the effect of which is that the company is at liberty to go on with its business as if the debentures did not exist, until possession is taken under them. From that time the company cannot deal with its assets as against the title of the debenture-holders; up to that time it can deal with them in every legitimate way of business. Therefore the date to be regarded is the time of taking possession. A conclusion that set-off could not arise during the period before taking possession would be injurious to debenture-holders, for it would hamper the company in carrying on its business, and so injure the debenture-holders, whose interest is that the company should carry on a prosperous business. There was an inchoate right of set-off at the time when the receiver was appointed; and that, and not the time of issuing the debentures, is the time to be looked to. The debentures must be regarded as incomplete assignments which do not become complete until the time when the receiver is appointed . . .

LINDLEY LJ delivered a concurring judgment.

Crystallisation of floating charges

A floating charge will crystallise, and become a fixed charge attaching to the assets of the company at that time: (i) when a receiver is appointed; (ii) when the company goes into liquidation (since the licence to deal with the assets in the ordinary course of business will then necessarily terminate); (iii) when the company ceases to carry on business (see [12.13]) or sells its business (*Re Real Meat Co Ltd* [1996] BCC 254); (iv) in the case where the debenture empowers the charge holder to convert the floating charge into a fixed charge by giving the company 'notice of conversion', and such a notice is given (see [12.13]); and (v) where an event occurs which under the terms of the debenture causes 'automatic' crystallisation.[20]

[20] A majority of the court in *Fire Nymph Products Ltd v Heating Centre Pty Ltd* (1992) 7 ACSR 365 (NSWCA) held that a floating charge also crystallises when the charged assets are dealt with otherwise than in the ordinary course of business. This might well be the case where the assets concerned comprised all or a substantial part of the company's property, or the whole of the assets affected by the charge, but it is doubtful that the *dictum* would apply to the disposal of individual items.

This last ground (automatic crystallisation) depends upon there being a provision in the document creating the charge which states that the charge will crystallise on the happening of some particular event—for example, if a creditor of the company should levy execution against its property, or if the company should give security over assets covered by the charge to a third party without the charge holder's consent.

Historically, these automatic crystallisation clauses generated considerable controversy, both as to their legality and as to whether, as a matter of policy, their use should be prohibited or subjected to restrictions by law.[21] However, they are now generally accepted as part of the architecture of floating charges (see *Re Brightlife Ltd* [12.12]).

A floating charge crystallises according to the terms of any automatic crystallisation clause.

[12.12] Re Brightlife Ltd [1987] Ch 200 (Chancery Division)

HOFFMANN J: . . . [Counsel] said that public policy required restrictions upon what the parties could stipulate as crystallising events. A winding up or the appointment of a receiver [should this happen to the company during its lifetime] would have to be noted on the register. But a notice [of conversion of a floating charge to a fixed charge] need not be registered and a provision for automatic crystallisation might take effect without the knowledge of either the company or the debenture-holder. The result might be prejudicial to third parties who gave credit to the company. Considerations of this kind impressed Berger J in the Canadian case of *R v Consolidated Churchill Copper Corpn Ltd*[22] where the concept of 'self-generating crystallisation' was rejected.

I do not think that it is open to the courts to restrict the contractual freedom of parties to a floating charge on such grounds. The floating charge was invented by Victorian lawyers to enable manufacturing and trading companies to raise loan capital on debentures. It could offer the security of a charge over the whole of the company's undertaking without inhibiting its ability to trade. But the mirror image of these advantages was the potential prejudice to the general body of creditors, who might know nothing of the floating charge but find that all the company's assets, including the very goods which they had just delivered on credit, had been swept up by the debenture-holder. The public interest requires a balancing of the advantages to the economy of facilitating the borrowing of money against the possibility of injustice to unsecured creditors. These arguments for and against the floating charge are matters for Parliament rather than the courts and have been the subject of public debate in and out of Parliament for more than a century.

Parliament has responded, first, by restricting the rights of the holder of a floating charge and secondly, by requiring public notice of the existence and enforcement of the charge. For example, priority was given to preferential debts . . . [Hoffmann J continued with other examples of the restrictions imposed by statute on floating charge holders] . . .

These limited and pragmatic interventions by the legislature make it in my judgment wholly inappropriate for the courts to impose additional restrictive rules on grounds of public policy. It is certainly not for a judge of first instance to proclaim a new head of public policy which no appellate court has even hinted at before . . .

---

[21] The Cork Committee (Cmnd 8558, 1982, paras 1578–1579) considered that automatic crystallisation was 'not merely inconvenient', but that there was 'no place for it in a modern insolvency law'. The Committee recommended that the circumstances in which a floating charge crystallised should be defined by statute, and that all other ways (including automatic crystallisation) should be banned.

[22] [1978] 5 WWR 652.

A floating charge crystallises when the company ceases to carry on business.

[12.13] Re Woodroffes (Musical Instruments) Ltd [1986] Ch 366 (Chancery Division)

The company had given a first floating charge to its bank and a second floating charge to Mrs Woodroffe. A provision in the latter instrument empowered Mrs Woodroffe, by giving notice to the company, to convert the charge into a fixed charge, and this she did on 27 August 1982. The bank appointed receivers on 1 September 1982. In this action, which was brought to establish the priorities as between the two debenture holders and the company's other creditors, Nourse J held that Mrs Woodroffe's notice did not have the effect of crystallising the bank's charge, as well as her own, on 27 August. He also ruled that the bank's charge would have crystallised if the company had ceased to carry on business at any time between 27 August and 1 September, but that there was not sufficient evidence that this had happened.

NOURSE J: On what date did the bank's floating charge crystallise? Mr Jarvis, for the bank, supported by Mr Marks, for Mrs Woodroffe, arguing in favour of 27 August, submit in the first instance that the effect of Mrs Woodroffe's notice of conversion was to crystallise not only her own charge, but also the bank's. They say that the notice, by determining Mrs Woodroffe's licence to the company to employ the assets subject to the charge in the ordinary course of its business, rendered any further use of those assets unlawful and impracticable, with the result that the company's business must be taken to have ceased at that time. Consequently, they submit that there was a crystallisation of both charges.

I find myself quite unable to accept that submission, which appears to me to run contrary to fundamental principles of the law of contract. I do not see how the determination of Mrs Woodroffe's licence can in some way work a determination of the bank's, or produce the effect that the bank has had its charge crystallised over its head and possibly contrary to its own wishes. The relationship between the company and the bank was governed by the [bank's] debenture, which, although it contained a prohibition against creating any subsequent charge without consent—see clause 5—did not provide for the bank's floating charge to crystallise either on the creation or crystallisation of a subsequent charge.

On analysis it appears to me that the arguments of Mr Jarvis on this point are founded, and can only be founded, on an implied term in the [bank's] debenture . . . It does not seem to me to be at all clear that a term to the effect contended for by Mr Jarvis must be implied. Why should it be assumed that the bank and the company, in particular the bank, intended that the crystallisation of a subsequent charge should in all circumstances cause a crystallisation of the bank's? No doubt it might suit the bank's interests in the great majority of circumstances, but that does not mean that it can be assumed in all. For example, the bank might have taken the view that it was in its own interests that the business of the company should continue. Unless Mrs Woodroffe had either appointed her own receiver, or had applied for an injunction restraining it from dealing with its assets in contravention of her own fixed charge, I can see no reason why the company could not have continued to carry on its business. True it could only have done so in breach of its contract with Mrs Woodroffe, but the bank might have been prepared to indemnify it against that liability or even to pay off Mrs Woodroffe. I can see no ground for any species of implication to the effect contended for . . .

The question whether the cessation of the company's business causes an automatic crystallisation of a floating charge is one of general importance upon which there appears to be no decision directly in point. Such authorities as there are disclose a uniform assumption in favour of crystallisation. There is a valuable discussion of them in *Picarda on The Law Relating to Receivers and Managers*, pp 16–18. One of the questions there raised is whether there is any distinction for this purpose between a company ceasing to carry on business on the one hand and ceasing to be a going concern on the other. My own impression is that these phrases are used interchangeably in the authorities . . . but whether that be right or wrong, I think it clear that the material event is a cessation of business and not, if that is something different, ceasing to be a going concern.

[His Lordship referred to a number of authorities, and continued:] It is unnecessary for me to examine any of those cases in detail, or to quote extracts from the judgments of the many judges who decided them. They all, to a greater or lesser extent, assume that crystallisation takes place on a cessation of business . . .

[His Lordship then held that the evidence did not support the view that the company had ceased business before 1 September.]

Relevant assets received by the company after the floating charge crystallises automatically become subject to the (now fixed) charge over the company's property.

[12.14] NW Robbie & Co Ltd v Witney Warehouse Co Ltd [1963] 1 WLR 1324 (Court of Appeal)

The plaintiff company had given a debenture, secured by a floating charge, to the Bank of Ireland. The bank put in a receiver, who continued to carry on the company's business. The company sold goods to the defendants worth in all £1,346, and in this action the receiver claimed payment of the price. The defendants had in the meantime taken an assignment of a debt of £852 due by the company to English Spinners Ltd, and claimed to be entitled to set off this sum against the £1,346 sued for. It was held that the claim failed, because the debenture holder's equity had priority. In particular, each debt accruing due to a company after a floating charge which affects its future property has crystallised becomes immediately fixed with an equity in favour of the debenture holder. No debt arising, or first coming into the hands of a creditor, after crystallisation may be set off by that creditor so as to give him priority over the debenture holder.[23]

RUSSELL LJ: The first question for consideration is whether on the true construction of the debenture the debt owed by the defendants as it arose became a chose in action of the company subject to an equitable charge in favour of the debenture-holders.

I consider that it did.

The relevant clauses and conditions of the debenture have already been referred to . . . There is under clause 3 a charge on all future assets of the company without restriction: that amounts to an agreement for valuable consideration to charge all such future assets, which agreement enables equity to fasten a charge on those future assets when they arise: and every such equitable charge as it arises operates as an equitable assignment to the debenture-holders of that asset . . . The fact that [the floating charge has crystallised and is now fixed] . . . in no way justifies the conclusion that the field of the charge is in any way restricted: it only means that after this particular quality disappears equity will fasten the charge directly upon all assets thereafter coming into existence as soon as they do so . . .

If that be a correct view of the construction of the debenture, then the choses in action consisting of the debts now sued upon became as they arise subject to an equitable charge—an equitable assignment—to the debenture-holders . . .

Thus far, in my judgment, by force of the debenture charge an equitable charge attached in favour of the debenture-holders not only on the £95 debt existing at the date of the appointment

---

[23] Exceptionally, such a debt may be set off if it arises out of the same contract as that which gives rise to the assigned debt, or is closely connected with that contract: *Business Computers Ltd v Anglo-African Leasing Ltd* [1977] 2 All ER 741 at 748, per Templeman J.

of the receiver and manager, but also upon the other debts constituting the total of £1,346 as they came into existence on delivery of goods to the defendants after such appointment. These choses in action belonging to the company became thus assigned in equity to the debenture-holders, at times when the defendants had no cross-claim of any kind against the company and consequently no right of set-off. Before the defendants acquired by assignment this cross-claim the defendants must be fixed with knowledge of this equitable assignment to the debenture-holders (by way of charge) of the debt owed by the defendants to the company. A debtor cannot set off his claim against X against a claim by X against him which the debtor knows has been as-signed by X to Y before the debtor's claims arose. Just as an assignee of a chose in action takes subject to an already existing right of set-off, so a debtor with no existing right of set-off cannot assert set-off of a cross-claim which he first acquires after he has notice of the assignment of the claim against him: here, for instance, no part of the £852 could have been set off against the £95.

Applying these considerations to the present case, at the time when the defendants first ac-quired the claim for £852, the choses in action sought to be enforced against the defendants had been assigned to the debenture-holders by way of charge, but the £852 claim in no way involved the debenture-holders . . .

SELLERS LJ delivered a concurring judgment.

DONOVAN LJ dissented.

> ### ➤ Question

Contrast this case with the *Biggerstaff* case **[12.11]**, and also see *Rother Iron Works Ltd v Canterbury Precision Engineers Ltd* [1974] QB 1, CA. What is the essential difference that explains the contrasting outcomes?

Priorities as between the floating charge, even after crystallisation, and other interests are determined by the usual rules.

[12.15] George Barker Ltd v Eynon [1974] 1 WLR 462 (Court of Appeal)

The case concerned a priority dispute between the holder of a contractual lien and the holder of a floating charge. The claimants had a contractual lien over the goods of a meat-importing company whose indebtedness to a bank was secured by a mortgage debenture creating a floating charge. The debenture holder's rights crystallised on the appointment of a receiver, but the Court of Appeal held that the lien took priority because the contractual rights arose even earlier, before the appointment of the receiver and so before crystallisation of the charge. This was notwithstanding that the claimants did not acquire actual possession of the goods until three days after the receiver's appointment.

STAMP LJ: . . . Shorn of the arguments supporting it, the receiver's contention before this court was that this is a case of priorities. The lien was a possessory lien which did not come into exist-ence until the carriers were in possession of the goods. Before the carriers came into posses-sion of the goods the charge in favour of the debenture holder crystallised by the effect of the appointment of the receiver. The goods had become the subject of an equitable assignment to the debenture holder and the lien could not come into existence as against the debenture holder.

These submissions are not, in my judgment, well founded. What is in law described under the convenient label of a 'lien' is in relation to a carrier . . . the contractual right to hold the goods which have been carried in respect of the debt for the carriage and in respect of the debts of the same character previously contracted. The duty of the carriers here was to carry the goods and deliver them, or they might say after they had carried them, 'We will hold these goods in exercise of the right to do so conferred by the contract of carriage until we have been paid,' and they might say, 'Moreover, we will, unless we are paid within a reasonable time, in exercise of our right under the contract, sell the goods and pay ourselves out of the proceeds. These are the terms upon which we carried the goods.' In my judgment, these rights did not arise or come into existence at the time the carriers took possession of the goods . . . The rights were rights created by the contract which became exercisable at the moment of time when the goods had been carried. The rights which were conferred on the carriers by condition 13 of the contract are conveniently and accurately described as a 'lien,' but you do not by so describing them alter their character. They are conveniently described as 'a possessory lien,' because it is only if the carriers have possession that they can be exercised. But to say that a lien, because it is so described, does not come into existence until possession is assumed is to reason falsely. Contractual rights come into existence at the time of the contract creating them notwithstanding that they may not be exercisable except upon the happening of a future event . . .

There was nothing remarkable about the contract. It was simply a contract for the carriage of goods incorporating the Conditions of Carriage of the Road Haulage Association. It was, in my judgment, clearly a contract into which, so long as the charge created by the debenture was a floating charge, the company could, consistently with the terms of the debenture, properly enter into. It was, as I have indicated, a contract which was not determined by the effect of the appointment of the receiver. The receiver might, so I will assume, have repudiated it before the carriers started the journey, so preventing the carriers obtaining possession of the goods and carrying out their obligations under it. He did not do so. How then could the receiver or the debenture holder as assignee of the goods and of the rights of the company under the contract be in any better position than would the company have been to insist at the end of the journey that the goods be handed over without making the payments for which condition 13 provided? In my judgment, Mr. Tugendhat was right in his contention that the assignment to the debenture holder brought about by the appointment of the receiver was subject to the rights already given by the company to other persons under ordinary trading contracts. As against the company, the carriers on arriving at the door of the consignees at Gravesend could have withheld the goods against payment, and in my judgment, the debenture holder as assignee from the company can be in no better position. The debenture holder as assignee of the company's rights under the contract can be in no better position than any other assignee of the company's rights under the contract . . .

Treatment of floating charges on the company's liquidation

The point has already been made that floating charges can be a vulnerable form of security. Certain statutory provisions cut down the effectiveness of the floating charges on liquidation or administration, by giving priority to other debts (eg the costs of liquidation and administration, preferred debts and unsecured debts (at least to the extent of a statutory proportion of the floating charge assets)): the statutory provisions are noted at 'Debenture holders' remedies and the protection afforded by charges', pp 626ff, and their effect is considered in more detail in Chapter 16.

In addition, IA 1986 s 245 avoids certain floating charges not given for 'new consideration' in the run-up to liquidation or administration. The intention is to prevent unsecured creditors from securing existing debts when the company is in difficulty, and thus obtaining an advantage over other unsecured creditors. IA 1986 s 245 provides that, subject to certain qualifications, a *floating* charge (not a *fixed* charge) that is created within 12 months of a liquidation or an administration shall be invalid except to the extent that the charge holder advances 'new money' or supplies goods or services to the company. This rule does not apply, at least in the normal case, if it is shown that the company immediately after the creation of the charge was solvent. But stricter conditions are applicable where the floating charge is given in favour of a person who is 'connected' with the company (see IA 1986 s 435, including, eg, a director or major shareholder, or a close relative of either, or an associated company). In this case the 12-month period is extended to two years, and the exemption on the ground of solvency is not available.

A floating charge which has already been redeemed cannot be attacked under IA 1986 s 245, but the payment of the debt may be open to challenge as a preference.

[12.16] Re Parkes Garage (Swadlincote) Ltd [1929] 1 Ch 139 (Chancery Division)

On 15 June, the (insolvent) company executed a floating charge to secure debts owed to a group of its creditors. On 27 July, the company received a sum of money from the purchaser of part of its business, and used this sum to pay off the group of creditors, who endorsed a memorandum of discharge on the debenture. On 14 September, a winding-up order was made on the petition of another creditor. It was held that the then equivalent of IA 1986 s 245 could not be invoked to compel repayment of the moneys once the debenture had been redeemed, but the court indicated that it was open to the liquidator to challenge the transaction as a fraudulent preference.[24]

EVE J: Having regard to the facts which I have stated, about which there is no dispute, it is quite obvious that the learned county court judge had no option but to declare the charge to be invalid, and he so did. That part of his judgment, however, was not of much practical importance, because the charge had been satisfied by the payments which had been made, and it was then argued that the declaration of invalidity involved the further question: whether the debenture was still subsisting for any purpose, and if so were the simple contract debts, to secure which it had been issued, merged in the covenant contained in the debenture. An argument on those lines was addressed to the learned judge, at the conclusion of which he held that the simple contract debts were merged, and forgetting for the moment the limited extent to which he had declared the debenture invalid, he referred to the whole debenture as invalid, and held that the simple contract debts having been merged, and the debenture being invalid, the creditors were not entitled to retain the money paid to them through their trustee on 27 July.

At the first hearing the learned judge had not declared, nor could he declare, the debenture invalid; all he could declare invalid was the charge therein contained. The rest of the document, the covenants to pay principal and interest, survived and was valid, for nothing in s 212 [IA 1986 s 245] affects them. The position therefore was that the simple contract creditors, by their trustee, who was the covenantee, were entitled to the benefit of the covenants to pay principal and interest, and on 27 July, when the company was in sufficient funds to pay the principal and interest, they had no alternative but to pay the same, and the trustee cannot on this summons be ordered to repay. But having regard to what has been disclosed in these proceedings, that the company was hopelessly insolvent from the beginning of March down to the date of the winding-up order, and that the effect of the payments to these half-dozen creditors on 27 July was to apply the whole available assets of the company to the payment of their debts in full and to leave other creditors whose debts largely exceeded the aggregate amount paid to the half-dozen unprovided for, raises a doubt whether the whole transaction, which culminated in the payments on 27 July, was not in the nature of a fraudulent preference. We desire therefore to give the liquidator an opportunity of considering the position from this standpoint, and in allowing this

---

[24] The statute did not then provide remedies against non-fraudulent preferences. Now see IA 1986 ss 238–241, and *Re MC Bacon Ltd* [16.15].

appeal to state that the order is without prejudice to any application to set aside the payments or to question the validity of the debenture on the ground of its being a fraudulent preference or on any other grounds which the liquidator may think fit to advance . . .

MAUGHAM J concurred.

➤ Note

Re Parkes Garage was followed in *Mace Builders (Glasgow) Ltd v Lunn* [1987] Ch 191, [1987] BCLC 55, where the debenture holder had put in a receiver to enforce the charge and the receiver had sold the charged assets before the commencement of the winding up. Although the charge had been created within 12 months of the liquidation, and at a time when the company was insolvent, it was held that the provision corresponding to IA 1986 s 245 (Companies Act 1948 (CA 1948) s 322) was inapplicable: transactions completed before the liquidation were not affected by the section.

The phrase 'money[25] ***paid to the company' in IA 1986 s 245 includes cheques met by a bank on the company's behalf.***

[12.17] Re Yeovil Glove Co Ltd [1965] Ch 148 (Court of Appeal)

The company had gone into liquidation having unsecured debts totalling £94,000 and an overdraft with the National Provincial Bank Ltd amounting to £67,000. This overdraft was secured by a floating charge given less than 12 months previously. During the currency of the charge the bank had met cheques drawn by the company amounting to £110,000, and received some £111,000 for payment into the company's account. (There were in fact four accounts, but this is not important.) The unsecured creditors attacked the security under CA 1948 s 322 (broadly comparable with IA 1986 s 245), alleging that no 'cash' had been 'paid to the company' by the bank within the meaning of that section; but the court treated the bank's acts in meeting the company's cheques as equivalent. It followed that, by virtue of the rule in *Clayton*'s case,[26] the bank could claim that the whole of the £67,000 was cash advanced subsequently to the creation of the charge, so that the security was valid for this sum.

HARMAN LJ: [The] only question which arises is whether there was cash paid to the company at the time of or subsequently to the creation of, and in consideration for, the charge. It was admittedly created within twelve months of the winding up at a time when the company was insolvent. It is further agreed that so far as the overdraft was incurred before the date of the floating charge, the charge would not be a valid security for it. The liquidator's claim is a simple one, namely, that as neither cash nor a covenant to pay cash was made at the time of the execution of the document, there was no consideration for it in the legal sense of that term except the bank's immediate forbearance. This seemed to me, I confess, an attractive argument . . .

It was argued that consideration in law is a well-known term and ought to receive its ordinary meaning, and that subsequent payments provided by the bank to defray the company's day-to-day outgoings or wages or salaries or indebtedness to its suppliers by cheque would not be consideration in law for the execution of a charge bearing an earlier date unless those payments

---

[25] Prior to IA 1986, the legislation used the phrase 'cash paid to the company': but it would appear that the decision in *Re Yeovil Glove Co Ltd* is not affected by the change in wording.

[26] (1816) 1 Mer 572, under which the earliest payments into an account are set off against the earliest payments out, and vice versa.

were made in pursuance of a promise contained in, or made at or before the date of, the charge itself. It was, however, pointed out that such subsequent payments would in fact not be made in consideration for the charge, but in consideration for the promise.

Now it is apparent on the fact of the section that cash subsequently paid to the company may be within the exception if so paid in consideration for the anterior charge, and the argument is that the words 'in consideration for' in this section cannot, therefore, be used in the technical sense, but mean 'by reason of' or 'having regard to the existence of' the charge. Oddly enough, there is no reported decision on these words, nor are they discussed in any of the well-known textbooks. There has, however, come to light a decision of Lord Romer, when a judge of first instance, in *Re Thomas Mortimer Ltd*,[27] in 1925, a decision on the corresponding section of the Companies (Consolidation) Act 1908, which was in the same terms as the present section except that the period was three instead of twelve months. A transcript of this judgment was before us. The facts of that case were, I think, indistinguishable from those of the present, and Romer J held that payments by the bank after the date of the charge were made in consideration for the charge . . .

That decision, if right, is enough to cover the present question, and Plowman J [at first instance] so held . . .

In the instant case some £111,000, representing its trading receipts, was paid into the no 1 account by the company between the date of the charge and the appointment of the receiver, and the bank paid out during the same period about £110,000. Those payments were either made directly to or to the order of the company, or were transfers to the no 3 and no 4 accounts against advances previously made to the company to defray wages or salaries. All the company's accounts were at all times overdrawn, so that every payment was a provision of new money by means of which, on the figures, it is overwhelmingly probable that all the creditors existing at the date of the charge were in fact paid off.

There arises at this point the consideration which has given me most trouble in this case, namely, that as the no 1 account was carried on after as well as before the charge in precisely the same way, the bank would be entitled in accordance with the rule in *Clayton's* case, to treat payments in as being in satisfaction of the earliest advances made. The result is startling, for thus the bank pays itself out of moneys received subsequent to the charge for the whole of the company's indebtedness to it prior to the charge, and which was admittedly not covered by it. The result is that the whole of the pre-charge indebtedness is treated as paid off, and the bank is left bound to set off against its post-charge advances only the excess received after satisfying the company's pre-charge indebtedness. This would seem largely to nullify the effect of the section in the case of a company having at the date of the charge a largely overdrawn account with its bank, and which continues to trade subsequently. Of course, if at the date of the charge a line were drawn in the bank's books and a new account opened, then the company could successfully argue that payments out by the bank subsequent to the charge were, within a few hundred pounds, wholly repaid by the company from its trading receipts, with the result that no substantial sum would be due on the charge. It was, however, held by Romer J in *Re Thomas Mortimer Ltd* that *Clayton's* case be applied with the result stated, and I can see no escape from it, nor in spite of frequent pressing by the court did the appellant's counsel put forward any alternative . . . [It] follows, if the decision in *Re Thomas Mortimer Ltd* be right, that there is admittedly nothing left for the unsecured creditors. In my judgment Romer J's decision was right, and was rightly followed by Plowman J in the present case.

fallacy in the appellant's argument lies, in my opinion, in the theory that, because the company's payments into the bank after the date of the charge were more or less equal to the payments out by the bank during the same period, no 'new money' was provided by the bank.

[27] (1925), reported [1965] Ch 186n.

> This is not the fact. Every such payment was in fact new money having regard to the state of the company's accounts, and it was in fact used to pay the company's creditors. That the indebtedness remained approximately at the same level was due to the fact that this was the limit set by the bank to the company's overdraft. I can find no reason to compel the bank to treat all payments in after the charge as devoted to post-charge indebtedness. The law is in fact the other way . . .
>
> WILLMER and RUSSELL LJJ delivered concurring judgments.

> ## Note

The exception to IA 1986 s 245 discussed in the *Yeovil Glove* case applies only where the money in question is paid, or the goods or services supplied, to the company 'at the same time as, or after, the creation of the charge' (s 245(2)). There has recently been some debate in the cases about the meaning of this phrase: how nearly contemporaneous must the payment and the execution of the charge document be? In the past, this question was treated rather loosely, a delay of even two months or so being thought unimportant if the payment was made in anticipation of and in reliance on the creation of the charge. But in *Power v Sharp Investments Ltd* [1994] 1 BCLC 111, CA (also known as *Re Shoe Lace Ltd*), the Court of Appeal, agreeing with Hoffmann J in the court below, held that, while the question was one of fact and degree, a delay of any substantial length—although not, perhaps, the time taken to have a coffee-break—would be fatal to the application of the exception.

> ## Questions

1. What do you think are the policy reasons behind the enactment of IA 1986 s 245?

2. What do you think are the policy reasons behind the enactment of IA 1986 s 40 (see 'Distribution of assets subject to the receivership', pp 832ff)?

Distinguishing between fixed and floating charges

The previous sections indicate the need to distinguish between fixed and floating charges, and the substantial attractions to the charge holder in having a charge classified as fixed rather than floating. Lenders therefore devote considerable energy to drafting charges that will be construed as fixed rather than floating. Before considering the case extracts, several general points can be made.

(i)   Prior to 1986, it was possible for the holder of a floating charge to evade the disadvantageous statutory rules simply by showing that the charge had crystallised (and thereby become a *fixed* charge) before the commencement of the liquidation or other relevant statutory date.[28] This loophole was quickly eliminated by IA 1986 s 251, which provides that 'floating charge' means 'a charge which, *as created*, was a floating charge'. Despite this setback, lenders have not been discouraged from seeking to achieve the same end result with ever more astutely worded documents.

---

[28] This was the case in *Re Brightlife Ltd* [12.12], where the debenture holder had given the company a notice converting the floating charge into a fixed charge a week before a resolution for voluntary winding up was passed. The court held that the preferential creditors no longer had any right to be paid in priority to the charge.

(ii)   In *Agnew v Commissioner of Inland Revenue (Re Brumark)* **[12.19]** (one of the lead-ing cases in this area), the Privy Council held that, in analysing a charge agree-ment to determine whether it creates a fixed or a floating charge, the court's task is not to discover whether the parties *intended* to create a fixed or floating charge and then give effect to their intention. The court's task is to discover what *rights* the parties intended to create, and then to decide whether, as a matter of law, those rights constitute a fixed or a floating charge. See Lord Millett at **[12.19]**.

(iii) In the Irish case *Re Armagh Shoes Ltd* [1984] BCLC 405, Hutton J held that the fact that a document by its express words purports to create a fixed or specific charge does not prevent the court from construing the charge as a floating one. The judge in that case was also prepared to infer from the terms of the charge as a whole that the company had a licence to deal with the assets charged in the or-dinary course of its business, even though this was not stated. More unusually, the courts have also held that a charge described as floating could, as a matter of law, be fixed: *Russell Cooke Trust Co Ltd v Elliott* [2007] EWHC 1443 (Ch), [2007] 2 BCLC 637.

(iv)   In *Re Brightlife Ltd* **[12.12]**, in considering the scope of the freedom to deal with the charged assets, Hoffmann J held that a charge over book debts which was expressed to be a fixed charge, and imposed some restrictions on the use of the charged assets, was in reality a floating charge. He said, at 209:

> Although clause 3(A)(ii)(a) speaks of a 'first specific charge' over the book debts and other debts, the rights over the debts created by the debenture were in my judgment such as to be catego-rised in law as a floating charge . . .
>
>   It is true that clause 5(ii) does not allow Brightlife to sell, factor or discount debts without the written consent of Norandex [the debenture-holder]. But a floating charge is consistent with some restriction upon the company's freedom to deal with its assets. For example, floating charges commonly contain a prohibition upon the creation of other charges ranking prior to or *pari passu* with the floating charge. Such dealings would otherwise be open to a company in the ordinary course of its business. In this debenture, the significant feature is that Brightlife was free to collect its debts and pay the proceeds into its bank account. Once in the account, they would be outside the charge over debts and at the free disposal of the company. In my judgment a right to deal in this way with the charged assets for its own account is a badge of a floating charge and is inconsistent with a fixed charge.

(v)   On the other hand, some degree of freedom to deal with the charged assets is not incompatible with a charge being a fixed charge. *Re Cimex Tissues Ltd* [1994] BCC 626 is typically cited: there a charge over plant and machinery was held to be a fixed charge even though it was contemplated that some of the items of plant might be replaced from time to time as they wore out. However, the case is difficult on its own terms, and even more difficult after the *Brumark* **[12.19]** and *Spectrum* **[12.20]** decisions. Replacing worn parts in machinery subject to a fixed charge is one thing, but if the chargor has the power to sell the charged machinery and purchase re-placements at will, then modern cases suggest the charge must then be floating.

(vi)   It is precisely this issue of control over the use of the charged assets which plagues analysis (along with the related issue of control over their proceeds, as, eg with a charge over book debts, where it is relevant to look at the related control over their proceeds). Suppose the charge holder is a bank with a charge over a company's book debts: if use of the proceeds of the book debts is not controlled at all, then the charge is floating (*Re Brightlife Ltd* **[12.12]**, although in this case the chargee was not itself a bank); and if use of the proceeds is completely restricted, then the charge is fixed (*Re Keenan Bros Ltd* [1986] BCLC 242, where the chargee bank stipulated that the account could not be drawn against without the counter-signature of one of its officers). But if neither the freedom nor the control is absolute, then a judgement is required. In *Siebe Gorman & Co Ltd v Barclays Bank Ltd* [1979] 2 Lloyd's Rep 142, for example, the company was forbidden to deal with the book debts *before collection* in certain specified ways but not in every conceivable way; there was also a right to obtain absolute control by giving notice, but this right was never exercised. The charge was held by Slade J to be a fixed charge, but his decision was overruled 25 years later by the House of Lords in *Spectrum* **[12.20]**.

(vii)   Clearly there are limits to what can be achieved by drafting alone. In *Royal Trust Bank v National Westminster Bank plc* [1996] 2 BCLC 699, CA, an instrument creating a charge over book debts gave the chargee bank the *right* to demand that the company should open a dedicated account and pay all moneys received on the collection of the debts into that account, but the bank never exercised this right, and in practice moneys collected went into the company's ordinary trading account. The charge was held by Millett LJ to be floating. (All three members of the court concurred in the result; Nourse LJ on other grounds, and Swinford Thomas LJ without giving reasons.)

(viii)   Similarly, in *Re Double S Printers Ltd* [1999] 1 BCLC 220 the chargee, as a director of the company, had *de facto* control over the proceeds of the charged book debts since he had actual control of the bank account, but this was not backed by any contractual restraint on their disposal in the instrument itself. As in the *Royal Trust Bank* case, it was held that the company's freedom (at least in law) to deal led to the conclusion that the charge was floating.

(ix)   More imaginative structures have been adopted. Perhaps the most notorious is that which was successfully proposed in *Re New Bullas Trading Ltd* **[12.18]** (although subsequently held to be wrong by the Privy Council in *Brumark* **[12.19]**, and now overruled by the House of Lords in *Spectrum* **[12.20]**). In *New Bullas*, the company granted a charge over book debts which was expressed to be a fixed charge over the uncollected book debts and a floating charge over their proceeds. The Court of Appeal, overruling Knox J, held that this was possible. The decision caused a good deal of controversy. It was followed in Australia (*Whitton v ACN 003 266 886 Pty Ltd* (1996) 42 NSWLR 123) but disowned by the New Zealand Court of Appeal (*Re Brumark Investments Ltd, Commissioner of Inland Revenue v Agnew* [2000] 1 BCLC 353, [2000] 1 NZLR 223). The Privy Council subsequently upheld the *Brumark* ruling, and held that *New Bullas* was wrongly decided: see **[12.19]**.

(x)   It is apparent from all of this that, of the three attributes of the floating charge identified by Romer LJ in *Re Yorkshire Woolcombers Ltd* (cited in **[12.04]**), it is the third—the trading power—which is normally regarded as crucial. The other two features, while characteristic of most floating charges, are less essential: in *Bond Worth* **[12.07]** two of the classes of assets affected were not 'present and future' but exclusively present (the goods) and exclusively future (the proceeds) respectively. And in *Welch v Bowmaker (Ireland) Ltd* [1980] IR 251 the second of the criteria—the expectation that the class of assets would be turned over in the course of business—was lacking: a charge over a parcel of land presently owned by the company was ruled to be a floating charge.

(xi)   This makes it rather extraordinary that in *Re Atlantic Computer Systems plc* [1992] Ch 505, CA (followed on similar facts in *Re Atlantic Medical Ltd* [1993] BCLC 386), the Court of Appeal appears to have been influenced almost entirely by the fact that the property affected by the charge was specific (rental moneys payable to the company under existing, identified computer-leasing agreements) in holding that the charge was a fixed charge. The fact that this property was not 'ambulatory and shifting in nature' seems to have been regarded as conclusive in itself, even though the rental moneys when received by the company were used by it in the ordinary course of business and the instrument did not prohibit this. Since this is a ruling of the Court of Appeal, it must be accorded due weight; but after the decisions of the Privy Council in *Brumark* **[12.19]** and the House of Lords in *Spectrum* **[12.20]** (neither of which referred to these cases), their authority must now be regarded as questionable.

A fixed charge may be created over book debts, including future book debts, but will be treated as a floating charge if the chargor is free to realise or collect the debts for his own account.

[12.18] Re New Bullas Trading Ltd [1994] 1 BCLC 485 (Court of Appeal)

This case, now overruled, is not extracted here, but given its notoriety and the continued reference to it in subsequent cases, it seems sensible to give it some attention. The case was decided on the basis of the contractual freedom of the parties to do what they proposed, in the absence of contrary arguments based on public policy. Notice carefully the response to this argument in the *Brumark* **[12.19]** and *Spectrum* **[12.20]** decisions. Reaction to the Court of Appeal decision was probably the impetus for the subsequent radical overhaul and a more tightly reasoned judicial approach to this area.

The company had executed a security document in favour of 3i plc which purported to create a fixed charge over book debts, so long as they remained uncollected, but when the proceeds of the debts had been collected and paid into a designated bank account the moneys so received were released from the fixed charge and became subject to a floating charge (unless written instructions to the contrary were given by 3i). At first instance, Knox J held that the charge was a floating charge throughout and that in consequence the company's preferential creditors were entitled in a receivership to priority under IA 1986 s 40 as regards the uncollected debts. The Court of Appeal reversed this decision, holding that there were commercial advantages for both parties in these arrangements (having a fixed charge over the uncollected debts and a floating charge over the proceeds when collected); that the parties were free to agree to such terms; and that the wording of the debenture did have the effect of making the security over the uncollected book debts a fixed charge.

➤ Note

The ruling in this case was strongly criticised by Professor Goode ('Charges over Book Debts: A Missed Opportunity' (1994) 110 LQR 592). In his view, it is not possible to create separate security interests over a debt and its proceeds: all that it is possible to have is a single, continuous security interest which moves from debts to proceeds. If the chargee does not retain sufficient control over the proceeds when collected, the charge, *'as created'*, must be regarded as a floating charge. This is because 'the distinctive feature of debts as an object of security is that they are realised by payment, upon which they cease to exist'.

Goode's view later received support from Millett LJ in *Royal Trust Bank v National Westminster Bank plc* [1996] 2 BCLC 682, where he said (at 704): 'while it is obviously possible to distinguish between a capital asset and its income, I do not see how it can be possible to separate a debt or other receivable from the proceeds of its realisation'.

New Bullas drew comment from other academic commentators. Griffin (1995) 46 *Northern Ireland Law Quarterly* 163, in reply to Professor Goode, condemned the notion that a charge over book debts and their proceeds must always be of an indivisible nature as 'misconceived'. A similar view was taken by McLauchlan in (2000) 116 LQR 211. Worthington, in contrast, in (1997) 113 LQR 563, agreed that a book debt and its proceeds do not constitute an indivisible asset, but considered this did not answer the question in issue; the conclusion reached in *New Bullas* was wrong simply because the security arrangement (the charge over the book debts) had left the chargor free to remove the charged assets from the ambit of the security without recourse to the chargee. *That* question could only be answered by asking what the chargor could do with the book debts: the right to realise them and spend the proceeds at will was the mark of a floating charge over the book debts, not a fixed one.

In the event, it is this last view which has been upheld. The Privy Council, in an appeal from New Zealand in the case next cited, stated categorically that *New Bullas* was wrongly decided and so it must be taken as having been to all intents and purposes overruled.

[12.19] Agnew v Commissioner of Inland Revenue (Re Brumark Investments Ltd) [2001] UKPC 28, [2001] 2 AC 710 (Privy Council)

[See the shorter extract at [12.04].]

Brumark had given security over its book debts to its bank (Westpac) in terms which were indistinguishable from those in *New Bullas* [12.18]—that is, which purported to make the debts subject to a fixed charge so long as they were uncollected but a floating charge over the proceeds once they had been collected and received by the company. The company was free to collect the debts for its own account and to use the proceeds in its business. Brumark went into receivership and the receivers collected the outstanding debts. Fisher J at first instance held that, as uncollected debts, they were subject to a fixed charge (as the parties had agreed) and, as such, not subject to the claims of the company's preferential creditors. The New Zealand Court of Appeal, declining to follow *New Bullas*, held that the fact that the company was free to collect the debts for its own account (and so remove them from the bank's security) was inconsistent with the charge being a fixed charge. It was accordingly a floating charge and the preferential creditors had a prior claim to the proceeds. This ruling was affirmed by the Privy Council.

> The opinion of the Judicial Committee was delivered by LORD MILLETT: . . . The question in this appeal is whether a charge [described as fixed] over uncollected book debts of a company which leaves the company free to collect them and use the proceeds in the ordinary course of its business is a fixed charge or a floating charge.... This is a question of characterisation. To answer it their Lordships must examine the nature of a floating charge and ascertain the features which distinguish it from a floating charge . . . [His Lordship traced the history of the floating charge, referring to cases from *Re Panama, New Zealand and Australian Royal Mail Co*[29] to *Re Cosslett (Contractors) Ltd* [12.08], emphasising in particular the following passage from the judgment of Vaughan Williams LJ in *Re Yorkshire Woolcombers Association Ltd* (cited in *Re Cosslett (Contractors) Ltd* [12.08]):
>
> > '. . . but what you do require to make a specific security is that the security whenever it has once come into existence, and been identified and appropriated as a security, shall never

---

[29] (1870) 5 Ch App 318, CA.

thereafter at the will of the mortgagor cease to be a security. *If at the will of the mortgagor he can dispose of it and prevent its being any longer a security, although something else may be substituted more or less for it, that is not a "specific security"'* (emphasis added).]

[His Lordship referred to the wording of the debentures in this case and in *New Bullas* and continued:] The principal theme of the judgment [in *New Bullas*] . . . was that the parties were free to make whatever agreement they liked. The question was therefore simply one of construction; unless unlawful the intention of the parties, to be gathered from the terms of the debenture, must prevail. It was clear from the descriptions which the parties attached to the charges that they had intended to create a fixed charge over the book debts while they were uncollected and a floating charge over the proceeds. It was open to the parties to do so, and freedom of contract prevailed.

Their Lordships consider this approach to be fundamentally mistaken. The question is not merely one of construction. In deciding whether a charge is a fixed charge or a floating charge, the court is engaged in a two-stage process. At the first stage it must construe the instrument of charge and seek to gather the intentions of the parties from the language they have used. But the object at this stage of the process is not to discover whether the parties intended to create a fixed or a floating charge. It is to ascertain the nature of the rights and obligations which the parties intended to grant each other in respect of the charged assets. Once these have been ascertained, the court can then embark on the second stage of the process, which is one of categorisation. This is a matter of law. It does not depend on the intention of the parties. If their intention, properly gathered from the language of the instrument, is to grant the company rights in respect of the charged assets which are inconsistent with the nature of a fixed charge, then the charge cannot be a fixed charge however they may have chosen to describe it. . . . In construing a debenture to see whether it creates a fixed or a floating charge, the only intention which is relevant is the intention that the company should be free to deal with the charged assets and withdraw them from the security without the consent of the holder of the charge; or, to put the question another way, whether the charged assets were intended to be under the control of the company or of the charge holder.

[His Lordship considered and rejected an argument which had been upheld by the Court of Appeal in *New Bullas*: that the book debts did not cease to be subject to the charge at the will of the company but that they ceased to be subject to the charge because that was what the parties had agreed in advance when they entered into the debenture. He also rejected as irrelevant a distinction which Fisher J had drawn between a power on the part of the company to *dispose of* the debts (eg by factoring them) and a power to *consume* them (by realising them). He continued:] Their Lordships turn finally to the questions which have exercised academic commentators: whether a debt or other receivable can be separated from its proceeds; whether they represent a single security interest or two; and whether a charge on book debts necessarily takes effect as a single indivisible charge on the debts and their proceeds irrespective of the way in which it may be drafted.

Property and its proceeds are clearly different assets. On a sale of goods the seller exchanges one asset for another. Both assets continue to exist, the goods in the hands of the buyer and proceeds of sale in the hands of the seller. If a book debt is assigned, the debt is transferred to the assignee in exchange for money paid to the assignor. The seller's former property right in the subject matter of the sale gives him an equivalent property right in its exchange product. The only difference between realising a debt by assignment and collection is that, on collection, the debt is wholly extinguished. As in the case of alienation, it is replaced in the hands of the creditor by a different asset, viz its proceeds.

The Court of Appeal saw no reason to examine the conceptual problems further. They held that, even if a debt and its proceeds are two different assets, the company was free to realise the uncollected debts, and accordingly the charge on those assets (being the assets whose destination was in dispute) could not be a fixed charge. There was simply no need to look at the proceeds at all. . . .

If the company is free to collect the debts, the nature of the charge on the uncollected debts cannot differ according to whether the proceeds are subject to a floating charge or are not subject to any charge. In each case the commercial effect is the same: the charge holder cannot prevent the company from collecting the debts and having the free use of the proceeds. But it does not follow that the nature of the charge on the uncollected book debts may not differ according to whether the proceeds are subject to a fixed charge or a floating charge; for in the one case the charge holder can prevent the company from having the use of the proceeds and in the other it cannot. The question is not whether the company is free to collect the uncollected debts, but whether it is free to do so for its own benefit. . . .

To constitute a charge on book debts a fixed charge, it is sufficient to prohibit the company from realising the debts itself, whether by assignment or collection. But . . . it is not inconsistent with the fixed nature of a charge on book debts for the holder of the charge to appoint the company its agent to collect the debts for its account and on its behalf. *Siebe Gorman*[30] and *Re Keenan* ['Distinguishing between fixed and floating charges', point (vi), p 651] merely introduced an alternative mechanism for appropriating the proceeds to the security. The proceeds of the debts collected by the company were no longer to be trust moneys but they were required to be paid into a blocked account with the charge holder. The commercial effect was the same: the proceeds were not at the company's disposal. Such an arrangement is inconsistent with the charge being a floating charge, since the debts are not available to the company as a source of its cash flow. But their Lordships would wish to make it clear that it is not enough to provide in the debenture that the account is a blocked account if it is not operated as one in fact. . . .

Their Lordships consider that *New Bullas* was wrongly decided.

[12.20] Re Spectrum Plus Ltd [2005] UKHL 41, [2005] 2 AC 680 (House of Lords)

The company granted a charge over its book debts to the bank, expressed to be 'by way of specific charge', prohibiting disposal of the book debts and requiring the proceeds to be paid into an account with the chargee bank. The bank permitted the company to draw on these proceeds for use in the ordinary course of business, subject to certain restrictions. In its terms, the charge was in the same form as that which had been accepted by Slade J as a fixed charge in *Siebe Gorman*.[31] If it was a floating charge, the preferential creditors would be entitled to have their debts paid out of the proceeds of the book debts in priority to the bank (IA 1986 s 175); if not, the bank would be entitled to the whole of the proceeds. The amount at stake was relatively trivial (approximately £16,000). But the case was run as a test case, with several hundred liquidations held up pending the resolution of the issue. The debenture was in a form used by many banks and other commercial lenders. Indeed, the company had gone into liquidation and took no part in the proceedings; the case was argued between the bank (as the secured creditor) and the Crown (as preferential creditor in the liquidation (see 'Distribution of assets subject to the receivership', pp 832ff)).

LORD HOPE: . . . [I]t is competent for anyone to whom book debts may accrue in the future to create for good consideration an equitable charge upon those book debts which will attach to them as soon as they come into existence. But if this is to be effective as a fixed security

---

[30] [1979] 2 Lloyd's Rep 142.
[31] [1979] 2 Lloyd's Rep 142.

everything depends on the way the security agreement ensures that the charge over the book debts is fixed. It is not easy to reconcile the company's need to continue to collect and use these sums for its own business purposes with the lender's wish to escape from the priority which section 175(2)(b) of the 1986 Act gives to preferential debts . . .

There are, as Professor Sarah Worthington has pointed out, a limited number of ways to ensure that a charge over book debts is fixed: An 'Unsatisfactory Area of the Law'—Fixed and Floating Charges Yet Again (2004) 1 International Corporate Rescue 175, 182. One is to prevent all dealings with the book debts so that they are preserved for the benefit of the chargee's security. . . . One can, of course, be confident where this method is used that the book debts will be permanently appropriated to the security which is given to the chargee. But a company that wishes to continue to trade will usually find the commercial consequences of such an arrangement unacceptable. Another is to prevent all dealings with the book debts other than their collection, and to require the proceeds when collected to be paid to the chargee in reduction of the chargor's outstanding debt. But this method too is likely to be unacceptable to a company which wishes to carry on its business as normally as possible by maintaining its cash flow and its working capital. A third is to prevent all dealings with the debts other than their collection, and to require the collected proceeds to be paid into an account with the chargee bank. That account must then be blocked so as to preserve the proceeds for the benefit of the chargee's security. A fourth is to prevent all dealings with the debts other than their collection and to require the collected proceeds to be paid into a separate account with a third party bank. The chargee then takes a fixed charge over that account so as to preserve the sums paid into it for the benefit of its security.

The method that was selected in this case comes closest to the third of these. It was selected, no doubt, because it enabled the company to continue to trade as normally as possible while restricting it, at the same time, to some degree as to what it could do with the book debts. The critical question is whether the restrictions that it imposed went far enough. There is no doubt that their effect was to prevent the company from entering into transactions with any third party in relation to the book debts prior to their collection. The uncollected book debts were to be held exclusively for the benefit of the bank. But everything then depended on the nature of the account with the bank into which the proceeds were to be paid under the arrangement described in clause 5 of the debenture. As McCarthy J said in In re Keenan Bros Ltd [1986] BCLC 242, 247, one must look, not at the declared intention of the parties alone, but to the effect of the instruments whereby they purported to carry out that intention. Was the account one which allowed the company to continue to use the proceeds of the book debts as a source of its cash flow or was it one which, on the contrary, preserved the proceeds intact for the benefit of the bank's security? Was it, putting the point shortly, a blocked account?

I do not see how this question can be answered without examining the contractual relationship in regard to that account between the bank and its customer. An account from which the customer is entitled to withdraw funds whenever it wishes within the agreed limits of any overdraft is not a blocked account. In Agnew v Comr of Inland Revenue [2001] 1 AC 710, 722, para 22 Lord Millett said that the critical feature which led the Irish Supreme Court in In re Keenan Bros Ltd [1986] BCLC 242 to characterise the charge on book debts as a fixed charge was that their proceeds were to be segregated in a blocked account where they would be frozen and unusable by the company without the bank's written consent. I respectfully agree. . . . [He then considered the arrangements in Siebe Gorman and in this case, and decided that neither were effective to block the account in the way required. He then continued:]

Should Siebe Gorman be overruled?

Lord Phillips of Worth Matravers MR [in this case in the Court of Appeal] said that, even if Slade J's construction of the debenture in Siebe Gorman & Co Ltd v Barclays Bank Ltd [1979] 2 Lloyd's Rep 142 had appeared to him to be erroneous, he would have been inclined to hold that the form of the debenture had, by custom and usage, acquired the meaning and effect that he had attributed to it: [2004] Ch 337, 383, para 97. This was because the form had been used for 25 years under the understanding that this was its meaning and effect. Banks had relied upon this understanding, and individuals had guaranteed the liabilities of companies to banks on the understanding that the banks would be entitled to look first to their charges on book debts unaffected by the claims of preferred creditors. The respondents say that this is the course that ought now to be followed in the interests of commercial certainty.

. . . It is hard to think of an area of the law where the need for certainty is more important than that with which your Lordships are concerned in this case. The commercial life of this country depends to a large extent on the reliability of the security arrangements that are entered into between debtors and their creditors. The law provides the context in which these arrangements are entered into, and it lays down the rules that have to be applied when the arrangements break down. Mistakes as to the law can make all the difference between success and failure when the creditor seeks to realise his security. So a heavy responsibility lies on judges to provide the lending market with guidance that is accurate and reliable. This is so that mistakes can be avoided and transactions entered into with confidence that they will achieve what is expected of them.

These are powerful considerations, but I am in no doubt that the proper course is for the *Siebe Gorman* decision to be overruled. . . . This is not one of those cases where there are respectable arguments either way. With regret, the conclusion has to be that it is not possible to defend the decision on any rational basis. It is not enough to say that it has stood for more than 25 years. The fact is that, like any other first instance decision, it was always open to correction if the country's highest appellate court was persuaded that there was something wrong with it. Those who relied upon it must be taken to have been aware of this. . . .

[He therefore held *Siebe Gorman* was wrong and should be overruled, and allowed the appeal.]

LORD WALKER: [Describing the essential difference between a fixed charge and a floating charge:] Under a fixed charge the assets charged as security are permanently appropriated to the payment of the sum charged, in such a way as to give the chargee a proprietary interest in the assets. So long as the charge remains unredeemed, the assets can be released from the charge only with the active concurrence of the chargee. The chargee may have good commercial reasons for agreeing to a partial release. If for instance a bank has a fixed charge over a large area of land which is being developed in phases as a housing estate (another example of a fixed charge on what might be regarded as trading stock) it might be short-sighted of the bank not to agree to take only a fraction of the proceeds of sale of houses in the first phase, so enabling the remainder of the development to be funded. But under a fixed charge that will be a matter for the chargee to decide for itself.

Under a floating charge, by contrast, the chargee does not have the same power to control the security for its own benefit. The chargee has a proprietary interest, but its interest is in a fund of circulating capital, and unless and until the chargee intervenes (on crystallisation of the charge) it is for the trader, and not the bank, to decide how to run its business. . . .

[He therefore held *Siebe Gorman* was wrong and should be overruled, and allowed the appeal.]

BARONESS HALE and LORDS SCOTT, NICHOLLS, STEYN and BROWN all delivered concurring opinions.

> ### Notes

1. *Spectrum* **[12.20]** and *Brumark* **[12.19]** are worth reading in full for a proper appreciation of the area. The *Spectrum* case also addresses the issue of 'prospective overruling' by the House of Lords (pursuant to the argument put by the bank that even if *Siebe Gorman* were overruled, the overruling should only have an impact on charges created after the date of the decision). The Law Lords unanimously agreed the power existed, but refused to exercise it in the circumstances.

2. *Re SSSL Realisations Ltd* [2004] EWHC 1760 (Ch), confirmed, if that were necessary, that it is possible to create a charge only on the proceeds of collection of debts without charging the debts themselves at all.

3. In *Arthur D Little Ltd v Ableco Finance LLC* [2003] Ch 217, [2002] EWHC 701 (Ch), it was re-affirmed that a chargor may enjoy the 'fruits' of the property that has been subjected to a *fixed* charge, without thereby converting the charge to a floating charge. Mr Roger Kaye QC said:

> As Nicholls LJ put it in *Re Atlantic Computer Systems Plc* [1992] Ch 505 at 534G: 'A mortgage of land does not become a floating charge by reason of a mortgagor being permitted to remain in possession and enjoy the fruits of the property charged from time to time.' The receipt of dividends and other rights arising by virtue of the shares seem to me to be examples of exploitation of the principal subject matter of the charge, i.e. the shares. As Lord Millett again expressed in the *Brumark* case[32] at page 727, paragraph 37: 'The judge drew a distinction between a power of disposition and a power of consumption. There is nothing he suggested inconsistent with a fixed charge in prohibiting the Company from disposing of the charged asset to others, but allowing it to exploit the characteristics inherent in the nature of the asset itself. Their Lordships agree with this.'

4. The reach of *Spectrum* has been tested in numerous cases now. In *Re Rayford Homes Ltd (In Admin. Rec.)* [2011] EWHC 1948 (Ch), [2011] BCC 715, trustees involved in a priority dispute unsuccessfully argued that the bank's fixed charge over the company's future-acquired investment property was on a proper analysis a floating charge because when the property was sold, the company was free to draw on the proceeds and could keep any excess after repayment of the advances referable to the property in question. David Richards J held that these features did not affect the status of the charge as a fixed charge:

> 44. In my judgment, the essential difference between that case and the present lies in the difference in the ability of the chargor company to deal with the charged property. Spectrum Plus Ltd was entitled to collect book debts without any involvement or prior consent of the bank. In the present case, the company could not realise any freehold or leasehold property without a release by the bank of its legal charge and the fixed charge in the debenture. Indeed, assuming that the charges were registered at the Land Registry against the title to each property as they were required to be (see cl.5 of the legal charges and cl.3.4 of the debenture), the company could not make good title on an unencumbered transfer without the bank's release of its security.
>
> 45. By the terms of both the debenture and the legal charges, the charges stood as security for all monies due to the bank. The provisions of the facility letter are not in conflict with the debenture and legal charges. Paragraph 2.3.1 of the facility letter is a provision for repayment: the advances referable to a particular property must be repaid on a sale of that property. It does not affect the extent of the bank's security on the property. It does not modify the terms of the legal charges, so that they are fixed charges securing only repayment of the sums to which para. 2.3.1 refers.
>
> 46. It is always open to the holder of a fixed charge over property to release the charge on payment of less than is secured by the charge, as specifically mentioned by Lord Walker of Gestingthorpe in *Spectrum* **[12.20]** at [138]. The fact that the company is then free to use the surplus proceeds as it wishes does not affect the status of the charge on the property as a fixed charge. For these reasons I conclude that the fixed charge on future-acquired property in the debenture and the legal charges were and are effective as fixed charges securing all monies due from the company to the bank.

---

[32] [2001] 2 AC 710.

5. Just as *Cosslett* **[12.08]** was something of a wake-up call in reminding parties that charges may arise when not intended (and worse, turn out to be void), so too in *Gray v G-T-P Group Ltd* [2010] EWHC 1772 (Ch). In an action by the liquidators (G), Vos J applied the *Spectrum* **[12.20]** reasoning to hold that a *declaration of trust* entered into between the company in liquidation (F) and the respondent (G) was void as an unregistered floating charge on F's property. F sold laminated floors; G supplied store debit card services. Sums paid by F's customers using the debit cards were paid into a designated bank account. G held these balances on trust for F, and it was agreed that 'except in the circumstances referred to in clause 3' F was to have effective control over the account. Clause 3 gave G access to the account to recoup sums owed to it in defined circumstances, including F's breach or F's insolvency. The judge concluded that Clause 3 created a charge, and that the charge was necessarily floating since F could draw on the account at will, and the assets subject to the charge defined in Clause 3 were not to be finally appropriated as a security for the payment of the debt until the occurrence of some future event.

> ➤ **Question**

Does it follow from these decisions that the commercial objectives which *New Bullas* sought to meet are now impossible to achieve? Draftsmen will clearly need to make sure that collections made by the company are held for the chargee's account (eg by being paid into a blocked bank account) and only after that released by an act of the chargee into the chargor's general funds. Can this be done in a way that is commercially attractive?

Avoiding the statutory regime for company securities

There are various practical mechanisms that can be adopted by way of 'quasi-security' in order to gain some of the benefits of being a secured creditor without the effort and expense (and possible disadvantages) of the fixed and floating charge regime just described. To this end, creditors use conditional sales, hire-purchase arrangements, trusts (eg building retention trusts, *Quistclose* trusts[33]), and other such devices.

Retention of title agreements are considered here, simply by way of illustration.

Retention of title agreements

Most trading companies use bank overdrafts to meet their short-term financial needs, and commonly also rely on bank loans for longer term credit. Almost invariably, such advances will be secured by floating charges over all the company's assets, and possibly by an array of fixed charges as well. In the event of insolvency, the bank and those creditors who are entitled to a statutory preference (see 'Distribution of assets subject to the receivership', pp 832ff) are likely between them to claim all that the company has, leaving ordinary trade creditors with nothing.

Many commentators have considered this situation to be unfair—see, for example, the Cork Committee's report (Cmnd 8558, 1982, para 1950) and the remarks of Templeman J in *Business Computers v Anglo-African Leasing Ltd* [1977] 1 WLR 578 at 580. Admittedly, some of these criticisms centred on the statutory provisions that accorded to the Crown status as a preferred creditor for many of the debts (including taxes) owed to the Crown.

---

[33] Named after the seminal case, *Barclays Bank Ltd v Quistclose Investments Ltd* [1970] AC 567, HL.

This preference was abolished by the Enterprise Act 2002 (see 'Application of assets by the liquidator', p 867).

Nevertheless, even as regards the normal operation of floating charges, there is particular unfairness in relation to those who supply the company with goods on credit—perhaps the raw materials needed for its manufacturing processes. The goods delivered become subject immediately to the floating charge (if, as is usual, it affects future property), even though it is the seller and not the bank who is providing this particular asset by way of credit. So suppliers have endeavoured to protect themselves by 'retention of title' clauses. There is nothing novel about this: the familiar hire-purchase agreement serves the same purpose. A Dutch supplier succeeded in defeating the claims of a receiver in this way in the celebrated *Romalpa* case **[12.21]** in 1976.

[12.21] Aluminium Industrie Vaassen BV v Romalpa Aluminium Ltd [1976] 1 WLR 676 (Chancery Division and Court of Appeal)

Aluminium foil was supplied by the plaintiffs, a Dutch company, to the defendants for processing in their factory. It was stipulated in the contract of sale that ownership of the foil should not be transferred to the buyers (the defendant purchasing company) until the price had been paid in full; that products made from the foil should be kept by the buyers as bailees (the contract, which was a translation from a Dutch draft, used the un-English expression 'fiduciary owners') separately from other stock, on the supplier's behalf, as 'surety' for the outstanding price; but that the buyers should have power to sell the manufactured articles in the ordinary course of business, such sales to be made by them as the suppliers' agents. Mocatta J, whose judgment was affirmed by the Court of Appeal, held that the retention of title clause was effective to retain legal title to the aluminium in the hands of the supplier; in addition, the suppliers could trace the price due to them into the proceeds of sales of the finished goods made by the buyers, ahead of the latter's secured and unsecured creditors.[34]

> MOCATTA J: The preservation of ownership clause contains unusual and fairly elaborate provisions departing substantially from the debtor/creditor relationship and shows, in my view, the intention to create a fiduciary relationship to which the [tracing] principle stated in *Re Hallett's Estate*[35] applies. A further point made by Mr Pickering was that if the plaintiffs were to succeed in their tracing claim this would, in effect, be a method available against a liquidator to a creditor of avoiding the provisions establishing the need to register charges on book debts: see s 95(1), (2)(e) of the Companies Act 1948 [now see CA 2006 s 859A]. He used this only as an argument against the effect of clause 13 contended for by Mr Lincoln. As to this, I think Mr Lincoln's answer was well founded, namely, that if property in the foil never passed to the defendants with the result that the proceeds of sub-sales belonged in equity to the plaintiffs, s 95(1) had no application.
>
> The plaintiffs accordingly succeeded and are entitled to the reliefs sought.
>
> [The decision of Mocatta J was affirmed by the Court of Appeal.]

➤ Notes

1. Since this decision, draftsmen of suppliers' contracts have endeavoured to adopt and improve upon 'Romalpa clauses' with varying success. In those cases where the goods sold are still in the hands of the company and identifiable, the supplier has usually been successful. But in other cases the danger is that the court will hold that a charge has been

---

[34] This second aspect of the decision is now regarded as justifiable, if at all, on the special terms of the contract. But the analysis in relation to basic retention of title clauses stands firm, and is much used in commercial practice.
[35] (1880) 13 Ch D 696.

created, which may be void in a subsequent insolvency for non-registration under CA 2006 ss 859Aff and will, in any event, probably rank after the bank.

2. The reach of retention of title clauses is a matter of contractual interpretation. In *Sandhu (t/a Isher Fashions UK) v Jet Star Retailer Ltd (In Administration)* [2011] EWCA Civ 459, CA, the Court of Appeal rejected the seller's claim for conversion/wrongful interference of goods subject to a retention of title clause. An express clause enabled the seller to withdraw the buyer's authority to deal with the goods in the ordinary course of business. However, until such withdrawal was made, on a proper construction, the court was satisfied that it had been the parties' contemplation that the buyer be permitted to continue to deal with the goods (in whatever ways it desired) even after it had become insolvent. By contrast, in *Wincanton Group Ltd v Garbe Logistics UK 1 SARL, Jenks Sales Brokers Ltd (In Administration)* [2011] EWHC 905 (Ch), it was agreed that title to certain industrial storage racks would not pass to Wincanton until *all* outstanding debts in relation to certain works had been met. The condition was not satisfied, so W could not claim title.

3. Recently, some interesting and important issues concerning 'Romalpa clauses' arose in *FG Wilson (Engineering) Ltd v John Holt & Co (Liverpool) Ltd* [2013] EWCA (Civ) 1232, [2014] 1 WLR 2365. The seller supplied generators and parts to the buyer. The buyer fell behind in payment, and the seller sought to exercise its rights under the retention of title clause. The buyer had already sold the parts to its subsidiary. The seller sued for the price. The main issues were (i) the construction of the retention of title clause and (ii) whether the seller could sue for the price under s 49 of the Sale of Goods Act 1979 if title in the goods has not passed to the buyer as a result of the retention of title clause.

On issue (i), the Court of Appeal, by majority (Patten and Floyd LJJ; Longmore LJ dissenting), construed the relevant clause as creating a fiduciary agent relationship between the seller and the buyer. Hence, the buyer sold as agent in the sub-sale, and is accountable to the seller-principal for the sale proceeds. On issue (ii), the Court of Appeal was unanimous that s 49 was the exclusive means for a seller to sue for non-payment of price.

Both aspects of the Court of Appeal's decision have been criticised by Louise Gullifer (2014) *Lloyd's Maritime and Commercial Law Quarterly* 564. On the construction point, Gullifer argued that the 'agency' construction is uncommercial because the agent's duty to account to its principal is vastly different from a buyer's obligation to pay the price to the seller. The seller would receive a 'windfall' if the buyer sub-sells (as agent) at a profit. Conversely, if the buyer did not sub-sell, the duty to account for the proceeds would not arise at all. This argument also casts much doubt on the correctness of *Romalpa* itself, which relied on similar 'fiduciary agent' reasoning.

On the s 49 point, Gullifer argued that there is no good reason why parties cannot depart from the Sale of Goods Act, which provides a default code only. Also, the mischief that s 49 is meant to protect the buyer against is a buyer's action for price where the goods are not delivered, as opposed to where property does not pass. Where the goods are delivered, the buyer has received what he contracted for, and a suit for the price should lie.

4. *Re Bond Worth Ltd* **[12.07]** established that an attempt to reserve a mere equitable title (at least in a case where the buyer was free to resell) created a charge in the nature of a floating charge, which was void unless registered; and later cases have held that the same result follows where the manufacturing process is such as to destroy the identity of the raw material which was originally supplied: *Borden (UK) Ltd v Scottish Timber Products Ltd* [1981] Ch 25 (resin used in making chipboard); *Re Peachdart Ltd* [1984] Ch 131 (leather used for handbags).

5. In regard to claims against the proceeds of sale, suppliers have not been successful unless the clause has created a duty to keep the moneys separate from other funds: *Hendy Lennox (Industrial Engines) Ltd v Grahame Puttick Ltd* [1984] 1 WLR 485. Even then, the natural inference is that a charge has been created, since almost invariably the amount

of the price owing to the supplier will be part only of the proceeds of resale: *E Pfeiffer Weinkellerei-Weineinkauf GmbH & Co v Arbuthnot Factors Ltd* [1988] 1 WLR 150, [1987] BCLC 522; *Compaq Computers Ltd v Abercorn Group Ltd* [1993] BCLC 603.

6. There have been pleas for reform of the law so as to make all contracts containing retention of title clauses (and presumably also hire-purchase and leasing contracts) registrable as charges. The Diamond Report (1989), paras 17.8ff and 23.6.10, proposed that a distinction should be drawn between 'simple' clauses, which do no more than retain title to the actual goods sold, or their proceeds if resold, but only in regard to a claim for the original price, and more complex clauses, such as those which purport to assert title to a manufactured product. Professor Diamond recommended that the law should be clarified by a statutory provision which declares the latter category to be registrable as charges and the former to be exempt. These recommendations have not been taken up by the legislature, and the question has been left in limbo during the past two decades and more while various groups have been debating possible reforms to the charges registration system (see 'Further reform of the registration system', pp 630ff).

7. IA 1986 s 15 empowers an administrator, with the leave of the court, to sell property affected by such contracts free from the supplier's interest on terms that the net proceeds are paid in discharge of the debt due to the supplier. (See, eg, *Sandhu (t/a Isher Fashions UK) v Jet Star Retailer Ltd (In Administration)* [2011] EWCA Civ 459, CA.)

▓ **Further reading**

ATHERTON, S and MOKAL, RJ, 'Charges over Chattels: Issues in the Fixed/Floating Jurisprudence' (2005) 26 *Company Lawyer* 163.

BERG, A, 'The Cuckoo in the Nest of Corporate Insolvency: Some Aspects of the *Spectrum* Case' [2006] JBL 22.

GOODE, R, 'The Case for the Abolition of the Floating Charge' in J Getzler and J Payne (eds), *Company Charges: Spectrum and Beyond* (2006), ch 2.

LOI, K, 'Quistclose Trusts and Romalpa Clauses: Substance and Nemo Dat in Corporate Insolvency' [2012] LQR 412.

PENNINGTON, R, 'Recent Developments in the Law and Practice Relating to the Creation of Security for Companies' Indebtedness' (2009) 30 *Company Lawyer* 163.

WORTHINGTON, S, 'An "Unsatisfactory Area of the Law"—Fixed and Floating Charges Yet Again' (2004) 1 *International Corporate Rescue* 175.

13

REMEDIES FOR MALADMINISTRATION OF THE COMPANY

General issues

The earlier chapters illustrate that either the directors or the members in general meeting (but generally the directors) have responsibility for the affairs of the company. This includes pursuing claims against outside parties who have caused the company harm. Where the harm is caused by insiders, however, then litigation is more difficult: vested interests may try to prevent claimants seeking recovery. That is the focus of this chapter, which looks at who can seek remedies, against whom, if the company is poorly run, and which matters are the legitimate subject of complaint.

A number of preliminary points can be made at the outset. First, legitimate claims of 'poor management' or 'maladministration' must be distinguished from simple disgruntlement (even justified disgruntlement) over the outcome of decisions which are properly subject to majority rule or other agreed constitutional arrangements (see 'Why is shareholder litigation such a problem?', pp 667ff). Secondly, poor management often harms both the company and its members. If compensating the company will also effectively compensate the members, then we would expect a rule against double recovery. But in the corporate context the law goes further, and in most circumstances allows *only* the company's claim, not the member's (see 'The "no reflective loss" principle', pp 706ff). Thirdly, despite the power of the principle of majority rule, both courts and statute are alert to its potential abuse. To address this, we will see that although the company can typically only make complaints against its insiders about 'legal wrongs'—negligence, breach of statutory duty, etc—the members can sometimes call on more general issues of perceived 'maladministration', including management approaches that are simply not in accordance with expectations. As might be expected, this avenue is tightly circumscribed (see 'Unfairly prejudicial conduct of the company's affairs', pp 715ff and 'Compulsory winding up on the "just and equitable" ground', pp 840ff).

In reading what follows, it is important to keep clear the distinctions between different types of claims (by the company or by members), the different ways they might be brought, their different pre-requisites and their different remedies.

Pursuing claims for maladministration

In pursuing claims for maladministration, the usual problem, of course, is that the people causing harm to the company (whether the directors or the majority shareholders) are usually also the people in control of the company. They are unlikely to pursue litigation against themselves. The relevant company law rules must address this difficult issue, while at the same time avoiding the problem of allowing every vexatious or litigious member to complain about activity that is to all intents and purposes acceptable to the company's various participants and interest groups.

The types of action examined in this chapter fall into slightly overlapping categories (the overlaps caused in large measure by statutory interventions).

Actionable wrongs committed against the company

If an actionable wrong has been done to the company, then the company has a cause of action which it may pursue in legal proceedings, just like any other legal person. Again, like any other legal person, it is not obliged to pursue every possible claim it has. Where the company's claim is against its own directors, however, it is clearly unsafe to leave the decision about whether the company should sue in the hands of those same directors. Accordingly, one special rule that allows members to pursue these company claims in very tightly defined circumstances has been added to the general rules in an attempt to address this problem. In sum, and including the special rule, the company may pursue its own legal claims (in its own name in all but point (iv)) by means of a decision to do so taken by:

(i)   The company's directors, acting within their normal powers of management of the company (if, as is usual, this is what the articles provide by way of power sharing within the company). Pragmatically, if the action is against one or more of the company's own directors, then such a decision to sue is only likely if the majority of directors is not aligned with the wrongdoers (even though the wrongdoers remain in post), or if a new board has taken over the management of the company and the old directors have been ousted. See, for example *John Shaw and Sons (Salford) Ltd v Shaw* **[4.07]** and *Regal (Hastings) Ltd v Gulliver* **[7.26]**.

(ii) The company's administrator or liquidator (in an administration or a winding up), since neither is likely to be diverted by personal allegiances to past directors.

(iii) The general meeting, in those rare cases where it seems that the general meeting has either primary or residual control over the company's power to litigate (but see *Breckland Group Holdings Ltd v London & Suffolk Properties Ltd* [1989] BCLC 100 (Ch)).

(iv) Individual members, using the statutory procedure that allows them to take a '*derivative action*': Companies Act 2006 (CA 2006) ss 260ff. A derivative action is taken in the name of the member, but in pursuit of a claim that belongs to the company, and for a remedy that will accrue to the company and not to the member as an individual. The company is brought before the court compulsorily (and so as a *defendant*, rather than a claimant), so as to ensure that it is subject to the jurisdiction and orders of the court in circumstances where those with actual power to cause the company to pursue its own claims are resisting this option.[1]

---

[1] See 'Company claims and the statutory derivative action: CA 2006 ss 260ff', pp 671ff.

(v)   The Secretary of State, under powers set out in the Companies Act 1985 (CA 1985) s 438 (see 'Public investigation of companies', pp 770ff; note, these few CA 1985 provisions remain operative).

Actionable wrongs committed against individual members

If a wrong has been done to the member personally (rather than to the company), then the member may pursue his or her claim against the company, or against the other (ie majority) members in the company, by way of:

(i)   A *personal action* (or a *representative action*[2]) based on the contract the member has with the company as set out in the company's constitution (CA 2006 s 33) (see 'Members' personal rights', pp 261ff).

(ii)   A *personal action* (or a *representative action*) based on other contracts the member may have with the company or with the body of members (see 'Shareholders' agreements', pp 256ff).

(iii)   A *statutory action* permitted by certain specific provisions in CA 2006 (see, eg, the provisions applying to reductions of capital or variation of class rights at 'Permitted reductions of capital', pp 534ff and 'Variation of class rights', pp 587ff).

(iv)   A statutory action to remedy '*unfair prejudice*' (CA 2006 s 994) (see 'Unfairly prejudicial conduct of the company's affairs', pp 715ff).

(v)   A statutory action to *wind the company up on the just and equitable ground* (IA 1986 s 122(1)(g)) (see 'Compulsory winding up on the "just and equitable" ground', pp 840ff).

It is not necessary to examine all of these options in detail in this chapter. However, it is necessary to be alert to the range of different procedures that are available for remedying different forms of maladministration. Where the normal process for pursuing well-recognised legal claims is adopted (as where the *company* sues its directors for *negligence*), then nothing more needs to be added to the earlier discussion of how a company acts (see 'General issues', pp 326ff) and what constitutes directors' negligence (see 'Duty to exercise reasonable care, skill and diligence: CA 2006 s 174', pp 375ff). Similarly, where the company or an individual pursues claims that are based on special statutory rights, it is not necessary to re-examine those special rights described earlier (eg individual member's rights of action based on the statutory contract with the company, or the statutory right to complain about reductions of capital or variation of class rights, see 'Members' personal rights', pp 261ff, 'Permitted reductions of capital', pp 534ff and 'Variation of class rights', pp 587ff). This chapter therefore focuses only on the availability of special rights of access to the court (see company claims in points (iii) and (iv) in the previous list), and special grounds of complaint (see members' claims at point (iv), while point (v) is considered in Chapter 16, along with the other grounds for the winding up of companies) in relation to maladministration.

Some of the issues addressed in this chapter were previously dealt with under quite different common law rules (especially the rule in *Foss v Harbottle* [13.01]), now replaced by provisions in CA 2006. Care must therefore be taken in referring to older authorities.

---

[2] A 'representative action' is a court procedure allowing one or more individuals to appear as claimants or defendants on behalf of a larger number of people having an identical interest in the proceedings, and so obtain a remedy (or provide a defence) for the entire class of them, as individuals, without each appearing individually before the court. See the Civil Procedure Rules 1998 (CPR) r 19.6; also see fn 39, p 702.

Why is shareholder litigation such a problem?

The practical problem which the law has to deal with in this area is balancing the risk that too little litigation is pursued because the wrongdoers are in control, or that too much litigation is pursued because vexatious individuals are disaffected with the majority-determined status quo. The law must therefore define proper limits to litigation control and majority rule. At the same time, it must be conceded that the general rule *is* majority rule, whether by directors or by members (sometimes, in the latter case, with the added protection of super-majorities, or segregated classes of interest groups), so there is always the likelihood of disaffected dissenting minorities. 'Majority rule' applies not only to decisions to pursue business activities, but also to decisions *not* to pursue corporate wrongdoers (especially directors). The practice of proper majority rule is therefore especially important in this chapter.

We have already seen that the law normally allows members to treat their rights to vote as an incident of property which they may prima facie exercise for their own advantage (*Peters' American Delicacy Co Ltd v Heath* [4.26]). Further, it is established that even the strict fiduciary duties of directors do not go so far as to prohibit them altogether from acting in matters where their own personal interests are affected by what they do as directors (*Mills v Mills* [7.10]), still less from voting as they like in their capacity as members (*North-West Transportation Co Ltd v Beatty* [4.34]) (although now contrast CA 2006 s 239). The three cases just referred to, and many others, also illustrate the traditional unwillingness of the courts to review matters of commercial judgement or policy, or of internal administration. 'This Court,' said Lord Eldon, 'is not to be required on every Occasion to take the Management of every Playhouse and Brewhouse in the Kingdom'.[3]

The time-honoured and democratic principle of majority rule, backed by these other factors, necessarily means that quite substantial power is placed in the hands of those who control more than half of the votes on the board or at a members' meeting. Indeed, where shares are widely dispersed among a large number of members, comparable power can be wielded with command of a good deal less than 51% of the votes.[4] Minority members must, in principle, accept the decisions of the majority and must also acknowledge that the power lawfully enjoyed by their more numerous associates is a fact of business life. In theory it is, of course, open to them to seek to bring about change by the normal democratic processes of persuasion, lobbying, publicity and so on; and it may sometimes be appropriate to argue that members who do not agree with the policy of those in control should sell their shares and invest their money elsewhere. In reality, however, neither of these courses may offer a practical solution. Minority members may not have the resources and will often lack access to the necessary information to mount a successful campaign against those in the seat of power. And in a smaller company there will almost always be no market for their shares: the only available buyers (assuming that they are interested) will probably be the very majority members with whom they are in disagreement, and they are likely to offer only a derisory price.[5]

---

[3] *Carlen v Drury* (1812) 1 Ves & B 154 at 158.

[4] This is because the controllers can usually count on a high degree of apathy and inertia on the part of the small 'armchair' investor. In addition, various devices such as 'pyramid', circular and cross-holdings of shares between companies can be used to concentrate power: see the classic analysis of A Berle and G Means, *The Modern Corporation and Private Property* (1932) and MA Pickering, 'Shareholders' Voting Rights and Company Control' (1965) 81 LQR 248. More generally, see JE Parkinson, *Corporate Power and Responsibility* (1993), pp 241–259.

[5] By contrast, in public companies where there is a ready market for shares, and exit is a real possibility, it seems that the chance of UK directors being sued by their companies is 'virtually nil': J Armour et al, 'Private Enforcement of Corporate Law: An Empirical Comparison of the UK with the US' (2009) 6 *Journal of Empirical Legal Studies* 687, available at: http://papers.ssrn.com/sol3/papers.cfm?abstract_id=1105355.

In such circumstances, frustrated minority members may turn to the law for help. Clearly, the law must provide some remedies to meet those cases in which majority power has been abused. There cannot be power—including the power of control over other people's investments—without corresponding responsibility. But the law has to strike a delicate balance. If it too readily supports the majority and is prepared to condone unfair and wrongful acts and decisions on their part, the minority will be prejudiced and, in a small company, 'locked in' with an unrealisable investment which the majority can exploit to its own advantage. If, on the other hand, too great indulgence is shown to complaining minorities, they will be able to obstruct the company's legitimate business with tiresome requisitions and objections, and exploit their nuisance value.

Both the legislature and the judiciary have made attempts to reconcile the opposing needs and interests of controllers and minorities.

Statutory protection is given to minorities by formalities of various kinds, for example:

(i)   requiring a special resolution rather than a simple majority vote in important matters, such as constitutional alterations;

(ii) requiring the court's sanction, in matters like a reduction of capital or scheme of arrangement; and

(iii) giving dissentients a right to apply to the court to have a resolution cancelled, for example in a variation of class rights, and sometimes empowering the court to order, alternatively, that they be bought out.

To balance this, some checks are imposed on the use of these measures by safeguards such as a requirement that dissentients applying to the court must have at least 15% support from their fellows.

Other statutory provisions give members direct access to the courts. Foremost among these are the right to petition to have a company compulsorily wound up (Insolvency Act 1986 (IA 1986) s 124) (see 'Compulsory winding up generally', pp 834ff) and the right to seek relief for 'unfairly prejudicial' conduct (CA 2006 s 994) (see 'Unfairly prejudicial conduct of the company's affairs', pp 715ff).

The judges for their part have also developed rules which are aimed at curbing the abuse of power by those with control. The directors, for example, are restrained by their fiduciary duties and by the 'bona fide' and 'proper purposes' principles. Majority members, at least in the context of an alteration of articles and a variation of class rights, are also constrained to act bona fide and in the common interest. But apart from these well-recognised (though not necessarily well-defined) limitations, the courts have by and large allowed laissez-faire principles to reign and majority rule to operate unchecked. They have thus avoided putting themselves into the position which so alarmed Lord Eldon, although in earlier chapters we have seen the increasing importance of this means of judicial review (see 'Duty to act for proper purposes: s 171(b)', pp 342ff).

All this aside, it remains true that, at least historically, a significant problem for members seeking to cure maladministration of the company by legal action is that the courts strongly resist hearing such claims. Various reasons are given. These include arguments that members' access to the courts will open the floodgates to a multiplicity of claims; that companies by their nature rely on majority rule, and therefore any disputes should be settled internally, by the general meeting, where majority rule should prevail; and, finally, that the courts cannot be asked to adjudicate on matters of business policy rather than matters of law.

The main judicial instrument by which this policy of non-intervention was maintained was a rule not of substance but of procedure, which all company lawyers knew as the rule in *Foss v Harbottle* [13.01]. Minority members who complained of a wrong or irregularity may well have found this a formidable, and perhaps an insurmountable, barrier to their quest for justice, even where they had a real and well-founded grievance. The rule attracted criticism from across the Atlantic both because of its complexity[6] and because it is considered unjust to recognise a substantive right but deny a remedy on procedural grounds.[7] The rule is outlined briefly in the following section, given how frequently it is still referred to in litigation, before then turning to the modern common law and statutory rules now enshrined in CA 2006.

The old common law rule in *Foss v Harbottle*

The rule in *Foss v Harbottle*

The 'rule in *Foss v Harbottle*'[8] provides that, *subject to certain limited exceptions*:

(i) the proper claimant in an action for a wrong alleged to have been done to the company is the company itself (the '*proper claimant principle*'); and

(ii) if the alleged wrong is a matter which it is competent for the company to settle itself (the '*internal management principle*') or, in the case of an irregularity to ratify or condone by its own internal procedure (the '*irregularity principle*'), then no individual member may bring action.

Notice that the rule has an impact on potential court actions in pursuit of wrongs done to a company *and* wrongs done personally to the members of the company. In both cases the rule restricts litigation by individual members unless they can bring themselves within the exceptions to the rule.

The 2006 statutory amendments now appearing in CA 2006 ss 260ff (providing for statutory derivative actions) only affect claims for wrongs done *to* the company, and even then, only claims for wrongs done *by* directors (s 260(5)). Personal claims by members remain subject to the common law, and in particular to the restrictions in point (ii) of the previous list. Recall the impact of the 'internal management' and 'irregularity' principles in the context of litigating to enforce the s 33 contract: see 'Deemed authority III:...the "indoor management rule"', pp 116ff, and also see Further notes following *Pender v Lushington* **[13.23]**, pp 704ff.

[13.01] Foss v Harbottle (1843) 2 Hare 461 (Chancery Division)

The case was brought by two shareholders in the Victoria Park Co (incorporated by statute) against the company's five directors and others, alleging that the property of the company had been misapplied and wasted and certain mortgages improperly given over the company's property. It asked that the defendants should be held accountable to the company, and also sought the appointment of a receiver. The Vice-Chancellor ruled that it

---

[6] RWV Dickerson, JL Howard and L Getz, in *Proposals for a New Business Corporation Law for Canada* (1971), §482, called it an 'infamous doctrine' which they recommended should be 'relegated to legal limbo without compunction'. In England, by contrast, the rule has been defended with enthusiasm by the Court of Appeal in cases such as *Prudential Assurance Co Ltd v Newman Industries Ltd (No 2)* [1982] Ch 204, which itself was cited with approval in the House of Lords decision in *Johnson v Gore Wood and Co* **[13.26]**.

[7] GD Hornstein [1967] JBL 282.

[8] (1843) 2 Hare 461. For further reading, see especially AJ Boyle, 'The Minority Shareholder in the Nineteenth Century' (1965) 28 *MLR* 317; Lord Wedderburn, 'Shareholders' Rights and the Rule in *Foss v Harbottle*' [1957] CLJ 194; [1958] CLJ 93 (a classic); LS Sealy, 'Problems of Standing, Pleading and Proof in Corporate Litigation' in *Company Law in Change* (1987), p 1.

was incompetent for the plaintiffs to bring such proceedings, the sole right to do so being that of the company in its corporate character.

> WIGRAM V-C: It was not, nor could it successfully be, argued that it was a matter of course for any individual members of a corporation thus to assume to themselves the right of suing in the name of the corporation. In law the corporation and the aggregate members of the corporation are not the same thing for purposes like this; and the only question can be whether the facts alleged in this case justify a departure from the rule which, prima facie, would require that the corporation should sue in its own name and in its corporate character or in the name of someone whom the law has appointed to be its representative . . .

Exceptions to the rule in *Foss v Harbottle*

This 'proper claimant' rule, if applied rigorously, would certainly ensure that few wrongs committed by directors would be pursued in the courts. Inevitably, therefore, common law 'exceptions' emerged, being instances where members, acting alone or together, were permitted to sue. These exceptions, where shareholders *could* sue, were usually grouped under four heads:[9]

(i)   the act complained of is *ultra vires* or illegal;

(ii) the matter is one which could validly be done or sanctioned only by some special majority of members;

(iii) the personal and individual rights of the claimant as a member have been invaded; or

(iv) what has been done amounts to a 'fraud on the minority'[10] and the wrongdoers are themselves in control of the company.

Of course, it is plain that only the fourth exception in this list is a true exception in litigating to remedy wrongs to the company. In pursuing the limits of this exception, the common law then proceeded to tie itself in knots in determining what constituted wrongdoer control,[11] and what counted as a 'fraud on the minority', and in particular whether it concerned types of *wrongs* or types of *decision processes*, or some combination of both.[12] For a summary of some of these issues, see *Abouraya v Sigmund* **[13.22]**.

It was therefore a relief for all when CA 2006 s 260ff was introduced, providing a mandatory statutory procedure for derivative actions. Some of the old notions still remain relevant, but used in the exercise of structured judicial discretion, not by way of binding rule. Sadly, however, the statutory provisions have been interpreted in a way which ensures they are not comprehensive: some types of derivative claim fall outside the statutory scheme, and in those cases the courts have held that the old common law regime continues to operate in the margins (see 'Residual use of common law derivative claims', pp 695ff).

---

[9] These are the heads used as a basis for discussion by KW Wedderburn, 'Shareholders' Rights and the Rule in *Foss v Harbottle*' [1957] CLJ 194 at 203. The same exceptions are listed (in a different order) by Jenkins LJ in *Edwards v Halliwell* [1950] 2 All ER 1064, CA.

[10] More properly described in most cases as a fraud on the *company*: see *Prudential Assurance Co Ltd v Newman Industries Ltd (No 2)* [1981] Ch 257 (Ch, Vinelott J), the most significant case on this issue and on the rule in *Foss v Harbottle*.

[11] See especially *Prudential Assurance Co Ltd v Newman Industries Ltd (No 2)* [1981] Ch 257 (Ch, Vinelott J); and *Smith v Croft (No 2)* **[13.19]**.

[12] See the detailed discussion in the 9th edition of this book, at Chapter 12.

It might be asked whether all this effort is necessary. The justification is perhaps best put by Lord Denning MR, in *Wallersteiner v Moir (No 2)* [1975] QB 373, 390:

> It is a fundamental principle of our law that a company is a legal person, with its own corporate identity, separate and distinct from the directors or shareholders, and with its own property rights and interests to which alone it is entitled. If it is defrauded by a wrongdoer, the company itself is the one person to sue for the damage. Such is the rule in *Foss v. Harbottle* (1843) 2 Hare 461. The rule is easy enough to apply when the company is defrauded by outsiders. The company itself is the only person who can sue. Likewise, when it is defrauded by insiders of a minor kind, once again the company is the only person who can sue. But suppose it is defrauded by insiders who control its affairs—by directors who hold a majority of the shares—who then can sue for damages? Those directors are themselves the wrongdoers. If a board meeting is held, they will not authorise the proceedings to be taken by the company against themselves. If a general meeting is called, they will vote down any suggestion that the company should sue them themselves. Yet the company is the one person who is damnified. It is the one person who should sue. In one way or another some means must be found for the company to sue. Otherwise the law would fail in its purpose. Injustice would be done without redress.

Company claims and the statutory derivative action: CA 2006 ss 260ff

In outline

CA 2006 ss 260ff has changed the common law fundamentally, and abolished the rule in *Foss v Harbottle* so far as it applies to litigating for most of the wrongs done to the company.[13] The Act provides a new derivative procedure (supplemented by amended Civil Procedure Rules (CPR)[14]). It sets out what sorts of company claims can be pursued, and when.

It defines a 'derivative claim' (CA 2006 s 260(1)), and then provides that such claims may *only* be brought under these statutory provisions (CA 2006 ss 260ff) or in pursuance of a court order granted in CA 2006 s 994 'unfair prejudice' proceedings:[15] CA 2006 s 260(2).[16] It then passes the 'gatekeeper' role in derivative corporate claims to the court, which must exercise a structured discretion on grounds laid out (non-exhaustively) in CA 2006. This involves a two-stage process. The court is first required to establish that there is a prima facie case for permission to be granted to continue the derivative claim (CA 2006 s 261(2)). If so, then the second stage is for the court to determine whether or not permission should be granted to continue the claim (CA 2006 s 263): in some circumstances permission *must* be refused (s 263(2)); otherwise the court has a discretion to allow continuance, but must take into account a number of specified considerations (s 263(3) and (4)).

---

[13] Although note that the Explanatory Notes to the 2006 Act specifically state at para 491 that, 'The sections in this Part do *not* formulate a substantive rule to replace the rule in *Foss v Harbottle*, but instead reflect the recommendations of the Law Commission that there should be a "new derivative procedure with more modern, flexible and accessible criteria for determining whether a shareholder can pursue an action" (*Shareholder Remedies*, paragraph 6.15)' (emphasis added).

[14] See CPR 1998 r 19.9–19.9F (subject to transitional provisions specified in SI 2007/2204, r 21).

[15] See 'Unfairly prejudicial conduct of the company's affairs', pp 715ff.

[16] But see the judicial expansion now in 'Residual use of common law derivative claims', pp 695ff.

There are further special rules where the application is not original, but is instead a request for permission to continue a claim initially brought by the company or by another member (ss 262 and 264 respectively).

Grounds for bringing a derivative claim and parties to the claim

CA 2006 broadens (but also makes exclusive[17]) the grounds upon which a derivative claim (as defined in s 260(1)) is available to members.[18] Under s 260(3), a cause of action arising from an actual or proposed act or omission *by a director* involving negligence, default, breach of duty or breach of trust are recognised as the only basis upon which to commence such a claim. Perhaps not all the wrongs which a director could conceivably commit against the company are included in the section, but breach of duty includes the newly codified directors' duties examined in Chapter 7, and 'director' for these purposes includes both former directors and shadow directors. Breach of duty presumably also includes other breaches under the Act (beyond the directors' general duties), and breaches of common law duties not within the Act at all.

Provided the cause of action is in respect of a relevant breach by a director, third parties may also be made defendants in the derivative claim, either in lieu of or in addition to the wrongdoing director (s 260(3)): for example, see *Iesini v Westrip Holdings Ltd* **[13.10]**. The general rules on third party liability in respect of breaches of duty by the directors are not set out in the Act, but rely on the common law rules on dishonest assistance and knowing receipt ('Secondary liability (liability of third parties associated with directors' wrongs)', pp 468ff).

It does not matter whether the cause of action arose before or after the person seeking to bring the derivative claim became a member (s 260(4)).

➤ Question

If the facts in *Estmanco (Kilner House) Ltd v Greater London Council* [1982] 1 WLR 2 were to arise now, litigation could not be pursued in derivative form by the members under the CA 2006 rules since the wrong in question was not committed by the directors, but by the majority shareholders voting to break an agreement. How will remedies now be provided in this type of case?

Common law derivative actions are not permitted at all in respect of 'derivative claims' as defined in s 260(1): see s 260(2).[19] And statutory derivative actions are only permitted in respect of claims arising from breaches of directors' duties: see s 260(3).[20]

What policy lies behind this limitation? See *Iesini v Westrip Holdings Ltd* **[13.10]**, and the dismissal of claims for restitution as not being claims in respect of breach of fiduciary duty:

> 103. The restitutionary claim is pleaded in the draft amended Particulars of Claim as follows:
>
>> '105. Further or in the alternative, in the belief that it owned the licences Westrip [the company] incurred expenditure in developing the Tanbreez licence as set out above. If…it

---

[17] Although see the previous footnote.

[18] A 'member' is defined in CA 2006 s 112, and is not restricted to a shareholder. Also, there is no further discussion here of s 260(2)(b).

[19] Although see 'Residual use of common law derivative claims', pp 695ff, for claims falling outside s 260(1).

[20] Or in pursuance of a court order in proceedings under s 994 (unfair prejudice): s 260(2)(b).

> incurred that expenditure acting under a mistake [then R and H would, on the facts] be unjustly enriched at the expense of Westrip ...
>
> 106. The Claimants, on behalf of Westrip, therefore seek an order for restitution of the value of the benefit conferred on [R and H] ...'

104. The striking point about this plea is that it contains no allegation of default or breach of duty (etc.) on the part of any director of Westrip. The cause of action does not arise out of the default or breach of duty (etc.) of a director. As pleaded, therefore, it is not a derivative claim which can be brought under Chapter 1. It must be brought, if at all, pursuant to an order of the court made in proceedings under section 994. [And, similarly, a breach of trust claim discussed at [105].]

Standing to take proceedings—permission will rarely be granted to a majority shareholder. Is this the statutory counterpart of the earlier common law's 'wrongdoer control'?

[13.02] Cinematic Finance Ltd v Ryder [2010] EWHC 3387 (Chancery Division)

Section 260(1) refers quite generally to 'a member'. Here, the corporate claimant had become a majority shareholder in various investment companies set up for film financing when those companies failed to repay loans the claimant had made to them. The claimant alleged various breaches of duty by the defendant directors and shadow directors. The directors responded that this was not an appropriate case for a derivative action, given the claimant's control over the companies in question. The judge exercised his discretion under s 261(3) to refuse permission to continue the derivative claim.

> ROTH J:
>
> 11. I accept that proceedings for a derivative claim are now comprehensively governed by the Act. But in my judgment the Act is not seeking to change the basic rule that a claim that lies in a company can be pursued only by the company or to disturb the fundamental distinction between a company and its shareholders. There is nothing to suggest that the Act intended such a radical reversal of long-standing and fundamental principles. It is relevant that this part of the Act has its genesis in the Report of the Law Commission on Shareholder Remedies, Law Commission No. 246 (1997). That report states at the outset in paragraph 1.2:
>
> > 'The focus of the project was on the remedies available to a minority shareholder who is dissatisfied with the manner in which the company of which he is a member is run.'
>
> 12. The Report proceeded to set out 'Guiding Principles' that the Law Commission applied as governing its proposals for reform of the law. The first of these is expressed as follows at paragraph 1.9:
>
> > '(i) *Proper plaintiff* Normally the company should be the only party entitled to enforce a cause of action belonging to it. Accordingly, a member should be able to maintain proceedings about wrongs done to the company only in exceptional circumstances.'
>
> 13. Although this part of the Act does not completely mirror the approach to be found in a combination of the Law Commission's draft bill and draft procedure rules, it clearly reflects the overall approach in the Law Commission's proposal and, in my view, one would expect very different language in the Act if it were adopting such a radically different approach that involved discarding the Guiding Principle that I have quoted. Indeed, in the Act the governing provision for the grant of permission by the court to continue a derivative claim is section 261(4) which makes clear that this is a discretion resting in the court.

14. Whilst the discretion must, of course, be exercised in accordance with established principles, in my judgment this is one such principle. I would not go so far as to say that it could never be appropriate for a derivative claim to be brought by a shareholder holding the majority of the shares in a company. A judge must be cautious about using the word 'never' when faced with a statutory discretion and when this is not one of the enumerated circumstances in section 263(2) in which permission must be refused. And faced only with the facts of the instant case, it is impossible to envisage all the factual circumstances that might arise in other cases. But in my judgment, only in very exceptional circumstances could it be appropriate to permit a derivative claim brought by a shareholder in control of the company. For my part, I find it difficult to envisage what those exceptional circumstances might be.

➤ Note

See, too, the *obiter* comments of HHJ Pelling QC (sitting as a judge of the High Court) in *Stimpson v Southern Private Landlords Association* **[13.09]**:

46. There remains one final factor that is significant. Under the old law if there was no wrongdoer control of the company, permission would be refused for the obvious reason that in the circumstances there was no need for derivative proceedings to be commenced. It was submitted on behalf of the claimant that these principles do not appear in the statute and therefore are no longer relevant. I am doubtful if that is correct. If the statute is followed strictly, the court is required to consider whether a prima facie case is established—see s 261(2). In considering that question, the court is bound to have regard, not merely to the factors identified in ss 263(3) and (4), but to any other relevant consideration since ss 263(3) and (4) are not exhaustive. It is open to the first claimant to requisition an EGM, obtain if he can a replacement Board and that Board can if it judges it appropriate to do so, applying the duties imposed upon them by s 172, authorise the litigation. This factor is at least a powerful one that negatives the giving of permission and may be overwhelming. However, I make clear that I have reached my conclusions for each of the reasons I have identified and that I would have reached the same decision irrespective of this last point.

➤ Questions

1. Compare Roth J's comments in *Cinematic Finance Ltd v Ryder* **[13.02]** with his comments in *Stainer v Lee* **[13.04]**. Has there been a change in attitude to the statutory derivative claim?

2. *Is* the above approach the appropriate way to import what was an important underlying common law requirement of 'wrongdoer control'?

Court permission to continue a derivative claim

Compulsory refusal of permission

At the first stage, s 261(2) requires the court to dismiss the application if the claimant's evidence does not disclose a prima facie case. At the second stage, s 263(2) then sets out the only three further matters that are complete bars to pursuit of a derivative claim:

(i)   a person acting in accordance with s 172 (ie the duty to promote the success of the company) would not seek to continue the claim (s 263(2)(a)); or

(ii) the proposed conduct constituting the wrongdoing has been authorised by the company (s 263(2)(b)); or

(iii) the wrongdoing has occurred, but was previously authorised or subsequently ratified by the company (s 263(2)(c)).

1. The action is not designed to promote the success of the company

Section 260(2)(a) reflects the fundamental philosophy of the derivative claim (and, it might be hoped, of the rule in *Foss v Harbottle*): a member ought to be permitted to pursue a derivative claim *because* this is for the benefit of the company, not because this is for the benefit of the member personally.[21] But the test that must be applied by the court is not quite as tough as this. The court does not have to decide whether a hypothetical director (subject to the duty in s 172) *would* think the claim worth pursuing (although that is relevant under s 263(3)(b)); the court merely has to refuse permission if it considers (on the balance of probabilities, presumably) that such a director would *not* seek to continue the claim. It remains to be seen whether the courts will use this power simply to order refusal in cases that are patently not in the company's interest, or whether it will engage in more 'commercial' deliberations, and order refusal in cases that it considers, on a more finely tuned balance, are not in the company's interests.

2. Proper authorisation or ratification

Section 263(2)(b) and (c) follows logically from the fundamental philosophy outlined previously: if an act has been *properly* authorised or ratified, then it no longer constitutes a wrong to the company, and the company cannot pursue a claim in relation to it, either through a derivative claim or otherwise.

The issue of proper authorisation and ratification is thus brought centre stage. This is a difficult and controversial area of law.[22] CA 2006 makes some specific provisions (see especially ss 175 and 180 on authorisation and s 239 on ratification), and, crucially, both ss 175 and 239 indicate that the votes of the 'wrongdoers' are not to count in determining the outcome in the decision-making body (the board of directors and the general meeting, respectively). This provides welcome clarification in an area where there had been great uncertainty.[23] These sections impose further requirements. Beyond that, however, the common law rules are preserved (see ss 180(4) and 239(7)), with all their complications and uncertainties. In particular, the question of whether the particular wrongs committed by the directors *can* be authorised[24] or ratified[25] remains a live issue.[26]

Discretionary refusal of permission

If the court does not refuse permission to continue the derivative action under s 263(2), then it must exercise its discretion in deciding whether to grant permission to the member to continue with the derivative claim. In exercising this discretion, the court *must* take into account, 'in particular' the non-exclusive list of matters provided in s 263(3).

In addition, s 263(4) requires the court to have 'particular regard' to any evidence of the views of members of the company who have no direct or indirect personal interest in the

---

[21] The possibility of personal benefit should be addressed via personal claims, either at common law or under the statutory 'unfair prejudice' provisions in CA 2006 s 994.

[22] See Chapter 7, and the cases and articles cited.

[23] See the cases cited in Chapter 7, and also *Smith v Croft (No 2)* [13.19].

[24] See the law on authorisation by the board or the general meeting in Chapter 7.

[25] The question is whether there are any 'non-ratifiable wrongs', see Notes following *Franbar Holdings Ltd v Patel* [13.13], pp 687ff.

[26] In *Franbar Holdings Ltd v Patel* [2008] EWHC 1534 (Ch), [2009] 1 BCLC 1, the court interpreted s 239(7) as requiring it to decide whether the purported ratification was such as to improperly prevent the member from bringing a claim on behalf of the company. This approach focuses not on the nature of the wrong done to the company, but on the quality of the approval/ratification decision.

matter. This effectively adopts the *Smith v Croft (No 2)* **[13.19]** test as a relevant factor in the exercise of the court's discretion.

➤ Questions

1. Is the order of the list in s 263(3) significant? In particular, is it significant that the views of the 'hypothetical director' are not given greater prominence?

2. Does segregation of s 263(4) from the list of issues provided in s 263(3) indicate that the views of disinterested members should have *more* or *less* influence than the other matters on the court's decision?

3. Is an agreed hierarchy of discretionary considerations essential? What is a court likely to do if, for example, the member is *not* acting in good faith, but a 'hypothetical director' *would* think the claim likely to promote the success of the company?

4. Do the older common law cases suggest additional factors that might be relevant to exercise of the court's discretion? In particular, what has happened to the idea of 'control' of the company by the wrongdoers?

Illustrations of the courts' exercise of control over applications

The legislative adoption of a statutory derivative claim underscores a theme that runs through CA 2006, namely, the strengthening of legal measures to counteract wrongdoing on the part of directors. The following extracts illustrate the application of the statutory provisions to typical factual scenarios.

Thresholds to be reached at the mandatory first stage (s 261(2)), the mandatory second stage (s 263(2)) and the discretionary second stage (s 263(3) and (4)) in order to obtain permission to continue the derivative claim.

The practical problem here is for the court to provide a gate-keeping role, and to do so fairly on the evidence, but also to do so without allowing the 'permission' stage to turn into a mini-trial or a rehearsal of the entire litigation.

[13.03] Iesini v Westrip Holdings Ltd [2009] EWHC 2526 (Chancery Division Companies Court)

The facts are irrelevant. Also see **[13.10]**.

LEWISON J:

78. The Act now provides for a two-stage procedure where it is the member himself who brings the proceedings. At the first stage, the applicant is required to make a *prima facie* case for permission to continue a derivative claim, and the court considers the question on the basis of the evidence filed by the applicant only, without requiring evidence from the defendant or the company. The court must dismiss the application if the applicant cannot establish a *prima facie* case. The *prima facie* case to which s 261(1) refers is a *prima facie* case 'for giving permission'. This necessarily entails a decision that there is a *prima facie* case both that the company has a good cause of action and that the cause of action arises out of a directors' default, breach of duty (etc.).

[13.04] Stainer v Lee [2010] EWHC 1539 (Chancery Division)

The facts are irrelevant at this stage, but see **[13.16]**.

ROTH J:

29. As regards the standard to be applied generally [at the second stage] under section 263, Lewison J [in *Iesini v Westrip Holdings Ltd* **[13.03]**] held that something more than simply a *prima facie* case must be needed since that forms the first stage of the procedure; and that while it would be wrong to embark on a mini-trial the court must form a view on the strength of the claim, albeit on a provisional basis: see at [79]. It seems to me possible, with respect, that the court might revise its view as to a *prima facie* case once it has received evidence and argument from the other side, so the antithesis between section 261(2) [the first stage] and 263 [the second stage] may not be so stark. But in any event, I consider that section 263(3) and (4) do not prescribe a particular standard of proof that has to be satisfied but rather require consideration of a range of factors to reach an overall view. In particular, under s 263(3)(b), as regards the hypothetical director acting in accordance with the s 172 duty, if the case seems very strong, it may be appropriate to continue it even if the likely level of recovery is not so large, since such a claim stands a good chance of provoking an early settlement or may indeed qualify for summary judgment. On the other hand, it may be in the interests of the Company to continue even a less strong case if the amount of potential recovery is very large. The necessary evaluation, conducted on, as Lewison J observed, a provisional basis and at a very early stage of the proceedings, is therefore not mechanistic.

[13.05] Kleanthous v Paphitis [2011] EWHC 2287 (Chancery Division)

The facts are irrelevant at this stage, but see **[13.17]**.

NEWEY J: [After contrasting Lewison J's view in *Iesini v Westrip Holdings Ltd* **[13.03]**, [79], that at the second stage 'something more than a prima facie case' is required with Roth J's views in *Stainer v Lee* **[13.04]**, and noting that CA 2006 does not in terms provide that a claim must reach a specific threshold, he continued:]

41. Roth J's observations are consistent with the Law Commission's intentions. In paragraph 6.72 of its report on shareholder remedies (number 246), on which the relevant provisions of the 2006 Act are to a considerable extent based, the Law Commission recommended that 'there should be no threshold test on the merits'. Roth J's views are in keeping, too, with comments made in a Scottish case, *Wishart v Castlecroft Securities Ltd* [2009] CSIH 65. Lord Reed, giving the opinion of the Inner House, there said (in paragraph 40):

'[S]ection 268 [i.e. the Scottish equivalent to section 263] does not impose any threshold test in relation to the merits of the derivative proceedings. As we have explained, the Law Commission recommended that there should be no such test, partly in order to avoid the risk of a detailed investigation into the merits of the case taking place at the leave stage, and partly to avoid the drawing of fine distinctions based on the language of a particular rule. Section 268, and the parallel provision for England and Wales and Northern Ireland in section 263, do not depart from that recommendation. That is consistent with the nature of the factor to be considered under section 268(2)(b): it is possible to conceive of circumstances in which a director acting in accordance with section 172 might attach great importance to raising proceedings which were merely arguable, and of other circumstances in which a director might have sound business reasons for attaching little importance to raising proceedings which had good prospects of success.'

42. In the circumstances, it seems to me that the Court can potentially grant permission for a derivative claim to be continued without being satisfied that there is a strong case. The merits of the claim will be relevant to whether permission should be given, but there is no set threshold.

➤ Note

In some cases, the court has been inclined to merge the two stages into one, and to consider the application for permission in one single hearing: *Mission Capital plc v Sinclair* **[13.07]**; *Franbar Holdings Ltd v Patel* at [24] **[13.08]**; *Stimpson v Southern Private Landlords Association* at [3] **[13.09]**; *Bridge v Daley* **[13.06]** at [9]. In such cases, it is arguable that the distinction between the requisite thresholds becomes of little significance, as the judge will simply embark on an overall analysis of the evidence and submissions put by both sides in order to decide whether permission should be granted. Whether the threshold in the second stage is higher than that required in the first stage, therefore, is neither here nor there, because there will not be a second stage in some of these cases.

The court must refuse permission to continue the claim if a person acting in accordance with s 172 (duty to promote the success of the company) would not seek to continue the claim (s 263(2)(a)). If that hurdle is met, then, in exercising its discretion to grant permission, the court must consider the importance that a person acting in accordance with s 172 would attach to continuing it (s 263(3)(b)).

[13.06] Bridge v Daley [2015] EWHC 2121 (Chancery Division)

Mr Bridge (the claimant) brought a derivative action against four directors of the company, alleging breaches of their directors' duties covering, amongst others, unfair share purchase, dissemination of information and market manipulation. Judge Hodge QC refused Mr Bridge's permission to continue the claim primarily on the ground that no reasonable director would support continuation of the litigation under s 263(2)(a).

HODGE QC:

74. Moreover, what I am satisfied of is that an independent board of directors has properly considered the claim and has decided that it should not be pursued. As Mr Miall has accepted, the court is unable to undertake a mini-trial. Nevertheless, I am satisfied [on the evidence before me] that the nature and strength of the claims, when viewed in the light of the evidence filed by the defendants and the difficulties in establishing loss to the company, are such that no reasonable directors would support the continuation of this litigation.

75. It is inappropriate for me to go into the merits of the claim generally. It is sufficient for me to say that, in relation to Mr Franklin, I can see absolutely no answer to the provisions of the settlement agreement, which operate as an absolute bar to the claim against him. And in the case of each of Mr Acland and Mr Wilson, I do not consider that there are any pleaded allegations specifically directed to them which amount to any prima facie case of breach of duty which has caused loss to the company in any actionable sense.

76. . . . [A]nd in the light of [there being no prima facie case], no reasonable director could countenance the continuation of the claim against any of them. I do not consider that it is sufficient for Mr Bridge to say that 'they are all in it together'. I accept the submission that the claim against each of the directors has to be viewed individually. . . It has to be specifically pleaded in relation to each of them individually as to what they knew about any asserted wrongdoing on the part of Mr Daley, and that has not been done. . . .

81. I am entirely satisfied that on the evidence there is no sufficiently clear and identifiable benefit [to the company, as distinct from benefits to particular shareholders] from the claim that would override the potential risks and costs of this litigation, not just financially in terms of the potential liability to the defendants if they are successful, but also in terms of the reputational damage to the company and the diversion of management time and effort.

[13.07] Mission Capital plc v Sinclair [2008] EWHC 1339 (Chancery Division)

Two former executive directors (S) (father and daughter) unsuccessfully sought permission to continue a derivative claim. M, via its three non-executive directors, had terminated S's employment and dismissed them as directors on the basis that they had failed to meet financial forecasts and submit important financial information to the board. S brought a derivative claim against M, the non-executive directors and their replacement director (P), claiming that M would suffer damage from their wrongful dismissal, and that P would act improperly.

> FLOYD J:
>
> 43. Although I could not be satisfied that the notional s 172 director would not continue the claim, I do not believe that he would attach that much importance to it. Would a company which had wrongfully dismissed a director normally take action against those responsible for the damage that it has suffered? It would depend, but I suspect that the action it would take in preference would be to replace the directors. Moreover, on the evidence before me the damage the Company will suffer is somewhat speculative—another reason why the s 172 director would not attach great weight to it. [And in any event, S could seek a remedy under s 994 (unfair prejudice) for the harm suffered.]

[13.08] Franbar Holdings Ltd v Patel [2008] EWHC 1534 (Chancery Division)

Medicentres (M) was a company established to provide primary health care and medical services. It was wholly owned by Franbar (F) until July 2005, when F sold 75% of the shares in M to Casualty Plus (C). F and C entered into a shareholders' agreement pursuant to which C appointed two directors to M (Mr Patel and Dr du Plessis (P)) and F appointed one (Mr Lalani (L)). The agreement also gave each party an option to sell or call for the remaining shares at a price nine times M's earnings before interest, tax, depreciation and amortisation as derived from its most recent audited accounts. F brought derivative proceedings against C and P, claiming negligence, default and various breaches of duty of care owed by P to M, including claims that P drove down M's share price by driving business away from it. William Trower QC, sitting as a deputy judge of the High Court, refused permission to continue the claim because he thought that a person acting under s 172 would not attach *great* importance to the claim, and that there were alternative modes of redress which would enable Franbar to claim what it was now seeking.

> MR WILLIAM TROWER QC:
>
> 28. The duty under s 172 to act in the way that the director considers, in good faith, would be most likely to promote the success of the relevant company for the benefit of its members as a whole, having regard amongst other matters to a number of listed criteria. Mr Sisley [counsel] has sought to persuade me that I can be satisfied that directors acting in accordance with s 172 would not seek to continue the claim because Franbar has not established a sufficiently cogent case on the merits to lead a reasonable director to conclude that the continuation of the claim would be in the best interests of Medicentres. In particular, he submits that the evidence in Mr Lalani's witness statement is of such low quality that the hypothetical director would not seek to continue the claim on that ground alone. . . .
>
> 29. Franbar contends to the contrary. It says that the allegations made are so serious and have caused such serious losses that the hypothetical director contemplated by s 263(2) would undoubtedly seek to continue the claim. . . .

30. In my judgment, this is one of those cases in which there is room for more than one view. Directors are often in the position of having to make what is no more than a partially informed decision on whether or not the institution of legal proceedings is appropriate, without having a very clear idea of how the proceedings will turn out. Some directors might wish to spend more time investigating and strengthening the company's case before issuing process, while others would wish to press on with proceedings straight away; in a case such as this one, both approaches would be entirely appropriate. It is my view that there is sufficient material for the hypothetical director to conclude that the conduct of Medicentres' business by those in control of it had given rise to actionable breaches of duty. As it seems likely that Mr Patel and Dr du Plessis were behind much of that conduct, I cannot be satisfied that a hypothetical director acting in accordance with s 172 would conclude that the case advanced was insufficiently cogent to justify continuation of the claim. Even though he may take a healthily sceptical approach to Medicentres' ability to prove the allegations at trial, it does not follow that the claim should not be continued on that ground alone. [So the first hurdle was met.] . . .

36. In my judgment, the hypothetical director acting in accordance with s 172 would take into account a wide range of considerations when assessing the importance of continuing the claim. These would include such matters as the prospects of success of the claim, the ability of the company to make a recovery on any award of damages, the disruption which would be caused to the development of the company's business by having to concentrate on the proceedings, the costs of the proceedings and any damage to the company's reputation and business if the proceedings were to fail. A director will often be in the position of having to make what is no more than a partially informed decision on continuation without any very clear idea of how the proceedings might turn out.

37. Franbar asserts that great importance would be attached to continuing the claim because there is no other means of securing compensation for the breaches of duty that it pleads. In my judgment, the difficulty with this submission is that the complaints are not yet in a form in which the hypothetical director might be expected to conclude that there were obvious breaches of duty which ought to be pursued and that the recovery to be expected in consequence of those breaches would be substantial. I also think that it is likely that the hypothetical director would be more inclined to regard pursuit of the derivative claim as less important in the light of the fact that several of the complaints are more naturally to be formulated as breaches of the Shareholders' Agreement and acts of unfair prejudice which are already the subject matter of proceedings commenced by the minority shareholder. I accept Mr Sisley's submission that, in the present case, where all parties seek and have offered (as the case may be) a buy-out of the minority by the majority and the principal issue is one of valuation, that means that the hypothetical director would be less likely to attribute importance to the continuation of the derivative claim. [And, accordingly, he refused permission to continue.]

[13.09] Stimpson v Southern Private Landlords Association [2009] EWHC 2072 (Chancery Division)

Southern Private Landlords Association (first defendant) was a non-profit company limited by guarantee, whose function it was to represent the interests of private landlords. The sixth defendant was also a company limited by guarantee, and who performed similar services, but on a large scale. The first claimant was the founding president and a director of the first defendant whose voting capacity was, however, limited to breaking deadlocks on the board. The remaining defendants were statutory (or, in the case of the fifth director, shadow) directors of the first defendant. In this application under s 261, the claimants alleged that the director defendants had engineered the transfer of all the assets of the first defendant to the sixth defendant, in breach of their duties. Taking into account the merits and value of the claim, as well as the likely costs of the litigation and that the first claimant would seek to recover his outlay from the first defendant, HHJ Pelling QC (sitting as a judge of the High Court) refused the application under s 263(2) on the basis that a hypothetical director acting under s 172 would not seek to continue the derivative claim.

HHJ PELLING QC (sitting as a judge of the High Court):

24. Thus the real first question to which I now turn is whether a hypothetical director acting in accordance with s 172 of the 2006 Act would not seek to continue the claim. . . .

26. Section 172(1) refers to the requirement that a director must act in a way he considers would most likely promote the success of the company for the benefits of its members as a whole. However, that provision has to be read subject to s 172(2). This provision contemplates two different situations—that where the objects of the company consist of purposes other than the benefit of its members and that where the purposes of the company include purposes other than the benefit of its members. In relation to the first of these situations, s 171(1) is to be read as providing that a director must act in a way that he considers in good faith would be most likely to achieve those purposes. Although it was suggested by the defendants that the first of these constructions applies to both of the situations I have identified and that such a construction would have an impact in the circumstances of this case, I reject that submission. To adopt such an approach would be to apply a test that would be entirely inappropriate to a company with mixed objects because it would require the benefit of its members to be ignored (even though the benefit of members was one of its objects) or suborned to the other objects. Such a test would be progressively more inappropriate depending on how relatively unimportant the other objects were both on a consideration of the relevant objects clause and as a matter of practicality. In my judgment s 172(1) is to be construed as meaning that a director of a company with mixed objects must act in a way that he considers in good faith would most likely promote the success of the company for the benefit of its members as a whole whilst at the same time achieving its other purposes. Where there is a conflict between promoting the success of the company for the benefit of its members and the achievement of the other objectives, a balancing exercise will be required. . . .

28. Deciding whether a hypothetical director acting in accordance with s 172 of the 2006 Act would not seek to continue the claim necessarily involves considering those issues identified by Mr Trower QC in *Franbar* **[13.08]** . . . However, that list is not and was not intended to be comprehensive. In a case such as this answering the question under consideration also involves considering the ability of the company to provide benefits to its members after completion of the litigation, the degree to which delay in completing the litigation would affect the ability of the company to provide services for its members at all, and the degree to which the company can expect to retain members during the litigation, or regain them after it has been completed, bearing in mind that the only income that the first defendant has ever had is its subscription income.

[13.10] Iesini v Westrip Holdings Ltd [2009] EWHC 2526 (Chancery Division Companies Court)

Also see **[13.03]** and 'Grounds for bringing a derivative claim . . .', p 672 (where Lewison J held that the restitution claim was not a valid ground for a derivative application). This case concerned allegations of asset-stripping. Mr Iesini and his co-claimants were shareholders and ex-directors in Westrip, a company formed as a vehicle to find funding for the development of a valuable mineral exploration licence (the 'Tanbreez licence'), worth about $900 million. They applied for permission to continue a derivative claim on behalf of Westrip, in which they sought by various means to reverse the alleged stripping of Westrip's assets.

LEWISON J:

85. As many judges have pointed out (e.g. Warren J in *Airey v Cordell* [2007] BCC 785, 800 and Mr William Trower QC in *Franbar Holdings Ltd v Patel* **[13.08]**) there are many cases in which some directors, acting in accordance with s 172, would think it worthwhile to continue a claim at least for the time being, while others, also acting in accordance with s 172, would reach the opposite conclusion. There are, of course, a number of factors that a director, acting in accordance with s 172, would consider in reaching his decision. They include: the size of the claim; the strength of the claim; the cost of the proceedings; the company's ability to fund the proceedings; the ability of the potential defendants to satisfy a judgment; the impact on the company if it lost the claim and had to pay not only its own costs but the defendant's as well; any disruption to the company's activities while the claim is pursued; whether the prosecution of the claim would damage the company in other ways (e.g. by losing the services of a valuable employee or alienating a key supplier or customer) and so on. The weighing of all these considerations is essentially a commercial decision, which the court is ill-equipped to take, except in a clear case.

86. In my judgment therefore (in agreement with Warren J and Mr Trower QC) s 263(2)(a) will apply only where the court is satisfied that *no* director acting in accordance with s 172 would seek to continue the claim. If some directors would, and others would not, seek to continue the claim the case is one for the application of s 263(3)(b). Many of the same considerations would apply to that paragraph too. . . .

102. In my judgment this is a clear case. The strength of the claim against the board is so weak that I conclude that no director, acting in accordance with s 172, would seek to continue the claim against the directors in respect of their actions in accepting the rescission of the SSA. If I am wrong about that, the case is so weak that a person acting in accordance with s 172 would attach little weight to continuing it.

[13.11] Kiani v Cooper [2010] EWHC 577 (Chancery Division)

Mrs Kiani (claimant) and Mr Cooper (first defendant) were the sole directors and shareholders of a property development company. In this application, Mrs Kiani alleged that Mr Cooper had acted in breach of his fiduciary duties owed to the company. These allegations concerned, first, sums claimed by Mr Cooper personally as a creditor of the company; secondly, Mr Cooper's failure adequately to handle and defend claims made by DPM (third defendant), of which Mr Cooper was a director and majority shareholder; and, thirdly, sums transferred out of the company's bank account by Mr Cooper to another company, which was allegedly owned beneficially by Mr Cooper himself. Proudman J concluded that Mr Cooper had a strong case to answer and he had not yet at any rate answered it. Taking this and the other statutory considerations into account, permission to continue the claim was granted, but only down to disclosure in the action, because further disclosure of documents would reveal the real strength of Mrs Kiani's case, and thus whether a director acting in accordance with s 172 would wish to continue the claim.

PROUDMAN J:

43. Mr Irvin [counsel for Mr Cooper] submitted under this head that the case is one for mandatory dismissal. He prayed in aid the fact that the company is deadlocked and development cannot continue. The company has ceased trading. He submitted that liquidation in one form or another was the only realistic option and the proper person to take decisions about whether there has been any breach of duty is a liquidator. I observe that although this could have been a case for the court to appoint a receiver, neither side has requested such an appointment. The evidence of Mr Rubin, an insolvency practitioner, given on the basis of information provided by Mr Cooper, is that the company may be cash flow insolvent, although it seems to be common ground that

on a balance sheet basis there is a surplus of assets over liabilities. Mr Irvin submitted that faced with the practical options a director would not expend money in what might be very considerable costs of these proceedings. One of the factors specified in section 172 is the need to act fairly between members of the company. In any event Mr Irvin submitted that it would be grossly unfair to pursue Mr Cooper in circumstances where even if he won he would be bearing a significant proportion of the costs of the proceedings.

44. However, taking all the factors I have stated into account, it seems to me that so far from there being a mandatory bar on the application, a director acting in accordance with his section 172 duties would decide to continue the proceedings on the basis that at present there is some strong evidence in favour of the case advanced by Mrs Kiani. The notional director would take into account the size of the claim in relation to the payments to Cranham Facilities Limited (some £296,000), which if successful would be bound to ensure full return for all creditors. Mr Irvin submitted that the costs of such an action would be disproportionate. However, that depends on the ability to recover in full.

45. I believe that a director acting in accordance with his duty would wish to continue the claim down to disclosure. Mr Cooper says he has supporting documentation and that is the time to assess what documentation he can in fact produce. . . .

> Note

In *Stainer v Lee* **[13.04]**, Roth J also granted permission to continue the claim only up to the conclusion of discovery.

> Question

Is the possibility that the claimant shareholder has other avenues for seeking a remedy a good reason for refusing permission to continue a derivative claim? What does CA 2006 say? (See s 263(3)(f).) What do the judges do?

[13.12] Cullen Investments Ltd v Brown [2015] EWHC 473 (Chancery Division)

Cullen (the claimant) and Mr Brown were the shareholders of a company set up as a vehicle for a joint venture. Brown was one of the directors. Cullen alleged that Brown had breached his fiduciary duty by taking an opportunity to invest in the German residential market himself. Brown alleged that the opportunity had been offered to and turned down by Cullen, and that the terms of the joint venture agreement permitted this course of action. Mark Anderson QC concluded that permission would not be refused under s 263(2) since it had not been established that no director acting in accordance with s 172 would seek to continue the claim, nor that the acts complained of had been authorised by the company. Then, taking into account the factors in s 263(3), in particular the good faith of the claimant, the importance a director acting in accordance with s 172 would place on the claim, and the need for derivative proceedings as a precaution against potential injustice, he granted permission to continue the claim.

ANDERSON QC:

Strength of the claim

38. Mr Davies [counsel] submits that the claim is so weak and its quantum so paltry that no hypothetical director would allow it to proceed. He relies heavily on the email of 22nd January 2009 quoted in paragraph 17 above. He submits that that email demonstrates that Mr Brown had

already been given permission to take the German Opportunity for his personal benefit, and that the failure by any of its recipients to reply, still less to gainsay what he said, was further evidence of, and in itself amounted to, such permission....

40. However I consider that the hypothetical director would think that there were good prospects of establishing that Mr Brown chose deliberately not to mention his personal involvement in more explicit terms and therefore did not make the full and frank disclosure which he would need to demonstrate to be released from his fiduciary or similar duties. This is because of the evidence, which to me at this preliminary stage on paper seems strong, that he deliberately concealed his involvement thereafter...

45. However the issue of express authorisation arising from or evidenced by the email of 22nd January 2009 is not Mr Brown's only answer to this claim. He also argues that the terms of the JVA [joint venture agreement] itself provide Cullen's authority for his personal investment in the German Opportunity...

46. However the terms of the JVA are not agreed. In my judgment the hypothetical director would conclude at this stage that if Mr Brown had genuinely thought that there were terms of his contract with Cullen which provided him with authority to invest personally, he would not have thought it necessary to conceal his investment from Cullen. On the contrary, as he promised in the email of 22nd January 2009, he would have kept Cullen informed. Moreover the contention that he did not need express authority would face the difficulty that he considered it necessary to claim that he had sought it and received it in text messages on 16th January 2009 which, on the evidence as it stands today, appear not to have been sent.

47. In my judgment a director would be advised, and would conclude, that the outcome of this dispute will probably depend on the simple issue of whether Mr Brown was given express authority to take the German Opportunity for himself, as he claims; and that the most likely answer at this preliminary stage is that he was not.

48. The next argument advanced by Mr Davies for Mr Brown is that the quantum of the claim is very small....

50. In my judgment at this preliminary stage the claim looks to be worth at least the amount of the profit made by Mr Brown from the German Opportunity. There is scant evidence of the amount and such evidence as there is comes from Mr Brown himself, and so would be treated with some scepticism by the hypothetical director. The Kauri CAB website boasts of a large number of developments and it is at least possible that these have yielded healthy profits. The extent of Mr Brown's entitlement to those profits can only be a matter of speculation at this stage but his decision not to give a full account of those profits is a matter which the hypothetical director would weigh in the balance: if Mr Brown had made such a small amount that it was not worth suing for, he would surely have said so and proved it by now. Taking that factor into account, and upon being advised that it is quite usual in this sort of case for quantum to be obscure until the litigation is well advanced, I do not think that the hypothetical director would be put off by the risk that the litigation might result in judgment for an amount which is not worthwhile.

51. Similar considerations apply to Mr Brown's ability to satisfy a judgment. A hypothetical director would always be reluctant to sue a defendant who was not good for the money, but I have seen no material to suggest that that is the position here.

Section 263(2)

52. For reasons which will by now be obvious, I reject the contention made on behalf of the defendants that permission to continue this claim must be refused under section 262(2). I am not satisfied that no director complying with section 172 would seek to continue the claim. Neither can I be satisfied on the current evidence that the acts complained of were authorised by the company.

Section 263(3)

...

54. In deciding how important it is to continue the claim, a hypothetical director would consider, in the words of section 172, whether the claim would be 'likely to promote the success of the company for the benefit of its members as a whole'. Of the six specific matters mentioned in sub-paragraphs (a) to (f) of section 172(1), only (a) and (f) are of potential relevance on the facts of this case, and subparagraph (f) seems to me to be neutral since (subject to what I say below about alternative remedies) my decision either way will disappoint half the shareholders and please the other half in equal measure.

55. Since Kauri is no longer trading, it seems to me that the question which the hypothetical director would ask is whether and to what extent the company's funds available for distribution to its members are likely to be enhanced or diminished by continuing the litigation. In this regard it is important to note that Cullen does not seek an order that the company fund the litigation, nor an indemnity against any adverse costs orders. Since the litigation is to be funded entirely by Cullen, and since Cullen and not Kauri will be liable for the adverse costs consequences in the event of failure, it is difficult to see any reason why a hypothetical director would not want to continue the litigation. Its funds cannot be diminished but may very well be enhanced, possibly to a very significant extent. In those circumstances in my judgment a hypothetical director would attach considerable importance to continuing the proceedings for the purpose of remedying the wrong which, on the claimant's case, has been perpetrated by the defendants.

The court must refuse permission to continue proceedings if the actual or proposed wrong has been properly authorised or ratified by the company: s 263(2)(b) and (c). If that hurdle is met, then, in exercising its discretion to grant permission, the court must consider whether the company has decided not to pursue the claim: s 263(e).

Care must be taken here. The authorisation (ie before the wrongdoing) or ratification (ie after the wrongdoing) must be proper. The rules for each are different.

In the absence of specific statutory provisions, *authorisation* is granted according to common law rules (s 180(4)), and these seem to permit the wrongdoing directors to vote (see the following Notes, p 687). Such authorisation may be derived from the terms of a prior agreement, such as a joint venture agreement where the company was set up as a vehicle for joint venture (see the unsuccessful argument in *Cullen Investments v Brown* **[13.12]**).

On the other hand, where *ratification* is in issue, s 239 applies, which adopts the common law rules with all their poorly defined limitations on what may be ratified by whom (s 239(7)), and then adds the further requirement that the wrongdoers cannot vote to ratify (unlike the common law), although they may count in the quorum and participate in the proceedings (s 239(4)). See *Franbar* **[13.13]** and the following Notes, p 687.

It should be noted that a decision by the company not to pursue the claim should be given very little weight where the defendant directors constitute a majority of its directors (*Cullen Investments v Brown* **[13.12]**).

[13.13] Franbar Holdings Ltd v Patel [2008] EWHC 1534 (Chancery Division)

For the facts, see **[13.08]**. Also see **[13.14]**.

MR WILLIAM TROWER QC:

38. As all of the acts and omissions relied on by Franbar have already occurred, the third relevant factor is whether those acts and omissions could be ratified, or in the circumstances would be likely to be ratified by Medicentres. Although Casualty Plus has a significant number

of outside shareholders, that fact of itself does not cause me to consider that it would not vote in favour of ratification of any of the breaches of duty to Medicentres pleaded against Mr Patel and Dr du Plessis. Mr Sisley (who is also instructed by Casualty Plus in the s 994 petition and the shareholders' action) told me that this was Casualty Plus' intention. I am satisfied that Casualty Plus will, if necessary, take steps to procure a resolution ratifying the conduct complained of against Mr Patel and Dr du Plessis.

39. Any such ratification must of course be effective; merely purporting to do so cannot amount to ratification sufficient to render permission to continue inappropriate, or at least less appropriate than would otherwise be the case. Provision for the ratification by a company of conduct by a director amounting to negligence, default, breach of duty or breach of trust is made by CA 2006 s 239, although it applies only to conduct by a director on or after 1 October 2007 (Schedule 3 paragraph 17 of The Companies Act 2006 (Commencement No 3 Consequential Amendments, Transitional Provisions and Savings) Order 2007 SI 2007/2194). Conduct prior to that date is subject to the law relating to ratification applicable immediately before that date. In the present case, some of the conduct of which complaint is made occurred prior to 1 October 2007 and some occurred thereafter.

40. The ratification must be effected by a resolution of the company's members. The material part of s 239 is in the following terms. . .:

41. The effect of these provisions is that the vote (in his capacity as a member) of the director whose conduct is in issue and the vote of any member connected with him must be left out of account when determining whether an effective resolution ratifying that conduct has been passed. Whether a member is a connected person for these purposes is set out in CA 2006 ss 252 and 254, the material parts of which are as follows: . . . [And then holding that Casualty Plus was not such a person.]

43. I shall revert shortly to Mr Matthias' submissions on whether or not a particular aspect of the conduct of Mr Patel and Dr du Plessis is capable of ratification. Before doing so, I should deal with a submission made by Mr Sisley that the introduction by section 239 of an obligation to disregard connected votes means that what he describes as the 'untainted majority' can ratify any act which is not *ultra vires* the company. He contended that the connected person provisions in section 239 have replaced the principle that breach of duty by a director is incapable of ratification where it constitutes a fraud on the minority in circumstances in which the wrongdoers are in control of the company. This submission can only relate to conduct which occurred after 1 October 2007.

44. In my judgment, that is not the correct approach. Section 239(7) explicitly preserves any rule of law as to acts that are incapable of being ratified by the company. This will include acts which are *ultra vires* the company in the strict sense, but it seems to me that it will also include acts which, pursuant to any rule of law, are incapable of being ratified for some other reason. If Mr Sisley were right, the effect of section 239 would be to restrict the types of circumstance in which ratification is not possible because of wrongdoer control to those in which the connected person requirements of section 239(3) and (4) are satisfied. He did not suggest any policy reason why that might have been the Parliamentary intention and the passages from *Gore-Browne on Companies* . . . and *Palmer's Company Law* . . . suggest that it was not. In summary, I agree with the editors of *Palmer* that the connected person provisions in section 239(3) and (4) impose additional requirements for effective ratification which draw on existing equitable rules but which impose more stringent demands (*Palmer's Company Law* (25th edn) at paragraph 8.3412).

45. It follows that I consider that the words of Sir Richard Baggalay, delivering the advice of the Privy Council in *North-West Transportation Company v. Beatty* **[4.34]**, 594, describing the circumstances in which a company cannot ratify breaches of duty by its directors, remain good law:

> '. . . provided such affirmance or adoption is not brought about by unfair or improper means, and is not illegal or fraudulent or oppressive towards those shareholders who oppose it.'

It follows that, where the question of ratification arises in the context of an application to continue a derivative claim, the question which the court must still ask itself is whether the ratification has the effect that the claimant is being improperly prevented from bringing the claim on behalf of the company (c.f. Knox J in *Smith v. Croft (No 2)* **[13.19]**, 185B). That may still be the case where the new connected person provisions are not satisfied, but there is still actual wrongdoer control pursuant to which there has been a diversion of assets to persons associated with the wrongdoer, albeit not connected in the sense for which provision is made by section 239(4).

46. Mr Matthias submitted that the acts complained of are incapable of ratification because their effect was to oppress the minority by driving down the value of Franbar's minority interest, in any event when seen against the background of the options contained in the Shareholders' Agreement. This might be correct in relation to a number of the breaches alleged against Mr Patel and Dr du Plessis, but it cannot sensibly be said that every breach of duty pleaded in the derivative claim is incapable of ratification merely because it caused sufficient loss to Medicentres to have an effect on the value of Franbar's shares. In my judgment, that would be to give a meaning to the concept of minority oppression which is not justified by the authorities.

47. I do, however, accept that some of the complaints made by Franbar may well be incapable of ratification. It seems to me that, if Franbar were to establish its claim that some part of the business of Medicentres, or some business opportunity which properly belonged to it, had been diverted to Casualty Plus at the suit of Mr Patel or Dr du Plessis, that may well amount to a breach of duty incapable of ratification on the votes of Casualty Plus, more particularly if it was done with the intention of driving down Medicentres' earnings and reducing the amount payable to Franbar on exercise of the option. Despite Mr Sisley's comprehensive submissions on the improbability of any such breach being established, I am unable to say at this stage that he is right. In my judgment it is possible that Franbar will establish at trial that, in all the circumstances of the case, some of the breaches alleged will prove to be incapable of ratification. In this, as in many cases, it is only possible to say at this stage that, while it is likely that an attempt will be made to ratify all of the breaches, it is no more than a possibility that ratification of all of the breaches will prove to be effective.

48. The fourth relevant matter of which I am required to take particular account is whether Medicentres has decided not to pursue the claim. Mr Matthias submitted that Medicentres has made no such decision and Mr Sisley did not contend that it had. I am able to infer, however, that if it were to engage in a formal consideration of whether or not to pursue the claim, Medicentres would decide not to do so. In a case such as the present, this seems to me to add little to the issue of ratification which I have already considered.

➤ Question

The previous case suggests that not only are the wrongdoers and connected persons barred from the ratification vote (CA 2006 s 239), but that certain wrongs are simply 'unratifiable', even by an untainted majority. Which wrongs are 'unratifiable'? Are such wrongs unratifiable because of the nature of the wrong or because of the nature of the ratification decision? *Should* any wrongs be unratifiable? Where a wrong *is* ratifiable, how does effective ratification take place? See the following Notes.

➤ Notes

1. In *Cook v Deeks* **[7.25]**, at 564, Lord Buckmaster took the view that if:

the contract in question was entered into under such circumstances that the directors could not retain the benefit of it for themselves, then it belonged in equity to the company and ought to have been dealt with as an asset of the company. Even supposing it be not *ultra vires* of a company to make a present to its directors, it appears quite certain that directors holding a majority of votes would not be permitted to make a present to themselves. This would be to allow a majority to oppress the minority. To such circumstances the cases of *North-West Transportation v Beatty* **[4.34]** and *Burland v Earle* [1902] AC 83, PC, have no application.

2. In *Daniels v Daniels* [1978] Ch 406, three minority shareholders brought an action against Mr and Mrs Daniels, the two directors and majority shareholders of the company, alleging *negligence* (rather than breach of the conflicts rules), in that they had negligently caused the company to sell land to Mrs Daniels at a fraction of its true value. In preliminary proceedings, Templeman J held that the plaintiffs had standing to sue, notwithstanding *Foss v Harbottle*. He said:

> The authorities which deal with simple fraud on the one hand and gross negligence on the other do not cover the situation which arises where, without fraud, the directors and majority shareholders are guilty of a breach of duty which they owe to the company, and that breach of duty not only harms the company but benefits the directors. In that case it seems to me that different considerations apply. If minority shareholders can sue if there is fraud, I see no reason why they cannot sue where the action of the majority and the directors, though without fraud, confers some benefit on those directors and majority shareholders themselves. . . . To put up with foolish directors is one thing; to put up with directors who are so foolish that they make a profit of £115,000 odd at the expense of the company is something entirely different. The principle which may be gleaned from *Alexander v Automatic Telephone Co*[27] (directors benefiting themselves), from *Cook v Deeks* **[7.25]** (directors diverting business in their own favour) and from dicta in *Pavlides v Jensen*[28] (directors appropriating assets of the company) is that a minority shareholder who has no other remedy may sue where directors use their powers, intentionally or unintentionally, fraudulently or negligently, in a manner which benefits themselves at the expense of the company.

3. *Daniels v Daniels* is always contrasted with *Pavlides v Jensen* [1956] Ch 565 where a minority shareholder unsuccessfully attempted to bring an action against the directors alleging negligence in the sale of an asbestos mine to an associated company at a gross undervalue. The directors objected that the shareholder had no right to sue, and the court agreed, there being no evidence of fraud or personal benefit.[29] Is the case legitimately distinguishable on this basis?

4. Is it true that *Cook v Deeks* **[7.25]** and *Daniels v Daniels*, in the previous Notes, represent a category of 'unratifiable wrongs'? If so, *should* this be allowed, or should it be left to CA 2006 s 239 to deal straightforwardly with these cases, and cases such as *Regal (Hastings) Ltd v Gulliver* **[7.26]** (corporate opportunity) and *North-West Transportation v Beatty* **[4.34]** (self-dealing)? (While noting s 239(7)!)

---

[27] [1900] 2 Ch 56, CA.

[28] [1956] Ch 565.

[29] This distinction between different forms of negligence is eliminated in CA 2006 ss 260ff, where, prima facie, all claims based on negligence can be pursued by way of derivative action, although the relevance of proper confirmation by the general meeting remains: see 'Grounds for bringing a derivative claim and parties to the claim', p 672.

The court must consider whether the member has alternative personal claims which could be pursued in his own right rather than on behalf of the company: s 263(3)(f).

[13.14] Franbar Holdings Ltd v Patel [2008] EWHC 1534 (Chancery Division)

For the facts, see **[13.08]**. Also see **[13.13]**.

MR WILLIAM TROWER QC:

50. . . . What is required is for the act or omission of which complaint is made to give rise to a cause of action available to the member in its own right. Doubtless such a cause of action will sometimes be a claim seeking relief against the same director defendants, but I do not read the subsection as being limited to such claims. In my view, the only limitation is that the cause of action should arise out of the same act or omission; where that act or omission gives rise to both a claim for unfair prejudice against a member and a claim for breach of duty against a director, s 263(3)(f) is engaged. The adequacy of the remedy available to the member in his own right is, however, a matter which will go into the balance when assessing the weight of this consideration on the facts of the case. Even if this is wrong as a matter of strict construction of the subsection, I consider that it is relevant in the present case for the court to see whether the acts or omissions in respect of which the derivative claim is brought give rise to a cause of action that the member can bring against another person. That is a consideration of some significance where that other person is the majority shareholder with close connections to the directors concerned, and where the buy-out offer which has already been made is made on behalf of all of the Defendants.

51. I can well understand why Mr Matthias accepted the extent of the overlap between the s 994 petition and the derivative claim and I think that he was right to do so. In my view most, if not all, of the allegations of breach of duty to Medicentres (and certainly all those which are even arguably incapable of ratification) are likely to be relevant to Franbar's complaint of unfair prejudice. Furthermore, the losses which Medicentres might have sustained as a result of the breaches of duty pleaded in the derivative claim are relevant to the fair value of Franbar's shares and to the question of what factual assumptions should be made on the valuation to ensure that Franbar is put into the position that it would have been in but for the unfair prejudice which it will (on this hypothesis) have established. I can see no reason why Franbar should not be granted such relief on the unfair prejudice petition as may be necessary to ensure that the interest which it seeks to realise is valued on a basis which takes full account of the value of the complaints it wishes to pursue on behalf of Medicentres in the derivative claim.

52. In the end, it was clear that Franbar's real concern was that Casualty Plus might not be in a position to pay a fair value for Franbar's shares in Medicentres (having regard to the value of Medicentres' claims against Mr Patel and Dr du Plessis), while a judgment against Mr Patel and Dr du Plessis is one which is more likely to be satisfied, or in any event gives Franbar an extra string to its bow. There is some foundation for this concern because it seems possible that Casualty Plus will have to raise additional capital to fund its purchase of Franbar's shares and may have difficulty in doing so, although I give this consideration less weight in the light of the fact that the open offer to purchase is one to which each of the Defendants is a party.

53. Franbar also submits that continuation and consolidation will be a cost effective and pro-portionate way of resolving all claims between the parties. It is said that this is a more efficient way of dealing with the dispute than leaving over the possibility that a derivative claim might have to be pursued in due course, once unfair prejudice has been established. I cannot rule out the possibility that a derivative claim may need to be pursued at a later stage, but I am bound to say that it seems to me most unlikely that this will be necessary. In this particular case, the availability (and indeed use) of both the s 994 petition and the shareholders' action weigh in the balance

against the grant of permission to continue the derivative action. Any possible future difficulty in enforcing a buy-out order against Casualty Plus is not, anyway at this stage of the proceedings, a sufficiently powerful basis for taking another view. I also take into account the fact that continuing with a further set of proceedings at this stage might well give rise to unnecessary further complexity in the future, even if those proceedings were to be consolidated with the s 994 petition and even though Franbar has now abandoned (in any event for the present) its application for an indemnity from Medicentres in respect of its costs.

[13.15] Kiani v Cooper [2010] EWHC 577 (Chancery Division)

For the facts, see **[13.11]**.

PROUDMAN J:

38. Another factor prescribed by s 263(3) is the availability to Mrs Kiani of an alternative remedy in respect of the alleged breaches of duty. Mr Irvin submits that one proper remedy would be a personal action under the shareholders' agreement. However, it seems to me that such an action could meet real difficulties in that the loss claimed could be viewed as loss reflective of the company's loss, irrecoverable under the principle enunciated in *Johnson v Gore Wood* **[13.26]**.

39. Mr Irvin's principal submission is however that Mrs Kiani's proper remedy is an unfair prejudice petition under CA 2006 s 994. Under s 994 the court has a very wide discretion as to the relief it may grant, including, by s 996(2)(c), authorising civil proceedings in the name of and on behalf of the company.

40. There is a lot to be said for this procedure in a case of a two-person company where the real dispute is between those two persons alone. However, the jurisdiction to make an order under s 996(2)(c) can only be exercised if the court is first satisfied that the unfair prejudice petition is well-founded. Mrs Kiani would not therefore have standing on behalf of the company to restrain a winding up petition. It may well be the case that the court would have jurisdiction on her application to restrain a winding up petition pending the outcome of s 994 proceedings. I have not been addressed on that issue. Moreover, yesterday Mr Cooper and DPM, through Mr Irvin, said for the first time that they were willing to offer an undertaking not to present creditors petitions pending s 994 proceedings.

41. Taking all those factors into consideration, it seems to me that Mrs Kiani's position is this. She says that she and the company have been deprived of the opportunity to pursue the development venture. She does not want the company to be wound up on the petition of Mr Cooper, at whose door she places responsibility for the deadlock which has occurred. She wants her opportunity to be preserved. She wishes to pursue Mr Cooper on behalf of the company in a derivative action. It seems to me that the fact that she could in a more roundabout way achieve the relief she seeks does not mean that she ought not to be granted permission in the present case. It is merely one of the factors that I have to take into account.

[13.16] Stainer v Lee [2010] EWHC 1539 (Chancery Division)

Also see **[13.04]**.

A minority shareholder (S) in company C was permitted to continue a derivative claim against two of C's directors in respect of what appeared to be substantial interest-free loans made by C to company E which was owned by one of those directors. E had been established as a special purpose vehicle (SPV) for the acquisition of shares in C. By 2002, it had acquired a 65% shareholding in C with the aid of a bank loan exceeding £4 million. This debt was repaid out of interest-free loan funds from C to E. The failure to obtain interest for C over a period of almost nine years on lending to E that rose from £4.6 million to £8.1 million constituted very strong grounds for a claim that the directors were in breach of their fiduciary duties. The judge held that it was therefore appropriate to grant S permission to continue the derivative claim until the conclusion of disclosure.

ROTH J:

50. The Respondents also contend that this is a case that the Applicant could pursue by an 'unfair prejudice' petition under section 994, and thus in his own right, which is a relevant consideration under section 263(3)(f). As Lewison J observed in *Iesini* **[13.10]** the availability of the alternative remedy is included under sub-section 263(3) not 263(2) and is accordingly a discretionary consideration not an absolute bar.

51. In many cases, an allegation of breach by directors of their fiduciary duties could found an unfair prejudice petition as well as a derivative action. But that should not disguise the fundamentally different nature of the two forms of proceedings. As Millett J explained in *Re Charnley Davies Ltd (No 2)* [1990] BCLC 760 at 784:

'The very same facts may well found either a derivative action or a s [994] petition. But that should not disguise the fact that the nature of the complaint and the appropriate relief is different in the two cases. Had the petitioners' true complaint been of the unlawfulness of the respondent's conduct, so that it would be met by an order for restitution, then a derivative action would have been appropriate and a s [994] petition would not. But that was not the true nature of the petitioners' complaint. They did not rely on the unlawfulness of the respondent's conduct to found their cause of action; and they would not have been content with an order that the respondent make restitution to the company. They relied on the respondent's unlawful conduct as evidence of the manner in which he had conducted the company's affairs for his own benefit and in disregard of their interests as minority shareholders; and they wanted to be bought out. They wanted relief from mismanagement, not a remedy for misconduct.'

52. In the present action, the Applicant is not seeking to be bought out. He commenced these proceedings, with the support of 35 other minority shareholders, seeking financial remedies for misconduct against the two directors personally, and now an order for restitution from Eldington. Such orders could not be made on an unfair prejudice petition, albeit that the court could by way of remedy authorise the bringing of proceedings in the name of the company by the petitioner: section 996(2)(c). But that would then give rise to a subsequent and further set of proceedings. I consider that given what is at the heart of the present case, a derivative action is entirely appropriate and therefore the theoretical availability to the Applicant of proceedings by way of an unfair prejudice petition is not a reason to refuse permission.

[13.17] Kleanthous v Paphitis [2011] EWHC 2287 (Chancery Division)

Also see **[13.05]**.

Mr Kleanthous was a shareholder in Ryman Group Limited (RGL), the three subsidiaries of which were engaged in the fields of stationery, lingerie and mobile telephone businesses respectively. Mr Kleanthous complained that the other directors had breached their fiduciary duties owed to RGL, by virtue of their decision to enable one of their number, Mr Paphitis, to acquire La Senza, a listed company also engaged in the lingerie business. Mr Kleanthous argued that Mr Paphitis and his company had been enabled to develop this opportunity as well as to use assets of RGL for their own benefit. It was further contended that the defendants had made very substantial profits which resulted in enormous loss to RGL. Newey J refused permission to continue the claim on the basis that the claim was not of such strength and size as could make it appropriate for permission to be granted when (i) that course was strongly opposed, on a reasoned basis, by the Ryman Companies' independent committees as well as by Mr Childs (who was accepted by the court as being disinterested in the alleged conflicts); (ii) that other means of redress were available under CA 2006 s 994; and (iii) much of the money recovered by the company from the director defendants could be expected to be returned to them by way of distribution.

NEWEY J:

78. In *Franbar Holdings Ltd v Patel* **[13.14]**, Mr William Trower QC, sitting as a Deputy High Court Judge, gave considerable weight to the fact that the Claimant should be able to achieve all that it could properly want through a s 994 petition and shareholders' action which were already on foot (see paragraphs 53 and 54). In *Iesini v Westrip Holdings Ltd* **[13.10]**, Lewison J said (in paragraph 126) that the availability of an alternative remedy under s 994 was one of the factors which would have led him to the conclusion that, had he not adjourned the matter, it would not have been appropriate to allow a derivative claim to proceed.

79. In contrast, the availability of an alternative remedy under s 994 did not appear to the Inner House to be a compelling consideration on the facts of *Wishart v Castlecroft Securities Ltd* [2009] CSIH 65, where Lord Reed commented (in paragraph 46) that such proceedings would 'constitute, at best, an indirect means of achieving what could be achieved directly by derivative proceedings'. Similarly, in *Stainer v Lee* **[13.16]** Roth J considered a derivative action 'entirely appropriate' and 'the theoretical availability to the applicant of proceedings by way of an unfair prejudice petition . . . not a reason to refuse permission'; the applicant was 'not seeking to be bought out' (paragraph 52).

80. In the present case, likewise, it was submitted on Mr Kleanthous' behalf that he was not seeking a buy-out of his shares. However, the evidence indicates that Mr Kleanthous is interested in being bought out. [The judge referred to various witness statements, and to proposed action under s 994.] . . . One is left with the suspicion that Mr Kleanthous has chosen to pursue derivative proceedings alone in the hope that he will be able to obtain a costs indemnity (with the result that the other shareholders in RGL would be likely to bear the bulk of the costs even if the claims against them failed).

81. In all the circumstances, I agree with Mr Todd that the availability of an alternative remedy in the form of an unfair prejudice petition is a powerful reason to refuse permission for the derivative claim to proceed in this case.

[13.18] Cullen Investments Ltd v Brown [2015] EWHC 473 (Chancery Division)

For the facts, see **[13.12]**.

ANDERSON QC:

58. Section 263(3)(f) requires me to consider whether the act or omission in respect of which the claim is brought gives rise to a cause of action that Cullen could pursue in its own right rather than on behalf of the company. It seems to me that this issue also arises under section 263(3)(b) since a director acting fairly as between the members would want to consider whether the shareholder, who wants the action to continue, really needs it to do so....

[After considering the uncertainty surrounding whether there *was* an alternative personal claim, and, even if it was, whether recovery would be barred as a result of the reflective loss principle as enunciated in *Johnson v Gore Wood & Co* **[13.26]** he continued:]

61. Even if an alternative remedy is available, that would not be decisive. It is but one consideration. Here, the alternative remedy is in fact Cullen's first remedy of choice, at least against

Julian Brown. It brings the derivative action in the alternative and only after service of a defence by Julian Brown which appeared to necessitate it. That strikes me as a conventional response to the risk that the company and not Cullen may be entitled to some or all of the relief which Cullen seeks. The derivative proceedings are a precaution against that potential injustice; and a precaution is worth taking notwithstanding that it is only that, and may never actually turn out to be necessary.

➤ Note

Where practical considerations demand, such as the urgent need for a summary judgment for the recovery of money misappropriated, and to stop more money from being taken, the claimant may be allowed to change his mind and bring a derivative action *in addition* to a s 994 petition: *Phillips v Fryer* [2012] EWHC 1611 (Ch).

➤ Question

Compare the previous cases. Are the courts' approaches consistent? What features render the alternative remedy more than a mere 'theoretical availability' (per Roth J in *Stainer v Lee* [**13.16**])?

In exercising its discretion, the court shall have particular regard to the views of the members of the company who have no direct or indirect personal interests in the matter: s 263(4).

[13.19] Smith v Croft (No 2) [1988] Ch 114 (Chancery Division)

This case pre-dates the CA 2006 changes, but reflects their import. The claimants were minority shareholders claiming (inter alia) to recover, on behalf of their company, sums which had been paid away in transactions which were both *ultra vires* and in breach of the statutory prohibition on financial assistance ('Financial assistance by a company for the acquisition of its own shares', pp 546ff). With their supporters, the plaintiffs had 14% of the voting rights in the company and the defendants 63%; and there were other shareholders commanding 21% of the votes who did not wish the litigation to proceed. Knox J held that: (i) a prima facie case of *ultra vires* and illegality had been made out, for which the company was entitled to relief; (ii) the plaintiffs accordingly had standing to bring a derivative action; but that (iii) the plaintiffs nevertheless had no right to sue if a majority of the shareholders who were independent of the defendants did not want the action to continue.

KNOX J: Another way of putting the question is to ask whether if a minority has been the victim of a fraud entitling the company in which they are shareholders to financial redress, the majority within that minority can prevent the minority within that minority from prosecuting the action for redress. The usual reason in practice for wanting to abandon such an action is that there is far more to lose financially by prosecuting the right to redress than by abandoning or not pursuing it, and that view will be reinforced in the minds of those who wish to abandon the claim if their opinion is that it is a bad claim anyway. . . .

Mr Potts [counsel] submitted that no reported authority held that in a case falling within the fraud on a minority exception to the rule in *Foss v Harbottle* the court should go beyond seeing whether the wrongdoers are in control and count heads to see what the other shareholders, ie those other than the plaintiff and the wrongdoers, think should be done. I accept that in many reported cases the court has not gone on to the second stage.

... Ultimately the question which has to be answered in order to determine whether the rule in *Foss v Harbottle* applies to prevent a minority shareholder seeking relief as plaintiff for the benefit of the company is 'Is the plaintiff being improperly prevented from bringing these proceedings on behalf of the company?' If it is an expression of the corporate will of the company by an appropriate independent organ that is preventing the plaintiff from prosecuting the action he is not improperly but properly prevented and so the answer to the question is 'No'. The appropriate independent organ will vary according to the constitution of the company concerned and the identity of the defendants who will in most cases be disqualified from participating by voting in expressing the corporate will. [His Lordship then held that a majority of shareholders, excluding the defendants but including the Wren Trust (which he ruled was 'independent'[30]) were opposed to continuing the action, and ordered that it should be struck out.]

Also see *Bridge v Daley* [2015] EWHC 2121 (Ch), [55]–[57] and [78], where the court paid particular attention to the commercial judgement of an independent board of directors, supported by the shareholders, opposed to the proposed claim. (Also see **[13.06]** on other issues.)

Costs.

[13.20] Kiani v Cooper [2010] EWHC 577 (Chancery Division)

For the facts and another part of the judgment, see **[13.11]**. Also see **[13.15]**.

PROUDMAN J:

47. That brings me to the second issue, which is the discrete one whether Mrs Kiani should be indemnified from the company's assets in respect of her costs. Mr Dougherty pressed me to make such an order. He said this is the usual order. He submitted that the claim is properly brought on behalf of the company in accordance with the statutory framework. The company is the loser as a result of the acts and defaults of the director and there is no justification for departure from the usual course. He prayed in aid the well-known comments of Lord Denning, Master of the Rolls, in *Wallersteiner v Moir (No 2)*.[31]

48. However, it seems to me that in a case of this kind, where the dispute is one between the two directors and shareholders, the court ought to take a realistic view. There are no significant unsecured creditors of which Mrs Kiani is aware whose interests come into the equation. There is some analogy with the trustee beneficiary who brings a *Beddoe* summons for directions to sue his fellow trustee beneficiary and asks for his costs of doing so out of the fund. In such circumstances the court is likely to refuse to force the defendant to fund proceedings against him. The claimant must take the risk as to costs.

49. On that basis I am prepared to make an order that Mrs Kiani's costs should be borne by the company, but I am not prepared to grant her an indemnity in respect of any adverse costs order, that is to say, any order that Mr Cooper or DPM should be entitled to costs. It seems to me that she should be required to assume part of the risk of the litigation. However, that part of the order will be subject to review after disclosure.

---

[30] His test of independence was: 'In my judgment in this case votes should be disregarded if, but only if, the court is satisfied either that the vote or its equivalent is actually cast with a view to supporting the defendants rather than securing benefit to the company ... The court should not substitute its own opinion but can, and in my view should, assess whether the decision making process is vitiated by being or being likely to be directed to an improper purpose' (at 186D–F).

[31] [1975] QB 173, CA.

Residual use of common law derivative claims

As noted earlier, the statutory derivative action provisions are not comprehensive. Where the proposed derivative claim falls within the definition in CA 2006 s 260, then the statutory regime is the *only* option open to a member. But where the proposed derivative claim falls outside that definition, then—if it is to be allowed at all—it must be brought under the old common law rules. See *UPMS Ltd v Fort Gilkicker Ltd* **[13.21]**. The 'residual category' governed in this way includes 'multiple' derivative claims (see *Bhullar v Bhullar* [2015] EWHC 1943 (Ch)) and claims concerning foreign-registered companies (see *Abouraya v Sigmund* **[13.22]**) and *Novatrust Ltd v Kea Investments Ltd* [2014] EWHC 4061 (Ch)).

Domestic companies and 'multiple' derivative claims

The statutory definition of the derivative claim in CA 2006 s 260(1) requires that the proceedings be brought 'by a member of a company . . . in respect of a cause of action vested in the company'. This seems to exclude what are commonly called 'multiple' derivative claims. This is the rather uninformative term for proceedings which are brought not by a member of the wronged company, but by a member of a member of the wronged company—typically, a member of the parent company of a wronged subsidiary or sub-subsidiary. The arguments for allowing such a claim are the same as those for allowing any derivative claim, that is, that the wrong to the subsidiary will go unredressed because neither the board of directors of the subsidiary nor its shareholders (the parent company) will sue.

As was explained by Lord Millett in the Hong Kong Court of Final Appeal in *Waddington Ltd v Chan Choo Hoo Thomas* [2009] 2 BCLC 82, such claims were permitted at common law, although without full analysis and justification (see, eg, *Wallersteiner v Moir (No 2)* [1974] 1 WLR 991). The Company Law Review (CLR) Steering Group recommended that these multiple derivative actions be brought within the statutory scheme (see *Developing the Framework* (2000), para 4.133), but this was not done. A very restrictive construction of s 260(1) and (2) would mean that such actions could not be brought either under the Act or at common law. In *UPMS Ltd v Fort Gilkicker Ltd* **[13.21]**, Briggs J regarded that conclusion as 'unpalatable', and devised a way around it.

There is a residual common law derivative claims category; CA 2006 is not comprehensive.

[13.21] Universal Project Management Services Ltd v Fort Gilkicker Ltd [2013] EWHC 348 (Ch), [2013] Ch 551 (Chancery Division)

BRIGGS J:

34. In my view, neither interpretation [of the Act] produces a result which is so obviously more satisfactory than the other for it to be safe on that ground alone to conclude that Parliament must have intended it. As will appear, a main purpose of the codification of derivative claims in Chapter 1 was to remove what were regarded (at least by the Law Commission in its report on shareholder remedies) as complicated, unwieldy and obscure provisions of the applicable common law and to replace them with a clear and transparent code. A conclusion that what Parliament in fact achieved in 2006 was to place a statutory code for derivative claims by members of the wronged company alongside a continued obscure, complicated and unwieldy common law regime for derivative claims by others does not commend itself as an exercise in commonsense. Conversely,

a conclusion that by narrowly defining *locus standi* for all company derivative claims to members of the wronged company Parliament abolished a convenient procedural device for doing justice in cases of wrongdoer control, in a modern context where multi-layered corporate structures with holding companies and subsidiaries are ever more common, hardly commends itself as an exercise in justice. There is, on the face of it, no persuasive reason why Parliament should have wished to provide a statutory scheme for doing justice where a company is in wrongdoer control, but none where its holding company is in the same wrongdoer control.

35. Neither counsel nor I can think of any third construction which would avoid all those unpalatable consequences. It might have been tempting to construe 'member of a company' in section 260(1) as including member of its holding company, but the express and inadequately narrow widening of the ordinary meaning of member in sub-section (5)(c) makes that impossible. . . .

44. I have come on balance to the conclusion that the 2006 Act did not do away with the multiple derivative action. My reasons follow. First, there was before 2006 a common law procedural device called the derivative action by which the court could permit a person or persons with the closest sufficient interest to litigate on behalf of a company by seeking for the company relief in respect of a cause of action vested in it. Those persons would usually be a minority of the company's members, but might, if the company was wholly owned by another company, be a minority of the holding company's members. These were not separate derivative actions, but simply examples of the efficient application of the procedural device, designed to avoid injustice, to different factual circumstances.

45. In 2006 Parliament identified the main version of that device, namely where *locus standi* is accorded to the wronged company's members, labelled it a 'derivative claim' and enacted a comprehensive statutory code in relation to it. As a matter of language, section 260 applied Chapter 1 of Part 11 only to that part of the old common law device thus labelled, leaving other instances of its application unaffected.

46. Applying the well established relevant principle of construction, Parliament did not expressly abolish the whole of the common law derivative action in relation to companies, even though by implication from the comprehensiveness of the statutory code it did do so in relation to derivative claims by members (as defined) of the wronged company. Beyond that, the assertion that the remainder of the common law device was abolished fails because abolition was neither express nor a clear or necessary implication.

47. Section 260 could so easily have been phrased to achieve precisely that result. Sub-section (1) could have excluded the phrase 'by a member of a company' and re-introduced it in sub-section (2) as a specific additional requirement in sub-sub-section (a) so that it read 'under this Chapter by a member of the company'. Alternatively, the whole of the common law derivative action in relation to companies could expressly have been abolished, as it was, for example, by section 236(3) of the Australian Corporations Act 2001 which provides that:

'The right of a person at general law to bring, or to intervene in, proceedings on behalf of the company is abolished.'

48. Neither Lord Millett nor any of the other academic writers who have concluded that the 2006 Act abolished multiple derivative actions have addressed the simple point of construction advanced by Mr Lightman,[32] Mr Hollington QC and by Mr Bailey in the present case, and it may be assumed that the editors of Palmer must have applied the same or a similar analysis.

49. I reach this conclusion with some relief. Not only does it address the manifest scope for real injustice which the abolition of any derivative action by members of a holding company would

---

[32] See too D Lightman, 'Two Aspects of the Statutory Derivative Claim' [2011] *Lloyd's Maritime and Commercial Law Quarterly* 142. For a comparative analysis of the appetite for multiple derivative claims in Hong Kong and England, see SH Goo, 'Multiple Derivative Action and Common Law Derivative Action Revisited: A Tale of Two Jurisdictions' (2010) *Journal of Corporate Law Studies* 255.

have entailed, and as graphically described by Lord Millett in his article,[33] but it ensures that English company law runs in this respect in harmony with the laws of Hong Kong, Singapore, Canada, Australia and New Zealand, all of which have, albeit by different methods, ensured that injustice of the type described by Lord Millett can properly be addressed.

This decision has since been followed, in particular in *Abouraya v Sigmund* **[13.22]**, and also see *Bhullar v Bhullar* [2015] EWHC 1943 (Ch) for a detailed application of the law to the facts.

➤ Question
Are you persuaded by the reasoning of Briggs J?

Foreign-registered companies

Claims concerning foreign-registered companies. A detailed summary of 'the rule in Foss v Harbottle*'.*

[13.22] Abouraya v Sigmund [2014] EWHC 277 (Chancery Division)

This double derivative action was brought by Mr Abouraya, a shareholder of Triangle HK, against the sole director of Triangle UK, a wholly owned subsidiary of Triangle HK, alleging misappropriation of funds and diversion of a business opportunity. In the following extract, Mr Justice David Richards reviewed the authorities on the 'fraud on a minority' exception and applied it to the facts of this case. The court refused permission on the ground that although a prima facie case that the company was entitled to the relief sought had been made out, the shareholder had failed to establish a prima facie case that the proposed action fell within the 'fraud on a minority' exception.

> MR JUSTICE DAVID RICHARDS:
>
> 16. It follows that the common law principles governing the circumstances in which the court will give permission for the commencement or continuation of a derivative claim apply to the present proceedings. The modern statement of these principles is contained in the judgment of the Court of Appeal in *Prudential Assurance Co Ltd v Newman Industries Ltd (No 2)* [1982] Ch 204, which repeated and built on the statement of principle contained in the earlier decision of the Court of Appeal in *Edwards v Halliwell* [1950] 2 All ER 1064, a case concerning a derivative claim by a member of a trade union. At p.222, the Court of Appeal in *Prudential Assurance* stated:
>
>> '... the plaintiff ought at least to be required before proceeding with his action to establish a prima facie case (i) that the company is entitled to the relief claimed, and (ii) that the action falls within the proper boundaries of the exception to the rule in *Foss v Harbottle*.'
>
> As summarised by the Court of Appeal at p.211, the exception arises:
>
>> 'where what has been done amounts to fraud and the wrongdoers are themselves in control of the company. In this case the rule is relaxed in favour of the aggrieved minority, who are allowed to bring a minority shareholder's action on behalf of themselves and all others. The

---

[33] 'Multiple Derivative Actions', in *The Gore-Browne Bulletin* for July 2010: see *Gore-Browne on Companies*, looseleaf edn, vol 1.

reason for this is that, if they were denied that right, their grievance could never reach the court because the wrongdoers themselves, being in control, would not allow the company to sue.'

17. It is common ground that for the purpose of the exception to the rule in *Foss v Harbottle*, the requirement for wrongdoer control is satisfied where control of the company entitled to the remedy is split 50:50 between the claimant and the alleged wrongdoer. It is not in issue that this requirement is satisfied in the present case. The defendant is the sole director of Triangle UK, in which any relevant cause of action is vested, and the only directors and shareholders of Triangle HK are the claimant and the defendant, with the result that the defendant can block any steps which might be taken to enable proceedings to be brought in the name of Triangle UK.

18. The scope of 'fraud' for the purposes of this exception has been considered in many cases. In *Daniels v Daniels* [1978] Ch 406, Templeman J reviewed the authorities to date on this subject. The nineteenth century authorities proceeded largely on the basis that the exception applied only to cases of what might be called actual fraud, that is to say deliberate and dishonest breaches of duty. The same is true of the celebrated passage in the advice of the Privy Council given by Lord Davey in *Burland v Earle* [1902] AC 83 at 93. However, derivative actions were permitted in *Alexander v Automatic Telephone Co* [1900] 2 Ch 56 and *Cook v Deeks* [1916] 1 AC 554, where allegations of fraud were rejected but the directors exercised their powers in a manner which conferred personal benefits on themselves at the expense of the company and the other shareholders.

19. In *Daniels v Daniels*, Templeman J held that a derivative action could be maintained against a director alleged to have negligently caused his company to sell to himself a valuable asset at a gross undervalue. He distinguished *Pavlides v Jensen* [1956] Ch 565 where a derivative claim alleging that directors had been guilty of negligence in selling a valuable asset at a gross undervalue to third parties was struck out as not coming within the exception to the rule in *Foss v Harbottle*. The distinction lay in the fact that the alleged negligence in *Daniels v Daniels*, if proved, resulted not only in harm to the company but personal benefit for the directors. The principle which Templeman J derived from the authorities was that:

'... a minority shareholder who has no other remedy may sue where directors use their powers, intentionally or unintentionally, fraudulently or negligently, in a manner which benefits themselves at the expense of the company.' (p.414D)

20. In reviewing the authorities in its Consultation Paper on Shareholder Remedies (Consultation Paper No 142, 1996), the Law Commission stated in para 4.9 that in this context fraud means fraud in 'the wider equitable sense of that term' (citing *Estmanco (Kilner House) Ltd v Greater London Council* [1982] 1 WLR 2 at 12) and, citing from Lord Davey's judgment in *Burland v Earle*, continued:

'Essentially, the term encompasses situations such as...where the majority are endeavouring directly or indirectly to appropriate to themselves money, property or advantages which belong to the company or in which other shareholders are entitled to participate...'

At para 4.11, the Law Commission stated:

'"Fraud" does not, however, cover the situation where the wrongdoers do not themselves benefit. Thus it does not include mere negligence on the part of the directors, so that a derivative action cannot be brought against directors who mismanage a company and cause it loss, even if they have control.'

21. An authority which may be said to extend the boundaries of the 'fraud' exception is the decision of Sir Robert Megarry V-C in *Estmanco*, referred to above. In that case, the GLC had formed the plaintiff company to regulate the management of a block of 60 flats being sold off to owner-occupiers, each of whom acquired one of the 60 shares in the company when the sale of a flat was completed. The GLC covenanted with the company to use its best endeavours to sell all the flats. Control of the GLC changed after the sale of 12 flats and, as a result of a change in

housing policy, the sale of the further flats, many of which had been agreed subject to contract, was halted and the flats were used to house disadvantaged families. The GLC had complete voting control of the company because, under the terms of its articles of association, the shares held by flat owners acquired voting rights only once all the flats had been sold. The three directors of the company who were all employees of the GLC took the view that the company ought to seek to enforce the contractual obligations of the GLC and acting on that view caused the company to issue proceedings. At a subsequent general meeting of the company, the GLC as the only member entitled to vote passed a resolution instructing the directors to withdraw the action. A flat-owner and member of the company applied for an order that she be substituted as plaintiff and that the action be permitted to continue in her name as a derivative action.

22. An unusual feature of the case was that the company was a non-profit making, non-trading company. Issues of financial benefit or loss to the shareholders could not arise, and as Sir Robert Megarry observed at p.13, the test of what was for the benefit of the company could not be a simple test of financial benefit for the company. Nonetheless, the evidence before the court satisfied the judge that the new policy of the GLC, and its decision to prevent the enforcement of the covenants given in favour of the company, involved the GLC and, it may be said, the company 'in depriving the purchasers of flats of their rights as shareholders, and in destroying the scheme under which they were induced to buy their flats' (page 15). Sir Robert Megarry concluded that the circumstances of the case brought it within the exception to the rule in *Foss v Harbottle*:

> 'There can be no doubt about the 12 voteless purchasers being a minority; there can be no doubt about the advantage to the council of having the action discontinued; there can be no doubt about the injury to the applicant and the rest of the minority, both as shareholders and as purchasers, of that discontinuance; and I feel little doubt that the council has used its voting power not in order to promote the best interests of the company but in order to bring advantage to itself and disadvantage to the minority. Furthermore, that disadvantage is no trivial matter, but represents a radical alteration in the basis on which the council sold the flats to the minority.'

The judge appreciated the difference between the minority's rights as shareholders and their rights as purchasers of flats but he considered, first, that the injury to the rights as shareholders sufficed in itself and, secondly, that their rights as shareholders formed such an integral part of the scheme as a whole as to make it unreal to consider those rights independently of their rights as purchasers: see p.16B.

23. *Estmanco* is not a case of financial gain to the majority and financial loss to the company and the minority members. It is, however, a case, and in his judgment Sir Robert Megarry V-C analysed it as being a case, in which the majority exercised their control of the company to advance their own interests as the local authority and, as a necessary result, to injure the interests of the company and its other members.

24. It is therefore the case that all the authorities on direct derivative actions have taken as a requirement that the alleged wrongdoing should result in a loss to the company and, hence, an indirect or reflective loss to the shareholders and also that the alleged wrongdoers should have personally gained from their breaches of duty. The same approach has been taken in double derivative actions. In all the cases of which I am aware, the alleged breach of duty by directors of the subsidiary has resulted in loss not only to the subsidiary but also to the holding company and therefore, indirectly, to the shareholders in the holding company. See, for example, the facts in *Universal Project Management Services Ltd v Fort Gilkicker Ltd* **[13.21]**, especially at [12]–[13]. This aspect was specifically addressed by Lord Millett in *Waddington Ltd v Chan Chun Hoo Thomas* at [74]–[75]:

> '[74] As I have said, the question is simply a question of the plaintiff's standing to sue. This would have been obvious when the procedure was for the proposed plaintiff to apply to the court for leave to use the company's name. On a question of standing, the court must ask itself whether the plaintiff has a legitimate interest in the relief claimed sufficient to justify

him in bringing proceedings to obtain it. The answer in the case of person wishing to bring a multiple derivative action is plainly "Yes". Any depletion of a subsidiary's assets causes indirect loss to its parent company and its shareholders. In either case the loss is merely reflective loss mirroring the loss directly sustained by the subsidiary and as such it is not recoverable by the parent company or its shareholders for the reasons stated in *Johnson v Gore Wood & Co* [2001] 1 BCLC 313, [2002] 2 AC 1. But this is a matter of legal policy. It is not because the law does not recognise the loss as a real loss; it is because if creditors are not to be prejudiced the loss must be recouped by the subsidiary and not recovered by its shareholders. It is impossible to understand how a person who has sustained a real, albeit reflective, loss which is legally recoverable only by a subsidiary can be said to have no legitimate or sufficient interest to bring proceedings on behalf of the subsidiary.

[75] This is not to allow economic interests to prevail over legal rights. The reflective loss which a shareholder suffers if the assets of his company are depleted is recognised by the law even if it is not directly recoverable by him. In the same way the reflective loss which a shareholder suffers if the assets of his company's subsidiary are depleted is recognised loss even if it is not directly recoverable by him. The very same reasons which justify the single derivative action also justify the multiple derivative action. To put the same point another way, if wrongdoers must not be allowed to defraud a parent company with impunity, they must not be allowed to defraud its subsidiary with impunity.'

25. It follows, on the authorities as they stand, that financial or other loss to the shareholders, albeit normally of a reflective character, is essential to give a claimant shareholder sufficient interest in the proceedings to make the shareholder an appropriate claimant on behalf of the company, whether he is a member of that company or of its holding company. Equally, the authorities require that, in the absence of actual fraud or an ultra vires act, the wrongdoers should themselves have benefitted from the wrongdoing. The significance of this requirement is that their breach of duty cannot be ratified by a majority vote which depends on the votes of the wrongdoers. It is essential to the exception to the rule in *Foss v Harbottle* that the alleged wrongdoing is incapable of lawful ratification: see *Smith v Croft (No 2)* **[13.19]**.

26. Satisfaction of the requirement for the claimant to establish a prima facie case both that the company is entitled to the relief claimed and that the action falls within the proper boundaries of the exception to the rule in *Foss v Harbottle* does not automatically entitle the claimant to permission to commence or continue the action. The court exercises a discretion whether to grant permission and will have regard to all relevant factors. This is illustrated by the authorities which establish that a claimant who has been involved in the alleged wrongdoing or who seeks to bring the proceedings for an ulterior purpose will not be regarded as an appropriate claimant and will not be given permission: see *Nurcombe v Nurcombe* [1985] 1 WLR 370 at 376 per Lawton LJ, *Barrett v Duckett* [1995] 1 BCLC 243 at 250 per Peter Gibson LJ. Above all, it is illustrated by the requirement that a reasonable board of directors would consider it to be in the best interests of the company to pursue the proceedings. [He then embarked on a detailed discussion of the application of these rules to the facts in issue, and concluded that permission to continue the present proceedings as a derivative action should be refused.]

Personal claims by members

The sources of members' personal rights

All these pitfalls associated with derivative claims can be avoided if members can pursue *personal* remedies for any wrongs done to them. Much of the relevant substantive law on members' rights has been addressed in earlier chapters. But we have so far omitted two very important rights. The first is an enormously significant one: members have a statutory right to complain to court that the company's affairs are being conducted in a manner that is unfairly prejudicial to the member's interests (CA 2006 s 994). This provision is commonly known as the *'unfair prejudice'* section. The court then has wide powers to make orders as it sees fit if a claim of unfair prejudice is made out (s 996). The second right, now of less importance given the impact of the first, is that members may petition for the company to be wound up on the 'just and equitable' ground.

Putting all this together, and indicating where the relevant discussion can be found, members' claims for a personal remedy are generally based on wrongs committed in relation to:

(i)   The contractual rights derived from the *company's constitution* (CA 2006 s 33).[34] Recall the difficult learning on the nature of the statutory contract, including the distinction between 'insider' and 'outsider' rights. In addition, these claims are subject to the 'internal irregularity principle' imposed by *Foss v Harbottle*: see *Macdougall v Gardiner* **[13.24]** and *Pender v Lushington* **[13.23]**. These rights are relevant in the pursuit of claims concerning amendments to the constitution, variations of class rights, capital reductions, etc, at least to the extent that the shareholder is not simply relying on specific statutory rights given to dissenting minorities to complain.

(ii) The contractual rights derived from outside contracts, especially *shareholders' agreements*:[35] see especially *Southern Foundries (1926) Ltd v Shirlaw* **[6.04]**, *Read v Astoria Garage (Streatham) Ltd* **[6.05]** and *Russell v Northern Bank Ltd* **[4.35]**.

(iii) The *duties owed by directors* to members individually, in those rare cases where this can be asserted successfully:[36] see especially *Percival v Wright* **[7.05]**; *Peskin v Anderson* [2001] BCLC 874, CA; *Coleman v Myers* [1977] 2 NZLR 225.

(iv) The entitlements inherent in the 'unfair prejudice' section (CA 2006 s 994).[37] This section provides a procedural mechanism for a member to raise a wide variety of complaints, including those noted in points (i)–(iii), although the court cannot give a remedy unless the 'unfair prejudice' basis is also established. But this section also permits shareholders to complain of, and obtain legal remedies for, acts and omissions that do not of themselves constitute legal wrongs.

(v)   The entitlements inherent in the 'just and equitable' winding-up provisions (IA 1986 s 122(1)(g)).[38]

The procedural form of members' personal claims

Two types of proceedings may be brought by shareholders to enforce *personal* rights, although note that these need to be distinguished from the derivative claims discussed earlier, which were to enforce the *company's* rights:

(i)   A member may sue alone to enforce some personal or individual right: for instance, in *Pender v Lushington* **[13.23]** the right to have a vote recorded or a proxy recognised. *Rayfield v Hands* **[4.39]** shows that the company is not a necessary party to

---

[34] See 'Members' personal rights', pp 261ff. See too CLR, *Completing the Framework*, paras 5.64–5.74; R Drury, 'The Relative Nature of a Shareholder's Right to Enforce the Company Contract' [1986] CLJ 219.

[35] See 'Shareholders' agreements', pp 256ff. See too E Ferran [1994] CLJ 343.

[36] See 'Duties to shareholders?', pp 338ff; and 'Offers to the public to purchase shares and remedies for misleading offers', pp 519ff.

[37] See 'Unfairly prejudicial conduct of the company's affairs', pp 715ff.

[38] These rules are discussed in detail in Chapter 16, along with the other winding-up rules: see 'Compulsory winding up on the "just and equitable" ground', pp 840ff.

such proceedings—unless, of course, it is claimed that the company is a party to the wrongdoing.

(ii) A member may sue alone, or with others, but in a *representative* capacity, claiming that a right has been infringed which, although affecting him as an individual member, also affects in a similar way either all or a number of the other members. Cases where a member has succeeded in a claim to have the directors observe the requirements of the Act or the constitution of the company itself are examples of this kind of action. This is a *representative action*.[39]

Establishing the member's personal right: personal and corporate claims can coexist

Sometimes it is very clear that the member has a personal right. But not all wrongs that a member complains of will be exclusively one thing or the other: an unconstitutional act by those in control may violate *both* shareholder's individual membership rights *and* those of the company, as has been recognised on many occasions: see, eg *Pulbrook v Richmond Consolidated Mining Co* [6.01] and *Pender v Lushington* [13.23].

It ought to be possible in such cases for an action to be brought in the name of either the member or the company (for different remedies), but unfortunately the courts have not always appreciated this. We find them giving an individual complainant short shrift and showing him the door of the court on the basis of a somewhat peremptory ruling that the wrong person has been named as plaintiff.[40] For example, see *Lee v Chou Wen Hsien* (Question 3 following *Pender v Lushington* [13.23], p 704); and contrast the views of Hoffmann J in *Re a Company* (Note 2 in Further notes following *Pender v Lushington* [13.23], p 703) with those expressed in *Bamford v Bamford* [1970] Ch 212 (see Note 1 in Further notes following *Pender v Lushington* [13.23], p 704). This sometimes seems to provide further proof of a *de facto* policy to discourage minority members from engaging in litigation. Added to this, there is the modern rule on '*reflective loss*', which aims to ensure that if both forms of action are possible, there is no chance of double recovery for the same loss (see 'The "no reflective loss" principle', pp 706ff).

An individual member whose personal rights have been infringed may pursue a personal claim even when the conduct complained of also constitutes a wrong to the company itself.

[13.23] Pender v Lushington (1877) 6 Ch D 70 (Chancery Division)

Pender had split his shareholding among nominees in order to defeat a provision in the articles that fixed the maximum number of votes to which any one shareholder was entitled. The chairman refused to accept the nominees' votes and accordingly declared lost a resolution proposed by Pender, which would otherwise have been carried. The Master of the Rolls granted Pender (who brought a representative action on behalf of himself and the

---

[39] This procedure allows one or more individuals to appear as claimants or defendants on behalf of a number of persons having an identical interest in the proceedings. It was developed by the courts of Chancery in the early nineteenth century especially to deal with the problems of large unincorporated associations. Now the procedural rules are found in CPR r 19.6 (Representation of parties with the same interest). It should be obvious that a *derivative* claim can be pursued by a shareholder acting in a *representative* capacity, so the two types of procedures may be in use at the same time.

[40] Although whether s 263(3)(f) will change this in favour of personal claims remains to be seen—see *Franbar Holdings Ltd v Patel* [13.13].

other shareholders, and also an action in the name of the company) an injunction restraining the directors from acting on the basis that the nominees' votes had been bad. He also held that Pender had a right to sue in the company's name, at least until a general meeting resolved otherwise,[41] and a further right to sue in his own name.

> JESSEL MR: But there is another ground [other than the claim in the company's name] on which the action may be maintained. This is an action by Mr Pender for himself. He is a member of the company, and whether he votes with the majority or the minority he is entitled to have his vote recorded—an individual right in respect of which he has a right to sue. That has nothing to do with the question like that raised in *Foss v Harbottle* and that line of cases. He has a right to say, 'Whether I vote in the majority or minority, you shall record my vote, as that is a right of property belonging to my interest in this company, and if you refuse to record my vote I will institute legal proceedings against you to compel you'. What is the answer to such an action? It seems to me it can be maintained as a matter of substance, and that there is no technical difficulty in maintaining it . . .

➤ Notes

1. The real problem in these cases is to determine whether a member *does* have a personal right, and one that can be pursued despite the 'irregularity principle' in *Foss v Harbottle*: see *Macdougall v Gardiner* **[13.24]**, which is difficult to reconcile with *Pender v Lushington*.

2. Personal rights do arise under some basic constitutional provisions, such as the right to vote or to exercise a pre-emptive power over a retiring member's share, and *Edwards v Halliwell* [1950] 2 All ER 1064, CA, illustrates the right in operation in a trade union context, protecting a member against having his dues raised without proper procedure and from unjustifiable expulsion. But all these 'constitutional' rights have an element of property linked with them, so it is easier to understand the readiness of the courts to come to the aid of a victimised member.

3. Where the complaint is about a mere matter of procedure, the courts seem much less willing to recognise a 'right to have the company observe the terms of its own constitution' which an individual member might invoke to claim standing to sue. One difficulty about such a supposed right is that it is balanced by an obligation to abide by majority decisions (see *Smith v Croft (No 2)* **[13.19]**). Another is that there are some constitutional irregularities which members may waive by a majority vote, or even, on the reasoning of *MacDougall v Gardiner* **[13.24]**, simply acquiesce in. Certainly, *obiter dicta* in cases such as *Re HR Harmer Ltd* [1959] 1 WLR 62, CA (see Note following *Scottish Co-operative Wholesale Society Ltd v Meyer* **[13.31]**, p 732), to the effect that members have a right to have their company conduct its affairs in accordance with its articles cannot be understood to apply without some such qualification.

4. Another difficulty concerns rights purportedly conferred on members by the company's articles, but not in their character as members. Cases like *Eley v Positive Life Assurance Co* **[4.37]** are accepted as laying down a rule that 'outsider rights' are not enforceable on a contractual basis by the member against the company. Nor can this rule be avoided simply by bringing an action as a 'member' to compel the company to comply with its 'constitutional obligations' to recognise the right. But the distinction between 'insider'

---

[41] The analysis is not persuasive, however, and in the light of the comments in the Notes following *Franbar Holdings Ltd v Patel* **[13.13]**, p 687, seems of doubtful authority.

and 'outsider' rights is not always clear. In *Pulbrook v Richmond Consolidated Mining Co* **[6.01]**, a director who had been excluded from board meetings was held to have suffered an individual wrong, and held able to sue in his own name; also see *Quin and Axtens Ltd v Salmon* **[4.06]**.

5. Of course, if the member *waives* the personal right, then there can be no complaint later on, even if it becomes apparent that the waiver was unwise. For example, in *Euro Brokers Holdings Ltd v Monecor (London) Ltd* [2003] EWCA Civ 105, special decision-making procedures were set out in a shareholders' agreement specifically to protect the interests of certain members. All the members nevertheless took a decision, unanimously, without following the special procedures. The decision was held valid. The key point in this case, however, was that the decision attracted the support of all members at the time, and the court therefore held that it should not be subsequently reviewable on the basis of non-compliance with some specified procedure. In *Edwards v Halliwell* [1950] 2 All ER 1064, CA, situations, it is precisely the lack of agreement to waive the special procedural requirements on the part of those protected by such requirements which gives rise to the arguments about personal rights and exceptions to the rule in *Foss v Harbottle*.

➤ Questions

1. In *Pender v Lushington* **[13.23]**, if a general meeting had been called and had voted against continuing the action, what would have happened to Pender's personal and derivative claims?

2. In *Devlin v Slough Estates Ltd* [1983] BCLC 497 a member sought a declaration that the directors had acted in breach of duty. He alleged that they had prepared accounts which failed to conform with the requirements of the Companies Acts, and also that they had failed to distribute accounts properly prepared in accordance with the Acts to the members in advance of the annual general meeting as required by the company's articles. Dillon J held that Devlin did not have standing to bring either a derivative action on the company's behalf or an action in his own right complaining that his personal rights as a member had been infringed. How, if at all, can Dillon J's decision be reconciled with *Edwards v Halliwell*, *Pender v Lushington* and the previous Note?

3. In *Lee v Chou Wen Hsien* [1984] 1 WLR 1202, the plaintiff sued in his own name complaining that he had been improperly removed as a director by his fellow directors, who had purportedly acted under a power conferred by the articles. The Privy Council took the view that if a wrong had been done, it was done to the *company*, and that the rule in *Foss v Harbottle* precluded any action by the director in his own name. Do you agree?

➤ Further notes

This area is difficult, and the cases are not easy to reconcile. Yet, if members are to pursue personal claims, then it is essential to know whether the wrong in question is one which has been done to the company or to the member personally, since in the latter circumstances the member, being the proper claimant, is able to sue, subject only to the 'internal management' and 'irregularity' principles (see 'The old common law rule in *Foss v Harbottle*', pp 669ff). The following examples further illustrate the courts' approach.

1. In *Bamford v Bamford* [1970] Ch 212 (for the facts and another part of the decision, see **[4.33]**), Russell LJ held that:

> The harm done by the assumed improperly motivated allotment is a harm done to the company, of which only the company can complain. It would be for the company by ordinary resolution to decide whether or not to proceed against the directors for compensation for misfeasance.

2. By contrast, in *Re a Company* [1987] BCLC 82, at 84, Hoffmann J said:

> Although the alleged breach of fiduciary duty by the board is in theory a breach of its duty to the company, the wrong to the company is not the substance of the complaint. The company is not particularly concerned with who its shareholders are. The true basis of the action is an alleged infringement of the petitioner's individual rights as a shareholder. The allotment is alleged to be an improper and unlawful exercise of the powers granted to the board by the articles of association, which constitute a contract between the company and its members. These are fiduciary powers, not to be exercised for an improper purpose, and it is generally speaking improper 'for the directors to use their fiduciary powers over the shares in the company purely for the purpose of destroying an existing majority, or creating a new majority which did not previously exist'. (See *Howard Smith Ltd v Ampol Petroleum Ltd* **[7.09]**.) An abuse of these powers is an infringement of a member's contractual rights under the articles.

3. Similarly, in *Residues Treatment and Trading Co Ltd v Southern Resources Ltd (No 4)* (1988) 14 ACLR 569, the Supreme Court of South Australia held that an action to challenge an allotment of shares on the ground that the directors had acted for an improper purpose came within the 'personal rights' exception to the rule in *Foss v Harbottle* **[13.01]** (as well as being a breach of duty to the company for which the company itself could have sued), since such an allotment brought about an impermissible dilution of the plaintiff member's voting rights. King CJ said, at 575:

> A member's voting rights and the rights of participation which they provide in the decision-making of the company are a fundamental attribute of membership and are rights which the member should be able to protect by legal action against improper diminution.

(He also expressed doubts whether *Bamford v Bamford*, Note 1, was correct in treating such an act on the part of the directors as ratifiable by the members, but it is suggested that *Bamford v Bamford* may be defended on this point.)

4. Finally, in *MacDougall v Gardiner* (1875) 10 Ch App 606, the member had an undoubted personal right under the articles, but the Court of Appeal nevertheless held that it had no jurisdiction to cure the improper denial of the member's right to call for a poll, since this was an irregularity which could be cured by the majority. James LJ drew attention to the good sense that lies behind the normal constitutional provisions which allow a meeting to be requisitioned, or conducted in a particular manner, only when a significant percentage of supporters can be mustered. (But contrast *Pender v Lushington* **[13.23]**.)

➤ Questions

1. Given the comments in Note 1 of the previous Further notes, was Russell LJ right to say that the harm done by an improperly motivated allotment was a harm to the company of which only the company could complain? Are these various views reconcilable?

2. Is it of any concern to a company who has control of it?

Can the member's personal right be enforced?

The 'irregularity principle'.

[13.24] MacDougall v Gardiner (1875) 1 Ch D 13 (Court of Appeal)

Gardiner, the chairman of the Emma Silver Mining Co, had adjourned a general meeting of the company without acceding to the request of a shareholder, MacDougall, and others, that a poll be held on the question of the adjournment. MacDougall now claimed a declaration that the chairman's action was improper, and an injunction restraining the directors from taking further action. The Court of Appeal held that this was a matter of internal management in which it should not interfere.

MELLISH LJ: In my opinion, if the thing complained of is a thing which in substance the majority of the company are entitled to do, or if something has been done irregularly which the majority of the company are entitled to do regularly, or if something has been done illegally which the majority of the company are entitled to do legally, there can be no use in having a litigation about it, the ultimate end of which is only that a meeting has to be called, and then ultimately the majority gets its wishes. Is it not better that the rule should be adhered to that if it is a thing which the majority are the masters of, the majority in substance shall be entitled to have their will followed? If it is a matter of that nature, it only comes to this, that the majority are the only persons who can complain that a thing which they are entitled to do has been done irregularly; and that, as I understand it, is what has been decided by the cases of *Mozley v Alston* (1847) 1 Ph 790 (Ch) and *Foss v Harbottle* **[13.01]**. In my opinion that is the rule that is to be maintained. Of course if the majority are abusing their powers, and are depriving the minority of their rights, that is an entirely different thing, and there the minority are entitled to come before this court to maintain their rights; but if what is complained of is simply that something which the majority are entitled to do has been done or undone irregularly, then I think it is quite right that nobody should have a right to set that aside, or to institute a suit in Chancery about it, except the company itself.

➤ Note

For a comment on this case, and a suggested reconciliation with the apparently contrary ruling in *Pender v Lushington* **[13.23]**, see C Baxter, 'Irregular Company Meetings' [1976] JBL 323, and the same author's 'The Role of the Judge in Enforcing Shareholder Rights' [1983] CLJ 96. His view is that 'the court will not interfere in the affairs of a company unless it is necessary to do so and that interference is always unnecessary when it has no practical consequence'. In the context of irregularities in company meetings, references to *Foss v Harbottle* are often gratuitous and irrelevant.

➤ Questions

1. The company's articles of association gave any five or more members the right to demand a poll, and MacDougall had the necessary support. Was there not a wrong done here to MacDougall, a denial of his rights as a member? If so, how do you think he might have enforced them?

2. Is the *ratio decidendi* of this case the same as that of the court in *Foss v Harbottle*?

The 'no reflective loss' principle

The 'no reflective loss' principle ensures that a defendant can be sued only once for the same loss, and, in ensuring that, prioritises the company's claim as a matter of principle, and disallows the member's claim. This is regardless of the type of claim (common law or equity), or the form of remedy (compensation or restitution), or the status of the member (majority or minority): the principle prevents a person other than the company suing for the loss even when the person has a cause of action against the defendant, and even if the cause of action is different from the company's.

A member has no right to sue in a personal capacity where the loss merely reflects the loss suffered by the company (the 'no reflective loss' principle).

[13.25] Prudential Assurance Co Ltd v Newman Industries Ltd (No 2) [1982] Ch 204 (Court of Appeal)

The plaintiff, a large institutional investor, held 3% of the shares in Newman. It brought an action against Bartlett and Laughton, two directors of Newman who, the plaintiff alleged, had defrauded Newman of over £400,000. These directors did not have a majority of the shares in Newman and so did not formally have 'control' of it. The transaction by which Newman had been allegedly defrauded had been approved by the shareholders in general meeting, but it was claimed that the shareholders had been misled into doing so. The plaintiff sought declaratory relief and damages on three grounds: (i) its own personal cause of action against the defendants (of interest here); (ii) its derivative claim against the defendants on behalf of Newman; and (iii) its representative claim on behalf of Newman shareholders. Vinelott J, after hearing all the evidence, found the case proved and held that there had been a 'fraud' by those in 'control' (in the sense that the wrongdoers had *de facto* control). The Court of Appeal allowed the appeal in part, and expressed the view that the plaintiff should not have been allowed to bring a derivative suit. Here, the Court of Appeal expressed the view that the plaintiff's claim in its own right was 'misconceived'.

[The judgment of the Court of Appeal (CUMMING-BRUCE, TEMPLEMAN and BRIGHTMAN LJJ) included the following:] In our judgment the personal claim is misconceived. It is of course correct, as the judge found and Mr. Bartlett did not dispute, that he and Mr. Laughton . . . owed the shareholders a duty to give . . . advice in good faith and not fraudulently. It is also correct that if directors convene a meeting on the basis of a fraudulent circular, a shareholder will have a right of action to recover any loss which he has been personally caused in consequence of the fraudulent circular; this might include the expense of attending the meeting. But what he cannot do is to recover damages merely because the company in which he is interested has suffered damage. He cannot recover a sum equal to the diminution in the market value of his shares, or equal to the likely diminution in dividend, because such a 'loss' is merely a reflection of the loss suffered by the company. The shareholder does not suffer any personal loss. His only 'loss' is through the company, in the diminution in the value of the net assets of the company, in which he has (say) a 3 per cent. shareholding. The plaintiff's shares are merely a right of participation in the company on the terms of the articles of association . . .

Counsel for the plaintiffs sought to answer this objection by agreeing that there cannot be double recovery from the defendants, but suggesting that the personal action will lie if the company's remedy is for some reason not pursued. But how can the failure of the company to pursue its remedy against the robber entitle the shareholder to recover for himself? What happens if the robbery takes place in year 1, the shareholder sues in year 2, and the company makes up its mind in year 3 to pursue its remedy? Is the shareholder's action stayed, if still on foot? Supposing judgment has already been recovered by the shareholder and satisfied, what then?

A personal action could have the most unexpected consequences . . .

The plaintiffs in this action were never concerned to recover in the personal action. The plaintiffs were only interested in the personal action as a means of circumventing the rule in *Foss v. Harbottle*. The plaintiffs succeeded. A personal action would subvert the rule in *Foss v. Harbottle* and that rule is not merely a tiresome procedural obstacle placed in the path of a shareholder by a legalistic judiciary. The rule is the consequence of the fact that a corporation is a separate legal entity. Other consequences are limited liability and limited rights. The company is liable for its contracts and torts; the shareholder has no such liability. The company acquires causes of action for breaches of contract and for torts which damage the company. No cause of action vests in the shareholder. When the shareholder acquires a share he accepts the fact that the value of his investment follows the fortunes of the company and that he can only exercise his influence over the fortunes of the company by the exercise of his voting rights in general meeting. The law confers on him the right to ensure that the company observes the limitations of its memorandum of association and the right to ensure that other shareholders observe the rule, imposed upon them by the articles of association. If it is right that the law has conferred or should in certain restricted circumstances confer further rights on a shareholder the scope and consequences of such further rights require careful consideration. In this case it is neither necessary nor desirable to draw any general conclusions . . .

The 'no reflective loss' principle.

[13.26] Johnson v Gore Wood and Co [2002] 2 AC 1 (House of Lords)

A company, WWH, commenced proceedings against a firm of solicitors, GW, for professional negligence related to the exercise of an option to purchase land. That claim was eventually settled. Subsequently, Johnson, a majority member in the company, commenced proceedings against the same firm for personal losses sustained which arose out of the same circumstances. It was argued by the firm that Johnson could not recover his own personal losses as these were essentially the same as the losses sustained by the company. The House of Lords explained the relevant legal rules.

LORD BINGHAM: . . . GW's first argument before the House . . . was in principle very simple. It was that this damage, if suffered at all, had been suffered by WWH, and Mr Johnson, being for this purpose no more than a shareholder in the company, could not sue to recover its loss. As the Court of Appeal pointed out in *Prudential Assurance Co Ltd v Newman Industries Ltd (No 2)* **[13.25]**, 210:

'A derivative action is an exception to the elementary principle that A cannot, as a general rule, bring an action against B to recover damages or secure other relief on behalf of C for an injury done by B to C. C is the proper plaintiff because C is the party injured, and, therefore, the person in whom the cause of action is vested.' . . .

Mr Johnson's response was equally simple. It was accepted, for purposes of the application to strike out the damages claim, that GW owed a duty to him personally and was in breach of that duty. Therefore, subject to showing that the damage complained of was caused by GW's breach of duty and was not too remote . . . he was entitled in principle to recover any damage which he had himself suffered as a personal loss separate and distinct from any loss suffered by the company.

[The authorities we were referred to] support the following propositions:

(1) Where a company suffers loss caused by a breach of duty owed to it, only the company may sue in respect of that loss. No action lies at the suit of a shareholder suing in that capacity and no other[42] to make good a diminution in the value of the shareholder's shareholding where that merely reflects the loss suffered by the company. A claim will not lie by a shareholder to make good a loss which would be made good if the company's assets were replenished through action against the party responsible for the loss, even if the company, acting through its constitutional organs, has declined or failed to make good that loss. So much is clear from *Prudential Assurance Co Ltd v Newman Industries (No 2)* **[13.25]** . . .

(2) Where a company suffers loss but has no cause of action to sue to recover that loss, the shareholder in the company may sue in respect of it (if the shareholder has a cause of action to do so), even though the loss is a diminution in the value of the shareholding . . .

(3) Where a company suffers loss caused by a breach of duty to it, and a shareholder suffers a loss separate and distinct from that suffered by the company caused by breach of a duty independently owed to the shareholder, each may sue to recover the loss caused to it by breach of the duty owed to it but neither may recover loss caused to the other by breach of the duty owed to that other . . .

[It follows that the task of the court is to] ascertain whether the loss claimed . . . is one which would be made good if the company had enforced its full rights against the party responsible, and whether (to use the language of *Prudential Assurance Co Ltd v Newman Industries (No 2)* . . . the loss claimed is 'merely a reflection of the loss suffered by the company'. In some cases the answer will be clear, as where the shareholder claims the loss of dividend or a diminution in the value of a shareholding attributable solely to depletion of the company's assets, or a loss unrelated to the business of the company. In other cases, inevitably, a finer judgment will be called for. . . . [Applying these principles to the facts, Lord Bingham held that, prima facie, the claim for sums which Mr Johnson, acting on GW's advice, invested in . . . companies and lost; the cost of personal borrowings made necessary because of other losses; the increased tax liability; and perhaps the diminution in value of his pension were all potentially recoverable; whereas the loss in value of his majority shareholding in WWH was merely a reflection of the company's loss and should be struck out.]

LORD MILLETT: . . . A company is a legal entity separate and distinct from its shareholders. It has its own assets and liabilities and its own creditors. The company's property belongs to the company and not to its shareholders . . . If the company has a cause of action, this represents a legal chose in action which represents part of its assets. Accordingly, where a company suffers loss as a result of an actionable wrong owed to it, the cause of action is vested in the company and the company alone can sue. No action lies at the suit of a shareholder suing as such, though exceptionally he may be permitted to bring a derivative action in right of the company and recover damages on its behalf: see *Prudential Assurance Co Ltd v Newman Industries Ltd (No 2)*. Correspondingly, of course, a company's shares are the property of the shareholder and not the company, and if he suffers loss as a result of an actionable wrong done to him, then prima facie he alone can sue and the company cannot. On the other hand, although a share is an identifiable piece of property which belongs to the shareholder and has an ascertainable value, it also represents a proportionate part of the company's met assets, and if these are depleted the diminution in its assets will be reflected in the diminution in the value of the shares. The correspondence may not be exact, especially in the case of a company whose shares are publicly traded, since their value depends on market sentiment. But in the case of a small private company like this company, the correspondence is exact.

---

[42] Ie suing personally or in a representative capacity, but not pursuing a derivative claim.

This causes no difficulty where the company has a cause of action and the shareholder has none; or where the shareholder has a cause of action and the company has none . . . Where the company suffers loss as a result of a wrong to the shareholder but has no cause of action in respect of its loss, the shareholder can sue and recover damages for his own loss, whether of a capital or income nature, measured by the diminution in the value of his shareholding. He must, of course show that he has an independent cause of action of his own and that he has suffered personal loss caused by the defendant's actionable wrong. Since the company itself has no cause of action in respect of its loss, its assets are not depleted by the recovery of damages by the shareholder.

The position is, however, different where the company suffers loss caused by the breach of a duty owed both to the company and to the shareholder. In such a case the shareholder's loss, in so far as this is measured by the diminution in value of his shareholding or the loss of dividends, merely reflects the loss suffered by the company in respect of which the company has its own cause of action. If the shareholder is allowed to recover in respect of such loss, then either there will be double recovery at the expense of the defendant or the shareholder will recover at the expense of the company and its creditors and other shareholders. Neither course can be permitted. This is a matter of principle; there is no discretion involved. Justice to the defendant requires the exclusion of one claim or the other; protection of the interests of the company's creditors requires that it is the company which is allowed to recover to the exclusion of the shareholder. These principles have been established in a number of cases, though they have not always been faithfully observed . . .

[After discussing two cases he regarded as incorrectly decided, he continued:] I cannot accept this reasoning as representing the position in English law. It is of course correct that the diminution in the value of the plaintiff's shares was by definition a personal loss and not the company's loss, but that is not the point. The point is that it merely reflected the diminution of the company's assets. The test is not whether the company could have made a claim in respect of the loss in question; the question is whether, treating the company and the shareholder as one for this purpose, the shareholder's loss is franked by that of the company. If so, such reflected loss is recoverable by the company and not by the shareholders.

[One of the judges in the cases criticised] acknowledged that double recovery could not be permitted, but thought that the problem did not arise where the company had settled its claim. He considered that it would be sufficient to make an allowance for the amount paid to the liquidator. With respect, I cannot accept this either. As Hobhouse LJ observed in *Gerber Garment Technology Inc v Lectra Systems Ltd* [1997] RPC 443, 471, if the company chooses not to exercise its remedy, the loss to the shareholder is caused by the company's decision not to pursue its remedy and not by the defendant's wrongdoing. By a parity of reasoning, the same applies if the company settles for less than it might have done. Shareholders (and creditors) who are aggrieved by the liquidator's proposals are not without remedy; they can have recourse to the Companies Court, or sue the liquidator for negligence.

But there is more to it than causation. The disallowance of the shareholder's claim in respect of reflective loss is driven by policy considerations. In my opinion, these preclude the shareholder from going behind the settlement of the company's claim. If he were allowed to do so then, if the company's action were brought by its directors, they would be placed in a position where their interest conflicted with their duty; while if it were brought by the liquidator, it would make it difficult for him to settle the action and would effectively take the conduct of the litigation out of his hands. The present case is a fortiori; Mr Johnson cannot be permitted to challenge in one capacity the adequacy of the terms he agreed in another . . .

For the reasons given by Lord Bingham, I too would strike out Mr Johnson's claims to damages for mental distress and anxiety and aggravated damages. Accordingly, I would dismiss the cross-appeal while varying the order of the Court of Appeal in the manner proposed . . .

Despite the 'no reflective loss' principle, if a company is unable to pursue its own cause of action precisely because of the actions of the wrongdoer, a member may be able to recover all the personal losses arising out of the same wrongdoing.

[13.27] Giles v Rhind [2002] EWCA Civ 1428, [2003] Ch 618 (Court of Appeal)

G and R had been members in a company which became insolvent following the diversion by R of a contract to a third party, in contravention of a shareholders' agreement. The company discontinued its proceedings against R as a consequence of its insolvency, but G sought to pursue in his own right damages against R. G contended that his claims were not merely reflective of the company's loss. Accepting this argument, the Court of Appeal held G had a cause of action against R separate from that of the company. In any case, with regard to G's losses which reflected those of the company, G was entitled to proceed with his personal claim, as the company had been prevented from pursuing its own action as a result of R's wrongdoing. Hence, this case can be distinguished from *Johnson v Gore Wood*, where additional claims by a member in relation to reflective losses were barred where the company was in fact able to pursue its own action (and had pursued it to settlement).

WALLER LJ: . . . There are certain facts which distinguish our present case from *Johnson v Gore Wood & Co* **[13.26]**. First, *Johnson v Gore Wood & Co* was a case as emphasised by Lord Bingham and Lord Millett where Mr Johnson carried on his business through a small private company. His position was practically indistinguishable from that of his company. It was a case where the depletion in the value of the assets reflected in the diminution in the value of the shares was likely to correspond exactly (in the words of Lord Millett at 121B). Second, W Ltd had brought an action and compromised the same; indeed Johnson was the directing mind of the company when it agreed to the compromise. There is no reason to think that the company would not have recovered if it had chosen to do so precisely that value which would have reflected the diminution in value of the shares which Johnson was claiming. There was no question of W Ltd having been disabled from bringing the claim by the very wrongdoing which by contract the defendant had promised the plaintiff he would not carry out. Third, the action was tried on the assumption that the solicitors owed an independent duty to Johnson, but the nature of the case was such that it was not easy to assume such a totally independent duty. Fourth, it could not be argued ultimately that the loss of value was other than reflective of the company's loss despite the way the claim was pleaded. But, so far as the damage in relation to investment in shares in this case is concerned, Mr Giles' losses are not as it seems to me 'merely reflective'. The shares became valueless on his case because the company's business as a whole was destroyed. Obviously the value of his shares reflect to some extent the value of the assets of the company but in his case they also reflect what Lord Millett described as market sentiment or what would have been considered their value because of the potential which the business had. Fifth, it certainly is not in my view in reality a case where Mr Giles is seeking to recover as damages, damages which the company could have recovered. The company's claim for damages for breach of contract would have been of a quite different nature based on an assessment of profits lost by virtue of the confidential information being used to take the Netto contract. Mr Giles' loss relates to the fact that the business as a whole was totally destroyed. Indeed even if the company had recovered damages the Netto contract would never have been restored, the business would never have been the same and Mr Giles' share would inevitably have been devalued by Mr Rhind's activities. The value of the shares when Mr Rhind obtained £300,000 for them in 1993 reflected not only the assets of the company but the good prospects of the company into the future and that loss of value could not be recovered by SHF in any action that it might have brought. . . .

. . . [N]either Lord Bingham nor Lord Millett would I think argue with the following propositions. First that the principle which *Johnson v Gore Wood & Co* establishes will not in the words of Sir Christopher Slade in *Walker v Stones* [2000] 4 All ER 412 at 438:

> 'operate to deprive a claimant of an otherwise good cause of action in a case where (a) the claimant can establish that the defendant's conduct has constituted a breach of some legal duty owed to him personally (whether under the law of contract, torts, trusts or any other branch of the law) *and* (b) on its assessment of the facts, the court is satisfied that such breach of duty has caused him personal loss, separate and distinct from any loss that may have been occasioned to any corporate body in which he may be financially interested.'

Second (as they both recognised) if shareholders have a cause of action in relation to damage suffered by the company in which they hold the shares where that company does not have a cause of action, the shareholders may bring a claim even if in reality they are claiming damages reflective of the loss suffered by the company. The logic of that second exception ought to be based on the injustice of a wrongdoer being able to defeat a claim by suggesting that the loss being suffered was suffered by the company and is thus irrecoverable by the shareholder although the company does not or may not have a cause of action. But it is right to say that Lord Millett justifies that exception on the basis that 'since the company itself has no cause of action in respect of its loss, its assets are not depleted by the recovery of damages by the shareholder'. Thus Lord Millett appears to have in mind the concept that the cause of action which a company has (if it has) is one which enables the company to bring about full recovery. . . .

In my view there are two aspects of the case which Mr Giles seeks to bring which point to Mr Giles being entitled to pursue his claim for the loss of his investment. First, as it seems to me, part of that loss is not reflective at all. It is a personal loss which would have been suffered at least in some measure even if the company had pursued its claim for damages. Second, even in relation to that part of the claim for diminution which could be said to be reflective of the company's loss, since, if the company had no cause of action to recover that loss the shareholder could bring a claim, the same should be true of a situation in which the wrongdoer has disabled the company from pursuing that cause of action. I accept that on the language of Lord Millett's speech there are difficulties with this second proposition, but I am doubtful whether he intended to go so far as his literal words would take him. Furthermore it seems to me that on Lord Bingham's speech supported by the others, it would not be right to conclude that the second proposition is unarguable. . . .

In my judgment Mr Giles should be entitled to pursue his head of damage relating to his case that his shares became valueless as a result of the activities of Mr Rhind.

As regards his other heads of loss, again on the basis that Mr Rhind disabled the company from pursuing any claim for damages, I would suggest that Mr Giles should not be precluded from proceeding with those claims. In any event I do not see that the other heads are pure 'reflective loss'. If Mr Giles had not been a shareholder but simply an employee or a lender with an enforceable covenant in his favour, those losses surely would have been recoverable. The fact that he is also a shareholder should not deny him his claims under those other heads. . . .

CHADWICK LJ: . . .

The first issue: is this a case in which the no reflective loss principle should be applied?

The paradigm case in which, by reason of the wrong done to it, the company is unable, in practice, to pursue its claim against the wrongdoer is one in which the company is obliged to abandon its claim because the wrong has deprived it of the funds needed for that purpose. *Johnson v Gore Wood* was not such a case. . . . [Consider whether it is likely that the law is such that] a wrongdoer who, in breach of his contract with the company and its shareholders, 'steals' the whole of the company's business, with the intention that the company should be so denuded of funds that it cannot pursue its remedy against him, and who gives effect to that intention by an application for security for costs which his own breach of contract has made it impossible for the company to provide, is entitled to defeat a claim by the shareholders on the grounds that their claim is 'trumped' by the claim which his own conduct was calculated to prevent, and has in fact prevented, the company from pursuing. If that were, indeed, the law following the decision in *Johnson v Gore Wood*, I would not find it easy to reconcile the result with Lord Bingham's observation, at [2002] 2 AC 1, 36C–D, that 'the court must be astute to ensure that the party who has in fact suffered loss is not arbitrarily denied fair compensation'.

In my view the reasoning in *Johnson v Gore Wood* does not compel the conclusion that the law requires that result. . . .

I confess that I have found it difficult to reconcile the point which Lord Millett appears to be making in the sentence 'The test is not whether the company could have made a claim in respect of the loss in question; the question is whether, treating the company and the shareholder as one for this purpose, the shareholder's loss is franked by that of the company' with the second of Lord Bingham's propositions [see **[13.26]**] or with the decision in *Gerber*,[43] which Lord Millett did not criticise. [He then discussed the various difficulties in detail, concluding that the practical and policy need to ensure that the company could enter into binding settlements—relevant in *Johnson v Gore Wood*—was not relevant here. He continued:] If that is a correct analysis of that passage, then the passage presents no difficulty in the case where the company has not settled its claim, but has been forced to abandon it by reason of impecuniosity attributable to the wrong which has been done to it. In such a case the policy considerations to which Lord Millett referred are not engaged. And it is difficult to see any other consideration of policy which should lead to the conclusion that a shareholder or creditor who has suffered loss by reason of a wrong which, itself, has prevented the company from pursuing its remedy should be denied any remedy at all. . . .

For those reasons, I am satisfied that the decision in *Johnson v Gore Wood* does not compel the conclusion . . . that the no reflective loss principle is applicable. . . .

The second issue: is the loss of future benefits properly to be regarded as reflective of the company's loss?

The question turns on whether the loss which Mr Giles has suffered as a result of the termination of his employment by the receivers is reflective of loss suffered by the company by reason of the wrong done to it by Mr Rhind. In my view the judge was wrong to hold that it was. I think that he fell into error by confusing the loss claimed under this head with the circumstances which had given rise to that loss. There is a distinction to be drawn between the claim for accrued remuneration under the first head and the claim for loss of future benefits under the second head. In the first case, the loss suffered by Mr Giles as an employee is reflective of the company's own loss; if the company had been able to enforce its rights against Mr Rhind, it would have the funds needed to pay its debts. In the second case, the loss suffered by Mr Giles is not reflective of any loss suffered by the company; it flows from the termination of his employment following the destruction of the company's business. If the company had been able to enforce its rights against Mr Rhind, following the destruction of its business, the damages which the company might recover would not compensate Mr Giles for the loss which flows from the termination of his employment. I would allow the appeal, in relation to the second head of loss, on this ground also. . . .

► Notes

1. In *Humberclyde Finance Group Ltd v Hicks* [2001] All ER (D) 202 (Nov), the court held that the 'no reflective loss' principle from *Johnson v Gore Wood* did not infringe the European Convention on Human Rights, as embodied in the UK's Human Rights Act 1998.

---

[43] *Gerber Garment Technology Inc v Lectra Systems Ltd* [1997] RPC 443.

This conclusion was affirmed in *Bank Mellat v HM Treasury* [2015] EWHC 1258 (Comm), where it was held that the European Court of Human Rights recognised a restriction on the damages recoverable which was equivalent to the English 'no reflective loss' rule.

2. Both *Johnson v Gore Wood* **[13.26]** and *Giles v Rhind* **[13.27]** were considered in *Gardner v Parker* [2004] EWCA Civ 781: G, the assignee of the rights of action of B, a company, sought recovery for an alleged breach of fiduciary duty by P (the sole director of B) and S, a second company in which B held a minority of shares. G claimed that P had sold an asset of S at an undervalue, forcing S into administrative receivership. G argued that the 'no reflective loss' principle should not apply where: (i) the shareholder's claim concerned a breach of fiduciary duty; (ii) P's actions had prevented S from commencing legal proceedings to recover its losses from P; and (iii) the shareholder's claim was in the capacity of creditor. Dismissing the case, the Court of Appeal held that: (i) the 'no reflective loss' principle was applicable where breaches of fiduciary duty were concerned, as the principle governed recovery for particular kinds of loss and thus the cause of action and relief sought in any particular case was irrelevant; (ii) a lack of evidence prevented the conclusion being drawn that P's actions precluded S from seeking recovery; and (iii) applying *Johnson v Gore Wood*, no reason existed to disapply the 'no reflective loss' principle where the shareholder's claim as creditor was based on his position as an employee. All these cases do, however, emphasise the need for careful assessment of the facts to determine accurately whether the loss being pursued is indeed a 'reflected' loss.

3. In *Perry v Day* [2004] EWHC 3372 (Ch), P and D were both shareholders in a private company. P sought damages from D for breach of a shareholders' agreement which bound the shareholders, inter alia, to use their 'best endeavours to promote the interests and prospects of the company'. D had sold a parcel of land to the company, but as the consequence of a mistake, an important strip of land had been excluded from the conveyance. The mistake only became evident when the company tried to sell the land to a third party, and then D would only agree to transfer the excluded strip of land on payment of further consideration. The court upheld P's claim on the basis that: (i) D's demand for more money was a clear breach of his obligations under the shareholders' agreement; (ii) it was only D's demand for more money in exchange for the transfer of the strip that caused the relevant loss, as the loss caused by the defective sale itself could be repaired by D's agreement to transfer the strip; and (iii) though P's loss was reflective of the company's loss, and the company could have successfully brought a claim for rectification of the title, the company was precluded from doing this because of D's wrongdoing. By demanding the company surrender its claim on terms generous to D, D had breached his obligations, and this constituted a wrongdoing sufficient to bring the situation within the parameters of the *Giles v Rhind* exception to the no reflective loss principle upheld in *Johnson v Gore Wood*.

4. By contrast, in *International Leisure Ltd v First National Trustee Co Ltd* [2012] EWHC 1971 (Ch), Mr Edward Bartley Jones QC (sitting as a Deputy High Court Judge) refused the application of the 'reflective loss' principle where the secured debenture holder (secured creditor) of a company had suffered loss as a result of the receiver's breach of his duties. Drawing a distinction between the position of secured and unsecured creditors, the judge held that the primary duty of an administrative receiver was owed to the debenture holder (see 'Receivership generally', pp 822ff), so the secured creditor here had a primary entitlement to obtain and retain all damages awarded for the breaches of duty, whereas the unsecured creditor's prejudice arose only through the depletion of the assets of the company. The court was also persuaded by policy considerations, recognising that invoking the reflective loss principle would have the deleterious effect of denying the secured creditor his right to pursue his claims directly and under his own control.

Unfairly prejudicial conduct of the company's affairs

So far in this chapter the focus has been on maladministration that constitutes a legal wrong, either to the company itself or to its members. CA 2006 ss 994ff give the court, on the application of a member, a wide-ranging power to remedy conduct of a company's affairs that is 'unfairly prejudicial to the interests of members generally or to some part of its members'.[44] The most common complaint is that a controlling majority has acted in a manner that is 'unfairly prejudicial' (the meaning of this term is explored later). The most common remedy sought is an order that the majority purchase the minority's shares at a price that reflects their proportion of the company's value. This is despite s 996(1), which gives the court the power to make 'such order as it thinks fit', with s 996(2) merely providing examples of possible orders, including compulsory share purchases. Most of the cases concern 'quasi-partnerships', although the provision has general application.

➤ Note

By way of linking the previous section on derivative claims to this one on 'unfair prejudice', note Lewison J in *Iesini v Westrip Holdings Ltd* **[13.10]**:

> 81. In parallel with a derivative action, there was (and is) the possibility of bringing a petition for unfair prejudice. This procedure is now governed by section 994 of the Companies Act 2006. The relief which the court may give under section 996 is very wide-ranging ('such order as it thinks fit'); but the section specifically provides that the court may require the company to do an act that the petitioner has complained that it has omitted to do; or authorise civil proceedings to be brought in the name and on behalf of the company by such person or persons and on such terms as it may direct. If a petition is brought the court will decide (on the balance of probabilities) in the course of the petition whether the affairs of the company have been conducted in a manner unfairly prejudicial to the petitioner. It is only if the court has decided that they have that it will go on to consider the appropriate relief. It will be noted that section 260(1) contains a general definition of 'derivative claim' and section 260(2) envisages two different ways in which such a claim may be brought. One is 'under this Chapter', in which case the restriction on the permissible cause of action contained in section 260(3) applies ('A derivative claim *under this Chapter* may only be brought . . .'). The other is pursuant to an order made in proceedings under section 994, in which case the restrictions in section 260(3) do not apply. In that case, the general definition in section 260(1) is the only relevant definition of a derivative claim.
>
> 82. Accordingly it seems to me that where the petitioner's complaint is that the company has failed to assert a good claim against a third party the court's powers under section 996 would include the making of an order requiring the company to assert that claim, if necessary by taking or defending proceedings. Since the company's claim would be a claim against a third party, once the court had decided that a failure to assert that claim had unfairly prejudiced the petitioner, the directors would not need to be parties to the subsequent claim against the third party. In addition the width of the court's jurisdiction under section 996 enables the joinder of third parties to the petition itself, at least where relief is claimed against them: *Re Little Olympian Each-Ways Ltd* [1994] 2 BCLC 420; *Lowe v Fahey* [1996] 1 BCLC 262.

---

[44] See the parallel provision applying to the acts and omissions of the administrator, which can be invoked by creditors as well as shareholders: IA 1986 Sch B1, para 74. This substitutes the word 'harm' for 'prejudice' (it is not clear whether this was intended to have substantive implications) and specifically allows for complaints that the administrator is not performing his functions 'as quickly or as efficiently as is reasonably practicable'.

> 83. On the other hand, it may be that the company's cause of action is a cause of action only against the directors for loss suffered as a result of their default or breach of duty (etc.). In such a case the directors will be necessary parties to the company's claim. It may be, therefore, that different procedural routes will be adopted depending on the company's underlying claim.

The pros and cons of CA 2006 s 994 claims

CA 2006 s 994 repeats CA 1985 s 459, so the doctrinal and practical learning on the earlier provision remains relevant. Indeed, some of the cases on the initial provision (Companies Act 1948 (CA 1948) s 210), which provided remedies for 'oppression' rather than unfair prejudice, are still considered influential.

CA 1985 s 459 was a popular provision, not least because the courts adopted a purposive approach and interpreted the section liberally where necessary in order not to stultify its development. Moreover, by its very terms the section clearly aimed to address management problems ranging well beyond traditional legal wrongs done to a company or its shareholders. But this popularity created problems of its own. The courts were required to handle large numbers of cases, each often demanding the hearing of a great deal of evidence and examination of the conduct of the parties, sometimes going back over many years. This caused costs to escalate, even though most cases concerned relatively small companies, where costs of full High Court hearings are discouraging, if not entirely prohibitive.[45]

In the light of these factors, there were frequent calls for reform (not least from the judges themselves). Both the Law Commissions and the CLR examined CA 1985 s 459 and proposed possible reforms.[46] The Law Commissions recommended that the excessive length and cost of many CA 1985 s 459 proceedings should be dealt with primarily by active case management by the courts. This happened. They also recommended encouraging the use of alternative dispute resolution procedures. Their other recommendations (not so far adopted) included:

(i)   making legislative provision for a statutory buy-out remedy (at a price reckoned on a pro rata and not a discounted basis) where a member of a private company with a shareholding of at least 10% has been excluded from participation in management, coupled with a presumption in such cases that the expulsion was unfairly prejudicial. Since research shows that the most common s 459 application is made in this kind of case, and that a buy-out is invariably ordered if the claimant is successful, it seems likely that a rule along these lines would lead to many cases being settled out of court;

(ii)   providing a time limit for bringing s 459 claims, to stop so much past history being put before the court;

---

[45] One unreported case (*Re Freudiana Music Co Ltd* (Ch, 24 March 1993)) lasted for 165 full court days, with the respondent awarded *costs* of £2 million. In *Re Elgindata Ltd* [13.29], costs totalling £320,000 were run up in a dispute over shares worth less than £25,000: see [1993] BCLC 119. The judgment of Arden J in *Re Macro (Ipswich) Ltd* [13.30] reviews the history of the company over a period of nearly 50 years and extends to 56 pages. In *Re Unisoft Group Ltd (No 3)* [1994] 1 BCLC 609 at 611, Harman J said: 'Petitions under s 459 have become notorious to judges of this court—and also to the Bar—for their length, their unpredictability of management, and the enormous and appalling costs which are incurred upon them.'

[46] See Law Commission, *Shareholder Remedies* (LCCP No 142, 1996), pp 55–102; and *Shareholder Remedies* (Law Com No 246, 1997), Pts 2–4 (for reform proposals); CLR, *Developing the Framework* (2000), paras 4.100–4.111; *Completing the Structure* (2000), paras 5.75–5.81, and *Final Report I* (2001), paras 7.41–7.45. Also see C Riley, 'Contracting Out of Company Law: Section 459 of the Companies Act 1985 and the Role of the Courts' (1992) 55 MLR 782.

(iii) adding a winding-up remedy to the remedies available under s 459 (but also providing that an application to seek this remedy should require the leave of the court);[47]

(iv) prohibiting advertisement (ie publicity) of s 459 proceedings, unless the court orders otherwise; and

(v) encouraging the use of 'shareholder's exit' articles in the constitutions of private companies (ie articles which settle in advance the terms on which members will leave the company in the event of future disputes), and providing such an article in the Model Articles for private companies.

The CLR gave these suggestions a cool reception, and expressly opposed recommendations (i) and (iii). It did, however, put forward one suggestion which features in the law of some other countries, but would be a novelty here: that is, that s 459 should apply not only to the abuse of power by a majority, but also to cases where a *minority* exercises its powers to block company decisions—for example, where it improperly prevents the passing of a special resolution which is demonstrably in the best interests of the company. As matters have emerged, CA 2006 has not taken up any of these suggestions, and CA 2006 s 994 adopts precisely the same form as CA 1985 s 459.

Although an enormous number of decisions are reported every year, not many repay prolonged study. Since the remedy is at the court's discretion, and depends upon the facts, there is often a lengthy account of all the evidence given in the case, but little chance of finding statements of principle of any significance. Included here are extracts from the few leading cases, and from a further selection of illustrative cases.

Basic principles: comprehensive overview

A very large number of cases have been reported under CA 1985 s 459 (the predecessor to CA 2006 s 994). However (no doubt out of a concern to save costs), many of them are rulings on preliminary points of law or on applications to strike out the proceedings, dealing with isolated issues, so that it is possible to identify the principles which are emerging only after fairly wide reading of the reports. But certain points as summarised in the following sections are now regarded as reasonably well settled. These principles can be assumed also to apply in full to CA 2006 s 994, since the wording is identical.

Who may apply

CA 2006 s 994 allows applications to court from:

(i) a member (s 994(1), as defined in CA 2006 s 112[48]), or members, including nominee shareholders,[49] not necessarily constituting a numerical minority,[50] but query the position of members holding a voting majority;[51]

(ii) a person to whom shares have been 'transmitted by operation of law' (s 994(2)), such as a trustee in bankruptcy or the personal representative of a deceased

---

[47] Since CA 2006 s 996 gives the court the widest possible discretion (as did CA 1985 s 461), this might seem unnecessary, but precedents suggested that courts could not make such an order, given that it would profoundly affect parties not before the court, without providing all the protections delivered by the IA 1986 procedures.

[48] Exceptionally, in *Re I Fit Global Ltd* [2013] EWHC 2090 (Ch), the court held that a person whose name was not entered in the company's register as required under s 112 was a shareholder and could bring a petition. This was because during the trading of the company, there had been wholly inadequate formal corporate documentation and records.

[49] *Atlasview Ltd v Brightview Ltd* [2004] EWHC 1056 (Ch).

[50] Eg in *Re HR Harmer Ltd* (see Note following *Scottish Co-operative Wholesale Society Ltd v Meyer* [13.31], p 732) the petitioners were majority shareholders but did not have voting control.

[51] The court may hold that a petition may not be brought by persons having voting control, since they may have recourse to domestic remedies (eg changing the directors) to remedy the conduct which is the source of complaint, and there may be no reason to also give them the benefit of a compulsory buy-out, eg: see *Re Legal Costs Negotiators Ltd* [1999] 2 BCLC 171, CA. Also see 'Relevance of alternative remedies', pp 726ff.

member: these people can apply even though they are not registered as members; but 'transmitted by operation of law' does not include persons holding by way of constructive trust (*Re a Company (No 007828 of 1985)* (1985) 2 BCC 98,951);

(iii) a person to whom shares have been 'transferred' (s 994(2)): these people can apply even though they are not registered as members, but the cases have drawn a line indicating that mere agreement to transfer will not suffice; there must be a proper instrument of transfer executed and delivered to either the transferee or the company (*Re Quickdome Ltd* [1988] BCLC 370; *Re McCarthy Surfacing Ltd* [2006] EWHC 832 (Ch); *Re Zetnet Ltd* [2011] EWHC 1518 (Ch)); or

(iv) the Secretary of State (s 995).

But a former member has no standing to apply, even if the conduct complained of occurred while he or she was a member *(Re a Company* [1986] 2 All ER 253). On the other hand, members (and presumably others) *with* standing can rely on conduct that predates their registration as shareholders (*Lloyd v Casey* [2002] 1 BCLC 454), unless that conduct had been authorised or ratified by the unanimous agreement of all the shareholders of the company (*Re Batesons Hotels* [2013] EWHC 2530 (Ch)).

Petitioners seeking relief need not 'come with clean hands', although their conduct may be relevant in deciding whether relief should be granted and what the nature of such relief should be: *Re London School of Electronics Ltd* [1986] Ch 211. In *Shah v Shah* [2010] EWHC 313 (Ch), for example, the petitioner 'clearly misconducted himself as employee', yet the learned judge nonetheless found that his attitude to the overall management of the company could not justify his exclusion [115]. In *Re Tobian Properties Ltd* [2012] EWCA Civ 998, the lower court had refused an unfair prejudice petition on the basis that the alleged wrongdoing had been disclosed in the company's accounts (available at Companies House). Arden LJ (with whom Aikens and Kitchin LJJ concurred) reversed the lower court's ruling, holding that this requirement was wrong in principle, as it would impose a new restriction on shareholders, namely that they would be at risk of losing their rights to protect their interests as minority shareholders if they failed to read filed accounts properly.

Although most s 459 petitions have been brought by shareholders in private companies, the jurisdiction does not exclude public companies from its scope. The same trend is likely with CA 2006 s 994 petitions.

Respondents

Normally, the respondents are the controlling members and/or directors. If the company is made a party, this is usually on a nominal basis. Several cases have held that it is improper for the controllers to use the company's funds to fight their case (see, eg, *Re a Company, ex p Johnson* [1992] BCLC 701).

Orders can, however, be sought against more remote respondents. In *Re Little Olympian Each-Ways Ltd (No 3)* [1995] 1 BCLC 636, the company's assets had been sold at an undervalue by those in *de facto* control to another company which was also controlled by them. It was held that an order could be made against the *second* company requiring it to buy out the petitioner's shares at a price which reflected their value before the wrongful sale.

And in *Re a Company* [1986] 1 WLR 281, Hoffmann J ruled that an order could be made against a former member, so ensuring that a potential respondent cannot escape liability by transferring his shares away before proceedings are commenced.

In *F&C Alternative Investments (Holdings) Ltd v Francois Barthelemy, Anthony Culligan* [2011] EWHC 1731 (Ch) at [1096], Sales J said the following:

> What is the relevant test of attribution of responsibility beyond the narrow class of case where an agency relationship exists? In my judgment, the test is whether the defendant in a s 994 claim is so connected to the unfairly prejudicial conduct in question that it would be just, in the context

of the statutory regime contained in ss 994 to 996, to grant a remedy against that defendant in relation to that conduct. The standard of justice to be applied reflects the requirements of fair commercial dealing inherent in the statutory regime. This is to state the test at a high level of abstraction. In practice, everything will depend upon the facts of a particular case and the court's assessment whether what was done involved unfairness in which the relevant defendant was sufficiently implicated to warrant relief being granted against him.

(This decision was later reversed by the Court of Appeal, but on a separate issue.)

Procedure

Since the introduction of the CPR, courts have started to take a much more vigorous and proactive stance (see, eg, *Re Rotadata Ltd* [2000] 1 BCLC 122). The Rules require the court to take the initiative from the outset and manage cases actively. The court registrar is required to consult the parties with a view to narrowing the issues, to consider bringing in outside experts and/or conciliators, etc, so as to minimise the length of any court hearing and cut down costs. The litigants are reminded that it is their duty to cooperate and to agree as much as possible on the issues in a constructive and sensible way. Recently, in *Re Tobian Properties Ltd* [2012] EWCA Civ 998, CA, at [27], Arden LJ made the following comments in relation to effective case management in s 994 proceedings:

Unfair prejudice proceedings generally raise numerous factual issues entailing examination of events over a considerable period of time. Just as defended divorces used to raise numerous issues, making trials long and complex, so trials of s 994 petitions can be long and complex. Thus a high degree of case management is required if the case is not to get out of hand. Effective case management means that, where possible, the court prevents unnecessary court time being spent on issues that are not capable of giving rise to relief. Thus a court will generally determine the issues necessary to determine whether a buyout order should be made at one hearing ('the liability hearing') and only proceed to a second hearing ('the quantum hearing'), at which evidence would be given relevant to establishing the value of the petitioner's shares, once it has determined that a buyout order should be made. Case management, however, must be consistent with both parties' right to a fair hearing.

In *Re Coroin Ltd* [2013] EWCA Civ 781, the Court of Appeal warned the judiciary to find ways and means of reducing hearing times for s 994 proceedings, and counsel to ensure their skeleton arguments were not over long.

In this area, combined claims can cause special problems. In particular, it is possible for a complaint under s 994 and an application for winding up[52] to be combined in the same petition. Since there are several reported cases in which a member has failed on the former ground but succeeded on the latter, judges could hardly complain when this became more or less standard practice. But since the presentation of a petition for winding up is likely to attract unfavourable publicity (and lead almost invariably to the freezing of the company's bank account), so putting considerable pressure on the controllers, this may give a minority shareholder an unfair bargaining advantage. In an attempt to counter this, Practice Direction [1999] BCC 741, para 9, requires petitioners to seek a winding-up order only where this is genuinely considered appropriate and, where they do, to consent to a standard-form interim order which enables the company to continue to trade and use its bank account pending the hearing of the case.

---

[52] The 'just and equitable' ground (IA 1986 s 122(1)(g)), see 'Compulsory winding up on the "just and equitable" ground', pp 840ff.

In *Re Abbington Hotel Ltd* [2012] 1 BCLC 410, an unfair prejudice claim was brought by the petitioner, while the respondent concurrently brought a cross-claim of unfair preju- dice against the petitioner. David Richards J was satisfied that both petitions established a case of unfairly prejudicial conduct of the company's affairs, and therefore ordered that relief be granted and one party was ordered to buy out the 50% holding of the other. This is a good example of effective case management where both complaints were disposed of in the course of one set of proceedings, especially where there was considerable overlap between the two claims.

Furthermore, the Court of Appeal held in the recent case of *Global Torch Ltd v Apex Global Management Ltd* [2013] EWCA Civ 819 that unfair prejudice applications should generally be heard in open court, even if reputational damage may be caused to the par- ties. This may have the effect of promoting early settlement of claims.

Grounds

CA 2006 s 994 requires the petitioner to show that 'the *company's affairs* are being or have been conducted in a manner that is *unfairly prejudicial* to the *interests of members* gener- ally or of some part of its members . . .' (s 994(1)(a)); or that 'an actual or proposed act or omission of the company . . . is or would be so prejudicial' (s 994(1)(b)). Each of the high- lighted requirements has proved troublesome.

Meaning of 'the company's affairs'

The complaint must be about the conduct of the company's affairs, not the conduct of the affairs of a member or director in a private capacity. So, in *Re Unisoft Group Ltd (No 3)* [1994] 1 BCLC 609, and again in *Re Leeds United Holdings plc* [1996] 2 BCLC 545, relief under s 459 was refused where the respondent was alleged not to have honoured a shareholders' agree- ment relating to the transfer of shares. But the leading case of *Scottish Wholesale Co-operative Society Ltd v Meyer* **[13.31]** shows that a broad view may also be taken of this requirement. And in *Re City Branch Group Ltd* **[13.32]**, it was held that 'the affairs of the company' could be interpreted widely, and could extend to the affairs of a subsidiary company, especially where, as in that case, the directors of the holding company and the subsidiary were almost identical. In *Re Abbington Hotel Ltd* [2012] 1 BCLC 410, it was held that the completion of the false minute by the respondent director seeking to agree a sale of the company, and in the hope of persuading the company's solicitor that he was acting with authority, occurred in the course of his conduct, albeit wrongful, of the company's affairs.

Furthermore, in *Graham v Every* [2014] EWCA Civ 191, it was held that breach of a pre- emption agreement governing the transfer of shares could be considered as conduct of a company's affairs in a 'quasi-partnership' company. At [40], Arden LJ held that:

> In the normal way, pre-emption agreements fall outside s.994(1) but in the present case the directors were, as I have explained, not to be remunerated by salary but by way of dividend. Thus the size of a director's shareholding would dictate his reward for his work on the company's busi- ness. How directors were to be remunerated and the company's distributions policy are within the conduct of the company's affairs. So, by denying Mr Graham's pre-emption right at a time when Mr Graham was still a director, Mr Every was arguably interfering with the way in which the parties had agreed that the company would remunerate its directors.

➤ Question

Consider *Re Home & Office Fire Extinguishers Ltd* [2012] EWHC 917 (Ch). HHJ Strauss QC found that a director/shareholder's physical attack on his brother/co-shareholder was part of the conduct of the company's affairs, not the conduct of the affairs of the director/ shareholder in his private capacity. This was because it constituted a breach of the implied understanding that the two brothers would act properly and in good faith towards each other. Further, the attack was a single event which made it impossible for them to continue their association as directors of, and shareholders in, the company; and that the attack arose as a reaction to the petitioner brother's refusal to lend money to the respondent (ie a decision concerning the company's finances). Are you persuaded by such a broad interpretation of 'company's affairs'? Is it true that most acts complained of in s 994 claims are 'personal' (even if not physical), and they make it impossible for shareholders to continue their association, which is why a s 994 petition is brought in most cases?

Meaning of 'unfairly prejudicial'

The conduct complained of must be both unfair *and* prejudicial, not merely unfair (*Re Saul D Harrison & Sons plc* **[13.33]**; *Rock Nominees Ltd v RCO* [2004] 1 BCLC 439), nor merely prejudicial (*Re London School of Electronics Ltd* [1986] Ch 211; *Nicholas v Soundcraft Electronics Ltd* ('Examples of "unfairly prejudicial" conduct', pp 727ff)).

The courts also stress that unfairly prejudicial conduct and wrongful or illegal conduct are separate concepts, each leading to its own remedies (*Re Charnley Davies Ltd* [1990] BCLC 760).

The test is objective, so the emphasis is not so much on the motive or intention of the controllers, as on the effect that the conduct has had on the complaining member (*Re Sam Weller & Sons Ltd* [1990] Ch 682). In *Re Guidezone Ltd* [2000] 2 BCLC 321 at 355, Jonathan Parker J said that *O'Neill v Phillips* **[13.34]** established that:

> 'unfairness' for the purposes of s 459 is not to be judged by reference to subjective notions of fairness, but rather by testing whether, applying established equitable principles, the majority has acted, or is proposing to act, in a manner which equity would regard as contrary to good faith.

In similar vein, Arden LJ in *Re Tobian Properties Ltd* [2012] EWCA Civ 998, CA, explained 'fairness' in this context as being 'flexible and open-textured but it is not unbounded. The courts must act on a principled basis even though the concept is to be approached flexibly. They cannot decide whether to grant or refuse relief from unfair prejudice on the basis of palm-tree justice'.

Further guidance on the meaning of 'prejudice' can be found in the following judgment of David Richards J in *Re Coroin Ltd* [2012] EWHC 2343 (Ch) (affd on appeal, [2013] EWCA Civ 781):

> 630. Prejudice will certainly encompass damage to the financial position of a member. The prejudice may be damage to the value of his shares but may also extend to other financial damage which in the circumstances of the case is bound up with his position as a member . . . The prejudice must be to the petitioner in his capacity as a member but this is not to be strictly confined to damage to the value of his shareholding. Moreover, prejudice need not be financial in character. A disregard of the rights of a member as such, without any financial consequences, may amount to prejudice falling within the section.
>
> 631. Where the acts complained of have no adverse financial consequence, it may be more difficult to establish relevant prejudice. This may particularly be the case where the acts or omissions are breaches of duty owed to the company rather than to shareholders individually. If it is said that the directors or some of them had been in breach of duty to the company but no loss to the company has resulted, the company would not have a claim against those directors. It may therefore be difficult for a shareholder to show that nonetheless as a member he has suffered prejudice . . .

Examples are given at 'Examples of "unfairly prejudicial" conduct', pp 727ff.

Meaning of 'interests of members'

The conduct must be unfairly prejudicial to the 'interests' of all or some part of the members. Whether the affected interests must be those of members, in their capacity as members, is considered later. But certainly the term 'interests' is wider than 'rights', and the cases show that regard can be had to 'legitimate expectations'[53] (particularly in a small company) that the member will be employed by the company, or have a say in its management, or receive some return in the form of dividends.

But the judge 'does not sit under a palm tree':[54] although the court may have regard to 'wider' equitable considerations beyond the parties' strict constitutional and statutory rights, it cannot simply add still further rights and obligations arising from its own concept of fairness (*Re JE Cade & Son Ltd* [1992] BCLC 213 at 227; *O'Neill v Phillips* **[13.34]**).

It follows that the more clearly and fully the parties have spelt out their arrangements, the less scope there will be for the court to find that there were other, unrecorded, 'legitimate expectations'. And if the company is a public company (more particularly if it has made a public issue of its shares) the court is most unlikely to take notice of any alleged arrangement that is not recorded in the company's published documents, for to do so would fly in the face of the principle that all material information must be disclosed to potential investors. Thus, in *Re Blue Arrow plc* [1987] BCLC 585 the court refused to grant any relief to a petitioner who alleged an agreement that she should remain in office as chairman; and in *Re Tottenham Hotspur plc* [1994] 1 BCLC 655 it declined to give effect to an alleged understanding that Terry Venables, the club's team manager, would continue to have a say in the company's management even after he had ceased to be a 50% shareholder.

Members in their capacity as members

A petitioner must show unfair prejudice in his or her character as a member and not, for example, as a director or creditor. *Re JE Cade & Son Ltd* [1992] BCLC 213 provides an illustration: the petitioner was a shareholder in a family farming company and was also the owner of land which the company held on an agricultural tenancy. The court found that his real object in bringing s 459 proceedings was not to obtain any relief in his capacity as a member but to obtain possession of the land, as landlord, and dismissed his claim.

But the rule is now applied more flexibly, following a lead given by the House of Lords in *Ebrahimi v Westbourne Galleries Ltd* **[16.13]**. In *Ebrahimi* the petitioner had been removed from office as a salaried director and so deprived of both his employment and any say in the management of the company, contrary to the basic assumptions on which this two-man company had been set up. In what is now the leading decision on the winding up of small companies, the House of Lords held that it was proper to have regard to 'wider' equitable considerations and not just the parties' strict legal rights in circumstances such as these, and granted him a winding-up order. But he failed on an alternative claim under CA 1948 s 210 (the forerunner of the present s 994) because, as that section was then construed, it was necessary for him to show that he had suffered oppression *as a member* rather than as a director or salaried employee. Soon after, s 210 was replaced and it was made clear that there would be a new departure: the same 'wider' equitable considerations would be applied in interpreting s 459 as the House of Lords had considered appropriate in the winding-up context in *Ebrahimi*.

---

[53] Lord Hoffmann in *O'Neill v Phillips* **[13.34]** expressed reservations about the use of this expression (borrowed from administrative law) in the s 456 (CA 2006 s 994) context, but it is fairly well established—and no one has yet suggested a better alternative.

[54] The expression used by Warner J in *Re JE Cade & Sons Ltd* [1992] BCLC 213 at 227.

For example, in *Re a Company* [1986] BCLC 376, Hoffmann J said (at 379):

> In the case of a small private company in which two or three members have invested their capital by subscribing for shares on the footing that dividends are unlikely but that each will earn his living by working for the company as a director . . . [the] member's interests as a member who has ventured his capital in the company's business may include a legitimate expectation that he will continue to be employed as a director and his dismissal from that office and exclusion from the management of the company may therefore be unfairly prejudicial to his interests as a member.

This reasoning resulted in the court issuing a buy-out order in *Re Eurofinance Group Ltd* [2001] BCC 551. And in *Re Phoenix Contracts (Leicester) Ltd* [2010] EWHC 2375 (Ch), Mr Shepherd was held to be entitled to be a working director, not merely a non-executive director, and so, accordingly, it was 'wholly artificial to draw a distinction between Mr Shepherd's role as an employee on the one hand and as a director and shareholder on the other' [115].

Use of CA 2006 s 994 to protect non-member interests

Using the unfair prejudice remedy to protect creditor interests.

[13.28] Gamlestaden Fastigheter AB v Baltic Partners Ltd [2007] UKPC 26 (Privy Council)

Gamlestaden was both a member and a creditor of Baltic. It sued under the Jersey equivalent of CA 2006 s 994, alleging unfair prejudice occasioned by the mismanagement of Baltic by its directors. It sought, by way of remedy, an order of the court that the directors pay damages to Baltic for their mismanagement. If successful, this claim would: (i) avoid possible limitation problems that existed in Baltic suing its own directors for their breach of duty; and (ii) put Baltic in funds which might be used to repay its creditors, including Gamlestaden, although not in sufficient funds to allow for any distribution to Baltic's members. The issue for the Board was whether the unfair prejudice provisions could deliver these ends.

> The decision of the Board was delivered by LORD SCOTT OF FOSCOTE: . . . Baltic is insolvent and the main issue for decision is whether it is open to a member of a company to make an unfair prejudice application for relief in circumstances where, as here, the company in question is insolvent, will remain insolvent whatever order is made on the application and where the relief sought will confer no financial benefit on the applicant *qua* member. . . .
>
>   The directors, however, applied to have the application struck out on the ground that it was bound in law to fail. They contended . . . that the alleged improprieties in the management of Baltic of which Gamlestaden complain cannot be shown to have caused Gamlestaden any financial loss in its capacity as shareholder. Its loss, if any, is suffered as a creditor. An application under Article 141 (or under section 459 of the 1985 Act) is, it is argued, a shareholder's remedy, not a creditor's remedy. Once it becomes clear that the only benefit to be derived from the relief sought in an unfair prejudice application would be a benefit to the company's creditors, and that no benefit would be obtained by the company's shareholders, it becomes clear that the application is an abuse of process, cannot succeed and should be struck out. The learned Bailiff agreed and struck out the application. The Court of Appeal dismissed Gamlestaden's appeal. The point is now before the Board for a final decision. [Then noting

that, on a strike-out application, the pleaded facts must be taken as true (save for any that can be shown by incontrovertible evidence to be untrue).] . . .

[Counsel's] submission comes to this, that it is a fatal and insurmountable bar in any and every application for Article 141 (or section 459) relief if the relief sought cannot be shown to be of some benefit to the applicant shareholder in his capacity as shareholder.

Mr Moss [counsel] supported his submission by reference, in particular, to the well established rule that a shareholder cannot petition for a winding-up order to be made in respect of a company that is insolvent. The reason is that the petitioning shareholder cannot obtain any benefit from the winding-up. . . . But there is a significant difference between a creditor's winding-up petition and an Article 141 (or section 459) application. . . . The former is . . . a public act or process in which the public has an interest. It seems to their Lordships quite right that a member with no financial interest in the process or its outcome should be denied *locus standi* to initiate the process.

Where relief is sought via an unfair prejudice application, on the other hand, the position is quite different. There is no public involvement or interest in the proceedings, other than the natural interest that may attend any proceedings heard in open court. The purpose of Article 141, or of section 459, or of their counterpart in Hong Kong, is to provide a means of relief to persons unfairly prejudiced by the management of the company in which they hold shares. If the company is a joint venture company and the joint venturers have arranged that one, or more, or all of them, shall provide working capital to the company by means of loans, it would, in their Lordships' opinion, be inconsistent with the purpose of these statutory provisions to limit the availability of the remedies they offer to cases where the value of the share or shares held by the applicant member would be enhanced by the grant of the relief sought. If the relief sought would, if granted, be of real, as opposed to merely nominal, value to an applicant joint venturer, such as Gamlestaden, in facilitating recovery of some part of its investment in the joint venture company, that should, in their Lordships' opinion, suffice to provide the requisite locus standi for the application to be made.

Mr Moss placed reliance on *Re J.E. Cade & Son Ltd* [1992] BCLC 213 where Warner J refused section 459 relief because the applicant was 'pursuing his interests as a freeholder of the farm and not his interests as a member of the company' (p 229). But there was no counterpart in that case with the feature in this case that the loans made by Gamlestaden were made pursuant to and for the purposes of the joint venture to be carried on by Gamlestaden and Mr Karlsten via Baltic.

There are several cases in which judicial approval is given to affording a wide scope to section 459. [His Lordship cited from several of them and continued:]

In their Lordships' opinion Articles 141 and 143 properly construed do not *ipso facto* rule out the grant of relief simply on the ground that the relief sought will not benefit the applicant in his capacity as member. In many cases such a feature might justifiably lead to the refusal of relief. . . . Their Lordships do not accept that the benefit must be a benefit to Gamlestaden in its capacity as a shareholder but they do accept that there must, where the only purpose of the application is to obtain payment of a sum of money to Baltic, be some real financial benefit to be derived therefrom by Gamlestaden. [This is] in agreement with the view expressed by Robert Walker J in relation to similar arrangements made by the applicant for section 459 relief in the *R&H Electric Ltd* case[55] . . .

[And so] this appeal against the strike-out of Gamlestaden's Article 141 application ought to be allowed. . . .

---

55 *R&H Electric Ltd v Haden Bill Electrical Ltd* [1995] 2 BCLC 280.

➤ Question

This case is likely to prove controversial. Is the legal analysis defensible? What practical consequences are likely to flow from this approach to the unfair prejudice provisions? Are these consequences either practically or commercially desirable?

Remedies

Section 996(1) gives the court the power to make 'such order as it thinks fit',[56] and s 996(2) provides examples of possible orders, including the commonly used compulsory share buy-back.

In particular, as indicated in s 996(2), the order may:

(i)   regulate the conduct of the company's affairs in the future (*Re HR Harmer Ltd* in the Note following *Scottish Co-operative Wholesale Society Ltd v Meyer* **[13.31]**, p 732; *Orr v DS Orr & Sons (Holdings) Ltd* [2013] CSOH 116);

(ii)   require the company to do or not to do some specified act (eg in *McGuinness, Petitioners* (1988) 4 BCC 161, the directors were ordered to comply promptly with a shareholders' requisition for the calling of a general meeting);

(iii) authorise civil proceedings to be brought in the name of the company (this is a possible way around the restrictions of *Foss v Harbottle* **[13.01]**; see, eg, *Bhullar v Bhullar* **[7.29]**;

(iv)   prohibit the alteration of all or a specified part of the company's constitution without the leave of the court; or

(v)   provide for the purchase of the shares of any members of the company by other members or by the company itself (see later).

Buy-out orders

In almost all successful cases brought under s 459, the court ordered one faction of shareholders to buy out the others. Section 994 is not proving any different. Usually, the majority is required to buy out the minority, although the reverse was ordered (on certain conditions) in *Re a Company, ex p Shooter* [1990] BCLC 384, where the controlling shareholder had shown himself unfit to continue to manage the business, and also in *Re Brenfield Squash Racquets Club Ltd* [1996] 2 BCLC 184. The court is not prevented from making this order even if the company subsequently becomes insolvent, provided the substantive relief had been asked for when the company was solvent, although this is a factor to be taken into account (*Re Via Servis* [2014] EWHC 3069 (Ch)).

Three questions arise. First, at what date should the valuation be made? Secondly, on what basis should the shares be valued and, in particular, should the holding be discounted to reflect the fact that it is a minority holding? Thirdly, should the conduct of the parties be taken into account in making the valuation?

As will be seen in 'Remedies: valuing shares in buy-out orders', pp 741ff, the courts have reserved to themselves a discretion as regards the first two questions, and have also held that the parties' conduct, and in particular their relative blameworthiness in the events leading to the breakdown in good relations between them, is a factor to be taken into account.

Although this may have some justification in logic, the consequences have been most unfortunate, for parties have felt obliged to make a s 459 hearing the occasion to review the whole of the company's history from its very beginnings and to reopen many old

---

[56] This means that the court is not limited to giving the relief asked for by the petitioner: *Hawkes v Cuddy* [2009] EWCA Civ 291.

battles, thus greatly adding to the length and cost of the case and, at times, attracting unfavourable comment from the judges concerned.

Finally, the prevalence of the courts' exercise of its discretion to order a buy-out once unfair prejudice has been proved appears, by weight of precedent, to be becoming a *right* accruing to the petitioner once the unfair prejudice grounds are established: see *Grace v Biagioli* [2005] EWCA Civ 1222, CA. There the Court of Appeal held that the trial judge had erred when he declined to issue a buy-out order in circumstances where unfairly prejudicial conduct (in this case, non-payment of a dividend) had been established. The trial judge had considered the request, but refused to make a buy-out order, and instead ordered payment of a sum representing the dividend plus interest. The Court of Appeal affirmed the broad discretion in CA 1985 s 461 (CA 2006 s 996), but nevertheless ordered a buy-out, holding that these orders were the usual remedy under s 459 for addressing disputes within small companies, and for good reason, since it was normally only this order that could achieve the full purpose behind the court's power to intervene.

In *Re Scitec Group Ltd* [2011] 1 BCLC 277, after conceding that there had been unfair prejudice against the petitioner, the respondent argued that he should not be *ordered* to purchase the petitioner's shares, as he was willing to do so anyway. The judge rejected this submission and held that 'it will ordinarily be appropriate that an order for purchase should be made', and that it was appropriate to do so here, taking into account the history of the dispute between the parties.

Relevance of alternative remedies

In *Re Baltic Real Estate Ltd (No 2)* [1993] BCLC 503 and *Re Legal Costs Negotiators Ltd* [1999] 2 BCLC 171 the court refused relief to a petitioner who was complaining about a situation which he could remedy by using his own votes. In *Re a Company, ex p Schwarcz (No 2)* [1989] BCLC 427 Peter Gibson J said:

> The developing jurisprudence on s 459 petitions has established that the court, even on a striking-out application, will consider whether the relief sought by a petitioner is inappropriate and whether it is unreasonable to pursue a petition when, for example, it is clear that the petitioner must leave the company and a fair offer has been made for the petitioner's shares (see, for example, *Re a Company (No 003843 of 1986)*[57]) [or] when a petitioner seeking an order for the sale of his shares might have achieved that result by invoking the transfer machinery available in the articles but failed to do so (see *Re a Company (No 007623 of 1984)*[58] and *Re a Company (No 004377 of 1986)*[59]). If the court is of the view that the relief sought is wholly inappropriate and the petitioner is acting unreasonably in pursuing the petition, it may stay or strike out the petition as being an abuse of the process.

A parallel may perhaps be drawn between these remarks and the approach of the courts in giving rulings under IA 1986 s 125(2), where a petitioner has sought the winding up of a company and it is contended that he ought to have pursued some other remedy: see Note 2 following *Loch v John Blackwood Ltd* **[16.12]**, p 846.

An alternative remedy may be provided by the articles; then the general approach of the courts is to leave the parties to their constitutional rights, unless there are special circumstances. For example, where the majority shareholders had followed a procedure laid down by the company's articles to deal with a breakdown in relations, Hoffmann J in *Re a Company* [1987] 1 WLR 102, [1987] BCLC 94 held that this was not unfairly prejudicial

---

[57] [1987] BCLC 562.
[58] [1986] BCLC 362.
[59] [1987] 1 WLR 102.

conduct. The procedure in this case provided for the remaining shareholders to purchase the minority member's shares at a price fixed by the company's auditors. In similar circumstances, in *Re a Company (No 00836 of 1995)* [1996] 2 BCLC 192, the court took the view that what was on offer under the articles would give the minority shareholder all the relief which he could realistically expect to obtain under s 459. But in several other cases it has been thought not unreasonable for a minority shareholder to persist in his desire to have his shares bought out on terms fixed by the court rather than at a price determined by the company's auditors, since he might have reason to fear that the auditors would not be wholly independent and objective. (See, eg, the longish list of cases (all reported as *Re a Company*) cited in the last-mentioned case, and compare the Court of Appeal's ruling in *Virdi v Abbey Leisure Ltd* (Note 2 following *Loch v John Blackwood Ltd* **[16.12]**, p 846), a winding-up case.)

Examples of 'unfairly prejudicial' conduct

The cases provide guidance. But note that many of the rulings are not given on the basis of real evidence, but on presumed facts on an application to strike out the proceedings as disclosing no cause of action, or on a preliminary point of law. Then the decision is no more than a ruling that the conduct in question is (or is not), in theory, *capable* of being unfairly prejudicial within CA 1985 s 459 (or CA 2006 s 799). This can at best provide only a rough guide.

Examples of conduct that has been held to be (or held capable of being) unfairly prejudicial, include:

(i)   exclusion from management (in a company formed as a quasi-partnership[60]): *Re RA Noble & Sons (Clothing) Ltd* [1983] BCLC 273 (Note 1 following *Loch v John Blackwood Ltd* **[16.12]**, p 846); *Re OC (Transport) Services Ltd* [1984] BCLC 251; *Re Phoenix Contracts (Leicester) Ltd* [2010] EWHC 2375 (Ch); *Re Abbington Hotel Ltd* [2012] 1 BCLC 410; *Re I Fit Global Ltd* [2013] EWHC 2090 (Ch); *Re J&S Insurance & Financial Consultants Ltd* [2014] EWHC 2206 (Ch); *Re Via Servis Ltd* [2014] EWHC 3069 (Ch);

(ii)   taking excessive remuneration: *Re Cumana Ltd* [1986] BCLC 430;

(iii)   diversion of a corporate asset or business opportunity: *Re London School of Electronics Ltd* [1986] Ch 211; *Re Via Servis Ltd* [2014] EWHC 3069 (Ch);

(iv)   not paying dividends: *Re a Company, ex p Glossop* [1988] 1 WLR 1068; *Re Sam Weller & Sons Ltd* [1990] Ch 682; *Grace v Biagioli* [2005] EWCA Civ 1222; *Re McCarthy Surfacing Ltd* [2008] EWHC 2279 (Ch); *Sikorski v Sikorski* [2012] EWHC 1613 (Ch); *Re J&S Insurance & Financial Consultants Ltd* [2014] EWHC 2206 (Ch);

(v)   making or proposing a rights issue which the minority cannot afford to take up: *Re Cumana Ltd* (see point (ii)); cf *Pennell Securities Ltd v Venida Investments Ltd* (25 July 1974, noted by Burridge (1981) 44 MLR 40);

(vi)   stacking the board with directors having interests adverse to the company: *Whyte, Petitioner* (1984) 1 BCC 99,044;

(vii)   failure on the part of the directors to advise the shareholders impartially on the merits of rival takeover bids (in one of which the directors were personally interested): *Re a Company* [1986] BCLC 382;

---

[60] Note that it is not necessary that the members of a 'quasi-partnership' should have equal shares in the venture: a junior partner in *Quinlan v Essex Hinge Co Ltd* [1996] 2 BCLC 417 successfully petitioned following his exclusion from management by a dominant senior partner.

(viii) misuse of fiduciary powers: *Scottish Co-operative Wholesale Society Ltd v Meyer* **[13.31]**;

(ix) mismanagement, but only if 'serious': *Re Macro (Ipswich) Ltd* **[13.30]**; contrast *Re Elgindata Ltd* **[13.29]**;

(x) failing to allow minority shareholders independent representation on the board when all control is in the hands of the majority faction which has potentially conflicting interests: *Re Macro (Ipswich) Ltd* **[13.30]**;

(xi) seeking to sell the company's assets (a hotel) contrary to the original agreement, and knowingly creating and putting forward a false minute for that purpose: *Re Abbington Hotel Ltd* [2012] 1 BCLC 410;

(xii) dilution of a shareholder's interest: *Re Zetnet Ltd* [2011] EWHC 1518 (Ch); *Re J&S Insurance & Financial Consultants Ltd* [2014] EWHC 2206 (Ch);

(xiii) physical attack on the petitioner shareholder with a hammer: *Re Home & Office Fire Extinguishers Ltd* [2012] EWHC 917 (Ch).

Examples of conduct which has been held *not* to be (or not to be capable of being) unfairly prejudicial include:

(i) declining to implement a scheme to make it possible for petitioners, 'locked in' to a private company, to realise their shares: *Re a Company* [1983] Ch 178 (Note 2 following *Loch v John Blackwood Ltd* **[16.12]**, p 846);

(ii) mere breakdown of confidence between the parties: *Re RA Noble & Sons (Clothing) Ltd* (Note 1 following *Loch v John Blackwood Ltd* **[16.12]**, p 846);

(iii) a situation which the petitioner could remedy by using his own votes: *Re Baltic Real Estate Ltd (No 2)* [1993] BCLC 503; *Re Legal Costs Negotiators Ltd* [1999] 2 BCLC 171;

(iv) the non-payment by a parent company of debts owing to a subsidiary when this course was considered to be in the interests of the group as a whole: *Nicholas v Soundcraft Electronics Ltd* [1993] BCLC 360; contrast *Scottish Co-operative Wholesale Society Ltd v Meyer* **[13.31]**;

(v) continuing to run a loss-making business when the minority shareholders stood to receive a substantial capital distribution if the company were wound up: *Re Saul D Harrison plc* **[13.33]**;

(vi) the dismissal of a member director of a quasi-partnership company as a result of his own misconduct, which jeopardised the company's ongoing survival: *Woolwich v Milne* [2003] EWHC 414 (Ch);

(vii) certain valuation offers, for example the valuation procedure at a discounted rate which underpinned the original offer made to Larvin in *Phoenix Office Supplies Ltd v Larvin* **[13.36]** and the offer made in accordance with a prior shareholders' agreement that the petitioner had entered into voluntarily in *Re Charterhouse Capital* [2015] EWCA Civ 536;

(viii) the company's decision to achieve, by legitimate means, a result which avoids the need for a special resolution, even though this disempowers the minority from opposing the intended result: *CAS (Nominees) Ltd v Nottingham Forest plc* [2002] BCC 145;

(ix) failure to issue a transfer notice where it should have been given, as this falls within the *personal* obligation of a shareholder: *Re Coroin Ltd* [2012] EWHC 2343 (Ch);

(x) past conduct to which all of the shareholders at the material time had expressly consented, unless the petitioner could point to some special facts which would have operated to render the unanimous consent of the shareholders ineffective: *Re Batesons Hotel* [2013] EWHC 2530 (Ch);

(xi)   requiring a member to transfer his shares for nominal consideration as contractually agreed between the parties: *Re LCM Wealth Management* [2013] EWHC 3957 (Ch);

(xii)   prejudicial conduct may not be unfair if it is objectively justified: *Re J&S Insurance & Financial Consultants* [2014] EWHC 2206 (Ch).

Analysis of conduct which amounts to 'unfair prejudice'

As a general rule, managerial decisions are unlikely to amount to unfairly prejudicial conduct.

[13.29] Re Elgindata Ltd [1991] BCLC 959 (Chancery Division)

Rowland, the petitioner, had invested in a company controlled by Mr and Mrs Purslow, taking a minority shareholding. The company had been in existence for over four years. The remarks of Warner J quoted here relate to the question whether mismanagement is capable of constituting unfairly prejudicial conduct.

WARNER J: [He referred to *Re Five Minute Car Wash Service Ltd* [1966] 1 WLR 745, a case under CA 1948 s 210 in which it had been held that mere mismanagement, however damaging, did not amount to 'oppression' for the purposes of that section, and continued:] I was referred, on this point also, to the judgment of Peter Gibson J in *Re Sam Weller & Sons Ltd* [61] at the end of which he said that he had no doubt that the court would ordinarily be very reluctant to accept that managerial decisions could amount to unfairly prejudicial conduct . . .

I do not doubt that in an appropriate case it is open to the court to find that serious mismanagement of a company's business constitutes conduct that is unfairly prejudicial to the interests of minority shareholders. But I share Peter Gibson J's view that the court will normally be very reluctant to accept that managerial decisions can amount to unfairly prejudicial conduct.

Two considerations seem to me to be relevant. First, there will be cases where there is disagreement between petitioners and respondents as to whether a particular managerial decision was, as a matter of commercial judgment, the right one to make, or as to whether a particular proposal relating to the conduct of the company's business is commercially sound . . . In my view, it is not for the court to resolve such disagreements on a petition under s 459. Not only is a judge ill-qualified to do so, but there can be no unfairness to the petitioners in those in control of the company's affairs taking a different view from theirs on such matters.

Secondly, as was persuasively argued by Mr Chivers, a shareholder acquires shares in a company knowing that their value will depend in some measure on the competence of the management. He takes the risk that that management may prove not to be of the highest quality. Short of a breach by a director of his duty of skill and care (and no such breach on the part of either Mr Purslow or Mrs Purslow was alleged) there is prima facie no unfairness to a shareholder in the quality of the management turning out to be poor. It occurred to me during the argument that one example of a case where the court might none the less find that there was unfair prejudice to minority shareholders would be one where the majority shareholders, for reasons of their own, persisted in retaining in charge of the management of the company's business a member of their family who was demonstrably incompetent. That of course would be a very different case from this. Mr Rowland deliberately invested in a company controlled and managed by Mr Purslow,

---

[61]   [1990] Ch 682.

whom he had known for five years or so. Indeed, he did so, despite Mr Purslow's reluctance to have him as a shareholder in his company. Mr Nourse submitted that Mr Rowland had a right to expect a reasonable standard of general management from Mr Purslow. In my view, he had no such right. He took the risk that Mr Purslow's management of the company might not be up to the standard that he, Mr Rowland, had hoped and expected . . .

However, exceptionally, significant and serious mismanagement may justify relief.

[13.30] Re Macro (Ipswich) Ltd [1994] 2 BCLC 354 (Chancery Division)

The applicants claimed that the two property-owning companies in which they were minority shareholders had suffered losses because a firm referred to as 'Thompsons' (the companies' property-managing agents) had committed various improprieties which Mr Thompson (an elderly, autocratic person who was the founder of Thompsons and the companies' sole director) had connived at or inadequately supervised. Arden J held that this was unfairly prejudicial conduct and ordered that the applicants' shares be bought out.

ARDEN J: . . . The question whether any action was or would be 'unfairly prejudicial' to the interests of the members has to be judged on an objective basis. Accordingly it has to be determined, on an objective basis, first whether the action of which complaint is made is prejudicial to members' interests and secondly whether it is unfairly so. Based on the findings of fact that I have made, I am satisfied that the companies suffered prejudice in consequence of failure to have a planned maintenance programme, the failure to supervise repairs, the failure to inspect properties regularly, the failure to let on protected shorthold tenancies, the taking of commissions from builders doing work for the companies by employees of Thompsons, the charging of excessive management charges and secretarial salary and the mismanagement of litigation. The absence of an effective system to prevent excessive amounts being retained on Thompsons' client account instead of paying it over to the companies is also in my judgment likely to cause loss to the companies in the future. All of these matters are within the responsibility of Thompsons as the companies' managing agent but they are attributable to the lack of effective supervision by Mr Thompson on behalf of the companies. It is this conduct of the companies' affairs by Mr Thompson which, in my judgment, is prejudicial in the respects I have mentioned. As the conduct is prejudicial in a financial sense to the companies, it must also be prejudicial to the interests of the plaintiffs as holders of its shares . . .

   [This] is not a case where what happened was merely that quality of management turned out to be poor (cf *Re Elgindata Ltd* **[13.29]**). This is a case where there were specific acts of mismanagement by Thompsons, which Mr Thompson failed to prevent or rectify. Moreover, several of the acts of mismanagement which the plaintiffs have identified were repeated over many years, as for example in relation to the failure to inspect repairs. In my judgment, viewed overall, those acts (and Mr Thompson's failures to prevent or rectify them) are sufficiently significant and serious to justify intervention by the court under s 461 . . .

➤ Note

Although there is no finding in the judgment that Mr Thompson was guilty of anything other than mismanagement, it is pertinent to note that, like the negligence of the directors in *Daniels v Daniels*,[62] there was a self-serving aspect to this mismanagement, since it was

---

[62] [1978] Ch 406, Notes 2 and 3 following *Franbar Holdings Ltd v Patel* **[13.13]**, p 688.

Mr Thompson's own firm which stood to gain from (inter alia) the excessive management charges.

> ➤ Question

In *Re Macro (Ipswich) Ltd* **[13.30]**, Arden J also said:

> Given the presence of minority interests, the absence of an independent director would in my judgment be prejudicial to the position of the plaintiffs as shareholders in the companies. If support were needed for such proposition, it can be found in the recent report of the Committee on the Financial Aspects of Corporate Governance (the Cadbury Committee) published in December 1992. This report, which has been accepted by, inter alia, the Stock Exchange, emphasises that no one individual within a company should have unfettered powers of decision and that, where the chairman is also chief executive, there should be a strong and independent element on the board. While that report is directed to listed companies, the desirability of having a truly independent board is applicable to all cases where there are minority shareholders. In my judgment neither Mr Thompson nor Mr Farley [Mr Thompson's proposed nominee] would be able to act independently of Mr Thompson's position as majority shareholder and sole proprietor of Thompsons. That situation would in my judgment not only be prejudicial to the interests of the minority shareholders, but unfairly so.

Does the modern law on private companies adopt this approach, or even suggest that it is best practice?

Nominee directors and conflicts that amount to 'oppression'.

[13.31] Scottish Co-operative Wholesale Society Ltd v Meyer [1959] AC 324 (House of Lords)

[This case was decided under the old CA 1948 s 210 'oppression' section, but is still regarded as influential. Despite the differences in the wording of CA 2006 ss 994 and 210, there can be little doubt that the same conclusion would be reached today.]

Scottish Textile & Manufacturing Co Ltd was a private company formed in 1946 by the appellant society and the respondents, Meyer and Lucas, to manufacture rayon cloth at a time when this product was subject to a system of state licensing. The society held the majority of the issued shares and had appointed three of its own directors to the board; the respondents, who held the rest of the shares, were joint managing directors and as such filled the remaining seats on the board. The society had formed this subsidiary because it could not have secured a licence to produce rayon cloth without experienced managers, and the respondents had the necessary experience. After licensing ceased in 1952, the society, by transferring the company's business to another branch of its organisation and cutting off the supply of raw materials on which the company was dependent, caused its activities to come to a standstill, with the result that it made no profits and the value of its shares fell greatly. The respondents petitioned for relief under s 210, and the House of Lords, confirming the decision of the Court of Session, ordered the society to purchase their shares at a fair price.

> LORD DENNING discussed the facts, and continued: Such being 'the matters complained of' by Dr Meyer and Mr Lucas, it is said: 'Those are all complaints about the conduct of the co-operative society. How do they touch the real issue—the manner in which the affairs of the textile company

were being conducted?' The answer is, I think, by their impact on the nominee directors. It must be remembered that we are here concerned with the manner in which the affairs of the textile company were being conducted. That is, with the conduct of those in control of its affairs. They may be some of the directors themselves, or, behind them, a group of shareholders who nominated those directors or whose interests those directors serve. If those persons—the nominee directors or the shareholders behind them—conduct the affairs of the company in a manner oppressive to the other shareholders, the court can intervene to bring an end to the oppression.

What, then, is the position of the nominee directors here? Under the articles of association of the textile company the co-operative society was entitled to nominate three out of the five directors, and it did so. It nominated three of its own directors and they held office, as the articles said, 'as nominees' of the co-operative society. These three were therefore at one and the same time directors of the co-operative society—being three out of twelve of that company—and also directors of the textile company—three out of five there. So long as the interests of all concerned were in harmony, there was no difficulty. The nominee directors could do their duty by both companies without embarrassment. But, so soon as the interests of the two companies were in conflict, the nominee directors were placed in an impossible position. It is plain that, in the circumstances, these three gentlemen could not do their duty by both companies, and they did not do so. They put their duty to the co-operative society above their duty to the textile company in this sense, at least, that they did nothing to defend the interests of the textile company against the conduct of the co-operative society. They probably thought that 'as nominees' of the co-operative society their first duty was to the co-operative society. In this they were wrong. By subordinating the interests of the textile company to those of the co-operative society, they conducted the affairs of the textile company in a manner oppressive to the other shareholders.

It is said that these three directors were at most only guilty of inaction—of doing nothing to protect the textile company. But the affairs of a company can, in my opinion, be conducted oppressively by the directors doing nothing to defend its interests when they ought to do something—just as they can conduct its affairs oppressively by doing something injurious to its interests when they ought not to do it . . .

Your Lordships were referred to *Bell v Lever Bros Ltd*,[63] where Lord Blanesburgh said that a director of one company was at liberty to become a director also of a rival company. That may have been so at that time. But it is at the risk now of an application under s 210 if he subordinates the interests of the one company to those of the other.

So I would hold that the affairs of the textile company were being conducted in a manner oppressive to Dr Meyer and Mr Lucas . . .

One of the most useful orders mentioned in the section—which will enable the court to do justice to the injured shareholders—is to order the oppressor to buy their shares at a fair price: and a fair price would be, I think, the value which the shares would have had at the date of the petition, if there had been no oppression . . .

VISCOUNT SIMONS and LORDS MORTON OF HENRYTON and KEITH OF AVONHOLM delivered concurring opinions.

> Note

The 'most useful' remedy of compulsory buy-out at a fair price, recognised in the extract, has become almost the only remedy called upon in these cases. *Re HR Harmer Ltd* [1959] 1 WLR 62, CA, remains notable for a more imaginative approach. The trial judge found that an autocratic father, in his role as 'governing director', was behaving 'oppressively'. He granted the sons relief, ordering, inter alia, 'that the company should contract for the services of the father as philatelic consultant at a named salary, that the father should not

---

[63] [1932] AC 161, HL.

interfere in the affairs of the company otherwise than in accordance with the valid decision of the board of directors, and that he should be appointed president of the company for life, but that this office should not impose any duties or rights or powers'. The order was upheld by the Court of Appeal.

Unfair prejudice in the conduct of the affairs of a subsidiary will suffice.

[13.32] Re City Branch Group Ltd [2005] 1 WLR 3505 (Court of Appeal)

This case was decided under CA 1985 s 459, and provides a modern example of what may constitute 'unfairly prejudicial' conduct. R and G each held 50% of the shares in a company, C. C had three wholly owned subsidiaries. All the business of C, which involved investment property portfolios, was carried out through its subsidiaries. C's business was effectively a quasi-partnership between R and G, which broke down following differences between them. R had applied for C to be wound up on the 'just and equitable' ground (see 'Compulsory winding up on the "just and equitable" ground', pp 840ff), and G had sought an order under CA 1985 s 459 on the ground that C's affairs had been conducted in a manner unfairly prejudicial to the interests of C, citing breaches of fiduciary duty and misappropriation of funds by R in respect of two of C's subsidiaries. On appeal, R argued that his alleged conduct related solely to C's subsidiaries and not to C itself, and therefore the petition could not succeed in relation to C. The Court of Appeal, dismissing the appeal, held that 'the affairs of the company' (in s 459) had a broad application and could include the affairs of a subsidiary, particularly as in the instant case where the directors of the holding company and the subsidiary were substantially the same.

SIR MARTIN NOURSE: . . . I now come to the main question. Does the court have power to make an order under section 459 in relation to a holding company where, first, it is the affairs of its wholly-owned subsidiary that are being or have been conducted in an unfairly prejudicial manner and, secondly, the directors of the holding company are also directors of the subsidiary? I emphasise that here Mr Gross and Mr Rackind are the only directors of the company and of Blaneland and are also directors of Citybranch, of which Mr Gerald Gross is an additional director.

There is no English authority which directly answers this question. . . . [He then examined various potentially relevant authorities, and continued:] [These observations] demonstrate that the expression 'the affairs of the company' is one of the widest import which can include the affairs of a subsidiary. Equally, I would hold that the affairs of a subsidiary can also be the affairs of its holding company, especially where, as here, the directors of the holding company, which necessarily controls the affairs of the subsidiary, also represent a majority of the directors of the subsidiary. (In the case of Blaneland they are identical). . . . [He then examined various Australian authorities, and continued:]

. . . The decision in *In re Norvabron (No 2)*[64] was followed and applied by Powell J, sitting in the Equity Division of the Supreme Court of New South Wales, in *In re Dernacourt Investments Pty Ltd* (1990) 2 ACSR 553 . . . It was held that the conduct of the affairs of the holding company towards a subsidiary may constitute the conduct of the affairs of the subsidiary and vice versa. Powell J said, at p 556:

'8. The words "affairs of the company" are extremely wide and should be construed liberally: (a) in determining the ambit of the "affairs" of a parent company for the purposes of section 320 [the equivalent of CA 1985 s 459], the court looks at the business realities of a situation and does not confine them to a narrow legalistic view; (b) "affairs" of a company

[64] (1986) 11 ACLR 279.

encompass all matters which may come before its board for consideration; (c) conduct of the "affairs" of a parent company includes refraining from procuring a subsidiary to do something or condoning by inaction an act of a subsidiary, particularly when the directors of the parent and the subsidiary are the same.' (Reference was there made to three authorities including *In re Norvabron (No 2)*.)

Powell J said, at p 561:

'although the relevant plaintiff must demonstrate that it is the relevant company's affairs which are being so conducted, I am prepared to proceed upon the bases, first, that, in an appropriate case, the conduct of a holding company, or of such of its directors who happen to be directors of the relevant subsidiary, towards a subsidiary, may constitute conduct in the affairs of that subsidiary (*Scottish Cooperative Wholesale Society Ltd v Meyer* **[13.31]**), and, secondly, that, in an appropriate case, the conduct of a subsidiary, or of some or all of its directors who happen as well to be directors of the holding company, may be regarded as part of the conduct of the affairs of the holding company: *In re Norvabron Pty Ltd (No 2)* 11 ACLR 279.'

In my view the second basis identified by Powell J, following and applying the decision in *In re Norvabron (No 2)*, is of great value in the decision of the present case. I accept that decisions of courts in other Commonwealth countries are of persuasive value only. But those two decisions certainly persuade me that the view taken by Judge Weeks QC, without their assistance, was correct . . . Those were considered judgments of judges of the Supreme Courts of Queensland and New South Wales respectively and they are directly in point. I would follow them accordingly. . . .

KEENE and JACOB LJJ concurred.

A special approach to 'legitimate expectations'?

'Legitimate expectations'.

[13.33] Re Saul D Harrison & Sons plc [1995] 1 BCLC 14 (Court of Appeal)

The petitioner held 'C' class shares in a company that made industrial cleaning cloths. The business had been founded by her great-grandfather in 1891. The 'C' class shares carried rights to dividends and to capital distributions in a liquidation, but no entitlement to vote. The company had substantial assets but had recently been run at a loss. The petitioner complained that the directors (her cousins) had unreasonably continued to run the business (and to pay themselves salaries, although the court ruled that these were not excessive), instead of closing the business down and distributing the assets to the shareholders. Vinelott J and the Court of Appeal held that the petitioner had no 'legitimate expectations' over and above an expectation that the board would manage the company in accordance with their fiduciary obligations and the terms of the articles of association and the Companies Act, and that no breach of these obligations had been shown.

HOFFMANN LJ: Mr Purle, who appeared for the petitioner, said that the only test of unfairness was whether a reasonable bystander would think that the conduct in question was unfair. This is correct, so far as it goes, and has some support in the cases. Its merit is to emphasise that the court is applying an objective standard of fairness. But I do not think that it is the most illuminating way of putting the matter. For one thing, the standard of fairness must necessarily be laid down by the court. In explaining how the court sets about deciding what is fair in the context of company management, I do not think that it helps a great deal to add the reasonable company watcher to the already substantial cast of imaginary characters which the law uses to personify its standards of justice in different situations. An appeal to the views of an imaginary third party makes the concept seem more vague than it really is. It is more useful to examine the factors which the law actually takes into account in setting the standard.

In deciding what is fair or unfair for the purposes of s 459, it is important to have in mind that fairness is being used in the context of a commercial relationship.[65] The articles of association are just what their name implies: the contractual terms which govern the relationships of the shareholders with the company and each other. They determine the powers of the board and the company in general meeting and everyone who becomes a member of a company is taken to have agreed to them. Since keeping promises and honouring agreements is probably the most important element of commercial fairness, the starting point in any case under s 459 will be to ask whether the conduct of which the shareholder complains was in accordance with the articles of association . . .

Although one begins with the articles and the powers of the board, a finding that conduct was not in accordance with the articles does not necessarily mean that it was unfair, still less that the court will exercise its discretion to grant relief . . .

Not only may conduct be technically unlawful without being unfair: it can also be unfair without being unlawful. In a commercial context, this may at first seem surprising. How can it be unfair to act in accordance with what the parties have agreed? As a general rule, it is not. But there are cases in which the letter of the articles does not fully reflect the understandings upon which the shareholders are associated.

[His Lordship referred to *Ebrahimi v Westbourne Galleries Ltd* [16.13], and continued:] Thus the personal relationship between a shareholder and those who control the company may entitle him to say that it would in certain circumstances be unfair for them to exercise a power conferred by the articles upon the board or the company in general meeting. I have in the past ventured to borrow from public law the term 'legitimate expectation' to describe the correlative 'right' in the shareholder to which such a relationship may give rise. It often arises out of a fundamental understanding between the shareholders which formed the basis of their association but was not put into contractual form, such as an assumption that each of the parties who has ventured his capital will also participate in the management of the company and receive the return on his investment in the form of salary rather than dividend . . .

Although the petition speaks of the petitioner having various 'legitimate expectations', no grounds are alleged for saying that her rights are not 'adequately and exhaustively' laid down by the articles. And in substance the alleged 'legitimate expectations' amount to no more than an expectation that the board would manage the company in accordance with their fiduciary obligations and the terms of the articles and the Companies Act . . .

Unfair prejudice and limiting the independent impact of legitimate expectations.

[13.34] O'Neill v Phillips [1999] 1 WLR 1092 (House of Lords)

This is a long extract, since this is the only House of Lords' decision in the area, and the issue is especially important in disputes in many small companies. In 1985 Phillips, who had owned all the shares in the company, gave a 25% share to O'Neill, its foreman and principal employee, and appointed him as a director. He told O'Neill that he hoped O'Neill would be able to take over the whole day-to-day management of the business, and on that basis he would be allowed to draw 50% of the profits. This in due course occurred and, indeed, Phillips retired from the board, leaving O'Neill as sole director. The company

---

[65] Note, however, that in *O'Neill v Phillips* **[13.34]** Lord Hoffmann states that 'conduct which is perfectly fair between competing businessmen may not be fair between members of a family', a consideration which weighed with the judge in giving a petitioner relief in *Brownlow v GH Marshall Ltd* [2000] 2 BCLC 655.

prospered for the next five years, during which time there were discussions about increasing O'Neill's shareholding to 50%. But then the construction industry went into recession and the company's fortunes declined. Phillips took back control of the business and reduced O'Neill's status to that of a branch manager, and also withdrew his share of the profits. O'Neill took steps to leave the company, and also issued a s 459 petition. Lord Hoffmann, with the support of all the other members of the House, held that there was no basis for a court to hold that Phillips had acted unfairly.

LORD HOFFMANN: . . .

'Unfairly prejudicial'

In [CA 1985] s 459 Parliament has chosen fairness as the criterion by which the court must decide whether it has jurisdiction to grant relief. It is clear from the legislative history (which I discussed in *Re Saul D Harrison & Sons plc* **[13.33]**) that it chose this concept to free the court from technical considerations of legal right and to confer a wide power to do what appeared just and equitable. But this does not mean that the court can do whatever the individual judge happens to think fair. The concept of fairness must be applied judicially and the content which it is given by the courts must be based upon rational principles. As Warner J said in *Re JE Cade & Sons Ltd* [1992] BCLC 213 at 227: 'The court . . . has a very wide discretion, but it does not sit under a palm tree.'

Although fairness is a notion which can be applied to all kinds of activities, its content will depend upon the context in which it is being used. Conduct which is perfectly fair between competing businessmen may not be fair between members of a family. In some sports it may require, at best, observance of the rules, in others ('it's not cricket') it may be unfair in some circumstances to take advantage of them. All is said to be fair in love and war. So the context and background are very important.

In the case of s 459, the background has the following two features. First, a company is an association of persons for an economic purpose, usually entered into with legal advice and some degree of formality. The terms of the association are contained in the articles of association and sometimes in collateral agreements between the shareholders. Thus the manner in which the affairs of the company may be conducted is closely regulated by rules to which the shareholders have agreed. Secondly, company law has developed seamlessly from the law of partnership, which was treated by equity, like the Roman *societas*, as a contract of good faith. One of the traditional roles of equity, as a separate jurisdiction, was to restrain the exercise of strict legal rights in certain relationships in which it considered that this would be contrary to good faith. These principles have, with appropriate modification, been carried over into company law.

The first of these two features leads to the conclusion that a member of a company will not ordinarily be entitled to complain of unfairness unless there has been some breach of the terms on which he agreed that the affairs of the company should be conducted. But the second leads to the conclusion that there will be cases in which equitable considerations make it unfair for those conducting the affairs of the company to rely upon their strict legal powers. Thus unfairness may consist in a breach of the rules or in using the rules in a manner which equity would regard as contrary to good faith.

This approach to the concept of unfairness in s 459 runs parallel to that which your Lordships' House, in *Ebrahimi v Westbourne Galleries Ltd* **[16.13]**, adopted in giving content to the concept of 'just and equitable' as a ground for winding up.

[His Lordship cited extracts from that case, and continued:] I would apply the same reasoning to the concept of unfairness in s 459. The Law Commission, in its report on Shareholder Remedies (Law Com No 246) (1997) para 4.11, p 43 expresses some concern that defining the content of the unfairness concept in the way I have suggested might unduly limit its scope and that 'conduct which would appear to be deserving of a remedy may be left unremedied'. In my view, a balance has to be struck between the breadth of the discretion given to the court and the principle of legal certainty. Petitions under s 459 are often lengthy and expensive. It is highly desirable that lawyers should be able to advise their clients whether or not a petition is likely to succeed. Lord Wilberforce, after the passage which I have quoted, said that it would be impossible 'and wholly undesirable' to define the circumstances in which the application of equitable principles might make it unjust, or inequitable (or unfair) for a party to insist on legal rights or to exercise them in particular way. This of course is right. But that does not mean that there are no principles by which those circumstances may be identified. The way in which such equitable principles operate is tolerably well settled and in my view it would be wrong to abandon them in favour of some wholly indefinite notion of fairness . . .

I agree with Jonathan Parker J when he said in *Re Astec (BSR) plc* [1998] 2 BCLC 556 at 588:

'. . . in order to give rise to an equitable constraint based on "legitimate expectation" what is required is a personal relationship or personal dealings of some kind between the party seeking to exercise the legal right and the party seeking to restrain such exercise, such as will affect the conscience of the former.'

This is putting the matter in very traditional language, reflecting in the word 'conscience' the ecclesiastical origins of the long-departed Court of Chancery . . . I have no difficulty with this formulation. But I think that one useful cross-check in a case like this is to ask whether the exercise of the power in question would be contrary to what the parties, by words or conduct, have actually agreed. Would it conflict with the promises which they appear to have exchanged? . . . In a quasi-partnership company, they will usually be found in the understandings between the members at the time they entered into association. But there may be later promises, by words or conduct, which it would be unfair to allow a member to ignore. Nor is it necessary that such promises should be independently enforceable as a matter of contract. A promise may be binding as a matter of justice and equity although for one reason or another (for example, because in favour of a third party) it would be enforceable in law . . .

I do not suggest that exercising rights in breach of some promise or undertaking is the only form of conduct which will be regarded as unfair for the purposes of s 459. For example, there may be some event which puts an end to the basis upon which the parties entered into association with each other, making it unfair that one shareholder should insist upon the continuance of the association. The analogy of contractual frustration suggests itself. The unfairness may arise not from what the parties have positively agreed but from a majority using its legal powers to maintain the association in circumstances to which the minority can reasonably say it did not agree: *non haec in foedera veni*.

Legitimate expectations

In *Re Saul D Harrison & Sons plc* I used the term 'legitimate expectation', borrowed from public law, as a label for the 'correlative right' to which a relationship between company members may give rise in a case when, on equitable principles, it would be regarded as unfair for a majority to exercise a power conferred upon them by the articles to the prejudice of another member. I gave as an example the standard case in which shareholders have entered into association upon the understanding that each of them who has ventured his capital will also participate in the management of the company. In such a case it will usually be considered unjust, inequitable or unfair for a majority to use their voting power to exclude a member from participation in the management without giving him the opportunity to remove his capital upon reasonable terms. The aggrieved member could be said to have had a 'legitimate expectation' that he would be able to participate in the management or withdraw from the company.

It was probably a mistake to use this term, as it usually is when one introduces a new label to describe a concept which is already sufficiently defined in other terms. In saying that it was 'correlative' to the equitable restraint, I meant that it could exist only when equitable principles of the kind I have been describing would make it unfair for a party to exercise rights under the articles. It is a consequence, not a cause, of the equitable restraint. The concept of a legitimate expectation should not be allowed to lead a life of its own, capable of giving rise to equitable restraints in circumstances to which the traditional equitable principles have no application. That is what seems to have happened in this case.

Was Mr Phillips unfair?

The Court of Appeal found that by 1991 the company had the characteristics identified by Lord Wilberforce in *Ebrahimi v Westbourne Galleries Ltd* as commonly giving rise to equitable restraints upon the exercise of powers under the articles. They were (1) an association formed or continued on the basis of a personal relationship involving mutual confidence, (2) an understanding that all, or some, of the shareholders shall participate in the conduct of the business and (3) restrictions on the transfer of shares, so that a member cannot take out his stake and go elsewhere. I agree. It follows that it would have been unfair of Mr Phillips to use his voting powers under the articles to remove Mr O'Neill from participation in the conduct of the business without giving him the opportunity to sell his interest in the company at a fair price. Although it does not matter, I should say that I do not think that this was the position when Mr O'Neill first acquired his shares in 1985. He received them as a gift and an incentive and I do not think that in making that gift Mr Phillips could be taken to have surrendered his right to dismiss Mr O'Neill from the management without making him an offer for the shares. Mr O'Neill was simply an employee who happened to have been given some shares. But over the following years the relationship changed. Mr O'Neill invested his own profits in the company by leaving some on loan account and agreeing to part being capitalised as shares. He worked to build up the company's business. He guaranteed its bank account and mortgaged his house in support . . .

The difficulty for Mr O'Neill is that Mr Phillips did not remove him from participation in the management of the business. After the meeting on 4 November 1991 he remained a director and continued to earn his salary as manager of the business in Germany. The Court of Appeal held that he had been constructively removed by the behaviour of Mr Phillips in the matter of equality of profits and shareholdings. So the question then becomes whether Mr Phillips acted unfairly in respect of these matters.

To take the shareholdings first, the Court of Appeal said that Mr O'Neill had a legitimate expectation of being allotted more shares when the targets were met. No doubt he did have such an expectation before 4 November and no doubt it was legitimate, or reasonable, in the sense that it reasonably appeared likely to happen. Mr Phillips had agreed in principle, subject to the execution of a suitable document. But this is where I think that the Court of Appeal may have been misled by the expression 'legitimate expectation'. The real question is whether in fairness or equity Mr O'Neill had a right to the shares. On this point, one runs up against what seems to me the insuperable obstacle of the judge's finding that Mr Phillips never agreed to give them. He made no promise on the point. From which it seems to me to follow that there is no basis, consistent with established principles of equity, for a court to hold that Mr Phillips was behaving unfairly in withdrawing from the negotiation. This would not be restraining the exercise of legal rights. It would be imposing upon Mr Phillips an obligation to which he never agreed. Where, as here, parties enter into negotiations with a view to a transfer of shares on professional advice and subject to a condition that they are not to be bound until a formal document has been executed, I do not think it is possible to say that an obligation has arisen in fairness or equity at an earlier stage.

The same reasoning applies to the sharing of profits. The judge found as a fact that Mr Phillips made no unconditional promise about the sharing of profits. He had said informally that he would share the profits equally while Mr O'Neill managed the company and he himself did not have to be involved in day-to-day business. He deliberately retained control of the company and with it, as the judge said, the right to redraw Mr O'Neill's responsibilities. This he did without objection in August 1991. The consequence was that he came back to running the business and Mr O'Neill was no longer managing director. He had made no promise to share the profits equally in such circumstances and it was therefore not inequitable or unfair for him to refuse to carry on doing so . . .

No-fault divorce?

Mr Hollington, who appeared for Mr O'Neill, said that it did not matter whether Mr Phillips had done anything unfair. The fact was that trust and confidence between the parties had broken down. In those circumstances it was obvious that there ought to be a parting of the ways and the unfairness lay in Mr Phillips, who accepted this to be the case, not being willing to allow Mr O'Neill to recover his stake in the company. Even if Mr Phillips was not at fault in causing the breakdown, it would be unfair to leave Mr O'Neill locked into the company as a minority shareholder.

Mr Hollington's submission comes to saying that, in a 'quasi-partnership' company, one partner ought to be entitled at will to require the other partner or partners to buy his shares at a fair value. . . .

I do not think that there is any support in the authorities for such a stark right of unilateral withdrawal. . . .

The Law Commission Report on Shareholder Remedies to which I have already referred considered whether to recommend the introduction of a statutory remedy 'in situations where there is no fault' (paragraph 3.65) so that members of a quasi-partnership could exit at will. They said, at p. 39, para. 3.66:

'In our view there are strong economic arguments against allowing shareholders to exit at will. Also, as a matter of principle, such a right would fundamentally contravene the sanctity of the contract binding the members and the company which we considered should guide our approach to shareholder remedies.'

The Law Commission plainly did not consider that section 459 already provided a right to exit at will and I do not think so either. . . .

The offer to buy

Mr Ralls, who appeared for Mr Phillips, submitted that even if his conduct had been unfairly prejudicial, the petition should have been dismissed because he had made an offer to buy the shares at a fair price, which was the whole of the relief to which Mr. O'Neill would have been entitled. In view of the conclusion I have reached about the absence of unfair prejudice, with which I understand your Lordships to agree, this point does not need to be decided. Nevertheless, the effect of an offer to buy the shares as an answer to a petition under section 459 is a matter of such great practical importance that I would invite your Lordships to consider it. . . .

The Law Commission Report on Shareholder Remedies, at pp. 30–37, paras. 3.26–56 has recommended that in a private company limited by shares in which substantially all the members are directors, there should be a statutory presumption that the removal of a shareholder as a director, or from substantially all his functions as a director, is unfairly prejudicial conduct. . . . [T]he unfairness does not lie in the exclusion alone but in exclusion without a reasonable offer. If the respondent to a petition has plainly made a reasonable offer, then the exclusion as such will not be unfairly prejudicial and he will be entitled to have the petition struck out. It is therefore very important that participants in such companies should be able to know what counts as a reasonable offer.

In the first place, the offer must be to purchase the shares at a fair value. This will ordinarily be a [pro rata] value . . . without a discount for its being a minority holding. [Although sometimes it will be fair to apply a discounted value.]

Secondly, the value, if not agreed, should be determined by a competent expert. . . .

Thirdly, the offer should be to have the value determined by the expert as an expert. I do not think that the offer should provide for the full machinery of arbitration or the half-way house of an expert who gives reasons. . . .

Fourthly, the offer should, as in this case, provide for equality of arms between the parties. Both should have the same right of access to information about the company which bears upon the value of the shares and both should have the right to make submissions to the expert, though the form (written or oral) which these submissions may take should be left to the discretion of the expert himself.

Fifthly, there is the question of costs. In the present case, when the offer was made after nearly three years of litigation, it could not serve as an independent ground for dismissing the petition, on the assumption that it was otherwise well founded, without an offer of costs. But this does not mean that payment of costs need always be offered. If there is a breakdown in relations between the parties, the majority shareholder should be given a reasonable opportunity to make an offer (which may include time to explore the question of how to raise finance) before he becomes obliged to pay costs. . . .

LORDS JAUNCEY OF TULLICHETTLE, CLYDE, HUTTON and HOBHOUSE OF WOODBOROUGH concurred.

> Notes

1. *O'Neill v Phillips* **[13.34]** is the first (and, to date, the only) House of Lords or Supreme Court case on the 'unfair prejudice' provisions (rather than the earlier CA 1948 s 210 'oppression' provisions). The case has generated a good deal of debate as to whether Lord Hoffmann (both in this case and in his earlier judgment in *Re Saul D Harrison & Sons plc* **[13.33]**) has given a restrictive interpretation to s 459 (and in particular to the concept of 'legitimate expectations'), so that the remedy is likely to be less readily available (as the Law Commissions seem to think), or whether the law remains substantially unchanged (as the CLR believes).

2. In *Re Coroin Ltd* [2012] EWHC 2343 (Ch) (the point not disturbed on appeal), David Richards J refused to recognise legitimate expectations where the founding members were:

a group of highly sophisticated and experienced business people and investors with a view to the purchase of a well-known group of hotels for a price running into many hundreds of millions of pounds and to retaining and managing some of those hotels. There was little prior relationship between many of the investors and some were unknown to each other until a few days before the company was formed. More importantly, articles of association and a shareholders' agreement were negotiated and drafted, containing lengthy and complex provisions governing their relations with each other and with the company. I find it hard to imagine a case where it would be more inappropriate to overlay on those arrangements equitable considerations of the sort discussed by Lord Wilberforce and Lord Hoffmann.

3. In relation to pre-trial offers to buy, in *Harborne Road Nominees Ltd v John Greenway Karvaski* [2011] EWHC 2214 (Ch), the court held that the rules in *O'Neill v Phillips* did not apply in the case of equal shareholders. In such cases, the question was whether the shareholder had been offered a sale on terms that gave him all the advantages he could reasonably expect to achieve from issuing an unfair prejudice petition: only then would it be an abuse to continue those proceedings in the face of such an offer. Furthermore, it was held in *Graham v Every* [2014] EWCA Civ 191 that the valuation used in pre-trial offers to buy should take account of the petitioner's allegations of unfair prejudicial conduct.

Remedies: valuing shares in buy-out orders

Relevance of parties' conduct to the valuation of shares.

[13.35] Bird Precision Bellows Ltd [1984] Ch 419 (Nourse J),
affd [1986] Ch 658 (Court of Appeal)

The only issue before the court was the issue of valuing shares when (in this case pursuant to an order made by consent) the petitioner's shares were to be purchased by the majority under CA 1980 s 75 [now CA 2006 s 994]. Nourse J, at first instance, held that the conduct of the parties could be relevant in determining whether the shares of the respective parties in the company were to be valued pro rata or whether the minority's interest should be discounted.

NOURSE J: Broadly speaking, shares in a small private company are acquired either by allotment on its incorporation or by transfer or devolution at some later date. In the first category it is a matter of common occurrence for a company to be incorporated in order to acquire an existing business or to start a new one, and in either event for it to be a vehicle for the conduct of a business carried on by two or more shareholders which they could, had they wished, have carried on in partnership together. Although it has been pointed out . . . that the description may be confusing, it is often convenient and it is certainly usual to describe that kind of company as a quasi-partnership. In the second category, irrespective of the nature of the company, it is a matter of common occurrence for a shareholder to acquire shares from another at a price which is discounted because they represent a minority holding. It seems to me that some general observations can usefully be made in regard to each of these examples . . .

I would expect that in a majority of cases where purchase orders are made under s 75 in relation to quasi-partnerships the vendor is unwilling in the sense that the sale has been forced upon him. Usually he will be a minority shareholder whose interests have been unfairly prejudiced by the manner in which the affairs of the company have been conducted by the majority. On the assumption that the unfair prejudice has made it no longer tolerable for him to retain his interest in the company, a sale of his shares will invariably be his only practical way out short of a winding up. In that kind of case it seems to me that it would not merely not be fair, but most unfair, that he should be bought out on the fictional basis applicable to a free election to sell his shares in accordance with the company's articles of association, or indeed on any other basis which involved a discounted price. In my judgment the correct course would be to fix the price pro rata according to the value of the shares as a whole and without any discount, as being the only fair method of compensating an unwilling vendor of the equivalent of a partnership share. Equally, if the order provided . . . for the purchase of the shares of the delinquent majority, it would not merely not be fair, but most unfair, that they should receive a price which involved an element of premium.

Of the other, I would expect more rare, cases in which the court might make a purchase order in relation to a quasi-partnership, the arguments of Mr Jacob require me to mention one. Suppose the case of a minority shareholder whose interests had been unfairly prejudiced by the conduct of the majority, but who had nevertheless so acted as to deserve his exclusion from the company. It is difficult to see how such a case could arise in practice, because one would expect acts and deserts of that kind to be inconsistent with the existence of the supposed conduct of the majority. Be that as it may the consideration of that possibility has been forced upon me by the agreement for the price to be determined by the court without any admission of unfairly prejudicial conduct on the part of the respondents. As will appear, Mr Jacob submitted that the petitioners did act in such a way as to deserve their exclusion from the company. He further submitted that it would therefore be fair for them to be bought out on the basis which would have been applicable if they had made a free election to sell their shares pursuant to the articles, ie at

> a discount. Assuming, at present, that the respondents can establish the necessary factual basis, I think that Mr Jacob's further submission is correct. A shareholder who deserves his exclusion has, if you like, made a constructive election to sever his connection with the company and thus to sell his shares.

On appeal, the Court of Appeal declined to interfere with the judge's approach, which was a matter for his discretion.

➤ Note

In *Re OC (Transport) Services Ltd* [1984] BCLC 251, Mervyn Davies J held that it was proper to backdate a valuation to the commencement of the 'unfairly prejudicial' conduct, so that the value of the shares would not be affected by the changes which that conduct had brought about. In this, he was following the approach of the House of Lords under the old s 210 in the *Scottish Co-operative* case **[13.31]**. Citing the position in *Re OC (Transport) Services Ltd*, Proudman J in *Re Phoenix Contracts (Leicester) Ltd* [2010] EWHC 2375 (Ch) was of the view that it would be required 'to specify an early valuation date where it was simply unclear whether the respondent's conduct after the date of unfairly prejudicial conduct caused the diminution in the value of the shares, on the basis that it was unfair for the petitioner to assume the burden of the risk' [150]. The learned judge therefore fixed the date of valuation as the date the petitioner was excluded from the company. Similarly, in *Re Abbington Hotel Ltd* [2012] 1 BCLC 410, David Richards J held that such a date 'meet[s] and provide[s] a remedy for the exclusion of Mr D'Angelo from the company' [140]. Also see *Attwood v Maidment* [2013] EWCA Civ 119 for discussion of other relevant issues.

Even in quasi-partnerships, purchase at an undiscounted price is not inevitable.

[13.36] Re Phoenix Office Supplies Ltd [2002] EWCA Civ 1740 (Court of Appeal)

P appealed against a decision ordering its two remaining directors to purchase the shares of a departing director, L, at their full undiscounted value. L had decided to leave his employment with P for personal reasons but had remained a director whilst seeking to sell his shareholding without a discount to reflect his minority holding. The remaining directors had refused L's request to pay one-third of the company's net asset value for the shares and had further rejected his requests for copies of management accounts. The Court of Appeal, allowing the appeal, held that a director leaving his position of his own volition was not entitled to have his shares bought out at their full undiscounted value: not every quasi-partnership entitles directors to a 'no fault divorce', and L could not 'put' his shares on the company.

> AULD LJ: Section 459 has two roles, as explained by Lord Hoffmann in *O'Neill v Phillips* **[13.34]** at 1098G–1099A. First, it protects shareholders against the breach of terms on which they have agreed the affairs of the company should be conducted, through the articles of association or, say, some collateral agreement. Second, it protects them against some inequity that makes it unfair for those conducting the company's affairs to rely upon their strict legal power, for example, a resolution by majority shareholders to remove a minority director under section 303 of the 1985 Act [see CA 2006 s 168]. As Lord Wilberforce had earlier explained in *In Re Westbourne*

Galleries Ltd **[16.13]**, the latter protection is the source of the notion of a relationship of quasi-partnership between shareholders . . .

[He then referred to various authorities, including *O'Neill v Phillips* **[13.34]**, citing some of the passages cited previously on 'legitimate expectations' and whether exclusion might be in breach of such expectations. He then continued:] Given the breadth of such propositions, it is important to keep in mind that section 459 is designed for the protection of the members of companies. It is in that capacity that they seek its protection, not as directors or employees, an important reminder where the provision is prayed in aid by a departing member who may also be a director or employee. And, as Lord Hoffmann indicated in *O'Neill v Phillips* at 1107B–C, where the member is departing because he has been excluded by other members from his involvement as a director and/or employee, the provision is aimed not at unfairness in such exclusion for its own sake, but at unfairness in his exclusion without a reasonable offer for his shares . . .

How then is the principle to be applied in a quasi-partnership company where the departing minority shareholder, not the majority shareholders, seeks to put an end to the association for personal reasons and take his investment in it with him, and where, as the Judge found, there was no agreement for such a 'no-fault divorce'? I have already indicated the answer in my summary of Lord Hoffmann's propositions, but here is the place to put it in his own words, at 1104D–1105B:

'Mr Hollington's submission comes to saying that, in a "quasi-partnership" company, one partner ought to be entitled at will to require the other partner or partners to buy his shares at a fair value. All he need do is to declare that trust and confidence has broken down . . .

I do not think that there is any support in the authorities for such a stark right of unilateral withdrawal. There are cases, such as *In re A Company (No. 006834 of 1988), Ex parte Kremer* [1989] BCLC 365, in which it has been said that if a breakdown in relations has caused the majority to remove a shareholder from participation in the management, it is usually a waste of time to try to investigate who caused the breakdown. Such breakdowns often occur . . . without either side having done anything seriously wrong or unfair. It is not fair to the excluded member, who will usually have lost his employment, to keep his assets lock[ed] in the company. But that does not mean that a member who has not been dismissed or excluded can demand that his shares be purchased simply because he feels that he has lost trust and confidence in the others. I rather doubt whether even in partnership law a dissolution would be granted on this ground in a case in which it was still possible under the articles for the business of the partnership to be continued. And as Lord Wilberforce observed in *In Re Westbourne Galleries Ltd* . . . [at] 380, one should not press the quasi-partnership analogy too far: "A company, however small, however domestic, is a company not a partnership or even a quasi-partnership . . ."

The Law Commission Report on Shareholder Remedies. . . considered whether to recommend the introduction of a statutory remedy 'in situations where there is no fault' (paragraph 3.65) so that members of a quasi-partnership could exit at will. They said, at p. 39, in para 3.66:

"In our view there are strong economic arguments against allowing shareholders to exit at will. Also, as a matter of principle, such a right would fundamentally contravene the sanctity of the contract binding the members and the company which we considered should guide our approach to shareholder remedies."

The Law Commission plainly did not consider that section 459 already provided a right to exit at will and I do not think so either.'

The [trial] Judge . . . ruled that a consequence of the quasi-partnership here was that Mr Larvin was entitled to the full undiscounted value of his shares. In so ruling, he appears to have proceeded as if it had been Messrs Parish and Ogden who had taken the initiative to sever the association rather than, as was the case, Mr Larvin. True it was that they refused to recognise him as a director or to give him access to certain company information, but that was only after he had made plain that he wanted to sever all relationship with the company and them and to take the value of his shareholding with him. In my judgment, this is not the sort of case that Lord Hoffmann had in mind when formulating his propositions applicable to excluded members. The Judge did not expressly refer to such propositions, but he appears to have had them in mind in the passages that I have emphasised . . .

Lord Hoffmann's different treatment of those cases where there is a withdrawal because of a sense of loss of trust and confidence applies *a fortiori* to a shareholder who, even without such a sense, but for other personal reasons, simply wishes to leave and take his investment in the company with him. Where, as here, the company is small and with only a few shareholders each holding a significant proportion of the company's issued capital, a sudden demand from one of them, for essentially personal reasons, to seek to withdraw his investment could be very damaging, even potentially ruinous, to them and the company.

As to the Judge's reliance on the 'lock-in' effect of Article 6 of the company's Articles of Association, I do not consider that the 'absolute discretion' it purported to give to the directors to decline to register any transfer of any share pointed to an intention that if any one of them wanted to move elsewhere, for whatever reason, he could be sure of realising the full value of his shareholding. Such an entitlement could, for the reasons I have just given, be ruinous to the company and its members. The company's directors have a fiduciary duty as such to act in the interests of the company. The power of veto on a transfer, despite its terms, is not absolute. It is subject to the equitable jurisdiction of the court to intervene by winding up the company on the just and equitable ground or to the provisions of section 459 itself. . . .

As Mr Crawford submitted, not every quasi-partnership company relationship gives rise to an entitlement to a 'no-fault divorce'; there must be something more. . . .

Accordingly, it does not follow from the fact that the company was a quasi-partnership that Mr Larvin was entitled to insist on leaving with an undiscounted value of his minority shareholding. . . .

Depending on the issues as they developed between the parties, there might have been a claim for an appropriately discounted value of his holding. Or Mr Larvin could have continued with his substantial minority holding, with a view eventually to agreeing a price with the others or for its transfer to a third party. Failing such agreement, he might have been able to seek such relief as might then be appropriate under s 459 or for the company to be wound up on the just and equitable ground. But that was not the basis of his petition. . . .

[He then went on to allow the appeal.]

CLARKE LJ concurred.

JONATHAN PARKER LJ delivered a concurring judgment.

➤ Note

By contrast, in *Strahan v Wilcock* [2006] EWCA Civ 13, CA, purchase at the undiscounted price was ordered. The company was held to be a quasi-partnership. This despite the facts that S had not participated in the business from the outset, had commenced the relationship as a consultant, had only later become a shareholder and manager, and had held only a minority of the shares. Given the quasi-partnership nature of the relationship at the time the shares were acquired, however, there were equitable considerations which bound W to purchase S's shares on a non-discounted basis once S had been dismissed by the company. S's departure from the company was involuntary. He did not take a unilateral decision to leave and nor was he guilty of misconduct. Fairness demanded that he should be entitled to claim back not simply the cost of acquiring the shares, but their value at the date of the buy-out order.

Indeed, in quasi-partnerships involving two shareholders with 50% shareholding each, the court will be reluctant to apply market discounts to the price at which 50% of the shares are purchased, even where the vendor shareholder has been found to be responsible for the breakdown of the 'partnership': *Re Home & Office Fire Extinguishers Ltd* [2012] EWHC 917 (Ch). To do so, in the learned judge's *dicta* at [77], 'when no loss has been proved, would be in effect to impose a penalty on the selling shareholder, and to give a windfall to the buying shareholder'.

Where the business of a company is dependent on the petitioner, who could conduct a competing business if he left, a discount should be applied.

[13.37] Re Via Servis [2014] EWHC 2069 (Chancery Division)

The facts are immaterial.

> JONES QC:
>
> 95. As to the second question, I note that Ms Skala may have been prepared to offer more than EUR 300,000 for Mr Traun's shares but he never named a higher price. This, of course, would have been on the basis of Ms Skala continuing to work in the Company and not running a competing business. And when Mr Traun told me in evidence that a fair offer for his shares would have been EUR 200,000 plus repayment of his loan that, of course, would have been on the basis that he sold his shares so, again, Ms Skala would continue to work for the Company and not for the competing business. So, as it seems to me, there has to be some discount for the fact that Ms Skala would no longer be employed by the Company and able to run a competing business on any sale of Ms Skala's shares....

In valuing shares, the valuer must consider whether his provisional valuation makes commercial or business sense.

[13.38] Chilukuri v RP Explorer Master Fund [2013] EWCA Civ 1307 (Court of Appeal)

The court considered the valuation of a minority shareholding in an incompetently managed company to ascertain damages payable for breach of a contractual obligation to transfer shares.

> BRIGGS LJ:
>
> 52. It is axiomatic that in any complicated process of valuation, the valuer must take the relevant aspects of the world as he finds them (unless constrained by his instructions), and that he must, after looking at each element of the process, stand back and ask himself whether his provisional valuation makes commercial or business sense, viewed in the round.
>
> 53. Standing back therefore, the putative market for this shareholding in July 2009 would have been offered a 26% minority holding in an apparently incompetently managed Indian company, the majority shareholders of which were close-knit private individuals with no reason to take any notice of the purchaser's views about the conduct of the company's affairs, with a track record of mismanagement, or non-management, of its principal asset which they had allowed to become dormant, in a deteriorating political and economic environment in the DRC [Democratic Republic of Congo], and who had allowed a winding up petition to be presented and served, with the immediate consequence of prohibiting the completion of any share sale transaction in any

event. The interested purchaser would have discovered, upon due diligence, that the supposedly valuable rights in the JVA were still inchoate as the result of the outstanding presidential decree, that attempts to fund the project had come to nothing, and apparently ceased a year previously, that the company lacked its own resources with which either to fund the project or to deal with its creditors, and that the commercial substratum upon which the JVA had been constructed, namely an immediate local demand in the DRC for bitumen needed in a large government road-building programme, had in all probability evaporated due to the deterioration in the political and economic state of that country.

54. In all the circumstances, I find myself quite unable to imagine any reasonably prudent and well-advised prospective purchaser paying anything for this 26% shareholding. In my judgment the only conclusion on the largely undisputed facts is that no such person would have touched these shares with a barge pole. It follows that, in my view, this appeal should be allowed, and that a substitution of nominal damages made for the substantial sum which the judge ordered.

[LEWISON LJ gave a short concurring judgment and RIMER LJ agreed with both.]

> ➤ Note

Although this case and the following three cases do not concern unfair prejudice petitions, it is submitted that general principles regarding the valuation of shares as reflected in these cases equally apply where shares have to be valued as part of an unfair prejudice petition.

Aside from making sure that the valuation makes commercial sense, the valuer must also adhere to his instructions strictly: *Begum v Hossain* [2015] EWCA Civ 717. In that case, an expert was appointed under a settlement agreement which stated that the expert was to have access to all of the records and documents in the company's control, including 'any handwritten takings'. In failing to take into account the handwritten takings, the expert was held to have exceeded his mandate and the valuation was set aside.

Furthermore, where the valuer is instructed to determine the fair value of shares, it should not adopt a valuation method that favours one party over the other: *Swain v Swain Plc* [2015] EWHC 600 (Ch).

Finally, in *Hut Group Ltd v Nobahar-Cookson* [2014] EWHC 3842 (QB), the parties agreed that shares comprised of the whole issued capital should be valued by reference to the effect on the company's earnings before interest, tax, depreciation and amortization (EBIDTA), while shares comprised of a minority interest should be valued using a discounted cash flow method.

Date of valuation.

[13.39] Profinance Trust SA v Gladstone [2002] 1 WLR 1024 (Court of Appeal)

The facts are immaterial.

ROBERT WALKER LJ for the court (SCHIEMANN and ROBERT WALKER LJ and LLOYD J): In our judgment the deputy judge was right in his view that an order for the equivalent of interest [ie a sum paid in addition to the settled price of the shares to be bought out, where the valuation has been carried out early] is not beyond the powers of the court under section 461(1) of the Companies Act 1985 [re-enacted in CA 2006 s 996]. The court has repeatedly emphasised the width of the discretion conferred by that subsection, which is not limited to the particular powers enumerated in subsection (2). The House of Lords has (in relation to the court's closely comparable powers under section 210 of the Companies Act 1948) approved the making of adjustments in the valuation process which mean that the court is actually valuing shares, not as they are, but as they would have been if events had followed a different course; and that practice is regularly followed by the court in orders under section 461(1). In these circumstances a denial of the court's power to award the equivalent of interest would come close to straining at a gnat.

It is however a power which should be exercised with great caution. Miss Newman [counsel] has rightly drawn attention to the need for lawyers to be able to advise their clients as to the likely range of outcomes of section 459 proceedings, in order to encourage compromise in an area in which litigation can be cripplingly expensive. If a petitioner seeking an order for the purchase of his shares contends (either as his only claim or in the alternative) that they should be valued at a relatively early date but then augmented by the equivalent of interest, he must put forward that claim clearly and persuade the court by evidence that it is the only way, or the best way, to a fair result. It should not be a last-minute afterthought (as it may have been, to some extent, in *In re Bird Precision Bellows Ltd* **[13.35]** and *Elliott v Planet Organic Ltd* [2000] BCC 610). Unless a petitioner is asking for no more than simple interest at a normal rate he should also put before the court evidence on which the court can decide what amount (if any) to allow. The exercise which the deputy judge undertook, as described in the last paragraph of his judgment, does not appear to have had a solid evidential basis. . . .

[And on the more general issue of valuation of shares, he continued:] The starting point should in our view be the general proposition stated by Nourse J in *In re London School of Electronics Ltd* [1986] Ch 211, 224: 'Prima facie an interest in a going concern ought to be valued at the date on which it is ordered to be purchased.' That is, as Nourse J said, subject to the overriding requirement that the valuation should be fair on the facts of the particular case.

The general trend of authority over the last 15 years appears to us to support that as the starting point, while recognising that there are many cases in which fairness (to one side or the other) requires the court to take another date. It would be wrong to try to enumerate all those cases but some of them can be illustrated by the authorities already referred to:

(i) Where a company has been deprived of its business, an early valuation date (and compensating adjustments) may be required in fairness to the claimant: see *Scottish Co-operative Wholesale Society Ltd v Meyer* **[13.31]**.

(ii) Where a company has been reconstructed or its business has changed significantly, so that it has a new economic identity, an early valuation date may be required in fairness to one or both parties: see *In re OC (Transport) Services Ltd* [1984] BCLC 251, and to a lesser degree *In re London School of Electronics Ltd* [1986] Ch 211. But an improper alteration in the issued share capital, unaccompanied by any change in the business, will not necessarily have that outcome: see *In re DR Chemicals Ltd* (1988) 5 BCC 39.

(iii) Where a minority shareholder has a petition on foot and there is a general fall in the market, the court may in fairness to the claimant have the shares valued at an early date, especially if it strongly disapproves of the majority shareholder's prejudicial conduct: see *In re Cumana Ltd* [1986] BCLC 430.

(iv) But a claimant is not entitled to what the deputy judge called a one-way bet, and the court will not direct an early valuation date simply to give the claimant the most advantageous exit from the company, especially where severe prejudice has not been made out: see *In re Elgindata Ltd* [1991] BCLC 959 **[13.29]**.

(v) All these points may be heavily influenced by the parties' conduct in making and accepting or rejecting offers either before or during the course of the proceedings: see *In re A Company (No 00709 of 1992)* [1999] 1 WLR 1092.

In our judgment the fairest course in this case would be to take the agreed value as at the time of the first instance hearing, that is £215,000. We allow this appeal and substitute an order that Mr Gladstone should purchase Profinance's 40% holding in the company for £86,000.

[13.40] Re KR Hardy Estates Ltd [2014] EWHC 4001 (Chancery Division)

This case concerned a family-run company. Ms Hardy (the petitioner) was a minority shareholder in the company and received a salary for an administrative position. In 2008, Ms Hardy's salary was stopped. In 2010, Ms Hardy sought legal advice in relation to her position as a shareholder and she rejected an offer from the first defendant (the other shareholder in the company) to buy her out. One of the issues before the court was the proper date for valuation of the shares.

MANN QC:

Valuation Date—conclusion

87. It has to be said that, while offering excellent guidance, none of the enumerated circumstances in *Profinance* can be said to obtain in the present case. Estates has not been deprived of its business. Even if there had been an unjustified value shift to Builders, it would still have its assets. Its business has not changed albeit its assets have been differently treated since 2011 in its financial statements for tax purposes. It is not suggested that there has been a fall in the market while the Petition has been on foot. The Offer might sensibly have been accepted but I have found in effect that Christine cannot be criticised for not doing so at the stage it was made.

88. At paragraph 67, I listed the candidate dates for valuation, as I see them, namely:

(a)　The date of the withdrawal of financial support for Christine;

(b)　The date any appreciable (i.e., more than minimal) unjustified 'value shift' first occurred;

(c)　The date on which the Offer was rejected;

(d)　The date on which the Petition was presented;

(e)　The date on which the Points of Defence were served;

(f)　The date of my order;

(g)　The date of actual valuation.

89. As regards (a), the withdrawal of the Benefits was clearly a significant event with serious consequences for Christine, viewing the matter from the perspective of her legitimate interest. However, it would not, in my judgment, be right to value her shares at this date, not least because she has adduced no evidence at all for not seeking to be bought out or presenting a petition much earlier than her first tentative approaches to Kenneth and Betty and then Richard and S&R through NLegal in 2010. Moreover, the withdrawal of the Benefits can only have had a positive impact, albeit very small, on the value of her shares. Furthermore, no evidence has been adduced tending to justify the selection of this date.

90. I have held as regards (b) that there has been neither an appreciable nor an unjustified value shift down to the year ended 31st December 2012. Accounts have not been adduced for either company for the year ended 31st December 2013 although, presumably, if they have not already been signed off, they soon will be. However, with the exception in Estates' financial statements of properties previously treated for tax purposes as stock held for development being transferred from stock to investments in 2011, the principles upon which the accounts for the earlier periods were prepared are now clear, so later accounts applying matching principles would have been unlikely had they been available to have affected either my reasoning or my conclusion. Accordingly (b) is not engaged.

91. As regards (c) to (e) inclusive, while there is force in Richard's contention for the selection of (e) rather than (c) and (d), I am not convinced, irrespective of the earlier delays, that Christine's legal and expert teams should have had been ready even by (e) to tender advice whether to concede and agree a valuation at this juncture.

92. The selection of (g) could serve as the date and would be consistent with principle yet suffers from uncertainty.

93. I have decided, therefore, in favour of (f), which has the advantage of certainty and in all the circumstances appears to me to be the most fair of all of these possible dates.

Unfair prejudice and other remedies

Before leaving this discussion of CA 2006 s 994, it is worth noting that this avenue for complaint by members might fruitfully be used to remedy a wide variety of wrongs that have been considered elsewhere in this book. Many of the cases traditionally located in some other part of the company law syllabus, such as those relating to the alteration of a company's articles, might well be decided differently today if proceedings were brought under this section. For example, consider the saga which culminated in the case of *Greenhalgh v Arderne Cinemas Ltd* **[4.27]** and **[11.09]**. Mr Greenhalgh might well have claimed (possibly with success) that he had been the victim of unfairly prejudicial conduct. It is also possible that minority shareholders who were in fact successful in some older cases might now choose to seek a remedy under CA 2006 s 994 rather than whatever was then available to them: for instance, the petitioners in *Loch v John Blackwood Ltd* **[16.12]** might well have preferred a buy-out rather than having the company compulsorily wound up.

On the other hand, where CA 2006 s 994 seems less than satisfactory, members might resort to petitioning the court for a winding-up order on the 'just and equitable' ground: see 'Compulsory winding up on the "just and equitable" ground', pp 840ff. There is also, at least in theory, the possibility of invoking the powers of the Department for Business, Innovation and Skills under CA 1985 Pt XIV (not re-enacted in CA 2006), to have the affairs of the company investigated (see 'Public investigation of companies', pp 770ff). In practice, the Department's powers are most commonly invoked in cases of insolvency, fraudulent trading and financial scandal—that is, in matters of interest to the investing public and to creditors—while minority shareholders who seek aid are sent away empty-handed. Mr Moir (see *Wallersteiner v Moir (No 2)* [1975] QB 373, cited at p 671) is reported to have made 15 unsuccessful requests to the Department (*Economist*, 8 February 1975).

Also note a recent decision by the Court of Appeal, in which it was held that members' rights to bring a petition under s 994 is not inalienable, in that members can agree to resolve such disputes through means of alternative dispute resolution, such as arbitration. No objection can be raised both as a matter of statutory construction, and on the ground of public policy: *Fulham Football Club (1987) v Richards* [2011] EWCA Civ 855, [2012] Ch 333: see H McVea, 'Section 994 of the Companies Act 2006 and the Primacy of Contract' (2012) 75 MLR 1123.

➤ Questions

1. Reconsider the cases on *directors'* decision-making (see Chapter 7) and assess the extent to which a *company* can complain that its directors have not acted bona fide, or not acted for proper purposes, and so impugn a decision on those grounds without having to prove that a particular *commercial* decision is inappropriate and in itself constitutes maladministration. Do the CA 2006 provisions on directors' duties strengthen the law in this regard?

2. Once you have read this entire chapter, assess the extent to which a *member* can complain about the sorts of directors' activities just described. If action *is* possible, is the remedy one for the company or one for the shareholders personally?

3. Reconsider the cases on *members'* decision-making (eg see 'Members' personal rights', pp 261ff, 'Permitted reductions of capital', pp 534ff and 'Variation of class rights', pp 587ff) and assess the extent to which a *company* can complain that its members have not acted bona fide, or not acted for proper purposes. Can *members* use this as a ground for complaint, in seeking a remedy for the company *or* a remedy for themselves personally?

▧ Further reading

ARSALIDOU, D, 'Litigation Culture and the New Statutory Derivative Claim' (2009) 30 *Company Lawyer* 205.

BAXTER, C, 'The True Spirit of *Foss v Harbottle*' (1987) 38 *Northern Ireland Law Quarterly* 6.

BAXTER, C, 'The Role of the Judge in Enforcing Shareholder Rights' [1983] CLJ 96.

BAXTER, C, 'Irregular Company Meetings' [1976] JBL 323.

BECK, SM, 'Shareholders' Derivative Action' (1974) 52 *Canadian Bar Review* 159.

BOYLE, AJ, 'The Minority Shareholder in the Nineteenth Century' (1965) 28 MLR 317.

DRURY, R, 'The Relative Nature of a Shareholder's Right to Enforce the Company Contract' [1986] CLJ 219.

GIBBS, D, 'Has the Statutory Derivative Claim Fulfilled its Objectives? A Prima Facie Case and the Mandatory Bar: Part 1' (2011) 32 *Company Lawyer* 41.

GIBBS, D, 'Has the Statutory Derivative Claim Fulfilled its Objectives? The Hypothetical Director and CSR: Part 2' (2011) 32 *Company Lawyer* 76.

GREGORY, R, 'What *is* the Rule in *Foss v Harbottle*?' (1982) 45 MLR 584.

GRIFFIN, S, 'Shareholder Remedies and the No Reflective Loss Principle—Problems Surrounding the Identification of a Membership Interests' [2010] JBL 461.

HANNIGAN, B, 'Drawing Boundaries between Derivative Claims and Unfairly Prejudicial Conduct' [2009] JBL 606.

HIRT, HC, 'The Company's Decision to Litigate against its Directors' [2005] JBL 159.

HIRT, HC, 'In What Circumstances Should Breaches of Directors' Duties Give Rise to a Remedy under ss 459–461 of the Companies Act 1985?' (2003) 24 *Company Lawyer* 100.

KEAY, A and LOUGHREY, J, 'Derivative Proceedings in a Brave New World for Company Management and Shareholders' [2010] JBL 151.

KOH, P, 'Derivative Actions "Once Removed"' [2010] JBL 101.

LIGHTMAN, D, 'The Role of the Company at the Permission Stage in the Statutory Derivative Claim' (2011) 30 CJQ 23.

MITCHELL, C, 'Shareholders' Claims for Reflective Loss' [2004] 120 LQR 457.

MUJIH, EC, 'The New Statutory Derivative Claim: A Delicate Balancing Act: Part 1' (2012) *Company Lawyer* 76.

MUJIH, EC, 'The New Statutory Derivative Claim: A Paradox of Minority Shareholder Protection: Part 2' (2012) *Company Lawyer* 99.

PARTRIDGE, RJC, 'Ratification and the Release of Directors from Personal Liability' [1987] CLJ 122.

PICKERING, MA, 'Shareholders' Voting Rights and Company Control' (1965) 81 LQR 248.

RILEY, C, 'Contracting Out of Company Law: Section 459 of the Companies Act 1985 and the Role of the Courts' (1992) 55 MLR 782.

SEALY, LS, 'Problems of Standing, Pleading and Proof in Corporate Litigation' in B Pettet (ed), *Company Law in Change* (1987), p 1.

SULLIVAN, GR, 'Restating the Scope of the Derivative Action' [1985] CLJ 236.

WEDDERBURN, KW, 'Derivative Actions and *Foss v Harbottle*' (1981) 44 MLR 202.

WEDDERBURN, KW, 'Shareholders' Rights and the Rule in *Foss v Harbottle*' [1957] CLJ 194 and [1958] CLJ 93.

WORTHINGTON, S, 'Corporate Governance: Remedying and Ratifying Directors' Breaches' (2000) 116 LQR 638.

14

PUBLIC DISCLOSURE, MARKET REGULATION AND PUBLIC INVESTIGATIONS OF COMPANIES

Public disclosure and the disclosure philosophy

It has long been recognised that the 'price' that companies must pay for the privileges of incorporation (separate personality) and limited liability is a fair degree of openness and publicity about their affairs. The Companies Acts have been largely based on this philosophy. Even the obligatory term 'Limited' is intended to achieve this purpose, warning those dealing with a company that its resources are finite.

In the ordinary course of business of a company, disclosure under the Act is secured by: (i) delivery of information to the Registrar of Companies; (ii) publication in the *Gazette*; (iii) information made available at the company's registered office; and (iv) notifications in various business documents. The Stock Exchange imposes additional obligations on listed companies. And, quite outside any legal regime, the market, and the financial press, may publicly disclose information considered significant.

Companies are also subject to special disclosure rules designed to give interested parties information on substantial share ownership in the company and to provide appropriate information to investors when new shares are issued to the public. Note, however, that courts have held that these powers to require disclosure must be used for 'proper purposes': see *Burry & Knight Ltd v Knight* [2014] EWCA Civ 604, where the Court of Appeal had to decide whether a member's request to inspect the register of members was made for improper purposes (see Question 3 following *Eclairs Group Ltd v JKX Oil & Gas Plc* **[7.11]**, p 355).

Finally, there are rules restricting the use of non-public information by those acquiring shares in the market.

General disclosure obligations

The Registrar of Companies

A company's obligation to make public disclosure is generally fulfilled by delivering the required information to the Registrar of Companies. Section 1061 of the Companies Act 2006 (CA 2006) confirms the role of the registrar, whose duties and functions date back to 1844.

There are three separate registrars, for England and Wales (situated in Cardiff), for Scotland and for Northern Ireland. The registrar maintains a file for every company and adds to it all the documents relating to that company as they are lodged for registration over the years. Files are open to public search, either electronically or using a microfiche system. Certain information delivered after 1 January 2007 must be filed electronically (CA 2006 s 1078); otherwise the filing mechanism is discretionary (s 1080).

All the company's most important documents relating to its constitution and its history subsequent to its incorporation, together with information about its membership, finances and management must be notified to the registrar with, as history shows, each successive Act stepping up the reporting obligations.

A person searching the records of a company at the registry will find the following documents available: the memorandum and articles of association, notices giving the situation of its registered office and details of its directors and secretary, particulars of charges over its property and trust deeds covering issues of debentures, copies of any prospectus or listing particulars that may have been issued, returns of allotments and lists of current members. In addition, there must be filed once a year an annual return (to be modified and renamed a 'confirmation statement') giving all the information specified by regulations (ss 854–856A,[1] and see s 858 for the consequences of non-compliance),[2] and various accounts and reports depending upon the size of the company (s 441), but generally including copies of the company's annual accounts (ss 394 and 399), together with the directors' report (s 415, unless the company qualifies as a 'micro-entity' under ss 384A and 384B), the auditors' report (ss 475 and 495–497, unless the company is exempt under s 477 or 480, although s 476, gives the members the power to require an audit in any event), and, for quoted companies, a directors' remuneration report (s 420).[3] Other events in the life of a company, both major ones such as alterations of its constitution (s 21) or the appointment of a receiver (s 871), and more minor ones where shares in public companies are issued for a non-cash consideration (ss 593 and 597), or where public companies agree to certain transfers of non-cash assets (ss 598 and 602), may trigger filing obligations. Today, company secretaries (or their equivalent for companies without secretaries) need the aid of very extensive checklists.

---

[1] The government recently amended these provisions, to the effect that companies which are already subject to other disclosure requirements (see later) by virtue of their shares being traded on a 'regulated market', a 'prescribed market' or any other market outside the UK, become subject to less stringent requirements on disclosing shareholder information under CA 2006. See BIS Explanatory Memorandum to Companies Act 2006 (Annual Returns) Regulations 2011, available at: www.gov.uk/government/uploads/system/uploads/attachment_data/file/31663/11-813-explanatory-memorandum-annual-returns-regulations.pdf.

[2] The proposed changes to the 'annual return', including its rebranding as a 'confirmation statement', were introduced by the Small Business, Enterprise and Employment Act 2015 (SBEEA 2015), and are intended to reduce bureaucracy and the filing burden on companies. When introduced, some time in 2016, they will simply require companies to confirm that all information required to be delivered by the company to the registrar in relation to the confirmation period has been delivered or is being delivered. See www.legislation.gov.uk/ukpga/2015/26/notes/division/5/8/1/1.

[3] See Chapter 5 on legislative changes on directors' remuneration and reporting on directors' pay. See also Enterprise and Regulatory Reform Act 2013.

In addition, SBEEA 2015 has added the requirement for a further register, a 'register of people with significant control', or a PSC Register, regulated under CA 2006 Pt 21A (ss 790Aff). Further details appear at 'Register of "people with significant control": the PSC Register', p 753.

The registration system is first and foremost an information service: not many legal consequences turn on the fact that a document has or has not been filed. Of these, the most important for our purposes are: (i) what remains of the constructive notice doctrine ('Reliance—no notice of the agent's want of actual authority and causal links', pp 112ff); (ii) the sanction of partial voidness which follows from the non-registration of charges ('Requirement to register charges', pp 627ff); and (iii) official notification (see the following section).

Although the information provided by the registration system was initially seen as a means of helping creditors to assess the risks of dealing with a limited company (the 'forewarned is forearmed' principle), the disclosure regime is now seen as increasingly essential in reducing the risks of managerial self-interest and incompetence, and facilitating the efficient operation of the capital markets.[4]

Errors on the register

Typically the person providing the information to the registrar is responsible for its accuracy, with criminal sanctions for knowingly or recklessly delivering documents which are misleading, false or deceptive in a material particular (CA 2006 s 1112).

But where the error is caused by the registrar, different rules apply. In *Sebry v Companies House* [2015] EWHC 115 (QB) the court held that the Registrar of Companies had a common law duty of care, when entering a winding-up order on the companies register, to take reasonable care to ensure that the order was not registered against the wrong company [118]. Here an innocent company had been forced into administration because a court order for the compulsory winding up of 'Taylor and Son Ltd' was negligently registered against a long-established company, 'Taylor and Sons Ltd', causing its bank and suppliers to refuse to deal with it on normal credit terms. The court emphasised that the duty was owed only to the company ([92], [96], [106]), not to all the many third parties who might rely on the register; and that it was a duty to take care in registering the information supplied to it—there was no duty to check the accuracy of the information itself ([108]–[118]).

Register of 'people with significant control': the PSC Register

From 2016, companies will have to disclose who is 'the power behind the throne'. They will have to compile a public register of 'people with significant control': a PSC Register (ss 790C(10), 790M).[5] This register must disclose the names of people who are able to exert 'significant influence or control' over the company's business—it matters not whether the 'person' is corporate or human, a company shareholder or not, and, if a shareholder, whether the legal owner of the shares or not.

This is a rather dramatic about-turn on the general rule in CA 2006 s 126, which prohibits trusts of any sort from being entered on the register of members. This had always meant that the 'real' owners of shares were not necessarily discoverable. The PSC Register goes even further, seeking to identify both shareholders and non-shareholders with control and

---

[4] See *Re Globespan Airways Ltd (In Liquidation)* [2012] EWCA Civ 1159, CA, where Arden LJ explained the significance of the filing system and described the role of the registrar within the process.

[5] The mechanics for achieving this objective are rather intricate. SBEEA 2015 inserts a substantial new Pt 21A (ss 790A–ZG) and Sch 1A into CA 2006, and that is supplemented by Regulations (Register of People with Significant Control Regulations 2016) and formal statutory Guidance. Interestingly, the information is not to be removed from the register until ten years after the person ceases to have such control (s 790U(1)).

influence. This has been done in the interests of making the control of companies more transparent, and also to prevent hidden operators misusing companies for illegal ends.

A person is deemed to have the necessary control (ie to be a PSC) if they meet at least one of the following five conditions:

(i)   directly or indirectly hold more than 25% of the nominal share capital; or

(ii) directly or indirectly control more than 25% of the votes at general meetings; or

(iii) directly or indirectly are able to control the appointment or removal of a majority of the board; or

(iv) actually exercise, or have the right to exercise, significant influence or control over the company; or

(v)   actually exercise or have the right to exercise significant influence or control over any trust or firm (which is not a legal entity) which has significant control (under one of the four conditions above) over the company.

These tests are amplified in the Act, the Regulations and formal statutory guidance. But their real breadth lies in defining 'significant influence or control' in (iv) and (v). Control and influence are alternatives, and it is the ability to exercise such power, not its actual exercise, which is the target. 'Control' indicates that the PSC is able to direct the company's activities; and 'influence' that the PSC can ensure (in fact, rather than as a matter of legal right) that the company follows the PSC's wishes. This might arise because the PSC owns important intellectual property, or was the company's founder, or is indeed a shadow director. The goal in this broad definition is to identify exactly who is pulling the corporate strings.[6]

The company has a duty to gather the necessary information and keep it up to date (ss 790D, 790E), and the requested parties a corresponding duty to supply the information and, again, keep it up to date (ss 790G, 790H).[7] The company's position in this task is strengthened, since it can disenfranchise shareholders who do not comply—so it is the non-shareholders who will prove more troublesome, and more difficult to discover.

Public access to the register is required, but is not unrestricted. Those seeking inspection must provide their name, address and the purpose for which they seek access (ss 790O(4), 790R). It is easy to see that without this restriction access might be abused, but it is also difficult to predict which purposes will be regarded as proper.[8] To support the restriction, the company is given a time-limited right to apply to court to seek an order that it need not make the requested disclosure (s 790P).

It is difficult to say what impact these disclosures will have, but they are clearly important, and certainly identify a different regulatory approach to issues of corporate control.

Publication in the *Gazette*

The registrar is obliged to give publicity in the *Gazette* to a company's incorporation (CA 2006 s 1064) and to various events affecting a company's administration or status—an alteration of its constitution or change in its directorate, for instance, or the appointment of a liquidator or redemption of shares out of capital. Most 'official notifications' in the *Gazette* are made under CA 2006 s 1077 in compliance with the First Company Law Directive (68/151/EEC).

---

[6] Accordingly, there are express exemptions where such power acceptably comes with particular roles—eg minority shareholder or managing director powers, or the powers of the company's professional advisers.

[7] With the sanction of a criminal offence (ss 790F, 790I and Sch 1B).

[8] However, see *Burry & Knight Ltd v Knight* [2014] EWCA Civ 604, where the Court of Appeal had to decide whether a member's request to inspect the register of members was made for improper purposes. This is likely to be informative in the PSC context.

These s 1077 notifications are really only token publicity, for very few copies of the special Companies Supplement to the *Gazette* (which is available only on microfiche) are sold. The Company Law Review (CLR) suggested electronic publication might be more effective (*Final Report* (2001), para 11.48). Accordingly, CA 2006 s 1116 provides a power for the Secretary of State to specify alternative means which the registrar may then approve for use. To ensure that any such change in current practice is itself publicised, s 1116(5) requires it to be announced first in the *Gazette*.

In contrast to the registers maintained at Companies House, legal consequences do flow from failures to secure the necessary official notification of specified events. These include the making of winding-up orders or appointments of liquidators in voluntary liquidations,[9] alteration of the company's articles, changes in the company's directors or changes in the company's registered office (at least for service of documents on the company). Third parties dealing with the company are protected by CA 2006 s 1079: it provides that the company cannot rely, as against a third party, on the happening of the specified events if, at the material time, the event had not been officially notified, unless the company can prove that the third party knew of the event at the material time.

On the other hand, notification in the *Gazette* is intended to protect third parties, not the company, so notification does not operate as constructive notice to third parties that the event has occurred: *Official Custodian for Charities v Parway Estates Developments Ltd* [1985] Ch 151, CA.

Publicity at the company's own registered office

Many of the statutory provisions requiring registration of matters at the Companies Registry are duplicated or supplemented by obligations to maintain copies of documents and other information at the company's own office, and to have facilities there for searching these records. Normally, this means public search, but sometimes the right is restricted to members of the company or to members and creditors. In practice, little use is made of these search facilities: people generally prefer the anonymity of the registrar's public office, even if it means getting less up-to-date or less detailed information.

Despite this, companies are required to keep registers of directors (s 162), directors' residential addresses (s 165—not open for inspection—see Pt 10, Ch 8), directors' service contracts (ss 228 and 229), secretaries (s 275—public companies only), members (ss 114, 116), members' substantial shareholdings (ss 808, 809; also see 'Transparency obligations: investigation and notification of major voting shareholdings in certain public companies', p 759), and debenture holders (s 743). CA 2006 no longer requires companies to keep a register of directors' interests in shares and debentures, or of company charges.

In some recognition of the effort of unnecessary duplication, SBEEA 2015 s 94 will insert a new Chapter into CA 2006 allowing private companies to elect formally (with the procedure for election specifically drafted) to keep its private registers (on members, PSCs, secretaries, directors and directors' residential addresses) on the central public register instead of with the company.

Specific provision of information to members

Most of the material which the Act requires a company to send to its members is linked to the annual general meeting. Copies of the accounts for the past year, the auditors' report and directors' report are required to be sent to members along with the notice summoning the meeting (ss 423 and 424). The confidentiality which one might associate with these essentially domestic reports is, however, destroyed by the statutory requirement that they

---

[9] See, eg, *Re Property Professionals + Ltd* [2013] EWHC 1903 (Ch).

also be filed with the registrar and made available at Companies House for public inspection. The directors' report, in particular, has in recent times become a vehicle for giving publicity to matters of general interest, such as the company's policy on employment or the environment. CA 2006 s 416 lists those items currently required to be covered, and allows the Secretary of State to make regulations as to other matters that must be disclosed. Unless the company is subject to the small companies' regime (s 381), the directors' report must include a 'strategic report' (s 414A) which is intended to inform members and help them to assess how the directors have performed in their duty to promote the success of the company (s 172). The strategic report must meet certain statutory requirements (s 414C) designed to ensure the report provides the shareholders with a fair and balanced analysis, consistent with the size and complexity of the business, of the development and performance of the company's business during the financial year; the position of the company at the end of the year; and a description of the principal risks and uncertainties facing the company.[10]

There are other scattered sections of the Act which make it obligatory to provide information to members, or to keep documents available for them to inspect, for example directors' service contracts (ss 228 and 229) and contracts relating to share repurchase (s 702).

Publicity on business documents

The Act may require a company to display its name outside its offices and places of business, and to state its name and registration details on its business letters and certain other business documents (s 82, authorising the Secretary of State to make appropriate regulations). In addition, if the company wishes to mention its share capital or directors' names on its business stationery, the Act may provide for the appropriate form. Finally, investment companies, charitable companies and insolvent companies must reveal that status on their business stationery.

Enforcement of the disclosure regime

CA 2006 seeks to secure compliance with these various disclosure obligations by a vast array of criminal sanctions (see the various penalties set out in the Act in relation to the individual sections noted later), which—depending upon the wording of the particular provision—may be imposed upon the company or its officers, or both. In practice, at least so far as the predecessor provisions in the Companies Act 1985 (CA 1985) were concerned, virtually no attempt was made to police or enforce any of these provisions except the requirements to file accounts (now CA 2006 ss 441 and 451–453) and annual returns (now CA 2006 ss 854 and 858).[11] Note the range of sanctions for failure to file accounts: the directors commit an offence and may be subjected to a fine (s 451), the company is automatically liable to a 'civil penalty' (which is a fine in all but name) (s 453) and the court may order immediate compliance with the statutory provision on pain of punishment for contempt of court (s 452).

Whether it makes best sense to use the criminal law to sanction compliance with a purely commercial regime—particularly if it is not enforced in practice—is a matter of debate. Some overseas systems largely manage without. The CLR reviewed the scheme, but saw advantages in retaining criminal sanctions: even though the number of prosecutions

---

[10] Financial Reporting Council (FRC) Staff Guidance Note: The Companies Act 2006 (Strategic Report and Directors' Report) Regulations 2013—Key Facts (www.frc.org.uk/Our-Work/Publications/Accounting-and-Reporting-Policy/FRC-Staff-Guidance-Note-Strategic-Report-Regulatio.pdf). Also see FRC Guidance on the Strategic Report (www.frc.org.uk/Our-Work/Publications/Accounting-and-Reporting-Policy/Guidance-on-the-Strategic-Report.pdf).

[11] Note that CA 2006 s 858(1) provides that 'for this purpose a shadow director is treated as a director'.

is relatively small, a high degree of compliance with the statutory filing obligations is achieved by the practice of sending pre-prosecution warning letters (threatening 'worse to come'). The CLR did, however, recommend that most of the criminal sanctions imposed on companies should be removed, and only the individual officers concerned should be made liable. CA 2006 has largely adopted this suggestion.

Listed companies and the Stock Exchange

Those companies whose shares are listed for dealing on the Stock Exchange (including the Alternative Investment Market (AIM)) are required, by the Listing Rules, as one of the conditions for the admission of their securities to listing, to undertake to make more frequent periodic disclosures about their financial and other affairs[12] to the Quotations Department and to the investing public (see 'Company investigations into share ownership and the disclosure register', pp 761ff). In addition, such companies are subject to a *continuing disclosure* obligation which requires them to ensure prompt publicity of any matters which are likely to have, when made public, a substantial effect on the price of the company's shares.

These enhanced disclosure requirements are motivated primarily by a desire to ensure accurate pricing by the market of the securities traded on it, so promoting investor confidence. The Companies Act 2006 (Strategic Report and Directors' Report) Regulations 2013 impose an even more stringent requirement on listed companies to include more information than was previously required in the then prescribed 'business review'.

Public regulation of securities markets

Most of the world's developed countries have a Securities Regulation Act of some kind. Uniquely, the control of securities dealing in the UK was traditionally not a matter for the law at all. Until relatively recently, it was largely left in the hands of 'self-regulatory' agencies such as the London Stock Exchange, with some informal backing from institutions like the Bank of England. For the enforcement of their rules, these bodies relied almost entirely on extra-legal sanctions, such as the disciplinary powers which they could exercise over their own members (eg stockbrokers) who acted as intermediaries in securities dealings, and the power to suspend or withdraw the listing of a particular company's securities. These sanctions were, on the whole, remarkably effective, but only because the self-regulatory bodies had virtual monopoly control of access to the securities markets. Supplementing this informal regime was a modest array of legislation, such as the Prevention of Fraud (Investments) Act 1958, which imposed limitations on the distribution of circulars and other inducements to invest.

Since then we have moved, in several steps, to the point where the conduct of financial investment businesses is now subject to an all-embracing, statute-based regime in the form of the Financial Services and Markets Act 2000 (FSMA 2000). This Act was in gestation from the earliest days of the Blair administration. The essence of the original scheme was the creation of a single regulator for financial businesses of every description—not just investment businesses, but fund managers, banking and insurance firms, clearing houses, building societies, friendly societies and so on. The Financial Services Authority

---

[12] Eg the Listing Rules require companies to state in their annual reports the extent to which they have complied with the UK Corporate Governance Code (see 'FRC and the UK Corporate Governance Code for listed companies', p 275).

(FSA) was the supreme regulator, and under the 2000 Act it had full statutory authority and corresponding accountability.

Such radical reform was inspired by a combination of factors. First, the proliferation of regulatory and self-regulatory bodies meant that there were some areas of overlap, some areas not covered and many inconsistencies; moreover, the fragmentation of management effort between these bodies was both inefficient and expensive. Secondly, many of the leading firms in the City were multifunctional, and under the earlier regime were required to seek multiple authorisations. Thirdly, there was a growing belief that self-regulation was no longer working well: there were well-publicised scandals to do with pensions mis-selling, Lloyd's insurance and the collapse of banks such as BCCI and Barings, and doubts whether foreign-based businesses could ever be effectively policed by a voluntary regime.

Under FSMA 2000 there was one 'super' regulator, one authorisation procedure, one rule book and one monitoring and disciplinary procedure. Overall responsibility lay with the Treasury, and little remained of the City's long-standing self-regulatory tradition.

Against this backdrop, and following the 2008 financial crisis, came yet another round of reforms which radically shook up the system once more. On 1 April 2013 the Financial Services Act 2012, came into force. It sought to strengthen the financial regulatory structure in the UK by making substantial changes to the previous system.

The unitary 'super regulator' structure under the FSA is now divided, and the Bank of England is required to play a far bigger role in financial regulation and stability. Rather than having the FSA as the supreme authority, three separate bodies have been created, each with defined and focused responsibilities. As described in policy documents issued by HM Treasury,[13] the Financial Policy Committee (FPC) within the Bank of England will be responsible for 'macro-prudential oversight' of the financial services system. For instance, s 3 of the Act inserts a new s 9(c) into the Bank of England Act 1993, which brings 'systematic risks attributable to structural features of financial markets' to the future agenda of the FPC. It is intended that the FPC will make use of Bank of England's expertise and experience to make independent decisions, free of undue political influence. Where the FPC disagrees and does not act in accordance with the recommendations of the Treasury, however, the FPC will be required to set out its reasons for taking such course of action.

At the same time, the Prudential Regulation Authority (PRA) has been created as a subsidiary of the Bank of England, and is charged with adopting a 'micro-prudential approach' in order to regulate firms which manage significant risks, and thus it is expected to harness the 'safety and soundness of individual firms'. The PRA is expected to intervene where necessary so as to ensure that firms satisfactorily address possible solvency and systemic risks, and mitigate costs that could otherwise be brought to their clients and the public in general.

Finally, outside the Bank of England structure, the Financial Conduct Authority (FCA) has been created. It acts as the regulator of business conduct. This means that the FCA is responsible for dealing with an extensive range of issues, from encouraging effective competition, to protecting consumers and providing for transparency, disclosure and access to information.

Overall, the spirit of these reforms places judgement and expertise at the heart of the financial regulatory regime. The aspiration is that these new regulators will take a more proactive and preventive role, in lieu of the 'box-ticking approach' evident in the lead up to the financial crisis. It remains to be seen, however, whether these reforms will be effective in instilling a new regulatory culture, and whether the new regulators are indeed able to take and maintain a hard line against some of the biggest financial institutions in the world. Perhaps the greatest challenge facing the new structure is how

---

[13] Available at: www.gov.uk/government/uploads/system/uploads/attachment_data/file/238240/8271.pdf.

the institutional elements will coordinate as between themselves so as to achieve a clear demarcation of functions and duties.

Transparency obligations: investigation and notification of major voting shareholdings in certain public companies

The Transparency Directive

The register of members of a company does not necessarily reveal the true identity of its shareholders: nominees often hold shares for unnamed beneficial owners. The Transparency Directive (2004/109/EC)[14] replaces earlier Directives (and corresponding provisions in CA 1985) and makes detailed provision for disclosure of substantial interests in the shares of public companies that are traded on regulated markets (ie not all public companies—see 'Company investigations into share ownership and the disclosure register', pp 761ff). The object of these measures is to enable both the company and the market to know who has a controlling interest, or who may be in a position to acquire such an interest in the company. More particularly, they enable a close eye to be kept on those who might otherwise obtain control without adhering to the principles laid down in the City Code on Takeovers and Mergers (see 'Takeovers', pp 796ff).

The Directive also makes provision for the periodic financial disclosures that must be made by issuers admitted to trading on a regulated market. The amended version however (subject to a residual discretion vested on member states) no longer requires companies to produce interim management statements or quarterly reports.

Substantial holdings

The Transparency Directive was implemented in the UK on 20 January 2007, and responsibility for major shareholding disclosures moved from the Department of Trade and Industry (DTI) (as BIS previously was, several iterations ago) to the FSA, and now to the FCA. According to the Directive, a notification requirement is triggered when the size of a shareholder's voting holdings reaches, exceeds or moves below certain thresholds stated in the Directive (5%, 10%, 15%, 20%, 25%, 30%, 50% and 75%). The shareholder is required to inform the issuer, and the issuer must then inform the market.

In preparation for this implementation, CA 2006 s 1266 inserted seven new sections into FSMA 2000 (ss 89A–89G). These new sections enabled new rules to be made by the FSA to implement the Directive. The UK's new rules, the Disclosure and Transparency Rules (DTR), Ch 5, go beyond those required by the Directive, in that the notification thresholds are tighter (3% then +/– every 1%), the range of issuers subjected to the disclosure obligations is more extensive (including both regulated markets and prescribed markets (such as AIM and PLUS)), and the time limitations for notification are stricter. These tighter rules substantially repeat the rules previously contained in CA 1985.

The thresholds and resulting notification requirements are subject to some practical exemptions and modifications:

(i)   clearing and settling—shares acquired for the sole purpose of clearing and settlement within the usual short settlement cycle will be exempt from the requirement to notify;

---

[14] As amended by Transparency Directive Amending Directive 2013/50/EU.

(ii) custodians—shares held by custodians in their custodian capacity will not be required to notify, provided that they can only exercise the voting rights attached to such shares under instructions given in writing or electronically;

(iii) market makers—market makers are exempt from the 5% threshold when acting in the capacity of market maker. This is provided that they are authorised under the Markets in Financial Instruments Directive (MiFID) (2004/39/EC) and do not intervene in the management of the issuer or exert any influence on the issuer to buy back shares or back the share price;

(iv) Investment Management Companies—the parent undertakings of management companies, as defined by the Transparency Directive, are not required to aggregate their holdings with those of their controlled undertakings. This is provided that the controlled undertaking exercises the voting rights independently from the parent.

Since the sections are concerned with questions of control, it is only voting shares that are affected, but in assessing this both options and rights convertible into shares are also covered (see s 1266, inserting s 89F into FSMA 2000).

In October 2011, the European Commission put forward proposals to amend the Transparency Directive. These seek to cure the 'notification gap'. They will mandate the disclosure of 'major holdings of certain types of financial instruments' that can be used to acquire economic interests in the subject listed companies. It is anticipated that even those who do not acquire the actual shares themselves may become subject to the disclosure requirements so as to prevent 'possible market abuse situations, low levels of investor confidence and the misalignment of investor intentions with long-term interests of companies'.[15]

Consequences of infringement of transparency obligations

If the FCA discovers that an issuer of securities admitted to trading on a regulated market (but not, it seems, other markets) has failed to comply with the various transparency rules, it may publicly censure the issuer (after a warning notice) and/or suspend or prohibit trading in the securities (s 1268, inserting ss 89K and 89L into FSMA 2000).

Liability for false or misleading statements concerning the transparency rules

The primary liability of issuers and directors for the accuracy of the required disclosures lies in criminal and administrative penalties under CA 2006 Pt 15 and FSMA 2000 Pt VI. In addition, restitution can be ordered by the court on the application of the FCA or the Secretary of State under FSMA 2000 s 382, or directly by the FCA under FSMA 2000 s 384.

CA 2006, through FSMA 2000, now also establishes a regime for civil liability to third parties in respect of disclosures that are made public in response to the transparency rules (including periodic financial disclosures) by issuers admitted to trading on regulated markets (CA 2006 s 1270 inserts ss 90A and 90B into FSMA 2000). The aim of this provision is to reduce the legal uncertainty as to whether any actionable duty is owed by issuers and their directors to investors. The section is intended to ensure that the potential scope of any civil liability is reasonable, and that the duties owed to investors are not extended unnecessarily, so that there is some protection for company members, employees and creditors. Clearly, however, there was some doubt about the potential impact of the new section, and FSMA 2000 s 90B enables the provision on liability to be amended if a wider or narrower civil liability regime is deemed appropriate. The 2007 *Davies Review*

---

[15] See: http://ec.europa.eu/internal_market/securities/transparency/index_en.htm and http://europa.eu/rapid/pressReleasesAction.do?reference=MEMO/11/734&format=HTML&aged=1&language=EN&guiLanguage=en.

of Issuer Liability proposed that issuers' liability to investors for breaches of their continuing disclosure obligations should be limited to cases where those responsible for the misstatement to the market had known that the statement was false, or were reckless in regard to its potential falsity, and where the claimant acted in reliance on the information in question.[16]

This new civil liability regime leaves undisturbed any other liability owed by directors to the issuer and to members of the company under UK and any other national law, and any liability under other FCA rules. It also leaves undisturbed any liability of the issuer in respect of any loss or damage arising other than as a result of acquiring securities in reliance on the relevant statement or report.

Company investigations into share ownership and the disclosure register

Although the disclosure obligations just noted are limited to issuers on regulated and prescribed markets, it is possible for every public company to obtain information about the voting control over its shares. Under CA 2006 s 793, a public company is empowered to require a person to inform it whether he or she has, or has had at any time within the past three years, an interest in its voting shares and, if so, to supply information about that interest. The information so obtained must be recorded on the company's register of interests in shares (s 808). These powers apply against anyone, not just to members. And members who themselves hold 10% or more of the voting shares may requisition the exercise of these powers by the company (s 803). For example, the members may want to act if they suspect that the directors are building up a holding behind the shelter of nominees.

These sections serve a different purpose from the automatic disclosure obligations discussed previously. They enable a company to discover the identity of those with direct or indirect voting rights that fall below the threshold for automatic disclosure, and to ascertain the underlying beneficial ownership of shares. To this end, the definition of an interest in shares is exceptionally wide (s 820): it includes the right to acquire or subscribe for shares (ss 824 and 821), and provides for indirect and family interests to be attributed to the same person (s 823).

If a person fails to give the company the information it requests, or gives false information, the person is not only subject to a penalty (s 795), but the company may apply to the court for an order directing that the shares be subject to restrictions (s 794) which may in effect freeze the right to transfer the shares and to receive dividends, vote and take advantage of rights offers (ss 797–802), and may even permit the sale of the shares with court approval (s 801). The restriction order can be a particularly effective sanction in the case where holdings of shares are being built up secretly through nominees based overseas, who are not easily made amenable to the local jurisdiction and who may be able to shelter behind laws in their own country which protect the confidentiality of nominee arrangements. The weakness of the sections is, however, that the company must know which of its shares are being affected by the scheme which it supposes to exist. In *Eclairs Group Ltd v JKX Oil & Gas Plc* **[7.11]**, the Supreme Court considered the purpose and scope of powers pursuant to the company's articles which provided the directors with rights corresponding to s 794 to impose restrictions on shares. Although the judgments may shed some light on the purpose and scope of the powers under s 794 (and, to a certain extent, s 793), care should be taken: Lord Mance JSC, at [34], noted that although there were some parallels in language, it might be unhelpful to the analysis he was undertaking to assume that the

---

[16] See PL Davies, 'Liability for Misstatements to the Market: Some Reflections' (2009) 9 *Journal of Corporate Law Studies* 295.

proper purposes contemplated in the articles were the same as those contemplated by the statutory provisions here; the reverse must then be equally true.

Disclosure and public offerings of shares

Companies wishing to raise capital may offer their shares for sale to the general public. To do this legally, the company must be a public company. The shares in public companies are often widely held, and individual members are usually more interested in capital and income returns than in close involvement in the management of the company. In order to make a company's shares more attractive to such investors, it is necessary to assure them that the initial sale is conducted on the basis of full and proper information, and that the new shares can easily be sold in the market to liquidate the investment, switch to a new investment or realise the capital gains.

These activities, and others, are regulated by FSMA 2000. This Act replaced the Financial Services Act 1986 and other legislation under which different aspects of the financial services industry were separately regulated by a mixture of public bodies, trade associations and professional institutes. Now there is a single regulator for these purposes, the FCA, with members of its board appointed by the Treasury. The FCA's duties are prescribed in FSMA 2000 s 1B (as amended by the Financial Services Act 2012). This section attempts a difficult balancing exercise between the FCA's strategic objective of ensuring that the relevant markets function well, and its three operational objectives of ensuring consumer protection (FSMA 2000 s 1C); protecting and enhancing the integrity of the UK financial system (s 1D); and promoting effective competition in the interests of consumers in the relevant markets (s 1E).

History

During the nineteenth century (and, indeed, for a considerable period before that), the formation of almost all companies was followed immediately by an appeal to the public to participate in the new venture by joining as members and subscribing for 'shares' in the 'joint stock'. The main reason for 'going public' in this way was to raise funds in the large amounts necessary for the enterprises of the period—often massive operations which built a large proportion of the world's railways, laid submarine cables, opened up trade and investment in distant parts and provided the banking, insurance and other services to support such activities. The promoters of the company would publish a 'prospectus', giving information about the undertaking and inviting subscriptions. This process is often referred to as a 'flotation' of the company or, more accurately, of its securities. Today, big business still has need of funding on a large scale, and this can be sought by the same process of appealing to the public to become investors in the enterprise. But it would be very unlikely nowadays that this would be attempted by the promoters of a new company immediately after its incorporation. The reason for this is that people will usually be prepared to become investors in shares or other securities only if they can be readily sold and turned back into cash, more or less at will. To meet this need there must be a 'market', available to all comers, where shares can be bought and sold and prices can fluctuate in response to supply and demand. Access to the share market is virtually indispensable if investors are to be attracted in any large numbers. And rules have been developed by the London Stock Exchange—the body which has for many years controlled the only markets of any significance in the country—which will not normally allow a company's securities to be accepted for dealing on the market unless it has an established business record. For a 'full' or 'official' listing on the Main Market this record must go back for at least three years. The requirements are less demanding, though still quite strict, if the listing is to be on AIM. Responsibility for the formulation of the Listing Rules was an 'in-house' matter for the Stock Exchange until October 1999 (originally, as a matter of self-regulation but later with the blessing of legislation). With the introduction of FSMA 2000, this function was taken over by the FSA and now passes to the FCA by virtue of the Financial Services Act 2012.

Securities markets

Securities markets make it easier for investors to buy and sell securities. These markets are regulated in the interests of investors, since attracting these people will maximise the amount of capital available to the issuers of the securities traded on the market. But this form of regulation imposes costs on the issuers, who must provide information and subject themselves to public scrutiny. The greater the regulation, the greater the cost. Regulators have therefore adopted a variety of regimes, so that the securities of larger, better-known and more stable companies can be traded on highly regulated exchanges, while the securities of smaller, less well-known and riskier companies can be traded elsewhere.

FSMA 2000 s 285 allows investment exchanges to become *recognised investment exchanges* (RIEs). To become recognised in this way, an exchange must have sufficient financial resources, be a 'fit and proper person' and ensure its business is conducted in an orderly manner so as to afford proper protection to investors (including deciding which investments should be 'admitted to trading' and what information should be made available to investors).

Exchanges that are not RIEs must obtain permission under FSMA 2000 Pt IV to carry on regulated activities, and are then subject to lesser regulation than RIEs. These exchanges are called *multilateral trading facilities*, following the transposition of MiFID into UK law in November 2007.

A RIE can operate a *'regulated market'* as defined in the Investment Services Directive (93/22/EEC), Art 16.[17] RIEs and alternative trading systems (ATSs) can also operate *'exchange-regulated markets'* that are regulated by the exchange itself. For example, the London Stock Exchange is an RIE, and it operates a number of markets subject to different regulatory regimes. The most significant are the Main Market, AIM and the Professional Securities Market (PSM). The Main Market is a 'regulated market'; AIM is an 'exchange-regulated market'.

The regulations operate at three levels: (i) at EU level for all securities admitted to trading on regulated markets (*'traded companies'*); (ii) at EU level for any security which is the subject of a public offer; and (iii) at national level (subject to EU minimum requirements) for listed securities on a domestic exchange (*'listed companies'*). In addition, *'quoted companies'* (CA 2006 s 385) are companies officially listed on various specified UK and other exchanges.

The London Stock Exchange's Main Market provides the most expensive and extensive form of regulation for listed securities. A company whose equity share capital is admitted to trading on this market is simultaneously listed, traded and quoted. A company whose shares are admitted to trading on AIM is not usually listed, traded on a regular basis or quoted.

---

[17] The UK list of 'regulated markets' are all operated by RIEs. 'Regulated market' is also sometimes used to refer to markets which are protected from insider trading by the Criminal Justice Act 1993 Pt V (see 'Insider dealing: criminal protection (Criminal Justice Act 1993 Pt V)', p 769).

Official listing

Official listing is an optional additional regulatory regime for securities markets. There are minimum EU standards for official listing (Listing Directive (2001/34/EC)), but the UK domestic rules (set out in the FCA's Listing Rules) are particularly extensive, and are said to contribute to the sound financial reputation of the London Stock Exchange's Main Market.

EU rules require an issuer to have a demonstrable track record, a certain financial size and a wide enough spread in public shareholdings to create a realistic market. In addition, the rules oblige publication of half-yearly reports. The Listing Rules impose additional obligations, requiring adherence to the Listing Principles, continuing obligations requiring extra information in annual accounts and reports, preliminary statements of annual results, compliance with the Model Code, which restricts dealings in securities by company managers and others, and compliance with the UK Corporate Governance Code (see Chapter 5) (or an explanation of non-compliance).

The FCA may permanently discontinue or temporarily suspend a listing, without notice, if it suspects irregularities that preclude normal dealings in the securities (FSMA 2000 s 77). It may also impose public censure or financial penalties, or launch a public investigation (FSMA 2000 ss 91 and 97).

Prospectuses

As it applies in the UK, the Prospectus Directive (2003/71/EC), implemented by FSMA 2000 Pt VI, provides that, with defined exceptions, whenever there is a public offer of securities or a request for admission of securities to trading on a regulated market, a prospectus approved by the FCA must be published (FSMA 2000 s 85). The prospectus must contain all the information required by investors to make an informed assessment of the securities. A person who contravenes the requirement for a prospectus commits an offence, and is liable to be sued for breach of statutory duty by anyone who suffers loss as a result of the contravention (s 85(3) and (4)).

These rules undergo periodic review. In mid-2010, for example, an Amending Directive (Directive 2010/73/EU) was approved by the European Parliament, and the changes thereof have now been implemented in the UK, through amendments made to the FSMA 2000, which came into force on 31 July 2012. Other changes were also introduced through Prospectus Regulations 2011 (SI 2011/1668) and 2012 (SI 2012/1538). In November 2015, a proposal was announced for a new regulation which will replace the Prospectus Directive, as the binding instrument on all member states. The revision exercise is said to pursue a simple goal: provide all types of issuers with disclosure rules which are tailored to their specific needs while making the prospectus a more relevant tool of informing potential investors. In consequence, the proposal puts special emphasis on four groups of issuers: (i) issuers already listed on a regulated market or a small and medium-size enterprise (SME) growth market who want to raise additional capital by means of a secondary issuance; (ii) SMEs; (iii) frequent issuers of all types of securities; and (iv) issuers of non-equity securities. It also intends to further incentivise the use of the cross-border 'passport' for approved prospectuses, which was introduced by the Prospectus Directive.[18]

When the FCA acts as the competent UK authority for these purposes, it sometimes uses the name United Kingdom Listing Authority (UKLA), and its rules on prospectuses are to be found in the Prospectus Rules Sourcebook (PR) in the FCA Handbook.

---

[18] European Commission Proposal dated 30 November 2015 (http://ec.europa.eu/finance/securities/docs/prospectus/151130-delegated-regulation_en.pdf). Also see http://ec.europa.eu/finance/securities/prospectus/index_en.htm. The draft details are available, but not discussed further here.

Restrictions on public offers by private companies

A private limited company is not permitted to offer its unlisted shares to the public (CA 2006 s 755, and s 756 for the meaning of 'offer to the public'), although an allotment following such an offer is not invalid (s 760).

Exceptions from the prohibition exist where the company acts in good faith in pursuance of arrangements to re-register as a public company before the shares are allotted, or as part of the terms of the offer it undertakes to and does in fact re-register as a public company (s 755).

The court may make an order restraining the company from contravening the prohibition, order the company to re-register as a public company, order it to be wound up or make a remedial order intended to put a person affected by the contravention in the position he or she would have been in had the contravention not occurred (ss 757–759).

Content of prospectuses

The prospectus must contain all the information required by investors to make an informed assessment of the securities, the rights attaching to them and the status of the issuer (assets and liabilities, financial position, profits and losses and prospects). This must be presented in a form that is easy to analyse and comprehend, and must contain a brief summary in non-technical language containing 'key information' which assists investors in deciding whether or not to invest in the subject securities. A definition for 'key information' is also provided, along with a list of information required thereof (FSMA 2000 s 87A (as amended in 2012)). Once approved in the issuer's home state, the prospectus is valid throughout the EU. This is to facilitate the development of a single European capital market in which an issue of shares can be offered to the public and traded throughout the EU.

If a significant new factor arises, or a material mistake or inaccuracy is noted, between the time of approval of the prospectus and the final closing of the offer of securities to the public or the beginning of trading on a regulated market, then a *supplementary prospectus* must be issued by way of correction (FSMA 2000 s 87G). Where the securities are both offered to the public and are to be admitted to trade on a regulated market, then the relevant period becomes the time of approval to either the closure of the public offer or the time when trading in the regulated market begins, whichever is later (FSMA 2000 s 87G(3A)).

Exemptions from the prospectus requirements

An approved prospectus need not be published if:

(i) the offer of securities is addressed solely to qualified investors (FSMA 2000 s 86(1)(a) and (7));

(ii) the offer of securities is addressed to fewer than 150 persons, other than qualified investors (FSMA 2000 s 86(1)(b) as amended by Prospectus Regulations 2011);

(iii) the total consideration for the offer is less than €5 million, with the exemption applying only once during a 12-month period, and applying on an EU-wide basis (FSMA 2000 ss 85(5)(a), 87, and Sch 11A, para 9);

(iv) the minimum consideration payable by each investor is €100,000 (or its equivalent in another currency), or the nominal value of each security is €100,000 (or its equivalent in another currency)[19] (FSMA 2000 s 86(1)(c) and (d));

(v) the additional shares being offered for trading (and not offered to the public, unless to existing or former directors or employees) are of the same class as existing shares and number less than 10% of those already admitted, with the 10% limit available once every 12 months (FSMA 2000 s 85(6)(b) and (5)(b));

---

[19] This exemption applies in practice to debt securities and convertibles intended for the wholesale market (professional investors) rather than the retail market (general public).

(vi)   the offer of securities is in exchange for shares of the same class already issued or admitted to trading, provided there is no increase in issued capital, or if the shares result from conversion or exchange of other transferable securities or from rights associated with such securities (FSMA 2000 s 85(5)(b) and (6)(b));

(vii)   the offer of securities is in connection with a takeover, merger or division, provided there is another document which the UKLA considers contains equivalent information (FSMA 2000 s 85(5)(b) and (6)(b));

(viii) the offer of securities is by way of bonus shares or shares issued in lieu of a dividend, provided there is a document explaining the offer (FSMA 2000 s 85(5)(b) and (6)(b)); or

(ix)   the shares have been admitted to trading on one EU regulated market for more than 18 months, and the proposal is to admit them on another regulated market (FSMA 2000 s 85(6)(b)).

In cases (i)–(iv), although the particular offer is exempt, it may still be necessary to publish a prospectus if the issuer wishes to obtain admission of the securities to trading on a regulated market (and exemptions (v)–(ix) do not apply).

FCA sanctions

The FCA has extensive powers to:

(i)   suspend or prevent a public offer of securities, or an application for admission to trading on a regulated market (FSMA 2000 ss 87K and 87L);

(ii)   publicly censure or impose a financial penalty (FSMA 2000 ss 87M and 91); or

(iii) instigate an investigation (FSMA 2000 s 97).

Liability for misleading statements and omissions in prospectuses

The primary object of the prospectus legislation (like the Listing Rules) is to ensure that potential investors in companies whose shares are offered to the public or traded on the market are provided with sufficient information to enable them to make informed decisions. Disclosure is the key. But the current legislation sets high standards; it imposes a *general* duty to ensure that the prospectus contains all such information as investors would reasonably require and reasonably expect to find there for the purpose of making an informed assessment of the financial position of the issuing company and the rights attaching to the securities.

If investors suffer a loss as a result of an untrue or misleading statement in, or omission from, a prospectus or supplementary prospectus, then, in addition to the various remedies available under the general rules described at 'Offers to the public to purchase shares and remedies for misleading offers', pp 519ff, certain specific remedies are available:

(i)   statutory compensation remedies under FSMA 2000 s 90(1) for losses caused by reliance on any untrue or misleading statements in the prospectus or supplement, or any omissions of matters required to be included by FSMA 2000 s 87A or 87G; or

(ii)   statutory remedies under FSMA 2000 s 90(4) for losses suffered in respect of failures to issue necessary supplementary prospectuses as required by FSMA 2000 s 87G.

'Compensation', under FSMA 2000 s 90(1) and (4), is likely to be assessed in the same way as damages for the tort of deceit (see *Clark v Urquhart* [1930] AC 28 in relation to predecessor provisions).

Under the FSMA 2000 provisions, compensation is payable by any person 'responsible for' the misleading prospectus (s 90(1)). This includes the company, every director at the time the prospectus was published (unless published without the director's knowledge or consent, and on becoming aware of it the director gave public notice to that effect as soon as practicable); every person named as being or having agreed to become a director (provided this statement was made with the person's consent); every person named as accepting responsibility for the prospectus (or the relevant specific parts of it); and every person who authorised the contents of the prospectus (or the relevant specific parts of it), although giving professional advice does not make a person responsible.

Certain defences are available to these potential defendants, including their own reasonable belief in the accuracy of the information, reasonable reliance on experts, reasonable efforts to effect corrections, or, alternatively, proof of the claimant's knowledge that the relevant statements were false or misleading or that there was a relevant omission (FSMA 2000 Sch 10).

It appears arguable that anyone who has 'acquired' shares, whether as the original allottee or on the market, is able to sue for compensation (FSMA 2000 s 90(1) and (4)). According to the common law, only the original allottees could sue, on the basis that a prospectus was intended for subscribers, not for subsequent purchasers (*Peek v Gurney* (1873) LR 6 HL 377). But Lightman J, in *obiter dicta*, suggested a different and broader approach to the FSMA 2000 provisions, on the basis that prospectuses are now intended to encourage subsequent trading in shares: *Possfund Custodian Trustee Ltd v Diamond* [1996] 1 WLR 1351. The decision is controversial.

Under-subscription for the new issue

Under CA 2006 ss 578–579, a company must not allot any shares unless the issue is fully subscribed or the offer makes it clear that some other conditions are to apply. If the issue is not fully subscribed (or other specified conditions are not met) within 40 days, then the subscribed funds must be returned to the investors forthwith, but without interest. Interest is payable after 48 days, with the directors becoming jointly and severally liable. Any attempt to contract out of this provision is void. If an allotment is made in contravention of this section, then the allottee may rescind the allotment within one month even if the company is in the course of being wound up.

Both the company and any allottee can recover any loss or damage sustained as a result of the contravention from any director who knowingly committed, permitted or authorised the contravention.

Market abuse: insider dealing and market manipulation

Controlling market abuse

Market confidence exists only if traders believe that market prices reflect the true value of what is bought and sold. Correct pricing is more likely if both buyers and sellers have all the relevant information to hand. Public confidence in the market is easily damaged if people close to the company use 'inside information' about the company to revalue the shares ahead of the market, and trade on that privileged basis (this is known as '*insider dealing*'). Public confidence is also damaged if false information about the value of shares is spread, creating a false market (this is known as '*market manipulation*').

Control of these forms of market abuse on regulated markets is required by the Market Abuse Directive (2003/6/EC),[20] and is implemented in FSMA 2000 Pt VIII (which extends to all markets operated by RIEs) by:

---

[20] The Commission has made proposals for a Regulation on insider dealing and market manipulation (market abuse) to strengthen the current provisions contained in the Market Abuse Directive. It is aimed that the rules as amended will prove more fitting in the modern markets, especially in relation to market abuse practices that take place in commodity and derivative markets.

(i)   penalising insider dealing and market manipulation;

(ii) requiring insiders to declare their trading; and

(iii) requiring companies to disclose price-sensitive information promptly to the market.

If the FCA discovers that a person has engaged in market abuse (on the balance of probabilities), it may request the court to issue an injunction restraining the activity, or order restitution or some form of mitigation, or issue a freezing injunction preventing the person dealing with his or her assets (FSMA 2000 ss 381 and 383–384). Alternatively, the FCA itself may impose a financial penalty or publicly censure the individual (FSMA 2000 s 123). The imposition of a penalty does not make the transaction void or unenforceable (FSMA 2000 s 131).

Following the LIBOR scandal and other problems in the market, these rules are to be strengthened. The current Market Abuse Directive will cease to have effect from 3 July 2016, as a result of a new Market Abuse Regulation (MAR). The new MAR updates and strengthens the existing framework to ensure market integrity and investor protection provided by the existing Directive. The new framework aims to ensure regulation keeps pace with market developments: it will strengthen the fight against market abuse across commodity and related derivative markets, explicitly ban the manipulation of benchmarks such as LIBOR and reinforce the investigative and sanctioning powers of regulators.[21] The UK Treasury is now in the course of preparing the necessary amendments or repeal of the existing legislation, so as to implement the new Regulation. The FCA has also published a consultation on possible changes to the FCA Handbook, which has been a supplementary instrument to the primary and secondary legislation.[22]

There is also a new EU Directive on Criminal Sanctions for Market Abuse (2014/57/EU) (CSMAD). However, the UK will opt out of CSMAD, and will instead update the domestic regime in order to retain flexibility. It is said that the domestic regime will go at least as far as the CSMAD.[23]

Insider dealing

There has been much interest in the past few decades in the topic of '*insider dealing*' or '*insider trading*'. These terms are used to describe the use (or, rather, the misuse) of confidential information by people who, as company officers or employees or as civil servants, avail themselves of knowledge which they acquire in the course of their work, or by reason of their office, to deal to their own profit in a company's securities. Most people regard this practice as unfair in itself and damaging to the confidence of investors in the integrity of the share market.

Insider dealing: common law protection

Until 1980, the only constraints available to deal with insider trading were those imposed extra-legally by the self-regulatory agencies of the City, and in particular by the Takeover Panel, and the possibility that there might be civil liability in at least some cases. It seemed that decisions like *Regal (Hastings) Ltd v Gulliver* **[7.26]** and *Boardman v Phipps* [1967] 2 AC 46 (see Note 1 following *Peso Silver Mines Ltd v Cropper* **[7.28]**, p 397) might be used as authority for making directors, and others similarly placed, liable to account to their company for any profit that they made, and indeed that is very

[21] http://europa.eu/rapid/press-release_MEMO-13-774_en.htm.
[22] www.fca.org.uk/your-fca/documents/consultation-papers/cp15-35.
[23] www.parliament.uk/business/publications/written-questions-answers-statements/written-question/Lords/2015-02-23/HL5099/.

much what happened in *Regal*. There was also the possibility of some form of liability for breach of confidence as an equitable remedy in its own right (*Seager v Copydex Ltd* [1967] 1 WLR 923). But all these possible claims are open to the criticism that in most insider dealing cases the company is not the real loser, and may have no incentive to pursue the wrongdoer. *Percival v Wright* **[7.05]** seems to bar the development of a claim based on breach of duty between the director (or other 'insider') and the person to whom he or she has sold or from whom he or she has bought the shares. However, there have been hints in cases such as *Coleman v Myers* ([1977] 2 NZLR 225) that a civil remedy for victims of insider trading could be developed, similar to that which has evolved in the United States through such cases as *SEC v Texas Gulf Sulphur Co* 401 F 2d 833 (1968) and *Diamond v Oreamuno* 24 NY 2d 494 (1969) (though the authority of the latter is questionable, since it was not followed in the company's home state, Florida: see *Schein v Chasen* 313 So 2d 739 (1975)).

All these questions centred on possible civil liability for insider dealing remain live issues, but they have had less of the limelight since 1980, when successive legislative provisions established both criminal and civil penalties for those guilty of the offences of insider dealing as there defined. Nevertheless, they remain important in cases where the statutory provisions do not apply (eg in cases of dealings in shares of private companies).

Insider dealing: statutory civil protection (FSMA 2000 s 118)

FSMA 2000 Pt VIII protects prescribed markets, being all regulated markets and markets operated by RIEs (and, under legacy provisions operating until 2008, all markets operated by UK RIEs and PLUS) (FSMA 2000 s 130A). Within these markets, it protects against three forms of insider dealing (FSMA 2000 s 118): dealing by an insider (s 118B) on the basis of inside information (s 118C) relating to the investment in question (*insider dealing*); improper disclosure by an insider otherwise than in the proper course of his or her duties (*improper disclosure* or *tipping*); and (only until 2008, under the legacy provisions) use by anyone of information not generally available (*misuse of information*).

Insider dealing: criminal protection (Criminal Justice Act 1993 Pt V)

The definitions of regulated market, inside information and insider dealing are all slightly different under the 1993 Act from the rules adopted in FSMA 2000. Within these definitions, and subject to limited exceptions, insiders cannot deal in the relevant securities, encourage others to deal, or disclose inside information to others. On indictment for an offence, the penalty can be imprisonment for up to seven years, and/or a fine for which there is no limit (Criminal Justice Act 1993 s 61(1)). Criminal proceedings may only be instituted by the FCA (FSMA 2000 s 402), or by, or with the consent of, either the Secretary of State or the Director of Public Prosecutions (Criminal Justice Act 1993 s 61(2)). A transaction entered into in contravention of the Criminal Justice Act 1993 is neither void nor voidable (s 63(2)), although, being illegal, it is unlikely to be enforced by any court.

Market abuse

FSMA 2000 s 118 identifies six forms of market manipulation as market abuse, all of which have the capacity to distort the market price of the relevant securities. The FCA provides some safe harbours for practices regarded as proper (eg company share buy-backs, or a public authority's pursuit of monetary or exchange rate policies).

The civil penalties for such conduct were outlined earlier (see 'Liability for false or misleading statements concerning the transparency rules', p 760). In addition, FSMA 2000 s 397 used to make creating a false market a criminal offence, but this has now been repealed and offences relating to financial services (including misleading statements) are now provided for under Part 7 of the Financial Services Act 2012[24]

For a recent illustration on the working of the market abuse provisions, see *David Massey v The Financial Services Authority* [2011] UKUT 49 (Tax and Chancery Chamber). Also see, for recent guidance on the definition of 'inside information', *Hannam v Financial Conduct Authority* [2014] UKUT 233 (TCC), citing a decision of the Court of Justice in *Gelti v Daimler AG* (Case C-19/11) [2012] 3 CMLR 32 in relation to s 118C(5)(a).

Public investigation of companies

The past 50 years have seen a continuing increase in the involvement of government in the affairs of companies. This reflects a long-held recognition that abuse of corporate power is unlikely to be adequately constrained by leaving all regulation and litigation to the company's members. It is further evidence of the loss of privacy that comes with limited liability. That said, the UK is one of the few jurisdictions to go further and provide for more controversial inspectorship provisions, allowing investigation of companies' affairs by the Companies Investigations Branch (CIB) of the Department for Business, Innovation and Skills (BIS), and providing for extensive powers to collect evidence and pass it on to regulatory or prosecuting authorities.

These powers of the Secretary of State to appoint inspectors to investigate the affairs of companies under CA 1985 Pt XIV (not transported to CA 2006, although CA 2006 ss 1035–1039 introduced certain amendments) may seem of little significance in comparison with the various forms of regulation ensuring control of fair practices, unfair competition, mergers and monopolies, takeovers (and mergers effected by takeover), and so on. Nevertheless, the possibility of such public investigation of companies sets them apart from individuals and partnerships. Investigations may be launched into the affairs of companies (CA 1985 ss 431 and 432) or into the membership and control of companies (CA 1985 s 442).

Powers of investigation

CA 1985 confers powers of investigation of two different kinds. The first is more formal. The Secretary of State may appoint inspectors 'to investigate the affairs of a company and to report on them in such manner as he may direct' (CA 1985 s 431(1)). The appointment may be initiated by the Secretary of State (see later). It may also be initiated on the application of the company itself, or by a requisition having the support of at least 200 members or members holding not less than one-tenth of the issued shares (CA 1985 s 432(2)), but then the applicants must show that they have good reason and be prepared to pay the costs. Not surprisingly, there are few occasions when this has been done. Alternatively, an investigation of this type may be ordered by the court (CA 1985 s 432(1)).

The mere announcement of an inspection is likely to have a substantial and detrimental impact on the company's standing and profit. The powers are therefore used sparingly,

---

[24] Note also EC Commission proposals on a uniform standard of criminal sanctions across member states, in order to increase the effectiveness of the criminal regime, and thus increasing the deterrent effect of such sanctions: http://ec.europa.eu/internal_market/securities/abuse/index_en.htm. It seems, however, that the UK will not directly apply the relevant regulations, but will instead enact domestic legislation meeting, as a minimum, the standard imposed by EU regulations.

and only in the most serious of cases, often after public outcry and extensive media coverage. In the past decade, only five or six investigations have been launched, often with long and expensive consequences. For example, the Mirror Group Newspapers trials lasted nine years and cost £9.5 million.[25]

Inspections are most commonly initiated by the Secretary of State. This may be done if the Secretary of State considers there is fraud or other improper conduct, or that the company's members have not been given all the information that they might reasonably expect (CA 1985 s 432(2)); or it is necessary to ascertain where the true ownership of shares or debentures or control of the company actually lies (CA 1985 s 442); or there has been insider dealing (FSMA 2000 s 168(3), also allowing the FCA to initiate such investigations).

In a straightforward case the inspectors may be officers in the Secretary of State's own department, but, for the more serious cases, it is usual to appoint a QC and a leading accountant. The report may be published, and usually is if the matter is one that has attracted public interest.

The second form of power held by the Secretary of State is lower key, allowing for an informal, unpublicised inquiry, requiring a company to produce specified documents for inspection by his officers or some other competent person, or, if they are not in its possession, to state where it believes they are (CA 1985 s 447). Failure to comply may be punished as contempt of court. This latter power (which avoids much expense and publicity) can be used alone, but is often used as a first step, before a decision is taken whether to set up a full-scale investigation under CA 1985 s 432(2). Use of this power is controversial. Many complain that the exercise is as detrimental, probing and traumatic as a formal inspection, yet often reveals no cause for follow-up. In 2005/2006, 3,702 companies were named in requests, but formal investigations were started in only 148 cases (ie in approximately 4% of cases). The investigations rarely concern the accountability of management to members, but almost always focus on fraudulent trading, theft, breach of disqualification orders and undertakings, and such like.

An investigation may lead to a number of consequences. If criminal conduct is revealed, or suspected, the inspectors' findings may be followed by a prosecution. The Secretary of State may apply for disqualification orders against directors and other persons involved in the management of the company (Company Directors Disqualification Act 1986 (CDDA 1986) s 8), or for the winding up of the company (Insolvency Act 1986 (IA 1986) s 124A), or for a remedy under CA 2006 s 995. Under CA 1985 s 438, the Secretary of State could institute proceedings for a civil remedy in the name of the company, but this provision has since been repealed under CA 2006 s 1176. Documents and information obtained during the investigation may be disclosed to regulatory authorities; comparable powers may also be used to assist certain overseas law enforcement and regulatory authorities (Companies Act 1989 (CA 1989) ss 82ff). If satisfactory information about the ownership or control of a company is not forthcoming, this may lead to the imposition of a 'freezing' order on the shares in question (CA 1985 s 445; see 'Company investigations into share ownership and the disclosure register', p 761).

Conduct of the investigation

The cases that follow illustrate aspects of the working of the investigatory powers in practice.

---

[25] Although the CLR found the length of investigations to be often necessary and certainly difficult to control, CA 2006 Pt 32 nevertheless indicates a legislative desire to control proceedings more closely and terminate them when necessary (see the new CA 1985 ss 446A and 446B inserted by CA 2006 s 1035).

In reaching a decision whether to appoint inspectors to investigate the affairs of a company, the Secretary of State is not bound by the rules of natural justice.

[14.01] Norwest Holst Ltd v Secretary of State for Trade [1978] Ch 201 (Court of Appeal)

The facts appear from the judgment.

LORD DENNING MR: Ever since 1948 there has been a valuable provision of the Companies Act by which the Board of Trade can appoint inspectors to investigate the affairs of a company. Many investigations have been held by inspectors, usually one of Queen's Counsel, and the other an accountant. In a case we had fairly recently, *Re Pergamon Press Ltd* **[14.02]**, we had to consider the position of the inspectors under such an inquiry. It was held by this court that the inspectors were under a duty to act fairly in the conduct of their inquiry.

Now we have to consider a different point. It is said that the minister himself has done wrong. His conduct is challenged. It is said that the minister has acted beyond his powers in appointing inspectors. He ought, it is said, to have warned the company beforehand and given them a chance of being heard. Furthermore, it is said that the minister exercised his discretion erroneously. He ought to have had sufficient reasons, and he had none in this case. It is said further that he is acting on the information of informers, which is inadmissible as being against the public interest.

On these grounds the company has brought an action to try to stop the inspectors proceeding with the inquiry. The minister applied to strike it out. Foster J struck it out. The company appeal to this court . . .

On 11 March 1977, the Secretary of State ordered the inquiry now in question. He did it under s 165(b)(ii) of the Companies Act 1948 [CA 1985 s 432(2)]. On 25 March 1977, the secretary of the group wrote:

'I am authorised to say that it does not appear to my board that there are any circumstances which would justify the exercise of your discretionary power under the section to appoint inspectors.'

He asked: What were the circumstances? Would they be disclosed? The Secretary of State declined to give that information . . .

As the minister gave no information, the company started this action. They delivered a statement of claim, which they afterwards amended. The burden of the statement of claim is that the company know of no wrongdoing which has been done by them or any of their people; and therefore it is wrong that the minister should appoint inspectors without, as they say, any proper justification. They put it in these words in their final amended pleadings:

'. . . It is implicit in the provisions of s 165(b)(ii) of the said Act that the discretionary power to appoint inspectors is to be exercised fairly and/or in accordance with the principles of natural justice.'

They ask for a declaration that the appointment or purported appointment was ultra vires and invalid.

It is important to know the background of the legislation. It sometimes happens that public companies are conducted in a way which is beyond the control of the ordinary shareholders. The majority of the shares are in the hands of two or three individuals. These have control of the company's affairs. The other shareholders know little and are told little. They receive the glossy annual reports. Most of them throw them into the wastepaper basket. There is an annual general meeting but few of the shareholders attend. The whole management and control is in the hands of the directors. They are a self-perpetuating oligarchy: and are virtually unaccountable. Seeing that the directors are the guardians of the company, the question is asked: *Quis custodiet ipsos custodes*—Who will guard the guards themselves?

It is because companies are beyond the reach of ordinary individuals that this legislation has been passed so as to enable the Department of Trade to appoint inspectors to investigate the affairs of a company. Mr Brodie, who appears for Norwest Holst Ltd, drew our attention to the practice of the Board of Trade from 1948 to 1962. It was given in evidence to Lord Jenkins' Company Law Committee (1962) (Cmnd 1749). The Board of Trade said (at p 79) that it was very necessary to hear both sides before deciding whether or not an inspector should be appointed. By so doing it is often possible in cases where no fraud is alleged to bring the parties together or for them to reach a mutually satisfactory arrangement so that an investigation is not necessary.

That was the practice before 1962. Mr Brodie submitted that that practice was required by the common law. He said that the principles of natural justice are to be applied; and, accordingly, both sides should be heard before an inspector is appointed.

That may have been the practice of the Board of Trade in those years; but I do not think that this was required by the common law. There are many cases where an inquiry is held—not as a judicial or quasi-judicial inquiry—but simply as a matter of good administration. In these circumstances there is no need to give preliminary notice of any charge, or anything of that sort. Take the case where a police officer is suspected of misconduct. The practice is to suspend him pending inquiries. He is not given notice of any charge at that stage, nor any opportunity of being heard. The rules of natural justice do not apply unless and until it is decided to take proceedings. Other instances can be given in other fields. For instance, the Stock Exchange may suspend dealings in a company's shares. They go by what they know, without warning the company beforehand.

Equally, so far as s 109 [CA 1985 s 447] is concerned, when the officers of the Department of Trade are appointed to examine the books, there is no need for the rules of natural justice to be applied. If the company was forewarned and told that the officers were coming, what is to happen to the books? In a wicked world, it is not unknown for books or papers to be destroyed or lost.

So also with the appointment of inspectors, under s 165(b)(ii). The inspectors are not to decide rights or wrongs. They are to investigate and report. This inquiry is a good administrative arrangement for the good conduct of companies and their affairs. It is not a case to which the rules of natural justice apply. There is no need for them to be given notice of a charge, or a fair opportunity of meeting it. I would say that, so long as the minister acts in good faith, it is not incumbent upon him to disclose the material he has before him, or the reasons for the inquiry.

ORMROD and GEOFFREY LANE LJJ delivered concurring judgments.

Inspectors appointed by the Secretary of State must act fairly, but their function is not judicial or quasi-judicial.

[14.02] Re Pergamon Press Ltd [1971] Ch 388 (Court of Appeal)

Maxwell and others, the directors of a company which was the subject of an investigation ordered under s 165(b) of the Act of 1948 [CA 1985 s 432(2)] had declined to answer questions unless they were first given assurances that, in effect, the proceeding would be conducted as if it were a judicial inquiry. The inspectors, acting under CA 1948 s 167(3) [CA 1985 s 436(2), (3)] referred this refusal to the court. The Court of Appeal, affirming Plowman J, held that the directors were not entitled to the assurances.

LORD DENNING MR: [Counsel for the directors] claimed that they had a right to see the transcripts of the evidence of the witnesses adverse to them...[and] to cross-examine the witnesses [and] that they ought to see any proposed finding against them before it was included finally in the report. In short, the directors claimed that the inspectors should conduct the inquiry much as if it were a judicial inquiry in a court of law in which Mr Maxwell and his colleagues were being charged with an offence.

It seems to me that this claim on their part went too far. This inquiry was not a court of law. It was an investigation in the public interest, in which all should surely co-operate, as they promised to do. But if the directors went too far on their side, I am afraid that Mr Fay, for the inspectors, went too far on the other. He did it very tactfully, but he did suggest that in point of law the inspectors were not bound by the rules of natural justice. He said that in all the cases where natural justice had been applied hitherto, the tribunal was under a duty to come to a determination or decision of some kind or other. He submitted that when there was no determination or decision but only an investigation or inquiry, the rules of natural justice did not apply . . .

I cannot accept Mr Fay's submission. It is true, of course, that the inspectors are not a court of law. Their proceedings are not judicial proceedings . . . They are not even quasi-judicial, for they decide nothing; they determine nothing. They only investigate and report. They sit in private and are not entitled to admit the public to their meetings . . . They do not even decide whether there is a prima facie case . . .

But this should not lead us to minimise the significance of their task. They have to make a report which may have wide repercussions. They may, if they think fit, make findings of fact which are very damaging to those whom they name. They may accuse some; they may condemn others; they may ruin reputations or careers. Their report may lead to judicial proceedings. It may expose persons to criminal prosecutions or to civil actions. It may bring about the winding up of the company, and be used itself as material for the winding up . . . When they do make their report, the Board are bound to send a copy of it to the company; and the Board may, in their discretion, publish it, if they think fit, to the public at large. Seeing that their work and their report may lead to such consequences, I am clearly of the opinion that the inspectors must act fairly. This is a duty which rests on them, as on many other bodies, even though they are not judicial, nor quasi-judicial, but only administrative: see *R v Gaming Board for Great Britain, ex p Benaim and Khaida*.[26] The inspectors can obtain information in any way they think best, but before they condemn or criticise a man, they must give him a fair opportunity for correcting or contradicting what is said against him. They need not quote chapter and verse. An outline of the charge will usually suffice.

That is what the inspectors here propose to do, but the directors of the company want more. They want to see the transcripts of the witnesses who speak adversely of them, and to see any documents which may be used against them. They, or some of them, even claim to cross-examine the witnesses.

In all this the directors go too far. This investigation is ordered in the public interest. It should not be impeded by measures of this kind. Witnesses should be encouraged to come forward and not hold back. Remember, this not being a judicial proceeding, the witnesses are not protected by an absolute privilege, but only by a qualified privilege . . . It is easy to imagine a situation in which, if the name of a witness were disclosed, he might have an action brought against him, and this might deter him from telling all he knew. No one likes to have an action brought against him, however unfounded. Every witness must, therefore, be protected. He must be encouraged to be frank. This is done by giving every witness an assurance that his evidence will be regarded as confidential and will not be used except for the purpose of the report. This assurance must be honoured. It does not mean that his name and his evidence will never be disclosed to anyone. It will often have to be used for the purpose of the report, not only in the report itself, but also by putting it in general terms to other witnesses for their comments. But it does mean that the inspectors will exercise a wise discretion in the use of it so as to safeguard the witness himself and any others affected by it. His evidence may sometimes, though rarely, be so confidential that

---

[26] [1970] 2 QB 417.

it cannot be put to those affected by it, even in general terms. If so, it should be ignored so far as they are concerned. For I take it to be axiomatic that the inspectors must not use the evidence of a witness so as to make it the basis on an adverse finding unless they give the party affected sufficient information to enable him to deal with it.

It was suggested before us that whenever the inspectors thought of deciding a conflict of evidence or of making adverse criticism of someone, they should draft the proposed passage of their report and put it before the party for his comments before including it. But I think this also is going too far. This sort of thing should be left to the discretion of the inspectors. They must be masters of their own procedure. They should be subject to no rules save this: they must be fair. This being done, they should make their report with courage and frankness, keeping nothing back. The public interest demands it. They need have no fear because their report, so far as I can judge, is protected by an absolute privilege . . .

SACHS and BUCKLEY LJJ delivered concurring judgments.

> Notes

1. In later proceedings (reported as *Maxwell v Department of Trade and Industry* [1974] QB 523), Robert Maxwell claimed that the inspectors had not acted fairly in that, before making their report, they had not first formulated their criticisms of him in tentative form and given him an opportunity of meeting them. The Court of Appeal, affirming Wien J, held that this procedure was unnecessary: it was sufficient that, in the course of the inquiry, all the matters which appeared to call for an explanation or an answer by a witness should have been put to him; and in substance this had been done.

2. In *R v Secretary for Trade, ex p Perestrello* [1981] QB 19, Woolf J held that there was a similar obligation to act fairly, but, again, no requirement to observe the rules of natural justice, in exercising the power to demand production of a company's books and papers under CA 1967 s 109 (CA 1985 s 447).

3. Recently, in *R (on the application of 1st Choice Engines Ltd) v Secretary of State for Business, Innovation and Skills* [2014] EWHC 1765 (Admin), it was held by His Honour Judge Platts (sitting as a Judge of the High Court) that a request under s 447 provides the Secretary of State with a very wide discretion 'for the very reason that he is acting in the public interest when exercising his powers to investigate companies' [34]. The learned judge had taken from *Perestrello* 'the principle that in theory a notice could be quashed if the court was satisfied that the documents sought were unreasonably wide and excessive in the circumstances' [28] and came to the view that the request for the document in question, though considered extremely wide, was not unreasonably excessive.

[14.03] Re an Inquiry into Mirror Group Newspapers plc [2000] Ch 194 (Chancery Division)

Nearly 30 years after *Pergamon Press Ltd* [14.02], and after Robert Maxwell's death and the collapse of his business empire, his son Kevin was the subject of a DTI investigation. The Secretary of State had appointed inspectors to look into the affairs of the company (MGN) of which Kevin Maxwell had been a director. Their investigation was put on hold until criminal proceedings against him (in which he was acquitted) had been concluded. Meanwhile, he had been cross-examined at the trial and questioned under other statutory procedures for a total of 61 days. The inspectors required Maxwell to sign an undertaking that he would not disclose information put to him in the course of their questioning, which he was unwilling to do. He also objected that the course which the inspectors proposed to take was unfair and unreasonable (especially since he had no legal representation), and in particular that they intended to question him at length on matters which had already been covered in the previous interrogations. Scott V-C ruled that his objections were largely justified.

SIR RICHARD SCOTT V-C: . . . There are two issues in this case. First, there is the issue of confidentiality. Are inspectors who have been appointed under Part XIV of the Companies Act 1985 entitled to demand of a person who is placed under a statutory obligation to attend before them and answer their questions that the person enter into an undertaking of confidentiality on the lines of that which Mr Maxwell was asked to sign or, indeed, any confidentiality undertaking at all?

This issue is one of general importance. As I have said, it appears to be the general practice of inspectors to insist on being given confidentiality undertakings. Are those who appear before them obliged to comply?

Second, there is an issue as to what, if any, limits there are on the right of inspectors to require officers and agents of a company under investigation to attend before them and assist them in their investigation. Is there a point at which the demands made by the inspectors become so onerous that a witness's refusal to co-operate becomes excusable? If there is such a point, has it been reached in the present case? . . .

The confidentiality issue

. . . I do not accept that the inspectors have any legal obligation to those from whom they obtain information or documents to insist on confidentiality undertakings being given by others before whom, for the purposes of their inquiry, they wish to put the information or documents. If they wish to preserve and protect the confidentiality of the information and documents, they need do no more than make sure that every person to whom the information is communicated, or before whom the documents are put, is on notice of their confidential character. Such a person would not be inhibited by being given such notice from making use of the information and documents for the purpose of answering the inspectors' questions. He could take advice from lawyers and others. He could consult others who had been involved, in order to check his recollection or remedy his lack of recollection. In doing so he would not, in my judgement, be in breach of any duty owed either to those from whom the information and documents had originated or to the inspectors. If, on the other hand, the new witness were to disclose the contents of the documents or information for a purpose not connected with the purposes for which they had been supplied to him, he would, in my view, prima facie commit a breach of duty to those from whom the information or documents had been obtained . . .

Unfairness and oppression

The starting point is the statutory obligation of persons such as Mr Maxwell to answer relevant questions put to them by Companies Act inspectors . . . None the less, the assistance that those on whom the statutory obligation is placed must give is not unlimited. They must give the assistance that they are 'reasonably able to give'. The word 'reasonably' limits the extent of their obligation. To put the point another way, the inspectors cannot place demands on them that are unreasonable, whether as to the time they must expend or the expense they must incur in preparation for the questions or in any other respect . . .

In my opinion, the inspectors should do their best to avoid questioning Mr Maxwell on topics on which he has been questioned before. They should, so far as possible, rely on the answers he has given in previous interrogations . . .

All the circumstances must, in my judgment, be taken into account in deciding whether or not assistance which a person is, in an absolute sense, able to give is also assistance which he is reasonably able to give. But, if, in all the circumstances, the demands made on the person go beyond what he is reasonably able to give, his failure to comply with the demands will not be a breach of his statutory duty and should not be treated as a contempt of court . . .

[His Lordship accordingly declined to rule that Maxwell had been in contempt.]

➤ Note

In *Re Attorney General's Reference (No 2 of 1998)* [2000] QB 412, CA, the court was asked to rule on the meaning of the phrase 'to provide an explanation' of documents which had been produced to inspectors under CA 1985 s 447. It was held that this was not limited to giving an exposition of the text of the document, but covered 'not only the contents, but also the date of creation, the authorship, provenance, accuracy, completeness, intended purpose, destination and significance of the document or its contents, and of the use to which it was in fact put', and also (subject to a test of reasonableness) to explain discrepancies between the documents and other evidence.

Inspections and the privilege against self-incrimination

A person who is being interviewed by inspectors has no privilege against self-incrimination. In *Re London United Investments plc* [1992] Ch 578 it was held that this common law privilege had been impliedly abrogated by CA 1985 Pt XIV. This means that the person is compellable to answer questions put to him, on pain of punishment for contempt of court if he refuses. There is similarly no privilege where a person is being examined (eg as to the causes of a company's insolvency) under the provisions of IA 1986 s 236: *Bishopsgate Investment Management Ltd v Maxwell* [1993] Ch 1, CA, with that case recently cited by the Supreme Court in *Beghal v DPP* [2015] UKSC 49 as illustrative of provisions which were clearly intended 'to impose an unqualified obligation to answer' [63].

Indeed, in *Re an Inquiry under the Company Securities (Insider Dealing) Act 1985* [1988] AC 660, HL, a journalist, Jeremy Warner, declined to answer questions put to him by inspectors because he felt obliged as a journalist to protect sources of information which had been given to him in confidence. The House of Lords held that this fact did not of itself provide a reasonable excuse, and that he was liable to punishment for contempt.

Inspections and subsequent fair trials—criminal and civil cases

Prior to 1994, courts had ruled in a number of cases that evidence given by a person during an investigation could be used against him in a subsequent criminal trial, or in proceedings brought to have a disqualification order made against him. This was so notwithstanding the fact that he was compellable to give the evidence, even if it was incriminating, on pain of punishment for contempt of court. Evidence obtained under compulsion in other statutory procedures (eg IA 1986 s 236) was the subject of similar rulings.

However, in 1994 the European Court of Human Rights (ECtHR) ruled in the *Saunders* case (*Saunders v United Kingdom* (1996) 23 EHRR 313) that the use of such evidence in a *criminal* prosecution violated the individual's right to a fair trial under Art 6 of the European Convention on Human Rights. Following this decision, the Crown changed its practice and ceased to use evidence so obtained in subsequent criminal trials. Now the law itself has been changed to reflect this: see CA 1985 s 434(5A) and (5B). (Note that notwithstanding the ruling by the Strasbourg Court, Saunders' conviction was upheld by the Court of Appeal: *R v Saunders* [1996] 1 Cr App Rep 463, CA.)

The protection is not absolute, however. For example, both the European Court and UK courts have ruled that disqualification proceedings are not criminal proceedings, but civil proceedings 'of a regulatory nature', in which the use of such evidence involves no infringement of Art 6.[27]

Although *Saunders* prompted legislative change, there is a lack of clarity in the case as to whether the right to silence and the right not to incriminate oneself are absolute rights. Four decisions, *Brown v Stott* [2001] 2 All ER 97, *R v Kearns* [2002] 1 WLR 2815, *Gray v News Group Newspapers Ltd* [2012] 2 WLR 848, CA, and a decision of the ECtHR, *O'Halloran v United Kingdom* (15809/02) (2008) 46 EHRR 21, all suggest that Art 6 may be limited if national authorities have a clear and proper public objective.

■ Further reading

ALCOCK, A, 'Liability for Misinforming the Market' [2011] JBL 243.

ALCOCK, A, 'Five Years of Market Abuse' (2007) 28 *Company Lawyer* 163.

DAVIES, PL, 'Liability for Misstatements to the Market: Some Reflections' (2009) 9 *Journal of Corporate Law Studies* 295.

DUFFY, M, 'Fraud on the Market: Judicial Approaches to Causation and Loss from Securities Nondisclosure in the United States, Canada and Australia' (2005) 29 *Melbourne University Law Review* 20.

GILOTTA, S, 'Disclosure in Securities Markets and the Firm's Need for Confidentiality: Theoretical Framework and Regulatory Analysis' (2012) 13 *European Business Organization Law Review* 45.

HAYNES, A, 'Market Abuse, Fraud and Misleading Communications' (2012) 19 *Journal of Financial Crime* 234.

HAYNES, A, 'Market Abuse: An Analysis of its Nature and Regulation' (2007) 28 *Company Lawyer* 323.

NORTH, G, 'Listed Company Disclosure and Financial Market Transparency: Is This a Battle Worth Fighting or Merely Policy and Regulatory Mantra?' [2014] JBL 484.

VILLIERS, C, 'Implementing the Transparency Directive: A Further Step towards Consolidating the FSAP' (2007) 28 *Company Lawyer* 257.

---

[27] See *DC, HS and AD v United Kingdom* [2000] BCC 710, ECtHR; and *Re Westminster Property Management Ltd* [2000] 2 BCLC 396, CA.

15

RECONSTRUCTIONS, MERGERS AND TAKEOVERS

General issues

Companies can generally undertake the full gamut of normal business activities using no more than basic company and common law rules, assisted by market forces: they can expand and contract, change business focus, undergo shifts in corporate control, and make various advantageous contractual arrangements with members and creditors and the like. But when companies want to act rapidly and decisively, or enter into arrangements with large numbers of members or creditors, or effect mergers with other corporate entities, or de-mergers of their own conglomerate business, then some more efficient way of proceeding is essential.

Modern company law provides three formal mechanisms to facilitate major corporate reconstructions:

(i)   arrangements or reconstructions under the Insolvency Act 1986 (IA 1986) ss 110–111 (see 'Schemes of reconstruction under IA 1986 ss 110–111', pp 781ff);

(ii)   arrangements, reconstructions, mergers or divisions under the Companies Act 2006 (CA 2006) Pts 26 and 27 (see 'Arrangements and reconstructions under CA 2006 ss 895–901', pp 784ff);

(iii) takeovers under CA 2006 Pt 28 (see 'Takeovers', pp 796ff).

Companies make use of these provisions for a variety of reasons. They may want to restructure the mutual rights and obligations of the company and its members or creditors. Economic motivations may prompt them to expand the company's business, whether by diversification, vertical integration (with companies performing other functions in the production process chain) or horizontal integration (with companies at the same stage in the production process). Alternatively, financial or fiscal considerations may prompt changes that will reduce liability to tax or improve the balance sheet.

Meaning of the terms

The terms employed in this chapter are commonly used without any great precision, but some generalisations are possible.

A *'reconstruction'* is usually the transfer of the undertaking and business of a company (or, sometimes, several companies) to a new company specially formed for the purpose. The old company is put into liquidation and its members, instead of being repaid their capital by the liquidator in cash, agree to take equivalent shares in the new company. The result of this is that the same members carry on the same or some part of the same enterprise through the medium of a new company. The simpler set of statutory provisions governing this procedure is contained in IA 1986 ss 110–111 ('Schemes of reconstruction under IA 1986 ss 110–111', pp 781ff).[1] The sanction of the court is not required, but a dissenting member may always require that he or she be paid out in cash rather than take the new shares. Creditors who do not agree to look to the new company for payment of their debts may prove in the liquidation of the old company.

This procedure is popular with private and family companies, and with investment trust companies undergoing restructuring. The process can enable the creation of a new company with wider or different objects, or a change in the rights of classes of members, or a necessary reorganisation prior to a de-merger which splits the company's businesses into more discrete units.

A *'merger'* or *'amalgamation'* takes place when the assets and undertakings of more than one company are brought under the ownership and control of a single company, which may be one of the companies involved or a new one. The result is that the shareholders who were members of the several amalgamating companies now together own and control the same enterprises as one aggregated venture. In a straightforward case, the procedure laid down by IA 1986 s 110 may be used. In more complicated cases, the other procedures are used.

Much the same consequences of merger and amalgamation may follow from a *'takeover'*, which is a general term used to describe the acquisition by one company (or by one or more individuals, or by a group of companies) of the share capital (all or part) and control of another, usually by buying all or a majority of its shares ('Takeovers', pp 796ff). In the ordinary case, the company taken over is the smaller; in a *'reverse takeover'*, a smaller company gains control of a larger one.[2] An offer addressed to all the shareholders of a company to buy the shares of each member at a stated price is known as a 'takeover bid'. It is usually expressed to be conditional upon a designated percentage of shares being accepted by a given date. This is commonly set at 51%, which is a sufficient majority for the bidder to replace the board of directors. Alternatively, it may be as high as 90%, because CA 2006 s 979 permits a company that has acquired 90% or more of a company's shares by a takeover bid to buy the remaining shares compulsorily, and conversely s 983 empowers the minority shareholders in such a situation to insist on being bought out.

Where the company making a takeover bid offers to exchange its own shares for those in the company being acquired, rather than make a bid for cash, the result is to all intents and purposes an amalgamation of the two companies as described earlier.

A *'scheme of arrangement'* or a *'reconstruction'* under CA 2006 Pts 26 and 27 (additional requirements for public companies) enables a company to effect mergers and amalgamations, and also to alter the rights of its members *or its creditors*, with the sanction of the court. The provisions are sufficiently wide to accommodate schemes having a considerable diversity of objectives and range of complexity, which may involve more than one company. The more elaborate kinds of merger will usually need to be dealt with under these sections, as will any scheme of reconstruction which is intended to affect creditors (and especially debenture holders) as well as shareholders. Unless the court orders otherwise,

---

[1] The other set is in CA 2006 Pts 26 and 27, see 'Arrangements and reconstructions under CA 2006 ss 895–901', pp 784ff.

[2] Paradoxically, however, if this is done by the bidding company exchanging its own shares for the shares of the target company, the former shareholders in the target will end up controlling the bidder.

the members or creditors who dissent are nevertheless bound to accept the terms of the scheme. In contrast with IA 1986 s 110, there is no liquidation of the company or companies involved.

Corporate businesses may, of course, be split up as well as aggregated. The most common procedure by which part of a company's assets and undertaking is sold off is usually referred to as 'hiving down'. The company forms a subsidiary and vests the assets in question in its name, or transfers the assets to an existing subsidiary, and sells the shareholding in that subsidiary to new owners. These may include the managers of that part of the business who have hitherto been employees of the vendor (a 'management buy-out'). Alternatively, there may be a simple sale of the assets, either for cash or in consideration of the allotment of shares in the purchasing company to the vendor, or to the shareholders of the vendor if it is a company. This last type of transaction, which is not common in this country, is known as a 'division'[3] or a 'de-merger'.

A merger or division that involves a public company and is achieved by a transfer of *assets and undertaking* in consideration of the allotment of shares in the transferee company to the former shareholders of the transferor must observe the requirements of CA 2006 Pt 27 (which modifies or excludes some of the provisions in Pt 26). These provisions implement the Third and Sixth EU Company Law Directives, although the independence requirements for experts and valuers in CA 2006 ss 936 and 937 are new, and correspond with the independence requirements for a statutory auditor (s 1214). The provisions have less impact than might be supposed, however, since the standard procedures for takeover and hiving down usually involve the purchase and sale of *shares* and not of assets.

Finally, the *economic* consequences of a merger may be such as to create a monopoly or other situation or one which distorts competition. Both the EU and successive governments in the UK have enacted measures which have as their object the control of mergers, as part of the wider legislation designed to promote competition and regulate restrictive and anti-competitive practices. These statutes and the associated regulations often impose additional restrictions, especially on large-scale mergers.

Schemes of reconstruction under IA 1986 ss 110–111

Under this type of reorganisation, the company resolves, first, to go into voluntary liquidation (members' or creditors'), and, secondly, to authorise by special resolution the transfer by the liquidator of the whole or part of the company's business or assets to another company (or limited liability partnership (LLP)) in consideration of shares in that company (or membership of the LLP).

The procedure provides a relatively simple method for reconstructing a single company or effecting a simple merger or takeover. Its advantage is that court approval is not generally required.[4] But its use is limited. The liquidator must ensure that the creditors' proved claims are met, and cannot rely on any indemnity given by the acquiring company.[5] And in a members' voluntary liquidation, dissenting members have a right to veto the scheme, or to be bought out at a price determined by agreement or arbitration (*an appraisal right*).[6]

---

[3] See CA 2006 Pt 27.
[4] It is required if the creditors' liquidation committee does not give approval: IA 1986 s 110(3)(b).
[5] *Pulsford v Devenish* [1903] 2 Ch 625.
[6] IA 1986 s 111.

A company cannot by a provision in its constitution authorise a scheme of reconstruction which disregards the rights of dissentients under IA 1986 s 111.

[15.01] Bisgood v Henderson's Transvaal Estates Ltd [1908] 1 Ch 743 (Court of Appeal)

The company in general meeting resolved to carry out a scheme whereby each fully paid £1 share was to be exchanged for one £1 share in a new company, to be credited as paid up to an amount of 87½p, leaving the outstanding balance 'on call' as a liability of the shareholders. Under the scheme, the 'new' shares of those who dissented were to be sold en bloc for what they would fetch, and the proceeds distributed pro rata amongst them. The company's memorandum and articles purported to authorise such a transaction; but it was held to be unlawful.

BUCKLEY LJ delivered the judgment of the court (COZENS-HARDY MR and FLETCHER MOULTON and BUCKLEY LJJ): The question involved is whether by clauses even in the memorandum of association of a company limited by shares the limit upon the shareholder's liability can be raised—whether the constitution of the company can provide that the majority may impose upon the minority a scheme under which the member must either come under an increased liability or accept such compensation as the scheme offers him. Section 161 of the Companies Act 1862 [IA 1986 s 111] protects the dissentient member by securing him the value of his interest to be determined by arbitration or agreement. The purpose of schemes such as that here in question is to evade or escape the provisions of that section. Their object is to impose upon the shareholders what is generally called an assessment—to require that in a limited company after the shares are fully paid the shareholder must either come under liability to make further contributions to capital or submit to take, not the value of his interest to be determined by arbitration or agreement, but such satisfaction as the scheme offers him. That satisfaction commonly means, and in substance means in this case, the surrender of his interest in the company . . .

The question is whether the reorganisation scheme [is intra vires merely because] it is justified by clauses in the memorandum of association . . .

[After discussing the purpose of the memorandum and articles, he continued:] . . . [T]he constitution of the company cannot provide that the corporator shall not enjoy rights and immunities which the statute gives him. [It follows that here] the articles cannot exclude a shareholder from his right of dissent under s 161 of the Companies Act 1862 . . . The question is not whether each individual corporator can bind himself in respect of his distributive share in the assets. The question is whether, consistently with the statutes, the constitution of the corporation can be such that every corporator shall in the matter of distribution—or *a fortiori* of distribution and further liability—be bound by the vote of the majority . . .

Shortly stated, the scheme is one under which the shareholder is told that he may take the share in the new company with its liability or sell the share in the new company with its liability, but he shall have nothing but the share in the new company or its proceeds; that he must be assessed or find some one who will take the new share with the assessment or take his chance that the liquidator may find someone who will do so, but that he shall have nothing else [and in particular shall not have his statutory rights]. In my opinion this is ultra vires. The plaintiff is, in my judgment, entitled to an injunction to restrain the defendants from carrying out the reorganisation scheme.

In a reconstruction under IA 1986 ss 110–111, the general meeting has no power to decide that the consideration received shall be distributed among the members otherwise than in accordance with their rights in a winding up.

[15.02] Griffith v Paget (1877) 5 Ch D 894 (Chancery Division)

The capital of the Argentine Tramways Co Ltd was divided into preferred shares and deferred shares each of a nominal value of £10, the former being entitled to a cumulative 12% preferential dividend. There was no provision as to the relative rights of the classes in a winding up. The preferred dividend had not been paid in full for many years. A scheme of reconstruction was proposed under which the shares in the existing company should be exchanged for shares, all of one class, in a new company, on a basis which gave the preferred shareholders approximately the par value of their existing holdings, but the deferred shareholders only about 15% of such value. The plaintiff, a preferred shareholder, who considered that this scheme gave the deferred shareholders more than the market value of their shares, objected that the general meeting had no power to fix the mode of distribution of the new shares; and the court upheld his view.

JESSEL MR: The question which is now raised, as far as I know for the first time, is this, whether in the case of a limited liability company, when there are two or more classes of shareholders having different rights inter se, and the powers conferred by the Companies Act 1862, s 161 [IA 1986 s 110], are exercised, the company can do more than decide on the nature of the consideration to be accepted, or whether it can, at the same time, by the statutory majority, decide as to the mode of distribution of the consideration so accepted between the two classes of shareholders. In my opinion it cannot do the latter at all.

I think the meaning of s 161, stated broadly, was this, that instead of disposing of the assets of the company, wound up under a voluntary winding up, for money, you may dispose of them for shares in any other company, or policies, or any like interest, or future profits or other benefit from the purchasing company, but that whatever the benefit was, in whatever shape it was taken, it was to be given, or paid, or handed over to the liquidators for the benefit of the contributories, if I may call them so, of the company wound up—of course subject to the payment of their debts; and that there was no authority conferred by the Act of Parliament on the general meeting, or rather the statutory majority, to direct a distribution as between those contributories otherwise than according to their rights inter se. I think that is tolerably plain from the nature of the case.

First, what is to become of the assets of the company when wound up voluntarily in the ordinary way? In that case we find, by s 133 [IA 1986 s 107], the property, after being applied in satisfaction of the liabilities, is to 'be distributed among the members according to their rights and interests in the company'. Therefore, if the liquidator sells the assets for money, there is no power given to a general meeting to alter the rights of the contributories inter se. They are to share according to their rights and interests . . .

➤ Note

There is an obvious advantage to a company in proceeding under CA 2006 Pts 26 and 27 (see 'Arrangements and reconstructions under CA 2006 ss 895–901', pp 784ff) rather than IA 1986 s 110, in that dissenting shareholders can be forced to accept a scheme under the former section, rather than being allowed to insist on their right under IA 1986 s 111 to be paid out in cash. In the next case cited, an attempt was made to formulate rules governing the freedom of a company to choose between the two forms of procedure.

Choosing between IA 1986 and CA 2006 procedures.

[15.03] Re Anglo-Continental Supply Co Ltd [1922] 2 Ch 723
(Chancery Division)

The facts are immaterial.

> ASTBURY J: As a result of his researches, Mr Maugham [counsel for the company] has formulated three propositions which, when expressed as follows, are in my judgment sound: (1) When a so-called scheme is really and truly a sale, etc under s 192 [IA 1986 s 110] simpliciter, that section must be complied with and cannot be evaded by calling it a scheme of arrangement under s 120 [CA 2006 Pt 26]: see per Warrington LJ in *Re Guardian Assurance Co.*[7] (2) Where a scheme of arrangement cannot be carried through under s 192, though it involves (inter alia) a sale to a company within that section for 'shares, policies and other like interests', and for liquidation and distribution of the proceeds, the court can sanction it under s 120 if it is fair and reasonable in accordance with the principles upon which the court acts in these cases, and it may, but only if it thinks fit, insist as a term of its sanction on the dissentient shareholders being protected in manner similar to that provided for in s 192. (3) Where a scheme of arrangement is one outside s 192 entirely, the court can also and a fortiori act as in proposition (2), subject to the conditions therein mentioned . . .

Arrangements and reconstructions under CA 2006 ss 895–901

The procedures in CA 2006 Pts 26 (ss 895–901) and 27 (applying to specific types of mergers and divisions of public companies only[8]) can be used to effect compromises or arrangements of one company with its members or its creditors,[9] but can also be used to amalgamate two or more companies, or to achieve the equivalent of a takeover.[10] The procedure requires:

(i)   a court order convening meetings of the appropriate classes of members or creditors who will be affected by the scheme;[11]

(ii) class meetings, seeking the approval of a majority in number *and* representing 75% in value of the groups affected by the proposal (ie members or classes of members, and creditors or classes of creditors[12]); and

(iii) sanction by the court of the approved scheme (CA 2006 s 899): the court must form its own judgement of the merits of the scheme, not simply confirm the view of the majority voters.[13]

---

[7] [1917] 1 Ch 431.

[8] See 'General issues', pp 779ff.

[9] Moratoria on debts and compromises with creditors (even, occasionally, including compromises that provide for different entitlements than those obtaining on winding up: *Anglo American Insurance Ltd* [2001] 1 BCLC 755) can be agreed under these provisions. However, a quicker and simpler alternative may be provided by company voluntary arrangements (see IA 1986 Pt I and Sch AI: see 'Company voluntary arrangements (CVAs)', pp 812ff).

[10] Such a scheme is also subject to the Takeover Code: see 'Takeovers', pp 796ff.

[11] The court has discretion as to the details of the meetings: *Re T & N Ltd* [2006] 2 BCLC 374.

[12] Companies Act 2006 (Consequential Amendments etc) Order 2008 (SI 2008/948) now enables a liquidator (if the company is being wound up) or an administrator (if the company is in administration) to apply to the court to order a meeting of creditors or members.

[13] CA 2006 s 899(2)(c) and (d) now enable a liquidator (if the company is being wound up) or an administrator (if the company is in administration) to apply to the court to sanction a compromise or arrangement (SI 2008/948).

The procedure has the advantage that, with court sanction, the proposed scheme is binding with only 75% approval, whereas a takeover leading to a compulsory buy-out requires 90% acceptance by the members being made the offer. The difference may be justified on the basis that the scheme procedure also requires court approval before the dissentients are bound. On the other hand, because the scheme is not binding until the vote and court approval, competing proposals can be organised to defeat the objectives. By contrast, takeover bidders can solicit irrevocable commitments even before the formal takeover offer is made.

What is a 'compromise or arrangement'?

A 'compromise or arrangement' under ss 895 and 899.

[15.04] Re Uniq plc [2011] EWHC 749 (Chancery Division, Companies Court)

For the facts, see Note 3 following *Brady v Brady* [**10.08**].

DAVID RICHARDS J:

24. Sections 895 and 899 require a scheme to constitute a compromise or arrangement between the company and its members or creditors, or classes of members or creditors. Where members or creditors give up all their rights and receive no benefit, there is no compromise or arrangement: *Re NFU Development Trust Ltd* [1972] 1 WLR 1548. If regard is had only to the terms of the scheme itself, the existing members see their 100% equity interest diluted to 9.8%, without any benefit to Uniq or themselves unless the restructuring as a whole is completed. If the restructuring is completed, a very substantial benefit is conferred on Uniq and, while the existing members' interests are reduced to 9.8%, they retain an interest in a viable company. It would, in my judgment, be artificial to confine the analysis to the terms of the scheme itself when the scheme forms an integral part of a restructuring which confers substantial benefit on the members bound by the scheme. I agree with the approach of Mann J in *Re Bluebrook Ltd* [2010] 1 BCLC 338 at [72] to [74].

25. It is true that it was possible for the scheme to come into effect but for the rest of the restructuring not to do so. This was neither intended nor likely, and it would not in my view be sensible or realistic to ignore the benefits flowing from the restructuring on the basis of this possibility.

➤ Notes

1. In *Re National Farmers' Union Development Trust Ltd* [1972] 1 WLR 1548, cited in *Re Uniq*, a non-profit-making company wished to write down its capital and reduce the number of its members from 94,000 to seven in order to reduce its administrative expenses. The proposal had the support of an 85% majority vote. But Brightman J held that he had no power to sanction the scheme under what is now CA 2006 s 899, since the statutory terms 'compromise' and 'arrangement' implied some element of accommodation on each side and were not appropriate to describe a scheme under which some members surrendered their rights altogether. Also see *Re Bluebrook Ltd* [2009] EWHC 2114 (Ch).

2. In *Re Lombard Medical Technologies Plc* [2015] 1 BCLC 656, applying *Re Uniq*, Henderson J sanctioned a scheme of arrangement that was still subject to the satisfaction of an outstanding condition, provided that clarity and certainty were present on the face of the scheme and that there was no new decision-making process following court approval.

3. A scheme which is designed to deal with and potentially alter the property rights of people who also happen to be creditors of the scheme company does not constitute

a compromise or arrangement within the scope of CA 2006 Pt 26: *Re Lehman Brothers International (Europe) (In Administration) (No 2)* [2009] EWHC 2141 (Ch), affd [2009] EWCA Civ 1161. See too *Re Welcome Financial Services Ltd* [2015] EWHC 815 (Ch) (Rose J).

4. The legislators are alert to what they regard as inappropriate use of combinations of these statutory provisions. See, for example, the recent amendments in CA 2006 s 641(2A) preventing a company using a scheme to reduce its share capital as part of a takeover scheme.[14]

Defining the classes for member or creditor meetings

The classic definition of a class is that of Bowen LJ in *Sovereign Life Assurance Co v Dodd*: a class consists of 'those persons whose rights are not so dissimilar as to make it impossible for them to consult together with a view to their common interest'.[15] This test sounds simple, but can be difficult to apply in practice, as the next extracts indicate. Notice how the issue is resolved in the modern cases: why is a simple answer so difficult? The practical consequences of different definitions of classes are also evident from these extracts—if two meetings need to give approval rather than only one, the scheme may founder.

Different classes—defined by different rights or different interests?

[15.05] Re Hellenic & General Trust Ltd [1976] 1 WLR 123
(Chancery Division)

Hambros Ltd, through a wholly owned subsidiary (referred to in the judgment as 'MIT') held 53% of the ordinary shares of the company, Hellenic & General Trust Ltd. A scheme of arrangement was proposed under which Hambros would acquire all the ordinary shares for a cash consideration of 48p per share. At a meeting of ordinary members, over 80% approved the scheme. MIT voted in support, but the National Bank of Greece, a minority shareholder holding some 14% of the shares, opposed the scheme because it would be liable to pay heavy taxes under Greek law. Templeman J refused to sanction the scheme, first, because he ruled that there should have been a separate 'class' meeting of those ordinary members who were not already a wholly owned subsidiary of Hambros and, secondly, because, although the scheme was objectively fair, it was as a matter of discretion, not fairness, to allow the use of CA 1948 s 206 (CA 2006 ss 895ff) to achieve the compulsory purchase of shares which could not be acquired by the use of the takeover procedure now contained in CA 2006 ss 974ff.

> TEMPLEMAN J: The first objection put forward is that the necessary agreement by the appropriate class of members has not been obtained. The shareholders who were summoned to the meeting consisted, it is submitted, of two classes. First there were the outside shareholders, that is to say the shareholders other than MIT; and secondly MIT, a subsidiary of Hambros. MIT were a separate class and should have been excluded from the meeting of outside shareholders. Although s 206 [CA 2006 s 896] provides that the court may order meetings, it is the responsibility of the petitioners to see that the class meetings are properly constituted, and if they fail then the necessary agreement is not obtained and the court has no jurisdiction to sanction the arrangement . . .

---

[14] See www.legislation.gov.uk/uksi/2015/472/contents/made.
[15] [1892] 2 QB 573 at 583. This was endorsed in *Re Hawk Insurance Co Ltd* **[15.09]**.

The question therefore is whether MIT, a wholly owned subsidiary of Hambros, formed part of the same class as the other ordinary shareholders.[16] What is an appropriate class must depend upon the circumstances but some general principles are to be found in the authorities. In *Sovereign Life Assurance Co v Dodd*,[17] the Court of Appeal held that for the purposes of an arrangement affecting the policyholders of an assurance company the holders of policies which had matured were creditors and were a different class from policyholders whose policies had not matured. Bowen LJ said: 'It seems plain that we must give such a meaning to the term "class" as will prevent the section being so worked as to result in confiscation and injustice, and that it must be confined to those persons whose rights are not so dissimilar as to make it impossible for them to consult together with a view to their common interest.' Vendors consulting together with a view to their common interest in an offer made by a purchaser would look askance at the presence among them of a wholly owned subsidiary of the purchaser...Mr Heyman, on behalf of the petitioners, submitted that since the parent and subsidiary were separate corporations with separate directors, and since MIT were ordinary shareholders in the company, it followed that MIT had the same interests as the other shareholders. The directors of MIT were under a duty to consider whether the arrangement was beneficial to the whole class of ordinary shareholders, and they were capable of forming an independent and unbiased judgment, irrespective of the interests of the parent company. This seems to me to be unreal. Hambros are purchasers making an offer. When the vendors meet to discuss and vote whether or not to accept the offer, it is incongruous that the loudest voice in theory and the most significant voice in practice should come from the wholly owned subsidiary of the purchaser. No one can be both a vendor and a purchaser and in my judgment, for the purpose of the class meetings in the present case, MIT were in the camp of the purchaser. Of course this does not mean that MIT should not have considered at a separate class meeting whether to accept the arrangement. But their consideration will be different from the considerations given to the matter by the other shareholders. Only MIT could say, within limits, that what was good for Hambros must be good for MIT . . .

Accordingly I uphold the first objection, which is fatal to the arrangement. But in view of the careful arguments put forward by both sides I will consider the other objections which are raised by Mr Wright and which are material if the class meeting in the present case, contrary to my view, was properly constituted.

The second objection is founded on the analysis of the arrangement as an offer by Hambros to acquire the ordinary shares for 48p. Section 209 [CA 2006 ss 974ff] provides safeguards for minority shareholders in the event of a takeover bid and in a proper case provides machinery for a small minority of shareholders to be obliged to accept a takeover against their wishes...If the present arrangement had been carried out under s 209, MIT as a subsidiary of Hambros would have been expressly forbidden to join in any approval for the purposes of s 209,[18] and in any event the objectors could not have been obliged to sell because they hold 10% of the ordinary shares of the company.

[It] seems to me that it is unfair to deprive the objectors of shares which they were entitled to assume were safe from compulsory purchase and with the effect of putting on the objectors a swingeing fiscal impost which, if the matter had proceeded under s 209, they could have avoided simply and quite properly by refusing to join in approving the scheme under that section.

Accordingly in the result, both as a matter of jurisdiction and as a matter of discretion, I am not prepared to make any order approving this scheme.

But contrast the next case.

---

[16] Note that this is not the same question as that arising under CA 2006 s 630, which speaks of rights 'attached to' a class of shares. Section 896 contemplates that creditors, as well as members, may fall into different classes.
[17] [1892] 2 QB 573.
[18] See now the more detailed provisions contained in CA 2006 ss 977(2) and 988.

Different classes: defined by rights; interests distinguished.

[15.06] Re BTR plc [1999] 2 BCLC 675 (Chancery Division)

A proposed scheme of arrangement, designed to effect a merger between BTR and another company, Siebe plc, had been carried by a 97% majority of BTR's ordinary shareholders at a single class meeting. Some dissenting shareholders contended that there should have been a separate class meeting for those BTR shareholders who already held shares in Siebe.

JONATHAN PARKER J [in rejecting the argument of the dissenting shareholders, said of *Re Hellenic & General Trust Ltd* **[15.05]**: For myself, I find it difficult to understand the concept of an interest arising out of a right as being something separate from the right itself. Nor do I think that such a process of analysis is necessary in relation to the *Hellenic* case where the majority of shares in the company the subject of the scheme were already held by a subsidiary of the intended purchaser. Templeman J effectively discounted the views of the registered holder of those shares and he did so, as I read the judgment, on the basis that in substance the scheme affected only the remainder of the shares. That is, in my judgment, the ratio of Templeman J's decision in so far as it addressed the question of separate classes . . .

It does not, as I see it, involve any analysis of interests and rights, nor is it inconsistent with the submission made by Mr Sykes (which I accept) that the relevant test is that of differing rights rather than differing interests. Nor do I agree with Mr Northcote that 'interest' in this connection is synonymous with right. Shareholders with the same rights in respect of the shares which they hold may be subject to an infinite number of different interests and may therefore, assessing their own personal interests (as they are perfectly entitled to do), vote their shares in the light of those interests. But that in itself, in my judgment, is simply a fact of life: it does not lead to the conclusion that shareholders who propose to vote differently are in some way a separate class of shareholders entitled to a separate class meeting. Indeed a journey down that road would in my judgment lead to impracticability and unworkability. In the course of his submissions Mr Northcote accepted that in the instant case it may well be that (if he is right) a very large number of separate class meetings would be required in order properly to reflect the differing interests of shareholders. The question then arises how the company could possibly reach an informed decision as to the division of shareholders into separate classes without first requiring a considerable amount of personal information from individual shareholders; a wholly unworkable, and highly undesirable, situation.

In my judgment, therefore, there was no warrant in this case for the convening of more than one meeting of the holders of the scheme shares, and I reject the submission that there are separate classes of holders of scheme shares for the purposes of this scheme . . .

Defining 'legal rights'; distinguishing 'interests'.

[15.07] Re UDL Holdings Ltd & Others (2001) 4 HKCFAR 358 (Hong Kong Court of Final Appeal)

The facts are immaterial.

LORD MILLETT NPJ: [He summarised the approach in distinguishing classes of rights (as opposed to interests) as follows (at [27]):]

(2) Persons whose rights are so dissimilar that they cannot sensibly consult together with a view to their common interest must be given separate meetings. Persons whose rights are

sufficiently similar that they can consult together with a view to their common interest should be summoned to a single meeting.

(3) The test is based on similarity or dissimilarity of legal rights against the company, not on similarity or dissimilarity of interests not derived from such legal rights. The fact that individuals may hold divergent views based on their private interests not derived from their legal rights against the company is not a ground for calling separate meetings.

(4) The question is whether the rights which are to be released or varied under the Scheme or the new rights which the Scheme gives in their place are so different that the Scheme must be treated as a compromise or arrangement with more than one class.

The modern resolution in defining classes?

[15.08] Re Apcoa Parking (UK) Ltd [2014] EWHC 997 (Chancery Division)

The facts are immaterial. Also see **[15.11]**.

HILDYARD J: [Clarifying the 'confusion and difficulty' arising out of the difference between rights and interests, and noting other 'blurred boundaries' in the purported distinction:]

50. The difference between rights and interests both before and after the relevant scheme has sometimes given rise to confusion and difficulty. Indeed, I suspect that the now approved approach of strictly confining class composition issues to questions as to different rights against the company, and thus reserving other matters to discretion rather than jurisdiction, is a relatively modern refinement, even if it is a refinement which has been built and justified by reference to older cases (see below).

51. My own sense is that, although the difference (which is plain) between legal rights against the company and personal interests or objectives in the case of particular creditors has always been recognised and emphasised, the importance attached to the difference has somewhat varied over the years. A tendency that developed was to regard Bowen LJ's classic test [in *Sovereign Life Assurance Co v Dodd*] as to the meaning of the term 'class' (see above) as connoting a single ultimate question, that is, whether the class constitution was such that any differences in the rights and the interests of the members of the proposed class were not such as to prevent them consulting together with a view to their common interests. Posed as a single question in that form, the test invites, indeed requires, consideration of interests.

52. The modern approach...is to break the question into two parts, and ask first whether there is any difference between the creditors in point of strict legal right, and only to proceed to the second question, at the Convening stage, if there is; and if there is, to postulate, by reference to the alternative if the scheme were to fail, whether objectively there would be more to unite than divide the creditors in the proposed class, ignoring for that purpose any personal or extraneous interest or subjective motivation operating in the case of any particular creditor(s)....

Some remaining confusion?

54. Be all this as it may, the confusion has largely been dispelled by a frank acknowledgment in later authorities that the language used had been 'imprecise' (see, for example, *per* Lord Millett NPJ sitting in the Hong Kong Court of Final Appeal in *Re UDL Holdings Ltd & Ors* **[15.07]**, [2002] 1 HKC 172 at 182B) and a reinstatement of orthodoxy which has been established since *Re Alabama, New Orleans, Texas and Pacific Junction Railway Co* [1891] 1 Ch 213. There Bowen LJ made clear that the fact that a member of a class comprised of persons all with the same legal rights had a different interest did not preclude it from being included in and

voting in that class, although that separate interest might lead the court to consider that the decision of the class was not in its interests, and on that basis to refuse to sanction the scheme as a matter of discretion. That chimes too, of course, with the inclination of judges to prefer the more flexible tool of discretion and an overall appreciation of fairness tested by reference to the real alternatives rather than the straight-jacket of jurisdiction, especially where rigidity may result in fragmentation of classes to avoid jurisdictional issues, but at the cost of enabling a small group to hold out unfairly against a majority.

55. I say 'largely been dispelled' because there remain, to my mind, some blurred boundaries, especially as to what meaning is to be given in the context to the term 'rights against the company'. Thus, for example, and as emphasised by Mr Snowden on behalf of FMS at the Convening Hearing, in the UDL case Lord Millett, when referring to Bowen LJ's analysis in *Re Alabama*, appeared to equate 'interests proceeding from rights' with 'rights' (see page 189I). He appears to treat the real distinction as being between such rights or derivative interests on the one hand, and 'different and potentially conflicting interests that arise from circumstances unconnected with their interests as members of the class' on the other. Lord Millett also later referred, in seeking to rationalise Templeman J's approach in *re Hellenic*, to 'different treatment' to be received under the scheme as going to the issue of class composition, without expressly confining the difference to a difference in legal rights. Indeed, he appears to have accepted that if the difference was that 'rights proposed to be conferred by the scheme' on one set of shareholders 'were commercially so dissimilar as to make it impossible for [that set and the other shareholders] to consult together with a view to their common interest', that would give rise to a jurisdictional issue (see page 181).

➤ Notes

1. Interestingly, in the same case, Hildyard J held that two grounds of creditors (albeit with different priority ranking) formed a single class because 'the advantage of avoiding insolvency and being able to share in a larger cake would sufficiently outweigh the wish to have a larger share than others in a much smaller cake' [116]. Thus, although 'the risk of imminent insolvency is not to be used as a solvent for all class differences', it would nevertheless in this case have caused reasonable creditors of a different ranking 'to unite in a common cause' [117].

2. On the other hand, Hildyard J also held that 'lock-up agreements' (ie agreements entered into by creditors agreeing to vote for the proposed scheme) do not render those creditors as a separate class. Such agreements do not affect the composition of classes, unless there is evidence to show that the creditors concerned would have voted differently in the absence of the agreement or that they have received special benefits not available to others (eg a retention of any special rights): [100]–[106].

3. Perhaps in a similar vein, the Court of Appeal confirmed that an offer of benefits for voting in favour of the scheme, to *all* those creditors belonging to the same class, was not in itself objectionable: see the discussion in Chapter 11, starting with *British America Nickel Corpn Ltd v O'Brien* [11.06].

4. It is also useful to bear in mind that, although the court in a convening hearing will not consider the merits or fairness of the proposed scheme, Norris J in *Re AI Scheme Ltd* [2015] EWHC 1233 (Ch), at [14], said:

[It is] important not to proceed with the scheme if it is plain, even at this stage, there is such a blot upon it that it has no real prospect of succeeding at the sanction hearing. That degree of initial oversight is, I think, particularly important in the case of a scheme of this sort, where the scheme creditors will be customers, each of whom has a relatively small claim and none of whom may have sufficient access to advice in relation to the complex issues arising.

Court intervention on its own motion.

[15.09] Re Hawk Insurance Co Ltd [2001] EWCA Civ 241 (Court of Appeal)

This was an appeal against a decision of the lower court refusing to sanction an unopposed scheme of arrangement under CA 1985 s 425 [CA 2006 s 895] on the ground that the court had no jurisdiction to do so because it was not satisfied that the creditors who had (without dissent) approved the scheme at a single meeting did, in fact, constitute a single class. The court allowed the appeal.

CHADWICK LJ:

The decision whether to summon more than one meeting

13. The decision whether to summon more than one meeting—and, if so, who should be summoned to which meeting—has to be made at the first stage [at the hearing for a court order summoning the meetings].... The relevant question is: between whom is the proposed compromise or arrangement to be made? There are, as it seems to me, three possible answers to that question. [He explained that this was on the basis that the compromise must be between the company and (i) all its creditors (ie one class meeting); (ii) one distinct class of creditors only (ie again, one class meeting); or (iii) two (or more) separate compromises or arrangements with two (or more) distinct classes of creditors (ie then requiring the appropriate number of class meetings). The last is clearly the one which causes problems, as here.]...

17. If the correct decision is not made at the first stage [ordering the meetings], the court may find, at the third stage [sanctioning the scheme], that it is without jurisdiction...That is what the judge [in the lower court] found to be the position in the present case.

18. It might be thought that the structure of the statutory provisions required the court to consider, at the first stage...whether the scheme proposed was a single compromise or arrangement...or was (on a true analysis) two or more linked compromises or arrangements...That has not been the practice in the Companies Court. [He then criticised this failing.]...

21. In my view an applicant is entitled to feel aggrieved if, in the absence of opposition from any creditor, the court holds, at the third stage and on its own motion, that the order which it made at the first stage was pointless. It is, to my mind, no answer to say that that is a risk which the applicant must accept. It may be inevitable that an applicant must accept the risk that a dissentient creditor will persuade the court at the third stage that the order which it made at the first stage (without hearing that creditor) was the wrong order. But that is not to say that the applicant must be required to accept that, when exercising what is plainly a judicial discretion at the first stage, the court will not address the question whether the order which it makes serves any useful purpose; or that, if it has addressed that question at the first stage, it will change its mind, of its own motion, at the third stage. [He continued, suggesting that the process could be improved, but that the question went to the court's jurisdiction to sanction, and so needed to be considered. However, on the facts here, he also held that separate class meetings were not required in the present case, and therefore allowed the appeal.]

PILL LJ gave a concurring judgment and WRIGHT LJ concurred with both.

➤ Notes

1. The risk that the classes have not been correctly identified so that, at the later stages, the court will not sanction the scheme has been reduced by a change in practice: see Practice Statement [2002] 3 All ER 96. This requires greater attention to the issues at the convening hearing, where application is made to the court for an order convening the necessary meetings. But, in addition, the courts have adopted the approach of Chadwick LJ in the previous extract, entitling them to find, on their own motion and without the intervention of dissentient voices, that the initial selection of classes was inappropriate.

2. By analogy with creditors' meetings in insolvency law, it is possible for the court to direct at stage 1 that split voting is possible at the creditors' meetings, particularly by nominee or trustee creditors, so that they might vote both for and against the scheme in relation to different parts of the value of that creditor's claim (*Re Equitable Life Assurance Society* [2002] BCC 319).

Court sanctioning of the scheme

The function of the courts in considering whether to sanction a scheme.

[15.10] Re Alabama, New Orleans, Texas and Pacific Junction Rly Co [1891] 1 Ch 213 (Court of Appeal)

The facts are immaterial.

> LINDLEY LJ: [What] the court has to do is to see, first of all, that the provisions of that statute have been complied with; and, secondly, that the majority has been acting bona fide. The court also has to see that the minority is not being overridden by a majority having interests of its own clashing with those of the minority whom they seek to coerce. Further than that, the court has to look at the scheme and see whether it is one as to which persons acting honestly, and viewing the scheme laid before them in the interests of those whom they represent, take a view which can be reasonably taken by businessmen . . .

Permitted judicial review of voting propriety.

[15.11] Re Apcoa Parking (UK) Ltd [2014] EWHC 997 (Chancery Division)

The facts are immaterial. Also see **[15.08]**.

> HILDYARD J:
> 129. These authorities make clear that the court must give full weight to the decision of the creditors, acting in their capacity as members of the class in which they are voting. It is not sufficient for the court to determine that it would not have reached the same decision as the creditors themselves reached. In the absence of some procedural or jurisdictional hurdle (or of some blot on the face of the scheme itself), the court should only decline to sanction the scheme if an intelligent and honest member of the relevant class acting in respect of his interest could not reasonably have approved it.
> 130. In particular, if an allegation is made that a creditor had improper regard to interests other than those of the class to which he belonged, it is necessary for there to be a 'but for' link

between the collateral interest and the decision to vote in the way that he did. The person challenging the relevant vote must therefore show that an intelligent and honest member of the class without those collateral interests could not have voted in the way that he did. It is not sufficient simply to show that the collateral interest is an additional reason for voting in the manner in which he would otherwise have voted.

➤ Notes

1. Also see *Re Hellenic & General Trust Ltd* **[15.05]**, the observations of Maugham J in *Re Dorman Long & Co* **[4.14]** and the more recent observations of Hildyard J in *Re Apcoa Parking Holdings GmbH* **[15.08]**.

2. The court has extensive powers under CA 2006 s 900 to make such ancillary orders as are necessary to facilitate implementation of any sanctioned scheme.

3. In *Re TSB Nuclear Energy Investment UK Ltd* [2014] EWHC 1272 (Ch), there was found to be no impediment to a scheme distributing assets of the company to its parent, since the proposal remained subject to obtaining the court's approval and the creditors' ability to dissent under CA 2006 s 900(2)(e).

4. In *In the Matter of Halcrow Holdings Ltd* [2011] EWHC 3662 (Ch), some 306 out of the 1,175 shareholders did not receive the scheme documents as a result of an accidental error in the printing process. Vos J held that the solicitors nonetheless had intended to notify all the shareholders and to provide all shareholders with copies of the scheme documents; and that the company took all reasonable steps to inform the relevant shareholders as soon as it had become aware of the mistake. The judge therefore held that the accidental omission could and should be waived under both CA 2006 s 313 and an 'accidental omission provision' in the company's articles.

5. In *Re La Seda De Barcelona SA* [2010] EWHC 1364 (Ch), Proudman J accepted that the court had jurisdiction to sanction a scheme which also provided for the release of liabilities on the part of a non-party to the scheme because the release fell within the 'requisite element of give and take between the scheme creditors and the company' [19]. The same considerations were applied by the same judge, more recently, in *Re Card Protection Plan Ltd* [2014] EWHC 114 (Ch).

Compulsory binding of dissentient minorities and the Human Rights Act 1998.

[15.12] Re Equitable Life Assurance Society [2002] EWHC 140 (Chancery Division)

Arguably the strength of Pt 26 lies in the ability to bind dissenting minorities. LLOYD J rejected the suggestion that compelling dissenting individuals to accept a scheme that alters their rights may be contrary to Art 1 of the First Protocol to the European Convention on Human Rights, as implemented by the Human Rights Act 1998:

> this type of rule, essential in a liberal society, cannot in principle be considered contrary to art 1 of the First Protocol, provided that the law does not create such inequality that one person could be arbitrarily and unjustly deprived of property in favour of another. It seems to me plain that, given the terms of s 425 [s 899] and the case law that has been established concerning its application, there is no possible argument for saying that the approval of a scheme under s 425, so as to bind dissentients among the relevant classes, breaches the rights afforded by

art 1 of the First Protocol...[In order to be sanctioned by the court] the scheme does both in law and in fact [have to] involve exchange of rights and thus consideration. No arrangement capable of being approved under s 425 could, in my view, amount to a confiscation such that art 1 would be infringed.

Compulsory binding of dissentient minorities and judicial review of majority determinations.

Re-read *Assénagon Asset Management SA v Irish Bank Resolution Corpn Ltd (formerly Anglo Irish Bank Corpn Ltd)* **[11.07]** and related cases.

➤ Question

You are consulted in advance of the meeting by the National Bank of Greece (in *Re Hellenic & General Trust Ltd* **[15.05]**), and asked to advise it whether it would be proper for the bank to consider its tax position in deciding how to cast its vote at the class meeting. What would your advice be? (See *Re Holders Investment Trust Ltd* **[10.04]**.)

Scheme jurisdiction: use of CA 2006 by foreign companies

There is a growing 'market' for English schemes used by foreign companies. In *Re Rodenstock GmbH* [2011] EWHC 1104 (Ch), the court, on its own motion, undertook a detailed review of the scheme jurisdiction and other issues arising from the fact that the company was located in Germany. Briggs J concluded that, analogous with the court's jurisdiction to wind up a foreign company, it must be demonstrated that the company whose scheme is subject to sanction has a sufficient connection with the English jurisdiction. Here, it was held that the Scheme Creditors' choice of English law and, for Senior Lenders, exclusive English jurisdiction, was a sufficient feature for establishing jurisdiction of the English court to sanction the scheme, which he then did, having established that the scheme was of sufficient merit, and that the sanctioning order could be effectively enforced in German courts.

Similarly, see the detailed analysis of this increasingly important jurisdiction by Snowden J in *Re Van Gansewinkel Groep BV* [2015] EWHC 2151 (Ch).

That said, it is often difficult to ascertain whether a 'sufficient connection' exists. See the subtle (hypothetical) drawing of boundary lines given by Hildyard J in *Re Apcoa Parking Holdings GmbH* **[15.08]** at [68]ff (not extracted).

Proposals for reform of the law

The Cork Committee on Insolvency made the following observations about the procedure under ss 425–427A [now CA 2006 Pt 26] and its utility in corporate insolvencies (Cmnd 8558, 1982, paras 406ff):

Because of the long and involved procedure, it is virtually impossible to shorten the period of time between initial formulation of a scheme of arrangement and its becoming effective by Court Order below eight weeks. During those eight weeks each individual creditor can exercise all the rights and remedies available to him against the company debtor . . .

The insolvent company's inability—particularly if it is a trading company—to hold the position (that is to prevent winding up or the random seizure of assets by individual creditors) during the period necessary for the devising and processing of a scheme, makes it extremely difficult for even the most uncomplicated scheme of arrangement to be launched. A straightforward moratorium on the payment of debts to unsecured creditors for a limited period, or such a moratorium coupled with a composition, say the reduction of all debts by 25%, may be the plainest good sense for all concerned, but it often cannot be done . . .

The Court is heavily involved in the procedure under section [425]. There are two distinct phases. First, the convening of the necessary meetings of creditors and contributories and, secondly, the petition to the Court for the sanctioning of the scheme as approved by the appropriate majorities at the meetings . . .

[We] believe that the Court procedure could be substantially streamlined and greatly improved. We cannot believe that there is the need for quite so many applications to, or attendances on, the Court. We doubt whether painstaking perusal of documents by Court officials with little or no experience of commerce or finance provides any real protection for creditors or contributories.

➤ Notes and Questions

1. The report of the Insolvency Service's Review Group on Company Rescue and Business Reconstruction Mechanisms (May 2000) proposed that consideration be given to augmenting what is now CA 2006 Pt 26 by introducing the option of a moratorium while a scheme for a composition between a company and its creditors is being put together. This idea has now been dropped. Is that wise?

2. The Company Law Review (CLR) queried whether there was any real point in preserving the distinction between the IA 1986 s 110 and the CA 2006 Pt 26[19] procedures, and suggested there might be a case for combining the two, giving the company the option of choosing between providing cash appraisal rights for dissenting members or seeking the sanction of the court.

3. The CLR doubted whether the IA 1986 s 111 system of cash appraisal which provides for compulsory arbitration without recourse to a court is compatible with the Human Rights Act.[20]

4. The CLR considered that there may be a case for introducing a statutory procedure (as is available in New Zealand) which would allow wholly owned companies within the same group to merge with each other or with their holding company without the need for court approval and with little more formality than the approval of all the directors, a declaration of solvency and appropriate notification to creditors.

There is no reform embedded in the new CA 2006 Pt 26 itself to meet these various criticisms. However, certain procedures introduced into IA 1986 over the years do meet some of the needs identified earlier. These measures include the statutory procedures for company voluntary arrangements (CVAs), with and without moratorium periods (IA 1986 Pt I and Sch A1), and also for administrations (IA 1986 Pt II): see 'General issues', pp 810ff.[21]

---

[19] Or, more accurately, its predecessor in CA 1985 s 425, which is in substantially the same form.

[20] IA 1986 s 111 invokes the arbitration provisions of the Companies Clauses Consolidation Act 1845, and does not specify the basis of valuation.

[21] See the broad and useful discussion in V Finch, *Company Insolvency Law: Perspectives and Principles* (2nd edn, 2009), pp 479–488.

Takeovers

Where a company acquires control over another by buying all or a majority holding of its shares, this is termed a '*takeover*'.[22] A general offer to buy addressed to all the members of a company is called a '*takeover bid*'. This is by far the commonest method used in this country for merging one corporate business with another. The two companies are usually referred to respectively as the '*offeror*' company or '*bidder*' and the '*target*' or '*offeree*' company.

If the target is a private company, control can usually only be exercised by a group holding more than 50% of the voting shares. Moreover, the target will probably have a provision in its articles authorising the directors to refuse to register a transfer of shares. It follows that a takeover of a private company usually requires the agreement of the directors.

On the other hand, if the target is a listed company, control can often be exercised by the holder of fewer than 50% of the voting shares because the other shareholders are either apathetic or lack coordination. But the bidder is unlikely to be able to acquire the necessary shareholding simply by purchases on the Stock Exchange. It is usually necessary to send a circular (a takeover bid) to the target's members offering to buy their shares.

For many years, economists have argued about whether takeovers and mergers are beneficial for the economy. The argument in favour is essentially that assets should be owned and/or managed in the most productive way possible: less productive or efficient ownership and/or management should be replaced by a more efficient one, via a takeover. Takeovers thus form part of the market for corporate ownership and control of assets.[23] On the other hand, empirical evidence suggests that underperforming management is not a primary inducement to a takeover, so the bids do not have a disciplining effect. And even where there is such an effect, the mechanism has been described as costly, disruptive and counterproductive in motivating long-term good corporate governance.[24]

Regulation of takeovers

CA 2006 Pt 28 deals with the regulation of takeovers. Apart from Ch 3,[25] its provisions are new.[26] It implements the European Directive on Takeover Bids (2004/25/EC) (the Takeovers Directive), takes account of criticisms and comments from the CLR and the Department of Trade and Industry,[27] and applies some of the rules beyond the sphere of operation required by the Directive.

The Takeovers Directive lays down, for the first time, minimum EU rules concerning the regulation of takeovers of companies whose shares are traded on a regulated market.

---

[22] For further reading, see N Boardman, 'What the Takeover Directive Means for the UK' (2006) 25(7) *International Financial Law Review* 174; M Mejucq, 'The European Regime on Takeovers' (2006) 3(2) *European Company and Financial Law Review* 222.

[23] See K Hopt and E Wymeersch (eds), *European Takeovers: Law and Practice* (1992), especially the chapters by R Romano, 'A Guide to Takeovers: Theory, Evidence and Regulation' and R Cranston, 'The Rise and Rise of the Hostile Takeover'.

[24] PW Moerland, 'Alternative Disciplinary Mechanisms in Different Corporate Systems' (1995) 26 *Journal of Economic Behavior and Organization* 17.

[25] This restates and amends CA 1985 Pt XIIIA.

[26] See DTI, *Implementation of the EU Directive on Takeover Bids—Guidance on Changes to the Rules on Company Takeovers* (URN 07/659, February 2007).

[27] DTI, *Company Law—Implementation of the European Directive on Takeover Bids* (January 2005).

It aims to strengthen the single market in financial services by facilitating cross-border restructuring and enhancing minority shareholder protection. It contains:

(i)   general principles that apply to the conduct of takeover bids;

(ii) a regulatory framework for bodies that supervise takeover bids (in the UK, the Panel on Takeovers and Mergers ('the Panel'));

(iii) basic rules about takeover bids (eg when a bid must be made, the price that must be paid to members, the contents of offer documents prepared by the bidder, requirements to inform employees and the time period a bid will be open for);

(iv) provisions restricting barriers to takeovers (eg action that might be taken to prevent a takeover by a company or its board of directors);

(v)   disclosure requirements for companies whose shares are traded on a regulated market; and

(vi) provisions dealing with the problems of, and for, residual minority members following a successful takeover bid (ie 'squeeze-out' and 'sell-out' provisions).

The Panel on Takeovers and Mergers

The Takeovers Directive requires certain significant structural changes to UK practices.

Since 1968, takeover regulation in the UK has been overseen by the Panel. The Panel's function is to ensure that shareholders are treated fairly and placed in a position to decide on the merits of a takeover, and that shareholders of the same class are afforded equivalent treatment by an offeror. The Panel administers rules contained in the City Code on Takeovers and Mergers ('the Takeover Code'), which historically had no legal force.[28] The Takeover Code was prepared and first issued in 1968 by representatives of various City bodies, including the Bank of England, the Stock Exchange and the Issuing Houses Association, as a statement of the principles of commercial morality which those taking part in a takeover were expected to follow. The Takeover Code is not concerned with the financial or commercial advantages of a takeover, nor does it seek to encourage or discourage takeovers in general. These are matters for the company and its shareholders. Wider questions of public interest are dealt with by the Competition Commission, the Office of Fair Trading, the Department for Business, Innovation and Skills (BIS) or the European Commission. The latest version of the Takeover Code (the 10th edition) is dated 19 September 2011.

There are six General Principles governing the Takeover Code:

(i)   All holders of the securities of an offeree company of the same class must be afforded equivalent treatment; moreover, if a person acquires control of a company, the other holders of securities must be protected.

(ii) The holders of the securities of an offeree company must have sufficient time and information to enable them to reach a properly informed decision on the bid; where it advises the holders of securities, the board of the offeree company must give its views on the effects of implementation of the bid on employment, conditions of employment and the locations of the company's places of business.

(iii) The board of an offeree company must act in the interests of the company as a whole and must not deny the holders of securities the opportunity to decide on the merits of the bid.

---

[28] Further information about the Panel and copies of the City Code on Takeovers and Mergers are available on the Panel's website (www.thetakeoverpanel.org.uk).

(iv) False markets must not be created in the securities of the offeree company, of the offeror company or of any other company concerned by the bid in such a way that the rise or fall of the prices of the securities becomes artificial and the normal functioning of the markets is distorted.

(v) An offeror must announce a bid only after ensuring that he or she can fulfil in full any cash consideration, if such is offered, and after taking all reasonable measures to secure the implementation of any other type of consideration.

(vi) An offeree company must not be hindered in the conduct of its affairs for longer than is reasonable by a bid for its securities.

The Takeovers Directive requires certain regulatory activities of the Panel to be placed within a legal framework. CA 2006 Pt 28 seeks to do this in a way that retains the considerable strengths of the previous system of takeover regulation overseen by the Panel, including:

(i)   flexibility, speed and certainty in decision-making;

(ii) independence and regulatory autonomy;

(iii) principles-based regulation;

(iv) involvement of key City and business participants in developing takeover rules and the regulatory framework;

(v)   professional expertise in regulatory activities, notably through Panel membership and secondments; and

(vi) consensual approach to regulation amongst those involved in the markets.

Part 28 therefore provides a statutory underpinning to the regulatory activities of the Panel, but leaves the Panel with considerable scope to decide its internal structures and operational framework. The Panel remains an unincorporated body. As such, it has rights and obligations under common law, supplemented by the relevant legislative provisions. It has power to make rules in relation to takeover regulation, and will continue to make rulings on the interpretation, application and effect of the Takeover Code and to give directions (CA 2006 ss 943–946).

Decisions of the Panel are in principle subject to judicial review. However, the court will not normally intervene while the Panel is actively dealing with a matter, but will only grant relief of a declaratory nature after the event.

[15.13] R v Panel on Take-overs and Mergers, ex p Datafin plc [1987] QB 815 (Court of Appeal)

The facts are immaterial, although some of the descriptions of the Panel are now out of date, given the changes implemented by CA 2006 Pt 28.[29]

> SIR JOHN DONALDSON MR: The Panel on Take-overs and Mergers is a truly remarkable body. Perched on the 20th floor of the Stock Exchange building in the City of London, both literally and metaphorically it oversees and regulates a very important part of the United Kingdom financial market. Yet it performs this function without visible means of legal support.
>
> The panel is an unincorporated association without legal personality... It has no statutory, prerogative or common law powers and it is not in contractual relationship with the financial market or with those who deal in that market.

---

[29] See Lord Alexander of Weedon, 'Judicial Review and City Regulators' (1989) 52 MLR 640.

[His Lordship read extracts from the City Code, and continued:] 'Self-regulation' is an emotive term. It is also ambiguous. An individual who voluntarily regulates his life in accordance with stated principles, because he believes that this is morally right and also, perhaps, in his own long-term interests, or a group of individuals who do so, are practising self-regulation. But it can mean something quite different. It can connote a system whereby a group of people, acting in concert, use their collective power to force themselves and others to comply with a code of conduct of their own devising. This is not necessarily morally wrong or contrary to the public interest, unlawful or even undesirable. But it is very different.

The panel is a self-regulating body in the latter sense. Lacking any authority de jure, it exercises immense power de facto by devising, promulgating, amending and interpreting the City Code on Take-overs and Mergers, by waiving or modifying the application of the code in particular circumstances, by investigating and reporting upon alleged breaches of the code and by the application or threat of sanctions. These sanctions are no less effective because they are applied indirectly and lack a legally enforceable base.

The principal issue in this appeal, and only issue which may matter in the longer term, is whether this remarkable body is above the law. Its respectability is beyond question. So is its bona fides. I do not doubt for one moment that it is intended to, and does, operate in the public interest and that the enormously wide discretion which it arrogates to itself is necessary if it is to function efficiently and effectively. Whilst not wishing to become involved in the political controversy on the relative merits of self-regulation and governmental or statutory regulation, I am content to assume for the purposes of this appeal that self-regulation is preferable in the public interest. But that said, what is to happen if the panel goes off the rails? Suppose, perish the thought, that it were to use its powers in a way which was manifestly unfair. What then? . . .

[His Lordship outlined the facts of the case and continued:] It will be seen that there are three principal issues, viz: (a) Are the decisions of the panel susceptible to judicial review? This is the 'jurisdictional' issue. (b) If so, how in principle is that jurisdiction to be exercised given the nature of the panel's activities and the fact that it is an essential part of the machinery of a market in which time is money in a very real sense? This might be described as the 'practical' issue. (c) If the jurisdictional issue is answered favourably to the applicants, is this a case in which relief should be granted and, if so, in what form? . . .

The jurisdictional issue

As I have said, the panel is a truly remarkable body, performing its function without visible means of legal support. But the operative word is 'visible', although perhaps I should have used the word 'direct'. Invisible or indirect support there is in abundance. Not only is a breach of the code, so found by the panel, ipso facto an act of misconduct by a member of the Stock Exchange, and the same may be true of other bodies represented on the panel, but the admission of shares to the Official List may be withheld in the event of such a breach. This is interesting and significant for listing of securities is a statutory function performed by the Stock Exchange in pursuance of . . . [and he went on to name various regulations and rules now incorporated in the Financial Services Act 1986].

. . . The picture which emerges is clear. As an act of government it was decided that, in relation to take-overs, there should be a central self-regulatory body which would be supported and sustained by a periphery of statutory powers and penalties wherever non-statutory powers and penalties were insufficient or non-existent or where EEC requirements called for statutory provisions . . .

The issue is thus whether the historic supervisory jurisdiction of the Queen's courts extends to such a body discharging such functions, including some which are quasi-judicial in their nature, as part of such a system. Mr Alexander, for the panel, submits that it does not. He says that this jurisdiction only extends to bodies whose power is derived from legislation or the exercise of the prerogative. Mr Lever, for the applicants, submits that this is too narrow a view and that regard has to be had not only to the source of the body's power, but also to whether it operates as an integral part of a system which has a public law character, is supported by public law in that public law sanctions are applied if its edicts are ignored and performs what might be described as public law functions.

[His Lordship referred to the analogous position of the Criminal Injuries Compensation Board, which had been considered by the Divisional Court in *R v Criminal Injuries Compensation Board, ex p Lain*,[30] and continued:] In fact, given its novelty, the panel fits surprisingly well into the format which this court had in mind in the *Criminal Injuries Compensation Board* case. It is without doubt performing a public duty and an important one. This is clear from the expressed willingness of the Secretary of State for Trade and Industry to limit legislation in the field of take-overs and mergers and to use the panel as the centrepiece of his regulation of that market. The rights of citizens are indirectly affected by its decisions…At least in its determination of whether there has been a breach of the code, it has a duty to act judicially and it asserts that its raison d'être is to do equity between one shareholder and another. Its source of power is only partly based upon moral persuasion and the assent of institutions and their members, the bottom line being the statutory powers exercised by the Department of Trade and Industry and the Bank of England. In this context I should be very disappointed if the courts could not recognise the realities of executive power and allowed their vision to be clouded by the subtlety and sometimes complexity of the way in which it can be exerted . . .

In reaching my conclusion that the court has jurisdiction to entertain applications for the judicial review of decisions of the panel, I have said nothing about the substantial arguments of Mr Alexander based upon the practical problems which are involved. These, in my judgment, go not to the existence of the jurisdiction, but to how it should be exercised and to that I now turn.

The practical issue

. . . In many cases of judicial review where the time scale is far more extended than in the financial markets, the decision-maker who learns that someone is seeking leave to challenge his decision may well seek to preserve the status quo meanwhile and, in particular, may not seek to enforce his decision pending a consideration of the matter by the court. If leave is granted, the court has the necessary authority to make orders designed to achieve this result, but usually the decision-maker will give undertakings in lieu. All this is but good administrative practice. However, against the background of the time scales of the financial market, the courts would not expect the panel or those who should comply with its decisions to act similarly. In that context the panel and those affected should treat its decisions as valid and binding, unless and until they are set aside. Above all they should ignore any application for leave to apply of which they become aware, since to do otherwise would enable such applications to be used as a mere ploy in take-over battles which would be a serious abuse of the process of the court and could not be adequately penalised by awards of costs.

[His Lordship referred to the various functions of the Panel and expressed the opinion that it was unlikely that the courts would often have occasion to intervene. He continued:] Nothing that I have said can fetter or is intended to or should be construed as fettering the discretion of any court to which application is made for leave to apply for judicial review of a decision of the panel or which, leave having been granted, is charged with the duty of considering such an application. Nevertheless, I wish to make it clear beyond a peradventure that in the light of the special nature of the panel, its functions, the market in which it is operating, the time scales which are inherent in that market and the need to safeguard the position of third parties, who may be numbered in thousands, all of whom are entitled to continue to trade upon an assumption of the validity of the

---

[30] [1967] 2 QB 864, [1967] 2 All ER 770.

panel's rules and decisions, unless and until they are quashed by the court, I should expect the relationship between the panel and the court to be historic rather than contemporaneous. I should expect the court to allow contemporary decisions to take their course, considering the complaint and intervening, if at all, later and in retrospect by declaratory orders which would enable the panel not to repeat any error and would relieve individuals of the disciplinary consequences of any erroneous finding of breach of the rules. This would provide a workable and valuable partnership between the courts and the panel in the public interest and would avoid all of the perils to which Mr Alexander alluded.

[His Lordship then ruled that a case for intervention in the present instance had not been made out.]

LLOYD and NICHOLLS LJJ delivered concurring judgments.

➤ Notes

1. On two occasions since *Datafin* the Court of Appeal has declined to intervene by way of judicial review in decisions of the Panel. See *R v Panel on Take-overs and Mergers, ex p Guinness plc* [1990] 1 QB 146, CA and *R v Panel on Take-overs and Mergers, ex p Fayed* [1992] BCLC 938, CA. However, in the *Guinness* case the Panel did not escape criticism, some of its decisions being condemned as 'insensitive and unwise'.

2. It should be borne in mind that not all takeovers are contested: many are settled by agreement between the respective boards and accepted by the members without opposition. Also (more particularly in the case of smaller companies), a change of control is commonly effected by a simple share sale and purchase agreement concluded between the outgoing and incoming members. (Although 'simple' may not be a particularly apt word to use here: the documents in these transactions often run to hundreds of pages!) For reference, see G Stedman, J Jones and J Cadman, *Shareholders' Agreements* (4th edn, 2003).

Restricting barriers to takeovers

The Takeovers Directive seeks to override certain steps that may be taken by companies both prior to and during a takeover bid which have the aim of frustrating a bid, including:

(i) Pre-bid defences (Takeovers Directive Art 11): this provides 'breakthrough provisions' that will defeat strategies including differential share structures under which minority shareholders exercise disproportionate voting rights, limitations on share ownership and restrictions on transfer of shares set out in the company's articles or in contractual agreements. Companies with voting shares traded on a regulated market may opt in to these breakthrough provisions should they wish to do so (CA 2006 ss 966–972); the Directive rules are not compulsory.

(ii) Post-bid defences (Takeovers Directive Art 9): the management of a target company cannot take action to frustrate a bid (eg by sale of the company's key assets) without the approval of the members at the time of the bid. The rules banning this type of defensive action are contained in the Takeover Code.

Disclosure requirements

CA 2006 Pt 28, Ch 4 (s 992) amends the 1985 Act in relation to the content of annual reports of companies traded on a regulated market, compelling disclosure of matters such as the share and control structures of companies. Note also the new requirements under the Takeover Code, namely in relation to the disclosure of offer-related fees and expenses, the

disclosure of financial and other information, and the public display of certain offer documents after the announcement of an offer. There are also additional rules requiring the
disclosure by offeror and offeree companies of the offeror's intentions and plans regarding
the offeree company and its employees.

'Virtual bids'

With a desire to counter prolonged 'virtual bid' periods—that is, where a potential offeror
announces its intention to make an offer but without providing a firm commitment to do
so—the recent amendments to the Takeover Code now require the offeree company to
make an announcement identifying any potential offerors (Rule 2.4). This is supplemented
by the 'put up or shut up' procedure (Rule 2.6(a)). Within 28 days from an announcement
under Rule 2.4, the identified potential offeror must publically provide a firm response,
that is, either make a formal offer, or announce that it does not seek to proceed forward. It
may, however, seek the Panel's consent for an extension of the deadline.

Mandatory offer rules

The Takeover Code recognises that a public company may be controlled by holders
of less than 50% of its voting rights. It therefore requires that a person (or persons
acting in concert) who gains 30% of the voting rights in a public company must make
a takeover bid for all the voting shares (Rule 9.1). The price that has to be offered is
the highest price at which the offeror (or persons acting in concert with it) has dealt in
the offeree's shares in the 12 months preceding the announcement of the mandatory
offer. This rule is designed to prevent an offeror obtaining a controlling interest at a
premium price from a few large members and then buying out the remaining small
members cheaply.

Deal protection measures and inducement fees

Previously, offeree companies might have provided offerors certain 'inducement fees'
(which payment may or may not be conditional upon the success of the takeover). The
latest edition of the Takeover Code, however, now prohibits (subject to five exceptions
contained in Rule 21.2(b)) any form of such payments. It is said that similar arrangements
may deter potential offerors (thus limiting available offer choices) and/or encourage offerors to put forward a less favourable offer (both, it seems, will go the detriment of the
offeree shareholders) (Rule 21.2).[31]

Position of minority members following a takeover

The concepts of *'squeeze-out'* and *'sell-out'*[32] are designed to address the problems of, and
for, residual minority members following a successful takeover bid. Squeeze-out rights (CA
2006 s 979) enable a successful bidder to purchase compulsorily the shares of remaining
minority members who have not accepted the bid. Sell-out rights (CA 2006 s 983) enable
minority members to require the majority member to purchase their shares. Because these
procedures involve compulsory sale or acquisition of shares against the will of the holder

---

[31] The Takeover Panel Executive has indicated that an irrevocable commitment or letter of intent may be given
by the shareholders of an offeree company who are also directors of the offeree company to accept an offer, but not
other kinds of offer-related arrangement with the offeror or any person acting in concert with the offeror. See, for
more detail, Practice Statement 29 as issued by the Takeover Panel (www.thetakeoverpanel.org.uk/wp-content/
uploads/2008/11/PS-29-New.pdf).

[32] Previously contained in CA 1985 Pt XIIIA.

or the acquirer, higher thresholds apply to the exercise of such rights, there are protective rules on the price that must be paid for the shares and the procedure can be challenged in the court (CA 2006 s 986).

CA 2006 Pt 28, Ch 3 introduces some changes to the 1985 Act to ensure compliance with the Takeovers Directive and to implement certain recommendations from the CLR. Chapter 3 applies to all companies and all bids within the ambit of Pt 28, whether or not the Takeovers Directive requires this.

Grounds on which the court will interfere in a squeeze-out.

CA 2006 s 986, like its predecessors, does not specify the grounds on which a court will interfere. Given the similar wording of the provisions, the earlier cases on this issue remain relevant.

[15.14] Re Grierson Oldham and Adams Ltd [1968] Ch 17 (Chancery Division)

The company, which dealt in wines and spirits, had been the subject of a successful takeover bid by John Holt & Co (Liverpool) Ltd. The offer made by Holts of 6s [30p] per 2s [10p] ordinary share had been accepted by 99.9% of the shareholders, and notice had been given of Holt's intention to acquire the remaining shares compulsorily at the same price pursuant to CA 1948 s 209 [CA 2006 ss 979 and 986]. The applicants, who had paid between 6s 7d [33p] and 6s 9d [34p] per share for their holdings, objected on the ground that the price offered was unfair to them; but the court declined to intervene.

> PLOWMAN J: The contentions which are put forward by the applicants fall under two main heads. In the first place it is said that the price of 6s a share is unfair, taking into account the assets and future prospects of the company and the advantages which will accrue to Holts by the take-over; and secondly, that it is unfair to the applicants that they should be compelled to sell their shares at a loss. Before considering those contentions in more detail, there are two or three general observations which I should make and which I think are justified by the authorities on this section to which I have been referred.
>
> The first general observation is that the onus of proof here is fairly and squarely on the applicants, and indeed they accepted that that is so. The onus of proof is on them to establish, if they can, that the offer was unfair . . .
>
> The second general observation which seems to me to be relevant is this: that since this is not a case of a purchase of assets, but of a purchase of shares, the market price on the stock exchange of those shares is cogent evidence of their true value; not conclusive evidence, of course, but cogent evidence . . . And in this case it is a formidable onus that the applicants have set out to discharge, bearing in mind that not only was the offer price above the stock exchange price, but that over 99% of the ordinary shareholders accepted the offer.
>
> The third general observation which arises out of the arguments that have been put forward concerns the question whether the test of the fairness of the offer is fairness to the individual shareholder or fairness to the body of shareholders as a whole. In my judgment, the test of fairness is whether the offer is fair to the offerees as a body and not whether it is fair to a particular shareholder in the peculiar circumstances of his own case . . . It would quite obviously be impossible, at any rate in most cases, for the offeror to know the circumstances of every individual shareholder and, therefore, to frame an offer which would necessarily be fair to every individual shareholder in the peculiar circumstances of his case.

The other general observation, which arises from the *Sussex Brick case*,[33] is that the fact that the applicants may be able to demonstrate that the scheme is open to criticism, or is capable of improvement, is not enough to discharge the onus of proof which lies upon them. Vaisey J said:

> I agree that certain criticisms set out in the applicant's affidavit show that a good case could be made out for the formulation of a better scheme, of a fairer scheme, of one which would be more attractive to the shareholders if they could have understood the implications of the criticisms. I have no doubt at all that a better scheme could have been evolved, but is that enough? . . .
>
> A scheme must be obviously unfair, patently unfair, unfair to the meanest intelligence. It cannot be said that no scheme can be effective to bind a dissenting shareholder unless it complies to the extent of 100 per cent with the highest possible standards of fairness, equity and reason . . .
>
> It must be affirmatively established that, notwithstanding the view of the majority, the scheme is unfair, and that is a different thing from saying that it must be established that the scheme is not a very fair one or not a fair one: a scheme has to be shown affirmatively, patently, obviously and convincingly to be unfair.

With those general observations, let me refer in a little more detail to some of the points which have been put forward on the part of the applicants. They have complained that the market price was substantially higher than 6s a share for a number of years [His Lordship cited prices ranging up to 9s 9d [49p]]; equally, as Mr Gurney-Champion said, in each of those years the lowest price for the shares was under 6s. But however that may be, it seems to me that the real point is, was 6s a fair price at the time when the offer was made, namely, in September 1965?

Then Mr Gurney-Champion submitted that it was unfair that he should be compelled to sell these shares at a loss, particularly having regard to the fact that the loss would be one which was not available for capital gains tax purposes, for the reason that he had bought the shares before 6 April 1965, and on that day the price of the shares was less than the purchase price. If I am right in thinking that the question of unfairness has to be judged without reference to the particular circumstances of the applicant, then it seems to me that this argument is irrelevant, and I am bound to reject it because I have already indicated the view that the particular circumstances of the applicant is not a matter with which the court is concerned. What the court is concerned with is the fairness of the offer as a whole . . .

Squeeze-out provisions in s 979 may not be used by majority shareholders to expropriate a minority.

[15.15] Re Bugle Press Ltd [1961] Ch 270 (Court of Appeal)

The £10,000 issued share capital of Bugle Press Ltd was held as to 4,500 £1 shares each by Shaw and Jackson ('the majority shareholders') and as to the remaining 1,000 shares by Treby. The majority shareholders formed a £100 company, Jackson & Shaw (Holdings) Ltd, which they caused to make an offer, addressed to the shareholders in Bugle Press Ltd, to purchase their holdings at £10 per share. After Shaw and Jackson had accepted this offer, and Treby had refused it on the ground that the price was too low, the offeror company gave Treby notice of its intention to purchase his holding compulsorily under

---

[33] *Re Sussex Brick Co Ltd* [1961] Ch 289n, [1960] 1 All ER 772n.

CA 1948 s 209 [CA 2006 ss 979 and 986]. The Court of Appeal, affirming Buckley J, exercising the discretion conferred by the section, declared that the scheme was not binding on Treby.

> LORD EVERSHED MR: Mr Instone [counsel for the offeror company] freely accepts that the mechanism of the section has here been invoked by means of the incorporation of this holding company, Jackson & Shaw (Holdings) Ltd, especially for the purpose, and in order to enable the two persons, Shaw and Jackson, to expropriate the shares of their minority colleague, Treby. He says that although that is undoubtedly true, nevertheless, in the result, the case does fall within the strict language of the section and falling within it the consequences must follow. If that argument is right, it would enable by a device of this kind the 90% majority of the shareholders always to get rid of a minority shareholder whom they did not happen to like. And that, as a matter of principle, would appear to be contrary to a fundamental principle of our law that prima facie, if a man has a legal right which is an absolute right, then he can do with it or not do with it what he will . . .
>
> [It] is, I think, relevant . . . to note that by the terms of the section itself one must have regard to what lies behind the invocation of the section . . . [It] seems to me plain that what the section is directed to is a case where there is a scheme or contract for the acquisition of a company, its amalgamation, reorganisation or the like, and where the offeror is independent of the shareholders in the transferor company or at least independent of that part or fraction of them from which the 90% is to be derived. Even, therefore, though the present case does fall strictly within the terms of s 209, the fact that the offeror, the transferee company, is for all practical purposes entirely equivalent to the nine-tenths of the shareholders who have accepted the offer, makes it in my judgment a case in which, for the purposes of exercising the court's discretion, the circumstances are special . . . It is no doubt true to say that it is still for the minority shareholder to establish that the discretion should be exercised in the way he seeks. That, I think . . . follows from the language of the section which uses the formula which I have already more than once read 'unless on an application made by the dissenting shareholder the court thinks fit to order otherwise'. But if the minority shareholder does show, as he shows here, that the offeror and the 90% of the transferor company's shareholders are the same, then as it seems to me he has, prima facie, shown that the court ought otherwise to order, since if it should not so do the result would be . . . that the section has been used not for the purpose of any scheme or contract properly so called or contemplated by the section but for the quite different purpose of enabling majority shareholders to expropriate or evict the minority; and that, as it seems to me, is something for the purposes of which, prima facie, the court ought not to allow the section to be invoked—unless at any rate it were shown that there was some good reason in the interests of the company for so doing, for example, that the minority shareholder was in some way acting in a manner destructive or highly damaging to the interests of the company from some motives entirely of his own . . .
>
> HARMAN LJ delivered a concurring judgment.
>
> DONOVAN LJ concurred.

➤ Notes

1. In most cases of substantial identity of interest, the accepting members will be 'associates' of the offeror (CA 2006 s 988), so their shares will not count in the calculation of the 90% acceptance limit.

2. Another special circumstance (beyond substantial identity of interest, as illustrated in *Re Bugle Press Ltd*) is where insufficient information has been given to the members to enable them to evaluate the offer properly: *Fiske Nominees Ltd v Dwyka Diamond Ltd* [2002] EWHC 770 (Ch), [2002] 2 BCLC 123. Note that the court may take into account the extent to which the bidder has made the disclosure required by the Takeover Code and otherwise complied with it, even where the company is a private company and so not

subject to the Code. It was recently held, therefore, that 'in order to be fair, an offer must be made in sufficient detail to enable an informed decision to be made. There is no positive duty to obtain advice on behalf of shareholders or to advise the shareholders nor is there a duty upon the directors to involve themselves in negotiations as to price': *Re Charterhouse Capital Ltd* [2014] EWHC 1410 (Ch) (Asplin J) at [276], affd [2015] EWCA Civ 536.

3. Technical failures can derail a squeeze-out. In *Chez Nico (Restaurants) Ltd* [1992] BCLC 192, the squeeze-out letters invited the remaining members to *offer* their shares for purchase, and were accordingly only invitations to treat. The court held that CA 1985 ss 428ff [CA 2006 ss 979 and 986] did not apply, since the 'bidders' had not made an offer.

Directors' role in a takeover

The duties imposed on directors apply with equal force during a takeover. The position of directors of the target company has been the subject of judicial consideration in a variety of contexts:

(i)   It is well established that directors may not use their powers (eg to issue further shares[34]) for improper purposes, and this may include their use as a defensive tactic to thwart a takeover bid (see *Hogg v Cramphorn Ltd* **[7.08]** and the other cases cited at 'Duty to act for proper purposes: s 171(b)', pp 342ff.[35] The use of *any* defensive tactics by directors without members' approval is forbidden by the Takeover Code, Rule 21.

(ii) In addition, the directors owe fiduciary duties to the company and cannot use their powers to further their own personal interests (see conflicts of duty and interest rules).

(iii) On the other hand, the ruling in *Heron International Ltd v Lord Grade* [1983] BCLC 244, CA, that the directors in that case owed fiduciary duties towards the company's *members* (as distinct from the company) cannot be taken to be of general application, since it turned upon the special article which gave the board control over the transfer of the voting shares.

(iv) In addition, in giving information relevant to the bid to their members—as they are required to do by the Takeover Code, for example—the directors must act in an honest way and not seek to mislead the members (*Gething v Kilner* [1972] 1 All ER 1166, [1972] 1 WLR 337). However, in forming its opinion on a particular offer, the board is not limited to consider a prescribed set of factors, and in particular, its opinion is not required to be based on the offer price as the determining factor (Rule 25.2, Note 1).

(v)   The directors must not exercise their powers in such a way as to prevent the members obtaining the best price for the shares (*Heron International Ltd v Lord Grade* [1983] BCLC 244, CA; *Re a Company (No 008699 of 1985)* **[15.16]**) although they are not under a positive duty to recommend and facilitate implementation of the highest offer (*Re a Company (No 008699 of 1985)* **[15.16]**; *Dawson International plc v Coats Patons plc* **[15.17]**).

The extracts which follow throw some light on the question, but each must be read in the light of the facts of the particular case.

---

[34] Although the pre-emption rights in CA 2006 s 561 have reduced the incidence of such cases.
[35] Note that there is no legal principle suggesting that it is inevitably improper for directors to take action designed to defeat a takeover bid: *Cayne v Global Natural Resources plc* [1984] 1 All ER 245, CA; *Darvall v North Sydney Brick and Tile Co Ltd* (1989) 16 NSWLR 260 at 325. But also see *Re a Company (No 008699 of 1985)* **[15.16]**, and *Dawson International plc v Coats Patons plc* **[15.17]**.

[15.16] Re a Company (No 008699 of 1985) [1986] BCLC 383, (1986) 2 BCC 99024 (Chancery Division)

Rival takeover bids had been made for the shares in a private company, one (referred to in the judgment as 'the N bid') by a company controlled by the target company's own directors and another, higher, bid by a trade competitor. The chairman had sent a circular to the members urging them to accept the N bid and explaining, with reasons, why the higher bid could not succeed. In these proceedings it was claimed that the directors had been in breach of duty in not recommending the higher offer and in not taking steps to facilitate the chances of that offer being successful, and that these breaches of duty had been unfairly prejudicial to the company's shareholders so as to justify relief under CA 1985 s 459 [CA 2006 s 994].

> HOFFMANN J: I cannot accept the proposition that the board must inevitably be under a positive duty to recommend and take all steps within their power to facilitate whichever is the highest offer. In a case such as the present, where the directors propose to exercise their undoubted right as shareholders to accept the lower offer in respect of their own shares and, for understandable and fully disclosed reasons, hope in their personal capacities that a majority of other shareholders will accept it as well, it seems to me that it would be artificial to say that they were under a positive duty to advise shareholders to accept the highest offer. The fact that they would get more money by taking the higher offer is hardly something which needs to be pointed out. I do not think that fairness can require more of the directors than to give the shareholders sufficient information and advice to enable them to reach a properly informed decision and to refrain from giving misleading advice or exercising their fiduciary powers in a way which would prevent or inhibit shareholders from choosing to take the better price. Thus I doubt whether it would have been unfair if the directors, on receipt of the rival bid, had issued a statement saying something along the following lines:
>
> > 'Shareholders will have received both bids. We think that they contain sufficient information to enable shareholders to reach a properly informed decision and there is nothing which the board wish to add. As individual shareholders, your directors propose to accept the N bid and hope that other shareholders who have no contrary fiduciary duties will have sufficient family loyalty to do so also.'
>
> [His Lordship held, however, that the circular which the directors had in fact sent to the members was arguably misleading and that accordingly the petition should be allowed to proceed.]

[15.17] Dawson International plc v Coats Paton plc 1993 SLT 80, [1988] 4 BCC 305 (Court of Session (Outer House))

The facts are immaterial.

> LORD CULLEN: At the outset I do not accept as a general proposition that a company can have no interest in the change of identity of its shareholders upon a take-over. It appears to me that there will be cases in which its agents, the directors, will see the take-over of its shares by a particular bidder as beneficial to the company. For example, it may provide the opportunity for integrating operations or obtaining additional resources. In other cases the directors will see a particular bid as not in the best interests of the company . . .
>
> I next consider the proposition that in regard to the disposal of their shares on a take-over the directors were under a fiduciary duty to the shareholders and accordingly obliged to act in such

a way as to further their best interests. It is well recognised that directors owe fiduciary duties to the company. Thus the directors have the duty of fiduciaries with respect to the property and funds of the company . . .

In contrast I see no good reason why it should be supposed that directors are, in general, under a fiduciary duty to shareholders, and in particular current shareholders with respect to the disposal of their shares in the most advantageous way. The directors are not normally the agents of the current shareholders. The cases and other authorities to which I was referred do not seem to me to establish any such fiduciary duty. It is contrary to statements in the standard textbooks...The absence of such a duty is demonstrated by the remarkable case of *Percival v Wright* **[7.05]**. I think it is important to emphasise that what I am being asked to consider is the alleged fiduciary duty of directors to current shareholders as sellers of their shares. This must not be confused with their duty to consider the interests of shareholders in the discharge of their duty to the company. What is in the interests of current shareholders as sellers of their shares may not necessarily coincide with what is in the interests of the company. The creation of parallel duties could lead to conflict. Directors have but one master, the company. Further it does not seem to me to be relevant to the present question to build an argument upon the rights, some of them very important rights, which shareholders have to take steps with a view to seeing that directors act in accordance with the constitution of the company and that their own interests are not unfairly prejudiced.

If on the other hand directors take it upon themselves to give advice to current shareholders, the cases cited to me show clearly that they have a duty to advise in good faith and not fraudulently, and not to mislead whether deliberately or carelessly. If they fail to do so the affected shareholders may have a remedy, including the recovery of what is truly the personal loss sustained by them as a result. However, these cases do not, in my view, demonstrate a pre-existing fiduciary duty to the shareholders but a potential liability arising out of their words or actions which can be based on ordinary principles of law. This, I may say, appears to be a more satisfactory way of expressing the position of directors in this context than by talking of a so-called secondary fiduciary duty to the shareholders.

➤ Note

There is a short summary of directors' duties in the context of takeovers by the Chancellor of the High Court, Etherton C, in *Arbuthnott v Bonnyman* [2015] EWCA Civ 536, CA (*sub nom Re Charterhouse Capital Ltd*) at [49]–[51].

Enforcement

The Panel is responsible for enforcing the rules contained in the Takeover Code. The Panel has power to order compensation in circumstances where a rule requiring the payment of money has been breached and to apply to the court to enforce its rulings and directions (CA 2006 ss 954 and 955). The Panel can also impose a range of sanctions upon persons who breach its rules, including reporting conduct to other regulatory authorities, such as the Financial Conduct Authority.

BIS is responsible for enforcement of other provisions in the Act, including the criminal offences created in connection with unlawful disclosure of information subject to secrecy provisions, bid documentation which fails to meet the standards required by the Takeovers Directive and where a company fails to notify relevant takeover authorities of its decision to opt in or out of the breakthrough provisions.

Further reading

BOARDMAN, N, 'What the Takeover Directive Means for the UK' (2006) 25 *International Financial Law Review* 174.

HANNIGAN, B, 'Altering the Articles to Allow for Compulsory Transfer—Dragging Minority Shareholders to a Reluctant Exit' [2007] JBL 471.

HOPT, K and WYMEERSCH, E (eds), *European Takeovers: Law and Practice* (1992), especially the chapters by R Romano, 'A Guide to Takeovers: Theory, Evidence and Regulation' and R Cranston, 'The Rise and Rise of the Hostile Takeover'.

LEIVESLEY, KJ, 'Financial Assistance: Why a *Uniq* Approach May Overcome *Chaston*' [2011] JBL 725.

MEJUCQ, M, 'The European Regime on Takeovers' (2006) 3 *European Company and Financial Law Review* 222.

PAYNE, J, 'Debt Restructuring in English Law: Lessons from the United States and the Need for Reform' (2014) 130 LQR 282.

ROBINSON, W, 'A Change in the Legal Wind—How a New Direction for Corporate Governance Could Affect Takeover Regulation' (2012) 23(9) *International Company and Commercial Law Review* 292.

TRIBE, J and ZHAO, J, 'Companies Act 2006 Schemes of Arrangement in Comparative Perspective' (2010) 25 *Butterworths Journal of International Banking and Financial Law* 15.

VAN DER ELST, C and VAN DEN STEEN, L, 'Balancing the Interests of Minority and Majority Shareholders: A Comparative Analysis of Squeeze-Out and Sell-Out Rights' (2009) 6 *European Company and Financial Law Review* 391.

16

RESCUE AND INSOLVENCY PROCEDURES

General issues

When a company is in financial difficulty, various procedures exist to effect either the timely rescue of viable commercial enterprises or the orderly and competent management of the company's affairs before the company's existence is brought to an end (by a process of *liquidation* or *winding up*: the terms are used interchangeably).

That said, it is worth noting that there is no necessary connection between *insolvency* and *winding up*: a very large number of companies are wound up whose balance sheets are in healthy surplus. A solvent company may be wound up because the business opportunity the company was formed to exploit has come to an end, or the members may wish to retire or reinvest their capital in other ventures, or there may be internal disputes. In this chapter, however, we concentrate on liquidations occasioned by insolvency.

With companies in difficulty, the important procedures include:

(i)   voluntary arrangements (see 'Company voluntary arrangements (CVAs)', pp 812ff);

(ii)   administration (see 'Administration', pp 813ff);

(iii)   administrative receiverships (see 'Administrative receivership', pp 824ff); and

(iv)   liquidations (including voluntary liquidations by the members[1] or creditors, and court-ordered liquidations) (see 'Liquidation or winding up', pp 834ff).

Each is considered in this chapter. In each case, the governance of the company is assumed by a qualified insolvency practitioner or (in compulsory liquidations, at least at the outset) an official receiver.[2] The role of the directors is, at least temporarily, displaced.

If the rescue procedure envisaged by the voluntary arrangement or administration is successful, or if the company survives receivership, then the company will continue in business. If not, then the company is likely to be put into liquidation. This is a process

---

[1] This procedure is only available to solvent companies.

[2] The official receiver attached to the court automatically becomes the company's liquidator in a court-ordered (compulsory) liquidation (see 'Liquidation or winding up', p 834), but the creditors, the Secretary of State or the official receiver himself can seek his replacement by an insolvency practitioner (IA 1986 ss 136 and 137).

by which the company's business is wound up, its contracts completed, transferred or brought to an end, and its assets and undertaking realised for the benefit of its creditors and (if there is a surplus of assets over liabilities) its members.[3] Finally, the company must be removed from the register of companies and dissolved.[4]

The Insolvency Service publishes quarterly statistics on insolvencies in England and Wales. Taking 2015 as illustrative, there were over 3.5 million companies on the register (with most being very small companies), and, very roughly, around 15,000 insolvencies for the year.

Insolvency and rescue

There are many ways of defining insolvency. For present purposes it is sufficient to note three. These serve to illustrate that when a company is in financial difficulty a judgement needs to be made about the likelihood of successful rescue, or alternatively the advisability of efficient liquidation. (As illustration, see Note 2 following **[16.09]**, p 840.)

'Commercial' insolvency

A company may be described as insolvent if it is unable to pay its debts as they fall due. In other words, even though its overall asset position may not be in deficit, it has cash-flow problems which prevent it from paying its way. This is the most common reason for the making of a compulsory winding-up order (Insolvency Act 1986 (IA 1986) s 122(1)(f)). There is a statutory definition of this type of insolvency (and also certain rules and presumptions relating to proof) in IA 1986 s 123(1).

'Balance sheet' insolvency

A company may also be said to be insolvent if the value of its assets is less than the amount of its liabilities. While the company is a going concern, an assessment of insolvency in this sense will depend upon the business judgement of those concerned. For this purpose it is proper to take account of the company's contingent and prospective liabilities (see IA 1986 s 123(2)), although the value of these will necessarily be difficult to estimate. A company which is insolvent in balance sheet terms will not necessarily be commercially insolvent: it may, for instance, have a heavy potential liability in tort and yet for the time being have a perfectly satisfactory cash flow. And, of course, it may happen that if its assets are realised there is in fact a surplus at the end of the day.

'Ultimate' insolvency

This definition of insolvency is based on the final position when the company's assets are sold up, for example by a liquidator, and there is not sufficient money realised to pay the creditors in full. This unhappy result may occur even though the company has previously seemed solvent under definitions (i) and (ii), for assets which are quite reasonably valued highly on a historic cost or going concern basis may fetch very little in a forced sale.

Statutory framework

The principal statute governing the procedures discussed in this chapter is IA 1986. This Act is a consolidation of the Insolvency Act 1985 and those parts of the Companies Act 1985 (CA 1985) which dealt with receivership and winding up (these provisions were not swept into CA 2006). The insolvency legislation of 1985 introduced comprehensive reforms to both the law of corporate insolvency and that of individual bankruptcy—the first major

---

[3] Unless the articles provide otherwise, as with charitable companies.

[4] There is statutory provision for restoration of companies to the register, if dissolution is later found to have been premature: see 'Restoration to the register', p 872.

overhaul of either subject for over a hundred years—based largely on the report of the Cork Committee (*Report of the Review Committee on Insolvency Law and Practice* (Cmnd 8558, 1982)). IA 1986 is supplemented by the Insolvency Rules 1986 (IR 1986) (SI 1986/1925 as amended), which specify the relevant procedural rules and requirements.

IA 1986 has been amended on various occasions, most significantly by:

(i)   Insolvency Act 2000, which introduced new rules on company voluntary arrangements, allowing for a moratorium;[5]

(ii) Enterprise Act 2002 (EA 2002), which provided a new regime for administration, restricted the right to appoint administrative receivers, and substantially changed the rules for distribution of company assets on liquidation.

Company voluntary arrangements (CVAs)

One of the most useful rescue mechanisms for a distressed company is the ability to make binding compromises or arrangements with all its creditors. IA 1986 now provides two mechanisms for this.[6] The first is an older, informal and relatively private procedure, open to all companies, introduced by IA 1986 Pt I, ss 1–7, under which a company may seek to achieve an accommodation with its creditors under the supervision of a 'supervisor', being a qualified insolvency practitioner. The arrangement is proposed by the company's directors (or its liquidator or administrator), reported to the court (but court approval is not necessary), and, if then approved by the requisite majority (over 75%) of unsecured creditors and members at separate single meetings, is binding on the dissenting minorities.

Some protection of minorities is provided by IA 1986 s 6, which allows the majority approvals to be challenged in court by anyone entitled to vote in the meetings, or by the supervisor or the liquidator or administrator, on the ground that the scheme is unfairly prejudicial or that there is some material process irregularity[7] affecting either of the meetings.

Although this procedure was a progressive one, enabling companies to continue trading while ensuring creditors received at least part of their debt, it got off to a slow start: only 21 arrangements were recorded in the first year of its operation and, although the number gradually increased, it has never reached more than a few hundred per annum, in contrast with the voluntary arrangement procedure for individuals, which is used in nearly a quarter of all personal insolvency cases. There are two main reasons for this: first, that a CVA cannot be made binding on secured or preferential creditors[8] without their consent; and, secondly, that (contrary to the Cork Committee's recommendation) the Act originally contained no provision for a moratorium to be put in place while the quite lengthy formalities are gone through: thus one impatient creditor could thwart the whole scheme.

A way round this second difficulty was, eventually, found, and a second option was introduced allowing for CVAs with a moratorium (IA 1986 Sch A1). But this was achieved only at the cost of making the whole procedure more elaborate, public and

---

[5] For an overview of the definition, role and policy justification for a moratorium in the insolvency context, see D Milman, 'Moratoria in UK Insolvency Law: Policy and Practical Implications' (2012) 317 *Company Law Newsletter* 1.

[6] Theoretically a scheme of arrangement, under Companies Act 2006 (CA 2006) s 895 provides a further alternative, but the process is generally considered too complex, time-consuming and expensive: see 'Arrangements and reconstructions under CA 2006 ss 895–901', p 784.

[7] Eg, see *Re Gatnom Capital & Finance Ltd* [2010] EWHC 3353 (Ch). The Companies Court reversed a previous decision approving the CVA in question, on the ground that the creditors' meeting to approve the CVA was carried only because of the votes based on certain sham liabilities.

[8] See IA 1986 s 175 and Sch 6. See 'Distribution of assets subject to the receivership', pp 832ff.

expensive. In addition, the option is only available to 'eligible companies' (primarily small private companies). The procedure allows for an automatic 28-day moratorium to come into force as soon as the documents containing a proposal for a CVA are filed in court. During this period (which may be extended for up to a further two months), the company may not be wound up and no steps may be taken, at least without the leave of the court, to enforce security over the company's property[9] or to take proceedings against it. The success of the much sought-after provision remains unclear, however. The advantages of the moratorium may be outweighed by the relative complexity (and cost) in terms of the companies which are eligible, the role of the supervisor, the restrictions on directors during the moratorium and the possible liabilities of directors and the supervisor for actions taken during the moratorium. In addition, even the advantages of the procedure pale in significance now that EA 2002 permits the appointment of administrators out of court (with their own associated moratorium provisions) (see 'Administration', pp 813ff).

On the other hand, the major attraction of CVAs, in either form, is that the directors remain in post, they retain control over the choice of the supervisor and the supervisor is not required to make a report of unfitness to the Insolvency Service under the Company Directors Disqualification Act 1986 (CDDA 1986). This remains so despite the amendments to CDDA 1986 introduced by the Small Business, Enterprise and Employment Act 2015 (see CDDA 1986 s 7A for the proposed reporting rules in other insolvency procedures).

The under-use of these CVA procedures must be a source of disappointment, particularly since much of the thrust of the reforms proposed by the Cork Committee was the fostering and promotion of a 'rescue culture' for failed (or failing) businesses: whereas the liquidation of a company frequently involves the break-up of its assets, the destruction of its goodwill and business connections, and the displacement of its employees, less drastic (and less costly) solutions can often be found if steps are taken in time to bring the affairs of the company under control with a view to ensuring the survival, if not of the entire concern, at least of the viable parts of it.

Administration

A statutory administration procedure has been in operation since IA 1986 was introduced, but EA 2002 made substantial amendments, and the new rules are now found in IA 1986 s 8 and Sch B1.[10] The amendments introduced fundamental changes in the purpose, appointment and powers of administrators, although the procedure remains open only to companies that are, or are likely to become, insolvent.[11]

Purpose of administration

Administration, after EA 2002, is explicitly designed to rescue an insolvent company, saving it from liquidation if at all possible. The amended IA 1986 Sch B1, para 3(1),

---

[9] And it is not possible for a floating charge holder to specify that obtaining or preparing for a moratorium crystallises the floating charge: IA 1986 Sch A1, para 43.

[10] The 'old' provisions on administration contained in IA 1986 Pt II are retained and apply to special categories of companies (water companies, railway companies, air traffic services companies, public–private partnership companies and building societies). They are not discussed here.

[11] For suggested reforms in the area of administration, see European High Yield Association (EHYA), *Submission on Insolvency Law Reform* (2009). And on evaluating the effectiveness of administration, see V Finch, *Corporate Insolvency Law: Perspectives and Principles* (2nd edn, 2009), pp 392–410.

specifies a hierarchy of purposes: administrators must perform their functions with the objective of:

(i) rescuing the company as a going concern;

(ii) achieving a better result for the company's creditors as a whole than would be likely if the company were wound up; or

(iii) realising property in order to make a distribution to one or more secured or preferential creditors.

Administrators must pursue (i) rather than (ii) unless it is not reasonably practicable to pursue (i), or unless (ii) would achieve a better result for the company's creditors as a whole. Moreover, administrators may only pursue (iii) if it is not reasonably practicable to achieve the other two objectives *and* the goal is pursued in such a way that it will not unnecessarily harm the interests of the creditors of the company as a whole. In addition, the administrator must act in the interests of the creditors as a whole (IA 1986 Sch B1, para 3(2)), and as quickly and efficiently as reasonably practicable (para 4).

Administration orders reflect the philosophical premise, held since the findings of the Cork Committee, that appointing a receiver and manager to a company (as was commonly done by floating charge holders) offered outstanding benefits to the commercial community and public as a whole, advancing the possibility of restoring an ailing enterprise to profitability, or disposing of a business as a going concern.[12] The administration procedure attempts to mirror this, allowing an ailing company an alternative to liquidation where there is a chance that it may be rehabilitated. In the light of the EA 2002 changes, administration has now largely replaced receiverships, at least for floating charge holders, and has the merit of being conducted in the interest of all concerned rather than only the secured creditor. The process is associated with a moratorium (Sch B1, para 43), so it also provides the company with breathing space, free from creditors' claims, where the administrator can determine the future of the company even where liquidation is inevitable, so that its assets can be realised to better advantage—ideally, by selling the business as a going concern.

Appointment of the administrator

An administrator may be appointed by the court (on the application of the company itself, or its directors, or a creditor)[13] or out of court (which is far more common) by the holder of a floating charge relating to the whole or substantially the whole of the company's property, by the company itself or by the company's directors. An out of court appointment must be reported to the court.[14] In each case, the company must be unable to pay its debts,[15] or likely to become unable to do so.

---

[12] *Report of the Review Committee on Insolvency Law and Practice* (Cmnd 8558, 1982), para 495.

[13] Where there is a difference in view as to the choice of administrator, all things being equal, the Companies Court in *Healthcare Management Services Ltd v Caremark Properties Ltd* [2012] EWHC 1693 (Ch) regarded the choice of the largest creditor (in terms of the value of the debt owed to it by the company) as being the 'tie-breaker'.

[14] 'Pre-packs' or arrangements under which the sale of all or part of the company's business or assets is negotiated prior to the appointment of an administrator and then effected shortly after the appointment, are increasingly common, but not considered here. See J Anderson, 'Minmar (2): Quite Possibly Mar!' (2012) 309 *Company Law Newsletter* 1. Pre-packs are frequently criticised for lack of transparency because creditors are often kept in the dark over sale terms. The *Graham Review into Pre-pack Administration*, published in June 2014, investigated these issues and considered that while pre-packs are often economical and efficient, stronger governance is required. Eg, it is suggested that the marketing of the business pre-'pre-pack' deals requires more publicity and transparency.

[15] For appointments by a floating charge holder, the floating charge must simply be enforceable.

Pre-conditions for a court order for administration: 'likely' and 'reasonably likely'.

For an administration order to be made by the court, the court must be satisfied that the company 'is or is likely to become' unable to pay its debts (Sch B1, para 11(a)), and that the administration order 'is reasonably likely' to achieve the purpose of the administration (Sch B1, para 11(b)). The next case pre-dates EA 2002, and the previous test was that the order be 'likely to achieve' the set purpose. The courts interpreted this as a requirement that there be 'a real prospect' (see later). It is not clear whether this remains the test, or whether there should be some lower threshold in recognition of Parliament's intention that administration be more readily available, especially as the administrator who cannot achieve the set purpose may always convert the administration into a creditors' voluntary winding up.

Even if this threshold is met, the court has a discretion as to whether to make the order, and will not do so where, weighing all the circumstances, this seems inappropriate (see later).

[16.01] Re Harris Simons Construction Ltd [1989] 1 WLR 368 (Chancery Division)

The facts appear from the judgment.

HOFFMANN J: The company carries on business as builders. Over the past four years there has been a spectacular increase in turnover, from £830,000 in the year to April 1985 to £17m in the year to April 1987 and £27m in the year to April 1988. Almost all of this increased turnover has come from one client, a property developer called Berkley House plc, with which the directors had a close relationship. Recently the relationship has turned sour. There are disputes over a number of contracts and Berkley House has purported to dismiss the company and require its employees to leave their sites. It is also withholding sums running into several million pounds which the company says are due and in respect of which Berkley House says it has cross-claims. The effect on the company's cash flow has been that it is unable to pay its debts as they fall due and several writs and a statutory demand have been served. If no administration order is made, the company cannot carry on trading. There is no debenture-holder who can be invited to appoint a receiver. The company will have to go into liquidation more or less immediately. The workforce will have to be dismissed and the contracts and work in progress will become a tangle of disputes and probably litigation. The report of the proposed administrator says that in those circumstances it would be extremely difficult to sell any part of the business.

If an administration order is made, the company will have what is usually called a breathing space but unless some source of funding can be found, will continue to have serious respiratory problems with its cash flow. It has however been able to negotiate at least an armistice with Berkley House by which the latter will, conditionally upon an administration order being made, provide sufficient funding to enable the company to complete four current contracts on condition that it quietly removes itself from the other sites in dispute. It is hoped that the four remaining contracts will produce a profit and that it may thereby be possible to stabilise and preserve a business which can either survive or be sold to a third party. In the meanwhile, it may be possible to arrive at a negotiated settlement of the underlying dispute with Berkley House. The administration order is therefore proposed to achieve two of the purposes specified in section 8(3) of the Act [IA 1986, but prior to the EA 2002 amendments]: '(a) the survival of the company, and the whole or any part of its undertaking, as a going concern;' and '(d) a more advantageous realisation of the company's assets than would be effected on a winding up' . . .

Section 8(1) gives the court jurisdiction to make an administration order if it '(a) is satisfied that a company is or is likely to become unable to pay its debts' and it '(b) considers that the making of an order...would be likely to achieve' one or more of the purposes specified in section 8(3). I am satisfied on the evidence that the company is unable to pay its debts. Whether the order would be likely to achieve one of the specified objects is not so easy to answer. When the statute says that I must consider it likely, what degree of probability does this involve? In *Re Consumer and Industrial Press Ltd*,[16] Peter Gibson J said:

> 'As I read section 8 the court must be satisfied on the evidence put before it that at least one of the purposes in section 8(3) is likely to be achieved if it is to make an administration order. That does not mean that it is merely possible that such purpose will be achieved; the evidence must go further than that to enable the court to hold that the purpose in question will more probably than not be achieved.'

He therefore required that on a scale of probability of 0 (impossibility) to 1 (absolute certainty) the likelihood of success should be more than 0.5. I naturally hesitate to disagree with Peter Gibson J, particularly since he had the benefit of adversarial argument. But this is a new statute on which the judges of the Companies Court are still feeling their way to a settled practice and I therefore think I should say that in my view he set the standard of probability too high. My reasons are as follows. First, 'likely' connotes probability but the particular degree of probability intended must be gathered from qualifying words (very likely, quite likely, more likely than not) or context. It cannot be a misuse of language to say that something is likely without intending to suggest that the probability of its happening exceeds 0.5, as in 'I think that the favourite, Golden Spurs at 5–1, is likely to win the Derby'. Secondly, the section requires the court to be 'satisfied' of the company's actual or likely insolvency but only to 'consider' that the order would be likely to achieve one of the stated purposes. There must have been a reason for this change of language and I think it was to indicate that a lower threshold of persuasion was needed in the latter case than the former....Thirdly, some of the stated purposes are mutually exclusive and the probability of any one of them being achieved may be less than 0.5 but the probability of one or other of them being achieved may be more than 0.5. I doubt whether Parliament intended the courts to embark on such calculations of cumulative probabilities. Fourthly, as Peter Gibson J said, section 8(1) only sets out the conditions to be satisfied before the court has jurisdiction. It still retains a discretion as to whether or not to make the order. It is therefore not unlikely that the legislature intended to set a modest threshold of probability to found jurisdiction and to rely on the court's discretion not to make orders in cases in which, weighing all the circumstances, it seemed inappropriate to do so. Fifthly, the Report of the Review Committee on Insolvency Law and Practice (1982), (Cmnd 8558), para 508, which recommended the introduction of administratorship, said that the new procedure was likely to be beneficial only in cases where there is a business of sufficient substance to justify the expense of an administration, and where there is a real prospect of returning profitability or selling as a going concern.

Elsewhere the report speaks of an order being made if there is a 'reasonable possibility' of a scheme of reconstruction. I think that this kind of phraseology was intended to be reflected in the statutory phrase 'considers that [it] would be likely' in section 8(1)(b).

For my part, therefore, I would hold that the requirements of section 8(1)(b) are satisfied if the court considers that there is a real prospect that one or more of the stated purposes may be achieved. It may be said that phrases like 'real prospect' lack precision compared with 0.5 on the scale of probability. But the courts are used to dealing in other contexts with such indications of the degrees of persuasion they must feel. 'Prima facie case' and 'good arguable case'

---

[16] [1988] BCLC 177 at 178.

are well known examples. Such phrases are like tempo markings in music; although there is inevitably a degree of subjectivity in the way they are interpreted, they are nevertheless meaningful and useful.

On the facts as they appear from the evidence before me, I think there is a real prospect that an administration order, coupled with the agreement with Berkley House, will enable the whole or part of the company's undertaking to survive or at least enable the administrator to effect a more advantageous realisation of the assets than would be effected in a winding up. Certainly the prospects for the company, its employees and creditors look bleak if no administration order is made and there has to be a winding up. Consequently, although I cannot say that it is more probable than not that one of the specified purposes will be achieved, I accept the opinion of the prospective administrator that 'the making of an administration order offers the best prospect for preserving the company's future and maximising the realisation of the company's assets for the benefit of its creditors.' I therefore make the order.

➤ Note

Other judges, including Peter Gibson J, have since followed the views expressed in this case. In *Re AA Mutual International Insurance Co Ltd* [2004] EWHC 2430 (Ch), [2005] 2 BCLC 8, Lewison J held that the test under the reformed provisions, IA 1986 Sch B1, para 11(a), was 'more probable than not', while for para 11(b) it was a 'real prospect' (as in **[16.01]**).

Powers and duties of the administrator

The first task of the administrator is to formulate a set of proposals for the company which must, within eight weeks, be submitted to the registrar and to the company's unsecured creditors, for approval within ten weeks by a simple majority in value of creditors present and voting in person or by proxy. If the creditors approve the proposals, the administrator must act accordingly. If they fail to approve them, the court may make any order it thinks fit, including terminating the administrator's appointment (Sch B1, para 55).

In the period between the appointment of the administrator and submission of proposals to the creditors' meeting, the administrator may exercise all of the exceptionally wide powers conferred by Sch B1, para 59 and Sch 1 (conferred by Sch B1, para 60). These include the power to sell the company's property (including the power to sell property subject to a floating charge, and, with court approval, property subject to any other charge[17]). Paragraph 59(1) provides that the administrator 'may do anything necessary or expedient for the management of the affairs, business and property of the company'. The administrator can act without the approval of the creditors, or the court, if he considers this is in the best interests of the creditors: *Re Transbus International Ltd* [2004] EWHC 932 (Ch); *Re Osmosis Group Ltd* [1999] 2 BCLC 329. The administrator is deemed to be an agent of the company (para 69).

The administrator's powers have been expanded by the Small Business, Enterprise and Employment Act 2015. This amends IA 1986, adding ss 246ZA–ZC, so as to allow administrators to bring actions against directors claiming compensation on behalf of the company for fraudulent or wrongful trading (see the parallel sections for liquidators in IA 1986 ss 213–215, and the discussion at 'The liquidator's ability to require wrongdoers to make personal contributions to the assets of the company', p 853, and *Re Produce Marketing (No 2)* **[16.16]** and the Notes following).

---

[17] Sch B1, paras 70 and 71, although the proceeds must be deployed according to the statutory priorities accorded to such chargees.

The administrator also has the benefit of the statutory moratorium (Sch B1, para 43). This prevents a winding up,[18] and prevents anyone taking action against the company, or any creditors from enforcing security, putting in execution, distraining on the company's goods, repossessing goods sold under hire-purchase, conditional sales, chattel-leasing or retention of title agreements, except, in every case, with the consent of the administrator or the permission of the court. The Court of Appeal has given guidance on exercising security rights against companies in administration: *Re Atlantic Computer Systems plc (No 1)* [1992] Ch 505 at 541–544.

Duties owed by the administrator to the company.

[16.02] Re Charnley Davies Ltd (No 2) [1990] BCLC 760 (Chancery Division)

The facts are immaterial.

MILLETT J: It was common ground that an administrator owes a duty to a company over which he is appointed to take reasonable steps to obtain a proper price for its assets. That is an obligation which the law imposes on anyone with a power, whether contractual or statutory, to sell property which does not belong to him. [See Note immediately following.] A mortgagee is bound to have regard to the interests of the mortgagor, but he is entitled to give priority to his own interests, and may insist on an immediate sale whether or not that is calculated to realise the best price; he must 'take reasonable care to obtain the true value of the property at the moment he chooses to sell it': see *Cuckmere Brick Co Ltd v Mutual Finance Ltd*.[19] An administrator, by contrast, like a liquidator, has no interest of his own to which he may give priority, and must take reasonable care in choosing the time at which to sell the property. His duty is 'to take reasonable care to obtain the best price that the circumstances permit': see *Standard Chartered Bank Ltd v Walker*.[20]

It is to be observed that it is not an absolute duty to obtain the best price that circumstances permit, but only to take reasonable care to do so; and in my judgment that means the best price that circumstances *as he reasonably perceives them to be* permit. He is not to be made liable because his perception is wrong, unless it is unreasonable.

An administrator must be a professional insolvency practitioner. A complaint that he has failed to take reasonable care in the sale of the company's assets is, therefore, a complaint of professional negligence and in my judgment the established principles applicable to cases of professional negligence are equally applicable in such a case. It follows that the administrator is to be judged, not by the standards of the most meticulous and conscientious member of his profession, but by those of an ordinary, skilled practitioner. In order to succeed the claimant must establish that the administrator has made an error which a reasonably skilled and careful insolvency practitioner would not have made . . .

➤ Note

This same duty to exercise reasonable care is equally applicable to liquidators (*Top Brands Ltd v Sharma* [2014] EWHC 2753 (Ch)). However, in *Rosserlane v Credit Suisse* [2015] EWHC 384 (Ch) (at [116]–[117]), Peter Smith J doubted Millett J's statement (the sentence noted in the extract above) insofar as it purports to assert a general duty on '*anyone with a power*

---

[18] Except on a public interest petition by the Secretary of State or the Financial Conduct Authority (Sch B1, para 42).

[19] [1971] Ch 949. See, however, 'Duties of administrative receivers', pp 827ff.

[20] [1982] 1 WLR 1410.

whether contractual or statutory to sell property which does not belong to him', and went on to hold that the defendant bank owed no duty of care to the claimants in exercising a contractual right of sale of the claimants' property.

No duty owed by the administrator to creditors.

[16.03] Kyrris v Oldham [2003] EWCA Civ 1506 (Court of Appeal)

The facts are immaterial.

JONATHAN PARKER LJ:

141. In my judgment it matters not whether one adopts the approach of the House of Lords in *Caparo Industries plc v Dickman* **[8.04]**, or the 'assumption of responsibility' approach which it adopted in *Henderson v Merrett*:[21] on either approach the result is the same, namely that, absent some special relationship, an administrator appointed under the 1986 Act owes no general common law duty of care to unsecured creditors in relation to his conduct of the administration.

142. In paragraphs 31 to 34 of his judgment in [*Peskin v Anderson*],[22] Mummery LJ said this:

'31. . . . [Counsel for the directors] accepted that the fiduciary duties owed by the directors to the company do not necessarily preclude, in special circumstances, the coexistence of additional duties owed by the directors to the shareholders. In such cases individual share-holders may bring a direct action, as distinct from a derivative action, against the directors for breach of duty.

32. A duality of duties may exist. In *Stein v. Blake & Ors (No 2)* [1988] 1 BCLC 573 at 576 Millett LJ recognised that there may be special circumstances in which a fiduciary duty is owed by a director to a shareholder personally and in which breach of such a duty has caused loss to him directly (e.g. by being induced by a director to part with his shares in the company at an undervalue), as distinct from loss sustained by him by a diminution in the value of his shares (e.g. by reason of the misappropriation by a director of the com-pany's assets), for which he (as distinct from the company) would not have a cause of action against the director personally.

33. The fiduciary duties owed to the company arise from the legal relationship between the directors and the company directed and controlled by them. The fiduciary duties owed to the shareholders do not arise from that legal relationship. They are dependent on establish-ing a special factual relationship between the directors and the shareholders in the particular case. Events may take place which bring the directors of the company into direct and close contact with the shareholders in a manner capable of generating fiduciary obligations, such as a duty of disclosure of material facts to shareholders, or an obligation to use confidential information and valuable commercial and financial opportunities, which have been acquired by directors in that office, for the benefit of the shareholders, and not to prefer their own interests at the expense of the shareholders.

34. These duties may arise in special circumstances which replicate the salient features of well-established categories of fiduciary relationships. Fiduciary relationships, such as agency, involve duties of trust, confidence and loyalty. Those duties are, in general, attracted by and attached to a person who undertakes, or who, depending on all the circumstances, is treated as having assumed, responsibility to act on behalf of, or for the benefit of, another person. That other person may have entrusted or, depending on the circumstances, may be treated as having entrusted, the care of his property, affairs, transactions or interests to him. There

---

[21] [1995] 2 AC 145, HL.
[22] [2001] BCC 87C, CA.

are, for example, instances of the directors of a company making direct approaches to, and dealing with, the shareholders in relation to a specific transaction and holding themselves out as agents for them in connection with the acquisition or disposal of shares; or making material representations to them; or failing to make material disclosure to them of insider information in the context of negotiations for a take-over of the company's business; or supplying to them specific information and advice on which they have relied. These events are capable of constituting special circumstances and of generating fiduciary obligations, especially in those cases in which the directors, for their own benefit, seek to use their position and special inside knowledge acquired by them to take improper or unfair advantage of the shareholders.'

143. It has not been suggested (nor could it be, in my judgment) that there is any relevant distinction for present purposes between a fiduciary duty and a common law duty of care. Further, I accept Miss Hilliard's submission that the position of an administrator appointed under the 1986 Act vis-à-vis creditors is directly analogous to that of a director vis-à-vis shareholders.

144. Section 8(2) of the 1986 Act defines an administration order as: '. . . an order directing that, during the period for which the order is in force, the affairs, business and property of the company shall be managed by a person ("the administrator") appointed for the purpose by the court.'

145. Section 14(1) of the 1986 Act confers on an administrator a number of specific powers of management set out in Schedule 1, including (in paragraph 14) a power to carry on the business of the company, together with a general power: '. . . to do all such things as may be necessary for the management of the affairs, business and property of the company'.

146. Given the nature and scope of an administrator's powers and duties, I can for my part see no basis for concluding that an administrator owes a duty of care to creditors in circumstances where a director would not owe such a duty to shareholders. In each case the relevant duties are, absent special circumstances, owed exclusively to the company.

147. It is also material, in my judgment, to consider the nature of the remedy provided by section 212 of the 1986 Act. Section 212(3) provides that on an application under the section the court may compel an administrator (among others):

'(a) to repay, restore or account for the money or property or any part of it, with interest at such rate as the court thinks just, or

(b) to contribute such sum to the company's assets by way of compensation in respect of the misfeasance or breach of fiduciary or other duty as the court thinks just.'

148. To my mind, this is a further indication that, absent some special relationship of the kind described by Mummery LJ in *Peskin v Anderson*, an administrator owes no general duty to creditors.

> ## Notes

1. This case has been followed in *Hague v Nam Tai Electronics* [2008] UKPC 13, PC (a case concerning a liquidator rather than an administrator) and *Fabb v Peters* [2013] EWHC 296 (Ch) (administrator successfully called for a strike out of the creditor's claim of breach of duty by the administrator).

2. In *Re Capitol Films Ltd (In Administration)* [2010] EWHC 3223 (Ch), after finding that the assets of the film company were only sufficient to meet the claims of secured creditors (or part thereof), Mr Richard Snowden QC held that the administration was therefore 'being conducted to make a payment to the secured creditors, and that it was, in essence, a substitute for each of the holders of fixed security conducting their own sales of the charged assets' [87]. Accordingly, given the administrators' failure to consider the interests of the secured creditors, and their failure to investigate the validity of a purported assignment of valuable rights in certain films executed prior to the company's insolvency, an application brought under IA 1986 Sch B1, para 71 (to dispose of the film rights in question as if they

were not subject to any fixed security to yield an overall greater return) had no real prospect of success. As such, it was neither reasonable nor rational for the administrators to have made this application; it was 'wrong to commence and pursue the application under paragraph 71 in the manner that they did' [94]. It followed that the administrators were ordered to pay the costs of the secured creditors who appeared to oppose the application. Indeed, their acts were held to be so 'out of the norm' and 'unreasonable to a sufficiently high level' as to justify an indemnity costs order [97].[23]

3. Given that the administrator is an agent of the company as principal, the court in a recent summary application accepted that an administrator acting in good faith in the course of his duties as administrator will not be held liable for procuring the breach of a contract between the company and a third party: *Lictor Anstalt v Mir Steel UK Ltd* [2011] EWHC 3310 (Ch) (affd on other grounds [2012] EWCA Civ 1397). This 'defence of justification' finds its roots in *Said v Butt* [1920] 3 KB 497, which referred to a director's role in causing his company to act in breach of contract.

Effect of appointment on directors

The appointment of an administrator leaves the directors with very limited authority (though they retain their statutory responsibilities). IA 1986 Sch B1, para 64 provides that any power of the company or its officers that could be exercised in such a way as to interfere with the exercise by the administrator of his powers is not exercisable except with the consent of the administrator.

Termination of administration

Administration ends automatically after one year, unless the term is extended by consent of the creditors or order of the court (Sch B1, para 76). Otherwise it can be terminated by the administrator (unilaterally or under directions from a creditors' meeting), or by a creditor on application to the court (Sch B1, paras 79–83).

Priority of expenses of administration

The expenses of an administration have priority over a debt secured by a floating charge (Sch B1, para 99). But debts or liabilities arising out of contracts entered into by the administrator (including contracts of employment adopted by the administrator so far as they relate to post-adoption work) have priority over the administrator's own remuneration and expenses ('super-priority') (Sch B1, para 99(3) and (4)).[24] This makes the classification of debts, and the distinction between debts and expenses, vitally important.

For a detailed consideration of the distinction between provable debts and expenses, see *Re Nortel GmbH; Re Lehman Brothers International (Europe)* [2013] UKSC 52, [2014] AC 209 3 (SC). The case arose out of the insolvency proceedings of Nortel and Lehman Brothers, and concerned the question of whether the company's liability arising after the insolvency event from a financial support direction (FSD) or a contribution notice (CN) pursuant to the Pensions Act 2004 constituted a 'necessary disbursement' of the liquidator or administrator. The Supreme Court overturned the lower courts' decisions and held that regardless of whether the FSD or CN was issued before or after the commencement

---

[23] This part of the proceedings dealt with the cost consequences following an earlier determination of the validity of a purported assignment.

[24] If a company in administration is in rateable occupation of property, the non-domestic rates payable during the administration are 'necessary disbursements by the administrator in the course of the administration' and, under IR 1986 r 2.67, rank for payment before the administrator's remuneration (*Exeter City Council v Bairstow* [2007] EWHC 400 (Ch)). This case has been highly criticised: see, eg, G Moss, 'Rescue Culture Speared by *Trident*' (2007) 20 *Insolvency Intelligence* 72.

of administration, it would be a provable claim, not a liquidation or administration expense.[25] This decision ameliorated several concerns.[26] First, the magnitude of liability from these FSDs and CNs may be enormous. If these liabilities are classified as expense with super-priority, the insolvent estate may be exhausted after satisfying these obligations, leaving the body of general creditors with nothing. Secondly, in the case of administration, the administrator may be forced to conclude that the goals of administration would not be served given such enormous liabilities. The Supreme Court in this ruling ensured that the rescue culture is not defeated by the rules regarding the classification of expenses and provable debts.

Further examples illustrate the courts' sensitivity to the commercial issues. In *Re Bickland Ltd* [2012] EWHC 706 (Ch), the court was willing to treat the costs of a director's dismissed application to appoint administrators (after a co-director had appointed administrators) 'as if' they were administration expenses, despite these falling out of the defined list under IR 1986 r 2.67.

The position of rent falling due before or after commencement of administration has also been rationalised: see *Jervis v Pillar Denton Ltd* [2015] Ch 87, CA, overruling earlier lower court authorities.[27] In short, if the office-holder retains or uses the property for the benefit of the winding up or administration, the rent for such use will be an administration expense (on a pro rata basis if necessary) whether the contract requires the rent to be paid in advance or in arrears.

However, compare this with the decision in *Laverty v British Gas Trading Ltd* [2014] EWHC 2721 (Ch), where Sir Terence Etherton C held that gas and electricity charges that had been incurred after companies had entered administration under deemed contracts with the suppliers ranked not as administration expenses, but as provable debts. IA 1986 does not permit suppliers of utilities (eg gas, electricity, water and communication services) to deny supply to companies in insolvency or administration, nor to compel the payment of charges incurred before the commencement of insolvency as a condition of continuing supply, although the legislation has now been amended to protect utility companies by permitting them to make it a condition of the supply that the office-holder provides a personal guarantee for the payment in respect of any supply made during the insolvency: see Insolvency (Protection of Essential Supplies) Order 2015 (SI 2015/989) which amends s 233 and introduces new s 233A as from 1 October 2015.

Receivership and administrative receivership

Receivership generally

Any secured creditor may enforce his security by the appointment of a receiver. So, for example, if a company has given a creditor a fixed charge over its book-debts, the appointment of a receiver will enable the debts to be collected and applied in satisfaction of the company's obligation. This may always be done by order of the court; but in practice the instrument by which the security is created will invariably confer on the holder of the

---

[25] See G Moss, 'Proof Positive—Supreme Court Expands Scope of Provable Contingent Liabilities' (2013) 26(7) *Insolvency Intelligence* 104.

[26] See I Fletcher, *The Law of Insolvency* (4th edn, 2nd Supplement, 2014), [16-147.1]; R Goode, *Principles of Corporate Insolvency Law* (4th edn, 2011), [8.37].

[27] *Re Luminar Lava Ignite Ltd* [2012] EWHC 951 (Ch); *Goldacre (Offices) Ltd v Nortel Networks UK Ltd* [2010] Ch 455.

security a power to appoint a receiver without recourse to the court. Receiverships (and administrative receiverships, to the extent that they still exist) are thus insolvency procedures operating largely without the involvement of the courts.[28]

Until the reforming insolvency legislation of 1985–86, the subject of receivership was largely a matter for the common law. There are now a number of provisions in IA 1986 Pt III which apply generally to receiverships: for example, there is a prohibition on the appointment of a body corporate or an undischarged bankrupt (ss 30–31); there must be notification on the company's stationery of the appointment of a receiver (s 39); and it is declared that normally a receiver is personally liable on any contracts he makes, but subject to a right of indemnity out of the assets under his control (ss 37(1) and 44).

A receiver appointed by the court is an officer of the court and accountable to it, and is not subject to direction or to dictation by the creditor in whose interests he has been appointed. A receiver appointed independently may in theory be the agent either of the company or of the creditor who appointed him: in practice, he is always expressly made the former (and this is now a statutory rule in the case of an *administrative receiver* (see the following section)). This agency (whether contractual or statutory) enables the receiver to enter into contracts in the company's name, employ staff and so on, but it ceases if the company goes into liquidation. From then on he continues to be competent to realise the company's assets for the purpose of discharging the secured debt, and to take any necessary steps to protect and preserve those assets, but he can no longer incur credit in the company's name or cause it to incur executory obligations. Note, however, the 'unusual' features in this agency relationship as enunciated in a recent case considering the duties owed by a firm of solicitors retained by the receivers of a company in receivership: *Edenwest Ltd v CMS Cameron McKenna (A Firm)* [2012] EWHC 1258 (Ch).

The primary duty of a receiver is to get in and, as necessary, realise sufficient of the company's assets and undertaking to satisfy the outstanding debt of the creditor on whose behalf he has been appointed. He does not owe duties of a fiduciary nature (in the fullest sense) to the company or the other creditors, although he may be liable to them if he uses his powers for an improper purpose (*Downsview Nominees Ltd v First City Corpn Ltd* **[16.05]**). He is under an obligation to keep and produce to the company proper accounts (*Smiths Ltd v Middleton* [1979] 3 All ER 842). In these respects his position may be contrasted with that of an administrator or a liquidator. A receiver's duties are owed first and foremost to the security holder who has appointed him, and the interests of the company, its trade creditors and any other person concerned can legitimately be subordinated to those of the security holder. An administrator or liquidator, however, is required to deal with the company's assets for the benefit of *all* the interested parties.

It is very common for an appointment to be made, not simply of a receiver, but of a *receiver and manager*—a twin office under which the appointee is empowered to manage the business and not just get in and sell off its assets. This is done in the hope either that the company may be able to trade its way back into profitability or, at the very least, that its business can be sold as a going concern rather than on a break-up basis and in that way fetch more. Of course, a power to manage 'the business' of a company can be given to a receiver only if the charge is over the whole of the company's undertaking—which means that it must be a floating charge.

The appointment of a receiver and manager puts an end to the directors' powers to manage the business, though they will revert once he has discharged his functions, so

---

[28] On the future of receivership generally, V Finch, *Corporate Insolvency Law: Perspectives and Principles* (2nd edn, 2009), pp 358–362.

long as the business or part of it has survived. But the directors do retain their *office*, and their other powers and functions: in *Newhart Developments v Co-operative Commercial Bank* [1978] QB 814, it was held that they had power to issue a writ claiming damages for breach of contract against the very creditor who had appointed the receiver. Likewise, the directors have the power to take proceedings to challenge the validity of the receiver's appointment, to oppose a petition to wind up the company or to cause the company to sue the receiver for breach of duty. [29]

A company that is in receivership may be put into liquidation. The liquidator has then, in principle, to allow the receiver to continue to act until the claims of his debenture holders or chargee are met out of the security. Conversely, a receiver may be appointed after a company has gone into liquidation; and, as we have seen, the fact of liquidation is itself effective to crystallise a floating charge.

Where a receiver is appointed to enforce a floating charge, the claims of certain preferential creditors (eg employees for certain claims) must be paid ahead of the debenture holder: IA 1986 s 40. In addition, a certain proportion must be set aside for the unsecured creditors: IA 1986 s 176A.

Administrative receivership

The main innovation made by the insolvency legislation of 1985–86 was the introduction of a separate category of receiver, the *administrative receiver*. Although this was a major innovation at the time, the reforms of EA 2002 signal the end for most administrative receiverships (see the following section).

An administrative receiver is defined by IA 1986 s 29(2). Essentially, administrative receivers are receivers and managers of the whole, or substantially the whole, of the property of a company appointed by or on behalf of the holders of a debenture of the company secured by a floating charge.[30] IA 1986 stipulates that administrative receivers must be qualified insolvency practitioners (ss 45(2) and 388–389), and confers on them a number of statutory powers (ss 42–43 and Sch 1). It also declares that they are deemed to be the company's agent, unless the company is in liquidation (s 44); this converts to a rule of law what was previously the standard practice under the usual terms of floating charge debentures before the Act.[31] The Act requires the directors to provide administrative receivers with information about the company by submitting to them a statement of affairs (s 47), but in turn requires the administrative receivers to keep the company's unsecured creditors informed about the progress of the receivership (s 48). This report must also be sent to secured creditors and to the registrar at Companies House.

Enterprise Act 2002 reforms—limited scope for administrative receiverships

After the reforms of EA 2002, it is not now possible to appoint an administrative receiver under a floating charge created on or after 15 September 2003 (IA 1986 s 72A; Insolvency Act 1986, Section 72A (Appointed Date) Order 2003 (SI 2003/2095)), except in special cases

---

[29] In *Closegate Hotel Development (Durham) Ltd v Mclean* [2013] EWHC 3237 (Ch), the court drew the distinction between (i) the statutory prohibition in IA 1986 Sch B1, para 64, which was primarily intended to bar the directors' exercise of powers where that could impede the exercise of similar powers by the administrators; and (ii) the directors' power to cause the company to bring claims in relation to the logically prior question of whether the administrators had any power at all (eg whether they had been validly appointed). Here the directors were pursuing the latter type of claim, for which they did have authority, and so no indemnity was required (as it would have been for claims under (i), according to *Tudor Grange Holdings Ltd v Citibank NA* [1992] Ch 53 (Browne-Wilkinson V-C)).

[30] Or a person who would be such a receiver but for the fact that there is someone else already in office as the receiver of part of the company's property under a prior-ranking charge.

[31] The practice was adopted to avoid the receiver being the agent of the chargee, and thus exposing the chargee to the onerous duties of a mortgagee in possession.

specified in IA 1986 ss 72B–72H.[32] Instead, the chargee has the right to appoint an administrator (IA 1986 Sch B1, para 14). Recall that an administrator is an officer of the court (Sch B1, para 5) who performs his functions in the interests of the company's creditors as a whole (Sch B1, para 3(2)).

Chargees with floating charges created before 15 September 2003 retain the right to appoint an administrative receiver, but also have the option to appoint an administrator. A chargee whose floating charge does not cover the whole or substantially the whole of the company's assets can still appoint a receiver, who will by definition not be an administrative receiver, but cannot appoint an administrator.[33] An administrator, administrative receiver or receiver cannot be appointed unless the charge is enforceable.

These EA 2002 reforms, largely doing away with administrative receivership, were intended to favour the rescue culture. An administrative receiver is entitled to put the secured creditor's interests first, and a suspicion prevailed that the interests of unsecured creditors and the company itself were not always best served; by contrast, an administrator must manage the company's affairs for the benefit of everyone concerned.

Powers of management—company contracts

An administrative receiver may cause the company to repudiate any contracts entered into before he was appointed. The only remedy the injured party will have is a claim against the company for breach of contract. If the claim sounds in damages only, then the company is unlikely to be able to pay once the claims of the secured creditor are met (*Airlines Airspares Ltd v Handley Page Ltd* [1970] Ch 193). If, on the other hand, the contract is one for which the court will award specific performance or an injunction, then the injured party is protected (*Freevale Ltd v Metrostores (Holdings) Ltd* [1984] Ch 199) since the company remains as liable to an order for specific performance as it would were it not in administration (*Re A/Wear UK Ltd (In Administration)* [2013] EWCA Civ 1626, CA).

An administrative receiver is personally liable on any new contract entered into in the performance of his functions, except insofar as the contract otherwise provides (IA 1986 s 44(1)(b)). So far as personal liability is assumed, the administrative receiver is entitled to an indemnity out of the assets of the company (s 44(1)(c)). In practice, he will also have an indemnity from the chargee. In the majority of cases, however, his aim will be expressly or impliedly to exclude all personal liability.

Employment contracts are a special class. Since the administrative receiver is the company's agent, the appointment does not automatically terminate these contracts. If the administrative receiver finds that the employees cannot be retained, he may dismiss them, and this will almost certainly not be unfair dismissal. On the other hand, if he wants to retain employees, he may either adopt their existing contracts or negotiate new ones on behalf of the company. An administrative receiver who adopts existing contracts is, by statute, and with no ability to contract out, personally liable in respect of services rendered wholly or partly after the adoption (IA 1986 s 44(1)(b) and (2A)–(2D)). He can, however, opt out of personal liability for newly negotiated contracts (s 44(1)(b)). Nothing the administrative receiver does in the first 14 days after appointment is taken as indicating adoption of existing contracts (s 44(2)), but if he continues to employ people and pay them according to their existing contracts after that time, he is taken to have impliedly adopted the contracts: *Powdrill v Watson* [1995] 2 AC 394.

---

[32] The exceptions relate to large-scale marketable loans, projects with step-in rights, financial market charges, registered social landlords and some utility companies.

[33] But note *Re Croftbell Ltd* [1990] BCLC 844, where a receiver appointed under a charge over 'the whole of [the company's] undertaking and all its property and assets' was held to be an administrative receiver notwithstanding that, at the time of appointment, the company's only asset (other than a small debt owed by the parent company) would not come into the receiver's control because it was separately charged to a third party.

The role of administrative receivers and their relationship to the company and its property.

[16.04] Re Atlantic Computer Systems plc [1992] Ch 505 (Court of Appeal)

The facts are immaterial.

NICHOLLS LJ: . . . Typically, when lending money to a company, a bank will take as security a charge over all or most of the assets of the company, present and future, the charge being a fixed charge on land and certain other assets, and a floating charge over the remaining assets. The deed authorises the bank to appoint a receiver and manager of the company's undertaking, with power to carry on the company's business. Such a receiver is referred to in the Act of 1986 as an 'administrative receiver'.

Normally the deed creating the floating charge and authorising his appointment provides that an administrative receiver shall be the agent of the company. Now the Act of 1986, in s 44(1)(a), provides that this shall always be so, unless and until the company goes into liquidation. For many years the position regarding a receiver appointed as agent of the company was that in general he was not personally liable for contracts entered into by him for and on behalf of the company. He was no more personally liable than was a director who entered into a contract for and on behalf of his company . . . The position now, with regard to administrative receivers, is set out in s 44(1) and (2) of the Act of 1986.[34] Under that section an administrative receiver is personally liable on (a) any contract entered into by him in the carrying out of his functions, except in so far as the contract otherwise provides, and (b) on any contract of employment 'adopted' by him in the carrying out of those functions. In the latter regard the administrative receiver has, in effect, a period of 14 days' grace after his appointment . . . In cases where he is personally liable an administrative receiver is entitled to an indemnity out of the assets of the company: s 44(1)(c). But even today an administrative receiver is not, in general, personally liable, and hence the statutory indemnity out of the assets of the company does not arise, in respect of contracts adopted by him in the course of managing the company's business, other than contracts of employment. With that one special exception, personal liability is confined, in general, to new contracts made by him. Thus he is not personally liable for the rent payable under an existing lease, or for the hire charges payable under an existing hire-purchase agreement. This is not a surprising conclusion. It does not offend against basic conceptions of justice or fairness. The rent and hire charges were a liability undertaken by the company at the inception of the lease or hire-purchase agreement. The land or goods are being used by the company even when an administrative receiver is in office. It is to the company that, along with other creditors, the lessor and the owner of the goods must look for payment.

Nor is a lessor or owner of goods in such a case entitled to be paid his rent or hire instalments as an 'expense' of the administrative receivership, even though the administrative receiver has retained and used the land or goods for the purpose of the receivership. The reason is not far to seek. The appointment of an administrative receiver does not trigger a statutory prohibition on the lessor or owner of goods such as that found in s 130 in the case of a winding-up order. If the rent or hire is not paid by the administrative receiver the lessor or owner of the goods is at liberty, as much after the appointment of the administrative receiver as before, to exercise the rights and remedies available to him under his lease or hire-purchase agreement. Faced with the prospect of proceedings, an administrative receiver may choose to pay the rent or hire charges in order to retain the land or goods. But if he decides not to do so, the lessor or owner of goods has his remedies. There is no occasion, assuming that there is jurisdiction, for the court to intervene and order the administrative receiver to pay these outgoings . . .

---

[34] Section 44 has since been amended: see the Note following.

➤ Note

IA 1986 s 44 has been amended since Nicholls LJ delivered his judgment in the *Atlantic Computer Systems* case, to meet the difficulties revealed in *Powdrill v Watson* and *Talbot v Cadge* [1995] 2 AC 394, HL (and more particularly in the rulings of the lower courts in these cases). The effect of this amendment (effected by the Insolvency Act 1994 s 2) is to make it clear that the receiver's personal liability is restricted to payments due to the employee in respect of services actually rendered during the receivership.

Duties of administrative receivers

This area of law remains troublesome. Clearly, the way in which an administrative receiver carries out his duties can have a profound and practical impact on the financial well-being of the security holder, the debtor company, any subsequent security holders with interests in the same assets, and any third parties who have guaranteed the secured debt. What duties, if any, does the administrative receiver owe to these parties?

[16.05] Downsview Nominees Ltd v First City Corpn Ltd [1993] AC 295 (Privy Council)

This case involved a claim by the second-ranked debenture holder (FCC) against the first-ranked debenture holder (Downsview) and its appointed receiver (Russell) claiming that their management of the receivership had caused loss to FCC. The borrower was a company that carried on a motor dealing and garage business in New Zealand. It had given a first debenture to the Westpac bank and a second debenture to FCC, each secured by a floating charge over all of its assets. It had defaulted under the second debenture and FCC had appointed receivers who formed the view that the company's business was unprofitable and that it should be closed down. The company's managing director appealed to Russell (the second defendant) for help. His response was (i) to procure Downsview (a company which he controlled) to take an assignment of W bank's first debenture and (ii) to have Downsview appoint himself as a receiver under that debenture. FCC's receivers were thus ousted from anything but a residual role. FCC at once offered to pay Downsview all the moneys owing under the first debenture, so that it would be redeemed and FCC's receivers could again take charge. But this offer was declined, and Russell continued to carry on the company's business, incurring further losses of over $500,000. The Privy Council held that: (i) Russell had used his powers not for the proper purpose of realising Downsview's security but in order to meet the managing director's wish that the company should continue trading; (ii) Downsview ought to have accepted FCC's offer to redeem; and (iii) each of them should compensate FCC for its losses. But it rejected the view of the trial judge and the New Zealand Court of Appeal that any liability lay in negligence.

> The opinion of the Judicial Committee was delivered by LORD TEMPLEMAN: . . . The second argument put forward on behalf of the first and second defendants [Downsview and Russell] is that though a mortgagee owes certain duties to the mortgagor [the borrowing company], he owes no duty to any subsequent encumbrancer [eg FCC], so the first and second defendants owed no duty to the first plaintiff. This argument also is untenable.... The mortgagor can mortgage the property again and again. A second or subsequent mortgage is a complete security on the mortgagor's interests subject only to the rights of prior encumbrancers. If a first mortgagee commits a breach of his duties to the mortgagor, the damage inflicted by that breach of duty will

be suffered by the second mortgagee, subsequent encumbrancers and the mortgagor, depending on the extent of the damage and the amount of each security. Thus if a first mortgagee in breach of duty sells property worth £500,000 for £300,000, he is liable at the suit of any subsequent encumbrancer or the mortgagor. Damages of £200,000 will be ordered to be taken into the accounts of the first mortgagee or paid into court or to the second mortgagee who, after satisfying, as far as he can, the amount of any debt outstanding under his mortgage, will pay over any balance remaining to the next encumbrancer or to the mortgagor if there is no subsequent encumbrancer . . .

The next submission on behalf of the first and second defendants is that, even if a mortgagee owes certain duties to subsequent encumbrancers, a receiver and manager appointed by a mortgagee is not under any such duty where, as in the present case, the receiver and manager is deemed to act as agent for the mortgagor. The fallacy in the argument is the failure to appreciate that, when a receiver and manager exercises the powers of sale and management conferred on him by the mortgage, he is dealing with the security; he is not merely selling or dealing with the interests of the mortgagor. He is exercising the power of selling and dealing with the mortgaged property for the purpose of securing repayment of the debt owing to his mortgagee and must exercise his powers in good faith and for the purpose of obtaining repayment of the debt owing to his mortgagee. The receiver and manager owes these duties to the mortgagor and to all subsequent encumbrancers in whose favour the mortgaged property has been charged.

The next question is the nature and extent of the duties owed by a mortgagee and a receiver and manager respectively to subsequent encumbrancers and the mortgagor.

Several centuries ago equity evolved principles for the enforcement of mortgages and the protection of borrowers. The most basic principles were, first, that a mortgage is security for the repayment of a debt and, secondly, that a security for repayment of a debt is only a mortgage. From these principles flowed two rules, first, that powers conferred on a mortgagee must be exercised in good faith for the purpose of obtaining repayment and secondly that, subject to the first rule, powers conferred on a mortgagee may be exercised although the consequences may be disadvantageous to the borrower. These principles and rules apply also to a receiver and manager appointed by the mortgagee.

It does not follow that a receiver and manager must immediately upon appointment seize all the cash in the coffers of the company and sell all the company's assets or so much of the assets as he chooses and considers sufficient to complete the redemption of the mortgage. He is entitled, but not bound, to allow the company's business to be continued by himself or by the existing or other executives. The decisions of the receiver and manager whether to continue the business or close down the business and sell assets chosen by him cannot be impeached if those decisions are taken in good faith while protecting the interests of the debenture holder in recovering the moneys due under the debenture, even though the decisions of the receiver and manager may be disadvantageous for the company . . . But since a mortgage is only security for a debt, a receiver and manager commits a breach of his duty if he abuses his powers by exercising them otherwise than 'for the special purpose of enabling the assets comprised in the debenture holders' security to be preserved and realised'[35] for the benefit of the debenture holder. In the present case the evidence of the second defendant himself and the clear emphatic findings of Gault J show that the second defendant accepted appointment and acted as receiver and manager not for the purpose of enforcing the security under the Westpac debenture but for the purpose of preventing the enforcement by the plaintiffs of the [FCC] debenture.

---

[35] The quotation is from the judgment of Jenkins LJ in *Re B Johnson & Co (Builders) Ltd* [1955] Ch 634 at 662–663.

This and other findings to similar effect establish that, ab initio and throughout his receivership, the second defendant did not exercise his powers for proper purposes. He was at all times in breach of the duty, which was pleaded against him, to exercise his powers in good faith for proper purposes.

Gault J rested his judgment not on breach of a duty to act in good faith for proper purposes but on negligence. He said:

'on an application of negligence principles, a receiver owes a duty to the debenture holders to take reasonable care in dealing with the assets of the company... [The first defendant's] position is merely a specific example of the duty a mortgagee has to subsequent chargeholders to exercise its powers with reasonable care . . .'

Richardson J, delivering the judgment of the Court of Appeal, agreed that duties of care in negligence as defined by Gault J were owed by the second defendant as receiver and manager and by the first defendant as first debenture holder to the plaintiffs as second debenture holders. Richardson J agreed that the second defendant was in breach of his duty but, differing from Gault J, held that the first defendant had committed no breach.

The general duty of care said to be owed by a mortgagee to subsequent encumbrancers and the mortgagor in negligence is inconsistent with the right of the mortgagee and the duties which the courts applying equitable principles have imposed on the mortgagee. If a mortgagee enters into possession he is liable to account for rent on the basis of wilful default; he must keep mortgage premises in repair; he is liable for waste. Those duties were imposed to ensure that a mortgagee is diligent in discharging his mortgage and returning the property to the mortgagor. If a mortgagee exercises his power of sale in good faith for the purpose of protecting his security, he is not liable to the mortgagor even though he might have obtained a higher price and even though the terms might be regarded as disadvantageous to the mortgagor. *Cuckmere Brick Co Ltd v Mutual Finance Ltd*[36] is Court of Appeal authority for the proposition that, if the mortgagee decides to sell, he must take reasonable care to obtain a proper price but is no authority for any wider proposition. A receiver exercising his power of sale also owes the same specific duties as the mortgagee. But that apart, the general duty of a receiver and manager appointed by a debenture holder... leaves no room for the imposition of a general duty to use reasonable care in dealing with the assets of the company. The duties imposed by equity on a mortgagee and on a receiver and manager would be quite unnecessary if there existed a general duty in negligence to take reasonable care in the exercise of powers and to take reasonable care in dealing with the assets of the mortgagor company . . .

A mortgagee owes a general duty to subsequent encumbrancers and to the mortgagor to use his powers for the sole purpose of securing repayments of the moneys owing under his mortgage and a duty to act in good faith. He also owes the specific duties which equity has imposed on him in the exercise of his powers to go into possession and his powers of sale. It may well be that a mortgagee who appoints a receiver and manager, knowing that the receiver and manager intends to exercise his powers for the purpose of frustrating the activities of the second mortgagee or for some other improper purpose or who fails to revoke the appointment of a receiver and manager when the mortgagee knows that the receiver and manager is abusing his powers, may himself be guilty of bad faith but in the present case this possibility need not be explored.

The liability of the second defendant in the present case is firmly based not on negligence but on the breach of duty. There was overwhelming evidence that the receivership of the second defendant was inspired by him for improper purposes and carried on in bad faith, ultimately verging on fraud. The liability of the first defendant does not arise under negligence but as a result of the

---

[36] [1971] Ch 949.

first defendant's breach of duty in failing to transfer the Westpac debenture to the first plaintiff at the end of March 1987. It is well settled that the mortgagor and all persons having any interest in the property subject to the mortgage or liable to pay the mortgage debt can redeem. It is now conceded that the first plaintiff was entitled to require the first defendant to assign the Westpac debenture to the first plaintiff on payment of all moneys due to the first defendant under the Westpac debenture . . .

The first defendant was from the end of March 1987 in breach of its duty to assign the Westpac debenture to the first plaintiff. If that debenture had been assigned, the second defendant would have ceased to be the receiver and manager and none of the avoidable losses caused by the second defendant would have been sustained . . .

➤ Notes

1. In *Cukurova Finance International Ltd v Alfa Telecom Turkey Ltd* [2013] UKPC 2, [2015] 2 WLR 875, it was held by the Privy Council that, 'more generally, if a chargee enforces his security for the proper purpose of satisfying the debt, the mere fact that he may have additional purposes, however significant, which are collateral to that object, cannot vitiate his enforcement of the security' [78]. Thus, in this case, the appropriation of the charged shares (to enable the obtaining of control over the subject companies, instead of selling the shares onto the market) could not be said to constitute an exercise of the power of enforcement for a collateral purpose.

2. In *Co-operative Bank plc v Phillips* [2014] EWHC 2862 (Ch), the court applied the principles in *Downsview* and concluded that the second chargee bank (which had brought, but later discontinued, proceedings for possession of the two secured properties) had brought the proceedings for proper purposes. Morgan J, at [67]–[68], said:

I am not able to decide that the Bank wanted to sell or let the properties. I am not [however] persuaded that the Bank was acting irrationally and without any purpose at all. I consider that, on the balance of probabilities, the Bank brought the proceedings to put pressure on Mr Phillips which the Bank considered, or at any rate hoped, would produce some payment which the Bank would be able to appropriate to the sums secured by the charges. The Bank's view was in the event borne out to the extent of the offer of £50,000 made by Mr Phillips' daughter...I also hold that the bringing of these possession proceedings for the purpose of putting pressure on Mr Phillips in that way was for the purpose of obtaining repayment of the sums secured by the charges and was therefore a permissible purpose.

A receiver who is appointed to manage the business of the chargor has a duty to do so with due diligence.

[16.06] Medforth v Blake [2000] Ch 86 (Court of Appeal)

Medforth was a pig farmer on a very large scale: his annual turnover was over £2 million. He ran into financial difficulties and his bank appointed receivers, who ran the business for four-and-a-half years, until Medforth was able to find a new source of finance and repay the bank. Although Medforth repeatedly told the receivers that they could claim large discounts from the suppliers of feedstuffs, amounting to some £1,000 a week, they failed to do so. The court held that the receivers owed a duty (subject to their primary duty to the bank) to manage the business with due diligence, and that for breach of this duty they were liable to Medforth.

SIR RICHARD SCOTT V-C: . . . As a Privy Council case, the *Downsview Nominees* case **[16.05]** is not binding but, as Mr. Smith submitted, is a persuasive authority of great weight. But what did it decide as to the duties owed by a receiver/manager to a mortgagor? It decided that the duty lies in equity, not in tort. It decided that there is no general duty of care in negligence. It held that the receiver/manager owes the same specific duties when exercising the power of sale as are owed by a mortgagee when exercising the power of sale. Lord Templeman cited with approval the *Cuckmere Brick* case [1971] Ch 949 test, namely, that the mortgagee must take reasonable care to obtain a proper price . . .

The *Cuckmere Brick* case test can impose liability on a mortgagee notwithstanding the absence of fraud or mala fides. It follows from the *Downsview Nominees* case and *Yorkshire Bank plc v Hall* [1999] 1 WLR 1713 that a receiver/manager who sells but fails to take reasonable care to obtain a proper price may incur liability notwithstanding the absence of fraud or mala fides. Why should the approach be any different if what is under review is not the conduct of a sale but conduct in carrying on a business? If a receiver exercises this power, why does not a specific duty, corresponding to the duty to take reasonable steps to obtain a proper price, arise? If the business is being carried on by a mortgagee, the mortgagee will be liable, as a mortgagee in possession, for loss caused by his failure to do so with due diligence. Why should not the receiver/manager, who, as Lord Templeman held, owes the same specific duties as the mortgagee when selling, owe comparable specific duties when conducting the mortgaged business? It may be that the particularly onerous duties constructed by courts of equity for mortgages in possession would not be appropriate to apply to a receiver. But, no duties at all save a duty of good faith? That does not seem to me to make commercial sense nor, more importantly, to correspond with the principles expressed in the bulk of the authorities . . .

I do not accept that there is any difference between the answer that would be given by the common law to the question what duties are owed by a receiver managing a mortgaged property to those interested in the equity of redemption and the answer that would be given by equity to that question. I do not, for my part, think it matters one jot whether the duty is expressed as a common law duty or as a duty in equity. The result is the same. The origin of the receiver's duty, like the mortgagee's duty, lies, however, in equity and we might as well continue to refer to it as a duty in equity.

In my judgment, in principle and on the authorities, the following propositions can be stated. (1) A receiver managing mortgaged property owes duties to the mortgagor and anyone else with an interest in the equity of redemption. (2) The duties include, but are not necessarily confined to, a duty of good faith. (3) The extent and scope of any duty additional to that of good faith will depend on the facts and circumstances of the particular case. (4) In exercising his powers of management the primary duty of the receiver is to try and bring about a situation in which interest on the secured debt can be paid and the debt itself repaid. (5) Subject to that primary duty, the receiver owes a duty to manage the property with due diligence. (6) Due diligence does not oblige the receiver to continue to carry on a business on the mortgaged premises previously carried on by the mortgagor. (7) If the receiver does carry on a business on the mortgaged premises, due diligence requires reasonable steps to be taken in order to try to do so profitably . . .

[His Lordship accordingly ruled that the trial judge had rightly held the receivers liable for breach of duty.]

SWINTON THOMAS and TUCKEY LJJ concurred.

➤ Questions

1. Does the duty described in *Downsview* **[16.05]** meet commercial needs and expectations? Does it contribute to a 'rescue culture'? See G Lightman, 'The Challenges Ahead: Address

to the Insolvency Lawyers' Association' [1996] JBL 113 at 119–120; contrast H Rajak, 'Can a Receiver be Negligent?' in B Rider (ed), *The Corporate Dimension* (1998).

2. Does it matter whether the receiver's duty is an equitable duty or a common law duty?[37]

3. What difference does it make to say that the receiver owes a duty of good faith, rather than a duty of care, to the company and to subsequent encumbrancers or guarantors?[38]

4. What duty does the *chargee* owe in deciding *when* or *whether* to appoint a receiver? See *Shamji v Johnson Matthey Bankers Ltd* [1986] BCLC 278, Ch, affd [1991] BCLC 36, CA. If an offer is made to redeem the secured debt (thereby extinguishing the charge), must the debenture holder accept it?

5. What duty does the *receiver* owe in deciding *whether* to exercise the power of sale or continue the business, and in deciding *when* to sell? See *Cuckmere Brick Co Ltd v Mutual Finance Ltd* [1971] Ch 949, CA.

6. Is the duty owed by the receiver when exercising the power of sale or the power to carry on the business one of good faith, due diligence or reasonable care? See LS Sealy, 'Mortgagees and Receivers—A Duty of Care Resurrected and Extended' [2000] CLJ 31; S Frisby, 'Making a Silk Purse Out of a Pig's Ear—*Medforth v Blake*' (2000) 63 MLR 413.

➤ Notes

1. Also see *International Leisure Ltd v First National Trustee Co Ltd* [2012] EWHC 1971 (Ch), [2013] Ch 346, discussed in the context of 'reflective losses', at Note 4 following *Giles v Rhind* **[13.27]**, pp 714.

2. In *Glatt v Sinclair* [2011] EWCA Civ 1317, applying the general principles governing the receiver's duties to the principal, the Court of Appeal ruled that there was at least an arguable case that a receiver appointed by the court pursuant to the Criminal Justice Act 1988 had committed a breach of duty in failing properly to market the property in question, given that the same property was re-advertised and re-sold by the purchaser with an uplift of nearly 38%.

Distribution of assets subject to the receivership

If there is more than one charge over the secured assets, then priority as between chargees depends upon rules discussed earlier (see 'Registration, priority and constructive notice of registered charges', pp 629ff). IA 1986 s 43 provides for sale of the secured assets by a receiver other than one appointed by the chargee with first claim on the proceeds.

If the charge over the secured assets is floating, then various claims rank ahead of the secured creditor's claim to have the secured debt repaid. This is one of the disadvantages of floating charges. The order of payment out of the realisations is as follows:

(i) The *expenses of winding up* (including the remuneration of the liquidator),[39] *if* the company goes into liquidation at any time while the administrative receiver

---

[37] See the earlier case of *Standard Chartered Bank Ltd v Walker* [1982] 1 WLR 1410, CA, discussing the duty as if it were a common law duty; contrast *Downsview* **[16.05]**.

[38] Contrast *Standard Chartered Bank Ltd v Walker* [1982] 1 WLR 1410, CA, and *Downsview* **[16.05]**; the conclusion in the former case must now be regarded as wrong, given the decision in *Downsview*.

[39] IA 1986 s 115 (and s 156 for compulsory liquidations), and IR 1986 r 4.218, defining both what counts as a liquidation expense (according to *Re Toshoku Finance UK plc, Kahn v IRC* [2002] UKHL 6, [2002] 1 WLR 671, HL), and setting out the order of priority in which they are to be paid.

has in his possession undistributed realisations from the charged assets—see CA 2006 s 1282, inserting a new provision in the IA 1986 s 176ZA,[40] providing that property subject to a floating charge may, where necessary, be used to fund the general expenses of winding up in priority to the floating charge holder and to any preferential creditors entitled to be paid out of the property, but not providing for payment of these expenses out of the statutory share of assets for the unsecured creditors (see point (iii)). IA 1986 s 176ZA also provides for the power to make rules requiring the authorisation or approval of the floating charge holder, or the preferential creditors, or the court, to the expenditures in certain circumstances.

(ii)   The *expenses of receivership*: these are payable in priority to the other preferred claims, on the basis that the person who has produced a fund for distribution should have the costs of doing so paid in priority. But the receiver has a duty not to incur expenses if this would lessen the amount available for the preferred creditors (see point (iv)): *Woods v Winskill* [1913] 2 Ch 303.

(iii) The *statutory share of assets (the 'prescribed part') for unsecured creditors*: a prescribed percentage of floating charge asset realisations must be set aside to pay the company's unsecured creditors—see IA 1986 s 176A, and Insolvency Act 1986 (Prescribed Part) Order 2003 (SI 2003/2097) art 3.[41] The prescribed percentage is: (a) 50% of the first £10,000; and (b) 20% or the remainder, up to a maximum grand total of £600,000.[42] The rule does not apply if the company's net assets are worth less than £10,000 (s 176A(3)(a)), or if the costs of distribution to unsecured creditors would be disproportionate to the benefits (s 176A(5)).

(iv)   The *'preferential debts'*[43] (now primarily owed to employees, since EA 2002 abolished Crown priority), being debts that Parliament has decided should be paid in priority to all other debts, other than the expenses of winding up—see IA 1986 ss 40 and 175(2)(b). Any payment of preferential debts may be recouped out of the assets of the company available for the payment of unsecured creditors (if there are any such assets remaining in the company's insolvency) (IA 1986 s 40(3)).

(v)   Finally, the *debt owed to the charge holder*.

By contrast, if the charge over the secured assets is fixed, rather than floating, then the property cannot be used to pay off the debts in points (i), (iii) and (iv). This is so even if the charge secures the same debt to the same charge holder as a floating charge in the creditor's favour expressed to be over all the company's assets and undertaking. This distinction between treatment of fixed and floating charge realisations is one reason why creditors expend such efforts in drafting charges that are classified as fixed rather than floating (see 'Distinguishing between fixed and floating charges', pp 650ff). It also explains why creditors adopt the practice of taking a fixed charge over as many assets as possible and an equally ranking floating charge over whatever assets remain. The same

---

[40] So reversing the controversial decision in *Re Leyland DAF Ltd, Buchler v Talbot* [2004] UKHL 9, [2004] 2 AC 298, which denied priority to liquidation expenses (and which had itself overruled the long-standing Court of Appeal authority allowing such priority: *Re Barleycorn Enterprises Ltd* [1970] Ch 465).

[41] And floating charge holders cannot claim against this fund, as 'unsecured creditors', for any shortfall in the recovery of their secured debts (for the simple reason that they are not 'unsecured creditors'): *Re Airbase (UK) Ltd* [2008] EWHC 124 (Ch), [2008] BCC 213. On the other hand, a secured creditor can waive or forego its security entirely, so that it becomes an unsecured creditor who is then entitled to participate in the 'prescribed part' as with other unsecured creditors: *Re JT Frith Ltd* [2012] EWHC 196 (Ch); *Kelly v Inflexion Fund 2 Ltd* [2010] EWHC 2850 (Ch). Secured creditors may be motivated to take this step where their security rights are subordinated, and there are insufficient funds to repay both debts.

[42] It is possible to vary this rule by means of a CVA: IA 1986 s 176A(4).

[43] Defined in IA 1986 s 386 and Sch 6, although the Crown preference was abolished by EA 2002 reforms.

receiver can then be appointed over both classes of assets, but the distributions will follow quite different rules.

Liquidation or winding up

Both solvent and insolvent companies may be wound up. In the *winding up* or *liquidation* (the terms are synonymous), the company gives up its business, sells off its assets, pays its debts (or, if it is insolvent, does so to the extent that its funds allow) and distributes whatever surplus remains amongst its members or otherwise as its constitution may provide. The event must be notified in the *Gazette* (see 'Publication in the *Gazette*', p 754).

The conduct of the winding up is placed by law in the hands of a *liquidator*; and on his appointment the directors' power to manage the business of the company ceases.[44]

The company continues in being throughout the process of winding up: there is still a corporate personality and all corporate acts in the course of the liquidation, such as the transfer of property and the institution of legal proceedings, are done in its name rather than by the liquidator in his own name. The company ceases to exist only by the formal act of *dissolution* (IA 1986 ss 201ff) after the winding-up procedure has been completed (see 'Dissolution of the company', p 871).

A company may be wound up *compulsorily*, that is, by court order, or *voluntarily*, as a consequence of an extraordinary resolution passed by the members.

Voluntary winding up

In a voluntary winding up, following a special resolution passed by the members (IA 1986 s 84, also indicating limited exceptions), the liquidator is appointed by the members if the directors are able to declare that the company will be able to meet its debts in full (a '*members' voluntary winding up*') (IA 1986 ss 89 and 91 setting out the detailed requirements); if not, the company's creditors have the power of appointment and exercise general control over the conduct of the liquidation (a '*creditors' voluntary winding up*') (IA 1986 ss 90 and 96).

The court need not be involved in a voluntary winding up, although court confirmation gives a creditors' winding up recognition throughout the EU, which is important if the company has assets in other EU states (IR 1986 r 7.62).

Compulsory winding up generally

In a compulsory (or court-ordered) winding up the Official Receiver[45] automatically becomes the liquidator and is in law regarded as an officer of the court acting under its direction and control. Various people are entitled to petition the court for the compulsory

---

[44] By statute in voluntary liquidations (IA 1986 s 90(2)), and by common law in compulsory liquidations (*Re Farrow's Bank Ltd* [1921] 2 Ch 164).

[45] The Official Receiver is a public officer who is appointed by the Secretary of State to act in the administration of bankruptcies and company liquidations. There are in fact many Official Receivers, each attached to a particular court. Since the coming into force of IA 1986, many more bankruptcies and liquidations have been placed in the hands of private insolvency practitioners than was the case under the former law, so enabling the Official Receiver to devote his attention to the larger or more complex insolvencies, and in particular those in which fraud or other wrongdoing is suspected.

liquidation of a company (IA 1986 s 124, and note the conditions specified), including company creditors (who bring almost all petitions), the company itself and the company's directors. The Secretary of State may petition for winding up, in the public interest, generally in cases of notoriety, most often following an investigation of the company's affairs under CA 1985 Pt XIV or the Financial Services and Markets Act 2000 (see 'Public investigation of companies, pp 770ff) (IA 1986 ss 124(4) and 124A). By way of additional protection, these people may also petition for the appointment of a *provisional liquidator*, as an interim measure designed to maintain the status quo and prevent prejudice to any party pending the court's decision on the petition itself (IA 1986 s 135). See too *HMRC v Rochdale Drinks Distributors Ltd* [2011] EWCA Civ 1116; *HMRC v SED Essex Ltd* [2013] EWHC 1583 (Ch); *Parkwell Investments Ltd v Wilson* [2014] EWHC 3381 (Ch).

A company may be wound up by the court only if it is shown that one of the circumstances listed in IA 1986 s 122(1) exists. In practice, companies are usually wound up because the company is unable to pay its debts (s 122(1)(f)), or because the court is of the opinion that it is 'just and equitable' to do so (s 122(1)(g)).[46] IA 1986 s 123 describes circumstances that a court will take as sufficient evidence of a company's inability to pay its debts.

Permitted petitioners for a compulsory winding up

Every contributory has a statutory right[47] *to petition for a winding up, which cannot be excluded or limited by any provision in the articles.*

[16.07] Re Peveril Gold Mines Ltd [1898] 1 Ch 122 (Court of Appeal)

The company's articles provided that no member should petition for the winding up of the company unless (i) two directors had consented in writing, or (ii) a general meeting had so resolved, or (iii) the petitioner held at least 20% of the issued capital. A member presented a petition without satisfying any of these conditions. It was held that the articles were ineffective to prevent him from doing so.

LINDLEY MR: Anyone who is familiar with the Companies Act knows perfectly well that these registered limited companies are incorporated on certain conditions; they continue to exist on certain conditions; and they are liable to be dissolved on certain conditions. The important sections of the Act of 1862, with regard to dissolution, are ss 79 and 82 [IA 1986 ss 122 and 124]. Section 79 states the circumstances under which such a company may be dissolved by the court, and s 82 states the persons who may petition for a dissolution. Any article contrary to these sections—any article which says that the company is formed on the condition that its life shall not be terminated when any of the circumstances mentioned in s 79 exist, or which limits the right of a contributory under s 82 to petition for a winding up, would be an attempt to enforce on all the shareholders that which is at variance with the statutory conditions, and is invalid. It is no answer to say that the right to petition may be waived by any contributory personally. I do not intend to decide whether a valid contract may or may not be made between the company and an individual shareholder that he shall not petition for the winding up of the company. That point does not arise now. But to say that a company is formed on the condition

---

[46] The 'just and equitable' ground is less common now that CA 2006 s 994 provides better and more tailored remedies.

[47] Although note the conditions in IA 1986 s 124(2) and (3). 'Contributory' refers to members and some former members: IA 1986 s 79.

that its existence shall not be terminated under the circumstances, or on the application of the persons, mentioned in the Act is to say that it is formed contrary to the provisions of the Act, and upon conditions which the court is bound to ignore. The view taken by Byrne J was right, and the appeal must be dismissed.

CHITTY LJ delivered a concurring judgment.

VAUGHAN WILLIAMS LJ concurred.

➤ Questions

1. Lindley MR left open the question whether a contract outside the articles between the company and a member that he would not petition for a winding-up order was enforceable. Is it? (An analogy might be drawn with *Fulham Football Club (1987) Ltd v Richards* [2011] EWCA Civ 855, [2012] Ch 333, CA, at [82], where the court upheld an agreement to refer unfair prejudice allegations to arbitration, ie a statutory right was compromised by private agreement.)

2. Would a contractual promise by a company that it would not petition for its own winding up be binding? Consider *Russell v Northern Development Corpn Ltd* **[4.35]**.

3. Would an agreement between a shareholder and an outsider, or between several or all of the shareholders *inter se*, containing a promise that none of the parties would petition for a winding-up order, be upheld?

A member cannot petition for a winding up unless there are assets available for distribution to members.

[16.08] Re Rica Gold Washing Co (1879) 11 Ch D 36 (Court of Appeal)

The facts appear from the judgment.

> JESSEL MR: This is an appeal from the decision of Vice-Chancellor Hall dismissing a petition to wind up the company, on the ground that it was not a bona fide petition, and that the petitioner, as I read the judgment, had not sufficient interest to support it . . .
>
> Now I will say a word or two on the law as regards the position of a petitioner holding fully paid-up shares. He is not liable to contribute anything towards the assets of the company, and if he has any interest at all, it must be that after full payment of all the debts and liabilities of the company there will remain a surplus divisible among the shareholders of sufficient value to authorise him to present a petition. That being his position, and the rule being that the petitioner must succeed upon allegations which are proved, of course the petitioner must show the court by sufficient allegation that he has a sufficient interest to entitle him to ask for the winding up of the company. I say 'a sufficient interest', for the mere allegation of a surplus or of a probable surplus will not be sufficient. He must show what I may call a tangible interest. I am not going to lay down any rule as to what that must be, but if he showed only that there was such a surplus as, on being fairly divided, irrespective of the costs of the winding up, would give him £5, I should say that would not be sufficient to induce the court to interfere in his behalf . . .
>
> I cannot believe that a shareholder who has 75 £1 paid-up shares can imagine that he has sufficient interest to make it worth his while to present a winding-up petition . . . I have no doubt that, as the Vice-Chancellor says, this is not a bona fide petition, but a petition

presented with a very different object than that of obtaining for the petitioner, the £75, or any part of it. In my opinion it is either presented for the purpose of obtaining costs, or for the purpose of annoyance to some other person or persons; and I entirely agree with the Vice-Chancellor that it is not a bona fide petition. Therefore I think we must dismiss this appeal.

BRETT LJ delivered a concurring judgment.

BRAMWELL LJ concurred.

➤ Questions

1. What is the *ratio decidendi* of this case?

2. If a petition for winding up is presented by a holder of a small parcel of fully paid shares on facts similar to *Re German Date Coffee Co* (1882) 20 Ch D 169, CA, or *Re Thomas Edward Brinsmead & Sons* **[16.10]** should the court apply the *Rica Gold* rule?

3. The Jenkins Committee (Cmnd 1749, 1962, para 503(h)) recommended the reversal of this rule by statute. In *Re Chesterfield Catering Co Ltd* [1977] Ch 373, the decision was affirmed as being still good law, notwithstanding an argument by counsel that in the light of *Ebrahimi v Westbourne Galleries Ltd* **[16.13]** the principle of *Rica Gold* should be regarded not as a strict rule, but merely as one of the considerations for the court to take into account in assessing whether it was just and equitable to order a winding up. Is this logic persuasive?

4. Given the imposition of filing fees to lodge a winding-up petition, plus legal fees (a hefty sum for a contested case), plus the chance that a petition which is not well founded may be dismissed with an order that the petitioner pay the company's costs, or may be struck out as vexatious (see *Charles Forte Investments Ltd v Amanda* [1964] Ch 240 at 'The courts' discretion to order a compulsory winding up', p 850), does the law need the rule in *Rica Gold*?

➤ Notes

1. Note the other restrictions on the circumstances in which a contributory can bring a petition: IA 1986 s 124(2)–(4A).

2. The petitioner is not required to prove a tangible interest if the petition is based on, or alleges, company defaults that themselves make it impossible to determine whether there is a surplus for contributories: *Re Wessex Computer Stationers Ltd* [1992] BCLC 366.

3. By contrast, and subject to the wishes of the class of creditors, an unpaid creditor of an insolvent company will not be refused an order on the ground that there are no assets, unless it is shown that making the order would be pointless: *Re Crigglestone Coal Co Ltd* [1906] 2 Ch 327 at 336; IA 1986 ss 195 and 125(1).

➤ Question

In *Bell Group Finance (Pty) Ltd v Bell Group (UK) Holdings Ltd* [1996] 1 BCLC 304, Chadwick J granted a winding-up order to a petitioning creditor where the company had no assets, so that the liquidator could investigate whether there had been impropriety in the conduct of the company's affairs. Is there any reason in principle for having one rule for a creditor (see earlier) and an opposite rule for a member **[16.08]**?

Grounds for compulsory winding up

Compulsory winding up because the company is unable to pay its debts

A winding-up order will not be made on the basis of a debt which is bona fide disputed.

[16.09] Stonegate Securities Ltd v Gregory [1980] Ch 576 (Court of Appeal)

Prior to the presentation of a petition to wind up the plaintiff company, the defendant, in accordance with the Companies Act 1948 (CA 1948) s 223(a) [IA 1986 s 123], served a notice on the company demanding the payment of a debt within 21 days. The company, while accepting that there was a contingent or prospective liability to the defendant, denied that the debt was presently due. It issued a writ and sought interlocutory relief restraining the defendant from presenting a petition. The trial judge found that there was a bona fide dispute whether the defendant was a creditor for a sum presently due and granted an injunction restraining the defendant from presenting a petition in respect of the alleged debt provided that, within three weeks, the directors of the plaintiff company made a declaration of solvency of the company. The company successfully appealed.

> BUCKLEY LJ: . . . The relevant statutory provisions are contained in sections 222, 223 and 224 of the Companies Act 1948 [IA 1986 ss 122, 123 and 124]. Section 222, as is very familiar, provides that a company may be wound up by the court if '(e) the company is unable to pay its debts.' Section 223 provides that a company shall be deemed to be unable to pay its debts if, among other things, a creditor to whom the company is indebted in a sum exceeding £50 [now £750] then due—and I emphasise those last two words—has served a statutory demand upon the company and the company has failed for three weeks to comply with it. That provision has no application to a case in which the creditor is a creditor in respect of a sum which is not presently due . . .
>
> . . . [I]n my opinion, the expression 'contingent creditor' means a creditor in respect of a debt which will only become due in an event which may or may not occur; and a 'prospective creditor' is a creditor in respect of a debt which will certainly become due in the future, either on some date which has been already determined or on some date determinable by reference to future events.
>
> Where a creditor petitions for the winding up of a company, the proceedings will take one of two courses, depending upon whether the petitioner is a creditor whose debt is presently due, or one whose debt is contingent or prospective . . . If the creditor petitions in respect of a debt which he claims to be presently due, and that claim is undisputed, the petition proceeds to hearing and adjudication in the normal way; but if the company in good faith and on substantial grounds disputes any liability in respect of the alleged debt, the petition will be dismissed or, if the matter is brought before a court before the petition is issued, its presentation will in normal circumstances be restrained. That is because a winding up petition is not a legitimate means of seeking to enforce payment of a debt which is bona fide disputed.
>
> Ungoed-Thomas J. put the matter thus in *Mann v Goldstein* [1968] 1 WLR 1091, 1098–1099:
>
> 'For my part, I would prefer to rest the jurisdiction directly on the comparatively simple propositions that a creditor's petition can only be presented by a creditor, that the winding up jurisdiction is not for the purpose of deciding a disputed debt (that is, disputed on substantial and not insubstantial grounds), since, until a creditor is established as a creditor he is not entitled to present the petition and has no locus standi in the Companies Court; and that, therefore, to invoke the winding up jurisdiction when the debt is disputed (that is,

on substantial grounds) or after it has become clear that it is so disputed is an abuse of the process of the court.'

I gratefully adopt the whole of that statement, although I think it could equally well have ended at the reference to want of locus standi. In my opinion a petition founded on a debt which is disputed in good faith and on substantial grounds is demurrable for the reason that the petitioner is not a creditor of the company within the meaning of section 224(1) at all, and the question whether he is or is not a creditor of the company is not appropriate for adjudication in winding up proceedings.

The circumstances may, however, be such that the company adopts an intermediate position, denying that the debt is presently due but not denying that it will or may become due in the future—in other words, accepting it as a contingent or prospective debt. The present case is of the last-mentioned kind and the present appeal involves consideration of what is proper in such a case.

. . . The company now admits that the defendant is a contingent creditor at any rate in a sum of £33,000, but not that any part of that sum is immediately due . . . and the defendant now accepts that there is a bona fide dispute as to whether any part of the £33,000 is now due, and he further admits that in so far as the debt is contingent, the relevant contingency may never happen. So the situation is such that the defendant cannot petition to wind the company up on the basis that he is a debtor for a sum which is presently due [ie via the statutory demand that had been issued], because that position is disputed in good faith and on substantial grounds; but he is competent to petition as a contingent creditor . . .

If the only established footing upon which the defendant can petition to wind up the company is as a contingent or prospective creditor, the burden rests on him to show prima facie that there is a case for winding up the company . . . If the ground for seeking a winding up order is that the company is unable to pay its debts—and no other ground is suggested here—it would be incumbent on the defendant to establish a prima facie case that this was so. The condition [imposed in the trial judge's injunction, requiring the directors to make a declaration of solvency] seems to me to reverse this burden of proof, for if the condition is not complied with it would be open to the defendant as a petitioner to rely upon that fact as some evidence of the company's inability to pay its debts; and moreover, having regard to the nature of the declaration of solvency . . . the condition imposes upon the company, through its directors, a heavier burden of proof than the burden of establishing merely that the company is not commercially solvent; it imposes the burden of proof of establishing that the company will ultimately be solvent on the basis of a prospective liquidation within 12 months. It seems to me that such a condition cannot be supported in principle . . .

The whole of the doctrine of this part of the law is based upon the view that winding up proceedings are not suitable proceedings in which to determine a genuine dispute about whether the company does or does not owe the sum in question; and equally I think it must be true that winding up proceedings are not suitable proceedings in which to determine whether that liability is an immediate liability or only a prospective or contingent liability . . .

GOFF LJ and SIR DAVID CAIRNS delivered concurring judgments.

➤ Notes

1. Exceptional circumstances may, however, justify the making of a winding-up order even if the debt is bona fide disputed. See the judgment of Warren J in *Lacontha Foundation v GBI Investments Ltd* [2010] EWHC 37 (Ch), where this exception is summarised:

84. The law today, which I regard as clear, is that there is no absolute jurisdictional bar to a petition being allowed to proceed, or indeed the making of winding-up order, where the debt on which the petition is founded is *bona fide* disputed on substantial grounds.

85. However, before the Companies Court will make a winding-up order or even allow a petition to proceed where the debt is *bona fide* disputed on substantial grounds, there have to be exceptional circumstances. The Privy Council in *Parmalat*[48] declined to give any guidance on the limits of the discretion. But some guidance can be obtained from two other authorities.

86. The first is *Claybridge*,[49] where a departure from the usual rule was said to be justified where the company was a foreign company and the petitioner would otherwise be without a remedy or otherwise injustice would result or for some other sufficient reason the petition should proceed.

. . .

88. The second authority is *Alipour v Ary*.[50] In that case, the company was a foreign company. The petitioner originally claimed to be the registered holder of 10 shares in a foreign company and subsequently wished to claim instead to be the original allottee of the shares having accepted that his claim to be a registered shareholder could not be maintained. The court summarised the position in this way:

> 'The position as we see it, in the light of the authorities as affected by the current procedures of the Companies Court, is this. (1) A creditor's petition based on a disputed debt will normally be dismissed. (2) It will not be dismissed if the petitioning creditor has a good arguable case that he is a creditor and the effect of dismissal would be to deprive the petitioner of a remedy or otherwise injustice would result or for some other sufficient reason the petition should proceed. (3) On a contributory's petition where the *locus standi* of the petitioner is disputed, the court will consider all the circumstances, including the likelihood of damage to the company if the petition is not dismissed, in determining whether to require the petitioner to seek the determination of the dispute outside the petition.'

2. Deciding when a company is unable to pay its debts can be difficult. There are deeming provisions in s 123(1)(a)–(d), a 'cash-flow' test (used to examine the short-term future of the company) in s 123(1)(e), and a 'balance-sheet' test (used to examine the long term prospects of the company) in s 123(2). On s 123(2), the Supreme Court in *BNY Corporate Trustee Services Ltd v Eurosail-UK 2007-3BL plc* [2013] UKSC 28, at [48], has insisted that the words of the section (requiring the petitioner to satisfy the court, on the balance of probabilities, that the company has insufficient assets to be able to meet all its liabilities, including prospective and contingent liabilities) should not be paraphrased as a ' "point of no return" (test reached by a company) because of an incurable deficiency in its assets'.[51] And in *Bucci v Carman (Liquidator of Casa Estates (UK) Ltd)* [2014] EWCA Civ 383, elaborating on the test in *Eurosail*, Lewison LJ (at [29]) held that the balance-sheet test 'is not excluded merely because a company is for the time being in fact paying its debts as they fall due', and that 'the two tests feature as part of a single exercise, namely to determine whether a company is unable to pay its debts.'

Compulsory winding up on the 'just and equitable' ground

Members are entitled, as 'contributories', to petition for the compulsory winding up of the company (IA 1986 s 124). They are not restricted to using the 'just and equitable' ground[52]

---

[48] [2008] UKPC 23.
[49] [1997] 1 BCLC 572, CA.
[50] [1997] 1 WLR 534.
[51] The test advocated in the Court of Appeal: [2011] EWCA Civ 227, CA, [47]–[49] (Lord Neuberger MR).
[52] On the 'just and equitable' ground generally, see BH McPherson, 'Winding Up on the Just and Equitable Ground' (1964) 27 MLR 282, suggesting that the decided cases fall into three broad categories: (i) where it initially

(and nor is this ground restricted to members), but this is the one most commonly used by members who find themselves unable to proceed on the basis of a special resolution for the voluntary winding up of the company (IA 1986 s 84(1)(b)).

A company formed for a fraudulent purpose may be wound up on the 'just and equitable' ground.

[16.10] Re Thomas Edward Brinsmead & Sons [1897] 1 Ch 406 (Court of Appeal)

Three men named Brinsmead, former employees of John Brinsmead & Sons, the well-known piano makers, formed the present company to make pianos which were to be passed off as the product of the older established firm. An injunction had been obtained, restraining the company from this action; but meantime shares in the company worth many thousands of pounds had been subscribed for by the public in a promotion fraud instigated by the Consolidated Contract Corporation. On this evidence, it was held to be just and equitable to grant a winding-up order.

> The judgment of the court (LINDLEY, AL SMITH and RIGBY LJJ) was read by AL SMITH LJ: In our judgment it has been proved that this company—ie Thomas Edward Brinsmead & Sons Limited—was initiated to carry out a fraud, and that, until restrained by injunction, it continued therein; and that a strong prima facie case has been made out that the Consolidated Contract Corporation are at the present moment dishonestly keeping the shareholders' money to which the shareholders, and not they, are entitled, and are resisting the petition to wind up in order to continue to do so. If the sums which they have improperly obtained from the company can be recovered from them, there will probably be something to distribute among the shareholders and, although the petitioner is a fully paid-up shareholder, he cannot be said to have no locus standi. The company is hopelessly embarrassed by the actions already brought against it, and there will, no doubt, be many more of the same sort if this petition is dismissed; and if it is not wound up the £35,000 obtained from it by its promoters will remain in their hands.
>
> Although the words 'just and equitable' have had a narrow construction put upon them,[53] they have never been construed so narrowly as to exclude such a case as this. If ever there was a case in which it was just and equitable that a company should be wound up by the court, we cannot doubt that the case is this case. For the reasons above, we dismiss this appeal with costs.

➤ Note

The entire scheme for the company must be fraudulent in order to justify liquidation under this principle. Usually if the company itself has been defrauded, or if subscribers for shares have been misled or defrauded, these parties must simply apply for a remedy against the wrongdoer; the company will not be wound up.

---

is, or later becomes, impossible to achieve the objects for which the company was formed; (ii) where it has become impossible for the company to carry on its business; and (iii) where there has been serious fraud, misconduct or oppression in regard to the affairs of the company.

53 This narrow construction was later rejected: see the *Ebrahimi* case [16.13].

It is just and equitable to wind up a company when its 'substratum' or principal object has failed.

[16.11] Re Kitson & Co Ltd [1946] 1 All ER 435 (Court of Appeal)

The company was incorporated in 1899. The first two sub-clauses of the objects clause in its memorandum read as follows:

(i)   To acquire and take over as a going concern the business now carried on at Airedale Foundry, Hunslet, in the city of Leeds, under the style or firm of 'Kitson & Co', and all or any of the assets and liabilities . . .

(ii) To carry on the business of locomotive engine manufacturers, iron-founders, mechanical engineers and manufacturers of agricultural implements and other machinery, tool makers, brass founders, metal workers, boiler makers . . .

In July 1945, the company agreed to sell the goodwill and assets of the engineering business which was carried on at the Airedale foundry, and acquire the assets of a subsidiary ('Balmforth') and to continue an engineering business. It was held that the substratum had not gone.

LORD GREENE MR: [The] form of the memorandum is the common form where a business is being acquired. It sets out in the usual way the acquisition of the business as the first step which the company is going to undertake. We are not considering now whether failure in 1899 to acquire the business of Kitson & Co would have destroyed the substratum of the company. It might possibly have been thought that unless it got this business it was not really starting its career in the way in which the shareholders bargained it should be started; but the question we have to decide is whether, that business having been acquired, forty-six years ago, the disposal of it last year amounted to a destruction of the substratum. In my opinion, the main and paramount object of this company was to carry on an engineering business of a general kind. It was such a business that was carried on by Kitson & Co, and I cannot bring myself to construe this memorandum as limiting the paramount object and restricting the contemplated adventure of the shareholders to the carrying on of what could be called the business of Kitson & Co. The impossibility of applying such a construction seems to me to be manifest when one remembers that a business is a thing which changes. It grows or it contracts. It changes; it disposes of the whole of its plant; it moves its factory; it entirely changes its range of products, and so forth. It is more like an organic thing. Counsel for the respondents quoted to us a number of very well-known authorities on which it has been held that on particular facts the substratum of particular companies had gone. I do not propose to examine those authorities because they do not assist me in construing this particular memorandum. It must be remembered in these substratum cases that there is every difference between a company which on the true construction of its memorandum is formed for the paramount purpose of dealing with some specific subject-matter and a company which is formed with wider and more comprehensive objects. I will explain what I mean. With regard to a company which is formed to acquire and exploit a mine, when you come to construe its memorandum of association you must construe the language used in reference to the subject-matter, namely, a mine, and, accordingly, if the mine cannot be acquired or if the mine turns out to be no mine at all, the object of the company is frustrated, because the subject-matter which the company was formed to exploit has ceased to exist. It is exactly the same way with a patent, as in the well-known *German Date Coffee* case.[54] A patent is a defined subject-matter, and, if the main object of a company is

---

[54] *Re German Date Coffee Co* (1882) 20 Ch D 169, CA.

to acquire and work a patent and it fails to acquire that patent, to compel the shareholders to remain bound together in order to work some other patent or make some unpatented article is to force them into a different adventure to that which they contracted to engage in together; but, when you come to subject-matter of a totally different kind like the carrying on of a type of business, then, so long as the company can carry on that type of business, it seems to me that prima facie at any rate it is impossible to say that its substratum has gone. So far as this stage of the argument is concerned, it is to my mind quite impossible upon the true construction of this memorandum of association to limit the paramount object of this company to the specific business of Kitson & Co, so as to lead to the result that as soon as Kitson & Co's business was sold the substratum of the company had gone . . .

MORTON and TUCKER LJJ delivered concurring judgments.

> Note

In *Re Tivoli Freeholds Ltd* [1972] VR 445 (SC Vic) a winding-up petition was granted on the just and equitable ground. The main objects of the company had been to own and build theatres and to carry on theatrical and similar entertainment businesses. An outside group acquired control of the company and, having realised nearly all of its assets, used the funds so raised to mount corporate raids on other firms. (These activities were quite profitable and dividends were regularly paid on the strength of the profits, so an alternative petition based on alleged oppression of the minority members (see 'Unfairly prejudicial conduct of the company's affairs', pp 715ff) was rejected by the judge.) Although it was not contended that the company could not, if it chose, have continued to pursue its original objects, the court accepted that the evidence showed that the business for which the company was formed had been conclusively abandoned, and granted relief on a basis analogous to a failure of substratum.

It is just and equitable to wind up a company when there is a complete deadlock in the management.

What is meant by 'deadlock' is not completely clear from the cases. Deadlock requires at least an impasse in the corporate decision-making process. But in most cases the courts will hold that there is no deadlock if a legal means exists to get decisions made, using some procedure under either the company's constitution or the general law. On the other hand, in quasi-partnerships, it may be unjust or inequitable to leave one faction to exercise its legal rights over the other (see the *Ebrahimi* case **[16.13]**).

It is just and equitable to wind up a company where there is such a justifiable (and, it seems, insoluble) lack of confidence in the management of the company's affairs that it is unjust and inequitable to require the petitioner to remain a member.

[16.12] Loch v John Blackwood Ltd [1924] AC 783 (Privy Council)

The engineering business of John Blackwood had, after his death, been formed into a company and run by one of his trustees, McLaren, for the benefit of the three beneficiaries in his estate: McLaren's wife (who was to take one-half), Mrs Loch (one-quarter) and Rodger (since deceased, one-quarter). The business had been run very profitably by McLaren, but (as is described in the judgment) he had run it in a manner which was oppressive to the beneficiaries other than his wife. They accordingly petitioned for the winding up of the company on the ground that it was just and equitable to do so. The

Chief Justice of Barbados made an order, which was reversed by the West Indian Court of Appeal but restored by the Privy Council. The remaining facts appear from the judgment.

The opinion of the Privy Council was delivered by LORD SHAW OF DUNFERMLINE: The board of directors now consists of Mr McLaren, his wife Mrs McLaren, who was appointed in 1913, and Mr Yearwood. Under this directorate the business of the company appears to have been energetically managed and to have amassed considerable profits.

The arrangement of the capital was this: the total amount was 40,000 in £1 shares; 20,000 of these were allotted to Mrs McLaren; of the remaining 20,000, 10,000 should have gone to Mrs Loch and 10,000 to Mr Rodger. Mrs Loch, however, was allotted 9,999; Mr Rodger, 9,998; and the three shares left over were allotted one to Mr McLaren and one each to Mr Yearwood and Mr King (Mrs McLaren's nominees; the first being Mr McLaren's clerk and the second his solicitor). This was quite a natural and proper arrangement; but, of course, in the event of a division of opinion in the family between what may be called the McLaren interest on the one hand, and the interest of the nephew and niece on the other, the preponderance of voting power lay with the former. It is thus seen that although taking the form of a public company the concern was practically a domestic and family concern. This consideration is important,[55] as also is the preponderance of voting power just alluded to.

In the petition for winding up eight different reasons are assigned therefor. The first is: that the statutory conditions as to general meetings have not been observed; the second that balance-sheets, profit and loss accounts and reports have not been submitted in terms of the articles of the company; and the third is that the conditions under the statute and articles as to audit have not been complied with. All these allegations are true, and it seems naturally to follow from the preponderance already alluded to, that there is at least considerable force in the fifth reason that it is impossible for the petitioners to obtain any relief by calling a general meeting of the company. There are further submissions—namely, that the company and the managing director, Mr McLaren, have refused to submit the value of the shares to arbitration, and that without winding up it is impossible for the petitioners to realise the true value of their shares. But the principal ground of the petitioner is that in the circumstances to be laid before the court it is just and equitable that the company should be ordered to be wound up. This last ground was affirmed by the Court of Common Pleas.

With regard to the first three submissions made in the petition, it was strenuously argued on behalf of the company, which practically means the directorate or the McLaren interest, that however true it might be that owing to the informal way in which the books of the company had been kept it appeared as if both the statute and the articles of association had been violated in various particulars and that no general meetings of the company had been held, and no auditors properly appointed, and it was certain that no balance-sheets, profit and loss accounts and reports had been submitted for the critical years 1919 and 1920, still these were no grounds for winding up. Other applications, it was said, might competently be made to the court to compel the statute and articles to be properly complied with. It may be doubtful whether such a course of conduct lasting in several particulars since its inception until now, would be insufficient as a ground for winding the company up. But their Lordships think it unnecessary to give any separate decision upon such a point.

In their opinion, however, elements of that character in the history of the company, together with the fact that a calling of a meeting of shareholders would lead admittedly to failure and be unavailable as a remedy, cannot be excluded from the point of view of the court in a consideration of the justice and equity of pronouncing an order for winding up. Such a consideration, in

---

[55] Although an important factor, it is probably not vital. In some jurisdictions overseas it has been held that the principle is not confined to domestic companies: see *Re Wondoflex Textiles Pty Ltd* [1951] VLR 458; *Palermo v Palermo (No 2)* [2014] WASC 6; *Re RJ Jowsey Mining Co Ltd* [1969] 2 OR 549.

their Lordships' view, ought to proceed upon a sound induction of all the facts of the case, and should not exclude, but should include circumstances which bear upon the problem of continuing or stopping courses of conduct which substantially impair those rights and protections to which shareholders, both under statute and contract, are entitled. It is undoubtedly true that at the foundation of applications for winding up, on the 'just and equitable' rule, there must lie a justifiable lack of confidence in the conduct and management of the company's affairs. But this lack of confidence must be grounded on conduct of the directors, not in regard to their private life or affairs, but in regard to the company's business.[56] Furthermore the lack of confidence must spring not from dissatisfaction at being outvoted on the business affairs or on what is called the domestic policy of the company. On the other hand, wherever the lack of confidence is rested on a lack of probity in the conduct of the company's affairs, then the former is justified by the latter, and it is under the statute just and equitable that the company be wound up . . .

Mr McLaren, for reasons not unnatural, had come to be of opinion that the business owed much of its value and prosperity to himself. But he appears to have proceeded to the further stage of feeling that in these circumstances he could manage the business as if it were his own. Had Mrs Loch and Mr Rodger, or after his death Mr Rodger's executor, obtained a dividend which year by year represented in any reasonable measure a just declaration out of the undoubted profits of the concern, they might no doubt have been content to allow this state of matters to go on; but although on one or two occasions, Mr McLaren paid trifling and fragmentary sums to Mrs Loch, neither she nor the Rodger family have ever obtained any dividend at all. And it is not to be wondered at that in the transaction now about to be mentioned they completely lost confidence in Mr McLaren, and had only too great justification for doing so . . .

[His Lordship then referred to a decision of the directors to pay McLaren an increased salary and to transfer to him £12,500 War Loan stock, and continued:] No notice was given to the respondents, as shareholders, of this piece of business being contemplated, and no notice was given of what had been done. Four days after this extraordinary transaction, Mr McLaren wrote to Mrs Loch's husband a letter dated 5 May 1920 proposing to her that £10,000 should be given by him as the cumulative value of Mrs Loch's shares and Mr JB Rodger's executor's shares. These shares in all amounted to one-half of the capital of the company—namely, £20,000—and, as already mentioned, it is evident that the true value of assets much exceeded this amount. The proposal was to buy Mrs Loch and the Rodger family out for £10,000. But a further suggestion, which in some ways seems to have been mixed up with the umbrage felt by Mr McLaren in regard to the contents of Mr Rodger's will, was made, and that was that Mrs Loch should be a participant in a scheme whereby the £10,000 to be paid should be distributed—£8,000 to herself and only £2,000 to the Rodgers family.

Their Lordships do not desire to characterise these suggestions in the language which perhaps they fully deserve. The Rodger family, entitled to one-fourth of the holding in the company, nominally £10,000, but in reality of a much higher value, were to be bought off for £2,000, and Mrs Loch was to be the agent in this scheme. No confidence in the directorate could survive such a proposal. To crown all this, as was afterwards discovered, the £10,000 could be comfortably paid by Mr McLaren out of the £12,500 which, four days before, he and his wife and clerk had voted to himself out of the funds of the company. Their Lordships express no surprise at the instant repudiation of Mr McLaren's proposals by Mrs Loch—a repudiation which is creditable to her—and at the application for a winding up of the company being made. Upon the principles already set forth in this judgment that application must succeed. The broad ground is that confidence in its management was, and is, and that most justifiably, at an end . . .

---

[56] Later cases, particularly those in which there has been a breakdown of personal relationships between the parties (eg a husband and wife who have divorced), seem to adopt a less restrictive approach: see, eg, *Belman v Belman* (1995) 26 OR (3d) 56, and cf the remarks of Lord Wilberforce in the *Ebrahimi* case [16.13], 'any circumstances of justice or equity which affect him in his relations . . . with the other shareholders'.

➤ Notes

1. In *Re RA Noble & Sons (Clothing) Ltd* [1983] BCLC 273, Nourse J held that, so long as the conduct of those in control has been 'the substantial cause' of the destruction of the mutual confidence between the parties, it is unnecessary to show either that that conduct has been in some way underhand or that the petitioner's own conduct has been above reproach. The Privy Council took a similar view in *Vujnovich v Vujnovich* [1990] BCLC 227.

2. But note that the court has a discretion under IA 1986 s 125(2) to refuse an order on the 'just and equitable' ground if the petitioner is acting unreasonably in seeking to have the company wound up instead of pursuing some other remedy. In *Re a Company* [1983] 1 WLR 927, Vinelott J held that a petitioner had acted unreasonably in refusing an offer made by the majority members to buy his shares, following a breakdown of confidence, and refused him a winding-up order. That case may be contrasted with *Virdi v Abbey Leisure Ltd* [1990] BCLC 342, CA, where the court exercised its discretion in the petitioner's favour on a similar issue.

It may be just and equitable to wind up a company where one party has simply exercised his or her legal rights, but in an unjust or inequitable way.

[16.13] Ebrahimi v Westbourne Galleries Ltd [1973] AC 360 (House of Lords)

This is probably the most cited case in this area. The company was formed in 1958 to take over a business which Nazar and Ebrahimi had run in partnership for over a decade. At first, the two were equal shareholders and the only directors, but soon afterwards Nazar's son joined the company as a director and shareholder, so that Ebrahimi found himself in a minority position both on the board of directors and at a general meeting. In 1969, after some disagreement between the parties, an ordinary resolution was passed under s 184 of the Act of 1948 [CA 2006 s 168], removing Ebrahimi as director. Ebrahimi sought relief under s 210, or, alternatively, s 222(f) of the 1948 Act [respectively CA 2006 s 994 and IA 1986 s 122(1)(g)]. Plowman J declined to make an order under s 210 because (inter alia) Ebrahimi's complaint was in his capacity as director rather than as member (see 'Members' personal rights', pp 261ff); but he did make a winding-up order. The Court of Appeal reversed the latter ruling, holding that the exercise by a majority of its constitutional and statutory rights, unless shown to be *mala fide*, was not a ground for 'just and equitable' relief under s 222(f). The House of Lords restored the decision of the trial judge.

LORD WILBERFORCE: My Lords, the petition was brought under s 222(f) of the Companies Act 1948 [IA 1986 s 122(1)(g)], which enables a winding-up order to be made if 'the court is of the opinion that it is just and equitable that the company should be wound up'. This power has existed in our company law in unaltered form since the first major Act, the Companies Act 1862. For some fifty years, following a pronouncement by Lord Cottenham LC in 1849, the words 'just and equitable' were interpreted so as only to include matters *ejusdem generis* as the preceding clauses of the section, but there is now ample authority for discarding this limitation. There are two other restrictive interpretations which I mention to reject. First, there has been a tendency to create categories or headings under which cases must be brought if the clause is to apply. This is wrong. Illustrations may be used, but general words should remain general and not be reduced to the sum of particular instances. Secondly, it has been suggested, and urged upon us, that (assuming the petitioner is a shareholder and not a creditor) the words must be confined to such circumstances as affect him in his capacity as shareholder. I see no warrant for this either. No doubt, in order to present a petition, he must qualify as a shareholder, but I see no reason for preventing him from relying upon any circumstances of justice or equity which affect him in his relations with the company, or, in a case such as the present, with the other shareholders.

One other signpost is significant. The same words 'just and equitable' appear in the Partnership Act 1890, s 35, as a ground for dissolution of a partnership and no doubt the considerations which they reflect formed part of the common law of partnership before its codification. The importance of this is to provide a bridge between cases under s 222(f) of the Act of 1948 and the principles of equity developed in relation to partnerships.

The winding-up order was made following a doctrine which has developed in the courts since the beginning of this century. As presented by the appellant, and in substance accepted by the learned judge, this was that in a case such as this the members of the company are in substance partners, or quasi-partners, and that a winding up may be ordered if such facts are shown as could justify a dissolution of partnership between them. The common use of the words 'just and equitable' in the company and partnership law supports this approach. Your Lordships were invited by the respondents' counsel to restate the principle on which this provision ought to be used; it has not previously been considered by this House. The main line of his submission was to suggest that too great a use of the partnership analogy had been made; that a limited company, however small, essentially differs from a partnership; that in the case of a company, the rights of its members are governed by the articles of association which have contractual force; that the court has no power or at least ought not to dispense parties from observing their contracts; that, in particular, when one member has been excluded from the directorate, or management, under powers expressly conferred by the Companies Act and the articles, an order for winding up, whether on the partnership analogy or under the just and equitable provision, should not be made. Alternatively, it was argued that before the making of such an order could be considered the petitioner must show and prove that the exclusion was not made bona fide in the interests of the company.

[His Lordship discussed a number of earlier cases and continued:] My Lords, in my opinion these authorities represent a sound and rational development of the law which should be endorsed. The foundation of it all lies in the words 'just and equitable' and, if there is any respect in which some of the cases may be open to criticism, it is that the courts may sometimes have been too timorous in giving them full force. The words are a recognition of the fact that a limited company is more than a mere legal entity, with a personality in law of its own: that there is room in company law for recognition of the fact that behind it, or amongst it, there are individuals, with rights, expectations and obligations inter se which are not necessarily submerged in the company structure. That structure is defined by the Companies Act and by the articles of association by which shareholders agree to be bound. In most companies and in most contexts, this definition is sufficient and exhaustive, equally so whether the company is large or small. The 'just and equitable' provision does not, as the respondents suggest, entitle one party to disregard the obligation he assumed by entering a company, nor the court to dispense him from it. It does, as equity always does, enable the court to subject the exercise of legal rights to equitable considerations, considerations, that is, of a personal character arising between one individual and another, which may make it unjust, or inequitable, to insist on legal rights, or to exercise them in a particular way.

It would be impossible, and wholly undesirable, to define the circumstances in which these considerations may arise. Certainly the fact that a company is a small one, or a private company, is not enough. There are very many of these where the association is a purely commercial one, of which it can safely be said that the basis of association is adequately and exhaustively laid down in the articles. The superimposition of equitable considerations requires something more, which typically may include one, or probably more, of the following elements: (i) an association formed or continued on the basis of a personal relationship, involving mutual confidence—this element will often be found where a pre-existing partnership has been converted into a limited company; (ii) an agreement, or understanding, that all, or some (for there may be 'sleeping' members), of the shareholders shall participate in the conduct of the business; (iii) restriction upon the transfer of the members' interest in the company—so that if confidence is lost, or one member is removed from management, he cannot take out his stake and go elsewhere.

It is these, and analogous, factors which may bring into play the just and equitable clause, and they do so directly, through the force of the words themselves. To refer, as so many of the cases do, to 'quasi-partnerships' or 'in substance partnerships' may be convenient but may also be confusing. It may be convenient because it is the law of partnership which has developed the conceptions of probity, good faith and mutual confidence, and the remedies where these are absent, which become relevant once such factors as I have mentioned are found to exist: the words 'just and equitable' sum these up in the law of partnership itself. And in many, but not necessarily all, cases there has been a pre-existing partnership the obligations of which it is reasonable to suppose continue to underlie the new company structure. But the expressions may be confusing if they obscure, or deny, the fact that the parties (possibly former partners) are now co-members in a company, who have accepted, in law, new obligations. A company, however small, however domestic, is a company, not a partnership or even a quasi-partnership and it is through the just and equitable clause that obligations, common to partnership relations, may come in.

My Lords, this is an expulsion case, and I must briefly justify the application in such cases of the just and equitable clause. The question is, as always, whether it is equitable to allow one (or two) to make use of his legal rights to the prejudice of his associate(s). The law of companies recognises the right, in many ways, to remove a director from the board. Section 184 of the Companies Act 1948 [CA 2006 s 168] confers this right upon the company in general meeting whatever the articles may say. Some articles may prescribe other methods: for example, a governing director may have the power to remove (compare *Re Wondoflex Textiles Pty Ltd*).[57] And quite apart from removal powers, there are normally provisions for retirement of directors by rotation so that their re-election can be opposed and defeated by a majority, or even by a casting vote. In all these ways a particular director-member may find himself no longer a director, through removal, or non-re-election: this situation he must normally accept, unless he undertakes the burden of proving fraud or mala fides. The just and equitable provision nevertheless comes to his assistance if he can point to, and prove, some special underlying obligation of his fellow member(s) in good faith, or confidence, that so long as the business continues he shall be entitled to management participation, an obligation so basic that, if broken, the conclusion must be that the association must be dissolved . . .

I come to the facts of this case. It is apparent enough that a potential basis for a winding-up order under the just and equitable clause existed. The appellant after a long association in partnership, during which he had an equal share in the management, joined in the formation of the company. The inference must be indisputable that he, and Mr Nazar, did so on the basis that the character of the association would, as a matter of personal relation and good faith, remain the same. He was removed from his directorship under a power valid in law. Did he establish a case which, if he had remained in a partnership with a term providing for expulsion, would have

---

[57] [1951] VLR 458.

justified an order for dissolution? This was the essential question for the judge. Plowman J dealt with the issue in a brief paragraph in which he said: 'while no doubt the petitioner was lawfully removed, in the sense that he ceased in law to be a director, it does not follow that in removing him the respondents did not do him a wrong. In my judgment, they did do him a wrong, in the sense that it was an abuse of power and a breach of the good faith which partners owe to each other to exclude one of them from all participation in the business upon which they have embarked on the basis that all should participate in its management. The main justification put forward for removing him was that he was perpetually complaining, but the faults were not all on one side and, in my judgment, this is not sufficient justification. For these reasons, in my judgment, the petitioner, therefore, has made out a case for a winding-up order.' Reading this in the context of the judgment as a whole, which had dealt with the specific complaints of one side against the other, I take it as a finding that the respondents were not entitled, in justice and equity, to make use of their legal powers of expulsion and that...the only just and equitable course was to dissolve the association . . .

LORD CROSS OF CHELSEA delivered a concurring opinion.

VISCOUNT DILHORNE, LORD PEARSON and LORD SALMON concurred.

➤ Notes

1. The *Ebrahimi* case **[16.13]** makes it clear that it may be just and equitable to wind up a company even though the controllers have acted within their strict legal rights.

2. The *Ebrahimi* case also makes it clear that it may be just and equitable to wind up a company when the complaint relates to behaviour that is contrary to the settled and accepted course of conduct between the parties, whether or not reinforced by contract or by the articles.

3. Many of the previous cases, especially the earlier ones, in which a winding-up order was made on the 'just and equitable' ground, might now be more appropriately made the subject of proceedings under CA 2006 s 994 (discussed at 'Unfairly prejudicial conduct of the company's affairs', pp 715ff). On the other hand, there are modern quasi-partnership cases where the courts refuse to find prejudicial conduct (under CA 1985 s 459, the predecessor of CA 2006 s 994), but will order a just and equitable winding up: for example, *Re RA Noble (Clothing) Ltd* [1983] BCLC 273.

4. *Hawkes v Cuddy* [2009] EWCA Civ 291 makes it clear that the winding-up and unfair prejudice jurisdictions overlap but are not identical.

➤ Question

In *Re Yenidje Tobacco Co Ltd* [1916] 2 Ch 426, CA, the Court of Appeal held that it was just and equitable to wind up a quasi-partnership company where there were sufficiently serious breaches of mutual understanding. The company had been formed by two tobacco manufacturers, Rothman and Weinberg, in order to amalgamate their businesses. They were the only members, with equal voting rights, and the only directors. The parties had been in a state of continuous quarrel for some time. Rothman had brought an action against Weinberg alleging fraud; they had spent over £1,000 (a substantial sum at the time) in litigation over the validity of the dismissal of a factory manager; had argued over the terms of employment of a traveller; and had been communicating with each other only through the secretary of the company. In this situation (despite the fact that the company was making larger profits than ever before), the court granted a winding-up order on Weinberg's petition. Would this case now be dealt with under CA 2006 s 994? What are the advantages and disadvantages of each option?

The courts' discretion to order a compulsory winding up

Once the petitioner has established the right to bring a petition, and proved the grounds alleged, the court has to decide whether or not to make the order to wind up the company. Normally their decision will follow from proof of the elements of the claim, but it is worth noting that:

(i)   On a member's or contributory's petition, the court has a statutory discretion to refuse the petition if some other remedy is available to the petitioners *and* it seems that the petitioners are acting unreasonably in seeking to have the company wound up rather than relying on that other remedy (IA 1986 s 125(2)). The court is frequently asked to exercise this discretion where minority shareholders seek an order on the grounds of 'unfair prejudice' (CA 2006 s 994, see 'Unfairly prejudicial conduct of the company's affairs', pp 715ff) and, alternatively, a winding up on the 'just and equitable' ground.

(ii) The court has an inherent jurisdiction to refuse a winding-up order brought for extraneous or improper purposes. In *Re Surrey Garden Village Trust Ltd* [1965] 1 WLR 974, Ch, Plowman J said '. . . I go further and say that in my judgment it is oppressive and an abuse of the process of the court for shareholders to make use of a winding-up petition for the purpose of seeking to facilitate the achievement of a purely sectional and extraneous object which . . . has no relevance to the interests of the members as such . . .'. Similarly, in *Re JE Cade & Sons Ltd* [1992] BCLC 213, a minority member owned the freehold of a farm which had been occupied under licence by the company for some years. He sought a winding-up order on the 'just and equitable' ground or, alternatively, relief under CA 1985 s 459 (CA 2006 s 994); but the court struck out his petition because his real object in bringing the proceedings was not to protect his interests as a member but to secure possession of the farm.

(iii) Finally, the court has an inherent jurisdiction to strike out a petition for winding up which is bound to fail, as an abuse of the process of the court, and it may grant an injunction to restrain the presentation of such a petition (see *Charles Forte Investments Ltd v Amanda* [1964] Ch 240, CA, where Amanda was attempting to use the winding-up procedure as a means of putting pressure on the directors to register certain share transfers; and compare *Amanda* with *Ebbvale Ltd v Hosking* [2013] UKPC 1 where the Privy Council distinguished the *Amanda* line of cases on the ground that the petitioner in *Ebbvale did* want the company to be wound up).

By invoking these statutory and inherent jurisdictions to have petitions dismissed, a company may avoid the unfavourable publicity that a winding-up petition inevitably attracts.

The functions, powers and duties of the liquidator

The basic duty of the liquidator is to wind up the company's affairs, collect in and realise the company's assets and undertaking, and make the appropriate distributions to the creditors and, if there is a surplus, to the shareholders.

The rules governing the functions, powers and duties of a liquidator are partly set out in IA 1986 and IR 1986, and partly established by the case law. The Act now makes it obligatory for a liquidator to be a qualified insolvency practitioner (s 230(3)). In a compulsory liquidation, the liquidator is also an officer of the court.

A liquidator acts in the name of the company (which continues to have a separate corporate personality) and not in his own name (except where he is exercising certain special statutory powers), although sometimes, exceptionally, an order of the court is sought vesting all or part of the company's property in the liquidator's name (IA 1986 s 145). This might be necessary, for example, to deal with the local assets of a foreign company which had already been dissolved in its home jurisdiction. Although a liquidator acts in the company's name and not in his own name, he can sometimes incur personal liability, for example where he institutes proceedings and the costs exceed the amount of the company's assets: *Re Wilson Lovatt & Sons Ltd* [1977] 1 All ER 274.

A liquidator owes his duties to the company, not to individual creditors or contributories (*Knowles v Scott* [1891] 1 Ch 717). He may be personally liable for breach of duty, and sued in misfeasance proceedings under IA 1986 s 212, if he:

(i) fails to comply with the strict statutory terms of his office (eg in wrongly admitting a claim by an alleged creditor: *Re Home and Colonial Insurance Co Ltd* [1930] 1 Ch 102; or in distributing the company's assets properly among the persons entitled: *Pulsford v Devenish* [1903] 2 Ch 625);

(ii) performs his functions negligently (*Re Windsor Steam Coal Co (1901) Ltd* [1928] Ch 609); or

(iii) breaches his fiduciary duties to the company by taking secret profits or placing himself in positions of conflict.

Certain statutory powers of a liquidator are conferred by IA 1986 ss 165ff and Sch 4. These, or rather the circumstances in which they may be exercised, vary slightly depending on the type of winding up. Other powers (eg to make calls upon the contributories) are given by the Act in the first place to the court but are then delegated to the liquidator by the rules, pursuant to s 160.

The conduct of the liquidation

The way in which a liquidation is conducted can be described in general terms, but there are differences in detail between compulsory and voluntary liquidations, and between a members' and a creditors' voluntary winding up, which can be discovered only from a study of the 1986 Act and the Insolvency Rules.

The Act confers a wide range of powers on a liquidator.[58] There is an extensive list of specific powers set out in Sch 4, for example the power to bring and defend proceedings, to carry on the company's business and to borrow and to charge the company's property as security. By ss 178ff a liquidator is empowered to 'disclaim' what are described as 'unprofitable contracts' and 'onerous property'—in other words, to wash his hands of any responsibility under the contract or any interest in the property. A common example is a lease of property which is let at a rental higher than the current market rate. Anyone who suffers loss as a result of a disclaimer can prove for it as a debt in the winding up, but will usually be an unsecured creditor with all the disadvantages that entails. Other powers (which are also given to an administrator) include the power to examine directors and other persons on oath in order to gain information about the company's affairs (s 236, see 'Investigating and reporting the affairs of the company', pp 870ff): recall that the person being examined cannot refuse to give answers even where they are incriminating (see 'Inspections and the privilege against self-incrimination', p 777).

'Commencement' of winding up

For many statutory purposes,[59] a winding up takes effect from its 'commencement', which may involve some backdating. IA 1986 s 86 provides that a voluntary winding up

---

[58] And on the accountability of liquidators post the Human Rights Act, see V Finch, *Corporate Insolvency Law: Perspectives and Principles* (2nd edn, 2009), p 569.

[59] But not all: eg, the value of a debt is reckoned for the purpose of proof at the date when the company goes into liquidation: *Re Lines Bros Ltd* [1983] Ch 1, CA (for a recent consideration of *Re Lines Bros Ltd* in the context of a solvent liquidation, see *Re Lehman Brothers International (Europe)* [2015] EWCA Civ 485); and the periods of time prescribed by the Limitation Act 1980 cease to run against the company's creditors (other than the petitioning creditor himself) on the making of the winding-up order: *Re Cases of Taff's Well Ltd* [1992] Ch 179, [1992] BCLC 11.

is deemed to commence at the time of the passing of the resolution for winding up. In the case of a compulsory winding up, the liquidation is deemed to commence at the time of the presentation of the petition (and not the making of the order itself), but if the company is already in voluntary liquidation when the petition is presented, the relevant time is when the winding-up resolution was passed (s 129).

These provisions have important consequences because from the date of commencement:

(i) dispositions of property by the company (in a compulsory winding up) are avoided, unless the court otherwise orders (s 127);[60]

(ii) attachments, distress and execution (in a compulsory winding up) which have not been completed are void (s 128);[61]

(iii) transfers of shares are avoided (ss 88 and 127);

(iv) transactions entered into within prescribed periods before that date may be invalidated as having been 'at an undervalue' or 'preferences' (ss 238–241: see *Re MC Bacon Ltd* [16.15]);

(v) a floating charge created within 12 months (or, in some cases, two years) of that date may be invalidated (s 245; see *Re Parkes Garage* [12.16], and *Re Yeovil Glove* [12.17]).

By contrast, some categories of creditor are given preferential rights in regard to debts incurred within prescribed periods before the date of the *order* (ss 175 and 386 and Sch 6) (see 'Application of assets by the liquidator', pp 867ff). Also see *Re Globespan Airways Ltd (in Liquidation)* [2012] EWCA Civ 1159, CA.

It is not easy to reconcile these 'backdating' provisions with those of CA 2006 s 1079, which aims to protect third parties without actual notice until 15 days after the 'official notification' in the *Gazette* of the making of a winding-up order or, in a voluntary liquidation, of the appointment of a liquidator (see 'Publication in the *Gazette*', p 754). It is plain that the full implications of this statutory misfit (which are the result of implementing the First EU Company Law Directive) have not been fully thought through by the legislators.

The liquidator's ability to 'claw back' property—unwinding transactions

The effect of the statutory provisions referred to in points (i), (ii), (iv) and (v) in the previous section, is to allow the liquidator to 'claw back' property which has been transferred away by the company, and to avoid some transactions which it has entered into in the period immediately preceding the winding up, thus increasing the assets available for distribution to the creditors generally.

IA 1986 dramatically extended the scope of these provisions by comparison with the previous law. The existing provisions do not depend upon proof of fraud and dishonesty, but simply require that there be '*transactions at an undervalue*' (s 238), or '*preferences*' (s 239). The rules also operate more strictly where the other party to the transaction is a person 'connected with' the company (eg a director or a substantial shareholder, or a close relative of such a person, or another company in the same group: for the full definition, see ss 249 and 435). Where a connected person is involved, the time limits may be extended (ss 240(1)(a) and 245(3)(a)), the onus of proof may be reversed (ss 239(6) and 249(2)), or a possible defence disallowed (s 245(4)). It goes without saying that a very careful reading of the Act is necessary to discover exactly which rules are applicable in a particular case.

---

[60] Also see *Leedon Ltd v Hurry* [2010] UKPC 27, where the Privy Council held that a clause in a shareholders' agreement granting pre-emption rights on the sale of the company's assets was not intended to be applied following liquidation of the company as the detailed and prescriptive requirements of the clause would prevent the liquidators from achieving a satisfactory realisation of the assets.

[61] In any case, the rights of creditors in levying execution etc, are restricted by ss 183–184 in every type of winding up.

The liquidator's ability to require wrongdoers to make personal contributions to the assets of the company

IA 1986 (in addition to imposing criminal liability for various forms of misconduct which may be revealed in the course of a winding up) contains a number of provisions under which the directors of a company in liquidation, and in some cases others, may be made liable to account, pay compensation or contribute to the assets of the company in the hands of the liquidator:

(i)   IA 1986 s 212 (commonly called the 'misfeasance' section) provides a summary remedy[62] for establishing accountability or assessing damages against delinquent officers (excluding administrators[63]). This is a purely procedural provision, which creates no new liabilities but provides a simpler mechanism for the recovery of property or compensation in a winding up. It does, however, give the court a discretion to require such compensation to be paid in full or in part, 'as the court thinks just', and does not specify conditions for the exercise of this discretion (s 212(3)).[64]

(ii) If, in the course of a winding up, it is found that any business of the company has been carried on with intent to defraud creditors or for any other fraudulent purpose ('*fraudulent trading*'), the court may order those who were knowingly parties to this misconduct to contribute to the company's assets (s 213). For the purposes of this provision, actual dishonesty must be proved (*Re Patrick and Lyon Ltd* [1933] Ch 786; *R v Hollier and Booth* [2013] EWCA Crim 2041, [28]–[29]). The sum to be contributed is assessed on a compensatory basis only, with no punitive element: *Morphitis v Bernasconi* [2003] EWCA Civ 289, [2003] Ch 552, CA.[65]

(iii) A director, former director or 'shadow director' of a company in liquidation may be ordered to contribute personally to the assets in the hands of the liquidator if there have been circumstances constituting '*wrongful trading*' (a phrase used in the side-note, but not the text, of the Act): s 214. The complex provisions of this section need careful study.

Prerequisites for liability are that (i) the person has been a director (or 'shadow director') and (ii) the company has gone into insolvent liquidation. The person must have known, or should have concluded, that there was no reasonable prospect that the company would avoid going into insolvent liquidation. However, he can avoid liability if the court is satisfied that he 'took every step with a view to minimising the potential loss to the company's creditors' that he ought to have taken. Only the liquidator has standing to bring proceedings.

Although described as 'wrongful trading', as noted earlier, the possible scope of this section is very wide indeed. It can cover passive inactivity just as much as positive wrong-doing; there need be no actual 'trading', but conduct such as allowing the payment of unjustified remuneration or dividends could be caught; and as s 214(4) makes clear, and, as the *Produce Marketing* case **[16.16]** confirms, the director's behaviour is to be judged by objective as well as subjective standards.

It has also been held, as a matter of law, that CA 2006 s 1157 (which empowers a court to relieve a director from liability for breach of duty where he has acted honestly and

---

[62] Note that the liquidator, too, may be sued under this provision, and may be sued by a creditor or any contributory.

[63] They are dealt with in IA 1986 Sch B1, para 75.

[64] Contrast CA 2006 s 1157.

[65] Also note the fraudulent trading provision in CA 2006 s 993, where *criminal* liability is imposed in circumstances not limited to winding up. This is the provision where penal remedies are appropriate.

reasonably and ought fairly to be excused) is not available to a director in s 214 proceedings, although the logic of that analysis appears questionable.[66] On the other hand,
s 214(1) itself allows the court to declare that the person is 'liable to make such contribution (if any) to the company's assets as the court thinks proper', so the court can exercise
a discretion in any event.

Although the statutory charge of *fraudulent* trading (s 213) remains on the books, the
introduction in 1986 of the concept of 'wrongful' trading, which can lead to the same consequences with a much lighter burden of proof, means that s 213 is only rarely invoked. It
is invoked, however, if the objective is to attach liability to defendants who are not subject
to s 214, which has a much narrower remit than s 213 (eg over the past decade, the liquidators of BCCI have made significant use of s 213). For a recent example, see *Bilta (UK) Ltd
(In Liquidation) v Nazir* [2015] UKSC 23, in which s 213 was held to have extra-territorial
effect.

Money that is ordered to be paid under ss 213 and 214 (and, similarly, ss 238 and
239) goes into the general assets of the company in the hands of the liquidator. It is not
awardable directly to those affected by the fraudulent or wrongful trading. This avoids the
danger that a particular creditor might bring pressure on the directors of a company that
was close to insolvency in order to induce them to pay him off out of their own pockets
and so gain an advantage over the other creditors. On the other hand, sums recovered
under s 212 are the product of a chose in action vested in the company prior to liquidation. Accordingly they are 'assets of the company', which are capable of being caught by
the provisions of an appropriately drafted charge (*Re Anglo-Austrian Printing & Publishing
Union* [1895] 2 Ch 891), or of being assigned by the company or its liquidator (*Re Oasis
Merchandising Services Ltd* [1998] Ch 170).

Finally, CDDA 1986 authorises the court to make a disqualification order against anyone
held liable for fraudulent or wrongful trading (and indeed against directors involved in
other defined ways in the management of domestic or overseas companies which have
become insolvent): see 'Directors' disqualification', pp 309ff.

Re-use of company names and the 'phoenix syndrome'

The Cork Committee, on whose recommendation the concept of wrongful trading was
introduced, were concerned also with another situation, popularly referred to as the 'phoenix syndrome'. This occurs where a person who had been trading through the medium
of a company allows it to go into insolvent liquidation and then forms a new company,
sometimes with a similar name, and carries on trading much as before. He might even
use assets in the new business which he had bought at a knock-down price in the liquidation of the old company, so that the old company's creditors subsidise his fresh start.
The Committee (Cmnd 8558, 1982, para 1827) recommended that such a person should be
personally liable for the second company's debts if it went into insolvent liquidation within
three years.

However, instead of this targeted liability, the Insolvency Act simply focuses on the re-
use of the name of a defunct company by a person who was one of its directors. Criminal
and civil liability follow: the behaviour is made a criminal offence (s 216) which, in *R v
Cole* [1998] 2 BCLC 234, CA, was held to be one of strict liability.[67] In addition, the director, without the need of any court order, is made personally liable, without limitation, for
the debts of the new business, whether or not it becomes insolvent (s 217). The conditions
for liability are stringently drawn, the criminal and civil consequences are severe and
liability is automatic: the court has no discretion to absolve the defendant (*Ricketts v Ad*

---

[66] *Re Produce Marketing Consortium Ltd (Halls v David)* **[16.16]**.
[67] Unless leave of the court has been obtained permitting such activity: s 216(3).

Valorem Factors Ltd [2003] EWCA Civ 1706, [2004] BCC 164). The provisions seem to be used increasingly frequently.

Insolvency and corporate groups

Another problem discussed by the Cork Committee was that of 'group trading'—the 'runt of the litter' situation criticised by Templeman LJ in *Re Southard & Co Ltd* ('Corporate groups: do they warrant special treatment?', p 51). Is it in keeping with commercial morality that a parent company can allow one of its subsidiaries to decline into insolvency while the rest of the group prospers? *A fortiori*, for the debts owed by the subsidiary to other members of the group to rank equally with those of outside creditors—or even, if secured, ahead of them? The Committee recommended (para 1963) that the law should be changed so that inter-company indebtedness could in some circumstances be postponed to the claim of outside creditors. But, it hesitated to follow the bolder reforms made in New Zealand and Ireland, which empower the court to order one company in a group to pay the debt of another in the insolvent winding up of the latter.

IA 1986 contains no special provisions relating to insolvent groups, although it may have met these problems in part by its 'wrongful trading' provisions (which might extend to a parent company as a 'shadow director') and by its measures to extend the circumstances in which floating charges given to 'connected persons' can be invalidated (companies within the same group are 'connected persons').

The common law 'anti-deprivation principle'

Re Harrison, ex p Jay **[16.17]** was one of the earliest cases to set out what is now known as the anti-deprivation principle. This is a common law principle which renders void contractual arrangements which provide for the forfeiture of proprietary interests where the forfeiture is triggered by the debtor's bankruptcy or liquidation.[68] These arrangements have re-emerged for judicial consideration in the fallout from the recent financial crisis, and in *Belmont Park Investments Pty Ltd v BNY Corporate Trustee Services Ltd and Lehman Brothers Special Financing Inc* **[16.18]** the issues were litigated all the way to the Supreme Court. The Supreme Court affirmed the existence of the principle, but attenuated its operation in ways which make any simple formulation now exceptionally difficult.

Cases illustrating the conduct of the liquidation

The cases which follow illustrate the operation in practice of some of the provisions of IA 1986 that are discussed previously.

Avoidance of property dispositions: IA 1986 s 127.

[16.14] Re Gray's Inn Construction Co Ltd [1980] 1 WLR 711
(Court of Appeal)

The company, which carried on a building business, was ordered to be wound up by the court. Between the time when the petition was presented and the date of the order its bank had allowed it to continue to operate its account. During this period it had traded unprofitably. The Court of Appeal held that both the amounts credited to the company's account and those debited to it constituted 'dispositions' of the company's property (although now see the Note following) and, in the exercise of its discretion under IA 1986 s 127, declined to validate most of these banking transactions. In the course of his judgment, Buckley

---

[68] Note that leases and licences which terminate on the insolvency of the debtor have never been regarded as subject to avoidance under this principle: see *Belmont* **[16.18]** at [84]–[88].

LJ enunciated some principles for the guidance of courts in relation to the jurisdiction under s 127.

BUCKLEY LJ: It is a basic concept of our law governing the liquidation of insolvent estates, whether in bankruptcy or under the Companies Acts, that the free assets of the insolvent at the commencement of the liquidation shall be distributed rateably amongst the insolvent's un-secured creditors as at that date...In a company's compulsory winding up [this] is achieved by section 227 [of CA 1948, equivalent to IA 1986 s 127]. There may be occasions, however, when it would be beneficial, not only for the company but also for its unsecured creditors, that the com-pany should be enabled to dispose of some of its property during the period after the petition has been presented but before a winding-up order has been made. An obvious example is if the com-pany has an opportunity by acting speedily to dispose of some piece of property at an exception-ally good price. Many applications for validation under the section relate to specific transactions of this kind or analogous kinds. It may sometimes be beneficial to the company and its creditors that the company should be enabled to complete a particular contract or project, or to continue to carry on its business generally in its ordinary course with a view to a sale of the business as a going concern. In any such case the court has power under section 227 of the Companies Act 1948 to validate the particular transaction, or the completion of the particular contract or project, or the continuance of the company's business in its ordinary course, as the case may be. In con-sidering whether to make a validating order the court must always, in my opinion, do its best to ensure that the interests of the unsecured creditors will not be prejudiced. Where the application relates to a specific transaction this may be susceptible of positive proof. In a case of comple-tion of a contract or project the proof may perhaps be less positive but nevertheless be cogent enough to satisfy the court that in the interests of the creditors the company should be enabled to proceed, or at any rate that proceeding in the manner proposed would not prejudice them in any respect. The desirability of the company being enabled to carry on its business generally is likely to be more speculative and will be likely to depend on whether a sale of the business as a going concern will probably be more beneficial than a break-up realisation of the company's assets. In each case, I think, the court must necessarily carry out a balancing exercise...Each case must depend upon its own particular facts.

Since the policy of the law is to procure so far as practicable rateable payments of the unse-cured creditors' claims, it is, in my opinion, clear that the court should not validate any transaction or series of transactions which might result in one or more pre-liquidation creditors being paid in full at the expense of other creditors, who will only receive a dividend, in the absence of special circumstances making such a course desirable in the interests of the unsecured creditors as a body. If, for example, it were in the interests of the creditors generally that the company's busi-ness should be carried on, and this could only be achieved by paying for goods already supplied to the company when the petition is presented but not yet paid for, the court might think fit in the exercise of its discretion to validate payment for those goods ...

It may not always be feasible, or desirable, that a validating order should be sought before the transaction in question is carried out. The parties may be unaware at the time when the transac-tion is entered into that a petition has been presented; or the need for speedy action may be such as to preclude an anticipatory application; or the beneficial character of the transaction may be so obvious that there is no real prospect of a liquidator seeking to set it aside, so that an application to the court would waste time, money and effort. But in any case in which the transaction is car-ried out without an anticipatory validating order the disponee is at risk of the court declining to validate the transaction. It follows, in my view, that the parties when entering into the transaction, if they are aware that it is liable to be invalidated by the section, should have in mind the sort of considerations which would influence the court's decision.

A disposition carried out in good faith in the ordinary course of business at a time when the parties are unaware that a petition has been presented may, it seems, normally be validated by the court...unless there is any ground for thinking that the transaction may involve an attempt to prefer the disponee, in which case the transaction would probably not be validated. In a number of cases reference has been made to the relevance of the policy of ensuring rateable distribution of the assets . . .

But although that policy might disincline the court to ratify any transaction which involved preferring a pre-liquidation creditor, it has no relevance to a transaction which is entirely post-liquidation, as for instance a sale of an asset at its full market value after presentation of a petition. Such a transaction involves no dissipation of the company's assets, for it does not reduce the value of those assets. It cannot harm the creditors and there would seem to be no reason why the court should not in the exercise of its discretion validate it. A fortiori, the court would be inclined to validate a transaction which would increase, or has increased, the value of the company's assets, or which would preserve, or has preserved, the value of the company's assets from harm which would result from the company's business being paralysed . . .

GOFF LJ and SIR DAVID CAIRNS concurred.

> Notes

1. The transactions which were challenged in this case were payments into and out of the company's bank account, and the court held, or accepted concessions made by counsel, that all such payments were 'dispositions' by the company within s 127. But later cases have shown that this is not always true. In *Re Barn Crown Ltd* [1994] 2 BCLC 186 it was held that there was no 'disposition', but only an adjustment of entries in the statement recording the accounts between the customer and the banker, when cheques belonging to the company were paid into an account which was already in credit. (However, Professor Goode, *Principles of Corporate Insolvency Law* (4th edn, 2011), paras 11.131ff, disagrees: if the bank were to become insolvent, the money would be lost, and accordingly there must have been a 'disposition'.) Subsequently, in *Hollicourt (Contracts) Ltd v Bank of Ireland* [2001] Ch 555, CA, it has been held that where a bank meets a cheque drawn by its customer (whether the account is in credit or overdrawn), it does so merely as the customer's agent. As a result, while there is clearly a disposition by the customer in favour of the payee, there is no disposition to the bank itself—as had been assumed in the *Gray's Inn* case. *Hollicourt* no doubt provides considerable comfort to the banking community, since it reduces concern about this type of restitutionary liability.

2. The policy underpinning IA 1986 s 127 was explained in *Wilson v SMC Properties* [2015] EWHC 870 (Ch), with Registrar Briggs holding that its function was twofold: preventing improper alienations of the insolvent estate (reducing the sums available to pay creditors); and ensuring rateable distribution amongst creditors of the same class (ie *pari passu* distribution).

Preferences and transactions at an undervalue: IA 1986 ss 239 and 238.

[16.15] Re MC Bacon Ltd [1990] BCLC 324 (Chancery Division)

The company, which carried on business as a bacon importer and wholesaler, had been profitable until it lost its principal customer. It continued trading on a reduced scale for a time, but eventually had to go into liquidation. This action was brought to challenge a debenture which had been given to its bank during this latter period, at a time when it was actually or virtually insolvent and could not have continued without the bank's support. Millett J held that the debenture was not liable to be struck down either (i) as a preference under IA 1986 s 239, since the directors in granting it had not been motivated by a desire to prefer the bank but only by a desire to avoid the calling in of the overdraft and their wish to continue trading, or (ii) as a transaction at an undervalue under s 238 because the giving of the security had neither depleted the company's assets nor diminished their value.

MILLETT J: . . .

Voidable preference

So far as I am aware, this is the first case under the section [s 239] and its meaning has been the subject of some debate before me. I shall therefore attempt to provide some guidance.

The section replaces s 44(1) of the Bankruptcy Act 1914, which in certain circumstances deemed fraudulent and avoided payments made and other transactions entered into in favour of a creditor 'with a view of giving such creditor...a preference over the other creditors'. Section 44(1) and its predecessors had been construed by the courts as requiring the person seeking to avoid the payment or other transaction to establish that it had been made 'with the dominant intention to prefer' the creditor.

Section 44(1) has been replaced and its language has been entirely recast. Every single word of significance, whether in the form of statutory definition or in its judicial exposition, has been jettisoned. 'View', 'dominant', 'intention' and even 'to prefer' have all been discarded. These are replaced by 'influenced', 'desire', and 'to produce in relation to that person the effect mentioned in sub-s (4)(b)'.

I therefore emphatically protest against the citation of cases decided under the old law. They cannot be of any assistance when the language of the statute has been so completely and deliberately changed. It may be that many of the cases which will come before the courts in future will be decided in the same way that they would have been decided under the old law. That may be so, but the grounds of decision will be different. What the court has to do is to interpret the language of the statute and apply it. It will no longer inquire whether there was 'a dominant intention to prefer' the creditor, but whether the company's decision was 'influenced by a desire to produce the effect mentioned in sub-s (4)(b)'.

This is a completely different test. It involves at least two radical departures from the old law. It is no longer necessary to establish a dominant intention to prefer. It is sufficient that the decision was influenced by the requisite desire. That is the first change. The second is that it is no longer sufficient to establish an intention to prefer. There must be a desire to produce the effect mentioned in the subsection.

This second change is made necessary by the first, for without it it would be virtually impossible to uphold the validity of a security taken in exchange for the injection of fresh funds into a company in financial difficulties. A man is taken to intend the necessary consequences of his actions, so that an intention to grant a security to a creditor necessarily involves an intention to prefer that creditor in the event of insolvency. The need to establish that such intention was dominant was essential under the old law to prevent perfectly proper transactions from being struck down. With the abolition of that requirement intention could not remain the relevant test. Desire has been substituted. That is a very different matter. Intention is objective, desire is subjective. A man can choose the lesser of two evils without desiring either.

It is not, however, sufficient to establish a desire to make the payment or grant the security which it is sought to avoid. There must have been a desire to produce the effect mentioned in the subsection, that is to say, to improve the creditor's position in the event of an insolvent liquidation. A man is not to be taken as desiring all the necessary consequences of his actions. Some consequences may be of advantage to him and be desired by him; others may not affect him and be matters of indifference to him; while still others may be positively disadvantageous to him and not be desired by him, but be regarded by him as the unavoidable price of obtaining the desired advantages. It will still be possible to provide assistance to a company in financial difficulties provided that the company is actuated only by proper commercial considerations. Under the new regime a transaction will not be set aside as a voidable preference unless the company positively wished to improve the creditor's position in the event of its own insolvent liquidation.

There is, of course, no need for there to be direct evidence of the requisite desire. Its existence may be inferred from the circumstances of the case just as the dominant intention could be inferred under the old law. But the mere presence of the requisite desire will not be sufficient by itself. It must have influenced the decision to enter into the transaction. It was submitted on behalf of the bank that it must have been the factor which 'tipped the scales'. I disagree. That is not what sub-s (5) says; it requires only that the desire should have influenced the decision. That requirement is satisfied if it was one of the factors which operated on the minds of those who made the decision. It need not have been the only factor or even the decisive one. In my judgment, it is not necessary to prove that, if the requisite desire had not been present, the company would not have entered into the transaction. That would be too high a test.

It was also submitted that the relevant time was the time when the debenture was created. That cannot be right. The relevant time was the time when the decision to grant it was made. In the present case that is not known with certainty...But it does not matter. If the requisite desire was operating at all, it was operating throughout.

[His Lordship ruled that the directors had been motivated by the desire to continue trading and not by a desire to give the bank a preference in the event of a liquidation. He continued:]

Transactions at an undervalue

Section 238 of the 1986 Act is concerned with the depletion of a company's assets by transactions at an undervalue. [His Lordship read s 238(4) and continued:]

The granting of the debenture was not a gift, nor was it without consideration. The consideration consisted of the bank's forbearance from calling in the overdraft and its honouring of cheques and making of fresh advances to the company during the continuance of the facility. The applicant relies therefore on para (b).

To come within that paragraph the transaction must be (i) entered into by the company; (ii) for a consideration; (iii) the value of which measured in money or money's worth; (iv) is significantly less than the value; (v) also measured in money or money's worth; (vi) of the consideration provided by the company. It requires a comparison to be made between the value obtained by the company for the transaction and the value of consideration provided by the company. Both values must be measurable in money or money's worth and both must be considered from the company's point of view.

In my judgment, the applicant's claim to characterise the granting of the bank's debenture as a transaction at an undervalue is misconceived. The mere creation of a security over a company's assets does not deplete them and does not come within the paragraph. By charging its assets the company appropriates them to meet the liabilities due to the secured creditor and adversely affects the rights of other creditors in the event of insolvency. But it does not deplete its assets or diminish their value. It retains the right to redeem and the right to sell or remortgage the charged assets. All it loses is the ability to apply the proceeds otherwise than in satisfaction of the secured debt. That is not something capable of valuation in monetary terms and is not customarily disposed of for value.

In the present case the company did not suffer that loss by reason of the grant of the debenture. Once the bank had demanded a debenture the company could not have sold or charged its assets without applying the proceeds in reduction of the overdraft; had it attempted to do so, the bank would at once have called in the overdraft. By granting the debenture the company parted with nothing of value, and the value of the consideration which it received in return was incapable of being measured in money or money's worth.

Counsel for the applicant (Mr Vos) submitted that the consideration which the company received was, with hindsight, of no value. It merely gained time and with it the opportunity to lose

> more money. But he could not and did not claim that the company ought to have received a fee or other capital sum in return for the debenture. That gives the game away. The applicant's real complaint is not that the company entered into the transaction at an undervalue but that it entered into it at all.
>
> In my judgment, the transaction does not fall within sub-s (4) . . .

➤ Notes

1. *Phillips v Brewin Dolphin Bell Lawrie Ltd* [2001] 1 WLR 143, HL, establishes that the consideration for a transaction may be provided by various parties, and that it may be appropriate to consider the details of a complex series of linked transactions to assess any 'undervalue'. Here, even doing that, the transaction was held to be one at an undervalue.

2. IA 1986 s 238(5) provides that the court shall not make an order in respect of a transaction at an undervalue if it is satisfied that the company entered into the transaction in good faith and for the purpose of carrying on its business, and that at the time it did so there were reasonable grounds for thinking that the transaction would benefit the company. This is clearly a difficult test to apply.

3. The time for judging whether the company was influenced by the requisite desire to improve the position of a creditor was recently considered in *Stealth Construction, Re* [2011] EWHC 1305 (Ch). The relevant time was held to be the time at which the decision to give the preference was made, not the time at which preference was actually given.

'Wrongful trading': IA 1986 s 214.

[16.16] Re Produce Marketing Consortium Ltd (No 2) [1989] BCLC 520 (Chancery Division)

This was the first reported case decided under IA 1986 s 214 ('wrongful trading'). The two directors, David and Murphy, had continued to run the company's fruit-importing business when they ought to have known that there was no prospect of avoiding insolvent liquidation. Knox J, in holding them liable for wrongful trading, emphasised that their conduct was to be judged, in part, by the objective standards laid down by s 214—that is, by more exacting criteria than those of the traditional common law, although CA 2006 s 174 now adopts this same s 214 standard (see 'The liquidator's ability to require wrongdoers to make personal contributions to the assets of the company', pp 853ff).

> KNOX J: The first question is whether [s 214(2)] applies to Mr David and Mr Murphy. There is no question but that they were directors at all material times and that PMC [the company] has gone into insolvent liquidation. The issue is whether at some time after 27 April 1986 and before 2 October 1987, when it went into insolvent liquidation, they knew or ought to have concluded that there was no reasonable prospect that PMC would avoid going into insolvent liquidation. It was inevitably conceded by counsel for the first respondent that this question has to be answered by the standards postulated by sub-s (4), so that the facts which Mr David and Mr Murphy ought to have known or ascertained and the conclusions that they ought to have reached are not limited to those which they themselves showing reasonable diligence and having the general knowledge, skill and experience which they respectively had, would have known, ascertained or reached but also those that a person with the general knowledge, skill and experience of someone carrying out their functions would have known, ascertained or reached . . .

The 1986 Act now has two separate provisions; s 213 dealing with fraudulent trading,...and s 214 which deals with what the sidenote calls 'wrongful trading'. It is evident that Parliament intended to widen the scope of the legislation under which directors who trade on when the company is insolvent may, in appropriate circumstances, be required to make a contribution to the assets of the company which, in practical terms, means its creditors.

Two steps in particular were taken in the legislative enlargement of the court's jurisdiction. First, the requirement for an intent to defraud and fraudulent purpose was not retained as an essential, and with it goes what Maugham J[69] called 'the need for actual dishonesty involving real moral blame'.

I pause here to observe that at no stage before me has it been suggested that either Mr David or Mr Murphy fell into this category.

The second enlargement is that the test to be applied by the court has become one under which the director in question is to be judged by the standards of what can reasonably be expected of a person fulfilling his functions, and showing reasonable diligence in doing so. I accept the submission of counsel for the first respondent in this connection, that the requirement to have regard to the functions to be carried out by the director in question, in relation to the company in question, involves having regard to the particular company and its business. It follows that the general knowledge, skill and experience postulated will be much less extensive in a small company in a modest way of business, with simple accounting procedures and equipment, than it will be in a large company with sophisticated procedures.

Nevertheless, certain minimum standards are to be assumed to be attained. Notably there is an obligation laid on companies to cause accounting records to be kept which are such as to disclose with reasonable accuracy at any time the financial position of the company at that time: see the Companies Act 1985, s 221(1) and (2)(a) [CA 2006 s 386]. In addition directors are required to prepare a profit and loss account for each financial year and a balance sheet as at the end of it: Companies Act 1985, s 227(1) and (3) [CA 2006 ss 394 and 399]. Directors are also required, in respect of each financial year, to lay before the company in general meeting copies of the accounts of the company for that year and to deliver to the registrar of companies a copy of those accounts, in the case of a private company, within 10 months after the end of the relevant accounting reference period (see the Companies Act 1985, ss 241(1) and (3) and 242(1) and (2)) [CA 2006 ss 437 and 441, providing different rules].

As I have already mentioned, the liquidator gave evidence that the accounting records of PMC were adequate for the purposes of its business. The preparation of accounts was woefully late, more especially in relation to those dealing with the year ending 30 September 1985 which should have been laid and delivered by the end of July 1986.

The knowledge to be imputed in testing whether or not directors knew or ought to have concluded that there was no reasonable prospect of the company avoiding insolvent liquidation is not limited to the documentary material actually available at the given time. This appears from s 214(4) which includes a reference to facts which a director of a company ought not only to know but those which he ought to ascertain, a word which does not appear in sub-s (2)(b). In my judgment this indicates that there is to be included by way of factual information not only what was actually there but what, given reasonable diligence and an appropriate level of general knowledge, skill and experience, was ascertainable. This leads me to the conclusion in this case that I should assume, for the purposes of applying the test in s 214(2), that the financial results for the year ending 30 September 1985 were known at the end of July 1986 at least to the extent of the size of the deficiency of assets over liabilities.

Mr David and Mr Murphy, although they did not have the accounts in their hands until January 1987, did, I find, know that the previous trading year had been a very bad one. They had a close

---

69 In *Re Patrick and Lyon Ltd* [1933] Ch 786 at 790.

and intimate knowledge of the business and they had a shrewd idea whether the turnover was up or down. In fact it was badly down in that year to £526,459 and although I have no doubt that they did not know in July 1986 that it was that precise figure, I have no doubt that they had a good rough idea of what it was and in particular that it was well down on the previous year. A major drop in turnover meant almost as night follows day that there was a substantial loss incurred, as indeed there was. That in turn meant again, as surely as night follows day, a substantial increase in the deficit of assets over liabilities.

That deals with their actual knowledge but in addition I have to have regard to what they have to be treated as having known or ascertained and that includes the actual deficit of assets over liabilities of £132,870…It was a deficit that, for an indefinite period in the future could not be made good even if the optimistic prognostications of level of turnover entertained by Mr David and Mr Murphy were achieved . . .

Counsel for the first respondent was not able to advance any particular calculation as constituting a basis for concluding that there was a prospect of insolvent liquidation being avoided. He is not to be criticised for that for in my judgment there was none available. Once the loss in the year ending 30 September 1985 was incurred PMC was in irreversible decline, assuming (as I must) that the respondents had no plans for altering the company's business and proposed to go on drawing the level of reasonable remuneration that they were currently receiving . . .

The next question which arises is whether there is a case under s 214(3) for saying that after the end of July 1986 the respondents took every step with a view to minimising the potential loss to the creditors of PMC as, assuming them to have known that there was no reasonable prospect of PMC avoiding insolvent liquidation, they ought to have taken. This clearly has to be answered No, since they went on trading for another year . . .

I am therefore driven to the conclusion that the court's discretion arises under s 214(1) . . .

In my judgment the jurisdiction under s 214 is primarily compensatory rather than penal. Prima facie the appropriate amount that a director is declared to be liable to contribute is the amount by which the company's assets can be discerned to have been depleted by the director's conduct which caused the discretion under sub-s (1) to arise. But Parliament has indeed chosen very wide words of discretion and it would be undesirable to seek to spell out limits on that discretion, more especially since this is, so far as counsel were aware, the first case to come to judgment under this section . . .

I take into account the following factors in addition to those set out above, which give rise to the existence of the court's discretion under s 214(1).

This was a case of failure to appreciate what should have been clear rather than a deliberate course of wrongdoing.

There were occasions when positive untruths were stated which cannot just be treated as unwarranted optimism . . .

The most solemn warning given by the auditor in early February 1987 was effectively ignored. The affairs of PMC were conducted during the last seven months of trading in a way which reduced the indebtedness to the bank, to which Mr David had given a guarantee, at the expense of trade creditors…The bank is, if not fully, at least substantially secured. If this jurisdiction is to be exercised, as in my judgment it should be in this case, it needs to be exercised in a way which will benefit unsecured creditors . . .

Taking all these circumstances into account I propose to declare that Mr David and Mr Murphy are liable to make a contribution to the assets of PMC of £75,000 . . .

➤ Note

See too *Brooks v Armstrong* [2015] EWHC 2289 (Ch), one of the rare successful cases for wrongful trading resulting in a compensatory award. It summarises the law on wrongful trading and makes it clear that once the elements of a wrongful trading claim are made out, the burden of proof is on the directors to show a defence.

➤ General notes

1. Recall that the 'fruits' of litigation instituted under s 214 are not at any time assets or property of the company, but the outcome of a power vested in the liquidator which only he can exercise. It follows that a charge over the company's assets—even if expressed to include its future assets—does not extend to sums ordered to be paid under s 214. The same reasoning applies to the various other 'clawback' provisions which vest similar powers in a liquidator, for example transactions at an undervalue (s 238) and preferences (s 239): *Re Yagerphone Ltd* [1935] Ch 392.

2. In contrast, it has been held that moneys recovered under the 'misfeasance' provision (s 212) are the fruits of a right of action which was vested in the company before it went into liquidation, and therefore an asset of the company capable of being caught by a suitably worded charge: *Re Anglo-Austrian Printing and Publishing Union* [1895] 2 Ch 891.

3. It is also possible for a charge to extend to money or property which was disposed of by the company between the presentation of a winding-up petition and the making of a winding-up order but, as a result of the disposition being declared void under IA 1986 s 127, comes back into its hands (*Mond v Hammond Suddards* [1996] 2 BCLC 470).

4. The 'charge' issue is only one aspect of the more general question raised by the meaning of the term 'assets (or property) of the company'. Schedules 1 and 4 to IA 1986 confer on an administrator and a liquidator respectively a statutory power to sell or otherwise dispose of 'the property of the company', and 'property' in this context plainly includes the right to bring proceedings to enforce any chose in action vested in the company (eg a right to sue a third party in tort: *Norglen Ltd v Reeds Rains Prudential Ltd* [1999] 2 AC 1, HL). In *Re Oasis Merchandising Services Ltd* [1998] Ch 170, CA, however, it was held that this power did not extend to an assignment by a liquidator of the 'fruits' of a s 214 action, since the right to bring such proceedings does not belong to the company but is conferred exclusively on the liquidator by the statute. It followed that there was no statutory authority justifying the assignment, and so it was liable to be held void at common law on the ground that it was champertous and against public policy. (Paradoxically, given the ruling in *Mond v Hammond Suddards* (Note 3), it has been held that the right to have dispositions of the company declared void under s 127 is also an incident of the office of liquidator which he cannot assign: *Re Ayala Holdings Ltd (No 2)* [1996] 1 BCLC 467.) For a critical analysis of the reasoning in *Re Oasis*, see LC Ho, 'Whose Claim Is It? A Critical Assessment of the *Re Oasis Merchandising Services* Orthodox' (2007) 23 *Tolley's Insolvency Law and Practice* 70.

5. In *Re DKG Contractors Ltd* [1990] BCC 903 the respondent was held liable to the company under IA 1986 s 212 (misfeasance), s 214 (wrongful trading) and s 239 (preference). The court ordered that these liabilities should not all be cumulative but that payments made under ss 212 and 239 should go towards satisfying the liability under s 214. The judge in *Re Brian D Pierson (Contractors) Ltd* [1999] BCC 26 was similarly considerate: not only did she rule that the respondents' liability for wrongful trading should not be increased by sums recoverable from them as preferences and on the ground of misfeasance, but she held also that the company's losses were in part due to extraneous factors, such as bad weather conditions, and reduced the contribution for wrongful trading by 30%. However, it is clear from other decisions that the jurisdiction is entirely discretionary, and that there is nothing to stop an order being made in an appropriate case which makes such liabilities cumulative (eg *Re Purpoint Ltd* [1991] BCLC 491).

6. A transaction at an undervalue may also be challenged under IA 1986 s 423 ('*transactions defrauding creditors*'), which replaces earlier legislation that can be traced back at least as far as 1571. Under this provision there are no time limits and the company need not be in liquidation or even insolvent. However, it must be shown that the transaction was entered

into *for the purpose* of putting assets beyond the reach of a creditor or potential creditor or of prejudicing the interests of such a person. For an example, see *Arbuthnot Leasing International Ltd v Havelet Leasing Ltd (No 2)* [1990] BCC 636, where a company's business and assets had been transferred on legal advice to an off-the-shelf company shortly before it went into receivership, and the court ordered the reversal of the transaction.

➤ Questions

1. What difference might the insolvency legislation of 1986 have made to the outcome of the following cases:

   (i)   *Salomon v Salomon & Co Ltd* **[2.02]**;

   (ii) the *Multinational Gas case* **[7.43]**;

   (iii) *Re Horsley & Weight Ltd* **[4.31]**;

   (iv) *Re Halt Garage (1964) Ltd* **[5.03]**.

2. Would any of the persons concerned in the cases (i) to (iv) have been liable to disqualification or compensation orders, as directors or shadow directors?

The common law 'anti-deprivation principle'.

[16.17] Re Harrison, ex p Jay (1879) 14 Ch D 19 (Court of Appeal)

A term in a building contract which provided for the forfeiture of the builder's materials to the landlord on the bankruptcy of the builder was held to be void, as contrary to the policy of the bankruptcy law, and accordingly, where the purported forfeiture had been triggered by that clause, the materials on the land did not thereby become the property of the landlord, but became instead the property of the trustee in bankruptcy in the builder's liquidation.

> JAMES LJ: The case has been very well argued. But it appears to me that it is governed by [earlier] decisions of this Court…which only followed much older decisions. The principle of those decisions is this, that a simple stipulation that, upon a man's becoming bankrupt, that which was his property up to the date of the bankruptcy should go over to some one else and be taken away from his creditors, is void as being a violation of the policy of the bankrupt law. Now that we have all the facts before us, I think we cannot escape from applying that principle to the present case. According to the debtor's own evidence everything that he was bound to do under the agreement had been performed by him up to the date of the bankruptcy, and therefore no right was vested in the lessor except by virtue of the bankruptcy. Her title is founded only on the stipulation that in the event of the builder's bankruptcy the materials which had been placed on the land should become her property. It seems to me impossible to distinguish the case from those authorities to which I have referred.

[16.18] Belmont Park Investments Pty Ltd v BNY Corporate Trustee Services Ltd and Lehman Brothers Special Financing Inc [2011] UKSC 38 (Supreme Court)

In the context of complicated derivative investments held by creditors of the Lehman Brothers Group, the Supreme Court held, amongst other matters, that a clause which flipped secured charge priority from one creditor (Lehman Brothers Special Financing

Inc) to another (Belmont Park Investments Pty Ltd) in the event of the original secured creditor's insolvency did not offend the common law anti-deprivation principle. The case is important. The seven judges were unanimous in their conclusions, although Lord Mance gave quite different reasons.

LORD COLLINS (with whom the majority agreed[70]):

75. From the earliest days of the [anti-deprivation] rule, it has been based on the notion of a fraud, or 'a direct fraud' (Lord Eldon LC in *Higinbotham v Holme* 19 Ves Jun 88, 92), on the bankruptcy laws, and that decision was taken to be authority for the proposition that where a person settles property in such a way that his interest determines on his bankruptcy 'that is evidence of an intention to defraud his creditors': *In re Stephenson; Ex p Brown* [1897] 1 QB 638, 640, per Vaughan Williams J. The overall effect of the authorities is that, where the anti-deprivation rule has applied, it has been an almost invariably expressed element that the party seeking to take advantage of the deprivation was intending to evade the bankruptcy rules; but that where it has not applied, the good faith or the commercial sense of the transaction has been a substantial factor. By contrast, in the leading pari passu principle case, *British Eagle* **[16.19]**, it was held by the majority that it did not matter that the clearing transaction was a sensible commercial arrangement not intended to circumvent the pari passu principle. . . .

78. Thus [after looking at a long line of authorities] there is an impressive body of opinion from some of the most distinguished judges that, in the case of the anti-deprivation rule, a deliberate intention to evade the insolvency laws is required. That conclusion is not affected by the decision in *British Eagle* **[16.19]**. The pari passu rule is clear. Parties cannot contract out of it. . . .

79. That does not mean, of course, that a subjective intention is required, or that there will not be cases so obvious that an intention can be inferred, as in *Ex p Jay* **[16.17]**. But it does suggest that in borderline cases a commercially sensible transaction entered into in good faith should not be held to infringe the anti-deprivation rule. Although he did not accept that absence of good faith was a necessary element, Neuberger J suggested in *Money Markets International Stockbrokers Ltd v London Stock Exchange Ltd* [2002] 1 WLR 1150, para 103 that if a deprivation provision, which might otherwise be held to be valid, could be shown to have been entered into by the parties with the intention of depriving creditors of their rights on an insolvency, then that might be sufficient to justify holding invalid the provision when it would not otherwise have been held invalid. . . .

80. By contrast with the pari passu principle, it is well established that if the deprivation takes place for reasons other than bankruptcy, the anti-deprivation rule does not apply. In *British Eagle* **[16.19]** the clearing house system was ineffective to avoid the pari passu principle, even though it applied throughout irrespective of whether the airlines went into liquidation. But the position is different with regard to the anti-deprivation rule, which is intended to operate only where provision is made for deprivation on bankruptcy. Thus in *Ex p Jay* **[16.17]**…both Brett and Cotton LJJ accepted, at p 26, that if forfeiture had taken place on the builder's breach (as the provision [also, in the alternative] envisaged) then it would have been valid . . .

➤ Note

Although the ancient and underutilised concept of anti-deprivation has now been given a new lease of life by the Supreme Court's decision, much work remains to be done in defining its precise modern scope and ambit. Relying on notions of 'good faith' and 'commercial reasonableness' may have their attractions in suggesting no intention to commit a fraud on

---

[70] Lord Walker agreed and added further points by way of 'footnote', while Lords Phillips, Hope and Clarke and Lady Hale agreed without further comment. Lord Mance delivered a separate judgment (not extracted here) which dissented from the majority in a number of crucially significant matters although not in its conclusion.

the statute,[71] but may also undermine much-needed certainty when not only are the deals typically commercial, but the parties' rights are in stark conflict given the insolvency context. Also see the recent decisions in *Lomas v JFB Firth Rixon Inc* [2012] EWCA Civ 419, CA; *Folgate London Market Ltd v Chaucer Insurance plc* [2011] EWCA Civ 328, CA; and *Revenue and Customs Commissioners v Football League Ltd* [2012] EWHC 1372 (Ch). For recent applications of *Belmont* in the context of termination rights, see *Re Pan Ocean Co Ltd* [2014] Bus LR 1041, [13]–[16]; and compare *Seawolf Tankers Inc and another v Pan Ocean Co Ltd* [2015] EWHC 1500 (Ch), [31]–[36].[72]

Assets available for distribution by the liquidator

The assets available to the liquidator in a winding up will include the following (or their proceeds after realisation):

(i)   all property beneficially owned by the company at the commencement of the winding up, apart from any property that the liquidator elects to disclaim under IA 1986 ss 178ff;

(ii) calls recovered from contributories;

(iii) moneys paid out of capital within the preceding 12 months for the repurchase of shares and recovered from past members and directors (s 76);

(iv) money or property recouped as a result of a court order nullifying a 'transaction at an undervalue' entered into within the preceding two years (ss 238 and 240);

(v)   property and money paid away by the company within the preceding six months (or, if the recipient is a 'connected person', two years) and recovered by the liquidator as a preference (ss 239 and 240);

(vi) property disposed of after the commencement of the liquidation under transactions which are invalidated by s 127, unless the court orders otherwise;

(vii) property not fully seized in execution or distress (s 183), or attached after the commencement of the winding up (s 128);

(viii) property recovered and compensation ordered to be paid by court order made against directors and others on the grounds of misfeasance (s 212), fraudulent trading (s 213) and wrongful trading (s 214).

The liquidator will take the assets—with one important qualification—subject to any security validly created in favour of a debenture holder or other creditor prior to the commencement of the winding up unless it is:

(i)   void against the liquidator for non-registration under CA 2006 s 874;

(ii) void as a preference under IA 1986 s 239;

(iii) a *floating* charge created within the preceding 12 months (or, if the chargee is a 'connected person', two years), except to the extent that it is valid under s 245.

The one qualification is that such security can be created only over *the property of the company* (present or future), and some of the categories of assets listed are regarded as

---

[71] Although, despite its name, a 'fraud on the statute' does not require any type of fraud or intention; the wrong is committed if the arrangement achieves an outcome contrary to the statute, regardless of good faith, etc.

[72] This issue has attracted a wealth of writing: S Worthington, 'Good Faith, Flawed Assets and the Emasculation of the UK Anti-Deprivation Rule' (2012) 75 MLR 112 and earlier articles cited there; R Goode, 'Flip Clauses: The End of the Affair' (2012) 128 LQR 171; T Cleary, 'Lehman Brothers and the Anti-Deprivation Principle: Current Uncertainties and Proposals for Reform' (2011) 6 *Capital Markets Law Journal* 411 (and a response by S Worthington, ibid, 450).

falling outside this description—for example, money recovered by the liquidator as a preference: see General notes 1 following **[16.16]**, p 863. These sums are therefore freely available for distribution among the company's unsecured creditors.

Property in the hands of the company will also be taken by the liquidator subject to any equities and set-offs enforceable against the company before it went into liquidation.

Application of assets by the liquidator

The claims of a secured creditor to the secured assets rank in principle ahead of any claim in the winding up—including even the costs of the liquidation. But recall that a *floating* charge holder must meet: (i) the claims of the unsecured creditors to a statutory share of the assets (IA 1986 s 176A, and Insolvency Act 1986 (Prescribed Part) Order 2003 (SI 2003/2097) art 3); (ii) the claims of the preferential creditors under s 175; and (iii) somewhat anomalously, the expenses of the winding up (including the liquidator's remuneration): see IA 1986 ss 175(2)(a) and 197ZA (see 'Distribution of assets subject to the receivership', p 832).

Assets will be applied, after the claims of secured creditors (other than holders of floating charges) have been satisfied, in the following order of priority:[73]

(i)   the expenses of the liquidation (including the liquidator's remuneration, post-liquidation debts and certain pre-liquidation debts) (s 115 (voluntary liquidations) and s 156 (compulsory liquidation)). What amounts to an expense of winding up has been the subject of major litigation: contrast *Re Toshoku Finance UK plc, Kahn v IRC* [2002] UKHL 6, HL, concluding that IR 1986 r 4.218 is a definitive statement of what counts as a liquidation expense[74] and of the priorities as between expenses; with the more functional and purposive approach in *Re Nortel GmbH* [2013] UKSC 52, [74]–[77] (see also [111] for discussion of *Toshoku*). For recent cases considering *Toshoku* and *Nortel* together, see *Re PGL Realisations plc* [2014] EWHC 2721 (Ch) and *Jervis v Pillar* [2014] EWCA Civ 180, [2015] Ch 87;

(ii)   the debts declared to be preferential debts by s 386 and Sch 6;

(iii)   floating charge holders (but see 'Distribution of assets subject to the receivership', pp 832ff, for the precise working out of this, including the statutory share to unsecured creditors, if the assets are not sufficient to meet (i)–(iii) in total);

(iv)   unsecured creditors—but note that some debts owed by the company to shareholders, such as moneys paid in advance of calls and sums due by way of dividends, are postponed to outside creditors (s 74(2)(f));

(v)   interest on all debts proved in the winding up (s 189);

(vi)   non-provable liabilities;

(vii)   money due to a member under a contract to redeem or repurchase shares which has not been completed prior to the winding up (CA 2006 s 735);

(viii) the debts due to members mentioned in (iv);

(ix)   repayment of capital to preference members; and

(x)   repayment of capital to ordinary members.

---

[73] See also *Re Nortel GmbH* [2013] UKSC 52, [39].

[74] And this rule has also been amended to cover litigation expenses under IA 1986 ss 213, 214, 238, 239, 242, 243 and 423, all of which are claims to recover assets or seek contributions to the company's assets, but where the *claims* are not 'assets of the company' (see General notes 1 following *Produce Marketing* **[16.16]**, p 863), and so litigation expenses relating to them were not previously allowed: *Re MC Bacon Ltd (No 2)* [1990] BCLC 607; *Re Floor Fourteen Ltd, Lewis v IRC* [2001] 2 BCLC 392, CA.

Any 'surplus assets' then go to whoever is entitled under the company's constitution; normally, this will be the ordinary members.

A Department of Trade and Industry review, now rather dated, suggested that average recovery rates in formal insolvency procedures were: 77% for the bank; 27% for preferential creditors; and virtually nil for unsecured creditors.[75]

A contract under which creditors agree to vary the statutory rules governing the distribution of a company's assets in a liquidation is contrary to public policy and void.

[16.19] British Eagle International Air Lines Ltd v Cie Nationale Air France [1975] 1 WLR 758 (House of Lords)

Many airlines set up a 'clearing house' scheme under which their mutual debits and credits were not set off one against another but were pooled with a third party, IATA. Under the agreement, participants could not claim against each other but only against IATA for any net balance due to the particular airline under the scheme. British Eagle went into liquidation at a time when it was a net debtor to the scheme in respect of its aggregated claims but, as between itself and Air France, it was a net creditor. The liquidator successfully challenged the legality of the clearing house arrangement.

> LORD CROSS OF CHELSEA: [What] the respondents are saying here is that the parties to the 'clearing house' arrangements by agreeing that simple contract debts are to be satisfied in a particular way have succeeded in 'contracting out' of the provisions contained in [CA 1948 s 302] [IA 1986, s 107] for the payment of unsecured debts 'pari passu'. In such a context it is to my mind irrelevant that the parties to the 'clearing house' arrangements had good business reasons for entering into them and did not direct their minds to the question how the arrangements might be affected by the insolvency of one or more of the parties. Such a 'contracting out' must, to my mind, be contrary to public policy. The question is, in essence, whether what was called in argument the 'mini liquidation' flowing from the clearing house arrangements is to yield to or to prevail over the general liquidation. I cannot doubt that on principle the rules of the general liquidation should prevail . . .
>
> LORDS DIPLOCK and EDMUND-DAVIES concurred.
>
> LORDS MORRIS OF BORTH-Y-GEST and SIMON OF GLAISDALE dissented.

➤ Notes

1. The Supreme Court reaffirmed the strictness of this rule, *obiter*, in *Belmont Park Investments Pty Ltd v BNY Corporate Trustee Services Ltd and Lehman Brothers Special Financing Inc* **[16.18]**.

2. There may be strong public policy arguments for allowing creditors to vary the statutory priorities by arrangement among themselves. One such situation is when the existing creditors of a company in difficulties are willing to let a new creditor advance money in an attempt to save the company from liquidation, on the understanding that if the attempt is unsuccessful the claim of the 'rescuer' should not rank equally with their own, but have priority. Following *British Eagle*, there was for a time considerable uncertainty whether such an arrangement—at least if effected by contract between the parties—would be lawful. There was pressure for legislation to be passed which would expressly

---

[75] Insolvency Service, *A Review of Company Rescue and Business Reconstruction Mechanisms: Report by the Review Group* (2000), para 57.

permit subordination agreements. However, in two decisions of Vinelott J, *Re British & Commonwealth Holdings plc (No 3)* [1992] BCLC 322 and *Re Maxwell Communications Corpn plc (No 2)* [1994] 1 BCLC 1 (where the agreements took the forms respectively of a trust and a contract), it was held that no violation of the *pari passu* principle is involved, where all that the subordinating creditor agrees to is that its rights in an insolvency shall be *less than* what would obtain under the statutory scheme. For a recent consideration (and implicit approval) of Vinelott J's decisions, see Re Lehman Brothers International (Europe) (In Administration) (No 4) [2015] Ch 1 (David Richards J), [81]–[86], affd [2015] EWCA Civ 485.

3. Special legislative provision has been made by Pt VII of CA 1989 (not moved to CA 2006) and the Financial Markets and Insolvency (Settlement Finality) Regulations 1999 (SI 1999/2979) to allow 'netting' arrangements of the type rejected in the *British Eagle* case to be used by investment exchanges, clearing houses and money market institutions and in banking and securities settlement arrangements.

4. It is also sometimes possible to avoid the application of the *British Eagle* ruling by establishing a *trust*, so that the sum which would ordinarily be payable as a debt to a particular creditor is held by the company as a trustee on his behalf: see *Re Kayford Ltd* [1975] 1 WLR 279; *Carreras Rothmans Ltd v Freeman Mathews Treasure Ltd* [1985] Ch 207. The courts have, on occasion, been prepared to *infer* the existence of a trust in such circumstances, for example *Barclays Bank Ltd v Quistclose Investments Ltd* [1970] AC 567, HL; *Mundy v Brown* [2011] EWHC 377 (Ch). But contrast the more robust approach in *Challinor v Juliet Bellis & Co* [2015] EWCA Civ 59, at [53]–[63], indicating how intentions are to be shown objectively.

5. The statutory rules as to set off,[76] like the *pari passu* distribution rule, are also regarded as mandatory and cannot be excluded by agreement between the parties (*National Westminster Bank Ltd v Halesowen Presswork and Assemblies Ltd* [1972] AC 785, HL), or under any discretionary power of the court (*Re Bank of Credit and Commerce International SA (No 10)* [1997] Ch 213).

6. In *Barclays Bank plc v British & Commonwealth Holdings plc* [1996] 1 BCLC 1 (on appeal, but not on this issue, [1996] 1 BCLC 1 at 26) Harman J held as unlawful a tripartite arrangement between a company, one of its members and a third party which breached, by an indirect route, the principle that a company may not return capital to its members except by a procedure authorised by statute (see 'Consequences of an unauthorised distribution', p 567). It was also a consequence of the arrangement that a sum of money which would have been repayable to the shareholder *qua* shareholder in a liquidation was replaced by an equivalent amount payable to the third party as a debt. In effect, this altered the statutory order of priorities in a liquidation (since creditors rank before shareholders) and was a further ground justifying the finding of illegality. By contrast, the court sanctioned three schemes of arrangement which, despite excluding the mezzanine lenders, were held not unlawful because those lenders had no economic interest in the company in any event: *Re Bluebrook Ltd* [2009] EWHC 2114 (Ch).

7. In the United States, the courts have developed an equitable jurisdiction under which they have a discretion to subordinate the claims of some creditors to others—for example, to postpone the claims of creditors who are members of the same corporate group. It would require legislation to bring about any reform along these lines in this country.

---

[76] All the various set-off rules have enormous practical importance: see, eg, *Fearns v Anglo-Dutch Paints & Chemical Co Ltd* [2010] EWHC 2366 (Ch) (legal set-off), *Geldof Constructivie NV v Simon Carves Ltd* [2010] EWCA Civ 667 (equitable set-off) and *Re Kaupthing Singer and Friedlander Ltd* [2010] EWCA Civ 518 (insolvency set-off), together with *Re Kaupthing Singer and Friedlander Ltd* [2011] UKSC 48 (set-off and the rule in *Cherry v Boultbee*).

Investigating and reporting the affairs of the company

In any of the insolvency or rescue procedures just noted, an insolvency practitioner must take charge of the affairs of the company and put himself in a position to take action quickly. IA 1986, therefore, makes special provision for acquisition of information by the office-holder. In addition, an insolvency office-holder is required to investigate potential wrongdoing in relation to the company's affairs, in particular for the purpose of action under CDDA 1986.

Investigations

The office-holder has available the following rights against specified persons involved in the management of the company:

(i)   The right to require a 'statement of affairs' verified by a statement of truth from persons connected with the company (IA 1986 ss 47, 99 and 131 and IR 1986 r 1.5).

(ii) Other than under CVAs, the right to require reasonable cooperation from persons connected with the company (IA 1986 ss 234(1) and 235). See *Bishopsgate Investment Management Ltd v Maxwell* [1993] Ch 1 at 57, for 'reasonableness'. Failure to comply without reasonable excuse is an offence (s 235).

(iii) Other than under CVAs, the right to require production of the company's books, papers and records (IA 1986 ss 234 and 246).

(iv) Other than under CVAs, the right to apply to court for an order requiring a 'private examination' (ie appearance for oral examination but with limited attendance); submission of an affidavit; or production of books, papers or other documents (IA 1986 ss 234, 236 and 237). An examinee is not entitled to privilege against self-incrimination (*Bishopsgate Investment Management Ltd v Maxwell* [1993] Ch 1; *Beghal v DPP* [2015] UKSC 49), so the statutory protection that followed from *Saunders v United Kingdom* (1996) 23 EHRR 313 applies (see 'Inspections and the privilege against self-incrimination', p 777). On the discretion to order a private examination, see *British and Commonwealth Holdings plc v Spicer and Oppenheim* [1993] AC 426; on the conduct of private examinations, see *Re Richbell Strategic Holdings Ltd (No 2)* [2000] 2 BCLC 794; and on the successful application for the production of documents pursuant to s 236 by a foreign company under the UNCITRAL Model Law on Cross-Border Insolvency, see *Re Chesterfield United Inc* [2012] EWHC 244 (Ch); *Re Corporate Jet Realisations Ltd* [2015] EWHC 221 (Ch); and *Re Comet Group Ltd* [2014] EWHC 3477 (Ch).

(v)   In compulsory (court-ordered) liquidations, the right of the official receiver (himself, or pursuant to a request by specified majorities of the company's creditors or contributories) to apply for a public examination of parties concerned in the promotion, formation or management of the company (IA 1986 s 133). Again, there is no privilege against self-incrimination (*Bishopsgate Investment Management Ltd v Maxwell* [1993] Ch 1). If the company is in voluntary liquidation, it seems a public examination may still be ordered (IA 1986 ss 122(1) and 133: see *Bishopsgate Investment Management Ltd v Maxwell* [1993] Ch 1 at 24, 46).

Reporting

When a company is subject to any of the insolvency or liquidation procedures other than a CVA, the relevant office-holder must submit a report to the Secretary of State on the conduct of any director whom the office-holder believes should be disqualified under CDDA 1986 s 6 (CDDA 1986 s 7(3)), and must, in any event, within six months of appointment, submit a return listing every director and stating whether a report has been made and, if not, why not (Insolvent Companies (Reports on Conduct of Directors) Rules 1996 (SI 1996/1909) r 4). Note that the current regime is to be superseded by amendments pursuant to the Small Business, Enterprise and Employment Act 2015, and s 7(3) will then be repealed. A new CDDA 1986 s 7A will require the office-holder to prepare a 'conduct report' about the conduct of *each* director on the insolvency date (defined in s 7A(10)), or at any time during the period of three years ending with that date (s 7A(1)). The office-holder must send the conduct report to the Secretary of State within three months from the insolvency date (s 7A(4)). (At the time of writing, these provisions are not yet in force other than to the extent necessary to make supporting rules and regulations.)

In compulsory liquidations, the official receiver has a duty to investigate the affairs of the company, and may make a report to the court (IA 1986 s 132(1)).

In any type of liquidation, the liquidator must report any criminal offences apparently committed in relation to the company by any past or present officers or members (IA 1986 s 118). This may lead to a public investigation of the company (see 'Public investigation of companies', pp 770ff).

Dissolution of the company

The corporate entity created under the Companies Act ceases to exist by the formal act of *dissolution*, effected by removing the name of the company from the register at Companies House. Dissolution ends the company's separate personality, terminates any legal relationships[77] and dissolves the relationship between the company and its members.

Dissolution may take place in a variety of ways (most requiring some form of publication in the *Gazette* at an appropriate stage in the process), including:

(i)   On completion of liquidation, automatically, three months after the registrar has been notified of the completion of the winding-up procedure (IA 1986 ss 94, 106, 172(8), 201 and 205). The processes vary slightly for voluntary and compulsory liquidations.

(ii) By the registrar, where the registrar has reasonable cause to believe that no liquidator is acting or the affairs of the company have been fully wound up, and yet the required returns (see (i)) have not been made for a period of six months (CA 2006 s 1001).

(iii) On application by the official receiver, automatically, three months after requesting early dissolution (unless some interested person intervenes in the meantime), if it appears that the realisable assets of the company are insufficient to cover the expenses of liquidation and that the affairs of the company do not require further investigation (IA 1986 s 202).

(iv) On completion of administration, three months after notification by the administrator that there is nothing to distribute to the creditors (IA 1986 Sch B1, para 84).

(v)   By order of the court, in conjunction with compromises, arrangements and reconstructions (CA 2006 s 900).

(vi) On application by the company itself, three months after publication of the application in the *Gazette* (CA 2006 s 1003). This option for voluntary striking off is subject

---

[77] So, eg, the company's property passes as *bona vacantia* to the Crown: CA 2006 s 1012.

to a wide variety of restrictions and conditions (CA 2006 ss 1004–1010), but it does enable the expense of a formal liquidation to be avoided.

(vii) By the registrar, exercising an administrative power to strike off (CA 2006 s 1000). In practice, the largest number of companies are dissolved by the simple administrative procedure of 'striking off the register'. CA 2006 s 1000 empowers the registrar to do this, after advertisement, if his inquiries show or suggest that the company has ceased to carry on business. This is a useful sanction in the case of a company which has failed to file accounts or annual returns.

Restoration to the register

Restoration of dissolved companies to the register may be necessary if, for example, further assets are discovered, or someone wishes to bring a damages claim for which the former company was insured.

There are two procedures available for restoring companies to the register:

(i) an administrative procedure, available when companies have been incorrectly struck off as defunct under CA 2006 s 1000 or 1001 (see points (ii) and (vii) in the previous section), requiring application to the registrar by the company's former directors or former members within six years of the date of dissolution (CA 2006 s 1024); and

(ii) a judicial procedure, requiring application to court (CA 2006 s 1029), in all other cases. The application may be made by a wide class of people (s 1029(2)), and must generally be made within six years of the dissolution of the company, although there are various exceptions. For example, there is no time limit where the application is for the purpose of bringing proceedings against the company for damages for personal injury (s 1030(1)). The court has wide powers to make restoration, including any case in which the court thinks it just to do so (s 1031(1)(c).

CA 2006 ss 1024–1034 provide detailed rules on the pre-conditions and consequences of the procedures, including special supplementary rules dealing with company names and with restoration of property that had vested in the Crown.

■ Further reading

ANDERSON, H, 'Receivership Preferential Creditors' (1994) 15 *Company Lawyer* 195.

DEAKIN, S and ARMOUR, JH, 'Norms in Private Insolvency: The "London Approach" to the Resolution of Financial Distress' (2001) 1 *Journal of Corporate Law Studies* 21.

DOYLE, LG, 'The Residual Status of Directors in Receivership' (1996) 17 *Company Lawyer* 131.

FERRAN, E, 'The Duties of an Administrative Receiver to Unsecured Creditors' (1998) 9 *Company Lawyer* 58.

FINCH, V, 'Corporate Rescue in a World of Debt' [2008] 8 JBL 756.

FRISBY, S, 'Making a Silk Purse Out of a Pig's Ear—*Medforth v Blake*' (2000) 63 MLR 413.

HANSMANN, H and KRAAKMAN, RH, 'The Essential Role of Organisational Law' (2000) 110 *Yale Law Journal* 387.

KASTRINOU, A, 'An Analysis of the Pre-Pack Technique and Recent Developments in the Area' (2008) 29 *Company Lawyer* 259.

KEAY, A, 'The Duty of Directors to Take Account of Creditors' Interests; Has It Any Role to Play?' [2002] JBL 379.

MOKAL, R, 'What Liquidation Does for Secured Creditors and What It Does for You?' (2008) 71 MLR 699.

SCHILLIG, M, ' "Deepening Insolvency"— Liability for Wrongful Trading in the United States?' (2009) 30 *Company Lawyer* 298.

WALTERS, A, 'Corporate Restructuring under Schedule B1 of the Insolvency Act 1986' (2005) 26 *Company Lawyer* 97.

WILLIAMS, R, 'Civil Recovery from Delinquent Directors' (2015) 15 *Journal of Corporate Law Studies* 311.

WORTHINGTON, S, 'Good Faith, Flawed Assets and the Emasculation of the UK Anti-Deprivation Rule' (2012) 75 MLR 112.

Index